T0145157

Lecture Notes in Computer Science 5716

Commenced Publication in 1973
Founding and Former Series Editors:
Gerhard Goos, Juris Hartmanis, and Jan van Leeuwen

Pasquale Foggia   Carlo Sansone
Mario Vento (Eds.)

Image Analysis and Processing – ICIAP 2009

15th International Conference
Vietri sul Mare, Italy, September 8-11, 2009
Proceedings

 Springer

Volume Editors

Pasquale Foggia
Mario Vento
Università di Salerno
Dipartimento di Ingegneria dell'Informazione e Ingegneria Elettrica
Via Ponte Don Melillo 1, 84084 Fisciano (SA), Italy
E-mail: {pfoggia, mvento}@unisa.it

Carlo Sansone
Università di Napoli Federico II
Dipartimento di Informatica e Sistemistica
Via Claudio 21, 80125 Napoli, Italy
E-mail: carlosan@unina.it

Library of Congress Control Number: 2009933192

CR Subject Classification (1998): I.4, I.5, I.3.5, I.2.10, I.2.6, F.2.2

LNCS Sublibrary: SL 6 – Image Processing, Computer Vision, Pattern Recognition, and Graphics

ISSN   0302-9743
ISBN-10   3-642-04145-0 Springer Berlin Heidelberg New York
ISBN-13   978-3-642-04145-7 Springer Berlin Heidelberg New York

springer.com

© Springer-Verlag Berlin Heidelberg 2009
Printed in Germany

Typesetting: Camera-ready by author, data conversion by Scientific Publishing Services, Chennai, India
Printed on acid-free paper   SPIN: 12750559   06/3180   5 4 3 2 1 0

Preface

This volume contains the papers presented at the 15th International Conference on Image Analysis and Processing (ICIAP 2009), held in Vietri sul Mare, Italy, September 8–11, 2009.

ICIAP 2009 was the 15th edition of a series of conferences organized every two years by the Italian group of researchers affiliated to the International Association for Pattern Recognition (IAPR). The aim of these conferences is to bring together researchers working on image analysis, image processing and pattern recognition from around the world. Topics for ICIAP 2009 included Image Analysis and Processing, Vision and Perception, Pattern Recognition, Multimodal Interaction and Multimedia Processing, and Applications.

There were 168 submissions. Each submission was reviewed by three Program Committee members. The committee decided to accept 107 papers, divided into 12 oral sessions (36 papers) and two poster sessions (71 papers).

The program included three invited talks by David Stork (Ricoh Innovations, USA), Bogdan Gabrys (Bournemouth University, UK) and Stan Matwin (University of Ottawa, Canada). For the latter two, the talks were organized in an unusual way: the two speakers presented a talk on the same topic as seen from their different point of views, with Bogdan Gabrys proposing a pattern recognition approach and Stan Matwin a machine learning approach. A stimulating comparison between the two approaches was made possible by the coordination and moderation by Floriana Esposito.

Two tutorials were offered, on "3D Video Processing for Immersive 3D Video-conferencing" (by Oliver Scheer) and on "Human-Centered Vision Systems" (by Hamid Aghajan and Nicu Sebe).

ICIAP 2009 also hosted the first edition of the Fingerprint Liveness Detection Contest (LivDet2009), organized by Fabio Roli, Stephanie Schuckers and Gian Luca Marcialis. The results of the contest were presented in a special contest session.

During the conference, the Caianiello Prize, in memory of Prof. E. Caianiello, was awarded to the best paper by a young author, as in the previous editions. Also, a prize was awarded to the best paper presented to the conference.

A special session was held to commemorate the achievements of our estimated colleague Vito Di Gesú, who recently left us. Prof. Di Gesú has always been an active and important presence in the GIRPR community. We missed him in ICIAP 2009, and we will surely miss him more and more in the future editions of ICIAP.

We wish to thank the Italian group of researchers affiliated to the International Association for Pattern Recognition (GIRPR) for giving us the possibility of organizing this conference. We also thank the International Association For Pattern Recognition for the endorsement of ICIAP 2009.

A special thank goes to the members of the Program Committee and to the reviewers that have contributed with their work to ensure the high-quality standard of the papers accepted to ICIAP 2009.

The organization of the conference would not have been possible without the financial and technical support of the University of Salerno, the Department of Electrical and Information Engineering (DIIIE), and of Citel Group S.r.l. and Nexera S.r.l.

The management of the papers, including the preparation of this proceedings volume, was assisted by the EasyChair conference management system. Local organization for events and accomodation was managed by Leader S.a.s. A special thank goes to the members of the Local Organizing Committee, Donatello Conte and Gennaro Percannella, and to Francesco Tufano for their indispensable contributions to the organization and their help and availability to solve the many practical problems arising during the preparation of ICIAP 2009.

September 2009

Pasquale Foggia
Carlo Sansone
Mario Vento

Organization

General Chair

Mario Vento   University of Salerno, Italy

Program Chairs

Pasquale Foggia   University of Salerno, Italy
Carlo Sansone   University of Napoli Federico II, Italy

Steering Committee

Virginio Cantoni (Italy)
Luigi P. Cordella (Italy)
Alberto Del Bimbo (Italy)
Vito Di Gesù (Italy)
Marco Ferretti (Italy)
Piero Mussio (Italy)
Gabriella Sanniti di Baja (Italy)

Program Committee

Jake K. Aggarwal (USA)
Maria Grazia Albanesi (Italy)
Edoardo Ardizzone (Italy)
Prabir Bhattacharya (Canada)
Giuseppe Boccignone (Italy)
Patrick Bouthemy (France)
Alberto Broggi (Italy)
Luc Brun (France)
Horst Bunke (Switzerland)
Paola Campadelli (Italy)
Aurélio Campilho (Portugal)
Luigi Cinque (Italy)
Isaac Cohen (USA)
Carlo Colombo (Italy)
Luciano da Fontoura Costa (Brazil)
Rita Cucchiara (Italy)
Leila De Floriani (Italy)
Massimo De Santo (Italy)

Luigi Di Stefano (Italy)
Floriana Esposito (Italy)
Mario Ferraro (Italy)
Francesc J. Ferri (Spain)
Robert Fisher (UK)
Gianluca Foresti (Italy)
Ana Fred (Portugal)
Andrea Fusiello (Italy)
Giovanni Gallo (Italy)
Giovanni Garibotto (Italy)
Giorgio Giacinto (Italy)
Georgy Gimel'farb (New Zealand)
Concettina Guerra (Italy)
Edwin R. Hancock (UK)
Tin K. Ho (USA)
Anil K. Jain (USA)
Xiaoyi Jiang (Germany)
Jean-Michel Jolion (France)

Graeme A. Jones (UK)
Josef Kittler (UK)
Walter Kropatsch (Austria)
Josep Lladós (Spain)
Luca Lombardi (Italy)
Brian C. Lovell (Australia)
Giuseppe Maino (Italy)
Stephen Maybank (UK)
Gerard Medioni (USA)
Stefano Messelodi (Italy)
Vittorio Murino (Italy)
Hirobumi Nishida (Japan)
Jean-Marc Ogier (France)
Marcello Pelillo (Italy)
Gennaro Percannella (Italy)
Fernando Pereira (Portugal)
Petra Perner (Germany)
Nicolai Petkov (The Netherlands)
Alfredo Petrosino (Italy)
Massimo Piccardi (Italy)

Matti Pietikainen (Finland)
Roberto Pirrone (Italy)
Carlo Regazzoni (Italy)
Vito Roberto (Italy)
Fabio Roli (Italy)
Arun Ross (USA)
Hideo Saito (Japan)
Raimondo Schettini (Italy)
Oliver Schreer (Germany)
Stefano Soatto (USA)
Pierre Soille (EU)
Guido Tascini (Italy)
Massimo Tistarelli (Italy)
Genoveffa Tortora (Italy)
Francesco Tortorella (Italy)
Alessandro Verri (Italy)
Marcel Worring (The Netherlands)
Yehezkel Yeshurun (Israel)

Local Organizing Committee

Donatello Conte   University of Salerno, Italy
Gennaro Percannella University of Salerno, Italy

Organized by

Dept. of Electrical and Information Engineering of the University of Salerno
GIRPR, the Italian group of researchers affiliated to the IAPR

Endorsed by

International Association for Pattern Recognition

Supported by

University of Salerno
Dept. of Electrical and Information Engineering of the University of Salerno
Citel Group S.r.l.
Nexera S.r.l.

Additional Reviewers

Davide Ariu
Nicole Artner
George Azzopardi
Lamberto Ballan
Sebastiano Battiato
Loris Bazzani
Luca Bianchi
Manuele Bicego
Battista Biggio
Samuel Rota Bulò
Vincenzo Cannella
Marco La Cascia
Elena Casiraghi
Umberto Castellani
Paul Chippendale
Anustup Choudhury
Andrea Colombari
Donatello Conte
Igino Corona
Marco Cristani
Luca Didaci
Nicola Di Mauro
Fabrizio Dini
Piercarlo Dondi
Aykut Erdem
Michela Farenzena
Giovanni Maria Farinella
Stefano Ferilli
Andreas Fischer
Fernando Franco
Volkmar Frinken

Maria Frucci
Giorgio Fumera
Orazio Gambino
Riccardo Gatti
Riccardo Gherardi
Ioannis Giotis
Thien M. Ha
Josh Harguess
Yll Haxhimusa
Changbo Hu
Adrian Ion
Charles Kervrann
Oswald Lanz
Alessandro Lanza
Michela Lecca
François Le Coat
Giuseppe Lipori
Luca Lombardi
Mario Molinara
Donato Malerba
Eric Marchand
Gian Luca Marcialis
Claudio Marrocco
Samuele Martelli
Alessandro Martinelli
Stefano Mattoccia
Giuseppe Mazzola
Etienne Mémin
Simone Merlini
Carla Maria Modena
Davide Moschini

Daniele Muntoni
Piero Mussio
Esther Antunez Ortiz
Giuseppe Papari
Patrick Perez
Alessandro Perina
Federico Pernici
Ignazio Pillai
Luca Piras
Marco Porta
Stella Pratissoli
Giovanni Puglisi
Pedro Quelhas
Giuliana Ramella
Ajita Rattani
Elisa Ricci
Kaspar Riesen
Christophe Rosenberger
Giuseppe Russo
Samuele Salti
Enver Sangineto
Lorenzo Seidenari
Giuseppe Serra
Jorge Silva
Christine Solnon
Roberto Toldo
Federico Tombari
Diego Tosato
Roberto Tronci
Michele Zanin

Table of Contents

2D and 3D Segmentation

Feature Extraction and Image Analysis

Object Detection and Recognition

Video Analysis and Processing

Pattern Analysis and Classification

Learning

Graphs and Trees

Applications

Shape Analysis

Face Analysis

Medical Imaging

Image Analysis and Pattern Recognition

Learning with Missing or Incomplete Data

Bogdan Gabrys

Smart Technology Research Centre
Computational Intelligence Research Group
Bournemouth University
bgabrys@bournemouth.ac.uk

Abstract. The problem of learning with missing or incomplete data has received a lot of attention in the literature [6,10,13,21,23]. The reasons for missing data can be multi-fold ranging from sensor failures in engineering applications to deliberate withholding of some information in medical questioners in the case of missing input feature values or lack of solved (labelled) cases required in supervised learning algorithms in the case of missing labels. And though such problems are very interesting from the practical and theoretical point of view, there are very few pattern recognition techniques which can deal with missing values in a straightforward and efficient manner. It is in a sharp contrast to the very efficient way in which humans deal with unknown data and are able to perform various pattern recognition tasks given only a subset of input features or few labelled reference cases.

In the context of pattern recognition or classification systems the problem of missing labels and the problem of missing features are very often treated separately.

The availability or otherwise of labels determines the type of the learning algorithm that can be used and has led to the well known split into supervised, unsupervised or more recently introduced hybrid/semi-supervised classes of learning algorithms.

Commonly, using supervised learning algorithms enables designing of robust and well performing classifiers. Unfortunately, in many real world applications labelling of the data is costly and thus possible only to some extent. Unlabelled data on the other hand is often available in large quantities but a classifier built using unsupervised learning is likely to demonstrate performance inferior to its supervised counterpart. The interest in a mixed supervised and unsupervised learning is thus a natural consequence of this state of things and various approaches have been discussed in the literature [2,5,10,12,14,15,18,19]. Our experimental results have shown [10] that when supported by unlabelled samples much less labelled data is generally required to build a classifier without compromising the classification performance. If only a very limited amount of labelled data is available the results based on random selection of labelled samples show high variability and the performance of the final classifier is more dependent on how reliable the labelled data samples are rather than use of additional unlabelled data. This points to a very interesting discussion point related to the issue of the trade-off between the information content in the observed data (in this case

P. Foggia, C. Sansone, and M. Vento (Eds.): ICIAP 2009, LNCS 5716, pp. 1–4, 2009.

available labels) versus the impact that can be achieved by employing sophisticated data processing algorithms which we will also revisit when discussing approaches dealing with missing feature values.

There are many ways of dealing with missing feature values though the most commonly used approaches can be found in the statistics literature. The ideas behind them and various types of missingness introduced in [20] are still in use today and the multiple imputation method is considered as state of the art alongside the Expectation Maximization (EM) algorithm [6,11,23,24]. In general the missing value imputation methods are the prevalent way of coping with missing data. However, as it has been pointed out in many papers [1,11,16,17,24] such a repaired data set may no longer be a good representation of the problem at hand and quite often leads to the solutions that are far from optimal.

In our previous work on the subject of learning on the basis of deficient data we have advocated a different, unified approach to both learning from a mixture of labelled and unlabelled data as well as robust approaches to using data with missing features without a need for imputation of missing values.

We argue that once the missing data has been replaced it can potentially result in overconfident decisions not supported by the discriminative characteristics of the observed variables and a different approach is needed.

One of the examples of such an approach not requiring imputation of missing values is based on hyperbox fuzzy sets and was presented in [8]. The General Fuzzy Min-Max (GFMM) algorithms for clustering and classification naturally support incomplete datasets, exploiting all available information in order to reduce a number of viable alternatives before making the classification decision. The GFMM algorithm is also able to learn from mixed supervised and unsupervised data, iteratively [9] or in an agglomerative manner [7] processing both types of patterns for adaptation and labelling of the fuzzy hyperboxes, thus falling into the semi-supervised category. The networks also posses the ability to quantify the uncertainty caused by missing data.

Such philosophy of dealing with both unlabelled and missing input data within a consistent, unified framework has also been pursued in our more recent work utilising the physical field based classifier, electrostatic charge analogy and a metaphor of data samples treated as charged particles which will be used here as the second example [3,4,22].

A number of simulation results for well-known data sets are provided in order to illustrate the properties and performance of the discussed approaches as well as facilitate the discussion.

References

1. Berthold, M.R., Huber, K.-P.: Missing values and learning of fuzzy rules. International Journal of Uncertainty, Fuzziness and Knowledge-Based Systems 6(2), 171–178 (1998)
2. Blum, A., Mitchell, T.: Combining labeled and unlabeled data with co-training. In: Proceedings of the eleventh annual conference on Computational learning theory, pp. 92–100. ACM, New York (1998)

3. Budka, M., Gabrys, B.: Electrostatic Field Classifier for Deficient Data. In: The sixth International Conference on Computer Recognition Systems, Jelenia Góra, Poland, May 25-28 (2009a)
4. Budka, M., Gabrys, B.: Mixed supervised and unsupervised learning from incomplete data using a physical field model. Natural Computing (submitted, 2009)
5. Dara, R., Kremer, S., Stacey, D.: Clustering unlabeled data with SOMs improves classification of labeled real-world data. In: Proceedings of the World Congress on Computational Intelligence, WCCI (2002)
6. Dempster, A., Laird, N., Rubin, D.: Maximum Likelihood from Incomplete Data via the EM Algorithm. Journal of the Royal Statistical Society. Series B (Methodological) 39(1), 1–38 (1977)
7. Gabrys, B.: Agglomerative Learning Algorithms for General Fuzzy Min-Max Neural Network. The Journal of VLSI Signal Processing 32(1), 67–82 (2002)
8. Gabrys, B.: Neuro-fuzzy approach to processing inputs with missing values in pattern recognition problems. International Journal of Approximate Reasoning 30(3), 149–179 (2002)
9. Gabrys, B., Bargiela, A.: General fuzzy min-max neural network for clustering and classification. IEEE Transactions on Neural Networks 11(3), 769–783 (2000)
10. Gabrys, B., Petrakieva, L.: Combining labelled and unlabelled data in the design of pattern classification systems. International Journal of Approximate Reasoning 35(3), 251–273 (2004)
11. Ghahramani, Z., Jordan, M.: Supervised learning from incomplete data via an EM approach. In: Cowan, J.D., Tesauro, G., Alspector, J. (eds.) Advances in Neural Information Processing Systems, vol. 6, pp. 120–127 (1994)
12. Goldman, S., Zhou, Y.: Enhancing supervised learning with unlabeled data. In: Proceedings of ICML (1998)
13. Graham, J., Cumsille, P., Elek-Fisk, E.: Methods for handling missing data. Handbook of psychology 2, 87–114 (2003)
14. Kothari, R., Jain, V.: Learning from labeled and unlabeled data. In: Proceedings of the 2002 International Joint Conference on Neural Networks, 2002. IJCNN 2002, vol. 3 (2002); Loss, D., Di Vincenzo, D.: Quantum computation with quantum dots. Physical Review A 57 (1), 120–126 (1998)
15. Mitchell, T.: The role of unlabeled data in supervised learning. In: Proceedings of the Sixth International Colloquium on Cognitive Science (1999)
16. Nauck, D., Kruse, R.: Learning in neuro-fuzzy systems with symbolic attributes and missing values. In: Proceedings of the International Conference on Neural Information Processing – ICONIP 1999, Perth, pp. 142–147 (1999)
17. Nijman, M.J., Kappen, H.J.: Symmetry breaking and training from incomplete data with radial basis Boltzmann machines. International Journal of Neural Systems 8(3), 301–315 (1997)
18. Nigam, K., Ghani, R.: Understanding the behavior of co-training. In: Proceedings of KDD 2000 Workshop on Text Mining (2000)
19. Pedrycz, W., Waletzky, J.: Fuzzy clustering with partial supervision. IEEE Transactions on Systems, Man, and Cybernetics, Part B 27(5), 787–795 (1997)
20. Rubin, D.: Inference and missing data. Biometrika 63(3), 581–592 (1976)
21. Rubin, D.: Multiple Imputation for Nonresponse in Surveys. Wiley-Interscience, Hoboken (1987)

22. Ruta, D., Gabrys, B.: A Framework for Machine Learning based on Dynamic Phys-
    ical Fields. Natural Computing Journal on Nature-inspired Learning and Adaptive
    Systems 8(2), 219–237 (2009)
23. Schafer, J., Graham, J.: Missing data: Our view of the state of the art. Psychological
    Methods 7(2), 147–177 (2002)
24. Tresp, V., Ahmad, S., Neuneier, R.: Training neural networks with deficient data.
    Advances in Neural Information Processing Systems 6, 128–135 (1994)

Image Analysis and Machine Learning: How to Foster a Stronger Connection?

Stan Matwin

School of Information Technology and Engineering (SITE)
University of Ottawa, Canada
stan@site.uottawa.ca

Abstract. In this talk I am trying to answer the question stated in its title. I discuss some of the challenges encountered in the use of Machine Learning in image analysis, including examples from our own work. In particular, I look at examples of successful recent research that uses advanced Machine Learning for specific image analysis tasks. I try to generalize lessons learned from this successful research. I argue that some of the reasons for these successes are consistent with the current research trends in Machine Learning. These new approaches resolve some of the difficulties encountered in the past between the two fields, e.g. in the area of feature selection. I look further at some of the recent research trends in Machine Learning (e.g. Active Learning), which might be interesting in image analysis and processing. I also speculate that the new research in cognitive neuroscience might provide interesting cues to Artificial Intelligence in general, and to Computer Vision and image analysis in particular.

P. Foggia, C. Sansone, and M. Vento (Eds.): ICIAP 2009, LNCS 5716, p. 5, 2009.
© Springer-Verlag Berlin Heidelberg 2009

Computer Analysis of Lighting in Realist Master Art:
Current Methods and Future Challenges

David G. Stork

Ricoh Innovations, 2882 Sand Hill Road, Menlo Park CA 94025, USA
and Department of Statistics, Stanford University, Stanford CA 94305, USA
artanalyst@gmail.com

Abstract. We review several computer based techniques for analyzing the lighting in images that have proven valuable when addressing questions in the history and interpretation of realist art. These techniques fall into two general classes: model independent (where one makes no assumption about the three-dimensional shape of the rendered objects) and model dependent (where one does make some assumptions about their three-dimensional shape). An additiona, statistical algorithm integrates the estimates of lighting position or direction produced by different such techniques. We conclude by discussing several outstanding problems and future directions in the analysis of lighting in realist art.

Keywords: computer vision, computer image analysis of art, occluding contour algorithm, cast shadow analysis, computer graphics constructions, *tableau virtuel*.

1   Introduction

In the past several years, algorithms from computer vision and image analysis have been extended and applied to an ever widening range of questions in the history of art. These algorithms have been applied to challenges in low-level imaging (to enhance the visibility of hidden or degraded passages, to predict the effects of conservatorial treatment of artworks, to identify pigments by spectral signature, to rejuvenate appearance by digitally reversing the fading of pigments, ...), stroke and mark analysis (to infer the marking tool, to date intaglio prints as the master wears, to identify the number of artists's "hands" in a given work, ...), perspective analysis (to reveal perspectival inaccuracies to test for artists' use of optical aids, ...), contour shape analysis (to test fidelity of art copies, ...), composition analysis (to infer compositional principles and detect forgeries, ...), computer graphics reconstructions (to infer sight lines, infer artists' studio practice, ...).

Another, important, general class of problems involve estimating the position or direction of illumination based on the image information in a painting, the class we consider here. Finding the direction or position of an illuminant can

P. Foggia, C. Sansone, and M. Vento (Eds.): ICIAP 2009, LNCS 5716, pp. 6–11, 2009.

help answer a number of problems in the history of art. For example, Johnson, Stork, Biswas and Furuichi estimated the direction of illumination in Jan Vermeer's *Girl with a pearl earring* using six semi-independent methods.[1] The excellent agreement among these estimates very strongly implies that Vermeer had an actual figure in his studio rather than worked from memory or created and ideal "fictive" figure. Stork and colleagues used several methods to estimate the location of the illuminant in Georges de la Tour's *Christ in the carpenter's studio* to test the claim that this painting was executed using optically projected images.[2,3,4,5] In those works, the illuminant could be assumed a point source, or fairly distant from the objects in question. Stork and Johnson extended the algorithms to the case of diffuse illumination, and tested paintings by the contemporary realist Garth Herrick, specifically *Apotheon* and *Human on my faithless arm* to reveal the painterly analogy of "compositing," here working from two photographic referents having different lighting conditions.[6]

Here we summarize some of the techniques and how they have addressed problems in the history of art.

The two general classes of methods are: model independent methods (where one makes no assumptions about the three-dimensional shape of the depicted objects) and model dependent methods (where one does make assumptions about the three-dimensional shape). We review these in Sects. 2 and 3, respectively, then turn in Sect. 4 to statistical and computational methods for integrating estimates from disparate information sources. We list some outstanding problems and future directions in Sect. 5.

2   Model Independent Methods

In model independent algorithms, one does not need to know or assume the three-dimensional shape of the depicted objects. All the visual information necessary for the algorithm can be extracted directly from the two-dimensional image itself. One may need to make assumptions or have other knowledge, for instance that the objects are of uniform albedo or reflectivity—but not assumptions about the shape.

2.1   Cast Shadow Analysis

The simplest technique for determining the direction of point-source illumination in the plane perpendicular to the light of sight is cast-shadow analysis. One merely identifies a point on an occluder, such as a tip of a nose or a finger, and its corresponding point on the cast shadow, draw a line linking them. This line, extended, should go through the two-dimensional location of the point-source illuminant.[7,2]

2.2   Occluding Contour Analysis

The occluding contour algorithm takes as input the measured lightness along the outer boundary or occluding contour of a three-dimensional object, and returns the direction to the illumination that best explains (in a least-square sense) this pattern. The algorithm can be applied only to contours of Lambertian surfaces (diffusely reflecting like cloth or skin, not shiny like glass or metal), and where the surface is of uniform albedo or reflectivity. Moreover, the contours must be convex and fairly far from other objects to avoid scattered light.[8]

Stork and Johnson pioneered the use of this algorithm in the study of art, showing that the illumination in the tableau in Georges de la Tour's *Christ in the carpenter's studio* came from the depicted candle, not (as had been claimed) from outside the picture, or from "in place of the other figure."[7,9] Johnson et al. applied the algorithm to Jan Vermeer's *Girl with a pearl earring* and found the direction to the illumination determined by this algorithm matched quite closely the directions estimated by several other methods.[1] This was an objective testament to both the power of these lighting estimation methods, but also to Vermeer's mastery in rendering the effects of light.

While the above work assumed, with great justification, that the light source was distance or a point source, most paintings depict scenes in which the tableau is illuminated by complex illumination. As such, Stork and Johnson extended the algorithms to this more complicated case, where the incident light could be represented as a series of five spherical harmonics. They used this representation to test paintings by Garth Herrick for consistency in lighting on different figures. The algorithm could indeed reveal that different figures had been rendered under different illumination conditions.[6] This technique might be applicable to other realist works, for instance Renaissance portraits containing multiple figures, where art historians are unsure how many artists—"hands"—executed the work.

3   Model Dependent Methods

As mentioned above, in model dependent algorithms, one knows or assumes the three-dimensional shape of the depicted objects. Sometimes the models are simple—as in a sphere or eyeball. Other times they can be quite complex—as in a full three-dimensional computer graphics model.

3.1   Specular Reflection

Specular reflections, such as the highlights on eyes, can be used to infer the direction of illumination. Johnson et al. used the highlights on the eyes in Jan Vermeer's *Girl with a pearl earring* to infer the direction of illumination.[1] They found this direction matched quite well the directions estimated from several other model and model independent methods.

3.2   Diffuse Reflection from Plane Surfaces

Yet another method for inferring the position of the illuminant is based on the pattern of lightness on planar surfaces, for instance a floor or wall. Stork and Kale derived the equations for the appearance model of a planar Lambertian surface (such as the floor inGeorges de la Tour's *Christ in the carpenter's studio* and used it to estimate the position of a point source consistent with the pattern of lightness found on the floor.[5,10] Although the results here were not as definitive as other methods in this painting, the results supported the claim that the light was in place of the candle rather than in place of the other figures.

3.3   Computer Graphics Rendering

Although computer graphics reconstructions have been used for exploring geometry, perspective, sight lines, and so on, these techniques have also been used to explore studio lighting conditions. Johnson et al. built a computer graphics model of *Girl with a pearl earring*,[1] Stork and Furuichi built a model of *Christ in the carpenter's studio*, Stork explored a model of Caravaggio's *Calling of St. Matthew*,[11] and finally Stork and Furuichi built a model of Diego Velàzquez's *Las meninas*.[12] In all these cases, the experimenters could adjust the location of virtual illuminants in the model (or *tableau virtuel*) until the rendered image matched the corresponding painting as closely as possible. In this way, these scholars could answer questions about studio practice, for instance whether some artists secretly traced optically projected images.

3.4   Shape from Shading

Johnson et al. exploited shape-from-shading methods to infer the direction of illumination in Vermeer's *Girl with a pearl earring*.[1] Because they did not have an accurate three-dimensional model of the girl's face, they adjusted a *generic* three-dimensional face model to match that of the girl. They temporarily assumed this was the actual model, and then inferred the direction of illumination that, for this model, best fit the measured lightness in the painting. This gave an initial estimate to the direction of illumination.

This iterative scheme is an example of the expectation-maximization (EM) algorithm, or more specifically the generalized expectation maximization (GEM) algorithm.[13] The direction they found closely matched that found using other lighting estimation methods, a testament to Vermeer's mastery in rendering the effects of light, and further corroboration that there was almost surely an actual model in his studio.

4   Integration of Lighting Estimates

Given several estimates of the direction or location of an illuminant, the problem arises how to integrate them to a single estimate. The principled, statistical method is Bayesian integration,[13] where here (under very reasonable assumptions) the integration is computed by:

$$p(\mathbf{x}|\mathbf{\Theta}) \propto \prod_i^k P_i p(\mathbf{x}|\theta_i). \tag{1}$$

That is, the probability density that the point illuminant is in spatial location
x given all the estimates, Θ, is proportional to the product of the densities
from each individual estimates, $p(\mathbf{x}|\theta_i)$, multiplied by their prior probabilities
or confidences, P_i. This method has been used to integrate estimates in de la
Tour's *Christ in the carpenter's studio*.[7]

5   Conclusions and Future Directions

There are a number of outstanding computational problems that must be solved
so as to extend the power of these methods and extend their applicability to a
wider range of artworks and problems in the history of art. The first is to get a
better estimate of the errors of each of the techniques when applied to a given
work. Some of the methods, such as the occluding contour algorithm and cast
shadow analysis, yield estimates of one spatial angle, perpendicular to the viewer's
(and artist's) line of sight, while others, such as shape-from-shading and computer
graphics modelling, yield estimates in two spatial angles. We need rigorous and
principled methods for integrating such estimates, particularly with their errors.
An intriguing problem is to generalize the occluding contour based methods in diffuse lighting environments to the case of multiple *colored* illuminants, for instance
an orange candle and blue sky flowing through a window.

This work in lighting in art is part of a broader research effort that is leading
to new techniques and shedding new light on art and art praxis.[14,15]

Acknowledgments

The author gratefully acknowledges insights provided by numerous scientists,
conservators, and historians of optics and art, as well as by anonymous reviewers,
and would also like to thank the Getty Research Institute, Santa Monica CA,
for extended reader's privileges in its superb research library.

References

1. Johnson, M.K., Stork, D.G., Biswas, S., Furuichi, Y.: Inferring illumination direction estimated from disparate sources in paintings: An investigation into Jan Vermeer's Girl with a pearl earring. In: Stork, D.G., Coddington, J. (eds.) Computer
   image analysis in the study of art, vol. 6810. SPIE/IS&T, Bellingham, 68100I–1–12
   (2008)
2. Stork, D.G.: Did Georges de la Tour use optical projections while painting Christ in
   the carpenter's studio? In: Said, A., Apolstolopoulos, J.G. (eds.) SPIE Electronic
   Imaging: Image and video communications and processing, vol. 5685, pp. 214–219.
   SPIE, Bellingham (2005)
3. Stork, D.G.: Locating illumination sources from lighting on planar surfaces in paintings: An application to Georges de la Tour and Caravaggio. In: Optical Society of
   American Annual Meeting, Rochester, NY, OSA (2008) (abstract)

4. Stork, D.G., Furuichi, Y.: Image analysis of paintings by computer graphics synthesis: An investigation of the illumination in Georges de la Tour's Christ in the carpenter's studio. In: Stork, D.G., Coddington, J. (eds.) Computer image analysis in the study of art, vol. 6810. SPIE/IS&T, Bellingham, 68100J–1–12 (2008)

5. Stork, D.G.: Locating illumination sources from lighting on planar surfaces in paintings: An application to Georges de la Tour and Caravaggio. In: Optical Society of American Annual Meeting, Rochester, NY, Optical Society of America (2008)

6. Stork, D.G., Johnson, M.K.: Lighting analysis of diffusely illuminated tabeaus in realist paintings: An application to detecting 'compositing' in the portraits of Garth Herrick. In: Delp III, E.J., Dittmann, J., Memon, N.D., Wong, P.W. (eds.) Electronic Imaging: Media forensics and security XI, vol. 7254. SPIE/IS&T, Bellingham, 72540L1–8 (2009)

7. Stork, D.G., Johnson, M.K.: Estimating the location of illuminants in realist master paintings: Computer image analysis addresses a debate in art history of the Baroque. In: Proceedings of the 18th International Conference on Pattern Recognition, Hong Kong, vol. I, pp. 255–258. IEEE Press, Los Alamitos (2006)

8. Nillius, P., Eklundh, J.-O.: Automatic estimation of the projected light source direction. In: IEEE Conference on Computer Vision and Pattern Recognition (CVPR 2001), vol. 1, pp. 1076–1083 (2001)

9. Stork, D.G., Johnson, M.K.: Computer vision, image analysis and master art, Part II. IEEE Multimedia 14(3), 12–17 (2006)

10. Kale, D., Stork, D.G.: Estimating the position of illuminants in paintings under weak model assumptions: An application to the works of two Baroque masters. In: Rogowitz, B.E., Pappas, T.N. (eds.) Electronic Imaging: Human vision and electronic imaging XIV, vol. 7240. SPIE/IS&T, Bellingham, 72401M1–12 (2009)

11. Stork, D.G.: New insights into Caravaggio's studio methods: Revelations from computer vision and computer graphics modeling. Renaissance Society of American Annual Meeting Los Angeles, CA, p. 102 (2009) (abstract)

12. Stork, D.G., Furuichi, Y.: Computer graphics synthesis for interring artist studio practice: An application to Diego Velázquez's Las meninas. In: McDowall, I.E., Dolinsky, M. (eds.) Electronic imaging: The engineering reality of virtual reality, vol. 7238. SPIE/IS&T, Bellingham, 7238061–9 (2009)

13. Duda, R.O., Hart, P.E., Stork, D.G.: Pattern classification, 2nd edn. John Wiley and Sons, New York (2001)

14. Stork, D.G., Coddington, J. (eds.): Computer image analysis in the study of art, vol. 6810. SPIE/IS&T, Bellingham (2008)

15. Stork, D.G., Coddington, J., Bentkowska-Kafel, A. (eds.): Computer vision and image analysis of art. SPIE/IS&T, Bellingham (forthcoming, 2010)

First International Fingerprint Liveness Detection Competition—LivDet 2009[*]

Gian Luca Marcialis[1], Aaron Lewicke[2], Bozhao Tan[2], Pietro Coli[1],
Dominic Grimberg[2], Alberto Congiu[1], Alessandra Tidu[1], Fabio Roli[1],
and Stephanie Schuckers[2]

[1] University of Cagliari - Department of Electrical and Electronic Engineering – Italy
{marcialis,roli,pietro.coli}@diee.unica.it
[2] Clarkson University - Department of Electrical and Computer Engineering – USA
{lewickat,tanb,sschucke}@clarkson.edu

Abstract. Fingerprint recognition systems are vulnerable to artificial spoof fingerprint attacks, like molds made of silicone, gelatin or Play-Doh. "Liveness detection", which is to detect vitality information from the biometric signature itself, has been proposed to defeat these kinds of spoof attacks. The goal for the LivDet 2009 competition is to compare different methodologies for software-based fingerprint liveness detection with a common experimental protocol and large dataset of spoof and live images. This competition is open to all academic and industrial institutions which have a solution for software-based fingerprint vitality detection problem. Four submissions resulted in successful completion: Dermalog, ATVS, and two anonymous participants (one industrial and one academic). Each participant submitted an algorithm as a Win32 console application. The performance was evaluated for three datasets, from three different optical scanners, each with over 1500 images of "fake" and over 1500 images of "live" fingerprints. The best results were from the algorithm submitted by Dermalog with a performance of 2.7% FRR and 2.8% FAR for the Identix (L-1) dataset. The competition goal is to become a reference event for academic and industrial research in software-based fingerprint liveness detection and to raise the visibility of this important research area in order to decrease risk of fingerprint systems to spoof attacks.

Keywords: Fingerprint, biometrics, spoofing, liveness detection, anti-spoofing protection, security.

1 Introduction

The widespread use of personal verification systems based on fingerprints has shown security vulnerabilities. Among the others, it is well-known that a fingerprint verification system can be deceived by submitting artificial reproductions of fingerprints

---

[*] LivDet 2009 Group is constituted by several Ph.D and under graduate students which con-tributed to the data set collection and LivDet09 web site managing (http://prag.diee.unica.it/ LivDet09).

P. Foggia, C. Sansone, and M. Vento (Eds.): ICIAP 2009, LNCS 5716, pp. 12–23, 2009.
© Springer-Verlag Berlin Heidelberg 2009

made up of silicon or gelatin to the electronic capture device. These images are then processed as "true" fingerprints.

A suggested solution to combat the use of artificial fingers in fingerprint verification is known as "liveness detection". In this, a standard verification system is coupled with additional hardware or software modules aimed to certify the authenticity of the submitted fingerprints. Whilst the hardware-based solution are the most expensive, the software-based ones attempt to measure liveness from characteristics of images themselves by simply integrating image processing algorithms. The problem of liveness detection is treated as a two-class classification problem (live or fake). An appropriate classifier is designed in order to extract the probability of the image vitality given the extracted set of features.

In order to assess the main achievements of the state of the art in fingerprint liveness detection, the Department of Electrical and Electronic Engineering of the University of Cagliari, in cooperation with the Department of Electrical and Computer Engineering of the Clarkson University, is proud to announce the first edition of the Fingerprint Liveness Detection Competition 2009 (LivDet 2009), which is held in the context of 15th International Conference on Image Analysis and Processing (ICIAP 2009). LivDet 2009 is open to all academic and industrial institutions which have a solution for software-based fingerprint vitality detection problem.

The goal of the competition is to compare different methodologies for software-based fingerprint liveness detection with a common experimental protocol and data set. As a reference event for academic and industrial research, the competition will raise the visibility of this important research area. The competition is not defined as an official system for quality certification of the proposed solutions, but rather, it hopes to impact the state of the art in this crucial field—security in biometric systems.

Each participant has been invited to submit its algorithm in a Win32 console application. The performance has been evaluated by utilizing a very large data set of "fake" and "live" fingerprint images captured with three different optical scanners. The performance rank has been compiled and the "best" algorithm has won the "Best Fingerprint Liveness Detection Algorithm Award" at ICIAP 2009. A Special Session of ICIAP 2009 has been devoted to present and discuss the experimental results.

In this paper, we summarize the competition characteristics and the final results achieved from the algorithms submitted by participants. Section 2 describes the problem of fingerprint spoofing. Section 3 is devoted to the competition results. Section 4 concludes the paper with some discussions on reported results. An appendix has been added after references in order to describe algorithms submitted by participants.

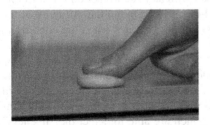

Fig. 1. Consensual method - the person puts his finger on a soft material

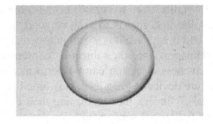

Fig. 2. Consensual method. The negative impression.

2 Background

The duplication of a fingerprint (also named "fingerprint spoofing") has remote origin from science fiction novels of the beginning of the twentieth century. In these last years this question is the focal point of numerous research groups, both academic and industrial. The first spoofing studies date back to 2000 and 2002 [1-2]. These works showed the possibility of the fingerprint reproduction and the defrauding of a biometric system. The steps to create spoof images are as follows: (1) The user puts his finger on a soft material to form the mold (Play Doh, dental impression material, plaster, etc.), see Figure 1. The negative impression of the fingerprint is fixed on the surface. (2) Silicone liquid or another similar material (wax, gelatin, etc) is poured in the mold or pressed in the mold (e.g., Play Doh), see Figure 2. When the liquid is hardened the spoof is formed, see Figure 3. This is the process was used to collect images from silicon, gelatin, and Play-Doh for the competition dataset.

Fig. 3. Consensual method - the stamp with the reproduction of the pattern

It is also possible to create fingerprint spoofs without cooperation with a latent print left by an unintentional user. The latent print is enhanced, photographed and printed in negative on a transparency. A mold is created by etching a printed circuit board and the spoof is formed by dripping a liquid (e.g., silicon, gelatine or wax) on the board.

When faced with this threat, a biometric device must decide if the finger on the acquisition sensors is from the authorized user present at the time of capture. In other words, the recognition process must be upgraded with an added function for detecting the "vitality" (or "liveness") of the submitted biometric. Due to the difficulty of the task, the first goal is to achieve good "liveness" detection rates when the consensual method is applied. It is worth noting that this method results in the best quality replica and images, since the subject is "consensual".

Liveness detection can be performed by adding some additional hardware to the capture device (e.g. for checking blood pressure, or heartbeat, which are not present in a "fake" finger), thus increasing their cost. Another solution is to integrate into standard fingerprint sensors additional algorithms which are able to detect the "liveness" degree from the captured image. They are so-called "software-based" approaches.

For software-based liveness, the question is: Are there biometric "liveness" measurements which can be extracted from captured images? Software-based liveness is the topic of this competition.

Several algorithms for detecting fingerprint liveness have been proposed [3-5], but the main problem is to understand how these algorithms may impact a fingerprint verification system when integrated. In particular, the objective of this competition is to evaluate various approaches' performance by a shared and well-defined experimental protocol, in order to assess the state of the art in the field on a common database.

3 Experimental Protocol and Evaluation

Due to the wide variety of current liveness detection algorithms, the competition defines some constraints for the submitted algorithms:

1) Methods must output, for each image, a "liveness degree" ranging from 0 to 100 (e.g. posterior probability of "true" class).
2) A training set of fake and live fingerprint images will be made available to each participant, freely downloadable from the LivDet site after the participant registration. These images are a subset (25%) of the entire data set.
3) Each submitted algorithm, as a Win32 console application, must follow the input and output sequence required.
4) Each submitted algorithm is tested using a withheld dataset that is the remaining 75% of the entire data set.

3.1 Participants

The competition is open to academic and industrial institutions. Each user receives, after his registration and information about the competition rules, a password to enter into the site and managing his personal information and uploaded files. In order to finalize the registration, it is necessary to submit a license agreement of the data set use. The filled and signed agreement is sent through fax and by mail. Once a signed consent form is obtained, a link for downloading the training set is given. Each participant gives their preference on whether to enter as anonymous. All results will be included in the final report. Results published at LivDet 2009 cannot be used for commercial purposes. The goal of the competition is merely to establish a baseline of the state-of-the-art.

3.2 Data Set

The data set for the final evaluation is constituted of three sub-sets, which contain live and fake fingerprint images from three different optical sensors. Table 1 lists the scanners we used for data collection and the image numbers in the total database.

Images have been collected by a consensual approach, as described in the Background section, using different materials for the artificial reproduction of the fingerprint (gelatin, silicone, play-doh). The downloadable training set is 25% of the above data. At the end of the competition, the entire data set will be made available by signing an appropriate license agreement. Fig. 4 shows example fake fingerprint images from the three optical scanners.

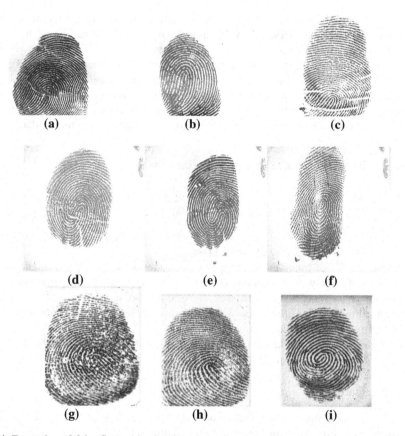

Fig. 4. Examples of fake fingerprint images, from Crossmatch: (a) Play-Doh, (b) gelatin, (c) silicone; from Identix: (d) Play-Doh, (e) gelatin, (f) silicone; from Biometrika: (g)-(i) silicone

Table 1. Fingerprint sensors and data collection for LivDet 2009

DATABASE	Scanners	Model No.	Resolution (dpi)	Image size	Live Samples	Fake Samples
Dataset #1	Crossmatch	Verifier 300 LC	500	480x640	2000	2000
Dataset #2	Identix	DFR2100	686	720x720	1500	1500
Dataset #3	Biometrika	FX2000	569	312x372	2000	2000

3.3 Algorithm Submission

Each submitted algorithm must be a Win32 console application with the following list of parameters:

LIVENESS_XYZ.exe [ndataset] [inputfile] [outputfile]

Each parameter, specified in Table 2, and related to the data set configuration and must be set before submission. Each user can configure his algorithm by the training set available after registration. Only Win32 console applications with the above characteristics will be accepted for the competition. Participants may publish also the source code of their algorithm, but this is not mandatory.

Table 2. Formats of submission requirements

Arguments	Description
LIVENESS_XYZ.exe	It is the executable name, where XYZ is the identification number of the participant. LIVENESS_XYZ.exe Format : Win32 console application (.exe)
[ndataset]	It is the identification number of the data set to analyse. Legend: 1=Crossmatch, 2=Identix, 3=Biometrika
[inputfile]	Txt file with the List of images to analyse. Each image is in RAW format (ASCII)
[outputfile]	Txt file with the output of each processed image, in the same order of inputfile. The output is a posterior probability of the live class given the image, or a degree of "liveness" normalized in the range 0 and 100 (100 is the maximum degree of liveness, 0 means that the image is fake). In the case that the algorithm has not been able to process the image, the correspondent output must be -1000 (failure to enroll).

3.4 Performance Evaluation

The parameters adopted for the performance evaluation will be the following:

Evaluation per sensor

- $Frej\_n$: Rate of failure to enroll for the sub-set n.
- $Fcorrlive\_n$: Rate of correctly classified live fingerprints for sub-set n.
- $Fcorrfake\_n$: Rate of correctly classified fake fingerprints for sub-set n.
- $Ferrlive\_n$: Rate of misclassified live fingerprints for sub-set n.
- $Ferrfake\_n$: Rate of misclassified fake fingerprints for sub-set n.
- ET: Average processing time per image
- MAM: Max. Allocated Memory while the algorithm is running.

Overall evaluation

- $Frej$: Rate of failure to enroll.
- $Fcorrlive$: Rate of correctly classified live fingerprints.

- *Fcorrfake_n*: Rate of correctly classified fake fingerprints.
- *Ferrlive_n*: Rate of misclassified live fingerprints.
- *Ferrfake_n*: Rate of misclassified fake fingerprints.

3.5 Declaration of the Winner

The winner will be awarded by simple averaging the overall classification errors on the three sensors. Only one winner will be awarded. The declaration will be made during the social dinner of ICIAP 2009. A Special Session of ICIAP 2009 will be devoted to present and discuss the performance of the proposed algorithms.

4 Results and Discussion

Four algorithm submissions successfully completed the competition at the time of submission of this paper: Dermalog Identification Systems GmbH (Dermalog), Biometric Recognition Group - ATVS at Universidad Autonoma de Madrid (ATVS), Anonymous (industry) and Anonymous 2 (academic). Details regarding the submitted algorithm from ATVS is given in the Appendix.

The rate of misclassified spoof fingerprints (*Ferrfake_n*) is given in Figure 5 and Table 3 and the rate of misclassified live fingerprints (*Ferrlive_n*) is given in Figure 6 and Table 3. The best results are for Dermalog algorithm on Identix dataset with 2.7% *Ferrlive* and 2.8% *Ferrfake*. Dermalog, ATVS, Anonymous, and Anonymous 2 achieved an average *Ferrfake* of 5.4%, 9%, 16%, and 16.0% respectively. Dermalog, ATVS, and Anonymous achieved an average *Ferrlive* of 20%, 30%, 33%, and 13.2% respectively.

For the majority of the algorithms, the liveness values are clustered around 0 or 100, so changing the threshold has little effect or no effect on *Ferrfake* and *Ferrlive*. Therefore we set the threshold to an arbitrary value of 50 to denote liveness. However, the results given by Anonymous 2 range fairly evenly between 40 and 60 so changing the threshold impacts the results. To determine a reasonable threshold, ROC curves of *Ferrfake* vs *Ferrlive* were generated for each data set for Anonymous 2 algorithm only. From these, thresholds were selected which minimizes both *Ferrfake* and *Ferrlive* simultaneously, resulting in a threshold of 72.9 for Identix, 63.9 for Crossmatch, and 73.9 for Biometrika.

Ferrlive for Biometrica was unexpectedly high for all algorithms. We hypothesize that this is related to the number of distinct live subjects in the training dataset, as well as the fact that the images were collected in a single session where as the other devices were collected over multiple sessions, as seen in Table 4. Both Crossmatch and Identix had over 35 and 63 unique individuals, respectively, in the training set, while Biometrica had only 13. In addition, for Crossmatch and Identix only four images per subject (2 fingers, 2 images) were collected during a single visit, while for Biometrica, all 40 images were collected during one visit. This highlights the importance of including a large number of unique individuals, as well as multiple visits for the

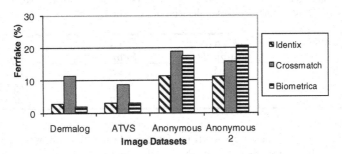

Fig. 5. Rate of misclassified spoof fingerprints (*Ferrfake_n*) for submitted algorithms, (left to right) Dermalog, ATVS, Anonymous, and Anonymous 2, for each of the image sets (Identix, Crossmatch, and Biometrica)

training live images. This creates a training dataset that is representative of the variability of live finger such that a liveness algorithm generalizable to unseen images can be developed.

Table 3. Rate of misclassified live fingerprints (*Ferrlive_n*) and rate of misclassified spoof fingerprints (*Ferrfake_n*) (%) for submitted algorithms (Dermalog, ATVS, Anonymous, Anonymous 2) for each dataset (Identix, Crossmatch, Biometrica), as well as average for each algorithm

Submitted Algorithms	Datasets							
	Identix		**Crossmatch**		**Biometrica**		**Average**	
	Ferrlive	Ferrfake	Ferrlive	Ferrfake	Ferrlive	Ferrfake	Ferrlive	Ferrfake
Dermalog	2.7%	2.8%	7.4%	11.4%	74.1%	1.9%	20.1%	5.4%
ATVS	9.8%	3.1%	8.8%	20.8%	71.7%	3.1%	30.1%	9.0%
Anonymous	15.2%	11.5%	27.1%	18.9%	56.0%	17.6%	32.8%	16.0%
Anonymous2	9.8%	11.3%	14.4%	15.9%	15.6%	20.7%	13.2%	16.0%

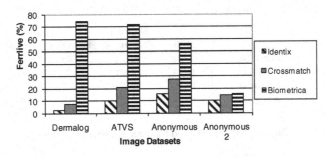

Fig. 6. Rate of misclassified live fingerprints (*Ferrlive_n*) for submitted algorithms, (left to right) Dermalog, ATVS, Anonymous, and Anonymous 2 for each of the image sets (Identix, Crossmatch, and Biometrica)

Table 4. Number of unique subjects in training and tests, as well as the average number of images per subject. It should also be noted that Identix and Crossmatch were collected over multiple visits, while Biometrica was collected during a single visit.

Scanners	# of Training Subjects	# of Testing Subjects	Aver Images / subject
Identix	35	125	18.75
Crossmatch	63	191	15.75
Biometrika	13	37	40.0

Failure to enroll rates are shown in Table 5. Some algorithms utilized this feature, most likely as a quality check. Images that had a failure to enroll were not included in the calculation of *Ferrlive* and *Ferrspoof*.

An alternative method of accounting for failure to enrol is to consider a false reject for a live individual an error; whereas for a spoof image, a failure to enrol would be a successful rejection of a spoof images, i.e., not an error. The overall classification error rates which considers all errors, as well as failure to enroll as described above, are given in Table 6.

Average processing time per image for each algorithm is shown in Table 7. The anonymous algorithm had the shortest processing time with average of 0.07 seconds per image. The algorithms that had longer processing time likely reflected that the algorithms were created in Matlab and compiled as an executable. Anonymous 2 algorithm had run-time problems such that elapsed time could not be estimated.

Table 5. Failure to enroll rates for submitted algorithms

		Data Sets		
		Identix	Crossmatch	Biometrica
Submitted	Dermalog	0.9%	1.1%	0.0%
Algorithms	ATVS	0.0%	0.0%	0.0%
	Anonymous	2.0%	2.2%	1.3%
	Anonymous 2	0.0%	0.0%	0.0%

Table 6. Overall classification error which considers rate of spoof and live classification errors, as well as errors where live images resulted in a failure to enroll

		Datasets			
		Identix	Crossmatch	Biometrica	Average
Submitted	Dermalog	3.6%	10.5%	37.9%	17.3%
Algorithms	ATVS	6.5%	14.8%	71.7%	31.0%
	Anonymous	14.2%	23.7%	37.2%	25.0%
	Anonymous 2	10.5%	15.2%	18.1%	14.6%

Table 7. Average elapsed time per image (in seconds)

Elapsed Time (s)		Data Sets		
		Identix	Crossmatch	Biometrica
Submitted	Anonymous	0.12	0.07	0.07
Algorithms	Dermalog	0.94	0.56	0.28
	ATVS	46.95	50.04	10.24

5 Conclusions

In summary, LivDet 2009 is the first international public competition for software-based fingerprint liveness detection.   Entries were submitted from four participants demonstrating the state-of-the art in fingerprint liveness. Best results achieved ~2.5% error. It is hoped that this first competition of fingerprint liveness detection is followed by a number of competitions such that further improvement in algorithm performance is encouraged. In particular, our expectation is that the proposed experimental protocol, data sets, and algorithm results, may become a standard reference point for the research community, such that increased algorithm performance can be achieved. An effective liveness detection algorithms is a key component to minimize the vulnerability of fingerprint systems to spoof attacks.

Acknowledgements

We would like to thank the funding support from Center for Identification Technology Research (CITeR) for the success of this project.

We also thank the ICIAP 2009 chairs, Mario Vento, Pasquale Foggia and Carlo Sansone, who kindly hosted the competition.

References

1. Ligon, A.: An investigation into the vulnerability of the Siemens id mouse Professional Version 4 (2002), http://www.bromba.com/knowhow/idm4vul.htm
2. Matsumoto, T., Matsumoto, H., Yamada, K., Hoshino, S.: Impact of artificial gummy fingers on fingerprint systems. In: Proceedings of SPIE, vol. 4677, Optical Security and Counterfeit Deterence Techniques IV, Yokohama
3. Tan, B., Schuckers, S.: A new approach for liveness detection in fingerprint scanners based on valley noise analysis. Journal of Electronic Imaging 17, 11009. SPIE (2008)
4. Chen, Y., Jain, A.K., Dass, S.: Fingerprint deformation for spoof detection. In: Biometric Symposium 2005, Cristal City, VA (2005)
5. Coli, P., Marcialis, G.L., Roli, F.: Fingerprint silicon replicas: static and dynamic features for vitality detection using an optical capture device. International Journal of Image and Graphics 8(4), 495–512 (2008)
6. Lim, E., Jiang, X., Yau, W.: Fingerprint quality and validity analysis. In: Proc. International Conference on Image Processing, ICIP, vol. 1, pp. 469–472 (2002)
7. Chen, Y., Dass, S., Jain, A.: Fingerprint quality indices for predicting authentication performance. In: Kanade, T., Jain, A., Ratha, N.K. (eds.) AVBPA 2005. LNCS, vol. 3546, pp. 160–170. Springer, Heidelberg (2005)
8. Chen, T., Jiang, X., Yau, W.: Fingerprint image quality analysis. In: Proc. International Conference on Image Processing, ICIP, vol. 2, pp. 1253–1256 (2004)
9. Hong, L., Wan, Y., Jain, A.: Fingerprint imagen enhancement: Algorithm and performance evaluation. IEEE Trans. on Pattern Analysis and Machine Intelligence 20, 777–789 (1998)

A Appendix: BRG-ATVS Submission to LivDet: System Description

Javier Galbally, Fernando Alonso, Julian Fierrez, and Javier Ortega

Biometric Recognition Group–ATVS, EPS, Universidad Autonoma de Madrid,
C/ Francisco Tomas y Valiente 11, 28049 Madrid, Spain
{javier.galbally,fernando.alonso,julian.fierrez,
javier.ortega}@uam.es

The proposed approach presented to LivDET uses a new parameterization based on quality measures for a software-based solution in fingerprint liveness detection. This novel strategy requires just one fingerprint image to extract the necessary features in order to determine if the finger presented to the sensor is real or fake. This fact shortens the acquisition process and reduces the inconvenience for the final user. A general diagram of the liveness detection system is shown in Fig. A. In the first step the fingerprint is segmented from the background. Once the useful information of the total image has been separated, ten different quality measures are extracted which will serve as the feature vector that will be used in the classification. Prior to the classification step, the best performing features are selected depending on the sensor that is used in the acquisition. Once the final feature vector has been generated the fingerprint is classified as real (generated by a living finger), or fake (coming from a gummy finger).

A.1 Feature Extraction

The parameterization used to solve the liveness detection problem comprises ten quality-based features. Image quality can be assessed by measuring one of the following properties: ridge strength or directionality, ridge continuity, ridge clarity, integrity of the ridge-valley structure, or estimated verification performance when using the image at hand. In the following, we give some details about the quality measures used in this paper. We have implemented several measures that make use of the above mentioned properties for quality assessment:

Ridge-strength measures. Orientation Certainty Level (Q_{OCL}) [6], Energy concentration in the power spectrum (Q_E) [7].

Ridge-continuity measures. Local Orientation Quality (Q_{LOQ}) [8], Continuity of the Orientation Field (Q_{COF}) [6].

Ridge-clarity measures. Mean (Q_{MEAN}) and standard deviation (Q_{STD}) values of the gray level image. Local Clarity Score (Q_{LCS1} and Q_{LCS2}) [8]. Amplitude and variance of the sinusoid that models ridges and valleys (Q_A and Q_{VAR}) [9].

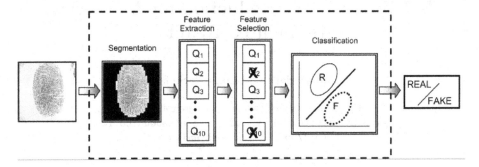

Fig. A. General diagram of the liveness detection system presented in this work

A.2   Feature Selection

Due to the curse of dimensionality, it is possible that the best classifying results are not obtained using the set of ten proposed features, but a subset of them. As we are dealing with a ten dimensional problem there are $2^{10} - 1 = 1,023$ possible feature subsets, which is a reasonably low number to apply exhaustive search as feature selection technique in order to find the best performing feature subset. This way we guarantee that we find the optimal set of features out of all the possible ones.

A.3   Classifier

We have used Linear Discriminant Analysis (LDA) as classifier. All the parameterized samples of a certain dataset are used to fit the two normal distributions representing each of the classes (real and fake). The sample being classified (which was left out of the training process) is assigned to the most probable class.

SVR-Based Jitter Reduction for Markerless Augmented Reality

Samuele Salti and Luigi Di Stefano

DEIS, University of Bologna, Bologna 40136, IT
samuele.salti@unibo.it, luigi.distefano@unibo.it
http://www.vision.deis.unibo.it

Abstract. The ability to augment a video stream with consistent virtual contents is an attractive Computer Vision application. The first Augmented Reality (AR) proposals required the scene to be endowed with special markers. Recently, thanks to the developments in the field of natural invariant local features, similar results have been achieved in a markerless scenario. The computer vision community is now equipped with a set of relatively standard techniques to solve the underlying markerless camera pose estimation problem, at least for planar textured reference objects. The majority of proposals, however, does not exploit temporal consistency across frames in order to reduce some disturbing effects of per-frame estimation, namely visualization of short spurious estimations and jitter. We proposes a new method based on Support Vector Regression to mitigate these undesired effects while preserving the ability to work in real-time. Our proposal can be used as a post processing step independent of the chosen pose estimation method, thus providing an effective and easily integrable building block for AR applications.

1   Introduction

Augmented Reality (AR) applications may be the killer technology of a new series of services yet to imagine. To have such an impact on our everyday life, we believe two major contributions are needed: as for hardware, devices, such as see-through visors, must evolve towards cheaper and more comfortable products; as for software, algorithms must provide in real-time a convincing and stable pose estimation even in presence of unpredictable user motion and illumination changes and without intrusive modification of the scene.

In this paper we focus on software issues. Some standard solutions to the markerless pose estimation problem are well known. We will describe a standard approach we have implemented in section 2. This approach suffers from a trade/off problem: in order to improve its frame-rate one has to sacrifice the stability of virtual contents. Such instability, even when not very relevant in metric units, turns out extremely disturbing for a human observer, especially when she/he stands still, and completely brakes the illusion of mixture between rendered and real world. We shortly refer to this effect as pose jitter and propose a new method based on Support Vector Regression (SVR) to reduce its effects while preserving the real-time behavior of the application (section 3).

P. Foggia, C. Sansone, and M. Vento (Eds.): ICIAP 2009, LNCS 5716, pp. 24–33, 2009.

Related works. The problem of jitter reduction is explicitly addressed in [1]. They estimate the pose for the current frame solving a non-linear minimization problem of re-projection errors. To regularize the pose across frames they add a term in the objective function that favors small camera motion between consecutive frames. In [2], pose is estimated by matching the current frame with a set of 3D registered keyframes of the reference object and providing these 3D-2D correspondences to an M-estimator. In order to obtain a smoother estimate, they extract correspondences between the current and the previous frame and simultaneously re-optimize the position of 3D points and the pose for the current and previous frame, thus merging measurement and regularization data. In [3] jitter is dealt with by performing a global bundle adjustment that optimizes both structure and motion on the whole sequence. When used on-line to augment a video, it requires a training sequence to reconstruct and bundle adjust the scene offline. Next, only the bundled 3D points are tracked during real-time operation. Unlike [1], [2] and [3], our proposal provides a general purpose solution because it completely decouples jitter reduction from pose estimation. Moreover, compared to [3], our proposal does not require an offline training sequence. General purpose solution for jitter reduction in AR systems based on Kalman Filtering [4] or Extended Kalman Filtering [5] have been proposed in literature. A major strength of our proposed SVR approach consists in not requiring specification of an arbitrarily constant motion model, the underlying model being dynamically learnt from the data.

2   A Typical Markerless Augmented Reality Application

The purpose of a markerless AR system is to recover in every frame the pose of the camera with respect to the scene. Given the relative pose, it is possible to render any virtual contents and, thus, create the illusion of augmentation.

A standard solution to build an AR system is to recover the pose with respect to a planar object. Given an image of the reference object, the problem is typically solved pursuing a two stages approach: i) correspondent points (i.e. projections on the two images of the same world point) are found between the reference image and the current frame using some invariant local features extraction and matching algorithm, such as [6]; ii)correspondences are used to robustly estimate the relative pose of the two planes.

Pose estimation given a set of correspondences between two views is a classical photogrammetry and computer vision problem (see [7] for a recent overview). In our solution we have adopted a slightly modified version of the ARToolkitPlus implementation [8] of the well known algorithm from [9], which is a state-of-the-art solution in the pose estimation problem from a planar object. This method performs a least squared minimization of a distance function in 3D space using all the input correspondences. Hence, it is very susceptible to wrong correspondences. To improve robustness, we have inserted between the two stages an outliers rejection phase. We have used RANSAC[10] to robustly estimate the homography between the reference image and the current frame given the correspondences. Only the subset of correspondences in agreement with the estimated transformation is used as input for the pose estimation stage.

3   SVR-Based Jitter Reduction

Two poses from consecutive frames are strongly correlated. In fact, it is reasonable to assume that the observer moves smoothly and so does the scene appearance in the image. The system for pose estimation described in the previous section, just as many other AR systems, does not take advantage of this temporal correlation. As a consequence, two likely sources of unrealistic rendering cannot be faced. First, in case of wrong correspondences, as it may happen on a very blurred or otherwise difficult to estimate frame, the resulting pose will be totally wrong and very far away from previous ones. Then, since feature extraction is affected by image noise, the estimated pose parameters exhibit oscillations of small amplitude and high frequency. This second effect produces vibrations of the virtual objects that are really disturbing for a human observer and may completely nullify the effort to hide the distinction between real and rendered parts of the scene. This pose jitter, as we shortly refer to it, is especially noticeable and annoying when the user stands still.

In order to overcome these problems and exploit the temporal consistency across frames we proposes to add to AR systems a pose regression module based on Support Vector Machine (SVM) used in regression mode [11]. When trained with the last values estimated for a pose component, e.g. the x coordinate of the translation, an SVM in regression mode can supply a prediction of the value for the next frame based on the learned temporal evolution for that component. Use of this prediction as the output value can i)avoid one-frame spikes in parameters value and ii) sensibly reduce jitter.

3.1   SVR in ϵ-Regression

SVMs are well known tools in pattern recognition based on the statistical learning theory developed by Vapnik and Chervonenkis. Their widespread use is due to their solid theoretical bases which guarantee their ability to generalize from training data minimizing the over-fitting problem. Their use as regressors is probably less popular but even in this field they obtained excellent performances [11].

To introduce SVMs as regressors, and in particular in ϵ-regression mode, let us have a quick look at the regression of a linear model given a series of data $(\mathbf{x_i}, y_i)$. In ϵ-regression mode the SVR tries to estimate a function of $\mathbf{x}$ that is far from training data y_i at most ϵ and is at the same time as flat as possible. This requirement of flatness comes from the theory of complexity developed by Vapnik and ensures that we will get a solution with minimal complexity (hence, with better generalization abilities). In the linear case, the model to regress is

$$f(x) = \langle \mathbf{w}, \mathbf{x} \rangle + b \tag{1}$$

(with boldface denoting vectors) and the solution with minimal complexity is given by the solution of the following convex optimization problem

$$min \tfrac{1}{2}||\mathbf{w}||^2$$

$$\begin{cases} y_i - \langle \mathbf{w}, \mathbf{x_i} \rangle - b \le \epsilon \\ y_i - \langle \mathbf{w}, \mathbf{x_i} \rangle - b \ge -\epsilon \end{cases}$$

(2)

Such a strict formulation may require a not existing function and make the problem infeasible. Moreover, it makes sense to accept errors greater than ϵ for some training data in order to have a globally better approximation of the underlying model. By introducing slack variables it is possible to relax the constraints, obtaining the standard formulation of a linear SVR problem:

$$min \tfrac{1}{2}||\mathbf{w}||^2 + C \sum_{i=1}^{l}(\xi_i + \xi_i^*)$$

$$\begin{cases} y_i - \langle \mathbf{w}, \mathbf{x_i} \rangle - b \le \epsilon + \xi_i \\ y_i - \langle \mathbf{w}, \mathbf{x_i} \rangle - b \ge -\epsilon - \xi_i^* \end{cases}$$

(3)

The constant C is an algorithm parameter and weights the deviations from the model greater than ϵ. The problem is then usually solved using its dual form, that is easier and extensible to estimation on non-linear functions (see [11] for more details). Beside using the dual form, in order to estimate a non-linear function it is necessary to introduce a mapping between the input space, where the function operates, and a feature space of greater dimension, where we will apply the linear algorithm developed so far. For example, the mapping

$$\Phi(x_1, x_2) = \left(x_1^2, \sqrt{2}x_1x_2, x_2^2\right)$$

(4)

allows us to use the linear algorithm in $\mathbb{R}^3$ to estimate a quadratic function in $\mathbb{R}^2$. Since the dual problem depends only on the dot products between data, it is possible to further simplify the problem choosing a mapping such that a function k that satisfies the following equation

$$k(\mathbf{x'}, \mathbf{x''}) = \langle \Phi(\mathbf{x'}), \Phi(\mathbf{x''}) \rangle$$

(5)

may be easily derived ($\mathbf{x'}, \mathbf{x''}$ representing generic vectors $\in \mathbb{R}^n$). Such a function is a crucial parameter of an SVR and is termed kernel function. Given the kernel function, a mapping is implicitly chosen. The choice of the kernel function is influenced by a priori knowledge on the model to estimate and on noise. In our scenario no knowledge is possible on this elements and the only requirement is to get an estimation from data that is smoother that the raw data. The suggested kernel function [11] is a Gaussian Radial Basis Function

$$k(\mathbf{x'}, \mathbf{x''}) = e^{-\gamma||\mathbf{x'}-\mathbf{x''}||^2}$$

(6)

Hence, another parameter to tune is γ, inversely related to the radius of the Gaussian functions.

3.2   SVR as Pose Regressor

In order to use SVRs to regress a smooth motion model a suitable pose parametrization must be adopted. Usually pose is provided as a rotation matrix and a translation vector, and so does [9]. We choose to operate on a different representation of rotations, i.e. quaternions [12]. A quaternion is a vector $\in \mathbb{R}^4$ and may be described as a scalar plus a 3D vector or as a complex number with three imaginary parts. By quaternion theory it is possible to define a bijective mapping between rotation matrices and unit quaternions. Hence, by applying regression independently to quaternion components it is then sufficient to divide the quaternion estimate by its norm in order to obtain a valid rotation. Instead, had rotation matrix elements been independently estimated, it would not be so direct and unequivocal how to asssembly and scale them in order to enforce orthogonality.

Summarizing, the whole method uses 7 SVRs, 4 to estimate quaternion components and 3 to regress translation. A sliding window approach is used: in every frame the current estimate is added to the set of correspondences $(f, \{q_f, t_f\})$ (where f indicates the frame number, q the quaternion and t the translation vector) used to estimate the model and the older is discarded. Then every SVR is trained and is required to provide its estimation for frame f.

Introducing the filtering effect of SVRs may result in a slow reaction to quick user movements. In order to immediately react, the system must detect this occurrence and favor the current measurement against the SVR output. Note that to detect this event one cannot use the output of the pose estimation, since this situation is indistinguishable from a spike in pose parameters due to a wrong estimation. Hence, the detection must be based on features only. In our system we detect such event by comparing the centroid of the features extracted in the current frame with the previous one. When this difference exceeds a threshold, we output the pose estimation directly. Moreover, we restart the accumulation of samples in the SVR training windows, in order to get smoothed values in accordance with the new state reached by the user after the quick move.

4   Results

Our system has been implemented in C++ under Windows®XP. In our implementation we have experimented with two feature extraction algorithms, SIFT [6] and SURF [13], both matched building a kd-tree on the reference image and traversing the tree using the best-bin-first (BBF) approximated strategy. SIFT support has been added using the GPL Rob Hess's implementation [14] and SURF was integrated wrapping the dll freely available for research purposes at the authors' website. We performed several tests, with different users and for different application scenarios, i.e. gaming [15], AR for aeronautical maintenance and AR for fruition of cultural heritage [16].

4.1 SVR Parameters Tuning

The best values of the parameters C and γ depend, of course, on the motion typically exhibited by the users for a specific application. Nevertheless, given some representative training sequences, it is possible to derive the best values for C and γ performing a grid-search in the 2D parameters-space using k-fold cross-validation. In our experiments we have used k = 10. The best values for the parameters have been estimated separately for the translation components and the quaternion components dynamics. To select the best configuration of parameters we have compared them using the Mean Squared Error (MSE) between prediction and input data in every frame. The best parameters for our sequences are C $= 2^{-3}$ and $\gamma = 2.0$ for translation and C $= 2^{-7}$ and $\gamma = 32.0$ for rotation. A limit of this type of tuning is that the search for the best parameters does not take place in the same conditions as their use at run-time. In fact, cross-validation, selecting random samples, does not generate predictions using only a sliding window of previous measurements, but from a mixture of past and future measurements spread across the temporal axis. Nevertheless, the estimated parameter values enable a satisfactory jitter reduction in our scenarios and, hence, we sticked to this technique. Moreover, we have experimentally verified that the method is not particularly sensible to parameters variation: parameters estimated in aeronautical maintenance scenario has been used with success in others. Together with its independence from the pose estimation algorithm, this absence of request for a fine parameter tuning allows this module to be used "plug'n'play" in almost every AR application.

4.2 Jitter Reduction and Error Recovering

In order to illustrate our results we present the progress for a complete test sequence (more than 1870 frames) of the X coordinate of the user centered reference system with respect to a point located at coordinates (20,20,20) in the virtual contents reference system. The choice of this point allows to convey with just one chart the combined effects of the estimation of the rotation matrix and the translation vector. The sequence deals with AR for aeronautical maintenance scenario [16] and shows the fuel tank lid cover of a Cessna airplane, the rendered content being a simple demo OpenGL object (see fig. 3). It is worth pointing out that the considered test sequence is particularly challenging for real-time pose estimation based on local features due to the small amount of texture on the reference object, the relatively fast camera movement and the wide range of camera poses. In absence of a real ground truth, results are compared with the best estimation our system can produce, namely that obtained using correspondences provided by SIFT with image doubling on full resolution images and shown as pink line in the four charts of fig. 1. By visual inspection, this reference estimate was found almost free of sharp pose errors and able to provide a very convincing effect of augmentation.

First of all, we compared SIFT and SURF to select the feature extraction algorithm. We carefully tuned the algorithms parameters to obtain acceptable

Table 1. Comparison between different local features algorithm

Features	RMSE (mm)	Max Error (mm)
SIFT 320x240 no Doubling	31.81	209.40
SURF 320x240 no Doubling	9.39	94.10
SURF + SVR	14.42	57.32
SURF + Kalman	18.99	63.53

correspondences in real-time. It turned out the best compromise for both algorithms was to not perform the initial image doubling proposed in the papers and to elaborate subsampled (320x240) versions of input frames. As can be seen from the error statistics listed in tab. 1 and the pictures in the first row of fig. 1, when constrained with lower resolution images and no initial image doubling, SURF seems to perform definitely better than SIFT. Therefore, given also its higher frame-rate (10 vs. 5.7 fps), we adopted SURF. Nevertheless, as already mentioned in sec. 3 and clearly shown by fig. 1, the output of pose estimation based on SURF correspondences is full of spikes and jitter that significantly disturb human perception. This is confirmed by the error statistics in the second row of tab. 1. In such circumstances the insertion of our filter can be crucial to make the system usable. In fact, as shown by the third chart of fig. 1, SVR filtering yields an estimation of the user movement that exhibits a realistic, smooth progress despite the spikes and jitter affecting the input provided by SURF correspondences. It is worth noticing that between frame 1250 and frame 1500 there were less than 4 features matched, not enough to allow for pose estimation. This shows up in the charts as a straight line, since the system maintains the old estimation until it can carry out a new one from the current frame: another proof of the difficulty inherent to this test case. Since, as suggested by a reviewer, the most disturbing errors might those affecting rotation parameters, we also provide

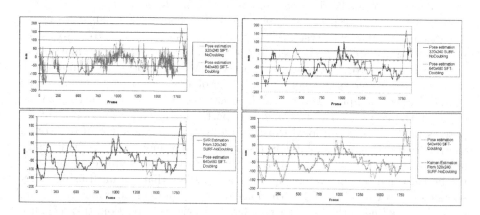

Fig. 1. Charts illustrating the temporal evolution of the x coordinate of the user reference system across a whole test sequence. From left to right and top to bottom: SIFT on 320x240 images and no image doubling; SURF with same settings; SVR with measurements provided by SURF; Kalman with measurements provided by SURF.

in the left column of fig. 2 charts showing the effectiveness of our proposal in mitigating this kind of errors.

As a closer look at the graph reveals, our proposal is able to solve the two problems that per-frame estimation cannot intrinsically face. In fig. 3 two close-ups of fig. 1 are shown, together with frames 205-210 from the original and the filtered sequences. On frame 207 the original sequence shows a sharp pose error that visual analysis of previous frames reveals but that the single frame estimator cannot detect. Moreover, frames 209 and 210 from the original sequence are clearly corrupted by jitter. All such shortcomings are filtered out effectively by the SVRs. Furthermore, the close-up on the charts shows the good behavior of our filter in mitigating the noise while keeping the estimation close enough to the ground truth. This is confirmed by the corresponding row of tab. 1, where we can see that because of the delay introduced by the filter the RMSE is higher than that of the original sequence, but the much lower value of the

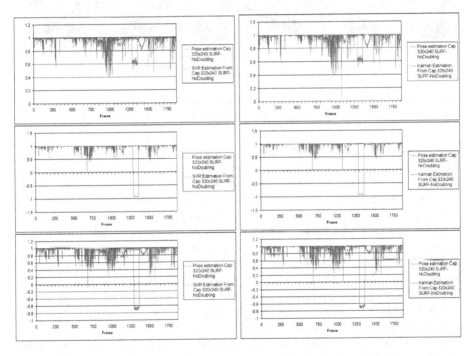

Fig. 2. Charts illustrating the temporal evolution of the rotations of the user reference system across a whole test sequence. Performance on jitter reduction for rotations are shown by plotting the cosines between the unit vectors of the ground truth reference system and the smoothed ones (i.e., cosines should be one in case of perfect estimation). From top to bottom, the three rows of the rotation matrix are sequentially analyzed. In the left column the comparison is between the rows of the rotation matrix regressed by the SVR with measurements provided by SURF on 320x240 images and no image doubling and those obtained directly from SURF; in the right column the comparison is between the rows of the rotation matrix regressed by the Kalman filter with same measurements and again those obtained from SURF.

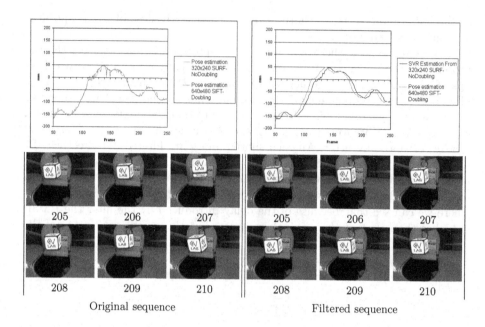

Fig. 3. Close-ups of the charts in fig. 1 and screenshots illustrating the temporal evolution of the rendered content from frame 205 to 210 of the test sequence

maximum error proves that SVRs filter out the most disturbing spikes in the output. The effectiveness of the proposed approach as well as the difficulties of the considered test sequence can also be assessed by watching the videos provided at http://vision.deis.unibo.it/AugRea-Figures/AR3D-SURF.avi and http://vision.deis.unibo.it/AugRea-Figures/AR3D-SIFT.avi.

Finally, we have also performed a preliminary comparison with a more conventional technique for jitter reduction, i.e. Kalman filtering with a drift process model. The Kalman Filter was tuned to obtain a level of regularization in the output comparable to the SVR-based method, as shown by the two charts in the second row of fig. 1 and by the right column of fig. 2. With this settings, our proposal yields lower error values than the Kalman filter (see tab. 1). This may be seen as a proof of the intuition that the ability of SVRs to dynamically learn a time-varying motion model can yield a significant advantage in pose regression for interactive applications.

5   Conclusions

We have presented a real-time method based on Support Vector Regression to stabilize the output of an AR system, so as to make it more usable and comfortable for the final user. So far, we have assessed that our approach is an effective, fast and almost parameters free solution for pose regularization across frames. In the future, we would like to investigate deeper on the benefits that the SVR generalization properties as well as its ability to estimate time-varying and possibly non-linear mappings can provide in order to make AR applications stable enough to be usable in difficult scenarios where it is not realistic to have a reliable estimation in every frame. This ability to deal with time-varying non-linear functions also suggests a direction where to go into more depth within the comparison with the Kalman Filter.

References

1. Gordon, I., Lowe, D.G.: What and where: 3d object recognition with accurate pose. In: Ponce, J., Hebert, M., Schmid, C., Zisserman, A. (eds.) Toward Category-Level Object Recognition. LNCS, vol. 4170, pp. 67–82. Springer, Heidelberg (2006)
2. Lepetit, V., Vacchetti, L., Thalmann, D., Fua, P.: Fully automated and stable registration for augmented reality applications. In: ISMAR 2003, Washington, DC, USA, p. 93. IEEE Computer Society, Los Alamitos (2003)
3. Cornelis, K., Pollefeys, M., Van Gool, L.: Tracking based structure and motion recovery for augmented video productions. In: VRST 2001, pp. 17–24. ACM, New York (2001)
4. Chia, K.W., Cheok, A.D., Prince, S.J.D.: Online 6 dof augmented reality registration from natural features. In: ISMAR 2002: Int. Symp. on Mixed and Augmented Reality, Washington, DC, USA, p. 305. IEEE Computer Society, Los Alamitos (2002)
5. Chai, L., Hoff, B., Vincent, T., Nguyen, K.: An adaptive estimator for registration in augmented reality. In: International Workshop on Augmented Reality, vol. 0, p. 23 (1999)
6. Lowe, D.G.: Distinctive image features from scale-invariant keypoints. Int. J. of Computer Vision 60(2), 91–110 (2004)
7. Moreno-Noguer, F., Lepetit, V., Fua, P.: Accurate non-iterative o(n) solution to the pnp problem. In: IEEE Int. Conf. on Computer Vision, Rio de Janeiro, Brazil (October 2007)
8. ARToolkitPlus, T.:
   http://studierstube.icg.tu-graz.ac.at/handheld_ar/artoolkitplus.php
   (last visited 19/01/2009)
9. Schweighofer, G., Pinz, A.: Robust pose estimation from a planar target. IEEE Trans. on Pattern Analysis and Machine Intelligence 28(12), 2024 2030 (2006)
10. Fischler, M.A., Bolles, R.C.: Random sample consensus: A paradigm for model fitting with applications to image analysis and automated cartography. Communications of the ACM 24(6), 381–395 (1981)
11. Smola, A.J., Olkopf, B.S.: A tutorial on support vector regression. Technical report, Statistics and Computing (1998)
12. Korn, G.A., Korn, T.M.: Mathematical Handbook for Scientists and Engineers. McGraw Hill, New York (1968)
13. Bay, H., Tuytelaars, T., Van Gool, L.: Surf: Speeded up robust features. In: Leonardis, A., Bischof, H., Pinz, A. (eds.) ECCV 2006. LNCS, vol. 3951, pp. 404–417. Springer, Heidelberg (2006)
14. Hess, R.: http://web.engr.oregonstate.edu/~hess/ (last visited 19/01/2009)
15. Azzari, P., di Stefano, L.: Vision-based markerless gaming interface. In: ICIAP 2009 (2009)
16. Azzari, P., di Stefano, L., Tombari, F., Mattoccia, S.: Markerless augmented reality using image mosaics. In: Elmoataz, A., Lezoray, O., Nouboud, F., Mammass, D. (eds.) ICISP 2008. LNCS, vol. 5099, pp. 413–420. Springer, Heidelberg (2008)

Re-photography and Environment Monitoring Using a Social Sensor Network

Paul Chippendale, Michele Zanin, and Claudio Andreatta

Fondazione Bruno Kessler, TeV Group,
Via Sommarive, 18, Povo, Trento, 38050 Italy
(chippendale,mizanin,andreatta)@fbk.eu

Abstract. This paper presents a technology capable of enabling the creation of a diffuse, calibrated vision-sensor network from the wealth of socially generated geo-referenced imagery, freely available on the Internet. Through the implementation of an accurate image registration system, based on image processing, terrain modelling and subsequent correlation, we will demonstrate how images taken by the public can potentially be used as a mean to gather environmental information from a unique, ground-level viewpoint normally denied non-terrestrial sensors (consider vertical or overhanging cliffs). Moreover, we will also show this registration technology can be used to synthesize new views using sections of photos taken from a variety of places and times.

Keywords: environmental monitoring, distributed sensors, geo-referencing, re-photography.

1 Introduction

Monitoring the environment, whether it be through vision, radar or a multitude of other technologies, has increased dramatically since the birth of satellite technology. The ability to view large swathes of the Earth in single orbits makes them ideal candidates for monitoring climactic changes in near real-time. The sensing technologies available to climatologists today are many; however the visual spectrum still has an important role to play in environmental observations. One good example is the monitoring of subtle vegetation colour changes over time which can signify variations in the onset of Autumn [1]. Furthermore, due to cloud cover and atmospheric attenuation, the planet's surface can rarely be visually observed with complete clarity from space.

The near ubiquitous ownership of digital cameras, their inclusion in virtually every mobile phone on the market combined with the speed at which an image can be taken and shared with the World (via 3G or WIFI and a multitude of photo websites) together promise a new paradigm in environmental observation. As the integration of GPS receivers into phones (and in the near future cameras) is becoming ever more common, the number of geo-referenced images taken and shared via Internet websites such as www.Flickr.com and www.Panoramio.com, often within minutes of capture, is increasing at a phenomenal rate. For example, the Flickr API tells us that over

P. Foggia, C. Sansone, and M. Vento (Eds.): ICIAP 2009, LNCS 5716, pp. 34–42, 2009.
© Springer-Verlag Berlin Heidelberg 2009

800,000 geo-referenced photos were taken in the Alps in 2008 (almost 27 millions worldwide). There is a clear trend: geo-tagging photos for the sole purpose of placing one's photos 'on the map', either automatically (via GPS) or manually (via GUIs in GoogleEarth), is becoming increasingly popular.

Geo-tagged photos alone are not a reliable resource to extract spatial information as their orientation and content is unknown. We therefore require the implementation of a system that can take such images and understand precisely their orientation at the time of capture and camera parameters so that registered orthophoto-like images can be generated.

However, image registration in an outdoor environment cannot exploit the established methods developed for indoor use, e.g. magnetic tracking, fiducial markers. Outdoor registration systems traditionally rely on GPS for position measurements combined with magnetic compasses and inertial sensors for orientation as used by Azuma et al. Examples of systems using such sensors include Columbia's Touring machine [2] and MARS [3], the Battlefield Augmented Reality System [4], work by Thomas [5], the Tinmith System [6] and to some extent Sentieri Vivi [7]. Although magnetic compasses, inertial sensors and GPS can be used to obtain a rough estimate of position and orientation, the precision of this registration method (using affordable devices) is insufficient to satisfy many Augmented Reality (AR) overlay applications. Unfortunately, these types of sensors are not yet to be found inside consumer electronics. Undoubtedly, one day they will become commonplace; until that day however, computer vision methods will have to suffice to estimate device orientation through the correlation of visual features with calibrated real-world objects.

In Microsoft's Photosynth [8], highly recognizable man-made features are detected, such as the architecture of Notre Dame de Paris, to align and assemble huge collections of photos. Using this tool, the relative orientation and position of a photo with respect to a calibration object can be calculated due to the scene's unique and unchanging nature. The University of Washington and Microsoft [9] took this idea one step further and created the tool 'PhotoTour' that permits the viewer to travel virtually from one photo into another. Viewfinder by the University of Southern California [10] and [11] are other research projects that aid users to spatially situate their photographs through the creation of alignment tools that interfaces with 3D models visualized inside GoogleEarth. Although their systems are essentially manual, a lot of the hard work of alignment is taken out of the registration process and the University claims that a 10-year-old should be able to find the pose of a photo in less than a minute.

Our approach to the problem of image registration tackles the challenge of the natural environment. We attempt to identify and align evident geographical photo features with similar ones generated in a synthetic terrain model. Extracting feature points from outdoor environments is however challenging, as disturbances such as clouds on mountain tops, foreground objects, large variations in lighting and bad viewing conditions in general such as haze, all inhibit accurate recognition. As a result, great care needs to be taken to overcome such inherent limitations and we attempt to compensate for this by combining different yet complementary methods.

Behringer's approach [12] is similar to ours, based on an edge detector to align the horizon silhouette extracted from Digital Terrain Model (DTM) data with video images to estimate the orientation of a mobile AR system. They demonstrated that a well-structured terrain could provide information to help other sensors to accurately estimate registration; their solution had problems with lighting and visibility conditions.

Our approach however incorporates an enriched set of feature points and a more accurately rendered terrain model enhanced by additional digital content such as: lake contours, GPS tracks, land-usage GIS layers, etc.

2 Photo Registration

We register photos by correlating their content against a rendered 3D spherical panorama generated about the photo's 'geo-location'. In essence we generate a complete 360° synthetic image of what an observer would see all around them at a given location. To do this we systematically load, scale and re-project DTM data (such as The Shuttle Radar Topography Mission data [13] freely available from NASA) onto the inside of a sphere using ray-tracing techniques. We render up to a distance dictated by the height of the observer above sea-level and the maximum theoretical visible distance due to Earth curvature and possible mountain heights (the maximum rendering distance for a ground-level observer is usually in the 200-550km range). In preparation for photo alignment the sphere is 'unwrapped' into a 360° by 180° rectangular window (a section of which is illustrated in Fig. 1); each synthetic pixel has its own latitude, longitude, altitude and depth.

Fig. 1. 70° wide by 40° tall section of unwrapped synthetic panorama, with intensity proportional to distance

Placing a photograph into this unwrapped space requires a deformation so that photo pixels are correctly mapped onto synthetic ones depending upon estimated camera parameters, such as pan, tilt, lens distortion, etc. The scaling parameter is extracted from the focal length meta-data contained within the EXIF JPEG data of the photo where available; otherwise it is estimated using an iterative strategy from a default value.

Our approach is structured into four phases: 1) extract salient points/profiles from a synthetic rendering, 2) extract salient points/profiles from the photo, 3) search for correspondences aiming to select significant synthetic/photo matches, 4) apply an optimization technique to derive the alignment parameters that minimize re-projection error.

The extraction of profiles from the synthetic panorama is relatively straightforward and is simply a matter of detecting abrupt depth discontinuities between adjacent pixels. In photos we have no prior knowledge of depth therefore we employ various image processing algorithms which analyze colour, texture and edge content to try to locate region interfaces and thus suspected depth changes in the real world. To place a different emphasis on the various types of profiles in the photo we attempt to locate sky regions (low detail zones with a hue in the blue range located towards the top of the image) and also estimate the presence of foreground objects (sharp and saturated regions starting from the bottom). The contribution of each type of profile is weighted differently; e.g. a land-sky interface is more reliable for correlation than a profile close to the observer.

The third step is hypothesis generation. From the synthetic panorama we generate a grid of match hypotheses by modifying the various camera parameters: the extrinsics such as pan, tilt and roll, and the intrinsics such as focal length and lens distortion. The initial hypotheses are generated with the intrinsic parameters set to a default value typical for that make of camera. The range over which yaw, pitch and roll vary depends upon the findings of a frequency analysis stage which evaluates the photo and synthetics sky/land interfaces. The most prominent/evident geographical peak or valley is used as a starting point for the search for a match.

As can be seen in Fig. 2a, the analysis algorithm follows the synthetic profile (red line) with a sliding window. The relevant features are locally computed inside the window in a multi-resolution manner in order to measure if there is a good correspondence between the synthetic profile and the real one. To do so, we examine the window to see if we have strong profiles in the photo and, moreover, if the profiles are of roughly the same angle. The alignment is measured considering the angle between the normal to the synthetic profile (green arrow) and the normal to the real one (black arrow).

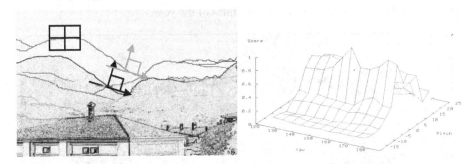

Fig. 2. (a) Correlation hypothesis test (synthetic profile in red) (b) Result of correlation search in the yaw - pitch parameters space

The results obtained from the series of 100 correlation tests can be seen in Fig. 2b. There is a distinctive peak at 150° pan and 10° tilt. The quality of this tentative alignment can be assessed visually in Fig. 3.

This automated brute force approach provides us with an initial 'best guess' alignment. Registration is refined in a following stage where the other parameters such as roll and lens distortion are adjusted using a minimization algorithm. All of the image analysis techniques involved are relatively fast and efficient; a necessity due to the sheer number of hypothesis to analyze.

Fig. 3. Result obtained from auto-alignment, with colour proportional to distance

3 Applications and Results

3.1 Creation of a Calibrated Social Sensor Network

Once a photo has been registered, a calibrated sensor network can be created by amassing a large number of similarly aligned images and then systematically draping their photo pixels onto a surface model generated from the DTM. In order to provide adequate spatio-temporal coverage of an area, photos need to be collected from different positions and orientations at various times of the year.

Fig. 4. Heat maps of 100 photo viewsheds combined, taken around the Matterhorn. The spatial resolution of each photo pixel varies in relation to camera-terrain distance, which is not expressed in this composite image.

To demonstrate the coverage obtainable, we downloaded and registered 100 georeferenced images taken in the area of the Matterhorn from Flickr. As can be seen in Fig. 4, (where red represents the terrain that features most often and blue the least), the coverage is quite extensive. In a previous paper [14], we went a step further with this Matterhorn data and explained how we could combine a viewshed with the social comments made about the photos themselves (number of views, comments, favourites, etc.) in order to estimate the 'attractiveness' of the terrain in question for photographers.

3.2 Generation, Analysis and Visualization of Environmental Content

Once a photo has been accurately registered, each photo pixel is assigned latitude, longitude, altitude and a distance from the camera. This geo-spatial information can be exploited in a variety of ways; for example we can generate new unique views from multiple images taken from a variety of places or we can extract environmental data such as the snowline.

To demonstrate how we can detect the snowline in aligned photos we selected an area of the Brenta Dolomites around Cima di Ghez, bound by the rectangle: 46.077032 < latitude < 46.159568 and 10.84653 < longitude < 10.92353. In this region the terrain altitude goes from 850m to about 3200m. Then we automatically generate a subset from our database of photos that in some part overlaps this area.

We then transform the photos into a top-down view-shed representation through the systematic projection of each terrain pixel from the 2D image plane (when registered these pixels also carry 3D information) into this new viewpoint. The colour of each mapped pixel is inserted into the appropriate position in a 0.2 seconds (about 7 m) resolution grid covering the area described.

In order to understand which pixels/regions from the selected images contain snow, we selected a reference image that adequately covered the region in question and was taken on a clear day in the summer (inferred from the photo's timestamp).

Next, from the DTM data, we generated a 3D representation of the landscape contained within the reference image and draped the photos for comparison onto this model. The results of this can be seen in Fig. 5.

(a) November

(b) September

(c) January

Fig. 5. Re-projection of aligned photos into the same viewpoint as the reference image

Fig. 6. Local terrain gradient map of the test region, viewed from reference image perspective

Our set of re-projected test photos is then subjected to a sigma filter to reduce noise. This averages the value of each pixel with its similar neighbours by analyzing the standard deviation σ. Thus it only averages those neighbouring pixels whose values lie within 2 σ of the central pixel value; where σ is calculated once for the entire image. This processing smoothes the images in an edge preserving manner.

Next we compare each image with the reference image; aiming to detect local differences using the L2 measure in RGB space with an adaptive local threshold (the threshold is computed in a sliding window considering the mean and variation of the colours among all the test images, thus reducing the impact of changes due to illumination variation).

Once the regions that differ from the reference image have been detected, we try to understand if this is due to the presence of snow. Snow is assumed to have a low saturation and high value in HSV space. As snow is unlikely to be seen on very steep mountain faces, we also take local gradient into account. Fig. 6 graphically illustrates the terrain gradients inside the test region, as seen from the reference perspective (black pixels are horizontal and white vertical).

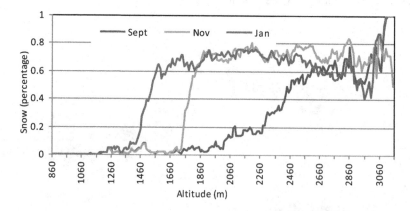

Fig. 7. Snowline detection using a summer image as a reference. The data is noisier at high altitudes: this is mainly caused by the fact that we have fewer pixels representing the highest part of the altitude range.

The saturation, luminance and terrain steepness distribution has been studied on a training set in order to model snow appearance using a multi-dimensional Gaussian distribution.

Fig. 7 shows the percentage of the pixels in the target images that differ from the reference and that have been classified as snow at a given altitude. The evident discontinuity from left to right represents the start of the snowline.

3.3 Re-photography

To further illustrate the re-photography potential of the system we generated two new 'virtual photos' based solely on the content of two images taken over 10km away. We chose an arbitrary point in space (lat. 46.096980, lon. 10.913257, alt. 1526m) and draped the view-sheds of the November and January images into GoogleEarth using the integrated photo overlay function. In this way we could precisely reproduce the same view point compared to GoogleEarth's. The two images, in the centre and on the right of Fig. 8, show the re-photography results.

Fig. 8. (a) GoogleEarth   (b) Image November re-projected, (c) Image January re-projected

As Fig. 8 shows, we are able to generate totally new views in GoogleEarth, representing different seasons and weather conditions through the gathering, registration and re-projection of public images shared openly on the Internet.

4   Conclusions

In this paper we have presented some of our current research in the field of photo registration, re-photography and environmental content generation (more details and constantly updated results are available at http://tev.fbk.eu/marmota). We have suggested how a widespread, calibrated network of ground-level vision sensors can be realized through the correlation of geo-referenced photos to the terrain, and have shown specific examples of how this 'composite-sensor' can be exploited. Initial observations suggest that areas close to attractions, honeypot villages, roads or popular footpaths are more heavily covered (down to a few centimetres per pixel) whilst more remote peaks are only covered at lower resolutions.

In the near future we plan to automatically monitor a wide variety of photo sharing websites on a daily basis for a specific area such as Trentino/Alto Adige and observe how extensive the photo coverage actually is.

We will then fuse our alignment results with existing orthophotos in order to investigate how we could improve their resolution and also fill in the many low resolution spots such as vertical cliffs. The user could also visualize such terrain and its changes over time. Registration of historical images taken at known locations will also enrich this temporal record of the environment.

To summarize, we have shown how a widespread vision sensor network can be created in an ad-hoc manner, which will naturally expand in time, improving in resolution and quality (through the availability of new devices) and which is, perhaps best of all, maintenance free and gratis.

References

1. Astola, H., Molinier, M., Mikkola, T., Kubin, E.: Web cameras in automatic autumn colour monitoring. In: IGARSS 2008 (2008)
2. Feiner, S., MacIntyre, B., Hollerer, T., Webster, A.: A touring machine: Prototyping 3D mobile augmented reality systems for exploring the urban environment. In: Proc. ISWC 1997, Cambridge, MA, USA, pp. 74–81 (1997)
3. Hollerer, T., Feiner, S., et al.: Exploring MARS: developing indoor and outdoor user interfaces to a mobile augmented reality system. Computer & Graphics 23, 779–785 (1999)
4. Baillot, Y., Brown, D., Julier, S.: Authoring of physical models using mobile computers. In: Proc. ISWC 2001, pp. 39–46 (2001)
5. Thomas, B., Demczuk, V., Piekarski, et al.: A wearable computer system with augmented reality to support terrestrial navigation. In: ISWC 1998, Pittsburgh, PA, USA, pp. 168–171 (1998)
6. Piekarski, W., Thomas, B.: Tinmith-metro: New outdoor techniques for creating city models with an augmented reality wearable computer. In: IEEE Proc. ISWC 2001, Zurich, Switzerland, pp. 31–38 (2001)
7. Sentieri Vivi (2008), http://www.sentierivivi.com
8. Snavely, N., Seitz, S., Szeliski, R.: Photo tourism: Exploring photo collections in 3D. In: Photo tourism: Exploring photo collections in 3D, SIGGRAPH Proceedings 2006, pp. 835–846 (2006)
9. Snavely, N., Garg, R., Seitz, S., Szeliski, R.: Finding Paths through the World's Photos. In: SIGGRAPH Proceedings 2008 (2008)
10. University of Southern California, Viewfinder - How to seamlessly Flickerize Google Earth (2008), http://interactive.usc.edu/viewfinder/approach.html
11. Chen, B., Ramos, G., Ofek, E., Cohen, M., Drucker, S., Nister, D.: Interactive Techniques for Registering Images to Digital Terrain and Building Models (2008), http://research.microsoft.com/pubs/70622/tr-2008-115.pdf
12. Behringer, R.: Registration for outdoor augmented reality applications using computer vision techniques and hybrid sensors. In: IEEE VR 1999, Houston, Texas, USA (1999)
13. The Shuttle Radar Topography Mission (SRTM) (2000), http://www2.jpl.nasa.gov/srtm/
14. Chippendale, P., Zanin, M., Andreatta, C.: Spatial and Temporal Attractiveness Analysis through Geo-Referenced Photo Alignment. In: International Geoscience and Remote Sensing Symposium (IEEE), Boston, Massachusetts, USA (2008)

Region-Based Illuminant Estimation
for Effective Color Correction

Simone Bianco, Francesca Gasparini, and Raimondo Schettini

DISCo (Dipartimento di Informatica, Sistemistica e Comunicazione),
Università degli Studi di Milano-Bicocca, Viale Sarca 336, 20126 Milano, Italy
{bianco,gasparini,schettini}@disco.unimib.it

Abstract. Several algorithms were proposed in the literature to recover
the illuminant chromaticity of the original scene. These algorithms work
well only when prior assumptions are satisfied, and the best and the worst
algorithms may be different for different scenes. In particular for certain
images a do nothing strategy can be preferred. Starting from these considerations, we have developed a region-based color constancy algorithm
able to automatically select (and/or blend) among different color corrections, including a conservative do nothing strategy. The strategy to be
applied is selected without any a priori knowledge of the image content
and only performing image low level analysis.

1 Introduction

The colors in a digital image depend not only on the surface properties of the objects present in the scene depicted, but also on the illuminant conditions (lighting
geometry and illuminant color) and the characteristics of the capturing device.
Unlike human vision, imaging devices (such as digital cameras) can not adapt
their spectral responses to cope with different lighting conditions; as a result,
the acquired image may have a cast, i.e. an undesirable shift in the entire color
range. Color constancy aims to estimate the actual color in an acquired scene
disregarding its illuminant. The different approaches can be broadly classified
into color invariant and illuminant estimation [1]. The former approaches derive
from the image data invariant color descriptors without estimating explicitly
the scene illuminant. The latter is actually a two stage procedure: the scene
illuminant is estimated from the image data, and the image colors are then corrected on the basis of this estimate to generate a new image of the scene as
if it were taken under a known, canonical illuminant. Many illuminant estimation solutions have been proposed in the last few years although it is known
that the problem addressed is actually ill-posed as its solution lack uniqueness
or stability. To cope with this problem, different solutions usually exploit some
assumptions about the statistical properties of the expected illuminants and/or
of the object reflectances in the scene. We have recently considered some well
known and widely used color constancy algorithms that are based on color image statistics, and we have shown that the best color correction algorithm with
respect to all the possible image typologies does not exist [2]. In particular color

P. Foggia, C. Sansone, and M. Vento (Eds.): ICIAP 2009, LNCS 5716, pp. 43–52, 2009.
© Springer-Verlag Berlin Heidelberg 2009

correction algorithms work well only when their prior assumptions are satisfied. Moreover in certain circumstances a do nothing strategy can be preferred with respect to a method that introduces a severe color distortion.

Most of the color correction algorithms based on a two step process, adopt for the color correction step a diagonal model of illumination change. This model is derived from the Von Kries hypothesis that color constancy is an independent gain regulation of the three cone signals, through three different gain coefficients [20]. The Gray World and the White Patch, which correspond respectively to average-to-gray and normalize-to-white, are perhaps the most commonly used. The Gray world algorithm assumes that, given an image with a sufficient amount of color variations, the mean value of the R, G, B components of the image will average out to a common gray value. Once we have chosen the common gray value, each image color component is scaled by applying a Von Kries transformation with coefficients:

$$
\begin{bmatrix} R \\ G \\ B \end{bmatrix}_{out} = \begin{bmatrix} Gray_R/R_{avg} & 0 & 0 \\ 0 & Gray_G/G_{avg} & 0 \\ 0 & 0 & Gray_B/B_{avg} \end{bmatrix} \begin{bmatrix} R \\ G \\ B \end{bmatrix}_{in} \tag{1}
$$

where $R_{avg}, G_{avg}, B_{avg}$ are the averages of the three RGB channels, and $Gray_R$, $Gray_G, Gray_B$ represent the gray value chosen. There are several versions of the white patch algorithm: the basic concept is to set at white a point or a region that appears reasonably white in the real scene. The skill lies in identifying this point or region in the acquired image. The Von Kries coefficients are evaluated

Fig. 1. Examples of different color corrections. First column: original images; second column: corresponding images processed by a white patch algorithm; third column corresponding images processed by a Gray World algorithm. Note that for certain images a do nothing strategy is preferred (for example for the image of the last row.)

setting respectively the maximum value of each channel or a potential white region at a reference white.

Example of images processed with these simple color correction algorithms are reported in Figure 1. In the first column original images are shown. In the second column the corresponding images processed by a White Patch algorithm are reported. While the third column refers to images processed by a Gray World algorithm. Note that for the image of the first row the White Patch algorithm could be considered a good processing, while for the second row image the Gray World performs better. For the image of the last row instead a do nothing strategy is preferred.

Starting from these considerations, we have developed a region-based color constancy algorithm able to automatically select (and/or blend) "do nothing strategy", Gray World and White Patch approach [10]. The selection/blending strategy to be applied is selected without any a priori knowledge of the image content and only performing image low level analysis.

2   Region-Based Color Correction

The region-based color constancy algorithm we propose is based on the Von Kries hypothesis. We look for what we have called the "White Balance Region (WBR)" i.e. the reference region to be neutralized to obtain the three gain coefficients. The idea is to select this region with respect to the color characteristic of the image so that the color correction will introduce less damage as possible. A dominant color in a scene could be a superimposed cast due to the illuminant, but it could also be the intrinsic color of the scene such as in the case of close-up images or portraits, or in case of images with a dominant portion of sky or sea or vegetation. We try to distinguish among true casts and intrinsic dominant colors without an image content analysis, but only analyzing the color distribution of the image in a proper color space with simple statistical tools. In this way it is possible not only to evaluate whether or not a cast is present, but also to classify it. The following color correction, (i.e. the estimate of the sensor scaling coefficients) is assimilated within the problem of quantifying the cast. Four cast classes are considered: i) no cast images; ii) evident cast images; iii) low cast images; iv) critical images: images with a predominant color that must be preserved or unclassifiable images. When we identify a cast, our approach tends to be a white patch approach, in case of low or ambiguous cast, we adopt a gray world like approach, while in the case of critical images (dominant intrinsic colors) or images without cast we adopt the do nothing strategy.

2.1   IPT Color Space

As we are interested in analyzing the image color distribution to correlate statistical measurements with the four cast classes defined above, we are interested in a color space that is possibly simple and perceptually uniform. With this aim we have adopted the IPT color space [11], that is more uniform in perceived hue than other commonly used color spaces, such as CIELAB or CIECAM97s. In the IPT color space lightness dimension is denoted as I, the red-green dimension is denoted as P,while the yellow-blue dimension is denoted as T. The model consists of a 3x3 matrix, followed by a nonlinearity, followed by another 3x3 matrix. The model assumes input data is in CIEXYZ for the 1931 2-deg. observer with an illuminant of D65. The color transformation is described by Equations 2:

$$
\begin{bmatrix} L \\ M \\ S \end{bmatrix} = \begin{bmatrix} 0.4002 & 0.7075 & -0.0807 \\ -0.2280 & 1.1500 & 0.0612 \\ 0.0000 & 0.0000 & 0.9184 \end{bmatrix} \begin{bmatrix} X_{D65} \\ Y_{D65} \\ Z_{D65} \end{bmatrix}
$$

$$
\begin{aligned}
L' &= L^{0.43}; L \geq 0 \\
L' &= -(-L)^{0.43}; L < 0 \\
M' &= M^{0.43}; M \geq 0 \\
M' &= -(-M)^{0.43}; M < 0 \\
S' &= S^{0.43}; S \geq 0 \\
S' &= -(-S)^{0.43}; S < 0
\end{aligned}
$$

$$
\begin{bmatrix} I \\ P \\ T \end{bmatrix} = \begin{bmatrix} 0.4000 & 0.4000 & 0.2000 \\ 4.4550 & -4.8510 & 0.3960 \\ 0.8056 & 0.3572 & -1.1628 \end{bmatrix} \begin{bmatrix} L' \\ M' \\ S' \end{bmatrix} \tag{2}
$$

2.2   Color Cast Image Classification

The basis of our procedure is that statistical analysis of image color distribution can provide information about the color image characteristics, permitting to automatically adapt the color correction process. We assume here that the images are coded in terms of RGB color coordinates. These RGB values are mapped first into the CIEXYZ color space and then into the IPT color space following the color transformation described by Equations 2. To classify the color cast of the image into the four classes defined above, we analyze the 2D histogram $F(P,T)$ of the chromatic components PT. If the histogram is concentrated and far from the neutral axis, the colors of the image are thus confined to a small region in the PT chromatic diagram. The images are likely to have either an evident cast (to be removed), or an intrinsic color (to be preserved: widespread areas of vegetation, skin, sky, or sea or close-up image). Color histograms uniformly distributed around the neutral axis ($P = 0$, $T = 0$), instead, correspond to images without cast. Examples of images respectively with a strong cast, with no cast and with an intrinsic color, together with their corresponding color histograms, are reported in Figure 2.

The statistical measures adopted to analyze the $F(P,T)$ color histogram are simply the mean and the variance of the 2D color histogram distribution. We define the mean values and the variances of the histogram projections along the two chromatic axes P and T as follows:

$$
\mu_k = \int_k k F(P,T) dk \tag{3}
$$

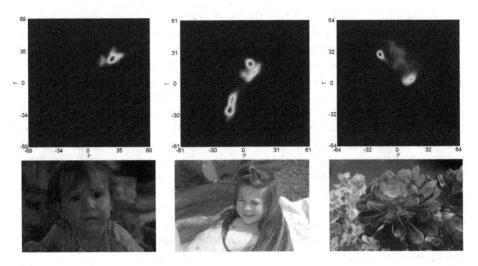

Fig. 2. Examples of 2D histogram of the chromatic components PT: evident cast (left), no cast (center), critical image (right)

and

$$\sigma_k^2 = \int_k (\mu_k - k)^2 F(P,T) dk \qquad (4)$$

with $k = P, T$. Using these measures we can associate to each image histogram an Equivalent Circle (EC) with center $C = (\mu_P, \mu_T)$ and radius $\sigma = \sqrt{\sigma_P^2 + \sigma_T^2}$. To quantitatively characterize the EC we introduce a distance D defined as $D = \mu - \sigma$, where $\mu = \sqrt{\mu_P^2 + \mu_T^2}$, and the ratio $D_\sigma = D/\sigma$. D is thus a measure of how far the whole histogram (identified with its EC) lies from the neutral axis ($P = 0$, $T = 0$), while σ is a measure of how the histogram is spread. The idea is that analyzing these measurements makes it possible to quantify the strength of the cast. For instance, if the histogram (and thus its corresponding EC) is concentrated (small value of σ) and far from the neutral axis (high value of μ and D_σ), the colors of the image are confined to a small region. This means that there is either a strong cast (to be removed), or what we have called a dominant intrinsic color (to be preserved). On the other hand, color histograms corresponding to spread EC (high values of σ), centered near the neutral axis (low value of μ and D_σ) could correspond to no cast or feeble cast images. The boundaries that distinguish among these cast classes in terms of mean, variance, D and D_σ, were determined applying the Particle Swarm Optimization method described in the next section, on a suitable training set.

3 Particle Swarm Optimization Description

The parameters for our Region-based color constancy are found using Particle Swarm Optimization (PSO)[3] over the set of feasible solutions. PSO is a population based stochastic optimization technique which shares many similarities with evolutionary computation techniques. A population of individuals is initialized as random guesses to the problem solutions; and a communication structure is also defined, assigning neighbours for each individual to interact with. These individuals are candidate solutions. An iterative process to improve these candidate solutions is set in motion. The particles iteratively evaluate the fitness of the candidate solutions and remember the location where they had their best success. The individual's best solution is called the particle best or the local best. Each particle makes this information available to its neighbours. They are also able to see where their neighbours have had success. Movements through the search space are guided by these successes. The swarm is typically modeled by particles in multidimensional space that have a position and a velocity. These particles fly through hyperspace and have two essential reasoning capabilities: their memory of their own best position and their knowledge of the global or their neighborhood's best position. Members of a swarm communicate good positions to each other and adjust their own position and velocity based on these good positions.

4   Experimental Results

4.1   Color Constancy Algorithms Used for Benchmarking

In this work, we chose for benchmark six widely used algorithms in the state of the art. These algorithms were chosen as exploiting only low-level image information.

These can be seen as different instantiations of a recently proposed equation[18] that unifies a variety of algorithms. The algorithms considered are:

1. Gray World (GW) algorithm [14], which is based on the assumption that the average reflectance in a scene is achromatic.
2. White Point (WP) algorithm [15], also known as Maximum RGB, which is based on the assumption that the maximum reflectance in a scene is achromatic.
3. Shades of Gray (SG) algorithm [16], which is based on the assumption that the $p-$th Minkowski norm of a scene is achromatic.
4. General Gray World (gGW) algorithm [17,18], which is based on the assumption that the $p-$th Minkowski norm of a scene after local smoothing is achromatic.
5. Gray Edge (GE1) algorithm [18], which is based on the assumption that the $p-$th Minkowski norm of the first order derivative in a scene is achromatic.
6. Second Order Gray Edge (GE2) algorithm [18], which is based on the assumption that the $p-$th Minkowski norm of the second order derivative in a scene is achromatic.

As can be noticed, four of the algorithms considered have one or two parameters that can be opportunely tuned for a particular image: SG has the $p-$th Minkowski norm, while gGW, GE1 and GE2 have both the $p-$th Minkowski norm and the smoothing parameter.

4.2   Dataset Selection

In our experiments we used a subset of the dataset presented by Ciurea and Funt [4]. The original dataset is commonly used in the evaluation of color constancy algorithms as it is labeled with the ground truth illuminants. In the dataset, 15 digital video clips were recorded (at 15 frames per second) in different settings such as indoor, outdoor, desert, markets, cityscape, etc... for a total of two hours of videos. From each clip, a set of images was extracted resulting in a dataset of more than 11,000 images. A gray sphere appears in the bottom right corner of the images and was used to estimate the true color of the scene illuminant. Since the dataset sources were video clips, the images extracted show high correlation. To remove this correlation, as already been done in [7,8], only a subset of images should be used from each set. Taking into account that the image sets came from video clips, we applied a two stage video-based analysis to select the image to be included in the final illuminant dataset.

In the first stage, a video clip is reconstructed from each set of images removing the right part of the images containing the gray sphere. The video clip is fed to a key frame extraction algorithm [5] which dynamically selects a set of candidate images by analyzing the visual contents of consecutive frames. Clips showing high variability in their pictorial contents will have a high number of images extracted while clips showing little or no variability will have only a single image extracted.

As a trade-off between the number of images to be included in the dataset and the correlation problem, we set the parameters of the key frame extraction algorithm so that the images extracted correspond to at least 10% of the clip size.

In the second stage, we further processed the extracted images with a visual summary post-processing algorithm [6]. For this work, we exploited only the key frame grouping processing step that eliminates pictorially similar images, using a hierarchical clustering algorithm.

The clustering algorithm further removes redundancies within the set of images. At each step one image is removed from the set and the clustering process stops when the number of remaining images is exactly 10% of the clip size. The final subset consists of 1,135 images.

4.3   Error Measure and Statistical Significance of the Results

To evaluate the performance of the algorithms on the dataset, we have used an intensity independent error measure. As suggested by Hordley and Finlayson [9], we use the angle between the RGB triplets of the illuminant color (ρ_w) and the algorithm's estimate of it ($\hat{\rho}_w$) as error measure:

$$e_{ANG} = \arccos\left(\frac{\rho_w^T \hat{\rho}_w}{\|\rho_w\|\|\hat{\rho}_w\|}\right) . \tag{5}$$

It has been shown also [9] that the median error is a good descriptor of the angular error distribution.

Our color constancy algorithms and four of the color constancy algorithms considered for comparison (SG, gGW, GE1, GE2), needed a training phase to opportunely tune their parameters. The best parameters chosen for the SG, gGW, GE1, GE2 are the same used in [7,8], where the median error has been used as a cost function and it was optimized using a Pattern Search Method (PSM)[12,13]. The training set consisted of 300 randomly extracted images from the 1,135 images of the illuminant dataset. The remaining 835 images were used as test set, on which the algorithm performance are assessed. In order to compare the whole error distribution between different algorithms, together with the median angular error, we used the Wilcoxon Sign Test (WST) [21]. A score is generated by counting the number of times that the performance of a given algorithm has been considered to be better than the others.

The results in terms of both the angular error and the Wilcoxon score for the training and test sets are reported in Table 1. For what concerns the training set, the performance of almost all the benchmark algorithms considered were statistically equivalent. Our region-based algorithm, instead, performed statistically better than all the benchmark algorithms considered. On the test set instead, the benchmark algorithms tend to form two different statistically indistinguishable groups. Our region-based algorithm was still statistically the best one.

Table 1. Median angular error obtained by the color constancy algorithms on the training and test set. The best results for each column are reported in bold.

Method	Training set		Test set	
	Median	WSTs	Median	WSTs
GW	5.62	1	5.95	0
WP	7.76	0	5.48	3
SG	5.56	1	5.80	0
gGW	5.57	1	5.80	0
GE1	5.45	1	4.47	4
GE2	5.47	1	4.65	4
Region-based	**3.89**	**6**	**3.74**	**6**

5   Conclusions

In this work we have proposed a new region-based illuminant estimation algorithm for an effective color correction. The algorithm proposed is able to automatically select among different color corrections, including also a conservative do nothing strategy. The strategy to be applied is selected without any a priori knowledge of the image content and only performing image low level analysis.

Experimental results, performed on a suitable subset of the widely used Funt and Ciurea dataset, demonstrate that our algorithm is able to improve the results with respect to widely used benchmark algorithms. From our experiments the region-based algorithm proposed reduced the median angular error by 19.6% with respect to the best benchmark algorithm considered.

As future work we plan to investigate if the results of the combination technique proposed can be improved using more performing illuminant estimation algorithms.

References

1. Hordley, S.D.: Scene illuminant estimation: Past, present, and future. Color Res. Appl. 31(4), 303–314 (2006)
2. Bianco, S., Gasparini, F., Schettini, R.: A consensus based framework for illuminant chromaticity estimation. Journal of Electronic Imaging 17, 023013-1–023013-9 (2008)
3. Kennedy, J., Eberhart, R.: Particle swarm optimization. In: Proc. IEEE International Conference on Neural Networks, vol. 4, pp. 1942–1948 (1995)
4. Ciurea, F., Funt, B.: A Large Image Database for Color Constancy Research. In: Proc. IS&T/SID 11th Color Imaging Conference, pp. 160–164 (2003)
5. Ciocca, G., Schettini, R.: An Innovative Algorithm for Key Frame Extraction in Video Summarization. Journal of Real-Time Image Processing 1(1), 69–88 (2006)
6. Ciocca, G., Schettini, R.: Supervised And Unsupervised Classification Post-Processing for Visual Video Summaries. IEEE Transactions on Consumer Electronics 2(52), 630–638 (2006)
7. Bianco, S., Ciocca, G., Cusano, C., Schettini, R.: Classification-based Color Constancy. In: Sebillo, M., Vitiello, G., Schaefer, G. (eds.) VISUAL 2008. LNCS, vol. 5188, pp. 104–113. Springer, Heidelberg (2008)
8. Bianco, S., Ciocca, G., Cusano, C., Schettini, R.: Improving Color Constancy Using Indoor–Outdoor Image Classification. IEEE Transactions on Image Processing 17(12), 2381–2392 (2008)
9. Hordley, S.D., Finlayson, G.D.: Re-evaluating Color Constancy Algorithms. In: Proc. 17th International Conference on Pattern Recognition, pp. 76–79 (2004)
10. Land, E.: The retinex theory of color vision. Scientific American 237(6), 108–128 (1977)
11. Ebner, F., Fairchild, M.D.: IDevelopment and Testing of a Color Space (IPT) with Improved Hue Uniformity. In: IS&T/SID Sixth Color Imaging Conference: Color Science, Systems and Applications, vol. 6, pp. 8–13 (1998)
12. Lewis, R.M., Torczon, V.: Pattern search algorithms for bound constrained minimization. SIAM Journal on Optimization 9, 1082–1099 (1999)
13. Lewis, R.M., Torczon, V.: Pattern search methods for linearly constrained minimization. SIAM Journal on Optimization 10, 917–941 (2000)
14. Buchsbaum, G.: A spatial processor model for object color perception. Journal of Franklin Institute 310, 1–26 (1980)
15. Cardei, V., Funt, B., Barndard, K.: White point estimation for uncalibrated images. In: Proc. IS&T/SID 7th Color Imaging Conference, pp. 97–100 (1999)
16. Finlayson, G., Trezzi, E.: Shades of gray and colour constancy. In: Proc. IS&T/SID 12th Color Imaging Conference, pp. 37–41 (2004)
17. Barnard, K., Cardei, V., Funt, B.: A comparison of computational color constancy algorithms; part two: Experiments with image data. IEEE Tansactions on Image Processing 11(9), 985–996 (2002)

18. van de Weijer, J., Gevers, T., Gijsenij, A.: Edge-based Color Constancy. IEEE Transactions on Image Processing 16(9), 2207–2214 (2007)
19. Funt, B., Barnard, K., Martin, L.: Is machine colour constancy good enough? In: Proc. 5th European Conference on Computer Vision, pp. 445–459 (1998)
20. Fairchild, M.D.: Color Appearance Models. Addison Wesley, Reading (1997)
21. Wilcoxon, F.: Individual comparisons by ranking methods. Biometrics 1, 80–83 (1945)

A New Technique for Image Magnification

Carlo Arcelli, Maria Frucci, and Gabriella Sanniti di Baja

Institute of Cybernetics "E. Caianiello", CNR, Pozzuoli (Naples), Italy
c.arcelli@cib.na.cnr.it, m.frucci@cib.na.cnr.it,
g.sannitidibaja@cib.na.cnr.it

Abstract. A discrete technique for image magnification is presented, which produces the resulting image in one scan of the input image and does not require any threshold. The technique allows the user to magnify an image with any integer zooming factor. The performance of the algorithm is evaluated by using the standard criterion based on the Peak Signal to Noise Ratio PSNR. The obtained results are visually good, since artifacts do not significantly affect the magnified images.

1 Introduction

Image magnification is a process that, starting from an input image at a given resolution, virtually generates a higher resolution image. This process is involved in a number of applications, e.g., for matching images captured by sensors with different capturing resolution, satellite image analysis, medical image display, entertainment, and image compression and transmission.

Among the many approaches to image magnification available in the literature, the most common ones are based on nearest-neighbor, bilinear, and bicubic interpolation [1]. The main drawback of the nearest-neighbor interpolation method is the too blocky appearance of the obtained higher resolution image, while bilinear and bicubic interpolations tend to blur the resulting image. Edge sharpness is better maintained if non-linear interpolation is adopted [2], or when more sophisticated methods are used, e.g., following the Bayesian maximum a posteriori approach [3], wavelet-based approach [4], fractal-based approach [5-7], and PDEs-based approach [8,9]. In any case, staircase artifacts affect the resulting image, especially when the magnifying factor is larger than 4. These artifacts can be reduced by adaptive techniques, which however often imply a significant increase in computational cost [10-12].

In the framework of interpolation methods, we introduce here a new technique to associate in the output image a block of size $n \times n$ (n integer) to each pixel p with gray level p in the input image. The gray level q to be assigned to each of the pixels in the $n \times n$ block associated to p is computed by taking into account a neighborhood of size $m \times m$ centered on q, where m is the smallest odd integer larger than n, i.e., $m = n + 1 + \mathrm{mod}(n,2)$. The $m \times m$ neighborhood is used, once the magnification factor is selected, only to determine the weights for the neighbors of p actually involved in the computation of each q. The gray level of q is computed as the weighted average of p and three suitable neighbors of p. The magnified version is computed in one scan of the input image.

P. Foggia, C. Sansone, and M. Vento (Eds.): ICIAP 2009, LNCS 5716, pp. 53–61, 2009.
© Springer-Verlag Berlin Heidelberg 2009

To evaluate the performance of our technique, we use as input an image whose resolution has been reduced starting from an original high resolution image and compute the Peak Signal to Noise Ratio (PSNR) by taking into account the original high resolution image and the high resolution image we generate. Then, we compare the resulting PSNR, to the PSNRs obtained when nearest-neighbor, bilinear and cubic interpolations are used. We show that the new technique generally increases the PSNR with respect to the compared ones, and produces visually appealing results.

The magnification procedure has been devised for gray level images, where the gray levels are in the range [0-255]. Work on its generalization to color images is in progress.

2 The Basic Algorithm

Let LR be a low resolution input image consisting of I×J pixels, and let n, with n integer, be the selected zooming factor. The reconstructed image HR at higher resolution will consist of $nI×nJ$ pixels.

The eight neighbors of a pixel $p_{i,j}$ of LR are denoted as tl (top left), t (top), tr (top right), r (right), br (bottom right), b (bottom), bl (bottom left) and l (left), by taking into account their positions with respect to $p_{i,j}$, as shown in Fig. 1.

tl	t	tr
l	$p_{i,j}$	r
bl	b	br

Fig. 1. The eight neighbors of $p_{i,j}$ in the low resolution input image LR

A block of $n×n$ pixels in HR is associated to each pixel $p_{i,j}$ of LR. The gray level of each pixel $q_{i',j'}$ in the $n×n$ block is computed in terms of the gray levels of $p_{i,j}$ and its neighbors in LR. To this aim, we introduce a mask of multiplicative weights, to be used for the gray levels of $p_{i,j}$ and its neighbors. To determine the values of the weights, for each pixel $q_{i',j'}$ of the block associated to $p_{i,j}$, we consider a neighborhood of size $m×m$. The value m is the smallest odd integer larger than n. For simplicity, let us suppose that the selected zooming factor is $n=4$. Hence, it is $m=5$ and the neighborhood centered on any $q_{i',j'}$ has size 5×5.

With reference to Fig. 2, the nine 4×4 blocks, framed by thick gray lines, correspond in HR to $p_{i,j}$ and to its eight neighbors in LR. The 5×5 neighborhood centered on $q_{i',j'}$ (the gray pixel in the central block) is framed by thick black lines. We observe that the 5×5 neighborhood of $q_{i',j'}$ partially overlaps the four blocks in HR associated with the pixels t, tr, r and $p_{i,j}$ in LR. Namely, the 5×5 neighborhood of $q_{i',j'}$ overlaps the block associated with t by 6 pixels, the block associated to tr by 4 pixels, the block associated to r by 6 pixels and the block associated to $p_{i,j}$ by 9 pixels. The values 6, 4, 6 and 9 are the multiplicative weights to be used for the gray levels of t, tr, r and $p_{i,j}$, respectively. The weighted average gray level is computed and assigned to the pixel $q_{i',j'}$. Of course, when another pixel $q_{i'',j''}$ is selected in the block, its neighborhood will possibly overlap blocks associated to different neighbors of $p_{i,j}$, or overlapping will involve a different number of pixels. Thus, proper weights have to be computed to determine the gray level to be assigned to each pixel belonging to the $n \times n$ block associated to $p_{i,j}$. The coordinates of each pixel $q_{i',j'}$ in the $n \times n$ block associated to $p_{i,j}$ in HR are computed as $i'= ni+k$, $j'= nj+h$, for $k=0....n$-1 and $h=0....n$-1.

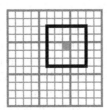

Fig. 2. The $n \times n$ blocks associated in HR to a pixel $p_{i,j}$ of LR and to its neighbors are framed by thick gray lines. The $m \times m$ neighborhood centered pixel $q_{i',j'}$ (gray square) belonging to the $n \times n$ block associated to $p_{i,j}$, is framed by thick black lines.

In LR, let z be any of the nine pixels in the 3×3 window centered on $p_{i,j}$, i.e., $z \in \{ tl$, t, tr l, $p_{i,j}$, r, bl, b, $br\}$. For every z, let $z\#$ denote the number of pixels in the intersection between the $n \times n$ block associated to z in HR and the $m \times m$ neighborhood associated to each $q_{i',j'}$ that has to be created in correspondence with $p_{i,j}$. In detail, $z\#$ is given by the following expressions:

$tl\# = a(k) \times a(h)$
$t\# = c(k) \times a(h)$
$tr\# = b(k) \times a(h)$
$l\# = a(k) \times c(h)$
$p_{i,j}\# = c(k) \times c(h)$
$r\# = b(k) \times c(h)$
$bl\# = a(k) \times b(h)$
$b\# = c(k) \times b(h)$
$br\# = b(k) \times b(h)$

where $a(x) = \max(0, \lfloor m/2 \rfloor - x)$, $b(x) = \max(0, x+m-n-\lfloor m/2 \rfloor)$ and $c(x) = m-a(x)-b(x)$, with $x \in \{k,h\}$

Then, the gray level of each $q_{i',j'}$ is computed as follows:

$q_{i',j'} = \Sigma(z\# \times z) / m \times m$

Obviously, special care should be taken to correctly compute the gray level $q_{i',j'}$ when $p_{i,j}$ belongs to the first and the last row or column of LR.

2.1 Improved Algorithm

The basic algorithm can be improved as follows, at the expenses of a modest increase in the computational cost. As soon as the block of $n \times n$ pixels associated to $p_{i,j}$ has been computed, the minimum gray level $qmin$ and the maximum gray level $qmax$ in the block are detected. Then, the gray level of each pixel $q_{i'j'}$ in the block is updated as follows:

if $p_{i,j} \leq qmin$, then $q_{i'j'} = (q_{i'j'} - \Delta)$, for any $q_{i'j'} > p_{i,j}$,

if $p_{i,j} \geq qmax$, then $q_{i'j'} = (q_{i'j'} + \Delta)$, for any $q_{i'j'} < p_{i,j}$,

where $\Delta = \min_{q_{i'j'} \neq p_{i,j}} \{|q_{i'j'} - p_{i,j}|\}$

In this way, if $qmin$ for a block is larger than or equal to the gray level of the pixel $p_{i,j}$ responsible of the block, the computed gray levels of the pixels $q_{i'j'}$ are lowered. In turn, if $qmax$ for the block is smaller than or equal to the gray level of the pixel $p_{i,j}$, the computed gray levels are increased. In any case, the amount for lowering/increasing is given by the minimal gray level discrepancy in the block with respect to $p_{i,j}$. The effect produced by this updating is to reduce the differences between the gray level of $p_{i,j}$ and the computed gray levels of the pixels $q_{i'j'}$, while preserving the relative gray level differences among the pixels $q_{i'j'}$. As a result, the improved algorithm is preferable to the basic algorithm as far as PSNR is concerned. Moreover, from a visual point of view, the effect produced by the updating is a reduction of blurring with a somehow better edge delineation.

3 Performance Evaluation

The algorithm has been tested on a large number of images with different resolution and by using different zooming factors. Here, the performance evaluation of the proposed technique is illustrated with reference to the set of 15 original images with resolution 512×512 shown in Fig. 3. In particular, the original images are reduced to LR images with resolution 128×128, to which the magnification procedure is applied with a zooming factor $n=4$ to obtain the reconstructed HR images.

Since the quality of LR images influences the quality of the reconstructed HR images, we use a decimation process that limits the presence of Moiré patterns in the LR images. To this aim, each pixel $p_{i,j}$ in LR is assigned a gray level equal to the average of the gray levels of the pixels in the block of the original 512×512 image from which $p_{i,j}$ is generated.

For each LR image, we compute the reconstructed HR images by our basic and improved algorithms, as well as by using nearest-neighbor, bilinear and cubic interpolation methods. To implement the latter methods, we have resorted to the standard OpenCV library. For each reconstructed image, the corresponding PSNR is computed to compare the original image to the reconstructed HR image. The PSNR is computed as follows:

$$PSNR = 20 \times \log_{10}\left(\frac{255}{\sqrt{MSE}}\right)$$

where $MSE = \frac{1}{H \times K} \sum_{i=1}^{H} \sum_{j=1}^{K} \left(v_{i,j} - w_{i,j}\right)^2$ and $v_{i,j}$ and $w_{i,j}$ belong to the original image and to the reconstructed image of size $H \times K$, respectively.

Fig. 3. Test images (512×512)

Table 1 summarizes the results. The highest PSNR value for each test image is in bold. The PSNR computed with the improved technique is always the highest one, except for the peppers image, for which the visual effect of the reconstruction obtained by using both bilinear interpolation and the improved algorithm is illustrated in Fig. 4.

Table 1. PSNR computed by using nearest-neighbor interpolation, bilinear interpolation, bicubic interpolation, the proposed basic algorithm and its improved version

	NN	BL	BC	Basic	Improved
airplane	24.693	25.485	23.158	25.215	**25.526**
aerial	21.714	22.117	20.348	21.885	**22.268**
boat	24.605	25.065	23.016	24.828	**25.141**
bridge	22.282	22.674	21.211	22.500	**22.737**
desert	22.760	22.854	21.917	22.734	**22.907**
dome	27.016	27.465	25.855	27.287	**27.537**
house	23.559	24.115	22.179	23.922	**24.148**
lake	23.630	24.437	22.070	24.153	**24.446**
lena	26.921	28.014	24.856	27.699	**28.053**
lighthouse	28.575	29.341	27.111	29.080	**29.414**
man	23.884	24.481	22.499	24.252	**24.535**
mandrill	20.849	20.887	20.095	20.778	**20.962**
peppers	25.999	**27.194**	24.418	26.957	27.152
soap	24.249	24.827	22.890	24.607	**24.867**
wedge	32.444	34.196	32.663	34.226	**34.893**

Fig. 4. The LR 128×128 input image, left, the 512×512 image reconstructed by bilinear inter-polation, middle, and by the improved algorithm, right

The comparison between the two 512×512 images in Fig.4 shows that, notwith-standing the smaller PSNR, the visual effect of our reconstructed image is still good, since one can appreciate a diminished blurring and a better edge delineation. See Fig. 5, where a real size close-up of two details of the two images is given.

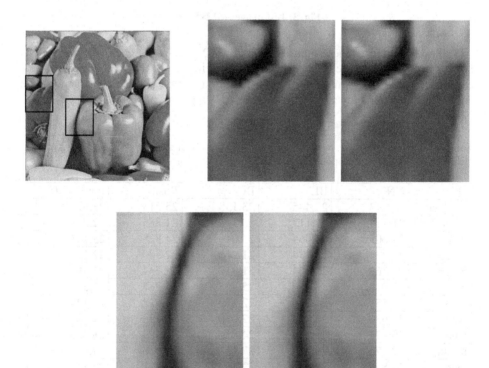

Fig. 5. The original 512×512 image, left, and a close-up of two details of the images, magnified from the 128×128 image, with bilinear interpolation, middle, and our technique, right

Though PSNR is widely used as a quantitative measure to evaluate the performance of magnification algorithms, we think that also qualitative ways should be taken into account. In fact, two reconstructed images with the same PSNR may have a different visual aspect, which is often important at least for display purposes. Thus, we have also computed the difference images, obtained by assigning to each pixel the absolute value of the difference in gray level pertaining that pixel in the original image and the reconstructed HR image. The difference images obtained by alternative magnification techniques are then compared to point out where discrepancies to the original images mainly occur. As an example, in Fig.6, we show two difference images obtained by bilinear interpolation and our improved algorithm. In both cases, for visualization purposes we have set to white all pixels for which the difference in gray level is at most equal to 25. We observe that the amount of pixels whose gray level in the HR images differs from the gray level in the original image is mostly the same in both cases and that differences concentrate along the edges.

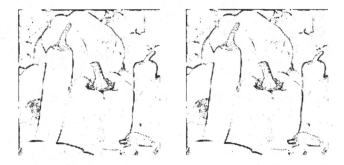

Fig. 6. The difference image for the peppers image obtained by bilinear interpolation, left, and by our improved algorithm, right

The difference image can be used to extract a number of features that could provide an alternative quantitative measure to evaluate the performance of a magnification algorithm. Some of the features that can be extracted from the difference image are: the percentage of modified pixels, i.e., pixels whose gray level in the reconstructed HR image differs from the gray level in the original image; the average gray level change of the modified pixels; the ratio between the number of pixels with a given discrepancy (or the number of pixels whose discrepancy has the highest frequency) and the number of modified pixels.

Experiments have been carried out with different integer values for the zooming factor n. As a result, we note that the PSNR obtained when magnification is performed with our technique still results to be generally higher than the PSNR with the other interpolation methods, as it is the case for the zooming factor $n=4$. Of course, to compute the PSNR, the original 512×512 images have to be reduced to LR images whose resolution is $1/n$ of the corresponding original image. As expected, the PSNR of the reconstructed image diminishes when the zooming factor increases. Actually, this is only partially due to the increase in the zooming factor n; in fact, the quality of the input LR image necessary to build the magnified HR image obviously worsens when n increases. In turn, we note that the visual aspect is not significantly affected for zooming factors slightly larger than 4, if the same LR image is used as input to our magnification procedure; as an example, in Fig.7, the HR images reconstructed from the 128×128 LR image peppers with $n=5$ and $n=6$ are shown.

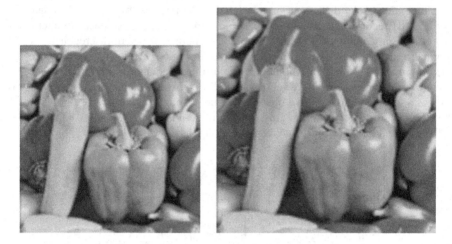

Fig. 7. Image reconstructed by the improved algorithm with $n=5$, left, and $n=6$, right

Finally, in Fig. 8 the magnification with a zooming factor $n=4$ of some particularly significant details of the original 512×512 lena image are given. We may note that staircase artifacts are not largely created (Fig. 8 left, portion of the hat and Fig. 8 middle, portion of the arm) in the presence of edges that are not aligned along the horizontal or vertical direction; we also note that thin image subsets with considerable variation of gray levels are reasonably well magnified (Fig. 8 right, feathers).

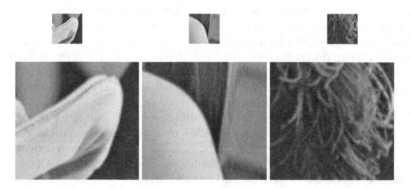

Fig. 8. Some particulars of the 512×512 original lena image, top, and their magnification with a zooming factor $n=4$, bottom

4 Concluding Remarks

We have introduced a discrete technique for image magnification, which is easy to implement and has a limited computational cost, since it requires only one scan of the LR input image. A relevant feature is that no threshold is necessary, so that the technique is fully automatic. Since the technique is discrete, only integer zooming factors can be used. Some blurring, especially with low quality input images, may occur. In turn, the visual aspect of the reconstructed image is appealing, when starting from a high quality low resolution input image, even if zooming factors larger than 4 are used.

Two versions of the algorithm have been presented. The basic algorithm has lower computational cost, while the results obtained by using the improved algorithm are characterized by a larger value of PSNR. The algorithms have been suggested for gray level images, but our approach can be extended to color images and work is currently in progress in this respect.

References

[1] Lehmann, T.M., Gonner, C., Spitzer, K.: Survey: interpolation methods in medical image processing. IEEE Trans. on Medical Imaging 18(11), 1049–1075 (1999)
[2] Zhang, L., Wu, X.: An edge guided image interpolation algorithm via directional filtering and data fusion. IEEE Trans. on Image Processing 15(8), 2226–2238 (2006)
[3] Schultz, R.R., Stevenson, R.L.: A Bayesian approach to image expansion for improved definition. IEEE Trans. on Image Processing 3(3), 233–242 (1994)
[4] Carey, W.K., Chuang, D.B., Hemami, S.S.: Regularity preserving image Interpolation. IEEE Trans. on Image Processing 8(9), 1293–1297 (1999)
[5] Mitra, S.K., Murthy, C.A., Kundu, M.K.: A technique for image magnification using partitioned iterative function system. Pattern Recognition 33(7), 1119–1133 (2000)
[6] Chung, K.H., Fung, Y.H., Chan, Y.H.: Image enlargement using fractal. In: Proc. IEEE Int. Conf. on Acoustics, Speech, and Signal Processing, pp. 273–276 (2003)
[7] Lai, C.M., Lam, K.M., Siu, W.C.: An efficient fractal-based algorithm for image magnification, proceedings. In: Proc. Int. Symp. on Intelligent Multimedia, Video and Speech Processing, pp. 571–574 (2004)
[8] Tsai, A., Yezzi Jr., A.: Curve evolution implementation of the Mumford–Shah functional for image segmentation, denoising, interpolation, and magnification. IEEE Trans. on Image Processing 10(8), 1169–1186 (2001)
[9] Tschumperle, D., Deriche, R.: Vector-valued image regularization with PDEs: a common framework for different applications. IEEE Trans. on Pattern Analysis and Machine Intelligence 27(4), 506–517 (2005)
[10] Thurnhofer, S., Mitra, S.: Edge-enhanced image zooming. Optical Engineering 35(7), 1862–1870 (1996)
[11] Battiato, S., Gallo, G., Stanco, F.: A locally adaptive zooming algorithm for digital images. Image and Vision Computing 20, 805–812 (2002)
[12] Zhang, X., Lam, K.-M., Shen, L.: Image magnification based on a blockwise adaptive Markov random field model. Image and Vision Computing 26, 1277–1284 (2008)

Nonlocal Similarity Image Filtering

Yifei Lou[1], Paolo Favaro[2], Stefano Soatto[1], and Andrea Bertozzi[1]

[1] University of California Los Angeles, USA
[2] Joint Research Institute on Image and Signal processing
Heriot-Watt University, Edinburgh, UK

Abstract. We exploit the recurrence of structures at different locations, orientations and scales in an image to perform denoising. While previous methods based on "nonlocal filtering" identify corresponding patches only up to translations, we consider more general similarity transformations. Due to the additional computational burden, we break the problem down into two steps: First, we extract similarity invariant descriptors at each pixel location; second, we search for similar patches by matching descriptors. The descriptors used are inspired by scale-invariant feature transform (SIFT), whereas the similarity search is solved via the minimization of a cost function adapted from local denoising methods. Our method compares favorably with existing denoising algorithms as tested on several datasets.

1 Introduction

Image "denoising" refers to a series of inference tasks whereby the effects of various nuisance factors in the image formation process are removed or mitigated. Like all inference tasks, denoising hinges on an underlying model – implicit or explicit – where nuisance factors are processes that affect the data, but whose inference is not directly of interest. The generic term "noise" then refers loosely to all unmodeled phenomena, so illumination could be treated as noise in one application, or signal in another.

In Computer Vision we are used to more explicit models of the underlying scene, and even simple ones such as "cartoon models" [1,2], occlusion "layers" [3], multi-resolution and scale-space processes [4] have had ramifications in image processing. However, one could argue that the image formation process is unduly complex, and modeling it explicitly just to remove noise or increase the resolution is overkill. This philosophy is at the core of so-called "exemplar-based methods," [5]: Instead of explicitly modeling the image-formation process, one can just "sample" its effects and manipulate the samples to yield the desired inference result. In the simpler forward problem, that of image synthesis, this philosophy has yielded so-called "procedural methods" in computer graphics, that have been rather successful especially in synthesizing complex textures (see [6] and references therein).

The basic model underlying nonlocal denoising [7] is that an image is generated by patches that are translated in different locations of the image, downsampled, and corrupted by additive noise. To perform denoising, then, one can search for all patches similar to the given one *up to translation*, then transform them, and then perform

P. Foggia, C. Sansone, and M. Vento (Eds.): ICIAP 2009, LNCS 5716, pp. 62–71, 2009.
© Springer-Verlag Berlin Heidelberg 2009

standard image processing operations. This model can be generalized, whereby the transformation undergone by patches is not just a translation, but any homeomorphic transformation of the image domain. The more complex the transformation, the more powerful the model, the more costly the inference process is. Which begs the question of what is the right trade off between modeling power (fidelity) and computational costs (complexity)[1].

We have therefore conducted empirical studies of various procedural, or exemplar-based, models and their effects on image denoising, and have converged to a *similarity model* as the desirable tradeoff. Furthermore, projective transformations can be approximated locally by similarity transformations, for which efficient detectors and descriptors are available [8]. In this manuscript we propose a denoising algorithm that operates on patches with scale and rigid invariance, hence extending recent results on nonlocal image filtering.

In our method, we consider equivalent all patches that are similarity transformations of a given pattern. This generates equivalence classes of patches, and one can define a metric and probabilistic structure on the equivalence classes, so that patches can be compared. This can be done as part of the matching process (by "searching" the equivalence class for all possible transformations of a given patch) or by defining "canonical representatives" of the equivalence class. This way, one can generate a "descriptor" for every equivalence class, and then endow the space of descriptors with a distance, without solving an optimization or search problem at every step. We choose this second option, where we compute – at each pixel – a similarity-invariant descriptor, similar to the scale-invariant feature transform (SIFT) [8].

In the next section we start from the general formulation of nonlocal filtering, then extend it to the similarity model. We then briefly review SIFT, and how it relates to our goals, and finally propose our algorithm in Sect. 3. We then present empirical results in support of our approach.

1.1 Related Work

A variety of methods are available for image denoising, such as PDE-based methods [9,10,11], wavelet-based approaches [12,13] and statistical filters [14,15]. Among all these methods, the most related one to ours is the nonlocal means filter [7]. It recently emerged as a generalization of the Yaroslavsky filter [16], but also taps on "exemplar-based" methods in texture synthesis [17] and super-resolution [5], as well as on "procedural methods" in computer graphics [6,18]. Buades *et al.* transposed the idea to image denoising. Its advantage is to exploit similar patches in the same image, without an explicit model of the image formation process. The approach is taken one step further in [19], where similarity is computed hierarchically and efficiently. Another accelerating method is proposed by Mahmoudi and Sapiro [20] via eliminating unrelated neighborhoods from the weighted average. There are several other methods based on the idea of nonlocal means filter [7]. For example, Kervrann, *et al.* [21] improve it by using an adaptive window size; [22,23] formalize a variational nonlocal framework motivated from graph theory [24]; Chatterjee, *et al.* [25] generalize nonlocal means to high-order

---

[1] As George E.P. Box said, "all models are wrong, some are useful," hence this question cannot be settled by means of analysis.

kernel regression. Nonetheless, all the methods interpret the concept of "similarity" only up to translation, while we extend it to a more general similarity transformation, *i.e.*, scaling and rotation.

2   Nonlocal Similarity Image Filtering

In the next subsection we review the method proposed by Buades *et al.*, then SIFT, and then propose our approach to image denoising and super-resolution.

2.1   Nonlocal Means Filtering

The key idea of the nonlocal means filter is that a given noisy image $f : \Omega \subset \mathbb{R}^2 \mapsto \mathbb{R}$ is filtered by

$$u(\mathbf{x}) = \int w_f(\mathbf{x}, \mathbf{y}) f(\mathbf{y}) d\mathbf{y} , \tag{1}$$

where $u : \Omega \mapsto \mathbb{R}$ is the denoised image and $w_f : \Omega \times \Omega \mapsto \mathbb{R}^+$ is a normalized weight function written as

$$w_f(\mathbf{x}, \mathbf{y}) \doteq \frac{e^{-\frac{d_f^2(\mathbf{x}, \mathbf{y})}{h^2}}}{\int e^{-\frac{d_f^2(\mathbf{x}, \mathbf{y})}{h^2}} d\mathbf{y}} , \qquad \text{for} \qquad d_f^2(\mathbf{x}, \mathbf{y}) \doteq \|f_\mathbf{x} - f_\mathbf{y}\|_{G_\sigma}^2 \tag{2}$$

is the L_2-norm of the difference of $f_\mathbf{x}$ (*i.e.*, f centered in $\mathbf{x}$) and $f_\mathbf{y}$ (*i.e.*, f centered in $\mathbf{y}$), weighted against a Gaussian window G_σ with standard deviation σ. The map $d_f(\mathbf{x}, \mathbf{y})$ measures how similar two patches of f centered in $\mathbf{x}$ and $\mathbf{y}$ are. If two patches are similar, then the corresponding weight $w_f(\mathbf{x}, \mathbf{y})$ will be high. Vice versa, if the patches are dissimilar, the weight $w_f(\mathbf{x}, \mathbf{y})$ will be small (but positive). While the parameter σ defines the dimension of the patch where we measure the similarity of two patches, the parameter h regulates how strict or relaxed we are in considering patches similar. The final result of the nonlocal means filter is that several (similar) patches are used to reconstruct another one.

Notice that the similarity of patches in d_f is defined up to translation. In other words, we can only match patches that are simply in different locations, but otherwise unchanged – with the same orientation and scale. This motivates us to consider the larger class of similarity measures that discounts scale and rotation changes, *i.e.*, a similarity-invariant measure. In theory, defining this measure is just a matter of introducing two more integrals in d_f and an inverse similarity-transformation in eq. (1) to align the patches being averaged. In practice, however, because this similarity has to be computed multiple times for each patch, this introduces considerable computational burden that makes the ensuing algorithm all but impractical. One way to address this problem is to find a function that estimates a rotation and a scale at each patch with respect to a common reference system, so that each patch can be transformed into a "canonical" patch. Once this is done, one can apply the original nonlocal means filter. In the next section we will describe one such function.

2.2 Scale-Invariant Feature Descriptors

The idea of determining when two regions are similar up to a similarity transformation has been widely explored in the past to solve several tasks including object recognition, structure from motion, wide-baseline matching, and motion tracking [26,8,27,28,29]. In this paper, however, we will exploit the same idea of matching similarity-invariant regions for the purpose of image denoising.

One of the most successful methodologies to match regions up to a similarity transformation is the Scale Invariant Feature Transform (SIFT) [8]. The main steps in computing SIFT are

- *Scale-space extrema detection:* Scale is identified at each point by searching for extrema in the scale-space of the image via a difference-of-Gaussian convolution.
- *Keypoint localization:* Keypoints are selected based on the stability of fitting a 3-D quadratic function (obtained via Taylor expansion of the scale-space of the image).
- *Orientation assignment:* A rotation with respect to a canonical reference frame is computed based on local image gradients.
- *Keypoint descriptor:* A vector composed of local image gradients is built, so that it is not sensitive to similarity transformations and, to some extent, changes in illumination.

More details on how each step is implemented in practice can be found in [8].

Notice that there is a fundamental difference in how SIFT is commonly used and how it is employed in our algorithm. In our case the *Keypoint localization* step is not implemented as we are interested in computing a SIFT descriptor and in obtaining some consistent estimate of scale and orientation at each pixel. From now on, therefore, we will define our SIFT filter to estimate scale and orientation as $\rho(\mathbf{x}) : \Omega \mapsto [0, \infty)$ and $\theta(\mathbf{x}) : \Omega \mapsto [0, \pi]$ respectively.

3 Nonlocal Similarity-Invariant Filtering

In this section we define our nonlocal similarity mean filter, which is a combination of nonlocal mean filtering and SIFT. The nonlocal means can be regarded as one step of a fixed point iteration to solve the optimality conditions of the following functional [30]

$$J(u) \doteq \int \left(u(\mathbf{x}) - u(\mathbf{y}) \right)^2 w_f(\mathbf{x}, \mathbf{y}) d\mathbf{x} d\mathbf{y} . \tag{3}$$

where w_f is defined in eq. (2). We reformulate the weight function to be similarity-invariant,

$$w_f(\mathbf{x}, \mathbf{y}) = \mathrm{e}^{-||P(\mathbf{x}) - P(\mathbf{y})||^2 / h^2} , \tag{4}$$

where $P(\mathbf{x})$ is the canonical form of the patch center at $\mathbf{x}$ and h is a parameter as in the Non-local means.

In Figure 1, we illustrate step-by-step how we align the patch to its canonical form: for each pixel $\mathbf{x}$,

1. Take a patch with size $\sim 10\rho(\mathbf{x})$ around the pixel;
2. Rotate this patch with the angle $\theta(\mathbf{x})$;
3. Extract the middle part with size $\sim 7\rho(\mathbf{x})$ for the boundary problem after rotating;
4. Down-sample to a uniform size (the smallest size among all patches) and save as $P(\mathbf{x})$.

In this way we can extract more meaningful patches than in previous nonlocal means methods, as shown in Figure 2. Since we assume additive Gaussian white noise, noise is invariant to rotation and scaling if the image is considered to be a continuous function. When aligning the patches, there are interpolation errors, but they are negligible two-pixels away from the center, if bilinear interpolation is used. We mitigate scale errors by using only patches that are larger, and therefore at higher resolution, than the reference patch.

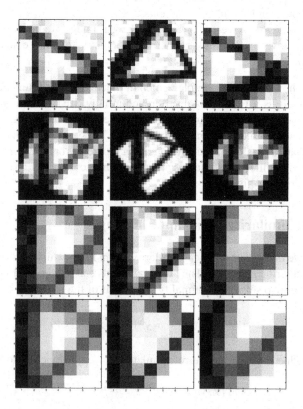

Fig. 1. Procedure to align patches. Three patches are selected to illustrate the alignment, as shown in the first row. From top to bottom: (1) noisy patches whose size corresponds to the scale of its center; (2) rotate the patch with the angle assigned by SIFT; (3) crop the black boundary due to the rotation; (4) down-sample to a uniform size patch 7×7.

Fig. 2. Fifteen most similar patches to the target one (red square on the left) are selected (middle) and aligned via similarity (right). On the right, the pose of the patch corresponds to the scale and orientation of its center as obtained by SIFT.

3.1 Denoising

We add a convex fidelity term to the nonlocal functional J in (3), yielding a denoising model

$$\hat{u} = \arg\min_{u} J(u) + \frac{\lambda}{2} \int (f(\mathbf{x}) - u(\mathbf{x}))^2 \, d\mathbf{x} \,. \tag{5}$$

To minimize the energy (5), we apply the gradient descent flow:

$$u_t(\mathbf{x}) = - \int (u(\mathbf{x}) - u(\mathbf{y}))w(\mathbf{x}, \mathbf{y})dy + \lambda(f(\mathbf{x}) - u(\mathbf{x})) \,. \tag{6}$$

Notice that the above equation is linear in $u(\mathbf{x})$, so an implicit time difference scheme is applied in order to make the iterations more stable.

$$\frac{u^{n+1}(\mathbf{x}) - u^n(\mathbf{x})}{dt} = - \int (u^{n+1}(\mathbf{x}) - u^n(\mathbf{y}))w(\mathbf{x}, \mathbf{y})dy + \lambda(f(\mathbf{x}) - u^{n+1}(\mathbf{x})) \,. \tag{7}$$

We can also extend this model to color image denoising in which the input image $f :=$ (f^R, f^G, f^B) is a three-channel signal. In a similar way, we can compute the weight $w_f(\mathbf{x}, \mathbf{y})$ using high-dimensional patches so that the weight is the same for all color channels. We express the total energy as follows,

$$\hat{u} = \arg\min_{u} \sum_{j=R,G,B} \int \left(u^j(\mathbf{x}) - u^j(\mathbf{y})\right)^2 w_f(\mathbf{x}, \mathbf{y})d\mathbf{x}dy + \frac{\lambda}{2} \int \left(f^j(\mathbf{x}) - u^j(\mathbf{x})\right)^2 d\mathbf{x} \,. \tag{8}$$

Notice that we can perform color image denoising by treating the three color channels independently.

4   Experiments

We compare the performance of our method to that of the PDE-based method [11], the wavelet-based method [12] and the original nonlocal means [7]. Other denoising methods are examined and compared in [7].

We present the nonlocal similarity filtering on two synthetic images which are corrupted by additive Gaussian noise with standard deviation $\sigma = 20$ (Fig. 3) and $\sigma = 40$ (Fig. 4) respectively. For each method, the residual image $f - u$ is shown. Both the PDE-based method [11] and the wavelet based method [12] fail to preserve structures as they are left in the residual image. The traditional nonlocal method fails to denoise the central part in Fig 3 since these regions in the residual image are almost flat.

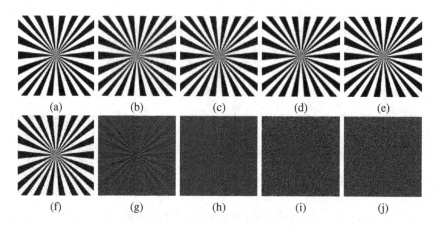

Fig. 3. Experiment with Gaussian noise: $\sigma = 20$. *Top: (a) original image, (b) PDE-based [11], (c) Wavelet-based [12], (d) nonlocal means and (e) NL similarity. Bottom: (f) noisy input f, (g)-(j) show the residual of each method (b)-(e) respectively. The flat regions in (h) show that the central part has not been denoised.*

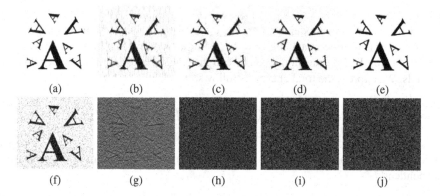

Fig. 4. Experiment with Gaussian noise: $\sigma = 40$. *Top: (a) original image, (b) PDE-based [11], (c) Wavelet-based [12], (d) nonlocal means and (e) NL similarity. Bottom: (f) noisy input f, (g)-(j) residual of each method (b)-(e) respectively. The flat regions in (h) show that the serifs of the A characters have not been captured.*

Fig. 5. Color image denoising with Gaussian noise with $\sigma = 30$. From left to right, top to bottom: (a) original image, (b) noisy input f, (c) nonlocal means u_1, (d) nonlocal Similarity u_2, (e) NL method noise $f - u_1$ and (f) NL similarity method noise $f - u_2$. The stripes tend to be restored better in (f) than in (e).

Table 1. Root mean square error for the input images and different denoising methods

RMS	Input	PDE-based [11]	wavelet-based[12]	NL means[7]	NL similarity
testpat	20.00	14.65	12.56	9.80	**6.74**
letter	40.00	20.05	13.57	12.42	**11.66**
flag (color)	30.00	N/A	N/A	10.43	**9.11**

An example of color image denoising is presented in Fig. 5. In computing the weight, the L_2 distance between 3-D patches (RGB) is used. As for denoising, we treat the three color bands independently. The results are presented in Fig. 5, which shows that our approach works better for stripes, while it is comparable to the original method for the stars.

We compare the quantitative evaluation of various denoising methods. Table 1 lists the root mean square (RMS) error of each method:

$$RMS(u) = \sqrt{\int_\Omega (I(x) - u(x))^2 dx / |\Omega|}, \qquad (9)$$

where I is the original image and u is the reconstruction of the method, both of which are defined on the image domain Ω.

5   Conclusions

We extended the nonlocal means filtering by a more general similarity measurement. In particular, we applied SIFT to estimate a rotation and a scale at each patch so that it can be transformed to a canonical form. Then we construct the weight based on the canonical form so that we could exploit more similar patches to help denoising. Experiments demonstrate that the proposed nonlocal similarity filtering outperforms the previous methods especially when applied to the restoration of patterns that are replicated with different scale and/or rotation.

Acknowledgement. This work is supported by NSF grant ECS-0622245, ONR grants N000140810363/N000140810414, and EPSRC grant EP/F023073/1(P). Dr. Favaro acknowledges the support of his position within the Joint Research Institute in Image and Signal Processing at Heriot-Watt University which is part of the Edinburgh Research Partnership in Engineering and Mathematics (ERPem).

References

1. Mumford, D., Shah, J.: Optimal approximation by piecewise smooth optimal approximation by piecewise smooth functions and associated variational problems. Commun. Pure Appl. Math. 42, 577–685 (1989)
2. Yin, W., Goldfarb, D., Osher, S.J.: Image cartoon-texture decomposition and feature selection using the total variation regularized l1 functional. In: Paragios, N., Faugeras, O., Chan, T., Schnörr, C. (eds.) VLSM 2005. LNCS, vol. 3752, pp. 73–84. Springer, Heidelberg (2005)
3. Wang, J.Y.A., Adelson, E.H.: Representing moving images with layers. IEEE Transactions on Image Processing Special Issue: Image Sequence Compression 3(5), 625–638 (1994)
4. Lindeberg, T.: Scale-space theory: A basic tool for analysing sturctures at different scale. Journal of Applied Statistics 21(2), 224–270 (1994)
5. Freeman, W.T., Jones, T.R., Pasztor, E.C.: Example-based super-resolution. In: IEEE Computer Graphics and Applications (2002)
6. Wei, L.Y., Levoy, M.: Fast texture synthesis using tree-structured vector quantization. In: Proc. of conf. on Computer Graphics and interactive techniques, pp. 479–488 (2000)
7. Buades, A., Coll, B., Morel, J.M.: On image denoising methods. SIAM Multiscale Modeling and Simulation 4(2), 490–530 (2005)
8. Lowe, D.G.: Distinctive image features from scale-invariant keypoints. International Journal of Computer Vision 60(2), 91–110 (2004)
9. Perona, P., Malik, J.: Scale space and edge detection using anisotropic diffusion. IEEE Trans. Pattern Anal. Math. Intell. 12, 629–639 (1990)
10. Rudin, L., Osher, S., Fatemi, E.: Nonlinear total variation based noise removal algorithms. Physica D 60, 259–268 (1992)
11. Chambolle, A.: An algorithm for total variation minimization and applications. Journal of Mathematical Imaging Vision 20, 89–97 (2004)
12. Portilla, J., Strela, V., Wainwright, M.J., Simoncelli, E.P.: Image denoising using scale mixtures of gaussians in the wavelet domain. IEEE Trans. Image Process. 12, 1338–1351 (2003)
13. Mignotte, M.: Image denoising by averaging of piecewise constant simulations of image partitions. IEEE Trans. Image Processing 16, 523–533 (2007)
14. Tomasi, C., Manduchi, R.: Bilateral filtering for gray and color images. In: Proc. International Conference Computer Vision, pp. 839–846 (1998)
15. Awate, S.P., Whitaker, R.T.: Unsupervised, information-theoretic, adaptive image filtering for image restoration. IEEE Trans. Pattern Anal. Mach. Intell. 28(3), 364–376 (2006)
16. Yaroslavsky, L.P.: Digital Picture Processing, an Introduction. Springer, Berlin (1985)
17. Efros, A.A., Leung, T.K.: Texture synthesis by non-parameteric sampling. In: ICCV, vol. 2, pp. 1033–1038 (1999)
18. Criminisi, A., Perez, P., Toyama, K.: Region filling and object removal by exemplar-based inpainting. IEEE Transactions on Image Processing, 1200–1212 (2004)

19. Brox, T., Cremers, D.: Iterated nonlocal means for texture restoration. In: Sgallari, F., Murli, A., Paragios, N. (eds.) SSVM 2007. LNCS, vol. 4485, pp. 13–24. Springer, Heidelberg (2007)

20. Mahmoudi, M., Sapiro, G.: Fast image and video denoising via nonlocal means of similiar neighborhoods. IEEE Signal Processing Letter 12, 839–842 (2005)

21. Kervrann, C., Boulanger, J.: Optimal spatial adaptatio for patch-based image denoising. IEEE Trans. Image Processing 15, 2866–2878 (2006)

22. Gilboa, G., Osher, S.: Nonlocal operators with applications to image processing. Technical report, UCLA CAM report 07-23 (2007)

23. Kindermann, S., Osher, S., Jones, P.: Deblurring and denoising of images by nonlocal functionals. SIAM Multiscale Modeling and Simulation 4(4), 1091–1115 (2005)

24. Zhou, D., Scholkopf, B.: A regularization framework for learning from graph data. In: ICML Workshop on Stat. Relational Learning and Its Connections to Other Fields (2004)

25. Chatterjee, P., Milanfar, P.: A generalization of non-local means via kernel regression. In: Proc. of SPIE Conf. on Computational Imaging (2008)

26. Schmid, C., Mohr, R.: Local greyvalue invariants for image retrieval. Pattern Analysis and Machine Intelligence (1997)

27. Tuytelaars, T., Gool, L.V.: Wide baseline stereo based on local, affinely invariant regions. In: British Machine vision conference, pp. 412–422 (2000)

28. Matas, J., Chum, O., Urban, M., Pajdla, T.: Robusts wide baseline stereo from maximally stable extremal regions. In: British Machine vision conference, pp. 384–393 (2002)

29. Vedaldi, A., Soatto, S.: Local features, all grown up. In: Proceedings of the IEEE Conf. on Computer Vision and Pattern Recognition (CVPR), pp. 1753–1760 (2006)

30. Gilboa, G., Osher, S.: Nonlocal linear image regularization and supervised segmentation. SIAM Multiscale Modeling and Simulation 6(2), 595–630 (2007)

FESID: Finite Element Scale Invariant Detector

Dermot Kerr[1], Sonya Coleman[1], and Bryan Scotney[2]

[1] School of Computing and Intelligent Systems, University of Ulster,
Magee, BT48 7JL, Northern Ireland
[2] School of Computing and Information Engineering, University of Ulster, Coleraine,
BT52 1SA, Northern Ireland

Abstract. Recently, finite element based methods have been used to develop gradient operators for edge detection that have improved angular accuracy over standard techniques. A more prominent issue in the field of image processing has become the use of interest point detectors and to this end we expand upon this research developing a finite element scale invariant interest point detector that is based on the same multi-scale approach used in the SURF detector. The operator differs in that the autocorrelation matrix is used to select the interest point location and the derivative and smoothing operations are combined into one operator developed through the use of the finite element framework.

1 Introduction

Local features such as corners or interest points have been used to find point correspondences between images as they are well suited to matching and robust to occlusion, clutter and content change [1,2]. The process of finding correspondences can be separated into three distinct stages: selection of interest points, description of interest points and finally, matching of interest points between different images. Here we focus on the first stage only, interest point detection.

Standard corner detectors, such as the Harris and Stephens corner detector [3], find points in an image at one particular scale, but points within an image may occur at many natural scales depending on what they represent. In order to deal with the natural scales at which features may be present recent corner detectors have been developed to work on multiple scales, thereby having the ability to detect all points no matter what scale they are represented at [1,2,4,5,6]. However, by representing the same feature at many scales we increase the difficulty of matching the interest points due to the increased numbers of points. A scale invariant approach seems more appropriate where the *characteristic scale* of the underlying feature is identified. This characteristic scale is the scale that best represents the scale of the feature, and it is not related to the resolution of the image, rather the underlying structure of the detected feature [6]. By using an operator to measure the response of the same interest point at different scales, the scale at which the peak response is obtained can be identified.

Many interest point detectors appear in the literature, and indeed many detectors do not even detect interest points, rather interesting regions corresponding

P. Foggia, C. Sansone, and M. Vento (Eds.): ICIAP 2009, LNCS 5716, pp. 72–81, 2009.

to features such as blobs, edges, or interest points. One example is the Harris-Laplace [6] that expands on the Harris and Stephens corner detector [3]. This detector uses a multi-scale approach to find Harris and Stephens corner points, which are then refined using a Laplacian scale selection to select the characteristic scale. The Hessian-Laplace detector [7] uses a similar multi-scale approach, although uses second-order derivatives for interest point selection leading to detection of blob and ridge type features. One of the most popular scale invariant detectors in the literature is the SIFT detector [5]. This implementation is very efficient where the Laplacian of Gaussian is approximated using a Difference of Gaussians. More recently the SURF detector [1] has been developed combining techniques from the Hessian-Laplace detector, the SIFT detector and using an novel image representation technique enabling improved computational performance, even over the already efficient SIFT detector.

In this paper we propose a scale invariant feature detector using the Linear^2-Gaussian corner detector [8,9,10] for interest point selection. This corner detector, developed through the use of the finite element framework, combines the separate derivative calculation and smoothing operations common to corner detectors such as the Harris and Stephens corner detector. We incorporate techniques from the Harris-Laplace detector and the SURF detector, allowing detection of point-like features rather than blob-like features, ensuring accuracy and efficient computation. In Section 2 we detail the proposed scale invariant detector, including construction of the point selection, and scale selection operators developed using the finite element framework. In Section 3 we perform comparative evaluation and provide a summary in Section 4.

2   A Finite Element Based Detector

The Harris-Laplace detector [2] uses a scale adapted Harris and Stephens corner detector to select the spatial location of interest points, and the scale adapted Laplacian of Gaussian to determine the peak response scale. Detected interest points are then refined using finer grained scales to obtain the interest point location where the Laplacian of Gaussian is maximum in scale. The SURF detector uses integral images with the Hessian matrix to determine interest point location. This approach allows for the detection of blob structures at a location where the determinant of the Hessian matrix is maximum. The finite element scale invariant detector (FESID) combines techniques from the Harris-Laplace detector and the SURF Fast Hessian detector. FESID uses the Linear^2-Gaussian corner detector [8,9,10] to detect interest points using a similar multi-scale approach to that used in the SURF detector. Selected interest points are then refined by rejecting points where the point scale (measured using a second-order finite element Linear-Gaussian operator) are not maximum. The integral image approach [11] used in the SURF detector is incorporated to increase computational efficiency.

2.1   First Order Linear²-Gaussian Operator

The Linear²-Gaussian operator [8] is developed through the use of the finite element framework and in the FESID detector is used to detect the location of the interest points. In [12], near circular Gaussian-based image derivative operators have be developed via the use of a virtual mesh and are proven to reduce angular errors when detecting edges over a range or orientations and in [9] the Linear²-Gaussian operator was shown to have comparable performance with the Harris and Stephens corner detector. The Linear²-Gaussian operator is based on the first directional derivative $\partial u/\partial b \equiv \underline{b} \cdot \underline{\nabla} u$ which measures a product of the directional derivative is approximated by the functional

$$H_i^\sigma (U) = \int_{\Omega_i^\sigma} \left(\underline{b}_i \cdot \underline{\nabla} U \right)^2 \psi_i^\sigma d\Omega_i. \tag{1}$$

We consider a locally constant unit vector $\underline{b}_i = (b_{i1}, b_{i2})^T$, where $b_{i1}^2 + b_{i2}^2 = 1$; $\underline{b}_{i1}$ and $\underline{b}_{i2}$ are each chosen to be along the $x-$ or $y-$directions depending on the operator being constructed. The image function u is approximated by a function $U(x,y) = \sum_{j=1}^N U_j \phi_j(x,y)$ where $\phi_i(x,y)$, $i = 1, \ldots, N$, are piecewise linear basis functions defined on a triangular mesh such that

$$\phi_i(x_j, y_j) = \begin{cases} 1 & \text{if } i = j \\ 0 & \text{if } i \neq j \end{cases} \quad i = 1, \ldots, N; \quad j = 1, \ldots, N \tag{2}$$

is centred on node i, and (x_i, y_i) are the coordinates of the nodal point j. In equation (1) $\psi_i^\sigma \in T_\sigma^h$ is a Gaussian test function confined to a neighbourhood Ω_i^σ surrounding node i that enables Gaussian smoothing to be built into the neighbourhood operator. We refer to the use of combination of two piecewise linear basis functions and one Gaussian test function as the Linear²-Gaussian operator.

     We use the Harris and Stephens [3] cornerness measure to measure the strength of the interest point thus it is required to compute the smoothed x^2, y^2, and xy-derivative values. As the Linear²-Gaussian operator combines two piecewise linear basis functions and one Gaussian test function it is possible to directly compute a smoothed product of the directional derivatives. For example, in the case of H_{xy}^σ we choose $\underline{b}_{i1}$ and $\underline{b}_{i2}$ to be along the $x-$ and $y-$coordinate directions respectively; and for $H_{x^2}^\sigma$ and $H_{y^2}^\sigma$ we choose $\underline{b}_{i1} = \underline{b}_{i2}$ along the $x-$ and $y-$coordinate directions respectively. Thus, we obtain directly measures of the products of the directional derivatives rather than from the product of measures of the directional derivatives. These can be defined by

$$K_{ij}^\sigma = \int_{\Omega_i^\sigma} \frac{\partial \phi_j}{\partial x} \frac{\partial \phi_j}{\partial x} \psi_i^\sigma \, dx dy, \ i, j = 1, \ldots, N \tag{3}$$

and

$$L_{ij}^\sigma = \int_{\Omega_i^\sigma} \frac{\partial \phi_j}{\partial y} \frac{\partial \phi_j}{\partial y} \psi_i^\sigma \, dx dy, \ i, j = 1, \ldots, N \tag{4}$$

and

$$M_{ij}^\sigma = \int_{\Omega_i^\sigma} \frac{\partial \phi_j}{\partial x} \frac{\partial \phi_j}{\partial y} \psi_i^\sigma dx dy, \ i,j = 1, \ldots, N. \tag{5}$$

The integrals are sums of the element integrals and are computed only over the neighbourhood Ω_i^σ, rather than the entire image domain Ω, as ψ_i^σ has support restricted to Ω_i^σ. Thus, by using two piecewise linear basis functions along with a Gaussian basis function, we generate the non-linear operators $H_{x^2}^\sigma$, $H_{y^2}^\sigma$, and H_{xy}^σ.

2.2 Second Order Linear-Gaussian Operator

A finite element based approach is again used to define and construct the second-order derivative Linear-Gaussian operators, again using a neighbourhood centred on node i and comprised of a set S_i^σ of elements, and supporting a Gaussian test function ψ_i^σ centred on the central node i, similar to the approach presented in Section 2.1 only using one piecewise linear basis function and one Gaussian test function. To construct the second order Linear-Gaussian operator, a second order directional derivative functional similar to that defined in equation (1) is used

$$Z_i^\sigma (U) = \int_{\Omega_i^\sigma} \underline{b}_i \cdot \underline{\nabla} U \cdot \underline{\nabla} \psi_i^\sigma d\Omega_i \tag{6}$$

Again we choose $\underline{b}_{i1}$ and $\underline{b}_{i2}$ to be along the $x-$ and $y-$coordinate directions depending on the the operator being constructed. Here we construct the operators N_{ij}^σ, O_{ij}^σ, and P_{ij}^σ representing the second order x-, y-, and xy-coordinate directions respectively.

$$N_{ij}^\sigma = \int_{\Omega_i^\sigma} \frac{\partial \phi_j}{\partial x} \frac{\partial \psi_i^\sigma}{\partial x} dx dy, \ i,j = 1, \ldots, N \tag{7}$$

and

$$O_{ij}^\sigma = \int_{\Omega_i^\sigma} \frac{\partial \phi_j}{\partial y} \frac{\partial \psi_i^\sigma}{\partial y} dx dy, \ i,j = 1, \ldots, N \tag{8}$$

and

$$P_{ij}^\sigma = \int_{\Omega_i^\sigma} \frac{\partial \phi_j}{\partial x} \frac{\partial \psi_i^\sigma}{\partial y} dx dy, \ i,j = 1, \ldots, N. \tag{9}$$

2.3 Image Representation

In order to provide an efficient image representation we have adopted the approach of integral images introduced by Viola and Jones [11]; more recently integral images have been a key aspect of the Speeded-Up Robust Features (SURF) detector [13]. Using integral images provides a means of fast computation when using small convolution filters.

If an intensity image is represented by an array of $n \times n$ samples of a continuous function $u(x, y)$ of image intensity on a domain Ω, then the integral image value

$I_{\sum}(\mathbf{x})$ at a pixel location $\mathbf{x} = (x, y)$ is the sum of all pixel values in the original image I within a rectangular area formed by the origin of the image and location $\mathbf{x}$, and can be described as,

$$I_{\sum}(\mathbf{x}) = \sum_{i=0}^{i \leq x} \sum_{j=0}^{j \leq y} I(i, j). \qquad (10)$$

The time and number of operations required to compute any rectangular area of the integral image is independent of the size of that region, as four memory reads and three additions are required to compute this region, or indeed any rectangular region regardless of its size.

2.4   Finite Element Scale Invariant Detector Operation

An integral image is constructed using the method outlined in Section 2.3 and the the interest point detection stage is then performed. Using the same multiscale approach as the SURF detector we first select the first filter size of 9×9. The 9×9 filter is partitioned slightly different from the approach used in the SURF detector as illustrated for the case of the y-direction filter in Figure 1.

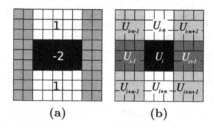

(a)   (b)

Fig. 1. 9×9 filter partitioning for (a) SURF and (b) FESID

This approach differs from the SURF detector in that we need to compute 9-regions for each operator, rather than the 3 or 4 regions that are computed with the SURF detector. The filter partitioning allows the operator values to be simply mapped to the appropriate 3×3 region on the 9×9 filter. The operator values, mapped from the Linear^2-Gaussian operator values obtained in Section 2.1, are then convolved with the sum of the pixel intensities from each of the areas U_{i-n-1}, U_{i-n}, U_{i-n+1}, U_{i-1}, U_i, U_{i+1}, U_{i+n-1}, U_{i+n}, and U_{i+n+1}, illustrated in Figure 1(b). The filter outputs are then used to compute the interest point strength using the function

$$R = \left(H_{U_{x^2}} H_{U_{y^2}} - \left(H_{U_{xy}} \right)^2 \right) - k \left(H_{U_{x^2}} + H_{U_{y^2}} \right)^2, \qquad (11)$$

over the complete integral image using the 9×9 box filter. This is repeated for all the scales using the same approach as the SURF detector, where for example filter sizes of 9×9, 15×15, 21×21, 27×27 are used within the first octave, creating a set of interest point strengths over the full range of scales.

Using the second-order operators from Section 2.2, the interest point scale strength is computed using a similar approach. Where an interest point is deemed to be present the scale strength is determined using the same method as the SURF detector, by constructing the Hessian matrix and computing the normalised determinant,

$$\mathbf{H} = \begin{bmatrix} H_{xx} & H_{xy} \\ H_{xy} & H_{yy} \end{bmatrix}. \tag{12}$$

$$\mathrm{Det}\,(H_{approx}) = H_{xx}H_{yy} - (0.9 \times H_{xy})^2 \tag{13}$$

where the value 0.9 in equation 13 is used to balance the Hessian matrix determinant [13]. Again, this is repeated for each of the octaves creating a set of interest point scale responses over the full range of scales. Interest points that are not local maxima in a $3 \times 3 \times 3$ neighbourhood or above pre-defined thresholds for both the interest point strength and the interest point scale response are rejected. Interest points are interpolated in 3D to localise the interest point's location, where rather than fitting the selected interest points with a 3D

Fig. 2. Example detected FESID interest points using the graffiti image [7]

quadratic function [5,13] to provide sub-pixel maxima, we simply interpolate in each direction $x-$, $y-$, and scale separately.

A circular region with a diameter that is $3\times$ the detected scale is then used to define the region around the interest point for computing descriptors, in a manner similar to the Harris-Laplace and the SURF detectors. Figure 2 illustrates an example image with detected interest points; in this image the threshold has been set higher than usual to limit the number of displayed points for visual clarity. It is interesting to note the Linear^2-Gaussian operator's susceptibility to detecting points around edge features as shown on the image.

3   Experimental Results

Evaluation of FESID was performed using the set of test images and testing software provided from the collaborative work between Katholieke Universiteit Leuven, Inria Rhone-Alpes, Visual Geometry Group and the Center for Machine Perception and available for download[1]. In the evaluation, the detectors used for comparison with FESID are limited to those that are most similar in terms of operation. A full evaluation of the different detectors using the same software and images has been carried out in [1,7], and the reader is refered to this work for full details.

Using the repeatability metric, first introduced in [14], we explicitly compare the geometrical stability of detected interest points between different images of a scene under different viewing conditions. In the FESID detector we describe a circular region with a diameter that is $3\times$ the detected scale of the interest point, similar to the approach in [7,13]. The overlap of the circular regions corresponding to an interest point pair in a set of images is measured based on the ratio of intersection and union of the circular regions. Thus, where the error in pixel location is less than 1.5 pixels, and the overlap error is below 60%, similar to the evaluation of the SURF detector[13], the interest points are deemed to correspond. For more information on how the detected regions are measured the reader is refered to [7].

The test image set consists of real structured and textured images of various scenes, with different geometric and photometric transformations such as viewpoint change, image blur, illumination change, scale and rotation and image compression. We have performed comparative evaluation with the SURF detector, Harris-Laplace detector, and Hessian-Laplace detector using the complete image dataset with different geometric and photometric transformations.

Figure 3 illustrates the repeatability of corresponding regions detected in each of the image sets. In all cases the thresholds used are those provided by the authors of the original detectors in the testing software, and in the case of the finite element scale invariant detector (FESID), a fixed threshold of 75 is used for the cornerness response, and a threshold of 50 is used for the determinant

---

[1] The images and testing software can be downloaded from:
http://www.robots.ox.ac.uk/~vgg/research/affine/

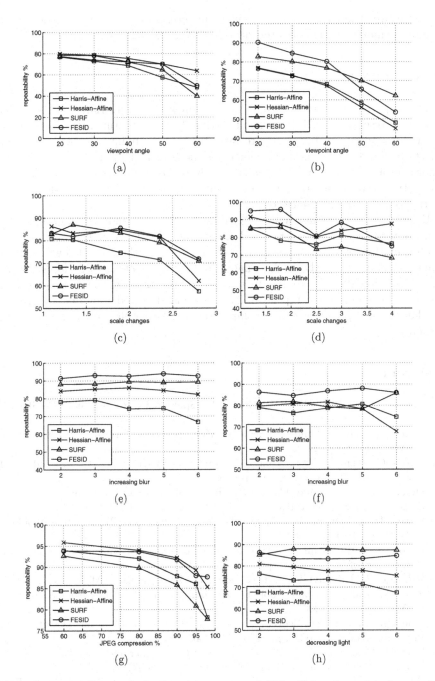

Fig. 3. Repeatability score for image sequences: (a) Graffiti - viewpoint change, (b) Wall - viewpoint change, (c) Boat - zoom and rotation, (d) Bark - zoom and rotation, (e) Bikes - image blur, (f) Trees - image blur, (g) UBC - JPEG compression, and (h) Leuven - illumination change

response over the complete image set. The threshold values where selected to achieve a similar number of interest points as the SURF detector.

4 Summary

In this paper we have introduced a finite element scale invariant interest point detector, presenting the finite element method for constructing first- and second-order derivative operators that are used for interest point selection and scale selection. We describe the finite element scale invariant interest point detector algorithm and show that the Harris and Stephens cornerness measure is used for spatial localisation of the interest point, and the determinant of the Hessian matrix is used for scale selection.

Use of the Linear^2-Gaussian corner detector with its built-in smoothing provides advantages over the standard Harris and Stephens detector. Comparative evaluation of FESID has been performed with other well known interest point detectors using the set of images and testing software developed in [7]. The evaluation illustrated that in most cases the finite element detector had improved or comparable repeatability rates and detected a similar or greater number of corresponding regions compared with other well known interest point detectors.

References

1. Bay, H., Ess, A., Tuytelaars, T., Gool, L.V.: Speeded-Up Robust Features (SURF). CVIU 110(3), 346–359 (2008)
2. Mikolajczyk, K., Schmid, C.: Scale & Affine Invariant Interest Point Detectors. IJCV 60(1), 63–86 (2004)
3. Harris, C., Stephens, M.: A combined corner and edge detector. In: Proceedings of Alvey Vision Conference, vol. 15, pp. 147–151 (1988)
4. Dufournaud, Y., Schmid, C., Horaud, R.: Matching images with different resolutions. In: Proceedings of IEEE CVPR, vol. 1, pp. 612–618 (2000)
5. Lowe, D.G.: Distinctive Image Features from Scale-Invariant Keypoints. IJCV 60(2), 91–110 (2004)
6. Mikolajczyk, K., Schmid, C.: Indexing based on scale invariant interest points. In: Proceedings of ICCV, vol. 1, pp. 525–531 (2001)
7. Mikolajczyk, K., Tuytelaars, T., Schmid, C., Zisserman, A., Matas, J., Schaffalitzky, F., Kadir, T., van Gool, L.: A Comparison of Affine Region Detectors. IJCV 65(1), 43–72 (2005)
8. Coleman, S., Kerr, D., Scotney, B.: Concurrent Edge and Corner Detection. In: Proceedings of IEEE ICIP, pp. 273–276 (2007)
9. Kerr, D., Coleman, S., Scotney, B.: Near-Circular Corner and Edge Detection Operators. In: Proceedings of IEEE IMVIP, pp. 7–14 (2007)
10. Coleman, S., Scotney, B., Kerr, D.: Integrated edge and corner detection. In: Proceedings of ICIAP (2007)
11. Viola, P., Jones, M.: Rapid object detection using a boosted cascade of simple features. CVPR 1, 511–518 (2001)

12. Scotney, B., Coleman, S.: Improving angular error via systematically designed near-circular Gaussian-based feature extraction operators. Pattern Recognition 40(5), 1451–1465 (2007)
13. Bay, H., Tuytelaars, T., Van Gool, L.: Surf: Speeded up robust features. In: Leonardis, A., Bischof, H., Pinz, A. (eds.) ECCV 2006. LNCS, vol. 3951, pp. 404–417. Springer, Heidelberg (2006)
14. Schmid, C., Mohr, R., Bauckhage, C.: Comparing and Evaluating Interest Points. In: Proceedings of ICCV, pp. 230–235. IEEE Computer Society Press, Los Alamitos (1998)

Conditions for Segmentation of 2D Translations of 3D Objects

Shafriza Nisha Basah[1], Alireza Bab-Hadiashar[1], and Reza Hoseinnezhad[2]

[1] Faculty of Engineering and Industrial Sciences, Swinburne University of Technology
[2] Melbourne School of Engineering, The University of Melbourne,
Victoria, Australia
{sbasah,abab-hadiashar}@swin.edu.au, rezah@unimelb.edu.au

Abstract. Various computer vision applications involve recovery and estimation of multiple motions from images of dynamic scenes. The exact nature of objects' motions and the camera parameters are often not known a priori and therefore, the most general motion model (the fundamental matrix) is applied. Although the estimation of a fundamental matrix and its use for motion segmentation are well understood, the conditions governing the feasibility of segmentation for different types of motions are yet to be discovered. In this paper, we study the feasibility of separating 2D translations of 3D objects in a dynamic scene. We show that successful segmentation of 2D translations depends on the magnitude of the translations, average distance between the camera and objects, focal length of the camera and level of noise. Extensive set of controlled experiments using both synthetic and real images were conducted to show the validity of the proposed constraints. In addition, we quantified the conditions for successful segmentation of 2D translations in terms of the magnitude of those translations, the average distance between the camera and objects in motions for a given camera. These results are of particular importance for practitioners designing solutions for computer vision problems.

Keywords: Motion segmentation, multibody structure-and-motion, fundamental matrix, robust estimation.

1 Introduction

Recovering structure-and-motion (SaM) from images of dynamic scenes is an indispensable part of many computer vision applications ranging from local navigation of a mobile robot to image rendering in multimedia applications. The main problem in SaM recovery is that the exact nature of objects' motions and the camera parameters are often not known a priori. Thus, a pure translation of 3D points needs to be modelled in the form of a fundamental matrix [12] (in the case where all moving points are in the same plane, the motion can be modelled as a homography). Motion estimation and segmentation based on the fundamental matrix are well understood and solved in the established work presented and

P. Foggia, C. Sansone, and M. Vento (Eds.): ICIAP 2009, LNCS 5716, pp. 82–91, 2009.

summarised in (Chpt.9-12,[6]). Soon after that work, researchers resumed to the more challenging multibody structure-and-motion (termed MSaM by Schindler and Suter in [10]) where multiple objects in motions need to be concurrently estimated and segmented. However, the conditions governing the feasibility of segmentation involving MSaM for different types of motions are yet to be established. These conditions are important as they provide information on the limits of current MSaM methods and would provide useful guidelines for practitioners designing solutions for computer vision problems.

Well known examples of previous works in motion segmentation using the fundamental matrix are by Torr [11], Vidal et.al [14] and Schindler and Suter [10]. Torr uses the fundamental matrix to estimate an object in motion and cluster it in a probabilistic framework using the Expectation Maximisation algorithm [11]. Vidal.et.al proposes to estimate the number of moving objects in motion and cluster those motions using the multibody fundamental matrix; the generalization of the epipolar constraint and the fundamental matrix of multiple motions [14]. Schindler and Suter have implemented the geometric model selection to replace degenerate motion in a dynamic scene using multibody fundamental matrix [10].

The focus of this paper is to study the feasibility to detect and segment an unknown 2D translation (of a rigid 3D object) in a dynamic scene (with images taken by an uncalibrated camera). The conditions for motion-background segmentation are established and provided by Basah et.al in [3]. In Section 2, we derive the conditions to detect and segment multiple 2D translations and provide quantitative measures for detectable translations using theoretical analysis. Section 3 details the experiments using synthetic and real images conducted to verify the theoretical analysis and the proposed conditions for successful segmentation of 2D translations. Section 4 concludes the paper.

1.1 Preliminary Information and Notations

This sections recalls some notations and equations governing motion segmentation using the fundamental matrix. Let $[X, Y, Z]^T$ and T refer to the location of a point and a translation in 3D world coordinate system and $[x, y]^T$ and t are their projected locations on a 2D image plane. The 3×3 rank 2 fundamental matrix F relates the epipolar geometry of homogeneous image points $m_{1i} = [x_{1i}, y_{1i}, 1]^T$ undergoing rotation and non-zero translation in world coordinate system to $m_{2i} = [x_{2i}, y_{2i}, 1]^T$ as [1,6,13,16]:

$$m_{2i}^T F m_{1i} = 0. \qquad (1)$$

The image sequence generally contains noise and mismatches which result in uncertainty and errors in the segmentation result. Thus, robust estimators are usually applied. There are numerous robust estimators developed for motion estimation and segmentation. Recent examples of robust estimators are pbM-estimator [5], TSSE [15] and MSSE [2]. The segmentation step of MSSE [2] is used because of its desired asymptotic and finite sample bias properties [7]. Although we use MSSE, the analysis is general and similar results will be obtained if other robust estimators are used.

The error measure is defined as a function of the distances such that the error is minimum for the target object (inliers) and larger for the rest (outliers). Thus, segmentation is based on automatic separation of small distances from the large ones. Four commonly used error measures to estimate F are the algebraic distance [12], geometric distance [6], Sampson distance [12,13] and Luong distance [9]. We adopt the Sampson distance [12,13]:

$$d_i = \frac{m_{2i}^T F m_{1i}}{\sqrt{\left[\frac{\partial}{\partial x_{1i}}^2 + \frac{\partial}{\partial y_{1i}}^2 + \frac{\partial}{\partial x_{2i}}^2 + \frac{\partial}{\partial y_{2i}}^2\right] m_{2i}^T F m_{1i}}}, \quad (2)$$

where d_i denotes the distance of the i-th matching points in the image from its epipolar lines. Sampson distance provides first order approximation to the geometric distance and it is computationally cheaper than geometric distance[12,13] and gives slightly better estimation results than Luong distance [16].

2   Separability Conditions for 2D Translations

Consider $n = n_i + n_o$ feature points belonging to two 3D objects $[X_i, Y_i, Z_i]^T$ undergoing pure translations in $X - Y$ plane denoted by T_a and T_b where $T_a = [T_{xa}, T_{ya}, T_{za}]^T$ and $T_b = [T_{xb}, T_{yb}, T_{zb}]^T$ with $T_{za} = T_{zb} = 0$ ($i = 0, 1 \ldots n_i$ denote the points belonging to T_a and $i = n_i + 1, n_i + 2 \ldots n$ denote points belonging to T_b). The location $[X_i, Y_i, Z_i]^T$ before and after the translations are visible on the image plane and are denoted by $[x_{1i}, y_{1i}]^T$ and $[x_{2i}, y_{2i}]^T$. All points in the image plane are contaminated by measurement noise e assumed to be independent and identically distributed (i.i.d) with Gaussian distribution:

$$x_{1i} = \underline{x}_{1i} + e_{ix}^1, \quad y_{1i} = \underline{y}_{1i} + e_{iy}^1, \quad x_{2i} = \underline{x}_{2i} + e_{ix}^2, \quad \text{and} \quad y_{2i} = \underline{y}_{2i} + e_{iy}^2, \quad (3)$$

where $e_{ix}^1, e_{iy}^1, e_{ix}^2$ and $e_{iy}^2 \sim N(0, \sigma_n^2)$ and σ_n is the unknown scale of noise. The underlined variables denote the true or noise-free locations of points in image plane. The relationship between all true matching points in the image plane and world coordinate points are:

$$\underline{x}_{1i} = \frac{fX_i}{Z_i}, \quad \underline{y}_{1i} = \frac{fY_i}{Z_i}, \quad \underline{x}_{2i} = \underline{x}_{1i} + \frac{fT_x}{Z_i} \quad \text{and} \quad \underline{y}_{2i} = \underline{y}_{1i} + \frac{fT_y}{Z_i}, \quad (4)$$

where f is the focal length of the camera matrix (equal focal length in X and Y directions is used and the offset distances are assumed zero for simplicity), $T_x = T_{xa}; T_y = T_{ya}$ for T_a and $T_x = T_{xb}; T_y = T_{yb}$ for T_b. In this scenario, we aim to segment matching points belonging to T_a from the mixture of matching points belonging to T_a and T_b in two images, thus the points undergoing T_a are the inliers and the points undergoing T_b are the outliers.

The fundamental matrix of point belonging to T_a is computed using:

$$F = A^{-T}[T]_x RA^{-1}, \tag{5}$$

where A is the camera matrix, R is the rotation matrix of the motion and $[T]_x$ is the skew symmetric matrix or a null vector of translation T [1,6,16]. For $T = [T_{xa}, T_{ya}, 0]^T$ and $R = I_3$ (representing zero rotation), equation (5) yields:

$$F = \frac{1}{f} \begin{pmatrix} 0 & 0 & T_{ya} \\ 0 & 0 & -T_{xa} \\ -T_{ya} & T_{xa} & 0 \end{pmatrix}. \tag{6}$$

If the fundamental matrix for T_a is known, d_i can be computed using (2). Substitution of real plus noise forms in (3) and true F in (6), yields:

$$d_i = \frac{T_{ya}(\underline{x}_{2i} + e_{ix}^2 - \underline{x}_{1i} - e_{ix}^1) + T_{xa}(\underline{y}_{1i} + e_{iy}^1 - \underline{y}_{2i} - e_{iy}^2)}{\sqrt{2(T_{ya}^2 + T_{xa}^2)}}. \tag{7}$$

For points belonging to T_a $(i = 0, 1 \ldots n_i)$, the expression without noise terms in (7) equal to zero according to equation (1) because the true F of T_a is used to compute the distances. Thus, equation (7) is simplified to:

$$d_i = \frac{T_{ya}(e_{ix}^2 - e_{ix}^1) + T_{xa}(e_{iy}^1 - e_{iy}^2)}{\sqrt{2(T_{ya}^2 + T_{xa}^2)}} \sim e(N(0, \sigma_n^2)). \tag{8}$$

Distances d_i's of the points belonging to T_a in (8) turn out to be a linear combination of the i.i.d. noises therefore, they are also normally distributed with zero mean. The variance of d_i's $(i = 0, 1 \ldots n_i)$ also equals σ_n^2 as the numerator and denominator cancel each other. The points belonging to T_a are to be separated from the points belonging to T_b. Thus, d_i's of points belonging to T_b $(i = n_i + 1, n_i + 2 \ldots n)$ with respect to F of T_a is calculated using (7) where $\underline{x}_{2i}$ and $\underline{y}_{2i}$ are replaced with the terms given in (4) for T_b yields:

$$d_i = \frac{f(T_{ya}T_{xb} - T_{xa}T_{yb})}{Z_i\sqrt{2(T_{ya}^2 + T_{xa}^2)}} + e, \tag{9}$$

where $e \sim N(0, \sigma_n^2)$. Based on (9) and the normality assumption, 99.4% of the points belonging to T_a will be correctly segmented from points belonging to T_b if the following condition is satisfied[1]:

$$\frac{|W|}{Z_i} \geq 5, \quad \text{where} \quad W = \frac{f(T_{ya}T_{xb} - T_{xa}T_{yb})}{\sqrt{2(T_{ya}^2 + T_{xa}^2)}\sigma_n}. \tag{10}$$

---

[1] From probability theory it is well known that if the means of two normal populations with the same variance σ^2 are at least 5σ away, then only 0.6% of the points of each population will overlap.

Alternatively W could be express in term of the direction of T_a and T_b as:

$$W = \frac{f}{\sqrt{2}\sigma_n}\sqrt{T_{yb}^2 + T_{xb}^2}\sin\left(\phi_a - \phi_b\right), \tag{11}$$

where $\phi_a - \phi_b$ are the angle between the T_a and T_b.

In most computer vision problems, the distance between the camera and the object in motion is roughly known. Therefore, the condition for segmentation in (10) can be expressed in term of average distance between camera and translating objects $\bar{Z}$:

$$\frac{|W|}{Z_i} \approx \frac{|W|}{\bar{Z}} \geq 5. \tag{12}$$

We assume an accurate estimate for F of T_a is given by minimising the cost function of a robust estimator. Having F of T_a, the distances d_i's of all matching points are computed. Then d_i^2's for all points are used as residuals for segmentation to segment points belonging to T_a using MSSE. In MSSE, d_i^2's are sorted in an ascending order and the scale estimate given by the smallest k distances is calculated using [2]:

$$\sigma_k^2 = \frac{\sum_{i=1}^{k} d_i^2}{k-1}. \tag{13}$$

While incrementing k, d_{k+1} is detected as the distance of the first outlier if it is larger than 2.5 times the scale estimate given by the smallest k distances:

$$d_{k+1}^2 > 2.5^2\sigma_k^2. \tag{14}$$

With the above threshold, at least 99.4% of the inliers will be segmented if there are normally distributed [2].

From our analysis, the separability of 2D translations depends on the magnitude of $|W|/\bar{Z}$ in (12). This is the basis of the Monte Carlo experiments presented in Section 3.1. We also aim to determine the condition for segmentation in term of minimum $|W|/\bar{Z}$ required for successful segmentation. The correctness of these conditions will be verified by studying the variance of the result of the Monte Carlo experiments. The condition for segmentation of 3D translations are too complex to be derived theoretically. However, the derived condition for segmentation of 2D translations is served as the basis of approximation for 3D translations when T_z are very small or close to zero.

3   Experiments

3.1   Monte Carlo Experiments with Synthetic Images

The Monte Carlo experiments with synthetic images were divided into two parts. The first part was to verify the separability condition in (12) for separating T_a from T_b. The second part of the experiments was designed to determine the conditions for successful segmentation in term of minimum $|W|/\bar{Z}$ required when the inlier ratio ϵ, noise level σ_n and the size of the objects in motions were varied.

In each iteration in those experiments, 2000 pairs of points in the world coordinate according to T_a (the inliers) were mixed with the pairs of matching points according to T_b (the number of matching points depends on ϵ). The X and Y coordinates of the matching points were randomly generated while Z coordinates were uniformly distributed according to $U(\bar{Z} - \sigma_Z, \bar{Z} + \sigma_Z)$. T_a and T_b (both with $T_z = 0$) were randomly selected based on $|W|/\bar{Z}$. Then, all matching points were projected to two images using a synthetic camera with equal focal length of 703 and offset distance of 256. Random noise with the distribution of $N(0, \sigma_n^2)$ were added to all points. Sampson distances were calculated using equation (2) based on the true F of T_a. After that, segmentation was performed using MSSE with d_i^2's as the segmentation residuals. The ratio of the number of segmented inliers over the true inliers ζ was calculated and recorded. Each experimental trial consists of 1000 experimental iterations and the mean and sigma of 1000 ζ's were recorded. The experiment trials were then repeated for various $|W|/\bar{Z}$, ϵ, σ_n and $\sigma_Z/\bar{Z}$ (representing different sizes of objects in motion).

The first part of the experiment was conducted with two cases of T_a and T_b randomly selected such that $|W|/\bar{Z} = 2$ and $|W|/\bar{Z} = 6$. The inlier ratios ϵ were 60%, $\sigma_n = 1$ and $\sigma_Z/\bar{Z} = 10\%$. The histogram of d_i^2 for all image points (the residuals for segmentation) are plotted in Fig.1(a) and 1(b). The ratio of segmented over true inliers ζ is 1.644 for $|W|/\bar{Z} = 2$, which means that 3288 points were segmented as belonging to T_a ($\zeta = 1$ and 2000 points for correct segmentation). In addition, the distribution of d_i^2 of T_a and T_b were well mixed and couldn't be distinguished from each other (as shown in Fig.1(a)). These observations show that points of T_a were not separable from the points of T_b when $|W|/\bar{Z} = 2$. As $|W|/\bar{Z}$ increased to 6, ζ reduced to 0.988 (1996 points segmented as belonging to T_a). Furthermore, the residuals (d_i^2's) of points belonging to T_a were easily distinguished from points belonging to T_b as shown in Fig.1(b). In this case, points belonging to T_a have successfully been identified and segmented. The result of possible segmentation when $|W|/\bar{Z} > 5$ in this case is consistent with our earlier separability analysis in (10) and (12).

In the second part of the experiments, the effect of varying parameters including $|W|/\bar{Z}$ (from 0 to 10), ϵ (from 30% to 80%), σ_n (from 0.25 to 1) and $\sigma_Z/\bar{Z}$ (from 5% to 20%) were examined. The mean and sigma of 1000 ζ's in each trial were recorded. Fig.1(c) and 1(d) show ζ versus $|W|/\bar{Z}$ when $\epsilon = 80\%$ and 50% while $\sigma_n = 1$ and $\sigma_Z/\bar{Z} = 10\%$. It was observed that, for small $|W|/\bar{Z}$ some points from T_b were mixed with points from T_a and segmented ($\zeta > 1$). In such cases, an inaccurate inlier-outlier dichotomy would result in an incorrect motion estimation and segmentation. As $|W|/\bar{Z}$ increased from 0 to 10, the mean of ζ reduced to 0.99 indicating accurate segmentation of T_a. Moreover, the very small sigma of ζ as $|W|/\bar{Z}$ increased indicated the consistency of the segmentation accuracy. The conditions for segmentation were then determined by interpolating $|W|/\bar{Z}$ when $\zeta = 0.994$ from Fig.1(c) and Fig.1(d). We found out that, the required condition for segmentation were $|W|/\bar{Z} \geq 4.25$ for $\epsilon = 80\%$

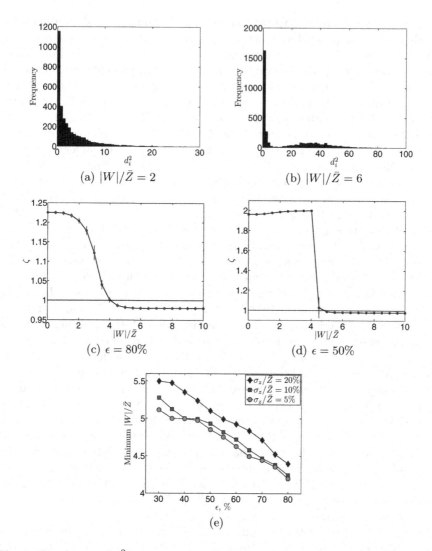

Fig. 1. Histogram of d_i^2's for all image points for ($T_a = [-5.4, 22.6, 0]$cm, $T_b = [15.1, -46.2, 0]$cm and $\zeta = 1.644$) in (a) and ($T_a = [-9.3, -10.5, 0]$cm, $T_b = [-22.8, -7.6, 0]$cm and $\zeta = 0.988$) in (b). The mean and sigma of ζ versus $|W|/\bar{Z}$ ($\sigma_n = 1$ and $\sigma_Z/\bar{Z} = 10\%$) are shown in (c) and (d). (e) shows the minimum $|W|/\bar{Z}$ required for segmentation for various σ_n and $\sigma_z/\bar{Z}$.

and $|W|/\bar{Z} \geq 4.93$ for $\epsilon = 50\%$ for 99.4% of T_a to be correctly segmented when $\sigma_n = 1$ and $\sigma_Z/\bar{Z} = 10\%$. The overall conditions for segmentation of T_a from T_b over ϵ, σ_n and $\sigma_Z/\bar{Z}$ are shown in Fig.1(e). It was observed that, the minimum $|W|/\bar{Z}$ for segmentations increased as ϵ decreased and $\sigma_Z/\bar{Z}$ increased and remain unchanged when σ_n was varied. More precisely, the segmentation of two translations becomes more difficult when more outliers were involved and the

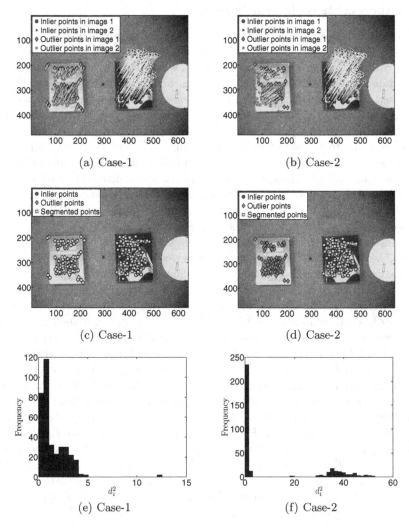

Fig. 2. Corresponding image points (the black book undergoing translation T_a (inliers) and the other book translated according to T_b (outliers)) superimposed in image-1 for Case-1 (T_a=[4.9, -7.0, 0]cm and T_b=[-1.0, 2.0, 0]cm) in (a) and Case-2 (T_a=[4.9, -7.0, 0]cm and T_b=[-3.0, 2.0, 0]cm) in (b), the segmented inliers in (c) and (d) and the histogram of d_i^2 for all image points in (e) and (f)

size of object belonging to the outlier translation was bigger. This is because as the contamination of outliers in image points increased and the size of object (outliers) was bigger, the density of outlier residuals became more spread and the likelihood of some of them to be included in inlier segment increased resulting in a higher magnitude of minimum $|W|/\bar{Z}$ required for correct segmentation.

3.2   Experiments with Real Images

The experiment with real images was set up using a commercial camera in a laboratory environment. The camera was calibrated using a publicly available camera calibration toolbox by Bouguet [4]. Two objects were moved according to 2D translations T_a and T_b and the images before and after the translations were taken. Then the corresponding image points were extracted from each pair of images using SIFT algorithm by Lowe [8]. Incorrect matches in each pair of images and background points were manually eliminated and the true image points belonging to the object moved according to T_a and T_b were manually extracted (in this case, points belonging to T_a was the inlier while points belonging to T_b was the outlier). Then, the true F for T_a was calculated using (5) with known T_a and the camera matrix. The segmentation step according to MSSE in (14) was performed to all image points to segment T_a (based on the Sampson distance d_i in (2) calculated using the true F for T_a). The segmented points was then compared with the true points belonging to T_a. The ratio ζ was computed and the histogram of d_i^2's of all image points were plotted.

The sample results of the experiment are shown in Fig.2 where the black book undergoes translation T_a while the other book moved according to T_b. The noise level σ_n during the experiment was about 0.75 (estimated using (13) and the true d_i's of points belonging to T_a) and the distance between the objects and camera was about 1.5m. The value $|W|/\bar{Z}$ was calculated using (10) from the magnitude of T_a and T_b, estimated σ_n, $\bar{Z} = 1.5$ and $f = 950.5$ according to camera calibration. In Case-1, ($|W|/\bar{Z} = 1.94$ in Fig.2(a)) it is observed that from Fig.2(c) and $\zeta = 1.463$ that the points belonging to T_a were incorrectly segmented. This is because the d_i^2's (the residuals for segmentation) of T_a were not distinguishable from the d_i^2's of T_b as shown in Fig.2(e). As $|W|/\bar{Z}$ increased to 7.73 in Case-2 as shown in Fig.2(b), the points belonging to T_a were correctly segmented as shown in Fig.2(d) and the ratio $\zeta = 0.996$. The successful segmentation of T_a was possible because d_i^2's of T_a could be easily distinguished from d_i^2's of T_b in Fig.2(f). These experimental results and observations are in agreement with the results of Monte Carlo experiments in Fig.1(a) and (b) and verify the segmentation analysis of 2D translations in (10) and (12).

4   Conclusions

The conditions for successful segmentation of 2D translations using the fundamental matrix depends on the term $|W|/\bar{Z}$ (consists of the magnitude of the translations, average distance between the camera and objects, focal length of the camera and level of noise). This relationship was explored both by theoretical analysis and experimentation with synthetic and real images. Monte Carlo experiments using synthetic images provided the required conditions for successful segmentation of 2D translations in term of the minimum $|W|/\bar{Z}$ required when the inlier ratio, noise level and the size of the objects in motion were varied. The minimum $|W|/\bar{Z}$ required for segmentations increased as the inlier ratio decreased and the size of the objects (belonging to the outliers) increased and remains unchanged when the noise level was varied. This is because, when the outlier contamination increased and became more spread, the likelihood for an outlier to be segmented as inlier increased resulting in a higher magnitude of minimum $|W|/\bar{Z}$ required for successful segmentation.

References

1. Armangue, X., Salvi, J.: Overall view regarding fundamental matrix estimation. Image and Vision Computing 21(2), 205–220 (2003)
2. Bab-Hadiashar, A., Suter, D.: Robust segmentation of visual data using ranked unbiased scale estimate. Robotica 17(6), 649–660 (1999)
3. Basah, S.N., Hoseinnezhad, R., Bab-Hadiashar, A.: Limits of Motion-Background Segmentation Using Fundamental Matrix Estimation. In: Proceedings of the Digital Image Computing: Techniques and Applications, pp. 250–256. IEEE Computer Society, California (2008)
4. Camera Calibration Toolbox for Matlab,
   http://www.vision.caltech.edu/bouguetj/calib_doc/index.html
5. Chen, H., Meer, P.: Robust regression with projection based M-estimators. In: Proceedings of the IEEE International Conference on Computer Vision (2003)
6. Hartley, R., Zisserman, A.: Multiple View Geometry in Computer Vision, 2nd edn. Cambridge University Press, Cambridge (2004)
7. Hoseinnezhad, R., Bab-Hadiashar, A.: Consistency of robust estimators in multi-structural visual data segmentation. Pattern Recognition 40(12), 3677–3690 (2007)
8. Lowe, D.G.: Distinctive image features from scale-invariant keypoints. IJCV 60(2), 91–110 (2004)
9. Luong, Q.T., Deriche, R., Faugeras, O.D., Papadopoulo, T.: Determining The Fundamental Matrix: Analysis of Different Methods and Experimental Results. INRIA (1993)
10. Schindler, K., Suter, D.: Two-view multibody structure-and-motion with outliers through model selection. PAMI 28(6), 983–995 (2006)
11. Torr, P.H.S.: Motion Segmentation and Outlier Detection. Phd Thesis, Department of Engineering Science, University of Oxford 28(6), 983–995 (1995)
12. Torr, P.H.S., Zisserman, A., Maybank, S.: Robust detection of degenerate configurations while estimating the fundamental matrix. CVIU 71(3), 312–333 (1998)
13. Torr, P.H.S., Murray, D.W.: The Development and Comparison of Robust Methods for Estimating the Fundamental Matrix. IJCV 24(3), 271–300 (1997)
14. Vidal, R., Ma, Y., Soatto, S., Sastry, S.: Two-view multibody structure from motion. IJCV 68(1), 7–25 (2006)
15. Wang, H., Suter, D.: Robust adaptive-scale parametric model estimation for computer vision. PAMI 26(11), 1459–1474 (2004)
16. Zhang, Z.: Determining the Epipolar Geometry and its Uncertainty: A Review. IJCV 27(2), 161–195 (1998)

Segmentation of Wood Fibres in 3D CT Images Using Graph Cuts

Erik L.G. Wernersson, Anders Brun, and Cris L. Luengo Hendriks

Centre for Image Analysis, Swedish University of Agricultural Sciences
Box 337, SE-751 05 Uppsala, Sweden
{erikw,anders,cris}@cb.uu.se
http://www.cb.uu.se

Abstract. To completely segment all individual wood fibres in volume images of fibrous materials presents a challenging problem but is important in understanding the micro mechanical properties of composite materials. This paper presents a filter that identifies and closes pores in wood fibre walls, simplifying the shape of the fibres. After this filter, a novel segmentation method based on graph cuts identifies individual fibres. The methods are validated on a realistic synthetic fibre data set and then applied on μCT images of wood fibre composites.

Keywords: microtomography (μCT), graph cuts, wood fibres, composite materials.

1 Introduction

This article addresses the problem of segmenting individual wood fibres in synchrotron radiation micro computed tomography (CT) images of wood fibre composites, which is solved in a two step procedure. The first step is to identify the void inside wood fibres called the lumen. It is a challenging task, particularly when the fibre wall does not separate the lumen from the background. This is the case when cracks have formed, or when the membranes of the fibre pores are damaged or thinner than the maximal resolution of the imaging modality, see Fig. 1. In the second step, the segmented lumens are used to guide the identification of individual fibres using a graph cut segmentation algorithm.

Wood fibres are relatively cheap to produce and thus interesting to use as bulk material in, for example, wood fibre reinforced composites. The wood fibre is a tree cell that mainly consists of cellulose ($40 - 44\%$), hemicellulose ($15 - 35\%$) and lignin ($18 - 35\%$) dry weight [1]. In a tree, it functions as a transporter of nutrition and water and is also the building block that gives wood materials their mechanical properties. It has an elongated shape with small pores, as seen in Fig. 1. However, during the manufacturing of bulk material, the cell structure may be damaged. The fibres sometimes break into small pieces and cracks appear in the fibre walls. This gives the material new mechanical properties and it introduces significant difficulties for segmentation algorithms.

P. Foggia, C. Sansone, and M. Vento (Eds.): ICIAP 2009, LNCS 5716, pp. 92–102, 2009.

(a)   (b)   (c)   (d)

Fig. 1. (A) A CT image with a cross section of a fibre with a pore in the middle. (B–D): Three hollow wood fibres extracted from a CT volume with the methods described in this article. A pore can be seen in the wall of fibre (D).

3D images of fibrous materials can be acquired in high resolution using confocal microscopy of 2D slices cut from the sample with a microtome and by CT of full 3D samples [2,3]. With the microscopy approach the resolution is seldom isotropic while the CT technique yields isotropic images and has also the advantage of being non destructive. Acquisition time varies from about one week for microtomy down to 20 minutes with the CT technique.

Wood fibre composites typically have a tight fibre network with many points of contact, which makes identification of individual fibres challenging. A complete segmentation is however necessary to understand the mechanical properties of the composites. One characteristic of the fibre that usually can be distinguished or identified is the lumen. We therefore follow the approach of first identifying individual lumen, and from there identify the corresponding fibres.

1.1 Previous and Related Work

Existing lumen segmentation methods are based on geometrical approaches and are designed for binarized 2D slices where each pixel is either fibre or background. In [4], lumen are identified as non fibre objects that have a certain area, ellipticity and mean curvature. This method is later used in [5] and [6], where a total number of ten fibres are segmented by applying this technique to sequential slices of a volume image. Pores in the cell walls do, however, result in many failed segmentations using this approach. To solve the problems with pores, Aronsson carried out some experiments with active contour models, snakes, steered by Gradient Vector Flow [7] but concluded that it was not very useful since the lumen often are far from elliptical in 2D slices. Hagen and Holen [8] developed a method that was later refined and automated by Bache-Wiig and Henden [9] to handle pores. Their method is based on a series of operations involving the constrained distance transform [10] and can not operate on single image slices. It is further restricted to small pores in fibres that shouldn't be much deformed.

A good lumen segmentation can be used as a seed for segmentation of individual fibres. Aronsson [4] has presented a method for this in which the constrained 3,4- chamfer distance transform is calculated from each lumen in the fibre material. The fibre wall thickness is then estimated from the histogram of the distance

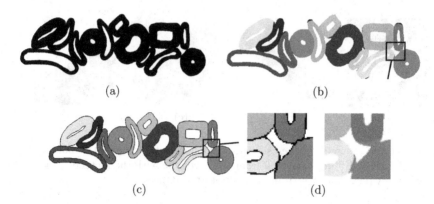

Fig. 2. (A) A synthetic image from [4] and (B) the corresponding segmentation result. (C), the result of our graph cut segmentation method. (D) A close up of the three fibres to the bottom right from (left) our method (right) Aronsson's method.

values. Based on that, a segmentation is performed. The method works under the assumption of uniform fibre wall thickness and was demonstrated on a synthetic image that we have reproduced in Fig. 2. Since the fibre wall thickness is not even, there is a need for other methods.

Another approach to fibre segmentation is by tracking, i.e. by non global methods that follow individual fibres from seed points. There is a method based on the Radon transform by Axelsson [11], a region growing approach by Svensson and Aronsson [6] and a maximally stable extremal regions based method by Donoser and Bischof [12]. We aim at global segmentation of full volume images, while the tracking methods aims at segmenting one fibre at a time and often require user interaction.

1.2 Contributions

A filter that identifies and closes pores in the fibre walls is presented, which has the advantage over previous methods that it works on a wide range of shapes and sizes of pores and cracks. A new method, based on graph cuts, to segment individual fibres in volume images is introduced. It has the advantage over the methods described above that the restriction to even fibre walls thickness is removed. Evaluations of methods designed to operate on images of wood fibres are hard to perform, since no ground truth usually exists but here we describe preliminary results on how to generate realistic synthetic 3D images of wood fibres for evaluation.

2 Methods

In this paper, we propose a filter that closes pores in cross sectional 2D images of fibrous materials, which is based on curvature calculations of the fibre wall boundaries. It identifies the opposite sides of pores as maxima in the curvature and connects suitable pairs of such points by line segments. We then segment individual fibres from 3D volumes using the lumen segmentation and graph cuts. The method transforms the volume image to a weighted graph structure and solves the segmentation problem in that domain before reconstructing the segmented volume image.

2.1   Closing Pores

In cross-sectional images of wood fibres, it is observed that the points of highest curvature at the boundaries are those at opposite sides of pores. Identifying pairs of points with high curvature and connecting them by line segments will thus close the pores.

The input data are binarized slices $I(x,y) \in \{0,1\}$ extracted from 3D volumes. For each object in the image, boundaries are extracted by using 8-connectivity (4-connectivity would give a more rugged boundary) and the pixel coordinates are stored in the arrays $\hat{x}(c)$ and $\hat{y}(c)$, where c is discrete. Anti clockwise direction is defined as positive on the outside of objects and the coordinate arrays are treated as cyclic. The coordinates are upsampled by a factor three and smoothed by a Gaussian kernel, G, with $\sigma = t/2$ to reduce unwanted details and digitization effects. The parameter t is the expected fibre wall thickness. This gives $b(c) = (G*\hat{x}(c), G*\hat{y}(c))$. We denote the first derivative $\hat{x}'(c)$, and the second derivative $\hat{x}''(c)$.

The curvature κ at a point c of a curve is a measurement on how bent the curve is [13]. As a comparison, a circle with radius r has a curvature of $1/r$ everywhere. In our case, the anticlockwise boundary extraction gives a positive curvature where the border is convex. Hence the curvature will have positive maxima at the opposite sides of the pores. We also use two distance measures for the identification of pores, the shortest distance along the boundary (the geodesic distance) $d_G(b(i), b(j))$ and the Euclidean distance $d_E(b(i), b(j))$.

However, to connect any two points where the curvature has a local maximum is not selective enough . First of all, if the fibre wall has a thickness, t, then the curvature at the pore is $2/t$ and we demand the curvature to be at least half of that. We do not let the distance along the boundary be longer than the maximal circumference of a lumen m_c and we do not let the Euclidean distance be larger than half of that. We also want the ratio between these distance values to be strictly different from 1 to avoid connecting corners of fibre walls with polygonal shape. We also not allow the straight lines between the points to overlap fibre material by more than four pixels.

Taking these considerations into account, we connect suitable points with line segments using Bresenham's algorithm [14]. We illustrate the method on a CT image of a fibre cross section in Fig. 3 and the complete algorithm is described in Algorithm 1. Note that the algorithm is performed in all three coordinate directions in the volume to achieve more directional invariance.

Data: (A 2D binary image)
Result: (A 2D binary image where pores are closed)
for *each object in the image* **do**
  extract the border to $(\hat{x}, \hat{y})$;
  $\tilde{x} = \hat{x} * G, \quad \tilde{y} = \hat{y} * G, \quad b(c) := (\tilde{x}(c), \tilde{y}(c))$;
  $\kappa(c) = \frac{\tilde{x}'(c)\tilde{y}''(c) - \tilde{x}''(c)\tilde{y}'(c)}{(\tilde{x}'(c)^2 + \tilde{y}'(c)^2)^{3/2}}$ (calculate the curvature);
  for *all c_i, c_j* **do**
    if $\kappa(c_i)$, $\kappa(c_j) \geq \frac{1}{t}$ *and* $\kappa(c_i)$, $\kappa(c_j)$ *are local maxima;*
    $d_G(b(c_i), b(c_j)) < m_c$ *and* $\frac{d_G(b(c_i),b(c_j))}{d_E(b(c_i),b(c_j))} \geq 1.2$ *and* $\int_{b(c_i)}^{b(c_j)} I(x,y)ds < 5$
    pixels **then**
      | connect $b(c_i)$ and $b(c_j)$ using Bresenhams algorithm;
    end
  end
end

Algorithm 1. The algorithm that closes pores

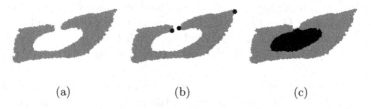

(a)   (b)   (c)

Fig. 3. (A) Cross section of a fibre with a pore. (B) There are many maxima in the curvature but in this case only three are strong enough and thus potential end points for lines that could close the pore. The location of those points are marked with black dots. (C) The line connecting the maxima at the gap is automatically selected and thus the fibre wall can be completed and the lumen correctly identified as the black region. More examples can be seen in Fig. 7.

2.2   Segmenting Lumen

The fibre walls will separate lumens from background when the pores are closed and thus, lumen can be segmented by labeling all non-fibre objects in 2D images. The standard procedure is then to classify the regions as background or lumen according to a few geometric features [4]. In our experiments, we simply classified objects as lumen or background depending on their area.

2.3   Automatic 3D Segmentation of Individual Fibres

It is possible to distinguish between fibre material and background in 3D CT images and from now on we also assume that individual lumen are segmented. When wood fibres are randomly distributed in some material, they have larger contact areas to their own lumen than to other fibres. As a consequence, when

Data: *vol* (a 2D or 3D fibre image);
lum (a lumen segmentation of *vol*);
capMap (an edge capacity map, see the text);
Result: *seg* (A segmentation of the fibres in *vol*)
for *each label in* lum **do**
> construct the graph, each pixel is a node and neighboring pixels share an edge with capacity according to *capMap*.;
> connect all voxels of the label to the *source* and remaining lumen voxels to the *sink*. ;
> solve the min-cut optimization problem and store in *MC* ;
> **for** *Each node in* MC **do**
>> **if** *the node is connected to the* sink **then**
>>> set the corresponding pixel in *seg* to the current label;
>>> remove the corresponding pixel in *vol* and *lum*;
>>
>> **end**
>
> **end**

end
set all voxels in seg that corresponds to any lumen in *lum* to zero;

Algorithm 2. The fibre segmentation algorithm. It uses a lumen segmentation as seed and divides the volume with graph cuts.

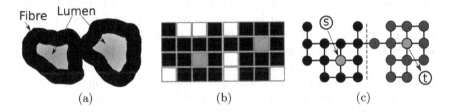

(a)   (b)   (c)

Fig. 4. After the image (A) is binarized into (B), each of the 25 object pixels is replaced by a node connected to its neighbours as in graph (C). The orange pixels in (B) represent lumen and we connect the left one to a special node, called the source and the right one to the sink, t. The minimal cut in the graph (C) is marked with a dashed line and separates the two fibres.

modeling the flow or transfer of something, say water, between different lumen in a fibre network; the fibre to fibre contact will limit the flow. Hence, to find such regions and cut there would also be to segment the individual fibres. Such modeling exists in graph theory and the solutions are called minimal cuts [15].

A volume image can be converted to a graph by letting each voxel be a vertex and connect each adjacent voxel by an edge. When constructing a graph, each edge is allowed to have an individual (directed) capacity. We take advantage of that in two ways. First, we must assure that the flow from small lumen is not restricted because the number of pixels around it increases with the distance. This is solved by letting the capacities of the edges decrease linearly with the distance from the lumen until a distance corresponding to the largest expected fibre width. We let the capacities increase linearly with the distance from the boundary between fibre and background. We call the result a capacity map for the graph structure. The full 3D algorithm is described in detail by Algorithm 2 and a 2D illustration is shown in Fig. 4.

3   Data

To validate our algorithms, they were tested on three types of data: synthetic 2-D images from a previous publication [4], realistic synthetic 3-D datasets of fiber materials recently developed in our lab and data from fibers scanned at ESRF in Grenoble, France.

3.1   Realistic Synthetic 3D Fibre Volumes

To validate our segmentation algorithm, we constructed a program to generate synthetic images of fibres in a volume with the dimensions $100 \times 100 \times 200$, where the fibres are aligned roughly along the last dimension. This is the case in paper and in many composite materials.

Each fibre is individually shaped from a set of variables that are uniformly distributed within an interval. The outer rim of the fibre cross section is modeled by a superellipse, $((x/r_1)^n + (y/r_2)^n)^{1/n} \leq 1$, where $n \in [2, 4]$. The two principal diameters of the ellipse are $r_1, r_2 \in [6, 16]$, the thickness of the fibre wall is $t \in [1.3, 2]$ and the fibre length is $L \in [100, 160]$. The bending of the fibre is modeled by aligning the fibre along a circle of radius $R \in [150, 300]$. The fibre is also twisted around the longitudinal axis, in total $f \in [0, 2\pi]$ radians, and randomly rotated around the same axis to make sure the bending of the fibre is applied in a random direction each time. Variations in the surface texture of the fibre were modeled by Perlin noise [16] and pores were added randomly to model irregularities and membranes in the fibre wall.

The fibres were stacked together by a simple procedure that placed each fibre inside the volume at a random position where it did not cover any other fibre, and then it was shifted by random steps in the two directions perpendicular to the fibre direction until it either reached the border of the volume or hit another fibre. In this manner, most fibres have contact with each other. Finally, the rendering of the fibre volume allowed us to extract different kinds of volume data: an anti-aliased gray-value model of the fibre volume similar to the CT images of fibres that we acquired; a thresholded image that has similar characteristics to the thresholded data sets we use for segmentation purposes; and finally, a volume where each voxel is labeled according to which fibre it belongs to. We also had the option to generate these images with or without pores, which was particularly useful to validate our pore-closing algorithm.

3.2   CT Images

The 3D CT images were imaged at the European Synchrotron Radiation Facility in Grenoble with a voxel size of $0.7 \times 0.7 \times 0.7\,\mu m$ after the reconstruction. For

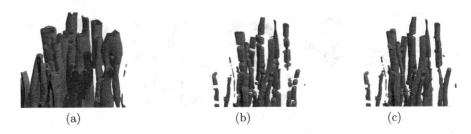

(a)   (b)   (c)

Fig. 5. A synthetic image is displayed in (A). A lumen extraction without closing the pores in the fibre walls gives the result shown in (B). If the proposed method is used, a better result, shown in (C), is obtained.

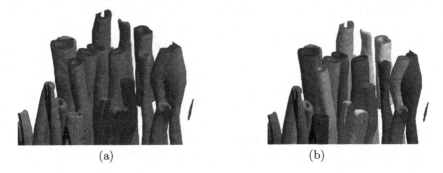

(a)   (b)

Fig. 6. Segmentation of fibres from the artificial volume with the proposed graph cut method. (A) The original volume from which lumen were segmented. (B): Each fibre is segmented, labeled and displayed.

our purposes, they are binarized by first applying a SUSAN filter [17] and then thresholding segmentation. Fibre material take up $\approx 17\%$ of the volumes. Parts of three extracted fibres can be seen in Fig. 1.

4   Results

The described methods were implemented for MATLAB (Release 2008b, The MathWorks) and MEX using C++ and run on a PC with 8 GB RAM under Red Hat Linux. The running time for the pore closing in Fig. 5 was less than 10 minutes. Segmentation of the fibres in Fig. 2 took less than a minute and for the 3D problem in Fig. 6 less than 5 minutes.

4.1   Closing of Pores

We let the method process each slice of the synthetic 3D volume in Fig. 5 where the fibre walls are full of pores. There are in total 144141 voxels that correspond to lumen in that volume (the number approximated by analyzing the same volume before the pores were created). Results from the experiment that show that the method is successful are displayed in Tab. 1.

Fig. 7. Results of the fibre closing method on cross sections of fibres from CT-images

Table 1. Evaluation results of the pore closing method on a synthetic 3D image. Missing voxels are those that should have been classified as lumen but were not. Surplus voxels are pixels falsely classified as lumen. Max overlap is the number of pixels with fibre material that lines connecting pores are allowed to pass through.

	No Closing	With Closing				
Max overlap	-	2	3	4	5	inf
Missing voxels	20891	16375	9599	8382	8572	9377
Surplus voxels	0	119	415	753	934	1055
Total pixel errors	14%	11%	7%	6%	7%	7%

Results of the closing method on single fibre cross sections from µCT data is shown in Fig. 7.

4.2   Individual Fibre Segmentation

We constructed the graph representations using 4- connectivity for plane image slices and 6- connectivity for volumes and used the MAXFLOW software [18] to solve the min-cut optimization problem.

The segmentation method was tried on the same 2D synthetic image as the method of Aronsson, see Fig. 2, where we first dilated each lumen as far as possible before it hit the background. In that case, our method is better since it does not leave any unassigned pixels and it resolves boundaries between fibres with less bleeding.

We have used the method on 3D images as well. For a synthetic volume, the segmentation worked excellently as shown in Fig. 6. We are also able to extract fibres from CT images, a few are shown in Fig. 1.

5   Discussion and Conclusion

The lumen closing method works best when the fibre direction is close to orthogonal to the slicing plane but is quite robust as seen in the example in Fig. 3 where the fibre clearly is not orthogonal to the plane. The method works on a wide range of shapes as seen in Fig. 7. The fibre closing can easily be extended to non-isotropic pixel sizes. The missing voxel errors in Tab. 1 are mainly due to multiple cracks in the fibres, in the same slice. The surplus voxels are created where the fibres are densely packed and small areas between them are classified as lumen. From Tab. 1, we conclude that the method works as expected. We think that the remaining 6% errors are due to pores larger than the fibre wall or when there are many of them in a single cross section.

The fibre segmentation will return one individual fibre per supplied lumen. Hence, good lumen segmentation is important.

From experience, we know that fibres show a great variation in morphology and at this early stage of the development of a synthetic dataset generator we are only able to model some aspects that are relevant for this particular segmentation task. The building of a more complete environment for simulation of wood fibre materials is a task for future work within the scope of our current research project.

Acknowledgments

The authors would like to thank Karin Almgren, Maria Axelsson, Gunilla Borgefors, Kristofer Gamstedt, Bjørn Steinar Tanem, Catherine Östlund and all other persons in the WoodFibre3D project. The CT images were acquired at EFSR in Grenoble, France. This work was funded through WoodWisdom-Net under project number 352006A.

References

1. Bowyer, J.L., Shmulsky, R., Haygreen, J.G.: Forest Products and Wood Science, an introduction, 5th edn. Blackwell Publishing, Malden (2007)
2. Donoser, M., Wiltsche, M., Bischof, H.: A new automated microtomy concept for 3D paper structure analysis. In: Proc. of the IAPR Conf. on Machine Vision Appl., pp. 76–79 (2005)
3. Samuelsen, E., Houen, P.J., Gregersen, O.W., Helle, T., Raven, C.: Three-dimensional imaging of paper by use of synchrotron x-ray microtomography. In: Proc. Int. Paper Physics Conf., pp. 307–312 (1999)
4. Aronsson, M., Borgefors, G.: 2D segmentation and labelling of clustered ring shaped objects. In: Scandinavian Conference on Image Analysis, pp. 272–279 (2001)
5. Lunden, J.: Image analysis methods for evaluation of fibre dimensions in paper cross-sections. Master's thesis, Royal Institute of Technology, Stockholm, Sweden (2002)
6. Svensson, S., Aronsson, M.: Some measurements of fibres in volume images of paper using medial representations detected on distance transforms. In: IEEE Computer Society Conf. Computer Vision Pattern Recognition., vol. 2 (2001)
7. Aronsson, M.: On 3D Fibre Measurements of Digitized Paper. PhD thesis, Swedish University of Agricultural Sciences (2002)
8. Holen, R., Hagen, M.: Segmentation of absorption mode x-ray micro tomographic images of paper. Master's thesis, Norwegian University of Science and Technology, Trondheim (2004)
9. Bache-Wiig, J., Henden, P.C.: Individual fiber segmentation of three-dimensional microtomograms of paper and fiber-reinforced composite materials. Master's thesis, Norwegian University of Science and Technology, Trondheim (2005)

10. Piper, J., Granum, E.: Computing distance transformations in convex and non-convex domains. Pattern Recognition 20(6), 599–615 (1987)
11. Axelsson, M.: 3D tracking of cellulose fibres in volume images. In: IEEE Int. Conf. on Image Processing, vol. 4, pp. 309–312 (2007)
12. Donoser, M., Bischof, H.: Efficient maximally stable extremal region (MSER) tracking. In: Proc. IEEE Conf. Computer Vision and Pattern Recognition, pp. 553–560 (2006)
13. Carmo, M.P.D.: Differential Geometry of Curves and Surfaces. Prentice Hall, Englewood Cliffs (1976)
14. Bresenham, J.E.: Algorithm for computer control of a digital plotter. IBM Systems Journal 4(1), 25–30 (1965)
15. Sonka, M., Hlavac, V., Boyle, R.: Chapter 7.6. In: Image Processing, Analysis, and Machine Vision, 3rd edn. Thomson Engineering (2008)
16. Perlin, K.: An image synthesizer. SIGGRAPH Comput. Graph. 19(3), 287–296 (1985)
17. Smith, S.M., Brady, J.M.: Susan - a new approach to low level image processing. Int. Journal of Computer Vision 23(1), 45–78 (1997)
18. Boykov, Y., Kolmogorov, V.: An experimental comparison of min-cut/max-flow algorithms for energy minimization in vision. IEEE PAMI (9), 1124–1137 (2004)

Semantic-Based Segmentation and Annotation of 3D Models

Laura Papaleo* and Leila De Floriani

Department of Information and Computer Science, University of Genova
Via Dodecaneso 35, 16100 Genova, Italy
{deflo,papaleo}@disi.unige.it
http://www.disi.unige.it

Abstract. 3D objects have become widely available and used in different application domains. Thus, it is becoming fundamental to use, integrate and develop techniques for extracting and maintaining their embedded knowledge. These techniques should be encapsulated in portable and intelligent systems able to semantically annotate the 3D object models in order to improve their usability and indexing, especially in innovative web cooperative environments. Lately, we are moving in this direction, with the definition and development of data structures, methods and interfaces for structuring and semantically annotating 3D complex models (and scenes) - even changing in time - according to ontology-driven metadata and following ontology-driven processes. Here, we concentrate on the tools for segmenting manifold 3D models and on the underline structural representation that we build and manipulate. We also describe the first prototype of an annotation tool which allows a hierarchical semantic-driven tagging of the segmented model and provides an interface from which the user can inspect and browse the entire segmentation graph.

Keywords: Shape segmentation and Structuring, Semantic-driven Annotation.

1 Introduction

In the last years, the amount of digital audio-visual information is huge and rapidly increasing. This data is available within digital libraries in a number of different formats (pictures, audio and, also, 3D shapes). Among them, the importance of 3D object models is augmenting: they are playing a preeminent role in application domains such as manufacturing, science and edu-entertainment and many more. Moreover, all these application domains are recently opening their activities to the web thanks also to the development of collaborative environments. In this context, efficient and effective methods to manage these data are becoming crucial. The most common and simple representation for a 3D object consists of a mesh of triangles discretizing the object boundary. Geometric meshes, as triangle meshes, provide unstructured descriptions of object shapes which, in general, are not sufficient for reasoning on them. The

---

* Corresponding author.

P. Foggia, C. Sansone, and M. Vento (Eds.): ICIAP 2009, LNCS 5716, pp. 103–112, 2009.

knowledge embedded into these digital representations can be better organized by using different levels of abstractions namely, *geometry*, *structure* and *semantics* [1]. At the geometric level, topological and geometric information are explicit but no further information is encoded in the model. At the structural level, meaningful parts of the shape are described together with their connections. Finally, the semantic level associates semantics to lower levels: the association can be done manually or through an automatic semantic annotation process. In order to reason and understand a given 3D model, all the information identifiable at the three different levels must be extracted and kept.

At the state-of-the art, there is a strong request of annotation tools capable of extracting semantics from complex 3D shapes and of enhancing digital representations with context-dependent metadata. Also, moving toward the Web 3.0, Internet is becoming a universal medium for data, information, and knowledge. To be really accessible and usable, multimedia data (as 3D shapes) must be represented accordingly. In this context, we designed (and we are developing) a system, called be-SMART[1], for inspecting complex (manifold and non-manifold) 3D shapes (and scenes) - even changing in time - and for structuring and annotating them using ontology-driven metadata. The idea behind our work is very interesting and promising, and different other systems with basically the same goal are growing in the last years. An example is the work presented in [6] where the concept of multi-segmentation is introduced in order to semantically annotate 3D meshes. In our case, the system has been designed to address not only 3D meshes but 3D scenes, even changing in time, and the choice of the X3D encoding for models and scenes makes the system particularly suited for web applications.

The contribution of this paper is basically related to the segmentation modules of our system as to the first prototype of the module for the semantic annotation. In particular, we developed different automatic and manual segmentation techniques with the mail goal of decomposing the input 3D model into *meaningful* parts. A model can be segmented automatically, according to geometric criteria, and manually, according to the user perception. We keep the semantic-based decomposition into a structural representation, in the form of a *segmentation graph*. In this graph, the nodes identify the portions of the model and the arcs the connections among these portions as the information of the shared boundaries. Our interface, developed in Java for portability issues, supports the use of X3D language [2] for the model encoding and allows the global visualization and inspection of the segmentation graph. We can also tag each portion of the model using a hierarchical semantic-based tagging procedure by which we are able to maintain the history of the segmentation. Once semantically annotated, the portions of the model can be saved all together or separately, preparing the basis of a semantic-based modeling-by-example environment.

The reminder of this paper is organized as follows. In Section 2 we present the related work on shape segmentation, in Section 3 we introduce the underlying structural representation we use for semantic annotation. Section 4 is dedicated to the presentation of our automatic segmentation tool, while Section 5 presents our tool for manual segmenting a 3D model by painting strokes on it. Section 6 will focus on the first prototype of our annotation tool. In Section 7 some concluding remarks are drawn.

---

[1] BEyond Shape Modeling for understAnding Real world represenTations.

2   Related Work

In this work, we basically focus on the segmentation modules of our system, thus, we present here related works on shape segmentation, outlining which methods we used and the extensions and adaptations we performed.

Mesh segmentation is, historically, one of the most ubiquitous technical problem in 3D model understanding. The problem of partitioning a 3D model into *meaningful pieces* has proved to be as difficult as other computational problems that attempt to mimic the capabilities of human perception. Shape understanding and semantic-based object representations rely on the segmentation of 3D meshes that represent objects. Shape segmentation techniques borrow from related fields, such as image segmentation, unsupervised machine learning and others. A complete survey of existing techniques can be found in [4]. The segmentation problem can be formulated as an *optimization problem*. Given a mesh M and the set of elements $S = \{V, E, F\}$, vertices, edges and faces of M respectively, the problem of segmenting M is equivalent to the problem of finding a disjoint partitioning S into $S_0, \ldots, S_{k-1}$ such that a given *criterion function* $J = J(S_0, \ldots, S_{k-1})$ is minimized (or maximized) under a set of specific constraints C. Shamir [4] provides a classification of the existing segmentation techniques into *part-type segmentations*, which segment an object into volumetric parts [18,24], and *surface-type segmentations*, which partition the boundary of the object into meaningful patches [20,7,10,23,5].

Also, different manual or user-guided segmentation techniques have been proposed in the literature [14,26,21,13,19,25,22,8,17] and they are rooted in the expert perception of the object. In this sense, the regions of interest are intrinsically guided by the semantic the user *recognizes* in the object model. In opposition to the automatic segmentation techniques, developed for a specific application context (e.g. CAD/CAM or biomedicine), manual segmentation methods are general purpose. We can divide the existing manual segmentation techniques into two main categories: *cut-based* methods and *region-based* methods. Algorithms belonging to the first category [26,21,13,19] allow the user to draw the cutting path on the model while those which belong to the second category let the user select the interesting regions, and they automatically compute the right position of the cut [25,22,8,17]. In [13], a so-called intelligent scissoring of 3D meshes has been presented in which the user paints *strokes* on the mesh surface to specify where cuts should be made.

For the automatic segmentation procedure, we used the method in [10] and a modification of the clustering method presented in [20] for the automatic region merging (Section 4). The manual procedure (Section 5), instead, has been implemented as an extension of the method described in [13] in order to deal also with non-triangular and not connected meshes, using in toto the expressiveness power of X3D encoding.

3   Underlying Structural Representation for Semantic Annotation

As we said before, our main objective is to develop a general framework for structuring and semantically annotating these complex shapes for improving their usability, indexing and retrieval. Semantic annotation can be performed if a structural representation underlying the input model (or scene) is used. In our case, the structural description has been defined as a *two-level graph* representation able to capture information in case of both manifold and non-manifold conditions. The first level, in case of non-manifold models, is a description of the decomposition of the shape into manifold components. Their structural interconnection is represented as a graph, that we call the *decomposition graph*, described as a hypergraph $H = (N,A)$ in which the nodes correspond to the components in the decomposition, while the hyperarcs catch the structure of the connectivity among the components or are self-loops. In this latter case, they represent the *non-manifold structure* of a single component and correspond to the duplicated non-manifold vertices and edges in the component. In the two-level graph representation, each manifold component (if further segmented) is structured in a *segmentation graph*. In this graph - used in the tools presented in this paper - the nodes identify the portions of the model and the arcs the connections among these portions. Formally, in the segmentation graph G, a node n_i represents a patch C of the input shape and an arc $a = (n_i, n_j)$ represents the adjacency relationship between the patches C_i and C_j and, thus, their shared boundary.

The two-level segmentation graph is also the *core* of a complex framework, called be-SMART, we designed for bridging Semantic Web technologies and shape analysis [11]. be-SMART has the objective to semantically annotate complex 3D shapes (even non-manifold meshes) using domain-specific ontologies and following domain-specific ontology-driven processes. Here, we present our first results regarding three main modules of be-SMART, namely the *Manual and Automatic Segmentation* modules (Section 4 and Section 5) for the manifold parts and a first prototype of the *Semantic Annotator* (Section 6) which adds semantic information to the recognized parts directly in the X3D model subparts. Thus, we will focus only on the updates and operations on the *segmentation graph G*, described above. In particular, in our implementation, G is represented using a standard adjacency list with additional information (also on the arcs) necessary for the clustering and the manual segmentation methods.

4   Combining Automatic Segmentation Methods

In this section we describe how we automatically segment a manifold 3D model. Specifically, we combine a segmentation and a clustering technique, namely the Variational Shape Approximation (*VSA*) presented in [10] and a clustering method inspired by [20]. In general, the system has been designed to the modular, thus allowing to import new automatic segmentation techniques, once implemented.

Given a manifold component M, the *VSA* algorithm segments M according to planarity criteria. Let R be a partition of M (initially the set of triangles in M). The idea is that every region $R_i \in R$ can be represented by a pair $P_i = (X_i, N_i)$, where X_i is the average center of R_i and N_i is the average normal. P_i is called a *shape proxy* of the region R_i. Thus, for any given partition of a surface in k regions, there is a set $P = \{P_i\}, i = 1 \ldots k$, of shape proxies that approximate the whole geometry. Partition R defines a *dual meta-mesh* [10] of the original: every shape proxy is a meta-face and the connectivity of the regions R_i defines the topology of the new mesh. The *VSA* algorithm first creates the set of seeds for activating a region-growing process. Then, from every seed s_i, a region R_i

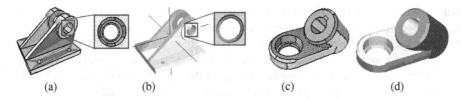

Fig. 1. (a)-(c) Segmentations of CAD models using the VSA method. Flat regions are segmented into single regions and cylindrical surfaces are segmented with many striped regions. (b)-(d) Refined segmentations via the clustering algorithm: cylindrical surfaces are partitioned with fewer regions.

is grown on the basis of specific conditions. In the process, the algorithm uses a priority queue Q, where the triangle T_i priority is equal to a specific distortion error E_{T_i} When Q is empty, the partition R is created. Successively, a fitting procedure is applied: for every region $R_i \in R$ the corresponding proxies P_i are updated in order to minimize the error $E(R_i, P_i)$. The clustering algorithm we have developed (fully described in [12]), extending and adapting the idea in [20] allows the refinement of the obtained segmentation by merging parts according to specific geometric conditions. It uses the *segmentation graph* G (Section 3): first, it considers every face of M as a patch C_i and then, at every step, it merges pairs of patches (C_i, C_j) creating a new patch C_{ij}. The choice of the patches to be merged is done according to *weights* assigned to the boundary of each patch. These weights are computed by combining geometric properties of the edges and faces sharing the boundaries. For example, the algorithm prevents the union of patches with *sharp corners* between them and avoids the existence of small patches. The clustering algorithm is applied by simply performing a *sequence of contractions* of the arcs in the graph G. The merging of a pair of patches C_i and C_j is done by contracting the corresponding arc $a = (n_i, n_j)$ in the graph G. This operation removes arc (n_i, n_j) from G, merges nodes n_i, n_j into a new node n_{ij} and transform the arcs incident in n_i and in n_j into arcs incident in node n_{ij}, inheriting the conditions and weights of the arcs and nodes involved. The result is a segmentation graph with the nodes corresponding to larger patches (shape regions). Figure 1(a) and (c) show two segmentations obtained by the VSA method for CAD (manifold) models. Flat surfaces are segmented as single regions, while cylindrical surfaces are segmented with many striped regions. Figure 1 (b) and (d) show the refined segmentations obtained by the application of our clustering approach: cylindrical surfaces are partitioned into fewer regions. Our tool, developed in Java, allows the user to perform a given number of step of the clustering algorithm and to assign specific weights to each geometric constraints to be considered in the computation of the weight W_a assigned to each border a of the segmentation. This is done via a user-friendly and portable interface.

5   Manual Segmentation by Strokes Painting

While automatic segmentation techniques - as those presented in the previous section - can be fast and precise, in some cases, the intervention of the user is fundamental, since modeling the human perception into an automatic system is still a open issue. For this reason, we believe that a combination of automatic and manual segmentations can be a real support to the user, when he points to semantically annotate a 3D model according to different criteria. These criteria can be *objective* (thus, based on specific, computable measures) and *subjective*, namely dependent on the user personal perception. The main goal is that the system can be able to associate different metadata to each patch of the model, allowing a hierarchical semantic organization of the identified portions.

In this sense, taking inspiration from the intelligent scissoring operation presented in [13], we developed a manual segmentation tool which enable the user to paint strokes on the mesh surface. By painting these strokes on the *visible* part of the model, the user specifies where cuts should be made and the system automatically computes the entire cut, splitting the selected portion of the model into two pieces and updating the *segmentation graph* accordingly. The general idea of the original method in [13] is the following: the user draws a stroke on the surface model. It has a specified width (r) representing a region of uncertainty within which the method should construct the cut, considering cuts along edges of the mesh. The stroke starts in a region (in which the algorithm selects an *initial* vertex a) and ends in another region (in which a *final* vertex b is selected). Successively, two edges paths (minimum paths) are computed: one front-side, involving edges touched by the stroke, and the other back-side. This last is the minimum path formed by edges *not visible* from the view point connecting the initial and the final vertices. Each minimum path is computed by the use of the Dijkstra's algorithm with a cost function which depends also on geometric properties of each edge involved (e.g. dihedral angles).

In our case, since X3D allows to define shapes using vertices and not edges, the use of an implementation of the original approach would have been computationally expensive. Every time the user would draw the stroke, the system should compute the intersection between a circle of radius r and all the edges present in the scene and projected on the viewplane. We decided to apply the algorithm on the vertices of the model. This change does not modify the general methodology, but it allows us to reduce the number of operations to be performed. With our choice, in fact, we do not have to compute intersections (solving linear systems) but only euclidean distances. Additionally, we have been able to extend the procedure to surface meshes which are not represented only by triangles, using in this way all the faces types defined by the X3D standard. Furthermore, we extended the method to special cases: we can treat the case in which, given a stroke (as a set of circles) there is no vertex inside it connecting the initial and final vertex of the stroke: each time we cannot find a connection inside the stroke, we search for the nearest point in the surface model and we let the path passing from it. This procedure solves also the case in which, given the stroke, the system cannot find an initial and/or final vertex. For automatic computation of the cut in the not visible part of the model, we improved the original method restricting the search of the connections to a subset of vertices. For doing this we compute the visibility of each vertex before performing the cut.

At structural level, our manual segmentation method performs an update operation on the *segmentation graph* G (Section 3), involving the region (node) C the user has cut. The graph is modified by creating two new nodes C_1 and C_2 and by eliminating the node C. The arcs having in C an extreme are updated accordingly. We will show in the

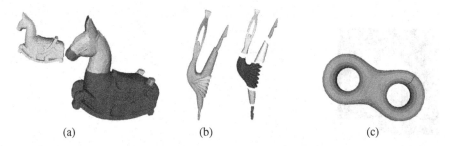

(a)   (b)   (c)

Fig. 2. (a)-(b) Segmentations obtained with our manual tool. (c) a case in which our tool cannot produce feasible results (blue stroke).

next section how the hierarchical semantic tagging, allows to maintain the history of the segmentation. In Figure 2 (a) and (b) we show two examples of segmentation obtained with our manual segmentation tool, while Figure 2 (c) shows a special case in which a complete cut cannot be found. In this case, the blue cut does not divide the model into two separate portions and multiple strokes should be used. We are working in order to support this type of functionality.

6   Global Inspection and Semantic-Based Hierarchical Tagging

As we mentioned in Section 3, the underlying structural representation for the segmentation procedures, performed on manifold models (or portions of models), is a graph that we called the *segmentation graph*. In the previous sections, we described also the updating operations we implemented in case of both the automatic and manual segmentation methods. Here, we present the interface we developed for inspecting and browsing the segmentation graph which is the basis for the semantic-based hierarchical tagging. Figure 3-(a) shows the overall interface. It has been implemented in Java extending the Xj3D browser [3] devoted to the visualization of X3D models. On the left, we have the canvas for model visualization and inspection and, on the right, we have placed the entire segmentation graph and the fields for semantic annotation. In particular, three different working tabs have been designed: for each node C of the segmentation graph G, one tab collects the geometrical information, automatically extracted (*geometry*); another tab (*adjacency*) describes the adjacency information, again automatically extracted. The last working tab (*semantic*) is, instead, devoted to the user-defined semantic annotation.

We have implemented a simple semantic tagging which allows the user to add information to a region. Every segmented region (node) C will contain in the name also the names of its ancestors with the following syntax: $ancestor_1 : ancestor_2 : \ldots ancestor_n : RegionName$. In this way, we are able to trace the entire segmentation process and we obtain two interesting results. On the one hand, using our tags - organized hierarchically - we are able to re-merge the segmented regions simply by checking the names of the regions and by merging their faces and vertices. On the other hand, looking at the name of a given region C we can access immediately to its history.

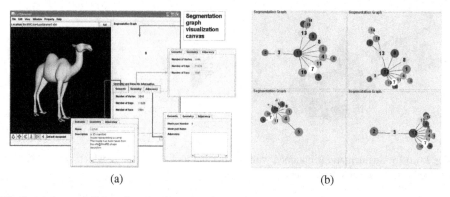

(a)   (b)

Fig. 3. (a) the overall interface for the manual segmentation. On the right the model, on the left the layer for visualizing the segmentation graph as for the semantic annotation. (b) an example of the global visualization and browsing on a complex segmentation graph. All the nodes are visible and the focus is on a specific node.

For the visualization of the segmentation graph, we decided to show it globally (Figure 3-(b)), where every node has a specific color (the same of the associated region) and a number. The user can browse the graph very intuitively. By clicking on a node C, the associated region in the Xj3D canvas will be highlighted and C will become the new visualization center of the hyperbolic graph. Also, the user can drag a node and the graph will change its shape accordingly. All the nodes will be always visible, but the focus will be on the active node and the nearest ones. Finally, when a node C is selected, all the associated information are shown in the working tabs described before.

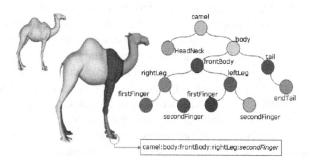

Fig. 4. A 3D segmented model representing a camel and the name given to a specific region, following our hierarchical tagging. In this case the second finger of the frontal right leg.

Figure 4 shows an examples of 3D model, its segmentations obtained via our tool and the associated segmentation graph. The interface has also some other functionalities. The segmentation can be rendered in an *expanded* or *not expanded* way, as shown in the examples depicted in Figure 2(a) and (b). Also, the user can save the entire segmented and annotated model in X3D format (using the tag Metadata and MetadataSet) or can select a portion of it, and saves it separately.

7   Concluding Remarks

In this paper, we presented different segmentation methods we have implemented in order to recognize meaningful portions of a 3D model. We focused also on how we maintain the decomposition into a structural representation and the updating operations we perform on it. Our interface allows the user to inspect both the segmented model and the segmentation graph. This has been done in order to support the user in the understanding of the overall model and to guide the user in the semantic annotation of each portion. We presented also our semantic-based hierarchical tagging by which we are able to maintain the history of the segmentation procedure. Once semantically annotated, the portions of the model can be saved all together or separately, preparing the basis of a semantic-based modeling-by-example environment. This work is part of a more complex Semantic Web system for inspecting complex 3D shape and for structuring and annotating them according to ontology-driven metadata.

Our future directions are multiple. For the automatic segmentation module, we are developing different other procedures, in order to cover several types of geometric constraints. The manual segmentation framework will be extended in order to solve the problem we showed in Section 5. Additionally, we are planning to implement innovative methods as those presented in [16,15,9] where the strokes are painted on the surface to identify meaningful portions (not the cut), and the system will automatically compute the right cut (according to the minimal rule).

The semantic annotator we presented is the basis of the annotation using ontological schema. We are actually working in order to interface our system with pre-defined ontologies. In this case, the semantics associated to the portions of the model will be saved also in separated RDF files, thus allowing to experiment the complete power of Semantic Web technologies.

Acknowledgments. This work has been partially supported by Project FIRB *SHALOM* funded by the Italian Ministry of Education, Research and University n.*RBIN04HWR*8. The authors thank Matteo Bertucelli and Nicoló Carissimi for the support in implementation. Some shapes in the paper are from the AIM@SHAPE shape repository [1].

References

1. The European Network of Excellence AIM@SHAPE - contract number 506766 (2004-2007), www.aimatshape.net
2. The web3d consortium x3d working group (2008), http://www.web3d.org/x3d
3. The xj3d project (2008), http://www.xj3d.org
4. Shamir, A.: A survey on mesh segmentation techniques. In: Computer Graphics Forum (2008)
5. Attene, M., Falcidieno, B., Spagnuolo, M.: Hierarchical mesh segmentation based on fitting primitives. The Visual Computer 22(3), 181–193 (2006)
6. Attene, M., Robbiano, F., Spagnuolo, M., Falcidieno, B.: Semantic annotation of 3d surface meshes based on feature characterization. In: Falcidieno, B., Spagnuolo, M., Avrithis, Y., Kompatsiaris, I., Buitelaar, P. (eds.) SAMT 2007. LNCS, vol. 4816, pp. 126–139. Springer, Heidelberg (2007)

7. Boier-Martin, I.M.: Domain decomposition for multiresolution analysis. In: Proc. of the EG Symposium on Geometry Processing, pp. 31–40. Eurographics Association (2003)
8. Brown, S.W.: Interactive part selection for mesh and point models using hierarchical graph-cut partitioning. Brigham Young University, PhD Thesis (2008)
9. Brown, S.W.: Interactive part selection for mesh and point models using hierarchical graph-cut partitioning. Brigham Young University, PhD Thesis (2008)
10. Cohen-Steiner, D., Alliez, P., Desbrun, M.: Variational shape approximation. ACM Trans. Graph. 23(3), 905–914 (2004)
11. De Floriani, L., Hui, A., Papaleo, L., Huang, M., Hendler, J.A.: A semantic web environment for digital shapes understanding. In: Falcidieno, B., Spagnuolo, M., Avrithis, Y., Kompatsiaris, I., Buitelaar, P. (eds.) SAMT 2007. LNCS, vol. 4816, pp. 226–239. Springer, Heidelberg (2007)
12. De Floriani, L., Papaleo, L., Carissimi, N.: A java3d framework for inspecting and segmenting 3d models. In: Proc. of the International Conference on 3D Web Technology (Web3D), pp. 67–74. ACM, New York (2008)
13. Funkhouser, T., Kazhdan, M., Shilane, P., Min, P., Kiefer, W., Tal, A., Rusinkiewicz, S., Dobkin, D.: Modeling by example. ACM Transactions on Graphics 23(3), 652–663 (2004)
14. Gregory, A.D., State, A., Lin, M.C., Manocha, D., Livingston, M.A.: Interactive surface decomposition for polyhedral morphing. The Visual Computer 15(9), 453–470 (1999)
15. Huaiyu, C., Jia, Q., Songde: A sketch-based interactive framework for real-time mesh segmentation. In: Proc. of the Computer Graphics International (2007)
16. Zhongping, J., Ligang, L., Zhonggui, C., Guojin, W.: Easy mesh cutting. Computer Graphics Forum 25(3), 283–292 (2006)
17. Lai, Y.-K., Hu, S.-M., Martin, R.R., Rosin, P.L.: Fast mesh segmentation using random walks. In: SPM 2008: Proceedings of the 2008 ACM symposium on Solid and physical modeling, pp. 183–191. ACM, New York (2008)
18. Katz, S., Tal, A.: Hierarchical mesh decomposition using fuzzy clustering and cuts. In: ACM SIGGRAPH Proceedings. ACM, New York (2003)
19. Sharf, A., Blumenkrants, M., Shamir, A., Cohen-Or, D.: Snappaste: an interactive technique for easy mesh composition. The Visual Computer 22(9-11), 835–844 (2006)
20. Sheffer, A.: Model simplification for meshing using face clustering. Computer-Aided Design 33(13), 925–934 (2001)
21. Weyrich, T., Pauly, M., Heinzle, S., Keiser, R., Scandella, S., Gross, M.: Post-processing of scanned 3d surface data. In: Symposium on Point-Based Graphics, pp. 85–94 (2004)
22. Wu, H.-Y., Pan, C., Pan, J., Yang, Q., Ma, S.: A sketch-based interactive framework for real-time mesh segmentation. In: Proceedings of the Computer Graphics International, CGI (2007)
23. Wu, J., Kobbelt, L.: Structure recovery via hybrid variational surface approximation. Computer Graphics Forum 24(3), 277–284 (2005)
24. Lee, Y., Lee, S., Shamir, A., Cohen-Or, D., Seidel, H.P.: Mesh scissoring with minima rule and part salience. Comput. Aided Geom. Des. 22(5), 444–465 (2005)
25. Zhongping, J., Ligang, L., Zhonggui, C., Guojin, W.: Easy mesh cutting. Computer Graphics Forum 25(3), 283–292 (2006)
26. Zöckler, M., Stalling, D., Hege, H.-C.: Fast and intuitive generation of geometric shape transitions. The Visual Computer 16(5), 241–253 (2000)

Reducing Keypoint Database Size

Shahar Jamshy[1], Eyal Krupka[2], and Yehezkel Yeshurun[1]

[1] School of Computer Science, Tel Aviv University, Tel Aviv 69978, Israel
{weasel,hezy}@post.tau.ac.il
[2] Israel Innovation Labs, Microsoft Israel R&D Center
eyalk@microsoft.com

Abstract. Keypoints are high dimensional descriptors for local features of an image or an object. Keypoint extraction is the first task in various computer vision algorithms, where the keypoints are then stored in a database used as the basis for comparing images or image features. Keypoints may be based on image features extracted by feature detection operators or on a dense grid of features. Both ways produce a large number of features per image, causing both time and space performance challenges when upscaling the problem.

We propose a novel framework for reducing the size of the keypoint database by learning which keypoints are beneficial for a specific application and using this knowledge to filter out a large portion of the keypoints. We demonstrate this approach on an object recognition application that uses a keypoint database. By using leave one out K nearest neighbor regression we significantly reduce the number of keypoints with relatively small reduction in performance.

Keywords: Keypoints, Saliency, Recognition, ALOI.

1 Introduction

Many fields in computer vision, such as object recognition [1,2], model based recognition [3,4], object tracking [5], and matching of stereo pairs [6,7] may benefit from the selection of salient areas in the image as the first step of their processing. The selection of salient areas focuses the task on similar areas in different images thus reducing computational complexity and increasing accuracy. These salient areas are often referred to as keypoints.

Various algorithms have been suggested in order to achieve this goal. These algorithms use different techniques such as corner detection [8], local symmetry detection [9,10], convexity estimation [11,12] or blob detection [7,13,14,15] in order to detect interest points in an image.

Since most applications compare keypoints from different images, where the same object may appear with different illumination, scale, orientation, or background, keypoints must be represented in a way that will be invariant to these differences. This representation is called keypoint descriptor (see [15,16,17] and [18] for comparison). For example, SIFT [15] describes the keypoint using a weighted histogram of the orientation of the gradient in the area of the keypoint.

P. Foggia, C. Sansone, and M. Vento (Eds.): ICIAP 2009, LNCS 5716, pp. 113–122, 2009.
© Springer-Verlag Berlin Heidelberg 2009

In order to compare keypoints from different objects and images the keypoints are stored in a labeled database and are then used as the basis for comparing, recognizing and tracking objects.

Even though there are many saliency operators intended to focus an image processing algorithm on salient areas in the image, state of the art operators (when used with parameters recommended by the authors) produce hundreds of keypoint for a single image which does not simplify the problem enough. Since different operators have different strengths and weaknesses (see [19] for comparison), it is common practice to use a combination of two or more operators [20], yielding more keypoints. Furthermore, it is another common practice to use a dense grid of keypoints (see [21,22]) instead of using a saliency operator, yielding an even larger number of keypoints.

When the number of images and objects grow the keypoints database becomes very large, which causes both time and space performance problems. In practice, a large number of the keypoints discovered are not actually helpful to the actual application (For example, if they belong to the background or to features common to many images and objects). Filtering the database and removing these redundant features we will reduce both time and space complexity of the application.

The rest of the paper is organized as follows: in Section 2 we give a general framework for filtering a keypoint database according to the specific requirements of the application. In Section 3 we show how to implement this framework for an object recognition application. Section 4 compares the results of filtering using our framework and random baseline filtering. We conclude in Section 5 with some further research directions.

1.1 Related Work

Most applications deal with the problems of large keypoint databases either by using a small scale implementation (order of hundreds of objects) to demonstrate their approach [2,4], or by reducing the complexity of the keypoint itself. A common approach (see [3]) uses Vector Quantizations and K-Means in order to reduce each keypoint to a single word in relatively small dictionary.

Another approach, described in [15], uses a hash function to approximate nearest-neighbor lookup. While this approach improves the time performance of the nearest neighbor search it does not reduce the memory required for a large database of keypoints.

Despite the large amount of literature on finding and describing keypoints little care has yet been given to the problem of directly reducing the number of keypoints or to working with databases that contain thousands of images.

2   Our Approach

We introduce a framework for filtering keypoints which is suitable for many computer vision tasks. The main notion of this framework is that an application can rank individual keypoints based on their usefulness. We use these ranks in order to learn the characteristics of keypoints useful to the application. Fig. 1 shows a general scheme of an application that uses keypoints. First, keypoints are extracted from the image, usually by using a saliency operator. The keypoints are then coded into descriptors, and then some application specific processing is done.

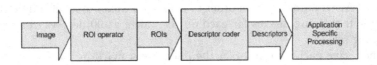

Fig. 1. General scheme of an application that uses keypoints

Our framework works in two stages: a training stage and a filtering stage. In the training stage the target application ranks each keypoint according to its usefulness. The ranks and the keypoints are used in order to train a keypoint filter, as shown in Fig. 2. For example, in an object recognition application, the application can rank the keypoints according to their ability to distinguish between the different objects. Highly distinctive keypoints will receive high grades and less distinctive keypoints will receive lower grades.

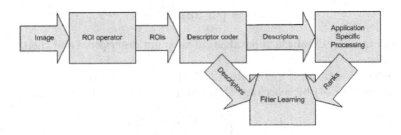

Fig. 2. Training Stage

In the filtering stage we use the rank based keypoint filter we built in the training stage in order to filter out less useful keypoints which reduces the number of keypoints the application needs to process, as shown in Fig. 3.

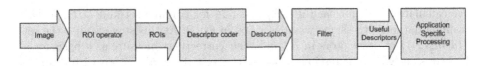

Fig. 3. Filtering Stage

3   Implementation

In order to demonstrate our framework we selected the SIFT based object recognition application described by Lowe in [15]. In this application keypoints are matched using a nearest neighbor database of keypoint descriptors, where the ratio between the distance from nearest neighbor and the first nearest neighbor from any other class is used to asses the distinctiveness of the match.

We used ALOI dataset [23] in order to train a database of labeled descriptors. We used four training images for each object, taken at 90 degrees difference as the training set.

We then gave each descriptor in the database a mark in the following way: Let $I_{i,j}$ be the j training image of object i. We denote $D(I_{i,j})$ the descriptors extracted from image $I_{i,j}$. For each descriptor $d \in D(I_{i,j})$ in the training set we define the correct label of the keypoint $l(d)$ by

$$l(d) = i \iff d \in D(I_{i,j}) \text{ for some } j \qquad (1)$$

Let n be the number of objects and k be the number of training images for each object we define

$$T = \bigcup_{i=1..n, j=1..k} D(I_{i,j})$$

to be a training set, and

$$DB_T = \left\{ (d, l(d)) \middle| d \in T \right\}$$

to be the training database, a database of keypoint descriptors and their respective labels.

For every descriptor d we denote $l(T, d)$ the label of the nearest neighbor of d in T (we find $l(T, d)$ by searching DB_T) and define the correctness measure:

$$m^c(d) = \begin{cases} 1 & l(T, d) = l(d) \\ -1 & l(T, d) \neq l(d) \end{cases} \qquad (2)$$

For each j we then break T into two parts: R_j - the descriptors extraced from the j training image for each object, and T_j - the rest of the descriptors in the training set. Formally:

$$R_j = \bigcup_{i=1..n} D(I_{i,j}) \text{ and } T_j = T \setminus R_j$$

We calculate $m^c_j(d)$ for each $d \in R_j$ using T_j for training set and DB_{T_j} as the training database the same way described in Eq. 2. At this stage we use the set $\left\{ (d, m^c_j(d)) \right\}$ of descriptors in R_j and their correctness measure as a basis for a K nearest neighbor regression database (we tested the algorithm with 3 and 5 neighbors) and find the regression value $m_j(d)$ for each $d \in T_j$.

Finally, we calculate the mark $m(d)$ for each descriptor $d \in I_{i,j}$:

$$m(d) = \sum_{j' \neq j} m_{j'}(d) \tag{3}$$

We then create a filtered training set T' and a filtered training database $DB_{T'}$ from T in the following way:

$$T' = \{ d \in T \mid m(d) > \phi \} \text{ for some } \phi$$

$$DB_{T'} = \{ (d, l(d)) \mid d \in T' \} \tag{4}$$

In order to test the performance of the database we used another image from each object. We extracted descriptors from each test image using SIFT and then matched each descriptor extracted to the database.

Let I_i^t be a test image and $D(I_i^t)$ be the descriptors extracted from I_i^t:

1. For each $d \in D(I_i^t)$ we calculated $l(T', d)$ by searching $DB_{T'}$.
2. For each $d \in D(I_i^t)$ we calculated the distinctiveness ratio suggested in [15]:

$$r(d) = \frac{\text{distance to the nearest descriptor in } T' \text{ labeled } l(T', d)}{\text{distance to the nearest descriptor in } T' \text{ not labeled } l(T', d)} \tag{5}$$

3. We calculated the label of I_i^t

$$l(I_i^t) = majority \left\{ l(T', d) \mid d \in D(I_i^t) \text{ and } r(d) > 1.5 \right\} \tag{6}$$

For each descriptor d in the test set, if $r(d) > 1.5$ we say that d was matched. If d was matched and $l(T', d) = l(d)$ we say that d was matched correctly.

4   Results

First, let's look at the performance of the original application without reducing the database size. Table 1 shows general statistics of the databases for 100, 200, and 500 objects. We can see that the precentage of matched keypoints is 16%-19% and the precent of correctly matched keypoints is 13%-18%. This shows that a large precentage of keypoints that were matched had a correct match. The distinctiveness ratio described in Eq. 5 is responsible for this high accuracy. We can also see that at most 20% of the keypoints were matched, showing the potential of using filtering in order to improve the performance of the application.

When looking at the result of the object recognition application described in Sec. 3 for 500 objects, we can see in Fig. 4 that in random filtering, in average, performs rather well by itself, losing only 5% accuracy when filtering 70% of the database showing the potential for reducing the database size. We can also

Table 1. General Statistics of Test Databases. Columns 1-3: quantities of objects, images and descriptors. Column 4-6: percent of matched discriptors, percent of correctly matched descriptors, and percent of mtched images using distinctiveness ratio of 1.5.

# of objects	# of images	# of descriptors	% descriptors matched	% descriptors matched correctly	% of images matched correctly
100	400	71214	19.7	17.6	92
200	800	122252	21.2	18.6	68.5
500	2000	278571	16.3	13.6	61.4

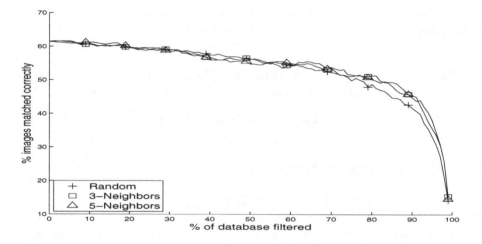

Fig. 4. Percent of matched images vs. filtering of the database for 500 objects, 3 and 5 nearest neighbors compared to averaged random filtering

see that when filtering up to 70% of the database our approach gives similiar results in a predictable way. In Fig. 5 we can see that when filtering 70%-95% percent of the database using our approach we achieve the same accuracy of the average random filtering with 2/3 the database size. For example, in order to match 45% of the images random filtering can filter 84% of the database leaving 16% of the descriptors, while with our approach we can filter 91% leaving only 9%.

Next, let's look at how filtering has affected the number of correctly matched descriptors. In order to assess our results we used an average of 20 random filtering of descriptors as reference. Figure 6 shows the result of filtering for 500 objects in relative percentage over the random reference. The main result these figures show is that when filtering 70%-95% of the database our filtering technique give an increase of 5%-20% percent correctlly matched descriptors relative to random filtering.

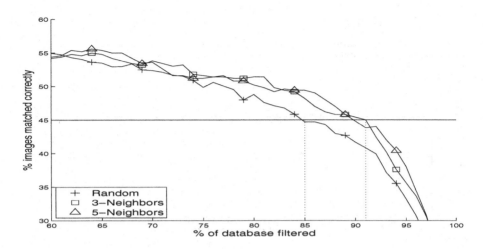

Fig. 5. Percent of matched images vs. filtering of the database for 500 objects, 3 and 5 nearest neighbors compared to averaged random filtering, when filtering 70%-90% of the database, showing we achieve the same accuracy of the average random filtering with less than 2/3 the database size

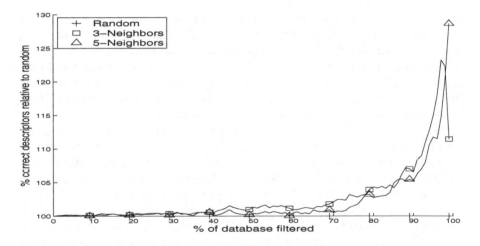

Fig. 6. Percent of matched descriptors relative to the random reference vs. filtering of the database for 500 objects, 3 and 5 nearest neighbors

Finally, when looking at the effect of our method on databases of different sizes, Fig. 7 shows that while for database of 100 and 200 objects our approach did not produce much improvement over random filtering, when database size was increased to 500 objects our approach produced much better results, emphasizing the benefit of our approach for large databases.

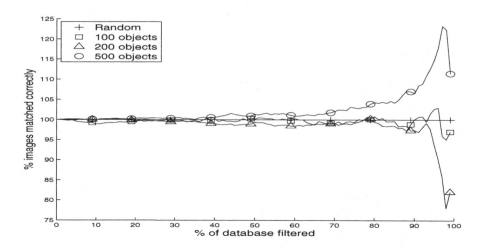

Fig. 7. Percent of matched descriptors relative to the random reference vs. filtering of the database for 100, 200, and 500 objects, 3 nearest neighbors

5   Conclusions and Future Work

In this paper we have proposed a new approach for filtering large databases of keypoints according to the needs of a specific application. We demonstrated this approach on an object recognition application. Using leave one out K nearest neighbor regression we learned the characteristics of useful keypoints and used this knowledge to filter the database. Our experiments have shown that when filtering using our approach we can achieve the same performance results with 2/3 the database size compared to random filtering.

Future research will concentrate on adapting our approach to other applications in computer vision. For example, in computer visions tasks that use the Bag of Keypoints approach (such as [3]) a keypoint filtering stage can be introduced before creating the Bag of Keypoints, filtering out less relevant keypoints and thus increasing accuracy. Tracking tasks can also benefit from our approach by deploying a keypoint filter that will learn to filter out keypoints that are less suitable for tracking. Other directions for future research are trying to improve the training stage by using different machine learning techniques such as SVM or RANSAC, and testing our approach on keypoint databases of even larger scale.

Acknowledgments. I would like to thank Ariel Tankus and Tania Barski-Kopilov for their valuable suggestions and support. In addition, I would like to thank Eddie Aronovich and the CS System Team for installing and supporting the Condor System [24] which made all the computations needed for this research possible.

References

1. Lowe, D.G.: Object recognition from local scale-invariant features. In: ICCV, pp. 1150–1157 (1999)
2. Obdržálek, S., Matas, J.: Object recognition using local affine frames on distinguished regions. In: Rosin, P.L., Marshall, A.D. (eds.) BMVC, British Machine Vision Association (2002)
3. Dance, C., Willamowski, J., Fan, L., Bray, C., Csurka, G.: Visual categorization with bags of keypoints. In: ECCV International Workshop on Statistical Learning in Computer Vision (2004)
4. Fergus, R., Perona, P., Zisserman, A.: Object class recognition by unsupervised scale-invariant learning. In: CVPR, pp. 264–271. IEEE Computer Society, Los Alamitos (2003)
5. Tissainayagam, P., Suter, D.: Object tracking in image sequences using point features. In: APRS Workshop on Digital Image Computing Online Proceedings, pp. 1197–1203 (2003)
6. Pritchett, P., Zisserman, A.: Wide baseline stereo matching. In: ICCV, pp. 754–760 (1998)
7. Matas, J., Chum, O., Urban, M., Pajdla, T.: Robust wide baseline stereo from maximally stable extremal regions. In: Rosin, P.L., Marshall, D. (eds.) Proceedings of the British Machine Vision Conference, London, UK, September 2002, vol. 1, pp. 384–393. BMVA (2002)
8. Harris, C., Stephans, M.: A combined corner and edge detector. In: Proc. 4th Alvey Vision Conf., Manchester, August 1988, pp. 189–192 (1988)
9. Reisfeld, D., Wolfson, H., Yeshurun, Y.: Detection of interest points using symmetry. In: ICCV, pp. 62–65 (1990)
10. Loy, G., Zelinsky, A.: Fast radial symmetry for detecting points of interest. IEEE Trans. Pattern Anal. Mach. Intell. 25(8), 959–973 (2003)
11. Tankus, A., Yeshurun, Y., Intrator, N.: Face detection by direct convexity estimation. Pattern Recognition Letters 18(9), 913–922 (1997)
12. Tankus, A., Yeshurun, Y.: Convexity-based visual camouflage breaking. Computer Vision and Image Understanding 82(3), 208–237 (2001)
13. Mikolajczyk, K., Schmid, C.: An affine invariant interest point detector. In: Heyden, A., Sparr, G., Nielsen, M., Johansen, P. (eds.) ECCV 2002. LNCS, vol. 2350, pp. 128–142. Springer, Heidelberg (2002)
14. Mikolajczyk, K., Schmid, C.: Scale & affine invariant interest point detectors. International Journal of Computer Vision 60(1), 63–86 (2004)
15. Lowe, D.G.: Distinctive image features from scale-invariant keypoints. International Journal of Computer Vision 60(2), 91–110 (2004)
16. Bay, H., Tuytelaars, T., Gool, L.J.V.: SURF: Speeded up robust features. In: Leonardis, A., Bischof, H., Pinz, A. (eds.) ECCV 2006. LNCS, vol. 3951, pp. 404–417. Springer, Heidelberg (2006)
17. Winder, S.A.J., Brown, M.: Learning local image descriptors. In: CVPR. IEEE Computer Society, Los Alamitos (2007)
18. Mikolajczyk, K., Schmid, C.: A performance evaluation of local descriptors. IEEE Transactions on Pattern Analysis & Machine Intelligence 27(10), 1615–1630 (2005)
19. Mikolajczyk, K., Tuytelaars, T., Schmid, C., Zisserman, A., Matas, J., Schaffalitzky, F., Kadir, T., Gool, L.J.V.: A comparison of affine region detectors. International Journal of Computer Vision 65(1-2), 43–72 (2005)

20. Ramisa, A., de Mántaras, R.L., Aldavert, D., Toledo, R.: Comparing combinations of feature regions for panoramic VSLAM. In: Zaytoon, J., Ferrier, J.-L., Andrade-Cetto, J., Filipe, J. (eds.) ICINCO-RA (2), pp. 292–297. INSTICC Press (2007)
21. Bosch, A., Zisserman, A., Muñoz, X.: Scene classification via pLSA. In: Leonardis, A., Bischof, H., Pinz, A. (eds.) ECCV 2006. LNCS, vol. 3954, pp. 517–530. Springer, Heidelberg (2006)
22. Bosch, A., Zisserman, A., Muñoz, X.: Scene classification using a hybrid generative/discriminative approach. IEEE Trans. Pattern Anal. Mach. Intell. 30(4), 712–727 (2008)
23. Geusebroek, J.M., Burghouts, G.J., Smeulders, A.W.M.: The Amsterdam library of object images. Int. J. Comput. Vis. 61(1), 103–112 (2005)
24. Litzkow, M., Livny, M., Mutka, M.: Condor - a hunter of idle workstations. In: Proceedings of the 8th International Conference of Distributed Computing Systems (June 1988)

Automatic Estimation of the Inlier Threshold in Robust Multiple Structures Fitting

Roberto Toldo and Andrea Fusiello

Dipartimento di Informatica, Università di Verona
Strada Le Grazie 15, 37134 Verona, Italy
roberto.toldo@univr.it, andrea.fusiello@univr.it

Abstract. This paper tackles the problem of estimating the inlier threshold in RANSAC-like approaches to multiple models fitting. An iterative approach finds the maximum of a score function which resembles the Silhouette index used in clustering validation. Although several methods have been proposed to solve this problem for the single model case, this is the first attempt to address multiple models. Experimental results demonstrate the performances of the algorithm.

1   Introduction

Fitting multiple models to noisy data is a widespread problem in Computer Vision. One of the most successful paradigm that sprouted after RANSAC is the one based on random sampling. Within this paradigm there are parametric methods (Randomized Hough Transform [1], Mean Shift [2]), and non parametric ones, (RANSAC [3], Residual histogram analysis [4], J-linkage [5]). In general the latter achieves better performances than the former and have a more general applicability, provided that the inlier threshold ϵ (also called *scale*), onto which they depend critically, is manually specified.

Some works [6,7,8,9] deal with the automatic computation of ϵ in the case of *one* model – i.e., in the case of RANSAC – but that are not extendible to the case of multiple models. In this paper we aim at filling this gap, namely at estimating ϵ when using a random sampling and residual analysis approach to fit *multiple instances* of a model to noisy data corrupted by outliers.

If ϵ is too small, noisy data points are explained by multiple similar well-fitted models, that is, the separation of the models is poor; if ϵ is too large, they are explained by a single poorly-fitted model, that is, the compactness of the model is poor. The "just right" ϵ should strike the balance between model separation and model compactness.

The degree of separation with respect to compactness is measured by a score very similar to the Silhouette index [10] for clustering validation. We compute the difference between the second and the first least model distance for each data point. The scale ϵ provides a normalizing denominator for the error difference. Consider some perturbation to the "just right" scale. As ϵ increases, a model recruits new data points, increasing the first error while decreasing the second error, causing the index to drop. As ϵ decreases, new models are created, decreasing the second error, causing the index to drop as well. Therefore, the "just right" scale is the one that yields the largest overall score from all the points.

P. Foggia, C. Sansone, and M. Vento (Eds.): ICIAP 2009, LNCS 5716, pp. 123–131, 2009.

We demonstrate our method in association with a baseline algorithm such as sequential RANSAC – sequentially apply RANSAC and remove the inliers from the data set as each model instance is detected – and with an advanced algorithm such as J-linkage [5], which have been recently demonstrated to have very good performances.

2   Fitting Validation

The inlier threshold (or scale) ϵ is used to define which points belong to which model. A point belongs to a model if its distance from the model is less than ϵ. The points belonging to the same model form the *consensus set* of that model. We define the "just right" ϵ as the smallest value that yields the correct models.

In this Section we shall concentrate on a method for estimating such value based on *validating* the output of the robust fitting, which consist in a grouping of data points according to the model they belong to, plus some points (outliers) that have not been fitted. The criterion for discarding outliers is described in Sec. 3.

The validation of the fitting is based on the concepts of *compactness* and *separation*, drawn from the clustering validation literature. In particular, our method stems from the following observation (see Fig. 1):

- if ϵ is too small a single structure will be fitted by more than one model, resulting in a low separation between points belonging to different models;
- if ϵ is too large the points fitted by one model will have a low compactness (or, equivalently, a high looseness), which produces a sub-optimal estimate. As an extreme case, different structures might be fitted by a single model.

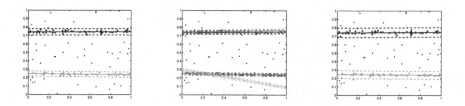

Fig. 1. From right to left: an optimal fit (according to our score), a fit with a smaller ϵ and a fit with a bigger ϵ. The dotted lines depicts the inlier band of width 2ϵ.

The "just right" ϵ has to strike the balance between these two effects. This idea is captured by the following index – which resembles the Silhouette index [10] – for a given point i:

$$r_i = \frac{b_i - a_i}{\epsilon} \tag{1}$$

where a_i is the distance of i to the model it belongs to (looseness) and b_i is the distance of i to the second closest model (separation). The global score, function of ϵ, is the average of r_i over all the points. We claim that the "just right" ϵ is the one that yields the maximum global score. Indeed, imagine to start with the "just right" ϵ. If we decrease it, a new model is created which causes the average separation b_i to drop. If ϵ is increased such that at least one new point is added to the model, this point will increase the average looseness a_i and decrease the average b_i, resulting in a decrease of the score (see Fig. 2). A score with a similar behavior (but slightly worse performances with very small ϵ) is the ratio b_i/a_i which resembles the ratio matching used in [11].

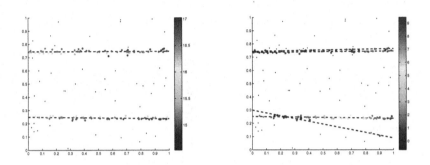

Fig. 2. This figure is best viewed in color. The left plot depicts a "good fit", whereas the right plot depicts a "bad fit" (the upper structure is fitted by two lines very close to each other). The color of the points encodes the score values, which are consistently lower in the "bad fit".

The algorithm for finding the optimal ϵ is iterative: the fitting algorithm is run several times with different ϵ and the value that obtained the higher score is retained.

3   Outliers Rejection

Sequential RANSAC and J-linkage – like clustering algorithms – in principle fit all the data. Bad models must be filtered out a-posteriori. Usually it is assumed that the number of models is known beforehand, but this assumption is too strong and we prefer not to rely on it. Thresholding on the cardinality of the consensus set may be an option, but this does not work if the number of data points supporting the different model instances are very different. A better approach would exploit the observation that outliers possess a diffused distribution whereas structures are concentrated. In particular, we used here a robust statistics based on points density.

Let e_i be distance of point i to its closest neighbor belonging to the same model. According to the X84 rejection rule [12], the inliers are those points such that

$$e_i < 5.2 \operatorname{med}_i |e_i - \operatorname{med}_j e_j|. \tag{2}$$

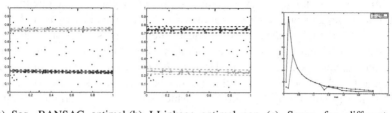

(a) Seq. RANSAC optimal (b) J-Linkage optimal con- (c) Score for different ϵ
configuration.   figuration.   values.

Fig. 3. Two lines example

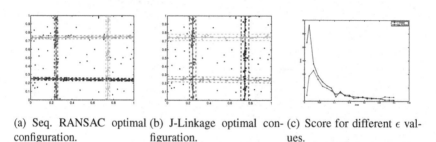

(a) Seq. RANSAC optimal (b) J-Linkage optimal con- (c) Score for different ϵ val-
configuration.   figuration.   ues.

Fig. 4. Four lines example

where med is the median. The models that are supported by the majority of outliers are discarded. Points that are classified as outliers but belongs to a "good" model are retained.

As the robust fit algorithm is executed repeatedly in order to estimate the best ϵ, the models that are fitted change, and hence changes the inlier/outlier classification.

4   Localized Sampling

The assumption that outliers posses a diffused distribution implies that the a-priori probability that two points belong to the same structure is higher the smaller the distance between the points [13]. Hence minimal sample sets are constructed in a way that neighboring points are selected with higher probability. This increases the probability of selecting a set of inliers [13,5]. Namely, if a point $\mathbf{x}_i$ has already been selected, then $\mathbf{x}_j$ has the following probability of being drawn:

$$P(\mathbf{x}_j|\mathbf{x}_i) = \begin{cases} \frac{1}{Z} \exp -\frac{||\mathbf{x}_j - \mathbf{x}_i||^2}{\sigma^2} & \text{if } \mathbf{x}_j \neq \mathbf{x}_i \\ 0 & \text{if } \mathbf{x}_j = \mathbf{x}_i \end{cases} \qquad (3)$$

where Z is a normalization constant and σ is chosen heuristically. Given an estimate α of the average inlier-inlier distance, the value of σ is selected such that a point at a distance α has a given probability P to be selected (we set $P = 0.5$).

$$\sigma = \frac{\alpha}{\sqrt{-log(P) - log(Z)}}. \tag{4}$$

The value of α is iteratively estimated as the outlier/inlier classification changes.

The normalization constant can be approximated as:

$$Z \simeq (1-\delta)e^{-\frac{\omega^2}{\sigma^2}} + \delta e^{-\frac{\alpha^2}{\sigma^2}} \tag{5}$$

where ω is the average inlier-outlier distance and δ is the lowest inlier fraction among the models.

The required number of samples that give a desired confidence of success is derived in [5].

5   Summary of the Method

The method that we propose can be seen as a meta-heuristic that is able to set automatically all the thresholds, perform outlier rejection and validate the final fitting. Any algorithm based on random sampling, from RANSAC to J-linkage, could fit.

The interval search for ϵ, $[\epsilon_L, \epsilon_H]$ must be specified.

Algorithm 1

1. Set $\alpha = \epsilon_H, \omega = 2\alpha$.
2. for $\epsilon = \epsilon_H$ to ϵ_L
   (a) Compute σ, using α and ω (Eq. 4);
   (b) Run multiple-models fitting (e.g. sequential RANSAC, J-linkage) using σ for sampling and ϵ for consensus;
   (c) Identify outliers (Sec. 3);
   (d) Compute the average score (Eq. 1);
   (e) Compute α, ω;
3. end
4. Retain the result with the highest score.

6   Experiments

We tested our scale estimation method with two different multiple models fitting algorithm based on random sampling: Sequential RANSAC and J-Linkage. The scale is

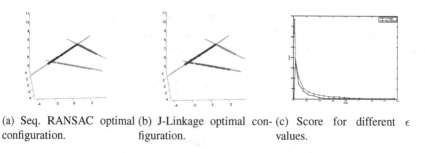

(a) Seq. RANSAC optimal (b) J-Linkage optimal con- (c) Score for different ϵ
configuration.   figuration.   values.

Fig. 5. Example of planes fitting in 3D from real data (castle)

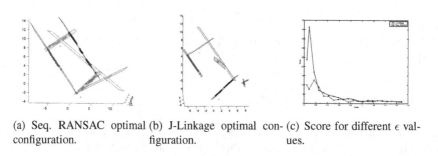

(a) Seq. RANSAC optimal (b) J-Linkage optimal con- (c) Score for different ϵ val-
configuration.   figuration.   ues.

Fig. 6. Example of planes fitting in 3D from real data (square)

initialized to a huge value such that in the first step only one model arises. Subsequently the scale is decreased by a constant value. We used the same number of samples generated (10000) for all the experiments.

The examples reported consist of both synthetic and real data. In the synthetic ones (Fig. 3 and Fig. 4) we used two and four lines in the plane, respectively The inlier points of the lines are surrounded by 50 pure outliers. Gaussian noise with standard deviation of 0.1 is added to coordinate of each inlier point.

In these experiments our meta-heuristic always proved able to converge toward a correct solution, provided that the underlying fitting algorithm (namely RANSAC or J-linkage) produced at least one correct fit.

In the real 3D data example (Fig. 5 and Fig. 6) planes are fitted to a cloud of 3D points produced by a Structure and Motion pipeline [14] fed with images of a castle and a square, respectively.

Finally, in the last two datasets (Fig. 7 and Fig. 8), SIFT features [11] are detected and matched in real images and homographies are fitted to the set of matches.

In the last three cases our scale estimation produced qualitatively different results when applied to sequential RANSAC or J-linkage, as not only the value of the optimal ϵ are different, but also estimated models are different. The J-linkage result is more accurate, but the output of sequential RANSAC is not completely wrong, suggesting that our meta-heuristic is able to produce a sensible result even when applied to a weak algorithm like sequential RANSAC.

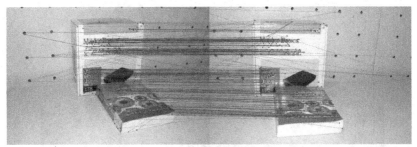

(a) SIFT Matches

(b) Seq. RANSAC optimal configuration (c) J-Linkage optimal configuration (points
(points membership is color coded).   membership is color coded).

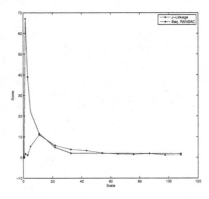

(d) Score for different ϵ values.

Fig. 7. Example of homography fitting (books)

(a) SIFT Matches

(b) Seq. RANSAC optimal configuration (c) J-Linkage optimal configuration (points
(points membership is color coded).   membership is color coded).

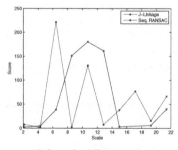

(d) Score for different ϵ values.

Fig. 8. Example of homography fitting (Valbonne)

7   Conclusions

In this paper we demonstrated a meta-heuristic for scale estimation in RANSAC-like approaches to multiple models fitting. The technique is inspired by clustering validation, and in particular it is based on a score function that resembles the Silhouette index. The fitting results produced by sequential RANSAC or J-linkage with different values of scale are evaluated and the best result – according to the score – is retained. Experimental results showed the effectiveness of the approach.

Future work will aim at improving the strategy for finding the optimal scale and smoothly cope with the special case of a single model instance.

References

1. Xu, L., Oja, E., Kultanen, P.: A new curve detection method: randomized Hough transform (RHT). Pattern Recognition Letters 11(5), 331–338 (1990)
2. Subbarao, R., Meer, P.: Nonlinear mean shift for clustering over analytic manifolds. In: Proceedings of the IEEE Conference on Computer Vision and Pattern Recognition, New York, USA, pp. 1168–1175 (2006)
3. Fischler, M.A., Bolles, R.C.: Random Sample Consensus: a paradigm model fitting with applications to image analysis and automated cartography. Communications of the ACM 24(6), 381–395 (1981)
4. Zhang, W., Kosecká, J.: Nonparametric estimation of multiple structures with outliers. In: Vidal, R., Heyden, A., Ma, Y. (eds.) WDV 2005/2006. LNCS, vol. 4358, pp. 60–74. Springer, Heidelberg (2007)
5. Toldo, R., Fusiello, A.: Robust multiple structures estimation with j-linkage. In: Forsyth, D., Torr, P., Zisserman, A. (eds.) ECCV 2008, Part I. LNCS, vol. 5302, pp. 537–547. Springer, Heidelberg (2008)
6. Fan, L., Pylvänäinen, T.: Robust scale estimation from ensemble inlier sets for random sample consensus methods. In: Forsyth, D., Torr, P., Zisserman, A. (eds.) ECCV 2008, Part III. LNCS, vol. 5304, pp. 182–195. Springer, Heidelberg (2008)
7. Wang, H., Suter, D.: Robust adaptive-scale parametric model estimation for computer vision. IEEE Trans. Pattern Anal. Mach. Intell. 26(11), 1459–1474 (2004)
8. Chen, H., Meer, P.: Robust regression with projection based m-estimators. In: 9th International Conference on Computer Vision, pp. 878–885 (2003)
9. Torr, P.H.S., Murray, D.W.: The development and comparison of robust methods for estimating the fundamental matrix. International Journal of Computer Vision 24(3), 271–300 (1997)
10. Rousseeuw, P.: Silhouettes: a graphical aid to the interpretation and validation of cluster analysis. J. Comput. Appl. Math. 20(1), 53–65 (1987)
11. Lowe, D.G.: Distinctive image features from scale-invariant keypoints. International Journal of Computer Vision 60(2), 91–110 (2004)
12. Hampel, F., Rousseeuw, P., Ronchetti, E., Stahel, W.: Robust Statistics: the Approach Based on Influence Functions. Wiley Series in probability and mathematical statistics. John Wiley & Sons, Chichester (1986)
13. Myatt, D.R., Torr, P.H.S., Nasuto, S.J., Bishop, J.M., Craddock, R.: Napsac: High noise, high dimensional robust estimation - it's in the bag. In: British Machine Vision Conference (2002)
14. Farenzena, M., Fusiello, A., Gherardi, R., Toldo, R.: Towards unsupervised reconstruction of architectural models. In: Deussen, O., Saupe, D., Keim, D. (eds.) Proceedings of the Vision, Modeling, and Visualization Workshop (VMV 2008), Konstanz, DE, October 8-10, 2008, pp. 41–50. IOS Press, Amsterdam (2008)

Integration of Contextual Information in Online Handwriting Representation

Sara Izadi and Ching Y. Suen

Concordia University, Montreal, Canada H3G 1M8
s_izadin@cs.concordia.ca, suen@cs.concordia.ca

Abstract. Robust handwriting recognition of complex patterns of arbitrary scale, orientation and location is yet elusive to date as reaching a good recognition rate is not trivial for most of the application developments in this field. Cursive scripts with complex character shapes, such as Arabic and Persian, make the recognition task even more challenging. This complexity requires sophisticated representations and learning methods, and comprehensive data samples. A direct approaches to achieve a better performance is focusing on designing more powerful building blocks of a handwriting recognition system which are *pattern representation* and *pattern classification*. In this paper we aim to scale up the efficiency of online recognition systems for Arabic characters by integrating novel representation techniques into efficient classification methods. We investigate the idea of incorporating two novel feature representations for online character data. We advocate the usefulness and practicality of these features in classification methods using neural networks and support vector machines. The combinations of proposed representations with related classifiers can offer a module for recognition tasks which can deal with any two-dimensional online pattern. Our empirical results confirm the higher distinctiveness and robustness to character deformations obtained by the proposed representation compared to currently available techniques.

1 Introduction

Handwriting is a natural way for humans to communicate and exchange information. Online handwriting recognition is used in the context of user interfaces for computing devices. For a variety of small devices such as hand-held computers and personal digital assistants (PDAs), keyboard-based data entry is not convenient. The ease of using a digital pen for writing also suits some larger devices such as tablet PCs and smart boards, which are designed for easy note taking in business, oce, clinic, and industry environments. The recognition of different forms of pen input such as mathematical equations and graphics, or of entire page layouts have attracted a lot of research attention. Interest in online handwriting recognition has increased due to market demand for both improved performance and for extended supporting scripts for those devices.

Handwriting recognition has still remained an active area of research to date [3, 5].This is because of the following main challenges: (1) low recognition rate

P. Foggia, C. Sansone, and M. Vento (Eds.): ICIAP 2009, LNCS 5716, pp. 132–142, 2009.

in general and only a reasonable recognition rate on highly restrictive classes of patterns which do not represent real handwriting data; (2) lack of enough data sets, especially for scripts such as Persian and Arabic; and (3) long recognition time (a few seconds). The main sources of difficulty in the recognition of handwriting patterns are variation and variability. Variation refers to the unique way of writing of each individual, while variability addresses the changes of a specific individual in producing different samples at different times under different conditions and moods. In online systems, variations in the number and the order of strokes introduce more variations in handwriting and should be taken into account. While not all of these subject-specific parameters are feasible to consider and carry useful information about the character identity, it is not still known which part of this information provides a parsimonious representation for recognition. There exist huge variability in Persian/Arabic scripts due to the facts that a letter can appear in up to four different forms: isolated, initial, medial, and final; there exist a large allographic variety for letters and combination of letters; and ane transformation includes main shape distortion and complementary part distortion.

Recognition methods try to tackle the variability problem to gain more accuracy. However, this may result in a long recognition time. Some techniques focus on the classification aspect of the recognition task by using a combination of classifiers, while others emphasize on data representation in order to obtain descriptive feature vectors. There has been relatively little work on feature representation which interact with direct shape of a character.

In this paper, we aim at improving time and accuracy of recognition of online isolated Arabic characters. We investigate novel approaches that target the challenges involved. This include improving the recognition accuracy of online isolated Arabic characters on existing databases by designing new features and improving the recognition speed using a suitable choice of classifiers. The main contributions of this paper is the design of two novel feature representations: relational histogram and relational context representations for isolated characters, and their corresponding extraction methods which suites two important supervised learning methods of neural networks (NNs) and support vector machines (SVMs) respectively. The idea behind our new feature representations is to consider measurements of local and global features which capture information related to the character shape.

2   Background

A typical online recognition system consists of three main building blocks: preprocessing, pattern representation and classification. In order to reduce the noise introduced by the digitizing device, preprocessing is performed. Patterns representation includes design and extraction of representative features. Features are most relevant information for classification purposes, in the sense of minimizing the within-class pattern variability while enhancing the between-class pattern variability. Features should be as invariant as possible to the expected distortions. Selecting the feature extraction method has been stated as the most important factor in achieving high recognition performance [16]. Features can be broadly divided into high-level (global) and low-level (local) features. High-level features extract a property related to the topology of the pattern using the whole sequence of trajectory points. Some of the frequently used global features for a stroke include: number of ascenders, descenders, cusps, loops, mass center, start or end points, and bounding box information. Low-level features are features which are calculated on a local area of the pattern, i.e. the trajectory points in a certain vicinity of a point for online handwriting. Local features (point features) are assigned to each point along a script trajectory. Some typical local features include: pen directional features, pen coordinate features, digital curvature, cumulative curve length, point aspect ratio, pen pressure, and ink related features such as point density. Global features may provide more descriptive information about a character than local features, usually for a higher computational cost. Global features are more powerful but less robust. The results of high level feature extraction tend to be highly erroneous due to large shape variations in natural cursive handwriting, especially among different writers [6].

In Perasian/Arabic online recognition, rule-based methods are the most widely used classification methods [14, 1, 4, 1]. These systems all share a similar pattern representation approach, which is to segment a stroke into some geometric primitives, and their recognition part is based on a set of fuzzy rules or variations of the traditional fuzzy theory. Neural networks have been used for isolated Persian and Arabic characters [9], however, these systems showed lower performances than the one-nearest-neighbor (1-NN) clustering method using the same features [12]. Besides, the neural networks classification becomes computationally expensive as the dimensions of the data increase, and the initial conditions change. The use of support vector machines (SVMs) classifiers has gained increasing attention in recent years due to excellent recognition results in various pattern recognition applications. However, this type of classifiers has never been used for online Arabic handwriting recognition. There has been some recent attempts for using SVMs in learning online Arabic handwriting recognition , but the choice of effective features is mandatory for boosting the performance of SVMs.

3 Relational Histogram Representation and Neural Network Classifiers

In this section we present our first proposed representation, *Relational Histogram*(RH). This representation is an adaptation of the shape context idea [2]. Shape context is a descriptor that has been proposed for measuring similarities in the shape matching framework. For a shape with N boundary points, a set of $N - 1$ vectors originating from each boundary point to all other sample points expresses the configuration of the entire shape relative to that point. A coarse histogram of the relative coordinates of those remaining $N-1$ points is defined as the shape context of that particular point. The representation and its matching method is computationally expensive. This is because a point correspondence must be formed between the points of each two shapes in order to measure the similarity between them. Shape context in its original form cannot be applied directly in online handwriting recognition since all computations need to occur in real time. The following algorithm presents our idea for using this concept in online handwritten data as follows:

Algorithm 1. Relational Histogram Feature Extraction
    INPUT: A set of re-sampled trajectory points S
    OUTPUT: Feature vector V
    Select an arbitrary set of reference points R
    Select an arbitrary set of r-bins: $r_1, r_2, ..., r_n$ and θ-bins: $\theta_1, \theta_2, ..., \theta_k$
    for all $r \in R$ **do**
      $Initialize(r - bins, \theta - bins)$
      for all $s \in S$ **do**
        Compute $dist(r, s)$
        Compute $angle(r, s)$
        $Assign(r - bins, \theta - bins, r, s)$
        $Update(r - bins, \theta - bins)$
      end for
    end for
    $V = count(r - bins, \theta - bins, r)$
    Return V

We normalize the character's trajectory points and denote them by a set P. Let R be a set of reference points . Our feature extraction method selects adequate features of the relational type. In the first part of this algorithm, we select an arbitrary and fixed set of points R. This set of reference points must not be outside the bounding box. The points in R may capture some interrelationship structures (for instance, symmetrical corners of the bounding box) or be random. The algorithm re-samples the normalized representation of the character P, as a set of equi-distanced points S. The surrounding area of each reference point that falls in the bounding box is divided into bins according to the distance and angle of each bin with respect to the reference point. The values of all the bins are initialized to zero for each reference point. Then, all the points in S are described from the view of each reference point and are placed into the corresponding bins. This is done by computing the distance and angle between the pair of points, $dist(r, p)$ and $angle(r, p)$, and updating the corresponding bin that this pair can be mapped into. After this step, the number of points in the bins provided by all the reference points will give a compact representation of the character. Using this system makes the descriptor more sensitive to differences in nearby points.

Figure 1 shows the log-polar histogram bins for computing the features of the Arabic character S, pronounced as "seen". We used the center point of a character bounding box as reference point in a log-polar coordinate system. The diagram has 5 bins in the tangential direction and 12 bins in the radial direction, yielding a feature vector of length 60. We capture the global characteristics of the character by this feature vector. In addition, we use a directional feature to

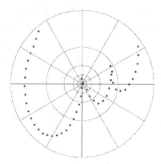

Fig. 1. Diagram of the log-polar bins around the center of the bounding box of the Arabic character "Seen" used for relational feature computation

extract the local writing directions as: $Arctan((x_i - x_{i-1}) + j(y_i - y_{i-1})) for i = 2 : N$. This allows for spatio-temporal data representation and augments the visual realism of the shape of a character.

We have used neural networks as the learning classifier method when trying our RH feature. This feature magnifies the differences between similar characters and improves learning in NNs. We train a Multi-Layer Perceptrons (MLP) classifier through a conjugate gradient method for classification using a three-layer network layout with 100 nodes in the hidden layer. Classification is obtained by adjusting the weights during the training using gradient descent optimization (back propagation method), where we calculate the derivatives of the cost function and find the weights in an iterative way. The evaluation of this system is presented in section 5.

4 Relational Context Representation and Support Vector Machine Classifiers

We call our second representation *relational context*(RC) since this representation uses the inclusion of the character context as the relative pairwise distances and angles. The idea is to use all pairs of points on the trajectory of a digital character to capture as much contextual information about the shape of a character as possible. The length of the RC feature for a trajectory of N sample points is $N(N - 1)$. We re-sample all characters with an equal number of points in order to make the feature vectors of the same length. We also preserve the order of the trajectory samples. Local relevance is captured by the representation of any single component of the character's shape feature vector. Neighborhood components capture the relationship between different parts of the character's shape. Preserving these relationships provides invariance with respect to different writing styles. In different writing styles, character points may have absolute information that is different from independent data points, however, the relative interrelationships on a set of points might not be different. Therefore, a small local change in the total shape of the character does not cause a large change in its representation. The global shape of the character is captured through all pairwise relationships between any two components. Different levels of details in the character's description can be selected by increasing or decreasing the trajectory point density. Figure 2 depicts some of these features for letter Y, pronounced *ye* in Arabic scripts. In this figure, the pairwise relationships are illustrated only for point P_J.

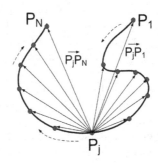

Fig. 2. Arabic letter "*ye*" in relative context feature representation

To extract RC feature, we use Algorithm 2. The length of the proposed RC feature can be potentially long for some very long trajectories with many points. Therefore, this feature, especially when used in fine level, may not be the best match with classifiers such as NNs in terms of required network complexity. However, for SVM classifiers, the size of the feature vector is not usually a practical constraint. The length is not a concern for the execution time since the number of descriptor data points, in the character level, is almost always very short, and the features extraction is of low-order polynomial. In our experience with RC, the number of support vectors required is low. As a consequence, the ultimate system will be very fast and practical with respect to memory constraints.

Algorithm 2. Relational Context Feature Extraction
  INPUT: A set of re-sampled trajectory points S
  OUTPUT: Feature vector V
  for all ordered pairs of data points $(a, b) \in combination(|S|, 2)$ **do**
      Compute $dist(a, b)$
      Compute $angle(a, b)$
  end for
  $V = (dist(a, b), angle(a, b))$
  Return V

The second supervised learning method we used for our recognition system with RC representation is a SVM classifier. A SVM was trained using RC feature on the currently largest database of isolated Arabic letters. The non-linear mapping is performed by using kernel functions. In order to extend SVM to be applied to a multi-class classification task, we have used one against all technique [10].

5   Empirical Results

Quantitative analysis of our feature representations is presented in this section with respect to recognition accuracy and time. In our evaluation studies, we used preprocessing operations in three steps: first smoothing, then de-hooking, and finally point re-sampling. We then normalize all characters to have the same heights, while their original aspect ratios remain unchanged, to achieve scale invariance.

In Table 1, the accuracy of our RH feature in an MLP-NN-based classifier for isolated Arabic characters is compared with the previous research on the same database in a NN-based system. It should be noted that in all tables, our results are reported as averages over 10 independent runs over 3-fold of the data. In each experiment, the dataset is randomly partitioned into disjoint training and test sets, using a fixed proportion (33% test and 66% training). The results are compared with the best previously existing results in the literature, on the same database, by Mezghani et. al. The recognition time for each character sample using the NN-based system is $23s$ with our relational feature approach, while this is $26s$ for the experiments in [12].

Table 1. Performance comparison of different recognition systems

Performance	1-NN	SOM [12]	RH-Tangent [8]
Recognition Rate	Ref	Ref-1.19%	Ref+4.22%
Training Time	-	2 hrs	7.5 min
Recognition Time	526 s	26 s	23 s

Our RC representation achieved a higher performance with a small number of support vectors, shown in Table2. The recognition time therefore, is remarkably low. According to our experimental results, it takes only $15ms$ for our system to recognize a character, while this time is reported in [12] as $26s$, which is orders of magnitude higher. This confirms an improvement in our method for speeding up the recognition process, and therefore proves the suitability of our approach for real time applications.

We are also interested to compare our features with previously used ones in the literature. The experimental settings (the dataset and the number of samples used in training and test sets), and the data preprocessing methods may differ among different researchers. Therefore, to have a fair comparison, we implemented these features and conducted experiments in the same setting as our proposed features. Measuring the representational power of a feature by using the same classifier is a standard approach in feature selection methods

Table 2. Experiments on isolated Arabic letters dataset

Approach	Accuracy	Settings	time
K.MAP [12]	94.6%	67% train; 33%test 432 sample/class	26 s
Bayes [13]	90.19%	67% train; 33%test 528 sample/class	-
RC-SVM	99.01%	67% train; 33%test 528 sample/class	0.015 s

Table 3. Features used for Arabic datasets. Each symbol is described by 6 points.

feature	dimension	error%
directional	10	2.7
positional	12	3.7
directional+positional	24	2.2
zone (3x3)	9	34.5
zone (10x10)	100	17.2
RC	30	0.91

[11,7,17]. We used SVM for these comparisons. Table 3 presents the results for Arabic characters. The combination of the directional and positional features shows the best performance on all datasets. However, the error rate by using our RC feature is still lower than other features, given the same data, the same preprocessing, and the same classifier. The results also show that the worst performances belong to zone features for all datasets. Such a low performance might be explained by the fact that a small number of points represent each symbol. However, even using a 30-point representation for each symbol, 3 × 3 zone features resulted in a high error rate of 17.2%. In this table, we also present the length of each feature vector. As we can see, the length of our RC feature is manageable in terms of the introduced complexity for all classifiers in the level of stroke recognition.

6   Discussion

The strength of the novel features presented in this paper can be summarized qualitatively according to several important properties: time complexity, uniqueness, performance accuracy, flexibility, ease of implementation, and memory issue. The recognition time is considered as a measure of performance since the training happens offline in a supervised classification. We demonstrated that the recognition time with SVMs is considerably short and the whole system with RC is very fast. Using a decreased resolution of RC features, even NNs are capable of providing faster results than the ones previously reported in the literature on the same data set [8].

Preserving all relationships between character points provides invariance with respect to similarity transformation, which could be decomposed into translation, scaling and rotation. Similarity transformation invariant is one kind of integral invariants. We can set the integral domain to be a segment of a curve [15]. Supposing each point p_i has coordinate $(x_i, y_i) = (r_i \times cos\Theta_i, r_i sin\Theta_i)$, we can express the three invariant geometric primitives in the plane with polar coordinates. We keep $(cos^2\Theta_i + sin^2\Theta_i)$ which is always 1 in the formula for a quick transformation to xy coordinates: $R(i) = (x_i^2 + y_i^2)^{1/2} = r_i(cos^2\Theta_i + sin^2\Theta_i)^{1/2}$; $A(O, i, j) = 1/2(x_i y_j - x_j y_i) = 1/2 r_i r_j sin(\Theta_j - \Theta_i)$; and $Dp(O, i, j) = (x_i, y_i)(x_j, y_j) = r_i r_j cos(\Theta_j - \Theta_i)$. In different writing styles, character points may have different absolute information of independent data points, however, the relative interrelationships on a set of points might not be different. Global shape of the character is also captured through all pairwise relationships between any two components.

Our proposed representations, in particular the RC feature, provide very well separated clusters with high margins in the feature space. The RC feature has the ability to incorporate a fair distribution of weights among all local and global features to be used in discriminating a character. We conjecture that RC feature combined by our choice of SVM kernel make the recognition system tolerant to Gaussian noise. This is an area of future investigation.

7   Conclusion and Future Work

We introduced in this paper new types of feature representations referred to as relational histogram and relational context. The strength of these representations resides in capturing contextual information related to the general shape of the characters. We successfully deployed our representations in neural networks and support vector machines classifiers. This was the first time that SVMs are used for recognition of online Arabic characters. Both systems showed superior results, compared to the state of the art methods for Arabic character recognition on the same database. The relational context feature not only outperforms the other approaches in recognition rate, but also provides a significant improvement in recognition time compared to the best existing results in the literature. The measured recognition speed makes the system a potentially perfect choice for the real-time applications. Future work includes the use of more sophisticated kernels for SVMs and extending our study to other series of recognition tasks such as the recognition of gestures, mathematical symbols, signatures, or any other shape or drawing. We also plan to check the ability of the proposed systems for sub-words and a limited dictionary size word recognition.

References

1. Baghshah, M.S., Shouraki, S.B., Kasaei, S.: A novel fuzzy classifier using fuzzy LVQ to recognize online persian handwriting. In: ICTTA 2006: The 2nd Information and Communication Technologies From Theory to Applications, April 2006, vol. 1, pp. 1878–1883 (2006)

2. Belongie, S., Malik, J., Puzicha, J.: Shape matching and object recognition using shape contexts. IEEE Transactions on Pattern Analysis and Machine Intelligence (PAMI) 24(4), 509–522 (2002)
3. Dinesh, M., Sridhar, M.K.: A feature based on encoding the relative position of a point in the character for online handwritten character recognition. In: ICDAR 2007: Proceedings of the 9th International Conference on Document Analysis and Recognition, pp. 1014–1017 (2007)
4. Halavati, R., Shouraki, S.B.: Recognition of Persian online handwriting using elastic fuzzy pattern recognition. International Journal of Pattern Recognition and Artificial Intelligence (IJPRAI) 21(3), 491–513 (2007)
5. Han, S., Chang, M., Zou, Y., Chen, X., Zhang, D.: Systematic multi-path HMM topology design for online handwriting recognition of east asian characters. In: ICDAR 2007: Proceedings of the 9th International Conference on Document Analysis and Recognition, pp. 604–608 (2007)
6. Hu, J., Rosenthal, A.S., Brown, M.K.: Combining high-level features with sequential local features for on-line handwriting recognition. In: ICIAP 1997: Proceedings of the 9th International Conference on Image Analysis and Processing, London, UK, vol. 2, pp. 647–654. Springer, Heidelberg (1997)
7. Huang, B.Q., Kechadi, M.-T.: A fast feature selection model for online handwriting symbol recognition. In: ICMLA '06: Proceedings of the 5th International Conference on Machine Learning and Applications, Washington, DC, USA, pp. 251–257. IEEE Computer Society, Los Alamitos (2006)
8. Izadi, S., Suen, C.Y.: Incorporating a new relational feature in Arabic online handwritten character recognition. In: VISAPP '08: Proceedings of the Third International Conference on Computer Vision Theory and Applications, PortugalMadeira, Portugal, January 2008, vol. 1, pp. 559–562. INSTICC - Institute for Systems and Technologies of Information,Control and Communication (2008)
9. Klassen, T.J., Heywood, M.I.: Towards the on-line recognition of arabic characters. In: IJCNN 2002: Proceedings of the 2002 International Joint Conference on Neural Networks, May 2002, vol. 2, pp. 1900–1905 (2002)
10. Kressel, U.H.G.: Pairwise classification and support vector machines. In: Advances in kernel methods: support vector learning, pp. 255–268 (1999)
11. Liwicki, M.M., Bunke, H.: Feature selection for on-line handwriting recognition of whiteboard notes. In: IGS 2007. The 13th Conference of the International Graphonomics Society, pp. 101–105 (2007)
12. Mezghani, N., Mitiche, A., Cheriet, M.: A new representation of shape and its use for high performance in online Arabic character recognition by an associative memory. International Journal on Document Analysis and Recognition (IJDAR) 7(4), 201–210 (2005)
13. Mezghani, N., Mitiche, A., Cheriet, M.: Bayes classification of online arabic characters by gibbs modeling of class conditional densities. IEEE Transactions on Pattern Analysis and Machine Intelligence (PAMI) 30(7), 1121–1131 (2008)
14. Randa, S.A.M., Elanwar, I., Rashwan, M.A.: Simultaneous segmentation and recognition of Arabic characters in an unconstrained on-line cursive handwritten document. International Journal of Computer and Information Science and Engineering (IJCISE) 1(4), 203–206 (2007)
15. Sluzek, A.: Using moment invariants to recognize and locate partially occluded 2d objects. Pattern Recognition Letters 7, 253 (1988)

16. Trier, O., Jain, A., Taxt, T.: Feature extraction methods for character recognition - a survey. Pattern Recognition 29(4), 641–662 (1996)

17. Verma, B., Ghosh, M.: A neural-evolutionary approach for feature and architecture selection in online handwriting recognition. In: ICDAR '03: Proceedings of the Seventh International Conference on Document Analysis and Recognition, Washington, DC, USA, pp. 1038–1042. IEEE Computer Society, Los Alamitos (2003)

Plant Leaf Identification Using Multi-scale Fractal Dimension

André R. Backes[1] and Odemir M. Bruno[2]

[1] Instituto de Ciências Matemáticas e de Computação (ICMC)
Universidade de São Paulo (USP)
Avenida do Trabalhador São-carlense, 400
13560-970 São Carlos SP Brazil
backes@icmc.usp.br
[2] Instituto de Física de São Carlos (IFSC)
Universidade de São Paulo (USP)
Avenida do Trabalhador São-carlense, 400
13560-970 São Carlos SP Brazil
bruno@ifsc.usp.br

Abstract. Taxonomical classification of plants is a very complex and time-consuming task. This is mostly due to the great biodiversity of species and the fact of most measures extracted from plants are traditionally performed manually. This paper presents a novel approach to plant identification based on leaf texture. Initially, the texture is modelled as a surface, so complexity analysis using Multi-scale fractal dimension can be performed over the generated surface, resulting in a feature vector which represents texture complexity in terms of the spatial scale. Yielded results show the potential of the approach, which overcomes traditional texture analysis methods, such as Co-occurrence matrices, Gabor filters and Fourier descriptors.

Keywords: plant identification, complexity, multi-scale fractal dimension, texture analysis.

1 Introduction

Many scientific problems related to biodiversity, ecology and pharmacology depend on plant identification. In Biology, this task involves the analysis of many organs, such as flowers, seeds, leaves and woody parts [1,2]. However, some characteristics depend on plant age or environment, what makes this task difficult to accomplish (e.g., flowers). Otherwise, leaves can be easily collected from most plants, including fossils or rare plants, so becoming a interesting source of information [3].

Plant leaf identification is a difficult task due to the wide pattern variation of its fundamental features. Variations in size, color, texture and shape, are found in leaves collected from a same plant (a response to different levels of maturity and sun exposure) or in samples from different plants (soil influence, climate or even environment).

P. Foggia, C. Sansone, and M. Vento (Eds.): ICIAP 2009, LNCS 5716, pp. 143–150, 2009.
© Springer-Verlag Berlin Heidelberg 2009

Texture is one of the most important visual attributes in images. It allows to describe the surface of a leaf in terms of the distribution of pixels over a region. Literature presents a wide number of approaches to describe texture patterns: second-order statistics [4,5], spectral analysis [6,7,8,9,10,11,12] and wavelet packets [13,14]. However, different of human-made textures, which present a detectable quasi-periodic structure, natural textures (such as, leaves texture) present a random but persistent pattern that results in a cloud like texture appearance [15,16].

An interesting alternative to these approaches is methods based on complexity analysis, such as fractal dimension. Fractals are objects which the dimension takes non-integer values (non-Euclidean geometry). Many natural phenomena and surfaces (e.g.,coastlines, brick, skin, rocks, etc) can be modelled using the fractal theory. Thus, by modelling the leaf texture as a surface it is possible to estimate its fractal dimension and, as a consequence, to describe its texture pattern in terms of space occupation and self-similarity [17,18,19].

This paper starts describing how texture analysis is performed by complexity (Section 2). A multi-scale approach for texture characterization is presented in Section 3. In Section 4, we describe how the leaf texture database was composed. Statistical analysis is employed to evaluate our approach. The results are presented and discussed in Section 5 while Section 6 concludes this paper.

2   Texture Analysis Based on Fractal Dimension

The fractal dimension has been widely used in literature to characterize both real and abstract objects in terms of complexity. While the topological dimension is defined by an integer value, which describes the number of dimensions where an object is inserted, the fractal dimension uses fractional values to describe an object in terms of space occupation and self-similarity [20,21,22,23,24,17,18].

Over the years, many approaches have been proposed to compute the fractal dimension. Bouligand-Minkowski method [18,21,25] has emerged as one of the most accurate methods and very sensitive to structural changes of the object. It is based on the study of the influence area of an object computed from its dilation. Let the gray-scale texture under analysis be represented in terms of the set $S \in R^3$ of the Cartesian coordinates. Each element $s \in S$, $s = (y, x, z)$, is defined by the pixel coordinates (y and x) in the original texture and the intensity z at this point. Let $S(r)$ be the dilation of S by a sphere of radius r:

$$S(r) = \left\{ s' \in R^3 | \exists s \in S : |s - s'| \leq r \right\},$$

where $p' = (x', y', z')$ is a point in R^3 whose distance from $p = (x, y, z)$ is smaller or equal to r (Figure 1).

The Bouligand-Minkowski fractal dimension D is defined as

$$D = 3 - \lim_{r \to 0} \frac{\log S(r)}{\log (r)},$$

where D is a number within $[0; 3]$ (i.e. considering a three-dimensional space).

Fig. 1. (a) Original Texture; (b) Texture modelled as Cartesian coordinates; (c) Dilation using $r = 10$

3   Multi-scale Fractal Dimension

Natural objects are not real fractals. They may present an infinite degree of details along the scales, although its self-similarity along these scales is not preserved. Usually, fractal dimension D is computed as the angular coefficient of the logarithm curve of the volume ($S(r)$) in terms of dilating radius, using linear interpolation. However, the logarithm curve computed presents more details than can be expressed by a single numeric value and, eventually, the fractal dimension D is not enough to represent all complexity of an object.

In order to provide a better description of objects in terms of its complexity, the Multi-Scale Fractal Dimension has been proposed [26,27,21]. This approach involves taking into the infinitesimal limit the linear interpolation by using the derivative, so achieving a function capable to express the complexity of an object in terms of the spatial scale (Figure 2). This function provides a more effective discrimination of the object, and it is defined as:

$$D(r) - 3 - \frac{d \log S(r)}{dr},$$

where $D(r)$ represents the complexity of the object at scale r.

4   Experiments

Experiments were conducted considering a texture leaf database built using 10 leaves species from Brazilian flora. A total of 3 leaves samples was manually collected for each species considered. Each leaf was washed to remove impurities that could act as noise in the texture pattern. The digitalization process was carried out by a scanner using a 1200dpi *(dots per inch)* resolution and leaves were oriented according to the central axis (line that connects the basal and apical ends) in a vertical position during this process.

From each digitalized leaf, a total of 5 texture windows of 128×128 pixels of size were extracted, totalising a database with 150 texture samples divided into

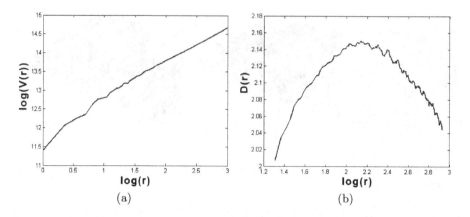

(a)   (b)

Fig. 2. (a) Log-log curve; (b) Multi-scale Fractal Dimension

10 classes (Figure 3). All color information was discarded, i.e., only the gray-scale information from the texture pattern was considered. It is important to emphasize that one single leaf may present a great variability of texture patterns (Figure 4). This variation in texture patterns can be caused by different factors, such as fungus, plague, injuries or even differences in the amount of light received by the leave during its lifetime. Thus, the selection of texture windows was guided to avoid such texture patterns that do not characterize the real texture of that leaf specie.

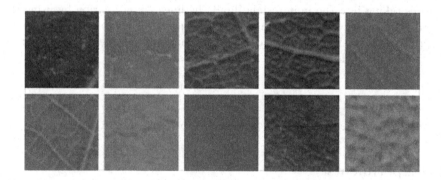

Fig. 3. Example of each texture class employed in the experiment

Evaluation of the Multi-scale curve was carried out using Linear Discriminant Analysis (LDA), a supervised statistical classification method [28,29]. LDA searches a linear combination of the descriptors (independent variables) that results in its class (dependent variable). Its main goal is to find a linear combination that minimizes the intra-classes variance while maximizes the inter-classes variance. The *leave-one-out cross-validation* strategy was also employed over the LDA.

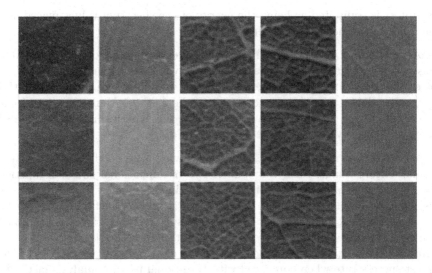

Fig. 4. Example of each texture class employed in the experiment. Example of texture variation in class (columns).

5 Results

Table 1 shows classification results yielded for the proposed approach. Multi-scale fractal dimension curves were computed from each texture pattern considered and best results were yielded considering dilation radius $r = 7$. Derivative was computed using the Finite Difference method [30], thus resulting in a Multi-scale curve containing 50 descriptors.

Table 1. Classification performance of different texture descriptors

Descriptor	No of Descriptors	Samples correctly classified	Success rate (%)
Gabor filters	16	114	76.00
Fourier descriptors	63	94	62.66
Co-occurrence matrices	16	130	86.66
M.S. Fractal Dimension	50	135	90.00

To provide a better performance evaluation, the proposed approach was compared with traditional texture analysis methods, such as Fourier descriptors [11], Co-occurrence matrices [4] and Gabor filters [8,9,31]. A brief description of the compared methods is presented as follows:

Fourier descriptors: The bi-dimensional Fourier transform is applied over the texture sample. Shifting operation is performed over the Fourier spectrum values, so that, low frequencies are placed at the center of the spectrum. A total of 63

descriptors is computed as being the energy of the spectrum values placed at a given radius distance from the center of the spectrum.

Co-occurrence matrices: This technique measures the joint probability distributions between pairs of pixels separated by a given distance and direction. Distances of 1 and 2 pixels with angles of $-45°$, $0°$, $45°$, $90°$ were considered in this paper, as well as a non-symmetric version of the method. Many descriptors can be computed from co-occurrence matrices. For the experiments, we considered energy and entropy, totalising a set of 16 descriptors.

Gabor filters: This approach consists of convolving a 2-D Gabor filter over the original texture image. Each Gabor filter is a bi-dimensional gaussian function moduled with an oriented sinusoid in a determined frequency and direction. In this paper, we employed 16 filters (4 rotation filter and 4 scale filters), with lower and upper frequencies equal to 0.01 and 0.3, respectively. Energy was computed from each convolved image, so resulting in a set of 16 descriptors.

Results show that the proposed method is more robust, as it presents the highest success rate when compared with traditional texture analysis methods. This is mainly due to the great sensitiveness of the method to changes in the texture behavior. According to the dilation radius r and the characteristics of the texture, the sphere produced by a pixel interferes on other spheres, and it disturbs the way the influence volume $S(r)$ increases. This disturbance in the influence volume allows to study pixels organization in the texture, as well as, its structural changes by complexity. Moreover, the use of Multi-scale Fractal dimension expands this analysis at different scales, so that, both micro and macro texture informations are considered and a better texture discrimination and classification are performed.

6   Conclusion

This paper presented a study of leaf texture classification based on complexity analysis. Leaf texture identification is a very difficult task due to the high similarity inter-classes and low similarity of intra-classes. Multi-scale Fractal Dimension computed from the Bouligand-Minkowski method was employed to output a curve that expresses the leaf texture complexity in terms of the spatial scale. These curves were evaluated in an experiment using linear discriminant analysis to classify a set of leaf texture previously selected. Results were compared with traditional texture analysis methods, and they show the great potential of the approach for natural texture analysis applications.

Acknowledgments

A.R.B. acknowledges support from FAPESP (2006/54367-9). O.M.B. acknowledges support from CNPq (306628/2007-4).

References

1. Judd, W., Campbell, C., Kellog, E., Stevens, P.: Plant Systematics: A Phylogenetic Approach. Sinauer Associates, Massachusetts (1999)
2. Kurmann, M.H., Hemsley, A.R.: The Evolution of Plant Architecture. Royal Botanic Gardens, Kew (1999)
3. Hickey, L.R.: Classification of archictecture of dicotyledonous leaves. Amer. J. Bot. 60(1), 17–33 (1973)
4. Haralick, R.M.: Statistical and structural approaches to texture. Proc. IEEE 67(5), 786–804 (1979)
5. Murino, V., Ottonello, C., Pagnan, S.: Noisy texture classification: A higher-order statistics approach. Pattern Recognition 31(4), 383–393 (1998)
6. Shen, L., Bai, L.: A review on gabor wavelets for face recognition. Pattern Anal. Appl. 9(2-3), 273–292 (2006)
7. Bianconi, F., Fernández, A.: Evaluation of the effects of gabor filter parameters on texture classification. Pattern Recognition 40(12), 3325–3335 (2007)
8. Jain, A.K., Farrokhnia, F.: Unsupervised texture segmentation using Gabor filters. Pattern Recognition 24(12), 1167–1186 (1991)
9. Daugman, J., Downing, C.: Gabor wavelets for statistical pattern recognition. In: Arbib, M.A. (ed.) The Handbook of Brain Theory and Neural Networks, pp. 414–419. MIT Press, Cambridge (1995)
10. Manjunath, B.S., Ma, W.-Y.: Texture features for browsing and retrieval of image data. IEEE Trans. Pattern Anal. Mach. Intell 18(8), 837–842 (1996)
11. Azencott, R., Wang, J.-P., Younes, L.: Texture classification using windowed fourier filters. IEEE Trans. Pattern Anal. Mach. Intell 19(2), 148–153 (1997)
12. Bajcsy, R.K.: Computer identification of visual surfaces. Computer Graphics Image Processing 2, 118–130 (1973)
13. Sengür, A., Türkoglu, I., Ince, M.C.: Wavelet packet neural networks for texture classification. Expert Syst. Appl. 32(2), 527–533 (2007)
14. Unser, M.: Texture classification and segmentation using wavelet frames. IEEE Trans. Image Processing 4(11), 1549–1560 (1995)
15. Huang, P.W., Dai, S.K., Lin, P.L.: Texture image retrieval and image segmentation using composite sub-band gradient vectors. J. Visual Communication and Image Representation 17(5), 947–957 (2006)
16. Kaplan, L.M.: Extended fractal analysis for texture classification and segmentation. IEEE Transactions on Image Processing 8(11), 1572–1585 (1999)
17. Schroeder, M.: Fractals, Chaos, Power Laws: Minutes From an Infinite Paradise. W.H. Freeman, New York (1996)
18. Tricot, C.: Curves and Fractal Dimension. Springer, Heidelberg (1995)
19. Backes, A.R., Bruno, O.M.: A new approach to estimate fractal dimension of texture images. In: Elmoataz, A., Lezoray, O., Nouboud, F., Mammass, D. (eds.) ICISP 2008 2008. LNCS, vol. 5099, pp. 136–143. Springer, Heidelberg (2008)
20. Chen, Y.Q., Bi, G.: On texture classification using fractal dimension. IJPRAI 13(6), 929–943 (1999)
21. de O. Plotze, R., Falvo, M., Pádua, J.G., Bernacci, L.C., Vieira, M.L.C., Oliveira, G.C.X., Bruno, O.M.: Leaf shape analysis using the multiscale minkowski fractal dimension, a new morphometric method: a study with passiflora (passifloraceae). Canadian Journal of Botany 83(3), 287–301 (2005)
22. Li, J., Sun, C., Du, Q.: A new box-counting method for estimation of image fractal dimension. In: International Conference on Image Processing, pp. 3029–3032 (2006)

23. da F. Costa, L., Cesar Jr., R.M.: Shape Analysis and Classification: Theory and Practice. CRC Press, Boca Raton (2000)
24. Carlin, M.: Measuring the complexity of non-fractal shapes by a fractal method. PRL: Pattern Recognition Letters 21(11), 1013–1017 (2000)
25. Bruno, O.M., de O. Plotze, R., Falvo, M., de Castro, M.: Fractal dimension applied to plant identification. Information Sciences 178, 2722–2733 (2008)
26. Emerson, C.W., Lam, N.N., Quattrochi, D.A.: Multi-scale fractal analysis of image texture and patterns. Photogrammetric Engineering and Remote Sensing 65(1), 51–62 (1999)
27. Gonzalez, R.C., Woods, R.E.: Digital Image Processing, 2nd edn. Prentic-Hall, New Jersey (2002)
28. Everitt, B.S., Dunn, G.: Applied Multivariate Analysis, 2nd edn. Arnold (2001)
29. Fukunaga, K.: Introduction to Statistical Pattern Recognition, 2nd edn. Academic Press, London (1990)
30. Smith, G.D.: Numerical Solution of Partial Differential Equations: Finite Difference Methods, 3rd edn., Oxford (1986)
31. Idrissa, M., Acheroy, M.: Texture classification using gabor filters. Pattern Recognition Letters 23(9), 1095–1102 (2002)

Detection of a Hand Holding a Cellular Phone Using Multiple Image Features

Hiroto Nagayoshi[1], Takashi Watanabe[1], Tatsuhiko Kagehiro[1],
Hisao Ogata[2], Tsukasa Yasue[2], and Hiroshi Sako[1]

[1] Central Research Laboratory, Hitachi Ltd., Tokyo, Japan
{hiroto.nagayoshi.wy,takashi.watanabe.dh,tatsuhiko.kagehiro.tx,
hiroshi.sako.ug}hitachi.com
[2] Hitachi-Omron Terminal Solutions, Corp., Aichi, Japan
{hisao_ogata,tsukasa_yasue}@hitachi-omron-ts.com

Abstract. Detection of a hand holding a cellular phone was developed to recognize whether someone is using a cellular phone while operating an automated teller machine (ATM). The purpose is to prevent money transfer fraud. Since a victim is told a bogus reason to transfer money and how to operate the machine through a cellular phone, detecting a working cellular phone is necessary.

However, cellular phone detection was not realistic due to variable colors and shapes. We assumed that a user's hand beside the face was holding a cellular phone and decided to detect it.

The proposed method utilizes color, shape, and motion. Color and motion were used to compare the input to the face. Shape was used to compare the input to the standard hand pattern. The experimental result was a detection rate of 90.0% and a false detection rate of 3.2%, where 7,324 and 20,708 images were used respectively.

Keywords: hand detection, multiple features, color, shape, motion, HOG, optical flow, face detection.

1   Introduction

"Money transfer fraud" that targets ATM users is a social problem in Japan. The number of cases increased substantially in 2005. The number of cases is now more than 10,000, and the financial loss is more than 25 billion yen per year.

In that type of fraud, criminals use a bogus reason to transfer money. For instance, they tell the victims that they can get a tax refund and ask them to go to an ATM. Then, the criminals show the victims how to operate the ATM through a cellular phone. Usually, the victims are those who are not familiar with that kind of electronic device. Therefore, the victims obey the instructions and operate the ATM without knowing that they are sending money to the criminals.

As described above, one of the specific features is that the victim uses a cellular phone. A system that can detect a working cellular phone and warn the victims is needed to prevent such a crime.

P. Foggia, C. Sansone, and M. Vento (Eds.): ICIAP 2009, LNCS 5716, pp. 151–160, 2009.
© Springer-Verlag Berlin Heidelberg 2009

We developed a system for that purpose using image recognition techniques. Other methods, such as detecting radio waves from the phone and voice recognition are also effective. However, the fact that many ATMs now have cameras makes it reasonable to use an image recognition based system.

One of the difficulties is that the colors and shapes of cellular phones are variable. In addition to that, the cellular phone is concealed by the hand. To avoid these problems, we focused on detecting the hand holding the cellular phone, rather than detecting the cellular phone itself. The variety of colors and shapes of hands is less than that of cellular phones.

One of the major applications of hand detection techniques is gesture recognition [1]. In that field, the environment sometimes can be modified to be appropriate for detection. For instance, a plain white or black background can be used. However, that is frequently impossible for a place such as an ATM booth. Therefore, a robust method against the variety of backgrounds is required.

Some robust methods were proposed which use color [2], hand contours [3,4], and spacial frequency of intensity [5]. Usually, shape detection is more robust against lighting variation. In particular, it gives the best performance when it captures the image of the fingers. However, in our application, the hand was in the shape of a fist, and sometimes fingers were concealed. Therefore, using complementary multiple images of different features was necessary.

This paper firstly describes the method to detect a hand utilizing multiple features such as color, shape, and motion. Then, the experimental results using the images that simulate real scenes are presented to show the validity of the proposed method.

2   Detection of a Hand Holding a Cellular Phone

2.1   Basic Idea

Fig.1 shows a person using a cellular phone. As described above, it is difficult to detect a cellular phone because of concealment by the hand and the variety of shapes and colors. Therefore, we decided to detect the hand beside the face, which can be recognized as a person using a cellular phone. Although there are other reasons for this hand position, such as scratching a cheek, it was possible to distinguish this because the duration was short.

The flow is shown in Fig.2. First, face detection is executed. We applied a face detector by Sochman et al., that was an improved version of [6]. Their method is characterized by WaldBoost classifier that gives optimal time and error rate trade-off. Then the feature value using color was calculated, and the positions of the hand candidate regions were revised using that value. The other feature values using shape and motion were calculated inside those candidate regions. The final decision was made using intermediate decisions based on each feature value.

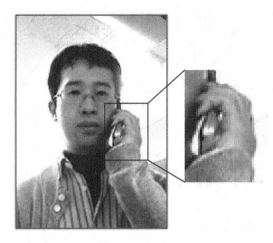

Fig. 1. A person using a cellular phone

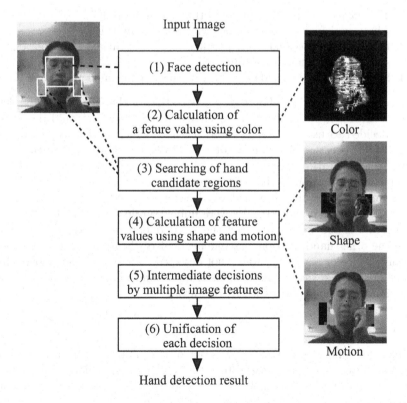

Fig. 2. Flow of the system

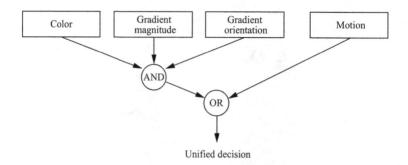

Fig. 3. Unification of decision for each feature

2.2   Image Features

To examine effective image features, we summarized the characteristics of a hand from the point of view of image processing.

1. The color of a hand is similar to that of the face [3].
2. The complexity of hand shapes will cause many thick edges.
3. Fingers not concealed make parallel edges. This means that the edges of the specific orientation are dominant.
4. Since the hand is beside the face, its motion is similar to that of the face.

For characteristic 1, similar color pixels to that of the face need to be detected. For 2 and 3, it was important to choose a method that could detect shapes. We decided to use a gradient based method, which is reported to be suitable for object detection [7]. One factor was gradient magnitude, and the other was gradient orientation. For 4, an optical flow was used to detect an object that had a similar motion to that of the face.

Using each feature, intermediate decisions showed whether a hand was detected. After that, those results were unified as shown in Fig.3. The results for color and shape were unified by the AND operator to reduce false detection. On the other hand, motion was independent of them. For instance, even if the results for color and shape were "not detected", an objects that moves the same way as the face should be recognised as a hand. This was why the result for motion was unified using the OR operator.

2.3   Color

The color similarity to the face was one of the important features. This feature had the advantage that it was robust to the variation in color of the environment because it used the face color as the standard. Even if the environment had changed, the hand and the face would still be very similar in color. However, the intensity between the face and the hand may be different because of shading. To avoid this problem, only hue and chroma components in the HSI color system were used.

The details of the method are as follows. First, the probabilistic distribution of the face color was calculated. This was implemented by hue-chroma histogram. Then, we calculated the likelihood that showed how similar each pixel was to that of the face (Fig.2(2)). The position of the candidate region was revised to where it had the maximum likelihood (Fig.2(3)), according to following the equation:

$$y_r = \arg\max_{y_s} \sum_{y=y_0+y_s}^{y_0+y_s+height} \sum_{x=x_0}^{x_0+width} L(x,y) \tag{1}$$

$L(x,y)$: Likelihood that shows how similar the pixel was to that of the face at position (x,y).

x_0, y_0 : The top-left position of a hand candidate region, which was determined by the size and the position of the detected face.

width, height : Width and height of candidate regions - they are proportional to those of the detected face.

Once we had hand candidate regions on both sides of a face, they were utilized in calculating feature values of shape and motion too.

To get the intermediate decision whether a hand was placed beside the face at this step (Fig.2(5)), the number of pixels whose likelihood is larger than a threshold was calculated first. Then, the decision "a hand is detected" was reached when the number exceeded a threshold.

2.4   Shape

One of the most effective methods to evaluate shape is HOG descriptors [7]. We used a more simple method for stability and computational cost. When using HOG descriptors, the target region is divided into many cells; here there was only one cell. As a hand holding a cellular phone is considered to be a solid object, one cell was enough.

The purpose of the shape feature was to detect the target that had thick edges and a specific bias of edge orientations. For the former, we simply calculated the average gradient magnitudes. For the latter, the orientation of each gradient was accumulated in a histogram weighted by its magnitude. The histogram had 8 bins for 8 orientations. Then, the feature vector of 8 dimensions was evaluated using Mahalanobis distance.

Two values were calculated. One was the average magnitude of the gradients. The other was a Mahalanobis distance that expressed the dissimilarity from the standard hand pattern. Intermediate decisions (Fig.2(5)) were made by applying the thresholding to each of them.

2.5   Motion

The hand that holds a cellular phone will be beside the face. This means that the face and the hand usually moved in the same direction. Therefore, detecting an object whose motion was similar to that of the face is the purpose of this section.

We applied the Lucas-Kanade method [8] to calculate the motion because its low computational cost was suitable for real time processing. When a pixel whose intensity value was $I(\boldsymbol{x}, t)$, was moving with velocity expressed as motion vector $\boldsymbol{v}$, the constraint equation is given as follows:

$$\nabla I(\boldsymbol{x}, t) \cdot \boldsymbol{v} = -I_t(\boldsymbol{x}, t) \tag{2}$$

where $\boldsymbol{x}$ denotes the position and t denotes the time. The assumption that the motion vector $\boldsymbol{v}$ is constant in the local area is introduced, and the following equation is given by using the least square method.

$$\boldsymbol{v} = \arg \min_{\tilde{\boldsymbol{v}}} \sum_{\boldsymbol{x}} \left[\nabla I(\boldsymbol{x}, t) \cdot \tilde{\boldsymbol{v}} + I_t(\boldsymbol{x}, t) \right]^2 \tag{3}$$

Then, the motion vector is given as follows:

$$\boldsymbol{v} = (A^T A)^{-1} A^T \boldsymbol{b} \tag{4}$$
$$A = [\nabla I(\boldsymbol{x}_1), \dots, \nabla I(\boldsymbol{x}_n)]^T \tag{5}$$
$$\boldsymbol{b} = [I_t(\boldsymbol{x}_1), \dots, I_t(\boldsymbol{x}_n)]^T \tag{6}$$

First, the motion vector was calculated inside a face region where the motion vector could be considered to be constant. The hand detection occurred only if the magnitude of a face motion vector exceeded a threshold. This is because when the face stopped, the hand would also stop, and it was impossible to distinguish it from the background.

The candidate region was divided into small cells. The motion vector in each cell was compared to that of the face using a similarity measure defined as follows:

$$s = \frac{\boldsymbol{v}_h(i) \cdot \boldsymbol{v}_f}{|\boldsymbol{v}_h(i)||\boldsymbol{v}_f|} \tag{7}$$

When the number of cells that exceeded a threshold was more than another threshold, the intermediate result in Fig.2(5) would be "hand detected".

3 Experiments

For an evaluation, 24 bit color images, which were compressed using motion JPEG format, were used. Those images were captured by USB cameras. The resolution was 320×240 pixels, and the frame rate was 15 frames per second. The number of frames are listed in Table 1. The A1 data is for evaluating the detection rate, and the B1-B3 data is for the false detection rate. The former data was collected when the person had a cellular phone while the latter data was collected when the person did not. We assumed that the camera was set at a position and an angle where it could capture the face of an ATM user head-on. In A1 and B1, the person looked straight at the camera and moved slightly. B2 and B3 include more variations. In B2, the person was standing in front of the camera but facing various directions. In B3, there were 3 people behind the

Table 1. Number of images for experiments

Database name	Situation	Number of frames	Number of frames where a face is detected
A1	facing the camera	10,789	7,324
B1	facing the camera	11,392	7,879
B2	facing various directions	3,954	1,874
B3	many people	14,805	10,955

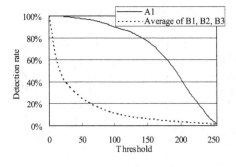

Fig. 4. Detection rate vs threshold (color)

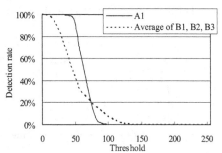

Fig. 5. Detection rate vs threshold (gradient magnitude)

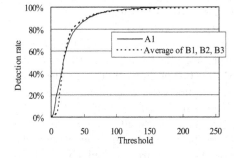

Fig. 6. Detection rate vs threshold (gradient orientation)

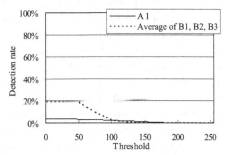

Fig. 7. Detection rate vs threshold (motion)

main person who stood in front of the camera. A1 and B1 consisted of 3 different sequences that captured 3 different people. B2 and B3 consisted of 5 sequences as well.

Using these data, the detection rate for each feature was evaluated. The results are shown in Fig.4-7. Solid lines indicate the detection rate evaluated using A1. Broken lines indicate the average rate of false detection evaluated using B1-B3. Comparing each result, the color feature gave the best result.

Table 2. Rate of correct and false detection using combinations of features

Data	C	C+Gm	C+Go	C+M	All features
A1	88.2%	87.3%	87.9%	88.4%	87.1%
average of B1, B2, B3	9.0%	4.3%	8.6%	10.0%	5.0%
B1	1.0%	0.2%	1.0%	1.3%	0.5%
B2	14.1%	3.5%	13.6%	16.3%	5.2%
B3	11.8%	9.2%	11.3%	12.4%	9.3%

*C: Color, Gm: Gradient magnitude, Go: Gradient orientation, M: Motion

Table 3. Rate of correct and false detection using multiple frames decisions

Data	C	C+Gm	C+Go	C+M	All features
A1	90.6%	90.0%	90.6%	90.8%	90.0%
average of B1, B2, B3	8.0%	3.1%	7.7%	8.5%	3.2%
B1	0.3%	0.1%	0.3%	0.4%	0.1%
B2	12.5%	0.7%	12.1%	13.6%	1.1%
B3	11.3%	8.7%	10.7%	11.6%	8.4%

*C: Color, Gm: Gradient magnitude, Go: Gradient orientation, M: Motion

Next, detection rates using combinations of features were evaluated. The thresholds were determined empirically. The results are shown in Table 2. The evaluated combinations of features are color, color and gradient magnitude, color and gradient orientation, color and motion, and all four features. The intermediate decisions for each feature were unified according to Fig.3.

From Table 2, gradient magnitude was the second best feature. It reduced false detections by 10.6 points in the B2 database while the correct detection rate went down by 0.9 points. Other features were less effective. Gradient orientation could reduce false detection in B2 and B4 by 0.5 points, while it reduced the correct detection rate by 0.3 points. Motion did not work well in this evaluation. However, motion can be used as a complementary feature for color and shape. For instance, when the user wore black gloves, it was difficult to detect the hand by color or shape. The reason for the worse performance may have been the instability of the motion vector. Especially, the small area size which was used to calculate the motion of hand would cause the unstable motion vector. More accurate techniques, such as introducing weight to each pixel according to its confidence are required.

The total accuracy was improved by using multiple frames. We introduced a decision rule that the final result was "detected" when a hand was detected in more than 4 of 10 successive frames. The result is shown in Table 3. The lowest average false detection was 3.1% using color and gradient magnitude while the correct detection rate was 90.0%. Using all four features gave a 90.0% detection rate and 3.2% false detection rate.

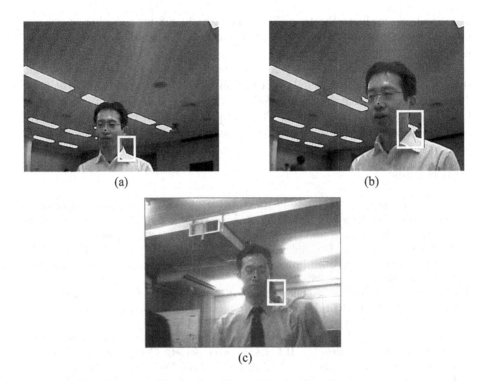

Fig. 8. Samples of false detection: (a),(b) samples from B2; (c) sample from B3

Some samples of false detection are shown in Fig.8. The falsely detected region included the cheek, neck, or other person's face. All of them are similar in color to that of the user's face. To reduce these false detections, shape and motion features need to be improved.

The computational time was fast enough for real time processing, 11.7 ms for each frame. The specification of the PC were Core 2 Duo 1.8 GHz, 3 GB RAM, where only one processor was used.

4   Conclusion

Detection of a hand that holds a cellular phone was developed to protect the ATM user from money transfer fraud. The reason for this is the victims usually indicated how to operate the ATM to a criminal through a cellular phone.

The detection method was based on image recognition techniques. The reason we focused on the detection of the hand is that the detection of cellular phones is very difficult due to the variety of colors and shapes.

Multiple features such as color, shape, and motion were used complementarily. To evaluate the detection rate, 7,324 images where a person faces the camera were used. To evaluate the false detection rate, 20,708 images where a person faced various directions were used. The results were a 90.0% correct detection rate and a 3.2% false detection rate.

One of our future tasks is to reduce false detection. The major reason was that the color of the cheek, neck, and other person's face is similar to that of the face. To resolve this problem, improving detection by shape will be effective. Another future task concerns the database. The proposed method was evaluated using limited databases. Preparing more databases from real situations is necessary.

References

1. Utsumi, A., Tetsutani, N., Igi, S.: Hand detection and tracking using pixel value distribution model for multiple-camera-based gesture interactions. In: Proceedings of IEEE Workshop on Knowledge Media Networking, pp. 31–36 (2002)
2. Girondel, V., Bonnaud, L., Caplier, A.: Hands detection and tracking for interactive multimedia applications. In: Proceedings of International Conference on Computer Vision and Graphics, pp. 282–287 (2002)
3. Ong, E.-J., Bowden, R.: A boosted classifier tree for hand shape detection. In: Proceedings of Sixth IEEE International Conference on Automatic Face and Gesture Recognition (FGR 2004), pp. 889–894 (2004)
4. Caglar, M.B., Lobo, N.: Open hand detection in a cluttered single image using finger primitives. In: Proceedings of IEEE Computer Society Conference on Computer Vision and Pattern Recognition Workshop (CVPRW 2006), p. 148 (2006)
5. Kolsch, M., Turk, M.: Robust hand detection. In: Proceedings of Sixth IEEE International Conference on Automatic Face and Gesture Recognition (FGR 2004), pp. 614–619 (2004)
6. Sochman, J., Matas, J.: Waldboost-learning for time constrained sequential detection. In: Proceedings of IEEE Computer Society Conference on Computer Vision and Pattern Recognition (CVPR 2005), vol. 2 (2005)
7. Dalal, N., Triggs, B.: Histograms of oriented gradients for human detection. In: Proceedings of IEEE Computer Society Conference on Computer Vision and Pattern Recognition (CVPR 2005), vol. 1, pp. 886–893 (2005)
8. Lucas, B.D., Kanade, T.: An iterative image registration technique with an application to stereo vision. In: Proceedings of 7th International Joint Conference on Artificial Intelligence, vol. 81, pp. 674–679 (1981)

Object Detection by Estimating and Combining High-Level Features

Geoffrey Levine and Gerald DeJong

Department of Computer Science
University of Illinois at Champaign-Urbana
Urbana, IL 61801
levine@cs.uiuc.edu, dejong@cs.uiuc.edu

Abstract. Many successful object detection systems characterize object classes with a statistical profile over a large number of local features. We present an enhancement to this method that learns to assemble local features into features that capture more global properties such as body shape and color distribution. The system then learns to combine these estimated global features to improve object detection accuracy. In our approach, each candidate object detection from an off-the-shelf gradient-based detection system is transformed into a conditional random field. This CRF is used to extract a most likely object silhouette, which is then processed into features based on color and shape. Finally, we show that on the difficult Pascal VOC 2007 data set, detection rates can be improved by combining these global features with the local features from a state-of-the-art gradient based approach.

1 Introduction

Recently, the field of computer vision has taken great strides in the area of object detection. Many of today's top performing systems perform recognition based on a constellation of local gradient features [1,2]. These systems have performed well on many of the latest object detection datasets [3,4]. However, the performance of these systems varies dramatically from object to object. For example, in the recent PASCAL VOC 2008 detection challenge [4], top performing local feature approaches performed very well on object classes with predictable structures such as bicycle, car and train. On the other hand, objects that are highly deformable and/or viewed from a diverse set of perspectives, such as bird, dog, and plant, were detected less than half as accurately.

In Figure 1 we show several false detections of one such approach [1]. This approach models object classes with a spatial histogram of gradients. Indeed, it is possible to see how in each case the local gradient features could confuse the detector. Still, to a human, these cases are not problematic as there are clear cues that the objects in question are not present.

In this paper, we present a more directed approach, in which high-level color and shape consistency features are estimated and utilized for object detection. We demonstrate that by combining these high-level features with confidence values from a state-of-the art object detection system, we are able to improve detection accuracy on the difficult subclass of animals from the PASCAL VOC 2007 dataset [3].

P. Foggia, C. Sansone, and M. Vento (Eds.): ICIAP 2009, LNCS 5716, pp. 161–169, 2009.
© Springer-Verlag Berlin Heidelberg 2009

Cat   Horse   Sheep

Fig. 1. False Positives (at equal error rate) of Felzenszwalb et al. [1]. The local features found by the gradient-based detector are consistent with the proposed class. However, in these cases, shape and color consistency can provide a strong cue that the object of interest is not present.

2 Approach

Our approach is illustrated in Figure 2. A black-box gradient-based object detector [1] is used to hypothesize object locations. We extract an image subwindow around each candidate detection, and construct a conditional random field probability model to estimate the most likely silhouette corresponding to each detection. These silhouettes are processed for global object shape and color features, which are amended to features available from the gradient-based detector, and a hybrid detector is trained to more accurately score candidate object detections.

Conditional Random Field. Conditional random fields [5,6,7], a probabilistic framework for classifying structured inputs, represent the conditional probability of a labeling, $\mathbf{Y}$, given structured data, $\mathbf{X}$, in the form of an undirected graphical model. The probability of a label sequence given observed data is equal to a normalized potential function:

$$P(\mathbf{Y}|\mathbf{X}) = \frac{e^{\psi(\mathbf{Y},\mathbf{X})}}{Z(\mathbf{X})} . \tag{1}$$

where $Z(\mathbf{X}) = \sum_{\mathbf{Y}} e^{\psi(\mathbf{Y},\mathbf{X})}$ is a normalization factor.

We utilize a conditional random field to estimate the most likely object silhouette within an image subwindow. The input, $\mathbf{X}$ is a graph (V, E), with one vertex corresponding to each pixel, and an edge between each adjacent pixel. $\mathbf{Y} = \{y_v, v \in V\}$ is the labeling of each pixel into one of two classes, object (1) or background (0). Additionally, we introduce a vector of unobservable index variables $\mathbf{W} = [w_f, w_b]$, related to the appearance of the foreground and background. Their role is described in the next section. The log potential function is then a sum of two terms, based on appearance and boundary.

$$\psi(\mathbf{Y}, \mathbf{W}, \mathbf{X}) = \psi^a(\mathbf{Y}, \mathbf{W}, \mathbf{X}) + \psi^b(\mathbf{Y}, \mathbf{X}) . \tag{2}$$

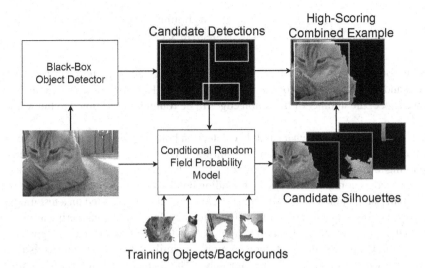

Fig. 2. Our approach

Appearance Potential. The appearance potential function must capture consistency between image pixel colors and the corresponding pixel label. It is important to note that object classes can be made up of a diverse set of individuals. Taking, for example, the variety of dog breeds, our probability model must assign high probability to labellings consistent with the coloring of either a German Shepherd or a Golden Retriever, but not when the foreground is a mixture of the two. For this reason we employ a nearest-neighbor like approach in our appearance potential function. We extract from the training images a set of object color histograms, one per individual, and introduce index variable w_f to represent the training individual to which the object labeled pixels are matched. Similarly, we introduce a second index, w_b, to represent the training background to which the background pixels match. Allowing w_f and w_b to vary separately allows us to correctly recognize cases where, for example, a Dalmatian is located outdoors, even if in training we only saw Dalmatians indoors and other dogs outdoors.

We define the appearance potential then as:

$$\psi^a(\mathbf{X}, \mathbf{W}, \mathbf{Y}) =$$
$$\frac{1}{|V|} \sum_{v \in V} \left((y_v) \phi \left(col(v), hist_{f,w_f} \right) + (1 - y_v) \phi \left(col(v), hist_{b,w_b} \right) \right) . \quad (3)$$

$$\phi(c, hist) = \theta_1 log(hist(c)) . \quad (4)$$

where $hist(c)$ is the value of the corresponding color histogram at color c. $\phi(c, hist)$ can be interpreted as the negative description length of color c given the color probability distribution implied by $hist$.

Boundary Potential. Relative to the total number of edges in $\mathbf{X}$, we expect the number of edges joining foreground and background pixels to be few, and thus we define the boundary potential function to penalize large numbers of boundaries:

$$\psi^b(\mathbf{X}, \mathbf{Y}) = \sum_{e=(v_i, v_j) \in E} \frac{\theta_2 \, \text{boundary}(y_i, y_j)}{\text{width}(\mathbf{X}) + \text{height}(\mathbf{X})} . \tag{5}$$

where $\text{boundary}(y_i, y_j) = 1$ if $y_i \neq y_j$ and 0 otherwise, width and height denote the width and height (in pixels) of the image subwindow. Here we normalize by their sum, as we expect the number of transition edges to be roughly proportional to this value.

CRF Construction. Given a candidate detection bounding box, we construct the input $\mathbf{X}$ for our conditional random field as follows. First we form an image subwindow by enlarging the bounding box by a factor of $\frac{1}{2}$ in each dimension in order to ensure that the entire object is contained should the bounding box be slightly too small. Because of the potentially large number of CRF's that are constructed and evaluated on a test image we employ the following approximations for efficiency. Instead of considering all possible $(0,1)$ labelings over all pixels, we first apply an off-the-shelf segmentation algorithm [8] to segment the pixels into contiguous regions of similar color. Then, all pixels in each segment are constrained to have the same label. The segmentation algorithm parameters are dependent on the size of the bounding box $((sigma, minsize)$ ranges from $(.5, 125)$ when bounding box < 16384 pixels to $(4, 1000)$ when bounding box > 65536 pixels). This strategy produces a roughly constant number of segments in the image subwindow, independent of its size (roughly 30 to 50). As we do not expect the object to extend into regions of the image outside of the CRF, all segments that extend beyond the image subwindow are constrained to be labeled as background.

Training. The individual object and background histograms are estimated from the silhouetted subset of training images from the PASCAL VOC 2007 dataset [3]. This is done simply by enlarging the annotated silhouette's bounding box as described above and recording each constituent pixel's color in the object or background color histogram. Colors are discretized into a 4096 bin smoothed histogram [9].

In order to learn CRF parameters θ, we construct a graphical structure and segmentation as described above for each object instance in the training images. Pixels are assigned foreground/background labels based on whether their associated segment is mostly in the silhouette or not. Thus we have a set $(\mathbf{X}^t, \mathbf{Y}^t), t = 1, ..., N$ of structured inputs and pixel-wise labelings. Indices w_{obj}^t and w_{back}^t are free parameters, but are constrained so as not to self-reference.

Ideally we could choose θ by maximizing the conditional log likelihood of the training data. Unfortunately, this requires calculating the normalizing factor $Z(\mathbf{X})$, which involves a sum over all pixel labelings, and so is not feasible. Thus, we employ an approximate method, contrastive divergence [10]. In contrastive divergence, a Markov chain is started at the correct labeling and run for a small number of steps (in our case one), and then the parameters are updated according to:

$$\theta^{s+1} = \theta^s + \lambda \left(\left\langle \frac{\partial \psi(\mathbf{X}, \mathbf{Y})}{\partial \theta} \right\rangle_{\mathbf{Y}^0} - \left\langle \frac{\partial \psi(\mathbf{X}, \mathbf{Y})}{\partial \theta} \right\rangle_{\mathbf{Y}^1} \right) . \tag{6}$$

where $\mathbf{Y}_0$ is the label distribution defined by the training data, and $\mathbf{Y}_1$ is the label distribution after one step in the Markov chain. This update has the effect of shaping the potential function locally to encourage the correct labeling. With the small number of parameters in our CRF model (two), we find that convergence is very fast (approximately 3000 iterations).

Application. For test images we proceed as follows. First the image is input to our black-box gradient based object detector, resulting in a set of candidate detections bounding boxes and associated scores, $\{(B_j, s_{B_j}), 1 \leq j \leq M\}$. This set is processed by a non-maximal suppression procedure, in which any candidate detections with stronger candidate detections nearby (overlapping by 80%) is removed. For each bounding box we construct a conditional random field by enlarging the bounding box and performing a size appropriate segmentation as described above.

The CRF defines a probability over all object/background labellings. Because of the large number of CRF's constructed (5 to 100 per image), evaluating each labeling is infeasible. Thus we find one high-probability labeling as follows. We initialize the labels such that all segments are assigned background except for those located entirely within the candidate bounding box B_j. w_f and w_b are chosen so as to maximize the color potential function. Then, segment labellings and indices are iterated through and changed as necessary so as to find a local maximum in the probability field. This set of $(\mathbf{X}, \mathbf{Y})$ pairs (one per candidate bounding box) is forwarded to the next stage for feature extraction.

3   High-Level Features

Color Consistency. Once the object silhouette, S, is estimated, we extract the foreground and background color histograms ($h_{S,f}$ and $h_{S,b}$). These histograms can then be compared to those from the training images. We generate two features (Equations 9 and 10) based on the consistency between these histograms and the matched training instances, and a third color feature to represent how salient the object/background distinction is (Equation 11):

$$f_{S,f,col} = - \left(\min_{w_f} D_{KL} \left(h_{S,f}, hist_{f,w_f} \right) \right) . \tag{7}$$

$$f_{S,b,col} = - \left(\min_{w_b} D_{KL} \left(h_{S,b}, hist_{b,w_b} \right) \right) . \tag{8}$$

where D_{KL} represents Kullback-Leibler divergence. Let $h_{S,all}$ be the histogram of all pixels in the candidate subwindow, and let $w_f = \arg\min_{w_f} D_{KL}(h_{S,f}, hist_{f,w_f})$ and $w_b = \arg\min_{w_b} D_{KL}(h_{S,b}, hist_{b,w_b})$. The saliency feature is then:

$$\begin{aligned} f_{S,colsal} = f_{S,objcol} &+ f_{S,backcol} \\ &+ D_{KL} \left(h_{S,all}, hist_{f,w_f} \right) + D_{KL} \left(h_{S,all}, hist_{b,w_b} \right) . \end{aligned} \tag{9}$$

Shape Consistency. We generate one feature $f_{S,shape}$ to represent the shape consistency between the estimated object silhouette and those seen in the training images. To do so, we first define a function, ShapeRep, that inputs a silhouette and outputs a 500 dimensional vector of shape characteristic features. ShapeRep operates by placing a 10 x 10 grid (indexed by (i,j)) over the silhouette's bounding box, and calculating 1 shape element, $e_{i,j}^{shape}$, and 4 boundary elements, $e_{i,j,k}^{boundary}$ ($k = \{up, down, left, right\}$), per cell. $e_{i,j}^{shape}$ equals the fraction of foreground pixels in cell (i,j), and $e_{i,j,k}^{boundary}$ equals the fraction of total boundary edges located in cell (i,j) with orientation k. Finally, the vector is normalized to length 1. Again, we utilize a nearest neighbor approach in defining $f_{S,shape}$,

$$f_{S,shape} = \max_{T \in D_{sil}} \text{ShapeRep}(S) \cdot \text{ShapeRep}(T) . \qquad (10)$$

where D_{sil} is the set of training silhouettes and their horizontal reflections.

Feature Combination. In order to combine the silhouettes/high-level features with the original set of bounding boxes/gradient scores, we define the following function:

$$\text{match}(B_j, S_i) = \frac{\text{IntersectionArea}(B_j, \text{Box}(S_i))}{\text{UnionArea}(B_j, \text{Box}(S_i))} . \qquad (11)$$

where $\text{Box}(S_i)$ returns the minimal size box fully enclosing silhouette S_i. The match function ranges from 0 to 1 and measures the compatibility between a bounding box and silhouette. For each bounding box B_j we first identify those silhouettes S_i for which $\text{match}(B_j, S_i)$ is greater than threshold α. Then, for each high level feature f_k, we set $f_{B_j,k}$ to the maximum value of f_k across all corresponding silhouettes.

Combined examples can then be assigned an overall confidence using a simple linear weighting of the bounding box score and high-level features of the combined example. In our empirical evaluations, detection methods are scored based on average precision over all recalls, and so we maximize this value over a set of withheld validation data (constraining all weights to be positive). Given the small number of features, we are able to implement this with a simple random walk through the weight space. Paramaeter α is optimized in this procedure as well.

4   Empirical Evaluation

We test our method on the set of animal categories from the PASCAL Visual Object Classes 2007 Detection Challenge dataset [3].[1] Animals (bird, cat, cow, dog, horse and sheep) are a difficult subclass of objects to detect because of their highly deformable nature. Object silhouettes are provided for roughly 5% of the images. As described in section 3.5, training image silhouettes are used to acquire object/background color

---

[1] We choose the 2007 dataset as the PASCAL VOC 2008 test data is not publicly available at the time of writing.

histograms and shape representations. This procedure results in approximately 50 training examples per class.

For the black-box gradient-based approach, we use the latest object detection system of Felzenszwalb et al., [1,11]. This system represents the state of the art earning the highest published overall detection rates for both the VOC 2007 and VOC 2008 detection challenges. We take advantage of their publicly available detection source code. While their model training code is unavailable at the time of writing, they made available models for each of the 20 VOC 2007 object classes. As the gradient based system has already been trained on all training images, in order to learn the linear combination parameters we randomly select half of the test images for validation. The parameters are chosen so as to maximize the average precision across the validation set. Finally, the combined approach is evaluated against the remaining test images. We repeat this process 6 times and take the average results.

In the VOC detection challenge, a correct detection is defined as one for which there exists an annotated ground truth bounding box of the same class such that $\frac{Area of Intersection}{Area of Union} > \frac{1}{2}$, however, only one detection is permitted for each ground-truth bounding box, all subsequent detections are considered false positives. We compare the performance of our combined approach (Low-level + High-Level Features) to that of the gradient based detector alone (Low-Level Features). For each system, the candidate detections are ranked based on confidence, non-maximal suppression is performed, and the average precision over all recalls is evaluated. Results appear in table 1.

Table 1. Our Detection Rates vs. [11](Average Precision). †: Best in VOC 2007 Detection Challenge (Cow, Horse) and VOC 2008 Detection Challenge (Bird).

Class	State of the Art (Low-Level) [11]†	Our System (Low-Level + High-Level)	Change
Bird	.0193	.0242	25.4%
Cat	.115	.120	4.3%
Cow	.148	.144	-2.5%
Dog	.098	.117	19.4%
Horse	.362	.372	2.9%
Sheep	.245	.248	1.4%

We see that the inclusion of high level features improves the results substantially for the two most difficult of the six classes (bird and dog). Potentially, the wide variety of perspective and poses for these objects renders the gradient based detector volatile, and the global color consistency features serve as an important cue. Improvements in other classes are modest (cat, horse, sheep), and the high-level features only decreases performance in one case (cow), and by a small amount. This is likely due to the low dimensional nature of the high-level features, which help the overall system resist overfitting the validation data. Example silhouettes are shown in Figure 3.

Image	Extracted Silhouette	Object Color Match	Background Color Match	Shape Match

Fig. 3. Example estimated object silhouettes. The last three columns illustrate the matched training instance for each of object color, background color, and object shape.

5   Conclusion

We present an approach to object detection that enhances the low-level local feature approach popular in today's literature with a high-level feature extraction stage to increase accuracy in object detection. In our approach candidate detections are fed into a conditional random field probability model to identify the most likely silhouette corresponding to each detection. Based on these silhouettes, color and shape consistency features are extracted and combined in a simple linear weighting for enhanced detection accuracy. We demonstrate the merit of our approach on the difficult animal classes from the PASCAL VOC 2007 object detection dataset.

References

1. Felzenszwalb, P., McAllester, D., Ramanan, D.: Discriminatively trained, multiscale, deformable part models. In: IEEE Conference on Computer Vision and Pattern Recognition (2008)
2. Zhang, H., Berg, A., Maire, M., Malik, J.: Svm-knn: Discriminative nearest neighbor classification for visual category recognition. In: IEEE Conference on Computer Vision and Pattern Recognition, vol. 2 (2006)
3. Everingham, M., Van Gool, L., Williams, C.K.I., Winn, J., Zisserman, A.: The PASCAL Visual Object Classes Challenge 2007 (VOC 2007) Results (2007),
   http://www.pascal-network.org/challenges/VOC/voc2007/
   workshop/index.html (accessed November 1, 2008)
4. Everingham, M., Van Gool, L., Williams, C.K.I., Winn, J., Zisserman, A.: The PASCAL Visual Object Classes Challenge 2008 (VOC 2008) Results (2008),
   http://www.pascal-network.org/challenges/VOC/
   voc2008/workshop/index.html (accessed November 1, 2008)
5. Lafferty, J., McCallum, A., Pereira, F.: Conditional random fields: Probabilistic models for segmenting and labeling sequence data. In: International Conference on Machine Learning (2001)
6. Quattoni, A., Collins, M., Darrell, T.: Conditional random fields for object recognition. In: Neural Information Processing Systems (2004)
7. He, S., Zemel, R., M., C.P.: Multiscale conditional random fields for image labeling. In: IEEE Conference of Computer Vision and Pattern Recognition (2004)
8. Felzenszwalb, P., Huttenlocher, D.: Efficient graph-based image segmentation. International Journal on Computer Vision 59(2) (2004)
9. Forsyth, D., Ponce, J.: Computer Vision: A Modern Approach. Prentice Hall, Englewood Cliffs (2003)
10. Hinton, G.: Training products of experts by minimizing contrastive divergence. Neural Comp. 14, 1771–1800 (2002)
11. Felzenszwalb, P., McAllester, D., Ramanan, D.: Discriminatively trained mixtures of deformable part models. In: PASCAL Visual Object Challenge (2008)

Video Event Classification Using Bag of Words and String Kernels

Lamberto Ballan, Marco Bertini, Alberto Del Bimbo, and Giuseppe Serra

Media Integration and Communication Center, University of Florence, Italy
{ballan,bertini,delbimbo,serra}@dsi.unifi.it

Abstract. The recognition of events in videos is a relevant and challenging task of automatic semantic video analysis. At present one of the most successful frameworks, used for object recognition tasks, is the bag-of-words (BoW) approach. However this approach does not model the temporal information of the video stream. In this paper we present a method to introduce temporal information within the BoW approach. Events are modeled as a sequence composed of histograms of visual features, computed from each frame using the traditional BoW model. The sequences are treated as strings where each histogram is considered as a character. Event classification of these sequences of variable size, depending on the length of the video clip, are performed using SVM classifiers with a string kernel that uses the Needlemann-Wunsch edit distance. Experimental results, performed on two datasets, soccer video and TRECVID 2005, demonstrate the validity of the proposed approach.

Keywords: video annotation, action classification, bag-of-words, string kernel, edit distance.

1 Introduction and Related Works

Recently it has been shown that part-based approaches are effective methods for object detection and recognition due to the fact that they can cope with the problem of occlusions and geometrical transformations [1,2]. These approaches are commonly based on the idea of modeling a complex object or a scene by a collection of local salient points. Each of these local features describes a small region around the interest point and therefore they are robust against occlusion and clutter. In particular, SIFT features by Lowe [3] have become the de facto standard because of their high performances and relatively low computational cost. In fact, these features have been frequently and successfully applied to many different tasks such as object or scene recognition.

In this field, an approach that recently has become very popular is the Bag-of-Words (BoW) model. It has been originally proposed for natural language processing and information retrieval, where it is used for document categorization in a text corpus, where each document is represented by its word frequency. In the visual domain, an image or a frame of a video is the visual analogue of a word and it is represented by a bag of quantized invariant local descriptors

P. Foggia, C. Sansone, and M. Vento (Eds.): ICIAP 2009, LNCS 5716, pp. 170–178, 2009.

(usually SIFT), called *visual-words* or *visterms*. The main reason of its success is that it provides methods that are sufficiently generic to cope with many object types simultaneously. We are thus confronted with the problem of generic visual categorization [4,5,6,7], like classification of objects or scenes, instead of recognizing a specific class of objects. The efficacy of this approach is demonstrated also by the large number of systems based on BoW representations that participate to the PASCAL VOC and TRECVID competitions. More recently, part-based and BoW models have been successfully applied also to the classification of human actions [8,9] and to video event recognition, typically using salient features that represent also temporal information (such as spatio-temporal gradients). These tasks are particularly interesting for video indexing and retrieval where dynamic concepts occur very frequently. Unfortunately, for this purpose the standard BoW model has shown some drawbacks with respect to the traditional image categorization task. Perhaps the most evident problem is that it does not take into account temporal relations between consecutive frames. Recently, few works have been proposed to cope with this problem. Wang *et al.* [10] have proposed to extend the BoW representation constructing relative motion histograms between visual words. In this way, they are able to describe motion of visual words obtaining better results on video event recognition. Xu *et al.* [11] represented each frame of video clips as a bag of orderless descriptors, applying then Earth Mover's Distance to integrate similarities among frames from two clips. They further build a multi-level temporal pyramid, observing that a clip is usually comprised of multiple sub-clips corresponding to event evolution over time; finally, video similarity is measured by fusing information at different levels.

In this paper, we present an approach to model actions as a sequence of histograms (one for each frame) represented by a traditional bag-of-words model. An action is described by a "phrase" of variable size, depending on the clip's length, providing so a global description of the video content that is able to incorporate temporal relations. Then video phrases can be compared by computing edit distances between them and, in particular, we use the Needleman-Wunsch distance [12] because it performs a global alignment on sequences dealing with video clips of different lenghts. Using this kind of representation we are able to perform categorization of video events and, following the promising results obtained in text categorization [13] and in bioinformatics (e.g. protein classification) [14], we investigate the use of SVMs based on an edit-distance based string kernel to perform classification. Experiments have been performed on soccer and news video datasets, comparing the proposed approach to a baseline kNN classifier and to a traditional BoW model. Experimental results obtained by SVM and string kernels outperform the other approaches and, more generally, they demonstrate the validity of the proposed method.

The rest of the paper is organized as follows: the techniques for frame and action representation are discussed in Sect. 2; the classification method, including details about the SVM string kernel, is presented in Sect. 3; experimental results are discussed in Sect. 4 and, finally, conclusions are drawn in Sect. 5.

2   Action Representation

Structurally an action is a sequence of frames, and may have different lengths depending on how the action has been carried out. We represent an action by a sequence of visual words frequency vectors, computed from the frames of the sequence (Fig. 1); we call this sequence (string) *phrase*, where each frequency vector is considered as a *character*.

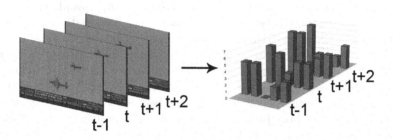

Fig. 1. Video clips are represented as a sequence of BoW histograms; actions are so described by a *phrase* (string) of variable size, depending on the clip's length

2.1   Frame Representation

Video frames are represented using bag-of-words, because this representation has demonstrated to be flexible and successful for various image analysis tasks [4,5,7]. First of all, a visual vocabulary is obtained by vector quantization of large sets of local feature descriptors. It is generated by clustering the detected keypoints (DoG in our case) in the feature space and using each cluster as a visual word; the size of the visual vocabulary is determined by the number of clusters and it is one of the main critical point of the model. A small vocabulary may lack the discriminative power since two features may be assigned to the same cluster even if they are not similar, while a large vocabulary is less generalizable. The trade-off between discrimination and generalization is highly content dependent and it is usually detemined by experiments [6]. Once a vocabulary is defined, a visual word frequency vector is computed for each frame, counting the number of occurrences of each visual word of the vocabulary in that frame. This frequency vector is used as frame representation and it can be fed to a classifier for classification. In this work we use SIFT features [3] as local salient points and k-means clustering for vocabulary formation.

2.2   Action Representation

As previously introduced, each video clip is described as a *phrase* (string) formed by the concatenation of the bag-of-words representations of consecutive *characters* (frames). To compare these *phrases*, and consequently actions and events, we can adapt metrics defined in the information theory.

(a) text example

		S	E	N	D
	0	1	2	3	4
A	1	1	2	3	4
N	2	2	2	2	3
D	3	3	3	3	2

(b) video example

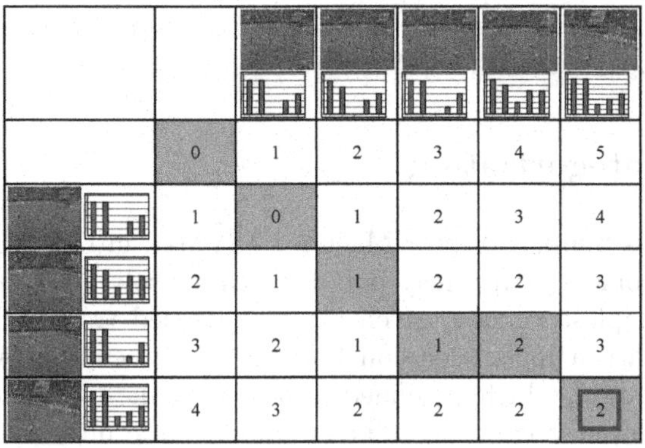

Fig. 2. Needleman-Wunsch edit distance: (a) text and (b) video examples

Edit distance. The edit distance between two string of characters is the number of operations required to transform one of them into the other (substitution, insertion and deletion). In particular our approach uses the Needleman-Wunsch distance [12] because it performs a global alignment that accounts for the structure of the strings and the distance can be considered as a score of similarity. The basic idea is to build up the best alignment through optimal alignments of smaller subsequences, using dynamic programming. Considering the cost matrix C that tracks the costs of the edit operations needed to match two strings, we can then write the cost formula for the alignment of the a_i and b_j characters of two strings as:

$$C_{i,j} = min(C_{i-1,j-1} + \delta(a_i, b_j), C_{i-1,j} + \delta_I, C_{i,j-1} + \delta_D)$$

where $\delta(a_i, b_j)$ is 0 if the distance between a_i and b_j is close enough to evaluate $a_i \approx b_j$ or the cost of substitution otherwise, δ_I and δ_D are the costs of insertion and deletion, respectively. Fig. 2 show an example of the evaluation of the Needleman-Wunsch distance for the case of text and soccer action, respectively. The distance is the number in the lower-right corner of the cost matrix. The traceback that shows the sequence of edit operations leading to the best alignement between the sequences is highlighted in each cost matrix. The algorithm is $O(mn)$ in time and $O(min(m,n))$ in space, where m and n are the lengths of the two strings being compared.

Measuring similarity between characters. A crucial point is the evaluation of the similarity among characters ($a_i \approx b_j$). In fact, when evaluating this similarity on text it is possible to define a similarity matrix between characters because their number is limited. Instead, in our case each frequency vectors is a different character, therefore we deal with an extremely large alphabet. This requires to define a function that evaluates the similarity of two characters. Since in our approach each character is an histogram we have evaluated several different methods to compare the frequency vectors of two frames, p and q. In particular we have considered the following distances: *Chi-square* test, *Kolmogorov-Smirnov* test, *Bhattacharyya, Intersection, Correlation, Mahalanobis.*

3   Action Categorization

In the latest years Support Vector Machines (SVMs), introduced by Vapnik *et al.* [15], have become an extremely popular tool for solving classification problems. In their simplest version, given a set of labeled training vectors of two classes, SVMs learn a linear decision boundary between the two classes that maximizes the margin, which is defined to be the smallest distance between the decision boundary and any of the input samples. The result is a linear classification that can be used to classify new input data. In the two classes classification problem suppose to have a training data set that comprises N input vectors $x_1, ..., x_N$, with corresponding target values $t_1, ..., t_N$ where $t_n \in \{-1, 1\}$. The SVMs approach finds the linear decision boundary $y(x)$ as:

$$y(x) = w^T \phi(x) + b \tag{1}$$

where ϕ denotes a fixed feature-space transformation, b is a bias parameter, so that, if the training data set is linearly separable, $y(x_n) > 0$ for points having $t_n = +1$ and $y(x_n) < 0$ for points having $t_n = -1$. In this case the maximum marginal solution is found by solving for the optimal weight vector $\mathbf{a} = (a_1, \ldots, a_N)$ in the dual problem in which we maximize:

$$\widetilde{L}(\mathbf{a}) = \sum_{n=1}^{N} a_n - \frac{1}{2} \sum_{n=1}^{N} \sum_{m=1}^{N} a_n a_m t_n t_m k(x_n, x_m) \tag{2}$$

with respect to $\mathbf{a}$, that is subject to the constraints:

$$\sum_{n=1}^{N} a_n t_n = 0, \quad a_n \geq 0 \quad \text{for} \quad n = 1, ..., N. \tag{3}$$

where $k(x_n, x_m)$, called kernel function, is defined by $k(x, x') = \phi(x)^T \phi(x')$. The parameters w and b are then derived from the optimal $\mathbf{a}$. The dual problem takes the form of a quadratic programming problem, which can be efficiently solved and any solution is a global optimum. Moreover, the SVM approach permits to use kernel techniques, so that the maximum margin classifier can be found efficiently in a feature space whose dimensionality exceeds the number of data points. Recently, many approaches in image categorization have successfully used different kernels such as linear, radial and chi-square basis functions; in particular the latter gives the best results. However these kernels are not appropriate for action classification. In fact these kernels deal with input vectors with fixed dimensionality, whereas action representation vectors usually have different lengths depending on how it is performed. Unlike other approaches that solve this problem simply by representing the clips with a fixed number of samples [16], we introduce a kernel that deals with input vectors with different dimensionality, in order to account for the temporal progression of the actions. Starting from a Gaussian Kernel that takes the form:

$$k(x, x') = exp(-\|x - x'\|^2 / 2\sigma^2).$$ (4)

we replace the Euclidean with the Needlmann-Wunsch distance. The proposed kernel is:

$$k(x, x') = exp(-d(x, x')).$$ (5)

where $d(x, x')$ is the Needlmann-Wunsch distance between x, x' input vectors. In this approach the structure of the string is evaluated by the edit distance and not by the kernel, that uses only the value of this distance. It has been demonstrated [17] that this type of kernels is suitable for classification of shapes, handwritten digits and chromosome images, despite the fact that the general edit distance has not been proved to be a valid kernel; this is confirmed in our experiments where all the pre-computed string kernels were checked to confirm their validity.

4   Experimental Results

We have carried out video event classification experiments to evaluate the general applicability and analyse the performance improvements achievable by the proposed method w.r.t. baseline kNN classifier and the standard BoW approach using a soccer videos and a subset of TRECVID 2005 video corpus. In the following sections, 4.1 and 4.2, the experiments and the two datasets used are described in details.

4.1   Comparing String-Kernel SVM Classifiers to Baseline kNN Classifiers on Soccer Videos Dataset

In this experiment we have compared the results of the proposed method with the baseline kNN classifier on a soccer video dataset. This dataset, available on request at our webpage[1], consists of 100 video clips in MPEG2 format at full PAL resolution (720 × 576 pixels, 25 fps). It contains 4 different actions: *shot-on-goal*, *placed-kick*, *throw-in* and *goal-kick*. The sequences were taken from 5 different matches of the Italian *"Serie A"* league (season 2007/08) between 7 different teams. For each class there are 25 clips of variable lengths, from a

---

[1] http://www.micc.unifi.it/vim

minimum of $\sim$ 4 sec (corresponding to $\sim$ 100 frames) to a maximum of $\sim$ 10 sec ($\sim$ 2500 frames). This collection is particularly challenging because actions are performed in a wide range of scenarios (i.e. different lighting conditions and different stadiums) and action classes show an high intra-class variability, because even instances of the same action may have very different progression. Videos are grouped in training and testing sets, composed by 20 and 5 videos respectively, and results are obtained by 3-fold cross-validation.

Results. Initially we have evaluated how different sizes of the visual vocabulary (30, 150, 300 visual words) affect the classification accuracy, obtaining the best result ($\sim$ 52%) with 30 words. In our test we observe that the increase of the codebook size does not improve the performance. This can be explained by analysing the type of views of the sport domain: actions are shown using the main camera that provides an overview of the playfield and of the ongoing action; thus the SIFT points are mostly detected in correspondence of playfield lines, crowd and players' jerseys and trousers and the whole scene can be completely represented using an histogram with a limited number of bins for the interest points. Increasing the number of bins risks to amplify the intra-class variability, even reducing the accuracy of classification, resulting also in higher computational costs. In another test we have evaluated what is the best metric to compare the characters (frequency vectors) and we have obtained the best accuracy using the Chi-square distance. Using the best dictionary size and metric selected with the previous tests we have finally compared the baseline kNN classifier and the proposed SVM with string kernel. The mean accuracy obtained by the SVM (0.73) largely outperforms that obtained using the kNN classifier (0.52). Fig. 3 reports the confusion matrices for kNN and SVM classifiers, respectively. A large part of the improvement in terms of accuracy is due to the fact that the SVM has a better performance on the two most critical actions: *shot-on-goal* and *throw-in*. This latter class has the worst classification results, due to the fact that it has an extremely large variability in the part of the action that follows immediately the throw of the ball (e.g. the player may choose several different directions and strengths for the throw, the defending team may steal the ball, etc.).

4.2 Comparing the Proposed Approach to a Baseline ("traditional") Bag-of-Words Representation on TRECVID 2005

In this experiment we show the improvement of the proposed approach with respect to a traditional BoW model. Experiments are performed on a subset of the TRECVID 2005 video corpus, obtained selecting five classes related to a few LSCOM dynamic concepts. In particular we have selected the following classes: *Exiting Car, Running, Walking, Demonstration Protest* and *Airplane Flying*. The resulting video collection consists of $\sim$ 180 videos for each class ($\sim$ 860 in total); experiments are performed again applying 3-fold cross-validation.

Results. As in the previous experiment, we have initially experimented different vocabulary sizes looking for the correct choice in this video domain. Results show that, in this case, a vocabulary of 300 words is a good trade-off between

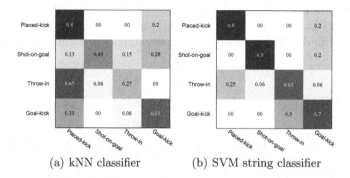

(a) kNN classifier   (b) SVM string classifier

Fig. 3. Confusion matrices of baseline kNN and SVM string classifiers; mean Accuracy for kNN is equal to 0.52 and 0.73 for SVM with string kernel

discriminativity and generalizability. Even in this case the metric used for comparing the similarity among characters within the N-W edit distance is the Chi-square (with a threshold of 4.5). Table 1 reports the comparison results between a traditional BoW aprroach and the proposed method; results are expressed in terms of Mean Average Precision (MAP) because it is the standard evaluation metric in the TRECVID benchmark.

Table 1. Mean Average Pracision (MAP) for event recognition in TRECVID 2005

	Exiting Car	Running	Walking	Demo. Protest	Airplane Flying	**MAP**
BoW	0.2	**0.49**	0.27	0.28	0.15	0.28
Our Approach	**0.37**	0.36	**0.29**	**0.38**	**0.34**	**0.35**

Our approach, on average slightly outperforms the traditional bag-of-words model (+7%) and it is also outperforming on four classes out of five.

5   Conclusions

In this paper we have presented a method for event classification based on the BoW approach. The proposed system uses generic static visual features (SIFT points) that represent the visual appearance of the scene; the dynamic progression of the event is modelled as a *phrase* composed by the temporal sequence of the bag-of-words histograms. Phrases are compared using the Needleman-Wunsch edit distance and SVMs with a string kernel have been used to deal with these feature vectors of variable length. Experiments have been performed on soccer videos and TRECVID 2005 news videos; the results show that SVM and string kernels outperform both the performance of the baseline kNN classifiers and of the standard BoW approach and, more generally, they exhibit the validity of the proposed method. Our future work will deal with the application of this approach to a broader set of events and actions that are part of the TRECVID LSCOM events/activities list, and the use of other string kernels.

Acknowledgments. This work is partially supported by the EU IST Vidi-Video Project (Contract FP6-045547) and IM3I Project (Contract FP7-222267). The authors thank Filippo Amendola for his support in the preparation of the experiments.

References

1. Mikolajczyk, K., Tuytelaars, T., Schmid, C., Zisserman, A., Matas, J., Schaffalitzky, F., Kadir, T., Van Gool, L.: A comparison of affine region detectors. International Journal of Computer Vision 65(1-2) (2005)
2. Mikolajczyk, K., Schmid, C.: A performance evaluation of local descriptors. IEEE Transactions on Pattern Analysis and Machine Intelligence 27(10) (2005)
3. Lowe, D.G.: Distinctive image features from scale-invariant keypoints. International Journal of Computer Vision 60(2), 91–110 (2004)
4. Sivic, J., Zisserman, A.: Video google: A text retrieval approach to object matching in videos. In: Proc. of ICCV (2003)
5. Fergus, R., Perona, P., Zisserman, A.: Object class recognition by unsupervised scale-invariant learning. In: Proc. of CVPR (2003)
6. Yang, J., Jiang, Y.G., Hauptmann, A.G., Ngo, C.W.: Evaluating bag-of-visual-words representations in scene classification. In: Proc. of ACM MIR (2007)
7. Zhang, J., Marszałek, M., Lazebnik, S., Schmid, C.: Local features and kernels for classification of texture and object categories: A comprehensive study. International Journal of Computer Vision 73(2), 213–238 (2007)
8. Dollar, P., Rabaud, V., Cottrell, G., Belongie, S.: Behavior recognition via sparse spatio-temporal features. In: Proc. of VSPETS (2005)
9. Niebles, J.C., Wang, H., Fei-Fei, L.: Unsupervised Learning of Human Action Categories Using Spatial-Temporal Words. International Journal of Computer Vision 79(3), 299–318 (2008)
10. Wang, F., Jiang, Y.-G., Ngo, C.-W.: Video event detection using motion relativity and visual relatedness. In: Proc. of ACM Multimedia (2008)
11. Xu, D., Chang, S.-F.: Video event recognition using kernel methods with multi-level temporal alignment. IEEE Transactions on Pattern Analysis and Machine Intelligence 30(11) (2008)
12. Needleman, S.B., Wunsch, C.D.: A general method applicable to the search for similarities in the amino acid sequence of two proteins. Journal of Molecular Biology 48(3), 443–453 (1970)
13. Lodhi, H., Saunders, C., Shawe-Taylor, J., Cristianini, N., Watkins, C.: Text classification using string kernels. Journal of Machine Learning Research (2002)
14. Leslie, C., Eskin, E., Weston, J., Noble, W.S.: Mismatch string kernels for SVM protein classification. In: Proc. of NIPS (2003)
15. Boser, B.E., Guyon, I.M., Vapnik, V.N.: A training algorithm for optimal margin classifiers. In: Proc. of ACM Workshop on Computational Learning Theory (1992)
16. Sadlier, D.A., O'Connor, N.E.: Event detection in field sports video using audio-visual features and a support vector machine. IEEE Transactions on Circuits and Systems for Video Technology 15(10), 1225–1233 (2005)
17. Neuhaus, M., Bunke, H.: Edit distance-based kernel functions for structural pattern classification. Pattern Recognition 39(10), 1852–1863 (2006)

Video Sequences Association for People Re-identification across Multiple Non-overlapping Cameras

Dung Nghi Truong Cong[1], Catherine Achard[2], Louahdi Khoudour[1],
and Lounis Douadi[1]

[1] French National Institute for Transport and Safety Research (INRETS),
20 rue Elise Reclus, 59650 Villeneuve d'Ascq, France
[2] UPMC Univ Paris 06, Institute of Intelligent Systems and Robotics (ISIR)
Case Courrier 252, 3 rue Galile, 94200 IVRY SUR SEINE, France

Abstract. This paper presents a solution of the appearance-based people re-identification problem in a surveillance system including multiple cameras with different fields of vision. We first utilize different color-based features, combined with several illuminant invariant normalizations in order to characterize the silhouettes in static frames. A graph-based approach which is capable of learning the global structure of the manifold and preserving the properties of the original data in a lower dimensional representation is then introduced to reduce the effective working space and to realize the comparison of the video sequences. The global system was tested on a real data set collected by two cameras installed on board a train. The experimental results show that the combination of color-based features, invariant normalization procedures and the graph-based approach leads to very satisfactory results.

1 Introduction

In recent years, public security has been facing an increasing demand from the general public as well as from governments. An important part of the efforts to prevent the threats to security is the ever-increasing use of video surveillance cameras throughout the network, in order to monitor and detect incidents without delay. Existing surveillance systems rely on human observation of video streams for high-level classification and recognition. The typically large number of cameras makes this solution inefficient and in many cases unfeasible. Although the basic imaging technologies for simple surveillance are available today, the reliable deployment of them in a large network is still ongoing research.

In this paper, we tackle the appearance-based people re-identification problem in a surveillance system including multiple cameras with different fields of vision. The video sequences capturing moving people are analyzed and compared in order to re-establish a match of the same person over different camera views located at different physical sites. In most cases, such a system relies on building an appearance-based model that depends on several factors, such as illumination conditions, different camera angles and pose changes. Thus, building an ideal appearance model is still a challenge.

A significant amount of research has been carried out in the field of appearance-based person recognition. Kettnaker and Zabih [1] exploit the similarity of views of

P. Foggia, C. Sansone, and M. Vento (Eds.): ICIAP 2009, LNCS 5716, pp. 179–189, 2009.

the person, as well as plausibility of transition time from one camera to another. Nakajima et al. [2] present a system which can recognize full-body people in indoor environments by using multi-class SVMs that were trained on color-based and shaped-based features extracted from the silhouette. Javed et al. [3] use various features based on space-time (entry/exit locations, velocity, travel time) and appearance (color histogram). A probabilistic framework is developed to identify best matches. Bird et al. [4] detect loitering individuals by matching pedestrians intermittently spotted in the camera field of view over a long time. Snapshots of pedestrians are extracted and divided into thin horizontal slices. The feature vector is based on color in each slice and Linear Discriminant Analysis is used to reduce the dimension. Gheissari et al. [5] propose a temporal signature which is invariant to the position of the body and the dynamic appearance of clothing within a video shot. Wang et al. [6] represent objects using histograms of oriented gradients that incorporate detailed spatial distribution of the color of objects across different body parts. Yang et al. [7] propose an appearance model constructed by kernel density estimation. A key-frame selection and matching technique was presented in order to represent the information contained in video sequences and then to compare them.

The research presented in this paper is the development of a multi-camera system installed on board trains that is able to track people moving through different sites. Different color-based features combined with invariant normalizations are first used to characterize the silhouettes in static frames. A graph-based approach is then introduced to reduce the effective working space and to realize the comparison of the video sequences.

The organization of the article is as follows. Section 2 describes how the invariant signature of a detected silhouette is generated. In Section 3, after a few theoretical reminders on the graph-based method for dimensionality reduction, we explain how to adapt this latter to our problem. Section 4 presents global results on the performance of our system on a database of given facts. Finally, in Section 5, the conclusion and important short-term perspectives are given.

2   Invariant Signature Extraction

2.1   Color-Based Feature Extraction

The first step in our system consists in extracting from each frame a robust signature characterizing the passage of a person. To do this, a detection of moving objects (silhouettes in our case), by using a background subtraction algorithm [8], combined with morphological operators is first carried out. Let us assume now that each person's silhouette is located in all the frames of a video sequence. Since the appearance of people is dominated by their clothes, color features are suitable for their description.

The most widely used feature for describing the color of objects is the *color histograms* [3]. Given a color image I of N pixels, the histogram is produced first by discretization of the colors in the image into M bins $b = \{1, ..., M\}$, and counting the number of occurrences per bin:

$$n_b = \sum_{k=1}^{N} \delta_{kb} \tag{1}$$

where $\delta_{kb} = 1$ if the kth pixel falls in bin b and $\delta_{kb} = 0$ otherwise. The similarity between two histograms can be computed using histogram intersection. Although histograms are robust to deformable shapes, they cannot discriminate between appearances that are the same in color distribution, but different in color structure, since they discard all spatial information.

A limited amount of spatial information of histograms can be retained by using *spatiograms* [9] that are a generalization of histograms, including higher order spatial moments. For example, the second-order spatiogram contains, for each histogram bin, the spatial mean and covariance:

$$\mu_b = \sum_{k=1}^{N} \mathbf{x}_k \delta_{kb} \, , \; \Sigma_b = \sum_{k=1}^{N} (\mathbf{x}_k - \mu_b)(\mathbf{x}_k - \mu_b)^T \delta_{kb} \tag{2}$$

where $\mathbf{x}_k = [x, y]$ is the spatial position of pixel k. To compare two spatiograms (S, S'), the following similarity measure is used:

$$\rho(S, S') = \sum_{b=1}^{M} \psi_b \rho_n (n_b, n_b') \tag{3}$$

where $\rho_n (n_b, n_b')$ is the similarity between histogram bins and ψ_b is the spatial similarity measure, given by:

$$\psi_b = \eta \exp \left\{ -\frac{1}{2} (\mu_b - \mu_b')^T \hat{\Sigma}_b^{-1} (\mu_b - \mu_b') \right\} \tag{4}$$

where η is the Gaussian normalization term and $\hat{\Sigma}_b^{-1} = \left(\Sigma_b^{-1} + (\Sigma_b')^{-1} \right)$.

Another approach for building appearance models is the *color/path-length feature* [7] that includes some spatial information: each pixel inside the silhouette is represented by a feature vector $(\mathbf{v}, l)$, where $\mathbf{v}$ is the color value and l is the length between an anchor point (the top of the head) and the pixel. The distribution of $p(\mathbf{v}, l)$ is estimated with a 4D histogram.

2.2 Invariant Normalization

Since the color acquired by cameras is heavily dependent on several factors, such as the surface reflectance, illuminant color, lighting geometry, response of the sensor..., a color normalization procedure has to be carried out in order to obtain invariant signatures. Many methods have been proposed in literature [10,11,12] and we tested most of them. In this paper, we only present the three invariances that lead to better results:

- Greyworld normalization [13] is derived from the RGB space by dividing the pixel value by the average of the image (or in the area corresponding to the moving person in our case) for each channel:

$$I_k^* = \frac{I_k}{mean(I_k)} \tag{5}$$

where I_k is the color value of channel k.

- Normalization using histogram equalization [11] is based on the assumption that the rank ordering of sensor responses is preserved across a change in imaging illuminations. The *rank measure* for level i and channel k is obtained with:

$$M_k(i) = \sum_{u=0}^{i} H_k(u) \bigg/ \sum_{u=0}^{Nb} H_k(u) \tag{6}$$

where Nb is the number of quantization steps and $H_k(\cdot)$ is the histogram for channel k.
- Affine normalization is defined by:

$$I_k^* = \frac{I_k - \mathrm{mean}(I_k)}{\mathrm{std}\,(I_k)} \tag{7}$$

Thus, the color normalization is applied inside the silhouette of each person before computing its color-based signature. A comparative study of the different color-based features combined with the invariant normalization procedures is presented in Section 4.

3   Dimensionality Reduction for Categorization

Dimensionality reduction is an important procedure employed in various high dimensional data analysis problems. It can be performed by keeping only the most important dimensions, i.e. the ones that hold the most information for the task, and/or by projecting some dimensions onto others. A representation of the data in lower dimensions can be advantageous for further processing of the data, such as classification, visualization, data compression, etc.

In recent years, a large number of nonlinear techniques for dimensionality reduction have been proposed, such as Locally Linear Embedding [14], Isomap [15], Laplacian Eigenmaps [16], Diffusion Maps [17]. These techniques can deal with complex nonlinear data by preserving global and/or local properties of the original data in the lower dimensional representation and therefore constitute traditional linear techniques.

In this paper, we only focus on Graph-based methods for nonlinear dimensionality reduction. Sometimes called Diffusion Maps, Laplacian Eigenmaps or Spectral Analysis [18], these manifold-learning techniques preserve the local proximity between data points by first constructing a graph representation for the underlying manifold with vertices and edges. The vertices represent the data points, and the edges connecting the vertices represent the similarities between adjacent nodes. After representing the graph with a matrix, the spectral properties of this matrix are used to embed the data points into a lower dimensional space, and gain insight into the geometry of the dataset.

3.1   Mathematical Formulation

Given a set of m frames $\{I_1, I_2, \ldots, I_m\}$, this set is associated to a complete neighborhood graph $G = (V, E)$ where each frame I_i corresponds to a vertex v_i in this graph. Two vertices corresponding to two frames I_i and I_j are connected by an edge that is weighted by $W_{ij} = K(I_i, I_j) = exp\left(-\frac{d(I_i, I_j)^2}{\sigma^2}\right)$, where $d(I_i, I_j)$ is the distance between two signatures extracted from these two frames, and σ is chosen as $\sigma = mean[d(I_i, I_j)]$, $\forall i, j = 1, \ldots, m$ $(i \neq j)$. The first step of dimensionality reduction consists in searching for a new representation $\{\mathbf{y_1}, \mathbf{y_2}, \ldots, \mathbf{y_m}\}$ with $\mathbf{y}_i \in \mathbb{R}^m$ obtained by minimizing the cost function:

$$\phi = \sum_{ij} \|\mathbf{y}_i - \mathbf{y}_j\|_2 W_{ij} \tag{8}$$

Let D denote the diagonal matrix with elements $D_{ii} = \sum_j W_{ij}$ and L denote the unnormalized Laplacian defined by $L = D - W$. The cost function can be reformulated as:

$$\phi = \sum_{ij} \|\mathbf{y}_i - \mathbf{y}_j\|_2 W_{ij} = 2\text{Tr}\left(\mathbf{Y}^T L \mathbf{Y}\right) \text{ with } \mathbf{Y} = [\mathbf{y}_1, \mathbf{y}_2, \ldots, \mathbf{y}_m] \tag{9}$$

Hence, minimizing the cost function ϕ is proportional to minimizing $\text{Tr}\left(\mathbf{Y}^T L \mathbf{Y}\right)$. Dimensionality reduction is obtained by solving the generalized eigenvector problem

$$Ly = \lambda Dy \tag{10}$$

for the d lowest non-zero eigenvalues.

Figure 1 presents an example of the results obtained by the graph-based approach for nonlinear dimensionality reduction. In order to make the representation easier to read, in this example, we use only the first two lowest eigenvectors to create the new coordinate system. The input of this test is a set of 120 frames belonging to 6 video sequences (20 frames per sequence). On the left-hand diagram, the frames are illustrated by points, while the points are directly illustrated by the corresponding silhouettes on the right-hand one. The first two sequences that are shown by the red and green points on the left-hand diagram belong to the same person captured by two cameras with different fields of vision. The other points correspond to the people similarly or differently dressed. One can notice that the new visualization of the frame sets in 2D space preserves almost all their original characteristics: frames belonging to one video sequence are represented by the neighbor points, while the space among the clusters varies according to the similarity of the color-based appearances of the silhouettes. The clusters corresponding to the two sequences of the same person strongly overlap, while the cluster belonging to person P3 who dresses very differently is well-separated from the others.

Hence, the representation of the frame set in the new coordinate system shows that, by evaluating how separate the clusters are, we can measure the similarities among the video sequences. In the following section, we describe how to apply it to our problem of people re-identification.

3.2 Implementation for People Re-identification

As mentioned in the introduction, the objective of this framework consists in re-identifying a person who has appeared in the field of one camera (e.g. camera 1)

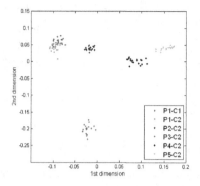 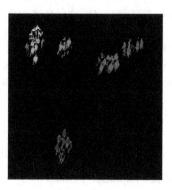

Fig. 1. Example obtained by the graph-based approach for nonlinear dimensionality reduction

and then reappears in front of another camera (e.g. camera 2). Thus, a set of m frames $\{I_1, I_2, \ldots, I_m\}$ belonging to p passages in front of camera 1 and the query passage in front of camera 2, is considered for the re-identification (let us notice that a passage is characterized by the concatenation of several frames of the sequence denoted by n). Thus, $m = n * (p + 1)$. By applying the graph-based method for nonlinear dimensionality reduction, we obtain the new coordinate system by considering the d lowest eigenvectors. In our current problem, we use the 20 lowest eigenvectors to create the new coordinate system. The dimensionality reduction operator can be defined as $h : I_i \rightarrow u_i = [y_1(i), \ldots, y_{20}(i)]$ where $y_k(i)$ is the ith coordinate of eigenvector y_k.

Since each passage is represented by the signatures of n frames, the barycentre of the n points obtained by projecting the n frames into the new coordinate system is calculated. The distance between two barycentres is considered as the dissimilarity measure between two corresponding people. The larger the distance, the more dissimilar the two people.

Hence, the dissimilarities between the query person detected in front of camera 2 and each candidate person of camera 1 are calculated and then classified in increasing order. Then, normally and in a perfect system, if the same person has been detected by the two cameras, the lowest distance between the barycentres should lead to the correct re-identification.

Figure 2 presents an example of the results obtained by such a procedure. In this example, we use only the first two principal components. In figure 2a, the query passage is shown by the red dots, while the candidates are represented by other color dots. Figure 2b is an illustration of the most interesting portion of figure 2a (surrounded by a square) enlarged to highlight more details. In figure 2b, the red dots correspond to the set of signatures belonging to the query passage; the green, cyan and yellow dots correspond respectively to the set of frames that have the nearest barycentres, in increasing order, when compared to the query barycentre. The silhouettes corresponding to these four sets of signatures are added in figure 2b. We notice that the silhouettes related to the query set and the nearest candidate set correspond to the same person, or, in other words, we get a true re-identification in this case.

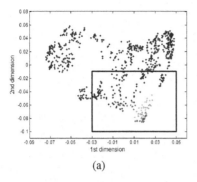 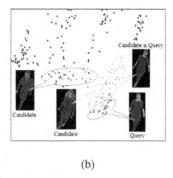

(a)   (b)

Fig. 2. Visualization of the set of signatures in the 2D space obtained by applying the graph-based dimensionality reduction method

4 Experimental Results

Our algorithms were entirely evaluated on real data sets containing video sequences of 35 people collected by two cameras installed on board a train at two different locations: one in the corridor and one in the cabin. This dataset is very difficult, since these two cameras are set up with different angles and the acquisition of the video is influenced by many factors, such as fast illumination variations, reflections, vibrations. Figure 3 illustrates an example of the dataset. For each passage in front of a camera, we extract 20 frames regularly spaced in which people are entirely viewed.

Fig. 3. Illustrations of the real dataset representing the same person in two different locations: in the cabin (left) and in the corridor (right)

In our experimentations, we calculate three types of signatures mentioned in Section 2: color histograms and spatiograms with 8 bins for each color channel, color/path-length descriptor with 8 bins per color channel and 8 bins for the path-length feature. For each silhouette, the illuminant invariant procedure is applied before extracting the signatures. Then, as described in section 3, for each query passage in front of one camera, the distances (i.e the dissimilarities) between the query person and each of the candidate people of the other camera are calculated. Distances are then classified in increasing order and the probability of correct re-identification at rank k is calculated.

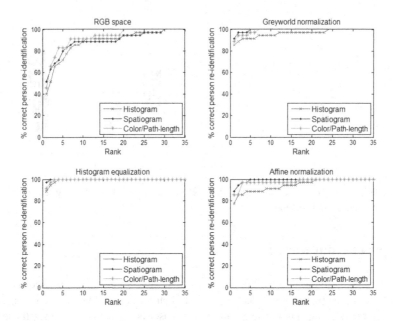

Fig. 4. CMC curves corresponding to four color spaces obtained by using the color-based signature coupled with the graph-based approach for comparing sequences

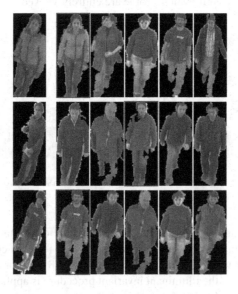

Fig. 5. Example of the top five matching sequences for several query passages

This leads to a Cumulative Match Characteristic (CMC) curve that illustrates the performance of our system.

Figure 4, which is divided into four parts according to the illuminant invariant, represents the CMC curves obtained by combining three color-based signatures with the graph-based method for dimensionality reduction. The rates of re-identification at the top rank are very satisfying: the best rate of 97% is obtained by combining spatiograms, normalization using histogram equalization and the graph-based method for sequence comparison. We note that the performance of color histograms is the worst. The others lead to better results thanks to the additional spatial information. The invariant normalizations have actually improved the results compared to the RGB space: the re-identification rate obtained by using spatiograms increases from 51% for RGB space to 97% for the histogram equalization.

Figure 5 shows an example of the top five matching sequences for several query passages. The query passages are shown in the left column, while the remaining columns present the top matches ordered from left to right. The red box highlights the candidate sequence corresponding to the same person of the query. In this figure, the two cases of the first and third rows correspond to a true re-identification, while the second row falls in a false re-identification (the correct match is not the nearest sequence).

5   Conclusion and Perspectives

In this paper, we have presented a novel approach for people re-identification in a surveillance system including multiple cameras with different fields of vision. Our approach relies on the graph-based technique for dimensionality reduction which is capable of learning the global structure of the manifold and preserving the properties of the original data in the low-dimensional representation. The first step of our system consists in extracting a feature that describes the person in each selected frame of each passage. Three color-based descriptors (histograms, spatiograms and color/pathlength) combined with several invariant normalization algorithms are utilized for this step. Since the passage of a person needs to be characterized by several frames, a large quantity of data has to be processed. Thus, the graph-based method for dimensionality reduction is applied to reduce the effective working space and realize the comparison of video sequences.

The global system was tested on a real data set collected by two cameras installed on board a train under real difficult conditions (fast illumination variations, reflections, vibrations, etc). The experimental results show that the combination of color-based features, invariant normalization procedures and the graph-based approach leads to very satisfactory results: 97% for the true re-identification rate at the top rank.

In order to further improve the performance of our system, the appearance-based features need to add more temporal and spatial information in order to be further discriminating among different people and to be unifying in order to make coherent classes with all the features belonging to the same person. The other features, such as camera transition time, moving direction of the individual, biometrics features (face, gait) should also be considered in order to improve the performance of the re-identification system, especially in the more challenging scenarios (multiple passages in front of cameras, many people wearing same color clothes, occlusion, partial detection, etc). More extensive evaluation also needs to be carried out. A good occasion will be to test them, more intensively, through BOSS European project. On-board automatic video surveillance is a challenge due to the difficulties in dealing with fast illumination variations, reflections, vibrations, high people density and static/dynamic occlusions that perturb actual video interpretation tools.

References

1. Kettnaker, V., Zabih, R.: Bayesian multi-camera surveillance. In: IEEE Computer Society Conference on Computer Vision and Pattern Recognition, vol. 2 (1999)
2. Nakajima, C., Pontil, M., Heisele, M., Poggio, T.: Full body person recognition system. Pattern Recognition 36(9), 1997–2006 (2003)
3. Javed, O., Rasheed, Z., Shafique, K., Shah, M.: Tracking across multiple cameras with disjoint views. In: Ninth IEEE International Conference on Computer Vision (2003)
4. Bird, N., Masoud, O., Papanikolopoulos, N., Isaacs, A.: Detection of loitering individuals in public transportation areas. IEEE Transactions on Intelligent Transportation Systems 6(2), 167–177 (2005)
5. Gheissari, N., Sebastian, T., Hartley, R.: Person reidentification using spatiotemporal appearance. In: Proceedings of the 2006 IEEE Computer Society Conference on Computer Vision and Pattern Recognition, Washington, DC, USA, pp. 1528–1535. IEEE Computer Society, Los Alamitos (2006)
6. Wang, X., Doretto, G., Sebastian, T., Rittscher, J., Tu, P.: Shape and appearance context modeling. In: IEEE 11th International Conference on Computer Vision, ICCV 2007, pp. 1–8 (2007)
7. Yu, Y., Harwood, D., Yoon, K., Davis, L.: Human appearance modeling for matching across video sequences. Machine Vision and Applications 18(3), 139–149 (2007)
8. Kim, K., Chalidabhongse, T., Harwood, D., Davis, L.: Background modeling and subtraction by codebook construction. In: International Conference on Image Processing, ICIP 2004, vol. 5 (2004)
9. Birchfield, S., Rangarajan, S.: Spatiograms versus histograms for region-based tracking. In: IEEE Computer Society Conference on Computer Vision and Pattern Recognition, vol. 2, pp. 1158–1163 (2005)
10. Gevers, T., Stokman, H.: Robust histogram construction from color invariants for object recognition. IEEE Transactions on Pattern Analysis and Machine Intelligence, 113–118 (2004)
11. Finlayson, G., Hordley, S., Schaefer, G., Yun Tian, G.: Illuminant and device invariant colour using histogram equalisation. Pattern Recognition 38(2), 179–190 (2005)
12. Madden, C., Piccardi, M., Zuffi, S.: Comparison of Techniques for Mitigating the Effects of Illumination Variations on the Appearance of Human Targets. In: Bebis, G., Boyle, R., Parvin, B., Koracin, D., Paragios, N., Tanveer, S.-M., Ju, T., Liu, Z., Coquillart, S., Cruz-Neira, C., Müller, T., Malzbender, T. (eds.) ISVC 2007, Part II. LNCS, vol. 4842, pp. 116–127. Springer, Heidelberg (2007)
13. Buchsbaum, G.: A spatial processor model for object color perception. Journal of the Franklin Institute 310(1), 1–26 (1980)

14. Roweis, S., Saul, L.: Nonlinear dimensionality reduction by locally linear embedding. Science 290(5500), 2323–2326 (2000)
15. Tenenbaum, J.B., de Silva, V., Langford, J.C.: A global geometric framework for nonlinear dimensionality reduction. Science 290(5500), 2319–2323 (2000)
16. Belkin, M., Niyogi, P.: Laplacian eigenmaps for dimensionality reduction and data representation. Neural Computation 15(6), 1373–1396 (2003)
17. Nadler, B., Lafon, S., Coifman, R.R., Kevrekidis, I.G.: Diffusion maps, spectral clustering and eigenfunctions of fokker-planck operators. In: Advances in Neural Information Processing Systems, pp. 955–962 (2005)
18. von Luxburg, U.: A tutorial on spectral clustering. Statistics and Computing 17(4), 395–416 (2007)

Shadow Removal in Outdoor Video Sequences by Automatic Thresholding of Division Images

Srinivasa Rao Dammavalam, Claudio Piciarelli, Christian Micheloni, and Gian Luca Foresti

University of Udine, Italy

Abstract. Several video-based applications, such as video surveillance, traffic monitoring, video annotation, etc., rely on the correct detection and tracking of moving objects within the observed scene. Even though several works have been proposed in the field of moving object detection, many of them do not consider the problem of segmenting real objects from their shadows. The shadow is considered part of the object, thus leading to possibly large errors in the subsequent steps of object localisation and tracking. In this paper we propose a shadow detection algorithm able to remove shadows from the blobs of moving objects, using division images and Expectation-Maximization histogram analysis. Experimental results prove that the use of the proposed method can significantly increase the performance of a video analysis system.

1 Introduction

Moving shadow detection and removal is a fundamental and critical task for accurate object detection in many computer vision applications, including visual traffic monitoring, automated remote video surveillance and people tracking. Shadow regions are usually adjacent to object points and in many commonly used segmentation techniques shadows and objects are merged in a single blob, causing errors in object tracking and classification.

The problem has generally been addressed by using geometric or photometric properties of shadows. Prati et al. [1] give a comprehensive literature survey of the available methods that deal with moving shadow identification. In [1] the requirements of moving shadow detection methods are detailed and quantitative and qualitative comparison between different known approaches are given. Bevilacqua [2] proposed a work on the detection of moving shadows in the context of an outdoor traffic scene for video surveillance applications. The proposed algorithm relies on some photometric properties concerning shadows; the method is mainly based on multi-gradient operations applied on the division image to discover the shadow regions. In [3] shadow detection for moving objects is done using a three-stage shadow identification scheme without imposing restrictions on the number of light sources, illumination conditions, surface orientations and object sizes. In the first step, background segmentation is done using a mixture of Gaussians technique; then, pixel-based decisions are made by comparing the

P. Foggia, C. Sansone, and M. Vento (Eds.): ICIAP 2009, LNCS 5716, pp. 190–198, 2009.

current frame with the background model to differ shadows from the actual foreground. Finally, the result is improved using blob-level reasoning which works on geometric constraints of identified shadow and foreground blobs. Cucchiara et al. [4] present a novel technique based on the HSV colour space for shadow detection and removal used in a system for moving object detection and tracking. In the Sakbot system [5] the technique has been exploited at two levels, both for improving segmentation and background update. In [6] Weiss proposed a technique to derive intrinsic, shadow-free images based on the concept of decomposing an image into its reflectance and illumination components; however it requires multiple images of a static scene under different lighting conditions and it is ineffective in removing vague shadows. In [7] a method is proposed in which invariant images are obtained by finding an image that is orthogonal to the direction of shadow intensity and colour change. In [8] Support Vector Machines (SVM) are used with a Gaussian kernel in order to find complex shadow boundaries; a co-training algorithm is used to improve the classification accuracy even when a small number of training examples is available.

As it can be seen, many relevant works on shadow detection and removal rely on radiometric properties of shadows, which can be used to extract invariant properties for the shadowed regions; however, these works often require the manual definition of fixed thresholds, thus limiting the general applicability of the method. In this paper we will propose a totally automated method for shadow detection and removal for outdoor scenes. The method uses division images in order to extract proper shadow features and performs Expectation-Maximization-based histogram analysis to automatically compute the required thresholds.

2   System Overview

The proposed shadow detection technique is developed in order to enhance the performance of a video surveillance system whose general architecture is shown in Figure 1. Images are acquired by a static colour camera and successively processed in order to identify zones of high intensity/chromatic variations (change detection). Even though the final aim of the change detection step is to identify the presence of moving objects in the scene, the shadows of moving objects are detected as well, thus causing erroneous data to be processed by the high-level modules; this justifies the introduction of a shadow detection and removal step.

Whenever a new image $I(x, y)$ is acquired, it is used to update a background model, this is an image of the scene without moving objects. We use a Gaussian model, in which each background pixel is represented by a running-average mean $\mu(x, y)$ and a variance $\sigma^2(x, y)$ computed using the previously acquired frames. Change detection is achieved by comparing the current frame with the background model according to the formula

$$M(x, y) = \begin{cases} 1 & \text{if } |I(x, y) - \mu(x, y)| > \sigma(x, y) \\ 0 & otherwise \end{cases}$$

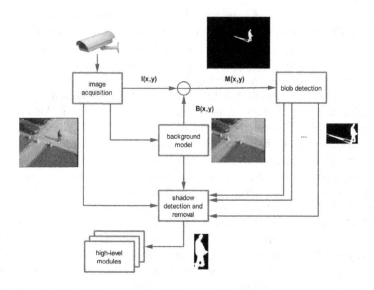

Fig. 1. System architecture

where $M(x, y)$ is the binary mask of foreground moving regions. Image M is processed in order to detect connected components and their bounding boxes, representing the moving objects within the scene. Each bounding box is processed by the shadow removal module in order to detect and remove the shadows included in the foreground mask. Once shadows have been removed, the high-level modules of the system can process the obtained data in order to perform visual surveillance tasks. These modules typically involve the classification and tracking of the moving objects, as well as a behaviour analysis step in order to detect potentially suspicious, dangerous or forbidden events [9].

3   Shadow Detection

As stated before, shadow detection and removal is a essential step in order to acquire good-quality data for the high-level processing modules. Many of the shadow detection algorithms described in section 1 take into account a priori information, such as the geometry of the scene and of the moving objects. In this method, we do not deal with geometric constraints, however we will assume that the sequences are acquired in outdoor environments under direct sunlight.

The proposed method is based on simple radiometry considerations about how light is spread across the scene when an object is lit by a light source [5]. We rely on the Lambertian model, in which the brightness of a lighted surface depends on the light source and object properties, but not on the position of the observer. The radiance (the amount of light reaching the camera) L at a given pixel (x, y) is thus defined as

$$L(x, y) = E(x, y)\rho(x, y) \tag{1}$$

where $E(x, y)$ is the irradiance, the amount of light coming from the light source and hitting the object at the point of coordinates (x, y) in the image plane, while $\rho(x, y)$ is the surface reflectance, an intrinsic property of the object about how much light it can reflect. While ρ depends exclusively on the lighted object, the irradiance depends both on the light source and its position respect to the surface normals. Moreover, we note that in real-world scenarios, irradiance depends on at least two light components, one coming directly from the main light source (e.g. the sun), and the other being the ambient light, a diffuse light coming from the surrounding environment (e.g. the sky) [4]. If no ambient light is considered, shadows would be totally black, which is generally not the case. We will call the light source intensity and the ambient light intensity respectively e_l and e_a. The irradiance can thus be defined as

$$E(x, y) = \begin{cases} e_a + e_l N(x, y) \cdot L & \text{for lit objects} \\ e_a & \text{for shadows} \end{cases} \tag{2}$$

where $N(x, y)$ and L respectively are unit vectors representing the surface normal and the light direction. The dot product shows how the irradiance depends on the angle between light rays and the surface normals; note that under the assumption of outdoor scenes with the sun as a primary light source, L can be considered constant.

Let now consider a frame $I(x, y)$, its foreground mask $M(x, y)$ and its corresponding background image $B(x, y)$. We introduce the notion of *division image*, a real-valued image defined as

$$D(x, y) = B(x, y)/I(x, y) \tag{3}$$

For each point (x, y), three cases can arise:

1. the point does not belong to the foreground mask, in this case $D(x, y) \approx 1$ (approximation is due to image noise);
2. the point is included in the foreground mask, and belongs to a shadow. In this case, by using eqs. 1 and 2, equation 3 becomes

$$D(x, y) = \frac{L_I(x, y)}{L_B(x, y)} = \frac{E_I(x, y)}{E_B(x, y)} = \frac{e_a + e_l N(x, y) \cdot L}{e_a} > 1 \tag{4}$$

   if we consider the case of a locally flat ground plane where the shadow is projected, then $N(x, y)$, and consequently D, are constant across all the shadow region;
3. the point is included in the foreground mask and belongs to a real moving object; in this case no hypotheses can be made on $D(x, y)$ since it will depend on the intensity/colour properties of the object itself.

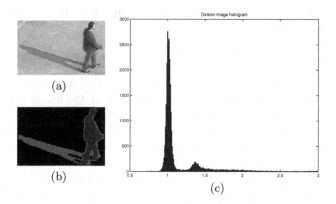

Fig. 2. Histogram of a division image

We thus hypothesize that the division image histogram will have two major peaks, one centred around 1 and denoting standard background pixels, one centred on a value greater than 1 and denoting shadows, as shown in Figure 2. No assumptions can be made on moving object pixels: they could produce a third peak in the histogram if both the background and the foreground objects have uniform colours, or more probably they will be scattered across the histogram without any particular distribution.

Even though some papers have already used this assumption [5], they relied on the detection of the shadow peak by manually defining two fixed upper and lower thresholds. This method requires manual tuning and it is not generic, since different scenes subject to different lighting conditions can require different thresholds. We here propose to automatically detect the peaks by using the Expectation-Maximization (EM) algorithm [10]. EM is a statistical, iterative method for finding maximum likelihood estimates of the parameters of a probabilistic model depending on latent variables. It is based on the iteration of two main steps: expectation, in which the hidden data are estimated based on the current parameters, and maximization, in which the parameters are estimated by likelihood maximization using the current hidden and known data. The process is iterated until convergence. In our case, the method is applied to a mixture-of-Gaussians model, in which the hidden data are the mean and variance of two Gaussians that must fit the division image histogram. By using EM, the two peaks can thus be detected; we also tested the case of 3 Gaussians (in order to model a possible peak due to the real moving object) but without noticeable performance improvement. Once the Gaussians are detected, the one with higher mean is associated to shadow pixels. Any pixel such that $|D(x, y) - \mu| < \sigma$ is then classified as a shadow pixel and removed from the foreground mask M; the resulting image is then enhanced by using morphological operators. The whole shadow detection procedure is depicted in Figure 3. Finally, note that the above procedure is defined for single-channel images, but the extension to the colour case is straightforward: the process can be applied separately to the three

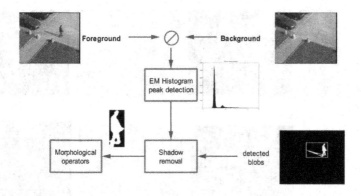

Fig. 3. The shadow detection process

red, green and blue channels, the pixel is finally classified as shadow only if all the three tests are positive (all the experiments proposed in sec. 4 have been performed on colour images).

4   Experimental Results

In order to evaluate the performance of the proposed shadow detection and removal system, we acquired several outdoor sequences during a sunny day, in order to have sharp shadows. All the sequences are composed of colour images acquired by a static camera at the resolution of 360×290 pixel, and involve a moving person within a passageway or in a parking lot. All the images are initially smoothed with a Gaussian kernel, and moving objects are detected using the technique described in section 2. Then, for each detected bounding box, shadow detection is applied in order to remove shadow pixels. Figure 4 allows a visual evaluation of the obtained results: some frames from the acquired sequences are shown together with the classification mask. In the mask, each non-black pixel was initially classified as foreground by the change detection module. The foreground pixels were then further classified as shadows (red pixels) or real moving objects (blue pixels). As it can be seen, the shadow detection technique managed to remove the shadows while keeping a large part of the original real moving object.

The main aim of our technique is to improve the performance of the subsequent high-level processing modules, in particular the tracking one. Since our tracking system is based on the shape and position of the bounding box rectangle for each moving object, it is a natural choice to use bounding boxes in order to give numerical measurements of the error introduced by our method. For each frame considered for performance evaluation, a bounding box enclosing the moving object is thus manually defined and used as ground truth. The ground truth is then compared both with the bounding box detected by the change detection module and the new bounding box after shadow removal: we want to prove that

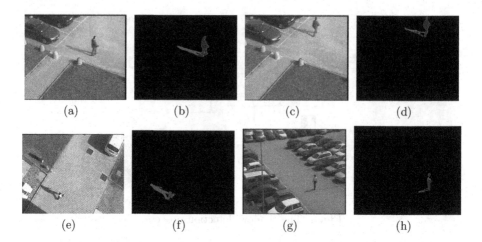

(a)   (b)   (c)   (d)

(e)   (f)   (g)   (h)

Fig. 4. Some example images. (a), (c), (e), (g): original images; (b), (d), (f), (h): the corresponding processed images, red areas are shadows, blue areas are foreground moving objects.

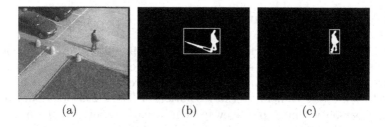

(a)   (b)   (c)

Fig. 5. Bounding boxes for a given moving object. (a) input frame; (b) detected bounding box without shadow removal; (c) detected bounding box with shadow removal.

the use of the shadow removal module always leads to better results if compared with the basic approach. An example of the data used in the evaluation is shown in Figure 5, where both the automatically computed bounding boxes are shown.

In order to numerically measure the difference between two bounding boxes, we used the same metric (the Dice coefficient) proposed in the ETISEO contest [11]. If two bounding boxes A and B are given, the Dice coefficient D is defined as

$$D = \frac{2|A \cap B|}{|A| + |B|}$$

where $| \cdot |$ is the area of a given bounding box. The results are given in table 1; the sequences used are the ones shown in figure 4 (sequence 1: figure (a) & (c), sequence 2: figure (e), sequence 3: figure (g))[1]. As it can be seen the

---

[1] Sequences available at
http://avires.dimi.uniud.it/papers/iciap09/sequences.zip

Table 1. Comparing the computed bounding boxes with ground truth data, 1 means perfect bounding box matching. The first column shows the results obtained without shadow removal; the second column refers to shadow removal with fixed thresholds as in [4]; the last column refers to shadow removal with the proposed method.

Sequence	no shadow removal	shadow removal (fixed thresholds)	shadow removal (proposed method)
seq 1, frame 160	0.3456	0.3529	0.7585
seq 1, frame 264	0.3160	0.3577	0.7578
seq 1, frame 570	0.4059	0.4153	0.7300
seq 1, frame 1055	0.4051	0.4480	0.7173
seq 1, frame 1156	0.3455	0.3829	0.8281
seq 1, frame 1371	0.3405	0.4460	0.8387
seq 1, frame 1478	0.3894	0.5124	0.8663
seq 1, frame 1807	0.3994	0.4100	0.8203
seq 1, frame 1878	0.3670	0.4348	0.8331
seq 1, frame 1926	0.3431	0.3936	0.8104
seq 2, frame 272	0.3858	0.4427	0.7669
seq 2, frame 297	0.3797	0.6781	0.7087
seq 2, frame 323	0.4494	0.5817	0.7778
seq 2, frame 579	0.4056	0.4233	0.8476
seq 2, frame 625	0.4006	0.5331	0.6180
seq 2, frame 704	0.4419	0.3934	0.8595
seq 2, frame 938	0.4159	0.4934	0.8942
seq 2, frame 1000	0.3817	0.4768	0.7120
seq 2, frame 1037	0.3794	0.4826	0.5845
seq 2, frame 1072	0.3564	0.6619	0.6947
seq 3, frame 329	0.3586	0.3840	0.3655
seq 3, frame 367	0.4018	0.4146	0.4846
seq 3, frame 556	0.3722	0.4706	0.5902
seq 3, frame 590	0.3537	0.3838	0.7490
seq 3, frame 764	0.3253	0.4437	0.5275
seq 3, frame 919	0.4308	0.4976	0.8759
seq 3, frame 1126	0.3030	0.4131	0.4545
seq 3, frame 1156	0.2941	0.4042	0.4632
seq 3, frame 1390	0.3856	0.3863	0.5042
seq 3, frame 1669	0.5197	0.5029	0.5422

introduction of the shadow removal step systematically leads to better results than the basic approach. Moreover, in table 1 we also give comparison with a fixed threshold approach, in which no EM histogram analysis is done in order to automatically detect the peaks in the histogram. In this experiment, we used the fixed thresholds proposed in [4]. Again it is evident that the automatic computation of the thresholds leads to better results than previously proposed methods.

5   Conclusions

In this paper, a novel approach for the detection and removal of moving shadows in outdoor video sequences has been presented and discussed. The approach relies on the use of division images, whose histogram gives strong hints on the possible classification of each pixel in the scene. The histogram peaks are automatically detected by means of Expectation-Maximization and allow the automatic detection of shadow pixels in foreground masks. The experimental results clearly show that the introduction of the proposed shadow removal technique gives a large improvement on the performance of the system.

Acknowledgements

This work was partially supported by the Italian Ministry of University and Scientific Research within the framework of the project "Ambient Intelligence: event analysis, sensor reconfiguration and multimodal interfaces" (PRIN 2007-2008). Srinivasa Dammalavam thanks the Italian Ministry of University and Research for the financial support.

References

1. Prati, A., Mikic, I., Trivedi, M.M., Cucchiara, R.: Detecting moving shadows: Algorithms and evaluation. IEEE Trans. on Pattern Analysis and Machine Intelligence 25(7), 918–923 (2003)
2. Bevilacqua, A.: Effective shadow detection in traffic monitoring applications. Journal of WSCG 11(1), 57–64 (2003)
3. Joshi, A.J., Atev, S., Masoud, O., Papanikolopoulos, N.: Moving shadow detection with low- and mid-level reasoning. In: IEEE International Conference on Robotics and Automation, Rome, Italy, pp. 4827–4832 (2007)
4. Cucchiara, R., Grana, C., Piccardi, M., Prati, A., Sirotti, S.: Improving shadow suppression in moving object detection with hsv color information. In: IEEE Proc. Intelligent Transportation Systems, Oakland, CA, USA, pp. 334–339 (2001)
5. Cucchiara, R., Grana, C., Piccardi, M., Prati, A.: Statistic and knowledge-based moving object detection in traffic scenes. In: IEEE Proc. Intelligent Transportation Systems, Dearborn, MI, USA, pp. 27–32 (2000)
6. Weiss, Y.: Deriving intrinsic images from image sequences. In: IEEE International Conference on Computer Vision, Vancouver, BC, Canada, pp. 68–75 (2001)
7. Finlayson, G.D., Hordley, S.D., Drew, M.S.: On the removal of shadows from images. IEEE Trans. Pattern Analysis and Machine Intelligence 28(1), 59–68 (2006)
8. Joshi, A.J., Papanikolopoulos, N.P.: Learning to detect moving shadows in dynamic environments. IEEE Trans. Pattern Analysis and Machine Intelligence 30(11), 2055–2063 (2008)
9. Micheloni, C., Piciarelli, C., Foresti, G.: How a visual surveillance system hypothesizes how you behave. Behavior Research Methods 38(3), 447–455 (2006)
10. Moon, T.: The expectation-maximization algorithm. IEEE Signal Processing Magazine 13(6), 47–60 (1996)
11. Nghiem, A., Bremond, F., Thonnat, M., Valentin, V.: ETISEO, performance evaluation for video surveillance systems. In: Proc. of Advanced Video and Signal-based Surveillance, London, UK, pp. 476–481 (2007)

A New Generative Feature Set Based on Entropy Distance for Discriminative Classification

Alessandro Perina[1], Marco Cristani[1,2], Umberto Castellani[1], and Vittorio Murino[1,2]

[1] Dipartimento di Informatica,
Università degli Studi di Verona,
Strada le Grazie 15, 37134 Verona, Italia
[2] Istituto Italiano di Tecnologia,
Via Morego 30, 16163 Genova, Italia
{alessandro.perina,marco.cristani,umberto.castellani,
vittorio.murino}@univr.it

Abstract. Score functions induced by generative models extract fixed-dimensions feature vectors from different-length data observations by subsuming the process of data generation, projecting them in highly informative spaces called score spaces. In this way, standard discriminative classifiers such as support vector machines, or logistic regressors are proved to achieve higher performances than a solely generative or discriminative approach. In this paper, we present a novel score space that capture the generative process encoding it in an entropic feature vector. In this way, both uncertainty in the generative model learning step and "local" compliance of data observations with respect to the generative process can be represented. The proposed score space is presented for hidden Markov models and mixture of gaussian and is experimentally validated on standard benchmark datasets; moreover it can be applied to any generative model. Results show how it achieves compelling classification accuracies.

1 Introduction

Pursuing principled hybrid architectures of discriminative and generative classifiers is currently one of the most interesting, useful, and difficult challenges for Machine Learning [1, 2, 3, 4]. The underlying motivation is the proved complementarity of discriminative and generative estimations: asymptotically[1] classification error of discriminative methods is lower than for generative ones [5]. On the other side, generative counterparts are effective with less, possibly unlabeled, data; further, they provide intuitive mappings among structure of the model and data features.

---

[1] In the number of labeled training examples

P. Foggia, C. Sansone, and M. Vento (Eds.): ICIAP 2009, LNCS 5716, pp. 199–208, 2009.

Among these methods, "generative score space" approaches grow in the recent years their importance in the literature. Firstly one usually has to learn an estimate of the parameters θ of the generative model; we refer with $\hat{\theta}$ to this estimate. Secondly, a score function $\phi(\mathbf{x}, \hat{\theta})$ is defined in order to map samples $\mathbf{x}$ in a fixed-size dimensional space built using the estimate of the parameters [1, 2]. After the mapping, a space metric must be defined in order to employ discriminative approaches.

Most of the literature on this topic exploits the hidden Markov models as generative frameworks, but any other generative methods can be employed [4].

In the literature, the most known score space is the Fisher space [2], in which a single model for all the classes or a set of per-class models are fit on the data. Then the tangent vector of the marginal log likelihood $\nabla_\theta \log p(x|\hat{\theta})$ is used as feature vector; the Fisher Kernel refers simply to the inner product in this space.

In general, the main intuition of generative score space approaches is to distill the contribution of each parameter θ_i in the generation of a particular sample.

Similarly to [2], other score spaces have been proposed, like the Top Kernel [1] derived from $\nabla_\theta(\log p(y = +1|x, \hat{\theta}) - \log p(y = -1|x, \hat{\theta}))^2$, the tangent vector of posterior log-odds, or the Fisher space variants presented in [3, 4].

Following this trend, in this paper we propose a novel feature extractor, introduced here for hidden Markov models, that extracts features from a learned generative model, moving the generative description of the data into a set of features that can be used in a discriminative framework. The idea is to capture the difference in the generative process between the samples, calculating a distance between the statistics collected over all the samples, encoded in the parameter estimate $\hat{\theta}$, and the individual j-th sample statistics $p(\mathbf{y}|x^{(j)})$, where $\mathbf{y}$ represent the set of hidden variables, possibly containing the class variable. The intuition is that the samples of a particular class have to differ in the same way (i.e., have to present the same generative behavior) from the parameters estimate $\hat{\theta}$.

The rest of the paper is organized as follows. In Sec. 2 technical preliminaries are reported. In Sec. 3, the proposed framework is introduced and several generalizations are discussed in Sec. 4. An exhaustive experimental section is presented in Sec. 5, and, conclusions are drawn in Sec. 6.

2   Hidden Markov Models

Hidden Markov models (HMMs) are generative models aimed at modeling sequential data. As visible in Figure 1, they are composed by a sequence of hidden state variables $\mathbf{S} = \{S_k\}_{k=1}^K$ and by a sequence of visible variables $\mathbf{O} = \{O_k\}_{k=1}^K$. In the case of a first-order hidden Markov model, each state variable S_k depends on the previous state variable S_{k-1} via a conditional dependency, and influences the visible observation variable O_k. Each value of k identifies a *slice* of the model. More formally, a HMM $\boldsymbol{\lambda}$ is defined by the number hidden states Q, and by the following parameters [6]:

---

[2] y is the label variable.

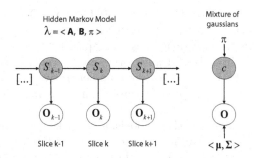

Fig. 1. On the left an hidden Markov model $\lambda = < \mathbf{A}, \mathbf{B}, \pi >$. On the right the graphical model that represent the mixture of Gaussians which can be viewed as a single slice of an hidden Markov model with gaussian emission.

1. A transition matrix $\mathbf{A} = \{a_{mn}\}$, $1 \leq m, n \leq Q$ representing the probability of moving from state m to state n,

$$a_{mn} = P(S_{k+1} = n | S_k = m), \quad 1 \leq n, m \leq Q, \quad \forall k = 1, \ldots, K$$

2. An emission matrix $\mathbf{B} = \{b_m(v)\}$, indicating the probability of emission of symbol $v \in V$ when the system state is m; V can be a discrete alphabet or a continuous set (e.g. $V = \mathbb{R}$) and, in this case, $b_m(v)$ is a probability density function.
3. $\boldsymbol{\pi} = \{\pi_m\}$, the initial state probability distribution, $\pi_m = P(S_1 = m)$

For convenience, we represent an HMM by $\boldsymbol{\lambda} = (\mathbf{A}, \mathbf{B}, \boldsymbol{\pi})$.

The learning problem. Given a model $\boldsymbol{\lambda}$ and a set of training observation sequences $\{\mathbf{O}^{(j)}\}_{j=1}^{J}$, the goal of a learning algorithm is to choose the values of the parameters $\boldsymbol{\lambda}$ that maximize the data likelihood $P(\{\mathbf{O}^{(j)}\}_{j=1}^{J} | \boldsymbol{\lambda})$. The procedure that exploits the model learning is a generalization of the well known Expectation-Maximization algorithm, known as Baum-Welch procedure [6].

The E-step consists in first calculating the standard forward and backward variables α and β using the *forwards-backwards procedure* [6]. From these variables key quantities can be obtained, such as the conditional probability of two consecutive hidden states in an observation sequence at site k, *i.e.*, $P(S_k = m, S_{k+1} = n | \mathbf{O}^{(j)}) = \xi_k^j(m, n)$ and the conditional $P(S_k = m | \mathbf{O}^{(j)}) = \sum_{n=1}^{L} \xi_k^j(m, n) = \gamma_k^j(m)$. In the M-step the prior distribution π and the transition $\mathbf{A}$ and the emission $\mathbf{B}$ matrices and are updated using these quantities.

3   Entropy Features for Hidden Markov Models

Given C hidden Markov models $\boldsymbol{\lambda}_1, \ldots, \boldsymbol{\lambda}_C$, to perform generative classification of a sequence $\mathbf{O}^{(j)}$, one has to solve the evaluation problem for each class $c = 1, \ldots, C$ obtaining $P(\mathbf{O}^{(j)} | \boldsymbol{\lambda}_c)$, and then assign the most likely class label $\hat{c}$, after computing the posterior distribution $P(c|\mathbf{O}^{(j)})$ via Bayes rule (*Maximum-a-posteriori* (MAP) classification). Nevertheless, as stated in [7], generative classification often yields to poor accuracies if compared with discriminative methods. To get the best from both frameworks, an alternative hybrid framework has been proposed: the idea is to exploit the generative process in a discriminative framework, trying to extract features from a generative model previously learned.

Here, we focus on hidden Markov models, and unlike generative classification, we want to move the focus from likelihoods, to the different behaviors of the samples under the generative model. To do this we learn a single hidden Markov model pooling all the samples of all C classes together, trying to capture the different generative process for each pair of examples $\mathbf{O}^{(j)}$ and $\mathbf{O}^{(h)}$ looking at their posterior distributions. The intuition is that the samples of the different classes have to "use" different paths over the hidden Markov models states S_k in order to fit the model parameters θ.

To catch this difference we use, as feature for a discriminative classifier, the distance between the posterior distribution of each sample $P(\mathbf{S}|\mathbf{O}^{(j)}, \boldsymbol{\lambda})$ and the joint distribution $P(\mathbf{S}, \mathbf{O}|\boldsymbol{\lambda})$ which is calculated collecting statistics over all the samples. In this way we can see *where* the samples of a class differentiate from the others.

Since we are calculating a distance between two distributions, we employ the entropy distance, defined as $\mathcal{H}(p, q) = -p \log q$; therefore the final feature vector becomes

$$
\begin{aligned}
\mathcal{H} &= -P(\mathbf{S}|\mathbf{O}^{(j)}, \boldsymbol{\lambda}) \log P(\mathbf{S}, \mathbf{O}|\boldsymbol{\lambda}) \\
&= -\sum_{[S_k]} P(S_k|\mathbf{O}^{(j)}, \boldsymbol{\lambda}) \log \left[\pi_1 \cdot \left(\prod_{k=2}^{K} a_{s_k, s_{k-1}} \right) \cdot \left(\prod_{k=1}^{K} b_{s_k}(v) \right) \right] \\
&= -\sum_{m=1}^{Q} P(S_1 = m|\mathbf{O}^{(j)}, \boldsymbol{\lambda}) \log \pi_m - \sum_{k=1}^{K} \sum_{m=1}^{Q} \sum_{v} P(S_k = m|\mathbf{O}^{(j)}, \boldsymbol{\lambda}) \log b_m(v) \\
&\quad - \sum_{k=2}^{K} \sum_{m,n=1}^{Q} P(S_k = m, S_{k+1} = n|\mathbf{O}^{(j)}, \boldsymbol{\lambda}) \log a_{m,n}
\end{aligned}
\tag{1}
$$

Instead of calculating the sums present in equation 1, we keep all the addends separated in order to have many descriptive features. In this way, for each j-th sample, we can extract a feature vector using the following three step procedure.

Transition probabilities. The statistics collected over all the sequences are encoded in the transition matrix $P(S_{k+1} = n|S_k = m) = a_{mn}$, which represent the probability of transition between states n and m. The same quantity, referred to a single sample j, is the probability that it moves from the state m to state n, i.e. $P(S_k = m, S_{k+1} = n|\mathbf{O}^{(j)}, \boldsymbol{\lambda}) = \xi_k(m, n)$. In this way we can calculate a entropic distance term for each slice k, for each couple of states m, n as

$$
\mathcal{H}_t(m, n, k) = -\xi_k(m, n) \cdot \log a_{m,n}
\tag{2}
$$

Emission probabilities. The probability that the hidden Markov model emits a symbol v being in the state m is $b_m(v)$, the statistics collected over a single sample is the probability that the sequence is in the state m if the current symbol is v, otherwise is 0. Therefore the distance between the generative process of a sample referring to the emission process and the emission matrix, can be calculated for each state m, for each symbol v and for each slice k as

$$\mathcal{H}_e(m, v, k) = -\gamma_k(m) \cdot \delta_{O_k^{(j)}, v} \cdot \log b_m(v) \tag{3}$$

where $\delta_{i,j}$ is the Kronecker delta.

Prior Probability. Similarly we can calculate a distance vector for each state value m between the sample posterior and the prior state distribution as

$$\mathcal{H}_p(m) = -\gamma_1(m) \cdot \log \pi_m \tag{4}$$

These distances can be concatenated and used as a feature vector for discriminative classification, since they encode the generative process that created the examples. Finally, we define the feature extractor ϕ that maps an observation $\mathbf{O}^{(j)}$ into a vector of entropy distances as:

$$\phi(\mathbf{O}^{(j)}, \mathbf{HMM}) : \mathbf{O}^{(j)} \rightarrow [\overbrace{\ldots, \mathcal{H}_e(m, v, k), \ldots}^{Q \cdot V \cdot K \ long}, \overbrace{\ldots, \mathcal{H}_t(m, n, k), \ldots}^{Q \cdot Q \cdot K \ long}, \overbrace{\ldots, \mathcal{H}_p(m), \ldots}^{Q \ long}] \tag{5}$$

The classification protocol is simple, an HMM λ is learned using the training data, then the extractor ϕ is applied to both training and testing data obtaining the data for the discriminative classifier.

4 Generalizations: Variable Length Sequences and Other Models

The major problem that (space) projection methods solve effectively is the classification of variable length sequences, such as audio recordings, DNA strings or shapes. Using the proposed feature extractor ϕ, each sequence is mapped in a space whose dimension depends on the length of the sample (see equations 2-3). In fact, if the j-th sample has length $K(j)$, the feature vector would be $Q \cdot K(j) \cdot (Q + V) + Q$ long, making it unusable for discriminative methods.

To solve this problem, we can simply sum over the slices $k = 1 \ldots K(j)$. Note how this operation is eligible and natural, since each piece of equations 2-4 is an entropy and so it is their sum. Therefore we define a second set of features as:

$$\overline{\mathcal{H}}_e(m, v) = -\sum_k \mathcal{H}_e(m, v, k), \quad \overline{\mathcal{H}}_t(m, n) = -\sum_k \mathcal{H}_t(m, n, k) \tag{6}$$

consequently, the mapping operator ϕ would result in

$$\phi(\mathbf{O}^{(j)}, \mathbf{HMM}) : \mathbf{O}^{(j)} \rightarrow [\overbrace{\ldots, \overline{\mathcal{H}}_e(m, v), \ldots}^{Q \cdot V \ long}, \overbrace{\ldots, \overline{\mathcal{H}}_t(m, n, t), \ldots}^{Q \cdot Q \ long}, \overbrace{\ldots, \mathcal{H}_p(m), \ldots}^{Q \ long}] \tag{7}$$

This framework can be further generalized to any generative model that contains a mixture variable that can separate the behaviors of the samples. Probably the most famous and simple generative model with such characteristics is the mixture of gaussians (MOG), which can be thought as a single slice of an hidden Markov model (see Figure 1).

Given a set of samples $\mathbf{X} = \left\{ \mathbf{X}^{(j)} \right\}_{j=1}^{J}$, the joint distribution of a mixture of gaussians is

$$P(C, \mathbf{X}) = \sum_c P(C = c) \cdot P(\mathbf{X}|C = c) = \prod_{j=1}^{J} \left(\sum_c \pi_c \cdot \mathcal{N}(\mathbf{X}^{(j)}; \mu_c, \Sigma_c) \right) \quad (8)$$

where C is the number of the mixture components. For each sample, in the E-step, the responsibilities $P(C = c|\mathbf{X}^{(j)})$ are calculated, then these statistics are collected to calculate the means μ_c and the covariance matrices Σ_c (M-step).

At this point, the derivation of the entropy features can be easily written as:

$$\mathcal{H}_\mu(c) = -P(C = c|\mathbf{X}^{(j)}) \cdot \log \mathcal{N}(\mathbf{X}^{(j)}; \mu_c, \Sigma_c) \quad \mathcal{H}_p(c) = -P(C = c|\mathbf{X}^{(j)}) \cdot \log \pi_c \quad (9)$$

leading to the following feature extractor operator:

$$\phi(\mathbf{X}^{(j)}, \mathbf{MOG}) : x^t \to [\overbrace{\ldots, \mathcal{H}_\mu(c), \ldots}^{C \ long}, \overbrace{\ldots, \mathcal{H}_p(c), \ldots}^{C \ long}] \quad (10)$$

5   Experiments

Having the feature set $\phi(\mathbf{X}, \cdot)$ been extracted, as discriminative classifier we employ support vector machines with gaussian RBF kernel [8] even though any other discriminative classifier could be employed. The choice of the particular kernel used, is guided by the fact that the feature vectors contain entropies, whose distance is usually calculated using the $\mathbb{L}_2$ norm [9].

5.1   Mixture of Gaussians

These experiments aim to show how the proposed features bring generative information to the discriminative classifiers boosting the classification accuracies. We compared the results with the MAP estimate of the generative model used to extract the features (**MOG**), with support vector machines (**SVM**) with RBF kernel, using directly the data as feature, and with an SVM on the proposed features ($\phi(\mathbf{X}, \mathbf{MOG})$ + **SVM**). For each experiment we learned a mixture of gaussians from the training data with C components[3], where C is the number of the classes of the particular dataset.

The first dataset is the Fisher's *Iris* dataset [10], perhaps the best known dataset in the pattern recognition. The data set contains 3 classes of 50 instances each, where each class refers to a type of iris plant.

---

[3] The number of classes in a classification task is a-priori known, so we do not have to investigate on C.

The second dataset is the *Wine* dataset [10]. Data points are the results of a chemical analysis of wines grown in the same region in Italy but derived from three different cultivations. The analysis determined the quantities of 13 constituents found in each of the 3 types of wines.

The *Blood* dataset [10] is composed by 748 samples described by 5 features. The associated task is to predict if samples had their blood drawn on a particular date (2 classes).

To perform generative classification, we learned a separate mixture of gaussian ($C = 2$) for each class, and we classify testing data using the Bayes rule. Results

Table 1. Mixture of gaussians numerical results. All the improvements are statistically significant however the main benefit of the method is that differently from **SVM**, it can deal with missing data or multiple length sequences (see Sec. 5.2).

Mixture of Gaussians

Dataset	Wine	Iris	Blood
Classes	3	3	2
MOG (MAP)	73,0%	87,1%	69,9%
SVM	83,1%	97,1%	76,3%
$\phi(\mathbf{X}, \mathbf{MOG}) + \mathbf{SVM}$	**86,6%**	**98,9%**	**78,3%**

for all datasets are shown in Table 1 and confirm that discriminative methods outperform generative classification, but the same discriminative method (SVM) obtains better performances when used with the proposed features since the mapping $\phi(\mathbf{X}, \mathbf{MOG})$ additionally encodes the generative process that created the data.

5.2   Hidden Markov Models

To evaluate our approach using HMMs, we focused on some standard datasets considering as comparative results, the classification accuracies reported by the dataset's authors, the generative classification based on likelihoods (**HMM**) and the Fisher and TOP Kernels [1, 2] in their original definition (indicated respectively with **FK** and **TK**).

The number of states of the hidden Markov model Q has been chosen using a validation set extracted from the training set and the same HMM used for generative classification is used for the extraction of the Fisher, Top and Entropy features.

In the first test we generated 800 fixed-length sequences, sampling 8 hidden Markov models (100 sequences per class). We classified the sequences using the 50% of the data for training and the rest for testing (50-50), repeating the process 10 times. The mean results are reported in table 2, where one can note that the improvement with respect to **HMM**, **FK** and **TK** is evident and statistically significant.

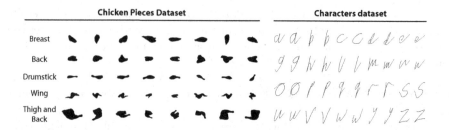

Fig. 2. On the left, examples from each of the 5 classes of the Chicken Pieces database. On the right examples from the Characters database.

The first dataset is the Chicken Pieces Database[4] [11], which consists of 446 binary images of chicken pieces, belonging to one of the five classes that represent specific parts of a chicken: "wing", "back", "drumstick", "thigh and back" and "breast". Despite the limited number of classes, this is a challenging dataset where the best result do not go over 81% of accuracy, at best of our knowledge.

The shapes are usually first described by contours, which are further encoded by suitable sequences; this makes the classification task even more difficult. In order to compute curvature sequences, the contours are first extracted by using the Canny edge detector, and the boundary is then approximated by segments of approximately fixed length. Finally, the curvature value at point x is computed as the angle between the two consecutive segments intersecting at x, resulting in continuous valued sequences of different length. Some images from this dataset are depicted in Figure 2.

Results published in [11] report a baseline leave-one-out accuracy of 67% by using the 1-NN on the Levenshtein (non-cyclic) edit distance computed on the contour chain code. In [12] the authors characterize the contour of each object using the multifractional Brownian motion (mBm), using Horst coefficients to derive a fixed length vector, which characterizes each shape. After that a 1-NN classifiers (with the Euclidean and the Minkowsky distance) is used. In [13] a kernel based method, based on a dissimilarity representation, was proposed. Note that each of these three methods employs a different technique to deal with variable length sequences. Moreover, we took as comparison the score space methods presented in [1, 2][5].

We compared our method with [11, 12] using leave-one-out (LOO) and with [1, 2, 13] using 50% of the data for training and the rest for testing (50-50), repeating the process 10 times. Results are reported in Table 2, confusion matrices are depicted in Figure 3; the proposed method strongly outperforms all the comparisons used.

The second dataset is the characters dataset used for a Ph.D. study on primitive extraction using HMM-based models [10, 14]. The data consists of 2858 character samples, divided in 20 classes (see Figure 2 for some example). Data

---

[4] http://algoval.essex.ac.uk:8080/data/sequence/chicken
[5] A brief description of the two methods can be found in Section 1.

was captured using a WACOM tablet. Three dimensions were kept: x, y, and pen tip force. Such data, captured at 200Hz, has been numerically differentiated and smoothed using a Gaussian with a sigma value equal to 2. This process results in a set of 3-dimensional continuous observations.

Classification has never been performed on this data, except some preliminary result over a restricted subset (p vs q).

Results are summarized in Table 2; also in this case the proposed approach outperforms the Fisher kernel [2], and generative classification with statistical significance. Top Kernel obtains slightly superior accuracy than the proposed method, but we cannot claim statistical difference between the two results. In Figure 3 we reported the confusion matrices.

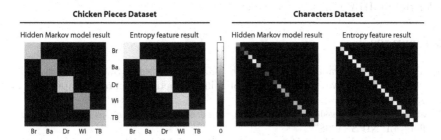

Fig. 3. Confusion matrices for generative hidden Markov classification and for the proposed approach for the chicken and the character datasets

Table 2. Hidden Markov Models numerical results for synthetic, chicken and character datasets. Differently from **MOG** experiments, discriminative methods cannot be applied directly here since the input sequences have different lengths. Best results are highlighted using bold numbers if they are statistically significant.

	Hidden Markov models			
Dataset	**Synthetic**	**Chicken pieces**		**Characters**
Feature - Classes	Continuous - 8	Curvature - 5		WACOM tablet - 20
Validation	50-50	50-50	LOO	50-50
$\phi(\mathbf{O}, \mathbf{HMM})$ + **SVM**	**88,43%**	**80,80%**	**81,21%**	**92,91%**
HMM (MAP)	71,31%	68,31%	-	57,30%
FK [2]	81,19%	79,12%	-	89,26%
TK [1]	82,95%	78,11%	-	**93,67%**
[11]		n.a.	$\approx 67\%$	
[12]		n.a.	76,5%	
[13]		74,3%	n.a.	

6   Conclusions

In this paper, we presented a novel generative feature set based on the differences in generative process. The features obtained by means of the proposed mapping

ϕ, encode ambiguity within the generative model, resulting from sub-optimal learning, but, at the same time, they mirror discrepancies of the test samples with respect to the generative data process. An large experimental section shows the goodness of the approach and exhibits more than promising performances. In almost all the tests performed our method achieves the best score, outperforming with a large margin, the generative model upon which the proposed feature are extracted. Moreover the tests show how the proposed method can successfully deal with either fixed or variable length data of different natures.

Acknowledgments

We acknowledge financial support from the FET programme within the EU FP7, under the SIMBAD project (contract 213250).

References

[1] Tsuda, K., Kawanabe, M., Rätsch, G., Sonnenburg, S., Müller, K.-R.: A new discriminative kernel from probabilistic models. Neural Comput. 14(10), 2397–2414 (2002)

[2] Jaakkola, T., Haussler, D.: Exploiting generative models in discriminative classifiers. In: NIPS (1998)

[3] Smith, N., Gales, M.: Using svms to classify variable length speech patterns. Technical Report CUED/F-INGENF/TR.412, University of Cambridge, UK (2002)

[4] Holub, A.D., Welling, M., Perona, P.: Combining generative models and fisher kernels for object recognition. In: ICCV, vol. 1, pp. 136–143 (2005)

[5] Ng, A.Y., Jordan, M.I.: On discriminative vs. generative classifiers: A comparison of logistic regression and naive bayes. In: Dietterich, T.G., Becker, S., Ghahramani, Z. (eds.) NIPS. MIT Press, Cambridge (2002)

[6] Rabiner, L.R.: A tutorial on Hidden Markov Models and selected applications in speech recognition. Proc. of IEEE 77(2), 257–286 (1989)

[7] Liang, P., Jordan, M.I.: An asymptotic analysis of generative, discriminative, and pseudolikelihood estimators. In: ICML 2008: Proceedings of the 25th international conference on Machine learning, pp. 584–591. ACM, New York (2008)

[8] Schölkopf, B., Smola, A.J.: Learning with Kernels: Support Vector Machines, Regularization, Optimization, and Beyond. The MIT Press, Cambridge (2001)

[9] Akhloufi, M.A., Larbi, W.B., Maldague, X.: Framework for color-texture classification in machine vision inspection of industrial products. In: ISIC, pp. 1067–1071 (2007)

[10] Asuncion, A., Newman, D.J.: UCI machine learning repository (2007)

[11] Mollineda, R.A., Vidal, E., Casacuberta, F.: Cyclic sequence alignments: Approximate versus optimal techniques. International Journal of Pattern Recognition and Artificial Intelligence 16, 291–299 (2002)

[12] Bicego, M., Trudda, A.: 2d shape classification using multifractional brownian motion. In: SSPR/SPR, pp. 906–916 (2008)

[13] Michel, N., Horst, B.: Edit distance-based kernel functions for structural pattern classification. Pattern Recogn. 39(10), 1852–1863 (2006)

[14] Williams, B.H., Toussaint, M., Storkey, A.J.: Extracting motion primitives from natural handwriting data. In: Kollias, S.D., Stafylopatis, A., Duch, W., Oja, E. (eds.) ICANN 2006. LNCS, vol. 4132, pp. 634–643. Springer, Heidelberg (2006)

A Hybrid Approach Handling Imbalanced Datasets

Paolo Soda

University Campus Bio-Medico of Rome, Integrated Research Centre, Medical
Informatics & Computer Science Laboratory, Rome, Italy
p.soda@unicampus.it

Abstract. Several binary classification problems exhibit imbalance in
class distribution, influencing system learning. Indeed, traditional machine learning algorithms are biased towards the majority class, thus
producing poor predictive accuracy over the minority one. To overcome
this limitation, many approaches have been proposed up to now to build
artificially balanced training sets. Further to their specific drawbacks,
they achieve more balanced accuracies on each class harming the global
accuracy. This paper first reviews the more recent method coping with
imbalanced datasets and then proposes a strategy overcoming the main
drawbacks of existing approaches. It is based on an ensemble of classifiers trained on balanced subsets of the original imbalanced training set
working in conjunction with the classifier trained on the original imbalanced dataset. The performance of the method has been estimated on six
public datasets, proving its effectiveness also in comparison with other
approaches. It also gives the chance to modify the system behaviour
according to the operating scenario.

1 Introduction

Class imbalance is considered a crucial issue in machine learning and data mining
since most learning systems cannot cope with the large difference between the
number of instances belonging to each class. A training set (TS) is imbalanced
when one of the classes is largely under-represented in comparison to the others.
According to previous works, we consider here only binary problems, namely
positive or negative. The former belong to the minority class, whereas the latter
to the majority one. Traditional algorithms are biased towards the majority
class, resulting in poor predictive accuracy over the minority one. Since classifiers
are designed to minimise errors over training samples, they may ignore classes
composed of few instances. The relevance of learning with imbalanced TS is
emphasised observing that it exists in a large number of real-world domains,
such as text classification, medical diagnosis, fraud detection, oil spills in satellite
images of the sea surface.

Research efforts dealing with imbalanced TSs in supervised learning can be
traced back to the following four categories: (i) undersampling the majority class
so as to match the size of the other class; (ii) oversampling the minority class

P. Foggia, C. Sansone, and M. Vento (Eds.): ICIAP 2009, LNCS 5716, pp. 209–218, 2009.

so as to match the size of the other class; (iii) internally biasing the discriminating process so as to compensate for the class imbalance; (iv) multi-experts system (MES) composed of multiple balanced classifiers. Despite several existing proposals [1,2,3,4,5,6,7,8,9,10,11,12], some issues remained opened. For instance, balancing the recognition accuracies achieved for each class very often decreases the global accuracy.

In order to overcome present limitations, we propose here an hybrid approach that uses the reliability of each classification act to combine the original imbalanced classifier (IC) with a MES trained on balanced subsets of the TS. The approach has been successfully tested on several public datasets, showing that it can overcome the drawbacks of the existing methods. A second contribution of the paper consists in reviewing the literature, particularly focusing on the MES approach, which has been proposed quite recently in the field of imbalanced datasets.

2   Background

This section first discusses performance metrics, then reviews the literature and finally presents the notion of classification reliability.

Performance measures. The confusion matrix is used to evaluate the performance of classification systems since its element describe the behaviour of the system. With reference to Table 1, which shows the confusion matrix for a two-classes problem, we denote as $n^- = FP + TN$ and $n^+ = TP + FN$ the number of samples in the negative and positive classes, respectively.

Classification accuracy is the traditional performance measure of a pattern recognition system. It is defined as $acc = (TP + TN)/(n^- + n^+)$. However, in case of imbalanced application the performance of a learning algorithm can not be measured in terms of classification accuracy only. For instance, consider a domain where the 3% of samples are positive: in this case, labelling all test patterns as negative will result in an accuracy of 97%, i.e. failing on all positive cases which is clearly meaningless.

Table 1. Confusion matrix for a two-classes problem

	Actual positive	Actual negative
Hypothesise positive	True Positive (TP)	False Positive (FP)
Hypothesise negative	False Negative (FN)	True Negative (TN)

Indeed, when the prior class probabilities are very different, measuring only the accuracy may lead to misleading conclusions since it is strongly biased in favor of the majority class. Such an observation can be easily explained observing that class distribution is the relationship between the first and the second column of the confusion matrix. Any performance measure based on values from both columns will be inherently sensitive to class skews, as accuracy is.

To this end, the most common performance metric for imbalanced datasets is the geometric mean (g) of accuracies, defined as [3]:

$$g = \sqrt{acc^+ \cdot acc^-} \tag{1}$$

where $acc^+ = \frac{TP}{TP+FN}$ is the *True Positive Rate* and $acc^- = \frac{TN}{TN+FP}$ is the *True Negative Rate*. The idea of such an estimator is to maximise the accuracy on each class while keeping these accuracies balanced. For instance, a high value of acc^+ by a low acc^- will result in a low g. Notice that such a measure is non-linear: a change in one of the two parameters has a different effect on g depending upon its magnitude. As an example, the smaller the value of acc^+, the greater the variation of g.

Techniques for Handling Imbalanced Datasets. This section reviews the four existing methods coping with imbalanced datasets, which have been introduced in the introduction.

Undersampling the majority class and oversampling the minority one so as to match the size of the other class have received great attention [1,2,3,4,6]. These methods resize the TS making the class distribution more balanced. Nevertheless, both have shown relevant drawbacks. On the one hand, undersampling the TS may remove potentially useful data. On the other hand, oversampling increases the number of samples of the minority class through the random replication of its elements, thus increasing the likelihood of overfitting [2,3]. Furthermore, it increases the time required to train the classifier since TS size grows up. Although this paper does not aim at providing a deep review of existing approaches of such types, it is worth observing that several papers have proposed various methods to reduce the limitations of both under and over sampling methods, such as [2,3,13,14].

Another approach to manage skewed TS consists in internally biasing the discrimination-based process so as to compensate for class imbalance. In [7] the authors proposes a weighted distance function to be used in the classification phase that compensates the TS imbalance without altering the class distribution since the weights are assigned to the respective classes and not to the individual examples. In [8] the authors assigned different weights to prototypes of the different classes. Ezawa et al. [15] biased the classifier in favour of certain attribute relationship, whereas Eavis et al. [9] presented a modified auto-encoder that allows for the incorporation of a recognition component into the conventional Multi-Layer Perceptrons (MLP) mechanism.

The last approach coping with imbalanced TS is based on multi-experts system, also known as ensemble of classifiers, where each composing classifier is trained on a subset of the majority class and on the whole minority class [10,11,12]. The idea is based on the widely accepted result that a MES approach generally produces better results than those obtained by individual composing experts, since different features and recognition systems complement each other in classification performance. Indeed, the MES takes advantage of the strengths of the single experts, without being affected by their weaknesses [16,17]. Furthermore, constructing balanced subsets of the original TS avoids the drawbacks of under and oversampling.

In [10] the authors generated as many training subsets as required to get balanced subsets from the given TS. The number of subsets was determined by the difference between the number of samples in majority and minority classes. Each classifier is trained with a learning set consisting of all samples of the minority class and the same number of training instances randomly selected from those of the majority one. As base classifiers, they employed Nearest Neighbour (NN) classifiers, combining their outputs by majority voting (MV). Their proposal has been tested on four datasets (Phoneme, Satimage, Glass and Vehicle) taken from the UCI Repository [18]. With respect to the original imbalanced classifier (IC), system performance, expressed in terms of geometric mean of accuracies, improves for three of the four datasets. Furthermore, in two cases the performance improves also in comparison with the approach reported in [3].

Molinara et al. [11] presented an approach similar to the previous one. In order to build a classifiers ensemble, they tested two splitting strategies which are based on clustering and random selection of the samples of the majority class. As base classifiers they have adopted Gentle AdaBoost, whereas dynamic selection, mean and MV have been used as criteria to aggregate individual decisions. They applied the approach to detect microcalcifications on a dataset of digital mammograms publicly available. The results reported in terms of accuracies on positive and negative samples showed that the former increases with respect to IC, whereas the latter decreases. Furthermore, such a paper studied how the behaviour of the MES system varies with respect to the number of base classifiers, in the range between one (i.e., the original imbalanced classifier) up to the ratio between majority and minority class cardinalities. Best performance has been achieved when the MES is composed of a number of base classifiers equal to the ratio between the number of majority and minority class samples.

In [12] the authors proposed a MES composed by a fixed number of base classifiers independently of sample distribution in the TS. As base learning systems they employed 5-NN, C4.5 decision tree and Naïve Bayes combined via the MV rule. The approach has been tested on eight UCI datasets showing that the MES improves geometric mean and accuracy on positive samples with respect to IC, while it decreases accuracy on negative patterns. Furthermore, it compares favorably with regard to other methods for handling imbalanced datasets, such as those based on the variation of weights assigned to the classes [19].

From the review reported so far, it is apparent that MES is a suitable alternative to cope with imbalanced dataset, outperforming also other approaches. However, most of the available methods including the MES approach, improve the accuracy on positive samples to the detriment of accuracy on negative samples, increasing g and lowering the global accuracy. Although the latter is not the unique measure to compare different methods handling imbalanced TS, nevertheless it is the ultimate parameter representing the global performance of a classifier. Moreover, to our knowledge, all the approaches provide "fixed" performance, i.e. certain values of g and acc, which are independent from the working scenario.

In this respect, this paper proposes a method that can overcome this limitations. Indeed, not only it can increase both g and acc in comparison with IC and MES approaches, but it also permits to tune the working point of the system on the basis of the operating context.

Reliability Estimation. Exploiting information derived from classifier output permits to properly estimates the reliability of the decision of each classification act [16,17]. Reliability takes into account the many issues that influence the achievement of a correct classification, such as the noise affecting the samples domain or the difference between the objects to be recognized and those used to train the classifier. The reliability assigned to a sample x, denoted as $\phi(x)$ in the following, typically varies in $[0,1]$. A low value of $\phi(x)$, i.e. $\phi(x) \to 0$, means that the crisp label allotted to x should be wrong. On the other side, $\phi(x) \to 1$ implies that the recognition system is more likely to provide a correct classification.

3   Methods

The original imbalanced classifier tends to classify test instances as negative since it is trained with a TS skewed toward that class. In this case, misclassifications mostly affect instances belonging to the minority class. Hence, it is reasonable to assume that IC classifier labels minority class samples with low reliability. However, this criterion is not sufficient to label a sample as positive, since low reliability can be measured also for majority class instances.

Previous works demonstrated that a MES trained on balanced subsets of the original TS better recognises minority class patterns than IC [10,11,12], as discussed in section 2. Based on these observations, the proposed method works as follows. When the reliability of the decision taken by IC on sample x is low, x is classified using the label provided by the MES, otherwise x is assigned to the class given by IC. To formally present this criterion let us denote as $O_{IC}(x)$, $O_{MES}(x)$ and $O(x)$ the labels provided by IC, MES and the overall system, respectively, and let t be a threshold value ranging in $[0,1]$. On this basis, the final label is given by:

$$O(x) = \begin{cases} O_{IC}(x) & \text{if } \phi(x) \geq t \\ O_{MES}(x) & \text{otherwise} \end{cases} \tag{2}$$

Since using either IC or MES depends on the reliability of sample classification, to refer to such a method we will use the term *Reliability-based Balancing* (RbB) in the rest of the paper. Fig. 1 graphically describes the RbB method, where the RbB block selects one of its inputs comparing $\phi(x)$ with the threshold t.

To measure the performance of the RbB system, we estimate both g and acc since the former represents the balancing between the two classes accuracies, while the latter the global performance of the classification system, respectively. In a plot where g and acc correspond to the X and Y axes, varying the threshold t in the interval $[0,1]$ returns a set of points that can be used to generate a

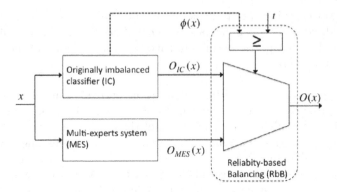

Fig. 1. Schematic representation of the proposed method handling with imbalanced TS. The sample x is given to IC, which provides both the label $O_{IC}(x)$ and the reliability measure $\phi(x)$.

curve. The curve extrema are given by the points corresponding to IC and MES performance, i.e. $t = 0$ and $t = 1$, respectively. Fig. 2 reports an instance of such a curve, whose data come from two experiments described in section 4. It is straightforward noting that the ideal point is $(1, 1)$; informally, the nearer the curve to this point, the better the performance obtained.

4   Experimental Evaluation

In this section, we experimentally prove that the RbB method can be used profitably with imbalanced dataset. To this aim, we perform tests on six UCI datasets [18], belonging to real-world problems. They show a variability with respect to the number of features and samples as well as in class distribution (Table 2). According to a general practice reported in previous works on imbalanced TS, for datasets having originally more than two classes we choose the class with fewer instances as the minority one (i.e. positive) and collapsed the others into the negative class. Hence, in the Glass set the problem was transformed to discriminate class 7 against all other classes, and in the Ecoli dataset the task consists in classifying class 4 against the others.

Support Vector Machine (SVM) with a Radial Basis Function (RBF) Kernel has been used as classifier for both IC and MES configuration. To evaluate the reliability of its decisions we use the distance of the pattern x from the optimal separating hyperplane in the feature space induced by the chosen kernel [20].

In order to build the MES composed of individual balanced classifiers, we randomly generate as many training subsets as is the ratio between the cardinalities of minority and majority classes, since this choice has been successfully adopted in previous works [10,11]. Hence, each base classifier is trained with a learning set composed of all negative samples and an approximately equal number of

Table 2. Summary of the used datasets

Dataset	Number of Samples	Number of features	Class Distribution (%) (minority, majority)
Ecoli	336	7	$(10.4, 89.6)$
Glass	214	9	$(7.9, 92.1)$
Hepatitis	155	19	$(20.8, 79.2)$
Pima	768	8	$(34.8, 65.2)$
Phoneme	5404	5	$(29.4, 70.6)$
Breast Cancer Wisconsin	699	9	$(34.5, 65.5)$

positive instances. The outputs of such classifiers are combined by the Weighted Voting (WV) rule, which weights the classification of each expert about the class by a reliability parameter.

4.1 Results and Discussion

Tests were performed using 5-folds cross validation and averaging the results over the runs. As performance parameters we measure the global accuracy, acc, and the geometric mean of accuracies, g, as motivated in section 3.

Table 3 reports for each dataset the results achieved by the originally imbalanced classifier (IC) and by the MES composed of several balanced classifiers.

Table 3. Results of the original imbalanced classifier (IC) and of the MES composed of several balanced classifiers as well as of RbB method, reported in terms of accuracy (acc) and geometric mean (g)

Dataset	Classifier	Accuracy (acc)	Geometric Mean (g)
Ecoli	IC	91.9%	72.4%
	MES Random	82.9%	88.9%
	RbB	92.5%	91.1%
Glass	IC	94.8%	87.4%
	MES Random	90.6%	87.6%
	RbB	94.8%	89.9%
Hepatitis	IC	85.6%	76.5%
	MES Random	76.6%	78.4%
	RbB	86.2%	78.8%
Pima	IC	77.7%	71.5%
	MES Random	74.3%	74.6%
	RbB	76.0%	74.8%
Phoneme	IC	75.6%	64.8%
	MES Random	69.9%	73.5%
	RbB	78.2%	75.1%
Breast Cancer Wisconsin	IC	96.5%	95.9%
	MES Random	97.0%	97.0%
	RbB	96.7%	97.1%

These results confirm previous findings since in five out of the six considered datasets balanced MES outperforms IC in terms of g, while the global accuracy decreases.

The same table reports the performance achieved applying the proposed method. The reported values correspond to the point of the curve closest to the upper right corner of the curve, which represents the best system performance as observed in section 3.

Figures 2 shows in the left and right panel the curves achieved varying t in case of Phoneme and Pima datasets , respectively. Other plots, where we observed similar trend, have been omitted for space reason. Points marked by IC, MES represent the performance of IC and MES solution, whereas point labelled as A corresponds to the performance of the RbB method reported in Table 3. In the left panel it is straightforward finding out the point corresponding to the best performance, which is the closest to the upper right corner. Right panel shows a less favourable case, where RbB does not outperform both IC and MES solutions, since its global accuracy is slightly smaller than IC one, but it provides a value of b higher than other solutions.

Data experimentally prove that RbB criterion has the valuable capability of improving both g and acc with respect to IC and MES in four out of the six datasets. In case of Breast Cancer dataset the MES itself outperforms IC and therefore RbB does not introduce any improvements. Furthermore, for Pima dataset RbB rule improves g in comparison with both IC and MES, while acc increases only with respect to MES configuration. Anyway, we deem that such findings can be regarded as positive results.

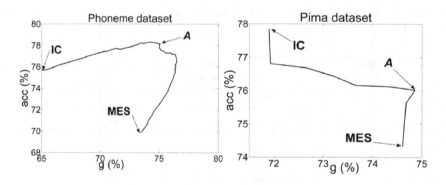

Fig. 2. Diagram of the RbB performance with respect to threshold variation in case of Phoneme and Pima datasets (left and right panel, respectively)

5   Conclusions

Methods handling imbalanced TS increase the geometric mean of accuracies harming the global accuracy. To overcome such a drawback, we have presented an approach integrating IC reliability and label with the decision taken by a

MES. This method increases in most cases both performance metrics as result of the estimation of the classification reliability. Furthermore, it returns a curve that can be used to set the operating point of the classification system on the basis of the domain peculiarities.

The interesting results achieved motivate us to further investigate such an approach, to develop an optimal rule to set the operating point, to analyse classifiers aggregation rules in case of imbalanced TS, and to extend the approach to problems with more than two classes. Furthermore, we are planning to compute the optimal threshold value on a validation set to provide a more careful evaluation of method performance.

References

1. Batista, G.E., Prati, R.C., Monard, M.C.: A study of the behavior of several methods for balancing machine learning training data. ACM SIGKDD Explorations Newsletter 6(1), 20–29 (2004)
2. Chawla, N.V., Bowyer, K.W., et al.: Smote: Synthetic minority over-sampling technique. Journal of Artificial Intelligence Research 16(3), 321–357 (2002)
3. Kubat, M., Matwin, S.: Addressing the curse of imbalanced training sets: One-sided selection. In: Machine Learning-International Workshop Then Conference, pp. 179–186. Morgan Kaufmann Publishers, Inc., San Francisco (1997)
4. Jo, T., Japkowicz, N.: Class imbalances versus small disjuncts. ACM SIGKDD Explorations Newsletter 6(1), 40–49 (2004)
5. Ling, C.X., Li, C.: Data mining for direct marketing: Problems and solutions. In: Proceedings of the Fourth International Conference on Knowledge Discovery and Data Mining, pp. 73–79 (1998)
6. Weiss, G.M., Provost, F.: Learning when training data are costly: the effect of class distribution on tree induction. Journal of Artificial Intelligence Research 19, 315–354 (2003)
7. Barandela, R., Sanchez, J.S., Garca, V., Rangel, E.: Strategies for learning in class imbalance problems. Pattern Recognition 36(3), 849–851 (2003)
8. Pazzani, M., Merz, C., Murphy, P., Ali, K., Hume, T., Brunk, C.: Reducing misclassification costs. In: Proceedings of the Eleventh International Conference on Machine Learning, pp. 217–225 (1994)
9. Eavis, T., Japkowicz, N.: A recognition-based alternative to discrimination-based multi-layer perceptrons. In: AI 2000: Proceedings of the 13th Biennial Conference of the Canadian Society on Computational Studies of Intelligence, pp. 280–292 (2000)
10. Barandela, R., Valdovinos, R.M., Sánchez, J.S.: New applications of ensembles of classifiers. Pattern Analysis & Applications 6(3), 245–256 (2003)
11. Molinara, M., Ricamato, M.T., Tortorella, F.: Facing imbalanced classes through aggregation of classifiers. In: ICIAP 2007: Proceedings of the 14th International Conference on Image Analysis and Processing, pp. 43–48 (2007)
12. Kotsiantis, S., Pintelas, P.: Mixture of expert agents for handling imbalanced data sets. Annals of Mathematics, Computing and Teleinformatics 1(1), 46–55 (2003)
13. Japkowicz, N.: Concept-learning in the presence of between-class and within-class imbalances. In: AI 2001: Proceedings of the 14th Biennial Conference of the Canadian Society on Computational Studies of Intelligence, pp. 67–77 (2001)

14. Laurikkala, J.: Improving Identification of Difficult Small Classes by Balancing Class Distribution. Springer, Heidelberg (2001)
15. Ezawa, K., Singh, M., Norton, S.: Learning goal oriented bayesian networks for telecommunications risk management. In: Machine Learning-International Workshop Then Conference, pp. 139–147 (1996)
16. Cordella, L.P., Foggia, P., Sansone, C., Tortorella, F., Vento, M.: Reliability parameters to improve combination strategies in multi-expert systems. Pattern Analysis & Applications 2(3), 205–214 (1999)
17. Kittler, J., Hatef, M., Duin, R.P.W., Matas, J.: On combining classifiers. IEEE Transactions on Pattern Analysis and Machine Intelligence 20(3), 226–239 (1998)
18. Asuncion, A., Newman, D.J.: UCI machine learning repository (2007)
19. Domingos, P.: Metacost: a general method for making classifiers cost-sensitive. In: KDD 1999: Proceedings of the fifth ACM SIGKDD international conference on Knowledge discovery and data mining, pp. 155–164. ACM, New York (2000)
20. Fumera, G., Roli, F.: Support Vector Machines with Embedded Reject Option. LNCS, pp. 68–82 (2002)

Nonlinear Embedded Map Projection for Dimensionality Reduction

Simone Marinai, Emanuele Marino, and Giovanni Soda

Dipartimento di Sistemi e Informatica - Università di Firenze
Via S.Marta, 3 - 50139 Firenze - Italy

Abstract. We describe a dimensionality reduction method used to perform similarity search that is tested on document image retrieval applications. The approach is based on data point projection into a low dimensional space obtained by merging together the layers of a Growing Hierarchical Self Organizing Map (GHSOM) trained to model the distribution of objects to be indexed. The low dimensional space is defined by embedding the GHSOM sub-maps in the space defined by a non-linear mapping of neurons belonging to the first level map. The latter mapping is computed with the Sammon projection algorithm.

The dimensionality reduction is used in a similarity search framework whose aim is to efficiently retrieve similar objects on the basis of the distance among projected points corresponding to high dimensional feature vectors describing the indexed objects.

We compare the proposed method with other dimensionality reduction techniques by evaluating the retrieval performance on three datasets.

1 Introduction

Objects in pattern recognition are frequently represented by means of feature vectors that allow us to imagine objects as belonging to a high dimensional vector space. To compare these representations in most cases the Euclidean distance in used. However, other measures can be considered especially when non-vectorial representations are adopted (e.g. in structural pattern recognition). Our main application domain is in the field of Document Image Retrieval (DIR) whose aim is to identify relevant documents considering image features only (e.g. considering layout-based retrieval or word indexing [1]).

In this paper we focus on the efficient retrieval of objects represented by n-dimensional points in suitable feature spaces. The framework that we consider is a query by example paradigm: given an n-dimensional query vector we look for most similar objects by searching the nearest points in the feature space. The simplest implementation relies on an exhaustive comparison of the query with all the indexed vectors, followed by a sorting of the computed distances. It is clear that this approach must be used with caution, for the high computational cost that it implies. To tackle this problem several multidimensional indexing methods have been proposed (e.g. X-tree) to index high-dimensional data more

P. Foggia, C. Sansone, and M. Vento (Eds.): ICIAP 2009, LNCS 5716, pp. 219–228, 2009.
© Springer-Verlag Berlin Heidelberg 2009

efficiently than the sequential scan. However, when dealing with "very high dimensional" data (hundreds or thousands of dimensions) many multidimensional indexes degenerate and perform poorly than the sequential scan for reasons that are generally attributed to the so called *curse of dimensionality* [2].

A complementary class of methods adopts a dimensionality reduction of the data as a preliminary processing step, before using a multidimensional index on the reduced space (e.g. [3]). Working on a reduced space the quality of the query results can be reduced, giving rise to wrong results both in terms of false hits and false dismissals ([4] pag 663).

In this paper we describe a dimensionality reduction technique designed to work in the DIR framework previously mentioned. The method is based on the use of Growing Hierarchical Self Organizing Maps (GHSOM) that cluster input vectors into a hierarchy of multiple layers consisting of several independent SOMs. The resulting tree is more deep in presence of more complex clusters. The GHSOM has been mainly used as a visualization tool exploring the maps independently one to each other. In our approach we embed the lower level maps in the root thus obtaining an unique low dimensional space where input patterns are projected by interpolation with respect to the cluster centers.

The basic embedding approach has been described in a recent work [5]. In this paper we focus on an improvement that relies on a non-linear placement of cluster centers in the root map. The Sammon's algorithm is used to place the neurons of the root map in R^2. We then compute the Voronoi diagram of the cluster centers to identify the regions in which to embed the second level maps by means of a projective transformation algorithm.

In Section 2 we analyze some methods for dimensionality reduction and we describe the basic characteristics of the Growing Hierarchical Self Organizing Map that are useful to understand the proposed method. In Section 3 we describe our previous approach, the Embedding Map Projection (EMP), and the Nonlinear Embedding Map Projection (NEMP). The experiments are described in Section 4 and some final remarks are drawn in Section 5.

2   Related Work

Dimensionality reduction techniques have been studied for a long time resulting in a large collection of methods available. In this section we do not aim at a broad literature survey, rather we summarize the methods that we considered for comparison with our approach.

Principal Components Analysis (PCA) performs dimensionality reduction by embedding the data into a low dimensional space finding a linear basis in which the variance in the data is maximal. PCA is based on the computation of the covariance matrix of the input data followed by the evaluation of the principal eigenvectors of the matrix, that will form the basis of the reduced space. The mapping of points in the reduced space can be computed in a straightforward way with a matrix multiplication. When dealing with real data non-linear mappings are frequently preferred to linear ones (such as PCA). In this framework both global and local techniques can be considered [6].

In the category of global techniques we consider autoencoders that have been used since the 1990's [7]. Autoencoders are Multilayer perceptrons (MLP) having the same number of input and output units and a reduced number of nodes in a hidden layer. During the training the network is forced to reproduce in the output layer the input patterns. The hidden units of a trained network describe the training data with few neurons, performing the desired non-linear dimensionality reduction. Similarly to other MLP-based architectures, large autoencoders can be difficult to train both for the computational cost and for the risk to get stuck in local minima. A new training strategy has been recently proposed [8] allowing large networks to be trained.

Local Tangent Space Analysis (LTSA) is a method that is based on the representation of the local geometry of the manifold using tangent spaces [9]. The local space is estimated by computing the PCA on the k nearest points of each input point and the local spaces are aligned to obtain the global coordinates of the data points. With LTSA it is not possible to embed additional data points in addition to those used to compute the transformation (*out-of-sample* extension) and it is not possible to index additional objects or to perform queries with objects not indexed.

Sammon mapping is a global non linear technique that maps the high-dimensional data representation to a low-dimensional representation while retaining the pairwise distances between the datapoints as much as possible [10]. The Sammon algorithm adjusts the input vectors in the output low-dimensional space trying to minimize a cost function. In Sammon technique, similarly to LTSA, the out-of-sample extension is not available. This limit does not affect PCA, autoencoders and the method proposed in this paper.

2.1 Growing Hierarchical Self Organizing Map

The Self-Organizing Map (SOM) is a clustering technique that can be considered in the artificial neural networks framework [10]. The SOM neurons are typically arranged in a two dimensional grid and each neuron is associated with a weight vector that corresponds to the cluster centroid. Two main limitations of the basic SOM algorithm are addressed by the GHSOM. First, at the beginning of the training it is required to define the map structure. Second, to accurately represent complex clusters, in some cases we need to build very large maps resulting in computational problems both for the map training and for its use. The GHSOM [11] dynamically models the training data and has been proposed to address the above mentioned problems. The GHSOM allows the network structure to grow in width and in depth, building a data structure with several layers consisting of independent SOMs. During the GHSOM training the map is adapted to the underlying distribution of training patterns.

3   Embedded Map Projection

Even if it is not easy to visualize data in high dimensional spaces, several studies have demonstrated that real patterns are unlikely to belong to uniform

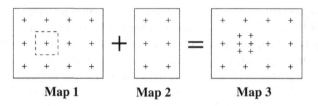

Fig. 1. Linear embedding of a second level SOM (Map2) into the parent one (Map1)

distributions in the vector space. The patterns can frequently be imagined as belonging to lower dimensional manifolds or to clusters. For instance, the Cluster Tree [12] has been proposed as an index strcture used to perform approximate search in high dimensional spaces on the basis of pattern clustering. In [13] we combined the SOM clustering with the PCA to efficiently index words represented by points in high dimensional spaces. Words in each cluster are projected in a low dimensional space with PCA to speed up the similarity search. In that work we did not use the topological order of clusters since complex patterns, such as words, can not be easily modeled by a single map. One solution is to use a larger SOM, but training such a map is not easy and the retrieval time risks to be very high, since the number of clusters quickly becomes very large. As an alternative approach we proposed in [5] to use the GHSOM hierarchy of maps to define a low dimensional space were input patterns can be projected. To give an idea of the type of maps that are built in the hierarchy, in the upper left part of Figure 3 we report the first level map and two sub-maps computed for the MNIST dataset. The basic idea of this approach is to embed lower maps in an output space that is defined by the first level map, subsequently projecting input points in this space. The GHSOM training, and embedded map building, is performed on a reduced number of points randomly selected from the collection to be indexed. The whole dataset is used in the projection step.

In Figure 1 we show the embedding of a second order map in the corresponding parent map as it is obtained by our previous method. The SOM cluster centers belong to a two-dimensional grid (represented by crosses in Map1). The cluster (1,1) (surrounded by a dashed box) is described with more details by a 3x2 map (Map2). Embedding Map2 into Map1 we obtain Map3 that describes with more resolution the region corresponding to the neuron (1,1) in Map1. The actual embedding is obtained by a recursive linear scaling of lower level maps in the main one. An actual embedded map computed with the MNIST dataset is shown in the upper part of Figure 3.

3.1   Nonlinear Embedded Map Building

Figure 2 depicts with one example the non-linear embedding proposed in this paper. After computing the GHSOM representing the input training patterns we re-arrange the neurons of the root level map using the Sammon mapping. The general idea behind this improvement is that a uniformly distributed grid of neurons does not necessarily reflect the similarity of cluster centers. We therefore

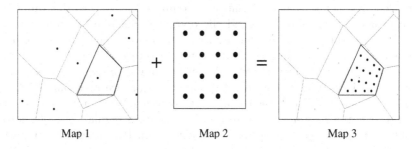

Fig. 2. Nonlinear embedding of a second level SOM (Map2) into the parent one (Map1)

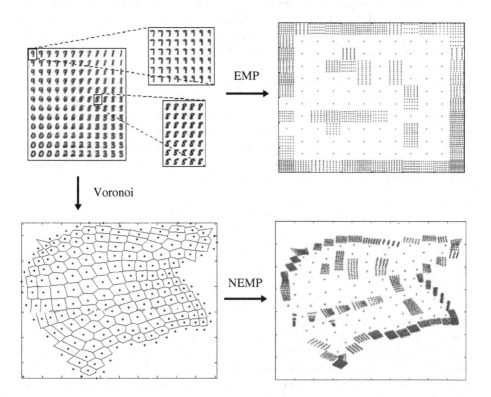

Fig. 3. Embedding obtained for the MNIST dataset. In the upper part we show the root GHSOM and two lower level maps and the linear embedding. The lower part contains the nonlinear embedding.

used the Sammon mapping to move closer clusters in the input space in near positions in the 2-d output space.

This adaptation is obtained by means of three steps that are summarized in the following and exemplified in Figure 2. First, we compute the Sammon mapping of the neurons in the root map. Second, in order to identify the regions where to embed the second level maps, we compute the Voronoi diagram of the root neurons. At this step, to avoid the open Voronoi polygons problem, before computing the Voronoi regions we add a frame of virtual points computed by an interpolation method (see the bottop-left picture in Fig. 3). Third, after computing the Voronoi diagram, we take into account the root neurons that are expanded in the GHSOM. For each expanded neuron, we find four points (P) belonging to the set of vertices of the corresponding Voronoi region. We then embed into P the neurons of the second level map, a regular grid of neurons, computing a projective homography transformation [14]. In the lower part of Figure 3 we show the embedding obtained with this algorithm in the MNIST dataset. On the left we report the new positions of root neurons after computing the Sammon mapping, together with the Voronoi regions and the virtual points. On the right we show the sub-maps embedded using the homography transformation. The NEMP method is a bit more computationally expensive than EMP method, and the adding computational load is only for the Voronoi computation.

After computing the embedded map we project all the input points in the previously defined two-dimensional space. Previous approaches to perform this projection worked with single SOMs [15], or with each individual map in the GHSOM [16]. The projection described here deals with the embedded map centroids and projects each input point x as follows (see also [5]). Let c_1 be the closest centroid to point x and c_2 and c_3 be the next closest centroids with distances $d_i = \| x - c_i \|$ $(i = 1, 2, 3)$. The three distances are ordered so that $d_1 \leq d_2 \leq d_3$ and x is placed between the three points according to:

$$x' = \frac{d_1^{-1} c_1 + d_2^{-1} c_2 + d_3^{-1} c_3}{d_1^{-1} + d_2^{-1} + d_3^{-1}}. \tag{1}$$

4   Experiments

We made several experiments on three datasets comparing some dimensionality reduction methods for similarity retrieval. The PCA, LTSA, and autoencoder software has been described in [17]. The proposed embedded map projection method has been implemented starting from the GHSOM Toolbox for Matlab [11]. In the experiments we used three datasets. The MNIST dataset is a widely used collection of handwritten digits containing 60,000 images. The COIL20 dataset contains images of 20 objects, depicted from 72 different viewpoints each. The WORDS dataset is a collection of digitized printed words normalized to fit a 12 x 57 grid. In this dataset we have 132,956 word images extrapolated from 1,302 pages that are part of an encyclopedia of the XIXth Century.

We first projected the input data of each dataset into a two dimensional space using the compared projection methods. Details of the parameters used for PCA, LTSA and autoencoders can be found in [5]. For the GHSOM training we evaluated several combinations of parameters, but for all the datasets the best results have been achieved with $\tau_1 = 0.6$ and $\tau_2 = 0.005$. The resulting maps have

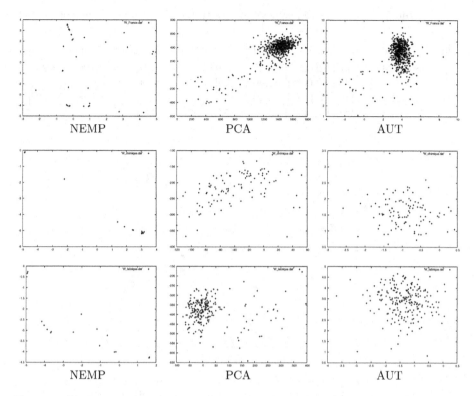

Fig. 4. Projection of the WORDS dataset for three words (*France*, *chimique*, and *fabrique*)

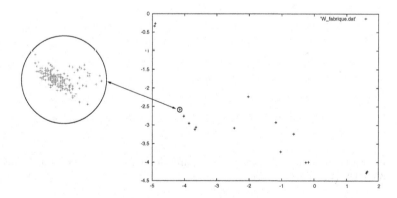

Fig. 5. Detail of the NEMP for the second word in Figure 4

Table 1. Precision at 0 percent Recall with the four compared methods

Dataset	n	Train	Indexed	NEMP	EMP	PCA	Autoencoder	Sammon	LTSA
MNIST	784	10,000	10,000	86.44	87.14	55.17	66.14	39.06	77.25
		10,000	60,000	84.00	84.56	53.55	64.66	–	–
COIL20	1024	1,440	1,440	86.59	85.59	71.68	82.35	63.58	43.68
WORDS	684	13,296	132,956	86.60	84.54	12.55	23.03	–	–

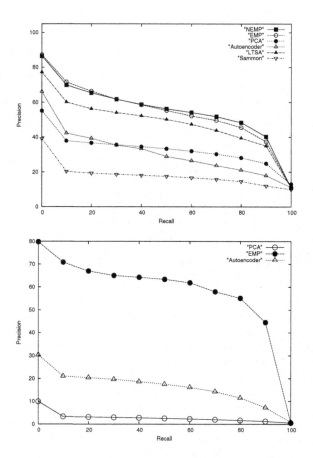

Fig. 6. Precision-Recall plots for the compared methods working on the MNIST (top) and WORDS (bottom) data-sets

the following features[1]: MNIST(2,60,2566), COIL20(4,70,395), WORDS(2,60, 2077). For the Sammon algorithm the iterative process for the minimization of the cost function was made with 100 epochs for all datasets.

---

[1] The notation used is DATASET(# levels, # maps, # clusters).

Figure 4 shows the projections of all the occurrences of three words (585 for *France*, 108 for *chimique*, 232 for *fabrique*) in the WORDS dataset with the proposed method (NEMP), PCA and the autoencoders. The NEMP method arranges the points of the words in narrow areas in the output space as it can be verified also by the detail in Figure 5. This feature is particularly useful for the use of dimensionality reduction to perform similarity search.

To obtain a numerical evaluation we measured the accuracy achieved by a query by example retrieval performed on the reduced space. We made several queries and we computed a Precision-Recall plot averaging each query. For the COIL20 dataset we used in turn each point as query evaluating the retrieval performance. For MNIST we used 10,000 queries randomly selected from the whole 60,000 patterns. In the case of the WORDS dataset we used the 111 most frequent words with a total of 24,050 occurrences. Also in this case we used in turn each word as a query with a significantly higher number of queries with respect to the experiments described in [5] (were we considered only 576 words).

Figure 6 shows the Precision-Recall plots for the MNIST and WORDS datasets. In the MNIST dataset we projected only the 10,000 training patterns, and therefore we have also a plot for LTSA and Sammon. In the WORDS dataset the LTSA and Sammon plots are missing, since we indexed all the 132,956 points, and as mentioned in section 2, the out-of-sample extension is not available for these methods. We summarize in Table 1 all the performed experiments reporting the Precision at Recall 0 in various cases (this value is obtained by an interpolation of the Precision Recall plots). In the table, n is the size of the input space. We report also the number of objects used for training ($Train$) and the number of indexed objects ($Indexed$). Summarizing, it is clear that the method described in this paper outperforms the other approaches and also the EMP one, in particular with the WORDS dataset. The increase in the computational cost with respect to the EMP is limited to the computation of the Voronoi diagram.

5   Conclusions

In this paper we propose a dimensionality reduction method that is based on the embedding of lower level maps of a GHSOM clustering of the input data. The method has been compared with other dimensionality reduction methods on a query by example retrieval application on three datasets. These preliminary results are encouraging, since the NEMP method outperforms the compared ones. Current work is addressing the extension of the approach to reduced spaces of size greater than two, in order to expand the possible range of applications.

References

1. Marinai, S., Marino, E., Soda, G.: Font adaptive word indexing of modern printed documents. IEEE Transactions on PAMI 28(8), 1187–1199 (2006)
2. Hastie, T., Tibshirani, R., Friedman, J.: The elements of statistical learning: data mining, inference, and prediction. Springer series in statistics, New York (2001)

3. Kanth, K.V.R., Agrawal, D., Singh, A.: Dimensionality reduction for similarity searching in dynamic databases. SIGMOD Rec. 27(2), 166–176 (1998)
4. Samet, H.: Foundations of multidimensional and metric data structures. Morgan Kaufmann, Amsterdam (2006)
5. Marinai, S., Marino, E., Soda, G.: Embedded map projection for dimensionality reduction-based similarity search. In: da Vitoria Lobo, N., Kasparis, T., Roli, F., Kwok, J.T., Georgiopoulos, M., Anagnostopoulos, G.C., Loog, M. (eds.) S+SSPR 2008. LNCS, vol. 5342, pp. 582–591. Springer, Heidelberg (2008)
6. van der Maaten, L., Postma, E., van den Herik, H.: Dimension reduction: A comparative review (preprint, 2007)
7. DeMers, D., Cottrell, G.: Nonlinear dimensionality reduction. In: NIPS-5 (1993)
8. Hinton, G.E., Salakhutdinov, R.R.: Reducing the dimensionality of data with neural networks. Science 313(5786), 504–507 (2006)
9. Zhang, Z., Zha, H.: Principal manifolds and nonlinear dimensionality reduction via local tangent space alignment. SIAM Journal of Scientific Computing 26(1), 313–338 (2004)
10. Kohonen, T., Kaski, S., Lagus, K., Salojarvi, J., Honkela, J., Paatero, V., Saarela, A.: Self organization of a massive document collection. IEEE Transactions on Neural Networks 11(3), 574–585 (2000)
11. Chan, A., Pampalk, E.: Growing hierarchical self organising map (ghsom) toolbox: visualisations and enhancements. In: Proceedings of the 9th International Conference on Neural Information Processing, 2002. ICONIP 2002, vol. 5, pp. 2537–2541 (2002)
12. Li, C., Chang, E., Garcia-Molina, H., Wiederhold, G.: Clustering for approximate similarity search in high-dimensional spaces. IEEE Transactions on Knowledge and Data Engineering 14(4), 792–808 (2002)
13. Marinai, S., Faini, S., Marino, E., Soda, G.: Efficient word retrieval by means of SOM clustering and PCA. In: Bunke, H., Spitz, A.L. (eds.) DAS 2006. LNCS, vol. 3872, pp. 336–347. Springer, Heidelberg (2006)
14. Hartley, R., Zisserman, A.: Multiple View Geometry in Computer Vision. Cambridge University Press, Cambridge (2003)
15. Wu, Z., Yen, G.: A som projection technique with the growing structure for visualizing high-dimensional data. In: Proceedings of the International Joint Conference on Neural Networks, 2003, vol. 3, pp. 1763–1768 (2003)
16. Yen, G.G., Wu, Z.: Ranked centroid projection: a data visualization approach with self-organizing maps. IEEE Transactions on Neural Networks 19(2), 245–258 (2008)
17. van der Maaten, L.: An introduction to dimensionality reduction using matlab. Technical Report Technical Report MICC 07-07 (2007)

A Riemannian Self-Organizing Map

Dongjun Yu[1,2], Edwin R. Hancock[2], and William A.P. Smith[2]

[1] School of Computer Science, Nanjing University of Science and Technology,
Nanjing 210094, China
njyudj@mail.njust.edu.cn
[2] Department of Computer Science, The University of York, York YO10 5DD, UK
{erh,wsmith}@cs.york.ac.uk

Abstract. We generalize the classic self-organizing map (SOM) in flat Euclidean space (linear manifold) onto a Riemannian manifold. Both sequential and batch learning algorithms for the generalized SOM are presented. Compared with the classical SOM, the most novel feature of the generalized SOM is that it can learn the intrinsic topological neighborhood structure of the underlying Riemannian manifold that fits to the input data. We here compared the performance of the generalized SOM and the classical SOM using real 3-Dimensional facial surface normals data. Experimental results show that the generalized SOM outperforms the classical SOM when the data lie on a curved Riemannian manifold.

1 Introduction

The self-organizing map (SOM) [1], also known as the topology-preserving map, can be used to learn the underlying topological neighborhood structure of the input space by applying a very simple adaptation rule. Because of its simplicity and effectiveness, the SOM has been widely used. However, the classical SOM can only reveal flat Euclidean topological neighborhood structure in the input space, and will fail to discover a non-Euclidean topological neighborhood structure of the input space [3].

To solve this problem, many researchers [3,4] have investigated how to combine the classical SOM with kernel methods and this has led to the Kernel-SOM. Different non-Euclidean topological neighborhood structures can be learned by applying different kernel functions, i.e. the resulting non-Euclidean topological neighborhood structure is kernel function dependent. Thus, when the data lie on a specific Riemannian manifold, the non-Euclidean topological neighborhood structure learned by Kernel-SOM is **not** the *intrinsic* topological neighborhood structure of the underlying Riemannian manifold on which the data reside.

In fact, in many real applications, the data may reside on some specific Riemannian manifold. For example, an unit surface normal of an object in $\mathbb{R}^3$ is a data point lying on unit 2-sphere manifold S^2. A set of unit surface normals of an object in $\mathbb{R}^3$ is a data point lying on Riemannian manifold $S^2(n)$, where n is the cardinality of the set. To learn the *intrinsic* topological neighborhood structure

P. Foggia, C. Sansone, and M. Vento (Eds.): ICIAP 2009, LNCS 5716, pp. 229–238, 2009.

of the underlying Riemannian manifold from such data, both the classic SOM and the Kernel-SOM do not apply. This paper aims to overcome this problem by generalizing the classical SOM onto a Riemannian manifold.

To the best of our knowledge, studies on this topic are far less extensive. Ritter [5] proposed method for learning a SOM in non-Euclidean space. However, it can only arrange the output neurons in a spherical or hyperbolic lattice topology, and still uses the Euclidean distance metric for locating the BMU. Shi [6] proposed a geodesic distance based SOM, referred to as GDBSOM. The GDBSOM uses a geodesic distance metric instead of a Euclidean distance metric to locate the BMU. However, when updating the codebook vectors, it does **not** consider how to guarantee that the updated codebook vectors still reside on the underlying manifold. Simila [7] incorporated manifold learning technique (such as LLE) into the classical SOM and proposed the M-SOM. In M-SOM, manifold learning is first applied to learn the internal coordinates on the underlying manifold, next the codebook vectors of the SOM are adapted in both the internal and observation coordinates, with similarities defined on the internal coordinates.

In this paper, we approach with this problem in a quite different style by directly generalizing the classical SOM onto a Riemannian manifold. More specifically, to locate the BMU, the Riemannian geodesic distance metric is applied. In the adaptation step, codebook vectors are adapted along the intrinsic geodesic curve with the aid of the Riemannian *Exponential* and *Log* maps.

2   Self-Organizing Map

The classical self-organizing map (SOM) in a flat Euclidean space (linear manifold) consists of a regular output grid (usually 1- or 2-dimensional), onto which the distribution of input vectors is projected nonlinearly [1]. The mapping tends to preserve the topological-metric relations between input vectors, i.e., similar inputs fed into the SOM will give similar outputs.

A SOM can be represented as a set of output neurons, denoted by $\{i\}_{i=1}^{K}$, on the output layer, where K is the number of neurons on the output layer. Each output neuron i is fully connected to all the input neurons and contains a d-dimensional *codebook* vector $\mathbf{w}_i \in \mathbb{R}^d$ (also referred to as a *prototype* vector). A SOM can be trained by iterative sequential or batch learning algorithms.

Sequential Learning Algorithm: Let $\{\mathbf{x}_i | \mathbf{x}_i \in \mathbb{R}^d\}_{i=1}^{N}$ be the learning dataset. One round of the sequential learning algorithm for SOM is briefly described as follow.

1) Choose the current learning sample: Randomly select a sample from the dataset $\{\mathbf{x}_i\}_{i=1}^{N}$ as the *current* learning sample $\mathbf{x}(t)$.

2) Locate the best-matching unit (BMU): The output neuron whose codebook vector is closest to the current learning sample $\mathbf{x}(t)$ is referred as the BMU, denoted by $c(\mathbf{x}(t))$ and satisfying $c(\mathbf{x}(t)) = \arg\min_{1 \leq i \leq K} \parallel \mathbf{x}(t) - \mathbf{w}_i(t) \parallel$.

3) Update the codebook vectors: The codebook vectors of the BMU and its topological neighborhood output nodes are updated using the following simple rule

$$\mathbf{w}_i(t+1) = \mathbf{w}_i(t) + \underbrace{\alpha(t) \cdot h_{c(\mathbf{x}(t)),i}(t) \cdot (\mathbf{x}(t) - \mathbf{w}_i(t))}_{\Delta}. \tag{1}$$

where t denotes learning step, which decreases monotonically with the learning steps and $\alpha(t)$ is the learning rate. The Gaussian neighborhood function defined as

$$h_{c(\mathbf{x}(t)),i}(t) = exp\left(-\frac{\|\mathbf{r}_i - \mathbf{r}_{c(\mathbf{x}(t))}\|^2}{2\sigma^2(t)}\right) \tag{2}$$

where $\mathbf{r}_i$ and $\mathbf{r}_{c(\mathbf{x}(t))}$ are the vector locations of neuron i and neuron $c(\mathbf{x}(t))$ on the output grid, respectively and $\sigma(t)$ is the width of the neighborhood function, which is also decreasing monotonically with the learning steps. Notice that the neighborhood function is not limited to be a Gaussian, and alternative neighborhood functions can also apply [1].

Batch Learning Algorithm: In the sequential learning algorithm, only a single learning sample is fed to the SOM at each learning step, and the codebook vectors of the BMU together with its topological neighborhood nodes are updated. However, in a batch learning algorithm, the entire learning dataset is fed to the SOM before any adaptations are made. The batch learning algorithm can effectively accelerate the leaning process and lessen the impact of the order of the sample data fed to the SOM. When the size of the learning dataset is large, batch learning is to be preferred.

3   Riemannian Manifolds

Let M be a Riemannian manifold. A Riemannian metric on M is a smoothly varying inner product $< \cdot, \cdot >$ on the tangent plane $T_w M$ at each point $w \in M$. The norm of a vector $v \in T_w M$ is given by $\|v\| = < \cdot, \cdot >^{\frac{1}{2}}$. Given a smooth curve segment on M, its length is computed by integrating the norm of the unit tangent vectors along the curve. Let w and x be two points lying on M, the Riemannian distance between them, denoted by $d(w, x)$, is defined as the minimum of lengths over all possible smooth curves between w and x. The *geodesic* is a smooth curve that locally minimizes the length between two points on M.

3.1   Riemannian *Exponential* Map and Riemannian *Log* Map

Let $v \in T_w M$ be a vector on the tangent plane to M at $w \in M$ and $v \neq 0$. γ_w^v be the geodesic that pass through point w (a.k.a. the base point) in the direction of v . The Riemannian *Exponential* map of v at base point w, denoted by $\mathrm{Exp}_w(v)$, maps v to the point, say x, on M along the *geodesic* at distance $\|v\|$ from w, i.e. $x = \mathrm{Exp}_w(v)$.

Note that the *Exponential* map preserves the geodesic distance from the base point to the mapped point, i.e. $d(w, x) = d(w, \text{Exp}_w(v)) = \|v\|$.

The Riemannian *Log* map is the inverse of Riemannian *Exponential* map, i.e. $v = \text{Log}_w(x)$.

3.2   Intrinsic Average and Weighted Intrinsic Average

The intrinsic average of the N points $\{x_1, x_2, \cdots, x_N\}$ lying on a Riemannian manifold M is defined as

$$\bar{x} = \textbf{IntrinsicAvg}(x_1; x_2; \cdots; x_N) = \arg \min_{x \in M} \sum_{i=1}^{N} (d(x, x_i))^2. \qquad (3)$$

Pennec [8] first proposed an iterative gradient-descent method to solve the aforementioned minimization problem

$$\bar{x}_{j+1} = \text{Exp}_{\bar{x}_j} \left(\frac{\tau}{N} \sum_{i=1}^{N} \text{Log}_{\bar{x}_j}(x_i) \right). \qquad (4)$$

where τ is the step size. The uniqueness of the solution can be guaranteed when the data are well localized.

Let w_i be the weight value of x_i, $w_i \geq 0$, $1 \leq i \leq N$. Likewise, the weighted intrinsic average $\bar{x} = \textbf{WIntrinsicAvg}(w_1, x_1; w_2, x_2; \cdots; w_N, x_N)$, can be computed using the following iteration equation:

$$\bar{x}_{j+1} = \text{Exp}_{\bar{x}_j} \left(\frac{\tau}{\sum_{i=1}^{N} w_i} \sum_{i=1}^{N} w_i \cdot \text{Log}_{\bar{x}_j}(x_i) \right). \qquad (5)$$

Embedding: Every Riemannian manifold M can be isometrically embedded into some Euclidean space $\mathbb{R}^d$, i.e., there exists embedding mapping $\Phi : M \to \mathbb{R}^d$, which embed M into its ambient Euclidean space $\mathbb{R}^d$. Under the embedding Φ, points on M can be depicted by corresponding vectors in the Euclidean space $\mathbb{R}^d$. For example, a unit 2-sphere manifold S^2 can be embedded into a 3-dimensional Euclidean space by defining embedding mapping $\Phi : M \to \mathbb{R}^3$. Under this embedding, data point w lying on manifold S^2 can be depicted by a corresponding vector $\mathbf{w}$ in 3-dimensional Euclidean space. From now on, data point on M, unless otherwise stated, is depicted by the corresponding vector in the ambient Euclidean space $\mathbb{R}^d$.

Exponential and Log maps on $S^2(n)$: We commence by considering how to implement Riemannian *Exponential* map and Riemannian *Log* map on a unit 2-sphere manifold S^2, which has been embedded into the Euclidean space $\mathbb{R}^3$.

Let point $\mathbf{p}_0 = (0, 0, 1)^T \in S^2$ be the base point, then a vector on the tangent plane $T_{\mathbf{p}_0}S^2$ can be written in the form of $\mathbf{v} = (v_x, v_y)^T$. Notice that here we choose the x and y axes of the ambient Euclidean space $\mathbb{R}^3$ as the coordinate system of $T_{\mathbf{p}_0}S^2$. Thus the Riemannian *Exponential* map on S^2 with base point $\mathbf{p}_0$ is given as [9]

$$\text{Exp}_{\mathbf{p}_0}(\mathbf{v}) = \left(v_x \cdot \frac{\sin\|\mathbf{v}\|}{\|\mathbf{v}\|}, v_y \cdot \frac{\sin\|\mathbf{v}\|}{\|\mathbf{v}\|}, \cos\|\mathbf{v}\| \right)^T. \qquad (6)$$

The corresponding Riemannian *Log* map for a point $\mathbf{q} = (q_x, q_y, q_z)^T$ on S^2 is given by

$$\mathrm{Log}_{\mathbf{p}_0}(\mathbf{q}) = \left(q_x \cdot \frac{\beta}{\sin \beta}, q_y \cdot \frac{\beta}{\sin \beta} \right)^T. \tag{7}$$

where $\beta = \arccos(q_z)$. Notice that the antipodal point $-\mathbf{p}_0$ is not in the domain of the Log map.

As stated above, a unit vector $\mathbf{p} \in \mathbb{R}^3$ can be considered as a point on the manifold S^2. Thus, a matrix $\mathbf{U} \in \mathbb{R}^{n \times 3}$, in which each row is a unit vector, can be considered as a point on manifold $S^2(n) = \prod_{i=1}^{n} S^2$. The *Exponential* and *Log* maps for $S^2(n)$ are just the direct products of n copies of the corresponding maps for S^2.

4   Learning SOM on Riemannian Manifold

In this section, we consider how to learn a SOM from data lying on a Riemannian manifold M. Note that the Riemannian manifold M has been embedded into an appropriate Euclidean space R^d by the embedding mapping $\Phi : M \to R^d$.

Sequential Learning Algorithm: First, we illustrate why the classic SOM can not *accurately* learn the *intrinsic* topological neighborhood structure of the underlying Riemannian manifold on where the data reside. Let us commence by starting from a simple case where the data reside on the Riemannian manifold S^2. Note that S^2 has been embedded into the Euclidean space $\mathbb{R}^3$ as shown in Fig.1.

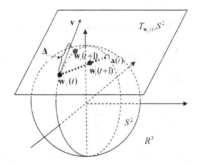

Fig. 1. Adaptation of codebook vector on S^2

To learn a SOM on S^2, if we use the classical updating equation (1), then the resulting effect is to move the *black* point corresponding to vector $\mathbf{w}_i(t)$ to the *blue* point corresponding to vector $\mathbf{w}_i'(t+1)$ by a distance of $\|\triangle\|$ along the direction of $\mathbf{x}(t) - \mathbf{w}_i(t)$, as shown in Fig.1. Note that the resulting data point corresponding to the updated codebook vector $\mathbf{w}_i'(t+1)$ is **not** guaranteed to still reside on the manifold S^2. Thus the classical SOM fails to accurately learn the *intrinsic* geometric and topological properties of data lying on S^2.

The correct procedure of for moving $\mathbf{w}_i(t)$ closer to the current learning sample $\mathbf{x}(t)$ is to move the *black* point corresponding to vector $\mathbf{w}_i(t)$ to the *red* point by a distance of $\|\triangle\|$ along the *geodesic* between $\mathbf{w}_i(t)$ and $\mathbf{x}(t)$. This can be implemented by three successive steps as follows

1) Map point $\mathbf{x}(t)$ to the vector $\mathbf{v}$ on the tangent plane using Riemannian *Log* map.

2) Calculate $\triangle = \alpha(t) \cdot h_{c(\mathbf{x}(t)),i}(t) \cdot \mathrm{Log}_{\mathbf{w}_i(t)}(\mathbf{x}(t))$, the magnitude and the direction of adjustment, with respect to $\alpha(t)$ and $h_{c(\mathbf{x}(t)),i}(t)$.

3) Map the $\triangle$ back to the point on manifold S^2 using the Riemannian *Exponential* map.

The aforementioned 3 steps can be formulated as the following update equation

$$\mathbf{w}_i(t+1) = \overbrace{\mathrm{Exp}_{\mathbf{w}_i(t)}\left(\underbrace{\alpha(t) \cdot h_{c(\mathbf{x}(t)),i}(t) \cdot \overbrace{\mathrm{Log}_{\mathbf{w}_i(t)}(\mathbf{x}(t))}^{\text{(step 1)}}}_{\text{(step 2)},\triangle}\right)}^{\text{(step 3)}}. \tag{8}$$

Batch Learning Algorithm: Likewise, for data that reside on a Riemannian manifold M, points corresponding to the updated codebook vectors are not guaranteed to still reside on M. In fact, batch learning algorithm for a SOM on a Riemannian manifold should first compute the *intrinsic* average $\overline{\mathbf{x}}_j$ of samples in each Voronoi region V_j, and then update the codebook vector to a *weighted intrinsic average* of $\overline{\mathbf{x}}_j, 1 \leq j \leq K$. More specifically, the update steps should be

$$\overline{\mathbf{x}}_j = \mathbf{IntrinsicAvg}(\mathbf{x}_1; \mathbf{x}_2; \cdots; \mathbf{x}_{n_j}). \tag{9}$$

$$\mathbf{w}_i(t+1) = \mathbf{WIntrinsicAvg}(w_{1i}, \overline{\mathbf{x}}_1; \cdots; w_{Ki}, \overline{\mathbf{x}}_K). \tag{10}$$

where w_{ji} is the weight value of $\overline{\mathbf{x}}_j$, defined as

$$w_{ji} = \frac{h_{ji}(t) \cdot n_j}{\sum_{j=1}^{K} h_{ji}(t) \cdot n_j}. \tag{11}$$

The right-sides of (9) and (10) can be solved by applying (4) and (5), respectively.

Initialization: Another key issue in our proposed learning algorithms is the initialization of the SOM. An appropriate initialization scheme must guarantee that the points corresponding to the initialized codebook vectors lie on the Riemannian manifold M, from where data are sampled.

We here present a simple randomized initialization scheme. When initializing the codebook vector $\mathbf{w}_i$, we first randomly select two samples, denoted by $\mathbf{x}$ and $\mathbf{y}$, from dataset $\{\mathbf{x}_i\}_{i=1}^N$. Then, $\mathbf{w}_i$ is initialized by taking the mid point between

$\mathbf{x}$ and $\mathbf{y}$ using $\mathbf{w}_i = \mathrm{Exp}_{\mathbf{x}}(\frac{1}{2} \cdot \mathrm{Log}_{\mathbf{x}}(\mathbf{y}))$. We repeat the above procedure K times until all the codebook vectors of the SOM have been initialized.

5   Experimental Results

In this section, we compare the performance between the classic SOM and the generalized SOM by performing experiments on both synthetic data and real word 3D facial shape data.

Synthetic Data: We use standard Swiss-roll datasets in this section. We randomly select 2000 points in Swiss-roll dataset. These points are used as training samples. After training, the distribution of the codebooks of the SOM are plotted.

Results are shown in Fig.2. The left plot in Fig.2 is the distribution of 2000 sample points, the center and right plots are the learning results of the classical SOM and the generalized SOM, respectively.

The center plot in Fig.2 clearly demonstrates that the updated codebook vectors in the classical SOM can not be guaranteed to still reside on the underlying manifold, as claimed in previous section. Thus, the resulting codebook vectors can not accurately reflect the structure of the underlying manifold. However, since the generalized SOM moves the codebook vectors along geodesics, they can be guaranteed to still reside on the underlying manifold, as depicted in the right plot in Fig.2.

From Fig.2, we can easily conclude that compared with the classical SOM, the generalized SOM can more accurately learn the topological neighborhood structure of the underlying manifold.

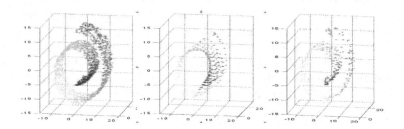

Fig. 2. Experimental results on Swiss-roll data. Left: samples of Swiss-roll data. Center: learning result of the classical SOM. Right: learning result of the generalized SOM.

Real Data: Our second application involves facial needle-map (a set of facial surface normals) as the representation of a 3D facial surface shape.

To explore the effectiveness of the generalized SOM, both facial needle-maps extracted from range images, referred as Dataset-I, and the facial needle-maps recovered from 2D brightness images using shape-from-shading, referred as

Dataset-II, are used in our experiments. Dataset-I contains range images obtained from UND database [10], and Dataset-II is a set of facial needle-maps recovered from FERET database by applying non-Lambertian shape-from-shading method, which was proposed by Smith&Hancock [11].

Dataset-I: Facial Needle-maps from UND: Dataset-I is obtained from the biometrics database from University of Notre Dame [10]. UND biometrics database provides both 3D range images and 2D face images for each subject. We select 200 range images for 200 subjects(100 females and 100 males, each subject has only one range image). Each selected 3D range image is geometrically aligned and get a corresponding facial surface height matrix $\mathbf{H}_{114 \times 100}$. Entry value $\mathbf{H}(i, j)$ is the facial surface height value corresponding to facial image location (i, j). The needle-map $\mathbf{N}_{114 \times 100 \times 3}$ then can be directly computed from the facial surface height matrix $\mathbf{H}_{114 \times 100}$ of the aligned 3D range image. More details about constructing Dataset-I can be found in Wu&Hancock [12].

Dataset-II: Recovered Facial Needle-maps from FERET: FERET [13] - the outcome of FERET program sponsored by DARPA - has become a standard face image database in the face recognition literatures. Each subject has different facial images with a variety of pose, angle of view, illumination, expression and age. Different gender and ethnicity categories are also covered by the database. In our experiments, 200 frontal facial images for 200 subjects are selected from FERET (103 females and 97 males, each subject has only one face image). Each selected image is pre-processed to a resolution of 142×124 by cropping, rotating, scaling and aligning. Face images are aligned with each other based on the central points of the left and right eyes.

After pre-processing, we use non-Lambertian shape-from-shading to recover the needle-map $\mathbf{N}_{142 \times 124 \times 3}$ for each facical image [11].

Results and Analysis: In the following experiments, the size of SOM is set to be 30×16 and the output neurons of the SOM are arranged in 2D hexagonal lattice structure. Batch learning algorithms for both the classical SOM and the generalized SOM are implemented. Note that 10-fold cross validation is applied.

Columns 2 and 3 of Table 1 show the experimental results for both the classical SOM and the generalized SOM on Dataset-I, while columns 4 and 5. Table present the experimental results on Dataset-II. From the table, it is clear that

Table 1. Number of erroneously classified needle-maps and corresponding accuracy rate

sub-block size	Method			
	classical SOM (I)	general SOM (I)	classical SOM (II)	general SOM (II)
$4 \times 4 \times 3$	31 (84.5%)	25 (87.5%)	34 (83.0%)	21 (89.5%)
$8 \times 8 \times 3$	36 (82.0%)	27 (86.5%)	37 (81.5%)	26 (87.0%)
$16 \times 16 \times 3$	50 (75.0%)	39 (80.5%)	37 (81.5%)	26 (87.0%)
$32 \times 32 \times 3$	53 (73.5%)	48 (76.0%)	55 (72.5%)	36 (82.0%)

both classical SOM and the generalized SOM achieve the best accuracy rates when the size of sub-block of is $4 \times 4 \times 3$. The best accuracy rate for the generalized SOM on Dataset-I is 87.5%, which is 3% higher than that (84.5%) obtained with the classical SOM. The best accuracy rate for the generalized SOM on Dataset-II is 89.5%, which is 6.5% higher than that (83.0%) obtained using the classical SOM.

We also carried out experiments by gradually changing the size of sub-block from $4 \times 4 \times 3$ to $32 \times 32 \times 3$. From the table the accuracy rates for both the classical SOM and the generalized SOM decrease when the size of sub-block becomes large. However, the generalized SOM consistently outperforms the classical SOM under different sub-block sizes on both datasets.

6 Conclusion

In this paper, we generalize the classical SOM from a flat Euclidean space to a curved Riemannian manifold. Both sequential and batch learning algorithms for learning a SOM on a Riemannian manifold are presented. We prove that the classic SOM learning algorithms are a special cases of the generalized learning algorithms of the generalized SOM. The generalized SOM can learn the *intrinsic* topological neighborhood structure of the underlying Riemannian manifold on where the data reside. We compare the generalized SOM with the classical SOM on both synthetic data and real world facial surface normal data. Experimental results show that the generalized SOM outperform the classical SOM when the data lie on curved manifold.

References

1. Kohonen, T.: Self-Organization and Associative Memory, 2nd edn. Springer, Berlin (1988)
2. Kohonen, T., Kaski, S., Lagus, K., Salojarvi, J., Honkela, J., Paatero, V., Saarela, A.: Self Organization of a Massive Document Collection. IEEE Transactions on Neural Networks 11(3), 574–585 (2000)
3. Andras, P.: Kernel-Kohonen Networks. Int. J. Neural. Syst. 12(2), 117–135 (2002)
4. Manuel, A.M., Alberto, M.: Extending the SOM algorithm to Non-Euclidean Distances via the Kernel Trick. In: 11th International Conference on Neural-Information-Processing, pp. 150–157. Springer, Calcutta (2004)
5. Ritter, H.: Self-organiring Maps on non-Euclidean Spaces. In: WSOM 99, pp. 1321–1344. IEEE Press, Espoo (1999)
6. Shi, C.Q., Zhang, S.L., Shi, Z.Z.: Geodesic Distance based SOM for Image Clustering. In: International Conference on Sensing, Computing and Automation, pp. 2483–2488. Watam Press, Chongqing (2006)
7. Simila, T.: Self-organizing Map Learning Nonlinearly Embedded Manifolds. J. Information Visualization 4, 22–31 (2005)
8. Pennec, X.: Probabilities and Statistics on Riemannian Manifolds: Basic Tools for Geometric Measurements. In: IEEE Workshop on Nonlinear Signal and Image Processing, pp. 194–198. IEEE Press, Antalya (1999)

9. Fletcher, P.T., Conglin, L., Pizer, S.M., Joshi, S.: Principal Geodesic Analysis for The Study of Nonlinear Statistics of Shape. IEEE Transactions on Medical Imaging 23(8), 995–1005 (2004)
10. Chang, K., Bowyer, K.W., Flynn, P.J.: Face Recognition using 2D and 3D Facial Data. In: ACM Workshop on Multimodal User Authentication, pp. 25–32. ACM Press, Santa Barbara (2003)
11. Smith, W.A.P., Hancock, E.R.: New Framework for Grayscale and Colour Non-Lambertian Shape-from-shading. In: ACCV, pp. 869–880. Springer, Heidelberg (2007)
12. Wu, J., Smith, W.A.P., Hancock, E.R.: Gender Classification using Shape from Shading. In: BMVC, UK, pp. 499–508 (2007)
13. Phillips, P.J., Moon, H., Rauss, P.J., Rizvi, S.: The FERET Evaluation Methodology for Face Recognition Algorithms. Transactions on Pattern Analysis and Machine Intelligence 22(10), 1090–1104 (2000)

Towards a Theoretical Framework for Learning Multi-modal Patterns for Embodied Agents

Nicoletta Noceti[1], Barbara Caputo[2], Claudio Castellini[3], Luca Baldassarre[1,4], Annalisa Barla[1], Lorenzo Rosasco[1,5], Francesca Odone[1], and Giulio Sandini[3,6]

[1] DISI - University of Genova
[2] IDIAP - Martigny
[3] DIST - University of Genova
[4] DIFI - University of Genova
[5] MIT, Cambridge, MA
[6] IIT, Genova
{noceti,baldassarre,barla,odone}@disi.unige.it,
bcaputo@idiap.ch, claudio.castellini@unige.it,
lrosasco@mit.edu, giulio.sandini@iit.it

Abstract. Multi-modality is a fundamental feature that characterizes biological systems and lets them achieve high robustness in understanding skills while coping with uncertainty. Relatively recent studies showed that multi-modal learning is a potentially effective add-on to artificial systems, allowing the transfer of information from one modality to another. In this paper we propose a general architecture for jointly learning visual and motion patterns: by means of regression theory we model a mapping between the two sensorial modalities improving the performance of artificial perceptive systems. We present promising results on a case study of grasp classification in a controlled setting and discuss future developments.

Keywords: multi-modality, visual and sensor-motor patterns, regression theory, behavioural model, objects and actions recognition.

1 Introduction

Multi-modal learning, that is, learning from sensorial patterns associated with very different kinds of sensors, is paramount for biological systems. Coupled acoustic and visual information is essential, for instance, for animals to determine whether they are facing a predator or a prey, as well as in courtship rituals. From the point of view of artificial intelligence, multi-modal learning is a potentially excellent way of enriching the input space of pattern recognition problems which could be otherwise more difficult. Indeed, sensorial inputs are available to biological systems in an endless, inextricably mixed flow coming from various sensorial apparatuses. It is not completely clear, then, *how* this information can be used to improve pattern recognition. For example, one could argue that the sight of a certain kind of predator is generally associated with a particular (set of) sound(s) and smell(s), and that animals learn to associate these multi-modal

P. Foggia, C. Sansone, and M. Vento (Eds.): ICIAP 2009, LNCS 5716, pp. 239–248, 2009.

patterns during their infanthood; later on, this fact is employed in recognising the associated danger in a dramatically better way. It seems apparent, then, that there is a mapping among sensorial modalities; e.g., the auditory stimulus corresponding to a predator should be reconstructible from its visual appearance. Therefore, even though not all modalities are always available, it should be possible to recover one from another, to various degrees of precision.

In this work we focus upon *active* perception modalities vs. *passive* ones. By active modality we mean perception arising from the *action* an embodied agent performs in its environment; by passive modality, we mean perception of stimuli which are independent from the agent's will. Our paradigmatic case is grasping for an embodied agent: objects must be grasped in the right way in order to use them as desired. According to the so-called *learning by demonstrations*, that is learning a grasp by observing someone doing it, we build a mapping from the object appearance to the grasping action and assess its ability to accurately describe the grasp type. In a multimodal setting, the estimated mapping could be used to predict the motor data when the corresponding channel is inactive.

In order to reconstruct actions from perception we draw inspiration from the work on *mirror neurons* [13,1]. Mirror neurons are clusters of neural cells which will fire if, and only if, an agent grasps an object *or* sees the same object grasped by another agent; they encode the semantics of an action associated to an object, and form the basis of *internal models* of actions, by which animals reconstruct the grasping and can therefore plan the grasp with greater robustness and effectiveness. Following the path laid out, e.g., in [14,17], where perception-action maps have been built into artificial systems, we hereby propose a theoretical framework for multi-modal learning in which an active modality is reconstructed via statistical regression from a passive modality. In the worked example, visual patterns describing the sight of an object are used to reconstruct the related grasping postures of the hand, with the hope that the use of *two* modalities, one active and one passive, instead of the passive one only, will aid the recognition of the object itself. This framework can be theoretically extended to any such active-passive coupling. The paper is organized as follows: in Section 2 we present the framework, discussing motivations and implementation choices; vision issues are tackled in Section 3 where we deal with objects modelling; the regression techniques used to build the perception-action map are in Section 4. In Section 5 we describe preliminary experiments that motivate the pertinence of our approach, while the last Section discusses future work.

2   A Theoretical Framework for Multi-modal Learning

As outlined in the Introduction, we assume that there exists a mapping between (sets of) patterns belonging to different modalities — here we focus upon the relations which exist between a passive and an active modality. In the aforementioned example dealing with objects (as seen) and grasping them, something like what is shown in Figure 1 is sought for.

In general, active modalities are not available to a biological system during the prediction phase, but only during the training phase. A paradigmatic example is

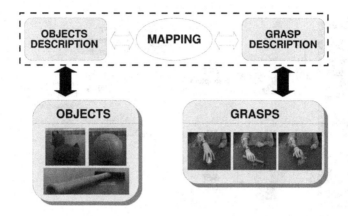

Fig. 1. An instance of the framework we propose: estimating a mapping between appropriate visual descriptions of objects and classes of grasp actions. For the time being, we assume that such relation is a one-to-one mapping.

that of a human infant learning how to grasp an object: by repeatedly trying to apply, e.g., a cylindric grasp to a bottle, he will learn not only to do it more and more efficiently, but also that a bottle is better be grasped cylindrically when moving it or bringing it close to the mouth. Later on, the sight of a bottle will remind the young human what one of the correct grasps is for that particular object. A *perception-to-action map* (PAM) is the equivalent of such training for a biological system: a model to reconstruct an active modality from a passive one. The PAM of our example is a mapping from visual features of an object to motor features of the grasping action used for that object. In general such a map is many-to-many: both a hammer and a bottle can be grasped cylindrically[1]), and as well a mug can be handled either cylindrically or by the handle. In this work we make the simplifying assumption that for a specific object there is just one acceptable grasping action — the PAM is one-to-one. A PAM is useful in passive pattern recognition (e.g., classifying an object just by seeing it) since it augments the input space with PAM-reconstructed active patterns (e.g., classifying the same object from its sight *and the associated grasp*). In this preliminary work we focus upon a simpler problem, namely that of checking whether, given the visual features of an object, the PAM-reconstructed grasp is (similar to) the one associated with that particular object. For example, we might train a PAM to reconstruct a pinch grip (hand posture) from the visual features of a pen; given then, in the prediciton phase, the visual features of another pen, will the PAM-reconstructed hand posture of a pinch grip look like a true pinch grip?

In particular, what is needed is: (*i*) a *vision unit* to extract visual features from an image or a series of images, and (*ii*) a *regression unit*, which will build the PAM.

---

[1] The nomenclature of grasp types loosely follows that of Cutkosky [16].

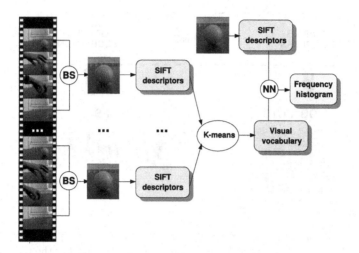

Fig. 2. A schema of the vision unit. First, suitable frames are extracted from the sequence and objects are located by means of background subtaction (BS). SIFT descriptors of a set of random points are input of a clustering step to get to the final visual vocabulary. Finally, each image is represented with respect to the vocabulary adopting a nearest neighbour (NN) strategy (see text for details).

3   Vision Unit

As we will discuss in Sec. 5, the system gathers, as one input, a video sequence acting as *spectator*, whose focus is on object appearance. The goal of the vision unit is to process the signal to obtain a global model of a set of given objects. Figure 2 shows the pipeline of the vision unit when considering only one object (the same procedure is applied to the whole set of objects). Among the sequence, we first select the frames showing only the object without any occlusion, then we locate more precisely its position by means of a simple background subtraction. Although in our application there is not an explicit object recognition step, it is clear from the architecture pipeline that a robust and specific object model is functional to subsequent analysis. It is worthwhile also to mention that with the terms *object recognition* we indicate the characterization of a specific object instance (aga5ints the concept of categorizing classes of objects). We adopt an approach based on local features to describe image structures: because of their popularity a rich variety of local measurements have been proposed in the literature [2,3,4] and applied successfully to objects recognition and categorization problems (see [6,7] just to name a few). Local approaches tipically include two distinct steps: keypoints extraction and description. However, in our case, a keypoint based-representation often ends up into a poor description due to the limited size of the images. We thus built our representation by extracting enough random points guaranteeing a more homogenous sampling. We chose to adopt

SIFT descriptors [4,5] to model image patches around these points, obtaining a set of *words* for each image.

To avoid redundancy and include some global information in our model, we apply k-means [15], following the well-known bag-of-words approach [6]. We thus build a *global* vocabulary, containing SIFT descriptions of all known objects. Image representation is obtained by means of frequency histogram of visual words, selecting for each random point extracted from the image the most similar visual word as nearest neighbor. A normalization step may be advisable for the subsequent data processing.

4 Regression Model

The mapping between object description and grasp description (Fig. 1) corresponds to a vector-valued regression problem. Given a training set of input-output pairs $\{(\mathbf{x}_i, \mathbf{y}_i) : \mathbf{x}_i \in \mathbb{R}^p, \mathbf{y}_i \in \mathbb{R}^d\}_{i=1}^n$, the aim is to estimate a deterministic map from images of objects to sensor values able to generalize on new data. In other words, we want to estimate a function $\boldsymbol{f} : \mathbb{R}^p \to \mathbb{R}^d$, where p is the number of features representing the input images and d is the number of sensors.

This requires an estension of supervised learning methods to the vector valued setting. Assuming that the data is sampled *i.i.d.* on $\mathbb{R}^p \times \mathbb{R}^d$ according to an unknown probability distribution $P(\mathbf{x}, \mathbf{y})$, ideally the best estimator minimizes the prediction error, measured by a loss function $V(\mathbf{y}, \boldsymbol{f}(\mathbf{x}))$, on all possible examples. Since P is unknown we can exploit the training data only. On the other hand, the minimization of the *empirical risk*: $\mathcal{E}_n(\boldsymbol{f}) = \frac{1}{n} \sum_{i=1}^n V(\mathbf{y}_i, \boldsymbol{f}(\mathbf{x}_i))$ leads to solving an ill-posed problem, since the solution is not stable and achieves poor generalization. Regularized methods tackle the learning problem by finding the estimator that minimizes a functional composed of a data fit term and a penalty term, which is introduced to favour smoother solutions that do not overfit the training data. The use of kernel functions allows to work with non-linearity in a simple and principled way. In [10] the vector-valued extension of the scalar Regularized Least Squares method was proposed, based on matrix-valued kernels that encode the similarities among the components f^ℓ of the vector-valued function $\boldsymbol{f}$. In particular we consider the minimization of the functional:

$$\frac{1}{n} \sum_{i=1}^n ||\mathbf{y}_i - \boldsymbol{f}(\mathbf{x}_i)||_d^2 + \lambda ||\boldsymbol{f}||_K^2 \qquad (1)$$

in a Reproducing Kernel Hilbert Space (RKHS) of vector valued functions, defined by a kernel function K. The first term in (1) is the *empirical risk* evaluated with the square loss and the second term is the norm of a candidate function $\boldsymbol{f}$ in the RKHS defined by the kernel K. The latter represents the *complexity* of the function $\boldsymbol{f}$, while the regularizing parameter λ balances the amount of error we allow on the training data and the smoothness of the desired estimator.

The representer theorem [11,10] guarantees that the solution of (1) can always be written as: $\boldsymbol{f}(\mathbf{x}) = \sum_{i=1}^n K(\mathbf{x}, \mathbf{x}_i)\mathbf{c}_i$, where the coefficients $\mathbf{c}_i$ depend on the data, on the kernel choice and on the regularization parameter λ. The minimization of (1) is known as Regularized Least Squares (RLS) and consists in inverting a matrix of size $nd \times nd$.

Tikhonov Regularization is a specific instance of a larger class of regularized kernel methods studied by [8] in the scalar case and extended to the vector case in [preprint]. These algorithms, collectively know spectral regularization methods, provide a computational alternative to Tikhonov regularization and are often easier to tune. In particular we consider iterative regularization methods with early stopping, where the role of the regularization parameter is played by the number of iterations. Besides Tikhonov regularization, in the experiments we consider L2 boosting (Landweber iteration) [18,8] and the ν-method [8].

5   Experimental Setup

The experimental phase aims at testing the proposed framework in a highly controlled environment, where we focus on learning the mapping between image descriptors and motor-sensor data to predict the grasp associated to each object. In the following we present the experimental setup and the regression results.

5.1   Data Acquisition Setup

Data were collected using two Watec *WAT-202D* colour cameras for the images and a Immersion *CyberGlove* with 22-sensors for the hand posture. An Ascension *Flock-Of-Birds* magnetic tracker mounted on the subject's wrist, and an additional standard force sensing resistor glued to the subject's thumb were used to determine the hand position and speed, and the instant of contact with the object.

The cameras return two video sequences, one placed laterally with focus on the object (the *spectator*) and one placed in front of the subject (observing the *actor*).

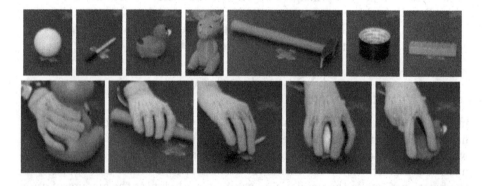

Fig. 3. Top row: the objects used in our experiments. Bottom, the grasp types we consider: *(left to right)* cylindric power grasp, flat grasp, pinch grip, spherical and tripodal grip.

We process only the *spectator* video sequence, because it supplies all the information required for preliminary testing. The video sequence is acquired at 25Hz by each camera, while the glove is sampled at 100Hz. Since the three devices are independent of one another a system of common time-stamps was used in order to synchronise the data.

The CyberGlove returns 22 8-bit numbers linearly related to the angles of the subject's hand joints. The resolution of the sensors is on average about 0.5 degrees. The sensors describe the position of the three phalanxes of each finger (for the thumb, rotation and two phalanxes), the four finger-to-finger abductions, the palm arch, the wrist pitch and the wrist yaw.

For these preliminary experiments we considered 7 objects and 5 grasping types identified by different hand postures (see Fig. 3); 2 subjects have joined the experiment: for each object, the actor was asked to perform the required grasping action 20 times.

5.2   Proof of Concept Experiments

Among the motor data, it is reasonable to consider only the 22 measures of hand joints as the most relevant for accurately describing the intrinsic properties of each grasping type. When a grasp occurs the pressure on the force sensing resistor increases, causing the signal to vary hence fixing the time-stamp of the event. Concurrently the values on each hand joint are stored as our output data.

By synchronising motor data and video sequence we select as input data the frames showing an object without clutter, going back along the sequence from the time-stamp in which the event occurs for a fixed amount of frames (see Fig. 2, left). Our data are thus generated as pairs of image descriptors and sensor-motor values, respectively input and output used to feed the regression model.

The regression methods discussed in Sec.4 are implemented in order to predict the expected sensor values of a grasp given the image of an object to be grasped. We compare four different image representations, based on bag-of-words descriptors where the histograms are computed for 20 and 50 words vocabularies on the entire image or on its four quadrants and then concatenated. We call the representations W20, W20conc, W50 and W50conc.

We consider two settings to evaluate the prediction performance of the proposed algorithms. In the first setting (V1-V2) we build training and test sets with the first and second volunteer's data respectively (140 examples each). In the second setting (MIXED) we mix the data of both volunteers and perform a 5 fold cross validation (5-CV). For both settings 5-CV on the training data only is used to select the regularizing paramenter for the RLS method and the stopping iteration for the Landweber [18,8] and ν-method [8]. The optimal regularization parameter is chosen among 25 values ranging from 10^{-6} to 10^{-2}, according to a geometric series. The maximum number of iterations for the iterative methods is set to 800. Tab.1 summarizes the prediction errors evaluated according to the square loss on all 22 components. The prediction errors are consistent among the three learning methods, homogenous with respect to the setting and there are no significant differences among the four representations. The values for the second setting are markedly lower because mixing the data of both volunteers reduces the variance between training and test sets in each split of the 5-CV. Therefore if we aim at building a model generalizing on several people, it is crucial to collect data from a large variety of volunteers.

Table 1. Data analysis results. We considered two different settings, which differ on the data splitting between training and test sets. Four distinct visual data representations are compared by feeding three learning methods, namely regularized least square (RLS), Landweber (Land) and ν-method (see text for details). For each method we report the prediction accuracies expressed as mean square error and the average number of iterations for the iterative methods. In the MIXED setting the associated variance is reported as well. Results are consistent among the different learning techniques.

Setting	Representation	RLS err $[10^3]$	Land err $[10^3]$	iterations	ν-method err $[10^3]$	iterations
V1-V2	W20conc	48	47	630	47	60
	W20	37	38	580	38	60
	W50conc	41	40	340	40	30
	W50	43	43	540	43	40
MIXED	W20conc	6.1(1.1)	6.4(1.2)	670	6.4(1.2)	80
	W20	7.9(1.3)	8.0(1.2)	630	8.0(1.3)	70
	W50conc	6.1(0.8)	6.1(0.9)	630	6.3(0.7)	70
	W50	7.4(2.0)	7.2(2.0)	620	7.3(2.0)	60

Finally, we aim at classifying the grasp type given the estimated sensor values. We restrict at the MIXED setting, using the best regression outcome case, W50conc/RLS. The input data are the sensor measures and the output data are the grasp classes. Again, a 5-CV is performed. For each split the training set is the actual set of measures from the sensors paired with the corresponding grasp type, while the test set is the set of estimated measures. We train a RLS classifier [20] in a One-vs-All configuration obtaining a prediction accuracy of 99.6 (0.8)%. This result indicates that the regression models perform well and guaranteeing the validity of the idea underlying the framework.

6   Discussion and Future Work

In this paper we proposed a general architecture for learning multi-modal patterns of data. The underlying assumption is that the system we want to model has several perceptual channels available, but among them some might be inactive. We adopted a regression-based approach to build a behavioral model of the system that can be exploited to amend such inactivity. As a validation attempt, we presented an application for grasp prediction by means of vector valued regression: the experimental phase produced very promising results that encourage us to further investigate this framework. Even though the regression problem is inherently vector-valued, we restricted our analysis to the simple scalar-valued case. A preliminary analysis on the covariance matrix of the sensors measures shows some correlation among the sensors, both positive and negative, pointing at the usefulness of a full-fledged vector-valued approach. Recently, much work has been devoted on how to best exploit the similarity among the components and learn all of them simultaneously. The main idea behind most of the literature is to use prior knowledge on the components relatedness to design a particular penalization term or a proper matrix-valued kernel [19]. In absence of prior knowledge, one approach is to design an heuristic to evaluate the similarity among the components from the available data, e.g. by computing the sample covariance of the sensor measures. Our current research is focused on how to translate this information into a viable matrix-valued kernel. Alternatively one can learn the vector structure directly in the training phase [21,22].

This multifaceted framework can be further extended in different directions. Regarding the experimental setup, we plan to enrich the dataset with a higher number of subjects, and multiple grasps for each object. Indeed, this will let us relax the one-to-one assumption we adopted in this paper and investigate a more realistic many-to-many mapping between objects and grasp classes. As anticipated in the introduction, the modeled mapping will be used in the context of multimodal learning to investigate whether, by reconstructing a missing modality, the object recognition rate improves. From the statistical learning viewpoint, we plan to explore new solutions drawing inspiration from the mentioned works on multitask learning.

Acknowledgments

This work was supported by the EMMA project sponsored by the Hasler Foundation (B. C.)

References

1. Rizzolatti, G., Craighero, L.: The Mirror-Neuron System. Annual Review of Neuroscience 27, 169–192 (2004)
2. Harris, C., Stephens, M.: A Combined Corner and Edge Detector. In: Proceedings of The Fourth Alvey Vision Conference, pp. 147–151 (1988)
3. Mikolajczyk, K., Schmid, C.: Scale and Affine Invariant Interest Point Detectors. IJCV 60(1), 63–86 (2004)
4. Lowe, D.G.: Distinctive Image Features from Scale-Invariant Keypoints. International Journal of Computer Vision 60(2), 91–110 (2004)
5. Mikolajczyk, K., Schmid, C.: A Performance Evaluation of Local Descriptors. Trans on PAMI 27(10) (2005)
6. Csurka, G., Dance, C.R., Fan, L., Bray, C.: Visual Categorization with Bag of Keypoints. In: ECCV (2004)
7. Ferrari, V., Tuytelaars, T., Van Gool, L.: Simultaneous Object Recognition and Segmentation from Single or Multiple Model Views. IJVC 67(2) (2006)
8. Lo Gerfo, L., Rosasco, L., Odone, F., De Vito, E., Verri, A.: Spectral Algorithms for Supervised Learning. Neural Computation 20(7) (2008)

9. Yao, Y., Rosasco, L., Caponnetto, A.: On Early Stopping in Gradient Descent Learning. Constructive Approximation 26(2) (2007)
10. Micchelli, C.A., Pontil, M.: On learning vector-valued functions. Neural Computation 17 (2005)
11. De Vito, E., Rosasco, L., Caponnetto, A., Piana, M., Verri, A.: Some Properties of Regularized Kernel Methods. Journal of Machine Learning Research 5 (2004)
12. Baldassarre, L., Barla, A., Rosasco, L., Verri, A.: Learning vector valued functions with spectral regularization (preprint)
13. Gallese, V., Fadiga, L., Fogassi, L., Rizzolatti, G.: Action Recognition in the Premotor Cortex. Brain 119, 593–609 (1996)
14. Metta, G., Sandini, G., Natale, L., Craighero, L., Fadiga, L.: Understanding Mirror Neurons: A Bio-Robotic Approach. Interaction Studies 7, 197–232 (2006)
15. Hartigan, J.A., Wong, M.A.: A K-Means Clustering Algorithm. Applied Statistics 28(1) (1979)
16. Cutkosky, M.: On grasp choice, grasp models and the design of hands for manufacturing tasks. IEEE Transactions on Robotics and Automation (1989)
17. Castellini, C., Orabona, F., Metta, G., Sandini, G.: Internal Models of Reaching and Grasping. Advanced Robotics 21(13) (2007)
18. Buhlmann, P.: Boosting for High-Dimensional Linear Models. Annals of Statistics 34(2) (2006)
19. Micchelli, C.A., Pontil, M.: Kernels for Multi-task Learning. In: NIPS (2004)
20. Rifkin, R., Yeo, G., Poggio, T.: Regularized Least-Squares Classification. In: Advances in Learning Theory: Methods, Models and Applications (2003)
21. Argyriou, A., Maurer, A., Pontil, M.: An Algorithm for Transfer Learning in a Heterogeneous Environment. In: ECML/PKDD (1), pp. 71–85 (2008)
22. Jacob, L., Bach, F., Vert, J.P.: Clustered Multi-Task Learning: a Convex Formulation. In: NIPS (2008)

The Impact of Reliability Evaluation on a Semi-supervised Learning Approach

Pasquale Foggia[1], Gennaro Percannella[1], Carlo Sansone[2], and Mario Vento[1]

[1] Dipartimento di Ingegneria dell'Informazione e di Ingegneria Elettrica,
Università di Salerno, Via Ponte Don Melillo, 1 I-84084 Fisciano (SA), Italy
{pfoggia,pergen,mvento}@unisa.it
[2] Dipartimento di Informatica e Sistemistica,
Università degli Studi di Napoli Federico II, Via Claudio, 21 I-80125 Napoli, Italy
carlosan@unina.it

Abstract. In *self-training* methods, unlabeled samples are first assigned a provisional label by the classifier, and then used to extend the training set of the classifier itself. For this latter step it is important to choose only the samples whose classification is likely to be correct, according to a suitably defined reliability measure.

In this paper we want to study to what extent the choice of a particular technique for evaluating the classification reliability can affect the learning performance. To this aim, we have compared five different reliability evaluators on four publicly available datasets, analyzing and discussing the obtained results.

1 Introduction

In the last years the Pattern Recognition community tried to use semi-supervised learning [2,11] to answer the needs of those real-life problems in which labeled data for training a classifier are usually a small proportion of the total available data [9]. This can happen when it is very difficult and time-consuming to obtain labeled objects [6,10] or when labeling is dangerous or even destructive [9].

A possible approach for building a better classifier by using large amount of unlabeled data together with the labeled data is in fact semi-supervised learning, that is "halfway between supervised and unsupervised learning" [2]. Among the various technique for semi-supervised learning, self-training is probably the earliest and also the most commonly used one [11], since it does not require any particular assumption. The approach that is typically followed by self-training methods is to augment the labeled training set of a classifier by using also those unlabeled samples that it classifies with the highest reliability [4,6,10,11]. In practice, the classifier is first trained with labeled data. Then, it is used to classify unlabeled data; the most confident unlabeled samples, together with their predicted labels, are added to the training set. This procedure is iterated until a stopping criterion is satisfied.

However, a problem that has been disregarded until now is how to choose a suitable approach for evaluating the classification reliability of unlabeled samples. In most papers [4,10] the authors simply suggest to select samples classified

P. Foggia, C. Sansone, and M. Vento (Eds.): ICIAP 2009, LNCS 5716, pp. 249–258, 2009.

with the highest confidence, even if there are several methods proposed so far for evaluating classification reliability (see for example [3,5,8]). A correct choice of the approach used for evaluating classification reliability should be instead of particular interest in the semi-supervised learning, since a classifier can also deteriorate when trained with unlabeled data. In fact, while some researchers demonstrate theoretically that, if the underlying model is guessed correctly, unlabeled data are expected to improve on the error [11], the use of unlabeled data may be more a damage than a benefit if there is a modeling error [9].

Starting from the previous considerations, in this paper we want to evaluate the impact of the choice of a proper reliability evaluation technique in the context of a particular semi-supervised approach, namely the self-training one. Moreover, we also tried to individuate some guidelines that could be used for individuating when a self-training procedure should produce a beneficial impact on the classifier performance. In order to do that, we compared on four publicly available datasets the performance of five different reliability evaluation techniques as the number of the labeled samples varies.

The rest of the paper is organized as follows: in Section 2, the considered self-training procedure is presented. Then, in Section 3 the selected methods for evaluating classification reliability are discussed in details, while the experimental comparative evaluation on some publicly available databases is reported in Section 4. Finally, some concluding remarks are drawn.

2   The Considered Semi-supervised Method

As we mentioned in the introduction, we will consider in this work the impact of reliability evaluation on a self-training semi-supervised learning algorithm. In Figure 1, an architectural overview of this algorithm is depicted.

In such a system, we have a classifier that is initially trained with the available labeled samples, and is used to classify the larger amount of unlabeled samples. The output of the classifier is fed into a *Reliability Evaluation* block, which estimates the reliability of each classification result, giving a numeric reliability value in the range between 0 (completely unreliable) and 1 (completely reliable). Then a *Thresholding* block divides the samples on the basis of a suitably tuned threshold τ on the reliability estimate. The ones with a reliability above the threshold are added to the training set, and the classifier is retrained. At this point the ones with a reliability below the threshold are processed again.

These steps are usually repeated until the system finds no more samples that can be added to the training set, although more complex termination conditions could be applied. After the termination of the algorithm, the trained classifier is ready for its use.

Any trainable classifier can be used with this algorithm, provided that a suitable reliability estimator can be defined. Most reliability estimation techniques, however, assume that the classifier delivers a vector of measures related to the likelihood of each class (*type 3* classifiers). Since we are interested in assessing the impact of the reliability evaluation on the performance of self-training

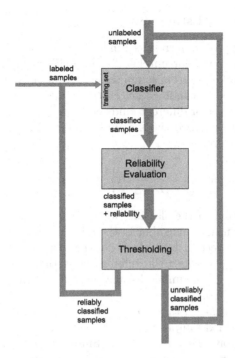

Fig. 1. Architecture of a self-training system based on reliability evaluation

algorithms, we will consider the simplest *type 3* classifier, that is the *Nearest Neighbor* (NN) classifier.

In the following section, we will describe the reliability estimation methods that we have considered for comparison.

3   The Reliability Evaluation Methods

For the Reliability Evaluation block, we have chosen three approaches that differ on the amount of training needed to perform the evaluation of the reliability. The considered options are: (i) *no training* (besides the setup of a global parameter), as represented by the ψ_A and the ψ_{med} estimators; (ii) *use of a reference set*, as exemplified by the Local_Distance-based_pre and Local_Distance-based_post estimators; (iii) *use of a trainable function estimator*, as represented by the ϵ-SVR estimators.

The following subsections will provide more details on each method. Notice that except for ψ_A and ψ_{med}, the definition of the considered reliability estimators is independent of the adopted classifier architecture. In the descriptions we will use the term *reference set* to denote the set of labeled samples available to the classifier, following the terminology commonly adopted for NN classifiers; however this does not imply that a different classification algorithm cannot be used.

3.1   The ψ_A and ψ_{med} Estimators

The first considered approach, introduced in [3], is based on the observation that there are two possible causes for unreliability in a classification: (i) the sample being classified is too different from samples the classifier has seen in the training phase; (ii) the sample being classified lies on the boundary between two classes. Thus, the authors propose for different kinds of classifiers two measures, ψ_A and ψ_B, that are related to the two types of unreliability. In particular, for a NN classifier, the measures are:

$$\psi_A = \max\left\{1 - \frac{O_{win}}{D_{max}}, 0\right\}; \psi_B = 1 - \frac{O_{win}}{O_{2win}}$$

where O_{win} is the output of the classifier for the winner class, i.e. the distance of the sample from its nearest neighbor in the reference set; O_{2win} is the output of the classifier for the second best class, i.e. the distance of the sample from the nearest neighbor belonging to a different class than the absolute nearest neighbor; and D_{max} is the maximum distance between a sample in the reference set and its nearest neighbor.

It can be easily seen that ψ_A takes into account the first cause of unreliability, since it is 1 if the classified sample is in the reference set, and becomes 0 as the sample gets farther from the reference set. Similarly, ψ_B reflects the second cause of unreliability, since it is 0 when the classified sample lies at the midpoint between two reference samples of different classes, and tends to 1 when the sample gets unambiguously closer to a single reference sample.

The authors of [3] suggests different ways of combining ψ_A and ψ_B to obtain a single, comprehensive estimator. For our evaluation we have chosen:

$$\psi_{med} = \frac{\psi_A + \psi_B}{2} \tag{1}$$

together with the use of ψ_A alone.

3.2   The Local_Distance-Based_Pre and Local_Distance-Based_Post Estimators

The second approach, introduced in [7], is based on an extension of the k-NN classification algorithm, combined with the *leave-one-out* technique used for the validation of classifiers. The underlying idea is that the samples in the reference set can be used to estimate the classifier reliability in the region surrounding them in the feature space (hence the term "local" in the name), on the basis of the correctness of their classification performed according to the *leave-one-out* method.

Before describing the estimators, we need to introduce some notational conventions. We indicate with $R = \{r_1, \ldots, r_n\}$ the reference set, and with $class(r_i)$ the true class of reference sample r_i. We denote as $l(r_i)$ the class that would be attributed to sample r_i by the classifier using $R-r_i$ as its reference set (this is the *leave-one-out* approach). Then we introduce the correct classification indicator p as the function:

$$p : r \in R \longrightarrow \begin{cases} 1 & \text{if } l(r) = class(r) \\ 0 & \text{if } l(r) \neq class(r) \end{cases}$$

Now, we can define the first reliability estimator, *Local_Distance-based_pre* (*LDpre* for short). Given the sample x under examination, we consider the set $N^k(x)$ formed by the k nearest neighbors to x in R. We have:

$$LDpre = \frac{\sum\limits_{r \in N^k(x)} p(r)/d(x,r)}{\sum\limits_{r \in N^k(x)} 1/d(x,r)} \tag{2}$$

where $d(x,r)$ is the distance in feature space (according to a suitably chosen metric) between the classified sample x and the reference sample r. In other words, *LDpre* is a weighted average of the correct classification indicator over the k nearest neighbors to x, using as weights the inverse of the distances.

The *LDpre* estimator does not take into account the class attributed to the classified sample x (hence the "pre" suffix in the name). In contrast, the *Local_Distance-based_post* estimator (*LDpost* for short) uses also this information in the reliability evaluation. Namely, instead of averaging the correct classification indicator over the k nearest neighbors in R, it considers the k nearest neighbors in the set $\{r \in R : l(r) = l(x)\}$, where, with a slight notational inconsistency, we denote by $l(x)$ the class attributed by the complete classifier to the sample x (recall that $l(r)$ is instead the class attributed to r by a *leave-one-out* approach).

In other words, the *LDpost* estimator only considers the reference samples that the *leave-one-out* classifier has attributed to the same class to which the complete classifier is assigning x. If we denote the k nearest neighbors in this subset of R as $N^k(x,l(x))$, then we can define *LDpost* as:

$$LDpost = \frac{\sum\limits_{r \in N^k(x,l(x))} p(r)/d(x,r)}{\sum\limits_{r \in N^k(x,l(x))} 1/d(x,r)} \tag{3}$$

3.3   The ϵ-SVR Estimator

The third reliability evaluation approach has been proposed in [5]. The basic idea in this approach is to use a trainable function estimator to *learn* the relation between the reliability and the region in classifier input/output space which the sample belongs to. In particular, the ϵ-*SVR* regression algorithm is used as the trainable function estimator.

After a learning phase, the ϵ-SVR receives as its input the feature vector concatenated with the response of the classifier (encoded as a vector of binary values), and produces as its output the reliability value.

In order to use as the reliability estimator a supervised learning algorithm such as the ϵ-SVR, there are two problems that must be faced: (i) the reliability estimator must be trained using a *validation set* containing both samples that are classified reliably and samples classified unreliably; the validation set must be different from the reference set, or else (at least for the NN classifier) it would contain only perfectly classified samples; (ii) for each sample in the validation set, a desired reliability value must be provided during the training of the reliability estimator; this value should reflect as close as possible the actual classification reliability of the sample.

The first problem is particularly hard in our context, since we assume that labeled samples are scarce. So we have adopted for training the ϵ-SVR a technique that is based on k-fold cross-validation. In particular, the reference set is randomly partitioned into F disjoint subsets $V_1, \ldots, V_F$ (called *folds*) of equal size. The samples of each V_i are then classified using $R - V_i$ as the reference set; for analogy with the previous subsection, we will denote as $l(v)$ the class assigned to sample $v \in V_i$ in this step, and as $p(v)$ the correct classification indicator, that is 1 if $l(v) = class(v)$, and 0 otherwise. At this point we can use all the samples of the reference set, together with the class labels $l(v)$ assigned by the folding procedure, for the training phase of the ϵ-SVR, since we expect that they will not be all correctly classified.

For the second problem (the definition of the desired reliability values), we have used $p(v)$ as the desired reliability value for sample v. While $p(v)$ only assumes the values 0 and 1, the generalization ability of the ϵ-SVR manages to interpolate other values inside the $[0, 1]$ interval.

4   Experimental Results

The questions raised in this paper can be summarized as follows: (i) what is the impact of the use of different reliability estimators on the recognition performance when the self-training procedure is used? (ii) how the performance of the self-training depend on the size of the training set?

In this section, we provide an answer to the above questions from an experimental point of view. In the design of the experimental protocol several aspects have been taken into account: the architecture of the base classifier, the settings of the reliability estimators, the criterion to stop the self-training procedure, the size of the training set, the value of the reliability threshold. The way these aspects have been taken into account in the tests is summarized in the following.

Base classifier: tests were carried out by using a Nearest Neighbor (NN). This choice is motivated by the fact that the NN does not require a training procedure, and is the simplest *type 3* classifier.

Reliability estimators: several preliminary tests have been carried out to determine the best setup of the *LDpre*, *LDpost* and ϵ-SVR reliability estimators: for the first two estimators the analysis has been carried out with respect to the number k of nearest neighbors, while for the latter we searched for the optimal number F of the folds the reference set is partitioned into. The results reported afterwards consider only the best configurations. The ψ_A and ψ_{med} did not require a setup procedure.

Self-training stopping criterion: we stop the self-training procedure when no more samples are available that can be added to the training set. This happens when the reliability of all the classified samples is below the threshold τ. However, our tests accounted also for the performance obtained by using an ideal stopping criterion, i.e. by stopping the self-training procedure when the minimum error rate is reached. This analysis is useful to highlight the potentiality of self-training using a certain reliability estimator, as it represents the highest performance that can be obtained. For simplicity, hereinafter we will refer to these stopping criteria as END and BEST respectively.

Training set size: we analyzed how recognition performance vary with the size of the dataset when using self-training with different reliability estimators. We considered several configurations where the reference set used by the NN ranges within 2% to 15% of the whole dataset.

Table 1. Characteristics of the employed datasets

Data set	letter	pendigits	spam	thyroid
# classes	26	10	2	3
# features	16	16	57	21
# patterns	20000	10992	4601	7200
# patterns used for test	2000	1100	460	3428

Table 2. Error rates obtained on the considered datasets by the base NN and by the NN after the self-training procedure using the different methods for reliability estimation. Performance improvements and decreases with respect to the base NN are reported with a plus (+) and minus (-) sign, respectively. The best result for each dataset is highlighted in bold.

	τ	letter	τ	pendigits	τ	spam	τ	thyroid
Base NN	-	35.2%	-	7.64%	-	19.13%	-	9.48%
ψ_A	0.90	**29.50%** (+)	0.85	**5.64%** (+)	0.90	22.39% (-)	0.95	9.31% (+)
ψ_{med}	0.85	30.70% (+)	0.80	5.82% (+)	0.90	20.87% (-)	0.95	**8.66%** (+)
LD-pre	0.27	34.75% (+)	0.70	8.37% (-)	0.85	20.65% (+)	0.55	8.91% (+)
LD-post	0.27	57.30% (-)	0.70	28.36% (-)	0.75	**18.91%** (+)	0.60	9.80% (-)
ϵ-SVR	0.90	32.60% (+)	0.85	7.37% (+)	0.85	21.74% (-)	0.65	9.16% (+)

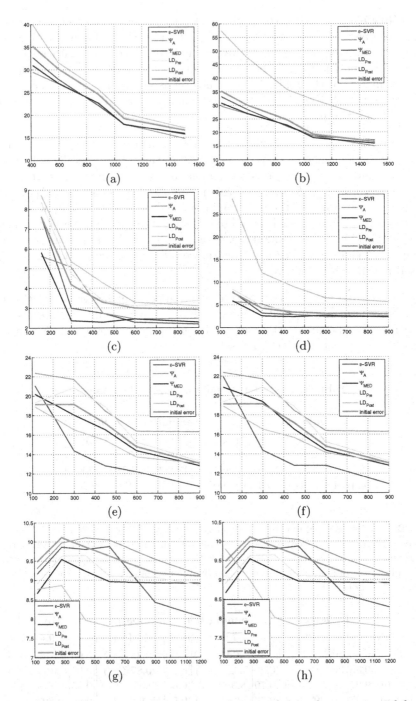

(a)

(b)

(c)

(d)

(e)

(f)

(g)

(h)

Fig. 2. Trends of error rate with respect to the size of the reference set used for the NN in case of *(a),(b) letter, (c),(d) pendigits, (e),(f) spam, (g),(h) thyroid* datasets. Curves in the left/right column are obtained using the BEST/END criterion.

Reliability threshold τ: for each reliability estimator we selected the value of the threshold τ that optimized the recognition performance when the reference set used by the NN is 2% of the whole dataset. Then, these optimal values were used for all the remaining experimentations.

We have considered four different datasets coming from the UCI Machine Learning Repository [1], i.e. *letter, pendigits, spam* and *thyroid*. Their characteristics are summarized in Table 1, where we have reported the number of the classes, of the features and of the samples within the whole dataset and those used for the test.

The results of the first experiment are reported in Table 2. Here, the error rates obtained by the NN after the self-training procedure using the different methods for reliability estimation on the considered datasets are reported together with the performance of the base classifier without semi-supervised training. The results refers to the case where the reference set used by the NN is 2% of the dataset (as in [9]). For each configuration of the self-training procedure and for each dataset the results shown in Table 2 represent the best performance with respect to the threshold τ defined in Section 2, whose optimal values are reported in the same Table.

The results in Table 2 clearly show that the use of the self-training procedure is beneficial on all the datasets: in all cases we observe the recognition rate increases with respect to the base NN. This observation, however, is not true if we consider each specific reliability estimator. For each estimator, in fact, there is at least a dataset where performance degrades.

In order to analyze how the performance of the NN classifier varies with the size of the training set when self-training with the different method for reliability estimation is adopted, we repeated the previous experiment by varying the size of the training set. The results, reported in Figure 2, are expressed in terms of the error rate and refer to the performance obtained using the BEST (left column) and the END (right column) criterion respectively.

As it can be expected, the error rates curves in Figure 2 decrease as the size of the training set increases. This behavior is still more evident for the ϵ-SVR (see Figures 2.f and 2.h) that benefits from the availability of more training samples to dramatically reduce its error rate. Another interesting element of discussion derives from the comparative analysis between the curves relative to the use of the BEST and the END criteria. In fact, at least for ϵ-SVR, ψ_A and ψ_{med}, in all cases the END criterion allows to perform as good as the BEST one. This can be explained by considering that the self-training procedure terminates after only few iterations (two or three).

5   Conclusions

In this paper we have assessed the impact of reliability evaluation on a semi-supervised learning approach, namely the self-training. The experimental analysis has been carried out on four publicly available datasets and was aimed at assessing the performance of five different reliability estimators. Even if the obtained results seem to confirm that self-training always (at least for the considered datasets) allows to increase the recognition rate with respect to the use of the base classifier, on the other side there is no reliability estimator that appears definitively the best. However, the behavior of the various methods when varying the size of the training dataset suggests that a simple definition of the reliability calculated using only the classifier output, as ψ_A or ψ_{med}, can be more adequate, while a trainable reliability estimator, as ϵ-SVR, can be preferred when the training set size tends to increase. The latter consideration seems to be particularly true when the number of classes is quite limited.

In this paper the robustness of the considered reliability estimators with respect to the reliability threshold τ has not been studied. It will be matter of further analysis in the future.

References

1. Blake, C., Keogh, E., Merz, C.J.: UCI Repository of machine learning databases. University of California, Department of Information and Computer Science, Irvine, CA, Irvine, CA (1998), http://www.ics.uci.edu/~mlearn/MLRepository.html
2. Chapelle, O., Zien, A., Schölkopf, B. (eds.): Semi-supervised learning. MIT Press, Cambridge (2006)
3. Cordella, L.P., Foggia, P., Sansone, C., Tortorella, F., Vento, M.: Reliability Parameters to Improve Combination Strategies in Multi-Expert Systems. Pattern Analysis and Applications 2(3), 205–214 (1999)
4. Didaci, L., Roli, F.: Using Co-training and Self-training in Semi-supervised Multiple Classifier Systems. In: Yeung, D.-Y., Kwok, J.T., Fred, A., Roli, F., de Ridder, D. (eds.) SSPR 2006 and SPR 2006. LNCS, vol. 4109, pp. 522–530. Springer, Heidelberg (2006)
5. Foggia, P., Percannella, G., Sansone, C., Vento, M.: Evaluating Classification Reliability for Combining Classifiers. In: Proceedings of the 14th International Conference on Image Analysis and Processing, Modena (IT), September 10-14, pp. 711–716 (2007)
6. Gargiulo, F., Mazzariello, C., Sansone, C.: A Self-training Approach for Automatically Labeling IP Traffic Traces. In: Kurzynski, M., Puchala, E., Wozniak, M., Zolnierek, A. (eds.) Computer Recognition Systems, vol. 2, pp. 705–717. Springer, Heidelberg (2008)
7. Giacinto, G., Roli, F.: Design of effective neural network ensembles for image classification purposes. Image Vision Computing 19(9-10), 699–707 (2001)
8. Woods, K., Kegelmeyer, W.P., Bowyer, K.W.: Combination of Multiple Classifiers Using Local Accuracy Estimates. IEEE Trans. Pattern Anal. Mach. Intell. 19(4), 405–410 (1997)
9. Kuncheva, L.I., Whitaker, C.J., Narasimhamurthy, A.: A case-study on naive labelling for the nearest mean and the linear discriminant classifiers. Pattern Recognition 41, 3010–3020 (2008)
10. Rosenberg, C., Hebert, M., Schneiderman, H.: Semi-supervised self-training of object detection models. In: Proceedings of the Seventh IEEE Workshop on Applications of Computer Vision, Breckenridge, USA, January 5-7 (2005)
11. Zhu, X.: Semi-supervised learning literature survey. Technical Report 1530, Computer Sciences, University of Wisconsin-Madison (2006)

On the Training Patterns Pruning for Optimum-Path Forest

João P. Papa and Alexandre X. Falcão

University of Campinas, Campinas SP 13083-970, Brazil
Institute of Computing, Visual Informatics Laboratory
{papa.joaopaulo,afalcao}@gmail.com

Abstract. The Optimum-Path Forest (OPF) classifier is a novel graph-based supervised pattern recognition technique that has been demonstrated to be superior to Artificial Neural Networks and similar to Support Vector Machines, but much faster. The OPF classifier reduces the problem of pattern recognition to a computation of an optimum-path forest in the feature space induced by a graph, creating discrete optimal partitions, which are optimum-path trees rooted by prototypes, i.e., key samples that will compete among themselves trying to conquer the remaining samples. Some applications, such that medical specialist systems for image-based diseases identification, need to be constantly re-trained with new instances (diagnostics) to achieve a better generalization of the problem, which requires large storage devices, due to the high number of generated data (millions of voxels). In that way, we present here a pruning algorithm for the OPF classifier that learns the most irrelevant samples and eliminate them from the training set, without compromising the classifier's accuracy.

1 Introduction

Recently, a novel approach for graph-based classifiers that reduces the pattern recognition problem as an optimum-path forest computation (OPF) in the feature space induced by a graph was presented [1]. The OPF does not interprets the classification task as a hyperplanes optimisation problem, but as a combinatorial optimum-path computation from some key samples (prototypes) to the remaining nodes. Each prototype becomes a root from its optimum-path tree and each node is classified according to its strongly connected prototype, that defines a discrete optimal partition (influence region) of the feature space. The OPF classifier has some advantages with respect to Artificial Neural Networks using Multilayer Perceptron (ANN-MLP) [2] and Support Vector Machines (SVM) [3]: (i) one of them is free of parameters, (ii) they do not assume any shape/separability of the feature space and (iii) run training phase faster. Notice that the OPF classifier has been extensively used for several purposes, including laryngeal pathology [4] and oropharyngeal dysphagia detection [5], fingerprint classification [6] and satellite-based rainfall estimation [7].

P. Foggia, C. Sansone, and M. Vento (Eds.): ICIAP 2009, LNCS 5716, pp. 259–268, 2009.
© Springer-Verlag Berlin Heidelberg 2009

Some specialist systems, such that image-based medical diagnosis systems, need to be constantly re-trained, allowing a better generalization performance. Parasitological systems, for instance, need to be regularly evaluated due to some diseases that occur in some periods of the year, in which we have a small amount of available information of such pathologies. The main problem of these systems is the limited storage capacity, which are extremely important in 3D datasets, such that in brain MRI (Magnetic Resonance Imaging) images. These images have millions of voxels to be stored, increasing the training set size exponentially, and have two main impacts: the large amount of information to be stored and the high computational effort for training classifiers. Despite of SVM good generalization capacity, its have a major drawback regarding its use in real applications: they are time consuming and demand a high computational burden. Artificial Neural Networks (ANN) are unstable classifiers, leading us to use collections of ANN [8] trying to improve their performance up to some unknown limit of classifiers, increasing their whole complexity.

The OPF classifier has been demonstrated to be similar and much faster than the aforementioned classifiers [1], which can be a very interesting approach in situations with large datasets. Based on this assumption, we propose here an OPF-based approach for training set pruning without compromising the classifier accuracy. A third evaluation set is used to identify the irrelevant training samples, which are further removed and the classifier re-trained with this reduced training set. The remainder of this paper is organized as follows: Sections 2 and 3 present, respectively, the OPF theory and its training set pruning algorithm. The experimental results are further discussed in 4 and the conclusions are stated in 5.

2   Optimum-Path Forest Classifier

Let Z_1, Z_2, and Z_3 be training, evaluation, and test sets with $|Z_1|$, $|Z_2|$, and $|Z_3|$ samples of a given dataset. We use samples as points, images, voxels, and contours in this paper. As already explained, this division of the dataset is necessary to validate the classifier and evaluate its learning capacity from the errors. Z_1 is used to project the classifier and Z_3 is used to measure its accuracy, being the labels of Z_3 kept unseen during the project. A pseudo-test on Z_2 is used to teach the classifier to identify the irrelevant samples of Z_1

Let $\lambda(s)$ be the function that assigns the correct label i, $i = 1, 2, \ldots, c$, of class i to any sample $s \in Z_1 \cup Z_2 \cup Z_3$, $S \subset Z_1$ be a set of prototypes from all classes, and v be an algorithm which extracts n features (color, shape, texture properties) from any sample $s \in Z_1 \cup Z_2 \cup Z_3$ and returns a vector $\boldsymbol{v}(s)$. The distance $d(s, t) \geq 0$ between two samples, s and t, is the one between their feature vectors $\boldsymbol{v}(s)$ and $\boldsymbol{v}(t)$. One can use any distance function suitable for the extracted features. The most common is the Euclidean norm $\|\boldsymbol{v}(t) - \boldsymbol{v}(s)\|$, but some image features require special distance algorithms [9]. A pair (v, d) then describes how the samples of a dataset are distributed in the feature space. Therefore, we call (v, d) a *descriptor* and the experiments in Section 4 use shape [10], texture [6] and color [11] descriptors based on this definition.

Our problem consists of projecting a classifier which can predict the correct label $\lambda(s)$ of any sample $s \in Z_3$. Training consists of finding a special set $S^* \subset Z_1$ of prototypes and a discrete optimal partition of Z_1 in the feature space (i.e., an optimum-path forest rooted in S^*). The classification of a sample $s \in Z_3$ (or $s \in Z_2$) is done by evaluating the optimum paths incrementally, as though it were part of the forest, and assigning to it the label of the most strongly connected prototype.

2.1   Training

Let (Z_1, A) be a complete graph whose nodes are the training samples and any pair of samples defines an arc in $A = Z_1 \times Z_1$. The arcs do not need to be stored and so the graph does not need to be explicitly represented. A path is a sequence of distinct samples $\pi_t = \langle s_1, s_2, \ldots, t \rangle$ with terminus at a sample t. A path is said *trivial* if $\pi_t = \langle t \rangle$. We assign to each path π_t a cost $f(\pi_t)$ given by a connectivity function f. A path π_t is said optimum if $f(\pi_t) \leq f(\tau_t)$ for any other path τ_t. We also denote by $\pi_s \cdot \langle s, t \rangle$ the concatenation of a path π_s and an arc (s, t). We will address the connectivity function $f_{\max}$.

$$f_{\max}(\langle s \rangle) = \begin{cases} 0 & \text{if } s \in S, \\ +\infty & \text{otherwise} \end{cases}$$
$$f_{\max}(\pi_s \cdot \langle s, t \rangle) = \max\{f_{\max}(\pi_s), d(s, t)\} \tag{1}$$

such that $f_{\max}(\pi_s \cdot \langle s, t \rangle)$ computes the maximum distance between adjacent samples along the path $\pi_s \cdot \langle s, t \rangle$. The minimization of $f_{\max}$ assigns to every sample $t \in Z_1$ an optimum path $P^*(t)$ from the set $S \subset Z_1$ of prototypes, whose minimum cost $C(t)$ is

$$C(t) = \min_{\forall \pi_t \in (Z_1, A)} \{f_{\max}(\pi_t)\}. \tag{2}$$

The minimization of $f_{\max}$ is computed by Algorithm 1, called OPF algorithm, which is an extension of the general image foresting transform (IFT) algorithm [12] from the image domain to the feature space, here specialized for $f_{\max}$. As explained in Section 1, this process assigns one optimum path from S to each training sample t in a non-decreasing order of minimum cost, such that the graph is partitioned into an optimum-path forest P (a function with no cycles which assigns to each $t \in Z_1 \backslash S$ its predecessor $P(t)$ in $P^*(t)$ or a marker *nil* when $t \in S$. The root $R(t) \in S$ of $P^*(t)$ can be obtained from $P(t)$ by following the predecessors backwards along the path, but its label is propagated during the algorithm by setting $L(t) \leftarrow \lambda(R(t))$.

Algorithm 1 – OPF Algorithm

INPUT: A training set Z_1, λ-labeled prototypes $S \subset Z_1$ and the pair (v, d) for
            feature vector and distance computations.
OUTPUT: Optimum-path forest P, cost map C and label map L.
AUXILIARY: Priority queue Q and cost variable cst.

1. *For each $s \in Z_1 \backslash S$, set $C(s) \leftarrow +\infty$.*
2. *For each $s \in S$, do*
3. $\quad$ └ $C(s) \leftarrow 0$, $P(s) \leftarrow nil$, $L(s) \leftarrow \lambda(s)$, *and insert s in Q.*
4. *While Q is not empty, do*
5. $\quad\mid\quad$ *Remove from Q a sample s such that $C(s)$ is minimum.*
6. $\quad\mid\quad$ *For each $t \in Z_1$ such that $t \neq s$ and $C(t) > C(s)$, do*
7. $\quad\mid\quad\mid\quad$ *Compute $cst \leftarrow \max\{C(s), d(s,t)\}$.*
8. $\quad\mid\quad\mid\quad$ *If $cst < C(t)$, then*
9. $\quad\mid\quad\mid\quad\mid\quad$ *If $C(t) \neq +\infty$, then remove t from Q.*
10. $\quad\mid\quad\mid\quad\mid\quad$ *$P(t) \leftarrow s$, $L(t) \leftarrow L(s)$ and $C(t) \leftarrow cst$.*
11. $\quad$ └ $\quad$ └ $\quad$ └ *Insert t in Q.*

Lines $1-3$ initialize maps and insert prototypes in Q. The main loop computes an optimum path from S to every sample s in a non-decreasing order of minimum cost (Lines $4-11$). At each iteration, a path of minimum cost $C(s)$ is obtained in P when we remove its last node s from Q (Line 5). Ties are broken in Q using first-in-first-out policy. That is, when two optimum paths reach an ambiguous sample s with the same minimum cost, s is assigned to the first path that reached it. Note that $C(t) > C(s)$ in Line 6 is false when t has been removed from Q and, therefore, $C(t) \neq +\infty$ in Line 9 is true only when $t \in Q$. Lines $8-11$ evaluate if the path that reaches an adjacent node t through s is cheaper than the current path with terminus t and update the position of t in Q, $C(t)$, $L(t)$ and $P(t)$ accordingly. One can use other *smooth* connectivity functions, as long as they group samples with similar properties [12].

We say that S^* is an optimum set of prototypes when Algorithm 1 minimizes the classification errors in Z_1. S^* can be found by exploiting the theoretical relation between minimum-spanning tree (MST) [13] and optimum-path tree for f_{max} [14]. By computing a MST in the complete graph (Z_1, A), we obtain a connected acyclic graph whose nodes are all samples of Z_1 and the arcs are undirected and weighted by the distances d between adjacent samples. The spanning tree is optimum in the sense that the sum of its arc weights is minimum as compared to any other spanning tree in the complete graph. In the MST, every pair of samples is connected by a single path which is optimum according to f_{max}. That is, the minimum-spanning tree contains one optimum-path tree for any selected root node.

The optimum prototypes are the closest elements of the MST with different labels in Z_1. By removing the arcs between different classes, their adjacent samples become prototypes in S^* and Algorithm 1 can compute an optimum-path forest in Z_1. Note that, a given class may be represented by multiple prototypes (i.e., optimum-path trees) and there must exist at least one prototype per class.

It is not difficult to see that the optimum paths between classes tend to pass through the same removed arcs of the minimum-spanning tree. The choice of prototypes as described above aims to block these passages, reducing the chances of samples in any given class be reached by optimum paths from prototypes of other classes.

2.2   Classification

For any sample $t \in Z_3$, we consider all arcs connecting t with samples $s \in Z_1$, as though t were part of the training graph. Considering all possible paths from S^* to t, we find the optimum path $P^*(t)$ from S^* and label t with the class $\lambda(R(t))$ of its most strongly connected prototype $R(t) \in S^*$. This path can be identified incrementally, by evaluating the optimum cost $C(t)$ as

$$C(t) = \min\{\max\{C(s), d(s,t)\}\}, \ \forall s \in Z_1. \tag{3}$$

Let the node $s^* \in Z_1$ be the one that satisfies Equation 3 (i.e., the predecessor $P(t)$ in the optimum path $P^*(t)$). Given that $L(s^*) = \lambda(R(t))$, the classification simply assigns $L(s^*)$ as the class of t. An error occurs when $L(s^*) \neq \lambda(t)$. Similar procedure is applied for samples in the evaluation set Z_2.

2.3   Accuracy Computation

The accuracies $\mathcal{L}(I)$, $I = 1, 2 \ldots, T$, are measured by taking into account that the classes may have different sizes in Z_3 (similar definition is applied for Z_2). If there are two classes, for example, with very different sizes and a classifier always assigns the label of the largest class, its accuracy will fall drastically due to the high error rate on the smallest class.

Let $NZ_2(i)$, $i = 1, 2, \ldots, c$, be the number of samples in Z_3 (similar procedure is applied to Z_2) from each class i. We define

$$e_{i,1} = \frac{FP(i)}{|Z_2| - |NZ_2(i)|} \quad \text{and} \quad e_{i,2} = \frac{FN(i)}{|NZ_2(i)|}, \ i = 1, \ldots, c \tag{4}$$

where $FP(i)$ and $FN(i)$ are the false positives and false negatives, respectively. That is, $FP(i)$ is the number of samples from other classes that were classified as being from the class i in Z_3, and $FN(i)$ is the number of samples from the class i that were incorrectly classified as being from other classes in Z_3. The errors $e_{i,1}$ and $e_{i,2}$ are used to define

$$E(i) = e_{i,1} + e_{i,2}, \tag{5}$$

where $E(i)$ is the partial sum error of class i. Finally, the accuracies $\mathcal{L}(I)$, $I = 1, 2 \ldots, T$, are written as

$$\mathcal{L}(I) = \frac{2c - \sum_{i=1}^{c} E(i)}{2c} = 1 - \frac{\sum_{i=1}^{c} E(i)}{2c}. \tag{6}$$

2.4   Complexity Analysis

The OPF algorithm, as aforementioned, can be divided in two phases: training and classification. In the training phase, essentially, we just need to compute the optimum prototypes (the closest samples in the MST) and after run the OPF algorithm (Algorithm 1). Let $|V_1|$ and $|E_1|$ be the number of samples (vertex) and the number of edges, respectively, in the training set represented by the complete graph (Z_1, A). We can compute the MST using the Prim's algorithm [13] with complexity $O(|E_1| \log |V_1|)$ and to find the the prototypes in $O(|V_1|)$.

The OPF algorithm (Algorithm 1) main (Line 4) and inner (Line 6) loops run in $O(|V_1|)$ times each one, because we have a complete graph. In this sense, the OPF algorithm runs in $O(|V_1|^2)$. The overall OPF training step complexity can be executed in $O(|E_1| \log |V_1|) + O(|V_1|) + O(|V_1|^2)$, which is dominated by $O(|V_1|^2)$.

The classification step can be done in $O(|Z_2| |V_1|)$, in which is $|Z_2|$ is the test set size. As aforementioned, a sample $t \in Z_2$ to be classified is connected to all samples in Z_1, and its optimum-path cost is evaluated. Since OPF classifier can be understood as a dynamic programming algorithm [13], we do not need to execute the OPF algorithm again in the test phase, because each node $s_i \in Z_1$, $i = 1, 2, \ldots, |Z_1|$ already has its optimum-path value stored. What we just need to do is to evaluate the paths from each node s_i until t. Finally, the overall estimated OPF complexity is $O(|V_1|^2) + O(|Z_2| |V_1|)$.

3 Pruning Algorithm

There are many situations that limit the size of Z_1: large datasets, limited computational resources, and high computational time as required by some approaches. Mainly in applications with large datasets, it would be interesting to select for Z_1 the most informative samples, such that the accuracy of the classifier is little affected by this size limitation. This section presents a pruning algorithm which uses a third evaluation set Z_2 to improve the composition of samples in Z_1 and reducing its size.

From an initial choice of Z_1 and Z_2, the algorithm projects an instance I of the OPF classifier from Z_1 and evaluates it on Z_2. As aforementioned in Section 2.2, we can identify the node $s^* \in Z_1$ that satisfies Equation 3. In that way, for each node $s^* \in Z_1$ that participated from some $t \in Z_2$ classification process, we mark them as relevant nodes and ate the final of evaluating Z_2, we remove the unmarked (irrelevant) samples and we re-trained the classifier. To ensure that this new instance of the trained classifier will be as most similar as possible to the initial instance (before pruning), we also mark the samples in $P^*(t)$), i.e., all samples from $P(t)$ until $R(t)$ (Section 2.2). The pruning algorithm is described below.

Algorithm 2 – OPF TRAINING PATTERNS PRUNING ALGORITHM

INPUT: Training and evaluation sets, Z_1 and Z_2, labeled by λ, and the pair
            (v, d) for feature vector and distance computations.
OUTPUT: The OPF pruned training set.
AUXILIARY: Arrays FP and FN of sizes c for false positives and false negatives
            and list LM of misclassified samples.

1. *Train OPF with Z_1.*
2. *For each sample $t \in Z_2$, do*

3.   *Use the classifier obtained in Line 1 to classify t with a label $L(t)$.*
4.   *While $P(t) \neq R(t)$*
5.   *Mark $P(t)$ as relevant*
6.   *$t \leftarrow P(t)$*
7.   *Mark $R(t)$ as relevant*
8.   *Remove the unmarked samples from Z_1*
9.   *Return the pruned training set Z_1*

Line 1 trains the OPF classifier using Algorithm 1. The main loop (Lines $2 - -7$) performs the classification step and the inner loop (Lines $4 - 6$) and Line 7 marks all nodes in $P^*(t)$. Lines $8 - 9$ remove the irrelevant samples and return the pruned training set Z_1.

Afterwards, by comparing the accuracies of the classifier on Z_3, before and after the pruning process, we can evaluate its reducing capacity without compromising its accuracy.

4 Experimental Results

We conducted two series of experiments: in the first one (Section 4.1) we evaluated the OPF algorithm against SVM and ANN-MLP in several public datasets using 50% for training and 50% for testing. These samples were randomly selected and each experiment was repeated 10 times with different sets Z_1 and Z_3 to compute mean (robustness) and standard deviation (precision) of the accuracy values. In the second round of experiments (Section 4.2), we evaluated the pruning algorithm capacity in reducing the training set size. The same datasets and similar procedure used as before was adopted: a training set Z_1 with 30% of the samples, an evaluation set Z_2 with 20% of the samples, and a test set Z_3 with 50% of the samples. These samples were randomly selected and each experiment was repeated 10 times with different sets Z_1, Z_2 and Z_3 to compute mean accuracy (robustness) and the mean pruning rate.

For SVM implementation, we use the latest version of the LibSVM package [15] with Radial Basis Function (RBF) kernel, parameter optimization and the one-versus-one strategy for the multi-class problem. The cross validation technique is used for selecting parameters that minimize the error rate in the training set. We use the Fast Artificial Neural Network Library(FANN) [16] to implement the ANN-MLP with learning by backpropagation algorithm. The network configuration is $x{:}y{:}z$, where $x = n$ (number of features), $y = |Z_1| - 1$ and $z = c$ (number of classes) are the number of neurons in the input, hidden and output layers, respectively. For OPF implementation we used the LibOPF package [17].

We used here six datasets with diverse types of samples. The dataset MPEG-7 [18] uses shape images and COREL [19] uses color images. These datasets allow to evaluate the performance of the classifiers using shape and color descriptors, respectively. The remaining datasets use the (x, y) coordinates of 2D points as features: Cone-Torus, Petals and Saturn [20]. For MPEG-7 dataset, we used two descriptors: FC (Fourier Coefficients) [21] and BAS (Beam Angle Statistics) [10]. For COREL dataset we used BIC descriptor [11].

4.1   Effectiveness of the Optimum-Path Forest Algorithm

We evaluated here the robustness the OPF classifier with respect to the SVM and ANN-MLP. Table 1 displays the results. We can see that OPF classifier outperformed SVM and ANN-MLP and all datasets, except for COREL-BIC. Some results show that OPF and SVM are similar if we consider the standard deviation.

Table 1. Mean accuracy results for different randomly generated training and test sets

Database	OPF	SVM	ANN-MLP
Cone-Torus	86.33%±0.1	78.41%±0.24	85.33%±2.21
Petals	100%±0.0	100%±0.0	100%±0.0
Saturn	82.88%±0.03	86.90%±0.05	83.60%±0.54
MPEG7-FC	71.71%±0.01	70.07%±0.01	57.28%±4.41
MPEG7-BAS	87.37%±1.21	87.05%±1.11	77.99%±3.41
COREL-BIC	86.88%±0.11%	90.65%±0.18	83.07%±1.41

4.2   Effectiveness of the Pruning Algorithm

We evaluated here the pruning algorithm capacity in reducing the training set size. Table 2 shows the results. We can see that we achieved good results with respect to the training set pruning rate. The MPEG-7 dataset was reduced up to 45% with its accuracy decreased up to 5%. The remaining datasets got lower compression rates, but their accuracies was decreased by only 1%-2%.

Table 2. Average pruning results for different randomly generated training, evaluating and test sets

Database	pruned Average	Accuracy before pruning	Accuracy after pruning
Cone-Torus	27.03%	86.33%	85.77%
Petals	17.06%	100%	98.88%
Saturn	32.00%	82.88%	76.22%
MPEG7-FC	48.09%	71.71%	65.66%
MPEG7-BAS	45.90%	87.37%	81.33%
COREL-BIC	39.12%	86.88%	85.11%

The most impressive results relie on the MPEG-7 dataset, which has 1400 samples distributed in 70 classes. The Corel dataset has 1603 colored images and its pruning rate was 39.12%. The lower pruning rate was achieved in the smallest dataset, Petals, which has only 100 samples.

5 Conclusions

We present here a novel training set pruning algorithm for OPF classifier, which is a new supervised approach for pattern recognition purposes that models the samples as nodes of a complete graph and tries to compute an collection of optimum-path trees (OPT) in this structure. Each OPT is rooted by its prototype, which offers optimum-path costs to the remaining nodes starting a competition process among all prototypes.

Some applications, such that automatic image-based diagnosis systems, need to be re-trained after some period to allow a better generalization performance. These kind of systems also suffer from the large amount of available data (3D MRI images), and the limited storage capacity of some devices is a problem that need to be considered. Based on this assumption, we proposed here an OPF pruning algorithm that can identify the training irrelevant samples using a third evaluation set, and further remove them from the training set. The results showed high pruning rates in some datasets (MPEG7-FC, MPEG77-BAS, COREL-BIC and Saturn). Currently, we are evaluating these results with respect to the computational effort (running time).

Acknowledgements

We would like to acknowledge the grants from projects BioCore (CNPq 550890/2007-6), CNPq 302617/2007-8 and FAPESP 07/52015-0.

References

1. Papa, J.P., Falcão, A.X., Suzuki, C.T.N., Mascarenhas, N.D.A.: A discrete approach for supervised pattern recognition. In: Brimkov, V.E., Barneva, R.P., Hauptman, H.A. (eds.) IWCIA 2008. LNCS, vol. 4958, pp. 136–147. Springer, Heidelberg (2008)
2. Haykin, S.: Neural networks: a comprehensive foundation. Prentice Hall, Englewood Cliffs (1994)
3. Boser, B.E., Guyon, I.M., Vapnik, V.N.: A training algorithm for optimal margin classifiers. In: Proceedings of the 5th Workshop on Computational Learning Theory, pp. 144–152. ACM Press, New York (1992)
4. Papa, J.P., Spadotto, A.A., Falcão, A.X., Pereira, J.C.: Optimum path forest classifier applied to laryngeal pathology detection. In: Proc. of the 15th Intl. Conf. on Systems, Signals, and Image Processing, vol. 1, pp. 249–252. IEEE, Los Alamitos (2008)
5. Spadotto, A.A., Pereira, J.C., Guido, R.C., Papa, J.P., Falcão, A.X., Gatto, A.R., Cola, P.C., Schelp, A.O.: Oropharyngeal dysphagia identification using wavelets and optimum path forest. In: Proc. of the 3rd IEEE Intl. Symp. on Communications, Control and Signal Processing, pp. 735–740 (2008)
6. Montoya-Zegarra, J.A., Papa, J.P., Leite, N.J., Torres, R.S., Falcão, A.X.: Learning how to extract rotation-invariant and scale-invariant features from texture images. EURASIP Journal on Advances in Signal Processing 2008, 1–16 (2008)

7. Freitas, G.M., Ávila, A.M.H., Pinto, H.S., Papa, J.P., Falcão, A.X.: Optimum-path forest-based models for rainfall estimation. In: Proceedings of the 14th IEEE Symposium on Computers and Communications (submitted, 2009)
8. Kuncheva, L.I.: Combining Pattern Classifiers: Methods and Algorithms. Wiley-Interscience, Hoboken (2004)
9. Wang, Y.P., Pavlidis, T.: Optimal correspondence of string subsequences. IEEE Transactions on Pattern Analysis and Machine Intelligence 12(11), 1080–1087 (1990)
10. Arica, N., Vural, F.T.Y.: BAS: A Perceptual Shape Descriptor Based on the Beam Angle Statistics. Pattern Recognition Letters 24(9-10), 1627–1639 (2003)
11. Stehling, R.O., Nascimento, M.A., Falcão, A.X.: A compact and efficient image retrieval approach based on border/interior pixel classification. In: Proceedings of the 11th International Conference on Information and Knowledge Management, pp. 102–109. ACM Press, New York (2002)
12. Falcão, A.X., Stolfi, J., Lotufo, R.A.: The image foresting transform: Theory, algorithms, and applications. IEEE Transactions on Pattern Analysis and Machine Intelligence 26(1), 19–29 (2004)
13. Cormen, T., Leiserson, C., Rivest, R.: Introduction to Algorithms. MIT, Cambridge (1990)
14. Rocha, A., Miranda, P.A.V., Falcão, A.X., Bergo, F.P.G.: Object delineation by κ-connected components. EURASIP Journal on Advances in Signal Processing 2008, 1–5 (2008)
15. Chang, C.C., Lin, C.J.: LIBSVM: A Library for Support Vector Machines (2001), http://www.csie.ntu.edu.tw/~cjlin/libsvm
16. Nissen, S.: Implementation of a Fast Artificial Neural Network Library (FANN), Department of Computer Science University of Copenhagen, DIKU (2003), http://leenissen.dk/fann/
17. Papa, J.P., Suzuki, C.T.N., Falcão, A.X.: LibOPF: A library for the design of optimum-path forest classifiers (2008), Software version 1.0, http://www.ic.unicamp.br/~afalcao/LibOPF
18. MPEG-7. Mpeg-7: The generic multimedia content description standard, part 1. IEEE MultiMedia 09(2), 78–87 (2002)
19. Corel Corporation. Corel stock photo images, http://www.corel.com
20. Kuncheva, L.: Artificial data. School of Informatics, University of Wales, Bangor (1996), http://www.informatics.bangor.ac.uk/~mas00a
21. Persoon, E., Fu, K.: Shape Discrimination Using Fourier Descriptors. IEEE Transanctions on Systems, Man, and Cybernetics 7(3), 170–178 (1977)

Learning Class Specific Graph Prototypes

Shengping Xia[1] and Edwin R. Hancock[2]

[1] ATR Lab, School of Electronic Science and Engineering,
National University of Defense Technology, Changsha, Hunan, P.R. China 410073
[2] Department of Computer Science, University of York, York YO10 5DD, UK

Abstract. This paper describes how to construct a graph prototype model from a large corpus of multi-view images using local invariant features. We commence by representing each image with a graph, which is constructed from a group of selected SIFT features. We then propose a new pairwise clustering method based on a graph matching similarity measure. The positive example graphs of a specific class accompanied with a set of negative example graphs are clustered into one or more clusters, which minimize an entropy function. Each cluster is simplified into a tree structure composed of a series of irreducible graphs, and for each of which a node co-occurrence probability matrix is obtained. Finally, a recognition oriented class specific graph prototype (CSGP) is automatically generated from the given graph set. Experiments are performed on over 50K training images spanning ~500 objects and over 20K test images of 68 objects. This demonstrates the scalability and recognition performance of our model.

1 Introduction

Local invariant feature based modeling from multi-view images has become a popular approach to object recognition. Lowe [9] presents a method for combining multi-views of a 3D object into a single model representation using so called SIFT (scale invariant feature transform) features [10]. Rothganger et al. demonstrate how to acquire true 3D affine and Euclidean models from multiple unregistered images, and perform recognition from arbitrary viewpoints [12]. Ferrari et al. present an approach, which includes a mechanism for capturing the relationships between multiple model views, and use the model to effect simultaneous object recognition and image segmentation [6]. Todorovic and Ahuja demonstrate the completely unsupervised extraction and learning of a visual category that occurs frequently in a given set of images [15]. This body of work has demonstrated impressive levels of performance and provide arguably the most successful paradigm for object recognition [4]. Recently, the methods for modeling and recognition have been extended to large image databases. For instance, Nister and Stewenius perform real-time object specific recognition using a database of 40,000 images [11] while Torralba et al. [16] have considered how to scale the methods to the internet.

P. Foggia, C. Sansone, and M. Vento (Eds.): ICIAP 2009, LNCS 5716, pp. 269–277, 2009.
© Springer-Verlag Berlin Heidelberg 2009

A limitation of these models is that only small variations in object viewpoint can be accommodated. A more significant limitation is the large number of parameters required and the assumptions imposed (such as the Gaussian nature of the data) which may not apply in practice [8][14]. To avoid these shortcomings, our goal is to derive a canonical model of visual category or class which is totally data driven and does not rely on limiting model assumptions.

One way to overcome these problems is to work with view-clusters and in this way deal with large variations in viewpoint [6][9][12]. For instance Lowe [9] clusters together training images from similar viewpoints into single model views. Each view cluster consists of the complete set of SIFT features extracted from the training views, along with a record of the location, orientation, and scale for each feature within that view. Object models can be incrementally updated and refined as recognition is performed. However, since the view clusters contain the union of the detected SIFT features encountered in the relevant set of training data, two potential pitfalls are encountered. The first of these is that the view-clusters contain an unmanageably large number of feature points. The second problem is that many of the feature points are not salient, and this gives rise to matching ambiguities or errors. Additional problems that remain to be solved are a) how to select the model views and b) how many views suffice. Our method can automatically select an irreducible set of image views, and then merge the information contained within the redundant image views into the most similar model views using a feature co-occurrence probability matrix.

Since the contents of each image can be captured using structured data in the form of SIFT features, attributed graphs provide a versatile and expressive representational tool [2]. There have been previous efforts aimed at generating a prototype graph from a set of training examples. For example, Crandall and Huttenlocher [3] use a graphical structure referred to as k-fans to model geometric constraints based on a statistical model. Here a Gaussian distribution is used to represent geometric relationships between the parts of an object. Jiang, Munger and Bunke [7] use a genetic search algorithm to learn a median graph from a training set. Torsello and Hancock [17] have constructed the class-prototype through tree-union and have performed clustering using a mixture of tree-unions controlled by a description length criterion. These ideas are taken further by Escolano and Lozano [1] who extended the methodology from trees to graphs, and used an EM algorithm for clustering. However, these approaches also only deal with a small range of views. Here we extend the methodology by developing a simple information criterion for learning the prototypes.

We commence by representing each image, or each region of interest in an image, with a graph which is constructed from a group of selected local invariant features. Using graphs alone, it is difficult to construct models from images containing large variations in viewpoint based on only one central prototype. Hence we turn to graph prototypes as a means of representing object models. Specifically, we aim to construct class specific prototype-graph (CSGP) for object recognition. A CSGP model is automatically generated from an arbitrary set of images of the relevant objects under significant or complex variations in imaging conditions. In a CSGP object model, a group of irreducible object views are selected by minimizing an information theoretic entropy criterion defined on a given training set. Each irreducible graph can be regarded as a central prototype used to seed an object model. The information contained in those graphs that are not selected as prototypes for model construction, and referred to as redundant graphs, is combined with the most similar prototype using node co-occurrence probabilities.

In previous work we have shown how the salient features required to construct such a representation can be extracted from images, and detail the representation of class prototypes [18,19]. The novel contribution of the current work is to show how the representation may be optimised with respect to both representational capacity and performance. The paper is organized as follows. In Section 2, we introduce some preliminaries, including how SIFT features are ranked, and present a pairwise graph matching method and the associated similarity measure required to merge graphs. In Section 3, we present the method used to learn CSGP models. We present experimental results in Section 4 and conclude the paper in Section 5.

2   Preliminaries

For an image, those SIFT [10] features that are robustly matched with the SIFT features in similar images can be regarded as salient representative features. Motivated by this, a method for ranking SIFT features has been proposed in [21]. Using this method, the SIFT features of an image $\mathcal{I}$ are ranked in descending order according to a matching frequency. We select the $\mathcal{T}$ best ranked SIFT features, denoted as $\mathcal{V}=\{V^t, t = 1, 2, ..., \mathcal{T}\}$, where $V^t = ((\overrightarrow{X}^t)^T, (\overrightarrow{D}^t)^T, (\overrightarrow{U}^t)^T)^T$. Here, $\overrightarrow{X}^t$ is the location, $\overrightarrow{D}^t$ is the direction vector and $\overrightarrow{U}^t$ is the set of descriptors of a SIFT feature. In our experiments, $\mathcal{T}$ is set to 40. If there are less than this number of feature points present then all available SIFT features in an image are selected. We then represent the selected SIFT features in each image using an attributed graph.

Formally, an attributed graph G [3] is a 2-tuple $G = (V, E)$, where V is the set of vertices, $E \subseteq V \times V$ is the set of edges. For each image, we construct a Delaunay graph G using the coordinates of the selected SIFT features. In this way, we can obtain a set of graphs $\mathbb{G} = \{G_l, l = 1, 2, ..., N\}$ from a set of images.

We perform pairwise graph matching (PGM) with the aim of finding a maximum common subgraph (MCS) between two graphs G_l and G_q, and the result is denoted as $MCS(G_l, G_q)$. In general, this problem has been proven to be NP-hard. Here we use a Procrustes alignment procedure [13] to align the feature points and remove those features that do not satisfy the spatial arrangement constraints.

Suppose that X_l and X_q are respectively the position coordinates of the selected features in graphs G_l and G_q. We can construct a matrix

$$Z = \arg\min \|X_l \cdot \Omega \cdot X_q\|_F, \ subject \ to \ \Omega^T \cdot \Omega = I. \tag{1}$$

where $\| \bullet \|_F$ denotes the Frobenius norm. The norm is minimized by the nearest orthogonal matrix

$$Z^* = \Psi \cdot \Upsilon^*, \; subject\; to \; X_l^T \cdot X_q = \Psi \cdot \Sigma \cdot \Upsilon^*. \tag{2}$$

where $\Psi \cdot \Sigma \cdot \Upsilon^*$ is the singular value decomposition of matrix $X_l^T \cdot X_q$. The goodness-of-fit criterion is the root-mean-squared error, denoted as $e(X_l, X_q)$. The best case is $e(X_l, X_q) = 0$. The error e can be used as a measure of geometric similarity between the two groups of points. If we discard one pair of points from X_l and X_q, denoted as $X_{l\to i}$ and $X_{q\to i}$, $e(X_{l\to i}, X_{q\to i})$, $i = 1, 2, ..., \|CS(G_l, G_q)\|$ can be obtained, where $CS(G_l, G_q)\|$ is the number of SIFT features between two graphs initially matched using the matching proposed in [18,19]. The maximum decrease of $e(X_{l\to i}, X_{q\to i})$ is defined as

$$\Delta e(\|CS(G_l, G_q)\|) = e(X_l, X_q) - \min\{e(X_{l\to i}, X_{q\to i})\} \tag{3}$$

if $\Delta e(\|CS(G_l, G_q)\|)/e(X_l, X_q) > \epsilon$, e.g. $\epsilon = 0.1$, the corresponding pair X_l^i and X_q^i is discarded as a mismatched feature pair. This leave-one-out procedure can proceed iteratively, and is referred as the iterative Procrustes matching of G_l and G_q.

Given $MCS(G_l, G_q)$ obtained by the above PGM procedure, we construct a similarity measure between the graphs G_l and G_q as follows:

$$R(G_l, G_q) = \|MCS(G_l, G_q)\| \times (\exp(- e(X_l, X_q)))^\kappa. \tag{4}$$

where $\|MCS(G_l, G_q)\|$ is the cardinality of the MCS of G_l and G_q, κ is the number of mismatched feature pairs discarded by iterative Procrustes matching, which is used to amplify the influence of the geometric dissimilarity between X_l and X_q.

We use the similarity measure to define a *Positive Matching Graph* (PMG) using the test

$$P(G_l, G_q) = \begin{cases} 1 & R(G_l, G_q) \geq R_{\tau 1} \\ 0 & else \end{cases} \tag{5}$$

where $R_{\tau 1}$ is a threshold on the similarity measure. If $P(G_l, G_q) = 1$, the two graphs G_l and G_q are called a PMG pair.

Finally, for the graph set $\mathbb{G} = \{G_q, q = 1, 2, ..., N\}$, for each graph $G_l \in \mathbb{G}$, and the remaining graphs in the set ($\forall G_q \in \mathbb{G}$), we obtain the pairwise graph similarity measures $R(G_l, G_q)$ defined in Equation (4). Using the similarity measures we rank in descending order all graphs G_q. The K top ranked graphs are defined as the K-nearest neighbor graphs (KNNG) of graph G_l, denoted as $\mathbb{K}\{G_l\}$.

3   Class Specific Graph Protypes

In this Section, we commence by showing how to construct an initial class specific graph prototype (CSGP). We then describe how to simplify such a CSGP model to obtain a compact model which suffice to capture structural variations from multiple views of objects of a particular class.

3.1   Construction of Initial CSGP

A Class Specific Graph Prototype (CSGP) is defined as 2-tuple $CSGP = (PV, PE)$, where 1) the prototype vertex $PV = \{ G_l, l = 1, 2, ..., N \}$ is a finite set of graphs forming the nodes of the CSGP; 2) the prototype-edge PE is the edge set of the CSGP. There is an edge between two nodes G_l and G_q, denoted by $Edge(G_l, G_q)$, if and only if $P(G_l, G_q) = 1$.

For efficiency, we use an incremental clustering tree-RSOM proposed in [20] for incrementally learning large corpus of SIFT descriptors and obtaining $K_\tau\{G_l\}$.

3.2   Learning a CSGP Model

Optimal Pairwise Clustering of CSGP. Suppose an initial CSGP model has been trained from a batch of images. In the CSGP model, the relationships of the graphs $K_\tau\{G_l\}$ have been encoded and will be updated with additional graphs. The number of the items in $K_\tau\{G_l\}$ is largely influenced by the threshold R_τ. We wish to obtain a compact representation from the initial CSGP. To this end we provide two basic definitions.

The siblings of G_l are defined as:

$$S\{G_l\} = \{G_q \in K_\tau\{G_l\} \mid P(G_l, G_q) = 1\} \triangleq S_{R_\tau}\{G_l\}. \tag{6}$$

For each graph $G_q \in S\{G_l\}$, the corresponding siblings can also be obtained. In this way, we can iteratively obtain a series of graphs which all satisfy consistent sibling relationships. The graph set, obtained in this way, is called a family tree of graph G_l.

Given a CSGP model, a Family Tree of a Graph (FTOG) of G_l with k generations and denoted as $F\{G_l, k\}$, is defined as:

$$F\{G_l, k\} = F\{G_l, k - 1\} \bigcup_{G_q \in F\{G_l, k-1\}} S_{R_\tau}\{G_q\}. \tag{7}$$

where, if $k - 1$, $F\{G_l, 1\} = F\{G_l, 0\} \bigcup S\{G_l\}$ and $F\{G_l, 0\} = \{G_l\}$; and the process stops when $F\{G_l, k\} = F\{G_l, k + 1\}$. An FTOG, whose graphs satisfy the restriction defined in Equation (6), is a sub-set of graphs in a CSGP model and can be regarded as a cluster of graphs. We refer to this process as pairwise clustering.

Consider a CSGP model, $\forall R_\tau, \exists G_{l_i}, i = 1, 2, ..., c$, subject to $F\{G_{l_i}, g\} \bigcap F\{G_{l_j}, g\} = \emptyset, i \neq j, i, j \in \{1, 2, ..., c \}$. We uniquely label these FTOG's as $L_1, L_2, ..., L_c$ and denote the cluster set as follows:

$$C_{R_\tau} = \{ F_{R_\tau}\{G_l, \infty\}\} \triangleq \{ F_l \mid l \in \{L_1, L_2, ..., L_c\} \}. \tag{8}$$

Clearly, the clustering result is influenced by threshold R_τ. Hence, we present a learning approach to obtain the optimal value of R_τ for a given CSGP model.

We can regard the above clustering process as a classification problem which gives rise to four possible outcomes, i.e a) true positive, b) false negative, c) true negative and d) false positive. The number of instances corresponding to the above four cases are separately denoted as $|TP|$, $|FN|$, $|TN|$ and $|FP|$. Accordingly a confusion matrix can be constructed representing the dispositions of the set of instances. This matrix forms the basis for computing many common performance measures [5], such as precision (p), recall (r) and the F-measure (f).

We denote the positive graph set as g^+, and the negative graph set g^-. We only consider those FTOGs generated from those graphs which belong to g^+. Suppose that $TP = |C_{R_\tau}\{g^+\}|$, $FP = |g^- \cap C_{R_\tau}\{g^+\}|$ and $|P| = |g^+|$. We define the precision, recall and the F-measure as $p\{R_\tau \mid g^+, g^-\} = TP/(TP + FP)$, $r\{R_\tau \mid g^+, g^-\} = TP/P$ and $f\{R_\tau \mid g^+, g^-\} = \frac{2}{1/p + 1/r}$. We define an entropy on $C_{R_\tau}\{g^+\}$ as follows.

$$E\{C_{R_\tau}\} = -\sum_{l=1}^{L_{N_c}}\{p_l \cdot \log p_l\} \quad where \quad p_l = \frac{\|F_l\|}{\sum_{l=1}^{L_{N_c}}\|F_l\|}, l = 1, 2, ..., L_c. \quad (9)$$

We wish to find the optimal threshold $R_{\tau_1} = \max\{\arg\min_{R_\tau} E\{C_{R_\tau}\}\}$ such that $f\{R_\tau \mid g^+, g^-\} > 1 - \varepsilon$, where the threshold ε is is heuristically set to 0.02 in our experiments. The smaller $E\{C_{R_{\tau_1}}\}$, the better. If $E\{C_{R_{\tau_1}}\} = 0$, then all the graphs in g^+ are clustered into a single FTOG, and the corresponding F-measure is greater than $1 - \varepsilon$. The optimal cluster membership is such that $C_{R_{\tau_1}}\{g^+\} \triangleq \{ F_l \mid l \in \{L_1, L_2, ..., L_c\}\}$.

In the above process, with the decrease of threshold R_τ, then $f\{R_\tau \mid g^+, g^-\}$ may decrease significantly. Namely, if $\exists G_q \in g^+$ and R_τ, subject to:

$$\lim_{\nabla R_\tau \to 0} \frac{\nabla f\{R_\tau \mid g^+, g^-\}}{\nabla R_\tau} \to \infty. \quad (10)$$

4   Experimental Results and Discussions

We have collected 53536 images as a training data set which spans more than 500 objects, including some human faces and scenes. From the training data we have obtained an RSOM clustering tree with 25334 leaf nodes using the method described in [20]. The method was implemented using Matlab 7.2 and run on a 2.14GHz computer with 2G RAM. In the incrementally training process, we have obtained $K_\tau\{G_l\}$ for each of the graphs. Following this, we individually train the CSGP models for the above 68 labeled object classes using the method presented in Section 3.2. For training a single specific object, the positive graphs are those of the desired class and all remaining graphs, labeled or unlabeled, are regarded as the negative set. This method is also adopted for recognition test.

The training process is incrementally carried out commencing from the first batch of 3600 graphs of A to all 50K graphs. For each object, the minimized entropy, and its accompanying F-measure and similarity threshold have been learned. As a second training stage, the similarity threshold for selecting irreducible graphs, the number and percentage of irreducible graphs are also learned. These parameters are part of the generated CSGP model and will be used for recognition and incremental training.

As distinct from most object recognition methods, where many implementation parameters can be varied, our method individually generate optimized models for each concerned object from given training data-sets.

Using the trained model, the F-measures of recognition test for Object 1 to Object 68 are shown in Table 1. It is interesting to note that the test recognition performance of Object B1 to B8 is very close to that obtained in [12] when only SIFT features are used (corresponding to the 8 objects marked magenta in Table 1. However, our results are obtained with large negative sample sets.

Table 1. F-measure f for given test set of Object 1~68

ID	f	ID	f	ID	f	ID	f	ID	f	ID	f	ID	f	ID	f	ID	f	ID	f
1	.996	2	.955	3	1.0	4	.983	5	1.0	6	1.0	7	1.0	8	.989	9	1.	10	1.0
11	.985	12	1.0	13	.987	14	1.0	15	1.0	16	1.0	17	1.0	18	.984	19	.979	20	1.0
21	.985	22	1.0	23	1.	24	1.0	25	1.0	26	1.0	27	.995	28	1.0	29	1.	30	1.0
31	1.0	32	1.0	33	.992	34	1.0	35	1.0	36	1.0	37	1.0	38	.993	39	.979	40	1.0
41	1.0	42	0.989	43	1.0	44	.995	45	.941	46	1.0	47	1.0	48	1.0	49	1.0	50	.988
51	.625	52	1.0	53	1.0	54	1.0	55	.714	56	1.0	57	.953	58	1.0	59	.992	60	.998
51	.625	52	1.0	53	1.0	54	1.0	55	.714	56	1.0	57	1.0	58	1.0				
61	.992	62	.997	63	.993	64	.983	65	.991	66	.989	67	.994	68	1.0				

The recognition result is largely determined by the training samples. Figure 1 (Left) shows how the F-measure is influenced by training samples for object C10. As a trend, the F-measure increases with the number of training samples. In our model, the F-measure is determined by the irreducible graphs. For objects A1 to A50, the average number of irreducible graphs are about 30% of the initial number of graphs. This means that 1 in 3 of the initial graphs are selected. This verifies the conclusion that an initial model view can be used to match and identify views of the object over a range of rotations of at least 20 degrees in any direction [9]. As an example, the F-measure of object B1 is low. The reasons include 1) B1 is an apple who lacks suitable texture; 2) Several of the test samples are largely occluded; 3) Both the test set (11 samples) and the training set (29 samples) are too small. Hence, for objects B1 to B8, the minimum number of graphs is only 16 and the maximum number of graphs is only 29, while the view variation is very large. Hence basically all graphs are irreducible. If the training and test graphs are obtained under similar imaging conditions (including the camera viewpoint), though the training set is small, we might still obtain good test result. If not, the F-measure tends to be low as shown in Figure 1 (Left).

For objects with complex appearance, we need a large training sample set. For each of the objects in C1 to C9, the number of irreducible graphs is comparatively large. However, for an increasing number of graphs, the number of new irreducible graphs, incrementally learned using our method, will decrease. As an example, only about 5% of the graphs are selected as irreducible graphs for object C10, shown in Figure 1 (Right). Using the redundant graphs, the node co-occurrence probability can be determined and used to locate the the most typical representative sub-graph (i.e. the median) of each irreducible graph. Hence each irreducible graph acts as a central prototype and a test graph, coming from the i.i.d. of an irreducible graph, is likely to be correctly recognized.

For a trained model $CSGP_k$ of object k, we define $\max_{G_q \in CSGP_k} R(G_l, G_q)$ as the similarity of a graph instance G_l to that model. For the above test set, as an example, the probability distribution (histogram) of the similarity of the positive set (the magenta part) and the negative set (the blue part) for object C10 are shown in Figure 1 (Right). This clearly illustrates the distinctiveness between negative and positive instances using our generated CSGP model. Hence we obtain high recognition performance for Object 68, as shown in Table 1.

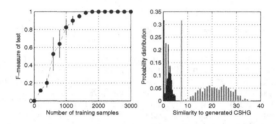

Fig. 1. Test result of object C10. F-measure of recognition test varies with the number of training samples is shown in the left sub-figure. For each number, we randomly select 10 different combinations and obtain the corresponding F-measures. The average of these F-measures is marked as '•', and the standard deviation of F-measure is marked as a vertical magenta line. Similarity distributions of negative and positive test set are shown in right sub-figure. The green line corresponds to the learned threshold R_{τ_1} of object C10.

5   Conclusion

This paper describes a framework for generating structural models from a large corpus of multi-view images. Our model is a comprehensive integration of the global and local information contained in local features from different views. The model is totally data driven. Using our method the precision of recognition can always be kept high while the recall can be improved with incremental training. Directions for future work include exploring the use of the method for image indexing and annotation. The most significant limitation of our approach is that it is best suited for objects that have some texture, much like the other local invariant feature of appearance based recognition schemes [6][12]. Hence we will combine some contour or edge based local invariant feature extractors for further research. We leave such problems as future work.

References

1. Bonev, B., Escolano, F., Lozano, M.A., Suau, P., Cazorla, M.A., Aguilar, W.: Constellations and the unsupervised learning of graphs. GbRPR 14(1), 340–350 (2007)
2. Chung, F.: Spectral graph theory. American Mathematical Society, Providence (1997)

3. Crandall, D.J., Huttenlocher, D.P.: Weakly supervised learning of part-based spatial models for visual object recognition. In: Leonardis, A., Bischof, H., Pinz, A. (eds.) ECCV 2006. LNCS, vol. 3951, pp. 16–29. Springer, Heidelberg (2006)
4. Everingham, M., Gool, L.V., Williams, C., Winn, J., Zisserman, A.: Overview and results of classification challenge, 2007. In: The PASCAL VOC 2007 Challenge Workshop, in conj. with ICCV (2007)
5. Fawcett, T.: Roc graphs: Notes and practical considerations for researchers (2004), http://citeseer.ist.psu.edu/fawcett04roc.html
6. Ferrari, V., Tuytelaara, T., Van-Gool, L.: Simultaneous object recognition and segmentation from single or multiple model views. IJCV 67(2), 159–188 (2006)
7. Jiang, X., Munger, A., Bunke, H.: On median graphs: properties, algorithms, and applications. PAMI 23(10), 1144–1151 (2001)
8. Li, F.F., Perona, P.: A bayesian hierarchical model for learning natural scene categories. CVPR 2(2), 524–531 (2005)
9. Lowe, D.: Local feature view clustering for 3d object recognition. CVPR 2(1), 1682–1688 (2001)
10. Lowe, D.: Distinctive image features from scale-invariant key points. IJCV 60(2), 91–110 (2004)
11. Nister, D., Stewenius, H.: Scalable recognition with a vocabulary tree. CVPR 2(2), 2161–2168 (2006)
12. Rothganger, F., Lazebnik, S., Schmid, C., Ponce, J.: 3d object modeling and recognition using local affine-invariant image descriptors and multi-view spatial constraints. IJCV 66(3), 231–259 (2006)
13. Schonemann, P.: A generalized solution of the orthogonal procrustes problem. Psychometrika 31(3), 1–10 (1966)
14. Sivic, J., Russell, B.C., Efros, A.A., Zisserman, A., Freeman, W.T.: Discovering objects and their location in images. ICCV 1(1), 872–877 (2005)
15. Todorovic, S., Ahuja, N.: Unsupervised category modeling, recognition and segmentation in images. PAMI (in press)
16. Torralba, A., Fergus, R., Weiss, Y.: Small codes and large image databases for recognition. In: CVPR (2008)
17. Torsello, A., Hancock, E.: Learning shape-classes using a mixture of tree-unions. PAMI 28(6), 954–967 (2006)
18. Xia, S., Hancock, E.R.: 3d object recognition using hyper-graphs and ranked local invariant features. In: da Vitoria Lobo, N., Kasparis, T., Roli, F., Kwok, J.T., Georgiopoulos, M., Anagnostopoulos, G.C., Loog, M. (eds.) S+SSPR 2008. LNCS, vol. 5342, pp. 117–126. Springer, Heidelberg (2008)
19. Xia, S., Hancock, E.R.: Clustering using class specific hyper graphs. In: da Vitoria Lobo, N., Kasparis, T., Roli, F., Kwok, J.T., Georgiopoulos, M., Anagnostopoulos, G.C., Loog, M. (eds.) S+SSPR 2008. LNCS, vol. 5342, pp. 318–328. Springer, Heidelberg (2008)
20. Xia, S.P., Liu, J.J., Yuan, Z.T., Yu, H., Zhang, L.F., Yu, W.X.: Cluster-computer based incremental and distributed rsom data-clustering. ACTA Electronica sinica 35(3), 385–391 (2007)
21. Xia, S.P., Ren, P., Hancock, E.R.: Ranking the local invariant features for the robust visual saliencies. In: ICPR 2008 (2008)

Tree Covering within a Graph Kernel Framework for Shape Classification

François-Xavier Dupé* and Luc Brun

GREYC UMR CNRS 6072,
ENSICAEN-Université de Caen Basse-Normandie,
14050 Caen France
{francois-xavier.dupe,luc.brun}@greyc.ensicaen.fr

Abstract. Shape classification using graphs and skeletons usually involves edition processes in order to reduce the influence of structural noise. On the other hand, graph kernels provide a rich framework in which many classification algorithm may be applied on graphs. However, edit distances cannot be readily used within the kernel machine framework as they generally lead to indefinite kernels. In this paper, we propose a graph kernel based on bags of paths and edit operations which remains positive definite according to the bags. The robustness of this kernel is based on a selection of the paths according to their relevance in the graph. Several experiments prove the efficiency of this approach compared to alternative kernel.

Keywords: Shape, Skeleton, Graph Kernel, Kernel Machines.

1 Introduction

Shape matching is a challenging problem in computer vision with many applications: indexing, classification, clustering... Many frameworks have been developed based on different point of views. Two types of methods can be distinguished: *model-based* methods [1] where each shape is compared to models or prototypes and *shape-based* methods where shapes are compared one to one. These last methods, are often based on the skeletons [2,3].

Usually, skeletons are transformed into graphs, translating the shape matching problem into the more general graph matching problem. Different works have been developed in order to tackle this last problem. For example Siddiqi [4] extracts shock graphs from shapes and uses a greedy algorithm for the comparison task. Pelillo [5] transforms graphs into trees and models the problem as a maximal clique problem. Goh [3] splits graphs into linear parts using heuristics and then directly compares their features. These methods operate directly inside the graph space which lacks many common mathematical tools.

One way to avoid this issue is to map graphs into a richer space. This is the purpose of graph kernels whose development is growing with the great interest

---

* This work is performed in close collaboration with the laboratory Cycéron and is supported by the CNRS and the région Basse-Normandie.

P. Foggia, C. Sansone, and M. Vento (Eds.): ICIAP 2009, LNCS 5716, pp. 278–287, 2009.

in kernel machines for the last ten years. The most famous graph kernels are the random walk kernel [6], the marginalized graph kernel [6] and the geometric kernel [6]. As the skeletonization process is not continuous, two graphs representing similar shapes can show severe structural differences. Since the above graph kernels implicitly reduce graphs comparison into paths comparison, graph perturbations modify the paths and thus lead to an inaccurate comparison.

Neuhaus and Bunke have proposed several kernels [7,8] based on the graph edit distance in order to reduce the influence of graph perturbations. However the graph edit distance does not usually fulfills all the properties of a metric and the design of a positive definite kernel from such a distance requires some precaution. Our approach is slightly different. Indeed, instead of considering a direct edit distance between graphs, our kernel is based on a rewriting process applied independently on some paths of the two graphs. Such a rewriting scheme is introduced within a more general graph kernel framework based on bags of paths.

Suard [9] introduced a new graph kernel framework based on an explicit encoding of bags of paths. This framework offers 3 degrees of liberty for the design of a graph kernel: 1) construction scheme of the bag of paths of a graph, 2) definition of a kernel between bags of paths and 3) definition of a kernel between paths. The contribution of this paper lies in two of these three points: we propose 1) a new algorithm for the construction of the bag of path based on an edge-covering algorithm and 2) a new bag of paths kernel based on the mean kernel. This bag of path kernel is combined with the edition path kernel first introduced in [10] and latter extended in [11].

This paper is structured as follows: first we present our graph construction scheme from a skeleton (Section 2). Then, a construction algorithm for bag of paths based on a tree-covering algorithm is proposed and analysed from a shape point of view (Section 3). Following that, we propose a new bag of paths kernel based on the mean kernel (Section 4). Then, we rapidly present the edition path kernel [10,11] which is based on a hierarchical comparison of paths. Finally, the performances of the resulting graph kernel are measured through experiments in Section 6.

2   Skeleton-Based Graph

The skeleton of a shape is usually constructed from the medial axis which is defined as the centers of the circles of maximal radius [2]. Many graphs may be associated to the skeleton of a shape. Our graph construction scheme follows the approach proposed by Siddiqi [4]. It considers the enriched translation of the skeleton structure to a graph structure: the terminal points, the junction points and any point encoding an important change of slope of the radius function along the medial axis define the nodes of the graph. The edges of the graph correspond to skeleton's branches between two nodes. The slopes can be obtained using regression methods based on first order splines [11,12]. Finally, for the sake of simplicity, we consider the maximal spanning tree of such graphs. Note that, as skeletonization is an homotopic transform, a shape with no hole leads directly to a tree.

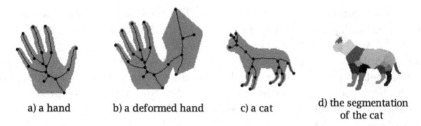

a) a hand   b) a deformed hand   c) a cat   d) the segmentation
                                                              of the cat

Fig. 1. Three examples of skeletons with their inflexion points

Fig. 1 shows three shapes with their inflexion points. The detection of these inflexion points may slightly vary according to the parameter of the regression method used to detect them. Such a variability of the graph should be compensated by the flexibility of our graph kernel.

The graph associated to a shape only provides information about its structural properties. Additional geometrical properties of the shape must be encoded using node and edge attributes in order to keep most of the shape properties. From a structural point of view, a node represents a particular point inside the shape skeleton and an edge a skeleton's branch. However, a branch also represents the set of points which are closer to the branch than any other branch. This set of points is defined as the *influence zone* of the branch and can be computed using a SKIZ transform [13] (Fig. 1d).

We have selected a set of attributes which provides a good approximation of the description of the shape. Torsello [14] proposes as edge attribute an approximation of the perimeter of the boundary which contributes to the formation of the edge, normalized by the approximated perimeter of the whole shape. This feature presents the double advantage of being additive and of encoding the relevance of edges inside graphs. Suard [15] proposes as node attribute the distance between the node position and the gravity center of the shape divided by the square of the shape area.

Two descriptors describing a branch of the skeleton and the evolution of the radius of the maximal circle along it are also considered. For each point $(x(t), y(t))$ of a branch, $t \in [0, 1]$, we consider the radius $R(t)$ of its maximal circle. In order to normalize the data, the radius is divided by the square root of the area of the influence zone of the branch. We also introduce $\alpha(t)$, the angle formed by the tangent vector at $(x(t), y(t))$ and the x-axis. Then the two considered descriptors are $(a_k)_{k \in \mathbb{N}}$ and $(b_k)_{k \in \mathbb{N}}$ the coefficients of two regression polynomials that fit respectively $R(t)$ and $\alpha(t)$ in the least square sense. If both polynomials are of sufficient orders, the skeleton can be reconstructed from the graph and so the shape. A more in depth analysis of this construction scheme of the graph may be found in [11].

Within Suard [9] framework, the comparison of 2 graphs requires to build their associated bags of paths. The construction of such bags remains problematic, if we want to keep the link between the graph and the represented shape. In the next section, we propose a method based on this link between the structure of the graph and its semantics.

3   Covering the Graph

The heuristic used to build a bag of paths from a graph constitutes a major step in the design of a graph kernel within the explicit bag of path framework. Paths extracted from a graph describe skeleton parts of the shape. So if a bag of paths contains all the paths of a graph (or all the paths up to a fixed length), it will describe several times the same part of the shape. This redundancy may be inaccurate since it artificially enforces the importance of some parts of the shape.

This last remark tends to prove that selecting paths for the bag opens a door to a more efficient comparison. One example of selection process is to keep only a fixed percentage of the paths amongst the weightier, however such a scheme induces a loss of some parts of the shape, since many edges may not be present inside such a bag of paths.

A proper solution would be to cut the shape into several parts and to consider only one path for each part. From a graph point of view, this algorithm is related to the tree covering [16] problem. More precisely, we would like to have the minimal sub-set of heaviest paths from a given set of paths which covers the set of edges of the graph. It is equivalent to the edge covering problem using a given set of paths with the constraints of minimal cardinality and maximum weight. Such a problem is NP-hard even for trees [16].

The exact algorithm proposed by Guo [16] is based on dynamic programming and computes the whole set of covering solutions from a given set of paths. This algorithm computes a vertex covering, but can be easily converted into an edge covering algorithm. We rapidly present the principle of this method: first, the authors root the tree using an arbitrary node and then apply an ascendant algorithm. At each step, a node is considered with all the paths which cover it, then for each combination of paths, the weight of the covering of the sub-tree rooted on the node is computed using information from children. The algorithm finishes at the root node and the result is given by taking only the solution of maximal weight (using a top-down approach). The final complexity of the algorithm is $\mathcal{O}(2^C C |V|)$ where $|V|$ is the number of vertices and C the maximal number of paths covering one node. The edge-covering version of this algorithm is built by 1) considering at each node the paths which cover the node and its parent and 2) adding a fictive path which links the root node to a fictive node, this fictive node does not appear in the covering but its presence is needed for the computation of the final covering.

Though the complexity of the algorithm is exponential according to the measure of redundancy C, the optimal solution is computable in reasonable time using a proper choice of the initial set of paths. In order to avoid the complexity issue, we use a simple heuristic in order to reduce the redundancy while constructing the input set of paths: first, we compute all the paths up to a fixed length (Fig. 2a), then the redundant paths with the smallest weight are removed until C is lower than a given threshold (Fig. 2b). By redundant paths, we mean paths which can be removed without breaking the covering clause i.e. all edges

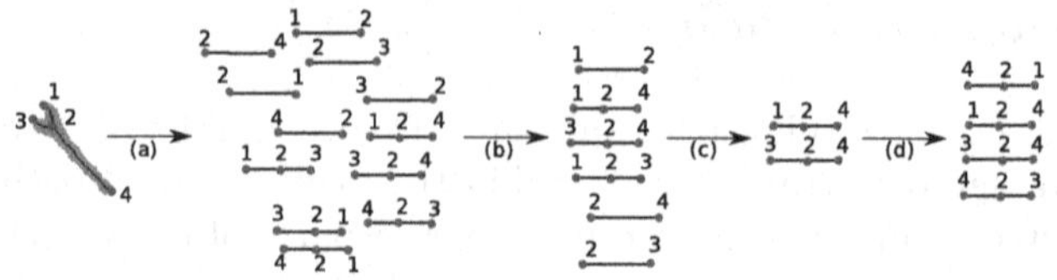

Fig. 2. Computation of the tree covering by paths: (a) Extraction of paths, (b) Reduction of redundancy, (c) Edge-covering, (d) Addition of the symmetric of the paths

must remain covered by at least one path. Finally, we run the covering algorithm on this last set of paths which produces the final bag of paths covering the whole graph (Fig. 2c).

For the sake of completeness, the symmetric of each path belonging to the bag is added to it (Fig. 2d). The symmetric of a path is the path which has the inverse route, i.e. the inverse of the path 124 is 421. Note, that the resulting bag of paths offers a complete representation of the shape as no edge is forgotten. The next section considers the construction of a bag of paths kernels.

4   Bag of Paths Kernel

Let us consider a graph $G = (V, E)$ where V denotes the set of vertices and $E \subset V \times V$ the set of edges. Let us additionally consider a bag of paths P associated to G, we denote by $|P|$ the number of paths inside P. We suppose that a positive definite path kernel, denoted K_{path}, is available.

By considering two bags of paths P_1, associated to a graph G_1 and P_2, associated to a graph G_2, as sets, we construct a bag of paths kernel by averaging the path kernel [15,9,10] results between all couples of paths from each bag:

$$K_{mean}(P_1, P_2) = \frac{1}{|P_1|} \frac{1}{|P_2|} \sum_{h \in P_1} \sum_{h' \in P_2} K_{path}(h, h'). \tag{1}$$

This kernel defines a positive definite kernel in the bag of paths domain [17]. However if the bags contain lots of paths, the kernel tends to average the information and so looses its efficiency. If the data follow a Gaussian law, a one-class SVM can be used to estimate the characteristics of the law. This leads to a kernel [10] based on the angle between the mean vectors which reduces the two bags of paths to their main characteristic, but is hence only positive semi-definite on the bags of paths.

We propose to control the average effect of the mean kernel by enforcing the weight of the paths near the mean path. This trick assumes that the distribution of the paths inside the bag almost follows a Gaussian law. Our kernel is thus constructed from the mean kernel with two additional control terms: first, we weight the paths by their relevance inside the graphs and second, we weight the paths by their distance to the center of their sets. These two weights lead to the following kernel:

$$K_{weighted}(P_1, P_2) = \frac{1}{|P_1|}\frac{1}{|P_2|}\sum_{h \in P_1}\sum_{h' \in P_2} <K_{path}(h, m), K_{path}(h', m')>^d \tag{2}$$
$$\frac{\omega(h)}{W}\frac{\omega(h')}{W'}K_{path}(h, h').$$

where $d \in \mathbb{R}^+$, m and m' denote the mean paths of P_1 and P_2, $\omega(h)$ (resp. $\omega(h')$) denotes the sum of the edge's weights of h (resp. h') and W (resp. W') the whole weight of the graph containing h (resp. h'). The value of the path kernel between a path and the mean path of its bag P is defined as: $K_{path}(h, w) = \frac{1}{|P|}\sum_{h_i \in P} K_{path}(h, h_i)$. The kernel $K_{weighted}$ is positive definite [17] and so defines a metric between bags of paths.

We directly use this last kernel, as graph kernel i.e. $K(G_1, G_2) = K_{weighted}(P_1, P_2)$ where P_1 (resp. P_2) is the bag of paths associated to G_1 (resp. G_2). Obviously, this graph kernel is only positive semi-definite as two similar bags of paths can be defined from two different graphs. However, the positive semi-definitiveness is not a real issue since shape graphs are closely characterized by their features attributed to edges and nodes. So equality between two bags of paths would mean that the two shapes share many common sub-parts and are therefore almost similar.

5   Hierarchical Kernel

Bags of paths kernel are built upon a path kernel. This kernel can be viewed as a similarity measure for paths. Kashima [18] proposes the following path kernel:

$$K_{path}(h, h') = K_v(\varphi(v_1), \varphi(v_1'))\prod_{i=2}^{|h|}K_e(\psi(e_{v_{i-1}v_i}), \psi(e_{v_{i-1}'v_i'}))K_v(\varphi(v_i), \varphi(v_i')), \tag{3}$$

where $\varphi(v)$ and $\psi(e)$ denote respectively the vectors of features associated to the node v and the edge e and K_v and K_e denote respectively vertices and edges kernels. This kernel is positive definite, if K_v and K_e are positive definite. Edges and vertices kernels are usually built using Gaussian radial basis kernel on the difference of feature vectors.

However, since graphs are constructed from shape skeletons, they are sensitive to shape perturbations. On complex shapes, severe shape modifications may lead to inaccurate comparison while working on paths. In order, to deal with this problem, we introduce an edit process inside the path kernel.

From a path point of view, the perturbation result in additional nodes and edges. Using this observation, we construct two elementary operations on paths: *node suppression* and *edge contraction*. The edit process is described in [11] and briefly recalled bellow for completeness.

Each edition corresponds to a deformation of the shape. Fig. 3 shows the effect of each edition operation on a simple shape (Fig. 3a): the suppression of a node

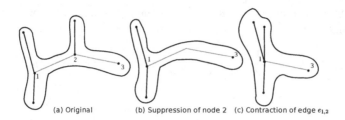

(a) Original   (b) Suppression of node 2   (c) Contraction of edge $e_{1,2}$

Fig. 3. Effect of the edit process

results in the partial loss of the shape (Fig. 3b) and the contraction of an edge results in the contraction of the shape (Fig. 3c). As these operations change the shape, all the attributes are updated using the new shape information. Finally, we construct a path kernel by comparing paths and their rewritings.

5.1   Edition Path Kernel

Let us denote by κ the function which applies the cheapest operation on a path [10,11] and D the maximal number of reductions. The successive applications of the function κ associates to each path h a sequence of reduced paths $(h, \kappa(h), \ldots, \kappa^D(h))$. A cost $cost_k(h)$ is associated to each reduced path $\kappa^k(h)$. This cost is defined as the sum of the costs of the k operations needed to obtain $\kappa^k(h)$ [11].

Using K_{path} as path kernel, the idea is to construct another path kernel with a control on the edition process. The kernel K_{edit} is defined as a sum of kernels between reduced paths thus leading to a hierarchical comparison of paths. Given two paths h and h', the kernel $K_{edit}(h, h')$ is thus defined as:

$$K_{edit}(h, h') = \frac{1}{D+1} \sum_{k=0}^{D} \sum_{l=0}^{D} \exp\left(-\frac{cost_k(h)+cost_l(h')}{2\sigma_{cost}^2}\right) K_{path}(\kappa^k(h), \kappa^l(h')), \quad (4)$$

where σ_{cost} is a tuning variable.

This kernel is composed of two parts: a scalar product of the edition costs in a particular space and a path kernel. For a small value of σ_{cost} the behavior of the kernel will be close to K_{path} as only low edition costs will contribute to the sum. For a high value every editions will contribute with an approximately equal importance. This kernel is positive definite on the domain of paths as it is a kernel between the hierarchies of paths (see [17,11] for more details).

6   Results

We perform in the following two experiments which compare the performances of 1) the mean kernels with the random walk kernel and 2) kernels based on different kind of bags of paths. For all these experiments, we used the following RBF coefficients (Section 2): for the perimeter: $\sigma_{perimeter} = 0.1$, for the distance of the coefficients of the order 2 polynomials describing the radius evolution: $\sigma_{radius} = 5.0$,

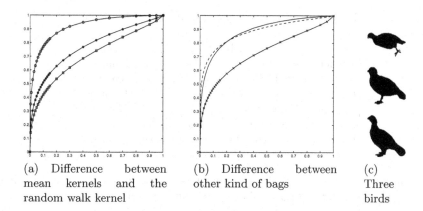

(a) Difference between mean kernels and the random walk kernel

(b) Difference between other kind of bags

(c) Three birds

Fig. 4. ROC curves: (a) using K_w (the curve with circles) and K_{unw} (the curve with squares) compared to the random walk kernel (the curves with the stars), (b) using K_w with all the paths (the curve with crosses), with only one percent of the heaviest paths (the solid curve) and only ten percent of the heaviest path (the dashed curve). (c) The three birds of the training set.

for the distance between the coefficients of the order 5 polynomials describing the orientation evolution: $\sigma_{orientation} = 2000$ and for the distance to the gravity center: $\sigma_{gravity\ center} = 0.5$. Each of these values have been set in order to provide the best results on average through several experiments. Concerning parameter used by several kernels, the best value of a coefficient for a particular kernel was also the best value for the remaining kernels. This last result may be explained by the fact that all the kernels share the same path kernel.

When building the different bags of paths, we only consider paths up to a length of three edges. For the edition process, we perform up to 3 editions on each paths [11] and fix the coefficient of the kernel over the edition cost as $\sigma_{cost} = 0.5$ (Eq. (4)). The weighted mean kernel is built using $K_{weighted}$ with $d = 5$ and is denoted by K_w and the unweighted mean kernel is built using $K_{weighted}$ with $d = 0$ and is denoted by K_{unw}.

For the following two experiments, we use the 216 shapes of the LEMS database [19] and consider the one-class classification of birds against all the shapes of this database. This classification is performed using the kernel PCA approach proposed by Hoffmann [20] and the results are used to built the ROC curves. The training set contains only three birds (Fig. 4c). The classification times for the different kernels are given in Tab 1.

6.1 Experiment I: Difference between the Mean Kernels and Random Walk Kernel

Fig. 4a shows the ROC curves obtained using the random walk kernel and the K_w and K_{unw} kernels combined with the covering algorithm for the construction of the bag of paths. K_{unw} shows the worst performance as the information is lost by the average. The random walk kernel shows an improvement compared

Table 1. Classification times: training and prediction

Kernel	Times
Random walk	12min40
K_{unw} combined with covering algorithm	3min50
K_w combined with covering algorithm	6min40
K_w using all the paths	153min50
K_w using 1 percent of the heaviest paths	10s
K_w using 10 percent of the heaviest paths	3min40

to the latter kernel, however since it considers all the walks of the graphs, it is sensitive to the structural noise. The best result is provided by K_w, as expected the average drawbacks are attenuated by the weighting.

6.2 Experiment II: Bag of Paths Kernels

Fig. 4b shows the ROC curves obtained using different bags of paths: one with all the paths, one with only 1 percent of the heaviest paths and the last one with 10 percent of the paths. All these bags of paths have been used with the weighted mean kernel K_w. The results prove that considering all the paths is not the best idea and the resulting kernel performs like K_{unw} combined with the covering algorithm, but requires more times to classify (Tab. 1). Using one percent of the heaviest paths or ten percent lead to similar results. This last result proves that most of the information is hold by the heaviest paths, however using the covering algorithm leads to better results as the description of shapes is more complete.

7 Conclusion

In this paper, we have defined a graph kernel based on an edition process and a selection of paths. Since the whole shape is covered by a set of paths with a minimal redundancy, the covering algorithm leads to accurate comparisons. Our results prove that removing redundancy inside the bag of paths leads to more efficient and faster kernel. In the future, we would like to improve the bag of paths kernel using more specialized set kernels.

References

1. Pope, A.R.: Model-based object recognition: A survey of recent research. Technical Report TR-94-04, University of British Columbia (1994)
2. Siddiqi, K., Bouix, S., Tannenbaum, A., Zucker, S.W.: Hamilton-jacobi skeletons. International Journal of Computer Vision 48(3), 215–231 (2002)
3. Goh, W.B.: Strategies for shape matching using skeletons. Computer Vision and Image Understanding 110, 326–345 (2008)

4. Siddiqi, K., Shokoufandeh, A., Dickinson, S.J., Zucker, S.W.: Shock graphs and shape matching. Int. J. Comput. Vision 35(1), 13–32 (1999)
5. Pelillo, M., Siddiqi, K., Zucker, S.: Matching hierarchical structures using association graphs. IEEE Trans. on PAMI 21(11), 1105–1120 (1999)
6. Vishwanathan, S., Borgwardt, K.M., Kondor, I.R., Schraudolph, N.N.: Graph kernels. Journal of Machine Learning Research 9, 1–37 (2008)
7. Neuhaus, M., Bunke, H.: Edit distance based kernel functions for structural pattern classification. Pattern Recognition 39, 1852–1863 (2006)
8. Neuhaus, M., Bunke, H.: Bridging the Gap Between Graph Edit Distance and Kernel Machines. World Scientific, Singapore (2007)
9. Suard, F., Rakotomamonjy, A., Bensrhair, A.: Kernel on bag of paths for measuring similarity of shapes. In: Proceedings of ESANN 2007, 15th European Symposium on Artificial Neural Networks, Bruges, Belgium, April 25-27, 2007, pp. 355–360 (2007)
10. Dupé, F.X., Brun, L.: Hierarchical bag of paths for kernel based shape classification. In: da Vitoria Lobo, N., Kasparis, T., Roli, F., Kwok, J.T., Georgiopoulos, M., Anagnostopoulos, G.C., Loog, M. (eds.) S+SSPR 2008. LNCS, vol. 5342, pp. 227–236. Springer, Heidelberg (2008)
11. Dupé, F.X., Brun, L.: Edition within a graph kernel framework for shape recognition. In: Torsello, A., Escolano, F., Brun, L. (eds.) GBR, pp. 11–20. Springer, Heidelberg (2009)
12. DiMatteo, I., Genovese, C., Kass, R.: Bayesian curve fitting with free-knot splines. Biometrika 88, 1055–1071 (2001)
13. Meyer, F.: Topographic distance and watershed lines. Signal Proc. 38(1) (1994)
14. Torsello, A., Hancock, E.R.: A skeletal measure of 2d shape similarity. CVIU 95, 1–29 (2004)
15. Suard, F., Rakotomamonjy, A., Bensrhair, A.: Mining shock graphs with kernels. Technical report, LITIS (2006),
    http://hal.archives-ouvertes.fr/hal-00121988/en/
16. Guo, J., Niedermeier, R., Uhlmann, J.: Two fixed-parameter algorithms for vertex covering by paths on trees. Information Processing Letters 106, 81–86 (2008)
17. Haussler, D.: Convolution kernels on discrete structures. Technical Report UCSC-CRL-99-10, Department of Computer Science, University of California at Santa Cruz (1999)
18. Kashima, H., Tsuda, K., Inokuchi, A.: Marginalized kernel between labeled graphs. In: Proc. of the Twentieth International conference on machine Learning, pp. 321–328 (2003)
19. LEMS: shapes databases, http://www.lems.brown.edu/vision/software/
20. Hoffmann, H.: Kernel PCA for novelty detection. Pattern Recognition 40, 863–874 (2007)

Vision-Based Markerless Gaming Interface

Pietro Azzari and Luigi Di Stefano

ARCES - DEIS, University of Bologna,
viale Risorgimento 2, 40125 Bologna, Italy
pazzari@unibo.it
http://www.vision.deis.unibo.it/

Abstract. The paper proposes a novel human machine interface for gaming applications based on computer vision. The key idea is to allow the user to interact with the game by simply moving a hand-held consumer grade camera. Detection of natural features in the incoming video stream avoids instrumenting the scene with optical markers while preserving real-time computation and accuracy. The paper presents also a prototype videogame developed as proof-of-concept of our camera-based gaming interface. Thanks to recent advances in real-time extraction and matching of natural features from images on mobile platforms, our proposal holds the potential to enable a new generation of camera-controlled videogames for hand-held mobile devices.

Keywords: human-machine interfaces, camera pose estimation, videogames, keypoint matching.

1 Introduction

The ever increasing pervasiveness of computer systems into our everyday environment calls for novel mechanisms of human-computer interaction. Interfaces to computerized equipment need to be straightforward and effective, the ability to interact using inexpensive tools being highly regarded.

In the last decades, keyboard and mouse have become the main interfaces for transferring information and commands to computerized equipment. In some applications involving 3D information, such as visualization, computer games and control of robots, other interfaces based on remote controller [16], joysticks and wands can improve the communication capabilities despite being sometimes impractical or limited.

Wearable and handheld devices, such as datagloves, "backpacks" [3] and haptics, are designed to be more user friendly, helping untrained users in performing complex tasks. On the other hand, the high cost and cumbersome hardware limit the field of usability of these solutions.

In daily life, however, vision and hearing are the main channels through which humans gather information about their surroundings. Therefore, the design of new interfaces that allow computerized equipment to communicate with humans by understanding visual and auditive input may conjugate effectiveness, naturalness and affordable prices.

P. Foggia, C. Sansone, and M. Vento (Eds.): ICIAP 2009, LNCS 5716, pp. 288–296, 2009.

Vision based interfaces hold the potential to communicate with computerized equipment at a distance and the machine can be taught to recognize and react to human-like feedbacks. Despite many advances have been recently reached in the field of human gesture, motion and behaviour understanding [10,20,11], engineers have been mostly focusing on marker-based tracking systems for human-computer interaction applications. The gaming industry is recently showing a deep interest in vision based interfaces, with many proof of concepts developed so far [7,21,2,17]. As a matter of fact visual markers can be reliably tracked [5] at low computational costs, nonetheless game boards or game controllers must be instrumented with them.

Conversely, this paper presents a novel vision-based gaming interface able to deliver position and orientation of the player by simply using a hand-held consumer grade camera and without requiring any visual marker. The proposed approach is straightforward since the movement of the camera directly translates into 3D commands to the game and requires no instrumentation of the environment. It is also very effective since camera pose is estimated with millimetric precision. Finally it is cheap since it relies on widely available low-cost cameras.

2   Related Work

Recent works in literature show that, to some extent, human behaviour understanding using imaging devices is attainable. Harville and al. [10] conceived a robust algorithm for 3D person tracking and activity recognition. The work by Viola and Jones [20] paved the way for sound automatic face detection. Isard and al. [11] demonstrated reliable tracking of deformable objects in presence of occlusion and cluttered environments. These outstanding achievements have inspired the works of Lu [15,14] on vision-based game interfaces controlled respectively by head and hands movements. Head, face and body position tracking for computer games was also successfully demonstrated in the work of Freeman et al. [6]. However, despite being very flexible and natural interfaces from a human perspective, the underlying technology is still too computational intensive to guarantee short latency time and smooth operations. Moreover precise handling and maneuvering tasks demand a detection and reconstruction accuracy that, in some cases, current algorithms may not deliver.

Tracking of optical markers has rapidly emerged as a fast and accurate alternative for conveying simplified information to computer systems. Although complex human behaviours cannot be captured, location and orientation information can be robustly retrieved in a wide variety of environmental conditions and at low computational cost. Examples of videogames built on top of optical marker trackers have been growing steadily in recent years. Cho et al. [2] described an augmented reality shoot-em-up game in which players aim at virtual opponents rendered on a game board filled with optical markers. Oda et al. [17] developed a racing game where users steer their virtual cars using controllers stuck with markers monitored with cameras. Govil and al. [7] designed a marker-based golf ball tracker used to set speed and direction of a virtual ball in a golf simulator.

By exploiting implementation of a markers tracker for portable devices, Wagner and colleagues [21] developed an Augmented Reality (AR) game where multiple players are allowed to interact using camera-equipped PDA devices.

Nonetheless, recent advances in the field of object recognition showed that accurate pose estimation and tracking can be achieved without the need of specific visual markers, but instead using keypoints extracted from textured areas [13]. In particular, the SURF (Speeded Up Robust Features) algorithm [1] reconciled accuracy and low computational cost for robust keypoints extraction and tracking.

In this paper we originally propose to deploy a camera pose estimation approach based on natural keypoints correspondences as a human-machine interface for gaming purposes. It is worth pointing out that camera pose estimation using natural keypoints on mobile phones has been recently demonstrated by Wagner et al. [22]. Hence, our proposal holds the potential for development of new camera-controlled gaming applications for hand-held mobile devices such as phones and PDAs. In the remainder of the paper we describe the camera pose estimation algorithm in terms of its key components and present a prototype videogame, dubbed Black Hole, developed so far as proof-of-concept of our proposed approach.

3   Markerless Pose Estimation

The interface consists essentially of an automatic camera pose estimation algorithm for scenes in which flat objects are present, therefore limiting the types of suitable scenes. In this case, however, the limitation is slight, since the requirements is that a plane be visible, even if partially occluded, in the scene. This is common in indoor environments, where a textured ceiling or ground plane is usually visible. Outdoors, even rough ground (grass, roads or pavements), provides also an acceptable reference for the system.

The pose recovery algorithm is largely inspired by the camera tracker illustrated by Simon et al. [19], for it delivers accurate estimation at low computational cost. However, differently from the original formulation, pose recovery is performed every time with respect to a reference frame (pose detection) instead of arising from the composition of multiple pairwise registration (pose tracking) among subsequent frames. Hence, pose detection tolerates failures since each frame is processed independently; besides it does not suffer from the dead reckoning issue typical of pairwise composition. On the other hand, pose detection requires a reference object to be known beforehand, i.e. the object with respect to which the pose is continuously computed. Moreover, pose jittering may arise since temporal correlation is usually not reinforced. In the rest of this section the solutions to these two problems are addressed and described.

Using natural keypoints instead of markers makes the instrumentation of the scene not needed anymore since any flat object can be a suitable reference. Just before starting a gaming session a brand new natural reference can be learnt on-the-fly by simply taking a snapshot of a textured planar object and extracting a vector of keypoints descriptors. The corresponding points of the reference keypoint set are searched within every new incoming frame and pairs of matching keypoints are likely to be detected even in case of large pose and illuminations changes, as shown in Fig. 1. Incorrect keypoints pairs can be easily detected and discarded using a RANSAC-based homography estimation step [9]. The remaining correspondences are fed to the pose estimation algorithm described in [19] in order to obtain a reliable estimation of the position and orientation of the camera with respect to the reference object.

Fig. 1. Tracking SURF keypoints in few snapshots taken from different viewpoints: correct (green) and incorrect (red) corresponding pairs

The way the pose is obtained is depicted in Fig. 2; keypoints m_i, located on the camera imaging sensor (bottom left plane), are in one-to-one correspondence with points M_i standing on a flat reference object (upper right plane). It can be assumed, without loss of generality, that the reference object lays on the $z = 0$ plane of the world coordinate frame, so that 2D points M_i can be augmented with a third null coordinate. The set of corresponding 2D-3D points (m_i, M_i), of which $\tilde{m}, \tilde{M}$ are just the homogeneous notations, are related by projective equations involving the internal camera matrix A, the rotation matrix R and the translation vector t

$$s\tilde{m} = A\,[Rt]\,\tilde{M} \tag{1}$$

Both R and t can be retrieved up to a scalar value s, by means of the method described in [19], provided that enough corresponding pairs (m_i, M_i) are available and the camera is internally calibrated.

Independent pose estimation computed at every frame exhibit an excellent accuracy with camera position usually estimated in the range of few millimeters from the true one. Nonetheless, since this approach does not exploit the temporal continuity of the camera trajectory, the sequence of estimated poses usually exhibit jitter effects. This problem manifests as small vibrations among

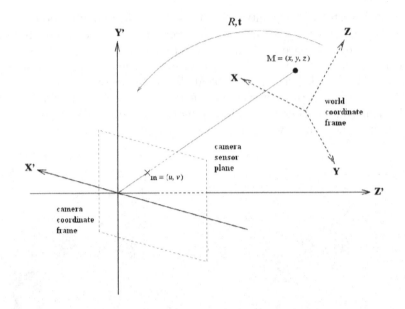

Fig. 2. Geometry of pose estimation from 2D-3D correspondences problem

subsequent estimations, such discontinuities being quite noticeable by a human observer and tending to degrade the gaming experience. In order to mitigate this effect a pose smoothing technique has been adopted. The developed approach, described in [18], consists in linking every new pose with those computed during a previous time window by exploiting a Support Vector Regression scheme as a temporal regularization term.

Natural keypoints correspondences and pose smoothing make the conceived pose estimation algorithm fast, robust and practical, thus providing accurate and jitter-free estimations without the need for fiducial markers placed all across the scene.

4   Game Sessions

A prototype videogames has been developed using as interface the vision-based pose estimation algorithm described previously. In addition, we integrated few third-party libraries for a number of specialized tasks, in particular:

- OpenGL (Open Graphics Library) [8], a portable and interactive 2D and 3D graphics library adopted for fast visualization and rendering.
- OpenCV (Open Computer Vision) [4], a collection of computer vision functions used for video capturing, keypoints detection and numerical optimization.
- Tokamak [12], an open-source real-time physics engine used for accurate simulation of dynamics of rigid body, gravity, friction ans so on.

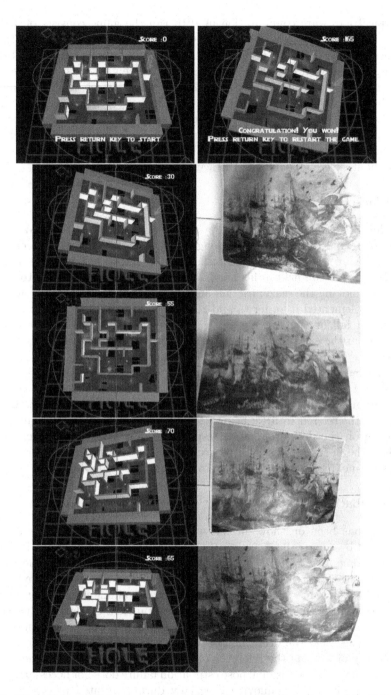

Fig. 3. Black Hole starting screen (top left) and game ending (top right). Below the snapshots depict the floating maze (left) tilting and panning according to the orientation of the camera with respect to the reference object (right).

The typical hardware configuration used to run the game consists of a single laptop pc powered by an Intel Core 2 CPU, equipped with 4 GB RAM and running Windows XP. The used video camera is a Logitech QuickCam Sphere grabbing color sequences at 640×480 resolution. The game has been developed in C++ using Microsoft Visual Studio 2005. Using this setting the frame rate ranges between 6 and 10 frames per second (FPS), keypoints extraction being the major bottleneck of the system. Although quite far from real-time processing, the system is responsive enough to allow for a satisfactory gaming experience. By reducing the camera resolution to 320×240 the frame rate increase to 9 - 15 FPS without severely penalizing the accuracy.

4.1   Black Hole

Black Hole is a puzzle game inspired by the dark atmosphere of Star Wars. The goal is to steer a R2D2-like ball through a Death Star maze till the endpoint avoiding the holes spread along the path. The user can slant and rotate the maze by moving a webcam held in his hand. Gravity effect allows the user to control the ball by moving the maze; friction and collision against maze walls and floor are also implemented in order to add realism. Every time the user loses a ball by letting it fall in a hole it obtains a number of points commensurate to the distance from the starting point. After three lost balls the game ends and the final score is the sum of the points obtained thus far.

Fig. 3 shows the starting and ending screens of Black Hole together with some screenshots taken during a gaming session. The Figure includes also the images coming from the webcam hand-held by the player in correspondence of each screenshot, the reference object being a textured picture printed on a paper sheet and laying on the desktop. The corresponding pairs screenshot-camera image show how the floating maze is tilted according to the instantaneous orientation of the hand-held camera with respect to the reference object.

4.2   Feedback and Observations

The game has been on show for few weeks in our laboratory rooms and has been played by some colleagues from other labs that gently provided feedbacks and suggestions. First of all, only a picture of a person pointing the camera to the reference pattern laying on the table, has been required by anybody to start playing the games. Such a limited amount of training information hints at the ease of use and naturalness of the conceived interface. Most of the players manage to get to the end of the game, this suggesting also good intuitiveness and friendliness. On the other hand several persons expressed concerns about the difficulty of keeping the reference object always in sight during the gaming session. Even though occasional pose estimation failure does not necessarily muck up the game, it can be ennoying especially during agitated phases. Another set of complains concerns the responsiveness of the gameplay which is mainly accountable to the high computational cost that the system incur when highly textured areas generate a large amount of keypoints.

5   Conclusions and Future Work

The ubiquitous presence of computerized equipments in everyday environment calls for conception and design of easy-to-use and natural human-machine interfaces. Practical, straightforward and inexpensive are the keywords for the next generation of interaction paradigms. Videogames are a challenging test ground since fast response and high accuracy are also required. Vision-based interfaces hold the potential to fulfill this expectation. In this paper a vision-based approach based on tracking natural features has been conceived as an interface for gaming applications. The proposed approach allows the user to interact with a videogame by simply moving a webcam pointing towards some planar textured object present in the scene. According to the feedback received by several users, the interface is intuitive, fast, responsive and, ultimately, enjoyable.

As for future directions of works, pose estimation from non-flat surfaces or larger-than-a-single frame object would prove useful to increase the possibility for the user to move around. Moreover, as for the difficulty of keeping the reference object always in sight, we wish to investigate on the possibility of enabling also a mixed-reality mode, in which the user would see the virtual objects of the game superimposed to actual video stream coming from the camera.

Eventually, the proposed approach is particularly suited to enable gaming applications on hand held devices such as phones and PDA, for the user may simply point the camera toward a textured plane and play by moving the device in his hand. Therefore, in the near feature we plan to port our gamimg interface on a state-of-the-art hand held device.

Acknoledgements

We would like to thank Marisa Panaccio for the development of the games, during her MS degree thesis, and for providing us with the images shown in Fig. 3

References

1. Bay, H., Ess, A., Tuytelaars, T., Van Gool, L.: Surf: Speeded up robust features. Computer Vision and Image Understanding 110(3), 346–359 (2008)
2. Cho, K., Kang, W., Soh, J., Lee, J., Yang, H.S.: Ghost hunter: a handheld augmented reality game system with dynamic environment. In: Proc. of Intl. Conf. on Entertainment Computing, pp. 10–15 (2007)
3. Close, B., Donoghue, J., Squires, J., De Bondi, P., Morris, M., Piekarski, W., Thomas, B.: Arquake: an outdoor/indoor augmented reality first person application. In: Proc. of IEEE Intl. Symp. on Wearable Computers, pp. 139–146 (2000)
4. Intel Corp. Opencv 1.1, open computer vision library (2000-2008), http://www.intel.com/technology/computing/opencv/
5. Fiala, M.: Artag, a fiducial marker system using digital techniques. In: Proc. of IEEE Intl. Conf. on Computer Vision, pp. 590–596 (2005)

6. Freeman, W.T., Tanaka, K., Ohta, J., Kyuma, K.: Computer vision for computer games. In: Proc. of Intl. Conf. on Automatic Face and Gesture Recognition, pp. 100–105 (1996)
7. Govil, A., You, S., Neumann, U.: A video-based augmented reality golf simulator. In: Proc. of ACM Multimedia, pp. 489–490 (2000)
8. Khronos Group. Opengl 2.1, open computer graphics library (1992-2008), http://www.opengl.org/
9. Hartley, R., Zisserman, A.: Multiple view Geometry in computer vision, 2nd edn. Cambridge University Press, Cambridge (2003)
10. Harville, M., Li, D.: Fast, integrated person tracking and activity recognition with plan-view templates from a single stereo camera. In: Proc. of Intl. Conf. on Computer Vision and Pattern Recognition, pp. 398–405 (2004)
11. Isard, M., Blake, A.: Condensation - conditional density propagation for visual tracking. Intl. Journal of Computer Vision 29(1), 5–28 (1998)
12. Lam, D.: Tokamak, open physics engine library, http://www.tokamakphysics.com/
13. Lowe, D.G.: Distinctive image features from scale-invariant keypoints. Intl. Journal of Computer Vision 60(2), 91–110 (2004)
14. Lu, P., Chen, Y., Zeng, X., Wang, Y.: A vision-based game control method. In: Proc. of Intl. Conf. on Computer Vision, Workshop on Human Machine Interaction, pp. 70–78 (2005)
15. Lu, P., Zeng, X.Y., Huang, X., Wang, Y.: Navigation in 3d game by markov model based head pose estimating. In: Proc. of Intl. Conf. on Image and Graphics, pp. 493–496 (2004)
16. Nintendo©. Wii, http://wii.nintendo.com/
17. Oda, O., Lister, L.J., White, S., Feiner, S.: Developing an augmented reality racing game. In: Proc. of Intl. Conf. on Intelligent Technologies for Interactive Environment (2008)
18. Salti, S., Di Stefano, L.: Svr-based jitter reduction for markerless augmented reality. In: Proc. of Intl. Conf. on Image Analysis and Processing (2008) (submitted paper)
19. Simon, G., Fitzgibbon, A.W., Zisserman, A.: Markerless tracking using planar structures in the scene. In: Proc. of Intl. Symposium on Augmented Reality, May-June 2000, pp. 120–128 (2000)
20. Viola, P., Jones, M.J.: Robust real-time face detection. Intl. Journal of Computer Vision 57(2), 137–154 (2004)
21. Wagner, D., Pintaric, T., Ledermann, F., Schmalstieg, D.: Towards massively multi-user augmented reality on handheld devices. In: Proc. of Intl. Conf. on Pervasive Computing, pp. 208–219 (2005)
22. Wagner, D., Reitmayr, G., Mulloni, A., Drummond, T., Schmalstieg, D.: Pose tracking from natural features on mobile phones. In: Proc. of Intl. Symp. on Mixed and Augmented Reality, pp. 125–134 (2008)

Quality Assessment of the MPEG-4 Scalable Video CODEC

Florian Niedermeier, Michael Niedermeier, and Harald Kosch

Department of Distributed Information Systems
University of Passau (UoP)
Passau, Germany
niederme@fim.uni-passau.de, niedermm@fim.uni-passau.de,
harald.kosch@uni-passau.de

Abstract. In this paper, the performance of the emerging MPEG-4 SVC CODEC is evaluated. In the first part, a brief introduction on the subject of quality assessment and the development of the MPEG-4 SVC CODEC is given. After that, the used test methodologies are described in detail, followed by an explanation of the actual test scenarios. The main part of this work concentrates on the performance analysis of the MPEG-4 SVC CODEC - both objective and subjective. Please note that this document is only a shortened version of the assessment. Further experimental results can be found in the extended version available at the Computing Research Repository (CoRR).

1 Introduction

As both high visual quality and low bandwidth requirements are key features in the emerging mobile multimedia sector, MPEG and VCEG introduced a new extension to the MPEG-4 AVC standard - scalable video coding (SVC). Its focus lies on supplying different client devices with video streams suited for their needs and capabilities. This is achieved by employing three different scalability modes: Spatial, temporal and SNR scalability. Because these new features are still in development and their impact on visual quality has not often been independently tested, this paper covers this subject. The performance evaluation is done using both objective and subjective methods. Additionally to the evaluations covering the matter of visual quality, test runs are performed to check the encoding speed of the SVC CODEC. The assessment is divided into two parts: The first is a MPEG-4 SVC stand-alone test, which examines the impact of different encoding settings on the CODEC's performance. The second part consists of a competitive comparison of the SVC reference CODEC, x264 (MPEG-4 AVC based) and Xvid (MPEG-4 ASP based), to analyze each CODEC's advantages and disadvantages.

2 Related Work

Some comparisons of subjective and objective assessment methods have been conducted, especially the CS MSU Graphics & Media Lab Video Group ran several evaluations concerning CODEC competitions [3] [2]. The emerging MPEG-4

P. Foggia, C. Sansone, and M. Vento (Eds.): ICIAP 2009, LNCS 5716, pp. 297–306, 2009.

SVC standard, however, has not been tested in such a manner. Although both objective [14] and subjective tests [5] have already been run separately, an analysis offering both test methodologies was yet outstanding. The MPEG-4 SVC CODEC was also evaluated in an official ISO test [7], which did however not assess a broad range of quality-impacting parameters. Another problem concerning this evaluation is that it only focused on the comparison of MPEG-4 SVC and its direct predecessor MPEG-4 AVC. In this paper, a broader range of quality-affecting settings and scenarios is assessed. Additionally, a comparative synthesis that comprises both subjective and objective test methods is conducted.

3   Used Test Methodologies

To provide comparable results, it is important for both objective and subjective assessments to be run under strictly specified conditions. This means for objective tests that the used metric and the encoding parameters are kept throughout the whole assessment. The subjective evaluations also need to have a fixed testing setup and environment as environmental influences can bias a users' opinion.

3.1   Objective Metrics

PSNR: The PSNR is the currently most widely used metric for quality evaluations of compression techniques. Even though this metric can be calculated for luminance as well as chrominance channels, it is common to just calculate the difference in luminance (Y-PSNR). The correlation of PSNR to subjective quality impression is discussed controversially: The results of the video quality experts group [4] come to the conclusion that PSNR correlation is on par with that of other metrics. In contrast, newer tests like [2] claim that the correlation of PSNR is significantly lower than that of the SSIM metric [13]. Still, PSNR is the standard metric used in most quality assessments and literature. To ensure comparability, this metric will be used in the following tests too.

PSNR adaption for temporally scaled videos: As shown in [6], normal PSNR calculation is not suitable for quality assessment of videos with temporal scalability. The calculated values are too low to accurately reflect perceived quality, so the following adapted quality score based on PSNR was proposed: $QM = PSNR + m^{0.38}(30 - FR)$. QM is the metrics score, FR is the framerate of the processed video. To calculate $PSNR$ in this equation, the frames of the temporally scaled video are repeated to match the frame count of the original sequence. Using this sequence, standard PSNR is calculated. The parameter m is the normalized average magnitude of large motion vectors, which is used to measure motion speed. The exact calculation is given in [6]. The equation was specifically designed for videos with a maximum framerate of 30 Hz. As the source videos used in the following work have different framerates, the following has to be considered: A simple adaption of the equation to fit the new source framerate ($QM = PSNR + m^{0.38}(60 - FR)$) does not lead to reasonable results, so the impact of temporal decimation is only considered if the framerate drops below 30 Hz. This means that sequences with a framerate of 30 Hz or lower are always compared against those with 30 Hz, so the metric described in [6] can be used without modification.

3.2 SAMVIQ

The Subjective Assessment Methodology for VIdeo Quality (SAMVIQ) is an invention of the EBU (European Broadcasting Union), which started in 2001 and finished in 2004. It is incorporated in ITU-R BT.700 by now [10]. SAMVIQ was developed because most other subjective test methodologies (for example DSIS, DSCQS, SSCQE and SDSCE) are specialized in rating videos shown on TV screens, and not on home computer or even mobile devices. At the beginning of the test process, the subject watches the reference sequence. After that the expert has to watch and rate all impaired sequences, which are randomly ordered and made anonymous to the expert by labeling them alphabetically. If required, every sequence may be repeated as often as the tester likes. It is also possible to change the rating of a sequence anytime. The reference is also hidden among the impaired sequences and is therefore rated as well. For voting, a linear, continuous scale with a range of 0 to 100 points is used, where a higher value represents better image quality and a lower one worse quality respectively [10] [8].

4   Test Setup

Selection of experts: A total of 21 persons of all age and working classes are included in the test. None of the experts was previously trained as a subjective tester or had a job associated with visual quality testing. However, before a person is approved as an expert in the evaluation, two aptitude tests are run: A visual acuity and a color blindness test. The visual acuity of every viewer is tested using the Freiburg Visual Acuity, Contrast & Vernier Test (FrACT). The process is thoroughly described in [1]. An acuity minimum of 1.0 is necessary to take part in the following quality evaluation. Vision aids like glasses are permitted in the test. The color perception is also an important factor when assessing graphical material. Persons with a visual impairment of the color perception are excluded from the test [9]. This test is executed using the standard Ishihara test charts. After these tests, one person had to be excluded, leaving 20 test subjects for the subjective assessment.

Subjective test environment: The testing environment is set up as follows: To prevent any unwanted display-related influences, the same device (a Samsung R40-T5500 Cinoso notebook, further technical details are shown in table 2) is used for every test session and expert. The black level and contrast of the display are adjusted using a PLUGE (Picture Line-Up Generation Equipment) pattern [12]. During the playback of the sequences the test room's background lighting is provided by a faint, artificial light source. The viewing distance is set concerning the rules of Preferred Viewing Distance (PVD) for an 15.4" LCD device. The display is aligned both horizontally and vertically to provide a viewing angle of $\leq 20°$ to the expert.

Encoder settings: Three CODECs are assessed in the comparison: Xvid 1.1.3 (MPEG-4 ASP), x264 core 59 r808bm ff5059a (MPEG-4 AVC) and the new MPEG-4 SVC reference encoder 9.12.2. All encoder parameters are kept at default settings except for the settings listed in table 1.

Table 1. x264 and SVC encoder settings

	x264		SVC	
Encoding Type	Single pass - bitrate-based (ABR)		GOPSize	4
Max consecutive	2		SearchMode	4
Threads	4		BaseLayerMode	2

The 'GOPSize' parameter is changed to a value of 4 to enable the usage of B frames. Encoding a video sequence without B frames would result in a significant drop in compression efficiency. The fast search algorithm is used, so 'SearchMode' is adjusted to 4. The parameter 'BaseLayerMode' is altered as the default setting is invalid.

5   Conducted Evaluations

The assessment is split in two separate evaluations: Firstly, the MPEG-4 SVC CODEC is tested in a stand-alone test, to document the impact of different encoder settings on the resulting quality and assess the CODEC's features. Secondly, the characteristics of the MPEG-4 SVC CODEC are compared to those of x264 and Xvid in a comparison test.

5.1   MPEG-4 SVC Stand-Alone Test

Quantization parameter test: During this test, the impact of the quantization parameter (QP) on the video quality is evaluated. The higher the QP value, the stronger is the quantization of the sequence and the lower is the resulting quality. The QP can either be a constant integer or - using rate control - automatically dynamically adjusted to match a selected bitrate. For the evaluation, the 'Foreman' (CIF, 30 Hz), 'Crew' (4CIF, 60 Hz) and 'Pedestrian Area' (720p, 25 Hz) sequences are each encoded with a single layer and constant QPs of 0, 10, 20, 30, 40 and 50. These sequences are used as they provide a wide range of different motion and spatial details. All other encoder settings are left at standard values.

CGS / MGS test: In the coarse grain scalability (CGS) / medium grain scalability (MGS) test, the impact of MGS on the video quality is assessed in comparison with CGS coding. To do so, the three sequences 'Foreman', 'Crew' and 'Pedestrian Area' are encoded with two layers. In CGS mode, only these two layers - using SNR scalability - can be extracted, while the sequence encoded with MGS additionally offers 4×4 MGS vectors to dynamically adjust to changing bandwidth needs. Except for the two layers, the standard encoding settings are employed. During the test, three different bitrates are compared.

Best extraction path test: The different video streams of a SVC bitstream are arranged in a spatio-temporal cube. The best extraction path test is conducted to determine which of the video streams is perceived as the optimal one for a given bitrate in terms of visual quality. To achieve this, the unimpaired original 4CIF sequences are encoded in three spatial (QCIF, CIF, 4CIF) and four temporal (7.5 Hz, 15 Hz, 30 Hz, 60 Hz) resolutions. The QP of each layer is adjusted to match the target filesize of 1000 KB. The outcome of the best extraction path test shows which of the three kinds of impairments (spatial, temporal or SNR) has the biggest impact on perceived quality and, as a result, if there is an extraction path which can generally be recommended.

5.2   Comparison of MPEG-4 SVC to MPEG-4 AVC/ASP

Quality comparison test: During the quality comparison test, nine test sequences are encoded with the three evaluated CODECs Xvid, x264 and SVC. The CIF sequences are encoded with 200 kbps, the 4CIF and HD sequences with 1000 kbps. In the subjective assessment, the experts are then asked to evaluate the sequences: In each test, the subject is first shown the uncompressed reference sequence. After that, the three impaired versions of the same sequence compressed with the three evaluated CODECs are compared to the original. During the objective evaluation, the three impaired sequences of each sequence are compared to the original.

Encoding speed test: In the encoding speed test, the time of each CODEC to encode a given sequence is measured. For this evaluation the standard encoder settings are employed. For the encoding process, three sequences ('Foreman', 'Crew' and 'Pedestrian Area') with different resolutions and a duration of 10 seconds each are used. The sequences are looped 3 times before the encoding process to reduce measuring inaccuracies.

6   Results

6.1   MPEG-4 SVC Stand-alone Test

First, the results from different tests regarding the SVC options are compared. It has to be mentioned that some tests could only be performed using objective metrics as the differences in quality are too small to be evaluated subjectively.

Quantization parameter test: After normalizing the both PSNR and ITU-R quality mark, the objective and subjective quality scores differ significantly. While the objective score degrades almost linearly with the rising QP value, the subjective score shows very little quality impairment up to a QP value of 30, but then quickly falls to a relative score of about 25% at QP 40. Apparently a certain amount of loss in high frequency information does not impair perceived quality much, but of course this loss is already picked up by the PSNR calculation.

CGS / MGS test: The CGS / MGS test showed similar results in both objective and subjective evaluation. At bitrates between the two SNR layers, MGS encoding can lead to a significant increase in quality. As the objective tests showed, the quality level assigner tool can be used to achieve an almost linear PSNR increase with a low number of MGS vectors.

Best extraction path test: While the results of the objective best extraction path assessment showed the best PSNR values for sequences encoded in 4CIF resolution and 30 / 60 Hz, in subjective testing, in contrast, especially the bitstream using the highest possible spatial and temporal level is rated very poor. This finding matches with the ones previously mentioned in the quantization parameter test, where the subjective quality ratings suddenly drops between QP 30 and 40, whereas the objective scores scaled almost linearly throughout the whole QP range. In the following figures, the numbers from 1 to 12 indicate the visual quality of each selectable bitstream, where 1 is the best and 12 the worst rating.

Apart from that, it is additionally visible that QCIF resolution, as well as all streams encoded with 7.5 Hz framerate received very low scores in both test runs. As a result, the selection of the lowest spatial and/or temporal resolution should be avoided if possible.

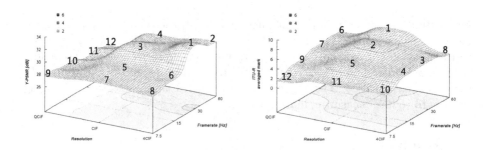

Fig. 1. Objective and subjective quality marks for different framerates and resolutions

6.2   Comparison of MPEG-4 SVC to MPEG-4 AVC/ASP

Quality comparison test: When looking at the quality comparison test, basically similar results could be observed in both subjective and objective testing.

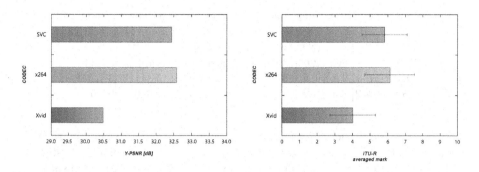

Fig. 2. Objective and subjective quality results of the quality comparison test

The overall visual quality of the three tested CODECs in the evaluated scenarios leads to the following ranking:

Under the described test conditions, the Xvid CODEC scores the lowest, which is most likely due to its MPEG-4 ASP base. The visual quality of x264 and SVC are nearly on par, which is expected as AVC is the direct predecessor of SVC. During the quality comparison, a particular flaw in the SVC CODEC became apparent: The rate control. Even though the requested bitrate is delivered in most cases quite accurately, the resulting quality can be unstable under certain conditions. While the maximum fluctuation amplitude of x264 is about 5 dB, the SVC CODEC reaches about 10 dB. Another significant flaw in SVC rate control is that in certain short sequences, the CODEC tends to distribute too much bitrate at the beginning of the sequence. This is followed by an excessive increase of quantization at the end of the file, leading to a significant quality decrease. It is however noteworthy that this behavior did not occur in every sequence.

Encoding speed test: The encoding time is measured on two different test systems to evaluate the impact of different CPU speeds and capabilities on SVC encoding. The details of both test systems are listed in table 2.

The following tables show the detailed results for both test systems. Both the absolute times and the relative speedup with System 2 as reference are given.

Table 2. Hardware configurations of the test systems

	System 1	System 2
OS	Microsoft Windows Vista Business 64-Bit, Version: 6.0.6001 SP1	Microsoft Windows Vista Business 32-Bit, Version: 6.0.6001 SP1
CPU	Intel® Core™ 2 Quad Q9450 4×2.66 GHz	Intel® Core™ 2 Duo T5500 2×1.66 GHz @ 1.00 GHz
RAM	4096 MB DDR2 800	2048 MB DDR2 667
HDD	Samsung Spinpoint T166, 320 GB, 7200 RPM, 16 MB Cache	Hitachi Travelstar 5K100, 100 GB, 5400 RPM, 8MB Cache

Table 3. Average encoding time on different computer systems in seconds

	CIF			4CIF			HD		
	Xvid	x264	SVC	Xvid	x264	SVC	Xvid	x264	SVC
System 1	1.1	0.9	387.7	12.1	7.8	2778.5	15.3	7.7	3902.1
System 2	4.1	7.2	947.8	42.1	60.8	8155.4	41.6	60.1	9575.8

As table 3 shows, there are significant differences in speedup between the different CODECs. SVC just seems to profit from the higher core clock of system 1, as the speed scales linearly with the core clock $\left(\frac{1.00GHz}{2.66GHz} = 0.376\right)$. Xvid speedup is slightly higher, maybe due to optimizations for the new SSE instruction sets implemented in the quadcore processors. The biggest speed gain can be observed using the x264 CODEC. This is because x264 is the only CODEC that supported multithreaded encoding at the time of testing, so the quadcore processor could be used to its full potential.

7   Current SVC Flaws

7.1   Improvement of Existing Features

While the new MPEG-4 SVC CODEC adds many useful features to its predecessor MPEG-4 AVC, some flaws could still be observed during the subjective as well as the objective evaluations. These are described in the next section.

More reasonable default configuration: Some parameters of the SVC configuration files are by default not reasonably adjusted. The most important is the value of 'BaseLayerMode', whose default value is '3', which is not even a defined setting. Although being allowed and defined, the value of '1' for the setting 'GOPSize' is also not reasonable, as it heavily cripples the amount of temporal scalability possible. Hence, a change of the default parameter to a value of '8' or '16' is purposed. Because the encoding speed of SVC is currently low, the default parameter '0' (= 'BlockSearch') of 'SearchMode' is also not considered to be reasonable and should be switched to '4' (= 'FastSearch').

Improve encoding speed: The previous test have shown that the current MPEG-4 SVC version has a much lower encoding speed than the other tested CODECs. Firstly, it needs to be mentioned again that this is to be expected, as SVC is still in development status, but two main reasons can be identified and are explained in the following.

Multithreading: The benefit of multithreading support becomes more and more visible in modern computer systems, because multicore configurations are already commonly found in private environments today. If a similar encoding speed gain as in x264 when using multithreading is proclaimed, the encoding speed would approximately be accelerated linearly with the number of available logical CPUs.

Motion estimation: To further decrease the encoding time needs, it would be essential to optimize the performance of the motion estimation algorithms. As already noted in [11], the currently employed motion estimation technique achieves the best quality possible. However, the computation complexity is very high, which obstructs it from practical use. [11] also proposes a fast mode decision algorithm for inter-frame coding as a solution, which achieves an average encoding time reduction of 53%.

Enhanced, stable rate control mechanism: As shown before, the SVC rate control feature still has minor flaws. Because the exact reasons for these behaviors could not be precisely pinpointed in the tests, no concrete proposal for improvement can be given here. Still, improvements in this area are regarded as necessary.

7.2   Additional Useful Features

In the next section, additional features, that are not implemented in the current SVC release, but would be useful, are described.

Variable, content-dependent framerate: As scalable video technology is especially advantageous in streaming media environments, a useful new technique would be content-aware variable framerate. The basic idea of variable content-dependent framerate is that a reduced temporal level does not impair scenes with no or very low movement, which was already proven by [6]. There could be two main positive results when reducing the framerate: Either the file size of the video sequence could be reduced, or - if the size remains constant - the SNR quality would benefit respectively.

2-Pass encoding mode: 2-pass encoding strategies have been implemented in most modern CODECs, for example Xvid or x264 which have been examined earlier. Implementing this feature into SVC would primarily benefit its suitability for archiving storage. Of course, the poor rate control of SVC would also benefit from the bitrate distribution algorithms in 2-pass mode. In spite of this fact, it is essential that single pass rate control of SVC is improved, as 2-pass encoding mode is not suited for realtime encoding.

7.3   Conclusion

The extensive tests conducted in this work show that the new scalable video coding extensions provide significant improvement in terms of adaptability of the video stream. Using the scalability features of SVC, both high quality and low bandwidth versions of a video stream can be delivered, while at the same time saving bitrate compared to the storage of separate videos. However, there are also several features that still need improvement. First and foremost, the encoding speed of the SVC reference encoder is far too slow. Two methods to speed up the encoding are already proposed before. Additionally, several optimizations and other new useful features are proposed in the previous section. Concluding, SVC is a promising new extension to the MPEG CODEC family.

References

1. Bach, M.: Freiburg Visual Acuity, Contrast & Vernier Test ('FrACT') (2002), http://www.michaelbach.de/fract/index.html
2. CS MSU Graphics & Media Lab Video Group. MOS Codecs Comparison (January 2006)
3. CS MSU Graphics & Media Lab Video Group. Video MPEG-4 AVC/H.264 Codecs Comparison (December 2007)
4. Rohaly, A.M., et al.: Video quality experts group: current results and future directions. In: Ngan, K.N., Sikora, T., Sun, M.-T. (eds.) Visual Communications and Image Processing 2000. Proceedings of SPIE, vol. 4067, pp. 742–753. SPIE (2000)
5. Barzilay, M.A.J., et al.: Subjective quality analysis of bit rate exchange between temporal and SNR scalability in the MPEG4 SVC extension. In: International Conference on Image Processing, pp. II: 285–288 (2007)
6. Feghali, R., Wang, D., Speranza, F., Vincent, A.: Quality metric for video sequences with temporal scalability. In: International Conference on Image Processing, pp. III: 137–140 (2005)
7. I.O. for Standardisation. Svc verification test report. iso/iec jtc 1/sc 29/wg 11 n9577 (2007)
8. Institut für Rundfunktechnik. ITU-R BT.500 Recommendation and SAMVIQ, ITU-R BT.700 (2005)
9. Rabin, J.: (Visual Function Laboratory Ophthalmology Branch / USAF School of Aerospace Medicine). Color vision fundamentals (1998)
10. Kozamernik, F., Steinman, V., Sunna, P., Wyckens, E.: SAMVIQ - A New EBU Methodology for Video Quality Evaluations in Multimedia, Amsterdam (2004)
11. Li, H., Li, Z.G., Wen, C.: Fast mode decision algorithm for inter-frame coding in fully scalable video coding. IEEE Trans. Circuits and Systems for Video Technology 16(7), 889–895 (2006)
12. W. Media. Pluge Test Pattern, http://www.mediacollege.com/video/test-patterns/pluge.html
13. Wang, Z., Bovik, A.C., Sheikh, H.R., Simoncelli, E.P.: Image quality assessment: From error visibility to structural similarity. IEEE Trans. Image Processing 13(4), 600–612 (2004)
14. Wien, M., Schwarz, H., Oelbaum, T.: Performance analysis of SVC. IEEE Trans. Circuits and Systems for Video Technology 17(9), 1194–1203 (2007)

An Automatic Method for Counting Annual Rings in Noisy Sawmill Images

Kristin Norell

Centre for Image Analysis, Swedish University of Agricultural Sciences
kristin@cb.uu.se

Abstract. The annual ring pattern of a log end face is related to the quality of the wood. We propose a method for computing the number of annual rings on a log end face depicted in sawmill production. The method is based on the grey-weighted polar distance transform and registration of detected rings from two different directions. The method is developed and evaluated on noisy images captured in on-line sawmill production at a Swedish sawmill during 2008, using an industrial colour camera. We have also evaluated the method using synthetic data with different ring widths, ring eccentricity, and noise levels.

1 Introduction

When sawing wood, the quality of the resulting product is related to the quality of the timber. The timber quality influences the price to wood suppliers as well as the usage. One parameter that is related to wood quality is the annual ring width, which is used at Swedish sawmills as a parameter for classification of the timber into different quality classes. The estimation of the annual ring width is made by visual inspection by a log scaler as the timber passes on a conveyor belt. An automatic system based on image analysis of timber end faces would reduce the work load for the log scaler and has the possibility to be more consistent and thus preferable over visual inspection.

The problem of measuring annual ring width using image analysis has been addressed before. The task has often been to measure the ring width for a dendrochronology application or to measure the amount of earlywood and latewood. In such cases, high resolution images depicting end faces with high readability are needed. Semi-automatic methods based on edge detection in high resolution microscopic images are presented in [1] and [2], as well as in [3] and [4], where sanded end faces are depicted using a scanner with 600 dpi resolution. The methods suggested in the mentioned papers are not applicable to our problem, as the quality of images that can be captured in an operating sawmill is much worse.

In [5] the images are captured in the field using a digital camera. Their method uses edge detection to find pixels that belong to the annual rings and fits polygons to the detected edges. The starting position for the polygon is the outer boundary of the end face and the polygon is then shrunken to detect the rings. In the trees considered here the annual rings are usually much narrower than in the example images shown in [5]. With only a few pixels separating each annual ring in combination with the images being noisy, this method is not applicable.

P. Foggia, C. Sansone, and M. Vento (Eds.): ICIAP 2009, LNCS 5716, pp. 307–316, 2009.

In [6] the annual rings are counted using the Fourier transform in a local region. The distance from the centre of the Fourier spectra to the maximum corresponds to the number of rings in the region. The number of annual rings along a path perpendicular to the annual ring pattern is computed by taking the Fourier transform of a number of pixels along the path and combining the results. A problem with this method is that only the dominating frequency influences the result. If the tree has been growing fast for one year, e.g., due to felling of surrounding trees, or slow due to a dry spring, this will not be visible in the spectrum. The resolution is also a problem in our case, since if the local region does not include more than about three rings, the maximum in the Fourier spectra will be difficult to distinguish from the high DC-component in the centre of the spectra.

We present an automatic method to compute the number of annual rings in end faces depicted in sawmill environment. Images of Scots pine are captured in on-line production at a sawmill, where all end faces are sawn with harvester or chain saw, stored in the forest for some time and then transported with truck to the sawmill. We compute the number of rings in images where the annual rings can be counted by visual inspection, as well as in synthetic images of different ring width and noise levels.

2   Data

End face images used in the development and evaluation of the method are captured at Setra Nyby sawmill in Sweden. The images are captured automatically at the sawmill measurement station while the logs pass on a conveyor belt with a speed of approximately 1.1 m/s. The camera is placed above the conveyor belt and captures images as the logs move away from the camera.

The camera is a colour camera suitable for industrial use, a PixeLINK PL-A782 with a CMOS sensor. A Bayer mosaic [7] pattern is used for capturing colour images. The imaging is performed using a rolling shutter technique, meaning that all pixels are not exposed in parallel, only a few pixel rows at a time. Images are 1800×1536 pixels, and the pixel size in the captured images is approximately 0.4 mm.

The camera is placed at the measurement station so that it is facing the log scaler. Unfortunately this placing means that it is impossible to use a flash in the imaging, since it would be a large disturbance for the log scaler. The rolling shutter technique in combination with a moving end face will therefore give motion blur in the image. The fact that the camera is placed above the conveyor belt means that we have an angle of approximately 20 degrees between the end face and the imaging plane which will create a distortion of the image, compressing it slightly in height. The motion blur and image distortion will result in the fact that each annual ring is more difficult to distinguish where the rings are horizontal, i.e., above and below the pith.

A training set of 24 images and an evaluation set of 20 images are drawn from images of Scots pine captured monthly during 2008. These are images in which the annual rings can be counted by visual inspection at least along some direction, which is not the case for all captured images.

2.1 Synthetic Data

A number of synthetic images were created for evaluation and testing of the proposed method. The synthetic images are based on a sinus signal modelling the annual ring pattern. A circular sinus pattern of frequency f can be created by applying a sinus function to the Euclidean distance from an image origin, p_0. To distort the perfectly circular pattern a 2D linear function is added to the distance image before applying the sinus function:

$$S(p) = \sin\left(2\pi f\left(\|x\| + k \cdot x\right)\right),\tag{1}$$

where p is a pixel, $x = p - p_0$ and k determines the slope of the linear function. The higher value of k, the more eccentricity of the rings. Random Gaussian noise with mean value 0 and standard deviation σ_n is added to the sinus pattern. The images are smoothed with a 2D Gaussian filter with standard deviation $\sigma = 2$ and scaled to the intensity range $50 - 115$ to resemble the captured end face images.

3 The Proposed Method

The goal of the method is to count the number of annual rings in correspondence with the instructions from the Swedish Timber Measurement Council. The annual rings should be counted in a region of 2-8 cm from the pith in the direction of the most sparse annual ring pattern. The area around the chosen direction is not permitted to include knots or other disturbances that influence the annual ring pattern [8]. To compute the number of rings in the direction with the most sparse rings, i.e., the lowest number of rings, requires knowledge of the annual ring pattern on the entire end face. At this point we do not attempt to compute the number of rings on the entire end face, but to automatically choose a direction proper for measuring the number of annual rings and compute the number of rings in that area. Such a direction shall have undisturbed annual rings with as high readability as possible. We will only consider annual rings in the area of 2 to 8 cm from the pith in the computations. We denote this area A_{2-8}.

3.1 Outline of the Method

The complete method consists of several steps:

1. Pith detection
2. Detection of proper region, P for measuring
3. Creation of a cost image, I in P
4. Detection of ring pattern in P
5. Computation of the number of rings.

The colour images are converted into grey level images before computations using the standard conversion $Y = 0.2989 \cdot R + 0.5870 \cdot G + 0.1140 \cdot B$ where R, G, and B represent the red, green and blue colour channels, respectively [9]. The signal to noise ratio in the blue channel of the captured images is low, therefore only the red and green channels are considered which is achieved by setting $B = 0$ before conversion.

No segmentation of the end faces is performed. The background in the images is dark, but not completely black, and do not disturb the analysis.

3.2 Pith Detection

The pith can be detected using the method described in [10] where local orientations in the image are detected and combined to estimate the pith position. See [10] for computational details.

3.3 Detection of Proper Region

To detect a suitable region for measurements is to detect a region with as clearly visible ring pattern as possible, without disturbances like knots, dirt, or snow. A clearly visible and undisturbed ring pattern is a region where, locally, the rings are parallel ridges, i.e., a 2D signal varying only in one direction. The direction of variation is ideally the direction towards the pith, i.e., the local orientation of the region is the direction towards the pith.

The local orientation, $\varphi(p)$, is computed for all pixels, p. Here we use the computation of local orientation that is included in the suggested pith detection method [10], with filters described in [11]. The computation of local orientation is fast and can be applied to the image even if another pith detection method is preferred. For each pixel, the angle from the detected pith is also computed and used as a reference, or ground truth, $\varphi_{gt}(p)$.

To detect the best direction for computations the image is divided into N overlapping regions, P_i, covering $4\frac{2\cdot\pi}{N}$ radians each. The regions are limited radially by the distance to the pith, considering only the area A_{2-8}. In each of the regions P_i an error is computed from the sum of the difference between detected local orientation and $\varphi_{gt}(p)$ for all pixels in the region

$$E_i = \sum_{p \in P_i} = |\varphi_{gt}(p) - \varphi(p)|, \tag{2}$$

where E_i is the error for region P_i. The direction D with the smallest error is chosen for further computations

$$D = j \mid E_j = \min_i(E_i), \quad i = 1, 2, \ldots, N. \tag{3}$$

Figure 1 shows the area A_{2-8} for an end face image with $N = 36$ different directions as well as the error, E_i for each region. Here $D = 14$ minimizes the error, giving the region P_{14} which is marked in the image with the limiting directions in white.

Due to the imaging technique giving motion blur and image distortion affecting mostly areas above and below the pith as described in Section 2, these regions are ignored when choosing a proper direction. This can easily be changed if another imaging technique is used.

3.4 Creating Cost Image

A cost image is needed in the further computations in which a clear annual ring pattern is wanted. The original image could be used but it is even better to use a contrast enhanced image. To improve the contrast in the images the method suggested in [12] is used, where local contrast enhancement is performed based on the local maximum,

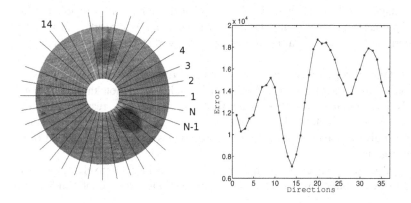

Fig. 1. An end face and the error computed for different regions. The limiting directions of P_{14} are shown as white lines.

minimum and average. The computations are made using a propagation scheme. A conductivity factor, C in the range 0 and 1 is used to determine the size of the propagation window, see [12] for computational details, and the image is enhanced depending on the range of the input image. If the range is smaller than a threshold, ω_0 the signal is considered as noise and the output range is compressed in this area. By visual inspection it was concluded that the suggested noise reduction does not improve the images in our case, thus $\omega_0 = 0$ is used. The parameter $C = 0.85$ has been chosen from experiments using the training data, described in Section 4. The contrast enhancement is computed in region P_D.

3.5 Detection of Annual Ring Pattern

The number of annual rings in region P_D can be estimated by applying the grey-weighted polar distance transform (GWPDT) described in [13]. The GWPDT is an anisotropic distance transform where the polar coordinates (r, θ) of the pixels are considered. By using different costs on propagation in the angular and radial direction, the distance propagates with different speed in the different directions. By setting the weight in the angular direction, ω_θ and the weight in the radial direction, ω_r, so that an angular step has lower cost than the radial, the distance will propagate faster in the angular direction.

We apply the GWPDT from both the directions

$$D_{-2} = D - 2 \quad \mathrm{mod}\ (N) \tag{4}$$

$$D_{+2} = D + 2 \quad \mathrm{mod}\ (N) \tag{5}$$

to the region P_D. We let the contrast enhanced image have the range $1 - 50$ and use it as a cost function in the GWPDT with weights $\omega_r = 5/r(p)$ and $\omega_\theta = 1$, where $r(p)$ is the radial coordinate for pixel p.

The cost image with low values in the dark parts of the annual rings together with the GWPDT propagating faster in angular direction than radial will result in fast propagation in dark parts of the annual rings, i.e., we get low distance values in the dark rings.

The two distance images that are the result from applying the GWPDT are analysed along a ray outwards in the direction D. We let S_{D-2} and S_{D+2} denote the one dimensional signals in direction D for GWPDT applied in D_{-2} and D_{+2}, respectively. For S_{D-2} and S_{D+2}, ideally, each local minimum corresponds to the dark part of an annual ring. This is not always the case however, since the images are noisy and annual ring pattern is far from ideal.

In the computations and analysis of the GWPDT we consider the pixels covering a distance of 1 to 9 cm from the pith to be certain to include rings close to the 2 and 8 cm limits.

3.6   Estimation of the Number of Annual Rings

Of the several local minima in S_{D-2} and S_{D+2} many correspond to annual rings, but not all. To count the local minima that correspond to annual rings we combine the result from the two distance transforms by performing elastic registration of the signals. In elastic registration both signals can be stretched or compressed along the signal indexes to best match each other. Here dynamic programming is used for the registration with the same approach as in [14], where the total cost for registration of signals R and S is given by the following:

$$C(R_1^i, S_1^j) = c(R_i, S_j) + \min \begin{cases} C(R_1^i, S_1^{j-1}) + g \\ C(R_1^{i-1}, S_1^{j-1}) \\ C(R_1^{i-1}, S_1^j) + g \end{cases} \tag{6}$$

where $C(R_1^i, S_1^j)$ is the total cost for registering signal R from index 1 to index i with signal S from index 1 to index j, $c(R_i, S_j)$ is the local cost between the signals at index i and j, respectively, and g is a penalty for compressing and stretching the signals. The local cost function

$$c(R_i, S_j) = (R_i - S_j)^2 \tag{7}$$

is used here. The value of the parameter $g = 0.2$ is determined using the training set, see Section 4.

Figure 2(a) shows parts of two signals S_{D-2} and S_{D+2}. Registration is performed to detect local minima, not general intensity, therefore the focus is on the local extrema. For each of the two signals considered, all values that are not local extrema are set to zero. The signals to register are then created by taking the difference between each local extrema and the previous one. The difference signals and registered signals are shown in Figure 2(b) and 2(c), respectively.

3.7   Detection of Rings

After registration, the signals are analyzed for the indexes covering pixels from 2 to 8 cm from the pith. All local minima that are registered to the same index are counted as

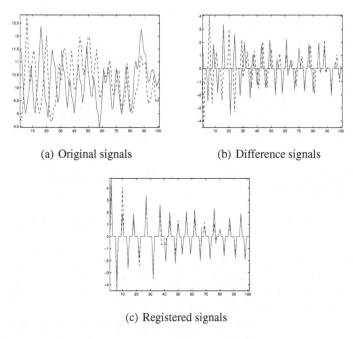

(a) Original signals   (b) Difference signals

(c) Registered signals

Fig. 2. Result from the elastic registration

rings. Other local minima are analyzed further: If there exist at least one local minimum in both signals between two registered minima it is counted as an annual ring. The number of extra rings between two registered minima is $\min(k, l)$ where k is the number of local minima in signal S_{D-2} and l is the number of local minima in signal S_{D+2}.

4   Results

The 24 images in the training set have been used to find proper values of the conductivity factor, C in the contrast enhancement and the cost, g in the registration of the signals. The result for different parameters are shown in Figure 3(a). For all combinations of parameters the number of detected rings, M, is compared with the ground truth, M_{gt} and summed, $e = \sum_{n=1}^{24} |M - M_{gt}|$. The ground truth have been established by visual inspection of the images in the automatically chosen directions. The parameters that gave the lowest error were $C = 0.80$ or $C = 0.85$ and $g = 0.2$, thus we have chosen to use $C = 0.85$ and $g = 0.2$ in all computations.

The results from the evaluation set is shown in Figure 3(b). The histogram shows the difference between the counted number of rings and the ground truth, $M - M_{gt}$. We can see that the proposed method underestimates the number of rings slightly.

We have tested the method on the synthetic images described in Section 2.1, using different values of the frequency f, the slope k of the linear function disturbing the circular pattern, and the noise level σ_n. We used $N = 36$ different regions, but computed the number of rings only in every other of them, i.e. in 18 directions. Figure 4(a) shows

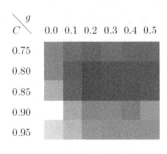
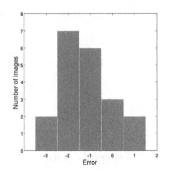

(a) Estimation of parameters from training data.

(b) Result for evaluation data, $M - M_{gt}$

Fig. 3. Parameters computed using training set and results for the evaluation set

the absolute value of the errors summed over all different directions $\sum_{d=1}^{18} |M^d - M_{gt}^d|$, where M^d is the number of detected rings in direction d. The result is shown for five different frequencies and six different values of the parameter k. All images have noise level $\sigma_n = 0.5$. Figure 4(b) shows results for images of frequency $f = 0.17$ with six different values of k and four different noise levels, σ_n. As can be expected high frequency, high noise level and high eccentricity gives considerable errors.

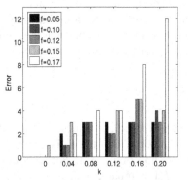
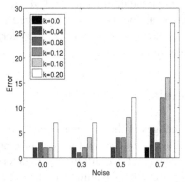
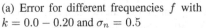

(a) Error for different frequencies f with $k = 0.0 - 0.20$ and $\sigma_n = 0.5$

(b) Error for frequency $f = 0.17$ of different k and different noise levels $\sigma_n = 0.0 - 0.7$.

Fig. 4. Results for synthetic images. Note the different scales on the vertical axis of the two plots.

The result for one of the real images from the evaluation set is shown in Figure 5(a). This is one of the end faces where the number of rings is underestimated by 2. The detected rings are shown as white pixels along the direction in which we computed the number of rings. The positions for the errors, i.e., non-detected annual rings, are marked with white arrows. Figure 5(b) shows the detected rings for a part of the synthetic image with $f = 0.17$, $k = 0.16$ and $\sigma_n = 0.7$. Detected rings are shown as black pixels. The local minima not registered to the same index are also marked using blue and red pixels for the different signals. The image shows one error which is marked with a white arrow. The positions with non-registered local minima that are correctly counted as rings are marked with black arrows. It can be seen from Figure 4(b) that the total sum of the errors for this image is around 17, i.e., the mean error for each direction is around 1.

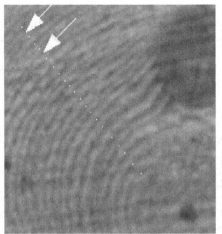
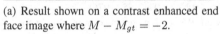
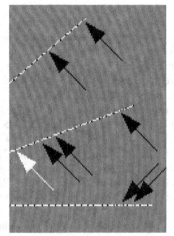

(a) Result shown on a contrast enhanced end face image where $M - M_{gt} = -2$.

(b) Result for a synthetic image with $f = 0.17$, $k = 0.16$, $\sigma_n = 0.7$.

Fig. 5. Example of results for one real and one synthetic image

5   Discussion

We have presented a method for automatic computations of the number of annual rings on end face images from Scots pine, taken in sawmill production. We have computed the number of rings in a training set and evaluation set from on-line captured images, as well as on synthetic data. The method has also been evaluated on synthetic images with different annual ring width, eccentricity and noise level.

In the future, the proposed method should be tested on more data and compared with a log scaler classifying the timber. The log scaler estimates the number of annual rings and classifies the logs into quality classes using the number of annual rings as one of the classification parameters. To compare that result with classification using the proposed method would be an interesting evaluation, and can show if the proposed method is suitable as an automatic method or as a tool to help the log scaler in the estimation. Comparisons should also be made with the exact number of rings, computed in the correct direction according to the instructions given by the Swedish Timber Measurement Council.

Acknowledgement

Thanks to Anders Brun and Gunilla Borgefors, Centre for Image Analysis, Swedish University of Agricultural Sciences, for scientific discussions. The project is partly financed by the Swedish Timber Measurement Council, VMU.

References

1. He, Z., Munro, M.A.R., Gopalan, G., Kulkarni, V., Schowengerdt, R.A., Hughes, M.K.: System and algorithm design for a new generation tree-ring image analysis system. Optical Engineering 47(2) (2008)
2. Conner, W., Schowengerdt, R., Munro, M., Hughes, M.: Design of a computer vision based tree ring dating system. In: 1998 IEEE Southwest Symposium on Image Analysis and Interpretation, pp. 256–261 (1998)
3. Laggoune, H., Sarifuddin, G.V.: Tree ring analysis. In: Canadian Conference on Electrical and Computer Engineering, May 2005, pp. 1574–1577 (2005)
4. Soille, P., Misson, L.: Tree ring area measurements using morphological image analysis. Canadian Journal of Forest Research 31, 1074–1083 (2001)
5. Cerda, M., Hitschfeld-Kahler, N., Mery, D.: Robust tree-ring detection. In: Mery, D., Rueda, L. (eds.) PSIVT 2007. LNCS, vol. 4872, pp. 575–585. Springer, Heidelberg (2007)
6. Österberg, P., Ihalainen, H., Ritala, R.: Robust methods for determining quality properties of wood using digital log end images. In: The 12th Int. Conf. on Scanning Technology and Process Optimization in the Wood Industry, ScanTech. (2007)
7. Bayer, B.E.: Color imaging array, U.S. Patent No. 3,971,065 (1976)
8. The Swedish Timber Measurement Council: Regulations for measuring roundwood (1999)
9. Sonka, M., Hlavac, V., Boyle, R.: Image Processing, Analysis, and Machine Vision. Brooks/Cole Publishing Company (1999)
10. Norell, K., Borgefors, G.: Estimation of pith position in untreated log ends in sawmill environments. Computers and Electronics in Agriculture 63(2), 155–167 (2008)
11. Bigün, J., Granlund, G.H.: Optimal orientation detection of linear symmetry. In: Proccedings of the first international conference on computer vision, pp. 433–438. IEEE Computer Society Press, Los Alamitos (1987)
12. Yu, Z., Bajaj, C.: A fast and adaptive method for image contrast enhancement. In: Int. Conf. on Image Processing (ICIP), pp. 1001–1004 (2004)
13. Norell, K., Lindblad, J., Svensson, S.: Grey weighted polar distance transform for outlining circular and approximately circular objects. In: Int. Conf. on Image Analysis and Processing (ICIAP), pp. 647–652. IEEE Computer Society, Los Alamitos (2007)
14. Nain, D., Haker, S., Grimson, W.E.L., Cosman Jr., E.R., Wells III, W.M., Ji, H., Kikinis, R., Westin, C.-F.: Intra-patient prone to supine colon registration for synchronized virtual colonoscopy. In: Dohi, T., Kikinis, R. (eds.) MICCAI 2002. LNCS, vol. 2489, pp. 573–580. Springer, Heidelberg (2002)

A License Plate Extraction Algorithm Based on Edge Statistics and Region Growing

Manuel Vargas, Sergio L. Toral, Federico Barrero, and Francisco Cortés

E. S. Ingenieros, University of Seville
Camino de los Descubrimientos s/n, 41092 Seville, Spain
{vargas,toral,fbarrero,fcortes1}@esi.us.es

Abstract. This paper presents a license plate extraction method for gray-scale images, based on a combination of edge statistics and a two-step seeded region growing algorithm. The proposed region growing algorithm uses a dual criterion based on edge density and gray-scale intensity affinity. The proposed method aims at achieving license plate segmentation that fits to the real plate boundaries better than existing methods. The robustness of the method has been tested with experimental results, including examples of low quality or poor-preserved plates and commercial or freight transport vehicles.

Keywords: Automatic License Plate Recognition (ALPR), plate localization, edge statistics, seeded region growing.

1 Introduction

Intelligent Transportation Systems (ITS) can be considered a global phenomenon, attracting worldwide interest from transportation professionals, the automotive industry, and political decision makers [1]. As a consequence, ITS involves a large number of research areas spread over many different technological sectors. One of the most important research issues is Automatic License Plate Recognition (ALPR), with important applications in areas like traffic surveillance, traffic control, vehicle tracking, localization, car park automation, electronic toll collection systems, and several other applications [2].

A typical ALPR system consists of three major phases: license plate detection, geometric correction, character segmentation, size or aspect ratio normalization, character recognition and application of grammatical rules [3], [4], [5]. Among them, a very critical step is the license plate location and segmentation, which directly affects the overall system performance.

A broad range of methods for license plate segmentation have been reported in the literature. A recent survey on this topic can be found in [6]. A first group of methods is based upon the combination of edge statistics and mathematical morphology [7], [8]. Other set of methods is based on color or gray-scale analysis [6]; they are based on scanning the image, looking for repeating contrast changes and counting edges [9]. In general, their performance and computational cost are worse than those provided by the first group of methods. Finally, classifiers based on statistical methods [10],

P. Foggia, C. Sansone, and M. Vento (Eds.): ICIAP 2009, LNCS 5716, pp. 317–326, 2009.

artificial neural networks [11], genetic programming [12] and genetic algorithms [13] have also been proposed in the literature.

The approach followed in this paper can be included in the first group of methods, that is, making use of edge statistics for plate location, combined with a two-step region growing algorithm, based on a dual (edge density / intensity affinity) criterion, with the aim of achieving a more accurate plate segmentation. The first region growing step uses just a gradient density criterion, leading to a typically elliptical region located at the core of the license plate. A simple statistical analysis is performed over this inner region in order to model the distribution of the plate background gray-level intensities. The objective of the second stage is growing from the inner region to include the whole license plate, adding a luminance criterion that tries to evaluate the affinity of gray-level intensities of the neighboring pixels with respect to the modeled plate background. The proposed method provides an accurate extraction of the plate region, reducing the task of false candidate rejection in subsequent stages.

2   License Plate Extraction Algorithm

The license plate of a vehicle contains rich edge information. Edge-based methods are based on this fact and the assumption that the areas containing a license plate will correspond to regions with higher edge density. Nevertheless, many false candidates can be obtained, and therefore, it is necessary to apply some morphological stages to choose the right ones. This decision making process will be greatly improved if the regions extracted are the most similar possible to the real plate dimensions and shape. In this paper, a processing stage based on a two-step region growing routine is proposed to accurate extract the plate region. The complete set of steps of the proposed method will be next listed and explained.

2.1 Vertical-Edge Image

Vertical edges are most prominent in the license plate region due to the contrasting vertical strokes of plate characters. On the opposite, the rear or front vehicle areas around the plate predominantly includes horizontal edges [14]. That is the reason why a vertical edge image is calculated as the first stage of the proposed method. Fig. 1 demonstrates the effect of applying a vertical edge 3x3 Sobel operator over the input image.

Fig. 1. Vertical-edge image

2.2   Binarization of Vertical-Edge Image

The vertical-edge image has to be binarized to highlight those edges to be considered relevant. According to [15], the threshold is obtained from the histogram of the vertical-edge image, as the value that guarantees that a $\alpha\%$ of the image values are above the chosen threshold. This thresholding mechanism has the advantage of being self-adaptive to different illumination and contrast conditions in the scene. Values around 5 or 6 for this parameter, α, have been empirically obtained, covering a wide range of illumination and contrast conditions. Fig. 2 shows the histogram and the resulting binarization, $B(x,y)=\{1,0\}$, for the previous vertical-edge image.

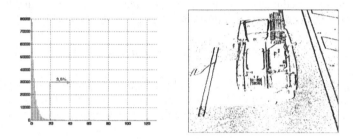

Fig. 2. Histogram and vertical-edge binarized image

2.3   Candidate Extraction Using Vertical-Edge Density

The region where the plate is located exhibits a high concentration of vertical edges. Consequently, a vertical-edge density image is next computed, in order to emphasize the location of candidate regions [16], [17].

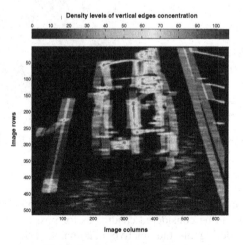

Fig. 3. Vertical-edge density image

If we define a density mask of dimension $w \times h$, a vertical-edge density image, $D(x,y)$, can be computed. The value of each pixel belonging to this image is calculated as the sum of the number of 1-valued pixels in image $B(x,y)$ inside the window:

$$D(x, y) = \sum_{i=x-w/2}^{x+w/2} \sum_{j=y-h/2}^{y+h/2} \frac{B(i, j)}{w \times h} \in [0,1]$$

Fig. 3 illustrates the vertical-edge density image as a thermographic map, where "hot" areas denote high-density areas. Obviously, the obtained result critically depends on a proper selection of the density mask dimension. It should be chosen according to the size, inter-distance and aspect ratio of license plate characters. Given the maximum and minimum expected plate character heights, h_M and h_m, respectively, and the character aspect ratio, r, the dimension of the density mask can be computed as:

$$h = \frac{h_M + h_m}{2} \cdot 0.85 ; \quad w = h \cdot r \cdot 0.7$$

This tuning rule has shown to work properly with very disparate values for expected character size, in particular: $h_M = 33$ (pixels) and $h_m = 10$ (pixels), while using a character aspect ratio: $r = 0.58$, corresponding to the old and new fashioned Spanish car plates.

The density image is used to locate those regions which are likely to include a license plate. First, candidate rows are searched by performing a unidimensional analysis of the density map. In particular, the variance of the density values along each row are obtained, leading to the vector $v(y)$ depicted in Fig. 4. Notice the two peak values around row 300 corresponding to the square (two lines) vehicle license plate.

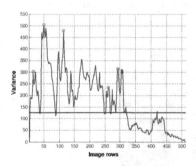

Fig. 4. Variance vector per rows of the vertical-edge density image

Fig. 5. Location of license plate candidates

Given the texture of license plates, the vertical-edge density, along a row belonging to a plate, typically exhibits higher variance values. Consequently, the relative maxima of the variance vector can be considered candidates for possible license plates. However, instead of considering all the relative maxima, a more selective procedure is followed. First, a set of intervals are defined (see Fig. 4) in the "image row" axis, then the absolute maximum inside each interval is taken as potential plate row (to be denoted as r_i^{cand}, for the i-th maximum). Each interval includes the set of adjacent rows whose variance is over a threshold, $\beta = k_\beta \, max(v(y))$ (blue line in Fig. 4), given by a percentage of the global maximum variance.

The intervals around each r_i^{cand} are then narrowed, in order to better fit to the plate vertical limits: $\left[r_i^{upp}, r_i^{bot} \right]$. r_i^{upp} is the first row towards the left of r_i^{cand} that does not fulfill: $v\left(r_i^{upp} \right) > k_\delta \cdot v\left(r_i^{cand} \right)$. Alternatively, r_i^{bot} is the first row towards the right of r_i^{cand} that does not fulfill the same condition.

For each candidate region, it is checked that its height is inside the range specified by the expected average size of the license plate characters.

A similar analysis is performed per columns, but only in those image stripes selected as possible candidates. Again, the relative maximum values of the variance c_i^{cand} for each of the possible candidates are searched, and the left and right limit columns are obtained: $\left[c_i^{left}, c_i^{right} \right]$. Fig. 5 illustrates the resulting candidate set after the described per-row and per-column edge-density variance analysis. Typical values for parameters $k_\beta=0.15$ and $k_\delta=0.3$ (in the case of the analysis per columns: $k_\beta=0.2$ and $k_\delta=0.25$).

2.4   Two-Step Region Growing

For each candidate region obtained in the previous step, a seeded region growing algorithm is performed, using as the initial seed the maximum density point inside the candidate bounding box. This process consists of incorporating neighbour points fulfilling a similitude criterion. A two-step procedure with a combined similitude criterion is proposed to improve the segmentation of plate candidates.

The first step employs a criterion based on an upper density threshold for region growing. This threshold is defined as a certain percentage α_1 of the maximum value corresponding to the initial seed. The result is a typically elliptic region centered on the license plate, but not reaching its limits.

As this region is expected to be located at the core of the plate, we will perform a simple luminance analysis, in order to classify those pixels owning to the background of the license plate from those belonging to the character strokes. On top of that, this analysis will allow distinguishing between white (light) background plates with black (dark) characters and the opposite.

The histogram of the previous region is obtained, $h(k)$. Then, on the one hand, the mean value of pixels' intensities μ is computed. On the other, an energy threshold, γ, is also computed, such that 75% of the histogram energy is under this threshold:

$$\gamma = \arg\min_{0 \leq i \leq 255} \left[\sum_{k=0}^{i} \left(\frac{h(k)}{N} \right)^2 \geq 0.75 \cdot E \right]$$

where N is the number of pixels of the analyzed region and E is the total histogram energy: $E = \sum_{k=0}^{255} \left(\dfrac{h(k)}{N} \right)^2$

Fig. 6 illustrates an example of the referred histogram. Two vertical lines are marking the two thresholds considered, the intensity mean value μ and the energy threshold γ. If $\gamma > \mu$, the region labeled as "B" in Fig. 6 corresponds to the plate background which is a white background with dark characters. Otherwise, it means this region is the dark background with white characters. In any case, the intensity distribution of the plate background can be modeled assuming a Gaussian probability density function, $N(\mu^B, \sigma^B)$, where μ^B is the mean background intensity value, and σ^B is the corresponding typical deviation.

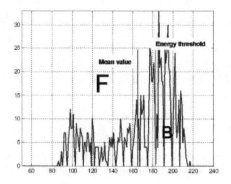

Fig. 6. Histogram of the resulting image after the first region growing process

The second stage of the region growing process consists of aggregating those pixels satisfying a combined criterion:

- Having a density level above a certain percentage α_2 of the maximum value corresponding to the initial seed, which constitutes a lower density threshold $(\alpha_2 \leq \alpha_1)$.
- Having an intensity level in an interval around the mean intensity value of pixels owning to the plate background. If $I^B(x, y)$ represents a plate background pixel, this can be described by:

$$I^B(x, y) \in \left[\mu^B - k \cdot \sigma^B, \mu^B + k \cdot \sigma^B \right]$$

Figures 7 and 8 illustrate two examples of the proposed two-step region growing algorithm ($\alpha_1 = 49\%$, $\alpha_2 = 31\%$, have been used in these and next experiments). It can be verified that the bounding box of the obtained region accurately fits to the plate limits, even in cases of bright vehicles bearing plates with a bright background.

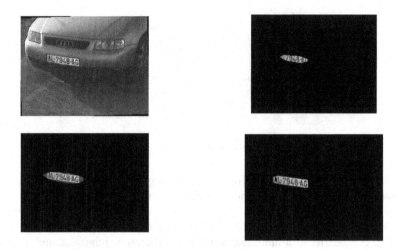

Fig. 7. From left to right and top to bottom: input image. First step (upper density threshold) region growing. Lower density threshold region growing. Two-step, combined-criterion (proposed) region growing.

Fig. 8. From left to right: First step (upper density threshold) region growing. Two-step, combined-criterion (proposed), region growing.

2.5 False Candidate Rejection

During the region growing steps, several parameters can be simultaneously computed, which provide useful information for false candidate rejection: maximum and minimum inertia axes, rectangularity, aspect ratio, etc. Although some false candidates can be identified using this information, a more precise analysis is usually required, in order to reduce the false positive ratio. The extended analysis includes the binarization of the region and the extraction and analysis of connected components.

The binarization can be performed using a global or an adaptive threshold. In general, the adaptive solution is more computationally expensive, but provides better results [18]. Niblack [19] proposed computing the adaptive threshold for each pixel, $T(x,y)$, using the median and standard deviation of the neighbourhood intensity values. A variation of this method, introduced in [20] will be used, considering the difference between the maximum and minimum neighbouring intensities, instead of the standard deviation:

$$T(x, y) = \mu(x, y) + k_T \cdot (M(x, y) - m(x, y))$$

Fig. 9. Binarization of candidate regions using adaptative thresholding

Fig. 9 shows the binarization of one candidate region using the described adaptive thresholding. A connected component labeling is then applied to distinguish the license plate characters from other objects [21] (size, aspect ratio). Then, only the reliable labeled objects are used in order to test some conditions over the license plate candidate: collinearity of a minimum number of characters, minimum and maximum number of allowed characters in a legal plate, etc.

3 Experimental Results

Experimental results have been performed on an Intel Pentium Core2 Duo at 1,7 GHz, 1 GB RAM. Two image sets have been used. The first one corresponds to 243 good quality/contrast grayscale images. The second set of images is constituted by 100 low quality/contrast grayscale images. The main part corresponds to commercial or freight transport vehicles. In the latter case, many license plates are badly-preserved or partially covered by other elements. Besides, the presence of printed text on the vehicle makes more difficult the license plate location.

The following parameters have been measured (see [22]), in order to evaluate the performance of the proposed method:

- *NRC:* Number of raw candidates provided by the algorithm.
- *NFC:* Number of candidates validated as license plates. This parameter can be decomposed in true positives (*TNFC*) and false positives (*FNFC*).
- *MR(%):* Miss rate.
- *FDR(%):* False detection rate.

Fig. 10. Left: Sample image from test set 1. Right: Sample image from test set 2.

Table 1. Metrics associated to two test sets

	Set 1	Set 2
NRC	967	867
NFC	241	108
TNFC	236	92
FNFC	5	16
MR (%)	2,88	8
FDR (%)	2,1	16

Table 1 details the performance of the proposed method using the two set of images considered. The second set of images exhibits a miss and false detection rate much higher than the first one, as expected, due to the low quality of images and to the numerous commercial vehicles which usually includes text and publicity labels that are possible license plate candidates.

4 Conclusions

This paper reports a method for license plate segmentation. The main contribution of the paper is the proposed two-step region growing procedure, combining density and intensity image information, which allow achieving a better fit to the true license plate region. As reported in the experiments, the proposed method achieves a good extraction of license plates.

Acknowledgments. This work has been supported by the Spanish Ministry of Education and Science (Research Project with reference DPI2007-60128), the Consejería de Innovación, Ciencia y Empresa (Research Project P07-TIC-02621) and ACISA R&D Department.

References

1. McQueen, B., McQueen, J.: Intelligent Transportation Systems Architectures. Artech House, Norwood (1999)
2. Walton, C.M.: The Heavy Vehicle Electronic License Plate Program and Crescent Demonstration Project. IEEE Transactions on Vehicular Technology 40(1), 147–151 (1991)
3. Caner, H., Gecim, H.S., Alkar, A.Z.: Efficient Embedded Neural-Network-Based License Plate Recognition System. IEEE Transactions on Vehicular Technology 57(5), 2675–2683 (2008)
4. Lopez, J.M., Gonzalez, J., Galindo, C., Cabello, J.: A versatile low-cost car plate recognition system. In: 9th Inl Symp. on Signal Processing and Its Applications ISSPA, pp. 1–4 (2007)
5. Comelli, P., Ferragina, P., Notturno Granieri, M., Stabile, F.: Optical Recognition of Motor Vehicle License Plates. IEEE Transactions on Vehicular Technology 44(4), 790–799 (1995)

6. Anagnostopoulos, C.-N.E., Anagnostopoulos, I.E., Psoroulas, I.D., Loumos, V., Kayafas, E.: License Plate Recognition From Still Images and Video Sequences: A Survey. IEEE Transactions on Intelligent Transportation Systems 9(3), 377–391 (2008)
7. Wang, S., Lee, H.: Detection and recognition of license plate characters with different appearences. In: Proc. Conf. Intell. Transp. Syst., vol. 2, pp. 979–984 (2003)
8. Ma, Z., Yang, J.: A license plate locating algorithm based on multiple Gauss filters and morphology mathematics. In: Proc. 24th IASTED Int. Multiconference, Signal Process., Pattern Recog. Appl., Insbruck, Austria, February 15-17, 2006, pp. 90–94 (2006)
9. Wang, T.-H., Ni, F.-C., Li, K.-T., Chen, Y.-P.: Robust license plate recognition based on dynamic projection warping. In: Proc. IEEE Int. Conf. Netw., Sens. Control, pp. 784–788 (2004)
10. Wu, Q., Zhang, H., Jia, W., He, X., Yang, J., Hintz, T.: Car plate detection using cascaded tree-style learner based on hybrid object features. In: Proc. IEEE Int. Conf. AVSS, Sydney, Australia, pp. 15–20 (2006)
11. Chen, Y.-N., Han, C.-C., Wang, C.-T., Jeng, B.-S., Fan, K.-C.: The application of a convolution neural network on face and license plate detection. In: Proc. 18th ICPR, Hong Kong, vol. 3, pp. 552–555 (2006)
12. Adorni, G., Cagnoni, S., Mordonini, M.: Efficient low-level vision program design using sub-machine-code genetic programming. In: Proc. Workshop sulla Percezione e Visione nelle Machine (2002)
13. Cui, Y., Huang, Q.: Extracting characters of license plates from video sequences. Machine, Vision and Applications 10(5/6), 308–320 (1998)
14. Zheng, D., Zhao, Y., Wang, J.: An efficient method of license plate location. Pattern Recognition Letters 26(15), 2431–2438 (2005)
15. Martín Rodríguez, F., Fernández Hermida, X.: New Advances in the Automatic Reading of V.L.P.'s (Vehicle License Plates). In: Proceedings de SPC 2000 (Signal Processing and Communications), Marbella (September 2000)
16. Hongliang, B., Changping, L.: A hybrid License Plate Extraction Method based on Edge Statistics and Morphology. In: Proc. of the 17th IEEE Conference on Pattern Recognition (ICPR 2004), Cambridge, U.K. (2004)
17. Shapiro, V., et al.: Adaptive License Plate Image Extraction. In: Proc. of the Int. Conference on Computer Systems and Technologies (2003)
18. Feng, M.-L., Tan, Y.-P.: Contrast adaptive binarization of low quality document images. IECICE Electronics Express 1(6), 501–506 (2004)
19. Niblack, W.: An Introduction to Digital Image Processing. Prentice Hall, Englewood Cliffs (1986)
20. Wolf, C., Jolion, J.-M.: Extraction and Recognition of Artificial Text in Multimedia Documents. Pattern Analysis & Applications 6(4), 309–326 (2003)
21. Chang, S.L., Chen, L.S., Chung, Y., Chen, S.: Automatic License Plate Recognition. IEEE Transactions on Intelligent Transportation Systems 5(1), 42–53 (2004)
22. Kim, K., Jung, K., Hyung, J.: Color Texture-Based Object Detection: An Application to License Plate Localization, pp. 293–309. Springer, Heidelberg (2002)

Boat Speed Monitoring Using Artificial Vision

Alberto Broggi, Pietro Cerri, Paolo Grisleri, and Marco Paterlini

VisLab - Dipartimento di Ingegneria dell'Informazione
Università degli Studi di Parma
43100 Parma, Italy
{broggi,cerri,grisleri,paterli}@ce.unipr.it
www.vislab.it

Abstract. This paper describes a method to detect, measure the speed, and extract statistics of boats moving on a wide water surface using a single image stream taken from grayscale camera. The approach is based on a background subtraction technique combined with classification and tracking to improve robustness; it provides a stable detection even with sea waves and strong light reflections. The method returns correct speed values within the range ±5% in the 97% of use cases. The algorithm has been integrated in a speed warning prototype system on the Burano island in Venice, monitoring a 250 m wide channel slice. Images are captured by a high resolution camera and processed on site in real-time. Processing results can be accessed remotely for monitoring purposes. The system has been up and running for more than two years.

1 Introduction

The city of Venice has a naval traffic made by an almost unique concentration of different types of boats whose length varies from few meters to more than one hundred meters, and their shape can heavily change from one type to another. Many vessels cross water channels navigating too fast and generating huge sea waves. Waves are a critical problem for the city: they can damage both the buildings and also the ecosystem that lives on the natural coasts and has the property to contrasts the lowering of ground's level. In order to solve this problem, a system to notify the boat drivers of their speed has been created with the aim of discouraging vessels driving too fast and therefore reducing the waves impact. Large speed panels are placed on the coast showing the current speed of boats passing through the channel. From the data collected during more than two years of continuous operation, it can be observed that boats reduce their speed after entering the measurement area.

The goal of monitoring vessel speeds can be reached also by analyzing data provided by a radar, but in this case the system would be much more expensive than using a single camera. An example of this application has been presented by Blake in [1] but unfortunately, like described in [2] and [3] using a radar-based method, it is difficult to recognize small boats, because their doppler spectrum is similar to sea waves' spectrum.

P. Foggia, C. Sansone, and M. Vento (Eds.): ICIAP 2009, LNCS 5716, pp. 327–336, 2009.

(a)   *(b)*

Fig. 1. The camera installed on Burano (Venice) island, a black arrow highlights the camera location *(a)*, and channel to monitor with indication of distance and field of view *(b)*

Vision based detectors offer great advantages since the classification capabilities are more precise than a radar (in a complex scene objects can be better distinguished and further classifications are possible).

Another system described in [10] has been realized in the city of Venice to monitor the traffic activity in the Grand Canal. The ARGOS system has a distributed structure, based on cells. Each cell has a vision sensor, a local processing unit, a Pan-Tilt-Zoom (PTZ) camera, and a wireless connection to a central server.

The system proposed in this work has been designed to work with a single camera. It can deal with different target lengths, from small boats to big vessels: it has been tested successfully with ferries more than 100 meters long (longer than the framed area). A single camera, covering about 7500 square meters is placed on the channel side, fixed on a 10 meters tall pole, as shown in figure 1.*a*. In figure 1.*b*: point A shows the camera location, B and C represent points with well-known GPS coordinates; the yellow area depicts the camera field of view. Notice that the camera is installed about 40 m far from the beginning of the detection area.

The camera is connected to a computer for local data processing. The system is connected through a standard ADSL line and can be monitored via browser thanks to a dedicated and integrated web server. The system collects statistics about the observed traffic and for each target it logs the speed of boats when entering the monitored area, when leaving it, the average speed, and the time of observation.

2   Boats Detection

This section describes the various phases of the detection algorithm.

The system, from a high level point of view, is organized into a three stages pipeline: the first stage takes a 256-levels grayscale image acquired from the camera as input and produces a 2 levels image representing pixels belonging to the background and pixels belonging to features of moving objects; the second section analyzes these 2-level images in the time domain to detect boats in the scene, tracking them, and calculating their speed, using camera calibration data. The assessment of determining the boat speed with a good accuracy requires the determination of the target position with high precision. A tide compensation procedure has also been introduced into the system to reduce errors due to incorrect positioning of the boat baseline. The third level carries over all other service tasks such as supervising the log composition and, publishing the output image on the web page.

2.1   Improving Background Subtraction

This section describes how to improve the well-known background subtraction technique to detect moving objects for this very specific application. The main issue consists in creating a suitable reference frame that is able to filter sea waves. In the literature different approaches are presented which describe how to detect moving object in indoor or structured outdoor scenes, but in this case we had to consider outdoor scenes, in which the background changes very quickly like water background.

Different statistical approaches has been proposed such as [4] and [5]. The algorithm described in this article draws on Alsaqre's[6] method to calculate a reference frame as the union between the current frame and the previous reference frame. Other more recent approaches like [11] are based on saliency.

In the proposed system raw images are processed to obtain the reference frame using equation (1), where r represents a pixel of the reference frame and, c a pixel of the current frame.

$$r = (1 - 0.25) * r + 0.25c \qquad (1)$$

By using equation (1), pixels representing sea and sea waves become similar. This is a useful result since waves disturb the detection of moving objects. The reference frame is shown in figure 2.b. Now, background subtraction is applied between the current frame and the reference frame, obtaining the image shown, with inverted colors, in figure 2.c.

After binarization some noise may still be present, as shown in inverted colors, in figure 2.d, mainly due to non completely filtered waves. To reduce and possibly remove it, the algorithm searches for connected regions larger than a fixed threshold and removes smaller regions.

Although the background subtraction method used here is simple and well known quite old it has been chosen over newest approaches available in literature thanks to its simplicity, the possibility to be executed in a short time, and eventually implemented in hardware.

Figure 2.e shows, in inverted colors, the resulting image after the filter application, with a strong noise reduction compared with the image shown in figure 2.d. Each connected region is then labeled using a unique bounding box that has a numeric identifier as shown in figure 2.f.

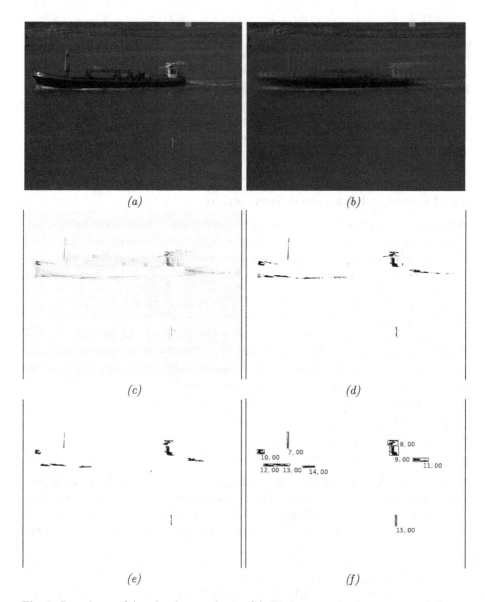

Fig. 2. Raw frame *(a)* and reference frame *(b)*. With inverted colors: difference frame *(c)* and binarized difference frame *(d)*. Connected regions *(e)* and bounding boxes *(f)*.

2.2 Tracking

This section explains how the tracking process is realized. The algorithm analyzes each connected region (i.e moving objects' features) searching for its movement from the previous frame to the current one. In particular, each feature in the current frame is compared to all those in the previous frame, in order to locate and match the very same feature. Similarity rules are used to evaluate the matching between two features are similar. Three parameters are used:

- Aspect ratio match,
- Area match,
- Content match.

Each comparison returns a floating point match value.

These values are then filtered using a triangular fuzzy function to normalize the results. The function slope has been adjusted during the in-lab development on pre-recorded sequences. After that, all these outputs are multiplied together, so that a single comparison match value equal to zero causes a null final match value.

The algorithm compares every bounding box of the current frame with every bounding box of the past frames. The average among the three match values was also considered, but it can lead to errors in some cases, so a new match value has been defined to be the final one.

The comparison process between bounding boxes has been extended up to the last five frames in the past, in order to reach a more robust result.

All match values are accumulated together to obtain a unique match value for each feature in the current frame. When possible, every feature in the current frame is linked to one feature only of the previous frame.

For each feature in the current frame, it is now possible to determine the correspondent motion vector, which links two bounding boxes' centers (figure 3) and which also has a weight, given by the features' characteristics. Vectors are clustered using similarity rules, depending on module and phase.

The time analysis of the motion vectors associated to each feature is the basis of the next high level processing step.

Fig. 3. Moving object features and corresponding motion vectors represented by red arrows

2.3   High Level Processing

The algorithm evaluates the motion vectors for each feature, looking for affinity in contiguous time steps. A new target is created when the algorithm finds similar vectors in contiguous time steps, meaning that two or more features are moving in the same fashion and are therefore clustered together.

This event implies a new target creation, which is identified by a bounding box and which has some distinctive features such as: unique identifier, geometric qualities, position coordinates, motion vector.

When new target features are identified, the target geometry changes.

The main purpose of the system is to measure the boat speed; this problem is directly mapped into measuring the speed of the boat features. The system provides a correct detection even if the silhouette of the boat is not completely visible, such as boats longer than 100 m which do not fit into the camera field of view.

The target base line, represented by the lower bound of the target's bounding box, is used to evaluate the target speed value. It is the only available means to estimate the distance between the target and the camera, since the system is based on monocular vision.

The baseline detection uses as features the wavelets at the boat base. This effects increase with the boat speed.

3   Speed Estimation

The module of the target's motion vector represents the speed value, measured in $pixel/frame$. Using camera calibration, frame rate, and the target's base line, it is possible to estimate the actual boat speed value measured in km/h.

Wrong estimations may occur when the algorithm is not able to correctly detect the target's base line. The use of a camera resolution of 1024×768 pixel makes it possible to decrease the probability of this kind of errors by hooking as features the small and regular wavelets the water shapes at the base of the boat. In figure 4.a, the x-axis plots the base line errors, measured in pixel; the y-axis represents the corresponding speed errors.

Many functions are plotted on the graph, depending on the current target's speed. For example when a target is moving at $45\,km/h$, a $+30$ pixels base line error (vertical) introduces a speed error of $4.9\,km/h$, about 5% of the actual speed. After a number of experimental tests carried over 3 months of tests it is possible to state that the maximum base line error is not higher than 5 pixels, corresponding to a 2% maximum speed error.

3.1   The Influence of Tide

A further source of errors is the tide level, that changes many times during the day, and that behaves differently depending on atmospheric conditions and season. In the gulf of Venice, the maximum tide range can reach $2\,m\,[-1\,m, +1\,m]$ under particular conditions. The water level acts as the reference plane: changing

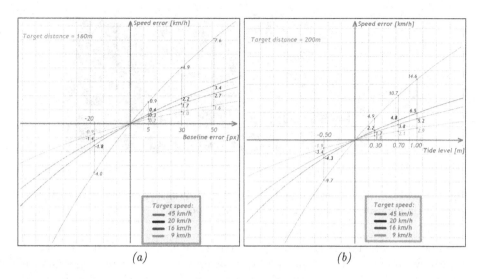

Fig. 4. Error produced by a wrong detection of the target's base line *(a)*. Error produced by the tide level *(b)*.

the water level is like changing the plane where targets are moving or changing the camera height. Errors due to tide level are described in figure 4.*b*: the x-axis plots the tide level, measured in meters; the y-axis indicates the corresponding speed errors. Many functions are plotted, depending on the target speed. For example, when a target is moving at $20\,km/h$, and the tide level is $70\,cm$, the error on the estimated speed for a boat $200\,m$ far from the camera will be $4.8\,km/h$, comparable to 24% of its actual speed. It is clear therefore that the tide's level can not be ignored. As mentioned, the tide level is given by the composition of two effects: astronomical effect (given by the specific position of the moon and the sun, which is predictable) and weather (especially wind blowing from south to north, which is unpredictable but measurable). In this work the tide level is provided by astronomical considerations, which represents a reasonable first order approximation. This is the easiest way to estimate the tide, because it does not imply any other tool installation, like for example a float sensor.

4 Results

Results tightly depend on the type of vessel entering the camera view, on vessels' shape and color, and lighting conditions; so it is therefore difficult to provide absolute results. Quantitative performance analysis has been carried out on different video sequences totaling about 1.5 hours which showed 87 correctly detected targets and only 2 missed over.

The system returns correct results with a very limited number of false positives; false negatives events are generally due to low lighting conditions. Results

(a)   (b)

Fig. 5. Successful operations during bad weather conditions *(a)*. A double vessel transition *(b)* in opposite directions: both speeds are reported.

are good even when more then one target enter the camera view shot. In case of adverse weather conditions, the algorithm also returns correct results, as shown in figure 5.*a* which was recorded during a snow storm with high winds blowing, generating both waves and a sensible camera pitch vibration.

When the boats direction is not orthogonal to the projection of the camera optical axis on the sea surface, boats can be seen as moving diagonally in the framed image, as that depicted in figure 5. In these cases, the speed measurement still remains below 5% boundary since the lower side of the bounding box surrounding the target has a corner belonging to the boat baseline.

Despite this, the geometry allows to correctly estimate the vessel speed. In correspondence to situations in which two vessels move in opposite directions, the algorithm returns two separate speed estimates which are displayed on two different panels. Figure 5.*b* shows two additional windows indicating the output values displayed on the hardware panels.

At the end of the development, the system was tested with motorboat equipped with a differential GPS. 8 hours of continuous tests with different speeds, distance from the camera, different scenario configurations (single boat, multiple boats with same and different directions), different illumination conditions have been concluded successfully. The error was measured to remain under the 5% of the GPS measurement.

5   Conclusion and Future Work

The system has been operational at the test site for more than two years and during this period the whole system has proven to be effective. From the logs analysis, the boats speed tends to be reduced as long as they pass in the monitored area. A further step of this work is the porting of the whole detection algorithm on an embedded architecture like a smart camera integrating both the sensor and an embedded processing system. This integration would allow to cut on price and simplify the system installation phase. Even if the proposed system has already reached significant results, some useful improvements can be made. First, automatic camera gain control process is needed to correct false negatives generated by low light conditions. The use of a second camera into the system may provide a number of improvements, solving for example errors generated by the tide level. In fact, stereo vision would make it possible to compute, the distance between the target and the camera with higher precision than a monocular-based system. On the other side, in order to detect targets placed 200 m far away from the camera system, it would be necessary to place the two cameras at a distance of about 2 m from each other. This implies to realize a tough infrastructure able to resist to adverse weather conditions, like high winds.

Acknowledgments

This work was funded by Ministry of Infrastructures and Transports - Magistrato delle acque through its concessionary "Consorzio Venezia Nuova" in the framework of the project "Interventi di protezione di margini barenali in erosione nell'area del canale di Burano. Progetto esecutivo Monitoraggio delle opere. Sperimentazione di un dissuasore di velocità natanti".

The authors also gratefully acknowledge the grant provided by Tattile and Thetis as a support to this research.

References

1. Blake, T.M.: Ship Detection and Tracking using High Frequency Surface Wave Radar. In: HF Radio Systems and Techniques, Nottingham, UK, lug., pp. 291–295 (1997)
2. Herselman, P.L., de Wind, H.J.: Improved covariance matrix estimation in spectrally inhomogeneous sea clutter with application to adaptive small boat detection. In: 2008 International Conference on Radar, Adelaide, Australia, September 2-5, 2008, pp. 94–99 (2008)
3. Herselman, P.L., Baker, C.J.: Analysis of calibrated sea clutter and boat reectivity data at c- and x-band in south African coastal waters. In: RADAR 2007 (2007)
4. Muller-Schneiders, S., Jager, T., Loos, H.S., Niem, W.: R.B. GmbH. Performance Evaluation of a Real Time Video Surveillance System. In: 2nd Joint IEEE International Workshop on VS-PETS, Beijing, China, October 2005, pp. 137–141 (2005)
5. Ohta, N.: A Statistical Approach to Background Subtraction for Surveillance Systems. In: IEEE International Conference of Computer Vision, pp. 481–486 (2001)
6. Alsaqre, F.E., Baozong, Y.: Multiple Moving Objects Tracking for Video Surveillance Systems. In: The 7th International Conference on Signal Processing (ICSP 2004), Beijing, China, pp. 1301–1305 (2004)
7. Seki, M., Fujiwara, H., Sumi, K.: A Robust Background Subtraction Method for Changing Background. In: IEEE Workshop Applications of Computer Vision, pp. 207–213 (2000)
8. Cucchiara, R., Grana, C., Piccardi, M., Prati, A.: Detecting Moving Objects, Ghosts, and Shadows in Video Streams. IEEE Transactions on Pattern Analysis and Machine Intelligence 25(10), 1337–1342 (2003)
9. Paterlini, M.: Progettazione e realizzazione di un algoritmo di visione artificiale per il monitoraggio della velocità dei natanti. Master Thesis. A.A. 2005-2006 Dip. Ing. Inf., Università degli Studi di Parma, Italy

10. Bloisi, D., Iocchi, L., Leone, G.R., Pigliacampo, R., Tombolini, L., Novelli, L.: A distributed vision system for boat traffic monitoring in the Venice Grand Canal. In: 2nd International Conference on Computer Vision Theory and Applications (VISAPP 2007), Barcelona, Spain, March 8-11 (2007)
11. Mahadevan, V., Vasconcelos, N.: Background Subtraction in Highly Dynamic Scenes. In: IEEE Conference on Computer Vision and Pattern Recognition. CVPR 2008, Anhorage, Alaska, June 23-28, 2008, pp. 23–28 (2008)
12. Ministry of Infrastructures and Transports - Magistrato delle acque through its concessionary "Consorzio Venezia Nuova" - Interventi di protezione di margini barenali in erosione nell'area del canale di Burano. Progetto esecutivo Monitoraggio delle opere. Sperimentazione di un dissuasore di velocità natanti

Theia: Multispectral Image Analysis and Archaeological Survey

Vito Roberto[1,2] and Massimiliano Hofer[1]

[1] Dipartimento di Matematica e Informatica
[2] Norbert Wiener Center
University of Udine, Italy
{vito.roberto,massimiliano.hofer}@dimi.uniud.it

Abstract. Theia is a software framework for multispectral image analysis. The design is grounded on the object-oriented approach and a model combining parallel computation with selective data processing. Multispectral images from the archaeological site of Aquileia, Italy, have been used as the experimental testbed in order to assess the effectiveness and performance of the system; satisfactory results are reported, and are quite promising towards the use of the framework as a dynamic, interactive interface to real-time data exploration and processing.

Keywords: Multispectral, Hyperspectral, Image Processing, Interactive, Visualization, Object Oriented Design, Cultural Heritage, Archaeological survey, Remote sensing.

1 Introduction

The analysis of multispectral images is a central issue in a number of research and management tasks, such as environmental planning, medical diagnosis, archaeological survey and surveillance for both military and civilian applications. Problems arise from the data acquisition by heterogeneous sensory systems; the massive data sets to be handled; the need for efficient algorithms for data visualization, filtering and mining.

As a consequence, a number of challenging topics are to be faced by the designers. Proprietary frameworks are available like ENVI® [2], or freeware like ISIS [3], which are the outcome of long-term research projects, and so are mature enough to address a large number of applications. More recent developments include Opticks [4] and Next ESA SAR Toolbox (NEST) [5].

However, most computers now process gigabytes of data in a second and load large data sets in the RAM; uniprocessor systems are being rapidly replaced by CMP, SMT and SMP architectures even in low-end hardware. Novel software systems should be put into operation to take advantage from this state of affairs [10]: new solutions can be explored towards real-time, dynamic processing of huge amounts of information, to be driven by fully interactive user interfaces.

On the other hand, the fast growth and differentiation of applications suggest to adopt well-posed criteria of software design – inspired by modularity

P. Foggia, C. Sansone, and M. Vento (Eds.): ICIAP 2009, LNCS 5716, pp. 337–345, 2009.

and openness – enabling the developer to re-use or embed new modules, and customize the core system to domain-specific applications.

Along these lines we designed and realized Theia, a software framework for image exploration and analysis, and the results are reported in the present paper. The next section introduces the system architecture, with details on the organization of modules and data flow; Sections 3 and 4 report two steps of the analysis of multispectral images taken for archaeological survey on the Aquileia area (Italy); Section 5 contains our conclusions.

2   Theia: Software Architecture and Implementation

The goals of the project are: Object-Oriented (O-O) design; portability among OS platforms; efficient use of parallel architectures; real-time processing of massive data sets; interactivity of the user interface; extendability with customized components.

Two architectural schemes are reported in Figure 1. Three functional blocks have been defined: data management; data processing; graphic user interfacing (GUI). The first includes data encoding and storing; the second, numerical processing and graphic rendering; the GUI manages the flow between user, events, components and processes. The accurate O-O design and interface definitions ensure that each block can be developed independently: for example, the GUI management block can be replaced by a scripting engine to drive the whole application.

In order to achieve efficiency, we adopted a computational model that combines selective (attentional) with parallel processing techniques; a scheme is reported in Figure 2. The management unit in the GUI performs the following steps: ▸ Notifies to update an image region; ▸ The visualization filter preprocesses data, if needed; ▸ The region is partitioned into tiles; ▸ Multiple threads are started, depending on the number of available CPUs; the tiles are inserted

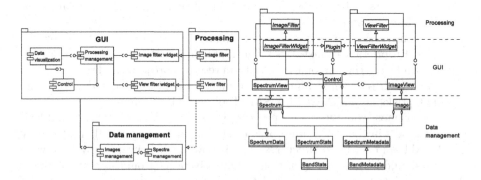

Fig. 1. General architecture of Theia, in UML 2 notation [12]. *Left:* Components organized into three functional blocks, and communications channelled through a few, well-defined interfaces. *Right:* Class diagram, with the same organization outlined.

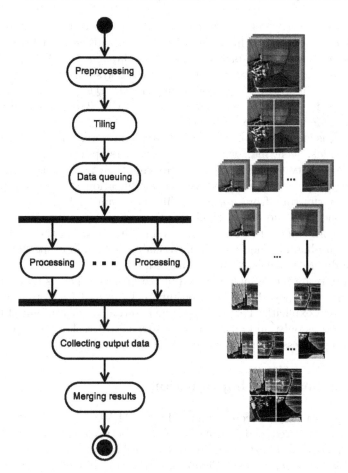

Fig. 2. UML 2 activity diagram of the parallel computations triggered by a screen update

into the input queue; ▶ Each thread pulls the tiles, processes them and pushes the results on an output queue, until the input is empty; ▶ The output is collected and dispatched to the GUI.

Theia addresses two basic tasks, image visualization and processing. The *Filter* is a central concept, mapped onto two modules: the *ViewFilter* and the *ImageFilter,* charged of visualization and numerical processing, respectively. They consist of three abtract classes: *Plugin,* exchanging parameters with the GUI; *Processor,* triggering the computations and providing results; *Widget,* customizing the GUI to a specified filter.

Theia has been implemented on the Linux[TM] OS (openSUSE 11.0, kernel 2.6.28) for x86-64 CPUs; the C++ language has been preferred to Java[TM] because of its higher efficiency in processing massive data sets; in addition, it allows a more effective use of the O-O and generic paradigms, by offering solutions such as multiple inheritance, virtual base classes and templates.

The infrastructure – not shown in Figure 1 – provides basic operations and support for common data formats (ENVI-BSQ [13], multichannel TIFF [7], PNG [14]). Standard transmission protocols like Web Map Service (WMS) [15] ensure the interconnection with network data sources and systems.

The system employs two cross-platform libraries: QT4 [1], v. 4.4.3, a framework for GUI development, distributed under GPL v. 2.0 or 3.0; and LibTIFF [6], v. 3.8.2 under the X11/MIT license.

Theia acts as an expandable core of software operators. The GUI is capable of handling plugins: event management, mouse ownership, drag-and-drop of basic data, switching between components and driving their placement and visualization. A new filter can be developed without modifications to the main program, and linked at run-time from a separate library; a minimal implementation requires just one class and one method.

All basic components to process images and show data in the GUI are fully re-usable by a plugin element: spectrum visualization components, for example, are used in different panels, as shown in Figures 4, 5.

Portability is another issue addressed in the project. Theia is coded in C++, which implies that portability between different OS and CPU architectures is to be addressed explicitly. For this sake, the external APIs are limited to cross-platform libraries only, and all architecture-dependent tasks – such as data encoding — are addressed within encapsulated common libraries.

3   Model-Based Orthoprojection

The multispectral images were acquired by the MIVIS airborne sensor system (Multispectral Infrared and Visible Imaging Spectrometer [16]). The data is subject to a systematic distortion due to the mechanical structure of the sensor system; a sketch is reported in Figure 3. A rotating mirror conveys radiation from the terrain into a detector. By taking repeated measurements at fixed time intervals, a strip of data of the terrain is acquired. The whole multispectral image is collected by an aircraft. In order to correct the distortions of this kind of sensor, we developed a mathematical model and designed a specific algorithm.

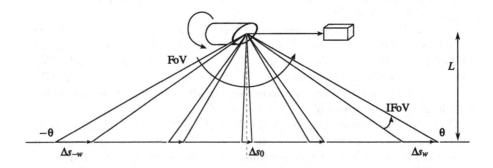

Fig. 3. Model scheme of the MIVIS airborne sensor system

We define *Field of View* (FoV) the angular width of the acquired data and *Instantaneous Field of View* (IFoV) the angular width of a single measure.

Let $\Delta s_i, i \in [-w, w] \cap \mathbb{N}$ be the $2w + 1$ samples collected at regular angular distances in the range $[-\theta, \theta]$ at an altitude L. The model in Figure 3 shows that the maximum resolution – expressed in $\frac{m}{pixel}$ – is reached in Δs_0.

The minimum and maximum angles corresponding to Δs_i are:

$$\left(\frac{2\theta(i+w)}{2w+1} - \theta, \frac{2\theta(i+1+w)}{2w+1} - \theta \right) \tag{1}$$

The minimum and maximum coordinates corresponding to Δs_i, then, are:

$$\left(L \tan\left(\frac{2\theta(i+w)}{2w+1} - \theta \right), L \tan\left(\frac{2\theta(i+1+w)}{2w+1} - \theta \right) \right) \tag{2}$$

We call *orthoprojection* the mapping between the vector of input values $\Delta \bar{s}$ and a new vector with components $\Delta o_j, j \in \left[-\frac{\tan\theta}{\theta} w, \frac{\tan\theta}{\theta} w \right] \cap \mathbb{N}$ of elements having the same resolution as Δs_0. The mapping is defined as follows:

$$\Delta o_j = \Delta s_{k_j} \text{ with } k_j = \left\lfloor \frac{w}{\theta} \tan^{-1}\left(\frac{\theta}{w} j \right) \right\rfloor \tag{3}$$

In order to check the validity of the model, we used four multispectral images acquired by MIVIS at the altitude $L = 1500$m. We compared them with georeferenced orthophotos with known precision and identified a set of common reference points (16 for each MIVIS image). We then computed the optimal least-square coefficients of a linear transform between the two coordinate systems.

The result provides us with georeferenced frames with a resolution between 2.45 and $3.70 \frac{m}{pixel}$, depending on the distance from the central axis, with standard deviation 8.61 m.

4   An Application to Archaeological Survey

Our framework has been tested on a multispectral image of Aquileia, an ancient roman city in the North-eastern Italy area.

A number of tasks have been implemented: ▶ Visualization and rendering: multispectral-to-RGB image mappings; real-time rendering of animated sequences. ▶ Processing: multispectral-to-multispectral mappings and filterings; band selection; pixel classifications and segmentation techniques [9]; model-based geometric transforms (othoprojection).

The tasks were carried out on a notebook equipped with 3 GB RAM and a dual core CPU with a 2 GHz clock. Each multispectral image consists of frames acquired in 102 wavelength bands between 433 and 12700 nanometers, with 755×4000 pixel resolution, 16–bit sample precision, and a load of 587 MB per frame.

The design solutions allowed us to explore and analyze data interactively. Frames were analysed by estimating distances with respect to reference spectra using appropriate measures [11]. Two such measures have been reported in

Table 1. Two spectral distance measures

Spectral angle	$\dfrac{\sum_{i=1}^{n} x_i y_i}{\sqrt{\sum_{i=1}^{n} x_i^2}\sqrt{\sum_{i=1}^{n} y_i^2}}$
Spectral information divergence	$\sum_{i=1}^{n} x_i \ln \dfrac{x_i}{y_i} - \sum_{i=1}^{n} y_i \ln \dfrac{y_i}{x_i}$

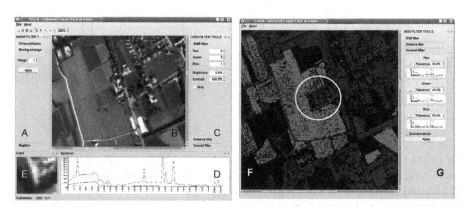

Fig. 4. Two screenshots of Theia, after processing frames of the same area of the roman city of Aquileia. *Left:* Moving average filtering in the visible energy band. Five panels at work: A) Processing filter parameters ; B) Output color frame; C) View filter parameters; D) Spectral data of a selected pixel: besides the true spectrum, two additional curves report the minimum and maximum values over all bands; horizontal scales are in nanometers; E) Magnified frame region surrounding the pixel (228, 1311). *Right.* The GUI has been reconfigured. Segmentation of the same frame into Voronoi regions; color rendering of stone (red) and two kinds of cultivated terrains (green, blue). F) Output frame, showing buried structures of a building (encircled), not distinguishable on the left frame; G) View filter configuration panel, reporting the reference spectral data.

Table 1. An advantage is that no calibration data are needed when extracting reference spectra from known areas within the image. Dozens of spectra could be tried in a few minutes to search for relevant patterns within the flood of data.

Interesting results have been obtained using the spectral angle distance [11] to highlight areas with strong matching with known archaeological findings. Novel evidences of buried structures were found in this way, and confirmed by expert archaeologists: two results have been reported in Figures 4, 5.

In all tests Theia exhibited a remarkable time efficiency: with a visible portion of 755×768 pixels, most visualization filters require a few tenths of a second for a

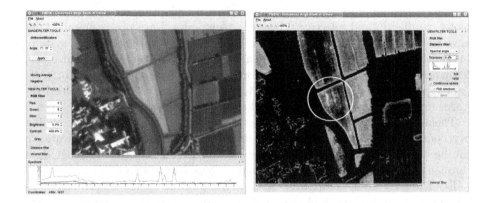

Fig. 5. *Left.* Orthoprojected frame in the visible band from a different area of Aquileia. *Right.* The same area. Spectral angle distance filtering of frames taken in the near infrared. The reference spectral data (panel on the right) are from a known building. A buried structure is apparent (encircled), not distinguishable in the visible band.

complete refresh; much less for the partial renderings needed while panning. The most CPU-intensive filters – e.g., false color segmentation – need at most 1.5 seconds for the first rendering, without activating multithreaded computations.

A measure in the case of a view filter with spectral angle distance, averaged over hundreds of proofs, yields the following results:

	1 thread	2 threads
CPU usage rate	0.98–1	0.72–0.75
Frames per second	2.6	4.3

This means that we reach 83% of the theoretical maximum efficiency.

5   Conclusions and Perspectives

We have designed, implemented and tested Theia, a software system devoted to the analysis of multispectral images. The results of our research work demonstrate that the goals listed in Section 2 are within reach.

The O-O software design provides effective solutions to address the project concerns: encapsulation allows for a clear-cut definition of modules at different granularity: classes, components, blocks; this yields a readable and reusable code. Portability is ensured by a careful implementation; porting on Windows 2000 and XP for i386 has been accomplished with little effort. We also verified that adding filters to the system or linking modules from separate libraries, are both readily affordable tasks.

Computational efficiency has been achieved by adopting a model which exploits parallelism and selective processing techniques. Data processing modules have been kept physically separate from the other ones throughout the system. In addition, features of the C++ language have been exploited to optimize performance, such as template specialization and inline method expansion for basic data types. As a consequence, satisfactory performance has been obtained towards interactive visualization and real-time data processing.

Theia is an open system under various respects: it can be extended by adding new components (e.g., image filters), in order to address specialized applications; can be integrated into a distributed network environment, so to exchange data through standard protocols with external sources, services and systems.

Realizing a system comparable with well-established software products was not the aim of our project. A considerable amount of work is needed for Theia to reach an adequate maturity with respect to the wide range of applications of multispectral analysis. Rather, after further systematic tests, Theia is expected to remain a light, open framework for exploring images and data, as well as developing specialized applications.

References

1. Qt, http://trolltech.com/products/qt
2. ENVI ITT Visual Information Solutions,
   http://www.ittvis.com/envi/index.asp
3. ISIS US Geological Survey, http://isis.astrogeology.usgs.gov/
4. Opticks Ball Aerospace & Technologies Corp., https://opticks.ballforge.net/
5. NEST Array Systems Computing Inc. under ESA Contract,
   http://www.array.ca/nest/
6. LibTIFF, http://www.libtiff.org/
7. Adobe Developers Association, TIFF Revision 6.0. (1992),
   http://partners.adobe.com/public/developer/en/tiff/TIFF6.pdf
8. Perrizo, W., Ding, Q., Ding, Q., Roy, A.: On mining satellite and other remotely sensed images. In: Proceedings of ACM SIGMOD Worksh. on Research Issues in Data Mining and Knowledge Discovery, pp. 33–40 (2001)
9. Landgrebe, D.: Some fundamentals and methods for hyperspectral image data analysis. In: Systems and Technologies for Clinical Diagnostics and Drug Discovery II. School of Electrical & Computer Engineering Purdue University, vol. 3603. SPIE (1999)
10. El-Ghazawi, T., Kaewpijit, S., Le Moigne, J.: Parallel and Adaptive Reduction of Hyperspectral Data to Intrinsic Dimensionality. In: Proceedings of the IEEE International Conference on Cluster Computing. The IEEE Computer Society, Los Alamitos (2001)
11. Sweet, J.: The spectral similarity scale and its application to the classification of hyperspectral remote sensing data. In: IEEE Worksh. on Advances in Techniques for Analysis of Remotely Sensed Data, pp. 92–99 (2003)
12. Eriksson, H.E., Penker, M., Lyons, B., Fado, D.: UML2^{TM} Toolkit. Wiley Publishing, Inc., Chichester (2004)
13. Frew, J.: Difficulties of dealing with large image cubes. In: Proceedings of AIAA Aerospace Sciences Meeting (1991)

14. Boutell, T., et al.: PNG (Portable Network Graphics) Specification Version 1.0. RFC 2083 (1997)
15. OpenGIS® Web Map Service (WMS) Implementation Specification. v. 1.3.0 Open Geospatial Consortium Inc. (2006)
16. Vagni, F.: Survey of hyperspectral and multispectral imaging technologies. Technical Report TR-SET-065-P3 NATO Research and Technology Organization (2007)
17. Boccardo, P., Mondino, E.B., Gomarasca, M.A., Perotti, L.: Orthoprojection tests of hyperspectral data in steep slope zones. In: ISPRS 2004, p. 872 (2004)

A Self-updating Multiexpert System
for Face Identification

Andrea F. Abate[1], Maria De Marsico[2], Michele Nappi[1], and Daniel Riccio[1]

[1] DMI - Dipartimento di Matematica e Informatica, Università di Salerno,
Fisciano (SA), Italy
{mnappi,driccio}@unisa.it
[2] DI - Dipartimento di Informatica, Sapienza Università di Roma, Italy
demarsico@di.uniroma1.it

Abstract. Multibiometric systems can solve a number of problems of single-biometry approaches. A source of flaws for present systems, both single-biometric and multibiometric, can be found in the lack of dynamic update of parameters, which does not allow them to adapt to changes in the working settings. They are generally calibrated once and for all, so that they are tuned and optimized with respect to standard conditions. In this work we investigate an architecture where single-biometry subsystems work in parallel, yet exchanging information at fixed points, according to the N-Cross Testing Protocol. In particular, the integrated subsystems work on the same biometric feature, the face in this case, yet exploiting different classifiers. Subsystems collaborate at a twofold level, both for returning a common answer and for tuning to changing operating conditions. Results demonstrate that component collaboration increases system accuracy and allows identifying unstable subsystems.

1 Introduction

Present biometric systems generally rely on a single classifier. The main drawback is that they are singly vulnerable to possible attacks, as well as little robust with respect to a number of problems (e.g. a voice altered by a cold or a dimly lit face). In the present work we will consider the combination of some popular classifiers to build a face identification system. We chose this biometry because it is contact-less, fast and fairly reliable. Face recognition, however, raises a number of non-easy to solve issues(pose, illumination or expression changes). Indeed, none of the existing approaches for face recognition is free from limitations when dealing with issues such as variation in expression, lighting, pose and acquisition time. Recognition techniques found in literature can be grouped in different classes. A first class includes linear methods. Among them, the two classic Principle Component Analysis (PCA) [1] and Linear Discriminant Analysis (LDA) [2] are widely used in the appearance-based approaches. They both solve the recognition problem within a representation space of lower dimension than image space. In general, LDA-based algorithms outperform PCA-based ones, but they suffer from the so-called *small sample size problem* (SSS) which

P. Foggia, C. Sansone, and M. Vento (Eds.): ICIAP 2009, LNCS 5716, pp. 346–354, 2009.

exists in high-dimensional pattern recognition tasks. Neighborhood Preserving Embedding (NPE) [3] differs from PCA because it aims at preserving the local manifold structure instead of the global Euclidean structure though maintaining linearity of the approach. A weight matrix is built which describes the relationships between the data points in the ambient space, so that each data point can be represented as a linear combination of the neighboring ones. Then an optimal embedding is computed such that the neighborhood structure can be preserved in the dimensionality reduced space. In [4] the authors introduce the Orthogonal Locality Preserving Projections (OLPP) method, producing orthogonal basis functions called Laplacianfaces. The manifold structure is modeled by a nearest-neighbor graph preserving the local structure of the image space. Each face image in the image space is mapped into a low-dimensional face subspace, obtained by OLPP. Fractals are largely exploited in image compression and indexing, so that they have also been investigated in the field of face recognition. In [5], the fractal code of a face image is only used for training a neural network, which works as a classifier on the face database, while in [6], the Partitioned Iterated Function Systems (PIFS) have been explicitly adapted to recognize face.

A multiexpert system provides an effective alternative, as flaws of an individual system can be compensated by the availability of a higher number of cooperating algorithms [7]. This is particularly true if the subsystems exchange information at different levels, as we shall see in presenting the N-Cross Testing Protocol. According to the above considerations, not all classifiers are equally reliable on any input image. In [8] System Response Reliability (SRR) indices have been introduced to evaluate the reliability of each response of single subsystems; responses are considered for fusion only if the corresponding SRR is higher than a given threshold *th*. This improves global system performance, but we argue that we can go even further by considering the "history" of the system. We assume the existence of a *supervisor module* exploiting not only single subsystems responses and their reliability, but also the final global response, to evaluate the overall system state and update reliability thresholds of single subsystems. Such module would allow overcoming the invariance of present multibiometric architectures, by implementing an algorithm converging to an optimal parameters configuration independently from the starting one. Each subsystem takes as input an image, pertaining to the corresponding biometry, and extracts salient features; the resulting feature vectors are used to compute similarity scores, to be inputted to the supervisor module, after a normalization step. In building our multiexpert/multiclassifier system, we chose each subsystem classification method from the most popular linear and non-linear techniques in the state of the art. We aimed at combining results which suffer with significantly different measures from the image variation problems: LDA [2], OLPP [4] and NPE [3].

2 The Integration Scheme

Our multiexpert system significantly differs from the state of art in literature. The algorithms implemented by the recognition subsystems to classify the input face are the ones presented above. The single subsystems cooperate at two different levels. In the first place, they exchange information about the produced subject lists. Such lists are the final result in traditional systems, while represent an intermediate result in our one. The exploited protocol is the N-Cross Testing Protocol [9]. Starting from this basic configuration, each subsystem can also return a measure of reliability for its own response, which can be used to better compute the global result. As a further increase in cooperation, a suitable supervisor module can further exploit reliability measures to obtain the final response and to update subsystems reliability parameters.

2.1   Reliability Margins

Subsystems involved in a multibiometric architecture might not be equally reliable, e.g. due to the possibly different quality of input. An unreliable response can trigger a further check. A *reliability* measure is then crucial for fusion. Some solutions use margins, measuring the "risk" associated to a single subsystem response after observing its scores. Poh and Bengio [10] introduce a confidence margin based on False Acceptance Rate (FAR) and False Rejection Rate (FRR). Many responses are marked as reliable, as the margin relies on an estimate of the actual distribution of genuine/impostor subjects' scores. This might be inappropriate when very high security is required. Moreover, frequentist approaches assume that the scores of the testing and development sets always originate from similar distributions. We adopt the new System Response Reliability (SRR) index [8], based on a system/gallery dependent metric, and measuring the ability of separating genuine subjects from impostors on a single probe basis. SRR can be computed by using as basic elements either the relative distance between the scores of the two first retrieved distinct identities, or the number of subjects near to the retrieved identity which are present in the gallery. SRR values always fall in the range $[0, 1]$. Each subsystem T_k computes, for each $s_{k,i}$, i=1, ..., in its set of responses, a *reliability measure* $srr_{k,i}$. Moreover, each subsystem T_k is characterized by an estimated threshold th_k, possibly updated over time [8], such that a response $s_{k,i}$ is considered as reliable only if $srr_{k,i} \geq th_k$. In general, th_k thresholds can be adjusted in a tuning phase, according to a set of samples with similar features to those of the set used for identification (the two sets should be different and disjoint). The limit is that thresholds do not take into account the performances of the other subsystems.

2.2   The Supervisor Module

A revisitation of the classical multibiometric schema, where subsystems act independently, given that a suitable fusion module is able to combine their single results, takes to global system self-tuning, with a much more flexible and robust architecture. One of the main limits of the subsystems combined within classical architectures, and also of the reliability measure in Section 2.1, is that they do not seize the main advantage of exploiting information coming from other subsystems. Each component works independently and final results give no feedback for the overall system. On the contrary, assume the existence of a *supervisor module*, which still exploits single subsystem responses and their reliability to compute the final global response, but which also uses the latter to evaluate the overall system state and update its parameters. Such module would implement an algorithm to update single thresholds also according to the behavior of the other subsystems, so converging to an optimal configuration independently from the starting $\{th_1, th_2, ...th_N\}$ configuration. The algorithm distinguishes two cases:

- More identities I_j, $j \in \{1, 2, \ldots, |H|\}$ share the same maximum number of votes, e.g. when retrieved identities are all different with 1 vote each. If at least one T_k in any such group has $srr_k > th_k$, the system returns the identity retrieved by the subsystem with the higher $srr_k > th_k$, and the response is marked as reliable, otherwise the response is marked as unreliable.
- One identity I_j gets more votes than the others. I_j is returned and the response is marked as reliable.

In both cases, if the response is reliable, each subsystem T_k voting for the returned identity is rewarded by lowering its threshold th_k by an updating step us, unless its current srr_k is already above its th_k. Each other subsystem T_k is penalized by increasing its threshold th_k by us, unless its current srr_k is already below its th_k. In this way the supervisor module lowers thresholds of subsystems voting in agreement, considering such behavior a confirmation of reliability, and increases thresholds of discordant ones, compensating possible distortions (local persistent distortions like lighting variations, dirt on lens).

Such an architecture does not need an adjustment phase, since the system can start from a default configuration of its parameters and converge in any case towards an optimal one. The speed to reach such latter configuration is a significant system feature, so that it is important to define how to measure it. As we want to simulate the dynamic behavior of an online identification system, we assume that system time is beaten by performed recognition operations; we define a *probe sequence* $P = \{p_1, p_2, \ldots, p_n\}$ as a series of n probes presented to the system, sharing the same acquisition characteristics (normal conditions, right light, earrings, dirty lens). A subsystem equilibrium state (*steady state*) is given by the consecutive instants when threshold fluctuations are lower than a fixed μ, while *convergence speed* of a subsystem λ_k is defined as the ratio between the total variation of its threshold between two steady states, and the number of instants needed to obtain such transition. Total system convergence speed is defined as the minimum speed among all its subsystems, i.e. $\lambda = min_k\lambda_k$, $k \in \{1, 2, 3\}$.

2.3 Integrating the Supervisor Module into the The N-Cross Testing Protocol

In this architecture, N subsystems T_k, k=1, 2,, N, work in parallel, first in identification mode and then in look-up mode, and exchange information in fixed

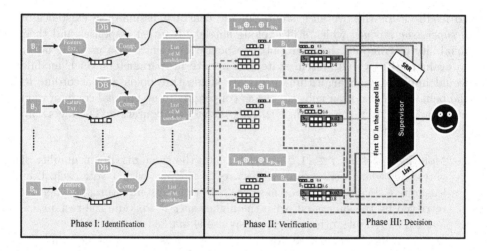

Fig. 1. The N-Cross Testing Protocol with SRR and Supervisor Module

points (Figure 1). At the beginning, each subsystem creates its own database of subjects, characterized by a peculiar set of image features. Face image data are then acquired for the probe subjects according to the specifications of each subsystem. We can identify three operation phases, namely identification, cross and testing. In identification phase, the N subsystems start up independently, by extracting biometric features and computing similarities according to the implemented classifiers. Each T_k, k=1, 2,, N, retrieves a list of candidate subjects from its specific database of enrolled subjects (gallery), ordered by similarity with the input: the lower the distance, the higher the similarity. All lists elements include the ID of a database subject and a numeric score for its similarity with the input. For a correct fusion, scores from different subsystems are made consistent through a suitable normalization function. Each subsystem also returns an estimate of its response reliability, namely a value for the SRR index. SRR is used in the cross operation. Afterwards the cross (verification) phase starts. Each T_k merges only lists coming from reliable companions. Subsystems with SRR value below their threshold still work during the fusion process, as they can receive and merge lists from reliable companions. We remind that each subsystem own list is not included in the merging operation in any case. In this way all subsystems produce a merged list, which only contains identities coming from reliable ones. A special case is when only one subsystem is reliable. During cross operation, all unreliable subsystems only receive its list, which so coincides with the merged one. The only reliable subsystem does not receive any list, so that it should return a null subject. This case is handled by adopting a specific rule, so that a reliable subsystem which does not receive any list during the cross phase can return its own list as the merged one. Shared subjects get a single score, which is the average of the original ones. Subjects belonging to only one list retain that score. The merged list is resorted. The SRR index assigned to the first retrieved identity in each merged list L_p, is given by the average of reliability indexes of subsystems in a set $\tilde{L}_p$, namely those contributing to such list (remind that they must all be reliable), and can be defined as:

$$LSRR_p = \frac{1}{|\tilde{L}_p|} \sum_{T_i \in \tilde{L}_p} SRR_i. \tag{1}$$

Each subsystem sends its list to the supervisor module, together with its reliability index and with the first element in its merged list. The supervisor module uses the latter two to compute the final response and to update system thresholds.

3   Experimental Results

Experimental tests have been conducted in order to asses the performance of the chosen classifiers when run alone or when combined in more collaborative architectures. The classification methods to use during the experiments were selected from those described in Section 1, due to their historical reference value or to their good performances in the two-dimensional setting. They are are LDA, OLPP, NPE and PIFS.

The sets of face images that have been considered as testing benchmark, were extracted from AR Faces database [11]. This database contains 126 subjects (70 men and 56 women) each of them was acquired in two different sessions with 13 image sets each. Sets differ in expression (1 neutral, 2 smile, 3 anger, 4 scream), illumination (5 left light, 6 right light, 7 all side light), presence/absence of occlusions (8 sun glasses, 11 scarf), or combinations (9 sun glasses and left light, 10 sun glasses and right light, 12 scarf and left light, 13 scarf and right light). Neutral images from the set 1 have been considered as the system gallery. Seven probes (2, 3, 4, 5, 6, 8, 11) have been used for testing. The face object detector that we used to locate the relevant regions is open source and based on Haar features [12], implemented in the OpenCV library [13]. Unfortunately, any automatic detector available nowadays makes some errors. As a matter of fact, detection methods make up a research issue by themselves. When errors happen, they are corrected by hand. After all, the focus of our work is rather on the ability by a collaborative system to enhance single classifiers performances. All tests performed on an Intel Pentium IV, 2.8Ghz with 512 Mb of RAM. Performances were measured in terms of Recognition Rate (RR), Equal Error Rate (EER), Cumulative Match Score (CMS), and, when using SRR index, Number of Reliable Responses (NRR).

The first experiment consisted in analyzing the performances of the different subsystems, which are summarized in Table 1. In the table, the better obtained results are in boldface for readability. We can notice that PIFS outperforms the other classifiers, on a regular basis in relation with RR and in most cases in relation with EER and CMS computed for rank 5. NPE appears as a fully complementary competitor, as it reaches the best performances of all classifiers,

Table 1. Performances of the single classifiers

DATASETS	CLASSIFIERS											
	LDA			OLPP			NPE			PIFS		
	RR	EER	CMS(5)	RR	EER	CMS(5)	RR	EER	CMS(5)	RR	EER	CMS(5)
SET 2	0.944	0.044	0.991	0.925	0.094	0.972	**0.953**	**0.028**	**1.000**	**0.953**	0.039	0.981
SET 3	0.822	0.075	0.944	0.879	0.135	0.925	0.869	0.043	**0.981**	**0.962**	**0.036**	**0.981**
SET 4	0.430	0.170	0.738	0.402	0.251	0.710	0.551	**0.091**	**0.850**	**0.588**	0.108	0.822
SET 5	0.626	0.095	0.841	0.879	0.102	0.972	0.262	0.118	0.617	**0.953**	**0.020**	**0.990**
SET 6	0.206	0.108	0.813	0.636	0.132	0.860	0.206	0.175	0.439	**0.869**	**0.076**	**0.934**
SET 8	0.290	0.208	0.579	0.393	0.232	0.617	0.374	0.127	0.664	**0.850**	**0.06**	**0.943**
SET 11	0.065	0.325	0.243	0.178	0.352	0.383	0.028	0.429	0.112	**0.803**	**0.123**	**0.906**

in relation with EER and CMS for rank 5 (see for example EER = 0.028 for smiling subjects in set 2) just where PIFS obtains suboptimal results, even if in all other cases it obtains changeable results. From this point of view LDA, OLPP and NPE all show performances that vary with their robustness to specific variations. For example, NPE badly reacts to changes in light (sets 5 and 6, with RR = 0.262 and RR = 0.206 respectively) and even worse to significant occlusions, with RR = 0.028 and CMS(5) = 0.112 for subjects with scarf in set 11. In the latter case, PIFS is the only classifier reaching more than acceptable results. Notice the scarce performances of all classifiers with screaming subjects in set 4. In this case, the best result in relation to RR is obtained by PIFS with RR = 0.588, which is far below its average behavior. This can be explained with the fact that, as for screaming subjects, the whole face expression undergoes a deformation process, especially the mouth region where we have something comparable to an occlusion. As a matter of fact, the same low performances are obtained by almost all classifiers with subjects wearing a scarf in set 11.

Given the discussed results, the following tests aimed at investigating if a more strict cooperation among subsystems running the given classifiers can improve the best performances obtained by the single methods. The results are reported in Table 2. We remind that NRR measures the number of reliable responses. As the simple NCT does not exploit reliability measures, the NRR column in that case always shows the total number of responses.

The basic N-Cross-Testing architecture provides worse performances than PIFS alone, as for RR at least, while EER follows an alternating trend. This is surely due to the fact that the global response is influenced by the scarce results obtained by the other classifiers. However, it is worth noticing how the result obtained for the screaming subjects of set 4 is better than PIFS one, that was the worst for this classifier, and the best till now for that set. In this particular case, were PIFS performances were low, the contribution of the other classifiers was significant. This seems to suggest that, when only one classifier shows a good behavior, its contribution might be overwhelmed by bad results from the others. However, in a situation where all classifiers encounter some

Table 2. Performances of N-Cross Testing in different cooperation settings

| DATASETS | ARCHITECTURES | | | | | |
| | SIMPLE N-CROSS-TESTING | | | SUPERVISED N-CROSS-TESTING | | |
	RR	EER	NRR	RR	EER	NRR
SET 2	0.962	0.018	126	**0.990**	**0.004**	121
SET 3	0.971	0.014	126	**0.989**	**0.005**	116
SET 4	0.652	0.17	126	**0.962**	**0.018**	94
SET 5	0.744	0.127	126	**0.940**	**0.029**	118
SET 6	0.584	0.207	126	**0.905**	**0.047**	112
SET 8	0.522	0.238	126	**0.849**	**0.075**	102
SET 11	0.359	0.320	126	**0.975**	**0.012**	94

troubles, unity is strength. The best performances are reached with supervised NCT, with the addition of a supervisor module providing dynamic feedback to the single subsystems about the global performances. Both RR and EER give better results in general, and most of all on the average, and the number of reliable responses significantly increases even in critical cases. The worst results are with set 4 and set 11, where about 75% of the responses were considered as reliable anyway. Notice the values obtained with screaming subjects of set 4. In this case we pass from RR = 0.588 and EER = 0.108 of PIFS alone (nevertheless, the best result among all classifiers) to RR = 0.962 and EER = 0.018 with supervised NCT, which is the higher proportional improvement obtained over all considered image sets. Again, the more critical are the identification conditions, the higher the advantage obtained by combining more classifiers. This latter results fully confirm our working hypotheses.

4   Conclusions

Biometric systems are generally somehow penalized from limits deriving from the adopted classification techniques. Multibiometric/multiclassifier systems resolve a number of problems of single-biometry ones, but suffer from the lack of communication among subsystems, and from the invariance of their parameters, making them unable to adapt to changes in the conditions of their working environment. In this paper, we propose an architecture aiming at overcoming such limitations, through the introduction of a collaboration protocol and of a supervisor module. Such additional component collects information from the different subsystems and exploits them to modify the internal conditions (parameters) of each subsystem, aiming at improving the global response. The experimental results show that the tighter is the cooperation among different classifiers, the better results are obtained. This work opens a line to further investigations, where aspects such as a deeper action of the supervisor module on the internal subsystems state, or template updating, represent potential integrations to the architecture presented herein.

Acknowledgements

This work has been partially supported by the Provincia di Salerno Administration, Italy.

References

1. Turk, M., Pentland, A.: Eigenfaces for recognition. Journal of Cognitive Neuroscience 3, 71–86 (1991)
2. Swets, D.L., Weng, J.J.: Using discriminant eigenfeatures for image retrieval. IEEE Trans. Pattern Analysis and Machine Intelligence 18, 831–836 (1996)
3. Yan, S., He, X., Cai, D., Zhang, H.-J.: Neighborhood preserving embedding. In: IEEE International Conference on Computer Vision, ICCV 2005, vol. 2, pp. 1208–1213 (2005)
4. Han, J., Cai, D., He, X., Zhang, H.-J.: Orthogonal laplacianfaces for face recognition. IEEE Transactions on Image Processing 15, 3608–3614 (2006)
5. He, F., Kouzani, A.Z., Sammut, K.: Fractal face representation and recognition. In: IEEE International Conference on Systems, Man, and Cybernetics, vol. 2, pp. 1609–1613 (1997)
6. Riccio, D., Tortora, G., Abate, A.F., Nappi, M.: Rbs: A robust bimodal system for face recognition. International Journal of Software Engineering and Knowledge Engineering 17, 497–514 (2007)
7. Ross, A., Jain, A.K., Qian, J.-Z.: Information fusion in biometrics. In: Bigun, J., Smeraldi, F. (eds.) AVBPA 2001. LNCS, vol. 2091, pp. 354–359. Springer, Heidelberg (2001)
8. Riccio, D., De Marsico, M., Abate, A.F., Nappi, M.: Data normalization and fusion in multibiometric systems. In: International Conference on Distributed Multimedia Systems, DMS 2007, pp. 87–92 (2007)
9. Riccio, D., De Marsico, M., Abate, A.F., Nappi, M.: Face, ear and fingerprint: Designing multibiometric architectures. In: Proceedings of the 14th International Conference on Image Analysis and Processing - ICIAP 2007, pp. 437–442 (2007)
10. Poh, N., Bengio, S.: Improving fusion with margin-derived confidence in biometric authentication tasks. In: Kanade, T., Jain, A., Ratha, N.K. (eds.) AVBPA 2005. LNCS, vol. 3546, pp. 474–483. Springer, Heidelberg (2005)
11. Martinez, A.M., Benavente, R.: The ar face database - cvc technical report n.24. Technical Report (1998)
12. Viola, P., Jones, M.: Rapid object detection using a boosted cascade of simple features. In: Proceedings of the IEEE Computer Society Conference on Computer Vision and Pattern Recognition (CVPR), vol. 1, pp. 511–518 (2001)
13. Opencv. Website, 2008-06-06

Characterisation of Retinal Feature Points Applied to a Biometric System

David Calvo, Marcos Ortega, Manuel G. Penedo, José Rouco,
and Beatriz Remeseiro

VARPA Group, Department of Computer Science, University of A Coruña, Spain
{dcalvo,mortega,mgpenedo,jrouco,bremeseiro}@udc.es

Abstract. In this work a methodology for the classification of retinal feature points is applied to a biometric system. This system is based in the extraction of feature points, namely bifurcations and crossovers as biometric pattern. In order to compare a pattern to other from a known individual a matching process takes place between both points sets. That matching task is performed by finding the best geometric transform between sets, i.e. the transform leading to the highest number of matched points. The goal is to reduce the number of explored transforms by introducing the previous characterisation of feature points. This is achieved with a constraint avoiding two differently classified points to match. The empirical reduction of transforms is about 20%.

Keywords: Retinal verification, Feature points characterisation, Registration.

1 Introduction

Retinal vessel tree pattern has been proved a valid biometric trait for personal authentication as it is unique, time invariant and very hard to forge, as showed by Mariño ct al. [1], who introduced a novel authentication system based on this trait. In that work, the whole arterial-venous tree structure was used as the feature pattern for individuals. One drawback of the proposed system was the necessity of storing and handling the whole vessel tree image as a pattern. Based on the idea of fingerprint minutiae [2], a more ideal and robust pattern was introduced and analysed in [3,4] where a set of landmarks (bifurcations and crossovers of retinal vessel tree) were extracted and used as feature points. In this scenario, the pattern matching problem is reduced to a point pattern matching problem. The matching is achieved by exploring the transform space to find the optimal transform in which the most points from both patterns are matched. The search is performed by forcing two matches between patterns, calculating the transform associated and calculating the additional matched produced. The matching between two points is accepted if once the transform is applied, both points are close enough.

This approach implies the exploration of a high number of transformations. The method proposed in this paper, classifies the feature points in the two

P. Foggia, C. Sansone, and M. Vento (Eds.): ICIAP 2009, LNCS 5716, pp. 355–363, 2009.

possible classes (bifurcations or crossovers) and introduces a constraint where two points with different characterisation can not match. This will allow to reduce the exploration in the transform space.

In the bibliography there are some works that approached this problem of characterisation of retinal points. The methods were not applied to a specific domain and the image processing techniques were more heavy computationally. For instance, the method proposed by Chia-Ling Tsai *et al.* [5], use vessel segments intersections as seeds to track vessel centre lines and classify feature points according to intersection angles. Another work, the proposed by V.Bevilacqua *et al.* [6], uses a small window to analyse the whole skeleton of the vascular structure. The main problem of this solution is the misclassification of crossovers, as they are only properly classified when the vessel segments intersect exactly in the same pixel. In order to correctly characterise the feature points, the methodology in this work takes advantage of the pattern extraction process and does not require additional processing of the original image. Feature points are classified according to a local analysis and a topological study.

The paper is organised as follows: in section 2 a general view of the retinal biometric system is explained. Section 3 introduces the methodology for characterisation of feature points. Section 4 shows the results of several experiments to test the classification performance and its impact in the biometric system. Finally, section 5 discusses some conclusions.

2   Retinal Recognition System

In the first step, to obtain a good representation of the tree, the creases of the image are extracted [7]. As vessels can be thought of as ridges or valleys seeing the retinal image as a landscape, creases image will consist in the vessels skeleton (Figure 1).

Using the whole creases image as biometric pattern has a major problem in the codification and storage of the pattern, as we need to store the whole image. To solve this, similarly to the fingerprint minutiae (ridges, endings, bifurcations

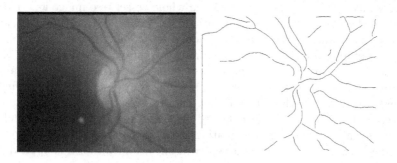

Fig. 1. Left, original image; Right, creases image extracted from original

in the fingerprints), the biometric pattern consists in a set of landmarks from the creases image. The most prominent landmarks in retinal vessel tree are crossovers (between two different vessels) and bifurcation points (one vessel coming out of another one). These are the feature points considered in the authentication system.

2.1   Biometric Pattern Extraction

To detect feature points, creases are tracked to label all of them as segments in the vessel tree, marking their endpoints. Next, bifurcations and crossovers are detected by means of relationships between endpoints. These relationships are extracted by finding segments endpoints close enough to each other and analysing orientations.

Due to quality or illumination issues in the images, there could be some discontinuities along a vessel so a relationship of union between segments must be considered to avoid detection of false feature points.

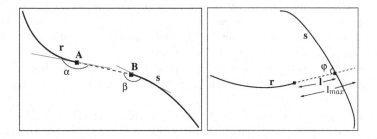

Fig. 2. Left, representation of an union relationship between segments r and s. Endpoints A and B are connected through a straight line and both their angles with that line are computed (α and β). Right, representation of a bifurcation between segments r and s. Segment r is prolongated for a maximum length l_{max} and, eventually, s is found forming a ϕ angle with r original endpoint direction.

An union happens when two adjacent segments belong to the same vessel. To detect an union between two segments, r and s, these are connected through a straight line between their closest endpoints (Figure 2, left). The angles formed by both endpoint directions and the straight line are calculated. Both angles should be closed to π radians to accept it as a union. A threshold θ is defined. To obtain the bifurcations, segments are prolongated through their endpoints direction to a maximum fixed length (l_{max}). If a pixel of another segment is found, the bifurcation is marked and the angle formed by both segments is calculated (Figure 2, right). Note that this method also allows to detect crossovers as they can be seen as bifurcations by both sides. Figure 3 shows two examples of biometric patterns obtained.

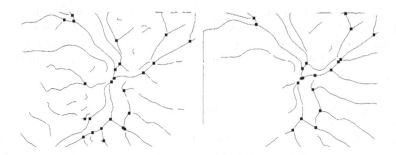

Fig. 3. Examples of feature points obtained in creases from the same individual extracted from images acquired in different times

2.2 Biometric Patterns Matching

In the matching process, the biometric pattern ν stored for a particular individual is compared to the pattern ν' extracted in the previous section when a user claiming that identity tries to be verified. Due to the eye movement during the image acquisition stage, it is necessary to align ν with ν' in order to be matched [8]. This movement of the eye consists basically only in translation in both axis, rotation and sometimes a very small change in scale. Considering this, a Similarity Transform schema (ST) is used to model pattern transformations [9]. It is also important to note that both patterns, ν and ν' could have a different number of points as showed in Figure 3.

To find the best transformation (i.e. the one with the highest similarity value associated, for a given similarity metric) a search is performed in the transformation space. In ST model, two points of each pattern are necessary to compute the transformation parameters and, thus, the maximum transformation space size (T) is given:

$$T = \frac{(M^2 - M)(N^2 - N)}{2} \tag{1}$$

where M and N represent the cardinality of ν and ν' respectively. Once both patterns are aligned, a point p from ν and a point p' from ν' match if $distance(p, p') < D_{max}$, where D_{max} is a threshold introduced in order to consider the quality loss and discontinuities during the creases extraction process leading to mislocation of feature points by some pixels. Therefore, for a given transformation the number of matched points between patterns can be calculated. Using this information, a similarity metric must be established to obtain a final criterion of comparison between patterns. In [10] a similarity measure between patterns, S_γ, is introduced based on a γ parameter:

$$S_\gamma = \frac{C^\gamma}{\sqrt{MN}} \tag{2}$$

where C is the number of matched points between patterns, M and N is the size of both patterns and γ is a parameter controlling the influence of matched points information.

The matching process weakness is the high amount of transformations that need to be calculated to find the optimal one. To reduce the number of calculations, more information about the domain is introduced. By characterising the feature points into crossovers and bifurcations, an efficient constraint can be added only allowing points of the same class (or unclassified) to match.

3   Feature Points Characterisation

This classification is done according to local features of those points and a topological analysis between them.

The first classification step is done according to local features of the points without considering, for it, the effect of the other points. So, to define a classification for a point the number of vessel segments that create the intersection is studied. Each detected feature point, F, is used as centre of a circumference with radius R_c used for the analysis. $n(F)$ gives the number of vessel segments that intersect the circumference being the point, F, such as a bifurcation corresponds to $n(F) = 3$ and a crossover to $n(F) = 4$. Fig.4 shows these two possible classifications. The images shows the blood vessels, the circumference used to do the analysis, and, coloured darker, the pixels where the vessels intersect the circumference.

By increasing R_C too much the circumference can be intersected by vessels that do not belong to the feature point. To avoid this problem a vote system with three radius sizes is used: R_c and two new radius defined around R_c, $R_1 = R_c - \rho$ and $R_2 = R_c + \rho$. In this work, $\rho = 5$. With these definitions, two values are calculated, $C(F)$ and $B(F)$, meaning the number of votes for a point F to be classified, respectively, as a crossover and a bifurcation:

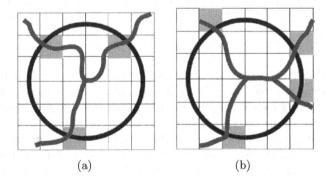

(a)   (b)

Fig. 4. Preliminary feature point classification according to the number of vessel intersections where (a) represents a bifurcation and (b) a crossover

$$C(F) = 2 * C(F, R_1) + C(F, R_c) + C(F, R_2) \tag{3}$$

$$B(F) = B(F, R_1) + B(F, R_c) + 2 * B(F, R_2) \tag{4}$$

where $C(F, R_i)$ and $B(F, R_i)$ are binary values indicating if F is classified, respectively, as a crossover or a bifurcation using a radius R_i. Note that the contribution of the small radius is more valuable, and therefore weighted, in the crossover classification while for bifurcations the big radius adds more information. F will be classified as a crossover when $C(F) > B(F)$ and a bifurcation otherwise.

Due to the representation of crossovers in the skeleton, this information is not enough to assure that a feature point is a crossover while being a necessary condition. According to this, a topological classification is needed analysing the feature points in pairs, (F_1, F_2), attending to their Euclidean distance $d(F_1, F_2)$. If both F_1 and F_2 are connected by a vessel segment and $d(F_1, F_2) <= 2 * R_c$, both points are merged into a crossover in the middle point between them.

For the rest of feature points not classified as crossovers, it can not be guaranteed they are bifurcations as for every real crossover not classified, two false bifurcations would be created. Because of this, it is necessary to use another threshold (R_b) to allow to take a decision of which points are accepted as bifurcations. This process is analogous to the previously presented for crossover classification. In this way, for each bifurcation its pair, understood as the connected bifurcation that minimises the Euclidean distance, is found. For each pair, a circumference with radius (R_b) centred in the middle point of the segment between the points is used. This circumference cannot contain both points.

Every pair of points not fulfilling the conditions is marked as not classified in the final result. This is due to the fact that points are not close enough to be considered as one crossover but not far enough to be considered as two independent bifurcations.

Note that R_c and R_b parameters allow to tune the system in terms of specificity and sensitivity as some domains would require different performances. In the next section, some experiments and performance results are shown.

4   Results

To perform the experiments a set of 30 images from 15 different individuals from VARIA database[11] were used. These images are centred in the optic disc with spatial resolution of 768x584 pixels and were labelled by medical experts to test the performance in the classification of feature points.

In the first test, the performance of the classification system was evaluated. The performance analysis is made as a function of R_c and R_b as they are the parameters that allow to tune the specificity and sensitivity of the system. specifically, R_c makes a direct impact in the crossover classification while R_b makes it in the bifurcations. For a right choice of the mentioned parameters a quantitative study according to the parameters is presented. The results allow to choose

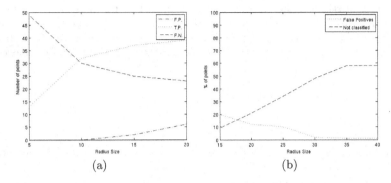

(a)   (b)

Fig. 5. Analysis of the influence of R_c for the crossovers, (a), and R_b for the bifurcations, (b) in the classification performance of the system

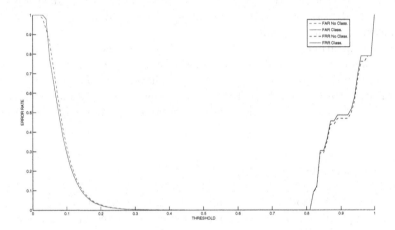

Fig. 6. FAR and FRR curves for using the test set. The system classification capability remains almost identical.

the adequate parameters for a specific domain where the desired sensitivity or specificity levels can change depending on the False Positives, True Positives and False Negatives as shown in Fig.5(a).

Fig.5(b) shows the results for bifurcation classification according to the chosen R_b radius. This figure displays a new category, the non classified points, that includes the points that fulfilling the morphology conditions are not close enough to be classified as crossover and not far enough not to be classified as independent bifurcations. The bigger radius, R_b, used the more number of points without classifying but the number of false positives will be below the 1%. Opposite to this, if a big level of true positives is needed with a small radius the sensitivity is over the 70%. Selecting $R_c = 10$ and $R_b = 30$, the global sensitivity of the system is 67% and the specificity 95%. The specificity is a highly important parameter

Table 1. Statistics on the transformations removed in the matching process. The columns refer to total possible transformations without considering the point classification restriction, the number of transformations avoided by including the restriction and the mean and standard deviation (std) percentages of transformation removed per image.

Total	Removed	Mean	Std
38617	7238	18.74%	5.97%

in this domain as a low rate indicates the chance to match two different points. This could lead to a bad performance of the recognition system.

In the second experiment this mentioned biometric system performance using the characterisation of points is tested. The goal is to check if the recognition rate is not diminished by the feature points classification errors. All the test images were compared versus all. Fig. 6 shows the False Acceptance (FAR) and Rejection (FRR) rate curves for the biometric system with and without using classification of feature points.

The classification performance of the system remains the same while reducing the computation load of the matching process by avoiding matches between differently classified points. This constraint removes a lot of irrelevant transformations from the computation. Table 1 shows the impact in the test set in terms of transformations removed. The average reduction of computed transformations was 18.74%.

5   Conclusions

In this work a methodology for characterisation of retinal vessel tree feature points is applied into a matching stage for a retinal recognition system. The matching process of two biometric patterns, i.e. two sets of feature points, involves the calculation of many possible similarity transforms where points from both patterns are matched. By characterising the points into crossovers or bifurcations, a constraint is added where two differently classified points can not match.

The methodology employed for the characterisation of points allows to tune the sensitivity and specificity values. Particularly in this domain, a high specificity is very valuable as this indicates the rate of misclassified points. The systems shows a specificity value of 95%. Because of this, the biometric system is improved in terms of computational optimisation while not reducing the high recognition rate.

In terms of transform operations reduction, the system computes a 18.74% less in the matching stage. The average execution time of the whole process in Pentium 4 Core Duo 2.4Ghz Desktop PC was 135ms, meaning a 12.78% faster than before adding the characterisation constraint. This supposes a great advantage specially in identification tasks where the same biometric pattern is compared with all the stored ones in the database of known users.

References

1. Mariño, C., Penedo, M.G., Penas, M., Carreira, M.J., González, F.: Personal authentication using digital retinal images. Pattern Analysis and Applications 9, 21–33 (2006)
2. Tan, X., Bhanu, B.: A robust two step approach for fingerprint identification. Pattern Recognition Letters 24, 2127–2134 (2003)
3. Ortega, M., Mariño, C., Penedo, M.G., Blanco, M., González, F.: Personal authentication based on featue extraction and optica nerve location in digital retinal images. WSEAS Transactions on Computers 5(6), 1169–1176 (2006)
4. Ortega, M., Penedo, M.G., Mariño, C., Carreira, M.J.: Similarity metrics analysis for feature point based retinal authentication. In: Campilho, A., Kamel, M.S. (eds.) ICIAR 2008. LNCS, vol. 5112, pp. 1023–1032. Springer, Heidelberg (2008)
5. Tsai, C.L., Stewart, C., Tanenbaum, H., Roysam, B.: Model-based method for improving the accuracy and repeatability of estimating vascular bifurcations and crossovers from retinal fundus images. IEEE Transactions on Information Technology in Biomedicine 8(2), 122–130 (2004)
6. Bevilacqua, V., Cambó, S., Cariello, L., Mastronardi, G.: A combined method to detect retinal fundus features. In: Proceedings of IEEE European Conference on Emergent Aspects in Clinical Data Analysis (2005)
7. López, A., Lloret, D., Serrat, J., Villanueva, J.: Multilocal creasness based on the level set extrinsic curvature. Computer Vision and Image Understanding 77, 111–144 (2000)
8. Zitová, B., Flusser, J.: Image registration methods: a survey. Image Vision and Computing 21(11), 977–1000 (2003)
9. Ryan, N., Heneghan, C., de Chazal, P.: Registration of digital retinal images using landmark correspondence by expectation maximization. Image and Vision Computing 22, 883–898 (2004)
10. Ortega, M., Penedo, M.G., Mariño, C., Carreira, M.J.: A novel similarity metric for retinal images based authentication. In: International Conference on Bio-inspired Systems and Signal Processing, vol. 1, pp. 249–253 (2009)
11. VARIA: Varpa retinal images for authentication, http://www.varpa.es/varia.html

Coastline Detection from SAR Images by Level Set Model

Maria Mercede Cerimele[1], Luigi Cinque[2], Rossella Cossu[1],
and Roberta Galiffa[1]

[1] Istituto per le Applicazioni del Calcolo "M. Picone" CNR, Roma
[2] Universitá degli Studi "Sapienza", Roma

Abstract. In this paper we present an innovative and automatic procedure which is used to extract the coastline from SAR (Synthetic Aperture
Radar) images by the level set model. This model consists in a PDE (Partial Differential Equation) equation governing the evolution of a curve
corresponding to the zero level of a 3D function, called level set function, until the curve reaches the edge of the region to be segmented. A
coastline is the boundary between land and sea masses. Detecting the
coastline is of fundamental importance when monitoring various natural
phenomena such as tides, coastal erosion and the dynamics of glaciers.
In this case SAR images show problems which arise from the presence
of the speckle noise and of the strong signal deriving from the rough
or slight sea. In fact in the case of heavy sea the signal determines an
intensity similar to the one of land, making it difficult to distinguish the
coastline.

1 Introduction

In this paper we present a level set method applied to the segmentation of
SAR (Synthetic Aperture Radar) images with the aim of extracting two regions
(land and sea) from them. This method, proposed by Osher and Sethian [1],
[2], [3], consists in the identification of an area of interest as the zero level set
of an implicit function that evolves according to the PDE (partial differential
equation) model with an appropriate speed function. This approach has many
advantages, for example the contours represented by the level set function can
split and merge naturally during the evolution and this allows the topological
changes to be controlled.

The interpretation of SAR images is an essential component of not invasive
monitoring in many fields such as urban planning, geology, for instance the
erosion of coast [4]. In particular detecting the coastline from SAR images is a
difficult problem because it is associated with the nature of the signal coming
from water and land regions. In fact, the signal return coming from the sea
can be frequently indistinct from one coming from the land. Nevertheless, the

P. Foggia, C. Sansone, and M. Vento (Eds.): ICIAP 2009, LNCS 5716, pp. 364–373, 2009.
© Springer-Verlag Berlin Heidelberg 2009

presence of speckle, modeled as a strong multiplicative noise, makes the coastline detection a very complicated issue.

The segmentation methods based on edge detection filters developed for SAR images [5], often show edges which may not form a set of closed curves surrounding connected regions. The traditional segmentation techniques of histogram thresholding and region-based need a preprocessing based on speckle reduction. Moreover, the region-growing techniques have the limit of depending on the selection of the starting points.

In recent years, active contours methods, based on the evolution of curves and on a *level set* approach have been an important tool for solving image segmentation problems. The active contours have been classified as parametric, also called *snakes*, or geometric depending on their representation and implementation. In particular, parametric active contours are explicitly represented as curves parameterized in a Lagrangian reference, while the geometric active contours are implicitly represented as two-dimensional functions, called *level sets* that evolve in an Eulerian reference. For SAR images, the parametric active contours were developed in [6],[7],[8].

In general, in order to extract the contour of a region, the *snake*-model type uses an algorithm that iteratively deforms an initial curve until it reaches the edge of the region to be segmented. However, this model presents several limitations. In fact, since the curve is represented in parametric form, it is discretized by a set of points, so that during the time evolution topological changes are difficult to compute. Moreover, the errors in the representation may be amplified during the numerical computation. Thus, these problems may affect the results of the segmentation process. Compared to the techniques of parametric active contours, the geometric active contours implemented by *level set* have the significant advantage of allowing natural and numerically stable topological changes.

In this paper we use the evolution of curves through *level set* to segment SAR images into two distinct classes, land and sea.

In particular a first approach developed is based on the assumption that each region to segment through *level set* is modeled by a Gamma distribution. In this case an expression of propagation speed of the front is obtained by computing intensity averages of the regions; the method does not need to reduce speckle noise [9].

A second approach takes into account the problem of filtering speckle noise in the image, which was faced with the application of the SRAD (Speckle Reducing Anisotropic Diffusion) technique to SAR image [10] [11].

Finally we propose an integrated procedure obtained by combining the two previous procedures, taking into account the advantages of the two approaches. The paper is organized as follows. In Section 2 level set method is described. In Section 3 speeds computation related to level set method and noise reducing are presented. Section 4 contains the description of proposed integrated procedure. A conclusion is drawn in Section 5.

2   Mathematical Approach

Let $\mathbf{I} : \Omega \rightarrow \Re^n$ be the intensity image function where $\Omega \subset \Re^2$.

The goal of image segmentation is to partition Ω in order to extract disjoint regions from image $\mathbf{I}$ such that they cover Ω.

The boundaries of these regions may be considered as curves belonging to a family in which time evolution is described by a level set equation. The main advantages of using the level set is that complex shaped regions can be detected and handled implicitly.

In order to obtain the governing equation of a front evolution, we consider a family of parameterized closed contours $\gamma(x(t), y(t), t) : [0, \infty) \rightarrow \Re^2$, generated by evolving an initial contour $\gamma_0(x(0), y(0), 0)$.

We underline that in the curves evolution theory the geometric shape of the contour is determined by the normal component of the velocity. Supposing that $\gamma(x(t), y(t), t)$ is a moving front in the image, if we embed this moving front as the zero level of a smooth continuous scalar 3D function $\phi(x(t), y(t), t)$, known as the level set function, the implicit contour at any time t is given by $\gamma(x(t), y(t), t) \equiv \{(x(t), y(t))/\phi(x(t), y(t), t) = 0\}$.

By differentiating respect to t the expression $\phi(x(t), y(t), t) = 0$ the equation for the evolution of the level set function may be derived

$$\frac{\partial \phi(x(t), y(t), t)}{\partial t} + \frac{dx(t)}{dt} \frac{\partial \phi(x(t), y(t), t)}{\partial x} + \frac{dy(t)}{dt} \frac{\partial \phi(x(t), y(t), t)}{\partial y} = 0 \quad (1)$$

We require that the level set function has to satisfy the condition $|\nabla \phi(x(t), y(t), t)| \neq 0$ for all $(x(t), y(t)) \in \gamma(x(t), y(t), t)$; this is possible because $\gamma(x(t), y(t), t)$ is a regular curve. Let $\mathbf{n} \equiv (n_1, n_2)$ be the normal vector to the curve $\gamma(x(t), y(t), t)$ defined as

$$n_1 = \frac{\frac{\partial \phi(x(t), y(t), t)}{\partial x}}{|\nabla \phi(x(t), y(t), t)|} \qquad n_2 = \frac{\frac{\partial \phi(x(t), y(t), t)}{\partial y}}{|\nabla \phi(x(t), y(t), t)|}$$

that is

$$\frac{\partial \phi(x(t), y(t), t)}{\partial x} = |\nabla \phi(x(t), y(t), t)| n_1 \qquad \frac{\partial \phi(x(t), y(t), t)}{\partial y} = |\nabla \phi(x(t), y(t), t)| n_2$$

substituting in (1)we obtain

$$\frac{\partial \phi(x(t), y(t), t)}{\partial t} + (n_1 \frac{dx(t)}{dt} + n_2 \frac{dy(t)}{dt}) |\nabla \phi(x(t), y(t), t)| = 0 \quad (2)$$

where $(n_1 \frac{dx(t)}{dt} + n_2 \frac{dy(t)}{dt})$ describes the curve evolution in the normal direction, so that we can write $(n_1 \frac{dx(t)}{dt} + n_2 \frac{dy(t)}{dt}) = \frac{d\gamma(x(t), y(t), t)}{dt}$ the (2) becomes

$$\frac{\partial \phi(x(t), y(t), t)}{\partial t} + \frac{d\gamma(x(t), y(t), t)}{dt} |\nabla \phi(x(t), y(t), t)| = 0 \quad (3)$$

or also

$$\frac{d\gamma(x(t), y(t), t)}{dt} = -\frac{\partial\phi(x(t), y(t), t)/\partial t}{|\nabla\phi(x(t), y(t), t)|} \tag{4}$$

In the following another important intrinsic geometric property will be used, that is the curvature of each level set given by

$$k = -\nabla \cdot \left(\frac{\nabla\phi(x(t), y(t), t)}{|\phi(x(t), y(t), t)|} \right)$$

and moreover we assume

$$\frac{d\gamma}{dt} = v.$$

3   Speed Computation

As mentioned above, the level set method starts from the definition of an initial curve in the domain of the image. In our case, the initial curve on the SAR images is placed so as to surround the object of interest (land). The evolution of the initial curve is determined by a speed function, which is a fundamental choice to achieve a good segmentation.

In this paper two different speed functions are introduced and compared.

The first uses a speed function based on modeling the intensity of image by a Gamma distribution. The second uses a speed function based on the computation of image gradient. Finally we propose an integrated procedure obtained by combining the two previous functions.

The SAR PRI (Precision Resolution Image) image here analyzed has been acquired during ERS2 mission. In Table 1 some annotations and calibration data are listed.

3.1   Average-Based Speed

The goal of the segmentation process in this work is to extract two types of regions representing land and sea R_i $i \in \{1, 2\}$).

Let be $I(\mathbf{x})$ the SAR image intensity which we model by a Gamma distribution.

After some probabilistic considerations and algebraic manipulations we obtain

$$v = \frac{d\gamma}{dt} = -\left(\log\mu_{R_1} + \frac{I(\mathbf{x})}{\mu_{R_1}} - \log\mu_{R_2} - \frac{I(\mathbf{x})}{\mu_{R_2}} + \lambda k \right) \tag{5}$$

where a λk is a regularization term, with λ a positive real constant and k the mean curvature function defined in Section 2, μ_{R_i} is the mean intensity given

$$\mu_{R_i} = \frac{\int_{R_i} I(\mathbf{x})d\mathbf{x}}{a_{R_i}} \tag{6}$$

and where the area a_{R_i} is given

$$a_{R_i} = \int_{R_i} d\mathbf{x}$$

Table 1. LOCATION: Sea between the Corsica and Tuscany coasts

$IMAGEUNIQUEID = ERS2 - 27574 - 02761 - B$	$SCENECENTRETIME= 29JUL2000$
$IMAGEWIDTH = 8000$ pixels	$PRF_HZ = 1679.9020$
$IMAGELENGTH = 8208$ pixels	$CALIBRATIONCONST = 944061.$
$MISSIONID = ERS2$	$CENTRELAT = 41.963$
$SENSORID = AMI$	$CENTRELON = 10.043$
$SENSORMODE = IMAGE$	$TOPLEFTLAT = 41.419$
$POLARISATION = VV$	$TOPLEFTLON = 10.485$
$PRODUCTTYPE = PRI$	$TOPRIGHTLAT = 41.602$
$ORBITDIRECTIONDESCENDING$	$TOPRIGHTLON = 9.336$
$SENSORPLATHEADIND = 194.31600°$	$BOTTOMLEFTLAT = 42.321$
$PIXELSPACING = 12.5m(S.R. = 25m)$	$BOTTOMLEFTLON = 10.757$
$AZIMUTHSTARTTIME = 29JUL2000$	$BOTTOMRIGHTLAT = 42.505$
$AZIMUTHSTOPTIME = 29JUL2000$	$BOTTOMRIGHTLON = 9.59$
$LOOKSIDE = RIGHT$	$REFINCANGLE = 23°$
$RANGESAMPLINGRATE = 18962467$ HZ	$NEARINCIDANGLE = 19.445999°$
$NEARZERODOPPLERRT = 0.0055504742$ s	$FARINCIDANGLE = 26.419001°$

From (3) we obtain the following level set equation

$$\frac{\partial\phi(x(t), y(t), t)}{\partial t} + v|\nabla\phi(x(t), y(t), t)| = 0 \qquad (7)$$

We have examined the behavior of the algorithm by using the averaged-based speed. In Figure 1 and Figure 2 the Tests A and B related to two different coastlines are shown: (a) and (b) identify a portion of the initial curves selected (initial data for the algorithm) and (c) and (d) show the respective results obtained when the convergence for the numerical approximation is satisfied (final contours).

From these tests it is evident that the results obtained depend on the initial position of the curve and in particular it has been obtained a better result as the initial curve is located near the coast.

3.2 Gradient-Based Speed

In this subsection the image gradient is used to identify the edges or contours. Indeed, if in a zone the value of the gradient is high then the related pixels correspond to an edge. The gradient-based speed function, in this case, is

$$v = -\frac{1}{1 + |\nabla I|^2} - \lambda k$$

where k is the curvature and $\lambda \in (0, 1)$ is a constant. Substituting this expression in (3) we obtain the corresponding level set equation. It is well known that in images corrupted by strong noise, the computation of gradient could detect false edges.

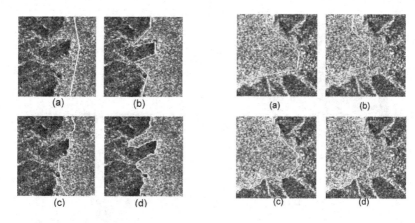

Fig. 1.
Test A: results by average-based speed

Fig. 2.
Test B: results by average-based speed

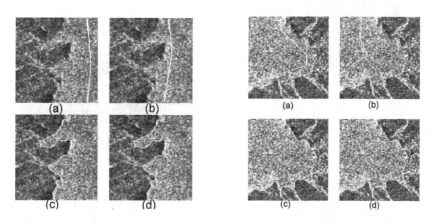

Fig. 3.
Test A: results by gradient based speed

Fig. 4.
Test B: results by gradient based speed

So that, because the SAR images are affected by speckle noise, they are pre-processed by means of the SRAD algorithm (Speckle Reducing Anisotropic Diffusion) which is an extension of Perona-Malik algorithm [10] [11]

$$\begin{cases} \frac{\partial I(\mathbf{x}(t),t)}{\partial t} = div[|c(q)|) \cdot \nabla I(\mathbf{x}(t),t)] \\ I(\mathbf{x}(0),0) = I_0 \end{cases}$$

where $c(q)$ is the diffusion coefficient.

So, the speed term is defined in such a way that the curve proceeds rather fast in low gradient zones, while it wades through next to high gradient ones. This strategy allows the contour to propagate until it achieves the limits of the

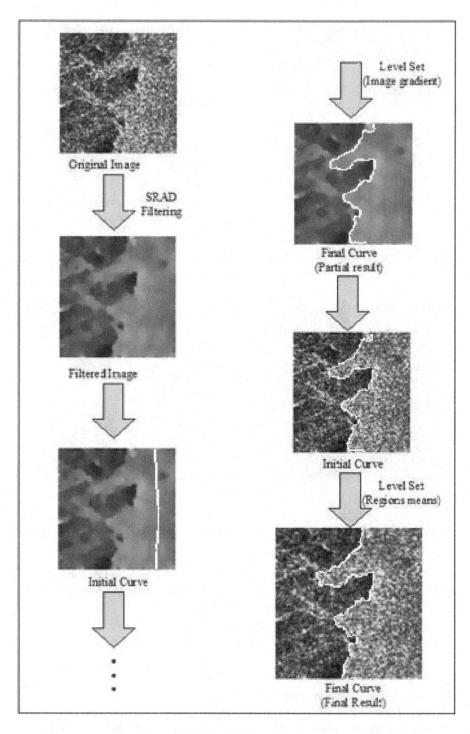

Fig. 5. Final result of integrated procedure

coastline in the image and then goes slowly close to those limits. In Figure 3 e Figure 4 two applications performed by gradient based speed are illustrated. Also in this case (a) and (b) represent a portion of initial curve selected (initial data for the numerical algorithm) while (c) and (d) show respectively the results (final boundaries) obtained when the convergence test is satisfied.

Unlike tests with average based speed, the same result is obtained from different initial curves.

4   Integrated Procedure

In order to obtain a more accurate result in the final position of the curve that identifies the coastline, an integration of both the procedures described above is proposed.

The implementation of Level Set with the speed based on regions means detects the coastline with more precision in terms of pixels, since the image is not dealt with filters for noise reduction. We observed that the best result is obtained by locating the initial curve as nearly as possible to the coastline, so that the final result depends on the position of the starting curve.

The implementation obtained by the speed based on image gradient is less accurate in terms of pixels than the previous one, because it works on the filtered image and not on the original one. However, this last approach is independent from the position of the initial curve.

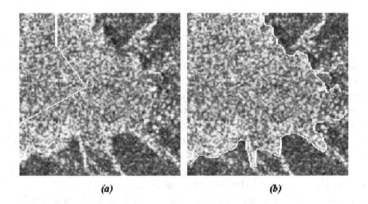

(a)   (b)

Fig. 6. Final result of integrated procedure

To obtain an automatic and accurate procedure, the two previous options have been integrated in the following way:

- The initial curve evolves applying the speed based on the image gradient to the image filtered by SRAD;
- The result is used as initial curve for the second application of level set to an original image by using the speed based on the means.

The proposed procedure integrates the two speed functions improving the segmentation results. In fact, the combined procedure allows the coastline to be identified *automatically* and *independently* from the initial location of the curve. In Figure 5 we describe the application of the proposed integrated procedure.

The Figure 6 shows the results of the procedure applied to the original image related to Test B.

5   Conclusion

In this paper we have faced the problem of detecting the coastline from SAR image by the level set model. Two distinct speed evolution functions have been examined. The first, based on the mean intensities of the regions, does not need to reduce speckle noise; the other, based on the image gradient, takes into account the problem to filter speckle noise by the SRAD technique. We proposed an innovative procedure that combines the two speed functions improving the two individual approaches. In fact, the integrated procedure allows the segmentation result to be independent by the initial location of the curve and moreover, it automatically stops when the curve achieves the coastline.

Acknowledgments. The authors wish to thank the Consortium for Informatics and Telematics "Innova" of Matera, which has provided the PRI (Precision Images) images of ERS Mission.

References

[1] Sethian, J.A.: Level Set Methods and Fast Marching Methods. Cambridge University Press, Cambridge (1999)

[2] Sethian, J.A.: Evolution, Implementation and Application of Level Set and Fast Marching Methods for Advancing Fronts. Journal of Computional Physics 169, 503–555 (2001)

[3] Osher, S., Fedkiw, R.: Level Set Methods and Dynamic Implicit Surfaces. Springer, New York (2002)

[4] Lee, J.-S., Igor, J.: Coastline Detection and Tracing in SAR. Images IEEE Transaction on Geoscence and Remote Sensing 28, 662–668 (1999)

[5] Dellepiane, S., De Laurentiis, R., Giordano, F.: Coastline Extraction from Sar Images and a Method for the Evaluation of the Coastline Precision. Pattern Recognition Letters 25, 146–147 (2004)

[6] Kass, M., Witkin, A., Terzopoulos, D.: Snakes: Active Contour Models. International Journal Vision 1, 321–333 (1988)

[7] Germain, O., Refregier, P.: Edge Location in SAR Images: Performance of the Likehood Ratio Filter and Accuracy Improvement with an Active Contour Approach. IEEE Trans. Image Processing 10, 72–77 (2001)

[8] Chesnaud, C., Refregier, P., Boulet, V.: Statistical Region Snake-Based Segmentation Adapted to Different Physical Noise Models. IEEE Trans. Pattern Analysis and Machine Intelligence 21, 1145–1157 (1999)

[9] Ben Ayed, I., Mitiche, A., Belhadj, Z.: Multiregion Level-Set Partitioning of Synthetic Aperture Radar Images. IEEE Trans. Pattern Analysis and Machine Intelligence 27, 793–800 (2005)

[10] Yu, Y., Acton, S.T.: Speckle Reducing Anisotropic Diffusion. IEEE Trans. on Image Processing 11, 1260–1270 (2002)

[11] Perona, P., Malik, J.: Scale Space and Edge Detection using Anisotropic Diffusion. IEEE Trans. Pattern Analysis and Machine Intelligence 12, 629–639 (1990)

Wavelet-Based Feature Extraction for Handwritten Numerals

Diego Romero, Ana Ruedin, and Leticia Seijas

Departamento de Computación, Facultad de Ciencias Exactas y Naturales,
Universidad de Buenos Aires
Pabellón I, Ciudad Universitaria (C1428EGA) Buenos Aires, Argentina
{dromero,ana.ruedin,lseijas}@dc.uba.ar

Abstract. We present a novel preprocessing technique for handwritten numerals recognition, that relies on the extraction of multiscale features to characterize the classes. These features are obtained by means of different continuous wavelet transforms, which behave as scale-dependent bandpass filters, and give information on local orientation of the strokes. First a shape-preserving, smooth and smaller version of the digit is extracted. Second, a complementary feature vector is constructed, that captures certain properties of the digits, such as orientation, gradients and curvature at different scales. The accuracy with which the selected features describe the original digits is assessed with a neural network classifier of the multilayer perceptron (MLP) type. The proposed method gives satisfactory results, regarding the dimensionality reduction as well as the recognition rates on the testing sets of CENPARMI and MNIST databases; the recognition rate being 92.60 % for the CENPARMI database and 98.22 % for the MNIST database.

Keywords: Continuous Wavelet Transform, Dimensionality Reduction, Pattern Recognition, Handwritten Numerals.

1 Introduction

Automatic recognition of handwritten numerals is a difficult task because of the wide variety of styles, strokes and orientations of digit samples. The subject has many interesting applications, such as automatic recognition of postal codes, recognition of amounts in banking cheques and automatic processing of application forms. Good results in numerals recognition have been obtained with neural networks among other classical learning procedures. The performance of these classifiers strongly depends on the preprocessing step. The choice of features to be extracted from the original data remains a challenge: it is not always clear which ones are to be selected to efficiently characterize their class, and at the same time provide a significant reduction in dimensionality.

Wavelet transforms have proved to be a powerful tool for image analysis, because of their capability to discriminate details at different resolutions. They have given good results in edge detection [1] and texture identification [2]. Discrete wavelet transforms (DWT) have been used to extract features for digit

P. Foggia, C. Sansone, and M. Vento (Eds.): ICIAP 2009, LNCS 5716, pp. 374–383, 2009.
© Springer-Verlag Berlin Heidelberg 2009

recognition. A 1D DWT [3] and a 1D undecimated multiwavelet transform [4] have been applied onto the previously extracted contour of the digits, and the result fed into a MLP classifier. Multirresolution techniques have also been used in conjunction with more complex classifiers: after applying a 2D DWT (3 different resolution levels) to the digits, a combination of multiple MLPs was used, each one being trained, with dynamic selection of training samples, for a specific level of (thresholded) approximation coefficients [5].

On the other hand, the 2D Continuous Wavelet Transform (CWT) performs a scale-space analysis on images, by calculating the correlation between an image and a 2D wavelet, at different scales and locations. It is more flexible than the DWT, and allows for scales that are non dyadic, providing greater frequential resolution. The 2D CWT has been extended by giving one principal orientation to the wavelet, via stretching one of its axes, and adding a rotational angle as a parameter to the transform [6]. It has translation, rotation and scale covariance [7] (the CWT is covariant under translations, because when applied to a translated image, it produces the translated CWT of the original image). This CWT has been applied for pattern recognition in images [8], and has given satisfactory results for digit recognition [9]. We use it here to extract a shape-preserving smaller version of the digits and to build a complementary vector with information on orientation, gradients and curvature at different scales.

We implemented the recognition system using a feed-forward neural network trained with the stochastic back-propagation algorithm with adaptive learning parameter. Our experiments were performed on 2 databases of handwritten digits: CENPARMI and MNIST.

This work is organized as follows: in Section 2 we introduce the 2 wavelets used in the CWT for the preprocessing step: the Mexican hat (in its isotropic and anisotropic versions) and the wavelet gradient. They are respectively based on the second and first derivatives of a Gaussian. In Section 3 we present our proposed feature extraction process, in Section 4 we describe the databases, and in Section 5 we give results and concluding remarks. Contributions and future work are briefly given in Sections 6 and 7.

2   2D Continuous Wavelet Transforms

The two-dimensional CWT is the inner product of an image s with a scaled, rotated and translated version of a wavelet function ψ [8]:

$$S_\psi(b, a, \theta) = a^{-1} \int_{\Re^2} \psi(a^{-1} r_{-\theta}(b - x))\, s(x)\, d^2x, \qquad (1)$$

where $x = (x_1, x_2)$, $b = (b_1, b_2) \in \Re^2$, $0 \le \theta \le 2\pi$, and

$$r_\theta(x) = (x_1 \cos\theta - x_2 \sin\theta, x_1 \sin\theta + x_2 \cos\theta). \qquad (2)$$

The wavelet ψ is highly localized in space; it is either compactly supported or has fast decay. Its integral is zero: for a given scale $a > 0$ the CWT behaves like a band-pass filter, providing information on where in the image we can find oscillations or details at that scale. At small scales the CWT captures short-lived variations in color such as thin edges; comparing the CWT at different scales reveals what kind of discontinuity is present; at large scales it blurs the image. If the wavelet is stretched in one direction, the CWT gives information on local orientation in the image.

2.1   2D Mexican Hat: Isotropic or Anisotropic

For our wavelet, we choose the Mexican Hat (MH), which is stretched in the direction of one of the axes in accordance with parameter ϵ [10]:

$$\psi_{MH}(x_1, x_2) = (2 - (x_1^2 + \frac{x_2^2}{\epsilon}))\ e^{-(x_1^2 + x_2^2/\epsilon)/2}. \qquad (3)$$

Note that when $\epsilon = 1$, ψ_{MH} is the Laplacian of $g(x_1, x_2) = e^{-(x_1^2 + x_2^2)/2}$, a bidimensional Gaussian; it is isotropic, and in that case the CWT gives no information on object orientation. When scaled, its essential support is a disk with radius proportional to the scale. If $\epsilon \neq 1$, we have the anisotropic MH, stretched out or shortened, and its support is an elipse.

The CWT has 4 parameters: scale, angle (orientation), and position $b = (b_1, b_2)$ in the image. For fixed a and θ, Eq. (1) gives the so-called position representation of the transform. By integrating the CWT' s energy over all positions, we have the scale–angle density [6]:

$$E(a, \theta) = \int_{\Re^2} |S_\psi(a, \theta, b)|^2 db_1\ db_2 \qquad (4)$$

2.2   The Wavelet Gradient

The first derivatives of g in each variable give 2 new wavelets:

$$\psi_1(x_1, x_2) = \frac{\partial g(x_1, x_2)}{\partial x_1}\ \text{ and }\ \psi_2(x_1, x_2) = \frac{\partial g(x_1, x_2)}{\partial x_2}, \qquad (5)$$

which have 2 vanishing moments and can be interpreted as a multiresolution differential operator. With both wavelets we construct the wavelet gradient [11] at scale a and at each position in the image:

$$T_\psi(b, a) = [S_{\psi_1}(b, a, 0), S_{\psi_2}(b, a, 0)]. \qquad (6)$$

$S_{\psi_1}(b, a, 0)$, the first component of $T_\psi(b, a)$ in Eq. (6), is the horizontal wavelet gradient. Integrating by parts we have

$$S_{\psi_1}(b, a, 0) = -\frac{1}{a} \int_{\Re^2} g(a^{-1}(b - x)) \frac{\partial}{\partial x_1} s(x)\, d^2 x, \qquad (7)$$

which is equal (except the sign) to the inner product of the first derivative of the image (with respect to x_1) and the scaled and translated Gaussian; in other words it averages the horizontal gradients smoothed with a Gaussian (with different widths), giving information on vertical edges at various scales. The same holds for the vertical wavelet gradient – the second component $S_{\psi_2}(b, a, 0)$, which gives information on horizontal edges at different scales. With the 2 components of the wavelet gradient vector, we may calculate both the absolute values

$$|T_\psi(b, a)| = \sqrt{S_{\psi_1}(b, a, 0)^2 + S_{\psi_2}(b, a, 0)^2}, \tag{8}$$

and the angles

$$\angle T_\psi(b, a) = arctan(S_{\psi_2}(b, a, 0), S_{\psi_1}(b, a, 0)) \tag{9}$$

of the transformed digit at each position. We then have the modulii and angular orientation of edges. (The sine and cosine are also calculated, and their signs are analyzed so as to give the angles in interval $[0 \ \ 2\pi)$.) Fig. 1 illustrates the wavelet gradient calculated on a MNIST digit, with $a = 1$.

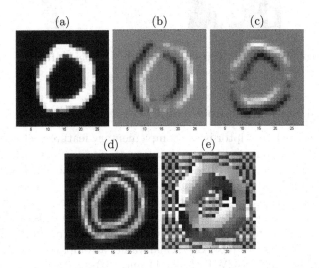

Fig. 1. Top row: (a) original digit, (b) horizontal wavelet gradient ($S_{\psi_1}(b, a, 0)$ in Eq. (6)), (c) vertical wavelet gradient ($S_{\psi_2}(b, a, 0)$ in Eq. (6)). Bottom row: (d) Absolute values (Eq. (8)), (e) angles (phase) (Eq. (9)) of the wavelet gradient.

In a similar way the second derivatives of the image may be estimated at different scales, and the curvature calculated.

3   Preprocessing of Handwritten Digits

3.1   First Step: MH-4 a Small Version with Smooth Edges

A low-level descriptor is extracted from the CWT, that preserves the structure and shape of the image, as well as spatial correlations in all directions: for this we select the isotropic MH wavelet given in Eq. (3) with ($\epsilon = 1$). By choosing a large scale ($a = 2.2$) to calculate the CWT we obtain a new version of the sample digit, in which the edges are smoothed out and filled in. To reduce dimensionality we subsample the transformed image by 2, by rows and by columns: for this we leave out the odd rows and columns of the transformed image. The result is a smoothed version of the digit, in size a fourth of the original one: we call this descriptor MH-4.

In Fig. 2 we observe an original digit from CENPARMI database, its CWT with isotropic MH, and the obtained small version with smooth edges.

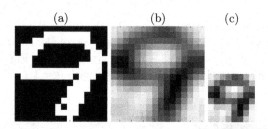

Fig. 2. (a) original digit, (b) result of applying the isotropic MH-CWT, (c) the same, subsampled (MH-4)

3.2   Second Step: A Complementary Feature Vector

A second high-level descriptor is the complementary feature vector (CFV). This vector has 85 components, averaging information on edges, orientations and curvature at different scales. It is the result of calculating 8 features [A]–[H] over the image, mostly extracted from 2 continuous wavelet transforms: the anisotropic MH-CWT and the gradient wavelet. Each feature is evaluated for different sets of parameters. To select the parameters we chose the ones giving best results, out of a limited set with which we carried out our tests. Each feature and set of parameters produces one scalar value, a component of the CFV.

In the case of the MH-CWT (Eqs. (1) and (3))– features [A] and [B]– this scalar value is obtained by means of the sum of squared values (over the transformed digit), which measures the energy, or by means of the entropy, which measures the dispersion of the related histogram.

In the case of the scale-angle density (Eqs. (1), (3) and (4))– feature [C]– $E(a, \theta)$ is calculated at different scales for a fixed set of angles. The scale giving the greatest energy values is chosen. For that chosen scale a, the entropy of $E(a, \theta)$ (varying θ) is calculated.

In the case of the wavelet gradient (Eq. (6)), the magnitudes and angles of the transformed digit are found (Eqs. (8), (9)). Either the sum of squared values or the entropy are calculated over the magnitudes – features [D] and [E]. Also the angles are quantized and the entropy of the resulting angles is calculated – feature [F]. The wavelet gradient is also used to calculate the mean curvature – feature [G].

The values of each component are scaled so that their ranges are approximately the same. For features marked with (*), calculations are performed twice for each set of parameters: first with no thresholding, second with a threshold equal to 30 % of the maximum value. The components of the CFV, grouped by features, are:

[A] (30 values) Sums of squares of absolute values of the anisotropic MH-CWT, with $e = 2.5$, and $a = 0.8$, at angles $\theta = i\,\pi/10$, $i = 0 \leq i \leq 9$. The same for $a = 1$ and $a = 1.8$.

[B] (30 values) Entropy of the absolute values of the anisotropic MH-CWT, with $e = 2.5$, and $a = 0.8$, at angles $\theta = i\,\pi/10$, $i = 0 \leq i \leq 9$. The same for $a = 1$ and $a = 1.8$.

[C] (4 values) Entropy of scale-angle density for a fixed scale at angles $\theta_i = i\,\pi/N$, $0 \leq i \leq N - 1$, for $N = 10$. The scale-angle density is calculated on the anisotropic MH-CWT with $e = 2.5$ ($e = 3.5$), at scales 0.8- 3.2 in steps of 0.4, and at angles as mentioned. The scale giving the greatest energy is chosen. The same, for $N = 15$.

[D] (4 values) Sums of squares of absolute values of wavelet gradient for $a = 1$ and 1.5 (*).

[E] (4 values) Entropy of the absolute values of the wavelet gradient, for $a = 1$ and 1.5 (*).

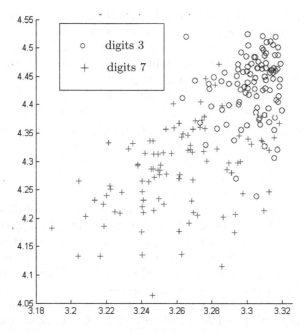

Fig. 3. Features [F] (y-axis) versus [C] (x-axis) for 200 digits from CENPARMI database

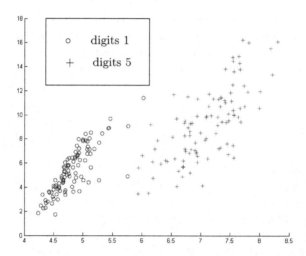

Fig. 4. Features [D] (y-axis) versus [E] (x-axis) for 200 digits from MNIST database

[F] (8 values) Entropy of the uniformly quantized angles (N classes) of the wavelet gradient at a fixed scale, for $a = 1$ and $a = 1.5$, for $N = 10$ and $N = 15$ (*).

[G] (4 values) Curvature calculated on wavelet gradient with $a=1$, $a = 1.5$ (*).

[H] (1 value) Curvature calculated on the original image.

In Figs. 3 and 4 we show how 2 components of the CFV (2 features for given parameters) separate 2 classes. The experiment is carried out with 100 digits from 2 distinct classes, and each point in the figures stands for one sample digit, its abscissa and ordinate being the values of the features. Parameters used in Fig. 3: for feature [F] : a=1.5 and 15 angles, for feature [C]: $e = 2.5$ and 10 angles. Parameters used in Fig. 4: for features [D] and [E], $a = 1.5$. Although in the figures the separation is not complete – the separation of classes is achieved with the complementary information of other features – it gives an idea of the efficiency of the features chosen to characterize the classes.

4   Databases

Our experiments were performed on the handwritten numeral databases CEN-PARMI and MNIST. These databases have been widely accepted as standard benchmarks to test and compare performances of the methods of pattern recognition and classification. Each database is partitioned into a standard training data set and a test data set such that the results of different algorithms and preprocessing techniques can be fairly compared.

MNIST is a modified version of NIST database and was originally set up by the AT&T group [12]. The normalized image data are available at webpage [13]. MNIST database contains 60,000 and 10,000 graylevel images (of size 28×28) for training and testing, respectively.

The CENPARMI digit database [14] was released by the Centre for Pattern Recognition and Machine Intelligence at Concordia University (CENPARMI), Canada. It contains unconstrained digits of binary pixels. In this database, 4,000 images (400 samples per class) are specified for training and the remaining 2,000 images (200 samples per class) are for testing. We scaled each digit to fit in a 16×16 bounding box such that the aspect ratio of the image would be preserved.

Because the CENPARMI database has less resolution, the database is much smaller, and the sampled digits are less uniform than in the MNIST database, the CENPARMI digits are more difficult to classify.

5   Results and Conclusions

In Table 1 the recognition rates of our proposed preprocessing technique on the CENPARMI database are listed, for the training set as well as for testing set. We give the recognition rates of the multilayer perceptron without preprocessing the sample digits. We also compare each step of our preprocessing technique (MH-4 and CFV) separately, and jointly. In the latter case, the smaller smooth image as well as the components of the CFV are fed into the neural network. We give the number of neurons in the first, hidden and final layers considered in the neural network's architecture; the number of neurons in the first layer being the dimension of the input. In Table 2 we have the same results for MNIST.

Notice the importance of preprocessing the digits, reflected by the higher recognition rates of MH-4 over no preprocessing. The CFV on its own, because it gives compact information on edges, orientations, curvature and scales, but lacks information on where they happen, gives lower recognition rates. However,

Table 1. Recognition rates for CENPARMI database

Preproc.	Network architecture	% Recog training set	% Recog test set
None	$256 \times 220 \times 10$	99.13	88.95
CFV	$85 \times 170 \times 10$	78.35	70.70
MH-4	$64 \times 150 \times 10$	99.22	91.95
MH-4 + CFV	$149 \times 200 \times 10$	99.22	92.60

Table 2. Recognition rates for MNIST database

Preproc.	Network architecture	% Recog training set	% Recog test set
None	$784 \times 110 \times 10$	99.29	97.06
CFV	$85 \times 110 \times 10$	79.88	80.85
MH-4	$196 \times 110 \times 10$	99.46	98.04
MH-4 + CFV	$281 \times 130 \times 10$	99.46	98.22

when added to the MH-4 representation, it improves the recognition rates and gives the best results.

Our proposed preprocessing technique, followed by a general purpose MLP classifier, achieved a recognition rate of 92.60 % on the test set for CENPARMI, and 98.22 % for MNIST. The combination of appropriate features and the reduction in the dimension of the descriptors with which the neural network was trained and tested, improved the performance and the generalization capability of the classifier.

Our results improved upon those mentioned in [3] and [4], the latter giving a recognition rate of 92.20 % for CENPARMI. In [5] the authors give a test error of 1.40 % for MNIST, which is better than ours; here it is difficult to evaluate the performance of our preprocessing method because their preprocessing is followed by a more complex classifier. Recently a classifier (with no preprocessing) was presented, based on the Bhattacharya distance and combined with a kernel approach [15], giving a test error of 1.8% for MNIST; our results are better than theirs. We plan to investigate further the properties of our preprocessing technique in order to reduce the error rate percentage.

6   Contributions

We present a novel preprocessing technique for handwritten numerals recognition, that relies on the extraction of multiscale features to characterize the classes. These features are obtained by means of different continuous wavelet transforms, which behave as scale-dependent bandpass filters, and give information on local orientation of the strokes.

The combination of appropriate features and the reduction in the dimension of the descriptors with which a multilayer perceptron neural network was trained and tested, improved the performance and the generalization capability of the classifier, obtaining competitive results over MNIST and CENPARMI databases.

7   Future Work

We plan to investigate further the properties of our preprocessing technique in order to improve the accuracy with which the features describe the original digits. We also plan to use more complex classifiers to obtain higher recognition rates. The application of this preprocessing technique to the problem of texture recognition is another goal in our research.

Acknowledgements

This work has been supported by grants UBACYT X166, X199 and BID 1728/ OC-AR-PICT 26001.
    The authors wish to thank the anonymous reviewer whose comments helped to improve the quality of this paper.

References

1. Mallat, S.: A theory of multiresolution signal decomposition: The wavelet representation. IEEE Trans. Pattern Analysis Machine Intell. PAMI-11(7) (1989)
2. de Ves, E., Ruedin, A., Acevedo, D., Benavent, X., Seijas, L.: A new wavelet-based texture descriptor for image retrieval. In: Kropatsch, W.G., Kampel, M., Hanbury, A. (eds.) CAIP 2007. LNCS, vol. 4673, pp. 895–902. Springer, Heidelberg (2007)
3. Wunsch, P., Laine, A.F.: Wavelet descriptors for multiresolution recognition of handprinted characters. Pattern Recognition 28(8), 1237–1249 (1995)
4. Chen, G., Bui, T., Krzyzak, A.: Contour-based handwritten numeral recognition using multiwavelets and neural networks. Pattern Recognition 36, 1597–1604 (2003)
5. Bhattacharya, U., Vajda, S., Mallick, A., Chaudhuri, B., Belaid, A.: On the choice of training set, architecture and combination rule of multiple MLP classifiers for multiresolution recognition of handwritten characters. In: 9th IEEE International Workshop on Frontiers in Handwritten Recognition (2004)
6. Antoine, J.-P., Murenzi, R.: Two-dimensional directional wavelets and the scale-angle representation. Signal Processing 52, 256–281 (1996)
7. Antoine, J., Vandergheynst, P., Bouyoucef, K., Murenzi, R.: Target detection and recognition using two-dimensional isotropic and anisotropic wavelets. In: Automatic Object Recognition V, SPIE Proc, vol. 2485, pp. 20–31 (1995)
8. Antoine, J.-P., Murenzi, R., Vandergheynst, P.: Directional wavelets revisited: Cauchy wavelets and symmetry detection in patterns. Appl. Comput. Harmon. Anal. 6, 314–345 (1999)
9. Romero, D., Seijas, L., Ruedin, A.: Directional continuous wavelet transform applied to handwritten numerals recognition using neural networks. Journal of Computer Science & Technology 7(1), 66–71 (2007)
10. Kaplan, L.P., Murenzi, R.: Pose estimation of sar imagery using the two dimensional continuous wavelet transform. Pattern Recognition Letters 24, 2269–2280 (2003)
11. Jelinek, H.F., Cesar Jr., R.M., Leandro, J.J.G.: Exploring wavelet transforms for morphological differentiation between functionally different cat retinal ganglion cells. Brain and Mind 4, 67–90 (2003)
12. LeCun, Y., Bengio, Y., Haffner, P.: Gradient-based learning applied to document recognition. Proceedings of the IEEE 86, 2278–2324 (1998)
13. LeCun, Y., Cortes, C.: The mnist database of handwritten digits, http://yann.lecun.com/exdb/mnist/index.html
14. Suen, C., Nadal, C., Legault, R., Mai, T., Lam, L.: Computer recognition of unconstrained handwritten numerals. Procs. IEEE 80(7), 1162–1180 (1992)
15. Wen, Y., Shi, P.: A novel classifier for handwritten numeral recognition. In: IEEE International Conference on Acoustics, Speech, and Signal Processing, pp. 1321–1324 (2008)

A Texture Based Shoe Retrieval System for Shoe Marks of Real Crime Scenes

Francesca Dardi, Federico Cervelli*, and Sergio Carrato

Dept. Electrical, Electronic and Information Engineering (DEEI)
University of Trieste, 34100 Trieste, Italy
federico.cervelli@deei.units.it

Abstract. Shoeprints found on the crime scene contain useful information for the investigator: being able to identify the make and model of the shoe that left the mark on the crime scene is important for the culprit identification. Semi-automatic and automatic systems have already been proposed in the literature to face the problem, however all previous works have dealt with synthetic cases, i.e. shoe marks which have not been taken from a real crime scene but are artificially generated with different noise adding techniques.

Here we propose a descriptor based on the Mahalanobis distance for the retrieval of shoeprint images. The performance test of the proposed descriptor is performed on real crime scenes shoe marks and the results are promising.

1 Introduction

Crime scene investigation is the starting point towards the identification of the culprit: only a great care and a careful analysis of the scene of crime allow the investigators to gain precious information about the criminal act. Among the activities to be performed by the crime scene experts we can recall the detailed documentation of the scene status, the search for fingerprints, shoeprints, biological fluids, chemicals and fire arms ammunition, and the collection of the items pertaining the crime for a later and deeper analysis in the laboratory [1].

In particular, shoe marks have a key role to understand the crime [2] and contain valuable information that can help investigators to unveil both the dynamics and the actors of the criminal action [3]: when no suspects or few elements are available to track investigation, knowing the make and the brand of the shoe sole that left the shoe mark on the scene can point a path; on the other side, if a suspect is given, the shoe mark can be compared to the shoes owned by the suspect, in order to formulate a statement about his or her involvement in the crime [4].

In this paper we deal with the first case: one or more shoe marks have been found on the crime scene and the make and model of the originating shoes must be found.

---

* Corresponding author.

P. Foggia, C. Sansone, and M. Vento (Eds.): ICIAP 2009, LNCS 5716, pp. 384–393, 2009.

The paper is organized as follows: in Sec. 2 we give the current state of the art of the research on automatic shoeprint matching, in Sec. 3 we describe the proposed descriptor and metrics, and in Sec. 4 we discuss the results. Finally in Sec. 5 we draw the conclusions and point out the future work.

2   Shoeprint Image Matching

We are interested in finding the make and the model of the shoe which produced a given shoe mark on the crime scene. In order to satisfy this request two different approaches can be followed:

1. a forensic shoeprint examiner analyzes the shoe mark and looks for the corresponding shoe on both digital and paper catalogs;
2. the crime scene shoe mark is queried using a reference database (DB) of known shoes, thanks to a content based image retrieval system, and the results of the query are then analyzed by the expert.

Some semi-automatic systems have been proposed to face the problem. In [5,6,7] shoe soles (and shoeprints more in general) are classified by a human expert which describes them with a series of geometric patterns.

Some automatic systems have also been proposed, but the field is still young. In [8] soles and shoeprints are described by a series of patterns automatically generated through a series of erosion-dilation steps. The Fourier components of the patterns are then calculated and chosen in order to be processed by a final classification through a neural network. Real crime scene shoeprints are used, but no performance results are given.

Fractals and mean square error are employed in [9] to represent and compare shoeprints, respectively. The DB is composed of 145 full print images, and is queried by the same images composing the DB but with added noise, rotation and translation. A 13 pixel translation result in a 10% accuracy of the results, and the algorithm needs the same size of the images for the mark and DB.

Fourier transform is implemented in [10]. The DB contains 476 full prints, which are correctly matched in the first 5% of the sorted DB patterns with an 85% score. Noisy images are not considered, and images are matched on themselves, to prove rotational and translational invariance.

Phase only correlation is employed in [11] to compare partial shoeprints produced starting from a 100 elements DB: these items are corrupted with noise or are added with some background texture images to simulate real case scenarios. The obtained simulated shoe marks are then queried to the DB, showing a satisfying performance.

More recently in [12] Hu's moment invariants are used on a DB containing 500 images, which are synthetically corrupted by noise and then queried against the full DB. Rotational robustness is tested in the range from -90° to +90°. The first returned image correctly matches the query image 99.4% of the time.

A Maximally Stable Extremal Region (MSER) detector is used in [13] to identify the features of the shoeprint and the Scale Invariant Feature Transform

(SIFT) algorithm is employed to describe them. After this first step a shorter list remains, and a finer search proceeds by comparing the shoeprints through a modified constrained spectral correspondence method. A query on the 374 elements in the DB gives a 92% top-eight rank. Also in this case the queried shoeprints are different print of varying quality of the same shoe model, i.e. they are not shoe marks coming from real crime scenes.

In this paper we have tested a new method over a reference DB of 87 known sole prints. Differently from all previous works, the query images used to evaluate the performance of the system are marks from real crime scenes.

3   The Proposed Shoeprint Image Retrieval System

A shoe sole is made with a distinguishing pattern which, in principle, can be thought as composed by a texture and a series of unique shapes (e.g. logos and other structures). Here, we focus on a proposal for the textured region descriptor and its recognition system. Obviously a full system would combine these results with those of a second algorithm based on the analysis of the unique shapes quoted above, in order to proceed with a finer search on the reduced cardinality DB.

3.1   Descriptor Selection and Calculation

In the following we describe a novel descriptor used to represent the texture region appearance in shoe sole marks found at crime scenes, on different types of background. This representation is based on the geometrical structures of objects, as proposed in [14] to detect human figures. As we can not assume particular pixel value patterns for objects like shoe marks found at crime scenes, we focus on geometrical structures observed as distances between pixel value patterns. Here, the pixel values are just labels making some regions stand out against other regions, because the variety of colors and textures of possible background where shoe marks can be found is enormous. Conversely, the relative positions and shapes of different parts in the sole print texture region are common for a given shoe model[1]. We select the proposed descriptor in order to focus more on geometrical entities rather than on pixel values themselves. So we extract the geometrical structures of our target object: this method is similar to edge based object recognition methods, but methods based only on edge detection are generally too sensitive to local information and are not robust against noise. In this work, we actually apply the proposed descriptor on gray scale shoeprint images either directly or after performing edge detection, in order to both overcome the aforementioned disadvantages of edge detection methods and improve recognition rate.

We briefly review the descriptor calculation. We divide a gray scale image area that we are interested in, into several sub-regions or blocks, and calculate

---

[1] We are not taking into account counterfeits reproducing the sole pattern of famous shoe makers.

the distances between all possible block pairs. More in detail, for an image $x(s,t)$ of size $m \times n$, we divide the area into small blocks of size $p \times q$. As a result we have M blocks in the horizontal direction and N blocks in the vertical direction. We first identify each block with a number ranging from 1 to MN in order to distinguish them as block $X_1, X_2, \ldots, X_{MN}$, and we compute the average vector, $\bar{x}_l$, and variance σ_l^2 for each block X_l.

We define the Mahalanobis distance [15] $d(i,j)$, with $i, j = 1, \ldots, MN$, between all possible block pairs:

$$d(i,j) = (\bar{x}_i - \bar{x}_j)(\sigma_i^2 + \sigma_j^2)^{-1}(\bar{x}_i - \bar{x}_j), \tag{1}$$

in order to determine the Mahalanobis map $\mathcal{M}$:

$$\mathcal{M} = \begin{pmatrix} 0 & d(1,2) & \cdots & d(1,MN) \\ d(2,1) & 0 & \cdots & d(2,MN) \\ \vdots & \vdots & \ddots & \vdots \\ d(MN,1) & d(MN,2) & \cdots & 0 \end{pmatrix}. \tag{2}$$

We used a 4×4 pixel block size for the calculation, for a total amount of 25×25 blocks (as our images are 100×100 pixel size wide).

Finally the descriptor of the mark and of the shoe sole in the DB is calculated as the Power Spectral Density (PSD) of $\mathcal{M}$, obtained as in [10]. In order to take care of the different noise sources affecting the shoe marks, the PSD is computed on the Mahalanobis map either calculated directly on the gray scale values of the image, or after the application of a suitable edge detection algorithm.

3.2   Similarity Metrics

In order to compare the input image (i.e. the shoe mark) with each of the images of the DB, a measure of similarity between the evaluated descriptors of the two images is required. The descriptor is calculated for each sole print image in the reference DB (corresponding to a different shoe make and model), and for the input shoe mark image; then the similarity measure between the descriptor of the mark and the descriptor of each item in the DB is computed and used to rank the results. The highest rank results are then supposed to be shown to a human expert who will select the database shoe that matches the shoe mark image (if a match exists).

The proposed measure of similarity between the shoe mark image and the image in the DB is their correlation coefficient. For 2D signals of size $r \times s$, $f_i(x,y)$, the correlation coefficient, $r_{i,j}$, is calculated using [17]:

$$\hat{f}_i(x,y) = [f_i(x,y) - mean(f_i)]/std(f_i) \tag{3}$$

$$r_{i,j} = \frac{1}{rs} \sum_{y=1}^{r} \sum_{x=1}^{s} \hat{f}_i(x,y)\hat{f}_j(x,y) \tag{4}$$

where $mean(f_i)$ is the average value of signal $f_i(x,y)$, and $std(f_i)$ is its standard deviation.

4   Results and Discussion

Performance testing of the proposed method was performed on a known shoe soles DB querying real marks coming from real crime scenes. The items were collected from the ENFSI[2] Working Group on Marks website [16] and then adapted as explained in the following.

Starting from the images available on the website, we built a reference DB made up of 87 known shoe soles, and a shoe marks list to query, made up of 30 items. The images were converted to gray scale and subjected to a rough resize and rotation, just in order to have an approximate correspondence in size and orientation between the soles and the marks.

Then one or more zones of interest of 100 × 100 pixel size were cropped and used for the test; in Fig. 1 some of the shoe soles and marks are shown. Some of the shoes from the reference DB were cropped in more than one image, in order to increase the reference DB dimension for testing purposes, Fig. 2.

Fig. 1. Examples of some shoe marks (top), and the expected matching shoes in the reference DB (bottom)

The descriptor described in Sec. 3.1 is computed either on the gray scale values of the image or after the application of a suitable edge detection algorithm. Fig. 3 shows the ranking results for each shoe mark queried, in case of both luminance values and two different edge detection algorithms (Laplacian and Canny). As can be seen, the 73% of the real case marks were found in the top-10 and their 100% in the top-19 shoes in at least one of the three used methods,

---

[2] European Network of Forensic Science Institutes, website: http://www.enfsi.eu/

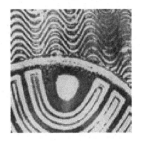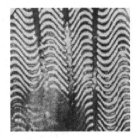

Fig. 2. Some shoeprints in the reference DB are cropped in more than one region, to increase the items number in the reference DB

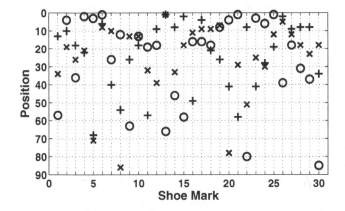

Fig. 3. The performance results are shown using the luminance image (∘), or using images processed by Laplacian edge detector (+), and Canny edge detector (×)

thus correctly excluding from the query results 89% and 78% of the known shoes DB, respectively. Fig. 4 is the same as Fig. 3 with only the best match shown for each show mark.

Finally, Fig. 5 represents the cumulative matching characteristics (CMC) [18] of each technique taken separately, while 6 shows the CMC obtained considering only the best ranking technique for each shoe mark. In both cases the horizontal axis of the graph is the percentage of the reference DB reviewed and the vertical axis is the probability of a match.

It has to be noted that no restoration and enhancement preprocessing methods have been employed, and that, as can be seen from Fig. 1, the repositioning, resizing and rotation during the shoe DB and marks list adaptation were performed without particular care; thus the results show that the system is able to face small rotations and has the ability to detect correlations even in case of shift and only partial overlapping between regions in the shoe mark and reference DB images.

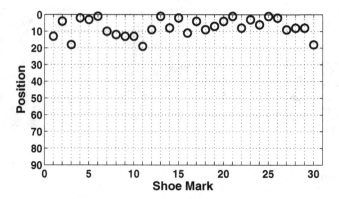

Fig. 4. Same as Fig. 3 with only the best match shown

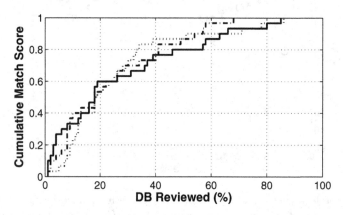

Fig. 5. Cumulative match score results using the luminance image (—), or using images processed by Laplacian edge detector (- -), and Canny edge detector ($\cdots$)

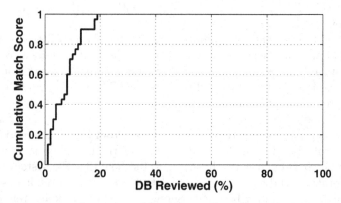

Fig. 6. Cumulative match score resulting by considering only the highest ranking technique for each shoe marks

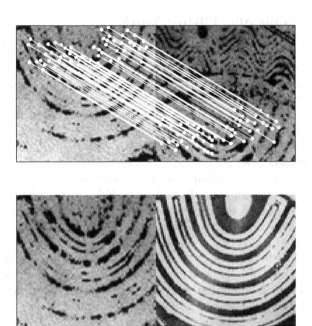

Fig. 7. The SIFT algorithm correctly matches (white lines show the corresponding features) the same shoe mark region with itself after a small translation (top), but is not able to match a shoe mark on the reference DB (bottom)

We would like to stress that this approach is taken to test the algorithm, while an operator oriented test would be instead performed using a different point of view, i.e. the one where the interest is in obtaining the right shoe, instead of the right region of the shoe.

Up to now none has reported on real shoe marks DB studies, thus none else has employed our known shoes DB and shoe marks list. The comparison of real crime scene shoe marks is a really demanding task, which can be simulated with great difficulty. We preliminary tested a SIFT matching algorithm [19], similar to the one employed in [13], on our marks and reference DB, and found that this algorithm is not likely to succeed without preprocessing in this case, Fig. 7.

The absence of a *de facto* standard reference DB with real crime scene marks seems to be, presently at least, a serious limit to any kind of performance comparison test. Thus, we have compared our system and the ones detailed in [10] and [11] on both synthetic and real shoe marks, showing that simulated shoe marks are not suited to test a footwear retrieval system aimed at finding the shoe make and model of a shoe mark found on the crime scene [20]: the algorithm in [11] outperformed the others on the synthetic test set, but it was on par with them when considering the results obtained on the real shoe marks set.

5   Conclusions and Future Work

In this paper, we consider a descriptor based on geometrical pixel structures, i.e. the Mahalanobis map applied following three different strategies, to recognize textures of shoe marks found at the crime scenes: such a performance evaluation has never been done in previous works, at the best of our knowledge. Results are encouraging, given the fact that no additional restoration and enhancement techniques have been used before querying the reference DB. However, we must note that a direct comparison with other works is not possible, given the lack of a standard reference DB for testing.

We believe we need to estimate the quality and nature (e.g. on sand, in blood, in the mud, etc.) of a shoe mark before it is fed into the process, to automatically select the best of the three proposed strategies required to optimize the performance of the system. Segmentation techniques could also be employed to separate textured regions from unique shapes (e.g. marks, logos, etc.). Thus future work will be devoted both to the investigation of suitable restoration and enhancement techniques for shoe mark images, and to enhance the performance of the system by combining the results of the proposed texture based algorithm with those of a suitable details extraction algorithm.

References

1. James, S.H., Nordby, J.J.: Forensic Science: an introduction to scientific and investigative techniques, 2nd edn. CRC Press, Boca Raton (2005)
2. Girod, A.: Shoeprints: coherent exploitation and management. In: European Meeting for Shoeprint Toolmark Examiners, The Netherlands (1997)
3. Bodziak, W.J.: Footwear impression evidence: detection, recovery and examination, 2nd edn. CRC Press, Boca Raton (1999)
4. ENFSI WGM Conclusion Scale Committee: Conclusion scale for shoeprint and toolmarks examiners. J. Forensic Ident. 56, 255–265 (2006)
5. Girod, A.: Computerized classification of the shoeprints of burglars' shoes. Forensic Sci. Int. 82, 59–65 (1996)
6. Sawyer, N.: SHOE-FIT a computerized shoe print database. In: Proc. Eur. Convention Secur. Detect., pp. 86–89 (1995)
7. Ashley, W.: What shoe was that? The use of computerized image database to assist in identification. Forensic Sci. Int. 82, 7–20 (1996)
8. Geradts, Z., Keijzer, J.: The image-database REBEZO for shoeprint with developments for automatic classification of shoe outsole designs. Forensic Sci. Int. 82, 21–31 (1996)
9. Bouridane, A., Alexander, A., Nibouche, M., Crookes, D.: Application of fractals to the detection and classification of shoeprints. In: Proc. Int. Conf. Image Processing, vol. 1, pp. 474–477 (2000)
10. De Chazal, P., Flynn, J., Reilly, R.B.: Automated processing of shoeprint image based on the fourier transform for use in forensic science. IEEE Trans. Pattern Analysis Machine Intelligence 27, 341–350 (2005)
11. Gueham, M., Bouridane, A., Crookes, D.: Automatic recognition of partial shoeprints based on phase-only correlation. In: Proc. Int. Conf. Image Processing, vol. 4, pp. 441–444 (2007)

12. Algarni, G., Amiane, M.: A novel technique for automatic shoeprint image retrieval. Forensic Sci. Int. 181, 10–14 (2008)
13. Pavlou, M., Allinson, N.M.: Automated encoding of footwear patterns for fast indexing. Image Vision Computing 27, 402–409 (2009)
14. Utsumi, A., Tetsutani, N.: Human detection using geometrical pixel value structures. In: Proc. 5th IEEE International Conference on Automatic Face and Gesture Recognition, pp. 39–44 (2002)
15. Gonzalez, R.C., Woods, R.E.: Digital image processing, 3rd edn. Pearson Prentice Hall, Upper Saddle River (2008)
16. Website: http://www.intermin.fi/intermin/hankkeet/wgm/home.nsf/
17. Russ, J.C.: The image processing handbook, 2nd edn. CRC Press, Boca Raton (2005)
18. Phillips, P.J., Moon, H., Rizvi, S.A., Rauss, P.J.: The FERET evaluation methodology for face-recognition algorithms. IEEE Trans. Patt. Anal. Mac. Intell. 22, 1090–1104 (2000)
19. Mikolajczyk, K., Tuytelaars, T., Schmid, C., Zisserman, A., Matas, J., Schaffalitzky, F., Kadir, T., Van Gool, L.: A comparison of affine region detectors. Int. J. Computer Vision 65, 43–72 (2005)
20. Cervelli, F., Dardi, F., Carrato, S.: Towards an automatic footwear retrieval system for crime scene shoe marks: Comparison of different methods on synthetic and real shoe marks. To be published in 6th Int. Symp. on Image and Signal Processing and Analysis (2009)

Encephalic NMR Tumor Diversification by Textural Interpretation

Danilo Avola and Luigi Cinque

University of Rome "La Sapienza", Department of Computer Science
Via Salaria 113, 00198 Rome, Italy
{avola,cinque}@di.uniroma1.it
http://w3.uniroma1.it/dipinfo/english/index.asp

Abstract. The novel technologies used in different application domains allow to obtain digital images with a high complex informative content. These meaningful information are expressed by textural skin that covers the objects represented inside the images. The textural information can be exploited to interpret the semantic meaning of the images themselves. This paper provides a mathematical characterization, based on texture analysis, of the craniopharyngioma pathology distinguishing it from other kinds of primary cerebral tumors. By this characterization a prototype has been developed, which has primarily allowed to identify potential abnormal masses inside the cerebral tissue and subsequently to possibly classify them as craniopharyngiomas.

Keywords: Medical image, texture analysis, pattern recognition, feature extraction, segmentation, classification, co-occurrence matrix.

1 Introduction

The novel image capture devices used in the different application domains allow to obtain images with high level details. These images often possess an informative content that goes beyond the simple visual representation. That is, by observing the relationships between pixels or clusters of pixels (that is, the texture) of the objects inside the images, it is possible to bring out the meaningful features through which to describe the semantic informative content of the images. In the last years, there have been many efforts to adopt the image analysis processes on medical images. The reason for this, comes from the need to get intelligent and automated systems for carrying out, in real time, several critical duties, such as: diagnosis, analysis, zones delineation, abnormal masses identification and irradiation, and so on. The making of these systems is still a hard task, and the current Decision Support Systems (DSSs) are still scanty tools.

This paper provides a concrete advancement of our results just shown in [1]. In particular, our previous work provided the numerical characterization, based on texture analysis, of each object represented in the NMR encephalic images (cerebral tissue, rest of skull, possible abnormal mass, and background). The step ahead of this paper has been to provide a further numerical class able to

P. Foggia, C. Sansone, and M. Vento (Eds.): ICIAP 2009, LNCS 5716, pp. 394–403, 2009.

distinguish the craniopharyngioma pathology from other kinds of primary cerebral tumors. There is an extensive heterogeneous literature on medical images analysis focalized on different aspects of medical image processing, such as: image segmentation, masses detection, and so on. In particular, these approaches are based on several principles related to the image understanding, but no so much works tend to exploit totally the morphological structure (given by texture analysis) of the objects inside the biomedical images, moreover there is no works about concrete mathematical characterization of a specific NMR brain tumor. In [2] an interesting approach of medical image processing is given, in particular the authors present a framework for multiple object segmentation in medical images that respects the topological properties and relationships of structures as given by a template. In [3] another framework for the segmentation of brain magnetic resonance imaging (MRI) is given. In particular, the authors provide an approach that combines atlas registration, fuzzy connectedness (FC) segmentation, and parametric bias field correction (PABIC) to perform automatically the segmentation task. A complex medical image processing system is shown in [4], in this work the authors present an approach, based on evolutionary computing, to medical image segmentation. In this approach the segmentation task, on sagittal brain magnetic resonance images (MRI), has been reached by complementing the image-pixel integration power of deformable shape models with the high-level control mechanisms of genetic algorithms (GAs). Diversely, the common approaches, such as [5], aim to exploit the well known features of the image content, such as: edge detection, boundary detection, model correlation-based, region-based, and so on. An alternative approach is also proposed in [6], in this approach the texture modeling is based on the implicit incorporation of spatial information through the introduction of particular matrixes that take into account the spatial relationships among pixels. Another interesting approach is proposed in [7], where the application, based on random neural network, accomplishes the texture classification and retrieval. In particular, in this context a neuron in the network corresponds to an image pixel and the neurons are connected according to neighboring relationship between pixels. In this way, a texture can be represented with the weights of the network. In [8] the authors give a last remarkable framework through which to perform brain MRI segmentation. In this approach the segmentation is performed by applying nonparametric density estimation, using the mean shift algorithm in the joint spatial-range domain.

Unlike the previous works, the proposed approach provides the identification of a well defined mathematical characterization, texture based, of the morphological structure of the craniopharyngioma pathology inside the encephalic NMR images. The paper is organized as follows. Section 2 introduces both the proposed image processing methodology and the numerical class representing the primary cerebral tumors. Section 3 introduces the numerical class about the craniopharyngioma pathology. Section 4 summarizes the medical cases study. Finally, Section 5 concludes.

2   Methodology and Designed Architecture

In order to determine the mathematical characterization related to the cranio-pharyngioma pathology (shown in the next section) we have exploited the classification obtained in our previous work [1]. Besides, also the adopted methodology as well as the used prototype coming from the same work. For this reason, this section shows the main aspects of the mentioned work.

With the purpose to obtain the preliminary textural mathematical characterization of the cerebral tissue necessary to subsequently distinguish craniopharyngioma pathology from other kinds of primary cerebral tumors has been adopted the methodology shown in Figure 1. Each one of the three modules will now be briefly explained.

Fig. 1. Methodology: the three modules

The recognition phase, applied on selected NMR images (chosen transversal T_1 weighted, with or without contrast) is designed to perform feature extraction activity on the following fix objects: object 1: possible cerebral anomaly (i.e.: primary cerebral tumor), object 2: cerebral tissue, object 3: rest of the image (i.e.: muscular and bony structure), object 4: background.

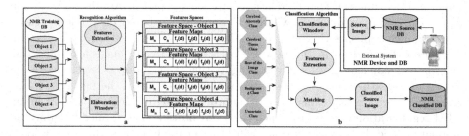

Fig. 2. Architecture: a) recognition phase b) classification phase

As shown in Figure 2-a, four different databases each one containing some images representing a collection of the same kind of objects have been used as training database. The feature extraction process has been performed by a pre-established elaboration window within which the feature extraction algorithm, based on textural statistical operators, worked to catch the different textural features. At the end of the recognition phase every image (in every database) provided several feature maps, these sets of feature maps, according to the specific objects, have constituted the feature spaces through which to provide the mathematical characterization of the objects themselves. The six textural statistical operators chosen to extrapolate the semantic meaning of the texture have been selected from the first and second order statistical class [9].

The operators belonging to the first order statistical class are: *N-Order Moment* (M_n) and *M-Order Central Moment* (C_m):

$$M_n = \sum_{i=0}^{N} i^n \times p(i), C_m = \sum_{i=0}^{N} (i - M_1)^m \times p(i) \tag{1}$$

Where: *p(i)* represents the probability that the gray level value i appears inside the elaboration window (E.W.). The following constraints must be respected:

$$0 \le p(i) \le 1 \; \forall i \in [0..255] \subset \mathrm{N}, \sum_{i=0}^{N} p(i) = 1, N = 255, n = 1, m = 2 \tag{2}$$

The remaining chosen four operators, co-occurrence matrix based, work according to the principle scheme shown in Figure 3.

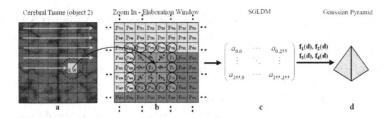

Fig. 3. NMR texture operators principle scheme

Figure 3-a represents the scanning (by Elaboration Window, E.W.) of an image belonging to sub-database object 2. Every square zone, where the arrow appears, identifies an elaborated image zone. The E.W. identifies the image zone under processing. The remaining image zones will be processed after the "actual" E.W.. In Figure 3-b can be observed that each pixel making up the elaboration window $(P_1..P_{16})$ will be considered as "the centre" of a "circle" whose radius value is predefined (called "d"). Every couple of points (centre point and each one on the boundary of the circumference) will increase by one frequency its coefficient on the co-occurrence matrix, Figure 3-c, at the coordinates (*row, column*) $a_{m,n}$ fixed through the gray tone level of considered points. The Figure 3-d shows the new image (feature map) that results after the full scanning.

Every E.W. that processes the image in Figure 3-a gives back (by the different operators) a single pixel that makes up the feature map. Thus, every feature map is sub-sampled (depending on the considered E.W. size) referring to the original image. This process can be repetitively performed on the obtained image. This working method is defined as "Gaussian Pyramidal Approach" [10], where every obtained image represents a level of the pyramid (original image is the pyramid base). Our approach considers, for every image in the whole NMR training DB two levels of the Gaussian Pyramid (L_0 and L_1). Also the two operators, belonging to the first order statistics, exploit the pyramidal approach.

The mentioned operators, belonging to the second order statistical class, are: *Homogeneity* ($f_1(d)$), *Contrast* ($f_2(d)$), *Inverse Difference* ($f_3(d)$), and *Entropy* ($f_4(d)$):

$$f_1(d) = \sum_{i=0}^{N} \sum_{j=0}^{N} [p_d(i,j)]^2, f_2(d) = \sum_{i=0}^{N} \sum_{j=0}^{N} (i-j)^2 [p_d(i,j)]^l$$
$$f_3(d) = \sum_{i=0}^{N} \sum_{j=0}^{N} \frac{[p_d(i,j)]^l}{1+(i-j)^k}, f_4(d) = -\sum_{i=0}^{N} \sum_{j=0}^{N} p_d(i,j) \log_n (p_d(i,j))$$

(3)

Where: $p_d(i,j)$ represents the probability that two points with distance "d" have respectively i and j gray value. The following constraints must be respected:

$$0 \le p_d(i,j) \le 1, \forall (i,j) \in [0....255] \times [0....255] \subset N^2$$
$$\sum_{i=0}^{N} \sum_{j=0}^{N} p_d(i,j) = 1, N = 255, k = 2, l = 1, n = 2$$

(4)

The operators ($f_1(d)$, $f_2(d)$), belonging to the Computer Vision (CV), are exploited to emulate human textural visual perception of two main parameters used by human analyst during NMR analysis: homogeneity and contrast. The operators ($f_3(d)$, $f_4(d)$) belonging to the Information Retrieval (IR) techniques, complete the feature extraction work. All four mentioned operators have been used with two different distance values "d" (d = 2, 3).

With the purpose of explaining both the way the mathematical classes have been built and how the original NMR images coming from the device have been classified, in Figure 2-b is shown the detailed software architecture of the NMR classification phase. In this phase, the feature spaces of each object (provided by recognition phase) have been carefully analyzed by grey tones histogram and correlated to others feature spaces belonging to the same objects. In this way four univocal mathematical characterizations, called *classes*, have been accomplished. As consequence, a class called *uncertain* is made up. It contains all those pixel configurations that are not included in the *classes*.

In this section (Figure 4-a) is shown only the mathematical class related to the possible cerebral anomaly (i.e.: primary cerebral tumors). The functions M_1, C_2, $f_1(d)$, $f_2(d)$, $f_3(d)$, and $f_4(d)$ are the operators used into the E.W. (where d = 2, 3). Moreover T_i, for $0 \le i \le 30$, are the extrapolation constants fixed to the following grey tone intensity values: $T_0..T_{30}$: 97, 18, 193, 33, 55, 140, 186, 8, 107, 120, 255, 55, 88, 121, 164, 6, 39, 70, 220, 25, 33, 71, 101, 198, 248, 110, 165, 80, 110, 45, 65. In Figure 5-a a visual example of the classes is shown.

The shown result is only related to the first level of the Gaussian Pyramid (L_0) (our algorithm takes into account (L_0) and (L_1)). In fact, this level represents the basic feature to distinguish the cerebral anomaly class from the other three *classes* (cerebral tissue class, rest of the image class, background class). By the

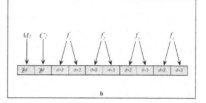

$E.W. \in \{Cerebral\ Anomaly\ Class\} \Leftrightarrow$

$(((C_2 \leq M_1 \leq T_0) \wedge (M_1 \geq T_0)) \wedge$

$(T_1 \leq f_1(2) \leq T_2) \wedge ((T_3 \leq f_1(3) \leq T_4) \vee ((T_5 \leq f_1(3) \leq T_6)) \wedge$

$((T_7 \leq f_2(2) \leq T_8) \vee (T_9 \leq f_2(2) \leq T_{10})) \wedge ((T_{11} \leq f_2(3) \leq T_{12}) \vee (T_{13} \leq f_2(3) \leq T_{14})) \wedge$

$((T_{15} \leq f_3(2) \leq T_{16}) \vee (T_{17} \leq f_3(2) \leq T_{18})) \wedge ((T_{19} \leq f_3(3) \leq T_{20}) \vee (T_{21} \leq f_3(3) \leq T_{22})) \wedge$

$((T_{23} \leq f_4(2) \leq T_{24}) \vee (T_{25} \leq f_4(2) \leq T_{26})) \wedge ((T_{27} \leq f_4(3) \leq T_{28}) \vee (T_{29} \leq f_4(3) \leq T_{30})))$

Fig. 4. a) Cerebral anomaly class b) Feature vector

formalized *classes* it is possible to explain how the original NMR images coming from the device have been classified.

As shown in Figure 2-b, the source images coming directly from the nuclear magnetic resonance device (NMR source database) are directly scanned, by a classification window (C.W. of the same size of the E.W.), in the same way as in the recognition phase. From each C.W. on these images a feature vector is extrapolated (features extraction). This vector, as shown in Figure 4-b, regards the same measures (operators) used for the recognition phase (with L_0 and L_1 levels). Each single feature vector, extracted from the original image, tries the matching (in the matching module) to the formalized classes. After the right class has been found, that particular cluster is assigned to the related class. After all source image clusters have been considered the image areas belonging to the same formalized classes are joined together. At the end of this process the outcome is that each zone of each image is classified as belonging to one of four formalized classes or (for exclusion) belonging to the *uncertain* class. Every classified image is arranged in the new database (NMR classified DB).

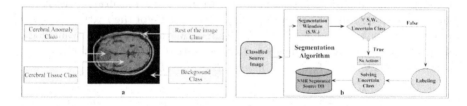

Fig. 5. a) Main classes b) Architecture: segmentation phase

The segmentation phase represents the last step of our image analysis process. In this phase two main tasks are accomplished. In the first a simple labeling process is performed on the classified source image. In the second the system solves all these image zones that belong to the *uncertain* class.

In Figure 5-b is shown the segmentation phase architecture. Each classified source image is directly scanned by a segmentation window (S.W. of the same size of C.W. and E.W.). As shown in Figure 5-b, if the pixels into the S.W. belong to one formalized class then all the pixels into the S.W. will be suitably labeled. Otherwise, no action is performed, and the system scans next S.W.. At the end of this first step a large amount of the image is labeled. In the second step, the unlabeled image zones are solved. The image zones belonging to the *uncertain* class are subdivided in two categories: not recognized zones (NRZs), spurious zones (SZs). Primarily, by context based algorithm, the first kind of ambiguity is solved. Subsequently, by decisional algorithm, also the second kind of ambiguity is solved. At the end of segmentation process every source image is perfectly labeled and arranged in NMR segmented source DB.

3   Craniopharyngioma Class

Once obtained the cerebral anomaly class (and related image segmentation), the framework can detect, as shown in Figure 6, the presence of abnormal masses inside the cerebral tissue. But it is not able to identify the kind of primary cerebral tumor.

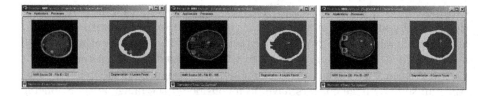

Fig. 6. Examples of detected primary cerebral tumors

The concrete advancement of the proposed work has been to distinguish the craniopharyngiomas pathology from other kinds of primary cerebral tumors. The first step to accomplish this task has been to find other textural statistical operators able to extrapolate the morphological structure of the texture expressed from the craniopharyngiomas tissue. Experimental observations have enabled to select, always belonging to the second order statistical class, the following two operators: *Correlation* ($f_5(d)$), *Difference Entropy* ($f_6(d)$):

$$f_5(d) = \sum_{i=0}^{N} \sum_{j=0}^{N} \frac{(i-\mu_x)(j-\mu_y)p_d(i,j)^l}{[\sigma_x \sigma_y]^m}, f_6(d) = -\sum_{i=0}^{N} p_{x-y}(i) \log_n[p_{x-y}(i)] \qquad (5)$$

Where:

$$\mu_x = \sum_{i=0}^{N} \sum_{j=0}^{N} i\,(p_d(i,j))\,, \sigma_x = \sqrt{\sum_{i=0}^{N} \sum_{j=0}^{N} (i-\mu_x)^2\,(p_d(i,j))}$$

$$\mu_y = \sum_{i=0}^{N} \sum_{j=0}^{N} j\,(p_d(i,j))\,, \sigma_y = \sqrt{\sum_{i=0}^{N} \sum_{j=0}^{N} (i-\mu_y)^2\,(p_d(i,j))} \qquad (6)$$

$$p_{x-y}(k) = \sum_{i=0}^{N} \sum_{j=0}^{N} [p_d(i,j)]^q, where |i-j| = k$$

Obviously, $p_d(i,j)$ has the same meaning and has to respect the the same constraints shown in the previous section. Moreover, experimental observations have fixed, on the two mentioned operators, the following parameters: $l = 1$, $m = 1$, $n = 2$, $q = 1$. More specifically, these two operators have been selected according to their capacity to catch both micro structural changes on texture with low level of stationarity and macro morphological pattern on texture with high level of entropy.

The two statistical operators $(f_5(d), f_6(d))$ have been used, by the methodology and the algorithms explained in the previous section, on the zones of images recognized as belonging to the cerebral anomaly class. In particular, the operators have been used with three different distance values "d" (d = 1, 2, 3). In this way, it has been possible to distinguish, within the cerebral anomaly class, the sub-class craniopharyngioma, as shown in Figure 7-a (it is shown only the results related to the first level of the Gaussian Pyramid (L_0)). In Figure 7-b is also shown the related feature vector.

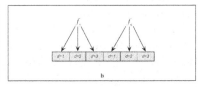

Fig. 7. a) Craniopharyngioma class. b) Feature vector

The functions $f_5(d)$, $f_6(d)$ are the operators used into the E.W. (where d = 1, 2, 3). Moreover T_i, for $31 \leq i \leq 54$, are the extrapolation constants fixed to the following grey tone intensity values: $T_{31}..T_{54}$: 25, 145, 198, 255, 33, 180, 220, 250, 23, 109, 148, 213, 70, 112, 160, 200, 34, 57, 100, 127, 110, 200, 220, 255.

4 Experimental Results

This section shows both the cases study through which the craniopharyngioma class has been built (NMR image recognition) and the case studies for the experimental phase (NMR image classification and segmentation).

The whole image set was made up of 1015 images provided by 255 selected patients. As in our previous work, the patients have been selected by a protocol in which was specified rules for patients inclusion or exclusion. Moreover, the protocol also specified particular texture requirements able to discard images where objects were represented by messy and/or ambiguous patterns of pixels. The main aim of the protocol was to avoid the introduction of unknown texture caused by several factors, such as: brain prostheses, recent brain operations, and so on.

All the used images have been selected according to the encephalic NMR diagnostic standard: depth 8 bit gray-scale, spatial resolution 512x512 pixels.

Table 1. Cases Study

Total Patients	Training DB		Source DB			Total Images
			PCT Patients (42% CRF patients)	3/5 images		
	CRF Patients	3/5 images		415		
				CRF Patients	PCT Patients	
255	150	600	105	175	240	1015

With these images the training DB and source DB have been built. In the Table 1 a short description case studies is shown. The total patients (255) have been subdivided into two groups: a first group (training DB) made up from 150 craniopharyngioma patients and the second group (source DB) made up from 105 primary cerebral tumor patients. The 42% of the patients belonging to the second group was affected by craniopharyngioma pathology. From each patient of the first and second group have been chosen respectively from 3 to 5 images (600 total images shown craniopharyngioma pathology), and from 3 to 5 images (415 total images, of which 175 shown craniopharyngioma pathology and 240 shown another kind of primary cerebral tumors).

Using the two classes shown in this work, our prototype has almost always correctly classified a craniopharyngioma pathology (success rate: 93%). In the remaining 7% of cases, the prototype always detected the presence of a primary cerebral tumor, but it failed during the classification process. The images for which the prototype fails have both a real small portion of pixel related the craniopharyngioma pathology and their position is almost ambiguous. This problem should be solved by using a whole set of images of a specific patient, and/or by enriching the operators used to define the craniopharyngioma class.

We have observed that the craniopharyngioma classification is reasonably independent from the height of the NMR scanning plan. Moreover, in the worst case, the difference between the real size of the craniopharyngioma pathology in the source image and the size of the labeled related object in the segmented image is about 9%.

5   Conclusion

This paper provides a mathematical characterization, based on texture analysis, of the craniopharyngioma pathology distinguishing it from other kinds of primary cerebral tumors. The developed prototype has shown the effectiveness of the obtained results.

By using all image categories (T_1, T_2, proton density, flair) and all scanning anatomic planes (sagittal, frontal, transversal) could be obtained several recognition/classification improvements, which should be aim to relax constraints of the protocol used to select patients and their images. More specifically, the prototype needs of a new advanced experimental session on a not controlled diagnostic environment.

The proposed approach can be also exploited to reach further advanced targets in NMR image analysis, such as: identification and classification of other kinds of primary cerebral tumors, 3D textural reconstruction, textural modeling of the brain and so on.

References

1. Avola, D., Cinque, L.: Encephalic NMR Image Analysis by Textural Interpretation. In: Proceedings of the 2008 ACM Symposium on Applied Computing, SAC 2008, pp. 1338–1342. ACM Press, New York (2008)
2. Bazin, P.L., Pham, D.L.: Topology Correction of Segmented Medical Images Using a Fast Marching Algorithm. Comput. Methods Prog. Biomed. 88(2), 182–190 (2007)
3. Zhou, Y., Bai, J.: Atlas-Based Fuzzy Connectedness Segmentation and Intensity Nonuniformity Correction Applied to Brain MRI. IEEE Transactions on Biomedical Engineering 54(1), 122–129 (2007)
4. McIntosh, C., Hamarneh, G.: Genetic Algorithm Driven Statistically Deformed Models for Medical Image Segmentation. In: ACM Workshop on Medical Applications of Genetic and Evolutionary Computation Workshop, MedGEC 2006, p. 8. ACM Press, New York (2006)
5. Yan, P., Kassim, A.A.: Medical Image Segmentation Using Minimal Path Deformable Models with Implicit Shape Priors. IEEE Transactions on Information Technology in Biomedicine 10(4), 677–684 (2006)
6. Zwiggelaar, R., Blot, L., Raba, D., Denton, E.R.E.: Set-Permutation-Occurrence Matrix Based Texture Segmentation. In: Perales, F.J., Campilho, A.C., Pérez, N., Sanfeliu, A. (eds.) IbPRIA 2003. LNCS, vol. 2652, pp. 1099–1107. Springer, Heidelberg (2003)
7. Teke, A., Atalay, V.: Texture Classification and Retrieval Using the Random Neural Network Model. Journal on Computational Management Science 3(3), 193–205 (2006)
8. Jimenez-Alaniz, J.R., Medina-Banuelos, V., Yanez-Suarez, O.: Data-Driven Brain MRI Segmentation Supported on Edge Confidence. IEEE Trans. Med. Imaging 25(1), 74–83 (2006)
9. Julesz, B.: Dialogues on Perception. Bradford/MIT Press, Cambridge (1995)
10. Heeger, D.J., Bergen, J.R.: Pyramid-Based Texture Analysis/Synthesis. In: Proceedings of the 22nd Annual Conference on Computer Graphics and Interactive Techniques, SIGGRAPH 1995, pp. 229–238. ACM Press, New York (1995)

Pathnodes Integration of Standalone Particle Filters for People Tracking on Distributed Surveillance Systems

Roberto Vezzani, Davide Baltieri, and Rita Cucchiara

Dipartimento di Ingegneria dell'Informazione - University of Modena and Reggio
Emilia, Via Vignolese, 905 - 41100 Modena - Italy
{roberto.vezzani,22218,rita.cucchiara}@unimore.it

Abstract. In this paper, we present a new approach to object tracking
based on batteries of particle filter working in multicamera systems with
non overlapped fields of view. In each view the moving objects are tracked
with independent particle filters; each filter exploits a likelihood function
based on both color and motion information. The consistent labeling of
people exiting from a camera field of view and entering in a neighbor
one is obtained sharing particles information for the initialization of new
filtering trackers. The information exchange algorithm is based on pathnodes, which are a graph-based scene representation usually adopted
in computer graphics. The approach has been tested even in case of
simultaneous transitions, occlusions, and groups of people. Promising
results have been obtained and here presented using a real setup of non
overlapped cameras.

Keywords: Pathnode, multicamera tracking.

1 Introduction

Probabilistic methods are widely used for people tracking. In presence of occlusions and crowd, it is worth to keep more than one hypothesis of the current
position of each tracked item: neighbor's body parts, noise, background objects,
and other distracters often mislead the tracking system, resulting in a wrong
state estimation and incorrect following. In a probabilistic framework the multiplicity of the state modes is faced with Mixtures of Gaussians or Particle Filtering. Particle Filtering has proven to be very successful for non linear and non
Gaussian estimation problems such as people tracking in presence of occlusions
and clutter. Thus, we propose a single camera tracking by particle filtering. This
solution also allows a multicamera tracking framework as extension of a set of
single camera systems.

2 Related Work

Approaches to multicamera tracking can be generally classified into three main
categories: *geometry-based*, *color-based*, and *hybrid* approaches [1]. The former

P. Foggia, C. Sansone, and M. Vento (Eds.): ICIAP 2009, LNCS 5716, pp. 404–413, 2009.

exploits geometrical relations and constraints between the different views to perform the consistent labeling process. They make use of known spatial information and relation among the set of available cameras. Two examples of this class are the work of Khan and Shah [2] and of Calderara et al [1]. Their approach is based on the computation of the so-called *Edges of Field of View*, i.e. the lines delimiting the field of view of each camera and, thus, defining the overlapped regions. Geometry-based approaches have been proved to be very reliable and effective, but they require at least a partial overlap between camera fields of view. In non overlapped camera frameworks, color-based approaches can be successfully applied, since the matching is essentially based on the color of the tracks. For example, in [3] a color space invariant to illumination changes is proposed and histogram-based information at low (texture) and mid (regions and blobs) level are adopted. Conversely, the work in [4] uses stereoscopic vision to match tracks, but when this matching is not sufficiently reliable, color histograms are used to solve ambiguities. Finally, Hybrid approaches, belonging to the third class, mix information about the geometry and the calibration with those provided by the visual appearance. These last methods are based on probabilistic information fusion [5] or on Bayesian Belief Networks (BBN) [6]. Our approach belongs to the hybrid class, since it makes use of a weak calibration in order to locate each camera in a global map of the environment. Geometrical information are used to make predictions as in [7], but they are not enough since the cameras are not overlapped. Then, color information are used to perform accurate track matches in different camera field of view.

3   Particle Filter for Single Camera Tracking

Goal of a single camera tracking system is to estimate the state $\mathbf{x}_t$ at frame t given the set of observations $\{\mathbf{z}_{1...t}\}$. At this stage we assume for simplicity that each tracked object is moving regardless of other people in the scene. Thus, an independent tracker is applied for each object in order to estimate its state $\mathbf{x}$, which we assume to be composed by the coordinates of the gravity center (x_c, y_c). In a probabilistic framework, $\mathbf{x}$ is a random variable, with the associated probability density function $p(\mathbf{x}|\mathbf{z})$ which we are interested on. The most likely position $\hat{\mathbf{x}}$ of each tracked person can be estimated at time t from the relative pdf as $\hat{\mathbf{x}}_t = E(\mathbf{x}_t)$. To this aim we adopted a generic particle filtering technique; for the sake of completeness we report here the base equations using the notation proposed by Arulampalam et al in their famous tutorial [8].

Let $\left\{\mathbf{x}^i, w^i\right\}_{i:1..N}$ be a characterization of the posterior probability $p(\mathbf{x}|\mathbf{z})$, where $\left\{\mathbf{x}^i, i = 1..N\right\}$ is the set of support points (particles) with their weights $\left\{w^i, i = 1..N\right\}$. The weights are normalized to add up to one. By means of this set of weighted particles the posterior probability can be approximated as:

$$p(\mathbf{x}|\mathbf{z}) \approx \sum_{i=1}^{N} w^i \delta\left(\mathbf{x} - \mathbf{x}^i\right), \quad w_t^i \propto w_{t-1}^i \cdot p\left(\mathbf{z}_t|\mathbf{x}_t^i\right) \tag{1}$$

Table 1. Pseudo-code of resampling and particle filter algorithms

RESAMPLING ALGORITHM

- Initialize the CDF: $c_1 = 0$
- FOR $i = 2 : N_s$
  - Construct CDF: $c_i = c_{i-1} + w_k^i$
- Start at the bottom of the CDF: $i = 1$
- Draw a starting point: $u_1 \sim \mathcal{U}[0, N_s^{-1}]$
- FOR $j = 1 : N_s$
  - Move along the CDF:
  $u_j = u_i + N_s^{-1}(j - 1)$
  - WHILE $u_j > c_i$
    * $i = i+1$
  - Assign sample: $\mathbf{x}_k^{j*} = \mathbf{x}_k^i$
  - Assign weight: $w_k^j = N_s^{-1}$

GENERIC PARTICLE FILTER

- FOR $i = 1 : N_s$
  - Draw $\mathbf{x}_k^i \sim q(\mathbf{x}_k | \mathbf{x}_{k-1}^i, \mathbf{z}_k)$
  - Assign the particle a weight, w_k^i according to Eq. (1)
- Normalize w_k^i such that $\sum_i w_k^i = 1$
- Calculate $\widehat{N_{eff}}$
- IF $\widehat{N_{eff}} < N_T$
  - RESAMPLING ALGORITHM

where we adopt as importance density the prior $p(\mathbf{x}_t | \mathbf{x}_{t-1}^i)$, and the resampling step is executed only if the measure of degeneracy $\widehat{N_{eff}} = \left[\sum_{i=1}^N (w^i)^2 \right]^{-1}$ is lower than a threshold N_T. The particle filter tracking can be described by the two pseudo-code algorithms reported in Tab. 1 (from Algorithms 2 and 3 in [9]). The adopted likelihood function and the new occlusion-based process model, instead, are fully described in the following.

3.1 The Likelihood Function

Similar to work of Li et al [10], for each object we store and keep updated a set of three appearance models $AM_t = \{am_t^1 \doteq F_t, am_t^2 \doteq A_t, am_t^3 \doteq D_t\}$. We assume that each pixel is independent of each other. The fixed model F_t contains the appearance of the tracked object stored at the initialization phase. The Adaptive model A_t stores the mean of N object appearances sampled at regular time steps. Finally, the Dynamic model D_t is estimated averaging D_{t-1} with the current frame. All these models can take advantage of a foreground segmentation of the current frame. Since in the regarded application we make use of fixed cameras, we process every frame with a background subtraction system, SAKBOT [11]. Only the image points classified as foreground pixels concur to the model estimation. Calling I_t the current frame, the model update equations are:

$$AM_t = \{am^1, am^2, am^3\} = \begin{cases} am^1 = F_t(\mathbf{x}) = F(\mathbf{x}) = I_{t_1}(\mathbf{x} - \hat{\mathbf{x}}_t) \\ am^2 = A_t(\mathbf{x}) = \frac{1}{N} \cdot \sum_{j=1}^{N} I_{t-j\Delta t}(\mathbf{x} - \hat{\mathbf{x}}_{t-j\Delta t}) \\ am^3 = D_t(\mathbf{x}) = \frac{1}{2} \cdot D_{t-1}(\mathbf{x}) + I_t(\mathbf{x} - \hat{\mathbf{x}}_t) \end{cases} \quad (2)$$

where I_{t_1} is the first frame of the i-th object, i.e. when it is entered the scene; the notation $\mathbf{x} - \hat{\mathbf{x}}_t$ is used to indicate the frame by frame alignment of the model using the estimated position of the target $\hat{\mathbf{x}}_t$.

On the whole, the state $\{\hat{\mathbf{x}}, AM\}$ of a tracked object is composed by $\hat{\mathbf{x}}$, i.e., the position of the center of mass in the image plane (estimated by particle filtering), and its appearance AM (updated using Eq. 2).

With the likelihood function we can estimate $p(\mathbf{z_t}|\mathbf{x_t})$, i.e., how likely a particular object position is to produce the current frame. Practically, we have to compare the estimated models for each object at the previous frame AM_{t-1} with the current image I_t. A pixel-wise comparison usually leads to errors if the model is not exactly aligned with the current frame, since a pixel-by-pixel distance is not a monotonic function. Therefore the distance measure between the model and the current observation is based on aggregate functions like color histograms.

Let be $RR_d\,(I, \mathbf{x})$ a rectangular region of the image I, centered around the point $\mathbf{x}$, fixed shape ratio and scale factor d derived from the previous background suppression phase. Let $H(\cdot)$ be the histogram of the image argument. Then, at sampling time one of the three appearance models $am^j \in AM_t$ is randomly selected for each particle. The likelihood value $p(\mathbf{z_t}|\mathbf{x_t})$ is extracted from a zero-mean normal distribution using the Bhattacharyya distance $\Phi(\cdot)$ between the color histogram from the current image $H\,(RR_d\,(I_t, \hat{\mathbf{x}}_t))$ and the selected model histogram $H(am^j)$ as in Eq. 3

$$p(\mathbf{z}_t|\mathbf{x}_t^i) = p(\mathbf{z}_t|\mathbf{x}_t^i, am^j) = \frac{1}{\sqrt{2\pi}\sigma} \exp^{-\frac{\Phi\left(H\left(RR_d(I_t,\hat{\mathbf{x}}_t)\right),H(am^j)\right)}{2\sigma^2}} \tag{3}$$

3.2   The Process Model

The motion of a person in a scene is difficult to predict and is seldom linear, in particular if the object position is measured in image coordinates. Therefore, usually the random walk equations are adopted for the state prediction step [12]. Our approach is slightly different and takes into account the previous movements of the person in addition to the Gaussian noise. We estimate the current person's speed my means of a exponentially weighted average schema:

$$\hat{\mathbf{v}}_t = \beta\hat{\mathbf{v}}_{t-1} + (1 - \beta)(\hat{\mathbf{x}}_t - \hat{\mathbf{x}}_{t-1}) \tag{4}$$

where β has been empirically set to $\frac{2}{3}$.

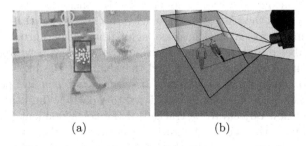

(a)   (b)

Fig. 1. Graphical representation of the tracked state through particle filter. Dots are the particles positions and the rectangle is the ROI for the likelihood computation and model update.

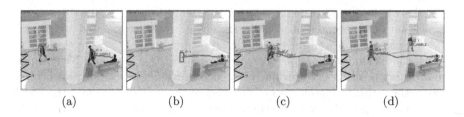

| (a) | (b) | (c) | (d) |

Fig. 2. Example of person tracking during a strong occlusion

$$\tilde{\mathbf{x}}_t^i = \mathbf{x}_{t-1}^i + \hat{\mathbf{v}}_{t-1} + \mathcal{N}(\mathbf{0}, \sigma \mathbf{I_2}). \tag{5}$$

The Gaussian noise of Eq. 5 should take into account the non linear nature of the human motion. Furthermore the tracker can be mislead by occlusions and shape changes. Thus, the Gaussian noise should be large enough to manage the unpredictable changes in speed and direction, but it does not set to naught the linear prediction. To this aim we propose a spherical covariance with a dynamic parameter σ_t which depends on the likelihood score computed at the previously estimated position $\mathbf{x}_{\hat{t}-1}$:

$$\sigma_t = \frac{\sigma_0}{(1 + \alpha p(\mathbf{z}_{t-1}|\hat{\mathbf{x}}_{t-1}))}. \tag{6}$$

where σ_0 is mandatory since the variance should be greater then zero and α is a predefined constant. During occlusions or quick motion changes the distance function computed in the estimated position grows; increasing the noise term. This will assure that particles will be much spread in the next step. Figure 2 reports an example of long-lasting occlusions. Even that, the tracker system can manage the label assignments after the occlusions thanks to the dynamic nature of the noise term.

3.3   Initialization

As above mentioned, each object is independently considered and tracked; every time a person enters the scene a new particle filter should be created and initialized. To this aim the foreground mask extracted from the background subtraction algorithm is labeled and unassigned blobs are classified as new objects. A blob is unassigned if no particle has required that blob for the likelihood function estimation. To avoid wrong assignments between new blobs and particles associated with other objects, a blob is associated to a particle (and then eliminated from the list of new objects to be tracked) if the correspondent Bhattacharyya distance is under a threshold. The initial position $\hat{\mathbf{x}}_0$ of the object is set equal to the blob gravity center and the three appearance models are initialized with the blob appearance.

4   Multi Camera Tracking

Let us suppose to have a wide space monitored by a set of non overlapped fixed cameras. If the fields of view of the cameras are close enough, it is plausible that a person exiting a camera field of view will soon appear on the field of view of a neighbor camera. Moreover, if the illumination conditions and the camera type are the same, a person will generate similar color histograms on different views. Information stored in the particle filter used to track a person in the source camera can be effectively used to initialize the tracking system of the destination camera.

We propose to exploit computer graphic techniques to manage the multicamera tracking problem. Interactions between different scenes and the movements of avatars are usually managed with graph models by the computer graphic and virtual reality communities. All the possible avatar positions (or rooms) are represented by nodes and the connecting arcs refers to allowed paths. The sequence of visited nodes is called *pathnodes*. A weight can be associated to each arc in order to give some measures on it, such as the duration, the likelihood to be chosen with respect to other paths, and so on. We empirically set the arc weights, but a learning phase can be established to automatically compute them.

In Fig. 3(a) a sample test bed is depicted; three cameras are installed and the correspondent fields of view are highlighted. A person walking in the represented scene can stay inside the field of view of the same camera, can move toward another one trough a transition zone or can definitely exits the area. According with the allowed paths, the overall area can be divided into three region types: A. Visible regions, corresponding to camera's fields of view; B. Non visible regions, i.e., transition areas between two or more visible regions; C. Forbidden or exit regions.

In particular we are interested to identify the boundaries of these regions. People inside visible regions can be detected and tracked by the corresponding single camera system; once they exit that region to enter in a non visible region, they will likely appear again in another visible region. The exit and the entry points are located on the boundaries between visible and non visible regions. If a person exits the entire scene walking through a forbidden region boundaries he will not be seen again. In other words, the state of a person can be estimated by the single camera tracker without exchanging information with the other systems during all his permanence on the field of view of a camera. If the person reach a boundary with a non visible region, his state should be propagated to the neighbor cameras in order to consistently label the person once he will appear again in another visible area. Finally, if the person crosses a forbidden or exit region boundary his state can be discarded since it is improbable that he will reappear in the scene (Fig 3(b)). Let us define the following symbols:

- $\{C^1 \dots C^K\}$: set of K installed cameras;
- $FoV(C^k)$: visible regions, i.e, the field of view of a camera C^k;
- $\{NVR^1 \dots NVR^L\}$: non visible regions;

– $\{FR^1 \dots FR^H\}$: forbidden or exit regions;
– $R^l \cap R^k$: boundary between two regions;

Through the Process Model described in Section 3.2 we can estimate $p(\mathbf{x}^i_{t+\Delta t}|\mathbf{x}^i_t)$ only for object positions inside the same camera field of view. Our goal is to extend that model for neighbor cameras, evaluating the probability of moving toward another camera FoV:

$$p(\mathbf{x}'^i_{t+\Delta t}|\mathbf{x}^i_t) \tag{7}$$

where $\mathbf{x}'$ and $\mathbf{x}$ are referred to two different FoV regions.

4.1   Pathnode Based Scene Representation

Due to preferential paths, perspective transformations, and scene nature, the probability of Eq. 7 cannot be expressed in analytical form. Following computer graphic techniques, we then generate a graph-based representation which can be considered an approximation of it. Actually, the domain of Eq. 7 can be restricted to the boundaries between visible and non visible regions.

We introduce the Pathnode based Scene Representation, composed by:

– $\Psi = \{\psi_i\}$: set of nodes $\psi_i \in \{FoV(C^k) \cap NVR^l, k = 1 \dots K, l = 1 \dots L\}$. Each node psi is associated to an object position $\mathbf{x}_\psi$ on the boundary between $FoV(C^k)$ and NVR^l;
– $\Gamma = \{\gamma_{i,j}\}$: set of weighted arcs $\gamma_{i,j} \subset \{\Psi \times \Psi\}$, corresponding to a possible path from two nodes ψ_i and ψ_j that people can follow. The weight $c(\gamma_{i,j}) \in \Re$ of each arc is proportional to the use frequency of the set of paths it represents:

$$c(\gamma_{i,j}) \propto p(\mathbf{x}_{t+\Delta t} = \mathbf{x}_{\psi_j}|\mathbf{x}_t = \mathbf{x}_{\psi_i}), \sum_i c(\gamma_{i,j}) = 1. \tag{8}$$

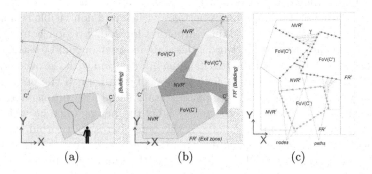

(a)   (b)   (c)

Fig. 3. A sample surveillance system. (a) FoV of three cameras, (b) region classification and graph-based representation with pathnodes.

4.2 Hand-off Management

Each time a tracked person approaches a boundary of the visible region, a new particle filter tracker is created on the cameras connected by at least one arc. Let us suppose that a person is exiting the field of view of the camera C^s. If a camera C^d is adjacent to C^s (i.e., at least one arc $\gamma_{i,j}$ connects one node of C^s to one node of C^d) a new particle filter is created in C^d, sharing the same appearance models and the same identifier of the source one, up to color transformations as afterwards described in Section 5.

The initial set of particles $\left\{ \mathbf{x}'^i, w'^i \right\}_{i=1..N}$ is sampled from the proposal distribution $q(\mathbf{x}'_t | \mathbf{x}_{t-\Delta t})$, where the position $\mathbf{x}'$ in the destination camera C^d is a function of the particle positions in the source one C^s.

$$q(\mathbf{x}'_t | \mathbf{x}^i_{t-\Delta t}) = \sum_{\psi_j \in C^d} \alpha_j \cdot \mathcal{N}(\mathbf{x}_{\psi_j}, \sigma) \tag{9}$$

$$\alpha_j = w^i \cdot \sum_{\psi_k \in C^s} c(\gamma_{k,j}) \cdot \delta_{\psi_k}\left(\mathbf{x}^i_{t-\Delta t}\right) \tag{10}$$

$$\delta_{\psi_k}\left(\mathbf{x}^i\right) = \begin{cases} 1 \text{ if } \left\| \mathbf{x}^i, \mathbf{x}_{\psi_k} \right\| \leq \beta \\ 0 \quad \text{otherwise} \end{cases} \tag{11}$$

5   Inter-camera Color Transformation

If the cameras are of different types or the illumination conditions are not uniform the main hypothesis of color portability is no more valid. Then, a inter-camera color calibration is required. To this aim different algorithms have been proposed, ranging from simple linear transformations to more generic solutions such as lookup tables. The two sample frames of Fig.4(a) show a situation in which the color calibration problem is particularly marked.

(a)   (b)

Fig. 4. a. A common problem: different views have different colors; b. Patterns used for the color calibration

For computational reasons we adopt a fast linear transformation, which consist in finding a matrix $\mathbf{M}$ able to model the space changes. In [13] Roullout shows that the linear algebraic model is the most natural model under the usual assumptions, providing the detailed mathematical justification. A set of couple

	#frames	FPS	#people	Correct	FN	FP	Double Assignment	Id exchange	Handoff errors	Precision	Recall
Video1	301	13,3	9	536	34	171	135	1	0,25	76%	94%
Video2	837	11,2	14	1119	75	134	90	4	0,44	89%	94%
Video3	500	11,5	12	547	35	48	48	1	0,00	92%	94%
Video4	1020	13,4	16	707	134	68	34	0	0,50	91%	84%
Video5	769	10,6	28	1547	161	196	30	1	0,00	89%	91%
Video6	633	12,1	10	435	113	3	2	0	0,30	99%	79%
	4060	12	89	4891	552	620	339	7	0,25	89%	90%

Fig. 5. Quantitative performance evaluation of the tracking system

of correspondent colors have been manually extracted from captured images of a color pattern as in Fig. 4(b). The matrix M is thus obtained with a least squares optimization.

6   Experimental Results

The proposed method has been implemented in C++, partially using the OpenCV libraries [14] and the Imagelab processing libraries. From a compu-tational point of view, the system with two running cameras is able to process 10 frames per second if the number of people in the scene is about ten, i.e., two background segmentation processing and ten particle filters are simultaneously working.

To test the application, we used some videos from the surveillance system installed in our department. The system is composed by four cameras: three of them are fixed and the forth is a PTZ dome camera. Three different scenarios obtained selecting couples of non overlapped views have been defined and used to generate the data set. A graphical interface allows to define the global map, the fields of view and the nodepaths.

We captured and tested the application on 6 videos of different complexity and we collected results in the table of Fig. 5. For each sequence we counted the number of appeared people. For each frame we identified the number of correct track assignments and the number of False Positives (FP) and False Negatives (FN) an their sum over the whole video are reported in the table. The mean precision and recall are 89% and 90% respectively for the in-camera tracking, while the consistent labeling task reaches a 80% precision rate. The different types of error are also reported in the table. As it is possible to see, most of the FP errors are due to double assignments, which are due to more than one particle filter being created for the same object, as a consequence of segmentation errors arising from the background suppression phase. Finally, there is an ID exchange each time the system fails to disambiguating after an interaction or a mutual occlusion among two or more people.

7   Conclusions and Future Work

In this paper we propose an integrated framework for in-camera and multi cam-era people tracking. First of all, a single camera particle filtering approach is proposed, in order to keep more than one hypothesis on the position of each tracked person. Such a condition is required in order to manage occlusions, group of people and color ambiguity. Experimental results on our real in-campus surveillance system show the validity and the robustness of the approach. Furthermore, the required computational load allows a real time implementation. Moreover, a new approach to multi camera tracking is the main contribution of this paper. Information embedded on each single camera tracker are diffused to other cameras, by means of a graph representation of possible connecting paths. The approach is very promising and the results on real datasets are good. Even so, color features are not enough distinctive and view invariant to be reliably transfered among different cameras. We proposed an inter-camera color transformation to reduce this problem, but it is still inadequate. We are currently working on finding more appropriate features and invariants.

References

1. Calderara, S., Cucchiara, R., Prati, A.: Bayesian-competitive consistent labeling for people surveillance. IEEE Trans. on PAMI 30, 354–360 (2008)
2. Khan, S., Shah, M.: Consistent labeling of tracked objects in multiple cameras with overlapping fields of view. IEEE Trans. on PAMI 25, 1355–1360 (2003)
3. Li, J., Chua, C., Ho, Y.: Color based multiple people tracking. In: Proc. of IEEE Intl Conf. on Control, Automation, Robotics and Vision, pp. 309–314 (2002)
4. Krumm, J., Harris, S., Meyers, B., Brumitt, B., Hale, M., Shafer, S.: Multi-camera multi-person tracking for easyliving. In: Proc. of IEEE Intl Workshop on Visual Surveillance, pp. 3–10 (2000)
5. Kang, J., Cohen, I., Medioni, G.: Continuous tracking within and across camera streams. In: Proc. of IEEE Int'l Conference on Computer Vision and Pattern Recognition., vol. 1, pp. 267–272 (2003)
6. Chang, S., Gong, T.H.: Tracking multiple people with a multi-camera system. In: Proc. of IEEE Workshop on Multi-Object Tracking, pp. 19–26 (2001)
7. Yue, Z., Zhou, S., Chellappa, R.: Robust two-camera tracking using homography. In: Proc. of IEEE Intl Conf. on Acoustics, Speech, and Signal Processing, pp. 1–4 (2004)
8. Arulampalam, S., Maskell, S., Gordon, N.: A tutorial on particle filters for online nonlinear/non-gaussian bayesian tracking. IEEE Transactions on Signal Processing 50, 174–188 (2002)
9. Doucet, A.: On sequential simulation-based methods for Bayesian filtering. Technical report (1998)
10. Li, A., Jing, Z., Hu, S.: Robust observation model for visual tracking in particle filter. AEU - International Journal of Electronics and Communications 61, 186–194 (2007)
11. Cucchiara, R., Grana, C., Piccardi, M., Prati, A.: Detecting moving objects, ghosts and shadows in video streams. IEEE Trans. on PAMI 25, 1337–1342 (2003)
12. Feller, W.: An Introduction to Probability Theory and Its Applications, vol. 1. Wiley, Chichester (1968)
13. Roullot, E.: A unifying framework for color image calibration. In: Proc. of IWSSIP 2008, pp. 97–100 (2008)
14. Bradski, G., Kaehler, A.: Learning OpenCV: Computer Vision with the OpenCV Library. O'Reilly, Cambridge (2008)

On Improving the Efficiency of Eigenface Using a Novel Facial Feature Localization

Aleksey Izmailov and Adam Krzyżak

Department of Computer Science and Software Engineering,
Concordia University,
Montreal, Canada H3G 1M8
izmailoff@gmail.com, krzyzak@cs.concordia.ca

Abstract. Face recognition is the most popular non-intrusive biometric technique with numerous applications in commerce, security and surveillance. Despite its good potential, most of the face recognition methods in the literature are not practical due to the lack of robustness, slow recognition, and semi-manual localizations. In this paper, we improve the robustness of eigenface-based systems with respect to variations in illumination level, pose and background. We propose a new method for face cropping and alignment which is fully automated and we integrate this method in Eigenface algorithm for face recognition. We also investigate the effect of various preprocessing techniques and several distance metrics on the overall system performance. The evaluation of this method under single-sample and multi-sample recognition is presented. The results of our comprehensive experiments on two databases, FERET and JRFD, show a significant gain compared to basic Eigenface method and considerable improvement with respect to recognition accuracy when compared with previously reported results in the literature.

1 Introduction

For many automated face recognition systems, the first step in the recognition process is to spatially locate the face in the image. This process is called *face detection*. The main challenge in face detection is the high degree of variation in facial appearance. The two main face detection methods are *feature-invariant* approach and *classification-based* approach. The former methods use those features of the face which can resist through appearance variations (such as eyes, mouth, face texture or color) as guidance to locate the face in the image. The latter methods consider a face detection problem as a binary classification, and train a classifier to filter out the non-face areas of the image. Image-based approaches were shown to be more effective in dealing with complex environments, varying illumination conditions, and cluttered backgrounds. The high computational cost is usually a major drawback of many face detection algorithms, especially for real-time applications. Viola and Jones [17], proposed a system using an ensemble learning approach which has received much attention due to its quick response time. Their

P. Foggia, C. Sansone, and M. Vento (Eds.): ICIAP 2009, LNCS 5716, pp. 414–424, 2009.
© Springer-Verlag Berlin Heidelberg 2009

method also has some features as multiple detection, and robustness to size variation and orientation (see [20] for a survey of face detection methods). We have used this method for the detection part in our system.

There have been a variety of face recognition methods proposed in the literature (see comprehensive surveys in [15,7,1]). These methods are categorized into three groups: holistic matching, feature-based matching, and hybrid methods [5]. Holistic methods use the full face area in recognition. Feature-based matching methods usually apply a structural classifier on extracted features such as mouth, eyes, nose, ears. Finally, hybrid methods combine holistic and feature-based methods in an attempt to employ the best properties of both. One of the best known face recognition methods is the *Eigenface algorithm* [16,6,14], which is based on Principal Component Analysis (PCA). The Eigenface technique has shown to be effective on images which are properly aligned, i.e. which are aligned so that fiducial points for all images are located at the same coordinates. It is often used for frontal face recognition since it is easy to align and there is no need to deal with head rotation. Like other holistic techniques, the Eigenface approach is sensitive to illumination and light intensity. This method operates on values of grey-scale pixels which are encoded as decomposition coefficients by comparing distances between vectors. Therefore, images produced with similar light intensities will tend to have lesser distances between them and because of that property might be misclassified. The Eigenface technique by itself does not work well in realistic environments with many dynamic factors, because captured images usually contain complicated background and occlusions.

In this paper, we present a face recognition system that is able to detect human faces, crop them, and perform recognition in real time. Eigenface recognition is integrated with our system. Variable illumination, pose, and background are hard problems in recognition with Eigenface approach. We are able to reduce the impact of these factors on recognition performance by our novel face cropping algorithm as well as carefully selected preprocessing techniques and parameters. Our system shows promising results and may be used in many practical areas such as security, entertainment and business.

2   Elliptical Facial Feature Localization (EFFL) Method

Our approach to localization is based on elliptical shape which represents a person's face. To be able to do this, we first find the location of eyes using Haar-like features in conjunction with Adaptive Boosting (AdaBoost) for detection of a pair of eyes [17,8]. Based on the location of eyes we calculate a point which we shall call face center point (FCP). The FCP represents center of a human face if we assume that it has elliptical shape. This point is later used to build an ellipse surrounding the face area. The area outside of the ellipse is considered as background and does not contain information useful for recognition. We eliminate background area by setting it's pixels to one constant value such as zero, thus producing an image containing only face and black region surrounding it. We applied cascades of boosted classifiers to detect face, one eye, two eyes, nose and lips in order to extract face area. During our experiments the most reliable results have been achieved by one classifier which was trained to detect frontal eyes. Thus we focused on face cropping based on aforementioned classifier.

The face center point is calculated by considering a rectangle $R = ABCD$ such that both eyes fall inside it (Figure 1). We denote the left and right upper corners of R as $A(x_A, y_A)$ and $B(x_B, y_B)$, respectively. These two points are the two vertices of a triangle that we form in order to find the center of the face. The third vertex of the equilateral triangle ABC, which we call the facial triangle, is point C. Point C is located in the mouth area. Figure 1 shows these stages involved in face localization and cropping. We define the centroid of ABC to be the center point of the face (O_f). We next use O_f to eliminate the background from the face image. By background we mean any part of the face image which is not a facial feature or skin area. For the purpose of background removal, we form an ellipse E around the face, which circumscribed area contains all facial features of interest such as lips, nose and eyes. Let face ellipse center O_E be the intersection point of its two major and minor axes. We choose the ellipse center O_E to be the same point as the face center O_f. The length and width of this rectangle are equal to the major and minor axes of the ellipse E as shown in Figure 1. The major and minor axes are calculated as follows:

$$\begin{aligned} ||a_1 a_2|| &= k_1 * ||AB|| \\ ||b_1 b_2|| &= k_2 * ||AB|| \end{aligned} \tag{1}$$

where k_1 and k_2 are fixed constants. These constants have been chosen carefully to build an ellipse so that we can eliminate as much background as possible, while preserving the facial features. k_1 and k_2 have been measured for an average typical person to provide a good ROI for the face recognition. We fill pixels that lie in the area outside of E and inside of ROI_C, with some constant C ($0 \leq C \leq 255$) which represents the gray scale color. The final result of this procedure can be seen in Figure 1.

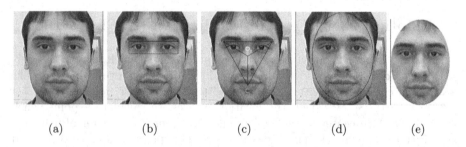

(a)   (b)   (c)   (d)   (e)

Fig. 1. The stages of face cropping procedure (a) original face image, (b) locating eyes (c) estimating face center O_f, (d) producing the face ellipse (e) cropping the face according to the face ellipse

3 Eigenface Recognition System with EFFL

In our face recognition process we use the Eigenface approach [16]. In order to recognize an unseen image, we proceed with automatic cropping of face according to the details described in Section 2. The same cropping and preprocessing should be applied to the testing and training images before recognition. Test images are represented in terms of eigenface coefficients by projecting them into face space (eigenspace) calculated during training. Test sample is recognized by measuring the similarity distance between the test sample and all samples in the training. The similarity measure is a metric of distance calculated between two vectors. We utilize some of the standard techniques used in image processing such as histogram equalization, and symmetrization. Histogram equalization redistributes the intensity values of pixels so that the distribution of intensities becomes uniform [4].

Symmetrization is a technique for recovering one part of an object from another symmetrical part. It can be applied to human faces to restore any shaded or occluded part. The axis of symmetry lies vertically along the nose line. Some promising results have been shown on finding this axis reliably, however there is still room for improvement [2]. Our approach to this problem, is to first find a bounding box around eyes as described in Section 2. We then build the center line as the line crosses the center of this rectangle and be parallel to short sides. Next we compute brightness of each side of the face as a function of sum of grayscale values of pixels. We compare relative brightness of the left and right side to some threshold ratio to determine if symmetrization is necessary. If the value exceeds the threshold we copy the brightest side to the darkest side, thus recovering it and making it more visible. Symmetrization works well only if the center line is determined very precisely. There are many factors that complicate the problem of finding a center line such as bad illumination, pose variation and facial expressions.

After the ellipse is extracted, we resize the resulting image to a predefined standard. This normalization step is necessary for Eigenface algorithm, as it requires that all vectors to be of the same dimensionality. We use bilinear interpolation to resize images, however other options are possible such as: nearest-neighbor interpolation, resampling using pixel area relation, and bi-cubic interpolation. Since detected features (such as eyes) for samples of the same class are practically located at the same coordinates of an image (fiducial points), we are able to automatically align images using these points and resizing. Alignment of the faces used for recognition is very important for Eigenface approach and improves recognition rate. As part of normalization we subtract average face image from all images in the training and testing set to normalize for lighting conditions [16].

Traditional Eigenface approach utilizes Euclidean distance [16]. Various experiments have been conducted by researches to measure performance of other distance measures [10]. Although in many cases Mahalanobis distance has outperformed Euclidian distance, not all studies agree on that matter. We investigate a variety of distance measures with Eigenface approach: squared Euclidean distance (in the forms of Sum Square Error and Mean Square Error), weighted SSE, Manhattan distance, weighted Manhattan distance, Mahalanobis distance, and Simplified Mahalanobis Distance (SMD). We report our results using these metrics in Section 4.

We perform a number of experiments in order to achieve best performance that method can provide on different datasets. We investigate what area of face is important for recognition, what number of eigenvectors are better to use, how normalization improves recognition and how to optimize between recognition performance and real-time performance by selecting proper image size.

4   Empirical Evaluation

We measure performance of our biometric system using algorithm-independent approach based on: False Acceptance Rate (FAR), False Rejection Rate (FRR), and Equal Error Rate (EER) [18]. We shall define in detail each measure according to specifics of our application. Note that each measure is calculated as personal rate, and the average result is reported as the final rate.

$$
\begin{aligned}
FAR &= \frac{\#\text{mis-recognized}}{\text{total recognition attempts}}, \quad FRR_1 = \frac{\#\text{frames without face}}{\text{total } \#\text{frames}} \\
FFR_2 &= \frac{\#\text{correctly recognized above threshold}}{\text{total } \#\text{detected faces}} \\
FFR_3 &= \frac{\#\text{frames without face + frames above threshold}}{\text{total } \#\text{frames}}
\end{aligned}
\tag{2}
$$

We define FAR as a ratio of mis-recognized samples which contain human face to total number of attempts to recognize a person. We define three FRR measures (FRR_1, FRR_2, FRR_3). FRR_1 is designed to show rejections only due to poor image quality. This includes absence of face in the image or inability of the program to locate face of desired size and location. FRR_1 is a ratio of number of frames where face is not found to total number of frames captured. FRR_2 serves to show the rate of false rejections due to thresholding after recognition to the total number of frames, where the face is found. Finally FRR_3 shows all rejections due to both reasons depicted in FRR_1 and FRR_2. It is defined as ratio of a number of false rejections due to thresholding plus number of frames where face is not found to total number of frames.

FRR_1 is convenient to use to see how sensitive the system is to user behavior. FRR_1 is more of a comfort criteria and can be reasonably low with collaborative user behavior. On contrary FRR_2 is a procedure that is free of quality rejection influence and thus serves as a true measure of system performance. It allows us to see how likely it is for the system to produce errors with "clean" data. FRR_3 is a good measure of overall system performance which takes into account user comfort as well. FRR and FAR by themselves do not provide a good comparison basis between systems. One usually determines a probability distribution function representing degree of similarity between test and reference samples. The most common approach is to calculate histograms which show frequency of incidence for every similarity rating.

Most similarity measures such as Euclidean distance or Mahalanobis distance return results which show how far one instance is from another one. Thus by setting threshold at a minimum distance value provided from false acceptance tests we can be "statistically" sure that there will be no false acceptance cases, i.e. if $FAR = 0$ then FRR most likely will be quite high. If we set threshold to obtain zero FRR then FAR might be unacceptably high. We also used Equal Error Rate EER, as a threshold representing the error at a point i where $FAR(i) = FRR(i)$.

4.1 Data

In our experiments we used two databases: FERET [3] and the extended version of JRFD [12]. JRFD consists of approximately 100 people. This database contains 16 frontal face images per individual (men and women of different age and race) taken by cellular phone camera. Images are taken in natural environment and faces are cropped to rectangular areas of 350x350 pixels. Images have prevalence of ambient light with left or right areas of the face occasionally being less illuminated.

4.2 Results

In this section we present final results on combination of methods tested in order to achieve highest recognition rate. We experiment with single and multi instance algorithms. A set of preprocessing techniques were applied to both databases and different criteria were examined as presented below.

Eigenvectors: Number of eigenvectors used for purposes of decomposition as well as similarity measure comparison is chosen. We select 150 top eigenvectors since this number produced the best result for both databases.

ROI: Cropping the whole face rather than eyes showed better performance. We believe that area containing both frontal eyes might be used for recognition only in very well controlled environment because the shape of the eyes changes due to different emotions, lighting, or blinking. These peculiarities produce high variance in pictures of eyes and make them less suitable for recognition.

Size: We select optimal size of the face. Since results of the experiments didn't vary much with image size we decided to choose the minimum size of the cropped face from JRFD (200x280) in order to gain recognition speed. It is also twice larger than that of FERET but smaller than it's maximum size.

Background: Our experiments show that the best value to fill out pixels outside the face area with, is zero. We present results for both all and averaged coefficients of a training class. For purposes of real-time system the use of averaged coefficients reduces time to compare test image coefficients to all training instances when finding smallest distance. However on modern computers with relatively small face databases the difference is hardly noticeable.

Brightness: We observed an improvement in accuracy by applying histogram equalization procedure to the cropped face. Another option besides regular intensity normalization techniques would be removing first eigenvector which provides less improvement in recognition rate. Hence we choose histogram equalization approach as a preprocessing step after face cropping.

Similarity measure: Euclidean distance, Mahalanobis distance and Manhattan distance showed good performance in different cases. We performed experiments using all three of these distances and compared results.

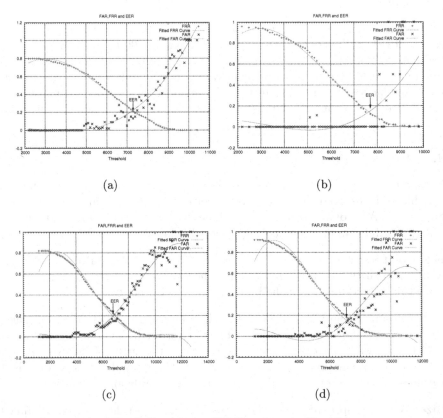

Fig. 2. Estimation of Equal Error Rate (EER) and tradeoffs of false acceptance and false rejection (FAR, FRR). Real data points as well as fitted curve are represented. (a) real person, single instance; (b) real person, multi instance; (c) database image, single instance; (d) database image, multi instance.

Multi instance: Recognition based on results combined from multiple images by selecting minimum weighted distance (described in Multi Instance Recognition section) showed best results. We present results for both single and multi instance recognition algorithms. Table 1 provides brief summary and statistics on our experiments.

Table 1. Experimental results for all performance rates defined in our experiments. EER estimated without curve fitting.

rate	test object	frames	threshold	EER	AVG	STDEV	MIN	MAX
FAR	person	multi	-	-	0.0529	0.1354	0.0000	0.4091
FAR	person	single	-	-	0.1861	0.1647	0.0234	0.5461
FAR	picture	multi	-	-	0.0923	0.1277	0.0000	0.7955
FAR	picture	single	-	-	0.1792	0.1466	0.0000	0.7744
FRR_1	person	multi	-	-	0.0000	0.0000	0.0000	0.0000
FRR_1	person	single	-	-	0.3278	0.1488	0.0298	0.5464
FRR_1	picture	multi	-	-	0.0000	0.0000	0.0000	0.0000
FRR_1	picture	single	-	-	0.1236	0.1565	0.0000	0.7583
FRR_2	person	multi	8019	0.0954	0.1235	0.2287	0.0000	0.6818
FRR_2	person	single	7445	0.1845	0.1697	0.2263	0.0138	0.7190
FRR_2	picture	multi	7363	0.1491	0.0664	0.0922	0.0000	0.4286
FRR_2	picture	single	7128	0.1804	0.1845	0.1785	0.0000	0.7143
FRR_3	person	multi	8019	0.0954	0.1235	0.2287	0.0000	0.6818
FRR_3	person	single	7445	0.1845	0.4523	0.1627	0.2914	0.8046
FRR_3	picture	multi	7363	0.1491	0.1533	0.1804	0.0000	0.8333
FRR_3	picture	single	7128	0.1804	0.2823	0.2025	0.0596	0.9205
FAR thresh	person	multi	8019	0.0954	0.0074	0.0222	0.0000	0.0667
FAR thresh	person	single	7445	0.1845	0.0524	0.0588	0.0000	0.1675
FAR thresh	picture	multi	7363	0.1491	0.0325	0.0951	0.0000	0.6591
FAR thresh	picture	single	7128	0.1804	0.0404	0.0941	0.0000	0.5219

We can conclude that our system has practical use and error proof even in realistic environment with complicated background and pose variations. Although experimental data shows that we can achieve $FAR = 0$ at tolerable FRR level we suggest long-term tests and further investigation to find possible problems in recognition.

Table 2. Comparison of recognition performance between different methods on FERET database

method	Accuracy%
Eigenface-(gray) [19]	35.00
Eigenface-(Gabor) [19]	36.05
TCF-CFA(N=3) [19]	94.18
Eigenface	48.89
Our method–single instance	84.18
Our method–multi-weighted	86.30

Table 3. Comparison of recognition performance between different methods on JRFD database

method	Accuracy%
multi-biometric [12](20 & 9 face & hand feature points)	99.54
Face [13](12 feature points)	98.85
Eigenface	89.46
Our method-single instance	98.34
Our method-multi-weighted	100.00

Table 2 shows results obtained on FERET database by other methods. First two eigenface methods are standard eigenface approaches. The sets of images used for these experiments are very similar but not identical. In all cases frontal face images were used. Although TCF-CFA method shows good performance it is based on precise locations of fiducial points which are established manually. Furthermore as reported its computational complexity is high. We would like to point out improvements made by our approach over the standard algorithm by

Table 4. JRFD - final recognition results with cropped face 200x280, 0 pixels - background, histogram equalized, with averaging coefficients, 150 eigenvectors

Distance Measure	Coef.Avg.	Accuracy(%) train-test:249-1025 JRFD	Accuracy(%) train-test:332-949 JRFD	Accuracy(%) train-test:2056-949 FERET	Accuracy(%) train-test:949-2056 FERET
Euclidean	no	97.66	98.20	82.51	68.24
Mahalanobis		97.46	97.77	82.51	67.70
Manhattan		98.34	97.66	84.18	70.18
Multi-weighted		100.00	100.00	84.18	86.30
Euclidean	yes	97.56	97.66	78.61	68.24
Mahalanobis		97.37	97.45	79.35	67.70
Manhattan		97.76	97.77	83.03	70.18
Multi-weighted		100.00	100.00	83.03	86.30

comparing results in the last three rows of Table 2. Original method performed poorly because no alignment or size normalization of the facial area is done. We would also like to note that 1-NN method is not restricted by thresholding in these experiments and accuracy can be further improved at the cost of FRR rate. We compare results on JRFD in Table 3 with the most statistically significant results reported in [11]. As you can see our fully automated system is only 0.51% less accurate than the manual face recognition system in [11]. Also it is only 1.2% worse that multi-biometric system. Our system outperforms [11] in case of multi-instance recognition. Overall we observe a drastic improvement in eigenface approach itself by almost 36% on FERET and 9% on JRFD databases. Moreover our results compare well to the state-of-the-art methods while those methods are not fully automatic.

In course of experiments using a set of preprocessing techniques on both databases we observed similar behavior of different techniques. Some researchers report in the literature significant improvements after applying symmetrization [9]. We did not obtain very precise results of symmetrization. This is mainly because minor shifts in center line would cause face to look less similar to original by shrinking or stretching lips and nose areas and changing the distance between eyes.

5   Conclusions

In this paper we developed a real-time face recognition response with a new automated face detection, which we called EFFL. It should be noted that very few existing applications automatically locate a face in the image and do automatic alignment. For many developed methods, faces should be manually located. This makes such systems impractical in real world applications. In our approach for face detection, if there exist more that one face in the image, our system selects the face that appears in the largest size or closest to the camera, for recognition or authentication. The face is then cropped and aligned by using our introduced background elimination method. An ellipse is fitted to the face area in order to minimize the effect of different hair styles while it preserves all fiducial features.

The face recognition module in our system uses Eigenface methodology. The Eigenface method has the shortcoming of reflecting variations of the background as well as variations of the face which can increase false matching. Our proposed face cropping procedure offers an efficient solution to this problem. We showed that performing face cropping prior to the recognition significantly improved the recognition accuracy (about 7% on JRFD database). In order to achieve a better performance, we also tried different distance metrics instead of the traditionally used Euclidian distance. Our results on two different face databases (FERET and JRFD) suggest that Manhattan distance is slightly superior. We also showed that performing histogram equalization on the cropped faces improves the overall system performance. We plan to continue our investigations with new symmetrization methods and eigenvectors. We also intend to expand our experiments to other databases and applications.

References

1. Abate, A.F., Nappi, M., Riccio, D., Sabatino, G.: 2d and 3d face recognition: A survey. Pattern Recog. Lett. 28(14), 1885–1906 (2007)
2. Chen, X., Flynn, P.J., Bowyer, K.W.: Fully automated facial symmetry axis detection in frontal color images. In: AUTOID 2005: Proceedings of the Fourth IEEE Workshop on Automatic Identification Advanced Technologies, Washington, DC, USA, pp. 106–111. IEEE Computer Society, Los Alamitos (2005)
3. FERET (October 2008), http://www.frvt.org/feret/default.htm
4. Gonzalez, R.C., Woods, R.E.: Digital Image Processing, 3rd edn. Prentice-Hall, Inc., Upper Saddle River (2006)
5. Hongtao, S., Feng, D.D., Rong-chun, Z.: Face recognition using multi-feature and radial basis function network. In: VIP 2002: Selected papers from the 2002 Pan-Sydney workshop on Visualisation, pp. 51–57. Australian Computer Society, Inc., Darlinghurst (2002)
6. Kirby, M., Sirovich, L.: Application of the Karhunen-Loeve procedure for the characterization of human faces. IEEE Trans. Pattern Anal. Mach. Intell. 12(1), 103–108 (1990)
7. Kong, S.G., Heo, J., Abidi, B.R., Paik, J., Abidi, M.A.: Recent advances in visual and infrared face recognition: a review. Comput. Vis. Image Underst. 97(1), 103–135 (2005)
8. Lienhart, R., Kuranov, A., Pisarevsky, V.: Empirical analysis of detection cascades of boosted classifiers for rapid object detection. In: Michaelis, B., Krell, G. (eds.) DAGM 2003. LNCS, vol. 2781, pp. 297–304. Springer, Heidelberg (2003)
9. Nakao, N., Ohyama, W., Wakabayashi, T., Kimura, F.: Automatic detection of facial midline as a guide for facial feature extraction. In: PRIS, pp. 119–128 (2007)
10. Perlibakas, V.: Distance measures for pca-based face recognition. Pattern Recog. Lett. 25(6), 711–724 (2004)
11. Rokita, J.: Multimodal biometric system based on face and hand images taken by a cell phone. Master's thesis, Computer Science Dept., Concordia University, Montreal, Quebec, Canada (March 2008)
12. Rokita, J., Krzyżak, A., Suen, C.Y.: Cell phones personal authentication systems using multimodal biometrics. In: International Conference on Image Analysis and Recognition, pp. 1013–1022 (2008)

13. Rokita, J., Krzyżak, A., Suen, C.Y.: Multimodal biometrics by face and hand images taken by a cell phone camera. International Journal of Pattern Recognition and Artificial Intelligence, 411–429 (2008)

14. Sirovich, L., Kirby, M.: Low-dimensional procedure for the characterization of human faces. Journal of the Optical Society of America 4(3), 519–524 (1987)

15. Tan, X., Chen, S., Zhou, Z.-H., Zhang, F.: Face recognition from a single image per person: A survey. Pattern Recog. 39(9), 1725–1745 (2006)

16. Turk, M., Pentland, A.: Eigenfaces for recognition. Journal of Cognitive Neuroscience 3(1), 71–86 (1991)

17. Viola, P., Jones, M.: Rapid object detection using a boosted cascade of simple features. In: CVPR, vol. 1, pp. 511–518 (2001)

18. Woodward, J.D., Orlans, N.M.: Biometrics. McGraw-Hill, Inc., New York (2002)

19. Yan, Y., Zhang, Y.-J.: Tensor correlation filter based class-dependence feature analysis for face recognition. Neurocomputing 71(16-18), 3434–3438 (2008)

20. Yang, M.-H., Kriegman, D.J., Ahuja, N.: Detecting faces in images: A survey. IEEE Trans. Pattern Anal. Mach. Intell. 24(1), 34–58 (2002)

Semiotic Design of a Hypermedia for Cultural Heritage

Vito Roberto[1,2] and Elio Toppano[1]

[1] Dipartimento di Matematica e Informatica
[2] Norbert Wiener Center
University of Udine, Italy
{vito.roberto,elio.toppano}@dimi.uniud.it

Abstract. The paper proposes a semiotic model inspired to the narrative, structural framework by A.J.Greimas, and applied to the design and analysis of a hypermedia. The framework is structured into four levels of signification and allows for a constructive process of semantic aggregation. We follow such a process in order to explore the conceptual organization of the model. We construct a hypermedia regarding a collection of ancient mosaics from a roman villa. Our results indicate that the proposed approach opens novel perspectives, and looks promising towards the definition of semiotic methodologies of hypermedia design.

Keywords: Semiotic, Design, Analysis, Hypermedia, Cultural, Heritage.

1 Introduction and Related Work

We address the issue of hypermedia design adopting a semiotic approach, with the aim of exploring its opportunities, and getting insights into possible advantages and limitations. Semiotics is a generic name for a set of disciplines that study the signs, the signification and sense-making processes, and the ways signs and signification take part in communication. Therefore, the focus is on how semantics is originated and can be assigned to the hypermedia, which will be regarded as a generic text – we shall use the terms 'hypermedia' and 'text' as synonyms throughout the paper – to which sense is given according to a constructive process. We adopt the semio-structural model by Greimas [7], [9] and follow the so-called *Generative Trajectory of Meaning,* which we shall detail and apply in the sequel. Using a plain language is a primary concern of the present paper: terms and techniques borrowed from Semiotics have been introduced and clarified. In order to provide our research with an experimental testbed, we designed and realized a hypermedia for education and entertainment. The aim is presenting a collection of ancient mosaics from the excavations of a roman villa near the city of Trieste, Italy.

Semiotics has slowly gained popularity in Computer Science during the last decade, in different domains of application. Semiotic Engineering is aimed at interpreting Human-Computer Interaction (HCI). Nadin [12] has analyzed computer interfaces; De Souza [15] has argued that Semiotics provides general and

P. Foggia, C. Sansone, and M. Vento (Eds.): ICIAP 2009, LNCS 5716, pp. 425–433, 2009.

motivated formulations of the interface guidelines. Nake [13] has mainly worked in the Interactive Graphics and given contributions to Computer Art. Andersen [1] has proposed a systematic analysis of interfaces as sign-complexes. In the field of Communication and Media theory, Semiotics has been used for analyzing new media and websites [3]. In the field of hypermedia design, attention has been devoted mainly on modelling global and local discourse coherence [11].

The paper is organized as follows. Section 2 introduces the main features of the framework adopted; the following Section details a process to construct a meaningful text; Section 4 applies the framework to the design of the hypermedia. Our conclusions are in Section 5.

2   The Semio-Narrative Framework

A narrative approach. Ever since a young age humans are exposed to narratives as a form of knowledge transfer. Therefore, narratives are perceived as natural and effective. The semiotician Roland Barthes (quoted in [2]) maintains that narrative is trans-cultural, trans-historical, trans-linguistic. It is suitable to be transposed from a dynamic medium to another, which makes narrative unique among the representation modalities. By narrating we impose an order; we transform a set of unstructured incidents into a sequence of continuous, closed and coherent events [14].

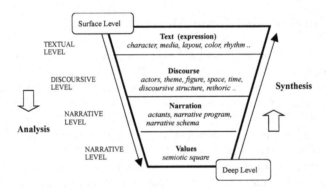

Fig. 1. A graphical scheme of the narrative-structural framework by Greimas

A structural approach. Greimas developed his theory [7] with the aim of analyzing narrative productions. Meaning takes form passing through four levels, as sketched in Figure 1: i) the deep semio-narrative structures, representing the fundamental values to be transferred, arranged into a scheme called *the semiotic square*; ii) the surface semio-narrative structure, with the conceptualizations describing the actions; iii) the discursive structure; iv) finally, the *textual structure,* the level of external manifestation. The framework was originally conceived to clarify the meaning of an existing text – e.g., an advertising – starting from

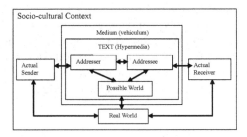

Fig. 2. The communication framework

its external manifestation and proceeding in a top-down fashion across the discoursive and semio-narrative structures. We claim that this view is helpful also for synthesis tasks, to build a meaningful hypermedia by visiting the structure in the opposite direction.

A communication model. Designer and user communicate through the hypermedia within a social and cultural context. Semiotics helps to put forward a thorough model, in which the potential interactions between user and artifact are fully *inscribed* into the text itself. The scheme in Figure 2 generalizes the original model proposed by Jakobson [10]. It considers the actual *(empirical)* sender (e.g., the designer) and the empirical receiver (the user). They are connected by means of an instrumental medium *(vehiculum)* – such as a PC connected to a network – which enables the circulation of the text within a socio- cultural context. The text includes two abstract rôles representing the *symulacra,* i.e., the images reflected onto the text of the empirical sender and receiver, named the *addresser* and the *addressee,* respectively. They establish a direct relationship with a possible world, i.e. a narrative universe that reproduces a portion of the real world. In this way, the dialogue between the empirical designer and user, mediated by the text, is inscribed within the text itself.

3   A Constructive Process of Signification

The semiotic square. It is the most abstract and elementary structure of signification. It is organized around a basic opposition *(contrariety)* relation between two conceptual categories, A and B, such as life and death. The square is defined as the logical articulation of this basic opposition; it comprises four terms — A, not-A, B, not-B — connected by three kinds of relations: - Contrariety: the relation between A and B; not-A and not-B; - Contradiction: between A and not-A; B and not-B; - Implication or complementarity: between not-B and A; not-A and B. The scheme has been largely used by the semioticians. Floch [5] individuated the basic values associated to a consumer product. Accordingly, there are four kinds of *exploitations* of an object by a user: *practical, critical, ludic and utopic.* The first one focusses on utility, effectiveness, usability and reliability of a product; the critical exploitation refers to its efficiency and economic convenience; the ludic one is related to the formal qualities, involving aesthetic pleasure and emotions; utopic exploitation refers to existential values, identity and social acknowledgement. We adopted the semiotic square of consumer values for the development of our instructional hypermedia, since it spans all the fundamental values we wish to communicate. We have specialized the terms in the square to the educational context, as shown in Figure 3.

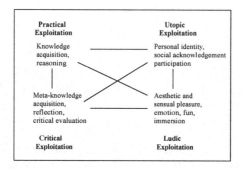

Fig. 3. The semiotic square of an instructional hypermedia

The semio-narrative level. The elements are: *Actants (A); Narrative Programs (NP); Narrative Structures (NS)* and the *Canonical Narrative Scheme (CNS).* An actant is something or somebody that acts or undergoes an action. An actant may correspond to an anthropomorphic being, a physical object, or a concept. A narrative program NP is an abstract formula to represent an action *(doing),* which is a transition between states in order to reach an value object O_v. The NP's are the building blocks of the narrative structures NS. A NS is composed of two or more narrative programs linked by temporal relations – succession, simultaneity,...– or logical ones – mutual exclusion, comparison,.... The Canonical Narrative Scheme CNS is a narrative structure including four phases: *Manipulation:* a sender transmits a message to a receiver/subject, for example the mission to act; *Competence:* the receiver/subject adheres to the sender's proposal and tries to achieve the resources that are necessary to execute the action; *Performance:* the subject executes the action and reaches the object of value from whom it was disjuncted; *Sanction:* the sender evaluates the subject's action, with a reward in case of success or punishment in case of failure. The canonical scheme represents the scaffolding of a narrative at a fully abstract level. The link between the narrative structure and the semiotic square is realized by associating the objects of value O_v within each narrative program, to the values V_i in the semiotic square.

The discoursive level. Adopts methods borrowed from the Structural Linguistics [4]. Each narrative program is mapped onto a discoursive structure, and each of the latter consists of groups of segments in sequential order; each sequence is given its value objective. Converting a narrative structure into a discoursive one entails two main processes: the identification of *themes* and *figures,* and the realization of the discourse structure. In a given universe of discourse, the figure is an element that evokes sensory perception, while the theme does not. Themes and figures translate the basic constituents of the narration: actants, narrative states and transitions. In this way, an abstract structure is translated into an ordered group of domain concepts – that is, a discourse structure – which is the conceptual organization of a presentation. The structures individuated so far follow a basic sequential order, involving logical and space-time relations. However, the process of sense-making at the discursive level is to be organized in a more complex fashion. Using rhetorical tropes makes more effective the transmission of contents; naturally, the choice of a trope depends on the contents themselves, and, in turn, influences the design choices at the textual level. Content-based rhetorical relations should be individuated as well.

The textual level. Concerns the perceptual characteristics of the visual and auditory signs used to present the hypermedia content *(substance of the expression),* as well as the ways signs are related in space and time *(form of the expression).* Discursive components such as actors, figurative and thematic elements, rhetorical tropes, are represented by specified media assets. The visual expression can be effectively approached using figurative and plastic semiotics [8].

4   A Hypermedia for Ancient Roman Mosaics

We designed a hypermedia devoted the presentation of a collection of ancient mosaics excavated from a roman villa near the city of Trieste, Italy. The document is addressed to the visitors of the collection, as well as students and teachers willing to learn how a mosaic should be inspected. The semiotic square reported in Figure 3 is the only conceptual scheme supporting the whole document. In Figure 4, NS_0 has been decomposed into three main substructures: NS_1, the introduction; NS_2, the body; NS_3 the conclusion. The body NS_2 has been further

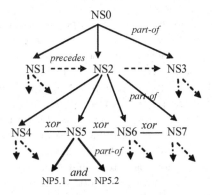

Fig. 4. Narrative structure of the hypermedia. Only the topmost elements have been reported.

decomposed into four substructures $NS_4, \ldots\ldots, NS_7$ which describe alternative paths within the hypermedia. The leafs of the tree are narrative programs, each one being associated to a single value objective/object.

4.1   The Catalog of Mosaics

The catalog of mosaics (CoM) is a tool accessible from all the substructures NS_1, NS_2 and NS_3. It contains the complete collection of the mosaics (over thirty pieces) in form of cards, with a picture and a short description. The CoM is intended to be a reference to be consulted during the hypermedia navigation. At the narrative level only the abstract action structure of the CoM is relevant. It can be viewed as a dialogue between the tool and the user.

Solutions at the discoursive level. Main themes are: spatial configuration of the mosaics, position, location, order, symmetry,... Figures are the roman villa, the catalogue,... Metaphors are of great help. The catalog itself is a metaphor, which can be enriched with other metaphors: for example, a magnifying glass can be used to signify the relation between two spatial scales. The mise-en-scene is consistent with the metaphors, and is given by a book the user can skim through, in order to acquire the information and the values specified at the level of semiotic square. Moreover, the user can inspect the mosaics at different scales, to single out graphic patterns or constructive details (tesserae).

Textual choices. We used textual media mainly to emphasize practical and critical values (Figure 3): introducing evaluation criteria of mosaics; conveying hystorical background. Instead, static and dynamic images – e.g., 3D animations – have been associated to ludic or utopic exploitations: to enhance enjoyment, to to support the user's experience of different space-time dimensions and enhance his/her sense of presence and immersion. Aesthetic (ludic) values are emphasized by letting the user explore the mosaics with a magnifying glass 5.

4.2   The Mosaics in Their Placements

The narrative structure NS5 (Figure 4) is composed by two programs, NP5.1 and NP5.2, linked by a logical AND. The former is associated, in the semiotic square, to a practical exploitation: teaching the user to look at the mosaics within their original locations in the roman villa. The latter program is associated to a utopic exploitation: letting the user make the experience of walking through the rooms of the villa, appreciating the patterns of the mosaics virtually replaced therein. At the discoursive level, the 'mise–en–scene' is the roman villa itself with its external location and internal arrangement of rooms. The helper (an actant) of program NP5.1 has been converted into a museum guide (an actor) providing information and knowledge necessary to achieve the desired practical values. In order to achieve the utopic values, a discourse concerning the space has been devised (trajectory of observation) to let the user relate external with internal spaces.

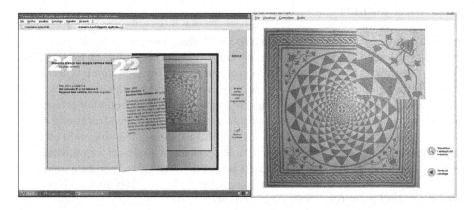

Fig. 5. Two screeenshots from the Catalog of Mosaics. *Left.* The user skims through the pages. *Right.* The user inspects the mosaic no.22 with the magnifying glass.

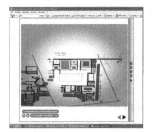  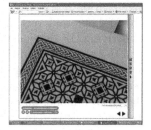

Fig. 6. Three screeenshots from the narrative structure NS5. *Left.* The planimetry of the roman villa. *Middle.* The apartments hosting the mosaics. 3D structures are emerging. *Right.* Moving in a room with a mosaic on the ground.

At the textual level the villa is represented by a 3D graphical model; the museum guide is translated into a narrative voice-over, while the trajectory of observation is realized by a set of camera viewpoints and movements. It starts with an aerial view showing a map (planimetry) of the villa (Figure 6, Left) and continues approaching the apartments hosting the mosaics. During this process, the 2D planimetry is transformed into a 3D model that gradually rises up (Figure 6, Middle). This corresponds to a transition from a symbolic/abstract representation (the map) to a concrete one (the virtual villa). Then, the camera moves inside the apartments in order to show details of the mosaics just as a 'model observer' would do (Figure 6, Right). In this way, empirical users are encouraged to identify themselves with the 'model observers', and feel like eye-witnesses of the villa reborn.

5 Conclusions

We have explored a semiotic approach to the design of hypermedia, and reported the practical experience of a document concerning a collection of mosaics. We adopted the narrative, structural framework proposed by A.J.Greimas, according to which the semantics is given a structure and assigned by means of a constructive process. We believe that the semiotic approach opens novel perspectives and offers profound, potentially fruitful suggestions. The semantic structure consists of four levels of signification, which are helpful in identifying the main steps of a possible process, and, at the same time, provide a clear-cut organization of concepts, relations and mechanisms to be used by the designer as a reference model. As much as the semiosis itself, semiotic design is likely to be a dynamic, structured and constructive process. It is well known that, in the design of hypermedia, semantic contents are to be kept separate from their expressive forms. However, this principle appears too vague and deserves further specifications. As a matter of fact, the current design methodologies seem to be confined – and constrained – around conceptual structures and their associations to multimedia objects. The semiotic approach allows to gain a deeper insight by adding new signification levels. Two semio-narrative structures support the upper discoursive and textual levels, and help the designer to make explicit the basic principles underlying the document: the profound values to be ultimately communicated, and the abstract narrative scheme to be adopted. We believe it is a substantial step towards the design of 'semantically-rich'– not merely media-rich – documents. Even in the attempt to make objective and reproducible the steps in the design, the model allows for an unlimited freedom in composing the text, and does not constrain to a serial production.

Semiotics is not a monolithic discipline, and several semiotics exist. *General Semiotics* is a kind of Phylosophy of Language, and *Specific Semiotics* concern peculiar sign systems, like Text, Music, Advertising, Fashion,... The language of each one tends to be a self-referential jargon, which is still a serious obstacle to the widespread diffusion of semiotic tools. For these reasons, transposing semiotic models into the domains of ICT is still at an exploratory stage, in spite of a few valuable attempts accomplished so far. The same happens for the domain of hypermedia, in which we are far from proposing a true semiotic methodology of design. In this respect, the present paper should be regarded as a further exploration effort. Several semiotic models should be investigated and applied to the hypermedia design, besides – possibly in contrast with – the narrative, structural approach which we propose. A systematic cross-disciplinary effort should be done in this respect. Our research will go further along these directions.

References

1. Andersen, P.B.: Theory of Computer Semiotics. Cambridge University Press, Cambridge (1997)
2. Chandler, D.: Semiotics for Beginners. e-book (1994),
   http://www.aber.ac.uk/media/Documents/S4B/semiotic.html

3. Chandler, D.: Personal Homepages and the Construction of Identities on the Web. In: Aberystwyth Post-Int. Group Conf. on Linking Theory and Practice. University of Wales, Aberystwyth (1998)
4. Fabbri, P., Marrone, G. (a cura di): Semiotica in Nuce. Meltemi, Roma (2000) (in Italian)
5. Floch, J.M.: Semiotics, marketing and communication: Beneath the signs, the strategies. Hampshire, Palgrave (2001)
6. Geurts, J., Bocconi, S., van Ossenbruggen, J., Hardman, J.L.: Towards ontology-driven discourse: from semantic graph to multimedia presentations. In: 2nd Int. Semantic Web Conference (2003)
7. Greimas, A.J., Courtés, J.: Semiotica. Dizionario Ragionato della Teoria del Linguaggio. La Casa Uscher, Firenze (1986) (in Italian)
8. Greimas, A.J.: Semiotica plastica e semiotica figurativa. In: Corrain, L., Valenti, M. (eds.) Leggere l'opera d'arte II. Esculapio, Bologna (1999) (in Italian)
9. Hebert, L.: Tools for text and image analysis: an introduction to Applied Semiotics. E-Book,
   http://www.revue-texto.net/Parutions/Livres-E/Hebert_AS/
   Hebert_Tools.html
10. Jakobson, R.: Saggi di Linguistica Generale. Feltrinelli, Milano (2002) (in Italian)
11. Mancini, C., Buckingham Shum, S.J.: Modelling discourse in contested domains: A semiotic and cognitive framework. International Journal of Human-Computer Studies 64(11), 1154–1171 (2006)
12. Nadin, M.: Interface design: a semiotic paradigm. Semiotica 69, 269–302 (1988)
13. Nake, F.: Human computer interaction: signs and signals interfacing. Languages of Design 2, 193–205
14. Scharfe, H.: Grand Principles of Narratology. In: Bas, I., Freeman, C. (eds.) Challenging the Boundaries, pp. 95–110. Rodopi, Amsterdam (2007)
15. Sieckenius De Souza, C.: The semiotic engineering of Human-Computer Interaction. The MIT Press, Cambridge (2005)

An Experimental Analysis of the Relationship between Biometric Template Update and the Doddington's Zoo: A Case Study in Face Verification

Ajita Rattani, Gian Luca Marcialis, and Fabio Roli

University of Cagliari – Department of Electrical and Electronic Engineering
{ajita.rattani,marcialis,roli}@diee.unica.it

Abstract. The problem of biometric template representativeness has recently attracted much attention with the introduction of several template update methods. Automatic template update methods adapt themselves to the intra-class variations of the input data. However, it is possible to hypothesize that the effect of template updating may not be the same for all the clients due to different characteristics of clients present in the biometric database. The goal of this paper is to investigate this hypothesis by explicitly partitioning clients into different groups of the "Doddington's zoo" as a function of their "intrinsic" characteristics, and studying the effect of state of art template "self update" procedure on these different groups. Experimental evaluation on Equinox database with a case study on face verification system based on EBGM algorithm shows the strong evidence of non-uniform update effects on different clients classes and suggest to modify the update procedures according to the client's characteristics.

1 Introduction

Recently, template representativeness has attracted much attention in the field of biometrics [1]. Often, the online operation of the biometric system encounters substantial intra-class variations in the input biometric data, due to the presence of several factors; like human-sensor interaction, environmental conditions, temporal variations (short term like scars in fingerprint surface and long term like aging in face) and other temporary variations like changes in facial expressions or rotation in fingerprint [2]. These variations make the initial enrolled templates, often captured in controlled environment, non-representative, thus resulting in degradation of the performance of the system.

To deal with this issue, novel solutions in the form of template update procedures have been introduced. Their aim is to adapt the enrolled templates to the intra-class variations of the input biometric data, on the basis of some learning methodologies like supervised [3] and semi-supervised learning [4-9]. Among these, supervised methods require the intervention of human experts for updating, thus making update procedure time consuming and inefficient task [3].

On the other hand, semi-supervised methods are automated systems that adapt themselves to the intra-class variations of the input biometric data. They derive their

P. Foggia, C. Sansone, and M. Vento (Eds.): ICIAP 2009, LNCS 5716, pp. 434–442, 2009.

name from the machine learning technique of semi-supervised learning that adapt the classifier through the joint use of initial labelled (templates) and unlabelled input biometric data. These data are available during the online operation, without the intervention of human supervisor [4-9]. Among others, self update is based on the self-training concept of semi-supervised learning, in which the input data recognized as highly confident are added iteratively to the template gallery set of the respective client [4-7].

Recently, self update procedure has gained much focus and the overall effectiveness of it has been proved experimentally in [4-7]. Also a serious issue of impostor's intrusion or "creep-in" errors, causing counter-productive effect, as an open issue has been pointed out in [9]. This problem of "creep-in" errors has also been recently investigated in detail [10] where the relationship between update errors due to impostor's introduction and performance degradation has been established. Ref [10] also suggested that the existence of creep-in of errors is also a function of user population characteristics apart from the basic FAR of the system or incorrect estimation of threshold parameters. Specifically in [10], the intrusion of impostors has been also correlated to clients which are intrinsically easy to "imitate", and clients "capable" to confuse themselves with other clients. These two groups have been called "lambs" and "wolves", respectively, according to the well-known concept of "Doddington's zoo" [11]. But their "presence" has not been recognized by using the rigorous definition given by Doddington et al. [11]. The presence of wolves, for example, has been detected by their repeated presence in different client's galleries at varying thresholds. Lambs have been identified by being attacked repeatedly at varying acceptance thresholds [10].

The aim of this paper is to extensively investigate the hypothesis that different types of clients as lambs, goats, wolves and sheeps [11] result in different updating effect on the application of self update procedure on the database, thus suggesting adaptation of template update methodology for each group of clients.

To this aim, user population is explicitly partitioned into different animal groups i.e., sheeps, lambs, wolves and goats using the definition of Doddington Zoo [11]. Then, the effect of global application of self update procedure has been studied on these classes of clients. Experimental evaluations are done on Equinox Database with 57 clients and 129 frontal face images per client [12]. The self update based technique has been used as a case study on face verification system based on Elastic Bunch Graph Matching (EBGM) [13]. Results pointed out that the effect of template update is different for each group, which confirms our hypothesis. This paper also mentions the counter-measures which may help to avoid the non-uniform effect of template update on these clients.

In Section 2, Self Update and its relation with Doddington zoo is described in detail. Section 3 reports the experimental results, and preliminary conclusions are drawn in Section 4.

2 Template Self Update and Doddington's Zoo

In the "online" template self update algorithm [4-7], a matcher adapts itself to the variations of the input data, available during the normal system's operation. The aim of these methods is to capture the temporal and temporary intra-class variations of the input data by modifying the templates, thus enhancing the generalization performance on the novel unseen data.

The general "online" self update method may involve two steps: 1. Initialization: where each user is enrolled with its templates to build the initial gallery and the initial system parameter ("updating threshold") is set; 2. Updating: where the input data is compared with the template(s) of the claimed identity's gallery to compute the matching score. If matching score is greater than the threshold, the template set of the respective client is updated by either fusing with the current template or adding that sample as another instance into the gallery set of the claimed identity. If the matching score is less than the threshold, that sample is rejected. The described process is repeated on each availability of input sample.

Self update techniques usually operate at stringent acceptance threshold and exploit (i.e. add to the clients' galleries) only the confidently classified samples in order to avoid the introduction of impostors into the gallery set of the client. But avoiding this problem is very difficult in a realistic verification system, and the impostor's introduction leads to the so-called "creep in" error which strongly decreases the effectiveness of the update procedure.

Apart from incorrect threshold estimation conditions, these creep-in errors are also due to the presence of variable clients, like wolves, lambs and goats, present in the Doddington zoo as identified and reported in [10]. The Doddington's definition of Wolves, Lambs, Goats are stated as follows [11]:

- Goats are clients intrinsically difficult to recognize: they exhibit a very high FRR;
- Lambs are clients easily imitable by other users: they exhibit a very high FAR;
- Wolves are the users (not necessarily clients) which have the capability to imitate other clients: i.e., when a wolf try to access as a certain client, it has a very high probability of success causing impostor's introduction [11].

Even with the operation at stringent threshold conditions, presence of wolves and lambs do result in impostor's intrusion. Work reported in [10] have discussed the threat of impostor's introduction into the client's galleries and highlighted that the presence of wolves and lambs cause the introduction of impostors into the gallery set of the clients even at the stringent threshold conditions. However, the presence of wolves and lambs have been shown on the basis of experimental evaluations, where wolves were determined by their repeated presence in the gallery set of other clients and lambs were identified by their repeated vulnerability to impostors at various threshold conditions. It was concluded that even with the operation at stringent threshold conditions, the intrusion of impostors is unavoidable due to the presence of clients like lambs and wolves in the biometric database [10]. Even, the unseen impostor input sample may also have the wolf characteristic apart from their presence in the database.

In this paper, we extend the above study and show explicitly the effect of update procedures not only for lambs and wolves but also for sheeps and goats. It has been hypothesized that due to the presence of these characteristic people in the database and the operation of the uniform self update procedure on them, goats may not be updated at the same strict threshold and lambs and wolves may attract impostors even at the strict threshold conditions. Thus the effect of self update is studied specifically for each group by the prior division of database into different animal groups according to the definition of Doddington zoo [11].

3   Experimental Results

3.1   Data Set

Equinox Corporation Database [12] consisting of 56 individuals with 129 face images per person with significant intra-class variations like illumination changes and variations in facial expressions etc, are used for experimental evaluation. The time span of the collected data sets is over one year. The self update based mechanism is used as a case study on face verification system based on Elastic Bunch Graph Matching [13]. Other face matching algorithm could be used as well.

3.2   Experimental Protocol

In a typical personal verification system, a different batch of unlabelled set (D_u), owing to different access attempts, is collected for each client over a period of time. In order to respect this simple evidence, the following protocol has been adopted in the literature [9-10]. We have also followed this protocol for our study.

(1) 56 initial templates are selected (one template for each client T). These are the initial template set consisting of a neutral image per client (T_{ca}). The threshold for self updating is always evaluated on this set, being the only set available in real environments. Threshold is evaluated on this template set by comparing each template to the templates (T) of all the other clients (T_{ca}) thus estimating the impostor distribution and selecting a threshold value at 0%FAR. These stringent starting conditions simulate the real environment where very less labelled data is available to set the system parameters.

(2) Remaining client images are subdivided in three sets with 25 images per client in in the prediction set and 25 in unlabelled set and remaining 78 face images in the test set. Prediction dataset is used to partition the database clients into different animal groups.

(3) The whole dataset (except for templates) is then randomly partitioned into 56 partitions, such that the c-th partition does not contain images of the c-th client. Each of these partitions, consisting of 128 images, represent the "impostor set" for the c-th client: 25 images are added to unlabelled set, 25 images to the prediction set and 78 face images in the test set. The same number of genuine and impostors are added to the unlabeled, prediction and test set to have equal priors for both the classes, i.e., genuine and impostor. The database is partitioned into different animal groups of Doddington's zoo using the samples from the prediction set. Then the unlabelled data set is used to update the enrolled templates using the self update procedure irrespective of the database partition. Then the test set is used to evaluate the actual improvement in performance gained

by the template self update algorithm. Then the performance of the updated system is evaluated using the test set for each partitioned group.

3.3 Rules for Identifying Different Animal Groups of Doddington's Zoo

This section presents the rules followed using the prediction set to divide the database into specific animals groups. Each client is enrolled using a single initial template. Note Ref [14] also partitions the database clients into different groups exhibiting variability on the basis of "sheepiness index" (sheeps are "well behaved" clients in the Doddington's zoo). However, the technique does not explicitly identifies which partition belongs to which specific animal group. It just partitions the database into different groups sharing the common characteristics. By considering the aim of this paper, we partitioned the database clients into specific animal groups according to the definition given by Doddington [11]. Thus:

- **Goats** are identified by evaluating FRR for each client at zeroFAR, which guarantees that no impostors are accepted. zeroFAR is calculated by matching each client's enrolled template to the relative impostor images of the prediction set. For each client, genuine samples belonging in the prediction set (25 samples) are matched with the initial enrolled template and FRR is evaluated for each client. Then, clients whose FRR exceeds a threshold value more than 0.5 are considered as "Goats".
- **Lambs** are identified by evaluating their FAR under an operational point of zeroFRR (zeroFRR is calculated by matching each enrolled template to the genuine samples of that client in the prediction set), which guarantees that no genuine users are rejected. Then for each client, a batch of impostor samples (25) from the prediction set are matched with the enrolled template and FAR is evaluated accordingly. Then, clients whose FAR exceeds a threshold value more than 0.5 are considered as "Lambs".
- **Wolves** are identified as follows. Each potential wolf (client) attacks all genuine samples (all 25 samples) of all the other clients in the prediction set. The operational point for each client is estimated at zeroFAR, calculated similarly as that for Goats. Candidate clients which are accepted even under this very stringent condition for more than 50% of the users are considered as "real" wolf.
- **Sheeps** are the clients which do not belong to any of the above presented group i.e., Lambs, Goats and Wolves.

Estimating zeroFRR is very difficult because of the small sample size affecting the data. However, by considering the goal of our study, the database partitioning has been made by considering quite large number of samples in order to have a good estimation of wolves, lambs and goats.

3.4 Results

The goal of the paper is to study the effect of template update procedure for different clients termed as members of Doddington's Zoo. Accordingly, first the biometric database is partitioned into different characteristics group of clients on the basis of definition of Doddington Zoo [11] (section 3.3) and then the effect of self update procedure (section 2), updating threshold is set at zeroFAR, is analyzed on these client's group.

Table 1 reports the statistics about the percentage of specific "animals" present in the database, found using the prediction set of the Equinox database (section 3.3).

Table 1. Percentage of different characteristic clients in the database

% Lambs	% Wolves	% Sheeps	% Goats
12	2	56	30

Table 1 shows that Equinox database comprises of 12% lambs, 2% wolves, 56% sheeps and 30% goats. It is worth noting that the most frequent class is that of "sheeps", that is, clients "easy" to recognize and also difficult to imitate. Goats appeared as the second most frequent class. This contradicts results found in other works [14-15] (Ref. 15 is about fingerprints), and pointed out how the frequency of these classes strongly depend on the variety of the user population, prediction rules adopted and cannot be referred to general "frequency rules". Lambs and wolves are the least frequent classes.

As second step, we evaluated the effectiveness of self update method for each group of clients. We computed the average % of unlabelled samples exploited from the batch of unlabelled set (section 3.2) and the average % of impostors introduced for each group (available in the same unlabelled set). These statistics, presented in Table 2, help to evaluate the behaviour of self update on different client's group.

Table 2. Average percentage of samples added to clients galleries, impostors introduced, and successful % of wolves attacks after self updating

Animal Type	(%) Samples Exploited (added to clients gallery)	(%) Impostors Introduced (among samples exploited)	(%) Wolves attacked (attack by all the detected wolves with 25 samples per wolf)
Wolves	56.0	37.0	-
Lambs	65.7	43.2	65.9
Goats	23.3	11.8	26.3
Sheeps	72.6	16.4	41.0

Table 2 shows the different percentage of impostors and available samples exploited, from the unlabelled batch, for each partitioned group. According to the statistics presented in Table 2, the following analysis can be done:

1) lambs, i.e. clients vulnerable to impostors, have introduced a high percentage of unlabelled samples, but about half of them are impostors. They are also strongly affected by detected wolves;

2) goats, i.e. clients difficult to be recognized, have exploited the lowest number of available samples, thus confirming their intrinsic characteristic according to the definition of Doddington. On the other hand, they are much less prone to impostors introduction (only 11.8% of added samples are impostors) than other classes of clients, and also are less prone to wolf attacks;

3) sheeps, i.e. well behaved clients, have exploited the largest number of samples and the % impostor introduction is also minimum for these clients. Even % of wolf attacks is minimum for these clients ;

4) wolves too are intruded by impostors. This class exhibits the additional feature that can attack other clients, namely, lambs, and can be confused with other impostors, even lambs. This confirms evidences in previous work [10], where it is stated that certain "lambs" may be "wolves" for other clients too [11].

3.5 Performance Enhancement Reported for Each Group of Clients

According to the statistics reported in section (3.5), it is evident that the effect of self update is different for each partitioned clients group. To provide a further evidence, the average performance attained due to updated templates after the self update procedure for each group of clients is reported in Fig. 1. Fig. 1 presents the ROC curves on test set, before (straight line) and after updating process (dotted line), for each group of clients. In ROC curves, x axis is % FAR and y axis % FRR.

As can be seen from Fig. 1, initial performances of the verification system for each client group (straight lines) is different and after the update procedure, the impact is different for each group of clients (dotted lines). Lambs (subplot 1), the clients vulnerable to impostors, have shown no substantial improvement, because of the large amount of impostors introduction into the galleries (table 2, second row, column 1). Sheeps, as expected, being well behaved clients, have upgraded in the performance after updating process. Nevertheless, they too have attracted impostors into galleries, but because of much more percentage of genuine samples introduced, the impact of impostors is less, hence the performance is upgraded (table 2, fourth row, column 1&2). Goats, difficult to recognize clients, have shown slight improvement in performance due to less capture of genuine samples, although very less percentage of impostor samples are added to the related gallery (table 2, third row, column 1&2). Finally, wolves appears to benefit from self update only at threshold value set at high-security level, where low FAR is expected. Different performances after updating and the statistics presented in table 2 clearly showed the different behaviour of self update procedure for the investigated groups of clients.

These evidences suggest that adjustable update procedures have to be adopted, depending on the clients class. In the following, we give some preliminary guidelines: (1) firstly, a user-specific update threshold can be adopted for each group of clients [10]; (2) lambs and wolves could be updated by adopting supervised methods, as even with the operation at stringent acceptance threshold, they are prone to impostors introduction. Thus, the manual assignment of labels to the samples utilized for updating may minimize the probability of impostors introduction [3]. We believe that manual assignment of label can be suitable, due to their small percentage in the user population: the cost of updating should be compensated by benefits in improving the performance; (3) goats may operate at relaxed updating threshold, say 1%FAR, for better capturing large intra-class variations [9], since they are less prone to impostors introduction.

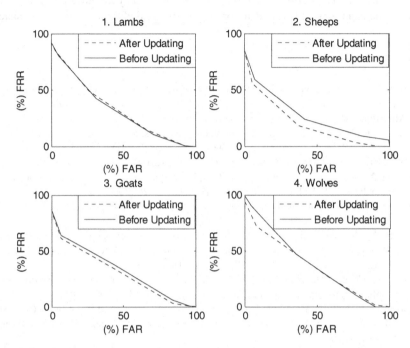

Fig. 1. ROC Curves showing the initial performance (straight line) and after template updating (dotted lines), on the test set, for each partitioned class of clients

4   Conclusions

This paper studied the hypothesis of different behaviour of the self update algorithm due to the presence of different characteristics of clients in the database. Accordingly using the Doddington's classification, the database is partitioned and self update process is applied. Our hypothesis has been confirmed by reported experimental results.

These preliminary results pointed out that the suitability of self update must be carefully analysed on the target user population, although no significant performance degradation have been noticed on the four identified groups of users, especially for "anomalous" clients (lambs and wolves). On the other hand, performance improvement for the most frequent classes, namely, sheeps and goats, has been pointed out. Since they result in covering about 80% of user population, applying update algorithms to these user appears to be worth-while. On the other hand, adjustable updating procedures may be taken into account for wolves and lambs. We suggested some "guide-lines" by considering the consistence of wolves, lambs, goats and sheeps in the user population at hand.

In our opinion, with regard to above guide-lines and their suitability, the main problem to solve is to clearly understand if frequency of users classes, which in our study did not partially agree with other achievements at the state of the art, is general. It can be easily supposed, and maybe verified, that this frequency may change as function not only of users, but also of selected biometric and prediction rules and the set used for clients partitioning. But, although frequency of different classes may change, the behaviour of self update for each partitioned class may remain consistent.

References

1. Roli, F., Didaci, L., Marcialis, G.L.: Adaptative Biometric Systems that Can Improve with Use. In: Ratha, N., Govindaraju, V. (eds.) Advances in Biometrics: Sensors, Systems and Algorithms, pp. 447–471. Springer, Heidelberg (2008)
2. Jain, A.K., Flynn, P., Ross, A.: Handbook of Biometrics. Springer, New York (2007)
3. Uludag, U., Ross, A., Jain, A.K.: Biometric template selection and update: a case study in fingerprints. Pattern Recognition 37(7), 1533–1542 (2004)
4. Jiang, X., Ser, W.: Online Fingerprint Template Improvement. IEEE Transactions on Pattern Analysis and Machine Intelligence 24(8), 1121–1126 (2002)
5. Ryu, C., Kim, H., Jain, A.K.: Template Adaptation based Fingerprint Verification. In: 18th ICPR 2006, vol. 4, pp. 582–585. IEEE Computer Society, Los Alamitos (2006)
6. Roli, F., Marcialis, G.L.: Semi-supervised PCA-based face recognition using self-training. In: Yeung, D.-Y., Kwok, J.T., Fred, A., Roli, F., de Ridder, D. (eds.) SSPR 2006 and SPR 2006. LNCS, vol. 4109, pp. 560–568. Springer, Heidelberg (2006)
7. Liu, X., Chen, T.H., Thornton, S.M.: Eigenspace updating for non-stationary process and its application to face recognition. Pattern Recognition, 1945–1959 (2003)
8. Roli, F., Didaci, L., Marcialis, G.L.: Template co-update in multimodal biometric system. In: Lee, S.-W., Li, S.Z. (eds.) ICB 2007. LNCS, vol. 4642, pp. 1194–1202. Springer, Heidelberg (2007)
9. Rattani, A., Marcialis, G.L., Roli, F.: Capturing large intra-class variations of biometric data by template co-updating. In: IEEE Workshop on Biometrics, International Conference on Vision and Pattern Recognition, Anchorage, Alaska, USA (2008)
10. Marcialis, G.L., Rattani, A., Roli, F.: Biometric template update: an experimental investigation on the relationship between update errors and performance degradation in face verification. In: da Vitoria Lobo, N., Kasparis, T., Roli, F., Kwok, J.T., Georgiopoulos, M., Anagnostopoulos, G.C., Loog, M. (eds.) S+SSPR 2008. LNCS, vol. 5342, pp. 684–693. Springer, Heidelberg (2008)
11. Doddington, G., Liggett, W., Martin, A., Przybocki, M., Reynolds, D.: Sheep, goats, lambs and wolves: A statistical analysis of speaker performance, NIST 1998 speaker recognition evaluation. In: Proceedings of ICSLP 1998 (1998)
12. http://www.equinoxsensors.com/products/HID.html
13. Wiskott, L., Fellows, J.-M., Kruger, N., von der Malsburg, C.: Face Recognition by elastic bunch graph matching, Tech. Report IR-INI 96-08 (1996)
14. Poh, N., Kittler, J.: A Methodology for Separating Sheep from Goats for Controlled Enrollment and Multimodal Fusion. In: 6th IEEE Biometric Symposium, Tampa, Florida, USA (2008)
15. Micklin, A., Watson, C., Ulery, B.: The Myth of Goats: how many people have fingerprints that are hard to match?, Tech. Rep. NISTIR 7271, NIST (2005)

Similarity Searches in Face Databases

Annalisa Franco and Dario Maio

DEIS – Università di Bologna, Viale Risorgimento, 2 – 40136 Bologna - Italy
{annalisa.franco,dario.maio}@unibo.it

Abstract. In this paper the problem of similarity searches in face databases is addressed. An approach based on relevance feedback is proposed to iteratively improve the query result. The approach is suitable both to supervised and unsupervised contexts. The efficacy of the learning procedures are confirmed by the results obtained on publicly available databases of faces.

1 Introduction

Face is one of the most studied biometric characteristics and a huge literature exists about face recognition approaches [12]. Face recognition relies on the availability of a labeled database of faces, i.e. the identity of each face image is known, thus allowing the creation of a template representative of the user; recognition is performed by comparing the unknown input face image with the stored templates. In this work a different scenario is addressed where a similarity search is more appropriate than a direct identification. Several real applications fall in this category. For example in video-surveillance applications usually large quantities of images are gathered and stored to be examined in case of need (e.g. image sequences acquired at a bank entrance could be analyzed after a robbery: an image of the robber could be compared with other images in the attempt of finding frames where the face is more clearly visible). Another important application in the law enforcement field is the typical mug-shot search problem where a witness has in mind the image of a subject and a support tool could help to leaf through a database of suspects. In this case a query image could not be available, so that typical face recognition approaches cannot be applied.

Our framework was designed with the objective of providing a valid and flexible tool to perform similarity searches in face databases. The proposed system exploits relevance feedback techniques to gradually improve the search result. The search process is iterative and the information obtained at each iteration is used to improve the result in the subsequent search steps. The proposed system is very flexible being able to work in different modalities: supervised by the user (with or without a query image) and unsupervised. In the former, like in traditional feedback techniques [13], the system gathers information from the user judgment to improve the results, in the latter, which represents the main contribution of this work, an unsupervised iterative mechanism is exploited to improve the initial result without requiring the user intervention. The two modalities can either work independently or be combined to reduce the user effort needed to obtain a satisfactory result.

P. Foggia, C. Sansone, and M. Vento (Eds.): ICIAP 2009, LNCS 5716, pp. 443–450, 2009.
© Springer-Verlag Berlin Heidelberg 2009

Many relevance feedback techniques have been proposed in the literature for similarity searches in generic image databases [13] where the user supervision is exploited
to gradually improve the performance. Quite a few works have been proposed to
address the specific problem of similarity searches in face databases. Supervised
feedback techniques for mental face retrieval have been proposed in [4] [2]. We believe that in this application the user supervision cannot be completely avoided, but
on the other hand some automatic mechanisms are needed to speed up the search
process in very large databases.

We previously proposed a supervised relevance feedback approach in [5] [6]. This
work starts from the same basic representation, but the method is here significantly
extended with the possibility of performing unsupervised feedback iterations that does
not require the user intervention. This paper is organized as follows: in section 2 the
proposed framework is described, in section 3 the experiments carried out and the
results obtained are presented, and finally in section 4 some concluding remarks are
given.

2   System Overview

The processing flow is analogous to that of a traditional system for similarity searches
based on relevance feedback. A query image is presented to the system that returns a
first set of results, based usually on a "nearest neighbor" criterion. The result is then
analyzed (either by the user in the *supervised* modality or automatically in the *unsupervised* one), thus determining an updating of the search parameters, subsequently
used to produce a new set of results.

In the supervised search the query image is optional: if it is not available the system randomly selects an initial set of images from the database and the user can start
directly indicating the most similar to the results he has in mind; this kind of search
allows to perform the so called *mental face retrieval*.

2.1   Query Representation

Similarly to [5], a vector model is adopted here, that is each image is represented as a
point in a multidimensional space, and a subspace-based representation is used for the
query. The information about the relevant images obtained at each iteration is organized in clusters and represented by a mixture of linear subspaces [7]. The use of a
mixture of linear subspaces allows to obtain a more robust representation and to deal
with the non-linearity that characterizes this problem [5]. A single KL subspace [7]
can be defined as follows. Let $P = \{x_i \in \Re^n | i = 1,..,m\}$ be a set of images
represented by n-dimensional feature vectors. The k-dimensional eigenspace S_P related to P is obtained by selecting the first k eigenvectors from the KL transformed
space of P, $S_P = [\bar{x}, \Phi, \Lambda, m]$, where $\bar{x}$ is the mean vector, Φ is the matrix of the first k
eigenvectors of the data covariance matrix and Λ the matrix of related eigenvalues.
The value of k is a parameter bounded by the dimension n of the feature space and the
number m of available samples. In our experiments no optimizations of the parameter
k have been conducted and it has been fixed to $min(3,m-1)$ for all the subspaces,
which is a reasonable value in consideration of the limited number of samples availa-

ble. Given a subspace S_P, the distance of a pattern from the subspace, called *distance from space*, is defined as:

$$d_{FS}(\mathbf{x}, S_P) = \sqrt{\|\mathbf{x} - \bar{\mathbf{x}}\|_2^2 - \|\Phi^T(\mathbf{x} - \bar{\mathbf{x}})\|_2^2}.$$

2.2 Feature Extraction

To represent the face images, texture features are used. No color information is exploited since the role of color in the analysis of faces is not as important as in typical image retrieval problems; indeed most of the face recognition approaches known in the literature use features derived from gray level images. The Local Binary Pattern operator (LBP) originally introduced in [9] is used in this work. The LBP operator was designed to operate on gray level images, so that if the database contains color images they have first to be converted to gray scale. The LBP operator analyzes the eight neighbors of a pixel, using the value of the central pixel as a threshold. If a neighbor pixel has a higher or equal gray value than the center pixel, then a 1 is assigned to that pixel, otherwise it gets a 0. The LBP code for the central pixel is then obtained by concatenating the eight 1 or 0 to a binary code. To obtain the final feature vector the approach proposed in [1] is used. The face image is divided into regions, and for each region a histogram with all possible labels is constructed. This means that every bin in a histogram represents a pattern and contains its frequency in the related region. The feature vector is then constructed by concatenating the local histograms to one global histogram.

2.3 Supervised Feedback

In the supervised modality, if a query image is available, the initial result is obtained by a simple nearest neighbor search in the feature space: the Euclidean distance between the images in the database and the query is calculated and the r nearest images are selected. If the query image is not available, a set of r random images are extracted from the database. As a future work more effective techniques to extract the initial image set will be studied to select heterogeneous images representative of the whole database content (e.g. men and women, young and old persons, etc.).

At each iteration the user can express a judgment about the result obtained, selecting the images considered "relevant" to the query. The images selected are organized in disjoint subsets according to a K-means clustering algorithm [8]; starting from each subset a KL subspace is calculated thus obtaining the mixture of linear subspaces constituting the new query representation. To obtain a new result the images in the database are compared to the mixture of subspaces according to the *distance from set of spaces* metric, and the r nearest images are selected.

2.4 Unsupervised Feedback

The procedure used in the unsupervised modality is more complicated and represents the main novel contribution of this work. In this case no interaction with the user is required, and the system has to automatically evaluate the result obtained at each iteration. A scoring mechanism has been designed for this purpose. At the beginning of a query, the score of each image is initialized to 0 and is successively updated according to different factors that will be detailed later. At the end of each iteration the *r* images with the highest score are shown in the result.

The scoring process is based on the assumption that the *r* images retrieved are very similar to the query. The images are thus organized into disjoint clusters which are sorted according to their distance from the query image. The distance of each image is then calculated taking into account its distance from the query and the position of the related cluster, thus rewarding the images in the clusters nearest to the query. Finally the *r* nearest images to the query, according to this distance are executed as second level queries: the images that belong to the result of both the original query and the second level query receive an additional score. This last step is outlined in Fig. 1.

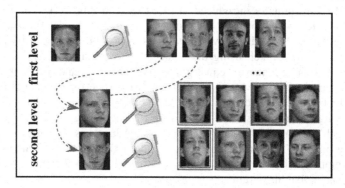

Fig. 1. Visual representation second level query step. The images with frame will receive an additional score

The detailed procedure is now described. Let's indicate with:

- $Y = \{\mathbf{y}_1, \mathbf{y}_2, .., \mathbf{y}_n\}$ the set of images in the database, where each image is represented by the LBP features extracted (section 2.2);
- $X^i = \{\mathbf{x}_1^i, .., \mathbf{x}_r^i\}, X^i \subseteq Y$ the set of *r* images retrieved at iteration *i*;
- $S^i = \{s^i(\mathbf{y}_1), s^i(\mathbf{y}_2), ..., s^i(\mathbf{y}_n)\}$ the set of scores accumulated by each image, respectively, during the *i* iterations;
- **q** the feature vector representative of the query image.
  The result X^{i+1} at iteration *i*+1 is calculated as follows:

- Partition the image set X^i into *p* disjoint subsets $P_1, P_2, ..., P_p$ using the K-means clustering algorithm [8];
- Calculate a KL subspace S_{P_i} for each subset $P_i, i = 1, .., p$;
- Sort the *p* subspaces according to their distance from the query $d_{FS}(\mathbf{q}, S_{P_i})$;
- For each image in the database $\mathbf{y}_i \in Y$ calculate the distance d_{ij} from each subspace S_{P_j} in the sorted list of subspaces ($d_{ij} = d_{FS}(\mathbf{y}_i, S_{P_j})$).

  Let $S_{P_{j^*}}$ be the nearest subspace to $\mathbf{y}_i$: $j^* = \underset{j}{argmin}\ d_{FS}\left(\mathbf{y}_i, S_{P_j}\right)$

- Calculate for each image $\mathbf{y}_i \in Y$ the composite weighted distance: $wd_i = \left(\frac{d_{ij^*} + \|\mathbf{q} - \mathbf{y}_i\|_2}{2}\right) \times \frac{j^*}{p}$

- Sort the images $\mathbf{y}_i \in Y$ in increasing order of distance wd_i, thus obtaining the sorted set $Y' = \{\mathbf{y}'_1, \mathbf{y}'_2, .., \mathbf{y}'_n\}$.
- Update $s^{i+1}(\mathbf{y}'_i) = s^i(\mathbf{y}'_i) + scoreFunc(i) \ i = 1, .., r$
- Take the first r images of $\mathbf{y}'_i \in Y', i = 1, .., r$ and find for each of them the $r1$ nearest images $Y'' \subseteq Y$, where $r1$ represents the number of images to score in the second level queries.
- Increase the score of each image $\mathbf{y}'_i \in (Y' \cap Y'')$ according to the following formula: $s^{i+1}(\mathbf{y}'_i) = s^i(\mathbf{y}'_i) + scoreFunc(i) \times \frac{1}{j^*+1}$

where j^* indicates the subspace $S_{P_{j^*}}$ nearest to $\mathbf{y}'_i$, and the subscript i refers to the position of the image $\mathbf{y}'_i$ in the sorted set Y'.

The new result X^{i+1} at iteration $i+1$ will include the r images with the highest score. The score function assigns a score according to the position i of an image in the result set. In this work the following formula has been used: $scoreFunc(i) = \frac{1}{c^i}$ where c is a constant value (5 in our experiments). This score function rapidly decreases thus rewarding mainly the images in the first positions.

3 Experimental Results

Some experiments have been carried out on two face databases:

- the ORL database of faces [10] containing 400 different images related to 40 individuals (10 images for each subject);
- the Faces96 database from the Essex facial images database [3] containing 3040 images of 152 individuals (20 per subject); the images are characterized by a complex background and large variations of head scale and position, image lighting and expression. The face has been automatically detected using the Viola Jones face detector [11].

In order to perform the experiments, the images in each database are partitioned into disjoint subsets containing respectively the first half and the second half of the images of each individual: the first one is used as database to search on, the second one is used as query set. The performance is measured in terms of *precision* defined as the percentage of relevant images returned by the system after a fixed number of iterations. An image is considered relevant to a query if it belongs to the same class. It is worth noting that the information about the class of the images is not used during the search process; it is only exploited to finally calculate the precision. The results reported refer to the average precision obtained over the query set.

The unsupervised search procedure is first analyzed. In particular in Fig. 2 the average precision is reported for different parameters setup as a function of the number of iterations for the two databases.

The two most critical parameters are considered in this experiment: the number r of images to retrieve, and the number $r1$ of images to score in the second level queries. Of course the precision is higher when a higher number of images is retrieved, but the results in the graph clearly show that, independently of the parameters setup, the unsupervised search procedure allows to gradually increase the precision. A term

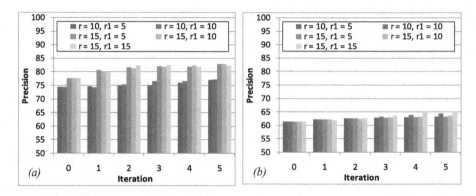

Fig. 2. Precision of the *unsupervised* search approach as a function of the number of iterations: *(a)* ORL database, *(b)* Faces96 database

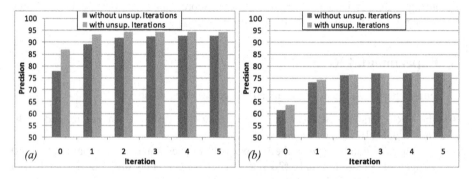

Fig. 3. Precision of the *supervised* search approach as a function of the number of iterations for the ORL *(a)* and Faces96 *(b)* databases. The result obtained with and without previous *unsupervised* iterations is given.

of comparison for the results of the *unsupervised* search is given by the performance measured for the *supervised* approach reported in Fig. 3.

In the second set of experiments the results obtained with the supervised feedback procedure are analyzed. To obtain objective and reproducible results, the supervised feedback has been simulated by automatically assigning a positive feedback to the images belonging to the same class of the query image. The final aim of our work is to reduce the effort required to the user to retrieve a satisfactory set of images; the advantage of the proposed approach is that a few unsupervised iterations can be performed before the user starts its interaction with the system. If the initial set of images is better, the number of supervised iterations needed to obtain a satisfactory result is lower. This evaluation is reported in Fig. 3. where the results obtained with a totally supervised search are compared to those obtained with a supervised search performed after 5 unsupervised iterations. The number of images to retrieve r was fixed to 15 in this test, and the number rl of images to score in the second level queries is 10. Analogous behaviors have been observed with other parameters setup.

The graph shows that the supervised search clearly benefits from some previous unsupervised iteration since the precision reached is higher, particularly in the first supervised iterations. This result is encouraging since it shows that the effort required to the user can be significantly reduced. The overall performance measured in the experiments are clearly higher for the ORL database where the images have been acquired under more controlled conditions; the Faces96 database contains very complex images and in some cases the automatic face detection provides inaccurate results. In both cases, however, the results confirm the efficacy of the proposed unsupervised feedback technique.

Experiments with the mental face retrieval (search without query image) require an extensive experimentation with several real users to provide reliable results, and will be thus performed in a future study.

4 Conclusions

In this paper a new approach for similarity searches in face database has been presented. The method exploits relevance feedback to gradually improve the quality of the result obtained. The feedback iterations can either be supervised by the user or be carried out automatically by the systems without requiring the interaction with the user. The two operative modalities can be combined to reduce the effort required to the user, obtaining at the same time satisfactory results.

This is only a preliminary work and the approach must be reinforced to better deal with typical changes in the face aspect that can make the search process more difficult. Moreover, the framework will be extended with the possibility of performing searches starting from sketches (as typically occurs when an identikit of a suspect is available).

References

[1] Ahonen, T., Hadid, A., Pietikäinen, M.: Face Recognition with Local Binary Patterns. In: Pajdla, T., Matas, J(G.) (eds.) ECCV 2004. LNCS, vol. 3021, pp. 469–481. Springer, Heidelberg (2004)

[2] Baker, E., Seltzer, M.: The Mug-Shot Search Problem. In: Proc. Vis. Int., pp. 421–430 (1998)

[3] Essex facial images database, http://cswww.essex.ac.uk/mv/allfaces/index.html

[4] Fang, Y., Geman, D., Boujemaa, N.: An Interactive System for Mental Face Retrieval. In: Proc. International Workshop on Multimedia information retrieval, pp. 193–200 (2005)

[5] Franco, A., Lumini, A.: Mixture of KL Subspaces for relevance feedback. Multimedia Tools and Applications 37(2), 189–209 (2008)

[6] Franco, A., Maio, D., Lumini, A.: A new approach for relevance feedback through positive and negative samples. In: Proc. ICPR, vol. 4, pp. 905–908 (2004)

[7] Fukunaga, K.: Statistical Pattern Recognition. Academic Press, San Diego (1990)

[8] MacQueen, J.B.: Some Methods for classification and Analysis of Multivariate Observations. In: Proc. Symp. on Math. Stat. and Probability, vol. 1, pp. 281–297 (1967)

[9] Ojala, T., Pietikainen, M., Harwood, D.: A comparative study of texture measures with classification based on feature distributions. Pattern Recognition 29(1), 51–59 (1996)

[10] ORL database of faces,
http://www.uk.research.att.com/facedatabase.html

[11] Viola, P., Jones, M.J.: Rapid object detection using a boosted cascade of simple features. In: Proc. of the IEEE ICCVPR, vol. 1, pp. 511–518 (2001)

[12] Zhao, W., Chellappa, R., Phillips, P.J., Rosenfeld, A.: Face recognition: a literature survey. ACM Computing Surveys 35(4), 399–458 (2003)

[13] Zhou, X.S., Huang, T.S.: Relevance feedback for image retrieval: a comprehensive review. Multimedia Systems 8(6), 536–544 (2003)

Vision-Based Motion Capture of Interacting Multiple People

Hiroaki Egashira[1], Atsushi Shimada[1], Daisaku Arita[1,2],
and Rin-ichiro Taniguchi[1]

[1] Department of Intelligent Systems Kyushu University
744, Motooka, Nishi-ku, Fukuoka, 819-0395, Japan
{aki,atsushi,rin}@limu.is.kyushu-u.ac.jp
[2] Institute of Systems, Information Technologies and Nanotechnologies
2-1-22, Momochihama, Sawara-ku, Fukuoka, 814-0001, Japan
arita@isit.or.jp

Abstract. Vision-based motion capture is getting popular for acquiring human motion information in various interactive applications. To enlarge its applicability, we have been developing a vision-based motion capture system which can estimate the postures of multiple people simultaneously using multiview image analysis. Our approach is divided into the following two phases: at first, extraction, or segmentation, of each person in input multiview images; then, posture analysis for one person is applied to the segmented region of each person. The segmentation is realized in the voxel space, which is reconstructed by visual cone intersection of multiview silhouettes. Here, a graph cut algorithm is employed to achieve optimal segmentation. Posture analysis is based on a model-based approach, where a skeleton model of human figure is matched with the multiview silhouettes based on a particle filter and physical constraints on human body movement. Several experimental studies show that the proposed method acquires human postures of multiple people correctly and efficiently even when they touch each otter.

1 Introduction

Motion capture systems (MCS) are useful tools for various interactive applications such as interactive animation, 3D virtual space operation, video game interface, etc. Especially, vision-based MCS is a smart and natural approach since it does not impose any physical restrictions on a user.

There are many researches into vision-based MCS: some of them employed a computation intensive approach to acquire precise motion information [1][2][3] and others made emphasis on real-time features so that it can be applied to interactive applications [4][5][6][7]. However, most of them handle posture estimation of just one person. From the viewpoint of human activity observation, it is also required to acquire motion information of multiple people who are interacting with each other.

To analyze the motion of multiple people, Tanaka et al. [8] employed an example-based approach. They made a database which consists of combined 3D

P. Foggia, C. Sansone, and M. Vento (Eds.): ICIAP 2009, LNCS 5716, pp. 451–460, 2009.
© Springer-Verlag Berlin Heidelberg 2009

shapes of two persons and their posture parameters, and estimated the postures by searching the database for observed 3D shapes. However, when multiple people are interacting with each other, the variation of the 3D shapes of the people becomes quite large and it is not easy to efficiently find a solution in such a large search space. This difficulty becomes larger when the number of persons becomes large. In contrast, we have employed another approach, where each person in the scene is segmented, and where the posture of the segmented person is analyzed by an ordinary one-person motion capture system. In this paper, we will present our motion capturing of multiple persons, emphasizing on the segmentation of the multiple persons using multiview image analysis. Also, we will show several experimental results showing the effectiveness of our algorithm.

In general, there are two approaches to segment human regions; one is segmentation in the 2D image space and the other is segmentation in the 3D space, where the 3D shape of the target object is reconstructed from multiview images. We have employed the latter approach, and the main issue is to assign a correct person identification label to each voxel, which represents the 3D shape of the reconstructed object. In this paper, we assume that there are two people in the observed space. When a person does not touch the other, it is easy to assign a unique label to each human region by finding a connected component of voxels [9,10]. However, when two people are interacting with each other, they often touch each other and their reconstructed 3D shape becomes one connected component. In this case, we have to segment the two persons. To solve this problem, we define an energy function that expresses the identifiability of the persons, which is assigned to each voxel of the reconstructed shape, and we realize the segmentation by minimizing the total energy assigned to segmented regions based on a graph cut algorithm [11].

2   Human Region Segmentation in the 3D Space

2.1   Outline

The goal of this human object segmentation is to extract regions each of which represents one person. In general, the segmentation in the 2D image is rather difficult because when we observe multiple persons, especially multiple persons interacting with each other, they usually make serious self-occlusion in the 2D image space. Here, since target people are observed by multiple cameras, we can construct their 3D shape from the acquired images, and it is much easier to classify the target region into separate human regions in the 3D space, each of which represents one person, although the computation time becomes larger due to the reconstruction process.

According to the above consideration, first, we reconstruct the 3D shape of the target from multiview images based on visual cone intersection [13], where the 3D shape is represented in terms of voxels. Then, we segment the reconstructed 3D target shape into separate 3D regions of the observed people. Visual cone intersection does not generate a precise 3D shape of the object but the purpose of the reconstruction here is just to acquire cues for multiple person segmentation.

From this point of view, we do not have to make the resolution of the voxel space high, and, thus, the computation cost is not increased heavily. After each person is segmented, a vision-based MCS for one person [7] is applied to the segmented data.

To partition the reconstructed 3D shape, we have employed an energy minimization framework. We attach a label, i.e., a person identifier, to each voxel, and we define an energy function that expresses the suitability of the person identifier attached to the voxel. To achieve its fast computation, we have segmented human regions by a graph cut algorithm [11,12] minimizing the total energy of all the voxels belonging to segmented regions. In general, the energy function can be defined based on the following information:

Temporal sequence information: the segmentation results in the previous frames are used to evaluate the validity of the current segmentation,

Visual features: 2D/3D visual features extracted from the images are referred to.

In the former, the difference of the voxels in the current frame and those in the previous frame is calculated, and each voxel of the detected difference is categorized according to its distance to the segmented regions in the previous frame. On the contrary, in the latter, each voxel is categorized according to its distance to detected robust visual features, i.e., skin-color blobs (shoe-color blobs for feet), of each person. Although the former is quite effective to reduce the computation cost and to realize real-time processing, it requires an initial segmentation and, more seriously, it tends to accumulate the segmentation error as the segmentation process proceeds into the succeeding frames. Therefore, here, we have not used the previous segmentation result, and we have segmented human regions based on the visual features extracted by image analysis.

2.2   Energy Minimization

The energy function we define consists of the data term and the smoothing term as follows.

$$E(X) = kG(X) + H(X) \tag{1}$$

$X = (X_1, \ldots, X_v, \ldots, X_{|V|})$ is a binary vector, where X_v is a label of a voxel v: person A or B[1], and V is a set of voxels to be labeled. $k(> 0)$ is the ratio of the data term $G(X)$ and the smoothing term $H(X)$. $G(X)$ is defined, referring to $g(X_v)$, the suitability of a given label, as follows:

$$G(X) = \sum_{v \in V} g(X_v) \tag{2}$$

$$g(X_v) = \begin{cases} g_A(v), & \text{if } X_v = A \\ g_B(v), & \text{if } X_v = B \end{cases} \tag{3}$$

---

[1] In this paper, we assume two persons are observed. However, the idea can be extended for analyzing three or more people.

where $g(X_v)$ denotes the likelihood of a given label. The detailed explanation will be given in the following subsection. On the other hand, $H(X)$ is defined, referring to $h(X_u, X_v)$, the consistency between neighboring pixels, as follows:

$$H(X) = \sum_{(u,v) \in N} h(X_u, X_v) \tag{4}$$

$$h(X_u, X_v) = \begin{cases} 1, & \text{if } X_u \neq X_v \\ 0, & \text{otherwise} \end{cases} \tag{5}$$

N is a set of all the neighboring pixel pairs in V here. We assign proper labels to the voxels which minimize the total energy $E(X)$, and it is solved by a graph cut algorithm.

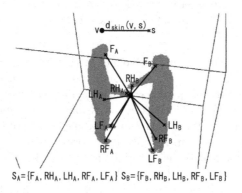

$S_A = \{F_A, RH_A, LH_A, RF_A, LF_A\}$ $S_B = \{F_B, RH_B, LH_B, RF_B, LF_B\}$

Fig. 1. 3D Positions of the Color Blobs

2.3   Human Region Segmentation Using Color Blob Information

Skin color blobs are good visual features for detecting people, and we have developed a segmentation method based on skin color blobs. We classify the voxels of reconstructed object shape, V, into person A or person B based on the distance to the color blobs of person A and those of person B. Blob identification is accomplished based on the blob positions in the previous frame, and basically the label of the nearest blob which has similar features in the previous frame is assigned to a given blob[2].

We obtain 3D positions of skin-color blobs (shoe-color blobs for feet) by multiview image analysis. Here, let a color blob be s, and a set of color blobs which belong to person A be S_A, and S_B for person B. A person has five color blobs; face (F), right hand (RH), left hand (LH), right foot (RF) and left foot (LF). Then, we calculate $g_A(v)$ as follows (see Fig.1).

---

[2] We assume, at beginning, the two persons do not touch each other and color blobs are easily classified into person A or B based on connected component analysis.

$$g_A(v) = \sum_{s \in S_B} \frac{1}{d_{skin}(v, s)} \tag{6}$$

$$S_B = \{F_B, RH_B, LH_B, RF_B, LF_B\} \tag{7}$$

$$d_{skin}(v, s) = D_E(P_V(v), P_S(s)) \tag{8}$$

Here, $D_E(\cdot, \cdot)$ denotes a Euclidean distance between the two points, $P_V(\cdot)$ the 3D position of the voxel, and $P_S(\cdot)$ is the 3D position of the color blob. If a voxel v is far from the color blobs of the other person, the value of $g_A(v)$ becomes small. We expect that segmentation results become good by considering all the color blobs belonging to the other person.

3   Human Posture Analysis

After the result of human region segmentation in the 3D space is projected to the multiview image space, we apply a one-person pose estimation method to each segmented human region. In our human posture analysis, to estimate full body human postures, we have introduced a skeleton model with 33 DOF (3DOF translation and 30 DOF orientation, see Fig.2). This model includes 4 DOF on the torso part, which enables the user to move flexibly, such as bending or leaning poses. We have established the human figure model relatively complex to make generated human postures natural.

Our algorithm is skeleton-based model fitting, in which the skeleton model of the human body is fit to the center of a human silhouette. In general, the model fitting approach for motion capturing iteratively synthesizes human models and analyzes their fitness based on image features, and it is usually time consuming because the human configuration space is very high dimensional. To solve this problem, we also use 3-D positional constraints among the body parts. For example, when we estimate the posture of the left arm, we can do much faster if the 3 D position of the left hand is known. The basic algorithm flow of our real-time motion capture system is as follows:

1. Detection of visual cues

   - Silhouette detection and skin-color blob (and shoe-color blob) detection.
   - Calculation of the 3-D positions of the color blobs using multiview fusion. The 3-D head position is also precisely estimated by Hough transform, which searches for a circular silhouette edge around the detected skin-color blobs.
   - Generating the distance-transformed image of the silhouette region for fast skeleton fitting in the next step.

2. Estimation of human posture
   Fitting the skeleton model of the human body to the center of silhouette using particle filter. Several constraints to narrow the search space have been introduced as follows:

constraints based on collision detection. The torso and the limbs cannot occupy the same place in 3-D space at the same time. We eliminate postures which have collisions among the torso and the limbs.

kinematic constraints. Human joints have movable limits. For example, the elbows cannot bend backward. We establish the limits on each joint angle based on anatomy to eliminate impossible postures and to prune the model configuration space.

Fig.3 shows the framework of our motion sensing. In the stage of posture estimation, first, we estimate the posture of the torso part. Next, four limb postures are estimated separately by using neck or waist position calculated in the previous step.

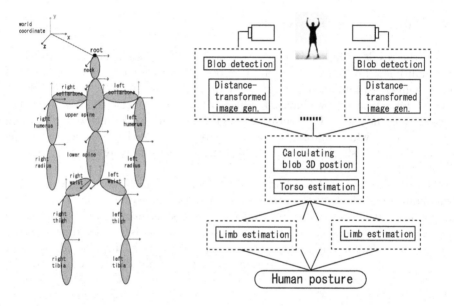

Fig. 2. Human Figure Model   **Fig. 3.** System Overview

4   Experimental Results

4.1   Human Region Segmentation

We have examined our algorithm using the following three video sequences which include scenes where a person touches the other:

Sequence1: person A shakes person B's hand (16frames).

Sequence2: person A touches, by his right hand, the left shoulder of person B (12frames).

Sequence3: person A kicks, by his right foot, person B on the left thigh (20frames).

In this experiment, we used 8 cameras (Dragonfly 2 of Point Grey Research) which had been calibrated in advance [14]. The sizes of captured images are 640×480 pixels and the resolution of the voxel space is $64 \times 64 \times 64$. We obtained segmentation results shown in Fig.4, 5 and 6, where typical three cases are shown.

Before touching: two people have not touched yet (the upper rows).
Just touching: two people are just touching (the middle row).
After touching: two people become untouched (the lower rows).

Segmentation referring to the 3D positions of the color blobs mostly succeeded, except the case that blobs of different persons are merged into one. In this case, we have to attach dual labels to the blob, by which the blob in the 3D space is projected onto both of 2D image regions corresponding the two persons.

The computational time for this segmentation is about 9ms/frame with Pentium4 3GHz CPU. Although the computational time to obtain the color blobs is not included, the color blob detection is also required in the human posture estimation phase, and it doe not become a large overhead of the system.

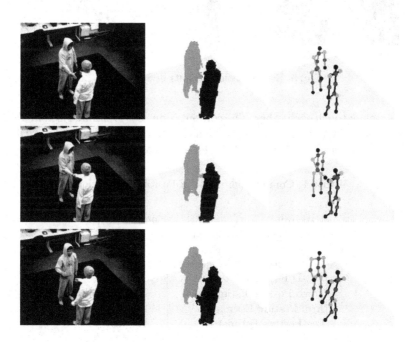

Fig. 4. Segmentation Results of Sequence1. Left: Input images, Middle: Segmentation results. Right: Estimated human postures.

4.2   Results of Human Motion Capturing

The right columns of Fig.4, 5, 6 show the results of human posture analysis of multiple people. They show that the postures of the people are correctly analyzed

Fig. 5. Segmentation Results of Sequence2

even when they touch each other. The computation cost is summarized in Table 1 (Pentium4 3GHz CPU), which shows the algorithm can be executed in real-time when we implement it on a parallel machine such as a PC-cluster [15].

Table 1. Computation Time of Posture Estimation

Category	Comp. Time
Visual Feature Extraction	
–Skin Blob Extraction	4msec
–Distance Image Generation	60msec
–3-D Position Estimation	21msec
Torso Posture Estimation	49 msec
Arm Posture Estimation	95 msec
Leg Posture Estimation	129 msec

Our human region segmentation relies on the blob detection, and therefore, when the blobs are not correctly detected, the result of human posture analysis is seriously affected. To apply our method to uncontrolled, i.e., complex background, we need robust color blob detection, and we have employed example-based color detection.

Fig. 6. Segmentation Results of Sequence3

5   Conclusion

In this paper, we have proposed a motion capture system to estimate the postures of interacting multiple people. To achieve the goal, we have constructed a two phase system, which consists of region segmentation of each person and human posture estimation of each segmented person. The segmentation is realized in the voxel space and a graph cut algorithm is employed to achieve optimal segmentation. Posture analysis is based on a model-based approach, where a skeleton model of human figure is matched with the multiview silhouettes. Experimental results have indicated the effectiveness of our method, showing that it acquires human postures of multiple people correctly and efficiently even when they touch each other.

In our future work, we are going to thoroughly evaluate the accuracy of the system, and to make the system more robust so that the system can be used in more practical environment with complex background. Also observing interacting people with tools or objects is the next goal.

References

1. Sundaresan, A., Chellappa, R.: Multi-camera Tracking of Articulated Human Motion Using Motion and Shape Cues. In: Narayanan, P.J., Nayar, S.K., Shum, H.-Y. (eds.) ACCV 2006. LNCS, vol. 3852, pp. 131–140. Springer, Heidelberg (2006)

2. Carranza, J., Theobalt, C., Magnor, M., Seidel, H.: Free-Viewpoint Video of Human Actors. In: Proc. of ACM SIGGRAPH, pp. 569–577 (2003)
3. Sand, P., McMillan, L., Popovic, J.: Continuous Capture of Skin Deformation. In: Proc. of ACM SIGGRAPH, pp. 578–586 (2003)
4. Date, N., Yoshimoto, H., Arita, D., Taniguchi, R.: Real-time Human Motion Sensing based on Vision-based Inverse Kinematics for Interactive Applications. In: Proc. of International Conference on Pattern Recognition, vol. 3, pp. 318–321 (2004)
5. Kehl, R., Bray, M., Van Gool, L.: Full Body Tracking from Multiple Views Using Stochastic Sampling. In: Proc. of Computer Vision and Pattern Recognition, pp. 129–136 (2005)
6. Bernier, O.: Real-Time 3D Articulated Pose Tracking using Particle Filters Interacting through Belief Propagation. In: Proc. of International Conference on Pattern Recognition, vol. 1, pp. 90–93 (2006)
7. Saiki, T., Shimada, A., Arita, D., Taniguchi, R.: A Vision-based Real-time Motion Capture System using Fast Model Fitting. In: CD-ROM Proc. of 14th Korea-Japan Joint Workshop on Frontiers of Computer Vision (2008)
8. Tanaka, H., Nakazawa, A., Takemura, H.: Human Pose Estimation from Volume Data and Topological Graph Database. In: Proc. of 8th Asian Conference on Computer Vision, pp. 618–627 (2007)
9. Sagawa, Y., Shimosaka, M., Mori, T., Sato, T.: Fast Online Human Pose Estimation via 3D Voxel Data. In: Proc. of IEEE/RSJ International Conference on Intelligent Robots and Systems, pp. 1034–1040 (2007)
10. Huang, K.S., Trivedi, M.M.: 3D Shape Context Based Gesture Analysis Integrated with Tracking using Omni Video Array. In: Proceedings of IEEE Workshop on Vision for Human-Computer Interaction, V4HCI (2005)
11. Boykov, Y., Kolmogorov, V.: An Experimental Comparison of Min-Cut/Max-Flow Algorithms for Energy Minimization in Vision. IEEE Trans. on Pattern Analysis and Machine Intelligence 26(9), 1124–1137 (2004)
12. Kolmogorov, V.:
    http://www.cs.ucl.ac.uk/staff/V.Kolmogorov/software.html
13. Martin, W.N., Aggarwal, J.K.: Volumetric Description of Objects from Multiple Views. IEEE Trans. on Pattern Analysis and Machine Intelligence 5(2), 150–158 (1983)
14. Tsai, R.Y.: A Versatile Camera Calibration Technique for High-Accuracy 3D Machine Vision Metrology Using Off-the-Shelf TV Cameras and Lenses. IEEE Journal of Robotics and Automation 3(4), 323–344 (1987)
15. Arita, D., Taniguchi, R.: RPV-II: A Stream-Based Real-Time Parallel Vision System and Its Application to Real-Time Volume Reconstruction. In: Schiele, B., Sagerer, G. (eds.) ICVS 2001. LNCS, vol. 2095, pp. 174–189. Springer, Heidelberg (2001)

Probabilistic Corner Detection for Facial Feature Extraction

Edoardo Ardizzone, Marco La Cascia, and Marco Morana

Università degli Studi di Palermo
DINFO - Dipartimento di Ingegneria Informatica
Viale delle Scienze - Ed.6 - 3° piano - 90128 Palermo, Italy
{ardizzon,lacascia,marcomorana}@unipa.it

Abstract. After more than 35 years of resrach, face processing is considered nowadays as one of the most important application of image analysis. It can be considered as a collection of problems (i.e., face detection, normalization, recognition and so on) each of which can be treated separately. Some face detection and face recognition techniques have reached a certain level of maturity, however facial feature extraction still represents the bottleneck of the entire process. In this paper we present a novel facial feature extraction approach that could be used for normalizing Viola-Jones detected faces and let them be recognized by an appearance-based face recognition method. For each observed feature a prior distribution is computed and used as boost map to filter the Harris corner detector response producing more feature candidates on interest region while discarding external values. Tests have been performed on both AR and BioID database using approximately 1750 faces and experimental results are very encouraging.

Keywords: Face detection, face recognition, features extraction, CBIR.

1 Introduction

After more than 35 years of resrach, face processing is considered nowadays as one of the most important application of image analysis and understanding. Even though automatic recognition of faces has reached satisfactory results on well constrained tasks, it is still a challenging problem.

Face processing can be considered as a collection of problems, i.e., *face detection, facial feature extraction, pose estimation, face validation, recognition, tracking, modelling* and so on, each of which can be treated separately.

Face recognition often represents the subsequent step of face detection and face normalization processes. Face detection aims to find the image position of a single face so it is usually the first step in any automated face processing system. Appearance-based approaches could then be used to compare detected faces against a database of known individuals in order to assign them an identity. Face normalization is required to support face recognition by normalizing a face for position so that the error due to face alignment is minimized.

P. Foggia, C. Sansone, and M. Vento (Eds.): ICIAP 2009, LNCS 5716, pp. 461–470, 2009.
© Springer-Verlag Berlin Heidelberg 2009

Some face detection (e.g., Viola-Jones face detector [1]) and face recognition (e.g. eigenfaces [2]) techniques have reached a certain level of maturity, however feature extraction still represents the bottleneck of the entire process.

In this work we present a novel facial feature extraction method to normalize Viola-Jones detected faces and let them be recognized by an appearance-based face recognition approach, e.g. Turk and Pentland eigenfaces.

We started by analyzing the Viola and Jones face detector and we noticed that the use of rectangle features creates some structure on facial features distribution over the detected faces. Thus, all faces are extracted in similar way and each feature locates inside a specific region. Thus, for each feature a prior distribution is computed and used as *boost map* to filter the Harris corner detector response so that thresholding produce a finer corner detection on interest region while discarding other values. Each corner can then be tested using SVMs to detect the presence of a facial feature.

The paper will show the following structure: an analysis of related work will be given (Sect. 2). The Sect. 3.1 will give an overview of Harris corner detector, while the proposed approach is described in Sect. 3.2. Experimental results are shown and discussed in Sect. 4. Conclusions will follow in Sect. 5.

2   Related Work

Automatic face processing for recognition [3] involves at least three different subtasks: *face detection, feature extraction, face recognition* and/or *verification*.

Up to the early '90s, most face detection algorithms were focused on images with single frontal face and simple backgrounds. A survey of these approaches was written by Samal and Iyengar [4].

Face recognition has received more attention especially in the last 10 years. Recent works based on face appearance train the detection system on large numbers of samples and perform really better than early template matching methods. State-of-the-art face detection tecniques can detect different faces in many poses and in cluttered backgrounds. A relevant survey of early face recognition methods was written by Yang et al. [5].

In this paper we propose a feature extraction technique based on Viola-Jones [1] face detector (VJFD), that is the most stable and used face detector both in academic and commercial systems. This is due to three key contributions: the first is *integral image* computation of *rectangle features* that allows for very fast feature evaluation; the second is an efficient classifier, based on AdaBoost [6], which selects a small number of critical visual features from a larger set; the third is an efficient method for discarding background regions which are unlikely to contain the object of interest.

However, many face recognition systems need facial features location to normalize detected faces avoiding degradation in recognition performance.

Early approaches focused on template matching to detect global features as eyes and mouth [7], while more recent models, i.e., ASM, AFM, AAM, offer more robustness and reliability working on local *feature point* position. Active Shape Model (ASM) [8] extends Active Contour Model [9] using a flexible statistical model to find feature point position in ways consistent with a training set. Active Appearance Model (AAM) [10] combines shapes with gray-level appearance of faces.

Face recognition still attracts researchers from both humanistic and scientific worlds. Zhao et al. [3] classify face recognition methods in *holistic matching methods, feature-based matching methods* and *hybrid methods*. In this work we use assume that face recognition step is based on a principal compenent analysis (PCA) technique: eigenfaces [2]. The reason for this choice is that eigenfaces is one of the most mature and investigated face recognition method and it performs well while normalizing faces with respect to scale, translation and rotation. PCA is applied on a training set of face images and eigenvectors (called eigenfaces) are computed. Thus, every face image can be represented as a vector of weights obtained by projecting the image into the "face space" and each new image is verified and identified calculating its distances to face space and to each known class respectively. Experiments performed by Turk and Pentland [2] report approximately 96% correct classification over lighting variation, while performance drops dramatically with orientation (85%) and size(64%) changes. For this reason face normalization is needed.

Berg et. al [11] proposed a *rectification* procedure to move each face image to a canonical frame by identifying five facial feature points (corners of the left and right eyes, corners of the mouth, and the tip of the nose) and then applying an affine transformation. Geometric blur feature [12] is used as input of five SVMs and each point in the entire image is tested to identify features. This approach gives good results, however $M \times N$ points need to be tested, where $M \times N$ is the image size.

In next section we propose a feature extraction method to localize facial features using a prior on location for each feature point and Harris corner detector [13].

3   Methods

3.1   Harris Corner Detector

Several interest point detection techniques have been proposed and evaluated [14], however the Harris corner detector is still one of the most used due to low numerical complexity and invariance to image shift, rotation and lighting variation.

Harris approach relies on the fact that at some image points, *corners*, the image intensity changes largely in multiple directions. Corners are captured by considering the changes of intensity due to shifts in a local window.

Let I is a gray-scale image; consider taking a window W and shifting it by $(\Delta x, \Delta y)$, the auto-correlation function[15] E is defined as,

$$E(x,y) = \sum_{W} (I(x_i, y_i) - I(x_i + \Delta x, y_i + \Delta y))^2 \tag{1}$$

where (x_i, y_i) are the points in the gaussian window centered on (x, y).

Approximating $I(x_i + \Delta x, y_i + \Delta y)$ by Taylor expansion,

$$I(x_i + \Delta x, y_i + \Delta y) \approx I(x_i, y_i) + (I_x(x_i, y_i) \, I_y(x_i, y_i)) \begin{bmatrix} \Delta x \\ \Delta y \end{bmatrix} \tag{2}$$

where $I_x = \frac{\partial I}{\partial x}$ and $I_y = \frac{\partial I}{\partial y}$ denote partial differentiation in x and y, we obtain

$$E(x,y) = \begin{bmatrix} \Delta x & \Delta y \end{bmatrix} M(x,y) \begin{bmatrix} \Delta x \\ \Delta y \end{bmatrix} \tag{3}$$

The matrix $M(x,y)$ captures the local intensity structure of the image and angle brackets denote summation over W.

Corner detection can be done by analyzing the eigenvalues of M for each point in the image, however this computation is computationally expensive. Harris suggested a measure based on the determinant and trace of M to find corners avoiding eigenvalue decomposition of M

$$\begin{aligned} R_H &= \alpha\beta - k(\alpha + \beta)^2 \\ &= Det(M) - kTr^2(M) \end{aligned} \tag{4}$$

where α and β are the eigenvalues of M.

A point $c(x,y)$ is then detected as corner if $R_H(x,y)$ is an 8-way local maximum.

3.2   Feature-Based Corner Detection

Harris corner detector performs well on different types of images, however it is not sufficient for facial feature extraction.

We want to obtain a set of points C_P that contains, among others, the true facial features so that each point in C_P can be tested using SVMs to detect facial features.

We started by analyzing Viola-Jones face detector and we noticed that the use of rectangle features creates some structure on facial features distribution over the detected faces. The reason for this is that each Viola-Jones face region is selected using the rectangle features [1] response to facial features (i.e. eyes, nose, mouth) position. Thus, all faces are extracted in similar way and each feature locates inside a well defined region, as shown in Fig. 1.

In order to reduce the computational cost and increase the rate of success of feature classification using SVMs, all points to be tested should represent true feature candidates. However Harris output is a "general-purpose" set of points, therefore many useless corners are detected and necessary ones are frequently missed. The proposed method is based on feature points distribution over

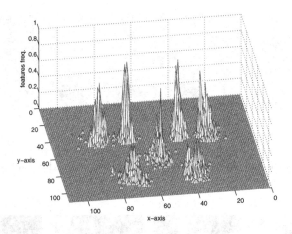

Fig. 1. 3-D distribution of 7 facial feature points over 400 Viola-Jones size-normalized faces (110x110 pixels)

size-normalized Viola-Jones detected faces. For each feature j a prior distribution B_j is used as *boost map* to filter Harris response:

1. reducing the number of corners outside the region of interested
2. increasing the number of corners inside the region of interested

Considering a training set of N face images of size $W \times L$ detected by VJFD, for each feature j the boost map B_j is given by:

$$B_j(x, y) = \frac{1}{N} \sum_{i=1}^{N} b_{ij}(x, y) \qquad (5)$$

where $1 \leq x \leq W$, $1 \leq y \leq L$ and

$$b_{ij}(x, y) = \begin{cases} 1 & if \ (X_{ij} = x) \, and \, (Y_{ij} = y) \\ 0 & otherwise \end{cases} \qquad (6)$$

Each point $B_j(x, y)$ represents the frequency with which observed features of coordinates (X_{ij}, Y_{ij}) fall in (x, y).

To reduce the dependence from training data, each B_j is approximated by a Thin Plate Spline (TPS) function [16]. Harris response R_H is then filtered using the corresponding *boost map* to obtain the feature-based corner detection.

$$R_j = B_j(x, y) R_H \qquad (7)$$

A feature point candidate $c_j(x, y)$ is finally detected as corner if $R_j(x, y)$ is an 8-way local maximum.

We refers at B_j as *boost map* since it boost the values in R_H according to the observed distribution of feature j. The values in B_j perturb the structure of R_H so that Harris thresholding produce a finer corner detection on interest region

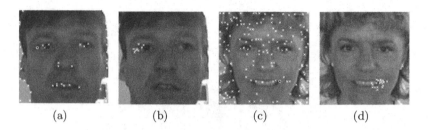

(a)   (b)   (c)   (d)

Fig. 2. Harris corner detection (a) and (c) compared with boost map-based facial feature detection (b) and (d). Detected corners are marked with x while a circle denotes the true feature position.

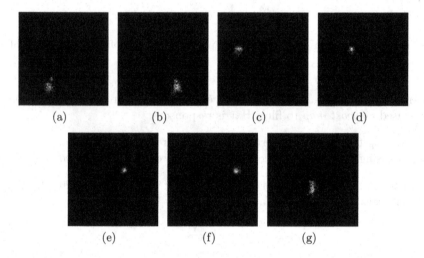

Fig. 3. Boost maps for right (a) and left (b) corners of the mouth, external (c-f) and internal (d-e) corners of the left and right eye, tip of the nose (g)

while discarding other values. TPS approximation allows to generalize training data while preserving the characteristics of the observed distributions. For this reason experimental results are very promising even using different training and test datasets.

4   Experimental Tests and Results

To enable detailed testing and *boost map* building we used two datasets manually annotated by Tim Cootes' staff [17]. In order to detect feature position for face normalization, 7 feature points have been selected from the 22 facial features available from the AR and BioID face database annotation. Face detection on both AR (359 labelled images) and BioID (1412 labelled images) datasets has been performed and 7 *boost maps* (Fig. 3) have been computed observing the position of the corners of the left and right eyes, corners of the mouth, and the tip of the nose on a 400 images subset.

To validate our method, several tests were conducted on the 1771 faces detected by VJFD. Our goal is to obtain feature candidates as close as possible to true feature point, so that for each feature we computed the corrispondent *boost map*-filtered Harris response. We then compared the known position of each feature with the nearest corner detected by Harris and proposed detector. Three test sessions have been run using different couples of training and test data:

- Test A: 359 images from AR database to build the *boost map* and 1412 BioID images as test set,
- Test B: 400 images from BioID database to build the *boost map* and the remaining 1012 images as test set,
- Test C: 400 images from BioID database to build the *boost map* and 359 AR images as test set.

Results of Test A, B and C are shown in Table 1, Table 2 and Table 3 respectively. Each column contains the number of images in which detected corners falls at distance m from the true feature position using Harris (H_m) and proposed *boost map*-based detector (B_m). We tested for distance $m = 0, 0 < m \leq 1, 1 < m \leq 2, 2 < m \leq 3, m > 3$, evaluating the ratio B/H for each m.

Each row contains results for the right (R) and left (L) corners of the mouth (mR,mL), external (E) and internal (I) corners of the left and right eyes(eER, eIR, eIL, eIR) and tip of the nose (n).

Positive ratio ($B/H > 1$) is obtained for $0 < m \leq 2$, that is the proposed approach performs better than Harris detector finding more corners in the radius of 2 pixels from the considered feature point.

Table 1. Test A - AR training (359 images) and BioID testing (1412 images). Results for Harris (H) and proposed approach (B) using 7 feature points.

	H_0	B_0	B/H	H_1	B_1	B/H	H_2	B_2	B/H	H_3	B_3	B/H	H_n	B_n	B/H
mR	62	168	2,71	813	804	0,99	466	421	0,90	60	18	0,30	11	1	0,09
mL	157	144	0,92	716	783	1,09	479	482	1,01	46	3	0,07	14	0	0
eER	29	127	4,38	77	286	3,71	413	755	1,83	468	216	0,46	425	28	0,07
eIR	47	83	1,77	109	228	2,09	493	707	1,43	382	364	0,95	381	30	0,08
eIL	18	117	6,50	63	210	3,33	366	673	1,84	482	261	0,54	483	151	0,31
eEL	27	92	3,41	130	269	2,07	641	719	1,12	390	268	0,69	224	64	0,29
n	9	71	7,89	143	259	1,81	374	711	1,90	349	230	0,66	537	141	0,26

Previous tests indicate system performance referring to the number of images in which a corner is found at distance m from the true feature position, while Fig. 4 shows previous values normalized to the number of corners detected by Harris (N_H) and proposed (N_B) method for each test set.

Experimental results showed that our *boost map*-based facial feature detector performs generally better than general purpose Harris corner detector. Even using different training and test data results are stable showing that each *boost map* attains an adequate level of generalization apart from used training data.

Table 2. Test B - BioID training (400 images) and BioID testing (1012 images). Results for Harris (H) and proposed approach (B) using 7 feature points.

	H_0	B_0	B/H	H_1	B_1	B/H	H_2	B_2	B/H	H_3	B_3	B/H	H_n	B_n	B/H
mR	88	194	2,20	618	550	0,89	274	262	0,96	28	6	0,21	3	0	0
mL	141	201	1,42	535	632	1,18	307	177	0,58	26	2	0,09	3	0	0
eER	37	129	3,50	82	199	2,43	338	500	1,48	323	150	0,47	232	33	0,14
eIR	49	103	2,11	120	183	1,52	369	481	1,30	243	198	0,82	232	47	0,20
eIL	31	115	3,67	83	172	2,08	274	509	1,86	328	190	0,58	297	26	0,09
eEL	16	134	8,38	115	177	1,54	421	553	1,31	287	139	0,48	173	9	0,05
n	2	106	45,29	94	228	2,42	300	574	1,92	174	90	0,52	442	14	0,03

Table 3. Test C - BioID training (400 images) and AR testing (359 images). Results for Harris (H) and proposed approach (B) using 7 feature points.

	H_0	B_0	B/H	H_1	B_1	B/H	H_2	B_2	B/H	H_3	B_3	B/H	H_n	B_n	B/H
mR	21	33	1,57	201	207	1,03	121	100	0,83	12	7	0,58	4	12	3,00
mL	20	37	1,85	206	188	0,91	122	129	1,06	7	4	0,57	4	1	0,25
eER	23	28	1,22	27	65	2,41	78	204	2,62	57	48	0,84	174	14	0,08
eIR	4	13	3,25	8	26	3,25	23	109	4,74	84	165	1,96	240	46	0,19
eIL	2	6	3,00	12	26	2,17	31	108	3,48	99	136	1,37	215	83	0,39
eEL	18	37	2,06	34	72	2,12	140	184	1,31	51	53	1,04	116	13	0,11
n	22	39	1,77	89	96	1,08	170	198	1,16	54	26	0,48	24	0	0

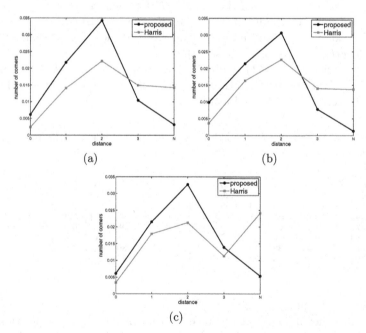

Fig. 4. Results for Harris and proposed approach normalizing to average number of corners detected for each image.(a) Test A: $N_H = 145796$, $N_B = 130375$. (b) Test B: $N_H = 100636$, $N_B = 99655$. (c) Test C: $N_H = 32194$, $N_B = 31563$.

Harris method detects more corners than proposed approach, moreover Harris corners are distributed over full image area while we detect corners just in features region as shown in Fig. 2. Thus, boost maps improve the SVMs point classification both reducing the number of points to be tested and increasing the quality/importance of those points.

Each face image is fully processed (i.e., detected, analyzed, recognized) in about 3 seconds using Matlab on a conventional 2,4 GHz Intel Pentium 4, however it does not represent a limit to the efficiency of Viola-Jones approach, since *face detection* is conceptually distinct from other face processing steps. Face detection aims to find the image position of a single face so it is anyway the first, necessary, step in any automated face processing system. The efficiency of Viola-Jones technique is required to quickly detect a face while discarding other regions, however detected faces need to be processed again to perform subsequent tasks, e.g., face recognition, face tracking, face modelling and so on. Thus, even if the proposed technique is not suitable for a real-time system, the computational cost is not prohibitive for online image analysis (e.g. image annotation, classification, recognition, etc.).

5   Conclusions

In this work was addressed the task of detecting facial featuers to normalize detected faces and perform face recogniton. We presented a novel facial feature extraction approach that could be used for normalizing Viola-Jones detected faces noticing that rectangle features creates some structure on features position over the detected faces. For each observed feature a prior distribution has been computed and used as *boost map* to filter the Harris corner detector response producing a finer corner detection on interest region while discarding external values. Experimental results are very promising using both AR and BioID face database. Further consideration could be done testing the proposed approach on natural images (i.e., personal photo album), however ground truth is needed and no more labelled datasets are currently available. This will be subject of future work.

References

1. Viola, P., Jones, M.: Rapid object detection using a boosted cascade of simple features. In: Proceedings of the 2001 IEEE Computer Society Conference on Computer Vision and Pattern Recognition, 2001. CVPR 2001, vol. 1, pp. 1:I–511–I–518 (2001)
2. Turk, M., Pentland, A.: Eigenfaces for recognition. Journal of Cognitive Neuroscience 3(1), 71–86 (1991)
3. Zhao, W., Chellappa, R., Phillips, P.J., Rosenfeld, A.: Face recognition: A literature survey. ACM Comput. Surv. 35(4), 399–458 (2003)
4. Samal, A., Iyengar, P.A.: Automatic recognition and analysis of human faces and facial expressions: a survey. Pattern Recogn. 25(1), 65–77 (1992)

5. Yang, M.-H., Kriegman, D.J., Ahuja, N.: Detecting faces in images: a survey. IEEE Transactions on Pattern Analysis and Machine Intelligence 24(1), 34–58 (2002)
6. Freund, Y., Schapire, R.E.: A decision-theoretic generalization of on-line learning and an application to boosting. In: Vitányi, P.M.B. (ed.) EuroCOLT 1995. LNCS, vol. 904, pp. 23–37. Springer, Heidelberg (1995)
7. Yuille, A.L., Cohen, D.S., Hallinan, P.W.: Feature extraction from faces using deformable templates. In: IEEE Computer Society Conference on Computer Vision and Pattern Recognition, 1989. Proceedings CVPR 1989, June 1989, pp. 104–109 (1989)
8. Cootes, T.F., Taylor, C.J., Cooper, D.H., Graham, J.: Active shape models—their training and application. Comput. Vis. Image Underst. 61(1), 38–59 (1995)
9. Kass, M., Witkin, A., Terzopoulos, D.: Snakes: Active contour models. International Journal of Computer Vision 1(4), 321–331 (1988)
10. Cootes, T.F., Edwards, G.J., Taylor, C.J.: Active appearance models. In: Burkhardt, H., Neumann, B. (eds.) ECCV 1998. LNCS, vol. 1407, pp. 484–498. Springer, Heidelberg (1998)
11. Berg, T.L., Berg, A.C., Edwards, J., Maire, M., White, R.: Names and faces in the news. In: Proceedings of the 2004 IEEE Computer Society Conference on Computer Vision and Pattern Recognition, 2004. CVPR 2004, vol. 2, pp. II–848–II–854 (2004)
12. Berg, A.C., Malik, J.: Geometric blur for template matching. In: Proceedings of the 2001 IEEE Computer Society Conference on Computer Vision and Pattern Recognition. CVPR 2001, vol. 1, pp. 1:I–607–I–614 (2001)
13. Harris, C., Stephens, M.: A combined corner and edge detection. In: Proceedings of The Fourth Alvey Vision Conference, pp. 147–151 (1988)
14. Schmid, C., Mohr, R., Bauckhage, C.: Evaluation of interest point detectors. International Journal of Computer Vision 37(2), 151–172 (2000)
15. Derpanis, K.G.: The harris corner detector (2004)
16. Duchon, J.: Spline minimizing rotation-invariant semi-norms on sobolev spaces. Lecture Notes in Math., vol. 571, pp. 85–100 (1977)
17. Cootes, T.F.:
http://personalpages.manchester.ac.uk/staff/timothy.f.cootes/

License Plate Detection and Character Recognition

Fabio Caccia, Roberto Marmo, and Luca Lombardi

Dip. Informatica e sistemistica, University of Pavia, Italy
marmo@vision.unipv.it
http://vision.unipv.it

Abstract. In this paper we describe an approach based on infrared camera and novel methods about how to detect license plates on rear-side of a vehicle in still image or video stream. Particular contribution is posed on discovering plate area by edge search on each side of plate and reconstruction of rectangular shape. The recognized plate area is rotated and adjusted for a better character separation. Top hat morphological operator is used to extract characters from plate background. Each single character inside plate area is separated even in case of tilted shape. This approach try to slice the plate vertically, and it follow the character profile that hit on his vertical path. Pattern matching based on modified Yule dissimilarity measure is used for character recognition. Performance on 200 images are discussed.

1 Introduction

License plate recognition regards completely automated system that can recognize the vehicle automatically. Without any added device installed inside the authorized car, we want to make possible to recognize each vehicle by reading automatically his plate. Numerous techniques have been developed in still images or video sequences, the purpose of survey paper [14] is to categorize and assess them. Issues such as processing time, computational power and recognition rate are also addressed. Even if the luminance conditions are optimal, problems exist about tilted character, rotated plates and different plate position on real images depending by car position and vehicle model.

2 Noise Removal

Software for character recognition must be able to elaborate images with different sort of noises due to low quality camera, environmental conditions, light levels too low or too high, dirty objects. Another problem regards the ground area that usually is unknown in outdoor scenes [11,3]. We adopt a fixed camera looking at a restricted region of interest with an unknown background: a tree with floating leafs, a street with people, a wall, etc. We cannot cut away the ground of image and get focus only on the car with simple comparison of two

P. Foggia, C. Sansone, and M. Vento (Eds.): ICIAP 2009, LNCS 5716, pp. 471–480, 2009.

frames and motion based segmentation. Many solutions has been found based on a smart segmentation of the image by supposing that plate is placed in the bottom centre of image, and using fuzzy logic to discover the white area with black character inside [13,12]. Other solutions are based on color base retrieval information as ground plate or character color, high contrast contours and areas filled with the same color [9], this approach consists to locate the car plate finding the edges. Acquisition noise is not considered due to high quality camera.

To reduce the price of camera we adopt an interpolated model, that acquires the frame with two scan of real scene: the first read the odd lines, the second the others. This acquisition must be corrected, otherwise is not unusable. Some solutions has been proposed when the image is corrupted and nothing more can be done to the source acquisition [15] but we can modify directly the original image because between odd and even lines there are not blur modifications. There is a visible difference between the two interpolated scans, so we discard an acquisition (the odd ones) ad copy twice each other line like stretching vertically the image. Our approach is not related on moving camera, so it is possible do not consider problems about line interpolation. Different light intensity are considered as a noise because the same plate seems to be different if acquired at 8.00 am or at 20.00 pm, and the software must recognize in the same way. This problem has been solved using: HSB color scheme, infrared camera, shape contours. Using an image codification like HSB we have three channel calculated from the RGB color scheme [5] because less sensible to light brightness. This solution was unused because we use infrared cameras that resolved the problem of varying illumination by hardware. This method emerged from the retroreflective material (this material returns the light back to the source and thus improves the contrast of the image) of plate surface and has already been tested [14] achieving a detection rate of 99.3% also in several commercial systems. An infrared hardware light up only the plate and make his contrast highest with the rest of the figure. This solution was good except the problem of lamp power consumption inside illumination unit. To ensure the correct illumination of the plate we had to keep on the lamp all the day and all the night. Using a second motion detector software that check if something is moving we switch on or off the lamp during the day, so the power consumption is lower. When the area is empty (nothing is moving), the lamp is switched off. During the night it is necessary to keep on the lamp or use magnetic sensors (generally, non optical sensors) that find the car passages and switch on the lamp. The camera are placed near the road in car park as restricted area. Since infrared light does not contain any of the colors visible to our vision system, the image acquired by camera is monochromatic.

3   Plate Detection

Now we extract the image area corresponding to a plate, even in case of different inclination or vehicle color. We convert the RGB scheme in YUV scheme and work on the Y (luminance) layer (U and V are used for color and saturation values, similarly to HSB). Using a threshold we obtain a monochromatic image of all shapes (Fig. 1) where white areas could contain the plate. Not all plates are well acquired and the algorithm try to restore the corrupted areas by filling empty black areas between edge white zones if there are more than 6/8 of white edge neighbors around the empty pixel group. These threshold has been estimated experimentally.

Fig. 1. Infrared image (left) and white areas detected by edge detection (right)

This approach need to distinguish the four corners plate and we adopt Sobel edge detector [5]. Horizontal and vertical masks have the same function, so we just describe the procedure for the horizontal one. First, the mask is convoluted on image and return a value positive or negative that represent the weighted distance between the pixel luminance under the area of the mask. This value is positive for areas that start from a dark color to a whitest color, and negative in other case, the absolute value of result is the contrast of pixel. Keeping the sign of the Sobel extraction we can distinguish the left side of the plate, from black to white is positive, and the right side, from white to black is negative. Similar for top and bottom side of the plate with the vertical mask. To make the contours less bold, skeletonization can create thinner segments without break their continuity. This algorithm can distinguish four different contours of the plate and any other rectangular object in the picture. Therefore, it is necessary to analyze inside each object.

4   Plate Recognition

We adopt the Italian plate that is a rectangular area with some specific geometric features. The height is more or less 1/4 of the weight and the longer side is the horizontal one, and these features are independent from the rotation of the plate. Contours are now covered with parts of borders and the omnipresent noise due to imperfection of the acquired image. Too many objects on image make more difficult to localize the real plate. We discard all small segment and all ambiguous elements. Usefulinformation about each single segment on image are stored in table: length, X and Y coordinates of the two vertex for each segment, inclination in degrees. Analyzing the table it is possible to detect segments with vertex coordinates near another segment in order to link them together, so lengths of the two segments are added together and a new segment take the place of them that are removed from table. Two segments are considered potentially near if there are no more than a small percentage of blank background in the gap between them. This threshold is based on length of two segments. When all segment near and similar has been linked and all others too small are discarded, we overlap the original contours on image using thin borders, obtaining an image with useful edges.

The analysis is now combined with table and obtained image of contours. Searching edges inclination, position and length in table, we can suppose that a particular area is a plate instead a mirror, a stripe or other rectangular objects. First, we find a left side (Fig. 2.A) corresponding to a vertical segment. If the segment is not composed by more than 10 pixels, we can suppose where could be the right side of the plate multiplying x4 the length of segment. In this supposed area we search a right side (Fig. 2.B). Now we return to image obtained from contours extraction and we check if there are enough pixels in top area (Fig. 2.C). If true, we search the same condition under top area and verify if there are enough pixels in the lower area (Fig. 2.D). These threshold has been estimated experimentally.

Fig. 2. Localization of segments around the plate and reconstruction of rectangular shape, from left side (A) to inferior side (D)

Now the plate is inside the region of interest located by: 4 vertex, inclination of horizontal and vertical sides. Plates of dark vehicles are easier to locate, because the distance between white and black area is more easy to localize, so segments are less fragmentized.

5   Plate Adjusting

Rotation of known angle is fundamental for pattern matching, in order to re-alignment of rows on image in case of rotated plate. Fig. 3 shows that after

Fig. 3. Leaned characters after plate rotation (left) and zoom on single character with little distortion (right), white line denotes the plate area and the angle of rotation

image rotation the characters are still leaned, due to half lines that we have acquired by interpolation problem. With only odd lines we discard 50% of vertical information and all objects are distorted.

Plate rotation is referred to center coordinates (X_0, Y_0) of plate rectangle, α is the inclination of horizontal side, (X_{IN}, Y_{IN}) coordinates of pixel by:

$$X_{IN} = (X_{OUT} - X_0)cos(-\alpha) - (Y_{OUT} - Y_0)sin(-\alpha) + X_0$$

$$Y_{IN} = (X_{OUT} - X_0)sin(-\alpha) - (Y_{OUT} - Y_0)sin(-\alpha) + Y_0$$

A pixel placed in (X_{OUT}, Y_{OUT}) originally blank is filled with the gray level in X_{IN}, Y_{IN}. Now we test the difference between horizontal and vertical inclination. In case of more or less 90 degrees, the vertical sides are not leaded, and that is correct. Otherwise, we have to adjust them (Fig. 4). Starting from the top of rotated plate, we shift on the rows by sh_x pixel and the angle value of adjusting is calculated by:

$$angRadV = 90 - abs(Horizontal\_side\_inclination - vertical\_side\_inclination)$$

$$sh\_x = abssin[(angRadV) * (y - Y_{IN})]$$

Two binary levels from the selected area are extracted: background (white) and symbol (black). Binarization algorithms needs a given value used for discrimination between two level of black and white [14]. This threshold changes in each image, so it is necessary a lot of test case. Our solution is the top hat morphological operator [5] applied to plate area, so we separate the inside characters from uniform background without a static threshold. The only value that we have to set up is the range of the mask, but experimentally there is not particular difference between results of bigger or smaller range of the masks. We delete noises on the top and the bottom of the plate by deleting horizontal black lines that are longer than 18 of plate width. Then we find the longer white lines

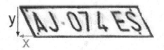

Fig. 4. Horizontal rows adjusted after left shift

Fig. 5. Noise removed around the characters (top), example of rotated plate and no noise on top and bottom of the characters after the cleaning (down)

on the top and the bottom of plate and delete the upper and lower side (Fig. 5). In some case we have vertical lines on left and right of plate area, we delete residual noise later.

6   Character Extraction

Now it is possible to separate characters by pattern matching [1,14]. Due to small percents of imperfection in the alignment algorithm and related inclination correction, it is not possible to separate character with an easy horizontal and vertical histogram projection [14].

We propose to correct all problems of sliced character and unaligned rows using "the falling pixel solution" due to his similitude to a small rock that fall from the top to the bottom and hit the characters on the way. This solution works fine on single line of characters on each plate, if we have two (or more) row of characters we must slice them in parts with only a character row each one. The assumption is that each character is a shape without interruption, character set like Chinese or Arabic need morphological operator [8,2,16,10,14]. In case of a string that are a bit tilted (Fig. 6), analyzing top-down the shape of plate we try to let fall a pixel. If the falling pixel locates an obstacle (black pixel) it change his direction to right, and try to fall again. If the falling is stopped, the method come back the falling pix to the top of shape and to left of previous starting point. In Fig. 6 character A is correctly sliced and in character X there are two attempts: the first ends in the V-hole of the character and does not slice it, the second one fall to the end, and the slice is correct. In case of a bad character extraction of L or J the algorithm can fail. Results good for plate acquired at a distance of 3 meters (9,84 feet) between the plate and the camera.

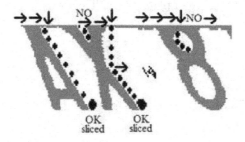

Fig. 6. Separation method based on falling pixel in unaligned characters (left) and output (right)

Fig. 7 shows shapes separation. The bottom one is a bit more unaligned than the top one, but the character separation works correctly looking at C and K symbols. Singles areas are recognized as uniform regions (character + ground) separated each others by a sort of wall due to falling pixel method. Looking at black and whites pixel inside the sliced areas we cam localize a character

Fig. 7. Failed acquisitions (top) and correct character separation (down), all these plates has been rotated and corrected. Gray box localizes a single character.

(40% black pixels) or discard a small black noise (less than 40% of black pixels). This algorithm can fail in case of acquisition is not good and the character is not closed. For example, the T letter could be sliced in a wrong way if the top part of the character is too thin. Fig. 7 shows some examples of good and bad acquisition after the falling pixel has sliced the characters.

7 Character Recognition

There are lots of methods about optical character recognition [4,14]. Our approach is based on comparison of acquired character to test set of Italian character that are was acquired apart. In case of similitude between a couple of character, probably they are the same shape and the output is the name of correspondent prototype. In order to match the character with a set of standard prototype characters using pattern matching, we align the acquired area to area of test set stretching the shape from original position to target position. If the target is larger than the original, some pixels must be copied more then one time (stretching), otherwise if the original is larger than the target some pixel must be ignored (compressing). This deformation step could modify the shape quality, therefore some areas of the acquired character could be ambiguous and the algorithm use a weight to calculate the precision of acquired sample character. Let a pixel on acquired character, b pixel on target position, A width of acquired character, B width of corresponding character in target set, the proportion is $a : A = b : B$ so $b = aB/A$ and similar approach is used for vertical reposition. The size of final character is 13 x 25 pixels. The character set is a text file obtained by the binarization of each character taken from plates. Fig. 8 shows the shape of a Z acquired: 0 corresponds to a single pixel of character, 1 corresponds to a single background pixel, 2 corresponds to no relevant pixel that can be considered as background or object and do not affect the character matching assuming different weight in next matching to avoid errors of matching between acquired character and prototype set [7] due to stretching and rotation step.

Each character of prototype set is labeled in same way. The distance measuring is often involved to match a known image with a set of unknown images and

Fig. 8. Labels on pixel describing the shape of the Z character: 0 is the bone of character, 1 is the background, 2 is ambiguous area

find out the most similar to the first one. The best way to return the most correct interpretation consists of checking correspondent pixels (black on black), correspondent ground pixels (white on white) and different pixels that does not have a match on image (black on white or vice versa). We adopt the Yule similarity measure [6] with changes about squared value for distance between responses and make sure that is not possible a division by zero:

$$D = ((N_{11} + N_{00})^2 - (N_{01} + N_{10})^2)/((N_{11} + N_{00})^2 + (N_{01} + N_{10})^2)$$

1. N_{00} = white on acquired image, white on test set: background match
2. N_{01} = white on acquired image, black on test set: no match
3. N_{10} = black on acquired image, white on test set: no match
4. N_{11} = black on acquired image, black on test set: object match

Pixels of prototype set marked as 2 are considered as a special pixel that increase N_{11} or N_{10}, but not affect value of N_{01} and N_{10}. In fact, black pixel on acquired image that match a label 2 on prototype set increases value of N_{11}, and a background white pixel on acquired image that match with label 2 on prototype set increases value of N_{10}. The shape contours may be different even in case of the character is the same, so this algorithm compare the acquired symbols to the entire set and return the most similar character.

8 Experimental Results

In case of shape not closed and has some breaks, falling pixel algorithm try to slice a symbol that is in effect unique. Test has been performed on 203 images of rear-side plates acquired from infrared camera placed at entry of car parking with different climatic factors like rain, fog and by night. Computing time is around

120 -500 milliseconds of execution on an AMD 64 bit (running on Ubuntu 6.4 x64) - 2.2 GHz. 200 plates has been found (99% of totality) and no false positive were found. About character extraction, there are some problems if the plate is too near or too far from the camera, it is possible to analyze a video stream and not a singular image. 50% of character are correctly found and the others are false positive. Vertical line on left and right sides of plates are often read like I or 1 characters. Sometime stretching the I and the 8 transform in shape similar to 1 and B.

9   Conclusions

In this paper we have presented an approach for the recognition of car license plates by infrared camera. The obtained results are satisfactory enough and make the system able to work efficiently in practice. This approach is suitable to localize and reading car plate area inside a larger image with any background and plate inclination less than 45 degrees or position. This strategy is only for car plates and not for scooters or other shape of plates different from the Italian standard car plate. For other shapes we change the proportion between width and height of the plate and the set of characters. Novel methods to recognize license concerns on discovering and adjusting the plate area, top hat morphological operator to extract characters, modified Yule dissimilarity measure for character recognition. In order to achieve best recognition it is possible to consider two solutions: give a weight to response and evaluate not only if a character is correct or not but if it is similar to it, to consider not only the most correspondent character by Yule measure but a set of first 3 characters that match with acquired symbol. A plate is now a fusion of all these set of candidates for each character of acquired plate and the number of false positive will decrease.

References

1. Barroso, J., Rafael, A., Dagless, E.L.: Number plate reading using computer vision. In: IEEE Intern. Symposium on Industrial Electronics, ISIE 1997 (1997)
2. Cowell, J., Hussain, F.: A fast recognition system fur isolated Arabic characters. In: Proc. Sixth International Conference on Infomotion and Visualisation, pp. 650–654. IEEE Computer Society, London (2002)
3. Uk, D., Hwan, Y.: Implementation of pre-processing independent of environment and recognition of car number plate using histogram and template matching. Journal of Korean Institute of Communication Sciences 23(1), 94–100 (1998)
4. Fujiyoshi, S.H., Umezaki, T., Imamura, T.: Area extraction of the license plate using artificial neural networks. Trans. Of the Institute of Electronics, Information and Communication Engineers D-11 JSOD-11, 1627–1634 (1997)
5. Gonzalez, R.C., Wood, R.E.: Digital Image Processing. Addison Wesley, Reading (1993)
6. Gower, J.C.: Metric and euclidean properties of dissimilarity coefficients. Journal of Classification 3, 5–48 (1986)

7. Hontani, H., Koga, T.: Character extraction method without prior knowledge on size and position information. In: Proc. IEEE Int. Conf. Vehicle Electronics, pp. 67–72 (2001)
8. Hsieh, J.-W., Yu, S.-H., Cben, Y.-S.: Morphology-based license plate detection from complex scenes. In: Proc. 16 International Conference on Pattern Recognition, vol. 3, pp. 176–179 (2002)
9. Kim, H.J., Kim, D.W., Lee, J.K.: Automatic Recognition of a Vehicle License Plate using Color Image Processing. Engineering Design and Automation Journal 3(1) (1997)
10. Lee, S.-H., Seok, Y.-S., Lee, E.-J.: Multi-National Integrated Car-License Plate Recognition System Using Geometrical Feature and Hybrid Pattern Vector. In: Conf. Circuits/Systems. Computers and Comm., Phuket, Thailand, pp. 1256–1259 (2002)
11. Naito, T., Tsukada, T., Yamada, K., Kozuka, K.: License plate recognition method for passing vehicles outside environment. In: Int. Conf. Quality Control by Articial Vision, pp. 86–93 (1998)
12. Nijhuis, J.A.G., Brugge, J.A.G.: Car license plate recognition with neural networks and fuzzy logic. In: Proc. Int. Conf. Neural Network, vol. 5, pp. 2232–2236 (1995)
13. Postolache, A., Trecat, J.: License Plate Segmentation Based on a coarse Texture Approach for Traffic Monitoring System. In: Proc. IEEE Benelux workshop on Circuits, Systems and Signal Processing, Mierlo, The Netherlands, pp. 243–250 (1995)
14. Psoroulas, D., Loumos, V., Anagnostopoulos, N., Anagnostopoulos, I.E.: License Plate Recognition From Still Images and Video Sequences: A Survey. IEEE Trans. Intelligent Transportation Systems 9(3), 377–391 (2008)
15. Sato, H., Ozawa, S., Komatsu, M., Kobayashi, A.: Motion blur correction of license plate images on running vehicle. Trans. IEE Japan 117-C(6), 777–784 (1997)
16. Yu, M., Kim, Y.: An approach to Korean license plate recognition based on vertical edge matching. In: IEEE Int. Conference on Systems, Man, Cybernerics, vol. 4, pp. 2975–2980 (2000)

Towards a Subject-Centered Analysis for Automated Video Surveillance

Michela Farenzena[1], Loris Bazzani[1],
Vittorio Murino[2], and Marco Cristani[2]

[1] Dipartimento di Informatica, Università di Verona, Italy
[2] IIT, Istituto Italiano di Tecnologia, Genova, Italy

Abstract. In a typical video surveillance framework, a single camera or a set of cameras monitor a scene in which human activities are carried out. In this paper, we propose a complementary framework where human activities can be analyzed under a subjective point of view. The idea is to represent the focus of attention of a person in the form of a 3D view frustum, and to insert it in a 3D representation of the scene. This leads to novel inferences and reasoning on the scene and the people acting in it. As a particular application of this proposed framework, we collect the information from the subjective view frusta in an Interest Map, i.e. a map that gathers in an effective and intuitive way which parts of the scene are observed more often in a defined time interval. The experimental results on standard benchmark data witness the goodness of the proposed framework, encouraging further efforts for the development of novel applications in the same direction.

1 Introduction

The visual focus of attention (VFOA) is a well-studied phenomenon in psychological literature, recently employed as strong social signal through which it is possible to robustly reckon social interest or the presence of an ongoing dialog. Social signaling aims to embed these psychological findings with computer science methods, in order to give robust insight about social activities (see [1] for a review). In this field, the use of the gaze direction as computational feature for the VFOA is widely accepted and tested. However, the main approaches in this area [2,3] focus mostly on meeting scenarios, in order to discover the addressee of a particular person, i.e. the subject one wants to address for a conversational exchange. Recently, Smith et al. [4] extend the VFOA problem to a wider scenario, estimating the gaze direction of people wondering freely in an outdoor scene. This paper goes in the same direction, widening the use of VFOA to the contest of automated video surveillance.

The main contribution of this paper is to translate the notion of VFOA into a feature that can be employed in a surveillance scenario. We claim that the three-dimensional (3D) space, not employed in [4], is the appropriate environment where to reason about this issue. Assuming that the monitoring camera is calibrated, we propose a novel feature, called *Subjective View Frustum* (SVF).

P. Foggia, C. Sansone, and M. Vento (Eds.): ICIAP 2009, LNCS 5716, pp. 481–489, 2009.

The SVF is an estimation of the view frustum of a single person. It is modeled as a 3D polyhedral whose volume represents the portion of the scene in which the subject is reasonably focused on. Having a rough 3D map of the scene being monitored, we consistently locate each person and its related SVF in the 3D space. Hence, we are able to satisfactorily analyze people attention in wide contexts, where several, overlapping people are present and in which the position of the video sensor does not permit a fully detailed acquisition of the human head.

More generally, the proposed framework provides a point of analysis that is different and complementary to the standard, third person point of view of a single camera or a set of cameras. This opens new perspectives on several interesting applications and inferences, in the direction of a subjects-centered understanding of human activities in surveillance contexts.

The second contribution of the paper is a visualization application of the proposed SFV-based framework, called the *Interest Map*. Since the part of the scene that intersects the SVF is the scene observed by the SVF's owner, we collect this information for each subject, over a given time interval. This permits to infer which are the parts of the scene that are more observed, thus more plausibly subjected to attention. The gathered information is visualized as a suitably colored map, in which hot colors represent the areas more frequently observed, vice versa for "cold" areas. This kind of inference is highly informative, at least for two reasons. The first one is diagnostics, in the sense that it gives us the possibility to observe which are the areas of a scene that arouse more attention in the people. The other one is prognostics, since it enables us to devise the parts of the scene that are naturally more seen, because for example they are the natural front of view in a narrow transit area, or for other reasons that this method cannot guess (the Interest Map only highlights the tangible effects). This application could be employed for a posteriori analysis. In a museum, for example, one may be interested in understanding which artworks receive more attention, or in a market which areas attract more the customers. In a prognostic sense it may be useful for marketing purposes, such as for example decide where to hang an advertisement.

A basic element of our scenario is a tracking module that is able to follow multiple objects, and deal with occlusions and overlapping people. It is based on the multi-object particle filtering platform proposed in [5] and it is described in Section 2. After that, Section 3 introduces the SVF model and explains how it is estimated. Section 4 describes how to build the Interest Map. Then we show the experimental results in Section 5 and we draw our conclusions in Section 6.

2   Hybrid Joint Separable Particle Filtering Tracker

The tracking module we employ is based on a particle filtering strategy. Particle filters offer a probabilistic framework for recursive dynamic state estimation. The approach was born originally for single-object tracking [6], then later it was extended to a multi-object tracking scenario [7]. Multi-object particle filters follow different strategies to achieve good tracking performances avoiding huge computational burdens. These are due primarily to the high number of particles required, which is (in general) exponential in the number of objects to track. Recently, an interesting yet general solution has been proposed by Lanz in [5]. He defined the Hybrid Joint-Separable (HJS) filter, that maintains a linear relationship between number of objects and particles.

The goal is to determine the posterior distribution $p(x_t|z_{1:t})$, where x_t is the current state, z_t is the current measurement, and $x_{1:t}$ and $z_{1:t}$ are respectively the states and the measurements up to time t. We refer to x_t as the state of single object, and $\mathbf{x}_t = \{x_t^1, x_t^2, \ldots, x_t^K\}$ the joint state (all objects). Finally, the posterior distribution $p(x_t|z_{1:t})$ is approximated by a set of N weighted particles, i.e. $\{(x_t^n, w_t^n)\}_{n=1}^N$.

The HJS approach represents a theoretical grounded compromise between dealing with a strictly joint process and instantiating a single, independent tracking filter for each distinct object. In practice, HJS alternates a separate modeling during the sampling step and a hybrid joint-separate formulation in the dynamical and observational steps.

The rule that permits the crossing over joint-separable treatments is based on the following approximation (see [5] for rigorous math details):

$$p(\mathbf{x}_t|z_{1:\tau}) \approx \prod_k p(x_t^k|z_{1:\tau}) \tag{1}$$

that is, the joint posterior could be approximated by the product of its marginal components. This assumption allows to sample the particles in the single state space (thus requiring a linear proportionality between number of object and number of samples), and to update the weights in the joint state space. The updating exploits a) a joint dynamical model that builds the distribution $p(\mathbf{x}_t|\mathbf{x}_{t-1})$, explaining how the system does evolve, and b) a joint observational model that provides estimates for the distribution $p(z_t|\mathbf{x}_t)$, explaining how the observations can be related to the state of the system. Both the models take into account the interactions among objects. In particular $p(\mathbf{x}_t|\mathbf{x}_{t-1})$ accounts for physical interactions between targets, thus avoiding track coalescence of spatially near targets.

The observational model $p(z_t|\mathbf{x}_t)$ quantifies the likelihood of the single measure z_t given the state $\mathbf{x}_t$, considering inter-objects occlusions. It is built upon the representation of the targets, that here are constrained to be human beings. The human body is represented by its three components: head, torso and legs. The observational model works by evaluating a separate appearance score for each object (summing then the contribute of the single parts). This score is encoded by a distance between the histograms of the model and the hypothesis (a sample), and it involves also a joint reasoning captured by an *occlusion map*. The occlusion map is a 2D projection of the 3D scene which focuses on the particular object under analysis, giving insight on what are the expected visible portions of that object. This is obtained by exploiting the hybrid particles set $\{x_p\}_{p=1}^{NK}$ in an incremental visit procedure on the ground floor. The hypothesis nearest to the camera is evaluated first. Its presence determines an occluding cone in the scene, with an associated confidence that depends on the observational likelihood achieved. Parts of other objects deeper in the scene that fall in the occlusion cone are considered less in their observational likelihood computation. The process of map building is iterated by going deeper in the scene.

In formulae, the observation model is defined as

$$p(z_t|x_p) \propto \exp\left(-\frac{fc_p + bc_p}{2\,\sigma^2}\right),$$
(2)

where fc_p is the foreground term, *i.e.*, the likelihood that an object matches to the model considering the unoccluded parts, and bc_p, the background term, accounts for the occluded parts of an object.

3 3D Modeling of the Subjective View Frustum

Once the tracks for one frame are available, the viewing direction of each tracked subject is derived and the information about the parts of the scene watched by him/her are suitably inserted in an accumulation matrix. This matrix will represent our Interest Map at the end of the computation. This reasoning goes by a sequence of 3D operations and the definition of the *Subjective View Frustum*, as detailed in the following.

3.1 3D Map Estimation

In this paper we suppose that the camera monitoring the area is fully calibrated, i.e. both internal parameters and camera position and orientation are known. For convenience, the world reference system is put on the ground floor, with the z-axis pointing upwards. This permits to obtain the 3D coordinates of a point in the image if the elevation from the ground floor is known. In fact, if P is the camera projection matrix and $\mathbf{M} = (M_x, M_y, M_z)$ the coordinates of a 3D point, the projection of $\mathbf{M}$ through P is given by two equations:

$$u = \frac{\mathbf{p}_1^{\mathsf{T}}\mathbf{M}}{\mathbf{p}_3^{\mathsf{T}}\mathbf{M}}, \quad v = \frac{\mathbf{p}_2^{\mathsf{T}}\mathbf{M}}{\mathbf{p}_3^{\mathsf{T}}\mathbf{M}}, \quad \text{with } P = \begin{bmatrix} \mathbf{p}_1^{\mathsf{T}} \\ \mathbf{p}_2^{\mathsf{T}} \\ \mathbf{p}_3^{\mathsf{T}} \end{bmatrix}.$$
(3)

(u, v) are the coordinates of the image point. Thus, knowing (u, v) and M_z it is possible to estimate the position of $\mathbf{M}$ in the 3D space.

A rough reconstruction of the area, made up of the principal planes present in the scene, can therefore be carried out. An example in shown in Figure 1. These planes represent the areas of the scene that are interesting to analyze. The Interest Map will be estimated on them only. In principle, a more detailed 3D map can be considered, if for example a CAD model of the scene is available or if a Structure-from-Motion (SfM) algorithm [8,9] is applied. In any case, this operation must be executed just once.

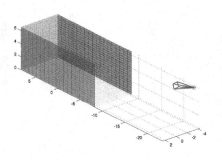

Fig. 1. 3D reconstruction of the area being monitored. On the left, the 3D map of the principal planes. The red cone represents the camera. On the right, the planes are projected through the camera and superimposed on one image.

3.2 Head Orientation Estimation

The tracking algorithm provides the position (x_{it}, y_{it}) of each person i present in the scene at a certain moment t. We need to calculate the head orientation in order to decide in which direction a person is looking. At the scale of a typical video surveillance scenario, tracking head direction is very difficult. Thus, are content with a rough estimator, that distinguishes among four possible directions (North, South, East, West) relative to the camera orientation.

In this paper we exploit the tracking information, i.e. the position of each person over the time. We calculate the angle between the motion direction and the camera orientation. The underlying assumption here is that the subject is looking in the direction towards which he/she is moving. This assumption is quite strong. It could be relaxed by employing a more sophisticated algorithm for head detection, such as [10], but it is beyond the purposes of this paper.

3.3 Subjective View Frustum

Once the view direction has been detected, a view frustum can be estimated. It represents the portion of 3D space seen by the subject. We call this portion *Subjective View Frustum* (SVF). Geometrically, we model the SVF as the polyhedron $\mathcal{D}$ depicted in Figure 2. It is composed by three planes that delimit the angle of view on the left, right and top sides, in such a way that the angle view is 60° horizontally and 120° vertically. If we take into account the maximum field of view of a human, the SVF should be much bigger (around 140° on both directions). However, we considered that the focus of attention, especially when a person is moving, reduces the actual field of view.

The 3D coordinates of the points corresponding to the head and the feet of a subject are obtained from the (x_{it}, y_{it}) coordinates given by the tracker, under the assumption that he/she walks on the ground floor and is 1.8 m tall.

The SVF $\mathcal{D}$ is computed precisely using Computational Geometry techniques. It can be written as the intersection of three negative half-spaces defined by

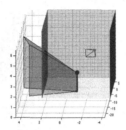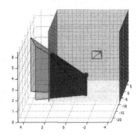

Fig. 2. SVF of the person detected in the frame on the left (blue square). At the center, a perspective view of the SVF (semi-transparent blue); on the right, the actual SVF inside the scene (solid blue).

their supporting planes respectively of the left, right and top side of the subject. Moreover, the SVF is also limited by the planes that set up the scene, according to the 3D map. The scene volume is similarly modeled as intersection of negative half-space. Thus, the exact SVF inside the scene can be computed solving a simple *vertex enumeration* problem, for which very efficient algorithms exists in literature [11].

4   Creation of the Interest Map

The SVF $\mathcal{D}$ represents the portion of 3D space seen by the subject. As mentioned before, we decided to concentrate our attention on the scene main planes only. A full volumetric reasoning could be tackled too, but this would capture other kinds of information, such as people interactions.

In order to record the SVF information, we project the SVF volume on each scene plane. This is equivalent to estimate the vertices of $\mathcal{D}$ lying on each plane, project these vertices on the image and select those pixels that lay inside the convex hull of the projected vertices. In this way the selected pixels can be inserted in an accumulation matrix, that is a 2D matrix of the same size of the camera frames. This also implies that the accumulation matrix is registered to the camera viewpoint. Two examples of this projection operation are shown in

Fig. 3. Two examples of projection of the SVF on the scene main planes. The 3D map permits to suitably model the interactions of the SVF with the scene.

Figure 3. The contributions provided by all tracked people in the whole sequence, or a set of sequences, are conveyed in the same accumulation matrix. This matrix, at the end of the observation time window, is our Interest Map.

5   Experimental Results

We perform some tests over the PETS 2007 sequence sets. This aims to show the expressiveness of our framework on widely known and used datasets. The sequences taken into account for the experiments are two. They both belong to the S07 dataset, in which an airport area is monitored. The first sequence is captured by Camera 2, the second one is captured by Camera 4.

Fig. 4. Some frames of the sequence from camera 2. The bounding boxes highlight the tracking results.

In Figure 4 we show some frames of the first sequence, with highlighted the tracking results. Totally, 1 minute of activity has been monitored, tracking continuously averagely 5 people at a time.

The resulting Interest Map is depicted in Figure 5, superimposed as transparency mask to an image of the scene. From this map interesting considerations can be assessed. The "hottest" area in the one closest to the camera, in the direction of the stairs on the left. Indeed in the sequence many people cross that area from right to left. Another interesting area is at the end of the corridor, while the entrance on the left end has never been watched. Indeed the other people detected throughout the sequence are on the right end, going north.

For the second sequence, captured by Camera 4, one minute is monitored, tracking averagely 4 people at a time. The SVF analysis produces the results shown in Figure 6. In this case the most seen area is the left end corner of the corridor. Indeed most of the people in the sequence give the back to the camera. The other "hot" area is the left front corner, due to a person loitering there most of the time interval considered. As a comparison we plot together (right picture of Figure 6) the tracking results. This representation is less meaningful from the point of view of people attention analysis. Our information visualization technique is instead intuitive and it captures in a very simple and richer way where people attention is focused.

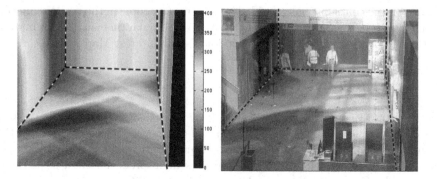

Fig. 5. On the left, the Interest Map for S07 sequence from camera 2. On the right, the same Interest Map superimposed on one frame of the sequence.

Fig. 6. On the left top, one frame of the second sequence, with highlighted the tracked people. On the right top, the Interest Map obtained. On the left bottom, the same Interest Map superimposed on one frame. On the right bottom, all the tracks estimated throughout the sequence displayed in the same frame.

6   Conclusions and Future Work

In this paper we proposed a complementary video surveillance framework focused on the subjective focus of attention. We showed that the 3D space is the appropriate environment for this issue: we model the view frustum of each person moving in the scene as a 3D polyhedral whose volume represents the portion of the scene in which the subject is reasonably focused on. As a particular application of this framework, we collect the focus of attention information in an Interest Map that gathers in an effective and intuitive way the information about the parts of the scene observed more in a defined time interval.

An interesting development toward a finer estimation of Interest Maps will be to employ a robust head pose estimator. Moreover, we plan to apply the SVF feature to investigate people interactions in wide areas.

Acknowledgements

This research is founded by the EU-Project FP7 SAMURAI, grant FP7-SEC-2007-01 No. 217899.

References

1. Gatica-Perez, D.: Automatic nonverbal analysis of social interaction in small groups: a review. Image and Vision Computing, Special Issue on Human Naturalistic Behavior (accepted for publication)
2. Jayagopi, D., Hung, H., Yeo, C., Gatica-Perez, D.: Modeling dominance in group conversations from nonverbal activity cues. IEEE Trans. on Audio, Speech, and Language Processing, Special Issue on Multimodal Processing for Speech-based Interactions 3(3) (2009)
3. Paul, C., Oswald, L.: Optimised meeting recording and annotation using real-time video analysis. In: Popescu-Belis, A., Stiefelhagen, R. (eds.) MLMI 2008. LNCS, vol. 5237, pp. 50–61. Springer, Heidelberg (2008)
4. Smith, K., Ba, S.O., Odobez, J.M., Gatica Perez, D.: Tracking the visual focus of attention for a varying number of wandering people. IEEE Transactions on Pattern Analysis and Machine Intelligence 30(7), 1–18 (2008)
5. Lanz, O.: Approximate bayesian multibody tracking. IEEE Transactions on Pattern Analysis and Machine Intelligence 28(9), 1436–1449 (2006)
6. Isard, M., Blake, A.: Condensation: Conditional density propagation for visual tracking. Int. J. of Computer Vision 29, 5–28 (1998)
7. Isard, M., MacCormick, J.: Bramble: A bayesian multiple-blob tracker (2001)
8. Snavely, N., Seitz, S.M., Szeliski, R.: Photo tourism: exploring photo collections in 3D. In: SIGGRAPH Conference Proceedings, NY, USA, pp. 835–846 (2006)
9. Farenzena, M., Fusiello, A., Gherardi, R., Toldo, R.: Towards unsupervised reconstruction of architectural models. In: Proceedings of Vision, Modeling, and Visualization 2008, pp. 41–50 (2008)
10. Stiefelhagen, R., Finke, M., Yang, J., Waibel, A.: From gaze to focus of attention. In: Huijsmans, D.P., Smeulders, A.W.M. (eds.) VISUAL 1999. LNCS, vol. 1614, pp. 761–768. Springer, Heidelberg (1999)
11. Preparata, F.P., Shamos, M.I.: Computational Geometry. An Introduction

Geometric-Aligned Cancelable Fingerprint Templates

Bian Yang[1], Christoph Busch[1], Mohammad Derawi[2], Patrick Bours[1],
and Davrondzhon Gafurov[1]

[1] Norwegian Information Security Laboratory at Gjøvik University College,
Teknologivegen 22, N-2815, Gjøvik, Norway
[2] Informatics and Mathematical Modelling at Technical University of Denmark,
DK-2800 Kongens Lyngby, Denmark
{bian.yang,christoph.busch,patrick.bours,
davrondzhon.gafurov}@hig.no

Abstract. A minutiae encryption algorithm based on geometric transformation of minutiae positions is proposed to generate cancelable fingerprint templates. A geometric transformation is used for alignment. A parameter-controlled minutiae encryption is performed within a local area to generate a cancelable minutiae template, and then all local encryption results are superimposed to form a protected template. Parameters to control the minutiae encryption are generated independent of the geometric-aligned minutiae, which ensures solid non-invertibility compared to those cancelable template generating algorithms with to-be-encrypted minutiae information as parameters.

Keywords: template protection, cancelable fingerprint template, fingerprint alignment, coordinate encryption.

1 Introduction

Biometric recognition is increasingly used as a strong security measure for authentication with the assumption that biometric characteristics are unique to a subject and cannot be forwarded to another individual. Thus a bypass of an existing security policy – that frequently happens with token or knowledge based authentication systems – can be avoided. However, from the view of data security and privacy, biometric templates are under potential compromise and therefore need careful protection, because biometric characteristics usually cannot be updated like normal passwords or PIN codes. Direct encryption of a biometric template by standard encryption algorithms (DES, AES, etc) is infeasible because the encrypted template needs decryption to invert to its plain-text for comparison. This happens during every verification process and is insecure, as full access to samples or unprotected biometric features are given to the potentially untrusted entity that conducts the comparison. It is better to run the comparison process in an encrypted domain to avoid decryption. However, standard encryption algorithms tolerate no fuzzy distortions inherent with biometric probes. Therefore, biometric template protection [1-19] was proposed, among which fingerprint template protection algorithms are intensively investigated [2,4-6,8-9, 13-15]. In general, there are three approaches to fingerprint template protection: the

P. Foggia, C. Sansone, and M. Vento (Eds.): ICIAP 2009, LNCS 5716, pp. 490–499, 2009.
© Springer-Verlag Berlin Heidelberg 2009

first approach directly extracts lumination features from fingerprint raster images by image processing techniques [4-5]; the second approach complements the minutiae with additional biometric features (such as ridge context) [6,16] to enhance biometric performance or security; and the third approach [2,9,13-15] aims at protecting plain-text minutiae templates that are already generated conforming to ANSI or ISO standards. A serious security leakage [12] was found in the fuzzy vault [2]. Although fuzzy extractor [13] and secure sketch [14] can alleviate this problem, they sacrifice comparison performance in some degree. Biotokens proposed in [17] exhibits good performance by exploiting enlarged feature space with large template size.

Cancelable fingerprint templates [9] was proposed to distort minutiae data in a non-invertible way which generates diversified protected templates via setting transformation parameters. As the protection mechanism is non-invertible, there is no way to launch the key-inversion attack [12] on the protected template. Furthermore, the generated cancelable fingerprint templates are compliant in format to the original minutiae template, making the state-of-art minutiae comparators applicable.

However, cancelable fingerprint templates [9] assume that all minutiae data (position and angle) are pre-aligned. Automatic pre-alignment such as core detection works well for a majority of samples, however a failure-to-align rate of approximately 10% is not unlikely to occur [20]. This will subject the comparison performance to the pre-alignment accuracy. Regarding non-invertiblity, the transformation parameters used in [9] depend on the to-be-transformed minutiae data themselves, which will decrease the number of unknown factors, and thus brute-force searching to generate the same cancelable template will be more likely to succeed.

In this paper, we analyze the non-invertible transformation parameter setting issues in section 2. To tackle the alignment and parameter setting problems of the algorithm in [9], we propose in section 3 our solution with geometric alignment and strong non-invertibility even under the assumption that the transformation parameter set is public.

2 Parameter Setting for Non-invertible Transformation

In [9], a protected template can be easily canceled and renewed by setting different parameters. Cancelable templates by non-invertible transformation can provide solid computational complexity against template inversion by keeping the transformation parameters secret and coordinates' perturbation large enough. But the surface functions used in [9] to scramble the coordinates and angles significantly depend on those to-be-transformed coordinates themselves. This has two limitations:

(1) Comparison performance degradation - because the to-be-transformed coordinates and angles themselves have inherent minor distortion, taking these fuzzy-distorted minutiae data as transformation parameters will cause potential comparison performance degradation. In this sense, it is better to use transformation parameters independent of the minutiae data themselves to avoid distortion amplification;

(2) Security against template inversion - although surface folding in [9] can increase overlapped positions by increasing the coordinates' perturbation or times of transformation, it is easy to find an original point as single solution in a coordinate space for some transformed points (x,y), i.e., overlapped positions cannot cover the

full original minutiae space even after multiple non-invertible transformation. If the parameters are compromised or required to be public, the transformed points with single solution can be identified. If the number of such single-solution points exceeds a threshold, the original minutiae template is compromised. Two methods can be used to strengthen the non-invertibility: a.) superimposition of minutiae points in new co-ordinate systems (as in Section 3.3), which ensures the solution number roughly equal to superimposition layers; b.) employment of independent transformation parameters, which increases unknown factors other than to-be-encrypted coordinates themselves to increase the solution number (as in Section 3.2). These two methods will roughly ensure that each transformed point will have multiple original points as solutions. This is a stronger non-invertibility compared to the surface folding function in [9]. Although the transformation parameters should be independent of the to-be-transformed minutiae, they are not necessarily to be secret keys stored independently.

3 Proposed Algorithm to Generate Geometric-Aligned Cancelable Fingerprint Template

We propose a geometric-aligned minutiae template protection algorithm as shown in Fig.1, where T and PT are the original unprotected minutiae template and the protected template respectively. S is the randomly bit stream generated from a pseudo-random number generator (PRNG), which is used to form the random quantization table QT containing $(N+1)$ quantization bins divided by N scales in a distance range $[0, D]$ (assuming D > largest distance between a minutia point position and the core[1] point in the original template). $\{m_a\}$ are geometric-aligned minutiae points set within the R-radial local disk area centering each original minutia point. Decided by the distance d_c between each original minutia point and the core point, a quantized index d_k and the corresponding coordinate offset (dx_k, dy_k) are selected to modify all

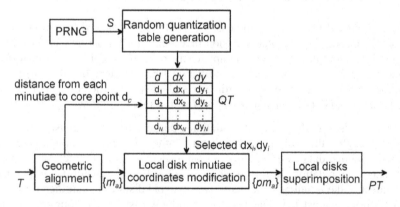

Fig. 1. Diagram of proposed minutiae template protection algorithm

---

[1] Core – singular point in the fingerprint, where the curvature of ridges reaches a maximum (according to ISO 19794-8).

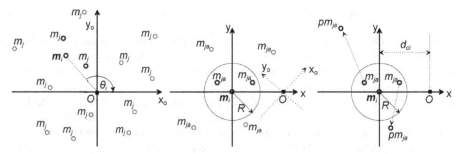

(a) Original minutiae template   (b) Geometric alignment to (c) Coordinates modification
                                  each minutia point m_i from m_{ja} to pm_{ja} as function of d_{ci}

Fig. 2. Geometric alignment and inside-disk-area minutiae coordinates' modification

minutiae coordinates within the local disk area. $\{pm_a\}$ are modified minutiae points set. After superimposition of all protected local disks, PT is obtained as the final protected template. We detail the whole process in Fig.1.

3.1 Geometric Alignment

Alignment is usually required for fingerprint template for both raster image [4] and minutiae coordinates [9]. Position and orientation of a core point can be detected as a reference point for alignment. However, the accuracy of core point detection remains to be a challenge, especially for the cases where multiple cores are found (e.g. twin loop fingerprint patterns). In such cases, we always choose the uppermost core as the reference point in our proposed algorithm. Another unstable factor is the core point's orientation, whose precision is differently defined by various standards and applications, such as $360°/256$ in ISO [21] and $360°/32$ in ANSI/NIST compatible software [22]. Unlike directly using core orientation in [4,9], we take only the position of a core as the reference for translation alignment of minutiae points but omit the detected orientation. Assuming there are totally M minutiae in the original template, each minutia $m_i(i=1,2,...,M)$ is set to be the new origin, and the line leading to the old origin O from m_i is set to be the new x-axis, and all other minutiae $m_j(i=1,2,...,M, j \neq i)$ can be correspondingly translation-and-rotation aligned to the new origin. Denote these $(M-1)$ geometric-aligned minutiae points as $\{m_{ai}\}(i=1,2,..,M-1)$, shown in Fig.2(a), where x_0-O-y_0 represents the old coordinate system. The alignment of $m_j(i=1,2,...,M, j \neq i)$ can be

$$\begin{bmatrix} m_{ja}(x) \\ m_{ja}(y) \end{bmatrix} = \begin{bmatrix} \cos(\theta_i - \pi) & \sin(\theta_i - \pi) \\ -\sin(\theta_i - \pi) & \cos(\theta_i - \pi) \end{bmatrix} \cdot \begin{bmatrix} m_j(x) - m_i(x) \\ m_j(y) - m_i(y) \end{bmatrix} \quad (1)$$

where $j=1,2,...,M$ but $j \neq i$, and $\angle m_i O x_0$ representing the angle decided by m_i's position in the old coordinate system x_0-O-y_0.

3.2 Minutiae Coordinates Random Modification in the Local Disk Area

After the minutiae points m_j(j=1,2,...,M, $j \neq i$) geometric alignment to the minutia point m_i, some scrambling effect has already been achieved to hide the original positions of m_j in the original template. Due to this alignment operation to every minutia point m_i(i=1,2,...,M) we can obtain M sets of aligned minutiae points $\{m_a\}_i$ (i=1,2,...,M). An intuitive idea can be to superimpose all the M sets $\{m_a\}_i$ (i=1,2,...,M) to form the final protected template, which is obviously a globally aligned version of the original template. However, this will dramatically increase the number of minutiae from M points in the original template to $M(M$-1) points in the protected template. Assuming averagely 30~50 minutiae points in one original template, the number reaches 870~2450 in the protected template. If we assume at least Q minutiae points out of the total P minutiae points in the $H \times W$ sized template need to match their mates for a successful comparison, the probability of success for a brute-force search attack is $\binom{P}{Q} \Big/ \binom{H \cdot W}{Q}$. Therefore a high density of resulting points (large value Q) definitely impacts a high probability for a false-match incident. In addition, a high number of resulting points will decrease the efficiency for compact template storage and also weakens the computational efficiency as the number of operational steps in minutiae template comparison increases. In order to reduce the total point number in the protected template, a local disk area with radius R can be defined to mask out those remote minutiae points (all m_{ja} with distance from m_i larger than R as shown in Fig.2.) and keep in the final protected template only those minutiae point inside the R-disk centering m_i.

Obviously, the kept minutiae points m_{ja} convey local topological information of the original template while the global topological information (local disks' orientation and distance to the old origin O) has been removed and thus secured by the previous geometric alignment step. To further secure the local topological relationship among the kept m_{ja} inside each local disk, the coordinates of all m_{ja} should be encrypted. For better comparison performance and stronger non-invertibility (as discussed in Section 2), we perturb m_{ja}'s coordinates by adding a random offset distance dx_k and dy_k (k=1,2,...,N) to x- and y- coordinates of m_{ja} respectively, where dx_k and dy_k are decided by quantizing the distance d_{ci} (between m_i, the center of ith local disk, and O, the old origin, shown in Fig.2) with a pre-generated random quantization table QT consisting of N distance values: $d_1, d_1, ..., d_N$, where N is a pre-set parameter. For each m_{ja} inside the ith local disk, the coordinates' perturbation can be formulated as

$$\begin{cases} pm_{ja}(x) = m_{ja}(x) + dx_K \\ pm_{ja}(y) = m_{ja}(y) + dy_K \end{cases} \tag{2}$$

where dx_K and dy_K are randomly generated offset values stored as the indexed content by the Kth item d_K in QT (shown in Fig.1) and K is decided by

$$K = \arg\min_k |d_k - QT(d_{ci})| \quad (k = 1,2,...,N) \tag{3}$$

Unlike directly using minutiae points coordinates as function parameters to encrypt minutiae points themselves in [9], we use a translation and rotation invariant - the distance value d_{ci} as the parameter to control random offset values' selection for encryption of the kept points' coordinates inside the ith local disk. The dependency between parameters and transformation input in [9] will definitely narrow the brute-force searching space and help find those security-concerned single solutions quickly. While in our algorithm, because d_{ci} is the removed global topological information of the original template and therefore independent of the local topological relationship among the kept points in the local disk, the single-solution security problem discussed in Session 2 can be effectively alleviated.

3.3 Local Disks Superimposition

In the above steps, all the minutiae points inside one disk are geometrically aligned to remove the global information of the disk's position in the original template, and then perturbed in coordinates to encrypt the local information. Now we superimpose all the M local disks with their perturbed points to obtain the final protected template. We consider only encryption of minutiae points' coordinates but not their orientation values because of their instability as discussed in Session 3.1.

4 Experimental Results

The proposed algorithm was tested with the public fingerprint database FVC2002 DB2_A. This database contains totally 800 gray-level fingerprint images sized 560×296 collected from 100 fingers with 8 samples for each finger. VeriFinger 6.0 from Neurotechnology [23] was used to detect the uppermost core and all minutiae from fingerprint images. We manually adjusted a portion of detected cores with obvious large error in position, but these cases account for less than 10%. Minutiae points extracted from all the 800 images were processed by the proposed algorithm and then 800 protected templates were obtained. To test the comparison performance of the proposed algorithm, the former 7 out of the 8 protected templates for each finger were evaluated to choose the most reliable one as the final reference template, and the 8th sample of each finger was used as a probe. For selecting the most reliable template, firstly we calculated the sum of distances (Hausdorff distance used here) between the minutiae set in one template and the 6 minutiae sets in the other 6 templates, and secondly we found the two templates with minimum distance sum values, and finally we selected the one with more minutiae points out of the two as the final reliable template. In this way 100 protected reference templates and 100 protected probes were obtained. To compare with the unprotected case, we tested the Neurotechnology comparator (called VeriFinger 6.0 Matcher) with the same database in which the first sample of all the fingers was used as the reference template and the 8th samples as a probe. This generated performance results without template protection.

False-match-rate (FMR) and false-none-match-rate (FNMR) were employed to evaluate the biometric performance defined as follows

$$FMR = \frac{number\ of\ accepted\ imposter\ attempts}{total\ number\ of\ imposter\ attempts} \tag{4}$$

$$FNMR = \frac{number\ of\ rejected\ genuine\ attempts}{total\ number\ of\ genuine\ attempts} \tag{5}$$

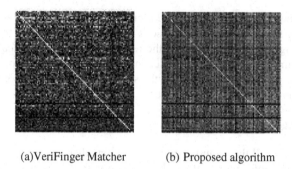

(a)VeriFinger Matcher   (b) Proposed algorithm

Fig. 3. Comparison scores matrix where brighter pixels indicate higher comparison scores. Vertical indices: probes and horizontal indices: reference templates.

where "accepted" and "rejected" are decided by thresholds calculated as the percentage of matched points in all the points in the protected template. A lower limit for number of matched points was also set to be 10 for a successful comparison.

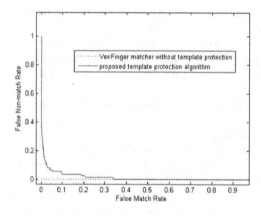

Fig. 4. Biometric performance (FNMR-FMR rate curve): VeriFinger Matcher without template protection (dotted-line) and the proposed template protection algorithm (solid-line)

In the experiments, we compare each of the 100 probes to all the 100 reference templates. The resulting comparison scores form a 256 gray-level (255 as highest and 0 as lowest) matrix in Fig.3, where (a) is the result from VeriFinger 6.0's matcher without template protection, and (b) our proposed algorithm with template protection. The vertical indices are the 100 probes ordered from top to bottom; the horizontal indices are the corresponding 100 templates ordered from left to right. The three dark horizontal lines in both Fig.3(a) and (b) are caused by the low number of detected minutiae in the probes (only 1,2, and 3 minutiae points detected in the 75th, 86th and 97th probes) which were regarded as non-match with comparison score zero.

The parameters we used for experiments are: local disk radius $R = 30$; total number of QT indices $N = 30$; all the $N = 30$ coordinate offset pairs (dx_k, dy_k) $(k=1,2,...,N)$ were randomly generated within the range [-100,100]. We use the simple Euclidean coordinate distance measure and assume that two points match with their distance < 8.

From the experimental results, out of the 100 fingers, 5 fingers had no core detected. We classified these 5 fingers as the case of failure to extract template, and excluded them in calculation of the FMR and FNMR. Another 5 probes had no core detected but their corresponding former 7 samples successfully contributed to a reference template. We excluded these 5 fail-to-extract-template probes from calculation of the FNMR, but included them for calculation of the FMR because they definitly contribute to the number of total imposter attempts. The biometric performance for both experiments are presented in Fig.4 by setting 500 thresholds in the normalized comparison scores range [0,1], where the dotted-curve is for the case by VeriFinger 6.0's Matcher without template protection and the solid-curve is for the case by the proposed template protection algorithm. From Fig.4 we can see that the result from our algorithm cannot reach the VeriFinger 6.0's result, which is probably due to VeriFinger Matcher's capability to exploit minutiae's orientation information, and its industry-level optimized comparator. We use Euclidean distance during verification and check the percentage of points' match in a protected probe template, and use this percentage value as the final comparison score. However, the biometric performance for protected minutiae templates indicates encouraging result and achieves highest Equal-Error-Rate (EER) of 0.0552 in our experiments. We suppose if a better comparator is employed, the comparison performance could be improved.

In our experiment, we generated 7 times of 100 potected templates and in each time different quantization tables were randomly generated. The EER values were slightly varied between 0.0552 and 0.0701.

5 Security Analysis

In our experiments, each transformed point's position could be originated from M possible local disks and each local disk could center on roughly 560×296 positions in an image, this equals to $M \cdot \binom{560 \times 296}{M}$ possibilities (more than 560×296 in the full search case) to guess one true original minutiae point. So it provides roughly $(560 \times 296)^Q = (560 \times 296)^{10} \approx 2^{173}$ possibilities to guessing $Q=10$ true minutiae points' positions from the original template. This is a strong non-invertiblity against the key-inversion attack [12] which undermines fuzzy vault and fuzzy commitment. To achieve non-invertibility from the encrypted template $\{pm_{ja}\}$ to the transformed template $\{m_{ja}\}$ against cross-match attack on the transformed template level, it further provides roughly $N^Q=30^{10} \approx 2^{49}$ possibilities to guess $Q=10$ true transformed minutiae m_{ja}' positions even with the transformation parameters (quantization table QT) public. Keeping the transformation parameters (QT) secret can effectively thwart the template reconstruction attack in which probes can be forged from the protected template by exploiting a public QT without need of inversion to the genuine original template. However, we still notice there is possibility to exploit correlations in topological relationship between encrypted points to gain some linkability between protected templates, which is caused by the simple translation operations via Eq.(2). This could be solvable with some non-linear transformations to replace Eq.(2) to destroy the local topological relationships.

6 Conclusion and Future Work

We proposed in this paper a geometric-alignment based local minutiae encryption algorithm to protect minutiae-based finger template. The proposed algorithm can preserve good comparison performance while providing strong non-invertibility for security enhancement compared to non-invertible transformation based cancelable biometrics proposed in [9]. The strong non-invertibility is assured by the independent information collected from minutiae templates to control encryption parameters. Since the proposed algorithm does not need any other live-captured features other than the minutiae data for security enhancement, it is compatible to both standard minutiae extractors and comparators and thus can work on minutiae templates which are already generated in the existing databases. Our future work will focus on enhancing the unlinkability between protected templates by replacing the employed simple translation operation on the minutiae coordinates with non-linear transformations which we expect to destroy the topological relationship among all the encrypted points in the local disk.

Acknowledgement

This work is supported by funding under the Seventh Research Framework Programme of the European Union, Project TURBINE (ICT-2007-216339). This document has been created in the context of the TURBINE project. All information is provided as is and no guarantee or warranty is given that the information is fit for any particular purpose. The user thereof uses the information at its sole risk and liability. The European Commission has no liability in respect of this document, which is merely representing the authors' view.

Thanks to Julien Bringer from Sagem Sécurité and Koen Simoens from Katholieke Universiteit Leuven for their security comments.

References

1. Juels, A., Wattenberg, M.: A Fuzzy Commitment Scheme. In: Sixth ACM Conference on Computer and Communications Security, Singapore, pp. 28–36 (1999)
2. Juels, A., Sudan, M.: A Fuzzy Vault Scheme. In: IEEE Inter. Symp. on Information Theory, Lausanne, Switzerland (2002)
3. Savvides, M., Kumar, B.V.K.V.: Cancellable Biometric Filters for Face Recognition. In: IEEE Inter. Conf. on Pattern Recognition, Cambridge, UK, vol. 3, pp. 922–925 (2004)
4. Tuyls, P., Akkermans, A.H.M., Kevenaar, T.A.M., Schrijen, G.-J., Bazen, A.M., Veldhuis, R.N.J.: Practical Biometric Authentication with Template Protection. In: Inter. Conf. on Audio- and Video-Based Biometric Person Authentication, USA, pp. 436–446 (2005)
5. Sutcu, Y., Sencar, H.T., Memon, N.: A Secure Biometric Authentication Scheme Based on Robust Hashing. In: ACM Multimedia and Security Workshop, USA, pp. 111–116 (2005)
6. Nagar, A., Nandakumar, K., Jain, A.K.: Securing Fingerprint Template: Fuzzy Vault with Minutiae Descriptors. In: Inter. Conf. on Pattern Recognition, Tampa, Florida, USA (2008)

7. Teoh, A.B.J., Goh, A., Ngo, D.C.L.: Random Multispace Quantization as an Analytic Mechanism for BioHashing of Biometric and Random Identity Inputs. IEEE Trans. on Pattern Analysis and Machine Intelligence 28(12), 1892–1901 (2006)
8. GenKey: System, Portable Device and Method for Digital Authenticating, Crypting and Signing by Generating Short-Lived Cryptokeys. US Patent 2006/0198514A1 (2006)
9. Ratha, N.K., Chikkerur, S., Connell, J.H., Bolle, R.M.: Generating Cancelable Fingerprint Templates. IEEE Trans. on Pattern Analysis and Machine Intelligence 29(4), 561–572 (2007)
10. Kelkboom, E.J.C., Gkberk, B., Kevenaar, T.A.M., Akkermans, A.H.M., Van der Veen, M.: "3D Face": Biometric Template Protection for 3D Face Recognition. In: 2nd Inter. Conf. on Biometrics, Seoul, South Korea (2007)
11. Lee, Y.J., Bae, K., Lee, S.J., Park, K.R., Kim, J.: Biometric Key Binding: Fuzzy Vault Based on Iris Images. In: 2nd Inter. Conf. on Biometrics, Seoul, South Korea, pp. 800–808 (2007)
12. Scheirer, W.J., Boult, T.E.: Cracking Fuzzy Vaults and Biometric Encryption. In: Biometrics Symposium (2007)
13. Arakala, A., Jeffers, J., Horadam, K.J.: Fuzzy Extractors for Minutiae-Based Fingerprint Authentication. In: 2nd Inter. Conf. on Biometrics, Seoul, South Korea (2007)
14. Chang, E.C., Roy, S.: Robust Extraction of Secret Bits From Minutiae. In: 2nd Inter. Conf. on Biometrics, Seoul, South Korea (2007)
15. Yang, B., Busch, C., Bours, P., Gafurov, D.: Non-Invertible Geometrical Transformation for Fingerprint Minutiae Template Protection. In: 1st Inter. Workshop on Security and Communication Networks, Trondheim, Norway (2009)
16. Lee, C., Choi, J.Y., Toh, K.A., Lee, S., Kim, J.: Alignment-Free Cancelable Fingerprint Templates Based on Local Minutiae Information. IEEE Trans. on Systems, Man, and Cybernetics – Part B: Cybernetics 37(4), 980–992 (2007)
17. Boult, T.E., Scheirer, W.J., Woodworth, R.: Revocable Fingerprint Biotokens: Accuracy and Security Analysis. In: IEEE Inter. Conf. on Comput. Vis. & Patt. Recog., USA (2007)
18. Breebaart, J., Busch, C., Grave, J., Kindt, E.: A Reference Architecture for Biometric Template Protection Based on Pseudo Identities. In: BIOSIG 2008, GI-LNI (2008)
19. Delvaux, N., Chabanne, H., Bringer, J., Kindarji, B., Lindeberg, P., Mdgren, J., Breebaart, J., Akkermans, T., Van der Veen, M., Vedhuis, R., Kindt, E., Simoens, K., Busch, C., Bours, P., Gafurov, D., Yang, B., Stern, I., Rust, C., Cucinelli, B., Skepastianos, D.: Pseudo Identities Based on Fingerprint Characteristics. In: IEEE Inter. Conf. on Intelligent Information Hiding and Multimedia Signal Processing, pp. 1063–1068 (2008)
20. Bazen, A.M., Veldhuis, R.N.J.: Likelihood-Ratio-Based Biometric Verification. IEEE Trans. on Circuits and Systems for Video Technology 14(1), 86–94 (2004)
21. ISO Standard. Information Technology - Biometric Data Interchange Formats - Part 8: Finger Pattern Skeletal Data. ISO/IEC 19794-8 (2006)
22. NIST Software Document, http://fingerprint.nist.gov/NBIS/nbis_non_export_control.pdf
23. VeriFinger Software, http://www.neurotechnology.com

A Hybrid Approach to Land Cover Classification from Multi Spectral Images

Primo Zingaretti[1], Emanuele Frontoni[1],
Eva Savina Malinverni[2], and Adriano Mancini[1]

[1] D.I.I.G.A., [2] DARDUS,
Università Politecnica delle Marche, Ancona - Italy
{zinga,frontoni,mancini}@diiga.univpm.it,
e.s.malinverni@univpm.it

Abstract. This work is part of a wider project whose general objective is to develop a methodology for the automatic classification, based on CORINE land-cover (CLC) classes, of high resolution multispectral IKONOS images. The specific objective of this paper is to describe a new methodology for producing really exploitable results from automatic classification algorithms. Input data are basically constituted by multispectral images, integrated with textural and contextual measures. The output is constituted by an image with each pixel assigned to one out of 15 classes at the second level of the CLC legend or let unclassified (somehow a better solution than a classification error), plus a stability map that helps users to separate the regions classified with high accuracy from those whose classification result should be verified before being used.

Keywords: Land cover - land use (LCLU), multispectral images, pixel-based and object-based classification, AdaBoost, stability map.

1 Introduction

Data classification has been used in several fields, from genetics to robotics and vision [11]. Image classification for the production of thematic maps, like Land Cover/ Land Use (LCLU) maps, is one of the most common applications of remote sensing.

LCLU is one of the most crucial properties of the Earth system. It is important from many points of view, such as its interaction with weather and climate prediction or with the carbon cycle (in particular, rates of deforestation and re-growth play a significant role in the release and sequestering of carbon and consequently affect atmospheric CO2 concentration and the strength of the greenhouse effect), but land cover also reflects the availability of food, fuel and other resources for human populations, and serves as a critical indicator of other ecosystem services such as biodiversity, urban development and agricultural productivity.

In 1985 the European Commission approved the CORINE programme, led by the European Environmental Agency (EEA) in coordination with the member countries, to compile, in a consistent and compatible way, information on certain topics with regard to the state of the environment. Among the results there was the definition of

P. Foggia, C. Sansone, and M. Vento (Eds.): ICIAP 2009, LNCS 5716, pp. 500–508, 2009.

CORINE Land Cover (CLC) inventories for all European countries based on a standard methodology and nomenclature, for use with remote sensing techniques. The CLC legend has a hierarchical structure on three levels, containing 44 land cover classes grouped into five major categories: 1. Urban Fabric, 2. Agriculture areas, 3. Forest and semi-natural areas, 4. Wetlands, 5. Water bodies [2]. With respect of this structure, the high ground resolution of current sensors, suitable for a map scale 1:10'000, suggested the introduction of fourth and fifth level categories.

For a long time, the LCLU classification methods were based only on the visual interpretation by specialists, i.e., derived by human photo-interpretation of satellite/aerial images. In recent years, partial or full automatic classification methods have been developed. The main characteristic of the former approach is a high accuracy (but strongly restricted by the experience of interpreters and their familiarity to the study area), while computer approaches allow quick map production but with relatively poor accuracy. Because of changes in time also LCLU maps created from human beings become soon of insufficient quality (in terms of time resolution) for operational applications an updating of these maps must be carried out on a regular basis to keep the databases up to date. So, automatic classification algorithms with improved accuracy become more and more desirable to reduce the high costs of photo-interpretation.

Automatic and semi-automatic classification starting from multi-spectral data can be divided into two major approaches: pixel based and object/region based [7]. Pixel-based classification approaches seek to identify the class of each pixel from its multispectral channel values and/or textural and contextual measures computed from those channels. Object-based approaches do not operate directly on individual pixels but on objects/regions consisting of many pixels that have been grouped together in a meaningful way by some image segmentation technique. Shape characteristics and neighbourhood relationships can then be added to spectral and textural information used in pixel-based classification methods to perform the classification.

Unfortunately, both these automatic classification methods cannot be used to create LCLU maps because of the lack in result accuracy. In the case of pixel-based approaches, which can exploit only spectral features, the cause is twofold: from one side, a same land cover type does not have unique spectral characteristics under different acquisition conditions, and, from another side, many different natural objects can have the same spectral response. In the case of object-based approaches the classification accuracy is heavily influenced by the quality of segmentation results.

During recent years, many techniques (e.g., fuzzy and neural classifiers, stepwise optimization approaches), some of which embedded in commercial software, allowed to improve greatly the accuracy of automatic classification, but the integration of object- and pixel-based classification seems the right way to follow [7, 10, 13].

The work here presented is part of a wider project whose general objective is to develop a methodology for the automatic classification, based on CLC classes, of high resolution multispectral IKONOS images.

The whole project is divided into four stages consisting of: i) pre-processing - including radiometric correction, orthorectification, etc., of the image dataset; ii) definition of training and control sample sets – an exhaustive number of samples, based on a hierarchical classification nomenclature, is the base for the training of algorithms and for accuracy assessment. The spectral analysis of the different channels of an image is also carried out to select optimal bands or combination of bands to be used in the classification process; iii) classification – using different supervised or rule-based classification methods; iv) accuracy assessment of classification results by a stability map – to estimate the accuracy of different classifications.

The specific objective of this paper is to describe a new methodology for producing really exploitable results from automatic classification algorithms.

The approach presented in this paper utilizes both pixel-based and object-based classification. Individual image pixels are first classified using an AdaBoost classifier that makes use of values of multispectral (red, green, blue and near-infrared) bands, eventually integrated with the Normalized-Difference-Vegetation-Index (NDVI), derived from the red and near-infrared bands, a Digital Terrain Model (DTM) of the area and pixel by pixel gradient values, derived by the DTM. The imagery is then segmented and spatial, texture and spectral attributes are derived for the resulting regions. The pixel classification is then used together with these additional object attributes with a set of rules to enhance the classification accuracy of image objects.

In Section 2 the proposed hybrid (pixel- and object-based) approach is described; in Section 3 the results obtained and in Section 4 some comments and conclusions.

2 Hybrid Approach Scheme

The hybrid approach here proposed for land cover classification based on multispectral bands of satellite or airborne digital images can be structured in different phases, as shown in Fig. 1.

First, the image dataset is created by applying the radiometric and geometric corrections, if not performed previously. The georeference procedure, assigning a coordinate system, allows to link data with other cartographic information available in the GIS, and to produce a correct overlay of the resulting thematic (LCLU) maps at the end of the workflow.

The classification process is at the central stage, where some other masks and textures, like one of the most widely known: the Normalized Difference Vegetation Index (NDVI), are added to the original spectral bands. Other types of features can also be derived performing a linear transformation of the spectral bands, using, for example, the Principal Component Analysis (PCA), so that the resulting components are uncorrelated. The multispectral classification is the process that assigns to the pixel an individual class if it satisfies a certain set of statistical criteria, based on the spectral characteristics of all pixels in the image. The classification process must be trained to recognize the pattern in the data. Supervised training is closely performed by an analyst, who have to select pixels that represent land cover features directly recognized on the original RGB or False Colour images, or identified by means of other sources, such as aerial photos, ground truth data or maps. Once defined the training and control samples, based on the hierarchical classification of the CLC legend, these are applied to train and check the automatic supervised classifier. Supervised classification refers to a wide variety of traditionally feature extraction approaches. In our work the AdaBoost algorithm described in the next section was adopted.

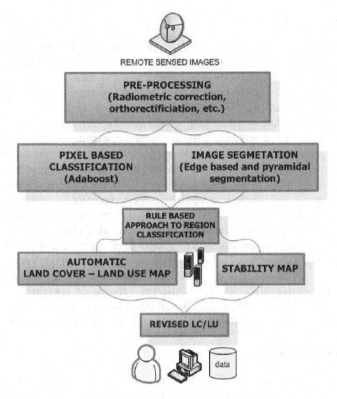

Fig. 1. The hybrid approach scheme

A multilevel segmentation is then performed to pass from pixel to object based classification. To label each segment with a land cover type, the above classification technique is combined with another form of classification: a specific decision rules system. The classification decision rules perform the sorting of pixels into distinct classes assigned to homogeneous regions. One of the major disadvantages of the per pixel techniques is that every pixel is analyzed without the contribute of additional information such as context, shape and proximity. The use of a rule-based approach introduces these criteria for a classification refinement and to realize a GIS ready mapping. This is applied on the multilevel segmentation performed on a RGB or false colour image.

The assessment of the classification accuracy is carried out comparing the classi-fied images with the control sample set. If the classification is accurate, the resulting classes represent the categories identified with the training samples.

Confidence values associated with each segment provide a stability map corre-sponding to the stability map of the final output classified image, which enable a quick validation of the final results allowing the identification of the problem-atic/confused areas. The quality of subsequent classification is directly affected by segmentation quality.

2.1 AdaBoost Classifier

One of the key problems to be solved in the automatic classification of data is to define a classifier that allows to categorize objects (pixels or regions) in the image according to a set of given categories. The approach here described applies an AdaBoost algorithm to learn a strong classifier from a large set of simple features with a decision tree as weak learner [8].

Boosting is a method of combining classifiers that are iteratively created from weighted versions of the learning samples, with the weights adaptively adjusted at each step to give increased weight to those samples that were misclassified in the previous step. The final predictions are obtained by weighting the results of the iteratively produced predictors. Boosting was originally developed for classification, and is typically applied for creating an accurate strong classifier by combining a set of weak classifiers. A weak classifier is only required to be better than chance, and thus can be very simple and computationally inexpensive. However, combining many of these simple and inexpensive classifiers results in a strong classifier, which often outperforms most "monolithic" strong classifiers such as Support Vector Machines and Neural Networks.. AdaBoost (short for "Adaptive Boosting") is presently the most popular boosting algorithm [3]. Different variants of boosting, e.g. Discrete Adaboost, Real AdaBoost (used in this paper), and Gentle AdaBoost [6], are identical in terms of computational complexity, but differ in their learning algorithm.

2.2 Image Segmentation

In object-based classification approaches segmentation is a preliminary activity to obtain a set of polygons that can be used to calculate spatial, spectral and texture attributes then used in the classification stage. The concept of region-based classification removes the sensibility of pixel-based classifiers to noise; however, for pixel based approaches there are available different techniques, as Winner Takes All (WTA) derived from mobile robotics, which can be applied to reduce the effect of above mentioned problem. In this case, the *winner* is the class that collects the majority of votes from each classified pixel inside a region.

A variety of segmentation techniques as region growing with edge detection [12], watersheds [5] and level-set [1],.have been applied to remote sensing imagery with varying degrees of success; Segmentation of remotely sensed images is a complex problem due to mixed pixels, spectral similarity, and the textured appearance of many land-cover types. Many segmentation algorithms are based on a region-growing approach where pixels are iteratively grouped into regions based on predefined similarity criteria.

The approach here followed to segment multi-spectral data fuses region growing and edge based methods. The advantage of using edges during the region growing process is the correct recognition of strong region boundaries and the robustness to noise inside the regions (e.g., spikes, small trees). The algorithm distinguishes between strong edges (boundary edges) from local edges (caused by noise). An example of edge detection with the difference in strength (DIS) algorithm [12] is shown in Fig. 2b, where edge pixels are associable to whiter pixels. The strength of an edge is determined by the presence or not of near edges. Near edges are points that during edge

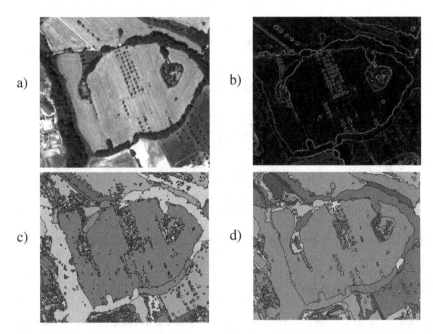

Fig. 2. Multi-spectral RGB high resolution aerial data processing: a) original image; b) edge detection results using the DIS algorithm; c) intermediate segmentation result after the region growing process; d) final segmentation result after the region merging process

extraction have a value greater than a proper threshold (calculated as the mean or median or mode of DIS map over all the image) and are in the proximity of strong edges. The great advantage of this algorithm is that the growing process stops when region reaches strong boundaries. Near edges also allow to connect strong pixels avoiding the presence of not-close boundaries.

At the end of the region growing there are a lot of small regions (Fig. 2c), caused by the presence of object noise in the image. To reduce the effect of over-segmentation a re-distribution stage, whose function is the merging of "similar" regions (Fig 2d), is applied.

The term "similar" must be defined by means of some metrics based on spatial, spectral and/or texture attributes. In the proposed scheme different re-distribution criteria were implemented (e.g., spectral difference, minimum area, perimeter, bounding box, compactness).

However, small regions can be also removed by using a multi-scale segmentation approach based on a pyramidal reduction from the lowest level 0 (original image) to chosen level N [9]. Segmentation starts at level N and regions can be merged using different criteria (spatial, spectral and textural). After the merging phase, image is projected into the neighbour level N-1; a skeleton operator is applied to keep minimal the size of borders. Process continues up to the level 0 is reached. A schematic description of this multi-scale approach is shown in Fig. 3.

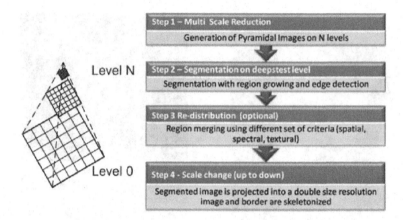

Fig. 3. Multi-scale pyramidal segmentation using region growing and edge detection

3 Classification Results

In this section, after a brief description of the dataset the obtained classification re-sults.are reported.

3.1 Dataset and Sample Definition

The case study refers to an area of approximately 150 km^2 located near the Ancona city, comprising both urban and rural environments, and with a topography that includes flat areas, but also the Natural Park of the Conero mountain, with a 550 m elevation range.

IKONOS images were acquired in July 2006, with a 29 degrees solar zenith angle. The dataset is composed by a panchromatic image at a ground resolution of 1m and multi-spectral 4m resolution data constituted by four bands: red, green, blue and near-infrared. These data were integrated by a Digital Terrain Model (DTM) of the area, derived from the Regional Technical Map at the scale 1:10'000, which, however, by definition, does not consider artificial structures. Additional features as gradient de-rived by the DTM, and the Normalized Difference Vegetation Index (NDVI) obtained from the red and near-infrared (were used to achieve better classification accuracy. A classification system should be informative, exhaustive and separable [4]. The first step to this aim is the definition of a hierarchical classification structure, mainly based on the user's needs and spatial resolution of remotely sensed data. To fit a standard classification system the CLC legend was chosen. The software training stage was carried out by means of about 100'000 sample points grouped in 130 training sites covering less than 1% of total area. A dedicated-GIS platform implementation stores and manages the collected samples by means of specific in field campaign and/or pan-sharpened IKONOS dataset visual interpretation.

3.2 Results

The performance of the classification algorithm at the second level of the CLC legend (15 classes), is analyzed in the following. The output is constituted by an image with each pixel assigned to one of the above classes or let unclassified (somehow a better solution than a classification error), plus a stability map.

Fig. 4 reports the classification results over a very small zone, but sufficient to show the differences among the three maps produced during the processing. In particular, in a) it is evident the noise present in the pixel based classification. After the shift to objects (polygons) it is important to evaluate the accuracy of the classification of each object and Fig. 4b shows in red the polygons with accuracy greater than 0.6 and in yellow the others, that is those for which the class assigned may not be considered stable enough. So the end user of the final LCLU map, shown in Fig. 4c, should take into account that some areas may not be correctly classified.

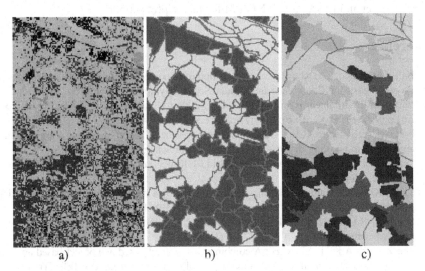

Fig. 4. Portion of classification results. a) pixel-based classification; b) stability map; c) Land cover - land use map.

4 Discussion and Conclusions

In this paper, a new method for high spatial resolution image classification is proposed; it integrates a pixel based classification method, using an AdaBoost classifier, with an object-based classification of the regions resulting from a multilevel segmentation that fuses region growing and edge based methods.

The output is constituted by an image with each pixel assigned to one of 15 classes at the second level of the CLC legend or let unclassified, plus a stability map that helps users to separate the regions classified with high accuracy from those whose classification result should be verified before being used. This last product is particularly important to overcome the problem that not accurate results totally prevent the use of the LCLU maps. In fact, if the end user simply knows that, on a static basis, the classification result is correct at, for example, 85% he cannot know where erroneously classified regions are located! On the contrary, owing to the stability map the end user knows them and he/she can decide to charge a photo-interpreter to complete the classification only for the remaining 15% (in the case hypothesized) of the area.

For similar reasons, the presence of not classified data constitutes a good quality of the AdaBoost approach; not classified data can be successively disambiguated using a second level classifier (different from the first one) or using a rule based approach.

In conclusion, even in presence of very small training sets the proposed approach works fine, so that exploring the use of more classes, that is at the third level of the CORINE legend, is a work in progress

Future works are steered to compare the results of different techniques to segment data; particular attention will be also focused on the definition of a set of rules to classify complex CLC classes as heterogeneous areas.

Acknowledgments. The authors would like to thank the Regione Marche for providing the dataset and DiSACS at UNIVPM for the helpful support.

References

1. Ball, J.E., Bruce, L.M.: Level set segmentation of remotely sensed hyperspectral images. In: Proceedings of Int. Geoscience and Remote Sensing Symposium, vol. 8, pp. 5638–5642
2. European Environment Agency (EEA), CLC 2006 technical guidelines - Technical report, http://www.eea.europa.eu/publications/technical_report_2007_17
3. Freund, Y., Schapire, R.E.: A decision-theoretic generalization of on-line learning and an application to boosting. J. of Computer and System Sciences 55(1), 119–139 (1997)
4. Landgrebe, D.A.: Signal Theory Methods in Multispectral Remote Sensing. John Wiley & Sons, Inc., Hoboken (2003)
5. Li, P., Xiao, X.: Multispectral image segmentation by a multichannel watershed-based approach. International Journal of Remote Sensing 28(19), 4429–4452 (2007)
6. Schapire, R.E., Singer, Y.: Improved boosting algorithms using confidence-rated predictions. Machine Learning 37(3), 297–336 (1999)
7. Shackelford, A.K., Davis, C.H.: A combined fuzzy pixel-based and object-based approach for classification of high-resolution multispectral data over urban areas. IEEE Transactions on Geoscience and Remote Sensing 41(10), 2354–2363 (2003)
8. Sutton, C.D.: Handbook of Statistics, vol. 24, cap. 11: Classification and regression trees, bagging, and boosting. Elsevier, Amsterdam (2005)
9. Tabb, M., Ahuja, N.: Multiscale image segmentation by integrated edge and region detection. IEEE Transactions on Image Processing 6(5), 642–655 (1997)
10. Wang, L., Sousa, W., Gong, P.: Integration of object-based and pixel-based classification for mangrove mapping with IKONOS imagery. Int. J. of Remote Sensing 25(24), 5655–5668 (2004)
11. Wood, J.: Invariant pattern recognition: a review. Pattern Recognition 29(1), 1–17 (1996)
12. Yu, Y.W., Wang, J.H.: Image segmentation based on region growing and edge detection. In: Proceedings of IEEE International Conference on Systems, Man, and Cybernetics, vol. 6, pp. 798–803 (1999)
13. Yuan, F., Bauer, M.E.: Mapping impervious surface area using high resolution imagery: A comarison of object-based and per pixel classification. In: Proceedings of ASPRS 2006 (2006)

Improving the Accuracy of a Score Fusion Approach Based on Likelihood Ratio in Multimodal Biometric Systems

Emanuela Marasco and Carlo Sansone

Dipartimento di Informatica e Sistemistica,
Università degli Studi di Napoli Federico II
Via Claudio, 21 I-80125 Napoli, Italy
{emanuela.marasco,carlosan}@unina.it

Abstract. Multimodal biometric systems integrate information from multiple sources to improve the performance of a typical unimodal biometric system. Among the possible information fusion approaches, those based on fusion of match scores are the most commonly used. Recently, a framework for the optimal combination of match scores that is based on the likelihood ratio (LR) test has been presented. It is based on the modeling of the distributions of genuine and impostor match scores as a finite Gaussian mixture models. In this paper, we propose two strategies for improving the performance of the LR test. The first one employs a voting strategy to circumvent the need of huge datasets for training, while the second one uses a sequential test to improve the classification accuracy on genuine users.

Experiments on the NIST multimodal database confirmed that the proposed strategies can outperform the standard LR test, especially when there is the need of realizing a multibiometric system that must accept no impostors.

1 Introduction

Nowadays, companies spend a lot of efforts in security concerns, such as access control. One of the means to guarantee such aspects is providing reliable authentication methods to identify an individual requesting services of critical applications. A Biometric System recognizes individuals by their biological or behavioral characteristics [1], such as fingerprints, iris, facial patterns, voice, gait, etc. [2]. There is a growing interest in industries towards biometrics because they offer the highest level of security. In fact, biometric features are typically a portion of the body belonging to the person to be authenticated, instead of something he/she knows (e.g., passwords) or he/she possess (e.g., keys or badges). So, they cannot be stolen or forgotten.

However, systems relying on the evidence of a single modality are vulnerable in real world applications, since: (i) the *distinctiveness* of a single biometric feature is limited [3], (e.g., twins are non distinguishable by using the face as biometric feature); (ii) *noisy sensed data*, captured in unfavorable ambient conditions, can

P. Foggia, C. Sansone, and M. Vento (Eds.): ICIAP 2009, LNCS 5716, pp. 509–518, 2009.

be incorrectly labeled, resulting in the rejection of a genuine user; (iii) there is the *non-universality* problem; it may not be possible to acquire meaningful data from a certain individual, because for such subject the quality of the features used to represent his/her required trait is not enough for a successful enrollment; (iv) finally, a biometric system have to face *spoofing* attacks, that can circumvent it by introducing fake biometric data that artificially reproduce physical traits.

The latest researches indicate that using a combination of biometric modalities, the human identification is more reliable [4]. A typical unimodal biometric system acquires the raw biometric data by an appropriate sensor module, extracts a feature set and compares it to the biometric sample (template) stored in a database, and then outputs a score used to establish the identity.

So, the information presented by multiple traits may be consolidated at various levels of recognition process. At feature extraction level, a new feature set is produced by fusing the features sets of multiple modalities, and this new feature set is used in the matching module. At match score level, the scores produced by multiple matchers are integrated, while at decision level the decisions made by the individual systems are combined. The integration at feature extraction level is expected to perform better, but the feature space of different biometric traits may not be compatible and most commercial systems do not provide access to information at this level. So, researchers found at score level a good compromise between the ease in realizing the fusion and the information content.

In literature three main approaches [5] are available to implement the fusion at score level [2]. First, the so called *Classifier-Based Scheme* [6] uses the output scores of each different matcher to construct a feature vector for training a classifier. This is accurate to correctly discriminate between genuine and impostor classes, regardless of the non-homogeneity of the score, but it typically requires a large training set. Second, the *Transformation-Based Scheme* [7] combines the match scores provided by different matchers: they are first transformed into a common domain (*score normalization*) and then are combined via a simple fusion rule such as *sum, min, max* or *weighted sum*. This approach is quite complex since it implicates a wide experimental analysis to choose the best normalization scheme and combination weights for the specific dataset of interest.

Last, the *Density-Based Scheme* [8] considers the match scores as random variables, whose class conditional densities are not *a prior* known. So, this approach requires an explicit estimation of density functions from the training data [2]. A recent method belonging to this category is the score fusion framework based on the Likelihood Ratio test, proposed by Nandakumar et al. in [5]. It models the scores of a biometric matcher by a mixture of Gaussians and perform a statistical test to discriminate between genuine and impostor classes. This framework produces high recognition rates at a chosen operating point (in terms of False Acceptance Rate), without the need of parameter tuning by the system designer once the method for score density estimation has been defined. Optimal performance, in fact, can be achieved when it is possible to perform accurate estimations of the genuine and impostor score densities. The Gaussian Mixture Model (GMM) lets to obtain reliable estimations of the distributions, even if the amount of data needed for it increases as the number of considered biometrics increases. Moreover, as noted by the authors in [5], the performance of their method can be improved by using a suitable *quality measure* together with each score. Most of the available biometric systems, however, do not provides such measures.

Starting from the last considerations, in this paper we present two novel score fusion strategies based on the likelihood ratio scheme, that can be used when an high security level is needed. We propose both a sequential test and a voting strategy. By using them, on one hand we tried to implicitly use the quality information embedded into the scores. On the other hand, we obtained a system that demonstrated to be more robust than the original one with respect to the lack of data for training.

The rest of the paper is as follows: in Section 2 the likelihood ratio test is reviewed. In Section 3 the proposed strategy are illustrated and motivated, while the experimental results are presented in Section 4. Finally, some conclusions are drawn in Section 5.

2 Background and Open Issues

2.1 The Likelihood Ratio Test

Nandakumar and Chen [5] formulate the problem of Identity Verification in terms of hypothesis testing: let Ψ denote a statistical test for deciding if the hypothesis H:{*the score vector* $\mathbf{s}$ *belongs to the Genuine class*} has been correctly formulated. The choice is based on the value of observed match score and it lies between only two decisions: accepting H or rejecting it. As it is known [9], different tests should be compared with respect to the concepts of *size* and *power*, that are respectively the probability of accepting H when it is false (also called *False Accept Rate* - FAR) and the probability of accepting H when it is true (also called *Genuine Accept Rate* - GAR) [9]. In the context of *prudential decision making* [10], the NP lemma [9] recognizes that, in choosing between a hypothesis H and an alternative, the test based on the Likelihood Ratio test is the best because it maximizes the *power* for a fixed *size* [9]. Let

$$LR(\mathbf{s}) = \frac{f_{gen}(\mathbf{s})}{f_{imp}(\mathbf{s})} \tag{1}$$

be the *Likelihood Ratio (LR)*, that is the probability of the observed outcome under H divided by the probability of assuming its alternative. As stated by the Neyman and Pearson theorem [9], the framework proposed by Nandakumar and Jain ensures that the most powerful test is the one, say $\Psi(\mathbf{s})$, that satisfies the equations (1) for some η

$$\Psi(\mathbf{s}) = \begin{cases} 1, & \text{when } LR(\mathbf{s}) \geq \eta \\ 0, & \text{when } LR(\mathbf{s}) < \eta \end{cases} \tag{2}$$

where $\mathbf{s} = [s_1, s_2, ...s_K]$ is an observed set of K match scores that is assigned to the genuine class if $LR(\mathbf{s})$ is greater than a fixed threshold η, with $\eta \geq 0$.

2.2   The Estimation of Match Score Densities

As it is known in biometric literature [2], it is hard to choose a specific parametric form for approximating the density of genuine and impostor match scores,
because the match distributions have a large tail, discrete components and not
only one mode.

Given a training set, density estimation can be done by employing parametric
or non-parametric techniques [11]. The non-parametric techniques do not assume
any form of the density function and are completely data-driven; on the contrary,
parametric techniques assume that the form of the density function is known
(e.g., Gaussian) and estimate its parameters from the training data. The power
of this scheme resides in its generality [12]: exactly the same procedure can be
used also if the known functions are a mixture of Gaussians. In [5] the authors
have proved the effectiveness of the GMM for modeling score distributions and of
the likelihood ratio fusion test in achieving high recognition rates when densities
estimations are based on GMM [5].

Let $\mathbf{s} = [s_1, s_2, ...s_K]$ denote the score vector of K different biometric matchers, where s_j is the random variable representing the match score provided by
the jth matcher, with $j = 1, 2, ..., K$. Let $f_{gen}(\mathbf{s})$ and $f_{imp}(\mathbf{s})$ denote the conditional joint density of the score vector $\mathbf{s}$ given respectively the genuine and
impostor class. The estimates of $f_{gen}(\mathbf{s})$ and $f_{imp}(\mathbf{s})$ are obtained as a mixture
of Gaussians:

$$\hat{f}_{gen}(s) = \sum_{j=1}^{M_{gen}} p_{gen,j} \Phi^K(s; \mu_{gen,j}, \Sigma_{gen,j}) \tag{3}$$

$$\hat{f}_{imp}(s) = \sum_{j=1}^{M_{imp}} p_{imp,j} \Phi^K(s; \mu_{imp,j}, \Sigma_{imp,j}) \tag{4}$$

where $\Phi^K(s; \mu; \Sigma) = (2\pi)^{-K/2}|\Sigma|^{-1/2}exp(-\frac{1}{2}(s - \mu)^T \Sigma^{-1}(s - \mu))$ denotes the
Gaussian density with mean μ and covariance matrix Σ, and M_{gen} (M_{imp}) represents the number of mixture components. Mixture parameters can be approximated by employing the fitting procedure of Figuereido and Jain [13], that uses
EM algorithm and Minimum Message Length (MML) criterion. It also estimates
the optimal number of Gaussians and is able to treat discrete values by modeling them as a mixture with a very small variance represented as a regularization
factor added to the diagonal of the covariance matrix.

Fusion based on GMM estimations achieves high performance [5], but there
is an important drawback. In practice, one has to determine reliable models for
estimations of genuine and impostor match score densities from the available
score to be used for training. In absence of a large database, it is hard to obtain
an accurate model, and this limitation is particularly true for multibiometric
systems, as the number of considered biometrics increases.

3   The Proposed Approaches

As said in the Introduction, the quality of the acquired biometric data affects the efficiency of a matching process [14]. When the samples presented to a matcher are of poor quality, it cannot reliably distinguish between genuine and impostor users. For example, some true minutiae may not be detected in noisy fingerprint images, and missing minutiae may lead to errors. Moreover, as stated in the previous Section, when several biometrics are available, a not huge dataset could be not sufficient for having a proper density estimate by means of the GMM. So, we propose the following two approaches for improving the performance of the standard LR test:

1. An analysis of how the exclusion of some biometric modalities affects the GMM estimate: this approach (hereinafter denoted as *voting LR*) can be associated to the attempt of implicitly individuating degraded quality samples, when the quality measures are not available. In practice, given a K-dimensional score vector, we estimate the K conditional class joint densities of K-1 scores, by using a GMM technique. Then, we fixed for each of the K estimates a threshold η on the training set that gives rise to a FAR equal to 0%. When we have to judge a new sample, K LR tests are made on the K densities and if at least one of the LR tests recognizes the sample as genuine it is declared as genuine by the system. The ratio of this procedure lies in the fact that we want to detect if a particular score, say s_i, coming from a genuine sample, could be affected by a low quality. In this case, it can be expected that all the score vectors including s_i it will result in a low LR value, giving rise to a false rejection. Only the K-1 dimensional score vector that do not include s_i could have a LR value able to overcome the threshold. So, if at least one test is passed, the sample with a single modality affected by low quality can be correctly recognized. The choice of fixing η on the training set so as to obtain a FAR equal to 0%, is motivated by the need of having a system characterized by a FAR as low as possible. Since this approach uses only K-1 dimensional score vectors, it should be also more robust to the lack of training data.

2. A sequential likelihood ratio test (hereinafter denoted as *Sequential LR*) that introduces the option of suspending the judgment if the hypothesis is accepted or rejected with a not sufficient degree of confidence. This is a sort of sequential probability test (as stated in [15] by Wald) that use additional data for taking the final decision, when it is not possible to make a decision with a sufficient reliability by only using the initial observation. In this case $LR(\mathbf{s})$ is first compared with two different thresholds, say A_k and B_k:

$$\Psi(\mathbf{s}) = \begin{cases} 1, & \text{when } LR(\mathbf{s}) > A_k \\ Suspension & \text{when } B_k \leq LR(\mathbf{s}) \leq A_k \\ 0, & \text{when } LR(\mathbf{s}) < B_k \end{cases} \qquad (5)$$

The thresholds A_k and B_k should be chosen so as to draw an uncertainty region around the value of the threshold η given by the standard LR test. In practice, a fraction ν of this threshold can be chosen, so as $B_k = (1 - \nu) \cdot \eta$ and $A_k = (1 + \nu) \cdot \eta$. If $LR(s) > A_k$, the decision is in favour of the genuine class, while if $LR(s) < B_k$, the decision is in favour of the impostor class. In the case of *suspension*, i.e., when $B_k \leq LR(s) \leq A_k$, the test procedure does not make any decision but activates a further step. The suspension of the judgment is motivated by the fact that samples that are quite near to the threshold could be misclassified due to the presence of one biometric trait acquired with a low quality. So, as a second step we propose to adopt the same approach presented in the previous case. In other words, K tests are made on score vectors of K-1 dimensions and the hypothesis is refused only if it is refused by all the K voting components.

4   Experimental Results

4.1   Dataset

The performances of our approaches are evaluated on a public domain database, namely, NIST-BSSR1 (Biometric Scores Set - Release 1). The BSSR1 is a *true* multimodal database i.e., the face and the fingerprint images coming from the same person at the same time. We performed experiments by employing the first partition made up of face and fingerprint scores belonging to a set of 517 people. For each individual, it is available a score coming from the comparison of two right index fingerprint, a score obtained by comparing impressions of two left index fingerprint, and two scores (from two different matchers, say C and G) that are the outputs of the matching between two frontal faces. So, in this case the match score for each modality indicates a *distance*. Then, our dataset consists in an unbalanced population composed by 517 genuine and 266,772 (517*516) impostor users.

4.2   Evaluation Procedure

We have performed a first experiment in which the training set is composed by half of the genuine and half of the impostor randomly selected from the dataset. The rest of the data are used as test set. The second experiment was directed to analyze how the reduction of the available scores for training affects the accuracy of the densities model. So, we performed another test in which the training set is halved with respect to the previous case, while the size of the test set remains unchanged. Both of these training-test partitioning have been randomly repeated 10 times and we report the average performance over the 10 runs.

4.3   Results

Tables 1 and 2 report the result of the two proposed approaches compared with the standard LR test. Moreover, we also report the K-1 dimensional score vector

Table 1. Test set results with a training set of equal size

	LR	LR on K-1 Matchers (LfInd,RxInd,FaceG)	Voting LR	Sequential LR $\nu = 0.2$	Sequential LR $\nu = 0.25$	Sequential LR $\nu = 0.30$
FAR	0.0%	0.0%	0.0%	0.0%	0.0%	0.000003%
GAR	95.60%	93.26%	97.77%	98.22%	98.22%	98.30%

Table 2. Test set results with a training set of halved size

	LR	LR on K-1 Matchers (LfInd,RxInd,FaceG)	Voting LR	Sequential LR $\nu = 0.2$	Sequential LR $\nu = 0.25$	Sequential LR $\nu = 0.30$
FAR	0.0%	0.0003%	0.0%	0.000009%	0.000011%	0.000011%
GAR	81.24%	95.35%	98.30%	88.09%	88.09%	88.01%

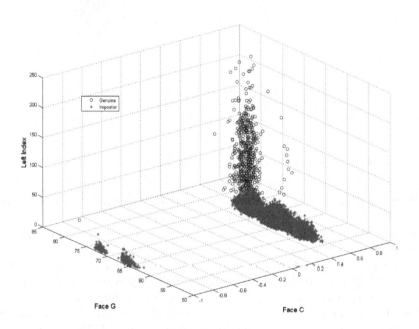

Fig. 1. Score distribution of Left Index, Face C and Face G from NIST-BSSR1

that allowed us to obtain the best results when used alone (in particular this score vector was composed by the outputs of the two fingerprint matchers and of the *Face G* matcher). Three values of ν have been considered, namely 0.2, 0.25 and 0.30.

Our system was designed for reducing to zero the number of accepted impostors. So, in order to have a fair comparison, the chosen operating point for each run of the standard LR test was obtained by fixing the FAR equal to 0% on the test set. The obtained threshold η is also used in the first step of the *sequential LR* approach.

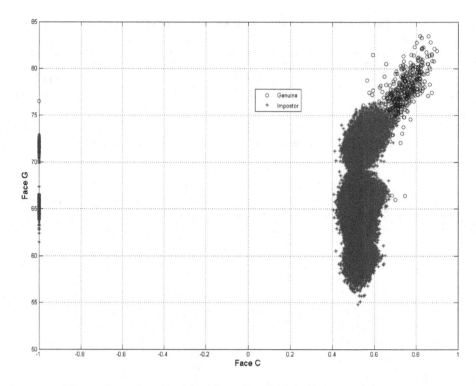

Fig. 2. Score distribution of Face C and Face G from NIST-BSSR1

From the previous tables it is evident that the *sequential LR* always improves the GAR obtainable with a standard LR, since its second stage is able to reduce misclassification of genuine samples with respect to the *pure* likelihood ratio, for those samples classified with a low degree of confidence.

Another interesting results is that the *voting LR* approach seems to be more robust with respect to the lack of training data. When only 25% of the data are used for training, in fact, it is able to significantly improve the GAR with respect to the standard LR approach. In this case, sequential LR is instead only able to slightly improve the LR performance in terms of GAR, but it also introduces few false accepted samples. On the contrary, when sufficient data for densities estimation are available, sequential LR achieves the best performance. All summarizing, it is worth noting that in both experiments the proposed approaches overperformed the standard LR test when a system at FAR=0% have to be realized.

Finally, is is interesting to consider the score distributions reported in Figures 1 and 2, where the joint distributions of *Left Index*, *Face C* and *Face G* and of *Face C* and *Face G* only are respectively shown. As it is evident (see also the considerations made by [16] on this problem), the use of only two modalities significantly reduces the possibility of distinguish between genuine users and impostors. This is why we did not propose to further iterate the sequential test by considering, for example, also the joint densities of all the possible score pairs.

5   Conclusions and Future Work

In this paper we have proposed two approaches for combining multiple biometric matchers, starting from a density-based approach that use a likelihood ratio (LR) test, in order to set-up a biometric system that minimizes the number of false accepted users. The first approach is based on a voting strategy, while the second one on a sequential probability test. As a result, we obtained that if the density estimate of the standard LR method is accurate, the sequential test can reduce the misclassified samples belong to the uncertainty region, giving rise to very good results in terms of GAR. On the contrary, if the estimate of the density function of the standard LR is not so accurate, it is convenient to implement a voting system for classifying all the samples.

As future work we planned to extend our study to other multimodal biometric datasets.

References

1. Jain, A., Ross, A., Prabhakar, S.: An introduction to biometric recognition. IEEE Transaction on Circuits and Systems for Video 14(1), 4–20 (2004)
2. Ross, A., Jain, A.: Handbook in MultiBiometrics. Springer, Heidelberg (2008)
3. Ross, A., Jain, A.: Information fusion in biometrics. Pattern Recognition Letters 24, 2115–2125 (2003)
4. Jain, A., Ross, A.: Multibiometric systems. Comm. ACM 47(1), 34–40 (2004)
5. Nandakumar, K., Chen, Y., Dass, S., Jain, A.: Likelihood ratio-based biometric score fusion. IEEE Transaction on Pattern Analysis and Machine Intelligence 30(2), 342–347 (2008)
6. Ma, Y., Cukic, B., Singh, H.: A classification approach to multi-biometric score fusion. In: Kanade, T., Jain, A., Ratha, N.K. (eds.) AVBPA 2005. LNCS, vol. 3546, pp. 484–493. Springer, Heidelberg (2005)
7. Nandakumar, K., Jain, A., Ross, A.: Score normalization in multimodal biometric systems. Pattern Recognition 38(12), 2270–2285 (2005)
8. Dass, S., Nandakumar, K., Jain, A.: A principled approach to score level fusion in multimodal biometric systems. In: Kanade, T., Jain, A., Ratha, N.K. (eds.) AVBPA 2005. LNCS, vol. 3546, pp. 1049–1058. Springer, Heidelberg (2005)
9. Graves, S.: On the neyman-pearson theory of testing. The British Journal for the Philosophy of Science 29(1), 1–23 (1978)
10. Lehmann, E., Romano, J.: Testing of Statistical Hypotheses. Springer, Heidelberg (2005)
11. Bishop, C.: Pattern Recognition and Machine Learning. Springer, Heidelberg (2006)
12. Duda, R., Hart, P., Stork, D.: Pattern Classification, 2nd edn. Wiley-Interscience, Hoboken (2001)

13. Figuereido, M., Jain, A.: Unsupervised learning of finite mixture models. IEEE Transaction on Patterns Analysis and Machine Intelligence 24(3), 381–396 (2002)
14. Nandakumar, K., Chen, Y., Jain, A., Dass, S.: Quality-based score level fusion in multimodal biometric systems. Pattern Recognition 4, 473–476 (2006)
15. Wald, A.: Sequential tests of statistical hypotheses. The annals of Mathematical Statistics 16(2), 117–186 (1945)
16. Tronci, R., Giacinto, G., Roli, F.: Combination of experts by classifiers in similarity score spaces. In: da Vitoria Lobo, N., Kasparis, T., Roli, F., Kwok, J.T., Georgiopoulos, M., Anagnostopoulos, G.C., Loog, M. (eds.) S+SSPR 2008. LNCS, vol. 5342, pp. 821–830. Springer, Heidelberg (2008)

A 3D Scanner for Transparent Glass

Gonen Eren[1,2,*], Olivier Aubreton[1], Fabrice Meriaudeau[1],
L.A. Sanchez Secades[1], David Fofi[1], A. Teoman Naskali[2],
Frederic Truchetet[1], and Aytul Ercil[2]

[1] University of Burgundy, Le2i Laboratory CNRS UMR 5158, Esplanade Erasme,
21000, Dijon, France
[2] Sabanci University, VPA Laboratory, Orhanli-Tuzla, 34956, Istanbul, Turkey
goneneren@su.sabanciuniv.edu

Abstract. Many practical tasks in industry, such as automatic inspection or robot vision, often require the scanning of three-dimensional shapes by use of non-contact techniques. However, few methods have been proposed to measure three-dimensional shapes of transparent objects because of the difficulty of dealing with transparency and specularity of the surface. This paper presents a 3D scanner for transparent glass objects based on Scanning From Heating (SFH), a new method that makes use of local surface heating and thermal imaging.

Keywords: Infrared imaging, Three-dimensional image processing, Carbon dioxide laser, Glass.

1 Introduction

Three-dimensional scanning has been widely used for many years for reverse engineering and part inspection. A good review of 3D model acquisition techniques can be found in [1]. However, most of these methods are designed to obtain the shape of opaque surfaces with Lambertian reflectance properties. Scanning of transparent objects cannot be properly achieved using these techniques. Figure 1 illustrates this fact and presents a transparent glass object and its reconstruction by a Minolta VI-910 Non Contact 3D Digitizer. The 3D reconstruction of the object is affected by internal refractions and specular reflections.

Researchers have proposed different approaches to deal with transparent objects. Miyazaki et al. have developed a method to determine the surface orientations of transparent objects based on polarization degrees in visible and infrared wavelengths [2,3]. Hata et al. have developed a shape from distortion technique to recover the surface shape of a glass object [4]. Ben-Ezra and Nayar estimated the parameterized surface shape of transparent objects using structure from

* We gratefully acknowledge the help of C. Oden, H. Isik, E. Dogan and G. Ciftci from Vistek A.S., M. Akay, H. Yuksek and H. Yavaslar from Sisecam A.S., E.D. Kunt and K. Cakir from AMS and O. Aygun from Flir Systems Turkey. This project was partially supported by SAN-TEZ(00335.STZ.2008-2) and SPICE(FP6-2004-ACC-SSA-2).

P. Foggia, C. Sansone, and M. Vento (Eds.): ICIAP 2009, LNCS 5716, pp. 519–527, 2009.
© Springer-Verlag Berlin Heidelberg 2009

(a)   (b)

Fig. 1. (a) Transparent glass object, (b) 3D reconstruction by Minolta VI-910 Non Contact 3D Digitizer

motion [5]. Additionally, an extension using optical flow formulations has been presented by Agarwal et al. [6]. Kutulakos and Steger investigated several applications of direct ray measurement [7]. Fanany et al. proposed a method based on a neural network scheme for transparent surface modeling [8]. Narita et al. used a range-finding approach [9]. Skydan et al. applied a fringe reflection technique to measure the 3D shape of automotive glass [10]. These approaches can deal relatively well with different sub-classes of objects. However, the algorithms are still very specific and not generally applicable. Furthermore, many techniques require considerable acquisition effort and careful calibration [11].

In this paper, a new 3D Scanner based on Scanning From Heating (SFH) method is presented. The paper is organized as follows. Section 2 presents the theory behind and describes the scanner. In Section 3, results are presented. Finally, Section 4 concludes the paper.

2 Scanner Design

2.1 Scanning From Heating (SFH) Method

The working principle of the method is illustrated on Figure 2. An infrared camera and a laser are placed on a moving platform. The surface of the object is localy heated at a point, using the laser. For each position of the moving platform a thermal image is acquired and pixel coordinates of the heated point are calculated ($P_{c1}(X_{c1}, Y_{c1})$ for Position 1 and $P_{c2}(X_{c2}, Y_{c2})$ for Position 2). The pixel coordinates of the heated point are obtained by smoothing the image with a Gaussian filter of 11x11 pixel size and $\sigma = 2.36$, then approximating by a quadratic polynomial in x and y, and finally examining the polynomial for local maxima. The process is repeated for several points by moving over the object to recover its surface shape. Knowing the intrinsic and extrinsic parameters of the acquisition system, and using the pinhole camera model [12], the 3D world coordinates are obtained as in Eq.(1).

$$\Delta Z = k.\sqrt{(X_{c2} - X_{c1})^2 + (Y_{c2} - Y_{c1})^2} \qquad (1)$$

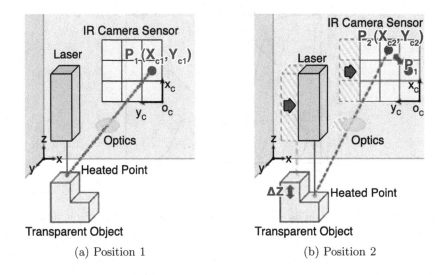

(a) Position 1   (b) Position 2

Fig. 2. Scanning From Heating method

where ΔZ is the variation of the depth between position 1 and 2. k is a constant which can be determined by an initial calibration, which consists of determining the camera coordinates of at least two points of a known object.

The camera observes the emission of the thermal radiation of the heated point once the laser has finished firing. It does not acquire the projection of the laser spot on the surface. Therefore, the method is not affected by the possible reflections of the laser beam on the surface of the glass.

To be able to heat the object with the laser, the object surface should be opaque to the laser source (i.e. the object should not transmit the laser beam through). Figure 3 illustrates the transmission of light as a percentage in the infrared domain of commonly used glasses. Presented glasses are opaque at wavelengths higher than 10 μm. Consequently, using a laser with a wavelength higher than 10 μm as heating source, the SFH method can be applied to transparent glass objects. We chose here to use a CO_2 laser at 10.6 μm.

Once the surface is heated, the thermal camera observes the emission of thermal radiation at the impact point of the laser on the surface. This emission should be omnidirectional so that the thermal camera can capture accurately the heated point on different curvatures of the surface. Figure 4 illustrates emissivity of a dielectric sphere like glass. The emissivity approaches an omnidirectional source.

The prediction of the heat distribution of the laser irradiation zone is important for accurate detection of the heated point. Additionally it is necessary to know the laser power to bring the surface of the object to a given temperature that is detectable by the thermal camera. A mathematical model proposed by Jiao et al. is used [15]. For a CO_2 laser beam traveling in direction x at a constant velocity v, we consider the laser power to have a Gaussian distribution

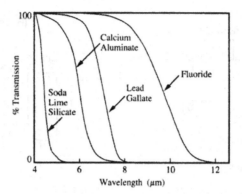

Fig. 3. Transmission of light as a percentage in the infrared domain of commonly used glasses [13]

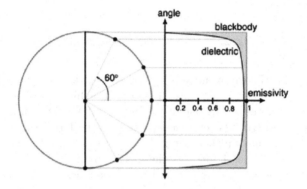

Fig. 4. Emissivity of a dielectric sphere like glass[14]

as in Eq. (2). We treat the CO_2 laser beam as a surface heating source, so the impulse function $\delta(z)$ is applied in Eq. (2).

$$I(x, y, z, t) = \frac{P_0}{\pi r^2} \exp\left(-\frac{(x - vt)^2 + y^2}{r^2}\right) \delta(z) \qquad (2)$$

where P_0 and r are the power and the radius of the CO_2 laser beam, respectively.

2.2   Technical Properties of the Scanner

The scanner has been designed to reconstruct models of large objects up to 80x150x30cm in size. A Synrad 48 Series 10W CO_2 Laser at 10.6 μm is used as the heating source. Thermal images are acquired with a Flir A320G LWIR Camera sensitive to 8 - 13 μm. The power of the laser is controlled by a Synrad UC2000 Laser Power Controller. The laser and thermal camera are placed on an XY positioning system, which is programmable to scan a given area in predefined

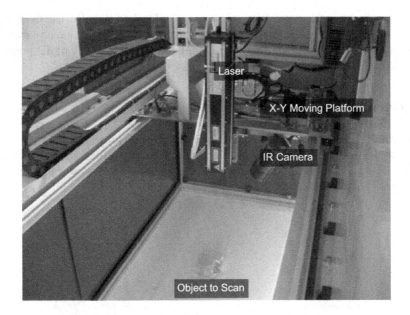

Fig. 5. CO_2 Laser, Thermal Camera and the X-Y Moving platform

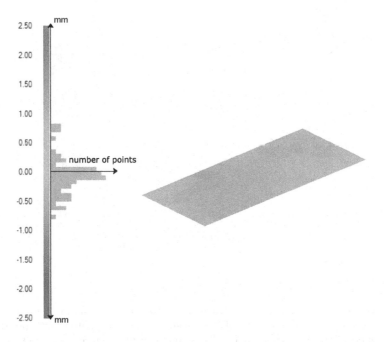

Fig. 6. 3D reconstruction of the transparent glass plate, compared to a perfect plane

steps of X and Y with a precision of 50 μm [Fig.5]. Additionally, the laser is set to fire continuously as it moves over the object during the scan, permitting acquisition of thermal images without stopping and the recovery of 3D points at the maximum speed of the camera (50 fps).

3   Results

This section presents results obtained from the SFH scanner.

Figure 6 illustrates the results obtained on a glass plate 10x5cm in size from 65 points. The reconstruction is compared to a perfect plane. The average deviation is $150\mu m$. This results allows us to validate the method.

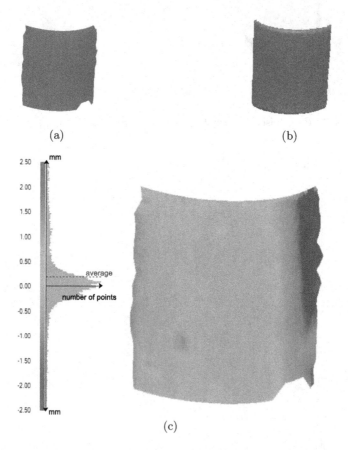

Fig. 7. (a) 3D reconstruction of the transparent glass cup presented in Fig.1 by the SFH Scanner, (b) 3D reconstruction of the transparent glass cup, after being powdered, by the Minolta 3D Laser Scanner, (c) 3D comparison of the reconstructions and the histogram of the deviation

(a) (b)

Fig. 8. (a) Transparent glass object, (b) 3D reconstruction by the SFH Scanner

(a) (b)

Fig. 9. (a) Transparent glass object, (b) 3D reconstruction by the SFH Scanner

Figure 7 illustrates the 3D reconstruction of the transparent glass cup presented in Figure 1 by the SFH Scanner and the reconstruction of the same cup, after being powdered, by the Minolta 3D Laser Scanner. In order to validate the efficiency and determine the accuracy of the method, results are compared and the average deviation is determined. Figure 7 presents 3D comparison of the reconstructions and the histogram of the deviation. The results fit reasonably well, and the average deviation is $210\mu m$. Differences between the two models are mostly located on the borders of the scanning region and are probably due to calibration errors in both reconstruction systems.

Figure 8 illustrates the results obtained from the scanning of a complex transparent glass object 7x7x15cm in size from 2100 points and Figure 9 illustrates the results obtained from another complex transparent glass object 9x9x14cm in size from 1300 points. Hence, the system is applicable to wide range of objects ranging from flat surfaces in the automotive industry to more complex objects in the packaging industry.

4   Conclusion

This paper presented a scanner for the 3-D shape measurement of transparent glass objects using the Scanning From Heating method. The scanner was implemented and tested on diverse glass objects. Experiments show that the quality of the reconstructed models is accurate as conventional laser scanners in the visible domain. Additionally, the obtained results demonstrated that the scanner has the capacity to scan different types of surfaces. The scanner holds promise for a wide range of applications in automotive and packaging industries. Future work will concentrate on extensions of the system, mainly oriented toward the projection of a specific pattern (e.g., line, grid, matrix of points) to improve the 3D point acquisition speed and precision. Initial tests on diverse transparent materials such as plastic have been performed and yield promising results. Further, an application for an industrial production line is planned.

References

1. Bernardini, F., Rushmeier, H.: The 3D Model Acquisition Pipeline. In: Computer Graphics Forum, vol. 21, pp. 149–172. Blackwell Synergy, Malden (2002)
2. Miyazaki, D., Ikeuchi, K.: Inverse Polarization Raytracing: Estimating Surface Shapes of Transparent Objects. In: IEEE Computer Society Conference on Computer Vision and Pattern Recognition, vol. 2, p. 910. Springer, Heidelberg (2005)
3. Miyazaki, D., Saito, M., Sato, Y., Ikeuchi, K.: Determining surface orientations of transparent objects based on polarization degrees in visible and infrared wavelengths. Journal of the Optical Society of America A 19(4), 687–694 (2002)
4. Hata, S., Saitoh, Y., Kumamura, S., Kaida, K.: Shape Extraction of Transparent Object Using Genetic Algorithm. In: International Conference on Pattern Recognition, vol. 13, pp. 684–688 (1996)
5. Ben-Ezra, M., Nayar, S.: What does motion reveal about transparency? In: Proc. IEEE International Conference on Computer Vision, pp. 1025–1032 (2003)
6. Agarwal, S., Mallick, S., Kriegman, D., Belongie, S.: On Refractive Optical Flow. LNCS, pp. 483–494. Springer, Heidelberg (2004)
7. Kutulakos, K., Steger, E.: A Theory of Refractive and Specular 3D Shape by Light-Path Triangulation. International Journal of Computer Vision 76(1), 13–29 (2008)
8. Fanany, M., Kumazawa, I., Kobayashi, K.: A neural network scheme for transparent surface modelling. In: Proceedings of the 3rd international conference on Computer graphics and interactive techniques in Australasia and South East Asia, pp. 433–437. ACM, New York (2005)
9. Narita, D., Baba, M., Ohtani, K.: Three-dimensional shape measurement of a transparent object using a rangefinding approach. In: Proceedings of the 20th IEEE Instrumentation and Measurement Technology Conference. IMTC 2003, vol. 2 (2003)

10. Skydan, O., Lalor, M., Burton, D.: 3D shape measurement of automotive glass by using a fringe reflection technique. Measurement Science and Technology 18(1), 106–114 (2007)
11. Ihrke, I., Kutulakos, K., Lensch, H., Magnor, M., Heidrich, W.: State of the art in transparent and specular object reconstruction. In: STAR Proc. of Eurographics (2008)
12. Forsyth, D., Ponce, J.: Computer Vision: A Modern Approach. Prentice Hall Professional Technical Reference (2002)
13. Shelby, J.: Introduction to Glass Science and Technology. Royal Society of Chemistry (2005)
14. Gaussorgues, G., Chomet, S.: Infrared Thermography. Springer, Heidelberg (1994)
15. Jiao, J., Wang, X.: A numerical simulation of machining glass by dual CO2-laser beams. Optics and Laser Technology 40(2), 297–301 (2008)

Red Eye Detection through Bag-of-Keypoints Classification

Sebastiano Battiato[1], Mirko Guarnera[2], Tony Meccio[1], and Giuseppe Messina[2]

[1] Università degli Studi di Catania
Dipartimento di Matematica
Viale A. Doria 6, 95125 Catania
[2] STMicroelectronics
Advanced System Technology
Stradale Primosole 50, 95121 Catania

Abstract. Red eye artifacts are a well-known problem in digital photography. Small compact devices and point-and-click usage, typical of non-professional photography, greatly increase the likelihood for red eyes to appear in acquired images. Automatic detection of red eyes is a very challenging task, due to the variability of the phenomenon and the general difficulty in reliably discerning the shape of eyes.

This paper presents a method for discriminating between red eyes and other objects in a set of red eye candidates. The proposed method performs feature-based image analysis and classification just considering the bag-of-keypoints paradigm. Experiments involving different keypoint detectors/descriptors are performed. Achieved results are presented, as well as directions for future work.

Keywords: Red Eyes, Feature Classification, SIFT, GLOH, SVM.

1 Introduction

The Red Eye phenomenon is a well-known problem which happens when taking flash-lighted pictures of people, causing pupils to appear red instead of black. This is expecially problematic in non-professional photography, where imaging devices are small in size. Thus, great need arises for a red eye removal system able to reliably detect and correct red eye artifacts without any user intervention [1].

Red eye artifacts are caused by direct reflection of light from the blood vessels of the retina through the pupil to the camera objective. High-end cameras often feature a separate flash with an extensible and steerable bracket (Fig. 1), which allows for more distance between the flash and the lens, thus reducing the probability for red eyes to appear. One preventive measure suitable to both high-end and low-end devices is to make additional flashes before actually taking the photograph. This method gives time to pupils to shrink in order to reduce the reflectance surface, thus making red eyes less likely. Despite the increased power consumption due to the additional flashes, this is a widespread feature of small digital cameras.

P. Foggia, C. Sansone, and M. Vento (Eds.): ICIAP 2009, LNCS 5716, pp. 528–537, 2009.

Fig. 1. Flash-gun light cone generated by reflection off the retina. If the angle α, representing the cone size, is greater than the angle β, between the camera lens and the flash-gun, then the red-eye artifact comes out.

In the easier cases, the small circle of the pupil is a clearly distinguishable red color disk instead of a normal black one. Usually a small white glint is also present, representing the direct reflection of the flash on the surface of the eye and giving the eye much more naturalness. However, red eye artifacts present a great degree of variability, as they may appear different in shape and color, and may also differ in position and size relative to the whole eye [2].

As the detection and the correction problems are well separable, lots of techniques exist which address only one of them. Typical red eye detection approaches involve extraction of "red" zones combined with template matching, face detection and/or skin extraction. Some approaches also make use of classifiers to better discriminate true eyes from false positives.

Patti et al. [3] used a nonstandard luminance-chrominance representation to enhance the regions affected by the red-eye artifact. After the detection of a block of maximal area, thresholding operation and a simple color replacement structure are employed. Most of the red eye detection algorithms apply some constraints to restrict possible red-eye regions in conjunction with reliable learning-based classifiers. Gaubatz and Ulichney [4] first applied a face detector and then searched for the eyes in the candidate face regions by using the constraints of color variance, red variance and glint. The results greatly depend on the face detector which only deals with frontal and upright faces.

Schildkraut and Gray [5] proposed an automatic algorithm to detect pairs of eyes, which is restricted to near-frontal face images. Ioffe [6] proposed a machine learning approach by combining two detectors. The first is the red-eye and non-red-eye classifier trained with boosting method on numerous training patches and the second is the face detector which is used to reduce the false positives. However, many photos have single red eyes (e.g., face partially screened). Zhang et al. [7] proposed a two-stage algorithm for red eye detection. At the first stage, red pixels are grouped and a cascade of heuristic algorithms based on color, size and highlight are used to decide whether the grouped region is red-eye or not. At the second stage, candidate red-eye regions are checked by the Adaboost classifier [8].

Though highlight is a good constraint for red eye detection, red eyes with no highlight region may occur when the eye direction does not face toward the camera/flash light. Luo et al. [9] proposed an algorithm that uses multi-scale square concentric templates to assess the candidate red-eye regions, followed by an Adaboost classifier.

Volken at al. [10] detect the eye itself by finding the appropriate colors and shapes. They use the basic knowledge that an eye is characterized by its shape and the white color of the sclera. Combining this intuitive approach with the detection of "skin" around the eye they obtain good results. Safonov [2] suggested to take into account color information via 3D tables and edge information via directional edge detection filters. For classification a cascade of classifiers including AdaBoost have been used. The approach proposed by Ferman [11] uses a novel unsupervised method to discover of red eye pixels. Analysis is performed primarily in the Hue-Saturation-Value (HSV) color space. A flash mask, which defines the regions where red-eye regions may be present, is first extracted from the brightness component. Subsequent processing on the other color components prunes the number of candidate regions that may correspond to red eyes.

In this paper we propose to attack the problem of red eye detection just using the bag-of-keypoints paradigm. It involves extraction of local image features, quantization of the feature space into a codebook through clustering, and extraction of codeword distribution histograms. A classifier is used to decide to which class each histogram, thus each image, belongs. Approaches of this kind have been shown to be able to recognize different kinds of images in a variety of applications [12] [13].

Our idea is to employ a classification technique to discriminate images representing red eyes from ones representing false candidates. In particular we propose to analyze the input dataset just considering a set of well-known keypoint detectors/descriptors [14] [15] [16] [17]. Support Vector Machine [18] [19] is used as final classifier. Such an approach is shape-based, thus robust to red image features which often cause false positives in color-based red eye detection algorithms, and is capable of detecting more complex features than most template-based methods. This, combined with a color-based red eye candidate extractor, and/or with a correction technique which leaves non-red zones untouched, may contribute to a full system robust to both color-based and shape-based false positives. Experiments confirm the effectiveness of the proposed pipeline.

This paper is organized as follows. Section 2 presents an overview of the proposed algorithm. Sections 3, 4 and 5 describe the feature extraction, quantization, and classification steps, respectively. Section 6 presents the results achieved, and in Section 7 suggestions for future work are given.

2   Algorithm Overview

The overall algorithm pipeline is depicted in Fig. 2. First, images are analysed with a local feature extraction method. This kind of methods scan the images for "interesting" points (keypoints) and compute the image information around the keypoints to associate to each a descriptor which is distinctive of the nature of the object(s) the keypoint belongs to. Keypoints are localized relative to their position, scale and orientation, and in some cases are normalized with respect to affine deformations, in order to make them invariant to as many variations as possible.

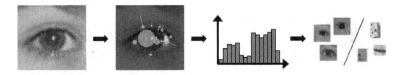

Fig. 2. The proposed algorithm pipeline. Left to right: Input image, feature extraction, feature quantization, classification.

In this application, the objects to describe are the various parts of the eye. Thus, it is fundamental to extract features distinctive of such parts, in order to well discriminate them from parts belonging to false candidates.

To compute a fixed-length vector from each image, local features extracted (which are variable in number) are counted into a histogram. Bins are distributed across the feature space in a way such that more populated portions of the space have more bins, in order to obtain more meaningful histograms.

Histograms are given as input to a classifier to separate the characteristics of the histograms of the two classes (eye and non-eye) and to discriminate them with high accuracy. A training set of labeled images is used to train the classifier and to find the optimal parameters for it.

3   Feature Extraction

The problems of keypoint detection and description can be treated independently. Experiments were made combining different detectors and descriptors, totalling 11 alternatives for image analysis.

As discussed in [15], the Harris corner detector [20] can be adapted to detect corners at multiple scales. To select only the most significant scale(s) for each feature, only corners for which the Laplacian-of-Gaussian operator attains a maximum over scale are selected (Harris-Laplace detector (HarLap)).

The Hessian-Laplace (HesLap) detector [16] looks for keypoints for which the determinant of the Hessian matrix, computed at different scales, attains a local maximum over space. In the same way as Harris-Laplace, the Laplacian-of-Gaussian operator is used to select the features at the most significant scale(s).

Since the Harris-Laplace and the Hessian-Laplace detectors are somewhat complementary to each other (corner-like vs. blob-like structures), it is possible to use both to obtain a richer representation (Harris-Hessian-Laplace detector (HarHesLap)).

Both the Harris-Laplace and Hessian-Laplace detectors can be further refined to detect affine invariant regions. To accomplish this, an iterative method is used to estimate the optimal shape adaptation matrix for each keypoint, thus extracting elliptical keypoints instead of circular ones (Harris-Affine (HarAff) and Hessian-Affine (HesAff) detectors). In these cases, the region underlying each keypoint is normalized to a circular/square one prior to computation of descriptors.

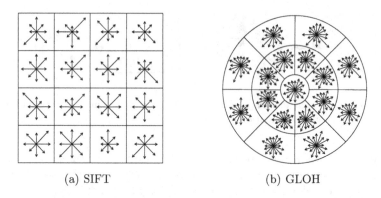

(a) SIFT   (b) GLOH

Fig. 3. Schematic representation of the two descriptors

One of the descriptors used to describe the extracted keypoints is the Scale Invariant Feature Transform (SIFT) descriptor [14]. It has been originally introduced for the SIFT image analysis technique. This method selects keypoints at different scales by computing a band-pass gaussian pyramid using the Difference-of-Gaussians (DoG) operator (an approximation of the Laplacian-of-Gaussian (LoG)), and local maxima and minima of the pyramid are selected as keypoints at the corresponding scale. Keypoints are filtered according to stability measures based on local contrast and "cornerness", and then orientations are assigned to them according to local image gradients in order to achieve rotational invariance. It is shown in [16] that the Hessian-Laplace detector responds to similar structures as the maxima of the Difference-of-Gaussians, but has high responses near corners and low responses near edges, making it unnecessary to filter keypoints on local cornerness. The SIFT descriptor is composed by a 4-by-4 grid of 8-bin local gradient orientation histograms. The grid is centered on the keypoint, sized accordingly to its scale and rotated accordingly to its orientation. The resulting 128-dimensional vector is normalized to unit Euclidean length in order to compensate for contrast variations (see Fig.3(a)).

The other employed descriptor is the Gradient Location and Orientation Histogram (GLOH) (see Fig.3(b)), a variant of the SIFT descriptor. Like the latter, it is a set of gradient orientation histograms, but instead of being a grid, it has a "crosshair"-like shape, with a central circular region and two external concentric rings each divided in the angular direction in 8 regions. This adds to 17 histograms, each consisting of 16 bins. The 272-dimensional vector is then reduced to 128 dimensions with PCA.

4   Feature Space Quantization

Clustering is used to select a meaningful subdivision of the feature space into histogram bins. Descriptors from the training set are clustered with the k-means algorithm [21], with k=50. The set of centroids found is used as a "codebook" of representative features, and one bin is assigned to each, thus obtaining a finer quantization in more populated regions of the feature space. Each descriptor contributes to the bin relative to the closest centroid.

In some cases, no keypoints are detected in a given candidate image. Since it almost always happens for false candidates, e.g., for blurry background objects, images without keypoints are considered non-eyes and are discarded from further consideration.

Prior to classification, histograms are normalized in order to make them less dependant to the number of keypoints detected. Then, since the classifier used (see below) considers euclidean distance between vectors, i.e. the 2-norm of the difference, a trasformation is performed to make this distance more meaningful: namely, histograms are transformed by taking the square root of each bin. This converts 1-norm normalized vectors into 2-norm normalized vectors. The dot product between two of these vectors, which is equivalent to the cosine of the angle between them, is the Bhattacharyya coefficient between the original (1-norm normalized) vectors [22]. This coefficient is a common measure of similiarity between frequency distributions, and it can be shown that the euclidean distance calculated this way is proportional to the metric commonly associated to the coefficient:

$$BC(\mathbf{v}, \mathbf{w}) = \sum_{i=1}^{n} \sqrt{v_i} \cdot \sqrt{w_i} \,. \tag{1}$$

$$d(\overline{\mathbf{v}}, \overline{\mathbf{w}}) = \sqrt{\sum_{i=1}^{n} (\overline{v_i} - \overline{w_i})^2} = \sqrt{\sum_{i=1}^{n} \overline{v_i}^2 + \sum_{i=1}^{n} \overline{w_i}^2 - 2 \cdot \sum_{i=1}^{n} \overline{v_i} \cdot \overline{w_i}} =$$

$$= \sqrt{\sum_{i=1}^{n} v_i + \sum_{i=1}^{n} w_i - 2 \cdot \sum_{i=1}^{n} \sqrt{v_i} \cdot \sqrt{w_i}} =$$

$$= \sqrt{2 - 2 \cdot BC(\mathbf{v}, \mathbf{w})} = \sqrt{2} \cdot \sqrt{1 - BC(\mathbf{v}, \mathbf{w})} \,. \tag{2}$$

In the above formulas, BC is the Bhattacharyya coefficient, d is the Euclidean distance, $\mathbf{v}, \mathbf{w}$ are 1-norm normalized vectors and $\overline{\mathbf{v}}, \overline{\mathbf{w}}$ are the corresponding 2-norm normalized vectors.

5   SVM Classification

Histograms are classified using a Support Vector Machine classifier [18] [19]. This classifier works by finding an optimal separation hyperplane between two different classes of labeled training vectors and specifying a small number of weighted vectors which lie on the boundaries of the classes (these vectors are called "support vectors"). Since a linear separation usually isn't meaningful, vectors are usually projected into a higher-dimensional space and then linearly classified in that space. However, computing the projected vectors explicitly can be expensive or even impossible. Instead, the problem can be expressed in a form where the projected vectors only appear in dot products between two of them. Thus, a common practice is to employ a function which, given two vectors in the original space, computes the dot product of their projections in the higher-dimensional space (usually in a much simpler way). This function is named "kernel", and this practice is named "kernel trick". It is proven that any continuous, symmetric, semidefinite positive function from $\mathbf{R}^n$ to $\mathbf{R}$ can be used as a classification kernel.

The kernel used in the experiments is the Radial Basis Function (RBF) kernel, which is a multidimensional non-normalized gaussian:

$$K(\mathbf{v}, \mathbf{w}) = e^{-\gamma \cdot \|\mathbf{v} - \mathbf{w}\|_2^2} \ , \ \gamma > 0 \ . \tag{3}$$

As shown above, the aperture of the gaussian function is controlled by a parameter γ. This is one of the parameters which must be adjusted in order to obtain the most accurate classification for each given training set. The other parameters to find, called C_1 and C_2, are penalty factors for outliers in the two classes of the training set. It is important to carefully adjust them in order to find an optimal tradeoff between accuracy of the classification and tolerance to outliers, which is important to prevent overfitting. The two parameters are adjusted independently to achieve more generality.

Optimal parameters are searched with a multi-level grid search using 8-fold cross-validation for training and testing: first, a grid of parameter triples, spaced evenly in a logarithmic scale, is tried, then a finer grid covering the parameters who gave the best results is tried, and so on, up to the fifth level of grid refinement.

6   Experimental Results

The proposed red-eye detection system has been trained on a data set of 4079 image patches, comprising 956 red eyes, and tested on a data set of 5797 image patches, comprising 234 red eyes. The sets has been collected from photographs taken with various sources, including DSLR images, compact cameras and Internet photos, and the image candidates have been extracted using an automatic red cluster detector [23]. This means that the "eye" class is mostly trained with red eye patches: however, since the method is shape-based, regular eyes are recognized as well, as red eye artifacts have little impact on the luminance. Training on red eyes allows to learn the slight differences in shape which occur (e.g. biggest and brightest pupils, different luminance distribution), while classifying regular eyes along with red eyes is not a problem, since regular eyes have no red pupils to correct, then a color-based correction algorithm can discard them easily, and a "blind" correction algorithm can desaturate them with almost no harm. Table 1 shows results achieved with the different detector+descriptor combinations. Hit rate is the percentage of eyes correctly classified out of the total number of eyes; False positives is the percentage of false candidates incorrectly classified out of

Table 1. Classification results for each detector/descriptor combination tested

Detector + Descriptor	Hit rate	False positives	Overall perf.	Accuracy
DoG + SIFT	83.3%	8.9%	87.20%	90.78%
HarLap + SIFT	78.2%	12.2%	83.00%	87.47%
HesLap + SIFT	71.8%	7.1%	82.35%	92.12%
HarHesLap + SIFT	82.9%	3.5%	89.70%	95.94%
HarAff + SIFT	70.1%	8.1%	81.00%	91.08%
HesAff + SIFT	82.9%	7.0%	87.95%	92.59%
HarLap + GLOH	75.2%	12.1%	81.55%	87.38%
HesLap + GLOH	80.3%	14.4%	82.95%	85.41%
HarHesLap + GLOH	76.9%	7.3%	84.80%	92.07%
HarAff + GLOH	73.5%	11.9%	80.80%	87.52%
HesAff + GLOH	69.2%	7.3%	84.80%	92.07%

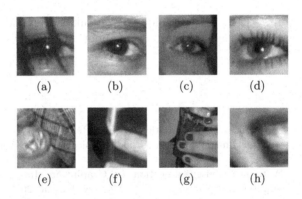

(a)   (b)   (c)   (d)

(e)   (f)   (g)   (h)

Fig. 4. Classification examples obtained with Harris-Affine + SIFT. Top row: (a), (b), (c) are eye patches correctly classified; (d) has been incorrectly classified as non-eye. Bottom row: (e), (f), (g) have been correctly classified as non-eyes; (h) is a false positive.

the total number of false candidates; Overall performance is (Hit rate + (100% - False positives))/2; Accuracy is the percentage of patches correctly classified out of the total number of patches.

It can be seen from the results that, while there are quite a significant amount of eyes that are missed, a restricted percentage of false candidates are misclassified as eyes (using the best performing detector+descriptor combinations). This is a remarkable result, since correction of false positives is one of the biggest problems in red eye removal, thus it is very important to keep false positives as low as possible. It is also evident how the blob-based detectors yielded better results than the corner-based detectors. This is not surprising, as many parts of the eye are more suitable to be extracted by a blob-like detector (expecially the iris and the pupil). Using both types of detector together, however, helps keep the false positives lower. SIFT performed better than GLOH.

Comparison with other red eye detectors cannot be made, since the proposed approach doesn't select candidates on its own. It cannot even be made with the classification phase of two-step detectors (candidate detection + classification), since in these cases the performance of the classifier is heavily influenced by the number of candidates extracted, and is also affected by how much the candidate detector and the classifier are "fine-tuned" for each other.

7   Conclusions and Future Work

In this work we showed the effectiveness of Bag-of-Keypoints-based classification in discriminating red eyes from false red eye candidates. Results are interesting, but improvement is needed. Further studies will be performed with different keypoints detectors/descriptors and other kind of image analyses, including spatial domain-based features.

Acknowledgments. The authors would like to thank Giovanni Maria Farinella and Giovanni Puglisi for their precious advice about image analysis, scene classification and SVM.

References

1. Gasparini, F., Schettini, R.: Automatic Red-Eye Removal for digital photography. In: Single-Sensor Imaging: Methods and Applications for Digital Cameras, pp. 429–457 (2008)
2. Safonov, I.V.: Automatic red-eye detection. In: GraphiCon., International conference on the Computer Graphics and Vision, Moscow, Russia (2007)
3. Patti, A.J., Konstantinides, K., Tretter, D., Lin, Q.: Automatic digital redeye reduction. In: IEEE International Conference on Image Processing (ICIP 1998), Chicago, Illinois, vol. 1, pp. 55–59 (1998)
4. Gaubatz, M., Ulichney, R.: Automatic red-eye detection and correction. In: IEEE International Conference on Image Processing (ICIP 2002), Rochester, New York, USA, vol. 1, pp. 804–807 (2002)
5. Schildkraut, J.S., Gray, R.T.: A fully automatic redeye detection and correction algorithm. In: IEEE International Conference on Image Processing (ICIP 2002), Rochester, New York, USA, vol. 1, pp. 801–803 (2002)
6. Ioffe, S.: Red eye detection with machine learning. In: IEEE International Conference on Image Processing (ICIP 2003), Barcelona, Catalonia, Spain, vol. 2, pp. 871–874 (2003)
7. Zhang, L., Sun, Y., Li, M., Zhang, H.: Automated red-eye detection and correction in digital photographs. In: IEEE International Conference on Image Processing (ICIP 2004), pp. 2363–2366 (2004)
8. Freund, Y., Schapire, R.E.: A decision-theoretic generalization of on-line learning and an application to boosting. Journal of Computer and System Sciences 55, 119–139 (1997)

9. Luo, H., Yen, J., Tretter, D.: An efficient automatic redeye detection and correction algorithm. In: IEEE International Conference on Pattern Recognition (ICPR 2004), pp. 883–886 (2004)
10. Volken, F., Terrier, J., Vandewalle, P.: Automatic red-eye removal based on sclera and skin tone detection. In: Third European Conference on Color in Graphics, Imaging and Vision (CGIV 2006), Society for Imaging Science and Technology, pp. 359–364 (2006)
11. Ferman, A.M.: Automatic detection of red-eye artifacts in digital color photos. In: IEEE International Conference on Image Processing (ICIP 2008), San Diego, California, vol. 1, pp. 617–620 (2008)
12. Battiato, S., Farinella, G.M., Gallo, G., Ravì, D.: Scene categorization using bags of textons on spatial hierarchy. In: International Conference on Image Processing, ICIP 2008 (2008)
13. Bosch, A., Zisserman, A., Munoz, X.: Scene classification using a hybrid generative/discriminative approach. IEEE Transactions on Pattern Analysis and Machine Intelligence 30 (2008)
14. Lowe, D.G.: Distinctive image features from scale-invariant keypoints. International Journal of Computer Vision 60, 91–110 (2004)
15. Mikolajczyk, K., Schmid, C.: Scale & affine invariant interest point detectors. International Journal of Computer Vision 60, 63–86 (2004)
16. Mikolajczyk, K., Schmid, C.: A performance evaluation of local descriptors. IEEE Trans. Pattern Anal. Mach. Intell. 27, 1615–1630 (2005)
17. Mikolajczyk, K., Tuytelaars, T., Schmid, C., Zisserman, A., Matas, J., Schaffalitzky, F., Kadir, T., Van Gool, L.J.: A comparison of affine region detectors. International Journal of Computer Vision 65, 43–72 (2005)
18. Boser, B.E., Guyon, I., Vapnik, V.: A training algorithm for optimal margin classifiers. In: COLT, pp. 144–152 (1992)
19. Cortes, C., Vapnik, V.: Support-vector networks. Machine Learning 20, 273–297 (1995)
20. Harris, C., Stephens, M.: A combined corner and edge detection. In: Proceedings of The Fourth Alvey Vision Conference, pp. 147–151 (1988)
21. Hartigan, J.A., Wong, M.A.: A K-means clustering algorithm. Applied Statistics 28, 100–108 (1979)
22. Comaniciu, D., Ramesh, V., Meer, P.: Kernel-based object tracking. IEEE Transactions on Pattern Analysis and Machine Intelligence 25, 564–575 (2003)
23. Battiato, S., Farinella, G.M., Guarnera, M., Messina, G., Ravì, D.: Red-eyes detection through cluster based linear discriminant analysis (to appear)

A New Large Urdu Database for Off-Line Handwriting Recognition

Malik Waqas Sagheer, Chun Lei He, Nicola Nobile, and Ching Y. Suen

CENPARMI (Centre for Pattern Recognition and Machine Intelligence)
Computer Science and Software Engineering Department, Concordia University
Montreal, Quebec, Canada
{m_saghee,cl_he,nicola,suen}@cenparmi.concordia.ca

Abstract. A new large Urdu handwriting database, which includes isolated digits, numeral strings with/without decimal points, five special symbols, 44 isolated characters, 57 Urdu words (mostly financial related), and Urdu dates in different patterns, was designed at Centre for Pattern Recognition and Machine Intelligence (CENPARMI). It is the first database for Urdu off-line handwriting recognition. It involves a large number of Urdu native speakers from different regions of the world. Moreover, the database has different formats – true color, gray level and binary. Experiments on Urdu digits recognition has been conducted with an accuracy of 98.61%. Methodologies in image pre-processing, gradient feature extraction and classification using SVM have been described, and a detailed error analysis is presented on the recognition results.

Keywords: Urdu OCR, Off-line Handwriting Recognition, Handwriting Segmentation, Urdu Digit Recognition.

1 Introduction

Off-line handwriting recognition has become an important area in the pattern recognition field and finding a good database for recognition is also a main issue. The writers of this Urdu database have been divided into three categories based on their genders, and writing orientations. For the Urdu language, this is the first known handwritten database and it can be used for multiple applications. The value of this Urdu database is based on the variety of its contents. The databases contain a large number of Urdu isolated digits and numeral strings of various lengths, including those with decimal points. This database can be used for various types of applications such as digit, letter, word, and cheque recognition as well as for word spotting applications.

Urdu is an Indo-European [1] language which originated in India. It is a popular language of the subcontinent. Urdu is one of the 23 official languages of India and is one of the two official languages of Pakistan. This language is also widely spoken in Dubai. It is one of the most spoken languages in the world.

Written Urdu has been derived from the Persian alphabet, which itself has been derived from the Arabic alphabet. Like Arabic, Urdu is written from right to left. However, Urdu has more isolated letters (37) than Arabic (28) and Persian (32). This fact

P. Foggia, C. Sansone, and M. Vento (Eds.): ICIAP 2009, LNCS 5716, pp. 538–546, 2009.
© Springer-Verlag Berlin Heidelberg 2009

makes Urdu different from Arabic and Persian in appearance in such a way that it uses slightly more complicated and complex script. Therefore, constructing an Urdu database for handwriting recognition was necessary.

The structure of this paper is divided into seven sections. In Section 2, we describe the data collection process. Section 3 comprises of data extraction and a description of preprocessing methods. In section 4, we discuss the overview of the database followed by descriptions of the datasets. We describe the ground truth data in Section 5. In section 6, experiments on Urdu isolated digits and their error analysis have been described. Finally, we discuss the conclusions as well as future work.

2   Data Collection Process

A two-page data entry form had been designed and used for the collection of handwritten data. The process of data collection was conducted in Montreal, Canada (30%) and Pakistan (70%). The first page of the form contains 20 Indian isolated digits (two samples of each digit), a freestyle written date, 38 numeral strings of various lengths, 43 isolated characters and 16 words. The second page includes the remaining 41 words and five special symbols. Fig. 1 shows a small portion of our form.

Fig. 1. Sample of Filled Form

So far, we collected handwriting samples from 343 different writers comprised of men and women from various professional backgrounds, qualifications, and ages. We were interested in keeping track of writer's gender, age, as well as whether they were right-handed or left-handed. Even though at this stage the writer information has no significance, it could be used in future research. The writers have been distributed into three categories as follows: 1) right-handed males (75.4%), 2) left-handed males (5.6%), and 3) right-handed females (19.0%). We can see that the number of left-handed subjects are far less than the number of right-handed ones.

3   Data Extraction and Preprocessing

We obtained digital copies of the forms by scanning and saving them as true color (24 Bit), 300 DPI lossless TIFF images. Basic noise removal was done at the form level before we applied our algorithm to remove the red lines from the forms. Removing these lines facilitates the extraction of the handwritten elements. Removing the lines requires careful inspection of the elements on the scanned page since some writers exceeded the field boundaries and overlapped the red line as seen in Fig. 2a-c. Furthermore, although the writers used either blue or black ink, if we zoom in some handwriting, as seen in Fig. 2d, we can see that some pen strokes contain traces of red (in different shades of red). Therefore, our algorithm had to carefully remove red lines without affecting the writing. Doing so would introduce salt and pepper noise and lose the true outline of the handwritten element.

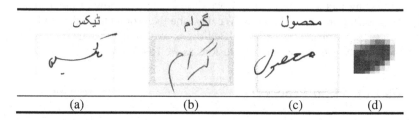

| (a) | (b) | (c) | (d) |

Fig. 2. Examples of Urdu Handwritten Elements Exceeding the Field Boundaries (a-c), and Close-up of Handwriting Displaying Several Colors

Removing the red lines involves analyzing each relevant pixel in the form. For each of these pixels, we determine if it should be removed by determining if its "redness" is within a range of red we had used for printing the forms. We then look at the neighboring pixels – if they are also red within the same range, then it could be potentially removed. If at least one bordering pixel is of handwriting colour, normally black or blue, then the pixel is kept, otherwise, it is considered a border pixel and is removed (replaced by white).

Several forms contained unwanted artifacts because of folding and crumpling of the paper mostly due to the handling by postal delivery from Pakistan to Canada. In addition, a number of forms had an overall dark background. In both cases, these problems had to be corrected before the forms were converted to grayscale. The cleaned forms were then passed to the handwriting extraction process.

For each handwritten sample, the box's coordinates were located. After extracting all the handwritten samples, a special filter was applied to remove the salt and pepper noise. Also, there was a great effort to manually clean those images. All the form images have been saved in three formats: true color, gray scale and binary. A special program was developed to automate the data extracting process from the true color forms. This program takes the coordinates of each box and extracts the box image in true color. The image from the same box numbers of each form is saved in a unique folder. All extracted handwritten items were then converted to grayscale and binary.

4 Database Overview

After creating the databases in true color, it was converted into gray scale and binary formats. Each database had six basic datasets which consisted of isolated digits, dates, isolated letters, numeral strings, words, and special symbols. For each dataset, the data was divided into training, validation, and testing sets by picking elements in the data using a ratio of 3-1-1. This resulted in an approximate distribution of 60%, 20%, and 20% for the training, validation, and testing sets, respectively. A complete description and statistics of each dataset are given in the following subsections.

4.1 Urdu Date Dataset

There are multiple standard ways to write dates in Urdu. Participants were given the freedom to write the dates in any format. Urdu follows the Gregorian calendar for writing dates. They used slash '/', hyphen '-'and dot '.' separate day, month and year. Some people drew a curvy line beneath the year (‏ـسخ··ـ‏), which represents سن (san) in Urdu, and signifies "the year" in English. Some people used the hamza 'ء' at the end of a year, which represents عیسوی (Aiswee) in Urdu and signifies "A.D." in the Gregorian calendar. Some people also wrote the name of a month in Urdu letters (جولۡ means July) instead of writing it in numeral format. From English influence, some people also used the dot to separate month, day and year. This is a challenge in date recognition since the dot is similar in shape with the Urdu digit zero. Some samples are shown in the Table 1. Of the 318 total date samples, 190 belong to the training set and 64 images to each of the validation and test sets.

Table 1. Different Samples of Urdu Dates

English Date	Urdu Date
12/2/2007	‎۱۲/.۲/۲..۷
7-7-2007	۷ —۷— ۲..۷
7 July, 2007	۷ جولۡ ۲..۷
16-Jul-2007 A.C	‎ـسخ··ـ جولۡ ۱۶
8.8.2007	۸.۸. ۲..۷

4.2 Indian Isolated Digit Dataset

Each form contains two samples of each isolated digit. In the numeral strings, each digit is repeated 14 to 18 times at different positions.

   We performed segmentation of the numeral strings by using a segmentation algorithm to separate and extract the digits. After segmentation, a set of isolated digits was created. Segmentation was performed on the grayscale and binary images. All other datasets are available in true color except isolated digits. We extracted a total of 60329 where 33974 were selected for training, 13177 for validation, and 13178 for test. A sample of each extracted digit is shown in Table 2.

Table 2. Sample of Indian Isolated Digits

Nine	Eight	Seven	Six	Five	Four	Three	Two	One	Zero
۹	۸	۷	۶	۵	۴	۳	۲	۱	.

4.3 Indian Numerical Strings Dataset

The data entry forms contain fields for 38 different numeral strings with varying lengths of 2,3,4,6 and 7 digits. Every digit, including the decimal point, is represented at least once in the strings. There are two ways in Urdu to write a decimal point; one way is to use dot (.) and the second is to use a hamza (ء). In most of the samples, the positions of the dot and hamza in numeral strings were located below the baseline. This could be a challenge in recognition of real strings as dot (.) looks like zero in Urdu. We divided this dataset into two sets – an integer set and a Real set. The latter includes decimal numbers of lengths 3 and 4. Samples for integer and real numeral strings are shown in Table 3 below. A total of 12914 strings were extracted which were divided into training (7750), validation (2584), and test (2580) sets.

Table 3. Sample of Different Numeral Strings

English (Numeral String)	Urdu (Numeral string)
47	٣ر
2460257	٢ر٤.٢٥ر
1.50	١ر۵.
1.50	١.۵•

4.4 Urdu Alphabet Dataset

The Urdu alphabet consists of 37 basic letters and some special characters (which consist of a combination of two letters). We added some of them as shown in Table 4. Similar to Arabic and Farsi [2] the words in Urdu are written in a cursive manner and the shape of a letter changes according to its position within a word. The data entry form includes one sample of each of the 37 Urdu isolated letters and each of the special letters. We have a total of 14890 letters with 8934 marked for training an 2978 for the validation and test sets each.

Table 4. Some Urdu Special Characters

Alif Mud AA	Bardi ye Hamza	Noon Guna	Chooti Ye Hamza	Hey Hamza
آ	ئے	ں	ئ	ۂ

4.5 Urdu Words Dataset

We selected 57 Urdu (mostly financial related) words for our word dataset. This dataset could help in recognizing new and different challenges in the recognition of Urdu handwriting and word spotting. It includes words for weights, measurements, and currencies. Samples of some of these Urdu words are shown in Table 5. The total number of images is 19432. These were divided into training (60%), validation (20%), and test (20%) sets.

Table 5. Sample of Urdu Words

Cash	Thousand	Cost	Decrease	Balance	Amount
لَقد	ہزار	لاَگت	کمی	میزان	رقم

4.6 Special Symbols Dataset

The data entry form also includes some special symbols that usually appear in any Urdu document. These symbols, which are also commonly used in other languages, are: comma (,), colon (:), at (@), slash (/), and pound (#). The total number of training samples is 1020. The validation set and the test set contain 340 and 345 images, respectively.

5 Ground Truth Data

For each folder that contains handwritten samples we have also included the ground truth data file. For each sample, the ground truth data file includes the following information: image name, content, number of connected components (CCs), writer number, length of a content, gender, and handwriting orientation. An example of the ground truth data for the numeral strings dataset is shown in Table 6.

Table 6: Examples of the Ground Truth data for Urdu Numeral String Dataset

Image Name	URD0110_P01_056.tif	URD0090_P01_029.tif
Content	0581294	47
Writer No.	URD0110	URD0090
Gender	F	M
Hand Orientation	R	R
Length	7	2
Length (No. of CCs)	7	2

6 Experiments and Error Analysis

6.1 Experiments

Recognition experiments have been conducted on the handwritten isolated Urdu digits. In image pre-processing, we did noise removal, grayscale normalization, size normalization, and binarization, etc. on all the grayscale images. In feature extraction, a 400D gradient feature based on Robert's operator [6] on each normalized image is extracted. In classification, a Support Vector Machine (SVM) using a Radial Base

Function (RBF) kernel function is applied. As a result, we have achieved an accuracy of 98.61% on the test set. The original Urdu Isolated numerals database includes the Training, the Validation, and the Test sets. Since we did nothing on the validation, we combine the Validation set to the Training set. Therefore, the number of samples in the Training set is 47, 151, and the number of the test samples is 13,178.

In image pre-processing, we did noise removal, grayscale normalization, size normalization, and binarization, etc. on all the grayscale images [4]. If the inputs were detected as binary images, they were converted to pseudo-grayscale images automatically. After removing the noise from a background-eliminated grayscale image, we cropped the image to remove the blank boundaries. Afterwards, we did size normalization using Moment Normalization (MN) [3] and grayscale normalization. Finally, we binarized the images based on the threshold calculated with the Otsu Method [5].

For extracting 32-direction gradient feature, the size of normalized image is set to 36 × 36 pixels. On each of 32 direction maps, 4 × 4 feature values are extracted in each block, and thus each image is divided to 9 × 9 blocks. Then, down sampling by Gaussian filtering is applied to reduce both the number of blocks and number of directions, and finally the feature dimensions is 400 (5 horizontal blocks × 5 vertical blocks × 16 directions) [6].

A Support Vector Machine (SVM) was chosen as a classifier for this research. An SVM constructs a separating hyperplane in the feature space, one which maximizes the margin between the data sets, and the kernel function chosen in this experiment is Radial Base Function (RBF). There are two parameters in RBF to be optimized: c and γ. c > 0 is the penalty parameter of the error term, and γ is the parameter in RBF. These two parameters can be are optimal chosen by the cross-validation. When lg(c) = 5 and lg(γ) = -7, the performance on training set achieve the highest recognition rate (97.60%). Thus, we set c = 32 & γ = 0.0078125, and then consider them as parameters in test.

6.2 Error Analysis

The recognition result has achieved accuracy with 98.61% (12995/13178) on the test set. ¾ errors can be grouped to four categories: (1) Almost ½ (88/183) errors occur among "2" (ʳ), "3" (ᵀ), and "4" (ʳ) because of their similar topologies. In this category of errors, half of them occur in "3", which are substituted by "2" since some "3" have small waves on their upper parts, shown in Figure 3. Moreover, some handwritten "2" (ʳ) and "4" (ᵛ) look the same in Urdu, so these make the recognition more difficult. (2) As "6" and "9" are similar in Urdu as well, some errors (33/183) are caused by the ambiguous of "6" and "9". All the substitution images are shown in Figure 4. (3) "5" and "0" in Urdu can have almost the same shapes which look like a circle, so the number of errors between these two classes is 12/183. Figure 5a shows all the errors between "6" and "9". (4) Some short strokes in "0" misrecognized as "1", and small "1" misrecognized as "0". All are shown in Figure 5b. Other substitution images are caused by variations of some individual's handwriting. For example, when the circles in "9" are very small (ʔ), they are misrecognized as "1". The confusion matrix is shown below (Table 7).

Table 7. Results of Handwritten Urdu Isolated Numeral Recognition on Test set

Truth Label	Output									
	0	1	2	3	4	5	6	7	8	9
0	2009	3		1		5				
1	7	1548	1				1	1		1
2			1930	12	13					
3			44	1015	6					
4			10	3	1541					
5	7			1	1	952		1	1	
6	2	2	3			1	969			19
7	3			1	1	1	970			
8	2	1			2				902	1
9	2	8		1		14				1159

Fig. 3. Some substituted images in "3" which were mis-recognized as "2"

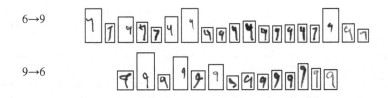

Fig. 4. All substitution images between "6" and "9"

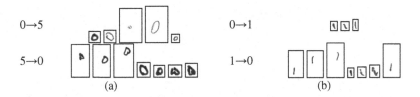

Fig. 5. All substitution images between "0" & "5" (a) and "0" & "1" (b)

7 Conclusion and Future Work

Although handwriting recognition has become a very popular area of Pattern Recognition for so many years, so far there exists no off-line Urdu handwriting database. Therefore, we created this comprehensive handwriting CENPARMI Urdu database which contains dates, isolated digits, numerical strings, isolated letters, a collection of

57 words, and a collection of special symbols. Experiments on the Urdu isolated digits have been conducted with a high recognition rate (98.61%). This database can be
used for the future research in multiple purposes in Urdu documents analysis, such as
Urdu word spotting, etc.

In the future, we will conduct more experiments on Urdu dates, numerical strings,
isolated letters, words, and even symbols recognition. In addition, we will do further
recognition on Urdu isolated digits. For example, we will analyze the errors especially
in the four categories shown above to verify the recognition results or even reject the
errors so that the recognition rate and/or reliability could be improved. We intend to
make this database publicly available in the future.

References

1. Anwar, W., Wang, X., Wang. X.-L.: A survey of automatic Urdu language processing. In:
   Proceedings of the Fifth International Conference on Machine Learning and Cybernetics,
   Dalian, China, pp. 13–16 (2006)
2. Dehghan, M., Faez, K., Ahmadi, M., Shridhar, M.: Handwritten Farsi (Arabic) word recognition: a holistic approach using discrete HMM. Pattern Recognition 34(5), 1057–1065
   (2001)
3. Liu, C.-L., Nakashima, K., Sako, H., Fujisawa, H.: Handwritten digit recognition: Investigation of normalization and feature extraction techniques. Pattern Recognition 37(2), 265–279
   (2004)
4. Liu, C.-L., Suen, C.Y.: A new benchmark on the recognition of handwritten Bangla and
   Farsi numeral characters. In: Proceedings of 11th International Conference on Frontiers in
   Handwriting Recognition (ICFHR), Montreal, Canada, pp. 278–283 (2008)
5. Otsu, N.: A threshold selection method from gray-level histogram. IEEE Trans. System
   Man Cybernet. 9, 1569–1576 (1979)
6. Shi, M., Fujisawa, Y., Wakabayashi, T., Kimura, F.: Handwritten numeral recognition using
   gradient and curvature of gray scale image. Pattern Recognition 35(10), 2051–2059 (2002)

Object Matching in Distributed Video Surveillance Systems by LDA-Based Appearance Descriptors

Liliana Lo Presti[1], Stan Sclaroff[2], and Marco La Cascia[1]

[1] Dipartimento di Ingegneria Informatica, University of Palermo
[2] Computer Science Department, Boston University
lopresti@dinfo.unipa.it, sclaroff@cs.bu.edu, lacascia@unipa.it

Abstract. Establishing correspondences among object instances is still challenging in multi-camera surveillance systems, especially when the cameras' fields of view are non-overlapping. Spatiotemporal constraints can help in solving the correspondence problem but still leave a wide margin of uncertainty. One way to reduce this uncertainty is to use appearance information about the moving objects in the site. In this paper we present the preliminary results of a new method that can capture salient appearance characteristics at each camera node in the network. A Latent Dirichlet Allocation (LDA) model is created and maintained at each node in the camera network. Each object is encoded in terms of the LDA bag-of-words model for appearance. The encoded appearance is then used to establish probable matching across cameras. Preliminary experiments are conducted on a dataset of 20 individuals and comparison against Madden's I-MCHR is reported.

1 Introduction

In a typical video-surveillance system, the tasks of object detection and tracking across the site are crucial for enabling event retrieval and a posteriori activity analysis. Detection and tracking can be quite challenging, depending on the type of setup available. In particular, for a multi-camera system the main problem is to establish correspondences among the observations from different cameras and consistently label the objects. When the cameras have overlapping fields of view, information about the geometrical relations among the camera views can be estimated and used to establish correspondences [1,2]. In the case of disjoint views, other information about the moving objects must be used to automatically identify multiple instances of the same object [3,4].

In a distributed video-surveillance system the detected objects should be represented by compact descriptors in order to allow efficient storage of the system state and compact communication between cameras to share knowledge and apply some cooperative strategy. Compact descriptors also enable event retrieval. One possible scenario is the search of all the nodes where a certain person appears; i.e., the identification of multiple instances of the same object in different

P. Foggia, C. Sansone, and M. Vento (Eds.): ICIAP 2009, LNCS 5716, pp. 547–557, 2009.
© Springer-Verlag Berlin Heidelberg 2009

locations and time instants. To be effective, the descriptor must also be sufficiently robust to the changes in resolution and viewpoint that occur as moving
object's orientation and distance from the camera continuously change.

A number of approaches, e.g., [5,6], learn the network topology or the activity
patterns in the site to predict probable correspondences among detected objects.
These systems simply use the probability that an action/event will be repeated
in the site during a predicted time period, and may perform not well in the case
of anomalies. These approaches do not consider that multi-camera system should
have a distributed knowledge of all the existent moving objects. This means that
every time an object is detected for the first time, all cameras in the system are
alerted about its presence in the site and wait for it reappears somewhere with
characteristics quite similar to those already observed.

In a distributed system, the nodes should work like independent and au-
tonomous agents monitoring their own FOV. Communications among nodes
should be done just when objects go outside the FOV and should consist of
a simple and compact appearance description related, for example, to the dress
of the detected person or his identity – when possible/applicable. This approach
does not require knowledge of the camera network's topology, although such
information could be used to limit the number of data transmissions in the net.

Appearance is difficult to represent. Detecting objects in a well-defined way
is often challenging, particularly in a cluttered environment; as a result, the information about an object is generally partial and noisy. As the object moves
continuously, its appearance depends on the object's orientation with respect
to the camera. Moreover, objects can move in a non-rigid way and can be
self-occluded, resulting in a loss of detail.

In this paper, we present a preliminary system to model object appearance
using latent features. Each object is assigned an "appearance topic" distribution
from a Latent Dirichlet Allocation (LDA) model that is maintained at each camera node. The object appearance models are propagated in the network and used
both to describe incoming objects and to establish correspondences. The resulting probable correspondences can be useful in constructing hypotheses about the
paths of objects in the site. These hypotheses can be pruned by using the accumulated information during the life of the system or by using spatiotemporal
constraints to guarantee consistency of hypotheses.

In Section 2 we describe works that use appearance information to establish
object correspondences. In Sections 3 and 4 we review the LDA model and
then formulate an LDA-based method that can describe objects and perform
matching. Finally, in Section 5 we report experiments and compare our method's
performance with that of [3].

2   Related Work

There are many kinds of approaches to establish correspondences among objects
in a multi-camera system. Some of these [1,2] are based on geometrical constraints, particularly for the case of calibrated cameras and overlapping FOVs.

Other approaches instead try to find correspondences by accumulating statistics about probable associations between cameras in the network.

In [5,6,8] first the topology is estimated, then transition probabilities are used to identify where/when an object can reappear in the camera network. In this kind of system, object correspondences are strongly related to the speed at which an object moves in the site. This can result in poor performance in anomalous cases, e.g., when people do not follow the expected trajectories in the site.

Some approaches perform consistent labeling by matching features as color or texture. In [3], correspondences are found by comparing compact color histograms of the major RGB colors in the image. To make the descriptors more robust, the histogram is computed on successive frames. More details about this method will be provided in Section 5.

In [7], a content-based retrieval system for surveillance data is presented. This system looks for all the sequences of a certain person by using tracking information and appearance model similarity. By using the estimated homographic relation among the camera FOVs, consistent labeling among all the tracks is performed by assigning to each unlabeled object the label of the nearest one with the highest appearance similarity. For each observation, the ten major modes are extracted from a color histogram; then the appearance model is computed by training a mixture of Gaussian on these modes.

In [4], each object is represented as a "bag-of-visterms" where the visual words are local features. A model is created for each individual detected in the site. When a new individual is detected, classification is performed to establish a potential match with previously seen objects. Descriptors consist of 128-dimensional SIFT vectors that are quantized to form visual words using a predefined vocabulary. The vocabulary is constructed during a training step by k-means clustering and organized hierarchically so to speed up the search. Object classification is performed by an incremental version of Adaboost in which, as new data is available, classifiers are added and trained. One-vs-one SVM classifiers are added at each round; thus, the number of classifiers can grow as a quadratic function of the number of observed objects. Furthermore, the system is centralized; making it distributed requires significant communication among the nodes with a master node tasked with continuously updating the object model.

In this paper, we adopt the strategy of modeling objects as bags of words in which a latent structure of features exists and must be discovered. This structure can enable compact object description and efficient object comparison. In our distributed system, each node processes individually and autonomously the data acquired by its own camera. Communications among nodes enable knowledge sharing and are performed every time a new object exits the camera FOV. Knowledge of the camera network topology is not required. During the start-up, each node detects people and trains an LDA model. The model is then used to describe objects appearing in the FOV. Correspondences with previously seen objects are computed by comparing the stored descriptors.

3   LDA Model

Latent Dirichlet Allocation (LDA), first introduced by Blei [9], is a generative model that can be used to explain how documents are generated given a set of topics and a vocabulary of words. In the LDA model, words are the only observable variables and they implicitly reflect a latent structure, i.e., the set of T topics used to generate the document. Generally speaking, given a set of documents, the latent topic structure lies in the set of words itself. Fig. 1(a) shows the graphical model for LDA. As the figure shows, in generating the document for each word-position a topic is sampled and, conditioned from the topic, a word is selected. Each topic is chosen on the basis of the random variable θ that is sampled – for convenience – from a Dirichlet distribution $p(\theta; \alpha)$ where α is a hyperparameter. The topic z conditioned on θ and the word w conditioned on the topic and on ϕ are sampled from multinomial distributions $p(z_n|\theta)$ and $p(w_n|z_n; \phi)$ respectively. ϕ represents the word distribution over the topics. The probability of a document can be computed as

$$p(\mathbf{w}) = \int_\theta \left[\prod_{n=1}^{N} \sum_{z_n=1}^{k} p(w_n|z_n; \phi) p(z_n|\theta) \right] p(\theta; \alpha) \, d\theta. \tag{1}$$

There are a number of different implementations of LDA. In [9], Blei, et al. present a variational approach to approximate the topic posterior with the lower bound of a more simple and computable function. In their implementation, α and ϕ are learnt by variational inference so to maximize the log likelihood of the data.

In another approach [10] a simple modification to the model enables easier computation of the posterior (cfr. Fig. 1(b)). A Dirichlet prior is introduced on the parameter ϕ, with hyper-parameter β. Despite this modification, computation of the conditional probability $p(\mathbf{z}|\mathbf{w})$ is still unmanageable. They propose to approximate it by Gibbs sampling based on the following distribution:

$$p(z_i = j|\mathbf{z_{-i}}, \mathbf{w}) \propto \frac{n_{-i,j}^{(w_i)} + \beta}{n_{-i,j}^{(\cdot)} + W\beta} \frac{n_{-i,j}^{(d_i)} + \alpha}{n_{-i}^{(d_i)} + T\alpha}. \tag{2}$$

This distribution represents the probability that word w_i should be assigned to topic j given all the other assignments z_{-i}. The quantities $n_{-i,j}^{(w_i)}$ and $n_{-i,j}^{(\cdot)}$ represent respectively the number of times word w_i has been already assigned to topic j and the total number of words assigned to topic j. The quantities $n_{-i,j}^{(d_i)}$ and $n_{-i}^{(d_i)}$ represent respectively the number of times the word w_i in the document d_i has been already assigned to topic j and the number of words in document d_i that are assigned to topic j. The hyperparameters α and β are computed using the method described in [10] ($\beta = 0.01$, $\alpha = 50/T$).

LDA has been applied with success in a number of computer vision scenarios. For instance, in [12] LDA is used in object segmentation and labeling for a large dataset of images. For each image in the dataset multiple segmentations are

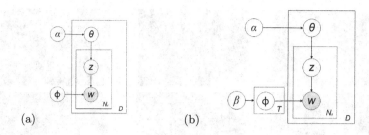

Fig. 1. Graphical models for LDA: (a) Blei's approach, (b) Griffiths' approach. In (b) a Dirichlet prior is introduced on ϕ.

obtained via different methods – these are treated as documents for LDA. An histogram of visual words (SIFT descriptors) is then computed for each segment-document. They then train an LDA model in order to discover topics in the set of documents. Segments corresponding to an object are those well explained by the discovered topics.

In other work [13], LDA is used for activity analysis in multi-camera systems. Activities are represented as motion patterns and the camera network topology is unknown. In this application, the documents are trajectory observations. Each trajectory is a set of words and a word is a tuple representing the camera, the position and the direction of motion for the observed object. Topics represent clusters of trajectories and, then, activities.

Our system detects and segments moving objects yielding their tracks in the monitored site. We define an object instance as the object segmented by background suppression from which a set of features can be extracted. Each track is a sequence of frames representing a particular instance of the object seen in different conditions, for example under different viewpoints. Indeed, during the track, objects approach or move away from the camera, are partially visible and, generally, they change their pose and/or orientation with respect to the camera.

We want to realize a system that can learn – in an unsupervised way the appearance of the object from its track by using an LDA model. For this purpose, we treat each object instance as a document and each extracted feature as a word. In this manner, each track is just a set of documents regarding the same object. With this analogy, each object instance has been generated first choosing a mixture of features – that is a topic – then choosing a particular feature on the basis of the underlying word-topic distribution.

An example of a feature-word that can be used in our model is the pixel color. Many representations in color space can be used: HSI, RGB, normalized RGB or invariant spaces. For the sake of demonstrating the general approach, we used RGB space. Other more sophisticated features as SIFT[14] or SURF[15], could be used too but, whilst they are locally scale and rotation invariant, they are not invariant to non-rigid transformations that are commonplace in human motion patterns. Instead, using many instances of the object while it is moving should permit to capture its appearance under different viewpoints and at several distances from the camera increasing the descriptor robustness to scale changes.

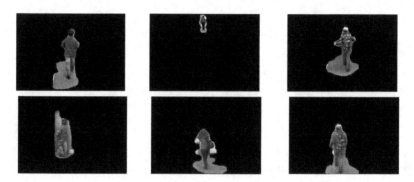

Fig. 2. Example images from the training set acquired with two different cameras. The images tend to be noisy and object resolutions differ significantly.

So, in our system each camera node computes an LDA model to capture the latent structure for the data it observes. We use the LDA method implemented by Griffiths[10]. Considering the full range of RGB colors could yield a vocabulary that is too broad; therefore, we restricted the set of words by scaling the RGB color resolution producing an 8x8x8 partition of the space. We have found in practice that this coarse uniform RGB partition tends to make the descriptor more robust to small illumination changes.

Once the model has been trained, a descriptor can be computed for every new object, based on the observed instances for the object in that camera view. As we can know the topic distribution for each object instance, we define the descriptor as the expected value of the topic distribution given the instance f. Assuming that the number of known instances is N, then our descriptor will be:

$$p(\mathbf{z}|\mathbf{Object}) = E[p(\mathbf{z}|f)] = \frac{1}{N}\sum_{i=1}^{N} p(\mathbf{z}|f_i). \qquad (3)$$

Fig. 2 shows example images from the training set that we use as documents to train the LDA model. Each frame contains one object instance and has been obtained by background suppression with hysteresis thresholding. As the figure shows, the images are quite noisy and part of the background is detected.

4   Matching Object Appearances

Every time a new object is seen, a distribution of the topics must be computed for that object. Given an object and an initial topic-assignment for it, the topic distribution can be estimated by appling a Gibbs sampler to Eq. 2 where, this time, the variables $n_{-i,j}^{(w_i)}$, $n_{-i,j}^{(\cdot)}$, $n_{-i,j}^{(d_i)}$ and $n_{-i}^{(d_i)}$ are updated so to consider also the current topic-word assignment in the analyzed document.

Each node estimates its own LDA model independently from the others on different training sets, and each camera can see different object views. Therefore, a topic association among LDA models is required in order to compare two topic distributions computed in different camera nodes. To do this, after the training is completed, the nodes propagate their own model over the camera network and then compute the topic association with each other.

Topic Association among Two LDA Models. In order to compute the topic association we consider two models, LDA1 and LDA2, with the same number of topics T and for each topic j we perform the following steps:

- we generate a document d_j by the model LDA1 using just the j-th topic; so, given $\delta_{i,j}$ is the Dirac's delta function, the topic distribution for d_j shall be

$$p_{LDA1}(z = i|d_j) = \delta_{i,j} \qquad i = 1..T \qquad (4)$$

- we compute the topic distribution of the previously generated document by using LDA2 in the manner described at the beginning of this section; i.e., we estimate $p_{LDA2}(\mathbf{z}|d_j)$.

Assuming a linear relation among the topics in the two models, performing the second step for each of the T generated documents results in a topic association matrix $\mathbf{M}$. In this manner, given a document **doc** the matrix $\mathbf{M}$ permits us to transform a generic topic distribution computed by the model LDA1 into a topic distribution $p^*_{LDA2}(\mathbf{z}|\mathbf{doc})$ valid for the model LDA2:

$$p^*_{LDA2}(\mathbf{z}|\mathbf{doc}) = \mathbf{M} \cdot p_{LDA1}(\mathbf{z}|\mathbf{doc}) \quad with \quad \mathbf{M} = \begin{bmatrix} p_{LDA2}(\mathbf{z}|d_1) \\ \vdots \\ p_{LDA2}(\mathbf{z}|d_T) \end{bmatrix}^T. \qquad (5)$$

Given this relation, for each object it is possible to compute two comparable distributions. Comparison is performed using the Jensen-Shannon (JS) divergence, which is a symmetric and normalized measure based on the Kullback Leibler divergence[11]. Defining $p = p_{LDA2}(\mathbf{z}|doc)$ and $q = p^*_{LDA2}(\mathbf{z}|doc)$, then the JS divergence

$$JS(p,q) = \frac{1}{2}\left[D(p, \frac{p+q}{2}) + D(q, \frac{p+q}{2})\right], \qquad (6)$$

where D is the Kullback Leibler divergence

$$D(p,q) = \sum_{j=1}^{T} p_j \cdot log_2(\frac{p_j}{q_j}). \qquad (7)$$

5   Experiments

To test our system we collected data using two cameras with non-overlapping fields of view. The training set comprises many different tracks of 20 different individuals acquired at approximately 15 fps, for a total of 1003 and 1433 frames for each camera. The test set comprises many different tracks of 20 individuals acquired at different time instants, for a total of 1961 and 2068 frames per camera. None of these individuals is in the training set. Among all the possible pairs, just 10 are true matches. The number of frames per track can vary considerably, ranging from 29 to 308 frames for both the test and training set. Fig. 2 shows example images used to train the models in our experiments. As can be seen, the images tend to be rather noisy and no shadow suppression has been applied. In the images of the training and test set, the object resolution varies greatly (examples are shown in Fig. 2). In acquiring the images, the cameras' auto-focus function has been disabled as it contributes to changes in the object's appearance.

Comparison. Comparison has been conducted against the I-MCHR method of Madden [3]. As explained in Sec. 2, this method computes an incremental histogram of the object's major colors. Given the first object instance, the method computes the bin centers of the color histogram in order to obtain a rough non-uniform partition of the RGB color space; this partition is then refined by k-means clustering. Only the modes that can represent 90% of the image pixels are retained. This RGB space partition is then used to compute an incremental histogram on all the successive frames. The authors utilize a symmetric similarity measure to compare two I-MCHR descriptors by considering the probabilities of the modes with distance less than a certain threshold. Distance among clusters is computed using a normalized distance metric in the RGB space. To address the problem of illumination changes, an intensity transformation is applied separately to each image channel, thereby yielding a "controlled equalization" of the image. This transformation scales and translates the histogram modes towards the lightest part of the intensity scale. The I-MCHR method gave us an accuracy of 84% on our dataset.

Results. We tested our system with different values of the hyperparameters α and β and different numbers of topics T. In this paper we report results obtained for several values of T; β and α have been set to 0.01 and $50/T$ respectively as proposed in [10]. Figure 3(a) shows the accuracy value obtained by changing the number of topics in the range [10; 50]. The best results are obtained by using 15 topics, which yields an accuracy of 94%. For values of T greater than 15, the accuracy decreases.

Fig. 3(b) shows the ROC curves computed for our method and Madden's I-MCHR on the test set. As the figure shows, performance of our method is generally better than that of Madden's method. As expected, the worst results are obtained for the nosiest images, for which correspondence is particularly ambiguous (many noisy objects tend to look similar). In addition, when people dress with almost the same colors, the system cannot reliably discriminate between these individuals. In such cases, additional information could be used by the system to make a decision – for instance body proportions, distinctive gait patterns, temporal constraints, etc. The matching errors can generally be ascribed both to illumination changes and to the scaled RGB resolution of the colors we

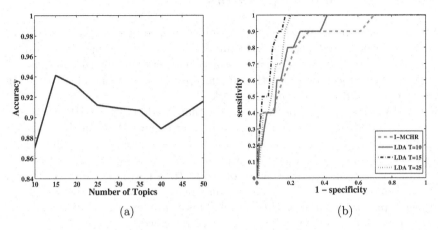

Fig. 3. (a)Accuracy of the method while the number of topics is changing; (b)ROC curves for our LDA based approach and for Madden's I-MCHR

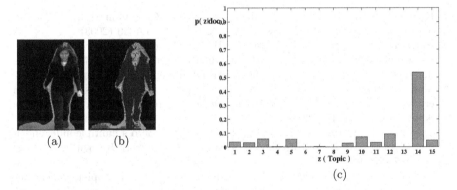

Fig. 4. Example of outputs from our method: a) the original image, b)the topic interpretation and c) the expected topic distribution (15 Topics)

used as input features to the model. Accounting for illumination variation, for instance with invariant descriptors, remains a topic for future investigation.

Nonetheless, taking into consideration that images are poorly processed and nothing is done to compensate for shadows, changes in the illumination and differences in the camera color calibrations, these preliminary results are quite promising. No doubt, further changes to the system to account for these issues can improve its overall performance.

Finally, in Figure 4 we present an example from the test set, the corresponding expected topic distribution and its topic interpretaton in false color. The latter image was obtained by associating at each pixel the most probable topic and so this image does not reflect the estimated topic distribution.

6   Conclusion and Future Work

In this paper we report the preliminary results obtained by considering an object as a bag of words and using a LDA model to infer the "appearance topic" distribution by which the object has been generated. This distribution is used to describe the object and also to establish probable correspondences among objects moving within the camera network.

Our LDA-based method performs better than Madden's I-MCHR in our experiments. Based on the preliminary study, we believe that the LDA model for appearance is promising. The formulation can be extended to include other features that describe an object's appearance, e.g., texture. In future work we intend to investigate the performance of the method in a more complex system setup with more than two cameras. We also plan to investigate the use of appearance topic distributions within a probabilistic framework for inferring likely trajectories of objects moving within the camera network.

References

1. Khan, S., Shah, M.: Consistent Labeling of Tracked Objects in Multiple Cameras with Overlapping Fields of View. IEEE PAMI 25, 1355–1360 (2003)
2. Calderara, S., Prati, A., Cucchiara, R.: HECOL: Homography and epipolar-based consistent labeling for outdoor park surveillance. Computer Vision and Image Understanding Special Issue on Intelligent Visual Surveillance, 21–42 (2008)
3. Madden, C., Cheng, E.D., Piccardi, M.: Tracking people across disjoint camera views by an illumination-tolerant appearance representation. Mach. Vision Appl. 18(3), 233–247 (2007)
4. Teixeira, L.F., Corte-Real, L.: Video object matching across multiple independent views using local descriptors and adaptive learning. Pattern Recogn. Lett. 30(2), 157–167 (2009)
5. Tieu, K., Dalley, G., Grimson, W.E.L.: Inference of non-overlapping camera network topology by measuring statistical dependence. In: IEEE Proc. of ICCV 2005, vol. 2, pp. 17–21 (2005)
6. Makris, D., Ellis, T., Black, J.: Bridging the gaps between cameras. In: IEEE Proc. of CVPR, vol. 2, pp. 205–210 (2004)
7. Calderara, S., Cucchiara, R., Prati, A.: Multimedia surveillance: content-based retrieval with multicamera people tracking. In: Proc. of the 4th ACM international workshop on Video surveillance and sensor networks, pp. 95–100 (2006)
8. Javed, O., Rasheed, Z., Shafique, K., Shah, M.: Tracking across multiple cameras with disjoint views. In: Proc. of ICCV 2003, vol. 2, pp. 952–957 (2003)
9. Blei, D.M., Ng, A.Y., Jordan, M.I.: Latent dirichlet allocation. Journal of Machine Learning Res. 3, 993–1022 (2003)
10. Griffiths, T., Steyvers, M.: Finding scientific topics. Proc. of the National Academy of Sciences 101, 5228–5235 (2004)
11. Griffiths, T., Steyvers, M.: Probabilistic Topic Models. In: Landauer, T., McNamara, D., Dennis, S., Kintsch, W. (eds.) LSA: A Road to Meaning
12. Russell, B.C., Freeman, W.T., Efros, A.A., Sivic, J., Zisserman, A.: Using Multiple Segmentations to Discover Objects and their Extent in Image Collections. In: IEEE Proc. of CVPR 2006, vol. 2, pp. 1605–1614 (2006)

13. Wang, X., Tieu, K., Grimson, E.L.: Correspondence-Free Activity Analysis and Scene Modeling in Multiple Camera Views. In: IEEE PAMI (accepted, 2009)
14. Lowe, D.G.: Distinctive Image Features from Scale-Invariant Keypoints. International Journal of Computer Vision 60, 91–110 (2004)
15. Bay, H., Ess, A., Tuytelaars, T., Van Gool, L.: Speeded-Up Robust Features (SURF). Comput. Vis. Image Underst. 110(3), 346–359 (2008)

Analysis and Classification of Crithidia Luciliae Fluorescent Images

Paolo Soda[1], Leonardo Onofri[1], Amelia Rigon[2], and Giulio Iannello[1]

[1] University Campus Bio-Medico of Rome, Integrated Research Centre, Medical Informatics & Computer Science Laboratory, Rome, Italy
[2] University Campus Bio-Medico of Rome, Integrated Research Centre, Immunology, Rome, Italy
{p.soda,leonardo.onofri,a.rigon,g.iannello}@unicampus.it

Abstract. Autoantibody tests based on Crithidia Luciliae (CL) substrate are the recommended method to detect Systemic Lupus Erythematosus (SLE), a very serious sickness further to be classified as an invalidating chronic disease. CL is an unicellular organism containing a strongly tangled mass of circular dsDNA, named as kinetoplast, whose fluorescence determines the positiveness to the test. Conversely, the staining of other parts of cell body is not a disease marker, thus representing false positive fluorescence. Such readings are subjected to several issues limiting the reproducibility and reliability of the method, as the photo-bleaching effect and the inter-observer variability. Hence, Computer-Aided Diagnosis (CAD) tools can support physicians decision. In this paper we propose a system to classify CL wells based on a three stages recognition approach, which classify single cell, images and, finally, the well. The fusion of such different information permits to reduce the misclassifications effect. The approach has been successfully tested on an annotated dataset, proving its feasibility.

1   Introduction

Systemic Lupus Erythematosus (SLE) is a chronic inflammatory disease of unknown aetiology affecting multiple organ systems. In Europe, SLE incidence and prevalence every 100000 inhabitants ranges between $1.9 - 4.8$ cases and $12.5 - 68$ cases, respectively [1]. Recent study has reported that 5 and 10 years survival ranges between $91\% - 97\%$ and $83\% - 92\%$ [2], respectively. Although SLE should be tagged as a rare illness due to its incidence, it is considered a very serious sickness further to be classified as an invalidating chronic disease.

The numerous and different manifestations of SLE make its diagnosis a burdensome task. The criteria of American College of Rheumatology require to perform autoantibodies tests for SLE diagnosis [3]. Indeed, it suggests to detect the presence of autoantibodies directed against double strand DNA (anti-dsDNA) due to the high specificity of the test (92%).

The recommended method to detect autoantibodies disorders is the Indirect ImmunoFluorescence (IIF) assay. IIF makes use of a substrate containing a specific antigen that can bond with serum antibodies, forming a molecular complex.

P. Foggia, C. Sansone, and M. Vento (Eds.): ICIAP 2009, LNCS 5716, pp. 558–566, 2009.

Then, this complex reacts with human immunoglobulin conjugated with a fluorochrome, making the complex observable at the fluorescence microscope. In order to detect SLE autoantibodies, IIF is performed using the Crithidia Luciliae (CL) substrate [4,5], since it includes a compressed mass of double strand DNA (dsDNA) named as *kinetoplast*.

However, the readings in IIF are subjected to several issues that limits the reproducibility and reliability of the method, such as the photo-bleaching effect and the inter-observer variability [6,7]. To date, the highest level of automation in anti-dsDNA tests is the preparation of slides with robotic devices performing dilution, dispensation and washing operations [8,9]. Although such instruments helps in speeding up the slide preparation step, the development of Computer-Aided-Diagnosis (CAD) systems supporting IIF diagnostic procedure would be beneficial in many respects.

To our knowledge, only recent papers dealing with CAD tools for autoantibodies tests based on the HEp-2 substrate[1] can be found in the literature [10,11,12,13,14]. In this paper we focus on the development of a decision system able to classify anti-dsDNA images based on the Crithidia Luciliae substrate. The system is usable in practice, capable of performing a pre-selection of the cases to be examined and serving as a second reader. The system has been successfully tested on an annotated dataset.

2   Background and Motivations

Current guidelines for SLE diagnosis recommend to use CL substrate diluted at 1:10 titer, prepared according to IIF method [5].

CL is an unicellular organism containing both the nucleus and the kinetoplast. The latter is composed of a strongly tangled mass of circular dsDNA, making this test highly specific. Hence, the fluorescence of kinetoplast is the fundamental parameter to define the positiveness of a well, whereas the fluorescence of other parts of CL cells, e.g. the basal body or the flagellum, is not a marker of anti-dsDNA autoantibodies and, consequently, of SLE. Fig. 1 shows five stylized cells representative of different cases.

Panels A and B depict positive cases. The former shows a cell where only the kinetoplast exhibits a fluorescence staining higher than cell body, while in the latter also the nucleus is highly fluorescent. The other three panels show negative cells. In panel C, the cell is clearly negative since all cell body has a weak and quite uniform fluorescence. Panels D and E depict cells where regions different from the kinetoplast exhibit strong fluorescence staining. Indeed, in panel D the basal body, which is similar to kinetoplast in size and type of fluorescence staining, is lighter than cell body. In panel E, one or more parts different from the kinetoplast has a strong staining. Finally, notice also that occasionally fluorescence objects, i.e. artifacts, may be observed outside cell body.

---

[1] IIF tests performed using HEp-2 substrate permits to detect antinuclear autoantibodies (ANA).

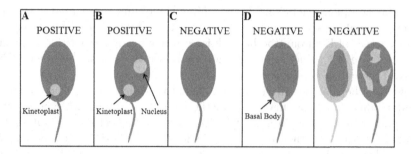

Fig. 1. Positive and negative cases depicted through stylized cells. Dark and light grey represent low and high fluorescence, respectively.

These observations suggest that several and different reasons of uncertainty can be observed in CL images, making the right determination of kinetoplast staining a demanding task. Such motivations are at the basis of CL tests inter-observer variability. Other reasons are the photo-bleaching effect that bleaches significantly the cells over a short period of time [7], as well as the lack of quantitative information supplied to physicians.

Developments in computer vision and artificial intelligence in medical image interpretation have shown that CAD systems can effectively support the special-ists in various medical fields. In particular, in the area of autoantibodies testing some recent papers have presented CAD tools for the classification of HEp-2 images [10,11,12,13,14], which are used to detect other autoimmune diseases. To our knowledge no works in the literature propose solutions for automatic classi-fication of CL slides. This paper therefore discusses a solution in this direction.

3   Methods

We aim at recognizing the positiveness or negativeness of a well, since it contains the serum of one patient. Due to microscope magnification typically used during the acquisition process, one digital image does not cover all the surface of one well. For this reason, several images are always collected. This feature permits us to exploit a certain degree of redundancy, integrating together the information extracted from different images of the same well. To recognize the staining of each well we initially classify the images acquired from the well under examination, and then label the well on the strength of the classification of its images (panel A of Fig. 2).

Panel B of Fig. 2 details the steps applied to label single images. The first one relies upon the observation that the kinetoplast fluorescence implies the presence in the image of a compact set of pixels brighter than other regions. Conversely, the absence of such a set suggests that the image is negative. For instance, the cell shown in panel C of Fig. 1 is classified as negative while the cells in the other panels contain regions candidate to be a kinetoplast and proceed in the next classification steps.

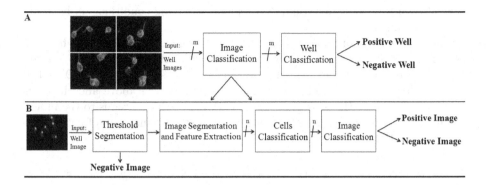

Fig. 2. Description of the classification approach

As a second step, we are interested in locating and classifying single cells. Hence, we segment only the images containing at least one set of pixels candidate to be a kinetoplast and, then, the segmented cells are classified. Finally, the staining of the image is computed on the basis of the labels of all cells.

In our opinion, the overall approach provides two benefits. First, the initial threshold segmentation allows a rapid classification of several images ($\approx 0.1s$ per image). Second, it is tolerant with respect to misclassifications in cells recognition: if enough cells per image are available, it is reasonable that misclassified cells, if limited, does not affect image classification. This permits to lower the effect of both erroneously segmented cells or artifacts. Notice also that a similar consideration holds also for well classification, where multiple images are available.

Following paragraphs focus on cell, image and well classification blocks, respectively.

Cell classification. The cells have been segmented using Otsu's algorithm [15]. Then, morphological operations, such as filling and connection analysis, output a binary mask for cutting out the cells from the image. Cells connected with the image border have been suppressed. From each segmented cell we extract a set of features belonging to different categories: (i) intensity histogram and co-occurence matrix, (ii) angular bin of Fourier Transform (FT) spectrum, (iii) radial bin of FT spectrum, (iv) wavelet transform, (v) Zernike moments, (vi) rectangle features, (vii) Local Binary Pattern both standard and circular as well as circular rotation invariant [16], (viii) morphological descriptors. The interested readers may refer to [17] for further details. Then, discriminant analysis permits us to identify the subset of most discriminant features.

Image classification. Each image contains several cells whose kinetoplasts can be positive or negative. According to previous considerations, as a first step we are interested in identifying clearly negative images, i.e. images that do not contain any compact fluorescent set of pixels. To this aim, we perform a threshold-based segmentation that looks for connected regions satisfying conditions on both intensity and dimension.

When the image contains regions candidate to be a kinetoplast, we have to determine if it is a true positive image. For istance, false positive images occur when there is a fluorescent mass inside cell body, as shown in panel D and E of Fig. 1. To this end, we classify single cells as reported above and then, on their basis, we apply the Majority Voting (MV) rule which assigns to the image the label corresponding to the class receiving the relative majority of votes. Ties lead to reject the image.

Well Classification. As reported at the beginning of the section, the class of the whole well is determined on the basis of the classification of its images. To this aim, we apply again the MV rule where the votes summation is performed at image level. In case of tie the system does not cast a decision on the well asking for specialist classification. Indeed, due to the high specificity of CL tests it is preferable to reject the well rather than risking a misclassification.

4   Data Set

Since, to our knowledge, there are not reference databases of CL images publicly available, we acquired and annotated 342 images, 74 positive (21.6%) and 268 negative (78.4%), belonging to 63 wells, 15 positive (23.8%) and 48 negative (76.2%). Furthermore, specialists label a set of cells since our approach requires their labels to train the corresponding classifier. This operation has been performed only on images where the threshold-based segmentation identifies fluorescent regions. At the end of such a procedure, the cells data set consists of 1487 cells belonging to 34 different wells. The cells are therefore labelled: 928 as positive (62.4%) and 559 as negative (37.6%).

5   Experimental Evaluation

In order to classify CL cells, we investigate the performance that could be achieved appealing to popular classifiers belonging to different paradigms, as reported below.

As a neural network, we use a Multi-Layer Perceptron (MLP) with one hidden layer. The number of neurons in input and output layers are equal to features number and two (i.e. we deal with a two-classes recognition task), respectively. Preliminary tests have permitted to determine the best configuration of the MLP in terms of neurons number in the hidden layer: specifically, configurations from 1 up to 50 neurons were tested.

As a bayesian classifier, we apply the Naïve Bayes classifier, which does not demand for specific set-up.

Support Vector Machine (SVM) is adopted as a kernel machine, using a Radial Basis Function kernel. We have performed a grid search to determine the best

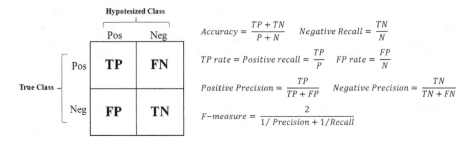

Fig. 3. Confusion matrix and derived performance metrics calculated for the two-classes recognition task. P and N represent the total number of positive and negative samples, respectively.

setup of the SVM in terms of Gaussian width, σ, and of regularisation parameter, C in the ranges $[0.01; 30]$ and $[0.1; 60]$, respectively.

AdaBoost is tested as ensemble of classifier, using decision stumps as base hypotheses and exploring different numbers of iterations (in the interval $[10; 100]$) to determine the best configuration.

In order to estimate the performance we measure the following common metrics: accuracy, recall, precision and f-measure, whose definition is reported in Fig. 3 together with the confusion matrix of a two-classes recognition problem. We measure also the area under ROC curve (AUC), since it permits to reduce the ROC performance to a single scalar value in $[0, 1]$: the more it approaches one, the better the performance [18].

5.1 Results and Discussion

In this subsection we present the results achieved in the classification of individual cells, images and whole wells.

Cell Classification. Table 1 reports the performance measures of the four classification paradigms tested in the recognition of positive and negative CL cells, estimated using 10-fold cross validation and randomly choosing training and test set elements.

These data point out that SVM classifier outperforms the others. They also show that accuracy is balanced over the two classes. This finding confirms previous papers reporting that SVMs have very good performance on binary classification task, since they have been originally defined for this type of problem [19].

Although these results are interesting, they do not accurately estimate the performance of the classifiers when the samples are outside the training set. Indeed, random cross validation does not take into account that cells belonging to the same well, and thus with not independent features, can be both in training and test sets. To overcome such a limitation, we divided the set of 1487 cells into 34 subsets, one for each well. We then perform a 34-folds cross validation using only SVMs, since they are the most performing classifier. Accuracy, negative

Table 1. Performance of the classifier recognizing positive and negative CL cells, estimated using 10-fold cross validation. In parenthesis we report the best configuration of each classifier: in case of MLP the number represents the hidden layer neurons, in case of SVMs the values are C and σ, and in case of Adaboost it is the iterations number.

		Recall(%)		Precision(%)		F-measure(%)		
Classifier	Accuracy(%)	Pos	Neg	Pos	Neg	Pos	Neg	AUC
Naive Bayes	89.4	88.3	91.2	94.4	82.4	91.2	86.6	0.938
MLP (40)	95.7	97.1	93.4	96.1	95.1	96.6	94.2	0.989
AdaBoost (50)	96.4	97.1	95.2	97.1	95.2	97.1	95.2	0.993
SVMs (17,1)	97.0	97.8	95.7	97.4	96.4	97.6	96.1	0.993

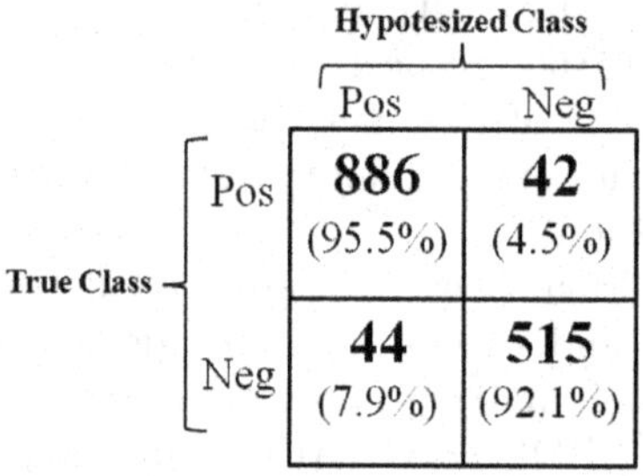

Fig. 4. Confusion Matrix of cells classification using SVM through 34-folds cross validation

and positive recall, negative and positive precision, negative and positive F-measure and AUC are now 94.2%, 92.1%, 95.5%, 92.5%, 95.3%, 92.3%, 95.4%, 0.984, respectively. Notice that the variation of such performance will not affect the results overall system results since the final classification depends on the classification of several cells.

Image Classification. The tests show that threshold-based segmentation does not exhibits FN, while 64.6% of images are correctly classified as negative (panel A of Fig. 5). The remaining 35.4% of images are then labelled having recourse to cell labels provided by 34-folds classification.

Panel B of Fig. 5 reports the confusion matrix achieved in the classification of such images, showing that only two of them have been misclassified. In conclusion, 340 images (99.4%) are correctly classified, attaining a positive and negative recalls of 98.6% and 99.6%, respectively.

Well Classification. With regard to well classification, we correctly classify 62 wells (98.4%) whereas only one well has been rejected since the same number of images have been labelled as positive and negative.

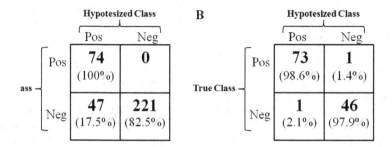

Fig. 5. Confusion Matrix of images classification. Panel A shows the result of threshold-based segmentation. Panel B shows the recognition result of the remaining images achieved using individual cells labels.

6 Conclusion

In this paper we have presented a system that can support the specialists in SLE diagnosis. As a novel contribution, this paper aims aims at classifying Chritidia Luciliae wells, since such a substrate is one of the most specific test to detect the considered disease. The proposed system is based on a three stages recognition approach, namely cells, images and well classification. It integrates several pieces of information providing a degree of redundancy that lowers the effect of misclassifications and permits us to achieve promising performance, even if improving tie breaking is the current challenge to make the system flexible to work in different operating scenario.We are currently engaged in populating a larger annotated database and testing the system in real-world tests to validate its use. The ultimate goal is the development of a CAD system providing the chance to automatically classify a panel of autoantibodies.

Acknowledgment

The authors thank Dario Malosti for his precious advices. This work has been partially supported by "Thought in Action" (TACT) project, part of the European Union NEST-Adventure Program, and by DAS s.r.l. of Palombara Sabina (www.dasitaly.com).

References

1. Lee, P.P.W., Lee, T.L., Ho, M.H.K., Wong, W.H.S., Lau, Y.L.: Recurrent major infections in juvenile-onset systemic lupus erythematosus–a close link with long-term disease damage. Rheumatology 46, 1290–1296 (2007)
2. Mok, C.C., Lee, K.W., Ho, C.T.K., et al.: A prospective study of survival and prognostic indicators of systemic lupus erythematosus in a southern chinese population. Rheumatology 39, 399–406 (2000)

3. Hochberg, M.C.: Updating the American College of Rheumatology revised criteria for the classification of systemic lupus erythematosus. Arthritis and Rheumatism 40(9), 1725 (1997)
4. Piazza, A., Manoni, F., Ghirardello, A., Bassetti, D., Villalta, D., Pradella, M., Rizzotti, P.: Variability between methods to determine ANA, anti-dsDNA and anti-ENA autoantibodies: a collaborative study with the biomedical industry. Journal of Immunological methods 219, 99–107 (1998)
5. Tozzoli, R., Bizzaro, N., Tonutti, E., Villalta, D., Bassetti, D., Manoni, F., Piazza, A., Pradella, M., Rizzotti, P.: Guidelines for the laboratory use of autoantibody tests in the diagnosis and monitoring of autoimmune rheumatic diseases. American Journal of Clinical Pathology 117(2), 316–324 (2002)
6. Song, L., Hennink, E.J., Young, I.T., Tanke, H.J.: Photobleaching kinetics of fluorescein in quantitative fluorescence microscopy. Biophysical Journal 68(6), 2588–2600 (1995)
7. Rigon, A., Soda, P., Zennaro, D., Iannello, G., Afeltra, A.: Indirect immunofluorescence in autoimmune diseases: assessment of digital images for diagnostic purpose. Cytometry 72(6), 472–477 (2007)
8. Das s.r.l.: Service Manual AP16 IF Plus. Palombara Sabina (RI) (March 2004)
9. Bio-Rad Laboratories Inc.: PhD System (2004), http://www.bio-rad.com
10. Perner, P., Perner, H., Muller, B.: Mining knowledge for HEp-2 cell image classification. Artificial Intelligence in Medicine 26(1-2), 161–173 (2002)
11. Sack, U., Knoechner, S., Warschkau, H., Pigla, U., Emmerich, F., Kamprad, M.: Computer-assisted classification of HEp-2 immunofluorescence patterns in autoimmune diagnostics. Autoimmunity Reviews 2(5), 298–304 (2003)
12. Hiemann, R., Hilger, N., Michel, J., Anderer, U., Weigert, M., Sack, U.: Principles, methods and algorithms for automatic analysis of immunofluorescence patterns on HEp-2 cells. Autoimmunity Reviews, 86 (2006)
13. Soda, P., Iannello, G., Vento, M.: A multiple experts system for classifying fluorescence intensity in antinuclear autoantibodies analysis. Pattern Analysis & Applications (2008)
14. Soda, P., Iannello, G.: Aggregation of classifiers for staining pattern recognition in antinuclear autoantibodies analysis. IEEE Transactions on Information Technology in Biomedicine 13(3), 322–329 (2009)
15. Otsu, N.: A threshold selection method from gray-level histograms. IEEE Transactions on Systems, Man, and Cybernetics 9(1), 62–66 (1970)
16. Ojala, T., Pietikäinen, M., Mäenpää, T.: Multiresolution gray-scale and rotation invariant texture classification with local binary pattern. IEEE Transactions on Pattern Analysis and Machine Intelligence 24(7), 971–987 (2002)
17. Onofri, L., Soda, P.: Feature extraction and selection for Chritidia Luciliae discrimination. Technical report, Università Campus Bio-Medico di Roma (December 2008)
18. Fawcett, T.: Roc graphs: Notes and practical considerations for researchers. HP Laboratories (2004)
19. Vapnik, V.N.: The nature of statistical learning theory. Springer, Heidelberg (1995)

Confidence Measures for Error Correction in Interactive Transcription Handwritten Text[*]

Lionel Tarazón, Daniel Pérez, Nicolás Serrano, Vicent Alabau,
Oriol Ramos Terrades, Alberto Sanchis, and Alfons Juan

DSIC/ITI, Universitat Politècnica de València
Camí de Vera, s/n, 46022 València, Spain
{lionel,nserrano,dperez,valabau,oriolrt,asanchis,ajuan}@iti.upv.es

Abstract. An effective approach to transcribe old text documents is to follow an interactive-predictive paradigm in which both, the system is guided by the human supervisor, and the supervisor is assisted by the system to complete the transcription task as efficiently as possible. In this paper, we focus on a particular system prototype called GIDOC, which can be seen as a first attempt to provide user-friendly, integrated support for interactive-predictive page layout analysis, text line detection and handwritten text transcription. More specifically, we focus on the handwriting recognition part of GIDOC, for which we propose the use of confidence measures to guide the human supervisor in locating possible system errors and deciding how to proceed. Empirical results are reported on two datasets showing that a word error rate not larger than a 10% can be achieved by only checking the 32% of words that are recognised with less confidence.

Keywords: Computer-assisted Transcription of Handwritten Text, User Interfaces, Confidence Measures.

1 Introduction

Transcription of handwritten text in (old) documents is an important, time-consuming task for digital libraries. It might be carried out by first processing all document images off-line, and then manually supervising system transcriptions to edit incorrect parts. However, state-of-the-art technologies for automatic page layout analysis, text line detection and handwritten text recognition are still far from perfect [1,2,3], and thus post-editing automatically generated output is not clearly better than simply ignoring it.

A more effective approach to transcribe old text documents is to follow an interactive-predictive paradigm in which both, the system is guided by the human supervisor, and the supervisor is assisted by the system to complete the

---

[*] Work supported by the EC (FEDER/FSE) and the Spanish MCE/MICINN under the MIPRCV "Consolider Ingenio 2010" programme (CSD2007-00018), the iTransDoc project (TIN2006-15694-CO2-01), the Juan de la Cierva programme, and the FPU scholarship AP2007-02867. Also supported by the UPV grant 20080033.

P. Foggia, C. Sansone, and M. Vento (Eds.): ICIAP 2009, LNCS 5716, pp. 567–574, 2009.

transcription task as efficiently as possible. This computer-assisted transcription (CAT) approach has been successfully followed in the DEBORA [4] and iDoc [5] research projects, for old-style printed and handwritten text, respectively. In the case of iDoc, a CAT system prototype called GIDOC (Gimp-based Interactive transcription of old text DOCuments) has been developed to provide user-friendly, integrated support for interactive-predictive page layout analysis, text line detection and handwritten text transcription [5].

Here we will focus on the handwriting recognition part of GIDOC. As in the most advanced handwriting recognisers today, it is based on standard speech technology adapted to handwritten text images; that is, HMM-based text image modelling and n-gram language modelling. HMMs and the language model are trained from manually transcribed text lines during early stages of the transcription task. Then, each new text line image is processed in turn, by first predicting its most likely transcription, and then locating and editing (hopefully minor) system errors. In [6], for instance, a transcription task is considered in which GIDOC achieves around 37% of (test) word error rate (WER) after transcribing 140 document pages out of a total of 764 (18%). Although a WER of 37% is not too bad for effective CAT, it goes without saying that considerable human effort has to be put into *locating* and *editing* systems errors, and this is true for handwritten text transcription tasks in general.

In this paper, we again resort to standard speech technology and, in particular, to *confidence measures (at word level)* [7,8], which are proposed for error (location and) correction in *interactive* handwritten text transcription. Although the use of confidence measures for offline handwritten text line recognition is not new (see [9] and the references therein), here we go a step further and confidence measures are proposed to guide the human supervisor in locating possible system errors and deciding how to proceed. For instance, if a small number of transcription errors can be tolerated for the sake of efficiency, then he/she might validate the system output after only checking those (few) words, if any, for which the system is not highly confident. On the contrary, if at a first glance no significant portion of the text line seems to be correctly recognised, then he/she might ignore system output and transcribe the whole text line manually. On the other hand and by contrast to previous works [9], here confidence measures are based on *posterior word probabilities* estimated from *word graphs* since, at least in the case of speech recognition, experimental evidence clearly shows that they outperform alternative confidence measures, and even posterior word probabilities estimated from N-*best lists* [7,8].

The paper is organised as follows. After a brief overview of GIDOC in Section 2, estimation of posterior word probabilities from word graphs is described in Section 3. Experiments are reported in Section 4, while conclusions and future work are discussed in Section 5.

2   GIDOC Overview

As indicated in the introduction, GIDOC is a first attempt to provide user-friendly, integrated support for interactive-predictive page layout analysis, text

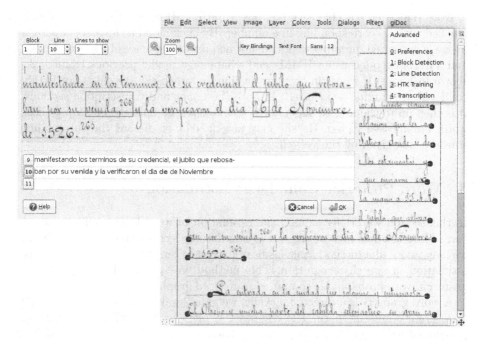

Fig. 1. Interactive transcription dialog over an image window showing GIDOC menu

line detection and handwritten text transcription [5]. It is built as a set of plug-ins for the well-known GNU Image Manipulation Program (GIMP), which has many image processing features already incorporated and, what is more important, a high-end user interface for image manipulation. To run GIDOC, we must first run GIMP and open a document image. GIMP will come up with its high-end user interface, which is often configured to only show the main toolbox (with docked dialogs) and an image window. GIDOC can be accessed from the menubar of the image window (see Figure 1).

As shown in Figure 1, the GIDOC menu includes six entries, though here only the last one, *Transcription,* is briefly described (see [5] for more details on GIDOC). The *Transcription* entry opens an interactive transcription dialog (also shown in Figure 1), which consists of two main sections: the image section, in the middle part, and the transcription section, in the bottom part. A number of text line images are displayed in the image section together with their transcriptions, if available, in separate editable text boxes within the transcription section. The *current* line to be transcribed is selected by placing the edit cursor in the appropriate editable box. Its corresponding baseline is emphasised (in blue colour) and, whenever possible, GIDOC shifts line images and their transcriptions so as to display the current line in the central part of both the image and transcription sections. It is assumed that the user transcribes or supervises text lines, from top to bottom, by entering text and moving the edit cursor with the arrow keys or the mouse. However, it is possible for the user to choose any order desired.

Note that each editable text box has a button attached to its left, which is labelled with its corresponding line number. By clicking on it, its associated line image is extracted, preprocessed, transformed into a sequence of feature vectors, and Viterbi-decoded using HMMs and a language model previous trained. As shown in Figure 1, words in the current line for which the system is not highly confident are emphasised (in red) in both the image and transcription sections. It is then up to the user to supervise system output completely, or simply those words emphasised in red. He/she may accept, edit or discard the current line transcription given by the system.

3   Word Posterior Confidence Estimation

In this section we briefly explain the estimation of word-level confidence measures. Taking advantage of the use of standard speech technology by GIDOC, we have adopted a method that has been proved to be very useful for confidence estimation in speech recognition. This method was proposed in [7] and uses posterior word probabilities computed from word graphs as confidence measures.

A word graph G is a directed, acyclic, weighted graph. The nodes correspond to discrete points in space. The edges are triplets $[w, s, e]$, where w is the hypothesized word from node s to node e. The weights are the recognition scores associated to the word graph edges. Any path from the initial to the final node forms a hypothesis $\boldsymbol{f}_1^J$.

Given the observations $\boldsymbol{x}_1^T$, the posterior probability for a specific word (edge) $[w, s, e]$ can be computed by summing up the posterior probabilities of all hypotheses of the word graph containing the edge $[w, s, e]$:

$$P([w, s, e] \mid \boldsymbol{x}_1^T) = \frac{1}{P(\boldsymbol{x}_1^T)} \sum_{\substack{\boldsymbol{f}_1^J \in G : \\ \exists [w', s', e'] : \\ w' = w, s' = s, e' = e}} P(\boldsymbol{f}_1^J, [w, s, e], \boldsymbol{x}_1^T) \qquad (1)$$

The probability of the sequence of observations $P(\boldsymbol{x}_1^T)$ can be computed by summing up the posterior probabilities of all word graph hypothesis:

$$P(\boldsymbol{x}_1^T) = \sum_{\boldsymbol{f}_1^J \in G} P(\boldsymbol{f}_1^J, \boldsymbol{x}_1^T)$$

The posterior probability defined in Eq. 1 does not perform well because a word w can occur in slightly different starting and ending points. This effect is represented in the word graph by different word edges and the posterior probability mass of the word is scattered among the different word segmentations (see Fig. 2).

To deal with this problem, we have considered a solution proposed in [7]. Given a specific word (edge) $[w, s, e]$ and a specific point in time $t \in [s, e]$, we compute the posterior probability of the word w at time t by summing up the posterior probabilities of the word graph edges $[w, s', e']$ with identical word w

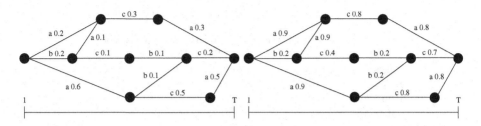

Fig. 2. Word graph with the word posterior probabilities computed as Eq. 1 (left) and as Eq. 3 (right)

and for which t is within the interval time $[s', e']$:

$$P_t([w, s, e] \mid x_1^T) = \sum_{t \in [s', e']} P([w, s', e'] \mid x_1^T) \qquad (2)$$

Based on Eq. 2, the posterior probability for a specific word $[w, s, e]$ is computed as the maximum of the frame time posterior probabilities:

$$P([w, s, e] \mid x_1^T) = \max_{s \leq t \leq e} P_t([w, s, e] \mid x_1^T) \qquad (3)$$

The probability computed on Eq. 3 is in the interval $[0, 1]$ since, by definition, the sum of the word posterior probabilities for a specific point in time must sum to one (see Fig. 2, left). The posterior probabilities calculated as Eq. 3 are used as word confidence measures (see Fig. 2).

Using these posterior probabilities, a word is proposed to the human supervisor if $P([w, s, e] \mid x_1^T)$ is lower that a certain threshold τ (cf. section 4.2).

4   Experiments

4.1   Databases

The IAM-DB 3.0 dataset [10] contains forms of handwritten English text, scanned at a 300dpi resolution and saved as PNG images with 256 gray levels. Feature extraction has been performed using the geometric-based method. HMMs have lineal topology composed of 7 states with a mixture of 16 gaussians per state. We have achieved a WER of 35.5% for IAM test corpus.

The GERMANA database is the result of digitising and annotating a 764-page Spanish manuscript written in 1891. Most pages only contain nearly calligraphed text written on ruled sheets of well-separated lines. GERMANA is a single-author book on a limited-domain topic. It has typical characteristics of historical documents that make things difficult: spots, writing from the verso appearing on the recto, unusual characters and words, etc. Also, the manuscript includes many notes and appended documents that are written in languages different from Spanish, namely Catalan, French and Latin. The manuscript was carefully

Table 1. Basic statistics of IAM and GERMANA

	IAM 20K Voc.			GERMANA 9.4K Voc.		
	Train	Val.	Test	Train	Val.	Test
Pages	747	116	336	94	36	38
Lines	6.161	920	2.781	2.131	811	811
Run.Words (K)	53.8	8.7	25.4	23.7	9.4	9.1
out-of-voc (%)	−	6.6	6.4	−	17.5	18.6

scanned by experts from the Valencian Library at 300dpi in true colours. The experiments have been performed using only the first 179 pages, which correspond to well structured pages written only in spanish. It is also worth noting that 68% of language model words occur once (singletons), and abbreviations appear in many different ways. Furthermore, 33% of words are incomplete since they are at the beginning or the end of lines. HMMs have lineal topology composed of 6 states with a mixture of 64 gaussians per state. We have achieved 42% of WER on the test set. See [6] for a full description.

4.2   Evaluation Measures

Let us assume that, after the recognition output is obtained, the system produces C correctly recognised words and I incorrectly recognised words. Using confidence measures, only words with confidence below on the decision threshold (see section 3) are suggested to the human supervisor for correction. We can distinguish two outcomes in this interactive paradigm:

- *True Rejection* (TR): words incorrectly recognised are suggested for correction.
- *False Rejection* (FR): words correctly recognised are suggested for correction.

When the human supervisor completes the revision of the suggested corrections, we are interested to evaluate the human effort along with the improvement achieved. For this purpose, we compute the ratio of words supervised by the human and the improvement on the system accuracy as a result of the interactive correction process.

$$Supervised = \frac{TR + FR}{I + C} \qquad Accuracy = \frac{TR + C}{I + C}$$

To provide an adequate overall estimation of these two measures, we need to compute both values for all possible decision threshold τ. This can be easily achieved based on a *Receiver Operating Characteristic* (ROC) curve. ROC curves are typically used to evaluate the performance of confidence measures. A ROC curve represents the *True Rejection Rate* (TRR) against the *False Rejection Rate* (FRR) for all possible values of τ. TRR and FRR are computed as:

$$TRR = \frac{TR}{I} \qquad\qquad FRR = \frac{FR}{C}$$

Let (frr,trr) be a point of the ROC curve, we can compute the supervision and accuracy measures for this decision threshold, as:

$$Supervised(frr, trr) = \frac{trr \cdot I + frr \cdot C}{I + C} \qquad Accuracy(trr) = \frac{trr \cdot I + C}{I + C}$$

Computing the Accuracy and Supervision as a function of the ROC curve allows to evaluate the impact of confidence measures over the trade-off accuracy-effort.

4.3   Results

The proposed approach has been tested using GIDOC toolkit along with the IAM and GERMANA corpora (described in Sec. 4.1).

For both corpus, a bigram language model and character-level HMMs have been obtained using the training set. Upper and lower case words were distinguished and punctuation marks were modelled as separate words. The validation set has been used to adjust the Grammar Scale Factor (GSF) and Word Insertion Penalty (WIP) recognition parameters. For confidence estimation, a parameter to scale the language model probabilities has been also optimized using the validation set. This scaling has an important impact on the performance of word posterior probabilities as confidence measures [7]. The optimized parameters have been used in the test phase.

The improvements on the transcription accuracy as a function of the ROC curve are shown in Figure 3. We have emphasised the supervision needed to achieve 80%, 90% and 95% of transcription accuracy.

The transcription accuracy baseline (without supervision) for the IAM corpus is about 69%. Confidence estimation allows us to improve it up to an 80% by supervising only 15% of recognised words. This figure increases to a nearly optimal 99% by supervising 69% of recognised words. In absolute terms, this implies a saving of $7k$ words to be supervised. Another view is that, when a small

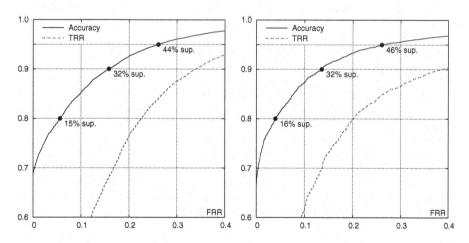

Fig. 3. ROC curve and Accuracy on IAM (left) and Germana (right) databases

number of transcription errors can be tolerated for the sake of efficiency, the use of confidence measures can help to reduce drastically the supervision effort. For the IAM, a 97% of accuracy is achieved by supervising half of the words.

Similar results have been obtained on the GERMANA corpus. The accuracy baseline (67%) is improved to an 80% by supervising only 16% of recognised words. Also, an accuracy of 96% is achieved by supervising half of the words.

5   Conclusions and Future Work

We have presented confidence estimation to reduce the supervision effort in interactive transcription of handwritten text. Posterior probabilities computed from word graphs have been used as confidence measures. The approach proposed have been tested using the GIDOC toolkit along with the IAM and GERMANA databases. We have shown how the use of confidence measures can help to reduce drastically the supervision effort improving the transcription accuracy. Experimental results show that the transcription accuracy can be higher than 95% while the user effort is reduced to the half. Future work should be explore new ways of using confidence measures in the interactive paradigm. Different criteria can be used to suggest for validation the words that are likely to be recognition errors. We plan to study the impact of these strategies over the supervisor effort.

References

1. Toselli, A.H., Juan, A., Keysers, D., et al.: Integrated handwriting recognition and interpretation using finite-state models. IJPRAI 18(4), 519–539 (2004)
2. Likforman-Sulem, L., Zahour, A., Taconet, B.: Text line segmentation of historical documents: a survey. IJDAR 9, 123–138 (2007)
3. Bertolami, R., Bunke, H.: Hidden markov model-based ensemble methods for offline handwritten text line recognition. Patter Recog. 41, 3452–3460 (2008)
4. Bourgeois, F.L., Emptoz, H.: DEBORA: Digital AccEss to BOoks of the RenAissance. IJDAR 9, 193–221 (2007)
5. Juan, A., et al.: iDoc research project (2009),
   http://prhlt.iti.es/projects/handwritten/idoc/
   content.php?page=idoc.php
6. Pérez, D., Tarazón, L., Serrano, N., Castro, F., Ramos, O., Juan, A.: The GERMANA database. In: Proc. of ICDAR 2009 (2009)
7. Wessel, F., Schlüter, R., Macherey, K., Ney, H.: Conf. measures for large vocabulary speech recognition. IEEE Trans. on Speech and Audio Proc. 9(3), 288–298 (2001)
8. Sanchis, A.: Estimación y aplicación de medidas de confianza en reconocimiento automático del habla. PhD thesis, Univ. Politécnica de Valencia, Spain (2004)
9. Bertolami, R., Zimmermann, M., Bunke, H.: Rejection strategies for offline handwritten text recognition. Pattern Recognition Letter 27, 2005–2012 (2006)
10. Marti, U.V., Bunke, H.: The IAM-database: an English sentence database for offline handwriting recognition. IJDAR, 39–46 (2002)

On the Quantitative Estimation of Short-Term Aging in Human Faces

Marcos Ortega, Linda Brodo, Manuele Bicego, and Massimo Tistarelli

[1] University of A Coruña, A Coruña, Spain
[2] Computer Vision Laboratory
University of Sassari, Italy

Abstract. Facial aging has been only partially studied in the past and mostly in a qualitative way. This paper presents a novel approach to the estimation of facial aging aimed to the quantitative evaluation of the changes in facial appearance over time. In particular, the changes both in face shape and texture, due to *short-time aging*, are considered. The developed framework exploits the concept of "distinctiveness" of facial features and the temporal evolution of such measure. The analysis is performed both at a global and local level to define the features which are more stable over time.

Several experiments are performed on publicly available databases with image sequences densely sampled over a time span of several years. The reported results clearly show the potential of the methodology to a number of applications in biometric identification from human faces.

1 Introduction

The demanding needs of the security industry as well as the introduction of electronic passports, increased the interest in automatic face identification and verification. In both operational modalities, digital patterns extracted from the face image are compared with similar patterns stored on the passport or in a database to validate the user's identity. A very challenging issue is the definition of the optimal face representation, either holistic (based on global features) or component-based (based on local features) [1,2,3]. Regardless of the adopted representation, biometric patterns are always affected by the changes in the face appearance due to aging. The impact on the intra-class variations can often spoil the distinctiveness of a face template even after a short time since the user's enrollment. It has been reported in several evaluation studies that, even a short time elapse of one or two weeks between acquisition sessions, can induce variations in the face appearance which degrade the performance of the recognition system. In order to overcome this problem a quantitative evaluation of the changes in the facial appearance over time as well as a regular update of the stored facial template are mandatory.

Only recently aging effects on face recognition have been rigorously studied, both for adult and young people faces[1] [4,5,6,7,8,9]. In general terms the analysis

---

[1] Face images of people from childhood into adulthood (18-20 years hold).

P. Foggia, C. Sansone, and M. Vento (Eds.): ICIAP 2009, LNCS 5716, pp. 575–584, 2009.

of the changes in the face appearance over time can be analyzed over two different time scales: *long-time* as opposed to *short-time* effects. As for the former, it involves gradual and deep modifications in the face structure and texture. These can be accounted for reduction in the fat tissue, progressive degradation of the skin elasticity, reduction of the tone of the facial muscles, development of the skull bones and non uniform pigmentation of the skin [10]. The short time effects can be either due to the same phenomena as well as to other, even transient, effects such as the change in facial tan, hair and beard growth, or small textural changes in the skin. As these are related to finer and sometimes temporary changes in the face appearance, they require a different methodology than the analysis of long time aging. First and outmost, long time changes can be analyzed from coarsely sampled face images over a considerably long time span (ten years or more), while short-time aging requires to analyze face images sampled very closely within a short time (one year or less).

In this paper a quantitative approach to facial aging is presented, where the evolution of changes in the face appearance are *measured* over a short time period. Most of the work reported in the literature is related to the analysis of long time variations. In [4,9] algorithms to simulate the age progression in adult face images are presented. In [8] a computer-based automatic aging simulation technique in 3D is described, with some qualitative results. The work in [6] describes the textural changes produced by three types of geometrical manipulations on face images, which are comparable to aging effects on the face appearance. In [11] an approach to automatically estimate age based on facial patterns is presented.

The most similar study to the one presented in this paper, is reported in [7]. In this case a quantitative approach is adopted to establish the identity between two age separated face images of an individual. The computational framework is based on Bayesian functions to estimate the intra-personal subspace (differences between two age separated faces of the same individual) and the extra-personal subspace (differences between different individuals). The estimated subspaces are used to correctly classify the face image of a given subject.

The estimation framework presented in this paper does not rely on a probabilistic measurement of the changes in the facial appearance but rather on the direct measurement of the time evolution of the face shape. In order to capture the global changes in the face an holistic approach is adopted. Given the short time variability and the transient nature of the analyzed changes, the physical phenomena underpinning the aging effects are not systematically analyzed in this paper. Rather, a global face map is computed, which allows to define the face areas showing the same *aging factor*. This estimation allows to determine the variability of facial features over time.

2   Estimation of Time-Related Face Variability

The primary objective of the proposed approach is to quantitatively measure the face changes, either local or global, within a given time interval.

The estimation is based on the algorithm presented in [12] to compute the most distinctive facial regions of an individual by comparing its face with a number of other faces. The concept of face differences is applied to define the distinctiveness of faces [13], where a feature is selected as distinctive if it is significantly different from any other feature in a given set (like a facial scar). In the context of short time aging, the same algorithm is then applied to a series of face images of the same person but sampled at different times. As a result, the facial regions which are more stable over time are located. These can be also considered as the most time-invariant regions in the face.

2.1 Computing Face Differences

The face difference process is defined in three steps: extraction of face patches, vectorization of each patch, and weighting of the patches. The weight represents a measure of the difference of the feature in one face from any other feature in the other face.

Since face analysis may involve processing information contained at a variety of spatial resolutions, the extraction of each patch is performed at multiple scales. Toward this end each patch is re-sampled using a log-polar mapping [14]. This mapping has been motivated by its resemblance to the distribution of the receptive fields in the human retina, where the sampling resolution is higher at the central fovea and decreases toward the periphery. The resulting sampling process ensures that each patch contains both low scale (fine resolution) and contextual (low resolution) information.

In principle, all the patches of the face may be equally useful for the analysis of the aging effects. To ensure translation-independence and to side-step coarse registration issues, the patches are extracted at the loci centered on the edges extracted from the image. In this way, translation-independence is enforced, while reducing the number of points.

It is worth noting that the use of edge points does not imply that the analysis occurs only at edges. The extracted points represent the center (the *fovea*) of the patches, which extends the sampled area also to the neighborhood. In particular, each face patch is re-sampled following a log-polar scheme representing a local space-variant remapping of the original patch. Analytically, the log-polar scheme describes the mapping postulated to occur between the retina (retinal plane (r, q)) and the visual cortex log-polar or cortical plane (x, h). As illustrated in Fig. 1(a) the size of the "receptive fields" follows a linear increment moving from the central region (fovea) outwards into the periphery.

The set of log-polar image patches, sampled at each point, are vectorized, e.g. a 20×20 pixels patch is transformed into a vector of 400 raw gray-level values which represents the face in the feature space.

Once vectorized, the patches of each face are weighted. Namely, the similarity between each patch in a face and all patches in the second face is computed. When projected to an higher dimensional space, the patches from one face image will tend to form their own cluster in the feature space, while those of the other face image ought to form a different cluster.

The degree of difference of each patch with respect to the other face can be related to its locus in the feature space. All patches of the first face, lying near

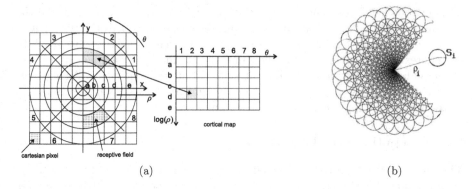

Fig. 1. (a) Log-polar sampling strategy and (b) the adopted log-polar model

the loci of a second face are not very different, and they may easily be confused with the patches of the second face. Conversely, a patch lying on the limb of its own cluster, that is most distant from any other cluster, turns out to be very different.

More formally, let P_1, P_2 be the set of patches of face 1 and 2, respectively. The weight of distinctiveness ω of a patch $p_{P_1}(x, y)$, centered at the position (x, y) in the face 1 is computed as:

$$\omega(p_{P_1}(x, y)) = d(p_{P_1}(x, y), P_2) \tag{1}$$

where

$$d(p_{P_1}(x, y), P_2) = \min_{(x', y')} d_M(p_{P_1}(x, y), p_{P_2}(x', y')) \tag{2}$$

where d_M is some distance metric between features vectors. Here, for clarity, we adopt an Euclidean metric. It might be worthwhile investigating other metrics, such as those due to transforming feature space via say a Principal Component Analysis or Linear Discriminant Analysis.

Another possibility for the extraction of weights is to train a classifier, which is able to separate the two sets P_1 and P_2 to compute the difference on the basis of the distance from the separating surface. This has been investigated in [12], using a Support Vector Machine with mixed results. However, SVM proved to be computationally demanding and much affected by the choice of the learning parameters. Still relaying on the same principle, in this paper a simpler approach is adopted to compute the facial differences which is easier to control and apply within the aging estimation context.

2.2   Face Evolution

The algorithm defined to computed the face differences can be applied to obtain a quantitative measure of the differences of the face over time. To apply the algorithm in this context, we first define the time evolution for two samples. The time evolution between two samples, I_1 and I_2, of the same face separated by a given time t is defined as the total difference between the two face appearance. Consequently, the difference between I_1 and I_2 is computed from the patch weights of both samples. The weights are averaged to obtain a single value of the difference.

The difference between I_1 and I_2 at a point (x, y) is computed considering only those patches extracted from I_1 and I_2 containing the point (x, y). Therefore, the difference $d_{I_1,I_2}(x, y)$, between two face samples I_1 and I_2 of a sequence of images from the same face, is defined by:

$$d_{I_1,I_2}(x, y) = \frac{1}{2} \left(\frac{1}{|P_{I_1}|} \sum_{p \in P_{I_1}} \omega(p) + \frac{1}{|P_{I_2}|} \sum_{q \in P_{I_2}} \omega(q) \right) \tag{3}$$

where P_{I_1} and P_{I_2} are, respectively, the sets of patches from I_1 and I_2 containing the point (x, y), $|P_{I_i}|$ represents the cardinality of the set P_{I_i} and w is the weight determining the distinctiveness of a patch.

The computed difference value can be used as a measure of the time evolution between two samples. In a sequence of faces $S = I_1, I_2, ..., I_t, ...$, the evolution for a point (x, y), within the time span t, can be computed using $d_{I_1,I_{t+1}}$, i.e. taking the initial sample as the reference point in time and computing the difference with the sample separated by the time t. A problem arising is that the results highly depend on the actual quality of both face samples being analyzed. Changes in illumination and image noise can introduce artifacts in the estimated time evolution. On the other hand, this approximation does not take advantage of the high temporal sampling of the sequences.

To overcome these issues, instead of a single difference value between two samples, the evolution within a time span is computed by considering a window of samples of size T and comparing each one of them with its respective sample separated by t. The average of the T differences returns a more robust evolution value, as noise and illumination changes are averaged out over time.

Following this concept, the evolution $E(x, y, t)$ in a sequence, for a point (x, y) and within the time span t, is defined by:

$$E(x, y, t) = \frac{1}{T} \sum_{i=1}^{T} d_{I_i,I_{i+t}}(x, y) \tag{4}$$

2.3 Evolution of Facial Regions

In order to assess the coherence of the aging-related differences in different subjects, the quantitative results for standard facial features are compared in sequences from different individuals. The value of the time evolution for a *standard* feature (either nose, eyes or mouth) of the same individual is expected to stay within a limited and small range. At the same time, when comparing samples from different individuals for the same feature, a substantial, consistent difference in the range of values is expected over time.

If the ranges of the time evolutions for different individuals can be separated, it would be possible to classify each individual on the basis of the face evolution as a signature. In order to verify these assumptions, six standard facial features are analyzed: the nose, eyes, mouth, chin, cheeks and subnasal area. In this case, a feature in the face is defined as a window in the image. For every feature (or landmark) L the evolution over time t is defined by:

$$E(L,t) = \frac{1}{w_L h_L} \sum_{(x,y) \in L} E(x,y,t)$$ (5)

where w_L, h_L are, respectively, the width and the height of the region around the feature L and $E(x,y,t)$ is the evolution function for an image point as defined in equation (4).

3 Experimental Evaluation

In order to analyze the effects of short-time aging and its implications, two experiments have been carried out using sequences of faces over a time frame from 1 to 4 years. The data used in the reported experiments were extracted from a series of publicly available videos which can be downloaded from few Internet web sites[2]. This data set was chosen because the high temporal sampling in the video streams allows to analyze the time evolution of facial features over a short time span. On the other hand, other publicly available databases, such as the MORPH [3] and the FG-NET databases, contain images of adults with a much larger time difference and therefore are not well suited to perform the analysis performed in this paper.

Three video sequences (S_1, S_2 and S_3) from three different individuals have been used. The resolution of the images in all the sequences is 352x240 pixels. In Fig. 2 some samples of the sequences are shown. S_1, S_2 and S_3 cover, respectively, a time span of 4, 3 and 1 year(s). As it can be noted, the faces have been acquired approximately centered in the image and with the head always in the same position and orientation. For this reason the position of facial features does not vary over time, thus simplifying the localization process. The data are highly sampled in time at a rate of one frame per day. This allows to process close in time images thus reducing the effects of noise and temporal aliasing. Only a very limited preprocessing was performed on the face images. In order to avoid face differences due to illumination changes, the samples are preprocessed with a standard histogram equalization. To minimize the influence of outliers, the images with extreme variations such as eyeglasses (weared just once) or long beard were removed from the sequence.

---

[2] The video streams are published as *Living my life faster*. Every subject acquired a picture of his/her face every day for a time period of one to eight years.

[3] http://faceaginggroup.com

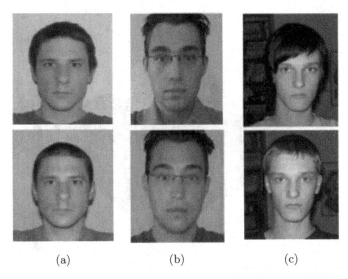

(a)   (b)   (c)

Fig. 2. Sample images extracted from the three image sequences used in the experiments. Images in (a), (b) and (c) correspond to images from sequence S_1, S_2 and S_3, respectively.

A first series of experiments was devoted to the analysis of the global evolution of the face appearance. Toward this aim, the methodology described in section 2.2 has been applied to the sequence S_1. In Fig. 3 the evolution for every face point over a time span of 4 years is shown. The brighter the value in the picture, the faster the temporal evolution of the point. These results are in line with the qualitative results reported in [10].

A second series of experiments was aimed to the analysis of the time evolution of specific, manually selected, facial regions. In particular, six regions were analyzed: the nose, eyes, mouth, chin, cheeks and subnasal area. The evolution value $E(L, t)$ has been computed for sequences S_2 and S_3. Another temporal evolution has been synthesized by crossing samples of both sequences into a single image stream. This procedure allows to compare the range of variability of the differences related to samples of the same individual, and of different individuals as well.

In Fig. 4 the results obtained analyzing different features over different time spans are shown. It is worth noting that the time evolution of every single feature, for the same subject, remains within a limited range. At the same time, the mean value of the temporal evolution of the same feature, but in different subjects, is always considerably different. The estimated difference in the range of values for different individuals is consistently in the order of 50% to 80%. This difference can be easily exploited to devise a robust template embedding the time evolution of each subject's feature for identification or verification purposes.

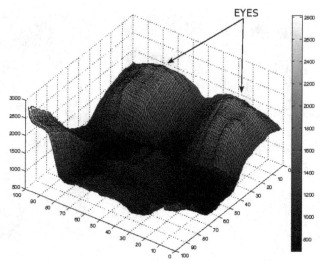

Fig. 3. Evolution for the subject in sequence 1 over 4 years. The area depicted corresponds to a 100x100 image window centered on the face. The elevation of each pixel represents the temporal evolution of the corresponding face point. As expected, the most variable regions (the most elevated in the face) appear to be those containing the eyes.

3.1   Discussion

Even the best learning algorithm can not cope for every possible variation in the face appearance. This is especially true for natural developments and changes due to aging. For this reason most identification algorithms fail to recognize individuals whenever the acquired face image is distant in time from the enrollment session. Sometimes even acquiring images of the same subject at different times in the day can result in noticeable changes in the face image. For these reasons, the analysis of long-time aging effects must be coupled with a short-time quantitative estimation of the time variability of facial features.

The quantitative results obtained in the experimental analysis can be further exploited in a number of practical applications of biometric identification from face images. As an example we may consider the following:

- The time evolution can allow to define the stability of facial features over time to devise more robust facial templates, which incorporate this measure in the face model.
- The analytical formulation of the temporal evolution of a subject's face may facilitate the update of a facial template. Both the global and local estimation of the temporal evolution can be applied as an indicator of the optimal time to update the template or part of it.

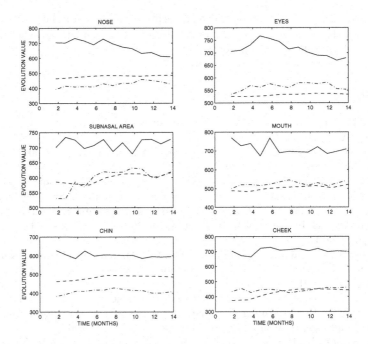

Fig. 4. Time evolution of facial differences obtained for six selected facial features: eyes, nose, mouth, chin, cheek and subnasal area. The solid lines report, for each facial feature, the differences between samples from sequences of different subjects. The dashed lines represent the computed differences between samples of sequence S_2 and the dash-dotted lines correspond to the computed differences between samples of sequence S_3.

- The quantitative evaluation of the temporal evolution for a subject may allow to forecast critical times when the template update or even re-enrollment would be required.

4   Conclusions

In this paper a novel approach to the quantitative estimation of facial aging has been presented. Differently from the majority of previous approaches, the proposed algorithm is aimed to the quantitative estimation of the temporal evolution of face patterns, within a short time span. The analysis has been performed both at a local and global scale allowing to define the time variability of individual facial features. Experiments have been performed on several sequences from different subjects highly sampled in time. The obtained results, not only demonstrate the possibility to quantitatively evaluate the temporal evolution of the face appearance over a short time scale, but also the high potential for applications to robust personal identity verification. As a further development of this work the application of the time evolution of facial features as a signature for personal identification will be exploited.

References

1. Zhao, W., Chellappa, R., Phillips, P.J., Rosenfeld, A.: Face recognition: A literature survey. ACM Computing Surveys 35(4), 399–458 (2003)
2. Zhao, W., Chellappa, R.: Face Processing: Advanced Modeling and Methods. Academic Press Inc., USA (2006)
3. Abate, A.F., Nappi, M., Riccio, D., Sabatino, G.: Face Recognition: A Survey on 2D and 3D Techniques Pattern Recognition Letters 28(14), 1885–1906 (2007)
4. Lanitis, A., Taylor, C.J., Cootes, T.F.: Toward Automatic Simulation of Aging Effects on Face Images. IEEE Transactions on Pattern Analysis and Machine Intelligence 24(4), 442–455 (2002)
5. Lanitis, A., Draganova, C., Christodoulou, C.: Comparing different classifiers for automatic age estimation. IEEE Transactions on Systems, Man and Cybernetics - Part B 34(1), 621–628 (2004)
6. Miyoshi, T., Hyodo, M.: Aging Effects on face images by varying vertical feature placement and transforming face shape. Proceedings of IEEE International Conference on Systems, Man and Cybernetics 2, 1548–1553 (2006)
7. Ramanathan, N., Chellappa, R.: Face verification across age progression. In: Proceedings of IEEE Computer Society Conference on Computer Vision and Pattern Recognition, vol. 2, pp. 462–469 (2005)
8. Park, U., Tong, Y., Jain, A.K.: Face Recognition with Temporal Invariance: A 3D Aging Model. In: Proceedings of IEEE Conference on Automatic Face and Gesture Recognition (to appear)
9. Wang, J., Shang, Y., Su, G., Lin, X.: Simulation of Aging Effects in Face Images. LNCIS, vol. 345, pp. 517–527. Springer, Heidelberg (2006)
10. Patterson, E., Sethuram, A., Albert, M., Ricanek, K., King, M.: Aspects of age variation in facial morphology affecting biometrics. In: Proceedings of IEEE Conference on Biometrics: Theory, Applications and Systems, pp. 1–6 (2007)
11. Geng, X., Zhou, Z.H., Smith-Miles, K.: Automatic age estimation based on facial aging patterns. IEEE Pattern Analysis and Machine Intelligence 29(12), 2234–2240 (2007)
12. Bicego, M., Grosso, E., Tistarelli, M.: On finding differences between faces. In: Kanade, T., Jain, A., Ratha, N.K. (eds.) AVBPA 2005. LNCS, vol. 3546, pp. 329–338. Springer, Heidelberg (2005)
13. Bicego, M., Brelstaff, G., Brodo, L., Grosso, E., Lagorio, A., Tistarelli, M.: Distinctiveness of faces: a computational approach. ACM Trans. on Applied Perception 5(2), 11:1–11:18 (2008)
14. Grosso, E., Tistarelli, M.: Log-polar stereo for anthropomorphic robots. In: Vernon, D. (ed.) ECCV 2000. LNCS, vol. 1842, pp. 299–313. Springer, Heidelberg (2000)

3D Neural Model-Based Stopped Object Detection

Lucia Maddalena[1] and Alfredo Petrosino[2]

[1] ICAR - National Research Council
Via P. Castellino 111, 80131 Naples, Italy
`lucia.maddalena@na.icar.cnr.it`
[2] DSA - University of Naples Parthenope
Centro Direzionale, Isola C/4, 80143 Naples, Italy
`alfredo.petrosino@uniparthenope.it`

Abstract. In this paper we propose a system that is able to distinguish moving and stopped objects in digital image sequences taken from stationary cameras. Our approach is based on self organization through artificial neural networks to construct a model of the scene background and a model of the scene foreground that can handle scenes containing moving backgrounds or gradual illumination variations, helping in distinguishing between moving and stopped foreground regions, leading to an initial segmentation of scene objects. Experimental results are presented for video sequences that represent typical situations critical for detecting vehicles stopped in no parking areas and compared with those obtained by other existing approaches.

Keywords: moving object detection, background subtraction, background modeling, foreground modeling, stopped object, self organization, neural network.

1   Introduction

Stopped object detection in an image sequence consists in detecting temporally static image regions indicating objects that do not constitute the original background but were brought into the scene at a subsequent time, such as abandoned and removed items, or illegally parked vehicles.

Great interest in the stopped object detection problem has been given by the PETS workshops held in 2006 [8] and in 2007 [9], where one of the main aims has been the detection of *left luggage*, that is luggage that has been abandoned by its owner, in movies taken from multiple cameras. Another example of strong interest in the considered problem is given by the *i-LIDS bag and vehicle detection challenge* proposed in the AVSS 2007 Conference [20], where the attention has been driven on abandoned bags and parked vehicles events, properly defined.

A broad classification of existing approaches to the detection of stopped objects can be given as *tracking-based* and *non tracking-based* approaches. In *tracking-based* approaches the stopped object detection is obtained on the basis

P. Foggia, C. Sansone, and M. Vento (Eds.): ICIAP 2009, LNCS 5716, pp. 585–593, 2009.

of the analysis of object trajectories through an application dependent event detection phase. Such approaches include most of the papers in [8,9,20]. *Non tracking-based* approaches include pixel- and region-based approaches aiming at classifying pixels/objects without the aid of tracking modules, and include [4,12,13,17,19].

Our approach to the problem is non tracking-based. The problem is tackled as *stopped foreground subtraction*, that, in analogy with the background subtraction approach, consists in maintaining an up-to-date model of the stopped foreground and in discriminating moving objects as those that deviate from such model. Both background subtraction and stopped foreground subtraction have the common issue of constructing and maintaining an image model that adapts to scene changes and can capture the most persisting features of the image sequence, i.e. the background and the stationary foreground, respectively. For such modeling problem we adopt visual attention mechanisms that help in detecting features that keep the user attention, based on a self-organizing neural network.

We propose to construct a system for motion detection based on the background and the foreground model automatically generated by a self-organizing method without prior knowledge of the pattern classes. The approach, that is a variation of the one proposed for background modeling [15,16], consists in using biologically inspired problem-solving methods to solve motion detection tasks, typically based on visual attention mechanisms [2]. The aim is to obtain the objects that keep the users attention by referring to a set of predefined features.

The paper is organized as follows. In Section 2 we describe a model-based pixelwise procedure allowing to discriminate foreground pixels into stopped and moving pixels, that is completely independent on the background and foreground models adopted. In Section 3 we describe the model for both background and foreground modeling that we adopted in our experiments. Section 4 presents results obtained with the implementation of the proposed approach and compares them with those obtained by other existing approaches, while Section 5 includes concluding remarks.

2   Stopped Foreground Detection

In this section we propose a model-based approach to the classification of foreground pixels into stopped and moving pixels. A foreground pixel is classified as *stopped* if it holds the same color features for several consecutive frames; otherwise it is classified as *moving*.

Assuming we have a model BG_t of the image sequence background, we compute a function $E(x)$ of color feature occurrences for pixel $I_t(x)$ as follows

$$E(x) = \begin{cases} \min(\tau_s, E(x) + 1) & \text{if} \quad I_t(x) \notin BG_t \quad \text{and} \quad I_t(x) \in FG_t \\ \max(0, E(x) - 1) & \text{if} \quad I_t(x) \notin BG_t \quad \text{and} \quad I_t(x) \notin FG_t \\ \max(0, E(x) - k) & \text{if} \quad I_t(x) \in BG_t \end{cases} \quad (1)$$

where model FG_t of the sequence foreground is iteratively built and updated using image pixels $I_t(x)$ for which $E(x) > 0$.

Every time pixel $I_t(x)$ belongs to the foreground model $(I_t(x) \in FG_t)$, $E(x)$ is incremented, while it is decremented if it does not belong to the foreground model. The maximum value τ_s for $E(x)$ corresponds to the *stationarity threshold*, i.e. the minimum number of consecutive frames after which a pixel assuming constant color features is classified as stopped. The value for τ_s is chosen depending on the desired responsiveness of the system.

On the contrary, if pixel $I_t(x)$ is detected as belonging to the background $(I_t(x) \in BG_t)$, $E(x)$ is decreased by a factor k. The decay constant k determines how fast $E(x)$ should decrease, i.e. how fast the system should recognize that a stopped pixel has moved again. To set the alarm flag off immediately after the removal of the stopped object, the value of decay should be large, eventually equal to τ_s.

Pixels $I_t(x)$ for which $E(x)$ reaches the stationarity threshold value τ_s are classified as stopped, and therefore the set ST_t defined as

$$ST_t = \{FG_t(x) : E(x) = \tau_s\}$$

supplies a model for the stopped objects, while the remaining part of FG_t represents moving objects.

The described procedure is completely independent on the model adopted for the scene background and foreground. The model that we have adopted for the background and the foreground will be described in the following section.

3   Background and Foreground Update

For background and foreground modeling we adopt here a variation of the model presented in [15,16], according to which a self-organizing neural network, organized as a 3-D grid of neurons, is built up. Each neuron computes a function of the weighted linear combination of incoming inputs, with weights resembling the neural network learning, and can be therefore represented by a weight vector obtained collecting the weights related to incoming links. An incoming pattern is mapped to the neuron whose set of weight vectors is most similar to the pattern, and weight vectors in a neighborhood of such node are updated.

Specifically, for each pixel $p_t = I_t(x)$ we build a neuronal map consisting of L weight vectors $c^l(p_t), l = 1, \ldots, L,$. Each weight vector $c^l(p_t)$ is represented in the HSV colour space, that allows to specify colours in a way that is close to human experience of colours, and is initialized to the HSV components of the corresponding pixel of the first sequence frame $I_0(p_t)$. The complete set of weight vectors for all pixels of an image I with N rows and M columns is organized as a 3D neuronal map $\tilde{B}$ with N rows, M columns, and L layers. An example of such neuronal map is given in Fig. 1, which shows that for each pixel $p_t = I_t(x)$ we have a weight vector $\tilde{B}_t(x) = (c^1(p_t), c^2(p_t), \ldots, c^L(p_t))$.

By subtracting the current image from the background model $\tilde{B}$, each pixel p_t of the t-th sequence frame I_t is compared to the current pixel weight vectors to determine if there exists a weight vector that matches it. The best matching weight vector is used as the pixel's encoding approximation, and therefore p_t is

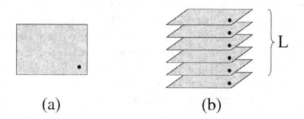

Fig. 1. A simple image (a) and the modeling neuronal map with L layers (b)

detected as foreground if no acceptable matching weight vector exists; otherwise it is classified as background.

Matching for the incoming pixel $p_t = I_t(x)$ is performed by looking for a weight vector $c^b(p_t)$ in the set $\tilde{B}_t(x) = (c^1(p_t), \ldots, c^L(p_t))$ of the current pixel weight vectors satisfying:

$$d(c^b(p_t), p_t) = \min_{i=1,\ldots,L} d(c^i(p_t), p_t) \leq \varepsilon \qquad (2)$$

where the metric $d(\cdot)$ and the threshold ε are suitably chosen as in [15].

The best matching weight vector $c^l(p_t) = \tilde{B}_t(x)$ belonging to layer l and all other weight vectors in a $n \times n$ neighborhood N_{p_t} of $c^l(p_t)$ in the l-th layer of the background model $\tilde{B}$ are updated according to selective weighted running average:

$$\tilde{B}_t^l(x) = (1 - \alpha_t(x))\tilde{B}_{t-1}^l(x) + \alpha_t(x)I_t(x), \quad \forall x \in N_{p_t} \qquad (3)$$

where $\alpha_t(x)$ is a learning factor, later specified, belonging to [0,1] and depends on scene variability. If the best match $c^b(p_t)$ satisfying (2) is not found, the background model $\tilde{B}$ remains unchanged. Such selectivity allows to adapt the background model to scene modifications without introducing the contribution of pixels not belonging to the background scene.

Spatial coherence is also introduced in order to enhance robustness against false detections. Let $p = I(x)$ the generic pixel of image I, and let N_p a spatial square neighborhood of pixel $p \in I$. We consider the set Ω_p of pixels belonging to N_p that have a best match in their background model according to (2), i.e.

$$\Omega_p = \{q \in N_p : d(c^b(q), q) \leq \varepsilon\} \ .$$

In analogy with [5], the *Neighborhood Coherence Factor* is defined as:

$$NCF(p) = \frac{|\Omega_p|}{|N_p|}$$

where $|\cdot|$ refers to the set cardinality. Such factor gives a relative measure of the number of pixels belonging to the spatial neighborhood N_p of a given pixel p that are well represented by the background model $\tilde{B}$. If $NCF(p) > 0.5$, most of the pixels in such spatial neighborhood are well represented by the background model, and this should imply that also pixel p is well represented by the background model. Values for $\alpha_t(x)$ in (3) are therefore expressed as

$$\alpha_t(x) = M(p_t)\ \alpha(t)\ w(x), \quad \forall x \in N_{p_t}, \tag{4}$$

where $w(x)$ are Gaussian weights in the neighborhood N_{p_t}, $\alpha(t)$ represents the learning factor, that is the same for each pixel of the t-th sequence frame, and $M(p_t)$ is the crisp hard-limited function

$$M(p_t) = \begin{cases} 1 & \text{if}\ \ NCF(p_t) > 0.5 \\ 0 & \text{otherwise} \end{cases} \tag{5}$$

that gives the background/foreground segmentation for pixel p_t, also taking into account spatial coherence.

The described model $\tilde{B}_t$ has been adopted for both the background model BG_t and the foreground model FG_t described in Section 2 for the classification of stopped and moving pixels.

4 Experimental Results

Experimental results for the detection of stopped objects using the proposed approach have been produced for several image sequences. Here we present results on parked vehicle sequences *PV-easy*, *PV-medium*, and *PV-hard* belonging to the publicly available *i-LIDS 2007* dataset[1]. Such scenes represent typical situations critical for detecting vehicles in no parking areas, where the street under control is more or less crowded with cars, depending on the hour of the day the scene refers to. For all the scenes the main difficulty is represented by the strong illumination variations, due to clouds frequently covering and uncovering the sun. For the purpose of the AVSS 2007 contest [20], the no parking area is defined as the main street borders, and the stationarity threshold is defined as $\tau_S = 1500$. This means that an object is considered irregularly parked if it stops in the no parking area for more than 60 seconds (scenes are captured at 25 fps).

Results obtained for sequence *PV-easy* are reported in Fig. 2. Since an empty initial background is not available for this scene, we artificially inserted 30 empty scene frames at the beginning of the sequence (starting from frame 251) in order to not be puzzled with bootstrapping problems for background modeling. As soon as the white van stops (starting from frame 2712) the function $E(x)$ described in Section 2 starts incrementing for pixels belonging to the van; such pixels are inserted into the foreground model FG_t and used for the model update. After approximately $\tau_S=1500$ frames, $E(x)$ reaches the stationarity threshold τ_S, thus signaling the first stopped object (frame 4119). From this moment till to the end of the stopped car event the stopped object model allows to distinguish moving objects from the stopped object. When the van leaves again (from frame 4875), the part of the scene uncovered by the van is again recognized as belonging to the background model, and previously stopped pixels are deleted from the stopped object model.

---

[1] ftp://motinas.elec.qmul.ac.uk/pub/iLids/

Fig. 2. Detection of stopped objects in sequence *PV-easy*. The van first stops in frame 2712. The first stationary object is detected in frame 4119; further stationary pixels are later detected, as shown in frames 4200 and 4875. The van is detected as a stationary object till to frame 4976, and no more stopped objects are detected till to frame 5290 (end of the sequence).

It should be stressed that illumination conditions have changed quite a bit between the stopping and leaving of the van. This results in an uncovered background very different from the background that was stored before the van stop. Our background model, however, could recognize it again as background since it includes a mechanism for distinguishing shadows and incorporating them into the background model (here not described for space constraints).

Moreover, it should be clarified that we do not identify the whole white van, but only its part belonging to the no parking area, since we restrict our attention only to the street including the no parking area (masking out the remaining part of the scene).

Results obtained for sequence *PV-medium* are reported in Fig. 3. In this case the empty scene available at the beginning of the sequence (starting from frame 469) allows to train a quite faithful background model. The role of the FG_t model is quite clear here, since many cars pass in front of the stopped car (e.g. in frame 2720, where the white car covers the stopped car) and, without a comparison with such model, could be taken erroneously as part of the stopped car.
Analogous considerations can be drawn by looking at results obtained for sequence *PV-hard*, whose images have not been reported here for space constraints.

We compared results obtained with our approach with those obtained with other approaches for the same sequences. Specifically we considered results obtained by four tracking-based approaches to the detection of stopped objects presented by Boragno et al. [1], who employ a DSP-based system for automatic visual surveillance where block matching motion detection is coupled with MOG-based foreground extraction; Guler et al. [11], who extend a tracking system, inspired by the human visual cognition system, introducing a stationary object

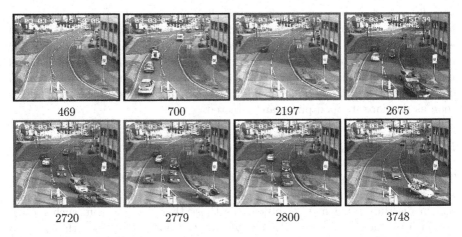

Fig. 3. Detection of stopped objects in sequence *PV-medium*. The car first stops in frame 700. The first stationary object is detected in frame 2197; further stationary pixels are later detected, even if the stopped object is occluded by foreground pixels (e.g. in frame 2720, where the white car covers the stopped car). The car is detected as stopped till to frame 2779, and no more stopped objects are detected till to frame 3748 (end of the sequence).

model where each region represents hypotheses stationary objects whose associated probability measures the endurance of the region; Lee et al. [14], who present a detection and tracking system operating on a 1D projection of images; and by Venetianer et al. [23], who employ an object-based video analysis system featuring detection, tracking and classification of objects.

In Table 1 we report stopped object event start and end times provided with the ground truth and those computed with all considered approaches. Corre-

Table 1. Comparison of ground truth (GT) stopped object event start and end times (in minutes) with those computed with our approach and with different approaches reported in [1,11,14,23], for considered sequences. Related absolute errors (ε) are expressed in seconds; total error is computed as the sum of absolute errors over the three sequences.

Sequence	Event	GT	Our	ε	[1]	ε	[11]	ε	[14]	ε	[23]	ε
PV-easy	Start	02:48	02:45	3	02:48	0	02:46	2	02:52	4	02:52	4
"	End	03:15	03:19	4	03:19	4	03:18	3	03:19	4	03:16	1
PV-medium	Start	01:28	01:28	0	01:28	0	01:28	0	01:41	13	01:43	15
"	End	01:47	01:51	4	01:55	8	01:54	7	01:55	8	01:47	0
PV-hard	Start	02:12	02:12	0	02:12	0	02:13	1	02:08	4	02:19	7
"	End	02:33	02:34	1	02:36	3	02:36	3	02:37	4	02:34	1
Total error				12		15		16		37		28

sponding absolute errors show that generally our approach compares favorably to the other approaches, and this is still more evident if we consider the total error over the three considered sequences. It should be emphasized that, since our approach to stopped object detection is pixel-based and no region-based post-processing is performed in order to identify objects, in our case a stopped object event starts as soon as a single pixel is detected as stopped and ends as soon as no more stopped pixels are detected.

5   Conclusions

The paper reports our approach to the problem of *stopped foreground subtraction*, consisting in maintaining an up-to-date model of the stopped foreground and in discriminating moving objects as those that deviate from such model. For such modeling problem we adopt visual attention mechanisms that help in detecting features that keep the user attention, based on a 3D self-organizing neural network, without prior knowledge of the pattern classes. The approach consists in using biologically inspired problem-solving methods to solve motion detection tasks, typically based on visual attention mechanisms [2]. The aim is to obtain the objects that keep the user attention in accordance with a set of predefined features, by learning the trajectories and features of moving and stopped objects in a self-organizing manner. Such models allow to construct a system able to detect motion and segment foreground objects into moving or stopped objects, even when they appear superimposed.

References

1. Boragno, S., Boghossian, B., Black, J., Makris, D., Velastin, S.: A DSP-based system for the detection of vehicles parked in prohibited areas. In: [20]
2. Cantoni, V., Marinaro, M., Petrosino, A. (eds.): Visual Attention Mechanisms. Kluwer Academic/Plenum Publishers, New York (2002)
3. Cheung, S.-C., Kamath, C.: Robust Techniques for Background Subtraction in Urban Traffic Video. In: Proceedings of EI-VCIP, pp. 881–892 (2004)
4. Collins, R.T., Lipton, A.J., Kanade, T., Fujiyoshi, H., Duggins, D., Tsin, Y., Tolliver, D., Enomoto, N., Hasegawa, O., Burt, P., Wixson, L.: A System for Video Surveillance and Monitoring. The Robotics Institute, Carnegie Mellon University, Tech. Rep. CMU-RI-TR-00-12 (2000)
5. Ding, J., Ma, R., Chen, S.: A Scale-Based Connected Coherence Tree Algorithm for Image Segmentation. IEEE Transactions on Image Processing 17(2), 204–216 (2008)
6. Elhabian, S.Y., El-Sayed, K.M., Ahmed, S.H.: Moving Object Detection in Spatial Domain using Background Removal Techniques - State-of-Art. Recent Patents on Computer Science 1, 32–54 (2008)
7. Elgammal, A., Duraiswami, R., Harwood, D., Davis, L.S.: Background and Foreground Modeling Using Nonparametric Kernel Density Estimation for Visual Surveillance. Proceedings of the IEEE 90(7), 1151–1163 (2002)
8. Ferryman, J.M. (ed.): Proceedings of the 9th IEEE International Workshop on PETS, New York, June 18 (2006)

9. Ferryman, J.M. (ed.): Proceedings of the 10th IEEE International Workshop on PETS, Rio de Janeiro, Brazil, October 14 (2007)

10. Fisher, R.B.: Change Detection in Color Images, http://homepages.inf.ed.ac.uk/rbf/PAPERS/iccv99.pdf

11. Guler, S., Silverstein, J.A., Pushee, I.H.: Stationary objects in multiple object tracking. In: [20]

12. Herrero-Jaraba, E., Orrite-Urunuela, C., Senar, J.: Detected Motion Classification with a Double-Background and a Neighborhood-based Difference. Pattern Recognition Letters 24, 2079–2092 (2003)

13. Kim, K., Chalidabhongse, T.H., Harwood, D., Davis, L.S.: Real-time Foreground-Background Segmentation using Codebook Model. Real-Time Imaging 11, 172–185 (2005)

14. Lee, J.T., Ryoo, M.S., Riley, M., Aggarwal, J.K.: Real-time detection of illegally parked vehicles using 1-D transformation. In: [20]

15. Maddalena, L., Petrosino, A.: A Self-Organizing Approach to Background Subtraction for Visual Surveillance Applications. IEEE Transactions on Image Processing 17(7), 1168–1177 (2008)

16. Maddalena, L., Petrosino, A., Ferone, A.: Object Motion Detection and Tracking by an Artificial Intelligence Approach. International Journal of Pattern Recognition and Artificial Intelligence 22(5), 915–928 (2008)

17. Patwardhan, K.A., Sapiro, G., Morellas, V.: Robust Foreground Detection in Video Using Pixel Layers. IEEE Transactions on PAMI 30(4), 746–751 (2008)

18. Piccardi, M.: Background Subtraction Techniques: A Review. In: Proceedings of IEEE Int. Conf. on Systems, Man and Cybernetics, pp. 3099–3104 (2004)

19. Porikli, F., Ivanov, Y., Haga, T.: Robust Abandoned Object Detection Using Dual Foregrounds. EURASIP Journal on Advances in Signal Processing (2008)

20. Proceedings of 2007 IEEE Conference on Advanced Video and Signal Based Surveillance (AVSS 2007). IEEE Computer Society (2007)

21. Radke, R.J., Andra, S., Al-Kofahi, O., Roysam, B.: Image Change Detection Algorithms: A Systematic Survey. IEEE Transactions on Image Processing 14(3), 294–307 (2005)

22. Toyama, K., Krumm, J., Brumitt, B., Meyers, B.: Wallflower: Principles and Practice of Background Maintenance. In: Proceedings of the Seventh IEEE Conference on Computer Vision, vol. 1, pp. 255–261 (1999)

23. Venetianer, P.L., Zhang, Z., Yin, W., Lipton, A.J.: Stationary target detection using the objectvideo surveillance system. In: [20]

24. Wren, C., Azarbayejani, A., Darrell, T., Pentland, A.: Pfinder: Real-Time Tracking of the Human Body. IEEE Transactions on PAMI 19(7), 780–785 (1997)

A New Linguistic-Perceptual Event Model for Spatio-Temporal Event Detection and Personalized Retrieval of Sports Video

Minh-Son Dao, Sharma Ishan Nath, and Noboru Babaguichi

Media Integrated Communication Lab. (MICL),
Graduate School of Engineering - Osaka University
2-1 Yamadaoka, Suita, Osaka 565-0871, Japan
{dao,sharma}@nanase.comm.eng.osaka-u.ac.jp,
babaguchi@comm.eng.osaka-u.ac.jp

Abstract. This paper proposes a new linguistic-perceptual event model tailoring to spatio-temporal event detection and conceptual-visual personalized retrieval of sports video sequences. The major contributions of the proposed model are hierarchical structure, independence between linguistic and perceptual part, and ability of capturing temporal information of sports events. Thanks to these advanced contributions, it is very easy to upgrade model events from simple to complex levels either by self-studying from inner knowledge or by being taught from plug-in additional knowledge. Thus, the proposed model not only can work well in unwell structured environments but also is able to adapt itself to new domains without the need (or with a few modification) for external reprogramming, re-configuring and re-adjusting. Thorough experimental results demonstrate that events are modeled and detected with high accuracy and automation, and users' expectation of personalized retrieval is highly satisfied.

Keywords: Video signal processing, String matching, Multimedia Information retrieval, Personalization.

1 Introduction

Sports have been known as the most exciting entertainment since the dawn of civilization. People always pay much attention to sports and tend to be involved in active (e.g. players, coaches, etc.) or passive (e.g. audiences, press, etc.) positions as much as possible. Nowadays, with dramatic development of digital technologies and data networks and with unlimited supports of broadcasting industry, audiences' requirements of entertainment have been almost satisfied. Unfortunately, due to different reasons, not all of audiences are ready to spend all their time to watch a full game in a certain sport. In fact, there are only few periods of time that can attract and excite audiences such as "goal" in soccer. These periods of time could be seen as "highlight" or "event".

P. Foggia, C. Sansone, and M. Vento (Eds.): ICIAP 2009, LNCS 5716, pp. 594–603, 2009.
© Springer-Verlag Berlin Heidelberg 2009

Although events could be defined as real-world occurrences that unfold over space and time, many existed methods heavily focus on and exploit the former information (e.g internal-spatial informations)[1]. Although Allen [2] proposed the temporal algebra to model optimally any temporal relation in reality, very little attention has been paid to utilize Allen's theory so far [1][3]. In video analysis, since most of methods dealing with capturing temporal information use only linear temporal relations, they lack the ability to represent temporal information of real complex events compared with Allen's [4][5]. Although there are a few methods that use Allen's algebra to model temporal relations of complex events [6][7], their ambiguous and complex structure representation lead to the increase in computational complexity as well as resources consuming.

In order to deal with one of crucial problems of video analysis: *semantic gap*, most of the existing methods are using supports from the domain knowledge. Since those methods relies heavily on the domain knowledge with significant human interference, it can be hardly applied as a generic framework for an arbitrary domain automatically [1][8].

Moreover, instead of receiving passively whatever products that are offered by broadcasters in one-to-many mode, consumers now tend to request such products that satisfy most of their preferences. The major challenge is the scalability of consumers' preferences. In another word, different users -with different needs and cultures, and accessing the service through heterogeneous terminals and connections- requires different products. Thus, providing tools by which users (both producers and customers) can produce a product based on their own queries related to their preferences seems to be the best solution to satisfy these advanced requirements [9].

In light of these discussions, this paper proposes a new linguistic-perceptual event model tailoring to spatio-temporal event detection and conceptual-visual personalized retrieval of sports video sequences. The major contributions of the proposed model are hierarchical structure, independence between linguistic and perceptual part, and ability of capturing temporal information of sports events. Thanks to these advanced contributions, it is very easy to upgrade model events from simple to complex levels either by self-studying from inner knowledge or by being taught from plug-in additional knowledge. Thus, the proposed model not only can work well in unwell structured environments but also is able to adapt itself to new domains without the need (or with a few modification) for external re-programming, re-configuring and re-adjusting. By taking benefit of the proposed event model, the spatio-temporal event detection method that can adaptively detect events by capturing and representing temporal information using Allen-based temporal algebra is introduced. Results of automatic event detection process are tailored to personalized retrieval via click-and-see style. Thanks to the proposed event model, users could retrieve events by using either conceptual or conceptual-visual fusion query schemes.

2   Linguistic-Perceptual Event Model

Since capturing and presenting temporal information are the core of this research, the temporal database scheme - inspired from Data Mining aspect - is chosen to store events' information. The temporal database contains given events, namely *target_event*, whose contents are the set of patterns that occur in various time periods. These patterns could be other (children) events or concepts, namely *basic_event*. In our method, the temporal database and events are described as follow:

Let $D = \{I\}$ denote the temporal database and

$$I = (target\_event\_name, basic\_event\_name, basic\_event\_interval) \qquad (1)$$

denote D's item, where

$$basic\_event\_interval = (time\_start, time\_end) \qquad (2)$$

be the time interval where such *basic_events* happens. The linguistic-perceptual event model is then defined in order to capture informations contained in the temporal database D as follow:

Definition 1 (Event Model)
Given an *target_event* A, the model of A is defined as follow:

$$model(A) \equiv \{(event\_id_i, event\_interval_i)\} \qquad (3)$$

$$event\_id_i = (event\_type_i, event\_property_i) \qquad (4)$$

$$event\_type_i \in \{codebook\_item_i\} \qquad (5)$$

$$event\_property_i \in \{(keyframe\_id_j, cluster\_id_j)\} \qquad (6)$$

$$codebook\_item_i = (basic\_event\_name, NATP\_id)_i \qquad (7)$$

where $i=1..n$, n is the number of basic events that constructed the target event, $j=1..m_i$, m_i is the number of *cluster_id* that belongs to *event_property_i*. The *event_type* is presented as symbols, called *linguistic part*, and the *event_property* captures the event's *perceptual part* that models multimedia patterns (e.g. audio, visual, textual, etc.) of the specializations of the concepts of the linguistic part. The *event_property* is presented by $(keyframe\_centroids, cluster\_id)$ where *cluster_id* is the name of cluster that contains similar keyframes (i.e. similarity distance among these frames is smaller than predefined threshold), and *keyframe_centroids* is the representation of these keyframes. The non-ambiguous temporal patterns (NATP) introduced by Wu et al [3] is applied to create a $NATP\_id$ of the *codebook*. For example: *(camera motion pan left, $a^{+1} < a^{-1}$)* is a vector of the codebook.

In other words, each real complex event *target_event* (model(A)) is recorded as the set of *basic_events* (*event_id*) that occur in complex and varied temporal relations with each other. Each *basic_event* can be low-level feature, mid-level

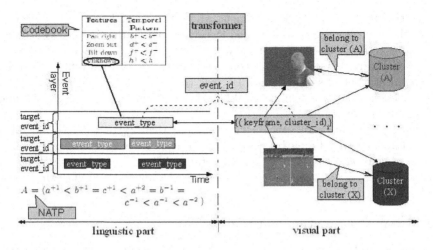

Fig. 1. Illustration of structures of linguistic part, perceptual part (visual concepts), transformer and their relationships of one event

feature, or high-level concept which can be easily extracted from draw video clip using multimedia processing techniques or inferred from simple semantic cues, even a *target_event* of other *basic_events*

Following sections explain how to apply the proposed event method to spatio-temporal event detection and personalized retrieval. Without loss of generality, in our study, soccer domain is chosen as the case study due to its loose structure of video, the diversification of events, and the highly random occurrence of events.

3   Spatio-Temporal Event Detection

The proposed method has three tasks as follow: (1) create a temporal database D by video-text analysis with supports of web-casting text; (2) represent complex events as temporal sequences, and discover temporal sequences that occur frequently in the temporal database D; and (3) detect events.

3.1   Video and Text Analysis

The purpose of this task is to build the temporal database D from a certain domain. Since this task is already done by authors in the previous works, only compact information which characterized how this task works is presented here. Please refer to [10] for details.

Step 1: Key-words by which events are labeled are extracted from web-casting text by using the commercial software, namely dtSearch[1]. At the end of this step, set of *target_event_id* is built.

Step 2: By linking the time stamp in the text event that is extracted from Web-casting text to the game time in the video that is detected by clock digits

---
[1] www.dtSearch.com

recognition technique [10], the moment where the event happens is detected. Then, the event boundary is extracted loosely by sliding the time backward and forward from the time-stamp in time interval t.

Step 3:The raw video clip that contains the just-extracted-event is then decomposed into set of simpler (basic) events that were defined beforehand (e.g. the codebook, other event models). When this step finishes, *event_interval* and *event_type* are determined.

Step 4: Key-frames of each basic event are then extracted and clustered into suitable cluster driven by judgment of predefined visual similar measure. *cluster_id* and *keyframe_centroids* are totally defined at the end. Principal Component Analysis and Spectral Clustering are applied for clustering these keyframes.

3.2   Event Presentation and Mining

The mission of this task is to solve the second issue raised in the previous section. In this task, only the conceptual events (i.e. linguistic part) are concerned. Therefore, this task is independent domain-knowledge.

Step 1: First, all *basic_events* of a certain event are mapped into the codebook to get their temporal patterns presentation. Then, these temporal patterns are aligned by their interval times in the same time axis. Finally, extended Allen temporal algebra is applied to present the certain event as a lexicon of NATP.

Step 2: First, results from the previous step are used to construct the training temporal patterns database (TTPD). Then, the modified NATP framework is used to mine all temporal patterns from TTPD. Since each event is treated as *ruleitem*, mining class association rules is used instead of mining normal association rules to mine temporal patterns (please refer to [10][3] for details).

3.3   Event Detection

We now turn to the problem of event detection from an unknown raw video both in offline case (e.g. video from storage equipments such as HDD, VideoTape, DVD, etc) , and online case (e.g. video as an online streaming from the Internet).

Let $S = S_1 \cup S_2 \cdots \cup S_n$ denote the classified temporal sequences database resulted from previous mining step, where S_i is a subset of S and contains TSs those have the same label i, $1 \leq i \leq n$. Let *maxlength* describe the number of patterns of the longest TS in S (in our method, the length of TS is counted by number of its patterns), and U represent an unknown raw video from which events will be detected.

The slide-window SW whose length equals *maxlength* is moved along U, each step equals to one camera motion pattern. All patterns occurring inside SW are used to construct a candidate TS γ. Then for every TS s in S, the containment is checked between s and γ. γ will be classified into class S_i if S_i contains one TS α that satisfies: (1) Containment(α, γ) = TRUE; (2) if β is the common part of γ and α (i.e all items of β appear both in γ and α), then (a) the length of β must be the longest; (b) the difference between lengths of γ and α is the smallest;

and (c) the *confidence* and *support* of β must satisfy predefined thresholds. Note that, γ could have more than one label.

There are two cases for the start position of SW: (1) if web-casting text does not exist, SW will start from beginning and go through a whole video; (2) otherwise SW jumps directly to video-event-timestamp pointed out by text-event-timestamp, then does to-and-fro motion around that timestamp with predefined number of steps.

4   Personalized Retrieval

Thanks to the event model of our method, we can build an event retrieval system that can work well with visual-based and concept-based queries instead of text-based query that is frequently used by most of existing multimedia retrieval systems.

4.1   Query Creating

From the Definition 1, it is not difficult to recognize that *event_id* can be defined by two ways: (1) using only conceptual items that are extracted from the codebook; or (2) using the fusion of conceptual items and visual items that are selected from key-frame database. Therefore, we can provide users two options to construct their own queries as follow: (See figure 1 for visualization of these tasks)

Conceptual query: First, from the codebook (items are showed by text), users select those basic events that - in users' mind - could be a part of an event they want to search. Then, for each *basic_event*, users arrange its interval time on the same time axis. Next, users confirm their query. Finally, the query is generated using the event model that is defined in Definition 1.

Fusion query: First, from the list of *keyframe_ids* of each basic event (items are showed by images), users select their preferred keyframes whose *event_types* are then automatically mapped using Equation 5. Then, *event_types* are put on the same time axis. Then, for each *basic_event* w.r.t *event_type*, users arrange its interval time on the same time axis. Next, users confirm their query. Finally, the query is generated using the event model that is defined in Definition 1.

4.2   Re-ranking

The re-ranking task is started when search engine returns results after the first query in order to make the better results in next queries. Set of retrieved results, namely R, are ranked by their confident scores and each result is assigned the **id** in its ranking order. Now, users can start re-querying by clicking on any keyframe of any result displayed on monitor as long as a visual content of that keyframe reflects user's imagination of what they want to query.

Let RC denote the set of results users clicked on, $RC = R_i$ where $i \in I$, and I is the set of results' **id** where users clicked on. Let S denote the new-query form

constructed by collecting information from users' clicks
$S = \{(event\_id, cluster\_id)\_m\}, m \in I$ so that
$\quad \forall (event\_id, cluster\_id)_m \in S, \exists (event\_id, cluster\_id)_k \in R_i$
so that $(event\_id, cluster\_id)_k = (event\_id, cluster\_id)_m$.

The similarity measure between the new-query S and an arbitrary $C_k \in R$ is defined as

$d(S, C_k) = (\frac{1}{\|S\|} \sum_{i=1}^{min(\|S\|, \|C_k\|)} (w_1.ES_i + w_2.CS_i)$ where
$ES_i = 1$ if S and C_k have the same $event\_id$, 0 otherwise
$CS_i = 1$ if S and C_k have the same $cluster_i d$, 0 otherwise
w_i are weight parameters that satisfy $w_1 + w_2 = 1$, $w_2 > w_1$.

R is then re-ranked according to the value of $d(S, C_k)$. This process is looped until users finish their searching progress.

5   Experimental Results

More than 30 hours of soccer video corpus captured at different broadcasters and conditions are used to evaluate the proposed method. Specifically, there are 26 packages of data. Each package contains triplex *(full matches, all events clips extracted from matches offered from broadcaster, web-casting text downloaded from the Internet)*, the second and third item are considered as the ground-truth. We have 20 packages from UEFA champion league, 5 packages from FIFA World Cup 2006, and 20 packages from YouTube (contains only events short clips). We use 10 UEFA, 5 FIFA, and 10 Youtube packages as training set, the rest is used as testing set. 10 students are invited as volunteers. Among them 4 persons are experters, and another 2 persons are naive and the rest are neutral to soccer.

At present, the proposed event model is tested with two levels: (1) *basic_event* level - each *basic_event* is visual or camera motion concept that are defined in the codebook denoted in Table 1; (2) the *target_event* level - we define 10 events that always appear in all soccer games as denoted in Table 2.

Event Detection - Quantity: This evaluation is performed in order to see how many putative events the proposed method could extract from the unknown raw video, and how many events in those putative events are classified into true

Table 1. The Codebook

basic_event_name	NATP_id	basic_event_name	NATP_id
Pan left	$a^+ < a^-$	Pan right	$b^+ < b^-$
Zoom in	$c^+ < c^-$	Zoom out	$d^+ < d^-$
Tilt up	$e^+ < e^-$	Tilt down	$f^+ < f^-$
Still	$g^+ < g^-$	Unknown	$h^+ < h^-$
Long view	$i^+ < i^-$	Medium view	$j^+ < j^-$
Close up	$k^+ < k^-$	Out of field	$l^+ < l^-$
Arc	$m^+ < m^-$	Replay	$n^+ < n^-$
Goal mouth	$o^+ < o^-$	Middle circle	$p^+ < p^-$

Table 2. Event detection evaluation

Event	Precision/Recall	Event	Precision/Recall	Event	Precision/Recall
Goal	100%/100%	Shot	98%/85.3%	Red card	100%/100%
Corner	100%/100%	Offside	100%/100%	Yellow card	100%/100%
Save	100%/100%	Free kick	92%/89%	Foul	83%/80%
Substitution	90%/83.2%				

class. It should be note that, there is a difference between the case where the input video has web-casting text and where that has not. With the former, since all events are marked exactly by keywords and time stamps that are extracted directly from web-casting text, there is no error or miss in detecting events. In this case, the precision and recall usually equal 100%. Therefore, only the case where there is no support of web-casting text is investigated. Table 2 illustrates the results of the proposed method in the case lack of web-casting text supports.

Event Detection - Quality: This evaluation is conducted to see how well the boundary of automatically detected event is. The Boundary Detection Accuracy (BDA) [4] is used to measure the detected event boundary compared with the ground-truth's. Moreover, the method in [4] that use web-casting text and Finite State Machine, and the method in [6] that utilize the Allen temporal algebra to detect event in sports are also used to compare with our method to distinguish which method is better. Table 3 shows that our method gains the better results than others. It should be noted that Snoek's method focuses on only three events (Goal, Yellowcard, and Substitution)

Personalized Retrieval: All volunteers are asked to query by using both conceptual and fusion queries to retrieve 10 events that are defined in 2 with highest similarity under their own conditions. Table 4 and Table 5 show the volunteers' feedback with respect to conceptual and fusion queries respectively. Most of volunteers satisfy after no more than 5 re-query times. It is easy to see that, naive users can satisfy with retrieval's results within 5 re-query times. Due to the high accuracy of event detection process, the proposed method has the ability to classify an unannotated event into a right class and return to users all data contained

Table 3. Event detection quality (Pr: the proposed method, Xu: Xu's method, Snoek: Snoek's method)

Event	BDA Pr - Xu - Snoek	Event	BDA Pr - Xu - Snoek
Goal	92% - 76% - 86%	Shot	88.2% - 83.1% - N/A
Corner	73.1% - 73% - N/A	Offside	89.1% - 85.2% - N/A
Save	92% - 90.7% - N/A	Free kick	44.2% - 43.5% - N/A
Foul	81% - 77.7% - N/A	Substitution	78% - 78.1% - 78.5%
Red card	83% - 82.5% - N/A	Yellow card	84.5% - 84% - 83%

Table 4. Evaluation of Personalized Retrieval: using Fusion Query and Re-ranking

Trial times	Expert	Naive	Neutral
< 5 times	71%	97%	85%
> 5 times and < 10 times	19%	3%	7%
> 10 times and < 20 times	11%	0%	6%

Table 5. Evaluation of Personalized Retrieval: using Conceptual Query and Re-ranking

Trial Times	Expert	Naive	Neutral
< 5 times	68%	94.2%	83.5%
> 5 times and < 10 times	23%	5.8%	8.3%
> 10 times and < 20 times	9%	0%	8.2%

in that class. Therefore, naive users who are not familiar with soccer, easily accept the retrieval's results without considering the visual similarity such as color of field, color of players' clothes or how the event happens. In contrast, expert users pay more attention in visual similarity so that they need more re-query times.

It is easy to see how query scheme effects the results. When using conceptual query, visual information that is easily recognized by human vision is neglected. This leads to the need of more re-ranking steps to make the final result similar to what users imagine both in conceptual and visual aspects. In contrast, when using fusion query, both conceptual and visual aspects are considered at the beginning. This leads to *near-perfect* result with respect to users' imagination. Thus, less re-ranking steps are needed to get the final result.

6   Conclusions

The new linguistic-perceptual event model is presented. By using the proposed event model, the new generic framework using non-ambiguous temporal patterns mining and web-casting text is built to detect event in sports video tailoring to personalized "click-and-see style" retrieval is presented. Unlike most of existing methods which neglect or use only linear temporal sequence to present temporal information, our method is able to capture and model temporal information of complex event. Moreover, due to the independence between linguistic and perceptual part of patterns, it is easy to deploy this framework to another domain (e.g football, baseball, etc.) with only a few modification of *perceptual part* and *transformer*. Results of automatic event detection progress are tailored to personalized retrieval via click-and-see style. Thanks to our new event model, users could retrieve events by using either conceptual or conceptual-visual fusion query schemes. Moreover, with support of re-ranking scheme, the results after doing query will be pruned to compact final results that are very similar to users' imagination.

In the future, more features and domain will be considered to find the optimal set of patterns by which the events will be detected in high accuracy. Moreover, more higher event levels will be defined to evaluate the ability of self-evolution of the proposed event model. Beside that, thorough comparisons with related methods will also be conducted to give better evaluation.

Acknowledgments

This research is financially supported by **Japan Society for the Promotion of Science (JSPS)**.

References

1. Xie, L., Sundaram, H., Campbell, M.: Event Mining in Multimedia Streams. Proceedings of the IEEE 96(4), 623–647 (2008)
2. Allen, J.: Maintaining knowledge about temporal intervals. Communications of the ACM 26(11), 832–843 (1983)
3. Wu, S., Chen, Y.: Mining nonambiguous temporal patterns for interval-based events. IEEE Trans. on Knowledge and Data Engineering 19(6), 742–758 (2007)
4. Xu, C., Wang, J., Kwan, K., Li, Y., Duan, L.: Live Sports Event Detection Based on Broadcast Video and Web-casting text. In: ACM International Conference on Multimedia, pp. 221–230 (2006)
5. Zhu, X., Wu, X., Elmagarmid, A.K., Feng, Z., Wu, L.: Video Data Mining: Semantic Indexing and Event Detection from the Association Perspective. IEEE Trans. on Knowledge and Data Engineering 7(5), 665–677 (2005)
6. Snoek, C.G.M., Worring, M.: Multimedia Event-Based Video Indexing Using Time Intervals. IEEE Trans. on Multimedia 7(4), 638–647 (2005)
7. Fleischman, M., Roy, D.: Unsupervised Content-based Indexing of Sports Video. In: ACM International Conference on Multimedia Information Retrieval, pp. 87–94 (2007)
8. Xiong, Z., Zhou, X., Tian, Q., Rui, Y., Huang., T.: Semantic retrieval of video. IEEE Signal Processing Magazine, 18–27 (2006)
9. Sebe, N., Tian, Q.: Personalized Multimedia Retrieval: The new trend? In: ACM International Conference on Multimedia Information Retrieval, pp. 299–306 (2007)
10. Dao, M.S., Babaguchi, N.: Mining temporal information and web-casting text for automatic sports event detection. In: International Workshop on Multimedia Signal Processing (2008)

Towards Protein Interaction Analysis through Surface Labeling

Virginio Cantoni[1,2], Riccardo Gatti[2], and Luca Lombardi[2]

[1] IEF Institut d'Électronique Fondamentale, Université Paris-Sud XI
[2] University of Pavia, Dept. of Computer Engineering and System Science
{virginio.cantoni,riccardo.gatti,luca.lombardi}@unipv.it

Abstract. The knowledge of the biological function of proteins would have great impact on the identification of novel drug targets, and on finding the molecular causes of diseases. Unfortunately, the experimental determination of protein function is a very expensive and time consuming process. As a consequence, the development of computational techniques to complement and guide the experimental process is a crucial and fundamental step for biological analysis.

The final goal of the activity here presented is to provide a method that allows the identification of sites of possible protein-protein and protein-ligand interaction on the basis of the geometrical and topological structure of protein surfaces. The goal is then to discover complementary regions (that is with concave and convex segments that match each others) among different proteins. In particular, we are considering the first step of this process: the segmentation of the protein surface in protuberances and inlets through the analysis of convexity and concavity. To this end, two approaches will be described with a comparative assessment in terms of accuracy and speed of execution.

Keywords: protein-protein interaction, surface labeling, heat diffusion.

1 Introduction

There are currently about 50,000 experimentally determined 3D structures of proteins deposited in the Protein Data Bank (PDB) [14]. However this set contains a lot of identical or very similar structures. The importance of the study of structural building blocks, their comparison and classification are instrumental to the study on evolution and on functional annotation, has brought about many methods for their identification and classification in proteins of known structure.

In particular, there are several methods for defining protein secondary structure, and the DSSP [16] method is the most commonly used. The DSSP defines eight types of secondary structures, nevertheless, the majority of secondary prediction methods further simplify to the three dominant states: Helix, Sheet and Coil. Unfortunately, no standard definition is available of what a structural motif, a domain, a family, a fold, a sub-unit, a class [15], etc. really is, so that assignments have varied enormously, with each researcher using its own set of criteria. There are several DBs for structural classification of proteins; among them the most commonly used are SCOP and CATH. They differ in domain and class definition and also because the former is more based

P. Foggia, C. Sansone, and M. Vento (Eds.): ICIAP 2009, LNCS 5716, pp. 604–612, 2009.
© Springer-Verlag Berlin Heidelberg 2009

on human expertise, whereas the latter is a semi-automatic classifier. Another well-known DB is FSSP, which is purely automatic [9].

An important research activity, with this large set of new proteins, is the prediction of interactions of these molecules by the discovery of similar or of complementary regions on their surfaces. When a novel protein with unknown function is discovered, bioinformatics tools are used to screen huge datasets of proteins with known functions and binding sites, searching for a candidate binding site in the new protein. More specifically, if a surface region of the novel protein is similar to that of the binding site of another protein with known function, the function of the former protein can be inferred and its molecular interaction predicted.

Much work has been done on the analysis of the binding sites of proteins and their identification, using various approaches based on different protein representations and matching strategies. The techniques employed are numerous ranging from geometric hashing of triangles of points and their associated physico-chemical properties [20], to clustering based on a representation of surfaces in terms of spherical harmonic coefficients [12] or by a collection of spin-images [2, 3] or by context shapes [10], to clique detection on the vertices of the triangulated solvent-accessible surface [1].

However, the shape descriptors used so far for surface matching are often too complex for real time analysis. A promising alternative approach, which we believe will be convenient to investigate, is the search for regions of interface that potentially correspond to the active sites, through the EGI introduced for applications of photometry by B. K. P. Horn [13] in the years '80 and which has been extended by K. Ikeuci [17, 21] in the years '90. To our knowledge the EGI has never been applied for protein representation.

The EGI is the histogram of the orientations placed on the unitarian sphere and it constitutes a compact and effective representation of a 3D object as a protein (or better the ligand that is usually a small molecule) or, as we plan to do, one of its part: the rotations of the object correspond to rotations of the EGI; the side surface of the object is the mass of the EGI; the barycentre of the EGI is in the sphere origin; every hemisphere is balanced by the complementary hemisphere; etc.. Just for these important properties, for the simplicity and the operational handiness on the unitarian sphere it is worth to verify if the conditions for docking conducted on the EGI are selective enough.

At the beginning, we do not think to adopt the extension of Ikeuci, Complex-EGI (C-EGI), because we consider that the hypothesis of model 'basically' convex (obviously, not always completely convex) can be applied in the search of matching between part of the proteins: the convexities of the ligand/protein and the complement to the concavity of the second protein. Moreover, also adopting the C-EGI, in presence of concavity [21], it is not guaranteed the biunivocity between C-EGI representation and 3D object.

For these reason, an effective way for computing the EGI representation is of great interest for the analysis of proteins convex and concave segments. The first phase of our planned activity for protein analysis that is presented in this paper is the development and the validation of algorithms to this purpose.

In literature, optimal 2D techniques for objects segmentation based on contour curvature, can be easily found. Nevertheless, their generalization to the 3D case is not trivial: an extra dimension will not only augment the computing time but due to the extension from contour points to border lines the problem become even more difficult because border lines are not necessarily flat!

We are presenting here two tentative approaches and a performance comparison. The first one is an extension of a technique that has been introduced for 2D segmentation a few years ago [6] and that later it has been extended for multi-resolution detection, i.e. for the parallel detection of concavities and convexities at different resolution scales [5]. The second approach is a new solution, very simple, based on trivial near neighbor operation that can be easily implemented with 'ad hoc' hardware.

2   Labeling through Heat Diffusion Process Simulation

The first proposed method is based on the analogy of a heat-diffusion process acting through a material. The digital volume of the protein is considered like a solid isotropic metal governed by the heat equation. The equation is used to determinate concavity and convexity as respectively cold and hot points. The heat equation is a partial differential equation:

$$\frac{\partial u}{\partial t} = k \left[\frac{\partial^2 u}{\partial x^2} + \frac{\partial^2 u}{\partial y^2} \right] \tag{1}$$

where k is the diffusion coefficient.

The procedure starts by assigning a constant value to all the border points of the object and zero inside the object. Then a limited sequence of an isotropic adiabatic three-dimension diffusion process is performed towards the interior of the object. For simulating a discrete heat-diffusion process, equation (1) is converted to the following difference equation (2):

$$u_{t+1}(p) = u_t(p) + k \left[\sum_{q \in N1} (u_t(p) - u_t(q)) + \sum_{q \in N2} \frac{1}{\sqrt{2}} (u_t(p) - u_t(q)) \right. \\ \left. + \sum_{q \in N3} \frac{1}{\sqrt{3}} (u_t(p) - u_t(q)) \right] \tag{2}$$

where $u_t(p)$ represents the value of voxel p at time t, and $u_t(q)$ represents the value of voxel q, near neighbor of voxel p, at time t. With N1, N2 and N3 we distinguish three sets of near neighbors (NN): N1 constitutes of the six neighbors that share one face and have distance equal to 1 from the voxel p, N2 includes the twelve neighbors that share only an edge and are at distance $\sqrt{2}$, and N3 includes the neighbors than share only a vertex and are at distance $\sqrt{3}$ always from voxel p (see figure 1). The different weights of equation (2) are determined by the inverse of the voxels distance; this in order to simulate an isotropic diffusion process. Something quite similar has been presented by Borgefors and Sanniti di Baja [4] in which a subset of the 3x3x3 neighborhood includes only the N1 and N2 sets.

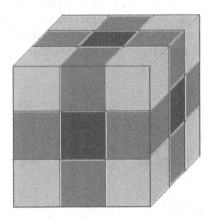

Fig. 1. Near neighbors of the voxel in the center of the elementary 3x3x3 cube: in evidence the three voxels of the set N1 in red; the nine voxels of the set N2 in blue; and the seven voxels of the set N3 in orange

At each iteration, new voxels, inside the object, are reached by the propagation process, according to equation 2. After a few number of iterations, the voxels that belong to local convexities will keep a higher value while those belonging to local concavities will have a value significantly reduced. Obviously, for t→∞ the object reaches a uniform heat distribution (i.e. constant temperature), so the number of step should be determined on the basis of the value of K (the diffusion coefficient) and of the size of the target details.

3   Iterative Detection of Convexities and Concavities

The Iterative Detection of Convexities and Concavities (IDCC) method here introduced is an algorithm that labels the voxels belonging to the border of the object according to their local convexities and concavities. Note that, also this approach constitutes a multi-resolution analysis: the higher the number of steps, the larger the receptive space involved for labeling the border voxels and the lower the details that can be analyzed. The approach is composed of two steps:

- the first step consists on labeling the border voxels of the object with the number of background voxels belonging to the 3x3x3 NN.[1]
- the second step consists on one to n iterations. At every sub-sequent step n, every border voxel is labeled with the sum of the labels at step n-1, within the 3x3x3 NN, divided by the number of the border voxels C, with label > 0 included in the NN.

---

[1] An alternative approach has been presented by Gallus and Neurath [11] in which the initial labeling is defined as the difference between the Freeman codes of pairs of successive contour points. Obviously this methods is not easily extendible in 3D.

The threshold $T = 9^n/ C$ partition the border Voxels in the convex set (voxels having a label greater than T) and in the concave set (voxels having a label lower than T). Note that n is the number of iteration step. For a direct interpretation of the algorithm, in Figure 2 a simple visual example of a 2D implementation is shown.

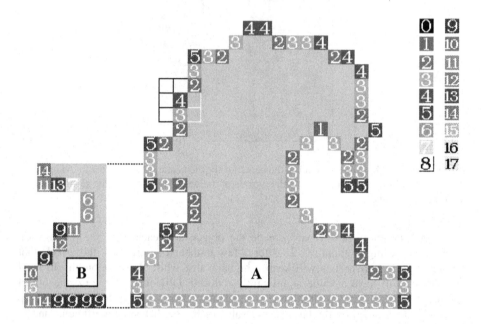

Fig. 2. Contour labeling of a 2D object by the IDCC algorithm. In A the first step is represented: the label of contour points, in 8-connection, is given by the number of background pixels (a 3x3 array is shown, putting in evidence the four background pixels). Pixels with a label greater than 3 are considered convex pixels, meanwhile pixels with label lower that 3 are considered concave pixels. In B the result obtained with the first iterative step is shown. The label of the contour point is given by the sum of the labels of the previous step, within the 3x3 surround. Pixels with a label greater than 9 are considered convex pixels, meanwhile pixels with label lower than 9 are considered concave pixels.

4 Experimental Results

Both algorithms are applied to the 'space-filling' representation of the protein, where atoms are represented as spheres with their Van der Walls radii (see figure 3). This representation is directly derived from PDB files which supply the ordered sequence of 3D positions of each atom's center. Figure 3 shows the image produced by our package for a molecule of 4PHV, a peptide-like ligand docked into HIV protease.

A first critical decision is the space resolution level for the analysis. For the first experiments we tried several voxels sizes ranging from 0.10 up to 0.75 Å, but the results here presented are given with a resolution of 0.25 Å that allows to the smallest represented atoms, a Van der Walls radius of more than five pixels. Obviously, the

Fig. 3. 'Space filling' representation of 4PHV protein. The colors follow the standard CPK scheme.

higher the voxel size, the lower the details on the surface representation, but the faster the algorithms convergence to an acceptable result. In figure 4.1, 4.2, 4.3 and 5.1, 5.2, 5.3 the results for IDCC and Heat Diffusion processes on the 4PHV molecule are shown for different numbers of iterations.

Let first point out that both the approaches lead to a segmentation useful for docking: as expected the small details that characterizes the original surface (with apexes and cusp at the convergence of different atoms spheres) of figure 3 are overcome as the iterations of the diffusion process reaches distances that are one order of magnitude of the Van der Walls radii, protuberances and fiords are well characterized and evident as well as than the site of possible protein-{ligand, protein} interaction.

The experiments show clearly that heat diffusion approach has a faster convergence to an acceptable solution, than the IDCC methodology. In fact, 300 iterations of IDCC method (figure 4.3) produce a result qualitatively similar to only 100 iterations of heat diffusion algorithm (figure 5.1). In other words, the two methods, with a suitable different number of iteration, reach almost the same result.[2]

Both algorithms were tested on a 2.20 GHz x86 Intel processor. A single iteration of heat diffusion algorithm takes on average 5.4 sec while a single iteration of IDCC takes 7.5 sec. This, combined with a faster convergence, makes, for standard hardware, the heat diffusion method a better approach than IDCC.

---

[2] The time performance of the IDCC method are improved limiting the calculus to the subset N1 and N2 as indicated above [4], reaching a reduction of the computation time of 40%. This is not sufficient to reach the performances of the heat diffusion approach. Note that not including the set N3 an extra number of iterations is required to reach the same results.

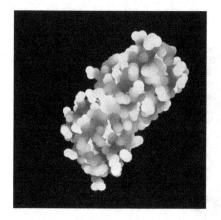

Fig. 4. 1

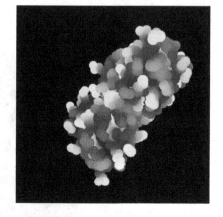

Fig. 4. 2

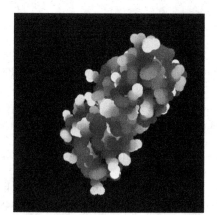

Fig. 4. 3

Fig. 4. Experimental results obtained with the IDCC approach. The values of the execution parameters are:

Voxel Side = 0.25 Å

Number of iterations: 100 (fig. 4.1), 200 (fig. 4.2), 300 (fig. 4.3)

Color scheme: intensity data using a "*Hot Iron*" color mapping, that is: yellow → white : higher convexities red → black: higher concavities

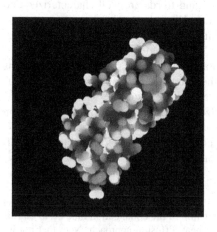

Fig. 5. 1

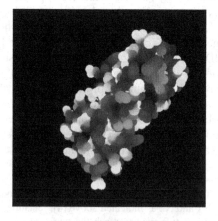

Fig. 5. 2

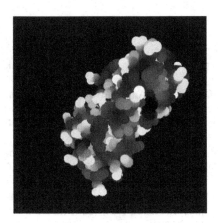

Fig. 5. Experimental results obtained with the Heat Diffusion approach. The values of the execution parameter are:

Voxel Side = 0.25 Å
K = 0.05
Number of iterations: 100 (fig. 5.1), 200 (fig. 5.2), 300 (fig. 5.3)

Color scheme: intensity data using a "*Hot Iron*" color mapping, that is:
yellow → white : higher convexities
red → black: higher concavities

Fig. 5. 3

Nevertheless, it is important to point out that both algorithms works locally and independently for each voxel. Therefore an implementation on a parallel architecture can be done without particular problem in partitioning the computation load and a great speed improvement can be easily obtained. Moreover, note that the IDCC approach looks suitable for a single chip implementation; in fact only trivial basic operations are required. This should be possibly taken into account in the future if the complete proteins interaction analysis will be successful.

5   Conclusion

The activities in proteomics are in an intensive development; for example the PDB has an annual growth rate that reaches the 3000 new proteins experimentally determined and deposited. So it is becoming increasingly necessary to reach high performance in research and analysis of these massive databases. Potential applications closely depend on the performance of the problem here discussed. The aim of our research is to provide a substantial increase of current performances for the comparison of protein surfaces through the development of new methods of analysis. The achieved results testify that the presented solutions are very promising.

References

1. Akutsu, T.: Protein structure alignment using dynamic programming and iterative improvement. IEICE Trans. Inf. and Syst. E78-D, 1–8 (1996)
2. Bock, M.E., Garutti, C., Guerra, C.: Spin image profile: a geometric descriptor for identifying and matching protein cavities. In: Proc. of CSB, San Diego (2007)
3. Bock, M.E., Garutti, C., Guerra, C.: Cavity detection and matching for binding site recognition. Theoretical Computer Science (2008), doi:10.1016/j.tcs.2008.08.018
4. Borgefors, G., Sanniti di Baja, G.: Analysing non-convex 2D and 2D patterns. Computer Vision and Image Understanding 63(1), 145–157 (1996)

5. Cantoni, V., Cinque, L., Guerra, C., Levialdi, S., Lombardi, L.: 2D Object recognition by multiscale tree matching. Pattern Recognition 31(10), 1443–1454 (1998)
6. Cantoni, V., Levialdi, S.: Contour labelling by pyramidal processing. In: Duff, M.J.B. (ed.) Intermediate-level Image Processing, ch. XI, pp. 181–190. Academic Press, New York (1986)
7. Coleman, R.G., Burr, M.A., Sourvaine, D.L., Cheng, A.C.: An intuitive approach to measuring protein surface curvature. Proteins: Struct. Funct. Bioinform. 61, 1068–1074 (2005)
8. Connolly, M.L.: Measurement of protein surface shape by solid angles. J. Mol. Graphics 4, 3–6 (1986)
9. Day, R., Beck, D.A., Armen, R.S., Daggett, V.: A consensus view of fold space: combining SCOP, CATH, and the Dali Domain Dictionary. Protein Sci. 12(10), 2150–2160 (2003)
10. Frome, A., Huber, D., Kolluri, R., Baulow, T., Malik, J.: Recognizing Objects in Range Data Using Regional Point Descriptors. In: Pajdla, T., Matas, J(G.) (eds.) ECCV 2004. LNCS, vol. 3023, pp. 224–237. Springer, Heidelberg (2004)
11. Gallus, G., Neurath, P.W.: Improved computer chromosome analysis incorporating preprocessing and boundary analysis. Phys. Med. Biol. 15, 435–445 (1970)
12. Glaser, F., Morris, R.J., Najmanovich, R.J., Laskowski, R.A., Thornton, J.M.: A Method for Localizing Ligand Binding Pockets in Protein Structures. PROTEINS: Structure, Function, and Bioinformatics 62, 479–488 (2006)
13. Horn, B.K.P.: Extended Gaussian images. Proc. IEEE 72(12), 1671–1686 (1984)
14. http://www.pdb.org/ (visited, April 2009)
15. Jacob, F.: Evolution and tinkering. Science 196, 1161–1166 (1977)
16. Kabsch, W., Sander, C.: Dictionary of protein secondary structure: pattern recognition of hydrogen-bonded and geometrical features. Biopolymers 22(12), 2577–2637 (1983)
17. Kang, S.B., Ikeuchi, K.: The complex EGI: a new representation for 3-D pose determination. IEEE-T-PAMI, 707–721 (1993)
18. Masuya, M.: Shape Analysis of Protein Molecule and Legand-Receptor Docking Studies Using Mathematical Morphology, Doctoral Thesis, The University of Tokyo (1996)
19. Nicholls, A., Sharp, K.A., Honig, B.: Protein folding and association: insights from the interfacial and thermodynamic properties of hydrocarbons. Proteins 11, 281–296 (1991)
20. Shulman-Peleg, A., Nussinov, R., Wolfson, H.: Recognition of Functional Sites in Protein Structures. J. Mol. Biol. 339, 607–633 (2004)
21. Shum, H., Hebert, M., Ikeuchi, K.: On 3D shape similarity. In: Proceedings of the IEEE-CVPR 1996, pp. 526–531 (1996)
22. Sridharan, S., Nicholls, A., Honig, B.: A new vertex algorithm to calculate solvent accessible surface area. Biophys. J. 61, A174 (1992)
23. Takeshi, K.: Multi-scale Pocket Detection on Protein Surface Using 3D Image Processing Technique. IPSJ SIG 2006(99) (BIO-6), 49–56 (2006)

A Semi-automated Method for the Measurement of the Fetal Nuchal Translucency in Ultrasound Images

Ezio Catanzariti[1], Giovanni Fusco[1], Francesco Isgrò[1], Salvatore Masecchia[1],
Roberto Prevete[2], and Matteo Santoro[2]

[1] Dipartimento di Scienze Fisiche
Università degli Studi di Napoli Federico II
Napoli, Italy
[2] Dipartimento di Informatica e Scienze dell'Informazione
Università degli Studi di Genova
Genova, Italy

Abstract. Nowadays the measurement of the nuchal translucency thickness is being used as part of routine ultrasound scanning during the end of the first trimester of pregnancy, for the screening of chromosomal defects, as trisomy 21. Currently, the measurement is being performed *manually* by physicians. The measurement can take a long time for being accomplished, needs to be performed by highly skilled operators, and is prone to errors. In this paper we present an algorithm that automatically detects the border of the nuchal translucency, once a region of interest has been manually identified. The algorithm is based on the minimisation of a cost function, and the optimisation is performed using the dynamic programming paradigm. The method we present overcomes several of the drawbacks present in the state of the art algorithms.

1 Introduction

It is getting more and more common for women to carry the pregnancy when over thirty. Since the risk of a foetus with chromosomal defects increases with the age of the mother [1], it is now very important to have screening techniques for detecting foetuses with chromosomal defects during early pregnancy.

There are two categories of screening procedures: invasive and non-invasive. Invasive diagnosis methods, as amniocentesis and chorionic villus sampling, do give a definitive answer, but need to be performed by trained and experienced operators, and studies have shown that they increase of about 1-2% the risk of fetal loss [2]. During the last thirty years research has aimed at developing non-invasive methods for prenatal diagnosis of fetal cells or cell-free DNA found in the maternal blood [2]. However the outcome is that the analysis of maternal blood is more likely to be used as a method for assessment of risk, rather than as a non-invasive prenatal diagnosis of chromosomal defects. Moreover different studies have brought contradictory evidence concerning the concentration of cell-free fetal DNA in trisomy 21 foetuses: some studies reported that the levels are

P. Foggia, C. Sansone, and M. Vento (Eds.): ICIAP 2009, LNCS 5716, pp. 613–622, 2009.
© Springer-Verlag Berlin Heidelberg 2009

increased and others reported that there is no difference from chromosomally normal pregnancies [2].

Despite the fact that no definitive non-invasive diagnosis is available at the moment, it is still possible to calculate a risk for chromosomal defects considering both patient-specific information and foetus related data. Among the former maternal age and the presence of previous affected pregnancies are the most significative. For the latter indicative data are the thickness of nuchal translucency (the sonographic appearance of sub-cutaneous accumulation of fluid behind the fetal neck in the first trimester of pregnancy) and/or the absence of the nose [3,2]. In fact it has been shown that about 75% of trisomy 21 foetuses have increased nuchal translucency thickness and 60-70% have absent nasal bone [2]. Studies in the mid 90s have shown that in normal pregnancies fetal nuchal translucency thickness increases with gestation during the first trimester [4], and that in trisomy 21 and other major chromosomal defects fetal nuchal translucency thickness is increased more than in normal pregnancies, and that the risk for trisomies can be derived by multiplying the a priori maternal age and gestational-related risk by a likelihood ratio, which depends on the degree of deviation in fetal nuchal translucency measurement from the normal median for that crown-rump length [2]. It was estimated that, in a pregnant population with a mean maternal age of 28 years, using the risk cut-off of 1 in 300 to define the screen positive group would detect about 80% of trisomy 21 foetuses for a false positive rate of 5% [5]. Therefore this test, together with other indicators, is used to check if the foetus can be at risk, and in the case of a positive answer it is suggested to take a chorionic villus sampling or amniocentesis for a definitive answer. These non-invasive diagnosis methods are used only to avoid amniocentesis when it is not necessary, that is when the risk of a trisomy 21 foetus is low enough.

Nuchal translucency (henceforth NT) is the subcutaneous fluid-filled space between the back of the neck of a foetus and the overlying skin [2]. In figure 1 it is shown an ultrasound image of the foetus with the NT highlighted, and the thickness measurement superimposed. The NT thickness is defined as the maximum thickness of the translucent space, that is the dark area between the two echogenic lines, the white borders delimiting the NT (see figure 1). Currently manual measurement is being performed by physicians using electronic callipers placed on the two echogenic lines on the screen of the sonograph [6] (see figure 1). The measurement takes an average of 15-20 minute for being accomplished, but it can take up to 35 minutes. There are two main reasons for this long amount of time. The first one is that that the NT thickness is measured in the saggital section of the foetus, and therefore the operator must look to find the correct position for the sensor and determine the best image for taking the measurement. The second one is that the measurement itself can be very tedious as the task of accurately placing callipers is very difficult. The measurement, that for its difficulty needs to be performed by highly skilled operators [6], is therefore prone to errors, and intra-observer and inter-observer repeatability can be questioned [7].

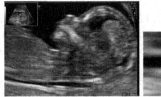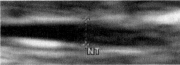

Fig. 1. Example of ultrasound image of the foetus. Left an image with the ROI containing the NT highlighted. Right the ROI with the result of manual measurement.

The research work presented in this paper is part of a work aiming to design and develop appropriate software tools capable to make the whole process of non-invasive screening easier for the operator, and, at the same time, more robust removing the issue of intra-observer and inter-observer repeatability. The advantage of an automated system is twofold. First, the measurement would become objective and repeatable, making the whole test more reliable, with the possible side effect of reducing the number of invasive screening. Second, with an automatic measurement the time necessary for a single diagnosis would be shortened, cutting down the amount of time patients have to wait before being examined, and at the same time, increasing the number of screenings that can be performed daily.

In this paper we present an algorithm for the automatic identification of the two echogenic lines and measurement of the NT thickness, once the human operator has identified a region of interest in the image. The algorithm presented starts from the work reported in [8] and overcomes some of the drawbacks present in the current literature . In particular the algorithm for the identification of the echogenic lines is an original piece of work, as it is based on the optimisation of a completely different cost function. The main advantages of our algorithm with respect to the previous work is that it is general, as it does not depend on weights that must be tuned for each image, and that always returns continuous borders.

The paper is organised as follows. The next Section reviews the related work. Section 3 describes the algorithm proposed in this paper, and Section 4 outlines the procedure for the automatic measurement of the NT thickness. Results are shown and discussed in Section 5. Section 6 is left to the final remarks.

2   Previous Work

Although the literature on medical image analysis is huge and covers a wide spectrum of topics (e.g., analysis of MRI images, mammograms) not so much work has been dedicated to automatic fetal measurements from ultrasound images; in fact the first few papers started appearing about 10 years ago [9]. The lack of too many scientific papers is due to the fact that ultrasound fetal images are very difficult data to deal with. The fetal ultrasound measurement considered in literature are typically: bi-parietal diameter, head circumference, abdominal circumference and femur length [9, 10, 11, 12], and the problem is still far from being solved, in particular because of the complexity of the object appearance, high presence of noise and shadows, and because of the amount of information that need to be processed.

Among the work done on automatic fetal measurements the topics of automatic measurement of the nuchal translucency thickness and of automatic detection of the nose bone have not been addressed by many authors. Actually we tracked down only two papers on the measurement of the nuchal translucency [13, 8] and none at all on the detection of the nose bone. The two papers mentioned, as the present one, differ in the method for determining the NT borders

The system in [13] helps the user determining the borders of the NT enhancing the edges with simple Sobel operator and using a threshold specified by the user on the magnitude of the gradient for detecting a variable number of image edges. The borders are identified manually selecting two point, one on each borders, and entirely determined via a flood-fill operation. The NT thickness is then automatically measured using the same algorithm adopted in [8] and in this work, and that will be outlined in section 4.

Less intervention of the operator is required for the method given in [8], where the image is first preprocessed with a CED filter [14] for reducing the speckle noise typical of ultrasound images. The NT borders detection on a ROI manually selected by an operator is addressed as a global optimisation problem based on the dynamic programming (DP) paradigm. The cost function adopted is

$$\sum_{j=1}^{k} w_1 f_1(p_j) + w_2 f_2(p_j) + w_3 f_3(p_j) + w_4 g(p_{j-1}, p_j) \tag{1}$$

where the w_i are weights. The terms $f_1(p)$ and $f_2(p)$ are respectively the average value of an interval of pixels above and below the pixel p, and are introduced to ensure that p is a transition point between a dark flat area and a bright flat area; $f_3(p)$ is the vertical component of the image gradient; the term $g(p_{j-1}, p_j)$ is a term introduced for ensuring border continuity, and is the distance of the pixel p from a reference line, which is chosen as a straight line when computing the lower border, and the lower border itself when computing the upper border. The weights are not necessarily the same for both borders. The choice of the cost function appears based on empiric considerations, and the quality of results is strongly dependent on the weights. In fact, our implementation of this method

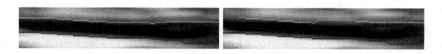

Fig. 2. Results from the algorithm in [8] with different weights. A not careful choice of the weights can produce discontinuous borders.

showed that a bad choice of the weights can lead to discontinuous borders as shown in figure 2.

3   NT Borders Estimation

The method for estimating the echogenic lines that we describe in this section overcomes some of the drawbacks of the algorithm presented in [8] and briefly reviewed in the previous section. Our method, summarised in table 1, is still semi-automatic, as it needs that the image region containing the NT is manually identified. Our algorithm differs from the one in [8] in several aspects. First, the cost function that we propose does not depend on any weight that need to be carefully tuned on each image, making the algorithm suitable for an automated system. Second, we introduce explicitly a term in the cost function that enforces the continuity of the border. Third, we substitute the terms f_1 and f_2 in equation 1 with a function of the zero-crossing direction that penalises edge points where the change between dark and bright pixels is not in the *right* direction. A last difference between the two algorithms is that we completely eliminated the g term when computing the lower border, and substituted it with a term that constrains the upper border to remain above the lower border.

The method we propose for estimating the borders of the NT in the selected ROI is as follows. Considering a ROI of dimensions NxM, borders are considered as polylines:

$$B_N = \{p_1, p_2, \cdots, p_{N-1}, p_N\}$$

where p_{j-1} and p_j are adjacent pixels and N is the total length of the border. The cost function we introduce for the detection of the upper and lower border are different from each other in signs and in number of terms. For the lower border, that is computed first, the cost function to minimise is:

$$\sum_{j=1}^{N} -\frac{\partial f}{\partial y}(p_j) + Z_l(p_j) + f_{adj}(p_j,$$

while for the detection of the upper border the cost function is:

$$\sum_{j=1}^{N} \frac{\partial f}{\partial y}(p_j) + Z_u(p_j) + f_{adj}(p_j, p_{j-1}) + f_{pos}(B_j^L, p_j).$$

The first term, common to both cost functions, consists of the image derivative along the vertical direction, in order to consider the energy deriving from the image features as edges or lines.

Second order derivatives are computed along the gradient direction θ_p, so that, by detecting zero-crossings, we can get more precise information about edges location, and taking account of their direction we can decide if they represent a transition from high intensity to darker region (upper border) or vice-versa

Table 1. Summary of the algorithm

---

1. Compute image gradient ∇f
2. For each point of p, compute gradient direction θ_p
3. Compute second order derivative $\frac{\partial^2 f}{\partial \theta_p^2}$ along gradient direction
4. Compute zero-crossing functions Z_u and Z_l as follows:

   (a) $Z_u(x,y) = \begin{cases} 0 \text{ if } \frac{\partial^2 f}{\partial \theta_p^2}(p) \times \frac{\partial^2 f}{\partial \theta_p^2}(q) < 0 \\ \zeta \text{ otherwise} \end{cases}$

   where q is the point preceding p along θ_p

   (b) $Z_l(x,y) = \begin{cases} 0 \ \frac{\partial^2 f}{\partial \theta_p^2}(p) \times \frac{\partial^2 f}{\partial \theta_p^2}(t) < 0 \\ \zeta \text{ otherwise} \end{cases}$

   where t is the point following along y and $\zeta > 0$.

5. Considering a border B as a polyline, $B = \{p_1, p_2, \cdots, p_N\}$, detect lower border using Dynamic Programming (DP):

   $C_l(B_1^L) = -\frac{\partial f}{\partial y}(p_1) + Z_l(x,y)$

   $C_l(B_n^L) = C_l(B_{n-1}) + \left\{ -\frac{\partial f}{\partial y}(p_n) + Z_l(p_n) + f_{adj}(p_n, p_{n-1}) \right\}$

   detect upper border using DP:

   $C_u(B_1^U) = \frac{\partial f}{\partial y}(p_1) + Z_u(x,y) + f_{pos}(B_1^L, p_1)$

   $C_u(B_n^U) = C_l(B_{n-1} + \left\{ \frac{\partial f}{\partial y}(p_n) + Z_u(p_n) + f_{adj}(p_n, p_{n-1}) + f_{pos}(B_n^L, p_n) \right\}$

   where

   $f_{adj}(p_n, p_{n-1}) = \begin{cases} 0 \text{ if } d(p_n, p_{n-1}) \leq 1, \\ \zeta \text{ otherwise} \end{cases}$ and f_{pos} is a sigmoid function of the vertical distance between a candidate point on the upper border and its corresponding on the lower border.

(lower border). The second term of the cost function consists of the non zero-crossings penalties in order that image points that are not on edges will have a high cost. These terms can be expressed for the upper border as

$$Z_u(p) = \begin{cases} 0 \text{ if } \frac{\partial^2 f}{\partial \theta_p^2}(p) \times \frac{\partial^2 f}{\partial \theta_p^2}(q) < 0 \\ \zeta \text{ otherwise,} \end{cases}$$

and for the lower border as

$$Z_l(p) = \begin{cases} 0 \ \frac{\partial^2 f}{\partial \theta_p^2}(p) \times \frac{\partial^2 f}{\partial \theta_p^2}(t) < 0 \\ \zeta \text{ otherwise} \end{cases}$$

where q is the pixel preceding p along the gradient direction, and t is the pixel next to p along the gradient direction, and $\zeta > 0$.

In order to enforce the continuity of the borders we introduce a third term, f_{adj}, in the cost function, that penalises a polyline where consecutive pixels have distance larger than one pixel:

$$f_{adj}(p_j, p_{j-1}) = \begin{cases} 0 \text{ if } d(p_j, p_{j-1}) \leq 1, \\ \zeta \text{ otherwise} \end{cases}$$

We also introduced a fourth term, f_{pos}, exclusively in the cost function used for the detection of the upper border. This term consists of a sigmoidal function which weighs the relative distance between candidate points of the upper border and the corresponding points on the lower border. In this way we strongly constrain the upper border to be made up of points that stay above the lower border.

The problem of the border detection is then solved optimising the cost functions C_l and C_u defined above. The solution has to be found globally in the ROI in order to avoid local minima that can be caused, for example, by residual speckle noise in the image.

4 NT Thickness Measurement

The last step is to estimate the maximum distance between the two borders we find. We achieve this using the same technique described in [13], and used in [8]. Let B_l and B_u be the lower and upper border respectively. The algorithm, depicted in figure 3 proceeds as follows.

1. Compute the median points m_j between $p_j \epsilon B_l$ and $q_j \epsilon B_u$;
2. Compute the line L_{j_U} using the points $p_i \epsilon B_l, i = j - 2, \cdots, j + 2$;
3. Compute the line L_{j_L} using the points $q_i \epsilon B_u, i = j - 2, \cdots, j + 2$;
4. Compute the line M_j using the computed median points $m_i, i = j-2, \cdots, j+2$;
5. Compute the line O_j orthogonal to M_j in m_j;
6. Compute the intersection points r_{j1} and r_{j2} between O_j and the two lines L_{jU} and L_{jL}, and store the distance $d_j = ||r_{j1} - r_{j2}||$;
7. Take the NT thickness as $\max_j(d_j)$; the relative points r_{j1} and r_{j2} are taken as the *artificial* position for the callipers.

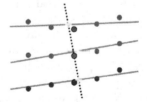

Fig. 3. Estimation of the NT thickness

5 Results

We run the algorithm on a set of ultrasound images, where the region of interests containing the NT have been identified by an expert physician. The images have been acquired using a GE Voluson E8, that automatically applies some digital filtering to the images for removing the noise. Unfortunately it was not possible to know what filtering is performed as the whole product is protected by a patent. After a few trials we decided not to use any kind of filtering, not even a

(a)   (b)

Fig. 4. Original image and result of our algorithm. The result of the algorithm in [8] is in figure 2.

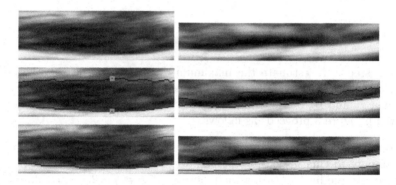

Fig. 5. Results of both algorithms for determining the NT borders. Top row original images. Middle row output of our algorithm. Bottom row result from the algorithm in [8].

smoothing filter, before calculating the gradient, relying entirely on the filtering operated by the system.

The data produced by the acquisition device are also in a proprietary format, so that we were not able to recover the real image resolution, necessary for testing the NT thickness recovered against the measure obtained manually by the physician. Moreover all the images appear to have different resolutions. Because of this technical difficulty we were able only to test our algorithm against the algorithm presented in [8], for the quality of the echogenic lines recovered. It is worth to point out that no quantitative analysis of the performance of the automatic measurement of the NT thickness has been published so far.

In figures 4 and 5 the results of our algorithm, with markers for the points r_{j1} and r_{j2}, are shown. In figure 4(a) is the original image relative to the results of our implementation of the algorithm in [8] shown in 2, and in figure 4(b) is the result of our algorithm. It can be noted how the border in figure 2 tends to be piecewise rectilinear, while the one produced by our algorithm follows the contour of the NT more closely. This difference in the performance is due to the g term in the cost function 1, that forces the lower border to be rectilinear, and therefore extends this behaviour to the upper border. The contour returned by our algorithm is not particularly smooth, and we are planning to introduce a smoothness term in the cost function.

A similar behaviour is shown in the examples displayed in figure 5, where on the top row are the original images, our result is in the middle row, and the

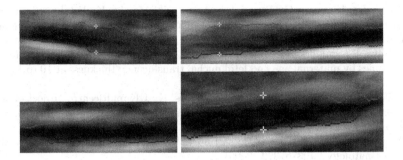

Fig. 6. Results of our algorithm for determining the NT borders

results from the algorithm in [8] is shown in the bottom row. It must be noted how the best result we managed to obtain with the competitor algorithm for the second image completely missed the NT.

In figure 6 a few more echogenic lines determined by our algorithm are shown.

6 Conclusions

In this paper we presented an algorithm for the automatic estimation of the borders of the nuchal translucency from ultrasound images of the foetus, that is a key step towards measurement of the NT thickness. The NT measure is obtained using a state of the art method. The main assumption we make is that the region containing the NT is manually identified.

This work is a first step of a larger work the aim of which is the realisation of a fully automated system for the trisomy 21 screening, that will include automatic identification of the NT, the NT thickness measurement, and the test for the presence of the nose bone.

Next steps in the pipeline will be an extensive validation of the automatic measurement method, that at the best of our knowledge, is missing in the literature, and the development of the automatic identification of the NT.

Acknowledgements

The authors wish to thank dr. Rosalia Musone and dr. Enrico Colosi for providing the images and for their kind technical help.

References

1. Hecht, C., Hook, E.: The imprecision in rates of down syndrome by 1-year maternal age intervals: a critical analysis of rates used in biochemical screening. Prenatal Diagnosis 14, 729–738 (1994)
2. Nicolaides, K., Sebire, N., Snijders, R.: The 11-14 weeks scan: the diagnosis of fetal abnormalities. Parthenon Publishing, New York (1999)

3. Nicolaides, K., Azar, G., Byrne, D., Mansur, C., Marrks, K.: Fetal nuchal translu-cency: ultrasound screening for chromosomal defects in first trimester of pregnancy. BMJ 304, 867–869 (1992)
4. Pandya, P., Snijders, R., Johnson, S., Brizot, M., Nicolaides, K.: Screening for fetal trisomies by maternal age and fetal nuchal translucency thickness at 10 to 14 weeks of gestation. BJOG 102, 957–962 (1995)
5. Snijders, R., Noble, P., Souka, A., Nicolaides, K.: UK multicentre project on asses-ment of risk of trimomy 21 by maternal age and fetal nuchal translucency thickness at 10-14 weeks of gestation. Lancet 352, 343–346 (1998)
6. Abuhamad, A.: Technical aspects of nuchal translucency measurement. Seminars in perinatology 29, 376–379 (2006)
7. Pandya, P., Altman, D., Brizot, M., Pettersen, H., Nicolaides, K.: Repeatability of measurement of fetal nuchal translucency thickness. Ultrasound in Obstetrics and Gynecology 5, 334–337 (1995)
8. Lee, Y., Kim, M., Kim, M.: Robust border enhancement and detection for mea-surement of fetal nuchal translucency in ultrasound images. Medical and Biological Engineering and Computing 45(11), 1143–1152 (2007)
9. Chalana, V., Winter, T., Cyr, D., Haynor, D., Kim, Y.: Automatic fetal head measurements from sonographic images. Academic Radiology 3(8), 628–635 (1996)
10. Hanna, C., Youssef, M.: Automated measurements in obstetric ultrasound im-ages. In: Proceedings of the International Conference Image Processing, vol. 3, pp. 714–717 (1997)
11. Carneiro, G., Georgescu, B., Good, S., Comaniciu, D.: Detection and measure-ment of fetal anatomies from ultrasound images using a constrained probabilistic boosting tree. IEEE Transactions on Medical Imaging 27(9), 1342–1355 (2008)
12. Pathak, S., Chalana, V., Kim, Y.: Interactive automatic fetal head measurements from ultrasound images using multimedia computer technology. Ultrasound in Medicine and Biology 23(5), 665–673 (1997)
13. Bernardino, F., Cardoso, R., Montenegro, N., Bernardes, J., de Sa, J.M.: Semiauto-mated ultrasonographic measurement of fetal nuchal translucency using a computer software tool. Ultrasound in Medicine and Biology 24(1), 51–54 (1998)
14. Weikert, J.: Coherence-enhancing diffusion filtering. International Journal of Com-puter Vision 31(2-3), 111–127 (1999)

Video Background Segmentation Using Adaptive Background Models

Xiaoyu Wu, Yangsheng Wang, and Jituo Li

Institute of Automation, Chinese Academy of Sciences
{xiaoyu.wu}@ia.ac.cn

Abstract. This paper proposes an adaptive background model which combines the advantages of both Eigenbackground and pixel-based gaussian models. This method exploits the illumination changes by Eigenbackground. Moreover, it can detect the chroma changes and remove shadow pixels using gaussian models. An adaptively strategy is used to integrate two models. A binary graph cut is used to implement the foreground/background segmentation by developing our data term and smooth term. We validate our method on indoor videos and test it on the benchmark video. Experiments demonstrate our method's efficiency.

Keywords: Background modeling, Background segmentation, Adaptive graph cut.

1 Introduction

Background segmentation seeks to automatically extract the foreground object from the background. As a fundamental part of high-level task such as object tracking and recognition, the technology of background segmentation is widely used in the multimedia, video surveillance,virtual reality, etc.

In this paper, we focus our research on monocular video background segmentation. In contrast to stereo depth information, monocular video background segmentation is much less constraints. Therefore, additional assumptions are often made to limit the solution space. The proposed assumptions are different dependent on the applications. In our case, the background scene is static and known , where the background modeling plays an important role in segmenting the foreground object.

Most background modeling methods are pixel-based which make use of statistical characteristic to model each pixel independently . Many representative pixel-level methods have been presented including unimodal Gaussian model in PFinder system [5], GMMs [1], W4 system, [2], non-parameter background modeling [3], mean-shift based modeling [4],etc. These methods are based on pixel-wise density estimation, which estimates the probability of an intensity or color value for each pixel. The density-based models have the advantage of extracting detailed shapes of moving objects and updating the models online for each pixel. However, their drawbacks are that the segmentation results are sensitive to noise, illumination change, and small movement of the background.

P. Foggia, C. Sansone, and M. Vento (Eds.): ICIAP 2009, LNCS 5716, pp. 623–632, 2009.
© Springer-Verlag Berlin Heidelberg 2009

On the other hand, eigenbackground modeling method [6]is also based on appropriate statistics of gray values over time at each pixel location. But its estimation technique is based on the principal component analysis that is different from pixel-wise probability density estimation. In Eigenbackground framework, the whole 2D images as vectors are collected to obtain principal components during the training phase. In the test phase, a new vectorized image is first projected onto trained eigenvector subspace and is reconstructed using the projected image and the principal components. The pixels will be considered as foreground points when their Euclidean distance difference between the input image and the the the reconstructed image are greater than a given threshold. This eigenspace model can well describe the range of intensity that have been observed(e.g., lighting variations over the trainging.), which will be explained in section 2.1. The advantage of this method lies in the simplicity and fastness comparing with pixel-wise density-based methods. However, it is not straightforward to integrate multi-channel data such as RGB color images without significant increase of dimensionality. Moreover, it is difficult to update eigen-background online during the detection procedure because the computational cost of recalculating eigenvectors is huge.

As mentioned above, the modeling method based on eigenspace analysis and the density-based methods have their pros and cons. Therefore, the combination of two types of methods should be considered to be complementary with each other. In this paper, we adopt the eigenspace model to build the intensity information for each pixel due to its satisfied description during the light variation. Unimodal gaussian density methods with less computational cost are used to describe color information for each pixel. The reason of using unimodal gaussian models is that the color information change little in most cases even if light varies much. In addition, it is easy to update unimodal gaussian modal online. An adaptive method is proposed to combine the unimodal gaussian model with the eigenspace model. The multi-channel data is used with less computation, and the mixture model can be updated partially .

The rest of the paper is organized as follows: Section 2 proposes how to build background model fusing eigenbackground with single gaussian models. Section 3 describes the segmentation method based on graph cut algorithm. Section 4 demonstrates experimental results. Conclusion is drawn in section 5.

2   Mixture Background Model

2.1   Eigenbackground

We build an eigenspace background model using the intensity information in a static background. The eigenspace model is formed by taking a set of N sample images,$\{I_t\}_{t=1,2,\cdots,N}$. From these images the mean background image μ_b is subtracted to get zero mean vector $\{X_i\}_{i=1,2,\cdots,N}$ where $X_t = I_t - \mu_b$. Then the covariance matrix C_b is computed by X_t and is diagonalized as: $L_b = \Phi_b C_b \Phi_b^T$,where L_b is the diagonal matrix with the corresponding eigenvalues. Φ_b is the eigenvector matrix that is calculated through the singular value decomposition(SVD). In order to reduce the dimensionality of the eigenvector space, only M largest eigenvalues are kept, resulting in Φ_{Mb}.

Once a new image, I_t, is available, it is first projected to the lower dimensional space expanded by the eigenbackgrounds images. In this reduction, only the static parts of the scene will be accurately described as a sum of the various eigenbackgrounds. The projected image,$I_t^B = \Phi_{Mb}(I_t - \mu_b)$,is now reconstructed as the background model for the new image. Finally we can determine the foreground points whose differences between the input image and the background image are greater than a given threshold θ :

$$D_t = \left| I_t - I_t^B \right| > \theta \tag{1}$$

The reason why this method works is that only the static parts of the scene will be accurately described as a sum of the various eigenbasis vectors. Moving objects will not appear in the same location of the sample images, so they contribute much less to the model than the static parts of the scene.

2.2 Single Gaussian Model

Similar to Pfinder[5], we learn the scene for N frames without the foreground object to build the density probability model for each pixel. Background representation is to use the normalized (r,g) space, where $r = R/(R + G + B)$ and $g = G/(R+G+B)$. The (r, g) color space we choose reflects the color information and is invariant to changes in brightness. Here, every channel of the color space is treated as independent to reduce the computation. By learning the scenes, we can obtain the parameter of model composed of the mean μ_i and covariance matrix σ_i for certain pixel i in the (r,g) color space.

If a new pixel value I_t belongs to the gaussian distribution at this point, the parameters are updated using the infinite impulse response filter as follows:

$$\begin{aligned}
\mu_{i,t} &= (1 - \alpha)\mu_{i,t-1} + \alpha I_{i,t} \\
\sigma_{i,t}^2 &= (1 - \alpha)\sigma_{i,t-1}^2 + \alpha(I_{i,t} - \mu_{i,t})^T(I_{i,t} - \mu_{i,t})
\end{aligned} \tag{2}$$

Here, α is the learning rate, which determines the speed of the distribution's parameters change. Note that I_t denotes (r_t^i, g_t^i) different from the intensity value in Equation 1.

If the problem of shadow removal is considered, (r, g) color space is helpful to detect shadow-pixels who are wrongly classified as object-pixels by Eigenbackground. As the literature [7] pointed out, the change in intensity by a shadow is expected to stay within a certain range. In other words, the ratio between the intensity value and the expectation value varies at some range. Under this circumstance, the (r, g) color value change little. So we can use this characteristic to distinguish the shadow pixels.

2.3 Combination of Two Background Models

Although Eigenbackground is more robust to the light variant, it doesn't make use of the color information and online-update is difficult. On the other hand, unimodal Gaussian model develop the color (r,g) space model without the intensity information because density-based unimodal Gaussian is sensitive to the light variant. Therefore, we combine two models to compensate for each other in the following way:

$$\begin{cases} D_i(B) = \lambda D_i(E) + (1 - \lambda)D_i(G) \\ D_i(E) = |I_i - B_i| \\ D_i(G) = (\frac{(I_{r,i} - \mu_r)^2}{\sigma_r^2} + \frac{(I_{g,i} - \mu_g)^2}{\sigma_g^2}) \\ \lambda = 1 - exp(-(I_i - \mu_i)^2/\eta^2) \end{cases} \quad (3)$$

Where $D_i(E)$ is the calculated background cost based on Eigenbackground method for the pixel i in Equation 1. $D_i(G)$ denotes the background cost based on Gaussian model in section 2.2. $D_i(B)$ is the combining cost of the pixel belonging to the background. I_i, $I_{r,i}$ and $I_{g,i}$ correspond to the illumination, normalized r and g value , respectively. λ is mixing factor that reflects the confidence in eigenspace model. η models the noise and is set as a priori. To maximize robustness, λ should be adaptively adjusted: if the intensity varies much, we should rely more on the eigenbackground model so that the whole system is robust to illumination changes of background; otherwise, we should rely more on per-pixel gaussian color models to detect R, G and B multi-channel color changes. Note that when the intensity I_i value is small and the input image is dark, it is better to only use $D_i(E)$ because the $(R + G + B)$ value is small and the $D_i(G)$ is not precise under this circumstance.

Figure 1 shows the experimental results using eigenbackground, single gaussian and mixture model, respectively. The fist column is the original test images. The second shows the results obtained by eigenbackground. The third column corresponds to the results using the single gaussian model. The last column gives the results by mixture background model. From Figure 1, we can find that the mixture models have the advantages of better segmentation results over the eigenbackground, and of less noise over the single gaussian model.

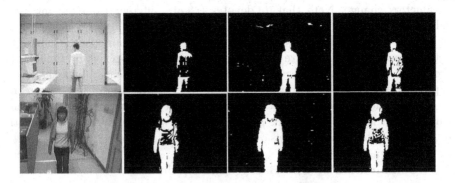

Fig. 1. The respective segmentation results using three methods

3   Background Segmentation Based on Graph Cut

Although we can obtain the segmentation results by setting the threshold to subtract the background in section 2, the results are not reliable because the threshold is very sensitive to noise and background illumination. Therefore, we hope to find an adaptively optimized method to determine the foreground object. The minimum graph cut algorithm based on a combinatorial optimization is an useful tool to image segmentation [8]. In graph cut framework, the observed image are divided into three labels by background model: the pixels with high background probability in the Equation 3 are the background(B). The pixels with low probability are the foreground(F). The rest are attached to the unknown label(U), which will be determined the background or foreground label by minimizing certain energy function using the min-cut algorithm. In the following, we will explain in detail how to label unclassified pixels by graph cut methods.

3.1   Graph Cut

Supposing that the input image of each frame is considered as a graph. All the image pixels are taken as the non-terminal nodes of the graph. The binary labels, namely foreground (B) and background (F), are taken as terminal nodes. Our goal is to assign the binary value to each pixel on a single frame by minimizing the following energy function:

$$E(X) = \sum_{i \in \mathcal{V}} D(x_i) + \rho \sum_{\{i,j\} \in \mathcal{E}} V(x_i, x_j) \qquad (4)$$

Here, the data term D measures the cost of assigning the label x_i to the pixel i given the observed data. x_i equals either F or B. Let $\mathcal{V}$ be the set of all pixels in the image. The link term V measures the cost of assigning the labels x_i, x_j to the adjacent pixels (i, j). The signal $\mathcal{E}$ denotes the set of all neighborhood pixels pairs (i, j). The coefficient ρ specifies the relative importance of the link term.

3.2   Setting Data Term and Link Term

The data term includes $D_i(B)$ and $D_i(F)$ cost, which corresponds to the cost of assigning the pixel i to background and foreground , respectively. we can set $D_i(B)$ that is the cost belonging to the background according to Equation 3. By this cost, the input image are divided into the definitely foreground for which $D_i(B)$ value is high, definitely background for which $D_i(B)$ value is small, and the reminder of pixels are uncertainty region. The cost $D_i(F)$ is set to be certain constant. Note that the normalized cost are used in Equation 4 so as to set coefficient ρ in the same quantity level with the link cost:

$$\begin{aligned} D_i(B) &= D(x_i = B) = \lambda D_i(E) + (1 - \lambda)D_i(U) \\ D_i(F) &= D(x_i = F) = \varphi^2 \end{aligned} \qquad (5)$$

Although the cost belonging to the foreground is estimated by a simple function, it is sufficient for the segmentation because the accurate per-pixel background model has been used. In contrast to the simple foreground cost, we develop a global foreground model to calculate the $D(x_i = F)$. Through experimental contrast, we find that similar segmentation is obtained by using simple foreground cost and global foreground model cost. However, the former has obviously less computation cost than the latter.

The link cost in Equation 4 is designed to keep the segmentation coherent across space. Only if two nodes are assigned to opposite labels, B and F, the link cost is non-zero. Otherwise, the cost of the link (i, j) is zero because of no contribution to the cost of the cut. So the link (i, j) is defined to be:

$$V_{ij}(x_i, x_j) = \begin{cases} \exp(-\frac{d_{ij}}{2\eta^2}) & \text{if } x_i \neq x_j \\ 0, & \text{if } x_i = x_j \end{cases} \quad (6)$$

Where, η can be estimated as "camera noise", which is set to 5 in practise. d_{ij} denotes the color different between two neighborhood pixels, which is designed referred the literatures [9] using the contrast attenuation.

$$d_{ij} = \|I_i - I_j\|^2 \cdot \cfrac{1}{1 + \left(\cfrac{\|I_i^B - I_j^B\|}{K}\right)^2 \exp(-\frac{z_{ij}^2}{\sigma_z})} \quad (7)$$

Where $z_{ij} = \max\{\|I_i - I_i^B\|, \|I_j - I_j^B\|\}$ measures the dissimilarity between pixel pair (I_i, I_j) in image I at the current frame and (I_i^B, I_j^B) in background image I^B obtained from the eigenbackground initialization. The improved link cost adaptively attenuates the contrasts in the background while preserving the contrasts across foreground/background boundaries.

After setting the data term and link term, we minimize the energy $E(X)$ in Equation 4 to achieve the segmentation using the implementation of dynamic graph cut algorithm [10]. Before getting the final binary segmentation results, we use region maker algorithm to remove the small regions.

Figure 2 shows the segmentation results on the original images using the graph cut. In contrast with the last column of the Figure 1, the results in Figure 2 demonstrate that the segmentations are improved by graph cut algorithm.

Fig. 2. The segmentation results using graph cut

4   Experimental Results

We validate our method on indoor video in our laboratory captured by a common web-camera. Meanwhile, our methods are tested on well-known benchmark videos[1]. The experimental results are shown from Figure 3 to Figure 6.

Fig. 3. Some segmentation results using graph cut

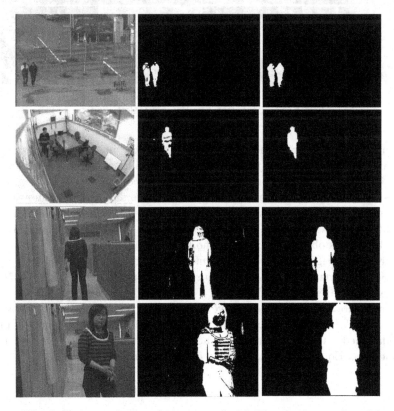

Fig. 4. Segmentation results compared with Eigenbackground model

[1] http://cvrr.ucsd.edu/aton/shadow

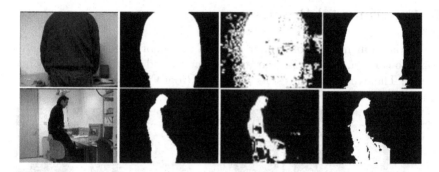

Fig. 5. The contrasted segmentation results between ours and wallflow

Fig. 6. Segmentation results on "JMleft" video

Figure 4 compare our method with the Eigenbackground model on public test image and sequence images in our lab. The second column gives the segmentation results by Eigenbackground model. The rightmost column shows the segmentation results through our adaptive background model and shadow removal.

In Figure 5, the first column is the original images. The second column is the ground truth data. The third is the results from the wallflow algorithm [11]. The last is the results obtained by our method

Figure 6 and Figure 8 give some segmentation result and quantitative evaluation. Some segmentation results by our method on the benchmark "$JMleft$" video from [12] are given in Figure 6.

Figure 7 shows the error rate curve that is drawn based on the segmentation results in the "$JMleft$" sequences from [12], which demonstrates that few pixels is misclassified and low error rate is achieved by our proposed method using multiple cues. Equation 8 gives how to calculate error rate.

$$Error\ rate = 100\% \times \left((FN + FP)/_{Image\ area} \right) \tag{8}$$

Where FP denotes the number of misclassified non-foreground points, and FN equals to the number of misclassified foreground points.

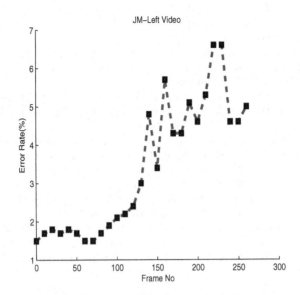

Fig. 7. Error rate curve on "JMleft" video

From Figure 3, Figure 5 and Figure 6, we can see that the proposed method can well obtain the better foreground segmentation on different videos in real time. In our experiment, the frame rate is about 16-18fames/seconds for a 320x240 video on a 3.0 GHZ laptop with 512MB RAM by using dynamic graph cut algorithm, which can meet the real-time requirement.

5   Conclusion

In this paper, we propose a mixture model that adaptively combines the eigen-background and single gaussian models. The proposed model is robust to noise and illumination change due to inheriting eigenbackground advantages. Meanwhile, it can make use of color information to detect multi-channel changes and remove the shadows by gaussian model. To avoiding the fixed threshold, we use the graph cut algorithm to obtain accurate binary label values. Experimental results on the benchmark video demonstrate that our methods are efficient.

References

1. Stauffer, C., Grimson, W.E.L.: Adaptive background mixture models for real-time tracking. In: IEEE Conference on Computer Vision and Pattern Recognition, pp. 246–252 (1999)
2. Haritaoglu, I., Harwood, D., Davis, L.S.: W4s: A Real-Time System for Detecting and Tracking People in 2 1/2 D. In: IEEE Transactions on Pattern Analysis and Machine Intelligence (1998)

3. Elgammal, A., Harwood, D., Davis, L.: Non-parametric Model for Background Subtraction. In: Proceedings of International Conference on Computer Vision, pp. 751–767 (1999)
4. Han, B., Comaniciu, D., Davis, L.: Sequential kernel density approximation through mode propagation: applications to background modeling. In: Asian Conference on Computer Vision, pp. 922–929 (2005)
5. Wren, C.R., Azarbayejani, A., Darrell, T., Pentland, A.P.: Pfinder: Real-Time Tracking of the Human Body. In: W4s: A Real-Time System for Detecting and Tracking People in 2 1/2 D, pp. 780–785 (1997)
6. Oliver, N., Rosario, B., Pentland, A.: A Bayesian Computer Vision System for Modeling Human Interactions. In: Int'l Conf. on Vision Systems, Gran Canaria, Spain (1999)
7. Schindler, K., Wang, H.: Smooth foreground-background segmentation for video processing. In: Narayanan, P.J., Nayar, S.K., Shum, H.-Y. (eds.) ACCV 2006. LNCS, vol. 3852, pp. 581–590. Springer, Heidelberg (2006)
8. Boykov, Y., Jolly, P.M.: Interactive Graph Cuts for Optimal Boundary & Region Segmentation of Objects in N-d Images. In: ICCV, pp. 102–112 (2001)
9. Sun, J., Zhang, W., Tang, X., Shum, H.Y.: Background cut. In: Leonardis, A., Bischof, H., Pinz, A. (eds.) ECCV 2006. LNCS, vol. 3952, pp. 628–641. Springer, Heidelberg (2006)
10. Kohli, P., Torr, P.H.S.: Efficiently solving dynamic Markov Random Fields Using Graph cuts. In: IEEE ICCV, pp. 922–929 (2005)
11. Toyama, K., Krumm, J., Brumitt, B., Meyers, B.: Wallflower: principles and practice of background maintenance. In: Proceedings of International Conference on Computer Vision, pp. 255–261 (1999)
12. Criminisi, A., Cross, G., Blake, A., Kolmogorov, V.: Bilayer Segmentation of Live Video. In: IEEE Conference on Computer Vision and Pattern Recognition, pp. 53–60 (2006)

A New Algorithm for Polygonal Approximation Based on Ant Colony Optimization

Cecilia Di Ruberto and Andrea Morgera

Dipartimento di Matematica e Informatica, Università di Cagliari, Cagliari, Italy

Abstract. In shape analysis a crucial step consists in extracting meaningful features from digital curves. Dominant points are those points with curvature extreme on the curve that can suitably describe the curve both for visual perception and for recognition. In this paper we present a novel method that combines the dominant point detection and the ant colony optimization search. The excellent results have been compared both to works using an optimal search approach and to works based on exact approximation strategy.

1 Introduction

Computer imaging has developed as an interdisciplinary research field whose focus is on the acquisition and processing of visual information by computer. Among all aspects underlying visual information, the shape of the objects plays a special role. In shape analysis an important step consists in extracting meaningful features from digital curves. Dominant points are those points that have curvature extreme on the curve and they can suitably describe the curve for both visual perception and recognition [1],[2]. There are many approaches developed for detecting dominant points. They can be classified into two main categories: corner detection approaches and polygonal approximation approaches. Corner detection approaches aim to detect potential significant points, but they cannot represent smooth curve appropriately. The performance of these detectors depends on the accuracy of the curvature evaluation [9],[10]. For polygonal approximation approaches, sequential, iterative and optimal algorithms are commonly used. Sequential approaches are simple and fast, but the results depend on the location of the point where they start the scan-along process and they can miss important features. The iterative approaches split and merge curves iteratively until they meet the preset allowances [7],[8]. Their results may be far from the optimal one if a poor initial segmentation is used. The optimal approaches tend to find the optimal polygonal approximation based on specified criteria and error bound constraints [4]-[6]. The idea is to approximate a given curve by an optimal polygon with the minimal number of line segments such that the approximation error between the original curve and the corresponding line segments is no more than a pre-specified tolerance. Local optimal methods are very fast but their results may be very far from the optimal one. However, an exhaustive search for the vertices of the optimal polygon from the given set of data points results in an

P. Foggia, C. Sansone, and M. Vento (Eds.): ICIAP 2009, LNCS 5716, pp. 633–641, 2009.

exponential complexity. However, there exist some heuristic approaches (genetic algorithms and tabu search) which can find solutions very close to the global optimal one in a relative short time. In this paper we present a method that combines the dominant point detection and the ant colony optimization search. The method is inspired by the ant colony search suggested in [6] but it results in a much more efficient and effective approximation algorithm. The excellent results have been compared to works using an optimal search approach and to works based on exact approximation strategy.

2   Ant Colony Optimization Algorithms

Ant Colony Optimization (ACO) firstly proposed by Dorigo in [3] is based on a computational paradigm inspired by the way real ant colonies function. The ants make use of a substance, called pheromone, to communicate information regarding shortest paths to food. A moving ant lays some pheromone on the ground, thus making a path by a trail of this substance. While an ant moves practically at random, it encounters a previously laid trail and can decide, with high probability, to follow it, thus reinforcing the trail with its own pheromone. The process is characterized by a positive feedback loop, where the probability with which an ant chooses a path increases with the number of ants that previously chose the same path. The ACO paradigm is inspired by this process. Artificial ants build solutions (tours) of a problem by moving on the problem graph from one node to another. The algorithm executes N_{max} iterations. During each iteration m ants build a tour in which a probabilistic decision rule is applied. If an ant in node i chooses to move to node j, the edge (i, j) is added to the tour under construction. This step is repeated until the ant has completed its tour. After ants have built their tours, each ant deposits pheromone on the visited edges to make them more desirable for future ants. The amount of pheromone trail τ_{ij} associated to edge (i, j) is intended to represent the learned desirability of choosing node j when in node i. The pheromone trail information is changed during problem solution to reflect the experience acquired by ants during problem solving. Ants deposit an amount of pheromone proportional to the quality of the solutions they produced: the shorter the tour generated by an ant, the greater the amount of pheromone it deposits on the edges which it used to generate the tour. This choice helps to direct search towards good solutions. The ACO algorithms have been applied to many different discrete optimization problems, like the travelling salesman problem and the quadratic assignment problem. Recent applications cover problems like vehicle routing, sequential ordering, graph coloring, routing in communications networks, and so on. In this work we use the ACO paradigm to solve the polygonal approximation problem.

3   The ACO-Based Proposed Method

We first define the problem of polygonal approximation in terms of optimization problem and then we describe how we use the ACO algorithm to solve it.

3.1   Problem Formulation and Graph Representation

Given a digital curve represented by a set of N clockwise-ordederd points, $C = \{c_1, c_2, ..., c_N\}$ where $c_{(i+1)mod N}$ is the succeeding point of c_i, we define arc $\widehat{c_i c_j}$ as the set of points between c_i and c_j, and chord $\overline{c_i c_j}$ as the line segment connecting c_i and c_j. In approximating the arc $\widehat{c_i c_j}$ by the chord $\overline{c_i c_j}$, we make an error, denoted by $e(\widehat{c_i c_j}, \overline{c_i c_j})$ that can be measured by a distance norm. We use the sum of squared perpendicular distance from every data point on $\widehat{c_i c_j}$ to $\overline{c_i c_j}$:

$$e(\widehat{c_i c_j}, \overline{c_i c_j}) = \sum_{c_k \in \widehat{c_i c_j}} d^2(c_k, \overline{c_i c_j}) \tag{1}$$

where $d(c_k, \overline{c_i c_j})$ is the perpendicular distance from point c_k to the corresponding chord $\overline{c_i c_j}$. The objective is to approximate a given curve by an optimal polygon with the minimal number of line segments such that the approximation error between the original curve and the corresponding line segments is less than a pre-specified tolerance. Formally, the aim is to find the ordered set $T = \{c_{p_1}, c_{p_2}, ..., c_{p_M}\}$ where $T \subset C$ and $M \leq N$ such that M is minimal and the set of M line segments, $P = \{\overline{c_{p_1} c_{p_2}}, \overline{c_{p_2} c_{p_3}}, ..., \overline{c_{p_{M-1}} c_{p_M}}, \overline{c_{p_M} c_{p_1}}\}$, composes an approximating polygon to the point set C with an error norm between C and P no more than a pre-specified tolerance, ϵ. The error between C and P, denoted by $E_2(C, P)$, is defined as the sum of the approximation errors between the M arcs $\{\widehat{c_{p_1} c_{p_2}}, \widehat{c_{p_2} c_{p_3}}, ..., \widehat{c_{p_{M-1}} c_{p_M}}, \widehat{c_{p_M} c_{p_1}}\}$ and the corresponding M line segments $\{\overline{c_{p_1} c_{p_2}}, \overline{c_{p_2} c_{p_3}}, ..., \overline{c_{p_{M-1}} c_{p_M}}, \overline{c_{p_M} c_{p_1}}\}$, with $c_{p_{M+1}} \equiv c_{p_1}$:

$$E_2(C, P) = \sum_{i=1}^{M} e(\widehat{c_{p_i} c_{p_{i+1}}}, \overline{c_{p_i} c_{p_{i+1}}}). \tag{2}$$

To apply the ACO paradigm, we need to represent our problem in terms of a graph, $G - (V, E)$. For the polygonal approximation problem, each point on the curve should be represented as a node of the graph, i.e. $V = C$. The edge set E is generated as follows. Initially, the set E is created as an empty set. Then, for every node $c_i \in C$, we examine each of the remaining nodes, $c_j \in C$, in clockwise order. If the approximation error between the arc $\widehat{c_i c_j}$ and the line segment $\overline{c_i c_j}$ is no more than ϵ, then the directed edge $\overrightarrow{c_i c_j}$ is added to the edge set E. Thus, we have:

$$E = \{\overrightarrow{c_i c_j} | e(\widehat{c_i c_j}, \overline{c_i c_j}) \leq \epsilon\}. \tag{3}$$

This means that E contains edges the error of which is smaller or equal to ϵ. The edge is directed to avoid the ants walking backward. Then, the problem of polygonal approximation is equivalent to finding the shortest closed circuit on the directed graph $G = < V, E >$ such that $E_2 \leq \epsilon$. In the following, the closed circuit completed by the ant k will be denoted by $tour_k$, its length will be $|tour_k|$ and the approximation error between the original curve C and the approximating polygon corresponding to $tour_k$ will be $E_2(C, tour_k)$.

3.2 Starting Node Initialization and Selection

During each cycle an ant chooses a starting node and sequentially constructs a closed path to finish its tour. To find the shortest closed tour, it is convenient to place the ants at the nodes with a high probability of finding such a tour, instead of a randomly distribution. For the selection of the starting nodes we propose two alternative strategies, we call *Selection_1* and *Selection_2*. They differ with respect to the way the initial set of starting nodes is defined. Let's describe the two algorithms in detail.

Selection_1. Shape signature is one of the most common shape descriptors and it is useful to understand the complexity of a shape. The more the extrema (maxima and minima) of the signature, the more articulated the object is. The number of signature extrema and the relative boundary points guide us to determine automatically the number of distributed ants and to select the nodes on the graph they choose to start their tour. In this algorithm the number m of distributed ants is equal to the number of the signature extrema and the m relative boundary points represent the m starting nodes at the beginning of the first cycle. In the next cycles, the ants are placed at the nodes with higher probability to find the shortest closed tour. We thus create a selection list for the starting nodes $T_i, i = 1, 2, ..., N$. Initially,

$$T_i = \begin{cases} 1 & \text{if } i \text{ is a starting node} \\ 0 & \text{otherwise} \end{cases} \tag{4}$$

The probability with which the node i is chosen as a starting node in the next cycles, denoted $Choose_i$, is estimated as the value T_i normalized by the sum of all values,

$$Choose_i = \frac{T_i}{\sum_{j=1}^{N} T_j} \tag{5}$$

At the end of each cycle, the value of $T_i, i = 1, 2, ..., N$ is updated. Let's denote by $Start\_Node_i$ the set of ants which start with the node i at the current cycle and by $|Start\_Node_i|$ its size. We update the value T_i making a trade-off between the average quality of current solutions constructed by the ants in $Start\_Node_i$ and the value of $Choose_i$ derived from older cycles. Thus, we let

$$T_i = \begin{cases} \frac{1}{|Start\_Node_i|} \sum_{j \in Start\_Node_i} \frac{1}{|tour_j|} + Choose_i & \text{if } i \text{ is a start node} \\ & \text{at current cycle} \\ T_i & \text{otherwise} \end{cases} \tag{6}$$

During the process, in the early iterations the ants will prefer the nodes which have not been chosen yet as starting nodes, by exploring new solutions. After all the nodes have been tested, they will be tend to choose the starting nodes which have more experiences of constructing shorter tours and enforce an exploitation search to the neighborhood of better solutions.

Selection_2. For each node $i, i = 1, ..., N$, of the graph we evaluate the greatest approximation error among all the directed edges departing from i. We generate a list of the N greatest errors sorted in ascending order. We select the first D edges, where D is a percentage on N (in all the experiments $D = 15$) and detect the nodes where these edges depart from. The list of such nodes, after eliminating duplications, represents the set of starting nodes at the beginning of the first cycle and its size is the number of the distributed ants. The selection phase continues as described previously.

3.3   Node Transition and Pheromone Updating Rules

According to ACO paradigm, the probability with which an ant k chooses to move from node i to node j is determined by the pheromone intensity τ_{ij} and the visibility value η_{ij} of the corresponding edge. In the proposed method, τ_{ij} is equally initialized to 1/N and is updated at the end of each cycle according to the average quality of the solutions that involve this edge. The value of η_{ij} is determined by a greedy heuristic which encourages the ants to walk to the farthest accessible node in order to construct the longest possible line segment in a hope that an approximating polygon with fewer vertices is obtained eventually. This can be accomplished by setting $\eta_{ij} = |\widehat{c_i c_j}|$, where $|\widehat{c_i c_j}|$ is the number of points on $\widehat{c_i c_j}$. The value of η_{ij} is fixed during all the cycles since it considers local information only. The transition probability from node i to node j through directed edge $\overrightarrow{c_i c_j}$ is defined as

$$p_{ij} = \frac{\tau_{ij}\eta_{ij}}{\sum_{\text{for all } \overrightarrow{c_i c_h} \text{ from} c_i} \tau_{ih}\eta_{ih}}. \tag{7}$$

At the end of each cycle we update the intensity of pheromone trails of an edge by the average quality of the solutions that use this edge. At the end of each cycle, the pheromone intensity at directed edge $\overrightarrow{c_i c_j}$ is updated by combining the pheromone evaporation and deposition as follows:

$$\tau_{ij} = \rho\tau_{ij} + \max(\sum_{k=1}^{m}\Delta_{ij}^{k}, 0) \tag{8}$$

where $\rho \in (0, 1)$ is the persistence rate of previous pheromone trails and Δ_{ij}^{k} is the quantity of new trails left by the ant k and it is computed by

$$\Delta_{ij}^{k} = \begin{cases} \frac{1}{|tour_k|} & \text{if the } \overrightarrow{c_i c_j} \in tour_k \text{ and } E_2(C, tour_k) \leq \epsilon \\ -\frac{E_2(C, tour_k)}{\epsilon N} & \text{if the } \overrightarrow{c_i c_j} \in tour_k \text{ and } E_2(C, tour_k) > \epsilon \\ 0 & \text{otherwise.} \end{cases} \tag{9}$$

According to the ACO paradigm, more quantities of pheromone trails will be laid at the edges along which most ants have constructed shorter feasible tours. As consequence, the proposed rule will guide the ants to explore better tours corresponding to high quality solutions.

3.4   Refinement of Approximation Polygon

On the detected dominant points we apply an enhancement process to refine their localization according to a minimal distance criterion. Let $T = \{c_{p_1}, c_{p_2}, ..., c_{p_M}\}$ the ordered set of detected dominant points. Considering the couple c_{p_i} and $c_{p_{i+2}}$, $i = 1, ..., M$, the refinement process consists in moving the intermediate point $c_{p_{i+1}}$ between c_{p_i} and $c_{p_{i+2}}$ in a new point by a local distance minimization. For all the points c_k on the arc $\overparen{c_{p_i}, c_{p_{i+2}}}$ we evaluate the sum of the approximation errors, $e(\overparen{c_{p_i}k}, \overline{c_{p_i}k}) + e(\overparen{kc_{p_{i+2}}}, \overline{kc_{p_{i+2}}})$. The new position for the point $c_{p_{i+1}}$ is chosen as follows:

$$c_{p_{i+1}} = \min_{c_k} e(\overparen{c_{p_i}c_k}, \overline{c_{p_i}c_k}) + e(\overparen{c_kc_{p_{i+2}}}, \overline{c_kc_{p_{i+2}}}) \tag{10}$$

The new point $c_{p_{i+1}}$ between c_{p_i} and $c_{p_{i+2}}$ is then used in the rest of the process. The refinement step is repeated for each pair $(c_{p_i}, c_{p_{i+2}})$, $i = 1, ..., M$.

4   Experimental Results and Conclusions

We present now the experimental results of the proposed approximation algorithm. In the following, we call by *Method_1* and by *Method_2* the methods based on *Selection_1* and *Selection_2* algorithms, respectively. The methods have been first tested on some real contours, showed in Fig.1. In Fig.2 we show the initial starting nodes, the approximating polygon before and after the refinement step by applying *Method_1* and *Method_2* for the aircraft curve. The performances have been compared to those of the method proposed by Yin [6] and presented in table 1. We have evaluated the initial number of points, N, the number of dominant points, Np, and the approximation error, E_2. For all the curves, our

Fig. 1. Some real world curves: fish, aircraft, hand, key

Table 1. The initial number of points, N, the number of dominant points, Np, and the approximation error E_2 for the real curves for our methods and Yin's algorithm. In bold the best approximation errors.

	N	Np	Method_1 before refine	Method_1 after refine	Method_2 before refine	Method_2 after refine	Yin [6]
Fish	325	25	172.45	102.03	171.10	**101.83**	176.19
F10	399	32	193.03	135.52	192.48	**134.28**	208.02
Hand	513	31	210.63	**149.56**	210.63	**149.56**	218.28
Key	257	16	116.14	**80.96**	117.85	82.79	121.25

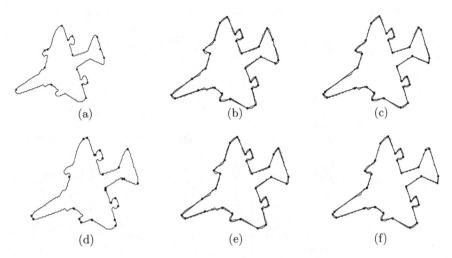

Fig. 2. F10 contour: the initial starting nodes, the polygonal approximation before and after refining the detected dominant points by applying *Method_1* in (a), (b), (c) and by applying *Method_2* in (d), (e), (f), respectively

Table 2. Comparison in terms of number of dominant points, Np, and E_2 on the benchmark curves

Curves	E_2	GA-based	TS-based	ACO_Poly	Method_1	Method_2
Leaf	150	17	11	13	9	9
$N = 120$	100	16	14	13	11	11
	90	17	15	14	12	11
	30	21	20	19	17	16
	15	23	23	23	19	19
Choromosome	30	7	6	6	6	6
$N = 60$	20	8	8	8	7	7
	10	10	11	11	11	9
	8	12	12	11	11	11
	6	15	14	14	13	12
Semicircle	60	13	11	10	10	10
$N = 102$	30	14	14	13	12	11
	25	17	15	13	12	12
	20	19	16	16	15	15
	15	23	18	18	17	16
Infinite	30	N/A	N/A	6	5	5
$N = 45$	20	N/A	N/A	7	6	6
	15	N/A	N/A	7	6	6
	10	N/A	N/A	7	7	7
	6	N/A	N/A	9	8	8
	3	N/A	N/A	17	10	10

Table 3. Comparison with other methods on the benchmark curves

Curves	Method	Np	E_2	$CR = N/Np$	E_2/CR	E_2/CR^2	E_2/CR^3
Leaf	Teh_Chin	28	15.43	4.286	3.600	0.840	0.196
$N = 120$	Cornic	N/A	N/A	N/A	N/A	N/A	N/A
	Ray-Ray	26	16.43	4.615	3.560	0.771	0.167
	Wu	24	15.93	5.000	3.186	0.637	0.127
	Marji-Siy	17	28.67	7.059	4.062	0.575	0.082
	Carmona	23	15.63	5.217	2.996	0.574	0.110
	Yin	24	13.73	5.000	2.746	0.549	0.110
	Our Method_1	24	10.62	5.000	2.124	0.425	0.085
	Our Method_2	24	10.62	5.000	2.124	0.425	0.085
Chromosome	Teh_Chin	16	6.40	3.750	1.707	0.455	0.121
$N = 60$	Cornic	17	5.54	3.529	1.570	0.445	0.126
	Ray-Ray	14	7.67	4.286	1.790	0.418	0.097
	Wu	16	4.70	3.750	1.253	0.334	0.089
	Marji-Siy	10	10.01	6.000	1.668	0.278	0.046
	Carmona	14	4.93	4.286	1.150	0.268	0.063
	Yin	14	6.41	4.286	1.496	0.349	0.081
	Our Method_1	14	5.39	4.286	1.258	0.293	0.068
	Our Method_2	14	5.39	4.286	1.258	0.293	0.068
Semicircle	Teh_Chin	22	20.61	4.636	4.445	0.959	0.207
$N = 102$	Cornic	30	9.19	3.400	2.703	0.795	0.234
	Ray-Ray	19	16.33	5.368	3.042	0.567	0.106
	Wu	26	9.04	3.923	2.304	0.587	0.150
	Marji-Siy	15	22.70	6.800	3.338	0.491	0.072
	Carmona	24	9.88	4.250	2.325	0.547	0.129
	Yin	23	10.50	4.435	2.368	0.534	0.120
	Our Method_1	23	6.28	4.435	1.416	0.319	0.072
	Our Method_2	23	6.28	4.435	1.416	0.319	0.072
Infinite	Teh_Chin	13	3.46	3.462	1.000	0.289	0.083
$N = 45$	Cornic	10	4.30	4.500	0.956	0.212	0.047
	Ray-Ray	12	3.75	3.750	1.000	0.267	0.071
	Wu	13	5.78	3.462	1.670	0.482	0.139
	Marji-Siy	N/A	N/A	N/A	N/A	N/A	N/A
	Carmona	10	5.56	4.500	1.236	0.275	0.061
	Yin	11	4.44	4.091	1.085	0.265	0.065
	Our Method_1	11	3.44	4.091	0.841	0.206	0.050
	Our Method_2	11	3.44	4.091	0.841	0.206	0.050

methods show a much better efficacy, both before and after the refining step. Also, our algorithms are less parameters dependent than Yin's one. Apart the ϵ-bound constraint and the number of the maximum cycles, Yin's method uses other five parameters. The detected approximating polygon is strongly dependent on the chosen parameter values. Our methods automatically choose the number of distributed ants and do not need any other parameter. We only define the maximum number of iterations and the ϵ-bound. Moreover, since the approach is non deterministic, different runs can lead to different solutions. We have approached this problem by choosing the initial set of starting nodes automatically and by introducing a refinement step to reduce the approximation error. Such two aspects are not present in Yin's approach. Finally, the approximation error levels off after only few iterations of the iterative process (in case of F10 curve after 3 iterations we achieve the best value $E_2 = 193.03$ and in case of hand curve just one iteration is needed to get $E_2 = 210.63$). This means that our methods are computationally more efficient, too. Our algorithms have been, also, tested on four commonly used curves (leaf, chromosome, semicircle and infinite). We have, first, compared our approach to other methods based on global search heuristic, like ACS_Poly method [6], the GA-based method [4] and the TS-based method [5]. The results confirm the superiority of our method both in effectiveness and in efficiency. The experimental results have been, finally, compared to many existing methods for dominant point detection. In table 3 for each algorithm we show the number of detected point, Np, the approximation error, E_2, the compression ratio, $CR = N/Np$, as suggested in [1] and [7] to measure the efficiency of the dominant point detectors and to compare them. Analyzing the table, we can affirm that the proposed approach is superior to many existing algorithms based on exact search methodology, too. Our future research will include the task of analyzing the stability of the proposed method with respect to affine transformations (rotation, scale, translation).

References

1. Carmona-Poyato, A., Fernández-García, N.L., Medina-Carnicer, R., Madrid-Cuevas, F.J.: Dominant point detection: A new proposal. Image and Vision Computing 23, 1226–1236 (2005)
2. Cornic, P.: Another look at dominant point detection of digital curves. Pattern Recognition Letters 18, 13–25 (1997)
3. Dorigo, M.: Optimization, learning, and natural algorithms. Ph.D. Thesis, Dip. Elettronica e Informazione, Politecnico di Milano, Italy (1992)
4. Yin, P.Y.: Genetic algorithms for polygonal approximation of digital curves. Int. J. Pattern Recognition Artif. Intell. 13, 1–22 (1999)
5. Yin, P.Y.: A tabu search approach to the polygonal approximation of digital curves. Int. J. Pattern Recognition Artif. Intell. 14, 243–255 (2000)
6. Yin, P.Y.: Ant colony search algorithms for optimal polygonal approximation of plane curves. Pattern Recognition 36(8), 1783–1797 (2003)
7. Marji, M., Siy, P.: A new algorithm for dominant points detection and polygonization of digital curves. Pattern Recognition 36, 2239–2251 (2003)
8. Ray, B.K., Ray, K.S.: Detection of significant points and polygonal approximation of digitized curves. Pattern Recognition Letters 22, 443–452 (1992)
9. Teh, C.H., Chin, R.T.: On the detection of dominant points on digital curves. IEEE Trans. on Pattern Analysis and Machine Intelligence 11(8), 859–871 (1989)
10. Wu, W.Y.: Dominant point detection using adaptive bending value. Image and Vision Computing 21, 517–525 (2003)

Recognition of Occluded Shapes Using Size Functions

Barbara Di Fabio[1], Claudia Landi[2,*], and Filippo Medri[3]

[1] Dipartimento di Matematica, Università di Bologna, Italy
difabio@dm.unibo.it
[2] Di.S.M.I., Università di Modena e Reggio Emilia, Italy
clandi@unimore.it
[3] Dipartimento di Scienze dell'Informazione, Università di Bologna, Italy
medri@cs.unibo.it

Abstract. The robustness against occlusions and the ability to perform not only global matching, but also partial matching are investigated in computer vision in order to evaluate the performance of shape descriptors. In this paper we consider the size function shape descriptor, and we illustrate some results about size functions of occluded shapes. Theoretical results indicate that size functions are able to detect a partial matching between shapes by showing a common subset of cornerpoints. Experiments are presented which outline the potential of the proposed approach in recognition tasks in the presence of occlusions.

Keywords: Size function, shape occlusion, cornerpoint, Hausdorff distance.

1 Introduction

Geometrical-topological methods for shape description and comparison are increasingly studied in computer vision, computer graphics and pattern recognition [1,4,6,7]. The common idea underlying the methods of this class is to perform a topological exploration of the shape according to some quantitative geometric properties provided by a real function chosen to extract shape features. For this reason they could be called shape-from-function methods. The attractive feature of shape-from-function techniques is that they concisely capture shape information, in a manner that can be robust to deformation while being able to cope with changes in object viewpoint at a multiresolution level [3]. In this context, size functions have been developed to analyze and compare multidimensional shapes, with application mainly to 2D digital shapes equipped with scalar functions [8,18,21] and 3D digital shapes (represented by surface or volume models) equipped with multivalued functions [2].

---

* Research partially carried out within the activities of ARCES, University of Bologna, Italy.

P. Foggia, C. Sansone, and M. Vento (Eds.): ICIAP 2009, LNCS 5716, pp. 642–651, 2009.
© Springer-Verlag Berlin Heidelberg 2009

Analyzing an image, occlusions can be found every time that foreground objects overlap other objects in the same scene. Therefore, occlusions understanding represents a crucial issue in computer vision.

Although in some contexts, such as stereo matching problems, the presence of occluding patterns may provide useful information (see e.g. [16]), in other settings, such as shape recognition and retrieval problems, the spotlight is on the background partially hidden object and the occlusion is considered to cause a loss of shape features information [19]. Therefore, the robustness of shape descriptors against occlusions is a common concern representing a widely researched topic. As far as point based representations of shape are concerned, works on the topic include the partial Hausdorff distance [15] by Huttenlocher et al. to compare portions of point sets, and Wolfson and Rigoutsos' use of geometric hashing [22] applied to point features. For shapes encoded as polylines, the Tanase and Veltkamp's approach [20] is that of computing the dissimilarity between multiple polylines and a polygon using the turning function, while Latecki et al. [17] propose a method based on removing certain parts of a polyline and see whether the objects become more similar without them. As for the region-based shape descriptors, Höynck and Ohm show that using central moments instead of the angular radial transform to extract features improves robustness to occlusions [14]. Regarding the shape-from-function methods, Biasotti et al. [5] automatically identify similar sub-parts exploiting a graph-matching technique applied to Reeb graphs.

In this paper we address the partial shape matching problem for size functions. In particular we illustrate the recent results proved in [11] on the behavior of size functions in the presence of occlusions, and their ability to preserve not only global, but also local information. The main result is that an occluded object and a fully visible object share a set of common features in the corresponding size functions. This property can be exploited to support recognition in the presence of occlusions, as shown by the experiments we present here.

The rest of the paper is organized as follows. Section 2 provides a brief overview on size functions. In Section 3 we summarize the relevant theoretical results obtained in [11]. Section 4 shows the potential of our approach applied to visible and invisible occlusions. Conclusions and suggestions on future developments end the paper.

2   Background on Size Functions

In Size Theory a shape is defined by a pair (X, φ), called a *size pair*, where X is a non-empty compact and locally connected Hausdorff topological space, and $\varphi : X \to \mathbb{R}$ denotes a continuous function, called a *measuring function*.

Shapes are studied through their lower level sets $X_u = \{p \in X : \varphi(p) \leq u\}$, u varying in $\mathbb{R}$. Indeed, denoting by Δ^+ the open half plane $\{(u, v) \in \mathbb{R}^2 : u < v\}$, size functions can be defined as follows.

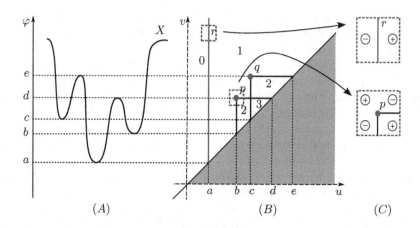

Fig. 1. (A) A size pair (X, φ), where X is the curve represented by a continuous line, and $\varphi : X \to \mathbb{R}$ is such that $\varphi(P) = y$ for every $P = (x, y) \in X$. (B) The size function associated with (X, φ). (C) Computation of multiplicities seen through lens.

Definition 1. *The* size function *associated with the size pair* (X, φ) *is the function* $\ell_{(X,\varphi)} : \Delta^+ \to \mathbb{N}$ *such that, for every* $(u, v) \in \Delta^+$, $\ell_{(X,\varphi)}(u, v)$ *is equal to the number of connected components in* X_v *containing at least one point of* X_u.

An example of size function is displayed in Fig. 1. In this example we consider the size pair (X, φ), where X is the curve of $\mathbb{R}^2$ represented by a solid line in Fig. 1 (A), and $\varphi : X \to \mathbb{R}$ is the function that associates to each point $P \in X$ its ordinate in the plane. The size function associated with (X, φ) is shown in Fig. 1 (B). Here, Δ^+, i.e. the domain of the size function, is divided by solid lines, representing the discontinuity points of the size function. These discontinuity points divide Δ^+ into regions where the size function is constant. The value displayed in each region is the value taken by the size function in that region. For instance, for $c \le v < d$, X_v has three connected components. Only one of them contains at least one point of X_u, when $a \le u < b$; two of them contain at least one point of X_u, when $b \le u < c$; all of them contain at least one point of X_u, when $c \le u < v < d$. Therefore, when $c \le v < d$, $\ell_{(X,\varphi)}(u, v) = 1$ for $a \le u < b$; $\ell_{(X,\varphi)}(u, v) = 2$ for $b \le u < c$; $\ell_{(X,\varphi)}(u, v) = 3$ for $c \le u < v$.

An equivalent representation of size function is given by countable collections of cornerpoints (proper and at infinity), with multiplicity [13]. A proper cornerpoint for $\ell_{(X,\varphi)}$ is a point $(u, v) \in \Delta^+$ encoding the level u at which a new connected component is born and the level v at which it get merged to another connected component. A cornerpoint at infinity just encodes the level u at which a new connected component of X is born. Formally they can be defined as follows.

Definition 2. *We call a* proper cornerpoint *for* $\ell_{(X,\varphi)}$ *any point* $p = (u, v) \in \Delta^+$ *such that the number* $\mu_X(p) = \lim_{\epsilon \to 0^+} \mu_X^\epsilon(p)$, *with* $\mu_X^\epsilon(p)$ *equal to*

$$\ell_{(X,\varphi)}(u+\epsilon, v-\epsilon) - \ell_{(X,\varphi)}(u-\epsilon, v-\epsilon) - \ell_{(X,\varphi)}(u+\epsilon, v+\epsilon) + \ell_{(X,\varphi)}(u-\epsilon, v+\epsilon),$$

is strictly positive. Moreover, we call a cornerpoint at infinity *for $\ell_{(X,\varphi)}$ any vertical line r, with equation $u = k$, such that the number $\mu_X(r) = \lim_{\epsilon \to 0^+} \mu_X^\epsilon(r)$, with $\mu_X^\epsilon(r)$ equal to*

$$\ell_{(X,\varphi)}(k + \epsilon, 1/\epsilon) - \ell_{(X,\varphi)}(k - \epsilon, 1/\epsilon),$$

is strictly positive.

Fig. 1 (C) zooms in on some cornerpoints to explain how their multiplicity is computed. For instance, the alternating sum of the size function values at four points around p is $2 - 1 - 1 + 1$, giving $\mu_X(p) = 1$. The alternating sum of the size function values at two points next to r is $1 - 0$, giving $\mu_X(r) = 1$.

Cornerpoints allow us to translate the comparison between size functions into distances between sets of points such as the Hausdorff metric or the matching distance, in a way that is robust against deformations [10,13].

From the computational point of view, the existing algorithm for computing size functions [9] requires the construction of a size graph (G, φ), where $G = (V(G), E(G))$ is a finite graph, with $V(G)$ and $E(G)$ the set of vertices and edges respectively, and $\varphi : V(G) \to \mathbb{R}$ is a measuring function labeling the nodes of the graph. In this paper we deal with binary 2D images, so $V(G)$ corresponds to image pixels and $E(G)$ represents the 8-neighborhood connectivity.

Once the size graph has been built, the computational complexity for computing the set of cornerpoints is $O(n \log n + m \cdot \alpha(2m + n, n))$, where n and m are the number of vertices and edges in the size graph, respectively, and α is the inverse of the Ackermann function.

Finally, in order to compare two size functions, encoded as collections of cornerpoints, each of cardinality N, the complexity of a simple implementation of the Hausdorff distance is $O(N^2)$, but a more efficient algorithm can reduce time complexity to $O(N \log N)$. We remark that, in general, N is always very much smaller than n and m.

3   Size Functions and Occluded Shapes

We model the presence of occlusions in a shape as follows. The object of interest A is occluded by an object B, so that $X = A \cup B$ is the object visible after occlusion. These sets are assumed to be locally connected compact Hausdorff spaces.

The shapes of X, A, and B are analyzed through the size functions $\ell_{(X,\varphi)}$, $\ell_{(A,\varphi|_A)}$, and $\ell_{(B,\varphi|_B)}$, respectively, where $\varphi : X \to \mathbb{R}$ is the continuous function chosen to extract the shape features.

The main theorem in [11] establishes a necessary and sufficient algebraic condition such that a (Mayer-Vietoris) relation exists among the size functions associated with X, A, B, and $A \cap B$. To be more precise, denoting by $\check{H}$ the Čech homology with coefficients in a field K, and by $\alpha_v : \check{H}_0((A \cap B)_v) \to \check{H}_0(A_v) \oplus \check{H}_0(B_v)$, $\alpha_{v,u} : \check{H}_0((A \cap B)_v, (A \cap B)_u) \to \check{H}_0(A_v, A_u) \oplus \check{H}_0(B_v, B_u)$ the homomorphisms belonging to the Mayer-Vietoris sequence of the triad (X_v, A_v, B_v) and to the relative Mayer-Vietoris sequence of the triad $((X_v, X_u), (A_v, A_u), (B_v, B_u))$, respectively, the following statement can be proved.

Theorem 1. *For every $(u, v) \in \Delta^+$, it holds that*

$$\ell_{(X,\varphi)}(u, v) = \ell_{(A,\varphi|_A)}(u, v) + \ell_{(B,\varphi|_B)}(u, v) - \ell_{(A\cap B,\varphi|_{A\cap B})}(u, v) \qquad (1)$$

if and only if $\dim \ker \alpha_v = \dim \ker \alpha_{v,u}$.

The relation among the size functions $\ell_{(X,\varphi)}$, $\ell_{(A,\varphi|_A)}$, $\ell_{(B,\varphi|_B)}$ and $\ell_{(A\cap B,\varphi|_{A\cap B})}$, stated in Theorem 1, can be translated into a relation among their cornerpoints. More precisely, the coordinates of cornerpoints for $\ell_{(X,\varphi)}$ are always coordinates of cornerpoints for $\ell_{(A,\varphi|_A)}$ or $\ell_{(B,\varphi|_B)}$ or $\ell_{(A\cap B,\varphi|_{A\cap B})}$ ([11], Thm. 5.4–5.5). Moreover, under proper assumptions, cornerpoints for $\ell_{(X,\varphi)}$ are cornerpoints for $\ell_{(A,\varphi|_A)}$ or $\ell_{(B,\varphi|_B)}$ or both ([11], Cor. 5.2). Fig. 2 illustrates these results on an example for which relation (1) holds everywhere in Δ^+.

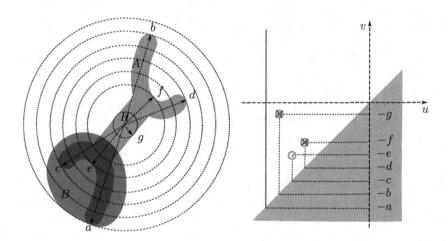

Fig. 2. Left: A "bone" shaped object A is occluded by another object B. The resulting occluded object $X = A \cup B$ is analyzed taking $\varphi : X \to \mathbb{R}$, $\varphi(P) = -\|P - H\|$. Right: The only cornerpoint at infinity for $\ell_{(X,\varphi)}$, $u = -a$, is also a cornerpoint at infinity for both $\ell_{(A,\varphi|_A)}$ and $\ell_{(B,\varphi|_B)}$; proper cornerpoints for $\ell_{(X,\varphi)}$ (×) belong to the set of cornerpoints for $\ell_{(A,\varphi|_A)}$ (○).

4   Experimental Results

In this section we are going to describe the results we have achieved in some preliminary experiments. In order to analyze the potential of our approach in the recognition of occluded shapes, we have considered both visible and invisible occlusions. To perform our tests we have worked with filled images from the MPEG-7 dataset [23]. In all the experiments, the occluding pattern is a rectangular shape occluding from the top, or the left, by an area we increasingly vary from 10% to 60% of the height or width of the bounding box of the original shape. For both the original shapes and the occluded ones, size functions are always computed with respect to a family of eight measuring functions having only the set of black pixels as domain. They are defined as follows: four of them as the distance from the line passing through the origin (top left point of the bounding box), rotated by an angle of 0, $\frac{\pi}{4}$, $\frac{\pi}{2}$ and $\frac{3\pi}{4}$ radians, respectively, with respect to the horizontal position; the other four as minus the distance from the same lines, respectively.

In the case of visible occlusions, with reference to the notation used in our theoretical setting, we are considering A as the original shape, B as a black rectangle, and X as the occluded shape generated by their union.

In Table 1 (column 3) a "device1" shape is depicted with one of its eight size functions. By comparison with the size function of the same object occluded from the top (column 1), or from the left (column 2), with respect to the same measuring function, it is easily seen that they present common substructures, since some cornerpoints are preserved after occlusions.

In Table 2, for different levels of occlusion, each 3D bar chart displays, along the z-axis, the percentage of common cornerpoints between the set of size functions associated with 70 shapes, each chosen from a different class of the MPEG-7 dataset (x-axis), and the set of size functions associated with the 70 occluded ones (y-axis). Note that, for each occluded shape, the highest bar is always on the diagonal, that is, where the occluded object is compared with the corresponding original one.

It has to be expected that, when a shape is not only occluded but also deformed, it will not be possible to find a common subset of cornerpoints between the original shape and the occluded one, since the deformation has slightly changed the cornerpoints position (see examples in Table 1, columns 3–5). To test the behavior of size functions when both occlusions and deformations are

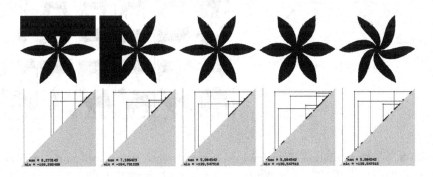

Table 1. Row 1: in columns 3–5, three "device1" shapes; in columns 1–2, the same "device1" shape as depicted in column 3, occluded from the top and from the left, respectively. Row 2: corresponding size functions associated with the same measuring function.

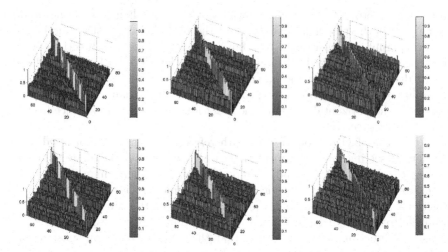

Table 2. 3D bar charts displaying, in the case of visible occlusions, the percentage of common cornerpoints (z-axis) between 70 occluded shapes (y-axis) and the 70 original ones (x-axis) correspondingly ordered. Row 1: Shapes are occluded from top by 20% (column 1), by 40% (column 2), by 60% (column 3). Row 2: Shapes are occluded from the left by 20% (column 1), by 40% (column 2), by 60% (column 3).

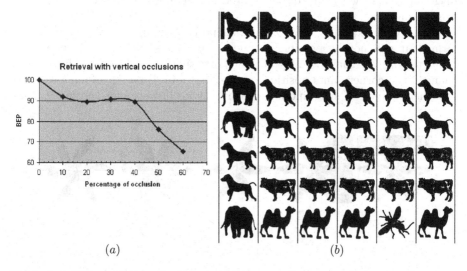

(a) (b)

Table 3. (a) The variation of retrieval performance when the occlusion area increases from the left; (b) Top retrieval results for a "dog" shape partially occluded from the left. Results are depicted in every column in increasing order of distance from the query.

introduced, we perform a retrieval test with the training set consisting of 75 images: three instances chosen from 25 different classes. The test set contains 25 occluded images, each taken from a different class. Each of them is taken

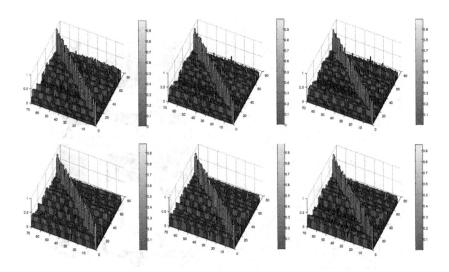

Table 4. 3D bar charts displaying, in the case of invisible occlusions, the percentage of common cornerpoints (z-axis) between 70 occluded shapes (y-axis) and the 70 original ones (x-axis) correspondingly ordered. Row 1: Shapes are occluded from top by 20% (column 1), by 30% (column 2), by 40% (column 3). Row 2: Shapes are occluded from the left by 20% (column 1), by 30% (column 2), by 40% (column 3).

as a query and is matched with all the images in the training set. Comparison is performed by calculating the sum of the eight Hausdorff distances between the sets of cornerpoints for the size functions associated with the corresponding eight measuring functions. The retrieval is evaluated using the *Bull's Eye Performance* (BEP) criterion. The BEP is measured by the correct retrievals among the top $2N$ retrievals, where N is the number of relevant (or similar) shapes to the query in the database. The effect of an increasing occlusion by a vertical rectangle on the retrieval performance is described by the graphs in Table 3 (a), while examples of query tests are exhibited in Table 3 (b).

When invisible occluding patterns are considered, with reference to the notation used in our theoretical setting, we take X as the original shape, A as the the occluded shape, and B as the invisible part of X. In this case, a comparison between cornerpoints of size functions, analogous to that of Table 2, is given in Table 4. The percentages of occlusion, from the top (row 1) and from the left (row 2), here vary from 20 to 40 (columns 1–3). Graphs in Table 5 (a) illustrate the recognition trend when, increasing the percentage of occlusion, we compare two shapes through the Hausdorff distance between their size functions, under the following convention. When the original shape is disconnected by the occlusion, we retain only the connected component of greatest area. This choice allows us to obtain always a finite Hausdorff distance, but determines a high loss of shape information even when the percentage of occlusion is low (see examples in Table 5 (b)).

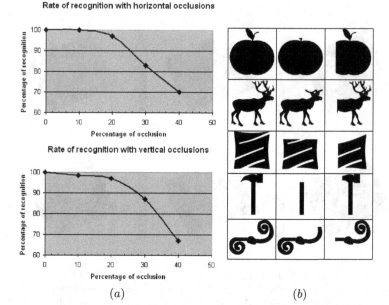

(a)   (b)

Table 5. (a) Recognition trend when the occluded area from the top and from the left increases. (b) The first column: some instances from the MPEG-7 dataset. The second and third columns: by 20% occluded from the top and from the left, respectively.

5   Discussion

In this paper we have proposed a method to assess partial matching using size functions. As demonstrated, recognition in the presence of occlusions amounts to detect common subsets of cornerpoints in size functions. The experimental results show that this method is effective both with visible and invisible occlusions. However, when deformations are added to occlusions, the Hausdorff distance between size functions seems not to be robust enough for recognition or retrieval tasks. The reason is that it works globally on the whole set of cornerpoints and therefore it is not able to detect substructures. As a consequence, an important open question is how to automatically detect similar substructures in size functions when cornerpoints can be distorted. This question could be addressed in a future research combining the results shown in this paper with the polynomial representation of size functions [12].

References

1. Biasotti, S., Cerri, A., Frosini, P., Giorgi, D., Landi, C.: Multidimensional Size Functions for Shape Comparison. J. Math. Imaging Vis. 32(2), 161–179 (2008)
2. Biasotti, S., Cerri, A., Giorgi, D.: k-dimensional size functions for shape description and comparison. In: Proc. of ICIAP 2007, pp. 345–352 (2007)

3. Biasotti, S., De Floriani, L., Falcidieno, B., Frosini, P., Giorgi, D., Landi, C., Papaleo, L., Spagnuolo, M.: Describing shapes by geometrical-topological properties of real functions. ACM Computing Surveys 40(4), 12:1–12:87 (2008)
4. Biasotti, S., Giorgi, D., Spagnuolo, M., Falcidieno, B.: Reeb graphs for shape analysis and applications. Theor. Comput. Sci. 392(1-3), 5–22 (2008)
5. Biasotti, S., Marini, S., Spagnuolo, M., Falcidieno, B.: Sub-part correspondence by structural descriptors of 3D shapes. Computer-Aided Design 38(9), 1002–1019 (2006)
6. Carlsson, G., Zomorodian, A., Collins, A., Guibas, L.: Persistence barcodes for shapes. International Journal of Shape Modeling 11, 149–187 (2005)
7. Cazals, F., Chazal, F., Lewiner, T.: Molecular shape analysis based upon the Morse-Smale complex and the Connolly function. In: Proc. of SCG 2003, pp. 351–360 (2003)
8. Cerri, A., Ferri, M., Giorgi, D.: Retrieval of trademarks images by means of size functions. Graphical Models 68, 451–471 (2006)
9. d'Amico, M.: A New Optimal Algorithm for Computing Size Functions of Shapes. In: Proc. of CVPRIP Algoritms III, pp. 107–110 (2000)
10. d'Amico, M., Frosini, P., Landi, C.: Natural pseudo-distance and optimal matching between reduced size functions. Acta Appl. Math. (digitally available)
11. Di Fabio, B., Landi, C.: Čech homology for shape recognition in the presence of occlusions (preprint),
http://arxiv.org/PS_cache/arxiv/pdf/0807/0807.0796v1.pdf
12. Ferri, M., Landi, C.: Representing size functions by complex polynomials. Proc. Math. Met. in Pattern Recognition 9, 16–19 (1999)
13. Landi, C., Frosini, P.: New pseudodistances for the size function space. In: Proc. SPIE, Vision Geometry VI, vol. 3168, pp. 52–60 (1997)
14. Höynck, M., Ohm, J.R.: Shape retrieval with robustness against partial occlusion. In: Proc. of IEEE ICASSP 2003, vol. 3, pp. 593–596 (2003)
15. Huttenlocher, D.P., Klanderman, G.A., Rucklidge, W.J.: Comparing images using the Hausdorff distance. IEEE Trans. PAMI 15, 850–863 (1993)
16. Intille, S.S., Bobick, A.F.: Disparity-space images and large occlusion stereo. In: Proc. of ECCV 1994, vol. II, pp. 179–186 (1994)
17. Latecki, L.J., Lakämper, R., Wolter, D.: Optimal partial shape similarity. Image Vision Comput. 23(2), 227–236 (2005)
18. Stanganelli, I., Brucale, A., Calori, L., Gori, R., Lovato, A., Magi, S., Kopf, B., Bacchilega, R., Rapisarda, V., Testori, A., Ascierto, P.A., Simeone, E., Ferri, M.: Computer-aided diagnosis of melanocytic lesions. Anticancer Res. 25, 4577–4582 (2005)
19. Veltkamp, R.C.: Shape matching: similarity measures and algorithms. In: Proc. of Shape Modeling International 2001, pp. 188–197 (2001)
20. Tanase, M., Veltkamp, R.C.: Part-based shape retrieval. In: Proc. of MULTIMEDIA 2005, pp. 543–546 (2005)
21. Uras, C., Verri, A.: Computing size functions from edge maps. Internat. J. Comput. Vis. 23(2), 169–183 (1997)
22. Wolfson, H.J., Rigoutsos, I.: Geometric Hashing: An Overview. IEEE Computational Science and Engineering 4(4), 10–21 (1997)
23. http://www.imageprocessingplace.com/root_files_V3/image_databases.htm

Discrete Distortion for Surface Meshes

Mohammed Mostefa Mesmoudi, Leila De Floriani, and Paola Magillo

Department of Computer Science, University of Genova
Via Dodecaneso n 35, 16146 Genova Italy
mmesmoudi@ac-creteil.fr,
{deflo,magillo}@disi.unige.it
http://www.disi.unige.it

Abstract. Discrete distortion for two- and three-dimensional combinatorial manifolds is a discrete alternative to Ricci curvature known for differentiable manifolds. Here, we show that distortion can be successfully used to estimate mean curvature at any point of a surface. We compare our approach with the continuous case and with a common discrete approximation of mean curvature, which depends on the area of the star of each vertex in the triangulated surface. This provides a new, area-independent, tool for curvature estimation and for morphological shape analysis. We illustrate our approach through experimental results showing the behavior of discrete distortion.

Keywords: Gaussian curvature, mean curvature, discrete curvature estimators, triangle meshes.

1 Introduction

Intrinsic properties of a surface, like genus, Euler-Poincaré characteristic, Betti numbers, orientability, serve to classify it topologically. Other properties, like tangent plane, normal vector at a point and the shape, serve to describe local geometry of the surface. Further properties, like first and second fundamental forms, principal curvature, Gaussian curvature, mean curvature, geodesic curvature, serve to study the surface from a metric point of view. In practical applications, we need to deal with discrete representations of surfaces, usually consisting of triangle meshes, called *triangulated*, or *polyhedral surfaces*. Metric properties of such surfaces have to be described in a discrete coherent way since they are usually known for smooth surfaces. From this point of view, many numerical methods are proposed in the literature, which often present problems in error control and estimation, and often have a high computational complexity.

Curvature plays a crucial role to understand the geometry and the topology of a surface. For analytic surfaces, the mathematical background is well developed [9], [16]. We find, thus, notions of geodesic, normal, principal, mean, Gaussian and total curvatures. All of them give a precise description of the local geometric shape of a surface in any direction.

In the discrete case, Gaussian curvature is generally estimated, according to the Gauss-Bonnet theorem, by computing the total angle at a vertex and by

P. Foggia, C. Sansone, and M. Vento (Eds.): ICIAP 2009, LNCS 5716, pp. 652–661, 2009.
© Springer-Verlag Berlin Heidelberg 2009

dividing it by the area of its neighborhood (see, for instance, [17]). All existing methods have approximation errors and many of them suffer from the convergence problem due to the choice of the neighborhood. This means that the curvature values strongly depend on the area of the local neighborhood of a point, and diverge generally when the area goes to 0 (by refining the mesh for example). The scale of curvature values depends generally on the method used. Moreover, those methods do not give importance the (local) geometric shape of the surface, while curvature is strongly related to it in the smooth case. Concentrated curvature [11], known also as the angle deficit method, is based only on angles estimation, and, thus, has many advantages: curvature values have a natural meaning, are accurate and simple to compute. Furthermore, concentrated curvature describes the global topology of the surfaces via a discrete equivalent version of Gauss-Bonnet theorem generally known for the smooth case. On the other hand, concentrated curvature does not describe the local geometric shape of the surface.

Mean curvature generally serves to identify some local geometric characteristics of the surfaces, namely ridges and ravines. Moreover, the combination of mean curvature combined and Gaussian curvature identifies morphological characteristics of the surface, such as convex and concave regions. A local geometric classification of points based on the sign of both Gaussian and mean curvature is presented in [16].

In a recent work [12], the authors have introduced a new notion, called *discrete distortion*, which is a local discrete approach to Ricci curvature for three-dimensional combinatorial manifolds. Discrete distortion has promising applications in many scientific fields (medical imagery, particle physics, general relativity, engineering mechanics,...). For three-dimensional manifolds with boundary, discrete distortion provides a new tool to explore the local geometry of surfaces viewed as boundary components of the 3-manifold.

The purpose of this work is to show that discrete distortion can be used as a tool for estimating mean curvature for triangulated surfaces. Specifically, distortion can be used to explore the morphology of a surface and to identify some of its features, such as ridges, ravines, convex and concave regions.

The remainder of this paper is organized as follows. In Section 2, we discuss related work on curvature estimation. In Section 3, we review fundamental notions related to discrete Gaussian and mean curvature and some notions related to spherical geometry. In Section 4, we recall the notions of discrete vertex and bond distortions for surfaces, and some of their properties. In Section 5, we investigate relations between discrete distortion and mean curvature. In Section 6, we present experimental results illustrating the behavior of distortion, and we compare it with a widely used mean curvature estimator. In Section 7, we draw some concluding remarks, and discuss our current and future work.

2 Related Work

Two major approaches exist in the literature to estimate curvature over triangulated surfaces: *analytic methods* and *discrete methods* [8]. Analytic approaches consist of interpolating over the vertices of the triangle mesh through smooth functions (generally quadratic functions) and of computing the curvature analytically on the resulting smooth approximation [7]. Analytic methods seem to perform quite well, but are computationally intensive, and, thus, not suitable for large-size triangulated surfaces.

Discrete approaches are numerous. They basically use discretization of derivatives of Gauss-Bonnet formula, or of Euler formula. Linearization of first and second derivatives is used in the first discrete approach to approximate, with some error estimates, curvature values [10]. Issues related to discrete approaches are error estimation and control, convergence problems over small areas or irregular meshes (see [8], [11], [13] for more details and discussion).

Concentrated curvature has been recently used by some authors [1,2] under the name of angle deflection and in [11] to define a discrete approximation of Gaussian curvature. In [11] a comparative study with the deficit angle method, mostly used in literature, has been performed. A purely combinatorial approach to concentrated curvature has been introduced in [3].

3   Background Notions

In this Section, we briefly review some notions related to discrete curvature and spherical geometry necessary for developing the material of this paper.

3.1   Discrete Mean Curvature

In computer graphics, smooth surfaces are approximated by discrete models, like clouds of points or triangle meshes. In mathematics, curvature is defined for smooth surfaces that are at least C^2 continuous. Hence, strictly speaking, curvature is not defined in the discrete case. In practice, techniques exist which provide curvature estimates for discrete surfaces. When the surface is represented by a triangle mesh, curvature at internal points of triangles has a null value. At points on triangulation edges, or at vertices, different methods exist to estimate the Gaussian and the mean curvatures. As discussed in Section 2, many problems exist for those methods which involve the area of a neighborhood of a point. A good, area-independent, alternative is presented in [11]. This curvature estimator is called, originally in mathematics [18], *concentrated curvature*.

Concentrated curvature at a vertex p is equal to the total curvature of a spherical cap approximating the surface, from its interior, around p. This quantity is expressed by means of the total angle at p. Thus, it is independent of the radius of the local neighborhood at p and hence of its area. Moreover, it has been shown that it satisfies a discrete version of Gauss-Bonnet theorem. Based on the idea of angle estimation, discrete distortion has been introduced in [12] for three-dimensional combinatorial manifolds. Its restriction to boundary surfaces is the purpose of this work.

In the discrete case, mean curvature at a vertex p of a polyhedral surface is usually defined [13] by

$$|H| = \tfrac{1}{4|A|} \sum_{i=1}^{n} \|\vec{e_i}\| |\beta_i|,$$ (1)

where $|A|$ is the the area of the Voronoi or barycentric region around p, e_i is one of the n edges incident in p, and β_i is the angle between the normal vectors of the two faces sharing edge e_i. If we denote with Θ_i the dihedral angle at e_i, then angle β_i is the supplementary angle of Θ_i, and Formula 1 becomes

$$|H| = \tfrac{1}{4|A|} \sum_{i=1}^{n} \|\vec{e_i}\| |\pi - \Theta_i|. \tag{2}$$

This formula can be justified as follows. Suppose that we want to approximate the surface at an edge e by a cylindric cap of radius r tangent to the surface from its interior at the faces adjacent to e. The total curvature of the circle arc generating the cap is equal to the absolute value of the supplementary angle β of the dihedral angle Θ at e (cf. [19] for a proof) and does not depend on the radius r. The curvature of any generating edge is null. Then the mean curvature at a point of the cylindrical cap is equal to $\frac{|\beta|+0}{2}$. Hence, the total mean curvature of the cylindrical cap is equal to $\frac{|\beta|}{2}$ multiplied by the length of the generating edge e. In general, the surrounding neighborhood of a vertex is taken to be the Voronoi area or the barycentric area around the vertex. Then only half of the incident edges of p are considered. This explain Formula 2.

However, there are two issues with the use of Formula 2 for a mean curvature estimator. The first issue is that its value depends on the length of the edges incident in vertex v, and thus it is area-dependent. The second issue is that such value is always positive since only absolute values are taken. This implies, for example, that the mean curvature of a saddle surface is always non-negative, which is clearly not true for analytic surfaces.

3.2   Spherical Geometry

Here, we briefly review some notions related to spherical geometry needed to introduce the notion of distortion.

Let T be a tetrahedron in the Euclidean space R^3. We refer to Figure 1. Let O be one of the four vertices of T. We consider the unit sphere centered at O, and the intersection points A, B, and C of the supporting half-lines of the three edges of T emanating from O. The trihedral angle, also called the *solid angle*, at O corresponds to the area of the spherical triangle ABC obtained from the intersection of the unit sphere centered at O with the cone $\prec (OABC)$. The trihedral angle at O is given by the formula

$$\widehat{A} + \widehat{B} + \widehat{C} - \pi, \tag{3}$$

where $\widehat{A}$, $\widehat{B}$, $\widehat{C}$, are the dihedral angles at vertices A, B and C. This formula is known to be *Girard's theorem* [14].

The dihedral angle between two adjacent faces is the supplementary of the angle between their normal vectors. It can easily be proven that a dihedral angle, without loss of generality let us say the one formed by the two faces incident in the edge containing A, that we denote with $\widehat{A}$, can be obtained by the following relation:

$$\cos(\widehat{A}) = \frac{\cos a - \cos b \cos c}{\sin b \sin c}, \tag{4}$$

where a, b and c are respectively the angles at O of the tetrahedron faces OBC, OCA and OAB, i.e., the lengths of the corresponding spherical arcs on the unit sphere. Each of them can be obtained from the inner product of the corresponding vectors.

Other trigonometric relations are available for spherical triangles [15].

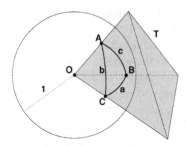

Fig. 1. Tetrahedron T, the unit sphere centered at vertex O of T, the spherical triangle ABC, and the three spherical arcs a, b, c

4   Discrete Distortion

In this Section, we discuss the notion of distortion for triangulated surfaces with some of its properties (see [12] for more details).

Let p be a vertex in a triangulated surface Σ. *Vertex distortion* at p is defined by the quantity

$$D(p) = 2\pi - S_p, \tag{5}$$

where S_p is the solid angle at p.

Similarly for each edge e of the mesh *Bond distortion* of edge e, is the quantity $\overline{D}(e)$ defined by

$$\overline{D}(e) = \pi - \Theta_e, \tag{6}$$

where Θ_e is the dihedral angle at edge e.

Theorem 1. *Vertex distortion at a vertex p is the sum of all bond distortions around edges incident to p. We have*

$$D(p) = \sum_{e \in St(p)} (\pi - \Theta_e), \tag{7}$$

where $St(p)$ is the one-ring neighborhood of p.

Note that, for the interior points of the triangles, the distortion is null since the area of spherical caps are semi-Euclidean spheres. For a point in the interior of an edge e, the spherical cap is a sphere segment delimited by the two faces adjacent to e. Its area is equal to twice the dihedral angle Θ at e. Thus, distortion of such points is given by

$$D(p) = 2(\pi - \Theta_e) = 2\overline{D}(e). \tag{8}$$

5   Discrete Distortion as a Mean Curvature Estimator

Let S be a smooth surface (at least C^2). Let p be a point of S and $S(p,r)$ be a sphere centered at p of radius $r > 0$. Surface S cuts $S(p,r)$ into two parts. Let $A(p,r)$ be the area of the cap contained within the internal volume of S. For r sufficiently small, the quantity

$$C(p,r) = \frac{A(p,r)}{r^2} \qquad (9)$$

is the value of the *Connolly function* at (p,r). This function has been introduced by Connolly in the seventies to study knobs and depressions of molecular shapes [4]. In the smooth case, for small values of r, this quantity is equivalent to 2π since the spherical cap converges to the half sphere located above the tangent plane. However, the convergence speed is proportional to the mean curvature as shown in the following Lemma:

Lemma 1 [4]. *There exists a C^∞ function ϵ defined on $S \times R^+$ such that ϵ tends to 0 when r goes to 0 and*

$$C(p,r) = 2\pi + \pi H(p)r + r^2\epsilon(p,r) \qquad (10)$$

where $H(p)$ is the mean curvature of S at p.

In the discrete case, for each vertex $p \in S$, there exists r_0 such that the intersection of the spheres $\left(S(p,r)\right)_{r \leq r_0}$ with surface S is located within the 1-ring neighborhood $St(p)$ of p and the Connolly function is constant. Then $D(p) = 2\pi - C(p,r)$ for any $r \leq r_0$. Combining this idea with Lemma 1, Connolly function (and thus distortion) can be used to estimate mean curvature values as explained below.

Under the assumptions of Lemma 1, the quantity $D(p,r) := 2\pi - C(p,r)$ at p is equal to

$$D(p,r) = -\pi H(p)r - r^2\epsilon(p,r) \qquad (11)$$

Specifically, for a fixed r

$$Grad_p(D) = -\pi r Grad_p(H) - r^2 Grad(\epsilon(p,r)) \qquad (12)$$

Formulas 11 and 12 allow us to find those points p for which $D(p,r)$ vanishes and the critical points of $D(p,r)$. Indeed, Formula 11 implies that, if $H(p) = 0$, then the values of $D(p,r)/r$ are close to 0 for sufficiently small r. This means that points with a null mean curvature are located in regions for which $D(p,r)/r$, and, hence, $D(p,r)$ is sufficiently close to 0. Conversely, if $D(p,r) = 0$, then Formula 11 gives $H(p) = \frac{r}{\pi}\epsilon(p,r)$, and this quantity is close to 0 if r is sufficiently small. Thus, points for which $D(p,r)$ vanishes are located in regions of small mean curvature.

Similar conclusions can be obtained from Formula 12, to find the critical points of $D(p,r)$ and $H(p)$ (i.e., points p for which $Grad_p(D) = 0$ and point p for which $Grad_p(H) = 0$).

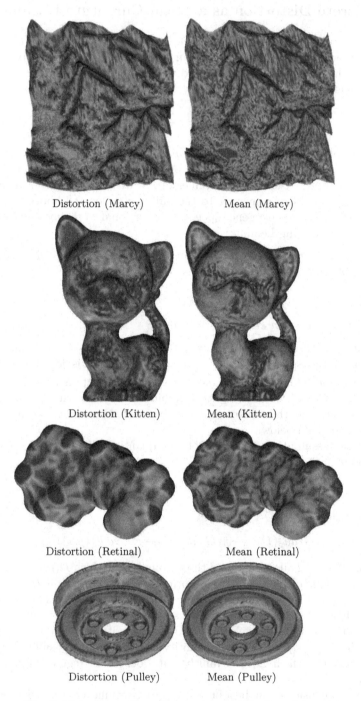

Distortion (Marcy)   Mean (Marcy)

Distortion (Kitten)   Mean (Kitten)

Distortion (Retinal)   Mean (Retinal)

Distortion (Pulley)   Mean (Pulley)

Fig. 2. Distortion and mean curvature on the four data sets

In the discrete case, where values can be considered as null for values of r below a certain threshold, theses properties allow localizing minimal surfaces (i.e., regions with null mean curvature), ravine and ridge regions by means of our discrete distortion. Furthermore, discrete distortion serves also to characterize convex and concave regions. Convex regions have positive distortion values, while concave regions have negative distortion values.

6   Experimental Results

We have implemented an algorithm that computes discrete distortion for surfaces. Here, we present experimental results to compare the behavior of discrete distortion and that of the mean curvature estimator expressed by Formula 2. We compare distortion and mean curvature on real data:

- Marcy (terrain, 128×128 vertices).
- Kitten (3D surface of a statue, 11039 vertices)
- Retinal (3D surface of a molecule, 3643 vertices)
- Pulley (3D surface of a mechanical piece, 25482 vertices)

We acknowledge Frederic Cazals for the Retinal mesh. The other three meshes are from the Aim at Shape Repository (`http://shapes.aim-at-shape.net/`).

In Figure 2 a rainbow-like color scale is used to map values: the minimum value of each measure is mapped to violet, the maximum value to magenta, and six intermediate values are mapped into blue, cyan, green, yellow, orange, and red.

Distortion seems better than the mean curvature estimator, in adapting smoothly to describe surface shape. It is less sensitive to noise in the data, and more effective in enhancing concave and convex areas. Note that the pulley mesh is not a CAD model but the result of scanning a real piece; distortion performs better in enhancing parts where the surface become irregular after long use.

As expected, both measures give large value to convex parts (peaks / ridges) and small values to concave parts (pits / ravines) of the terrain.

7   Concluding Remarks

We have presented the notion of discrete distortion for triangulated surfaces. We showed that distortion can be used as a good estimator of mean curvature. We discussed some issues related with the classical definition of discrete mean curvature mostly used in literature, and we showed that discrete distortion is more reliable. We have presented experimental results to illustrate the behavior of distortion and compare it with a mostly used discrete mean curvature estimator.

Our algorithm for computing discrete distortion can be used to simplify the algorithm in [4] that evaluates the Connolly function. The properties of discrete distortion make it suitable for use in many applications, such as physics of particles and chemistry. We are currently working on an algorithm that optimizes a triangulation using distortion as a metric. The optimized triangulation can be used to prove some properties that we conjecture for chemical reactions. It can also be used to for surface smoothing as discussed in [5].

Acknowledgments

This work has been partially supported by the National Science Foundation under grant CCF-0541032 and by the MIUR-FIRB project SHALOM under contract number RBIN04HWR8.

References

1. Alboul, L., Echeverria, G., Rodrigues, M.A.: Discrete Curvatures and Gauss Maps for Polyhedral Surfaces. In: Workshop on Computational Geometry, The Netherlands (2005)
2. Akleman, E., Chen, J.: Practical Polygonal Mesh Modeling with Discrete Gaussian-Bonnet Theorem. In: Proceedings of Geometry, Modeling and Processing, Pittsburg (2006)
3. Baues, O., Peyerimho, N.: Geodesics in non-positively curved plane tessellations. Advanced in Geometry 6, 243–263 (2006)
4. Cazals, F., Chazal, F., Lewiner, T.: Molecular Shape Analysis based upon the Morse-Smale Complex and the Connoly Function. In: Proceedings of SoCG 2003 (2003)
5. Dyn, N., Hormann, K., Sun-Jeong, K., Levin, D.: Optimizing 3D Triangulations Using Discrete Curvature Analysis. In: Oslo, T.L., Schumaker, L.L. (eds.) Mathematical Methods for Curves and Surfaces, pp. 135–146 (2000)
6. Eisenhart, L.P.: Riemannian geometry. Princeton Univ. Press, Princeton (1949)
7. Garimella, R.V., Swartz, B.K.: Curvature Estimation for Unstructured Triangulations of Surfaces. Los Alamos National Laboratory LA-03-8240 (2003)
8. Gatzke, T.D., Grimm, C.M.: Estimating Curvature on Triangular Meshes. International Journal on shape Modeling 12, 1–29 (2006)
9. Gray, A.: Modern Differential Geometry of Curves and Surfaces Introduction to Computer Graphics. CRC Press, Boca Raton (1993)
10. Mangan, A., Whitaker, R., Partitioning, R.: Partitioning 3D Surface Meshes Using Watershed Segmentation. IEEE Transaction on Visualization and Computer Graphics 5(4), 308–321 (1999)
11. Mesmoudi, M.M., De Floriani, L., Danovaro, E., Port, U.: Surface Segmentation through Concentrated Curvature. In: Proceedings of International Conference on Image Analysis and Processing, vol. 1, pp. 671–676. IEEE Computer Society, Los Alamitos (2007)
12. Mesmoudi, M.M., De Floriani, L., Port, U.: Distortion in Triangulated 3-Manifolds. Computer Graphics Forum (the International Journal of the EUROGRAPHICS Association) 27(5), 1333–1340 (2008)
13. Meyer, M., Desbrun, M., Schroder, P., Barr, A.: Discrete differential-geometry operator for triangulated 2-manifolds. In: Proceedings of VisMath 2002, Berlin, Germany (2002)
14. The area of a spherical triangle, Girard's Theorem,
    http://math.rice.edu/~pcmi/sphere/gos4.htm

15. Rousseau, J.-J., Gibaud, A.: Cristallographie Géométrique et Radiocristallographie. Dunod edn. (2007)
16. Spivak, M.: A comprehensive introduction to differential Geometry. Houston Texas (1979)
17. Stokely, E.M., Wu, S.Y.: Surface parametrization and curvature measurement of arbitrary 3-d objects: Five pratical methods. In: IEEE Transactions on pattern analysis and machine Intelligence, pp. 833–839 (1992)
18. Troyanov, M.: Les Surfaces Euclidiennes à Singularités Coniques. L'enseignement Mathématique 32, 79–94 (1986)
19. Port, U.: Shape Segmentation Algorithms Based on Curvature. Master Thesis, University of Genova, Italy (2007)

Webcam-Based Visual Gaze Estimation

Roberto Valenti[1], Jacopo Staiano[1], Nicu Sebe[2], and Theo Gevers[1]

[1] Faculty of Science, University of Amsterdam, The Netherlands
{rvalenti,staiano,gevers}@science.uva.nl
[2] University of Trento, Italy
sebe@disi.unitn.it

Abstract. In this paper we combine a state of the art eye center locator and a new eye corner locator into a system which estimates the visual gaze of a user in a controlled environment (e.g. sitting in front of a screen). In order to reduce to a minimum the computational costs, the eye corner locator is built upon the same technology of the eye center locator, tweaked for the specific task. If high mapping precision is not a priority of the application, we claim that the system can achieve acceptable accuracy without the requirements of additional dedicated hardware. We believe that this could bring new gaze based methodologies for human-computer interactions into the mainstream.

1 Introduction

Eye location and tracking and the related visual gaze estimation are important tasks in many computer vision applications and research [1]. Some of the most common examples are the application to user attention and gaze in driving and marketing scenarios, and control devices for disabled people. Eye location/tracking techniques can be divided into three distinct modalities [2]: (1) Electro oculography, which records the electric potential differences of the skin surrounding the ocular cavity; (2) scleral contact lens/search coil, which uses a mechanical reference mounted on a contact lens, and (3) photo/video oculography, which uses image processing techniques to locate the center of the eye. Unfortunately, the common problem of the above techniques is the use of intrusive and expensive sensors [3]. While photo/video oculography is considered the least invasive of the modalities, commercially available trackers still require the user to be either equipped with a head mounted device, or to use a high resolution camera combined with a chinrest to limit the allowed head movement. Furthermore, daylight applications are precluded due to the common use of active infrared (IR) illumination, used to obtain accurate eye location through corneal reflection. Non infrared appearance based eye locators [4,5,6,7,8,9,10,11] can successfully locate eye regions, yet are unable to track eye movements accurately.

The goal of this paper is to present a way to map eye gaze patterns on a screen. These patterns are detected based on a few ingredients: (1) an eye tracker that can quickly and accurately locate and track eye centers and eye corners in low

P. Foggia, C. Sansone, and M. Vento (Eds.): ICIAP 2009, LNCS 5716, pp. 662–671, 2009.
© Springer-Verlag Berlin Heidelberg 2009

resolution images and videos (i.e., coming from a simple web cam); (2) a scale space framework that gives scale invariance to the eye center and eye corners localization; and (3) a mapping mechanism that maps eye and corner locations to screen coordinates.

2   Isocenters Estimation

The isophotes of an image are curves connecting points of equal intensity. Since isophotes do not intersect each other, an image can be fully described by its isophotes. Furthermore, the shape of the isophotes is independent to rotation and linear lighting changes [12]. To better illustrate the well known isophote framework, it is opportune to introduce the notion of intrinsic geometry, i.e., geometry with a locally defined coordinate system. In every point of the image, a local coordinate frame is fixed in such a way that it points in the direction of the maximal change of the intensity, which corresponds to the direction of the gradient. This reference frame $\{v, w\}$ is referred to as the *gauge coordinates*. Its frame vectors $\hat{w}$ and $\hat{v}$ are defined as:

$$\hat{w} = \frac{\{L_x, L_y\}}{\sqrt{L_x^2 + L_y^2}}; \hat{v} = \perp \hat{w};$$ (1)

where L_x and L_y are the first-order derivatives of the luminance function $L(x, y)$ in the x and y dimension, respectively. In this setting, a derivative in the w direction is the gradient itself, and the derivative in the v direction (perpendicular to the gradient) is 0 (no intensity change along the isophote). In this coordinate system, an isophote is defined as $L(v, w(v)) = constant$ and its curvature κ is defined as the change w'' of the tangent vector w' which in Cartesian coordinates becomes [13,14,15]:

$$\kappa = -\frac{L_{vv}}{L_w} = -\frac{L_y^2 L_{xx} - 2L_x L_{xy} L_y + L_x^2 L_{yy}}{(L_x^2 + L_y^2)^{3/2}}.$$ (2)

Since the curvature is the reciprocal of the radius, we can reverse Eq. (2) to obtain the radius of the circle that generated the curvature of the isophote. The radius is meaningless if it is not combined with orientation and direction. The orientation can be estimated from the gradient, but its direction will always point towards the highest change in the luminance. However, the sign of the isophote curvature depends on the intensity of the outer side of the curve (for a brighter outer side the sign is positive). Thus, by multiplying the gradient with the inverse of the isophote curvature, the duality of the isophote curvature helps in disambiguating the direction of the center. Since the gradient can be written as $\frac{\{L_x, L_y\}}{L_w}$, we have:

$$D(x, y) = \frac{\{L_x, L_y\}}{L_w} \left(-\frac{L_w}{L_{vv}}\right) = -\frac{\{L_x, L_y\}}{L_{vv}}$$

$$= -\frac{\{L_x, L_y\}(L_x^2 + L_y^2)}{L_y^2 L_{xx} - 2L_x L_{xy} L_y + L_x^2 L_{yy}}.$$ (3)

where $D(x, y)$ are the displacement vectors to the estimated position of the centers, which can be mapped into an accumulator, hereinafter *"centermap"*. Since every vector gives a rough estimate of the center, we can convolve the accumulator with a Gaussian kernel so that each cluster of votes will form a single center estimate. Furthermore, the contribution of each vector can be weighted according to a relevance mechanism. The main idea is that by collecting and averaging local evidence of curvature, the discretization problems in a digital image could be lessened and accurate center estimation could be achieved.

In order to achieve this goal, only the parts of the isophotes which are meaningful for our purposes should be used, that is, the ones that follow the edges of an object. This selection can be performed by using the curvedness [16]:

$$curvedness = \sqrt{L_{xx}^2 + 2L_{xy}^2 + L_{yy}^2}. \tag{4}$$

We note that the curvedness has low response on flat surfaces and edges, whereas it yields high response in places where the isophote density is maximal. As observed before, the isophote density is maximal around the edges of an object, meaning that by selecting the parts of the isophotes where the curvedness is maximal, they will likely follow an object boundary and locally agree on the same center. The advantage of this approach over a pure edge based method is that, by using the curvedness as the voting scheme for the importance of the vote, every pixel in the image may contribute to a decision. By summing the votes, we obtain high response on isocentric isophotes patterns which respect the constraint of being near edges. We call these high responses *"isocenters"*, or ICs.

3   Eye Center Location

Recalling that the sign of the isophote curvature depends on the intensity of the outer side of the curve, we observe that a negative sign indicates a change in the direction of the gradient (i.e., from brighter to darker areas). Therefore, it is possible to discriminate between dark and bright centers by analyzing the sign of the curvature. Regarding the specific task of cornea and iris location, it can be assumed that the sclera is brighter than the cornea and the iris, so we should ignore the votes in which the curvature is positive, that is, where it agrees with the direction of the gradient. As a consequence, the maximum isocenter (MIC) obtained will represent the estimated center of the eye. The result of this procedure on an eye image is shown in Figure 1. From the 3D plot it is clear where the MIC is, but we can expect that certain lighting conditions and occlusions from the eyelids to result in a wrong eye center estimate. To cope with this problem, we use the mean shift algorithm for density estimation. Mean shift (MS) usually operates on back-projected images in which probabilities are assigned to pixels based on the color probability distribution of a target,

Fig. 1. The source image, the obtained centermap and the 3D representation of the latter

weighted by a spatial kernel over pixel locations. It then finds the local maximum of this distribution by gradient ascent [17]. Here, the mean shift procedure is directly applied to the centermap resulting from our method, under the assumption that the most relevant isocenter should have higher density of votes, and that wrong MICs are not so distant from the correct one (e.g., on an eye corner). A mean shift search window is initialized on the centermap, centered on the found MIC. The algorithm then iterates to converge to a region with maximal votes distribution. After some iteration, the isocenter closest to the center of the search window is selected as the new eye center estimate.

An extensive evaluation of the eye locator was performed in [15], testing the eye locator for robustness to illumination and pose changes, for accurate eye location in low resolution images and for eye tracking in low resolution videos. The comparison with the state of the art suggested that the method is able to achieve highest accuracy, but this is somewhat bounded by the presence of a symmetrical pattern in the image.

Figure 2 qualitatively shows some of the results obtained on different subjects of the BioID database. The dataset consists of 1521 grayscale images of 23 different subjects and has been taken in different locations and at different times of the day (i.e., uncontrolled illumination). We observe that the method successfully deals with slight changes in pose, scale, and presence of glasses (second row). By analyzing the failures (last row) it can be observed that the system is prone to errors when presented with closed eyes, very bright eyes, or strong highlights on the glasses. When these cases occur, the iris and cornea do not contribute enough to the center voting, so the eyebrows or the eye corners assume a position of maximum relevance.

4   Eye Corner Location

Unfortunately the eye center location is not enough for visual gaze estimation: there is a need for an accurate fixed point (or anchor point) in order to be able to measure successive displacements of the eye center independently of the face position. The common approach is to locate the position of the eyelids and

Fig. 2. Sample of success and failures (last row) on the BioID face database; a white dot represents the estimated center

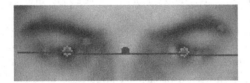

Fig. 3. Eye centers and corner candidates

the eye corners [18,19]. A fast and inexpensive way to locate such an anchor is to reuse the obtained centermap. As stated before, by analyzing the results of the eye locator we note that the largest number of mistakes in eye-center location are located on eye corners. This is due to the fact that the eye corners have a somewhat symmetrical structure: in blurred low resolution imagery, the junction between the eyelashes creates an almost circular dark structure which is in contrast with the brighter skin and the sclera and therefore receives higher response than the rest of the features. In this way we can exploit this problem to our advantage. Figure 3 shows the highest ICs obtained. Once the eye center is selected by the mean shift we can apply some geometrical constraints to find the most stable anchor. Experimentally, the external eye corner turned out to be the most stable isocenter. In order to find them we look for the furthest away isocenter that lays closer to the line created by connecting the two eye centers (shown in red in Figure 3). While this assumption is reasonable and showed quite stable results (see Figure 4), the process is bound to fail every time that the eye locator fails (last image in Figure 4). This problem could be solved by enforcing additional constrains on the movement.

Fig. 4. Examples of combined eye center (green) and eye corner (red) detection

5   Scale Space Framework

Although the proposed approach is invariant to rotation and linear illumination changes, it still suffers from changes in scale. While in the previous work [15] the scale problem was solved by exhaustively searching for the scale value that obtained the best overall results, here we want to gain scale independence in order to avoid adjustments to the parameters for different situations. Firstly, since the sampled eye region depends on the scale of the detected face and on the camera

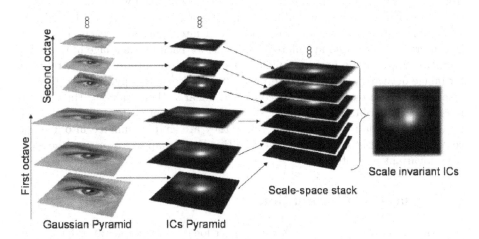

Fig. 5. The scale space framework applied to eye location: the grayscale image is downscaled to different octaves, each octave is divided into intervals. For each intervals, the centermap is computed and upscaled to a reference size to obtain a scale space stack. The combination of the obtained results gives the scale invariant isocenters.

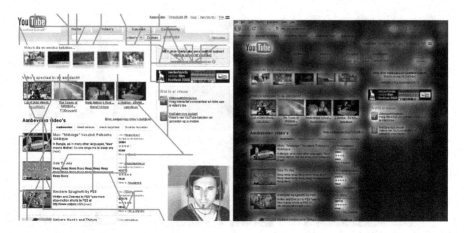

Fig. 6. Mapped visual gaze on an internet page and the associated heat map

resolution, to improve scale independency each eye region is scaled to a reference window. While this technique is expected to slightly decrease the accuracy with respect to the standard approach (due to interpolation artifacts), once the correct scale values are found for the chosen reference window, the algorithm can be applied at different scales without requiring an exhaustive parameter search. Furthermore, to increase robustness and accuracy, a scale space framework is used to select the isocenters that are stable across multiple scales.

The algorithm is applied to an input image at different scales and the outcome is analyzed for stable results. To this end, a Gaussian pyramid is constructed from the original grayscale image. The image is convolved with different Gaussians so that they are separated by a constant factor in scale space. In order to save computation, the image is downsampled into octaves. In each octave the isocenters are calculated at different intervals: for each of the image in the pyramid, the proposed method is applied by using the appropriate σ as a parameter for image derivatives. This procedure results in a isocenters pyramid (Figure 5). The responses in each octave are combined linearly, then scaled to the original reference size to obtain a scalespace stack. Every element of the scale space stack is considered equally important therefore they are simply summed into a single centermap. The highest peaks in the resulting centermap will represent the most scale invariant isocenters.

6   Visual Gaze Estimation

Now that we have the eye center and corner location available, in order to correctly estimate visual gaze it would be reasonable to consider the head position and orientation to give a rough initialization of the visual gaze, and then use the information about the eye centers and corners to fine tune the information. Unfortunately, head pose estimators often involve many assumptions in order to achieve a realistic modeling (i.e. the shape and size of the head, the possible rotation angles of the eye, etc.). Furthermore, the high computational requirements of head pose estimators are not in line with the lightweight requirements of our system. Finally small mistakes in pose estimation might introduce additional errors in the final visual gaze estimation. Other methods tend to simplify the problem by assuming that the eye does not rotate but it just shifts. This assumption is reflected in commercial eye trackers, which deal with high resolution images of the eyes. This simplification comes from the assumption that the face is always frontal to the screen so the head pose information can be discarded. Therefore, we used the linear mapping method suggested by [19] and the user needs to perform a calibration procedure by looking at several known points on the screen. A 2D linear mapping is then constructed from the vector between the eye corner and the iris center and recorded at the known position on the screen. This vector is then used to interpolate between the known screen locations. For example, if we have two calibration points P_1 and P_2 with screen coordinates α and β, and eye-center vector (taken with origin from the anchor point) x and y, we can interpolate a new reading of the eye-center vector to obtain the screen coordinates by using the following interpolant:

$$\alpha = \alpha_1 + \frac{x - x_1}{x_2 - x_1}(\alpha_2 - \alpha_1) \tag{5}$$

$$\beta = \beta_1 + \frac{y - y_1}{y_2 - y_1}(\beta_2 - \beta_1) \tag{6}$$

The advantage of this approach is its low computational cost and a decent accuracy with respect to more complex systems. In fact the reported error introduced by this approximation is just $1.2°$. Unfortunately, this method does not allow for large head movements, so the user will need to recalibrate in case of big horizontal or vertical shifts. However, in our case the distance from the screen and the camera parameters are known. So, we can compensate for this problem by remapping the calibration points accordingly with the registered displacement of the eyes. Therefore the final accuracy of the system is bounded just by the number of pixels that the eye is allowed to move. This generates some kind of *grid effect* on the recorded eye locations that can be seen in Figure 6.

While the final accuracy is bounded by the quality of the camera and the distance from it, we still believe that the system can be used for specific applications that do not require high level of accuracy (like changing the focused window or scrolling when looking outside the boundaries of the screen). The final outcome of the system can be visualized as a heat map (see Figure 6) which indicates the gaze patterns of the user. As can be seen from the figure our main goal is to use the system for qualitative investigation of the user interest while browsing a webpage and as such it is sufficient if we correctly identify the major sections of the webpage.

In order to evaluate the performance of our system, we asked 20 subjects to perform a simple task while looking at a webpage. The subjects were instructed to look and fixate at all the images displayed on a YouTube webpage (an example layout of such a page is displayed in Figure 6) starting from the higher left one and continuing to the right and below. We recorded the coordinates of their fixation and we checked if they fall within the corresponding image area. For such a simple task we obtained 95% accuracy.

In order to give the reader an idea of how our system is really working and its capabilities we have recorded two videos which can be accessed at:

http://www.science.uva.nl/~rvalenti/downloads/tracker.wmv
http://www.science.uva.nl/~rvalenti/downloads/tracking.avi

7   Conclusions

In this paper, we extended a method to infer eye center location to eye corner detection. Both eye center and eye corner can be detected at same time, do not require significant additional computation, and the detection can be scale invariant. We used the estimated locations to estimate the visual gaze of a user sitting in front of a screen. Although the accuracy of the system is bounded by the quality of the used webcam, we believe that the approximate gaze information can be useful for analyzing the gaze patterns of the subjects. The main advantage of our method is that is does not require any dedicated equipment, it does not use training which makes it very flexible, it is real-time, and it gives reasonable accuracy.

References

1. COGAIN: Communication by gaze interaction, gazing into the future (2006), http://www.cogain.org
2. Duchowski, A.T.: Eye Tracking Methodology: Theory and Practice. Springer, Heidelberg (2007)
3. Bates, R., Istance, H., Oosthuizen, L., Majaranta, P.: Survey of de-facto standards in eye tracking. In: COGAIN Conf. on Comm. by Gaze Inter. (2005)
4. Asteriadis, S., Nikolaidis, N., Hajdu, A., Pitas, I.: An eye detection algorithm using pixel to edge information. In: Int. Symp. on Control, Commun. and Sign. Proc. (2006)
5. Bai, L., Shen, L., Wang, Y.: A novel eye location algorithm based on radial symmetry transform. In: ICPR, pp. 511–514 (2006)
6. Campadelli, P., Lanzarotti, R., Lipori, G.: Precise eye localization through a general-to-specific model definition. In: BMVC (2006)
7. Cristinacce, D., Cootes, T.: Feature detection and tracking with constrained local models. In: BMVC (2006)
8. Cristinacce, D., Cootes, T., Scott, I.: A multi-stage approach to facial feature detection. In: BMVC, pp. 277–286 (2004)
9. Hamouz, M., Kittlerand, J., Kamarainen, J.K., Paalanen, P., Kalviainen, H., Matas, J.: Feature-based affine-invariant localization of faces. PAMI 27(9), 1490–1495 (2005)
10. Türkan, M., Pardás, M., Çetin, E.: Human eye localization using edge projection. In: Comp. Vis. Theory and App. (2007)
11. Zhou, Z.H., Geng, X.: Projection functions for eye detection. In: Pattern Recog., pp. 1049–1056 (2004)

12. Lichtenauer, J., Hendriks, E., Reinders, M.: Isophote properties as features for object detection. In: CVPR, vol. 2, pp. 649–654 (2005)
13. Dam, E.B., ter Haar Romeny, B.: Front End Vision and Multi-Scale Image Analysis. Kluwer, Dordrecht (2003)
14. van Ginkel, M., van de Weijer, J., van Vliet, L., Verbeek, P.: Curvature estimation from orientation fields. In: SCIA (1999)
15. Valenti, R., Gevers, T.: Accurate eye center location and tracking using isophote curvature. In: CVPR (June 2008)
16. Koenderink, J., van Doorn, A.J.: Surface shape and curvature scales. Image and Vision Computing, 557–565 (1992)
17. Comaniciu, D., Ramesh, V., Meer, P.: Kernel-based object tracking. PAMI 25(5), 564–577 (2003)
18. Zheng, Z., Yang, J., Yang, L.: A robust method for eye features extraction on color image. Pattern Recognition Letters 26, 2252–2261 (2005)
19. Zhu, J., Yang, J.: Subpixel eye gaze tracking. In: Face and Gesture Recogn. Conference, p. 131 (2002)

Real-Time Probabilistic Tracking
of Faces in Video

Giuseppe Boccignone, Paola Campadelli, Alessandro Ferrari, and Giuseppe Lipori

Dipartimento di Scienze dell'Informazione - Università degli Studi di Milano
via Comelico 39/41, 20135 Milano, Italy
{boccignone,campadelli,lipori}@dsi.unimi.it,
alessandro.ferrari3@studenti.unimi.it

Abstract. In this note it is discussed how real-time face detection and tracking in video can be achieved by relying on a Bayesian approach realized in a multi-threaded architecture. To this end we propose a probabilistic interpretation of the output provided by a cascade of AdaBoost classifiers. Results show that such integrated approach is appealing with respect either to robustness and computational efficiency.

1 Introduction

Face detection and tracking can be performed either according to a frame based approach (e.g., [1]) or according to a detection and tracking approach, where faces are detected in the first frame and tracked through the video sequence (for a review, refer to [2]). Clearly, in the first case, temporal information is not exploited, and the intrinsic independence among successive detections makes it difficult to reconstruct the *track* of each subject. In the second case a loss of information may occur (e.g., new faces entering the scene) and, in general, the output of face detection is used only at initialization, while tracking relies upon low level features (color histograms [3], contours [4], etc.) which are very sensitive to the conditions of acquisition. To overcome these drawbacks, a tighter coupling between face detection and tracking has been proposed [2]. Such an approach can be given a simple and elegant form in the Bayesian framework.

Each face is characterized at frame t of the video stream by a state vector $\mathbf{x}_t$, e.g., a face bounding box. The tracking goal is to estimate the correct state $\mathbf{x}_t$ given all the measurements $Z_t = \{z_1, \cdots, z_t\}$ up to that moment, or equivalently to construct the posterior probability density function (pdf) $p(\mathbf{x}_t \mid Z_t)$. The theoretically optimal solution is provided by recursive Bayesian filtering that in the *prediction* step uses the dynamic equation and the already computed pdf of the state at time $t-1$, $p(\mathbf{x}_{t-1} \mid Z_{t-1})$, to derive the prior pdf of the current state, $p(\mathbf{x}_t \mid Z_{t-1})$; then, in the *update* step, it employs the face likelihood function $p(z_t \mid x_t)$ of the current measurement to compute the posterior pdf $p(\mathbf{x}_t \mid z_t)$. Formally:

$$p(\mathbf{x}_t \mid Z_t) \propto p(z_t \mid \mathbf{x}_t) \int p(\mathbf{x}_t \mid \mathbf{x}_{t-1}) p(\mathbf{x}_{t-1} \mid Z_{t-1}) \mathrm{d}\mathbf{x}_{t-1}. \tag{1}$$

Thus, the key issue of a tight coupling approach is to provide a face detection algorithm suitable to calculate the face likelihood function $p(z_t \mid \mathbf{x}_t)$ and, if a Particle Filtering

P. Foggia, C. Sansone, and M. Vento (Eds.): ICIAP 2009, LNCS 5716, pp. 672–681, 2009.

(PF, [4]) implementation of Eq. 1 is adopted, to generate proper particle weighting. For instance, Verma et al. [2] adopt the Schneiderman and Kanade detector [5], which provides a suitable probabilistic output, but unfortunately is inadequate for real-time implementation.

A more appealing solution, which we propose here, could be the real-time face detection scheme proposed by Viola and Jones (VJ, [6]) - basically a cascade of AdaBoost classifiers - which is arguably the most commonly employed detection method [7]. Note that the combination of AdaBoost and PF has been proposed in [3], but detection results were heuristically combined in the proposal function, rather than being exploited to model a likelihood function in a principled way. In [8], PF is integrated with an AdaBoost monolithic classifier via the probabilistic interpretation given by Friedman et al. in [9]. Unfortunately tight coupling is spoiled by the introduction of a mean shift iteration, based on color features, to support the prediction of new hypotheses in adjacent regions.

Differently, we exploit the cascaded classifiers described in [10]. In this case, the probabilistic interpretation valid for monolithic classifiers does not apply directly; thus we work out a probabilistic interpretation of the VJ algorithm suitable to address Eq. 1 (Section 2).

Section 3 discusses the proposed PF implementation of Eq. 1 by defining the state parametrization and the adopted dynamical model. A PF may perform poorly when the posterior is multi-modal as the result of ambiguities or multiple targets, and issues such as appearance and disappearance of faces should be handled in a robust way. Interestingly enough, the latter issue, which is considered critical in PF based tracking, is very easily solved in human vision where multiple object tracking "runs" in parallel with background motion alerting processes capable of triggering, through pop-out effects, the tracking of new objects entering the scene and the loss of attention for disappearing objects. These problems have been tackled by incorporating such concurrency of processes in the system architecture. Experimental results and performance of the system are discussed in Section 4.

2   Face Likelihood: A Probabilistic View of Viola and Jones

AdaBoost classifiers are originally conceived for binary classification, attributing to an example $\mathbf{x}$ a label $y \in \{-1, 1\}$ according to the sign of the weighted sum $F(\mathbf{x}) = \sum_i w_i \cdot h_i(\mathbf{x})$, where h_i are the so called *weak classifiers* and w_i the associated weights. In our case a typical example is specified by a state vector $\mathbf{x} = \{x, y, width, height\}$ that indicates the location and size (in pixels) of a rectangular box surrounding the face. According to Friedman et al. [9], the following holds:

$$p(y = 1 \mid \mathbf{x}) = p\left(y = 1 \mid F(\mathbf{x})\right) = \frac{e^{F(\mathbf{x})}}{e^{F(\mathbf{x})} + e^{-F(\mathbf{x})}}. \tag{2}$$

In our interpretation, $p(z \mid \mathbf{x}) \simeq p(y = 1 \mid \mathbf{x})$ since the application of the face classifier is the means by which data are observed. Hence, for monolithic classifiers, Eq. 2 can be directly plugged in Eq. 1. Unfortunately, in case of a cascaded classifier, the likelihood estimate is not as immediate.

A cascaded classifier is obtained by chaining a set of monolithic classifiers or *stages* so to increase the specialization of the classifiers along the cascade. An example is classified as a positive if and only if it is judged so by all stages, while negative examples are discarded according to an *early reject* strategy. Along training, each stage falsely accepts a fixed ratio f of the non-face patterns in the training sample, while wrongly eliminating only a very small portion $1 - d$ of face patterns; formally:

$$p\left(F_i(\mathbf{x}) \geq 0 \mid F_{i-1}(\mathbf{x}) \geq 0, y = 1\right) = d \tag{3}$$

$$p\left(F_i(\mathbf{x}) \geq 0 \mid F_{i-1}(\mathbf{x}) \geq 0, y = -1\right) = f \tag{4}$$

where $F_i(\mathbf{x})$ is the weighted sum output by the i-th stage classifier, $i = 1, \ldots, k$, and k is the total number of stages. Denote F_i^+ the event $F_i(\mathbf{x}) \geq 0$ of positive classification at stage i and F_i^- the complementary event.

By applying the conditional rule of probability and recursively exploiting the Markovianity intrinsic to the cascade, the global detection and false acceptance rates of the trained cascade are easily derived as

$$d_g = p\left(F_k^+, \ldots, F_1^+ \mid y = 1\right) = d^k \tag{5}$$

$$f_g = p\left(F_k^+, \ldots, F_1^+ \mid y = -1\right) = f^k. \tag{6}$$

If the training examples are representative of the learning task, one could expect similar detection and false alarm rates also when applying the cascade to test examples.

We are interested in evaluating the likelihood of an example under the two possible outcomes of classification by the cascade, namely $p\left(y = 1 \mid F_k^+, \ldots, F_1^+\right)$ and $p\left(y = 1 \mid F_i^-, F_{i-1}^+, \ldots, F_1^+\right)$, $i = 1, \ldots, k$. By applying Bayes' rule, the conditional rule of probability, Markovianity and Eqs. 5 and 6:

$$p\left(y = 1 \mid F_k^+, \ldots, F_1^+\right) = \frac{p\left(F_k^+, \ldots, F_1^+ \mid y = 1\right) p(y = 1)}{\sum_{\bar{y} \in \{-1,1\}} p\left(F_k^+, \ldots, F_1^+ \mid y = \bar{y}\right) p(y = \bar{y})}$$

$$= \frac{d^k p(y = 1)}{d^k p(y = 1) + f^k p(y = -1)} \tag{7}$$

$$p\left(y = 1 \mid F_i^-, F_{i-1}^+, \ldots, F_1^+\right) = \frac{p\left(F_i^-, F_{i-1}^+ \ldots, F_1^+ \mid y = 1\right) p(y = 1)}{\sum_{\bar{y} \in \{-1,1\}} p\left(F_i^-, F_{i-1}^+, \ldots, F_1^+ \mid y = \bar{y}\right) p(y = \bar{y})}$$

$$= \frac{(1 - d)d^{i-1} p(y = 1)}{(1 - d)d^{i-1} p(y = 1) + (1 - f)f^{i-1} p(y = -1)} \tag{8}$$

The only unknown left is $p(y = 1)$, i.e. the probability of feeding the cascade with a true positive example; assuming once again that the cascade is applied to examples drawn according to the same distribution that generated the training set, one can force this value to the ratio between the cardinalities of the positive and negative classes in the training set.

It is worth spending some words about the assumption according to which the distributions over the training and test set are taken to be the same. On one side it is clear that this hypothesis does not hold strictly: it is sufficient to notice that, due to the nature of particle filtering, during tests many particles will be placed in the neighborhood of the face although not perfectly aligned with the pattern. Since the original training sample contains only perfectly aligned face regions, most of such particles are likely not to be classified as positives by a monolithic classifier. On the other hand, one can expect these examples to pass through a bigger number of stages (loosely inversely proportional to the degree of misplacement) with respect to true negative patterns, resulting in a higher likelihood and hence contributing to the correct estimation of the density distribution.

Moreover, the same issue applies also to particles generated under other circumstances which are not taken into account by the original training, such as out-of-plane rotations. One possible approach is that of [8], where out-of-plane rotations are embedded in the training set to extend the class of positives. In this spirit misalignment should be also included; we think that this approach would introduce too much variability for a learning technique which is based on Haar filter responses and is therefore highly dependent on the structure and relative arrangement of facial features.

In this work our interest is not that of fine tuning the face detector; instead, we intend to reuse the off-the-shelf detector described in [10] as a *plug-in* module into a PF scheme[1]. Rotations around the vertical axis are taken into account by means of combining the profile classifier; other out-of-plane rotations are considered in the same way as sequences of occlusions and treated as discussed in Section 4.

3   Face Tracking

Face tracking is accomplished via Particle Filtering [4]. The main idea of PF relies upon approximating the probability distribution by means of a set of weighted samples $S = \{(s^{(n)}, \pi^{(n)})\}$, $n = 1, \ldots, N$. A sample s represents a hypothetical state of the tracked object to which is associated a discrete sampled probability π, where $\sum_{n=1}^{N} \pi^{(n)} = 1$. The goal is to compute by sampling the posterior probability $p(s_t \mid Z_t)$ in place of $p(x_t \mid Z_t)$. That is, filtering is performed by rewriting Eq. 1 as $p(s_t \mid Z_t) \propto p(z_t \mid s_t) \int p(s_t \mid s_{t-1}) p(s_{t-1} \mid Z_{t-1}) ds_{t-1}$.

In our case $s_t = \{x, y, s, \theta\}$, where s is the side of the square face bounding box and θ indicates the face pose (rotation around the vertical axis) estimated as in [2] by interpolating the likelihood of the particle as measured by the frontal and profile classifier.

A filtering cycle starts with resampling S_{t-1} by extracting N particles with probability $\pi_{t-1}^{(n)}$ to populate the new set S_t, as described in [4]. Then prediction $p(s_t \mid s_{t-1})$ is obtained by diffusing each particle by a zero order dynamical model, with some adjustments w.r.t. [2]:

$$x_t = x_{t-1} + \mathcal{N}(0, \sigma_x^2) \cdot s_{t-1} \cdot \phi, \qquad y_t = y_{t-1} + \mathcal{N}(0, \sigma_y^2) \cdot s_{t-1} \cdot \phi$$

$$s_t = s_{t-1}(1.1)^{\lfloor 0.5 + \mathcal{N}(0, \sigma_s^2) \cdot \phi \rfloor}, \qquad \theta_t = \theta_{t-1} + \mathcal{N}(0, \sigma_\theta^2) \cdot \phi$$

---

[1] Any other classifier among those available in the OpenCV distribution for full, lower or upper body detection could be used equally well.

where σ_x and σ_y are percentage values to relate the diffusion to the particle size, and ϕ is a factor depending on the frame rate of acquisition. Subsequently, data observation is accomplished and the likelihood $p(z_t \mid \mathbf{s}_t)$ evaluated, as explained in Section 2. Eventually, the weighted mean state is computed as $\mu_{\mathbf{s}} = E[\mathbf{s}] = \sum_{n=1}^{N} \pi^{(n)} \mathbf{s}^{(n)}$, and this determines the estimated position of the face.

In principle, the original PF formulation [4] allows to track multi-target / multi-modal distributions. In practice, this requires to automatically identify and separate the different components (modes), ensuring that each has a sufficient number of particles to evolve correctly. To avoid this, we choose to keep the components separated by activating a different set of particles for every detected subject. To activate the PF cycle, initialization is triggered by a *motion detection* module [11], that executes as a background process (thread); the system stays in "stand-by" till a certain amount of motion is seen in the scene. In that case, the system runs a face detection scan over the regions which represent moving objects in order to locate the subjects, and then launches a new PF thread for each detected face. This mechanism allows to spare system resources by executing face detection only where and when needed, so avoiding periodic re-initialization as in [2] which would require exhaustive scans over the entire frame (all positions, all scales).

Once initialization is accomplished, all threads run in parallel. Similarly to [2], each sample of particles is constantly monitored in order to automatically detect when the face estimate looses track of the subject for some reason. In particular, a sufficient condition is whether the maximum likelihood over the sample is below a threshold p_{min} for more than N_1 of frames, or if the standard deviation over the sample of one of the state dimensions $\{x, y, s, \theta\}$ exceeds the corresponding threshold $\{x_{max}, y_{max}, s_{max}, \theta_{max}\}$ for more than N_2 of frames. In both cases, the PF thread tries to re-initialize the sample by performing face detection in a ROI including the recent movement of the subject; in case of failure for more than a certain number of trials, the thread exits and the sample dies out.

If desired, e.g. in situations where subjects can enter/exit only from outside the scene, the system can exploit a definition of *peripheral vision* to treat certain events such as the appearance of a new face in the scene, or the disappearance of a tracked face. The first situation takes place when the motion detector segments a blob of peripheral moving foreground with no intersection with the ROIs of existing trackers, therefore it is handled within the main thread by performing selective face detection on the blob to initialize a new PF thread. The second event involves a subject who is already being tracked, hence it is treated as a special case of track loss when the ROI including the recent movement of the subject terminated in the peripheral area of the frame. However, in more general scenarios where no assumption can be made about the entry/exit location of subjects (e.g. when monitoring a corridor), the notion of peripheral area can be disabled and all events are equally treated independently from their position, at the expenses of a minor increase in demand of computational resources.

The multi-threaded tracking system can run in two modalities: *unsynchronized* and *synchronized*. In the former, the main thread signals to the PF threads when a new frame is available from the streaming, but does not wait for them to complete execution of the filtering cycle. In case a PF thread loses one or more frames, it will adjust the prediction step by setting the diffusion parameter ϕ to the number of frames elapsed from the last cycle execution. In the synchronized case, the newly available frame is signaled only when all PFs have accomplished their task; this modality of execution can be simulated by a single-threaded system and will eventually slow down the global performance when several subjects are tracked simultaneously.

4 Experimental Setting and Results

Data set. We gathered two sets of short video sequences: 1) 16 validation sequences for tuning the main parameters 2) 5 test sequences to evaluate the global behavior of face tracking. The sequences have been shot in such a way to isolate the sources of variability, making the tuning of the different parameters as independent as possible. In particular, there are sequences of horizontal motion to tune σ_x, vertical motion for σ_y, motion in depth for σ_s, and sequences with face occlusions for p_{min}, x_{max}, y_{max}, s_{max}. For each sequence type we acquired 4 videos to enrich the sample variability, making a total of 16. Regarding each type of motion, we shot two sequences with uniform dynamics (one slower, one at normal speed), a sequence with speed discontinuities (pauses) and one with changes in direction. Regarding occlusions, the four sequences vary in the duration of the occlusion (23, 35, 50, and 80 frames), however never exceeding the parameters of tracking persistence (in our experiments $N_1 = N_2 = 100$). The cardinality of each sample is set to $N = 100$ particles.

Motion parameters. These were separately tuned in $[0.1, 0.5]$ with unform increment of 0.05; the optimal values are those that minimize the number of frames in which the tracking mean estimate is not well positioned and scaled over the subject face, as judged by visual inspection. Doing so, we set $\sigma_x = 0.15$ (0.3% of lost frames), $\sigma_y = 0.15$ (1%), and $\sigma_s = 0.4$ (15.7%). As expected, the scale dynamics is the most difficult to correctly predict. In our experience, this is mainly due to an inferior sensitivity of the face detector with respect to the scale parameter, which is compensated, in our system, by the re-initialization mechanism so that in no tuning sequences the tracking was definitely lost. Although it is convenient to tune each motion parameter separately to reduce the number of experiments, the results cannot be applied as they are on sequences with mixed dynamics because the different components of diffusion increase the sample variability in a non linear way. Therefore, we consider a joined reduction of the estimated diffusion parameters by about 50%, leading to the following configuration: $\sigma_x = 0.1$, $\sigma_y = 0.1$ and $\sigma_s = 0.25$.

Pose estimation. In the vein of [2], we exploit the combined application of two specialized classifiers, one for frontal and one for profile views, in order to estimate the correct pose angle of the tracked subjects. To do so, we used the classifiers made available in the OpenCV library distribution [12] with no need to retrain. Notice that the standard deviation of the pose parameter σ_θ is not subject to tuning since it does not contribute to the observation likelihood, hence the system is almost unaffected by variations of σ_θ (a little diffusion is still necessary for correct inference of pose side, so in our experiments $\sigma_\theta = 1°$).

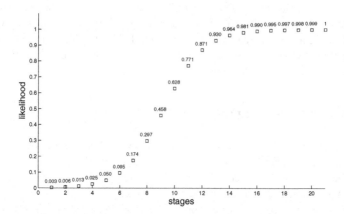

Fig. 1. The tabulated likelihood values in the event of rejection by the cascade (positions 1 to k) and in case of positive classification (position $k + 1$)

Observation likelihood computation. The method derived in Section 2 offers the advantage that the likelihood is estimated based only on training data, hence it can be pre-computed and stored in a look up table that contains at positions $i = 1, \ldots, k$ the likelihood associated to examples rejected by the i-th stage of the cascade, and (for convenience) at position $k + 1$ the likelihood of an example classified as a positive. Since we are using Lienhart's algorithms [10] as implemented in [12] we can straightforwardly refer to the training data reported in [10], namely $p(y = 1) = \frac{5}{8}$, $d = 0.999$, $f = 0.5$, $k = 20$ and hence $d_g \approx 0.98$, $f_g \approx 9.6e - 7$, yielding the weights in Fig. 1. These values refer to the training of the frontal classifier, while no mention is made to the corresponding values for training the profile classifier. For simplicity we assume it was trained over a sample with the same positive-to-negative ratio and with the same requirements d and f put on each stage.

Occlusions. We observed that during such an event all particles are attributed with equally low weights, which in turn results in an increasingly bigger dispersion of the sample. Following these considerations, we separately tuned the probability parameter, p_{min}, from the standard deviation thresholds, x_{max}, y_{max}, s_{max}. Regarding the former, the goal is to set the threshold in such a way that a tracker promptly reacts to occlusions of the face. To this end, we varied p_{min} among the likelihood values corresponding to the last 6 stages (Fig. 1) and chose the one that minimized the percentage of occluding frames not signaled as problematic, leading to $p_{min} = 0.999$ (0.5% of false detections). Regarding the standard deviations, we plot their values against time and chose the thresholds that best separated the intervals of occlusions from the other frames, leading to the following configuration: $x_{max} = 5$, $y_{max} = 5$ and $s_{max} = 3$.

Entry/exit events. There are no parameters directly involved in the strategy for entry/exit detection on/off the scene.

Results. After tuning, the method has been tested on 5 sequences of different types, for a total of 5327 frames. Results are measured by visual inspection and refer to the

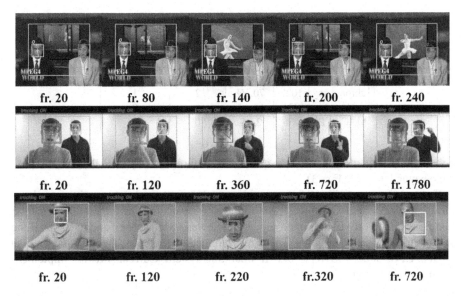

Fig. 2. Excerpts from the *news, dialogue* and *chroma key* sequences. Yellow box encloses the central area of vision as opposed to the peripheral.

following events: percentage of frames with erroneous estimate of the face, erroneous changes of identity (failed re-initializations), number of tracked false positives (which usually expire after $max(N_1, N_2)$ frames). Table 1 summarizes the obtained results and Figures 2 and 3 depict excerpts from the test sequences. The sequences cover various situations: face expression and verbalization (*dialogue, news, chroma key*), complex and moving background (*video clip, news*), entry in the scene (*video clip, MAC vs PC*), pose variations (*video clip, MAC vs PC*). The worst behavior was observed on the *chroma key* sequence, which is characterized by chaotic movements with sudden changes of direction, and quick motion in depth; the observed dynamics is far beyond the dynamics that can be modelled by our stochastic diffusion. Some problems were also observed on

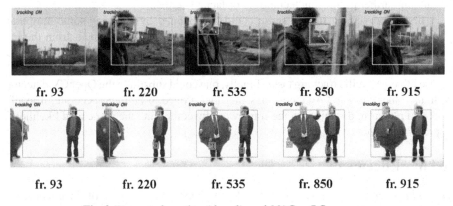

Fig. 3. Excerpts from the *video clip* and *MAC vs PC* sequences

Table 1. Results on test sequences

sequence	frames	track loss	ID changes	false positives
news	298	0%	0	0
dialogue	2495	0%	0	0
chroma key	1022	70.1%	2	1
video clip	921	14.4%	0	0
MAC vs PC	636	2.8%	0	4

the *video clip* sequence, in occasion of the subject turning away from the camera (pose angle beyond 90°, see Fig. 3).

The system runs at about 15 fps on videos of 320x240 pixels (minimal required resolution for faces is 20x20 pixels); the frame rate raises to 18 if the motion detection module is turned off (assuming no subjects are entering the scene), and to 64 fps if the pose estimation is also disabled. These measurements have been taken on a Pentium D 3.4GHz CPU, under MS Windows XP operating system. Current software implementation is in C++ language.

5   Conclusions

Main results achieved so far can be summarized as follows: 1) a principled integration of face detection and tracking steps, relying on a novel probabilistic interpretation of the VJ detection algorithm; 2) this turns into an efficient implementation of the likelihood computation in terms of look-up table; 3) introduction of a multi-threaded architecture which contributes to effective handling of event detections within the scene.

Preliminary results show that the proposed approach is appealing with respect to either robustness and computational efficiency. Concerning accuracy, that is the precision of the face estimate regarding position, scale and pose, it depends on the number of particles constituting every tracking sample, and especially on the virtues of the particular face detection technique employed in the PF scheme. It is generally believed that the Viola and Jones detector is a very efficient technique, but not as accurate; in fact, we observe that the tracking estimate is not always precise and cannot be used as it is for initializing further processing techniques of facial features.

A first improvement in that sense could be obtained by applying some temporal smoothing over the estimate. Moreover, the accuracy would also benefit from the introduction of a deterministic component in the prediction step to better condition the evolution; this component could be estimated online during execution, or even learned in case of very specific tracking tasks. Finally, one could substitute the OpenCV detector with any other cascaded Adaboost classifier that proved to be more accurate, if available, and plug it in directly into the framework by computing the associated likelihood as proposed in this article.

Acknowledgements

The authors acknowledge partial support by the PASCAL2 Network of Excellence under EC grant no. 216886. This publication only reflects the authors' views.

References

1. Boccignone, G., Marcelli, A., Napoletano, P., Di Fiore, G., Iacovoni, G., Morsa, S.: Bayesian integration of face and low-level cues for foveated video coding. IEEE Trans. Circ. Sys. Video Tech. 18, 1727–1740 (2008)
2. Verma, R., Schmid, C., Mikolajczyk, K.: Face Detection and Tracking in a Video by Propagating Detection Probabilities. IEEE Transactions on Pattern Analysis and Machine Intelligence 25(10), 1215–1228 (2003)
3. Okuma, K., Taleghani, A., de Freitas, N., Little, J., Lowe, D.: A Boosted Particle Filter: Multitarget Detection and Tracking. LNCS, pp. 28–39. Springer, Heidelberg (2004)
4. Isard, M., Blake, A.: CONDENSATION – Conditional Density Propagation for Visual Tracking. International Journal of Computer Vision 29(1), 5–28 (1998)
5. Schneiderman, H., Kanade, T.: A statistical method for 3D object detection applied to faces and cars. In: Proc. IEEE Conf. Computer Vision and Pattern Recognition (2000)
6. Viola, P., Jones, M.: Robust Real-Time Face Detection. International Journal of Computer Vision 57(2), 137–154 (2004)
7. Pantic, M., Pentland, A., Nijholt, A., Huang, T.: Human Computing and Machine Understanding of Human Behavior: A Survey. In: Huang, T.S., Nijholt, A., Pantic, M., Pentland, A. (eds.) ICMI/IJCAI Workshops 2007. LNCS (LNAI), vol. 4451, pp. 47–71. Springer, Heidelberg (2007)
8. Li, P., Wang, H.: Probabilistic Object Tracking Based on Machine Learning and Importance Sampling. In: Marques, J.S., Pérez de la Blanca, N., Pina, P. (eds.) IbPRIA 2005. LNCS, vol. 3522, pp. 161–167. Springer, Heidelberg (2005)
9. Friedman, J., Hastie, T., Tibshirani, R.: Additive logistic regression: a statistical view of boosting. Technical report, Stanford University (1998)
10. Lienhart, R., Kuranov, E., Pisarevsky, V.: Empirical analysis of detection cascades of boosted classifiers for rapid object detection. In: DAGM 25th Pattern Recognition Symposium (2003)
11. Elgammal, A., Duraiswami, R., Harwood, D., Davis, L.S.: Background and foreground modeling using nonparametric kernel density estimation for visual surveillance. Proceedings of the IEEE 90(2) (2002)
12. OpenCV library: http://sourceforge.net/projects/opencvlibrary/

A Robust Iris Localization Model Based on Phase Congruency and Least Trimmed Squares Estimation

Lili Pan, Mei Xie, Tao Zheng, and Jianli Ren

School of Electronic Engineering, University of Electronic Science and Technology of China,
No. 4, Section 2, Jianshe North Road, Chengdu, China
panlili8255@hotmail.com, xiemei@ee.uestc.edu.cn

Abstract. Iris localization is a crucial step in iris recognition. The previous proposed algorithms perform unsatisfactorily due to the disturbing of eyelash and variation of image brightness. To solve these problems, we proposed a robust iris position estimation algorithm based on phase congruency analysis and LTSE (Least Trimmed Squares Estimation). Through using the robust regression method to fit iris edge points we can solve the eyelash occlusion problem at a certain extent. The experimental results demonstrate the validity of this algorithm.

Keywords: Iris Segmentation, Phase Congruency, Least Trimmed Squares Estimation.

1 Introduction

As an important branch of biometric identification, iris recognition, which is regarded as the most secure personal identification method, attracted tremendous attention of more and more researchers and has developed rapidly over recent years[1][2][3]. A critical part influencing the performance of iris recognition is the demarcating of iris' inner and outer boundaries at pupil and sclera, for the error of this part will cause the non-iris region mapping in the normalization part. In fact, false non-match errors always arise due to the inaccuracy of localization. Therefore, a large number of iris localization algorithms having been proposed to reach the goal to localize iris boundary robustly and accurately.

The earliest iris localization algorithms, which we are most familiar with, were proposed by Daugman [4] and Wildes [5]. To reach the goal of robustness, an integrodifferential detector is adopted in [4] and Hough transform is employed in [5]. These two methods were frequently applied to the iris recognition system in the previous time; however the insufficiency in executing time and segmenting off-angle gazing iris image caused the emergence of some new methods [6-13]. These methods made progress to improve the speed and accuracy of iris segmentation a lot. Our previous attempts to iris localization are based on image intensity derivative and least squares estimation [14]. Although some progress has been made, some problems also exist. The most emergent problem needing us to solve is the tradeoff between efficiency and accuracy.

P. Foggia, C. Sansone, and M. Vento (Eds.): ICIAP 2009, LNCS 5716, pp. 682–691, 2009.
© Springer-Verlag Berlin Heidelberg 2009

In this paper, we propose a novel and robust iris localization algorithm based on phase congruency and least trimmed squares estimation. Phase congruency [15] [16] is a novel model for feature detection that populates features are perceived at points in an image where the Fourier components are maximally in phase. Compared with the gradient based edge detection method adopted in [4] [8-9] [14], it is not sensitive to variation in image illumination. Moreover, in this paper, we employ an improved method to compute phase congruency through automatically selecting the range of scales over which a locally one-dimensional feature exists [16]. LTS estimation [17] [18], as a robust regression method, can eliminate the influence of outliers that are produced on account of the eyelash at the time of curve fitting. It reduces the sensitivity of the fitting method [11], which is based on LSE, to fake iris edge points. Meanwhile, it improves the efficiency of the segmentation method [13] by avoiding detecting ellipse in a large region and complex iterative computation. Although, Jinyu Zuo [6] attempted to discard the worst 10% edge points to doing a fitting to increase the robustness and efficiency of the segmentation algorithm; however, this method depends heavily on the initial fitting result. The proposed algorithm of this paper solves this problem properly.

2 Iris' Inner and Outer Edge Points Detection

Iris' inner and outer edge point detection is the first step of iris localization and the distribution of these edge points determines the curve fitting result. Actually, for the intensity gradient based edge detection method, it is usually influenced by the variation of image illumination and contrast variation. Therefore; we select the phase congruency model for pupillary and limbic edge point detection.

2.1 Specular Highlights Removal and Pupillary Coarse Center Detection

As we know, most of iris images are captured under the NIR (near-infrared) illumination and the pupil area always contaminated by the reflections which are shown in Fig.1(a). These specular reflections always interrupt the pupillary edge boundary detection and reduce accuracy of segmentation. As most previous iris segmentation algorithms deal with this problem, we should firstly remove these reflection noises. In this paper, we firstly localize the reflections according to their intensity value, their location in the iris image and the sharpness of their boundaries. After we get the location of the reflection regions, we can fill these regions according to the morphological method that is proposed in [20]. One example of the reflection removal is shown in Fig.1(c).

After we remove the specular highlights, we need to find the coarse central point of the pupil to determine the region for searching pupillary and limbic edge points in the next step. The coarse central point of the pupil is an important location indication in such a dimensionless coordinate system. In order to improve the speed and accuracy of this indicating point detection, the original iris image is transformed to a binary image. The pixel, whose intensity value is below the threshold V_P and its 8 neighborhood's intensity values are all below the threshold V_P, is set to be 0 in the binary image. Other pixels are set to be 1. After this operation, almost only the pupil region is black in the binary iris image and the influence of eyelash can be reduced to the greatest extent. The threshold V_P is:

$$V_p = V_{\min} + V_{range} \qquad (1)$$

Where V_{min} is the beginning intensity value of the iris image and V_{range} is the intensity distribution range of the pupil region. It can be estimated as $k*V_{all}$ (a suitable value for k is set to be 0.04 through our experiments), where V_{all} is the intensity distribution range of the whole iris image. Then, we adopt a hierarchical grid searching method [21] to detect the coarse center of the pupil (x'_p, y'_p) in the binary image. Detection is carried out by scanning all possible image locations with a series circular template $\{S_1, S_2...S_N\}$ of radius $\{R_1, R_2...R_N\}$. At each location a matching score describes the similarity of the template and the underlying image patch. When the similarity score is lager than the threshold T_m, the underlying region is the candidate of pupil region. Through a coarse to fine manner, we can get the center location of pupil region whose similarity with the circular template is maximal. In addition, a down sampling operation to binary image is employed to increase the detection speed. In Fig. 1(c), the center and the width of the square are the coarse center of the pupil and the diameter of the matched template respectively.

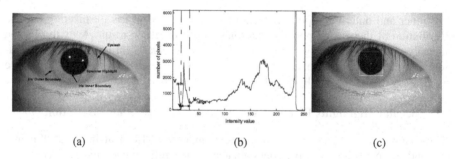

(a)   (b)   (c)

Fig. 1. (a) The original iris image that is acquired by the OKI's IRISPASS-h device. This equipment has two LED illuminators and generates two specular highlights in the pupil region of the image. (b) The intensity histogram distribution. (c) The reflection removal and the pupillary coarse center detection result.

2.2 Edge Points Detection Based on Phase Congruency of 1-D Signal

How to localize these edge points fast and precisely is a crucial problem. The shortage of the existing algorithms is that the edge point detection is always interrupted by illumination variation and contrast variation, and needs a comparatively long time to compute the edge map of the whole image [5] [10]. Phase congruency is an effective means for edge detection and will perform excellently when applied to iris edge point detection of course. In this work, in order to improve the speed of edge point detection, we only calculate the phase congruency of some rows in the vicinity of the pupillary coarse center and process the intensity value of a row as a 1-D signal.

Phase congruency is a relative new model for feature detection and invariant to changes in image brightness or contrast; hence, it provides an absolute measure of the significance of feature points. Generally speaking, the peaks of phase congruency correspond to significant feature points of an image. Peter Kovesi [21] described the phase congruency model for 1-D signal as follows:

$$PC(x) = \frac{\sum_n W(x) \lfloor A_n(x) [\cos(\phi_n(x) - \bar{\phi}(x)) - |\sin(\phi_n(x) - \bar{\phi}(x))|] - T \rfloor}{\sum_n A_n(x) + \varepsilon} \qquad (2)$$

Where $\lfloor \ \rfloor$ denotes that the enclosed quantity is equal to itself when its value is positive, and zero otherwise. A_n represents the amplitude of the nth Fourier component of the 1-D signal, and $\phi_n(x)$ represents the local phase of the Fourier component at position x. ε is a small constant to avoid division by zero. $W(x)$ is a phase congruency weighting function that is designed for sharpening the localization of features, especially those that have been smoothed and can be constructed as below:

$$W(x) = \frac{1}{1 + e^{\gamma(c - s(x))}} \qquad (3)$$

Where c is the cut-off value of filter response spread below which phase congruency values become penalized, and γ is a gain factor that controls the sharpness of the cut-off. $s(x)$ is a measure of filter response spread. The above parameter T is the total noise influence over all scales. In this work, the logarithmic Gabor function, which maintains a zero DC component, is selected to calculate the phase congruency.

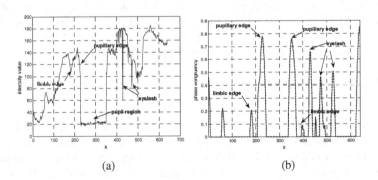

(a)   (b)

Fig. 2. (a) The intensity curve of one row near the coarse center of pupil in t Fig.1.(a). For testing the validation of the phase congruency model, we select an iris image shown in Fig.1 with relatively blurred limbic boundary to analyze. (b) The phase congruency of the left intensity curve.

In this paper, we employed the improved phase congruency algorithm proposed in [16] to localize the pupillary and limbic edge points. Compared with the limbic boundary, the pupillary boundary and eyelash is the more obvious feature in the iris image, and they give rise to peaks in phase congruency with high value which can be seen in Fig.2. There are two main steps to detect the pupillary edge points. First of all, we select a series of intensity values $S_y(x)$ of row y which is near the pupillary coarse center and compute its phase congruency. An important parameter for the phase congruency calculation is the scale spread. In this paper, we estimate this parameter by tracking the phase over scale and record the start-scale and end-scale λ_b and λ_e at which phase is congruent on the pupillary boundary. The influence of eyelash noises in the pupil region can be eliminated through setting the noise threshold T [15]. Over the selected range of scales, from λ_b to λ_e, we compute the phase congruency $PC_y(x)$ of $S_y(x)$ and the result is shown in Fig.2. Second, we need to localize the position of these peaks that correspond to the pupillary edge points. In section 2.1, the pupillary coarse center (x'_p, y'_p) is gained and the local maxima can be localized as below:

$$
\begin{cases}
\dfrac{\partial PC_y(x)}{\partial x} = 0 \\[2mm]
\dfrac{\partial^2 PC_y(x)}{\partial^2 x} < 0
\end{cases}
\tag{4}
$$

The pupillary edge points x_{pl} and x_{pr} in row y are the local maximal points of phase congruency which are nearest to the pupillary inner point (x'_p, y'_p) on the right and left respectively. Similarly, we can get a group of edge points of pupil in the rows which are near the pupillary inner point (x'_p, y'_p).

For the contrast of limbic boundary is not so great as the pupillary boundary, limbic edge point detection is much more difficult than the pupillary edge point detection. Furthermore, it is always disturbed by the obvious fleck and stripe texture of iris and eye lash. To avoid this interruption and emphasize the intensity change in the iris' outer boundary , we need to smooth the original intensity curve $S_y(x)$ and set the intensity value of the pupil region in row y to be the intensity value of iris region before calculating the phase congruency. The smooth operation is as below:

$$
S'_y(x) = S_y(x) * g(x, \sigma) = \int_{-\infty}^{+\infty} S_y(x - u) \cdot \frac{1}{\sqrt{2\pi\sigma}} \exp(-u^2 / 2\sigma^2) \, du
\tag{5}
$$

Where $g(x,\sigma)$ is the Gaussian smoothing function with deviation σ. σ has an important effect on the selection of phase spread parameter. As we calculate the phase congruency for pupillary edge point detection, we should select a range of scales to calculate the phase congruency according to the characteristic of limbic edge. The result is shown in Fig.3 and the limbic edge points have much higher phase congruency value. We can find that the limbic edge points of row y are the local maximal points which are nearest to the pupillary inner point (x'_p, y'_p). In the same way, we can get a group of limbic edge points through processing a number of rows which are not occluded by eyelash. We can determine whether one row is occluded by eyelash through calculate the number of peaks whose value is above 0.45 when compute the phase congruency for pupillary edge point detection because eyelashes are most obvious feature of an iris image.

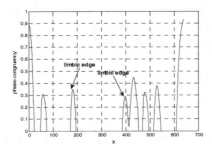

Fig. 3. The phase congruency of the smoothed intensity curve, in which the intensity values in pupil region are set to be the iris intensity value

3   Least Trimmed Squares Estimation

As we know, in the iris image, the boundaries of iris are almost circular contour at front-angle position. When the iris image is captured at off-angle position, the circular contour will become elliptical contour. Thus, we set two ellipses to fit iris' inner and outer boundaries. Although slight non-circular iris' boundaries exist, they won't cause any problem if we use the same approach to model the boundaries for both the enrolled and inquiry iris images. The most normal data fitting algorithm is the LSE (Least Squares Estimation) method which gives every sample the same weight. Actually, this method is notoriously sensitive to outliers, which are defined as the sample values that cause surprise in relation to the majority of the sample. In this work, the outliers are usually the no-iris edge points, such as the eyelash edge points, and even one outlier will give rise to the departure of position estimation. To increase robustness of the iris position estimation, the fitting method must be more forgiving about outlying measurements; therefore, the LTSE (Least Trimmed Squares Estimation) that is one of the robust regression methods is applied. The principle of LTSE is to minimize the sum of squares for the smallest h of residuals [17] [18].

Consider an ordinary robust regression model that can be described as the followed form:

$$Z = A\beta + v \tag{6}$$

$Z = [z_1, \ldots, z_m]^T \in R^m$ is a measurement vector, $A = [a_1, \ldots, a_m]^T \in R^{m \times n}$ is a design (or model) matrix with full column rank, $\in R^n$ is an unknown parameter vector to be estimated, and $v \in R^m$ is a random noise vector. For a given vector $\in R^n$, the residual vector is defined as $r(\ ) \equiv Z - A$, with i th element $r(\ )_i$. The robust least trimmed squares estimator for   is given by:

$$\min_{\beta} \sum_{i=1}^{h} r^2(\beta)_{i:m} \tag{7}$$

Where $r^2(\ )_{1:m} \leqslant \ldots \leqslant r^2(\ )_{i:m}$ are the ordered squared residuals, h is the trimming constant which can he set to a value in the range from $m/2$ to m. Thus there will be h

data points, out of m, used to estimate the parameters. LTSE also employs the random sampling technique to avert the dependence on the initial fitting result [6].

The iris position estimation according to the sampled edge pionts is an elliptical fitting problem. And we know the normal equation for an ellipse is:

$$\frac{(x\cos\theta + y\sin\theta - x_o\cos\theta - y_o\sin\theta)^2}{A} + \frac{(-x\sin\theta + y\cos\theta + x_o\sin\theta - y_o\cos\theta)^2}{B} = 1 \qquad (8)$$

Where (x_o, y_o) is central location of the ellipse and $\{A,B\}$ are the major and minor axes, and θ is the orientation of the ellipse. The equivalent function can be written as below:

$$ax^2 + bxy + cy^2 + dx + ey + f = 0 \qquad b^2 - 4ac < 0 \qquad (9)$$

In section 2.2, we obtain a number of pupillary edge points (x_1, y_1), (x_2, y_2), $\cdots$ (x_N, y_N) and the parameter a, b, c, d, e can be estimated according to the followed simultaneous Equations.

$$\begin{bmatrix} x_1^2 & x_1 y_1 & y_1^2 & x_1 & y_1 & 1 \\ x_2^2 & x_2 y_2 & y_2^2 & x_2 & y_2 & 1 \\ \vdots & \vdots & \vdots & \vdots & \vdots & \vdots \\ x_N^2 & x_N y_N & y_N^2 & x_N & y_N & 1 \end{bmatrix} \begin{bmatrix} a \\ b \\ c \\ d \\ e \\ f \end{bmatrix} = \begin{bmatrix} 0 \\ 0 \\ \vdots \\ 0 \end{bmatrix} \qquad (10)$$

Here, for the pupil position estimation problem, the vector of observation Z is $[0,0,...,0]^T$, the component of the matrix of observations on the explanatory variables a_i is $[x_i^2, x_i y_i, y_i^2, x_i, y_i, 1]$, and the vector of regression coefficients to be estimated β is $[a, b, c, d, e, f]$. According to the direct ellipse-specific fitting method that are introduced in [19], the estimation of β under the LTS principle is the solution of Equ.(12) subject to $\beta^T C \beta = 1$, where C is the matrix that expresses the constraint. From the above description, we can get that the weights for the outliers are 0 in the LTSE method, That is, the LTSE performs outlier rejection while fitting data. In the same way, we can get the estimation of iris position.

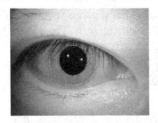 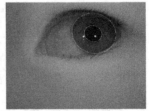

Fig. 4. The ellipse fitting results for the front-angle and off-angle captured iris image

4   Experiment Result

The database used to test this proposed algorithm includes three parts. One is the public database CASIA version 2.0, and others are CASIA version 3.0(Twins) and the private database founded by ourselves. The CASIA version 2.0 database contains 1200 images with a resolution of 640×480 from 60 live human test subjects (20 different images of each subject) over two visitors separated by 40 days. The CASIA Version 3.0(Twins) contains 100 pairs of twins' 3183 images(640×480 pixel resolution). The private database contains 3300 iris images (640×480 pixel resolution) of 115 persons and the image acquisition device is OKI's IRISPASS-h.

4.1   The Comparison of LSE and LTSE

Though we adopt some means to eliminate the influence of eyelash occlusion, the fake pupillary and limbic edge points appear sometimes on account of the multiple eyelashes, which are overlap in a small area. In order to eliminate the effect of the fake edge points when fitting circle, we choose the LTSE method that we introduce in section 3, which can endure 50% bad points. Fig.5 gives an example of the comparison between LSE and LTSE on the iris location estimation of the same image, whose pupil and iris region is occluded by multiple eyelashes. In Fig.5(a), the scattered points are the pupillary and limbic edge points and the two groups of ellipses are the LTSE and LSE fitting result. The test on the CASIA version 2.0 database, CASIA version 3.0(Twins) database, and our private database shows that the EER reduces by 68.2%, 66.8% and 76.5% respectively through using LTSE rather than LSE to fit the edge points that are detected by phase congruency analysis.

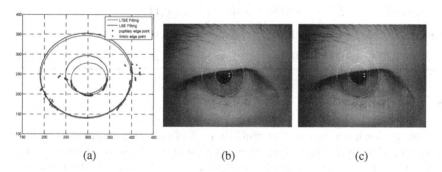

(a)   (b)   (c)

Fig. 5. The comparison of LSE and LTSE. (a) The edge point distribution and curve fitting result. (b) The iris localization result by using LTSE. (c)The iris localization result by using LSE.

4.2   The Test Result on CASIA Database and Our Private Iris Database

On the above database, the iris location estimation method based on phase congruency and LTSE is proved to be precise. Daugman's method [4], Wildes' method [5] and three other methods are implemented on the same database for the comparison.

To test the performance of the proposed algorithm objectively, we adopt different methods in the iris localization part and the same feature extracting and matching methods proposed by Daugman[4] to compare the different localization algorithms' performance. We give the comparing results of these five methods in Table1. PC+LSE means first detecting the iris' inner and outer edge point through phase congruency analysis and then doing ellipse fitting to these edge points based on LSE; PC+ILSE means first detecting the iris' inner and outer edge point through phase congruency analysis and then using Improved LSE, which is proposed in [6], to fitting these edge points; PC+LTSE means first detecting the iris' inner and outer edge point through phase congruency analysis and then using LTSE to fit ellipses to these edge points. All the experiments are performed in Matlab 2006 environment on a 3.98GHz duo CPU (1.99G per core) and 2G DDR memory computer. Our algorithm only needs 0.13s on average to localize one iris image. After we implement the proposed algorithm in C and optimize the code, its speed can reach 30ms/f, that is, it can satisfy the requirement of real time iris image processing system.

Table 1. The Comparison of Iris Localization Algorithms

	CASIA Version 2.0 Database		CASIA Version 3.0- Twins Database		Our Private Database	
	EER	Mean Speed	EER	Mean Speed	EER	Mean
Daugman [4]	2.12%	0.91s	2.89%	0.90s	1.23%	0.92s
Wides[5]	2.37%	0.97s	2.99%	0.98s	1.39%	0.95s
PC+LSE	3.75%	0.09s	4.04%	0.11s	2.77%	0.10s
PC+ILSE[6]	2.84%	0.09s	3.68%	0.10s	1.67%	0.11s
PC+LTSE	1.19%	0.13s	1.34%	0.14s	0.65%	0.13s

5 Conclusion

Iris recognition has a long and colorful history. So far, there are a plenty of algorithms having been proposed. In this paper, we propose a novel iris localization algorithm, which is basing on phase congruency analysis and least trimmed squares estimation. It performs robustly due to the robust regression of LTSE; moreover, it is invariant to image brightness and contrast. The experiments on three different iris databases show the validity of the proposed algorithm.

Acknowledgements

This work was supported by a grant from the National Nature Science Foundation of China (NO.60472046).

References

1. Jain, A.K., Flynn, P., Ross, A.A.: Handbook of Biometrics. Springer, Heidelberg (2008)
2. Jain, A.K.: Biometric recognition: Q&A. Nature 449(6), 38–40 (2007)
3. Bowyer, K.W., Hollingsworth, K., Flynn, P.J.: Image Understanding for Iris Biometrics: A Survey. Computer Vision and Image Understanding, 1–37 (2007)
4. Daugman, J.G.: High confidence visual recognition of persons by a test of statistical independence. IEEE Trans. Pattern Anal. Machine Intell. 15(11), 1148–1161 (1993)
5. Wildes, R.P.: Iris recognition: an emerging biometric technology. Proceeding of the IEEE 85(9), 1348–1363 (1997)
6. Zuo, J., Ratha, N.K., Connell, J.H.: A New Approach for Iris Segmentation. In: 2008 IEEE Computer Society Conference on Computer Vision and Pattern Recognition Workshop on Biometrics, pp. 1–6 (2008)
7. Nabti, M., Bouridane, A.: An Efficient and Fast Iris Recognition System based on a Combined Multiscale Feature Extraction technique. Pattern Recognition 41(3), 868–879 (2008)
8. Ren, X., Peng, Z., Zeng, Q., et al.: An Improved Method for Daugman's Iris Localization Algorithm. Computers in Biology and Medicine 38(1), 111–115 (2008)
9. Basit, A., Javed, M.Y.: Localization of Iris in Gray Scale Images Using Intensity Gradient. Optics and Lasers in Engineering 45(12), 1107–1114 (2007)
10. He, X., Shi, P.: A New Segmentation Approach for Iris Recognition based on Hand-held Capture Device. Pattern Recognition 40(4), 1326–1333 (2007)
11. Pundlik, S.J., Woodard, D.L., Birchfield, S.T.: Non-Ideal Iris Segmentation Using Graph Cuts. In: Pr2008 IEEE Computer Society Conference on Computer Vision and Pattern Recognition Workshop on Biometrics, pp. 23–28 (2008)
12. He, Z., Tan, T., Sun, Z., Qiu, X.: Towards Accurate and Fast Iris Segmentation for Iris Biometrics. To be appeared in IEEE Trans. Pattern Anal. Machine Intell. (2008)
13. Miyazawa, K., Ito, K., Aoki, T.: An Effective Approach for Iris Recognition Using Phase-Based Image Matching. IEEE Trans. Pattern Anal. Machine Intell. 30(10), 1741–1756 (2008)
14. Pan, L., Xie, M.: The Algorithm of Iris Image Preprocessing. In: Proceedings of the Fourth IEEE Workshop on Automatic Identification Advanced Technologies, pp. 134–138 (2005)
15. Kovesi, P.: Image features from phase congruency. Videre: A Journal of Computer Vision Research 1(3), 1–27 (1999)
16. Schenk, V.U.B., Brady, M.: Improving Phase-Congruency Based Feature Detection through Automatic Scale-Selection. In: Sanfeliu, A., Ruiz-Shulcloper, J. (eds.) CIARP 2003. LNCS, vol. 2905, pp. 121–128. Springer, Heidelberg (2003)
17. Wang, H., Suter, D.: LTSD: A Highly Efficient Symmetry-Based Robust Estimator. In: Proceeding of the Seventh International Conference on Control, Antomation, Robatlu and Vision, Singapore, pp. 332–337 (2002)
18. Bai, E.: Outliers: Inliers and the Squares Estimator in Generalized Least Trimmed System Identification. Journal of Control Theory and Application 1, 17–27 (2003)
19. Fitzgibbon, A., Pilu, M., Fisher, R.B.: Direct Least Square Fitting of Ellipse. IEEE Trans. Pattern Anal. Machine Intell. 21(5), 476–480 (1999)
20. Soille, P.: Morphological Image Analysis: Principles and Applications, pp. 173–174. Springer, Heidelberg (1999)
21. Froba, B., Emst, A., Kubleck, C.: Real-Time Face Detection Using Edge-Orientation Matching. In: The Third International Conference on Audio- and Video-Based Biometric Person Authentication, pp. 78–83 (2001)

Shape-Based Classification of 3D Head Data

Linda G. Shapiro, Katarzyna Wilamowska, Indriyati Atmosukarto, Jia Wu,
Carrie Heike, Matthew Speltz, and Michael Cunningham

University of Washington,
Seattle, WA 98195 U.S.A.
{shapiro,kasiaw,indria,jiawu}@cs.washington.edu,
carrie.heike@seattlechildrens.org,
{mspeltz,mcunning}@u.washington.edu

Abstract. Craniofacial disorders are one of the most common category
of birth defects worldwide, and are an important topic of biomedical research. In order to better understand these disorders and correlate them
with genetic patterns and life outcomes, researchers need to quantify
the craniofacial anatomy. In this paper we introduce several different
craniofacial descriptors that are being used in research studies for two
craniofacial disorders: the 22q11.2 deletion syndrome (a genetic disor-
der) and plagiocephaly/brachycephaly, disorders caused by pressure on
the head. Experimental results show that our descriptors show promise
for quantifying craniofacial shape.

Keywords: 3D shape, shape-based classification, craniofacial data.

1 Introduction

Researchers at the Seattle Children's Hospital Craniofacial Center (SCHCC)
study craniofacial disorders in children. They wish to develop new computational
techniques to represent, quantify, and analyze variants of biological morphology
from imaging sources such as stereo cameras, CT scans and MRI scans. The
focus of their research is the introduction of principled algorithms to reveal
genotype-phenotype disease associations. We are collaborating in two research
studies at SCHCC for the study of craniofacial anatomy. The first study is of
children with the 22q11.2 deletion syndrome, a genetic disease, which causes
abnormalities of the face, including such features as asymmetric face shape,
hooded eyes, bulbous nasal tip, and retrusive chin, among others (Figure 1a). The
second study is of infants with plagiocephaly or brachycephaly, two conditions in
which a portion of the child's head, usually at the back, becomes abnormally flat
(Figure 1b). Our objective is to provide feature-extraction tools for the study
of craniofacial anatomy from 3D mesh data obtained from the 3dMD active
stereo photogrammetry system at SCHCC. These tools will produce quantitative
representations (descriptors) of the 3D data that can be used to summarize the
3D shape as pertains to the condition being studied and the question being
asked.

P. Foggia, C. Sansone, and M. Vento (Eds.): ICIAP 2009, LNCS 5716, pp. 692–700, 2009.
© Springer-Verlag Berlin Heidelberg 2009

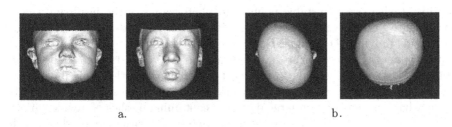

a.   b.

Fig. 1. 3D mesh data. a) Faces of 2 children with 22q11.2 deletion syndrome; b) Tops of heads of children with plagiocephaly (left) and brachycephaly (right).

This paper describes our work on extracting shape descriptors from 3D craniofacial data in the form of 3D meshes and using them for classification. Section 2 discusses related work from both medical image analysis and computer vision. Section 3 describes our procedures for data acquisition and preprocessing. Section 4 explains the descriptors we have developed for studies of the 22q11.2 deletion syndrome and related classification results. Section 5 discusses the descriptors we have developed for studies of plagiocephaly and brachycephaly and experimental results. Section 6 concludes the paper.

2   Related Work

There are two main classes of research related to this work: medical studies of craniofacial features and 3D shape analysis from computer vision. Traditionally, the clinical approach to identify and study an individual with facial dysmorphism has been through physical examination combined with craniofacial anthropometric measurements [6]. Newer methods of craniofacial assessment use digital image data, but hand measurement or at least hand labeling of landmarks is common.

With respect to 22q11.2DS, craniofacial anthropometric measurements prevail as the standard manual assessment method; automated methods for its analysis are limited to just two. Boehringer et al. [1] applied a Gabor wavelet transformation to 2D photographs of individuals with ten different facial dysmorphic syndromes. The generated data sets were then transformed using principal component analysis (PCA) and classified using linear discriminant analysis, support vector machines, and k-nearest neighbors. The dense surface model approach [3] aligns training samples according to point correspondences. It then produces an "average" face for each population being studied and represents each face by a vector of PCA coefficients. Neither method is fully automatic; both require manual landmark placement.

There has also been some semiautomated work on analysis of plagiocephaly and brachycephaly. Hutchison et al. [4] developed a technique called HeadsUp that takes a top view digital photograph of infant heads fitted with an elastic head circumference band equipped with adjustable color markers to identify landmarks. The resulting photograph is then automatically analyzed to obtain quantitative measurements for the head shape. Zonenshayn et al. [10] used a headband with two adjustable points and photographs of the headband shape to calculate a cranial index of symmetry. Both these methods analyze 2D shapes for use in studying 3D craniofacial anatomy

Computer vision researchers have not, for the most part, tackled shape-based analysis of 3D craniofacial data. The most relevant work is the seminal paper on face recognition using eigenfaces [7]. Work on classification and retrieval for 3D meshes has concentrated on large data sets containing meshes of a wide variety of objects. In the SHREC shape retrieval contest, algorithms must distinguish between such objects as a human being (in any pose!), a cow, and an airplane. A large number of descriptors have been proposed for this competition; the descriptor that performs best is based on the shapes of multiple 2D views of the 3D mesh, represented in terms of Fourier descriptors and Zernike moments [2].

3   Data Acquisition and Preprocessing

The 3D data used in this research was collected at the Craniofacial Center of Seattle Children's Hospital for their studies on 22q11.2 deletion syndrome, plagiocephaly, and brachycephaly. The 3dMD imaging system uses four camera stands, each containing three cameras. Stereo analysis yields twelve range maps that are combined using 3dMD proprietary software to yield a 3D mesh of the patient's head and a texture map of the face. Our project uses only the 3D meshes, which capture the shape of the head.

An automated system to align the pose of each mesh was developed, using symmetry to align the yaw and roll angles and a height differential to align the pitch angle. Although faces are not truly symmetrical, the pose alignment procedure can be cast as finding the angular rotations of yaw and roll that minimized the difference between the left and right side of the face. The pitch of the head was aligned by minimizing the difference between the height of the chin and the height of the forehead. If the final alignment is not satisfactory, it is adjusted by hand, which occurred in 1% of the symmetry alignments and 15% of the pitch alignments.

4   Shape-Based Description of 3D Face Data for 22q11.2 Deletion Syndrome

22q11.2 deletion syndrome has been shown to be one of the most common multiple anomaly syndromes in humans [5]. Early detection is important as many affected individuals are born with a conotruncal cardiac anomaly, mild-to-moderate immune deficiency and learning disabilities, all of which can benefit from early intervention.

4.1   Descriptors

Since 3D mesh processing is expensive and the details of the face are most important for our analysis, we constructed three different global descriptors from

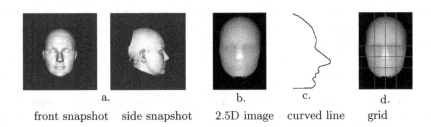

a.		b.	c.	d.
front snapshot	side snapshot	2.5D image	curved line	grid

Fig. 2. a) 2D snapshot of the 3D mesh from front and side views; b) 2.5D depth representation in which the value of each pixel is the height above a cutting plane; c) 1D curved line segment; d) grid of curved line segments

the 3D meshes: 2D frontal and side snapshots of the 3D mesh (Figure 2a), 2.5D depth images (Figure 2b), and 1D curved line segments (Figure 2c). The 2D snapshots are merely screen shots of the 3D mesh from the front and side views. The 2.5D depth images represent the face on an x-y grid so that the value of a pixel at point (x,y) is the height of the point above a plane used to cut the face from the rest of the mesh. The curved line segment is a 1D representation of the fluctuations of a line travelling across the face. Curved line segments were extracted in multiple positions in both the vertical and horizontal directions. We experimented with 1, 3, 5, and 7 line segments in each direction; Figure 2d shows a grid of 3 × 3 lines. The curved line shown in Figure 2c came from the middle vertical line of the grid. Each of the three descriptors was transformed using PCA, which converted its original representation into a feature vector comprised of the coefficients of the eigenvectors. Since there were 189 individuals in our full data set, this allowed for a maximum 189 attribute representation. Our analyses determined that the 22q11.2 syndrome, because of its subtle facial appearance, required the entire set of 189 coefficients.

We have also developed automatic detection and description of local features known to be common manifestations of 22q11.2DS. The bulbous nasal tip is a nasal anomaly, which is associated with a ball-like nasal appearance. The depth ND of the nose is detected as the difference in height between the tip of the nose and its base. A sequence of nasal tip regions NT_i are produced by varying a depth threshold i from ND down to 1, stopping just before the nasal tip region runs into another region (usually the forehead). For each NT_i, its bounding box BNT_i and an ellipse E_i inscribed in that box are constructed and used to calculate two nasal features, rectangularity R_i and circularity C_i, and a severity score S^f for each feature f.

$$R_i = area(NT_i)/area(BNT_i)$$
$$C_i = \big(area(NT_i) - area(E_i)\big)/area(BNT_i)$$
$$S^f = |\{i|f_i > f_t\}|/ND$$

where f_t is a threshold for feature f, empirically chosen to be stable over multiple data sets. The bulbous nose coefficient B is then defined as a combination of rectangularity and circularity: $B = S^{rect}(1 - S^{circ})$.

4.2 Classification Experiments

We have run a number of classification experiments using the PCA representations of the three descriptors. Our experiments use the WEKA suite of classifiers [9] with 10-fold cross validation to distinguish between affected and control individuals. We calculated the following performance measures: accuracy (percent of all decisions that were correct), recall (percentage of all affected individuals that are correctly labeled affected), and precision (percentage of individuals labeled affected that actually are affected).

Although testing on a balanced set is common practice in data mining, our data set only included a small number of affected individuals. The full data set included 189 individuals (53 affected, 136 control). Set *A106* matched each of the 53 affected individuals to a control individual of closest age. Set *AS106* matched each of the 53 affected individuals to a control individual of same sex and closest age. Set *W86* matched a subset of 43 affected self-identified white individuals to a control individual of same ethnicity, sex and closest age. Set *WR86* matched the same 43 affected white individuals to a control individual of same ethnicity, sex and age, allowing repeats of controls where same-aged subjects were lacking. The full data set obtained the highest accuracy (75%), but due to a large number of false positives, its precision and recall were very low (.56 and .52, respectively). The W86 data set achieved the highest results in precision and recall, and its accuracy was approximately the same as the full data set (74%); it was thus selected as most appropriate for this work.

Table 1. Comparison of 2D snapshots, 2.5D depth representations, vertical curved lines, and local nasal features using the Naive Bayes classifier on the W86 data set

	2D snap	2.5D depth	1 line	3 lines	5 lines	7 lines	Rect. Sev.	Circle Sev.	Bulb. Coef.	Nasal Feat.
Precision	0.88	0.80	0.81	0.88	0.88	0.79	0.67	0.71	0.77	0.80
Recall	0.63	0.69	0.68	0.70	0.73	0.62	0.59	0.63	0.58	0.67
Accuracy	0.76	0.76	0.75	0.80	0.82	0.72	0.64	0.68	0.70	0.75

For the human viewer, the 3D Snapshot is considered to hold much more information than the 2.5D representation. As shown in Table 1, we found no statistically significant difference in classifier performance for the two different representations. However, since the 2.5D representation retains the 3D shape of the face, it is better suited to developing algorithms for finding 3D landmarks used in local descriptor development. For the curved lines, the 3 and 5 vertical line descriptors performed the best, even outperforming the more detailed 2.5D depth image as shown in Table 1, while horizontal lines performed poorly. For the local nasal tip features, the combination of all three features gave the best performance. The local nasal tip results are promising considering that the nose is only one of several different facial areas to be investigated. The bulbous nasal tip features improve the results reported in [8].

5 3D Shape Severity Quantification and Localization for Deformational Plagiocephaly and Brachycephaly

Deformational plagiocephaly (Figure 3a) refers to the deformation of the head characterized by a persistent flattening on the side, resulting in an asymmetric head shape and misalignment of the ears. Brachycephaly (Figure 3b) is a similar condition in which the flattening is usually located at the back of the head, resulting in a symmetrical but wide head shape. Current shape severity assessment techniques for deformational plagiocephaly and brachycephaly rely on expert scores and are very subjective, resulting in a lack of standard severity quantification. To alleviate this problem, our goal was to define shape descriptors and related severity scores that can be automatically produced by a computer program operating on 3D mesh data.

Our original dataset consisted of 254 3D head meshes, each assessed by two human experts who assigned discrete severity scores based on the degree of the deformation severity at the back of the head: category 0 (normal), category 1 (mild), category 2 (moderate), and category 3 (severe). To avoid inter-expert score variations, heads that were assigned different scores by the two human experts were removed from the dataset. The final dataset for our experiments consisted of 140 3D meshes, with 50 in category 0, 46 in category 1, 35 in category 2, and 9 in category 3.

Our method for detecting plagiocephaly and brachycephaly on the 3D meshes uses 2D histograms of the azimuth and elevation angles of surface normals. The intuition is that on flat surfaces of the skull, which are approximately planar, all the surface normals point in the same direction. An individual with plagiocephaly or brachycephaly will have one or more such flat spots, and the larger they are the more surface normals will point in that direction (Figure 3c). Unaffected individuals are expected to have a more even distribution of surface normal directions, since their heads are more rounded (Figure 3d).

We calculate the surface normal at each point on the posterior side of the head and represent each by the azimuth and elevation angles, as shown in Figure 3e. Since our descriptors are histograms, the computed angles must be converted into a small number of ranges or bins. In our work we use 12 bins each for azimuth and elevation angles and construct a 144-bin 2D histogram. Each bin represents an azimuth/elevation combination that corresponds to a particular area of the head and contains the count of normals with that combination. We defined a severity score for the left and right sides of the back of the head using the appropriate bins. The left posterior flatness score is the sum of the histogram bins that correspond to azimuth angles ranging from $-90°$ to $-30°$ and elevation angles ranging from $-15°$ to $45°$, while the right posterior flatness score is the sum of the bins for azimuth angles ranging from $-150°$ to $-90°$ and

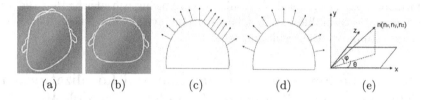

Fig. 3. (a) Example of plagiocephaly. (b) Example of brachycephaly ((a) and (b) are from www.cranialtech.com). (c) Surface normal vectors of points that lie on a flat surface and will create a peak in the 2D angle histogram. (d) Surface normal vectors of points that lie on a more rounded surface and will be spread out in the histogram bins. (e) Azimuth and elevation angles of a 3D surface normal vector.

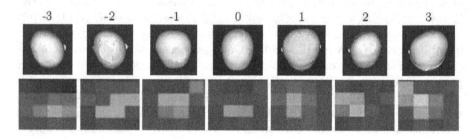

Fig. 4. Most relevant bins of 2D histograms of azimuth and elevation angles of surface normal vectors on 3D head mesh models. As the severity of flatness increases on the side of the head, the peak in the 2D histogram becomes more prominent.

elevation angles ranging from $-15°$ to $45°$. Figure 4 shows 16 relevant bins of the 2D histograms for 7 different individuals with expert scores ranging from -3 to 3; scores < 0 indicate left posterior flatness, while expert scores > 0 indicate right posterior flatness. The histogram for the unaffected individual (Expert score 0) has no bins with high counts. The histogram for individuals with right posterior flatness have high bin counts in columns 1-2 of the 2D histogram, while individuals with left posterior flatness have high bin counts in columns 3-4.

5.1 Classification Experiments

We have run a number of experiments to measure the performance of our shape severity scores in distinguishing individuals with head shape deformation. As in the 22q11.2 deletion syndrome experiments, we used accuracy, precision and recall to measure the performance of our method. The objective of our first two experiments was to measure the performance of our left and right posterior flatness scores. We calculated these scores for all the heads in our dataset and used an empirically obtained threshold of $t = 0.15$ to distinguish individuals with either left or right posterior flatness. As shown in Table 2, our left and right posterior flatness scores agree well with the experts, particularly on the left side. Note that the experts chose only the side with the most flatness to score, whereas

Table 2. Performance of left, right and asymmetry posterior flatness scores

	Left score	Right score	Asymmetry score
Precision	0.88	0.77	0.96
Recall	0.92	0.88	0.88
Accuracy	0.96	0.82	0.96

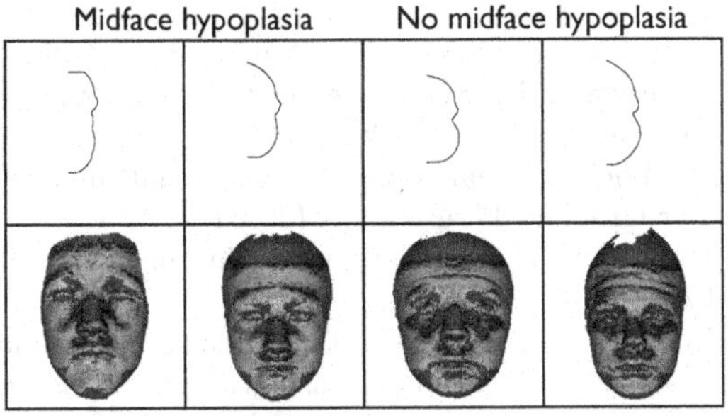

Fig. 5. Comparison of cheek lines and projected angle histograms for individuals with flat midface vs. unaffected individuals

the computer program detected flatness on both sides; this accounts for some of the discrepancy. For the third experiment, we calculated an asymmetry score as the difference between left posterior and right posterior flatness of the affected individuals and compared it to asymmetry scores provided by the experts. The results in Table 2 show that our method performs quite well. Furthermore, the bins with high counts can be projected back onto the heads to show doctors where the flatness occurs and for additional use in classification.

6 Generality of Approach and Conclusion

The descriptors we have developed were motivated by particular craniofacial disorders: 22q11.2 deletion syndrome and plagiocephaly/brachycephaly. The global descriptors are basic representations that we claim can be useful to quantify most, if not all, craniofacial disorders. In order to illustrate this point, we have begun a study of midface hypoplasia, a flattening of the midface of individuals, often present in 22q11.2DS, but of particular interest in those with cleft lip/palate. We used vertical curved lines in the midcheek area to produce one set of descriptors and the angle histograms projected onto the faces (instead of the backs of the heads) to produce a second set. Figure 5 illustrates the difference between two individuals without midface hypoplasia and two who are affected. The curved lines, which seem only slightly different to computer vision researchers, were considered to be highly differentiable by the craniofacial experts. The projection of the angle histograms to the faces shows an interesting pattern, whose 2D snapshot can be used in classification. We conclude that our descriptors are general representations that are useful in quantifying craniofacial anatomy for use by doctors and biomedical researchers.

Acknowledgment. This work was supported by NSF Grant DBI-0543631 and NIH grants DE013813-05, DC02310, and DE17741-2.

References

1. Boehringer, S., Vollmar, T., Tasse, C., Wurtz, R.P., Gillessen-Kaesbach, G., Horsthemke, B., Wieczorek, D.: Syndrome identification based on 2d analysis software. Eur. J. Hum. Genet. 14, 1082–1089 (2006)
2. Chen, D., Tian, X., Shen, Y., Ouhyoung, M.: On visual similarity based 3d model retrieval. Computer Graphics Forum 22(3) (2003)
3. Hammond, P.: The use of 3d face shape modelling in dysmorphology. Arch. Dis. Child 92, 1120–1126 (2007)
4. Hutchison, L., Hutchison, L., Thompson, J., Mitchell, E.A.: Quantification of plagiocephaly and brachycephaly in infants using a digital photographic technique. The Cleft Palate-Craniofacial Journal 42(5), 539–547 (2005)
5. Kobrynski, L., Sullivan, K.: Velocardiofacial syndrome, digeorge syndrome: the chromosome 22q11. 2 deletion syndromes. The Lancet (2007)
6. Richtsmeier, J.T., DeLeon, V.B., Lele, S.R.: The promise of geometric morphometrics. Yearbook of Physical Anthropology 45, 63–91 (2002)
7. Turk, M., Pentland, A.: Eigenfaces for regcognition. Journal of Cognitive Neuroscience 3(1), 71–86 (1991)
8. Wilamowska, K., Shapiro, L.G., Heike, C.L.: Classification of 3d face shape in 22q11.2 deletion syndrome. In: IEEE International Symposium on Biomedical Imaging (2009)
9. Witten, I.H., Frank, E.: Data mining: Practical machine learning tools and techniques (2005)
10. Zonenshayn, M., Kronberg, E., Souweidane, M.: Cranial index of symmetry: an objective semiautomated measure of plagiocephaly. J. Neurosurgery (Pediatrics 5) 100, 537–540 (2004)

Sudden Changes Detection in WCE Video

Giovanni Gallo[1], Eliana Granata[1], and Giuseppe Scarpulla[2]

[1] Dipartimento di Matematica e Informatica,
Viale A. Doria, 6, 95125 Catania, Italy
[2] Ospedale Maddalena Raimondi,
Via Forlanini, 5, 93017 San Cataldo (CL), Italy
{gallo,granata}@dmi.unict.it

Abstract. The direct visual inspection of WCE video by an expert is a tiring and cost activity and it is a true bottleneck to the widespread application of this diagnostic technique. In this paper we apply the texton approach to characterize with a numeric indicator the sub-sequences of a WCE that show sharp change and that are likely to represent relevant medical details. Experiments show that the proposed fully automatic technique may safely reduce the amount of frames that need further examination of up to 70%.

Keywords: Wireless Capsule Endoscopy (WCE), Video Segmentation, Textons, Video Classification, Gabor Filters.

1 Introduction

Wireless Capsule Endoscopy (WCE) is a recent technique which allows the visualization of the entire intestine without the need of any surgery. WCE has been proposed in 2000 [1] and it integrates wireless transmission with image and video technology. After FDA approved WCE in 2002 for the use in the US, this technique has been used routinely to examine the small intestine non invasively. WCE uses a small capsule of 11 mm diameter and 25 mm length. The front end of the capsule has an optical dome where white light illuminates the luminal surface of the intestine, and a micro colour camera sends images to a receiver worn by the patient. The camera takes 2 pictures per second. The stored data consists of about 50000 images, and is viewed as a video sequence using ad hoc software provided by the manufacturers [2]. The capsule contains a small battery that works for about 8 hours. The capsule is propelled through the intestine by normal peristalsis. This method has proved to be an important tool in the diagnosis of Crohn's disease [3], Celiac disease [4] and occult bleedings [5].

Medical specialists look for significative events in the WCE video stream by direct visual inspection, manually labelling clinical relevant frames. The time taken by this process, even for an experienced viewer, can be up to one or more hours. This is a bottleneck of this method, since it limits its general applicability and it incurs considerable costs. Labelling the video frames to automatically discriminate digestive organs such as esophagus, stomach, small intestine (duodenum, jejunum, ileum) and colon could hence be of great advantage. It would

P. Foggia, C. Sansone, and M. Vento (Eds.): ICIAP 2009, LNCS 5716, pp. 701–710, 2009.
© Springer-Verlag Berlin Heidelberg 2009

make possible to find event boundaries that indicate either entrance to the next organ or to find unusual events within the same organ, such as bleedings, intestinal juices or obstructions, etc.

Manufacturers provide, in a Windows application named *Rapid Reader*, some functionalities to automatically analyze single images. This is done using a suspected blood indicator, that reveals the position in the video of areas with active bleedings. This tool has been reported to produce many false positives while at the same time it misses a large percentage of relevant events [6]. *Rapid Reader* includes also the localization function, which displays the route and the relative position of the capsule on a graphical torso model. To enable this functionality the viewer must find and mark two important locations in the video: first, the pylorus (the valve between stomach and intestine), and the ileo-caecal valve (between intestine and colon). Finding these two loci is difficult even with direct visual analysis because the tissues before and after them are very similar in both cases. Indeed the method proposed in this paper has been proved helpful to this task.

Computer Vision research has devoted a lot of effort to classify frames in a video or to discriminate still images from a database within some semantic classes. One of the state of art techniques to solve this problem is the use of textons [7]. In this paper we advocate the use of textons for the automatic discrimination of abrupt changes within a WCE video. In particular, we consider for each frame the high-frequency energy content and the features related to the texture by means of the response of the images to a bank of Gabor filters. Using textons, it is possible to calculate distances between intervals of frames to find points with abrupt change in pattern.

The experiments to test the method have been conducted on ten video segments extracted from WCE videos of different patients, in which the significant events have been previously labelled by experts. Results have shown that the proposed method may eliminate up to 70% of the frames from further processing while retaining all the clinically relevant frames.

This paper is organized as follows: Section 2 discusses related works. Section 3 describes the methodology that we use to discriminate meaningful events in a WCE video. Section 4 reports experimental results. Finally Section 5 draws conclusions and future works.

2   Related Works

In [8], Lee at al. propose an algorithm to detect event boundaries based on the energy function in the frequency domain. The segmentation of the video is performed taking into account the high frequency content function (HFC) of each frame. To find exact boundaries of digestive organs a bottom-up approach is used to determinate the correlation between consecutive frames. Their experimental results show a recall of 76% and a precision of 51%: the energy is hence a good indicator for relevant frame detection.

In [9] Vilarino et al. propose a method based on anisotropic image filtering and efficient statistical classification of the contraction features. They apply the image gradient tensor to mine local directional information, and a sequence of descriptors to capture the star-pattern of the wrinkles that are the distinctive signature of contractions. Classification is performed with a SVM.

In [10] the previous authors observe that contractions represent only 1% of the entire video. They hence propose to use ROC curves together with simple and ensemble classifiers to identify the frames of contractions.

In [11] the same authors propose a method to reject part of the video with intestinal juices that are not meaningful for a diagnosis. They apply Gabor filters for the characterization of the frames containing intestinal juices.

In [12] Mackiewicz et al. describe a method that uses colour image analysis to discriminate the organs in WCE. The authors create a feature vector combining colour, texture and motion information of the entire image and valid sub-images. The video is segmented into meaningful parts using SVM and HMM.

Bleeding detection is investigated in [13], where multiple features are combined to analyze frames that present bleedings. A two steps process is proposed. The first step to discriminate images containing bleedings uses a block-based colour saturation method. The second step refines the classification using a pixel-based analysis of the luminance and colour saturation. The reported sensitivity in this case is of 88.3%.

3   Proposed Method

We consider the problem of classifying frames of a WCE video without imposing any constraints on the viewing or illumination conditions under which these images were specially obtained. The basic idea is that each digestive organ has a different visual pattern. Each pattern may be characterized by specific values of some observed features. Several candidate features may be considered: the texton method [7] allows to statistically combine all of them to produce a classifier. Our proposal integrates texture-based features (obtained as response to a bank of Gabor filters) with features like colour and luminance that are customarily of primary relevance to the clinician.

The general goal of automatic WCE segmentation is to split a video into shorter sequences each with the same semantic content. In the following we use the term "event" to indicate frame sequences of 6 consecutive frames that testify some abrupt and significative changes in the video. Our definition of "event" includes boundary transitions, intestinal juices, bile, bubbles, etc. We have make precise this term in accordance with medical experts that have manually labelled the test data. It should be pointed out that the term "event" has been used in the published research with different meanings than ours.

The features that we have chosen to build a classifier are: luminance and colour, energy and the responses to a bank of Gabor filters. These features are computed separately on frame sub-blocks. We apply k-means clustering to the set of feature vectors to build a texton dictionary. Frames are hence represented by mean of the histograms over the resulting dictionary. Comparison between histograms provides a way to assign a distance between frames.

3.1   Frame Pre-processing

The frames coming from the WCE videos have been pre-processed as described in this subsection in order to make further information extraction easier ad more reliable. The original frames have a dimension of 576×576 pixels. This includes a large black area and textual information. We restrict the Region Of Interest within the circular area of the video, hence for each frame only a sub-image of dimension 352x352 pixels is considered. (Fig. 1)

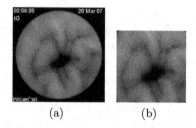

(a)   (b)

Fig. 1. (a) original image; (b) extracted ROI

Each extracted ROI has been in turn transformed in the HSI colour space. It is indeed well known that this colour space grants a greater robustness for analysis. Frames, moreover, are partitioned into 484 squares each of 16×16 pixels. For each one of these squared sub-images we extract the features used for classification as described below. Hence each frame is eventually represented by the collection of the values of the features over all its 484 blocks.

3.2   Colour Features

Direct visual inspection by clinicians is largely based on the consideration of the chrominance value of the frames. Unfortunately colour features althought informative do not provide sufficient clues to a classifier. Because of this we choose to include the average values of the hue, saturation and intensity of each of the 484 blocks of a frame among the representative features of the frame and to integrate them with more features as shown below.

3.3   Energy Features

Transitions, from an organ of the digestive tract to the next, are generally marked by frames that present a greater density of details. This fact has been exploited in [4] to characterize transitions. For this reason we include the high frequency content of blocks among the features used by the proposed classifier. Following [4] we consider the weighted sum of the energy function, linearly increased toward the high frequencies

$$HFC_i = \sum_{i=2}^{\frac{N}{2}+1} (|X_i(k)|^2 * k) \tag{1}$$

where the range $0 \cdots N$ is the index number range of the FFT frequencies in the frame; $|X_i(k)|^2$ is the squared module of the kth component of the FFT and k is a weight to increase the relevance of higher frequencies.

(In (1) we ignore the lowest two bins in order to avoid unwanted bias from low frequency components). We include the HFC of each 16x16 sub-image among the representative features of a frame.

3.4 Texture Features

Textures are powerful discriminators when one has to classify real world pictures. Indeed all the state of the art content based retrieval engines rely on texture analysis. It is natural to include texture descriptors among the features representing a WCE frame. Texture classification has a long history in Computer Vision, starting with Haralick [14] proposed features to the up today methods that use large sets of responses to family of linear filters. In this paper we choose a Gabor filter bank for texture representation. Full details about Gabor filter may be found in several signal processing textbooks, for example see the classical [15].

For the sake of the present application a Gabor filter is defined as follows:

$$H(u, v) = \frac{1}{2\pi\sigma_u\sigma_v} e^{-\frac{1}{2}\left[\frac{(u-u_0)^2}{\sigma_u^2} + \frac{(v-v_0)^2}{\sigma_v^2}\right]} \tag{2}$$

where $\sigma_u = \frac{1}{2\pi\sigma_x}$ and $\sigma_v = \frac{1}{2\pi\sigma_y}$ are the standard deviation of the Gaussian envelope along x and y directions. The set of parameters $(u_0, v_0, \sigma_x, \sigma_y)$ completely define a Gabor filter.

In particular in our usage we empirically found appropriate the following parameters set: $\sigma_x = \sigma_y = 2$; *phase* : $0, 2, 4, 8, 16, 32$ and four directions: $0°, 45°, 90°, 135°$. The rationale behind our choice has been to achieve a good compromise between the recall and precision of the resulting classifier. An optimal choice of the parameters set will be the subject of further investigations. Observe that also the response of a Local Binary Pattern operator, which can be seen as a special filter based texture operator, could be proved itself useful [16].

3.5 The Complete Features Vector

In our proposal a frame comes to be eventually represented as a vector of 28×484 components. The 28 features includes information about average colour and luminace (3 elements), HFC (1 element) and Gabor filter responses (24 elements) for each block.

3.6 The Texton Dictionary

In order to achieve a more abstract representation we pool together the vector of all of the 16x16 blocks of the frames in the video. In our experiments each of the videos is made of 500 frames. This leads to an ensamble of 242000 vectors.

The ensamble has been clusterized to get a small set of recurrent and typical "visual words". Clusterization is performed with a standard K-clustering. The number of clusters is choosen to optimize the ratio of dispersion between cluster centers over the dispersion within clusters. We empirically found that a suitable value for the number of clusters in our experiments is 100.

3.7   From Frames to Histograms

In this phase the dictionary obtained in section 3.6 provides the buckets to compute, for each frame, the relative frequencies of "visual word". In this way we come to a high level representation of a frame as a "bag of visual words". The problem of evaluating similarity between frames is hence turned into the computation of histograms distance. Among the several available choices for histogram distance estimation we choose the Bhatthacharya distance [17]. In this way we define $d(f_i, f_j)$, as the distance between frame f_i and f_j, the Bhattacharya distance between the corresponding histograms.

3.8   Finding Sudden Changes

Direct computation of the Bhattacharya distance of a pair of consecutive frames is generally a weak indicator of changes in the video. This happens because occasionally a frame can be quite different from the previous one just because of casual disturbances and trasmission noise. To have a more robust indicator of sudden changes in the video we consider for each frame f_i the function $C(i)$ defined as follows:

$$C(i) = \frac{1}{9} \sum_{k=i}^{i+2} \sum_{j=3}^{5} d(f_k, f_{i+j}) \qquad (3)$$

$C(i)$ averages the distances between frames in a short sequence and it provides high values when a sudden change is happening or low values in more homogeneous segments (Fig. 2).

   Thresholding the function $C(i)$ will naturally lead to select frames that are very likely to be loci of sudden changes (Fig. 4).

4   Experimental Results

To assess the validity of the use of the indicator function $C(i)$ to discriminate meaningful sudden changes in WCE videos we have analized the performance of this index over 10 manually labelled sequences. The 10 randomly selected sequences have all been obtained from patients of the Ospedale "M. Raimondi" in the period between 2005 and 2008. The manual labelling protocol has been the following. Let $(f_i...f_N)$ be the sequence of frames in a video. We have formed the sequence of intervals $(I_1...I_{\frac{N-3}{3}})$ where interval I_i is made of the six frames $(f_{3i-2}...f_{3i+3})$. For each interval the expert has judged if there is a significative change between the first 3 frames with respect to the last 3 frames. If this is

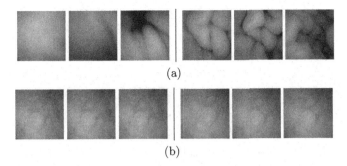

(a)

(b)

Fig. 2. The two rows represent two sequences of consecutive frames. The row (a) is relative to the pylorus: function $C(i)$ for it takes the value 0.41. The row (b) is relative to a smooth portion of stomach: the $C(i)$ takes the value 0.21.

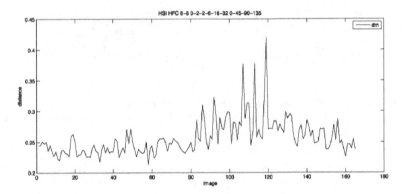

Fig. 3. Plot of the function $C(i)$ for a WCE video sequence; peaks indicate loci of sudden change. The sequence in the upper row of Fig. 2 corresponds to the maximum (interval of frames: 355-360) while the sequence in the lower row of Fig. 2 corresponds to the minimum (interval of frames: 172-177).

the case the interval has been labelled as an "event". In our setting hence an event is a relevant anatomical locus (esophagus, pylorus, etc.) or a pathological presence (bleedings, ulcerations, etc.) or a common non pathological disturbance (intestinal juices, bubbles, etc.) (Fig. 4). Observe that with this experimental framework we only need to compute function $C(i)$ (3) at the first frame of each interval. The typical graph of the $C(i)$ indicator is shown in (Fig. 3). The graph suggests that events may be found thresholding the indicator. However it is difficult at this stage of our research to automatically select a suitable threshold.

For this reason the performance of the index $C(i)$ has been tested as follows: intervals I_i of each video have been sorted according to the decreasing value of their $C(i)$ indicator. We have hence partitioned the sorted I_i's into ten groups of the same size. The first group contains the intervals with the top 10% $C(i)$ score, the last group contains the interval with the lowest 10% $C(i)$ score. For

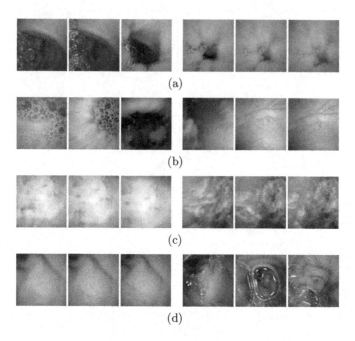

Fig. 4. Examples of events among the WCE video frames; the row (a) corresponds to a pylorus; (b) is relative to the ileo-caecal valve; (c) represents frames with faecal residuals; (d) show the presence of bubbles

Table 1. Percentage of events in the ten groups of intervals sorted by $C(i)$ value

Video	10th	9th	8th	7th	6th	5th	4th	3rd	2nd	1st
1	93%	81%	31%	0%	0%	0%	0%	0%	0%	0%
2	81%	69%	0%	0%	0%	0%	0%	0%	0%	0%
3	100%	100%	38%	6%	13%	0%	0%	0%	0%	0%
4	88%	69%	0%	0%	0%	0%	0%	0%	0%	0%
5	94%	81%	31%	6%	0%	0%	6%	0%	0%	0%
6	94%	88%	19%	0%	0%	0%	0%	0%	0%	0%
7	100%	63%	0%	0%	0%	0%	0%	0%	0%	0%
8	100%	88%	0%	0%	0%	0%	0%	0%	0%	0%
9	100%	75%	19%	0%	0%	0%	0%	0%	0%	0%
10	100%	50%	6%	0%	0%	0%	0%	0%	0%	0%
mean	95%	76%	14%	1%	1%	0%	1%	0%	1%	0%

each group we have counted the number of intervals that the expert labelled as event. The statistics relative to the test data are reported in Table 1 and Table 2. It is evident from the experimental data that the proposed method may safely provide a filter to the clinician that could indeed concentrate the visual inspection on the intervals that score at the top 30% of the $C(i)$ index. Althought this reduction is significative the number of intervals that have to

Table 2. Presence in % over the total number of events in the ten groups of interval sorted by $C(i)$ value

Video	10th	9th	8th	7th	6th	5th	4th	3rd	2nd	1st
1	45%	39%	15%	0%	0%	0%	0%	0%	0%	0%
2	54%	46%	0%	0%	0%	0%	0%	0%	0%	0%
3	39%	39%	15%	2%	5%	0%	0%	0%	0%	0%
4	56%	44%	0%	0%	0%	0%	0%	0%	0%	0%
5	43%	37%	14%	3%	0%	0%	3%	0%	0%	0%
6	47%	44%	9%	0%	0%	0%	0%	0%	0%	0%
7	62%	38%	0%	0%	0%	0%	0%	0%	0%	0%
8	53%	47%	0%	0%	0%	0%	0%	0%	0%	0%
9	50%	38%	9%	0%	0%	0%	0%	0%	3%	0%
10	64%	32%	4%	0%	0%	0%	0%	0%	0%	0%
mean	51%	40%	7%	1%	0%	0%	0%	0%	0%	0%

be examined is still high for a human observer but it may allow the realistic application of computationally more expensive pattern recognition algorithms to this restricted set of intervals.

5 Conclusions and Future Works

In this paper we have shown that a trasformation of the visual data coming from the WCE video into the space of textons opens up the possibility to robustly and effinciently discriminate eventful intervals of a diagnostic video. The proposed technique computes a suitable indicator of the presence of meaningful events. Experimental results show that all the relevant intervals are found among the 30% intervals when they are sorted according to the decreasing value of the proposed indicator. This percentage may be safely furtherly reduced optimizing the ROI selection, the parameters of the Gabor filter banks and the size of the visual dictionary. Future works will concentrate on this issues. Inclusions of the responses of non linear filters, like Local Binary Pattern, among the features will also be considered. The proposed technique may, especially if coupled with fast and effective tools for interactive exploration and visualization of the data, improve the applicability of WCE to clinical pratice.

References

1. Iddan, G., Meron, G., Glukhovsky, A., Swain, P.: Wireless Capsule Endoscopy. Nature 405, 725–729 (2000)
2. Given Imaging, Ltd Israel, http://www.givenimaging.com
3. Gay, G., Delvaux, M., Key, J.: The role of video capsule endoscopy in the diagnosis of digestive diseases: A review of current possibilities. Endoscopy 36, 913–920 (2004)
4. Swain, P.: Wireless capsule endoscopy and Crohns disease. Gut. 54, 323–326 (2005)

5. Culliford, A., Daly, J., Diamond, B., Rubin, M., Green, P.H.R.: The value of wireless capsule endoscopy in patients with complicated celiac disease. Gastrointestinal Endoscopy 62(1), 55–61 (2005)
6. Signorelli, C., et al.: Sensitivity and specificity of the suspected blood identification system in video capsule enteroscopy. Endoscopy 37, 1170–1173 (2005)
7. Varma, M., Zisserman, A.: A statistical approach to texture classification from single images. International Journal of Computer Vision 62 (2005)
8. Lee, J., Oh, J., Shah, S.K., Yuan, X., Tang, S.J.: Automatic classification of digestive organs in Wireless Capsule Endoscopy videos. In: SAC 2007: Proceedings of the, ACM symposium on Applied computing (2007)
9. Spyridonos, P., Vilarino, F., Vitri, J., Azpiroz, F., Radeva, P.: Anisotropic feature extraction from endoluminal images for detection of intestinal contractions. In: Larsen, R., Nielsen, M., Sporring, J. (eds.) MICCAI 2006. LNCS, vol. 4191, pp. 161–168. Springer, Heidelberg (2006)
10. Vilarino, F., Kuncheva, L.I., Radeva, P.: ROC curves and video analysis optimization in intestinal capsule endoscopy. Pattern Recognition Letters 27(8), 875–881 (2006)
11. Vilarino, F., Spyridonos, P., Pujol, O., Vitri, J., Radeva, P.: Automatic detection of intestinal juices in Wireless Capsule Video Endoscopy. In: ICPR 2006: The 18th International Conference on Pattern Recognition (2006)
12. Mackiewicz, M., Berens, J., Fisher, M.: Wireless Capsule Endoscopy Color Video Segmentation. IEEE Transaction on Medical Imaging 27(12) (December 2008)
13. Lau, P.Y., Correia, P.L.: Detection of bleeding patterns in WCE video using multiple features. In: Proceedings of the 29th Annual International Conference of the IEEE EMBS, August 23-26 (2007)
14. Haralick, R., Shapiro, L.: Image segmentation techniques. Comput. Vision Graphics Image Processing 29, 100–132 (1985)
15. Gabor, C.T., Sanjit, K.M.: Modern Filter Theory and Design. John Wiley & Sons, Chichester (1973)
16. Ojala, M.P.T., Maenpaa, T.: Multiresolution grey-scale and rotation invariant texture classification with local binary patterns. IEEE Trans. Pattern Anal. Mach. Intell. 24(7), 971–987 (2002)
17. Bhattacharyya, A.: On a measure of divergence between two statistical populations defined by probability distributions. Bull. Calcutta Math. Soc. 35, 99–109 (1943)

Denoising of Digital Radiographic Images with Automatic Regularization Based on Total Variation

Mirko Lucchese and N. Alberto Borghese

Applied Intelligent Systems Laboratory (AIS-Lab), Department of Computer Science,
University of Milano, Via Comelico 39, 20135 Milano, Italy
{mirko.lucchese,alberto.borghese}@unimi.it

Abstract. We report here a principled method for setting the regularization parameter in total variation filtering, that is based on the analysis of the distribution of the gray levels on the noisy image. We also report the results of an experimental investigation of the application of this framework to very low photon count digital radiography that shows the effectiveness of the method in denoising such images. Total variation regularization leads to a non-linear optimization problem that is solved here with a new generation adaptive first order method. Results suggest a further investigation of both the convergence criteria and/or the scheduling of the optimization parameters of this method.

Keywords: Digital radiography, total variation filtering, regularization, Bayesian filtering, gradient descent minimization.

1 Introduction

Radiographic images are produced by converting the number of X-ray photons that hit the sensor inside the area of each pixel, into a gray level. Thanks to the sensitivity of modern detectors, radiation dose is getting lower and lower: digital panoramic images are produced by a maximum photon count around 10,000 on 14 bits: an almost one to one correspondence between the number of photons and the gray levels. This greatly increases the resolution of the imaging system, but it requires also a careful noise elimination to make the images most readable to the clinicians.

In radiographic images noise is mainly introduced by errors in photon ount and it is therefore modeled through a Poisson distribution [1, 2]. Traditional denoising approaches like linear filtering are inadequate to remove this kind of noise, as they generally tend to smooth significantly the edges in the image and different approaches have been investigated. Among these, regularization theory is particularly suitable as it clearly expresses the two goals of a denoising process: obtain a function as close as possible to the measured data and penalize solutions that have undesirable properties. In this framework a cost function is written as a weighted sum of a distance between the measured and the true data and a function that penalizes "bad" solutions [3]. In the original formulation the squared function was used to express the difference between the true and the measured data and the squared of the gradient was used as a penalization term. This formulation leads to a squared cost function that is convex and calls

P. Foggia, C. Sansone, and M. Vento (Eds.): ICIAP 2009, LNCS 5716, pp. 711–720, 2009.

for an easy minimization. However, it was soon recognized that the weighting coefficient, called regularization parameter, was critical for the quality of the result.

More recently, a clear connection between regularization theory and Bayesian estimate has been described [4]. In the Bayesian framework, the distance between the true and the measured image is evaluated through the negative logarithm of the likelihood of the measured image given the true one, and the penalizing term is associated to a suitable prior distribution of the solutions, often in terms of an Gibbs distributions. The filtered image, $\mathbf{g_f}$, is therefore obtained as:

$$\begin{cases} \mathbf{g_f} = \arg\min_{\mathbf{g}}\left[J(\mathbf{g},\mathbf{g_n})\right] \\ J(\mathbf{g},\mathbf{g_n}) = L(\mathbf{g},\mathbf{g_n}) + \lambda \cdot R(\mathbf{g}) \end{cases} \tag{1}$$

where, i=1....N are the pixels in the image, $\mathbf{g} = \{g_i\}_{i=1..N}$ is the unknown, noiseless (true) radiographic image and $\mathbf{g_n} = \{g_{n,i}\}_{i=1..N}$ is the measured, noisy image. R(.) is the regularization term, function of $\mathbf{g}$ (often of its derivatives). λ is the regularization parameter and balances closeness to the data and reliability of prior distribution.

The statistical view allows incorporating an adequate noise model and a principled regularizer inside the cost function J(.). In particular, in X-ray radiography, Poisson noise is considered inside the first term. This leads to the following L(.) function:

$$L(\mathbf{g},\mathbf{g_n}) = \sum_{i=1}^{N}\left[-g_i + g_{n,i}\ln(g_i) - \ln(g_{n,i}!)\right] \tag{2}$$

This expression contains a factorial term, difficult to compute; therefore, (2) is often substituted by the ratio between $L(\mathbf{g},\mathbf{g_n})$ and $L(\mathbf{g_n},\mathbf{g_n})$, that is also called normalized Kullback-Liebler divergence:

$$KL(\mathbf{g},\mathbf{g_n}) = \frac{L(\mathbf{g},\mathbf{g_n})}{L(\mathbf{g_n},\mathbf{g_n})} = -\sum_{i=1}^{N}\left\{g_{n,i}\cdot\ln\frac{g_i}{g_{n,i}} + g_{n,i} - g_i\right\} \tag{3}$$

The expression of the penalization term, as the squared sum of the gradients, has been also questioned as it tends to over smooth the images. For this reason regularizers that increase less smoothly with the edge amplitude have been proposed. One of the most used is based on a total variation measure, defined as:

$$R(\mathbf{g}) = \sum_{i=1}^{N}\|\nabla g_i\| \tag{4}$$

where ∇g_i is the gradient of $\mathbf{g}$ computed in position i and ||.|| indicates its l_1 or l_2 norm. This approach has become recently popular also in the image processing field [5].

J(.) in (1) becomes strongly non linear with respect to $\mathbf{g}$, and iterative algorithms have been adopted for its minimization. Very recently improved first order methods have been proposed, and in particular the Scaled Gradient Projection Method [6] has shown superior convergence speed and it has been adopted here.

The most critical issue of a regularization approach is an adequate setting of the regularization parameter, λ. One possibility is to use the Mozorov discrepancy principle [7] that states that: the regularization parameter should be increased as much as possible until the difference between the filtered and original data match the noise covariance. This principle can be adopted in a straightforward way when noise is supposed Gaussian, as the covariance matrix, in this case, does not depend of the gray levels distribution. The adaptation of the discrepancy principle to the Poisson case is more difficult. Only very recently a first attempt in this direction has been recently proposed in [6], with an approximation of the likelihood function. We derive here a different method to set λ that is based on the properties of the Poisson distribution and does not require any approximation. We show that it behaves very similarly to [6] for most photon counts, while it is more accurate when photon count is very low.

2 Method

We have generated a set of simulated radiographic images of 512 x 512 pixels, with 16 bpp. First, an absorption coefficients map is created, with coefficients increasing from 0% for the left-most pixels to 100% for the right-most ones. Then, 50 different geometrical figures (circles and rectangles) were randomly positioned inside the map, and added to the background previously created. The circles have a random radius between 1 and 512 pixels; the rectangles sides have a random length between 1 and 512 pixels. Each time a circle or a rectangle is added to the map, all the absorption coefficients covered by the figure are modified as follows: either they are substituted by their complements with respect to 100%, or they are multiplied by a random value between 0 and 1, or a random value between 0% and 100% is added to them. In the latter case, the resulting absorption coefficients are always clipped to 100%. The choice among the three modalities is random.

original image - filtering with a 19x19 sliding window applied

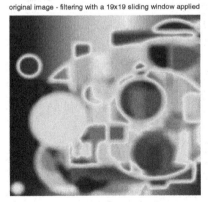 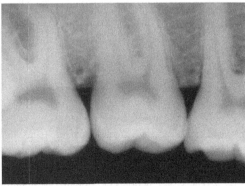

Fig. 1. A typical synthetic digital image used for testing is shown in panel (a). A typical intra-oral image on which total variation filtering was applied is shown in panel (b). It has dimension 1000 x 1387 on 14 bits. The image is shown applying a γ-correction with an exponent equal to 1.5 as usual in clinical practice.

The image is then filtered with a moving average (MA) filter, whose window size was set to 19 x 19 to obtain frequency content similar to that of X-ray digital images and panoramic images in particular. A maximum number of photons equal to 15,000 is considered here. A typical image of this type is shown in Fig. 1a (cf. [2]). A sensor gain equal to one and an offset equal to zero were adopted to guarantee that the gray levels coincide with photon counts. Noise is then added independently for each pixel, according to Poisson statistics (Fig. 1a). Sensor parameters and maximum number of photon counts were chosen such that sensor does not saturate.

These images were then filtered minimizing the cost function (1) through the Scaled Projected Gradient method introduced in [6]. This method adapts at each step the update amplitude analyzing the cost function value in two consecutive steps, applying the Barzilai and Borwein adaptation rule. Moreover, at each step, the cost function is compared to that of the previous step and the update can be decreased in order to keep the cost function decreasing (Armijo rule, [8]).

The following parameters were used according to [6]: the maximum absolute value of the scaling factor is set to L = 1000, the range of admissible step sizes, α_{min}, α_{Max} to: $[10^{-3} \ 10^{3}]$, the number of consecutive values of α stored is $M_{\alpha} = 10$, the rate of updating used to evaluate if the scale size has to be reduced is $\gamma = 10^{-4}$ and the reduction factor of the step size introduced by Armijo rule is $\theta = 0.4$. The α value used in the first iterate was set to $\alpha_{0} = 1.3$. The gradient in (4) was computed as the difference between the gray level of the pixel and that of the north and east pixels. To avoid possible singularity in the derivative of the gradient a value of small quantity is added to the absolute value of the gradient in (4), according to [4]. This small quantity has been chosen equal to one here.

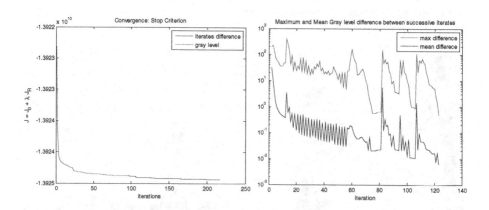

Fig. 2. The cost function (1) is plotted as iterations progresses on the left. The iterations in which the maximum difference of gray levels between two consecutive iterations is above half a gray level are plotted in red. On the right, the mean and maximum variation of gray levels between two iterates.

The following convergence criterion is adopted:

$$\frac{\left|J_k - J_{k-1}\right|}{J_k} < \tau \tag{5}$$

with k number of iteration. $\tau = 10^{-9}$ was set: we verified that the maximum variation of the grey levels when the optimization algorithm was stopped was never larger than half a gray level.

As shown in Fig. 2, the cost function (1) decreases smoothly as the iterations progresses. In particular condition (5) is met at 140 iterations, while a maximum increase between two consecutive iterates below half a gray level is achieved already after 62 iterations.

We repeated the minimization criterion for different values of the regularization parameter, λ, for this image and found that for $\lambda = 0.01$ the distance, measured through the normalized KL, between the filtered and the true image, $KL(g, g_{true})$, was the smallest as shown in Figs. 3. Different values of λ are found for different images although the values are generally quite similar.

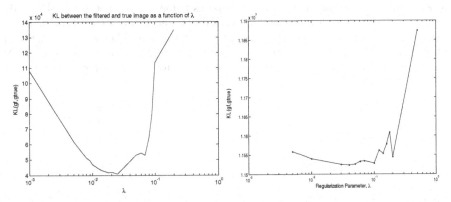

Fig. 3. $KL(g, g_{true})$ as a function of the regularization parameter λ for two different images of the data set. The minimum is achieved for $\lambda = 0.025$ in the first image, for $\lambda = 0.04$ in the second one. The stopping condition of Equation (5) is adopted here.

However, in real life, we usually do not have g_{true} (otherwise, there would be no need of filtering!) and the need of a suitable criterion to compute the optimal value of λ arises. Very recently, [6], an approach based on the Mozorov principle has been proposed: the KL in (1) is linearized around the true value g, obtaining the following Taylor expansion:

$$KL(g_n, g) = \frac{(g_n - g)^2}{2g} - \frac{(g_n - g)^3}{6g^2} + \frac{(g_n - g)^4}{12g^3} - \frac{(g_n - g)^5}{2g^4} + \ldots \tag{6}$$

The expected value of (6) can be computed from the gray value of the pixels in the image. Taking into account that the variance and the curtosis of a Poisson distribution are equal to the mean value [9], we obtain:

$$E\{KL(g_n,g)\}=\frac{1}{2}\left\{\frac{\sigma^2}{g}+\frac{1}{6g}-\frac{29}{6g^2}+....\right\} \tag{7}$$

The approximation gets better and better as photon count, g, increases, therefore, in [6], the expansion in (5) arrested at the first order derivative is considered:

$$E\{KL(g_n,g)\}=\frac{1}{2}\left\{\frac{\sigma^2}{g}+O\left(\frac{1}{g}\right)\right\} \tag{8}$$

Considering that in the real case, we have a finite number of pixels with the same gray level, but that this number can be sufficiently large to get a reliable estimate of KL(.), the following discrepancy principle has been proposed [6]:

$$D(g_n,g)=\frac{2}{n*m}\sum_{i=1}^{n}\sum_{j=1}^{m}\left(g_{n_{i,j}}\ \ln\left(\frac{g_{n_{i,j}}}{g_{i,j}}\right)+g_{i,j}-g_{n_{i,j}}\right) \tag{9}$$

This can be viewed as twice the average value of the normalized KL, averaged over all the pixels. The true value of D(.) is larger than 1 because of the term O(1/g) in (8), and it approaches 1 with the increase in the photons number as shown in Fig. 4. For the images containing very few photon, the possibility of measuring $g_n(.) = 0$ can be meaningful, in this case we assume that $g_n\log(g_n/g) = 0$ for $g_n = 0$ and therefore set the value of the generalized KL to 0 for those pixels for which the noisy image contains zero. As can be seen in Fig. 4, D(.) becomes very little reliable for very low photon counts.

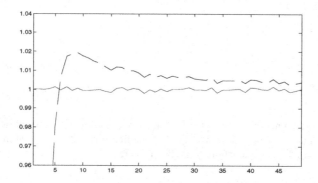

Fig. 4. The value of the discrepancy function in (9) as a function of the pixel counts is plotted in dashed line. Data are obtained from empty simulated digital images for which the same number of photons arrives in all the pixels. Results are averaged over 40 different images and are a good approximation of the expected value of D(.) for photon counts in the range between 0 and 100. The value of the discrepancy function D'(.) in (11) as a function of photon counts is plotted as a continuous line and it is almost constant and equal to 1.

We observe that D(.) derived in (7) is based on an approximation (Eq. (6)). A different discrepancy function is derived here that does not require any approximation. Let us consider the properties of the Poisson distribution, namely that the variance is equal to the expected value. From this observation, for each gray level, we can derive the simple relationship:

$$\frac{\sigma_{g_{true}}^{2}}{g_{true}} = 1 \tag{10}$$

which expresses the well known property that Poisson noise variance increases with the gray levels. We can specialize this property to the case in which we have many, although in finite number, of pixels for each gray level: we can write (10) as:

$$D'(g_n, g_f) := \frac{1}{n*m} \sum_{i=1}^{n} \sum_{j=1}^{m} \frac{\left(g_{n,i} - g_{f,i}\right)^2}{g_{f,i}} = 1 \tag{11}$$

The time course of D'(.) is very similar to that of D(.) in the examined images and the value computed for λ, in most of the gray levels range, is almost the same. Eq. (11) may produce a different, more appropriate, value of λ when images have a very low photon count as shown in Fig. 4.

We also notice that D'(.) is coincident with the second order approximation of the normalized KL. Therefore it seems that KL is equal to the normalized variance plus other terms: these additional terms constitute the difference between D(.) and D'(.) and tend to vanish increasing the photon count (cf. Equation (8)).

3 Results

Equation (11) can be used to automatically set the value of λ in (1) as follows: starting from a reasonable low value, λ is increased until the function D'(.) in (11), computed between the filtered and the noisy image, crosses the value of 1 ([6] and cf. Figs. 5).

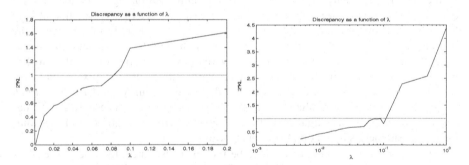

Fig. 5. The value of the function D(.) in (9) is reported as a function of λ for the same image of the leftmost panel of Fig. 3. Notice that the curve intersects the axis D(.) = 1 λ = 0.09, larger than the optimal one defined in Fig. 3.

As it can be seen the curve is quite smooth but the value of λ is slightly overestimated being set to λ = 0.09 versus the value of λ = 0.025 that results optimal from Fig. 3.

We have first investigated the sensitive of λ to the stopping conditions. If we stop the iterations when the maximum increment of the gray levels falls below half a gray level, KL(g_f, g) follows the curve reported in Fig. 6. This curve suggest a value λ = 0.2, and it is quite different from that reported in Fig. 3, where a maximum

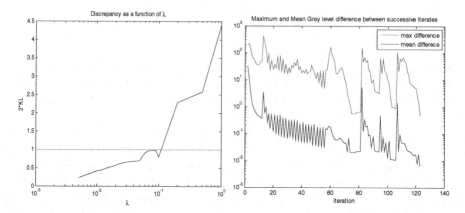

Fig. 6. The KL(g_f, g_{true}) as a function of λ for the same image in the upper panel of Fig. 3. Convergence was stopped when the maximum increment of the gray levels between two iterates falls below half a gray level. Notice the different shape of the curve, the minimum is achieved for $\lambda = 0.05$, about twice that found in Fig. 3.

normalized variation in the cost function was considered as a stopping criterion. When this second condition was adopted as stopping criterion, the value of $\lambda = 0,025$ was suggested, almost 8 times smaller.

Notice that, in Fig. 6, the behavior of D'(.) is not monotone and the risk of a double crossing of the horizontal line D'(.)=1 does exist. This would make the choice of λ not well behaving.

We have further analyzed the behavior of the minimization algorithm as the number of iterations progresses: we have plotted the mean and maximum variation of gray levels between two successive iterates in Fig. 2. Data are referred to the image in the bottom panel of Fig. 4. As it can be appreciated, although the cost function is monotonically decreasing (Fig. 2), there are large variations in the gray levels, of up to 100 gray levels, also close to convergence. This regards only a very few pixels and therefore it does not change significantly the overall cost function. A similar behavior can be noticed also in the normalized variation of the cost function. These data may suggest a more in depth investigation of the convergence criterion and/or of the scheduling of the parameters in the optimization algorithm.

Although the computation of λ has to be further investigated, the filtering result is quite good as it can be appreciated in Fig. 7. In particular the filter is able to remove most of the Poisson noise from the image, leaving the edges almost unchanged (Fig. 7c). We have compared the behavior of such filter with a popular non-linear edge preserving filter, the bilateral filter, implemented according to [10]. Results with this filter are reported in Fig. 7b and in Fig. 7d; they show that this filter does reduce the edges amplitude significantly. The better capability of removing Poisson noise by total variation can be appreciated by computing the standard deviation in a homogeneous region like the one delimited by a dashed square in Figs. 7a and 7b. This is 3.37 for the image obtained through total variation filtering and 9.34 for bilateral filtering. This result indirectly confirms the suitability of the method proposed here to set the value of λ.

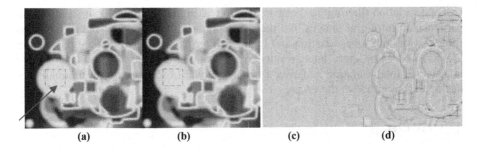

(a)   (b)   (c)   (d)

Fig. 7. The image in Fig. 1b, filtered through total variation is shown in panel (a) and filtered through the bilateral filter in panel (b), of 11x11 mask, a spatial standard deviation $\sigma_d = 3$, and an intensity standard deviation, $\sigma_r = 0,1$, that proved experimentally the best results. The difference between filtered images and the original noise-less image in Fig. 1a is shown in panels (c) and (d). Colors have been assigned by the colormap "jet" of Matlab software.

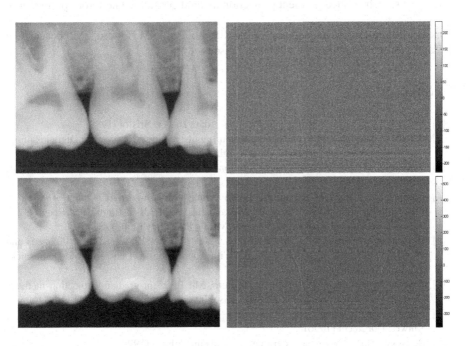

Fig. 8. In panel (a) the image in Fig. 10 filtered with total variation, the difference between the filtered and the original image is shown in panel (b), notice that noise removed is distributed homogeneously over the image. The same image in Fig. 1b, filtered with a bilateral filter, with the same parameters reported for Fig. 7. The difference between the image in panel (c) and the original image is reported in panel (d), notice a dependence of the filtered signal on the edge amplitude. Notice also that the difference in the gray levels in the image filtered with the bilateral filter is more than twice that of total variation filtering; this variation is concentrated in the edges.

Total variation filtering has been applied to real digital radiographic images, and in particular to intra-oral images like the one reported in Fig. 1b. The image has been filtered with both total variation and bilateral filtering and the results are reported in Fig. 8. As it can be appreciated, results are very similar to those obtained in simulated images and total variation achieves a better removal of Poisson noise minimally reducing the amplitude of the edges.

4   Conclusion

From these preliminary results, the ability of total variation filtering of removing Poisson noise from digital radiographs with low photon counts is evident. This confirms also the suitability of the method described here to compute the optimal value of the regularization parameter λ. The experimental results suggest a further investigation of both the convergence criteria and/or the scheduling of the optimization parameter inside the scaled gradient projection method considered here for optimization.

Acknowledgements. The authors would like to thank M.Bertero, P.Boccacci and L.Zanni, for the insightful and interesting discussions.

References

[1] Webb, S.: The Physics of Medical Imaging. Adam Hilger, Bristol (1988)
[2] Frosio, I., Borghese, N.A.: Statistical Based Impulsive Noise Removal in Digital Radiography. IEEE Transactions on Medical Imaging 28(1), 3–16 (2009)
[3] Tikhonov, A.N., Arsenin, V.A.: Solution of Ill-posed Problems. Winston & Sons, Washington (1977)
[4] Bertero, M., Lanteri, H., Zanni, L.: Iterative image reconstruction: A point of view. In: Proc. Interdisciplinary Workshop on Mathematical Methods in Biomedical Imaging and Intensity-Modulated Radiation, Therapy (IMRT), Pisa, Italy (2007)
[5] Hirakawa, K., Meng, X.L., Wolfe, P.J.: A Framework for Wavelet-Based, Analysis and Processing of Color Filter Array Images With Applications to Denoising and Demosaicking. In: ICASSP (2007)
[6] Zanella, R., Boccacci, P., Zanni, L., Bertero, M.: Efficient gradient projection methods for edge-preserving removal of Poisson noise, Inverse Problems (in press)
[7] Engle, H.W., Hanke, M., Neubauer, A.: Regularization of Inverse Problems. Kluwer, Dordrecht (1996)
[8] Bertsekas, D.P.: Nonlinear Programming, 2nd edn. Athena (1999)
[9] Johnson, N.L., Katz, S., Kemps, A.W.: Univariate Discrete Distributions. Wiley and Sons, New York (1993)
[10] Tomasi, C., Manduchi, R.: Bilateral filtering for gray and color images. In: Sixth International Conference on Computer Vision, 1998, pp. 839–846 (1998)

A Real-Time Occlusion Aware Hardware Structure for Disparity Map Computation

Christos Georgoulas and Ioannis Andreadis

Laboratory of Electronics
Department of Electrical and Computer Engineering, Democritus University of Thrace,
GR-67 100 Xanthi, Greece
{cgeorg,iandread}@ee.duth.gr

Abstract. Many machine vision applications deal with depth estimation in a scene. Disparity map recovery from a stereo image pair has been extensively studied by the computer vision community. Previous methods are mainly restricted to software based techniques on general-purpose architectures, presenting relatively high execution time due to the computationally complex algorithms involved. In this paper a new hardware module suitable for real-time disparity map computation module is realized. This enables a hardware based occlusion-aware parallel-pipelined design, implemented on a single FPGA device with a typical operating frequency of 511 MHz. It provides accurate disparity map computation at a rate of 768 frames per second, given a stereo image pair with a disparity range of 80 pixels and 640x480 pixel spatial resolution. The proposed method allows a fast disparity map computational module to be built, enabling a suitable module for real-time stereo vision applications.

Keywords: FPGA-hardware implementation, occlusions, real–time imaging, disparity maps, color image processing.

1 Introduction

An active area of research is the so-called correspondence problem. It comprises the detection of conjugate pairs in stereo image pairs, i.e. to find for each point in the left image, its corresponding in the right image [1]. The candidate matching points should be distinctly different from their surrounding pixels. Even two identical cameras have different sensor parameters, which introduces pixel intensity value variations for the same scene point. Thus, suitable feature extraction should precede stereo matching. The two major categories of feature extraction algorithms are: area-based [2, 3] and feature-based [4, 5]. Area-based algorithms use local pixel intensities as a distance measure and they produce dense disparity maps, i.e. process the whole area of the image pair. On the other hand, feature-based algorithms rely on certain points of interest. These points are selected according to appropriate feature detectors. Comparing the strengths and weaknesses of these two major categories, the main advantage of feature-based compared to area-based algorithms, is that they produce more accurate results. The disadvantages are that they are much slower and produce sparse disparity

P. Foggia, C. Sansone, and M. Vento (Eds.): ICIAP 2009, LNCS 5716, pp. 721–730, 2009.
© Springer-Verlag Berlin Heidelberg 2009

maps [4]. This makes area-based algorithms suitable for real-time applications [6]. A major problem though with area-based algorithms is that the computed disparity map contains an amount of false matched points due to uncertainty during the disparity selection stage, especially within featureless regions or at occlusion boundaries. This uncertainty cannot be easily handled by dense stereo algorithms. The occlusion problem in stereovision refers to the fact that some scene points are visible to one camera but not the other, due to the geometry of the scene and camera setup geometries. Many researches have focused on detecting and measuring occlusion regions in stereo imagery, and recovering accurate depth estimates for these regions, as evaluated in [7].

In our later work [8], a three-stage module addressing the stereo vision matching problem aimed at real-time applications was proposed and implemented in hardware. It employed an adaptive window constrained search as well as a Cellular Automata (CA) approach, as a post-processing step, for efficient false reconstructions removal, improving the accuracy of the resulting disparity maps. The work was further extended [9], implementing a Fuzzy Inference System (FIS) hardware structure, as a post processing step for performance and accuracy improvement.

In this paper, a novel three stage real-time hardware implemented disparity map computation module is proposed, extending our previous work [8, 9], both from qualitative and quantitative terms, concerning the quality of the produced disparity map and the frame rate output of the module. The proposed module can efficiently deal with speed demanding applications since disparity maps are computed at a rate of 768 frames per second for a 640x480 pixel resolution stereo pair. Its main advantage compared to previous algorithms is its high processing speed, which is crucial in real-time practical applications such as three-dimensional modeling, vision-guided mobile robots, object recognition and navigation, biometrics and many more. To eliminate false correspondences, an occlusion-aware module was implemented, concerning both left-right and right-left disparity consistency information. The above requires the initial computation of two disparity maps, in order to retrieve the inconsistent disparities, which comprise to occluded areas.

The paper is organized as follows: the proposed algorithm is described in Section 2, the proposed hardware structure is presented in Section 3, experimental results are shown in Section 4 and conclusions are provided in Section 5.

2 Proposed Algorithm

The disparity maps are initially generated with the use of Sum of Absolute Differences (SAD). Afterwards, the occluded areas and other false matched points are extracted from the previously calculated maps, to finally refine and obtain the resulting disparity maps. All three steps are fully implemented in hardware on an FPGA device.

2.1 Color SAD Window Based Technique

A color SAD window based algorithm was used for the disparity map generation. As in our later work [8, 9], this choice was made to increase speed. Sum of squared differences, correlation, or image moments, could also be used, but were not selected after considering speed issues, since greater computational complexity is involved in these metrics, enhancing their required processing times compared to SAD. Moreover, the SAD can be directly implemented in hardware, due to its simplicity. The SAD equations used can be seen below:

$$SAD(i, j, d)_{left-right} = \sum_{\mu=-w}^{w} \sum_{v=-w}^{w} \sum_{k=1}^{3} \left| I_l(i+\mu, j+v, k) - I_r(i+\mu, j-d+v, k) \right|, \tag{1}$$

$$SAD(i, j, d)_{right-left} = \sum_{\mu=-w}^{w} \sum_{v=-w}^{w} \sum_{k=1}^{3} \left| I_l(i+\mu, j+d+v, k) - I_r(i+\mu, j+v, k) \right|, \tag{2}$$

where w is the square window size fixed to 7x7 pixels, I_l and I_r denote the left and right image pixel grayscale values, d is the disparity range, and i, j, k are the coordinates (rows, columns, color component) of the center pixel of the window for which the SAD is computed.

Once the two SADs are computed for all pixels and for all disparity values, a similarity accumulator has been constructed for each pixel, for each consistency, which indicates the most likely disparity. A search in the SADs for all disparity values, (d_{min} up to d_{max}), is performed for every pixel, and at the disparity index where the SADs are minimum, these values are given as the corresponding pixel values for the left-right and right-left disparity maps:

$$D(i, j) = \arg \min_{d \in [d_{min}, d_{max}]} SAD(i, j, d). \tag{3}$$

2.2 Occlusion and False Matching Detection

There are three main classes of algorithms for handling occlusions: 1) methods that detect occlusions [10, 11], 2) methods that reduce sensitivity to occlusions [12, 13], and 3) methods that model the occlusion geometry [14, 15]. Considering the first class, left-right consistencychecking may also be used to detect occlusion boundaries. Computing two disparity maps, one based on the correspondence from the left image to the right image, and the other based on the correspondence from the right image to the left image, inconsistent disparities are assumed to represent occluded regions in the scene. Left-right consistency checking is also known as the "two-views constraint". This technique is well suited to remove false correspondences caused by occluded areas within a scene [11]. Due to its simplicity and overall good performance, this technique was implemented in many real-time stereo vision systems [16-18].

Disparity maps are usually corrupted due to false correspondence matches. There might be occluded areas in the scene, leading to false disparity assignment. Using the left-right consistency checking, valid disparity values are considered, only those that are consistent in both disparity maps, i.e. those that do not lie within occluded areas. A pixel that lies within an occluded area will have different disparity value in the left disparity map, from its consistent pixel in the right disparity map. For example, a non-occluded pixel in the left disparity image must have a unique pixel with equally as-signed disparity value in the right disparity map according to the following equations:

$$D_{left\text{-}right}(i,j) = D_{right\text{-}left}(i,j\text{-}d), \ (d = D_{left\text{-}right}(i,j)), \tag{4}$$

$$D_{right\text{-}left}(i,j) = D_{left\text{-}right}(i,j\text{+}d), \ (d = D_{right\text{-}left}(i,j)). \tag{5}$$

The same applies, for false matched points not exclusively due to occlusions, but due to textureless areas or sensor parameter variations. These points are assigned with a false disparity value during the disparity map assignment stage described by equation (3), since there might be more than one minimum SAD value for a given pixel, which leads to false disparity value assignment for that pixel. Thus, the disparity value assigned to some pixels does not correspond to the appropriate correct value.

Performing this consistency check, the occluded pixel along with the false matched points within the scene can be derived. These are depicted in Figure 1, (a) for left-right and (b) for right-left disparity map respectively.

2.3 Disparity Refinement

Once the occluded areas along with the false matched points have been extracted, the disparity maps are refined in order to improve their resulting quality. Considering the occluded and false matched pixels in the left-right disparity map, their value is being replaced by one of their neighboring pixels in the range (i,j-5) up to (i,j-1) according to which approximates best equation (4), after being crossed-checked with right-left disparity map corresponding pixels. In the case that the neighboring pixels are un-matched, disparity refinement cannot be performed for the given pixels. The proposed method thus yields semi-dense disparity results. The neighborhood size has been se-lected after a series of tests under various size configurations, to obtain adequate per-formance [19]. The right-left disparity map is refined in the similar manner according to equation (5). This improves the resulting disparity maps accuracy, since uncertainty can be eliminated by an appropriate disparity value assignment.

3   Hardware Description

The module implementation relies on the use of an FPGA device. Considering their flexibility in terms of reconfigurability and ease of use convenience, FPGAs

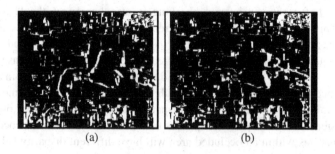

                 (a)   (b)

Fig. 1. Occluded and false matched pixels

have become very popular in digital systems synthesis, providing high performance at a reasonable price on digital system design [20]. The module was implemented in parallel pipelined architecture, realized on a single FPGA device of the Stratix IV family of Altera Devices. The typical operating clock frequency was found to be 511 MHz. The block diagram of the proposed module can be seen in Figure 2.

SAD calculation is required for a 7x7 pixel size window, throughout the whole image. 24-bit color depth images are used as inputs. The calculated disparity values are 7-bit binary words, since the proposed module was designed to operate for up to 80 disparity levels, (2^7= 128 different levels).

Two serpentine-type input register arrangements are used to temporally store the left and right image working windows. The serpentine input blocks are considered in order to increase the processing speed of the proposed module, since overlapping pixels usually exist between adjacent windows in window-based operations. This architecture is used to temporarily store overlapping pixels in order to reduce the clock cycles needed to load image pixels into the module. After an initial latency period which depends on the image size, output is provided once every clock cycle.

Two similar sets of registers are used to store d_{max} 3x7x7 working windows for the left and right image R, G and B components. The number of the registers concerning the image inputs, is proportional to the number of the disparity range; i.e. for a disparity range up to 80 and a working window of 7x7, [7x7 + ((80-1)x7)] = 602 registers are needed for each color component for each image input. A disparity selection input pin is used to enable the required number of registers according to the given disparity range, to increase the speed performance when operating at smaller disparity ranges, concerning the time needed to initially fill the required registers sizes with the image pixel values. The SADs for left-right and right-left disparity maps are computed according to equations (1) and (2). The disparity value, (d_{min} up to d_{max}), for which the SAD is minimum for each pixel, equation (3), is selected as the corresponding pixel value for disparity map, which is then fed to the occlusion/false match detector circuit.

A range of d_{max} disparity values is required by the occlusion/false match detector module. This is due to the fact that consistency checking is performed for all possible horizontal displacements according to equations (4) and (5). Therefore, for the case of an operating range of 80 disparity levels, for the left-right disparity map check, the $D_{left-right}(i,j)$ disparity value is checked against its unique consistent match which lies in the $D_{right-left}(i,j-80$ up to j) range. Every pixel is checked against its consistent match, and if equations (4) and (5) are not satisfied, the pixel is marked as occluded or false assigned. To enable such operation a set of 80 registers is used for each map, to store the necessary disparity values calculated from previous module stages.

Finally the disparity map refinement is performed by obtaining the occluded and false assigned pixels from previous stage and replacing their values considering the neighboring (i,j-5) up to (i,j-1) pixel range. A set of registers is used to store the data required to perform the disparity value replacement. A total of 5x7 bits are required from each consistency, which are fed into the disparity map refinement unit from the previous stage. Once the refinement is performed, the final 7-bit disparity value for both left-right and right-left consistency is obtained at the module output.

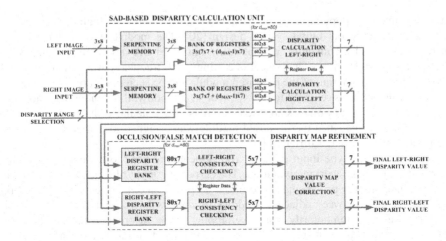

Fig. 2. Block diagram of the proposed module

The architecture presented in Section 3 has been implemented using Quartus II schematic editor by Altera. It has been then simulated to prove functionality, and once tested, finally mapped on an FPGA device. The analytical specifications of the target device are shown in Table 1.

4   Experimental Results

The proposed occlusion and false assignment detection provides satisfactory improvement in the accuracy of the resulting disparity maps, while preserving all the necessary details of the disparity map depth values. The resulting disparity maps are presented in Figure 3 along with original image pairs for (a) Tsukuba and (b) Cones.

The hardware implemented module enables an appropriate method in real-time demanding applications. The relationship between the number of frames processed per second and the processed image size, for an operating range of 80 disparity levels, is presented in Table 2. As it can be observed, the module presents real-time response even for high resolution images.

Compared to existing methods in terms of speed, it presents higher processing rates. Quantitative results of the proposed module under various configurations can be seen in Table 3, and compared to our previous methods [8, 9] and other existing methods [21-25], in Table 4. Compared to [8, 9,21-25], our method proves its performance, as it can be seen in Table 4. The Acc (accuracy) term, shown in Tables 3 and 4, states the ratio of the pixels given a correct disparity value (as compared with the ground truth) to the total assigned pixels, where the Cov (coverage) term states the percentage of the image total pixels, for which a disparity value has been assigned. The total accuracy (Tot Acc) term, shown in Table 4, is the percentage of the image total pixels, for which a correct disparity value has been assigned. The standard Non-occ, All and Disc parameters, that appear in Middlebury stereo evaluation webpage (http://vision.middlebury.edu/stereo/), were not followed since they correspond to dense disparity maps metrics, whereas the proposed method yields semi-dense results.

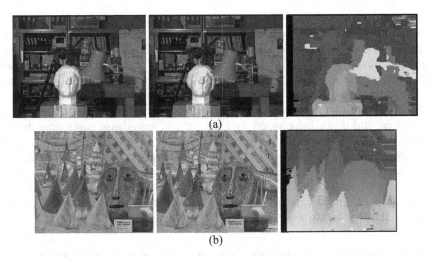

Fig. 3. Resulting disparity maps along with original image pairs for (a) Tsukuba (b) Cones

Table 1. Specifications of target device

Device	Block memory bits (%)	Registers	ALUTs (%)	LABs (%)	Pins (%)
EP4SGX290 HF35C2	<1 (192/ 13,934,592)	15,442	59 (143,653/ 244,160)	74 (9,036 /12,208)	10 (70/660)

Table 2. Frame rate output of realized module

Disp. levels	**80**				
Image size (pixels)	320x240	640x480	800x600	1024x768	1280x1024
Frames / sec	2042	768	550	375	251

The accuracy achieved by the proposed method along with the speed performance under various levels of disparity, enable an efficient module that can perform adequately enough in stereo vision applications, regarding less than 10% decrease in accuracy and more than a hundred times faster processing speed compared to previous algorithms [21-25], Table 4. Moreover, the proposed module exhibits real time speed response preservation even at practical stereo vision large disparity ranges, while other methods [21-25] present an exponential rise in time needed to compute larger disparity ranges. This can be seen in Table 4.

Compared to other FPGA-based approaches, with practical stereo image data, the proposed method presents higher processing rates. In [26], an FPGA-based module reaches 10 frames per second for a sub-sampled 640x480 pixel resolution image with a disparity range of 30 levels. In [27], a 3D-vision system implemented for tracking people, reaches 30 frames per second for a 512x480 pixel resolution image pair with 52 levels of disparity. In [28], an FPGA-based system achieves 19 frames per second for a 640x480 image pair resolution with 80 levels of disparity. Additionally in [29], a performance of 600 frames per second is reported, for a 450x375 pixel resolution image pair with a disparity range of 100 levels. The proposed method performs higher processing rates compared to [26-29], reaching 768 frames per second for a 640x480 pixel resolution image pair with 80 levels of disparity, as it can be observed in Table 2.

Finally, it must be noted that the proposed module results to semi-dense disparity estimation. The depth information loss due to the semi-dense results can be adequately balanced by the high output rate, since much more depth estimations are being carried out, and more importantly in real-time speeds. On the other hand, dense stereo algorithms are designed to perform better in the accuracy term, and to present much slower output rates. This occurs due to their design architecture complexity, that involves composite calculations and to their sometimes required repetitive behaviour to reach such highly accurate results.

Table 3. Quantitative results of the proposed module under various configurations

	Tsukuba		Venus		Cones		Teddy	
	Acc (%)	Cov (%)	Acc (%)	Cov (%)	Acc (%)	Cov (%)	Acc (%)	Cov (%)
Initial Disparity Map	94	77	93	75	99	80	98	77
Refined Disparity Map	95	91	95	92	94	93	92	95

Table 4. Quantitative results of the proposed module compared to previous algorithms

	Tsukuba (384x288, disp. levels = 16)				Venus (434x383, disp. levels = 20)				Cones (450x375, disp. Levels = 60)			
	Acc (%)	Cov (%)	Tot Acc (%)	Time (ms)	Acc (%)	Cov (%)	Tot Acc (%)	Time (ms)	Acc (%)	Cov (%)	Tot Acc (%)	Time (ms)
[8]	88	51	44.88	1.3	92	69	63.48	1.97	72	56	40.32	2
[24]	99.64	75	74.73	6,000	99.84	73	72.88	13,000	-	-	-	-
[25]	99.68	76	75.76	62	99.82	73	72.87	156	99.21	55	54.56	328
[9]	89	92	81.88	0.8	92	90	82.80	1.21	99	93	92.07	1.26
[21]	99.7	85	84.75	42	99.79	86	85.82	109	-	-	-	-
Proposed	**95**	**91**	**86.45**	**0.29**	**95**	**92**	**87.40**	**0.44**	**92**	**95**	**87.4**	**0.33**
[23]	99.47	93	92.51	178	98.91	93	91.99	216	95.02	78	74.11	293
[22]	99.76	95.2	94.97	4,400	99.91	92.9	92.82	11,100	-	-	-	-

(-) Not Provided

5 Conclusions

This paper presents a hardware implemented three-stage module, addressing the stereo vision matching problem aimed at real time applications, which extends our previous implemented algorithms [8, 9]. An SAD window based technique using full color RGB images as well as an occlusion detection approach to remove false matchings are employed. The architecture is based on fully parallel-pipelined blocks in order to achieve maximum processing speed. Depending on the required operational disparity range, the proposed module can be parameterized, to adapt to the given configuration. Both from qualitative and quantitative terms, concerning the quality of the produced disparity map and the frame rate output of the module, a highly efficient method dealing with the stereo correspondence problem has been proposed. Real-time speeds rated up to 768 frames per second for a 640x480 pixel resolution image pair with 80 disparity levels, are achieved, which enable the proposed module for real stereo vision applications. The proposed module maintains almost constant frame rate output, even for large disparity ranges, considering that disparity levels in most practical stereo vision applications range from 60 up to 100.Its maximum disparity operating range is designed up to 80 levels, but it can be straightforwardly implemented even further, to enable even larger disparity ranges.

Additionally, the proposed module design was targeted on a single Altera FPGA device. As a result, it could be applied to enable an efficient system including three-dimensional modeling, vision-guided mobile robots, object recognition and navigation, biometrics and many more. The proposed analysis and results confirm that semi-dense disparity maps can be efficiently calculated at real-time rates, whereas other methods have proved that the improvement in the disparity map quality results in speed reduction. This trade-off will always be present in this type of implementations. The proposed module can effectively be applied to practical real-time stereo vision applications due to its speed performance.

References

1. Barnard, S.T., Thompson, W.B.: Disparity analysis of images. IEEE Transactions on Pattern Analysis and Machine Intelligence 2, 333–340 (1980)
2. Di Stefano, L., Marchionni, M., Mattoccia, S.: A fast area-based stereo matching algorithm. Image and Vision Computing 22(12), 983–1005 (2004)
3. Muhlmann, K., Maier, D., Hesser, J., Manner, R.: Calculating dense disparity maps from color stereo images, an efficient implementation. Int. J. Comput. Vision 47(1-3), 79–88 (2002)
4. Jordan, J.R., Bovik, A.C.: Using chromatic information in edge-based stereo correspondence. Computer Vision, Graphics, and Image Processing: Image Understanding 54(1), 98–118 (1991)
5. Baumberg, A.: Reliable feature matching across widely separated views. In: Proceedings of the IEEE Conference on Computer Vision and Pattern Recognition, pp. 774–781 (2000)
6. Hirschmuller, H.: Improvements in Real-Time Correlation-Based Stereo Vision. In: Proceedings of IEEE Workshop on Stereo and Multi-Baseline Vision, pp. 141–148 (2001)
7. Brown, M., Burschka, D., Hager, G.: Advances in computational stereo. IEEE Transactions on Image Processing 25, 993–1008 (2003)
8. Georgoulas, C., Kotoulas, L., Sirakoulis, G., Andreadis, I., Gasteratos, A.: Real-Time Disparity Map Computation Module. Journal of Microprocessors & Microsystems 32(3), 159–170 (2008)
9. Georgoulas, C., Andreadis, I.: A real-time fuzzy hardware structure for disparity map computation. Submitted to Journal of Real-Time Image Processing

10. Chang, C., Chatterjee, S., Kube, P.R.: On an Analysis of Static Occlusion in Stereo Vision. In: Proceedings of Computer Vision and Pattern Recognition, pp. 722–723 (1991)
11. Fua, P.: A Parallel Stereo Algorithm that Produces Dense Depth Maps and Preserves Image Features. Machine Vision and Applications 6(1), 35–49 (1993)
12. Bhat, D.N., Nayar, S.K.: Ordinal Measures for Image Correspondence. IEEE Transactions on Pattern Analysis and Machine Intelligence 20(4), 415–423 (1998)
13. Sara, R., Bajcsy, R.: On Occluding Contour Artifacts in Stereo Vision. In: Proceedings of Computer Vision and Pattern Recognition, pp. 852–857 (1997)
14. Belhumeur, P.N.: A Bayesian Approach to Binocular Stereopsis. Int. J. Computer Vision 19(3), 23–260 (1996)
15. Birchfield, S., Tomasi, C.: Depth Discontinuities by Pixel-to- Pixel Stereo. In: Proceedings of the IEEE International Conference on Computer Vision, pp. 1073–1080 (1998)
16. Faugeras, O., et al.: Real-time correlation-based stereo: algorithm, implementations and application. Technical Report RR 2013, INRIA (1993)
17. Konolige, K.: Small vision systems: Hardware and implementation. In: 8th International Symposium on Robotics Research, Hayama, Japan, pp. 203–212. Springer, London (1997)
18. Matthies, L., Kelly, A., Litwin, T.: Obstacle detection for unmanned ground vehicles: A progress report. In: International Symposium of Robotics Research, Munich, Germany (1995)
19. Scharstein, D., Szeliski, R.: A taxonomy and evaluation of dense two-frame stereo correspondence algorithms. Int. J. Comput. Vision 47(1-3), 7–42 (2002)
20. Leeser, M., Hauck, S., Tessier, R.: Editorial: field-programmable gate arrays in embedded systems. EURASIP Journal on Embedded Systems (1), 11 (2006)
21. Gong, M., Yang, Y.H.: Near real-time reliable stereo matching using programmable graphics hardware. In: Proceedings of IEEE Conference on Computer Vision and Pattern Recognition, pp. 924–931 (2005)
22. Kim, J.C., Lee, K.M., Choi, B.T., Lee, S.U.: A dense stereo matching using two-pass dynamic programming with generalized ground control points. In: Proceedings of the IEEE Conference on Computer Vision and Pattern Recognition, pp. 1075–1082 (2005)
23. Gong, M., Yang, Y.H.: Real-Time Stereo Matching Using Orthogonal Reliability-Based Dynamic Programming. IEEE Transactions on Image Processing 16(3), 879–884 (2007)
24. Veksler, O.: Extracting Dense Features for Visual Correspondence with Graph Cuts. In: Proceedings of IEEE Conference on Computer Vision and Pattern Recognition, pp. 689–694 (2003)
25. Gong, M., Yang, Y.H.: Fast Unambiguous Stereo Matching Using Reliability-Based Dynamic Programming. IEEE Transactions on Pattern Analysis and Machine Intelligence 27(6), 998–1003 (2005)
26. Khaleghi, B., Ahuja, S., Wu, J.Q.M.: A new Miniaturized Embedded Stereo-Vision System (MESVS-I). In: Proceedings of Canadian Conference on Computer and Robot Vision, pp. 26–33 (2008)
27. Woodill, J.I., Buck, R., Jurasek, D., Gordon, G., Brown, T.: 3D Vision: Developing an Embedded Stereo-Vision System. IEEE Computer 40(5), 106–108 (2007)
28. Miyajima, Y., Maruyama, T.: A Real-Time Stereo Vision System with FPGA. In: Y. K. Cheung, P., Constantinides, G.A. (eds.) FPL 2003. LNCS, vol. 2778, pp. 448–457. Springer, Heidelberg (2003)
29. Ambrosch, K., Humenberger, M., Kubinger, W., Steininger, A.: SAD-based Stereo Matching Using FPGAs. In: Embedded Computer Vision part II, pp. 121–138. Springer, London (2009)

A Graph-Based Approach for Shape Skeleton Analysis

André R. Backes[1] and Odemir M. Bruno[2]

[1] Instituto de Ciências Matemáticas e de Computação (ICMC)
Universidade de São Paulo (USP)
Avenida do Trabalhador São-carlense, 400
13560-970 São Carlos SP Brazil
backes@icmc.usp.br
[2] Instituto de Física de São Carlos (IFSC)
Universidade de São Paulo (USP)
Avenida do Trabalhador São-carlense, 400
13560-970 São Carlos SP Brazil
bruno@ifsc.usp.br

Abstract. This paper presents a novel methodology to shape characterization, where a shape skeleton is modeled as a dynamic graph, and
degree measurements are computed to compose a set of shape descriptors. The proposed approach is evaluated in a classification experiment
which considers a generic set of shapes. A comparison with traditional
shape analysis methods, such as Fourier descriptors, Curvature, Zernike
moments and Multi-scale Fractal Dimension, is also performed. Results
show that the method is efficient for shape characterization tasks, in spite
of the reduced amount of information present in the shape skeleton.

Keywords: graph, Shape Analysis, Skeleton.

1 Introduction

Skeletonization is a method that transforms the shape into a simple structure,
which is capable of represent it. The goal of the method is to reduce the information of the shape, in order to make easier the process of recognition and
analysis. There are distinct methods for skeleton and most of them are based on
the Medial Axis Transform (MAT) originally proposed by Blum [1,2]. The MAT
of a shape consists of a set of center coordinates of circles that (i) have to be
bi-tangents to the shape and (ii) be completely inside of the shape.

The structure formed by the MAT is a set of interconnected points that represents the original shape with a reduced amount of information. Although the
skeleton of a shape is simpler than its contour, the nature of its structure is not
so easy to process, and it demands a special analysis. There are some traditional
approaches to analyze and recognize skeletons: (i) metrics, this is the simplest

P. Foggia, C. Sansone, and M. Vento (Eds.): ICIAP 2009, LNCS 5716, pp. 731–738, 2009.
© Springer-Verlag Berlin Heidelberg 2009

approach, and it consists of measuring the skeleton structure (i.e. , angles formed by lines, width and number of lines); (ii) signal processing based methods, where the contour of the skeleton structure is analyzed by signal processing techniques, such as Fourier transform or wavelets; (iii) fractals [3] and shape methods [4] and (iv) neural networks or other AI techniques, which consists in applying the skeleton directly into the input of a neural network [5,6].

In this work, we propose a graph-based approach to analyze the skeleton. The method was originally proposed to deal with shape contours [7] and in this work, we propose its use in the skeleton analysis. Experiments compare the method with contour based methods [8], signal processing [9] and fractal dimension [10]. Results demonstrate that the method is suitable to the skeleton analysis and overcome traditional contour approaches.

2   Shape Skeleton Graph

2.1   Shape Skeleton as a Graph

In order to represent the shape skeleton computed from a shape image as a graph (Figure 1), we consider skeleton information as a list of connected points S, $S = [s_1, s_2, ..., s_N]$, where N is the number of points in the skeleton and $s_i = (x_i, y_i)$ represents the discreet coordinate of the point i in the skeleton. A graph $G = (V, E)$ is built by considering each point $s_i \in S$ as a vertex in graph G, i.e., $V = S$. For each pair of vertices (v_i, v_j) a non-directed edge $e_{ij} \in E$ is built connecting these vertices. The weight of the edges is computed considering the Euclidean distance between each pair of points of the skeleton:

$$d(s_i, s_j) = \sqrt{(x_i - x_j)^2 + (y_i - y_j)^2}.$$

A $N \times N$ matrix W represents the weight of the edges between vertices

$$W(i, j) = w_{ij} = d(s_i, s_j),$$

where the weights are normalized into the interval $[0, 1]$,

$$W = \frac{W}{\max_{w_{ij} \in W}}.$$

The resulting graph presents a regular behavior as each vertex presents the same characteristic, such as number of connections, as other vertices. Hence, no relevant properties can be computed from this graph. Thus, a transformation must be applied over this graph to achieve relevant properties that can be used to characterize this graph structure and, as a result, the original shape skeleton. For this transformation, we propose to use the dynamic evolution of the graph.

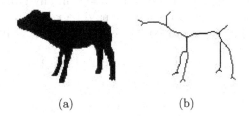

(a)   (b)

Fig. 1. (a) Original shape; (b) Shape skeleton

2.2 Dynamic Evolution

Graphs with different topological aspect present a large range in their characteristics. Besides, the interaction between structural and dynamical aspects improve graph characterization [11].

Modeling the dynamics of a graph is a difficult task. It may involve node addition or deletion, changes in edges positions or anything else, during a time period. However, the graph structure dynamics can be estimated by applying a transformation over the original graph. Then, properties from this new version of the graph are computed and used to characterize its dynamics [12].

A graph transformation can be performed in many ways. A very simple and straight approach is to apply a threshold t over the set of edges E to select E^*, $E^* \subseteq E$. By keeping the original set of nodes V, a new graph $G^* = (V, E^*)$, which represents an intermediary stage in graph evolution, is achieved.

In our approach, an edge belongs to E^* with its weight is equal or smaller than a threshold t (Figure 2). This δ_t transformation can be represented as

$$E^* = \delta_t(E) = \{e \in E | w(e) \leq t\}.$$

By applying different thresholds t over the original graph it is possible to provide a richer set of measurements, thus providing a better graph characterization.

2.3 Measurements

Graph theory provides numerous measurements that can be computed from a graph or network. The vertex degree is largely used in graph studies due to its

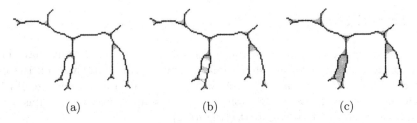

(a)   (b)   (c)

Fig. 2. Different stages in graph evolution. Edges in each graph are the only ones with weight smaller than a threshold t.

simplicity and for being a characteristic present in any graph. It is defined as the number of incident edges (or connections) in a vertex $v_i \in V$. The degree of a vertex v_i, $deg(v_i)$, indicates its connectivity and can be defined as:

$$deg(v_i) = |\{e \in E | v_i \in e\}| = |\{v_j \in V | \{v_i, v_j\} \in E\}| = |\partial v_i|,$$

with

$$\partial v_i = \{v_j \in V | (v_i, v_j) \in E\}$$

where ∂v_i is the set of neighbors of v_i and $|A|$ denotes the cardinality (number of elements) of a set A [13].

To characterize a graph, we propose to use global measurements computed from degree distribution analysis. Two measurements have been considered for this application: the *Average Degree*

$$Av(G) = \sum_{v_i \in V} \frac{deg(v_i)}{|N|},$$

and the *Maximum Degree*

$$Max(G) = \max_i deg(v_i).$$

3   Skeleton Graph Signature

We propose to perform skeleton characterization by using a signature which describes temporary characteristics of the computed skeleton graph. This signature is a feature vector φ composed by Average and Maximum Degree measurements computed from each transformed graph G^* achieved by applying a transformation δ_t over the original graph G, for different values of $t \in T$:

$$\varphi = [Av(G_{t_1}), Max(G_{t_1}), \ldots, Av(G_{t_M}), Max(G_{t_M})], t_i \in T,$$

where G_{t_i} is the graph G^* computed using a threshold t_i.

In order to avoid scale distortions, the proposed signature is normalized by the number of vertices present in the graph, N. So, degree measurements are represented as proportions of the original graph.

4   Experiments

To evaluate the performance of the proposed method, experiments have been done using a set of artificial shape images. This shape database consists of 9 different classes with 11 samples each, which makes a total of 99 images [14,15]. Each class groups different variations of a same shape structure, such as occlusion, articulation and missing parts (Figure 3).

Skeleton graph signature was computed considering different manifestations of the skeleton graph during its dynamic evolution. Thus, to compose the signature,

Fig. 3. Example of the artificial shapes used in the experiments

the thresholds $t \in \{0.1, 0.21, 0.32, 0.43, 0.54, 0.65\}$ were used. For each new graph achieved, the maximum and average degrees were computed to compose the skeleton signature, totalizing 12 descriptors.

The proposed signature was evaluated using Linear Discriminant Analysis (LDA) in a leave-one-out cross-validation scheme [16,17]. This method has as objective to find a linear sub-space to project the data where variance intra-classes is larger than inter-classes.

To provide a better evaluation, proposed signature was compared with traditional shape analysis methods from literature. So, the following methods were considered in this experiment:

Fourier descriptors: this approach uses a feature vector containing the 20 most significant coefficients of the Fourier Transform computed from the shape contour, as described in [9,18].

Zernike moments: a total of 20 moments (order $n = 0, \ldots, 7$) are used to compose a feature vector. Each represents the most significant magnitudes computed from a set of orthogonal complex moments of the shape image [19]

Curvature descriptors: this approach uses a curve to represent the contour of a shape. Maximum and minimum local points of this curve correspond to the direction changes in the shape contour [8].

Multi-scale Fractal Dimension: a curve is used to describe how the shape complexity changes along the scale. In this approach shape characterization is performed using the 50 most meaningful points of the curve [3,10].

Skeleton Paths: from a shape skeleton, this method uses the shortest path between each pair of *end Points* of the skeleton to describe it. Each shortest path is described by M equidistant skeleton points. Each point is represented by the maximum disc size associated to it. Unlike the other methods, LDA was not used for classification, but a graph matching approach which estimates the probability of one path belonging to a specific shape skeleton [20]. A total of 15 equidistant points was used to represent each path. The total number of descriptors of a shape skeleton varies according to the *(number of shortest paths in the skeleton)* $\times 15$.

5   Results

Table 1 shows the results yielded for each method in the proposed experiment. The proposed approach uses shape skeleton for characterization and identification of shape patterns. Its comparison was carried out considering contour-based approaches. Shape contours are able to represent more efficiently all details present in a shape than its skeleton. Besides, shape skeletons are more sensitive to variations or noise in the surface of the shape, i.e., small changes in the shape may produce abrupt changes in the skeleton. In our approach, we computed the shape skeleton using method by Choi et al. [21]. A pruning method [22] is applied over the resulting skeleton to minimize shape deformation and noise. Thus, only the most significant ending branches remain in the skeleton.

Results show that, in spite of the reduced amount of information present in the shape skeleton and its deficiencies in shape representation, the proposed method presents great capacity for shape recognition, overcoming traditional contour-based methods, such as Fourier descriptors, Zernike moments, Curvature descriptors and Multi-scale Fractal Dimension. Using simple degree-based measurements computed from the skeleton graph, the proposed approach can characterize different shape patterns with different variations in their structure (such as, occlusion, articulation and missing parts), confirming the great efficacy of the method.

The proposed approach also present a superior performance in comparison to another skeleton-based method, the skeleton paths. Our approach uses all skeleton points to compute a graph whose properties are used to describe it and, as a consequence, the original shape. The skeleton path method uses the shortest paths (sampled by M points) computed between two *end Points* to describe the skeleton. However, we have that skeletons from different shapes may present similar groups of paths (Figure 4). Thus, the information of how skeleton points are distributed over the skeleton is quite important to the effectiveness of the method. It is a characteristic present in our approach which explains the superiority of our approach to the skeleton paths method.

Table 1. Classification performance of various shape descriptors for the artificial shapes database

Shape Descriptor	Shapes correctly classified	Mean success rate (%)
Proposed Method	93	93.94
Fourier descriptors	83	83.84
Zernike moments	91	91.92
Curvature	76	76.77
M. S. Fractal Dimension	87	87.88
Skeleton Path	91	91.92

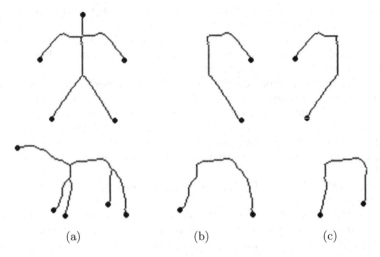

Fig. 4. (a) Skeletons of two different shapes; (b)-(c) Similar paths in the skeletons

6   Conclusion

Paper presents a novel approach for pattern characterization using shape skeletons. There, shape skeleton is represented and characterized as a graph in a dynamic evolution context. Degree based measurements (such as average and maximum degrees) are used to characterize this graph and, as a consequence, the original shape. Results reported a powerful potential of discriminating shape patterns, including those with different variations in their structure, overcoming traditional shape analysis (such as curvature, Fourier descriptors, Zernike moments and Multi-scale Fractal Dimension) and skeleton-based methods (Skeleton paths).

Acknowledgements

A.R.B. acknowledges support from FAPESP (2006/54367-9). O.M.B. acknowledges support from CNPq (306628/2007-4).

References

1. Blum, H.: A transformation for extracting new descriptors of shape. In: Wathen-Dunn, W. (ed.) Models for the Perception of Speech and Visual Forms, pp. 362–380. MIT Press, Amsterdam (1967)
2. Blum, H., Nagel, R.: Shape description using weighted symmetric axis features. Pattern Recognition 10(3), 167–180 (1978)
3. da S. Torres, R., Falcão, A.X., da F. Costa, L.: A graph-based approach for multiscale shape analysis. Pattern Recognition 37, 1163–1174 (2003)

4. Sebastian, T.B., Kimia, B.B.: Curves vs. skeletons in object recognition. Signal Processing 85(2), 247–263 (2005)
5. Wang, C., Cannon, D.J., Kumara, S.R.T., Guowen, L.: A skeleton and neural network-based approach for identifying cosmetic surface flaws. IEEE transactions on neural networks 6(5), 1201–1211 (1995)
6. Zhu, X.: Shape recognition based on skeleton and support vector machines. In: Third International Conference on Intelligent Computing, pp. 1035–1043 (2007)
7. Backes, A.R., Casanova, D., Bruno, O.M.: A complex network-based approach for boundary shape analysis. Pattern Recognition 42(1), 54–67 (2009)
8. Wu, W.Y., Wang, M.J.: On Detecting the dominant points by the curvature-based polygonal approximation. CVGIP: Graphical Models Image Process 55, 79–88 (1993)
9. Gonzalez, R.C., Woods, R.E.: Digital Image Processing, 2nd edn. Prentic-Hall, New Jersey (2002)
10. Plotze, R.O., Padua, J.G., Falvo, M., Vieira, M.L.C., Oliveira, G.C.X., Bruno, O.M.: Leaf shape analysis by the multiscale minkowski fractal dimension, a new morphometric method: a study in passiflora l (passifloraceae) 83, 287–301 (2005)
11. Boccaletti, S., Latora, V., Moreno, Y., Chavez, M., Hwang, D.U.: Complex networks: Structure and dynamics. Physics Reports 424(4-5), 175–308 (2006)
12. da F Costa, L., Rodrigues, F.A., Travieso, G., Villas Boas, P.R.: Characterization of complex networks: A survey of measurements. Advances in Physics 56(1), 167–242 (2007)
13. Wuchty, S., Stadler, P.F.: Centers of complex networks. Journal of Theoretical Biology 223, 45–53 (2003)
14. Sebastian, T.B., Klein, P.N., Kimia, B.B.: Recognition of shapes by editing their shock graphs. IEEE Trans. Pattern Analysis and Machine Intelligence 26(5), 550–571 (2004)
15. Sharvit, D., Chan, J., Tek, H., Kimia, B.B.: Symmetry-based indexing of image databases. Journal of Visual Communication and Image Representation 9(4), 366–380 (1998)
16. Everitt, B.S., Dunn, G.: Applied Multivariate Analysis, 2nd edn. Arnold (2001)
17. Fukunaga, K.: Introduction to Statistical Pattern Recognition, 2nd edn. Academic Press, London (1990)
18. Osowski, S., Nghia, D.D.: Fourier and wavelet descriptors for shape recognition using neural networks - a comparative study. Pattern Recognition 35(9), 1949–1957 (2002)
19. Zhenjiang, M.: Zernike moment-based image shape analysis and its application". Pattern Recognition Letters 21(2), 169–177 (2000)
20. Bai, X., Latecki, L.J.: Path similarity skeleton graph matching. IEEE Transactions on Pattern Analysis and Machine Intelligence 30(7), 1282–1292 (2008)
21. Choi, W.P., Lam, K.M., Siu, W.C.: Extraction of the euclidean skeleton based on a connectivity criterion. Pattern Recognition 36(3), 721–729 (2003)
22. Bai, X., Latecki, L.J., Liu, W.Y.: Skeleton pruning by contour partitioning with discrete curve evolution. IEEE Trans. Pattern Analysis and Machine Intelligence 29(3), 449–462 (2007)

Reconnecting Broken Ridges in Fingerprint Images

Nadia Brancati, Maria Frucci, and Gabriella Sanniti di Baja

Institute of Cybernetics "E. Caianiello", CNR, Pozzuoli (Naples), Italy
n.brancati@cib.na.cnr.it, m.frucci@cib.na.cnr.it,
g.sannitidibaja@cib.na.cnr.it

Abstract. In this paper, we present a new method for reconnecting broken ridges in fingerprint images. The method is based on the use of a discrete directional mask and on the standard deviation of the gray-levels to determine ridge direction. The obtained direction map is smoothed by counting the occurrences of the directions in a sufficiently large window. The fingerprint image is, then, binarized and thinned. Linking paths to connect broken ridges are generated by using a morphological transformation to guide the process.

1 Introduction

Fingerprints are widely used in biometric techniques for automatic personal identification, though a number of other techniques exist, which involve other biometric features such as face, iris, ear and voice. In fact, fingerprints of any individual are unique (even in the case of identical twins), remain the same over lifetime, and are easy to collect.

Fingerprints were initially introduced for criminal investigation, and their verification used to be performed manually by experts. Nowadays fingerprints are still used to identify suspects and victims of crimes, but are also involved in an increasing number of applications, such as physical access control, employee identification, and information systems security. Moreover, the tedious manual matching work has been replaced by automatic fingerprint identification systems, which can work with databases including even several millions records of fingerprint images. Most of the fingerprint matching algorithms follow the forensic procedure of matching particular features in a fingerprint image, called *minutiae*. The minutiae are local discontinuities of ridgelines in a fingerprint image. Though minutiae could be classified in several classes, it is standard practice to use a classification in two minutiae only, namely termination and bifurcation.

Fingerprints can be captured by different devices, each of which may produce a corrupted image. For automatic fingerprint identification, the quality of fingerprint images is of great importance, since low quality images severely affect the detection of the minutiae and, accordingly, a correct identification. For this reason, fingerprint images generally undergo a number of different processes, aimed at enhancement, computation of the ridge direction, thinning, and feature extraction.

Enhancement largely contributes to the robustness of a system for fingerprint verification/recognition and is a topic that has received much attention. In this paper, we focus on the problem of reconnecting broken ridges. We suggest a method based on

P. Foggia, C. Sansone, and M. Vento (Eds.): ICIAP 2009, LNCS 5716, pp. 739–747, 2009.

the use of a discrete 9*9 directional mask and on the standard deviation of the gray-levels to build an initial direction map. The final direction map is, then, obtained by counting the occurrences of the directions within a 45*45 window. The skeleton of the binarized fingerprint image is used, together with the watershed transform, computed by taking into account the end points and the isolated pixels of the skeleton, to generate linking paths and reconnect broken ridges.

2 Related Works

Enhancement of damaged fingerprint images has received much attention in the literature. Different techniques based, for example, on the use of Gabor filter, directional median filter, thresholding, wavelets, were suggested to improve the quality of the gray level fingerprint image [1-4]. Most of the existing methods can be classified in two categories, depending on whether frequency domain or spatial domain is considered.

In the frequency domain, enhancement methods are mainly based on the Fourier transform [5-7]. For example, the method suggested in [5] uses a bandpass filter to build 16 images filtered in 16 different directions. For each image, the inverse Fourier transform is computed and the 16 obtained images are suitably combined to get an enhanced image. In [7], enhancement is obtained without resorting to information derived from the directions along the ridges. The fingerprint image is divided into non-overlapping blocks of size 32*32 and the Fourier transform of each block is computed. The underlying idea is that the direction along the ridge is constant within each block. A drawback common to enhancement methods based on the Fourier transform is that short ridges are often filtered out. Thus, ridges that are broken in many small parts are not always reconstructed.

In the spatial domain, ridge directions are extracted from the gradient of the fingerprint image (see e.g., [8-10]), or by means of directional masks (see e.g., [11-14]). In [9], a bandpass filter is used to filter the image in 2 directions so as to reduce noise before computing the gradient. In [14], the fingerprint image is divided into non overlapping blocks, the direction of the central pixel is computed by using a directional mask and this direction is assigned to all pixels of the block, so generating a smoothed direction map. In [15], 16 directions are considered and the standard deviation of gray-levels of pixels aligned along them is computed. The direction to be assigned to each pixel p is found by selecting the pair of perpendicular directions for which the highest discrepancy is found: if the two standard deviations differ, the direction of p is the one with the smaller standard deviation, otherwise a special value is assigned to p. The basic idea is that along a ridge the standard deviation should be remarkably smaller than that in the perpendicular direction. Since pixels of the fingerprint image in correspondence with broken ridges are generally assigned the special value, windows of different sizes are used to compute the standard deviations and update the direction map. Gradient-based method may fail to detect correct directions in the ridge breakings areas. Methods based on directional masks to compute ridge direction and on the subdivision of the fingerprint image into non-overlapping blocks to get a smoothed direction map have the same drawback, since the direction map updating is done in a too global way. Methods like [15], where the direction map updating is done with local criteria, are more effective. The main problem is the selection of the size of the windows used for the updating.

3   The Suggested Method

Our method for reconnecting broken ridges is in the class of methods working in the spatial domain and on the use of directional masks. Our work has been inspired by the method suggested in [15] as concerns the construction of the direction map. The method has been tested on the fingerprint images used for the 'Fingerprint Verification Competition'(FVC) of years 2000, 2002 and 2004.

3.1   Building the Direction Map

Working in the discrete plane, the number of possible directions depends on the size of the selected directional mask. For a size $n*n$, $2*n-2$ directions are possible. In turn, the size of the directional mask should be selected by taking into account the thickness of the fingerprint ridges and of the valleys separating them. If a too small mask is centered on the innermost pixels in a ridge (valley), only very small gray-level changes would be detected along all directions, so that the innermost pixels could not be assigned any direction. In turn, if a too large mask is used, wherever the mask hits a portion of the image including both ridges and valleys, quite high gray-level variations would be detected, causing non-correct direction assignment.

We use, a directional mask of size 9*9, which is a reasonably good compromise for our dataset and, hence, 16 different directions result to be possible. The discrete directional mask is given in Fig. 1. A darker tone is used to identify the lines passing through the pixels along the direction in one of the two ways (positive) and a lighter tone to identify the lines in the opposite (negative) way.

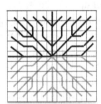

Fig. 1. The 9*9 discrete directional map

Our criterion to build the direction map is improved with respect to the one in [15]. For each pixel p in the fingerprint image, the standard deviation of the gray-levels of the pixels aligned along each of the above directions is computed in a 9*9 window. Let min be the minimum value of the standard deviation. The absolute value of the difference in standard deviation for each pair of perpendicular directions and the maximal value, max, of such a difference are also computed.

In principle, for a pixel p located along a ridge (valley) the standard deviation along the ridge (valley) direction should be the only one with value min. If this is the case, the unique direction with standard deviation min is by all means the direction to be assigned to p. However, when the ridge (valley) includes pixels with scarcely different gray-levels, the standard deviation can be equal to min in more than one direction and some ambiguity in the direction selection exists. We distinguish two cases. If the standard deviation is equal to min in all the principal (horizontal, vertical and

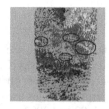

Fig. 2. A fingerprint, left, the initial direction map, middle, and the final direction map, right

diagonal) directions, we consider the direction for p as undetermined and assign to p a special value v in the direction map. Otherwise, we select the pair of perpendicular directions for which the absolute value of the difference in standard deviation is equal to *max*. If the difference *max* is found for only one pair of perpendicular directions, the direction characterized by the smaller value in that unique pair is assigned to p. Otherwise, a decision on the direction for p cannot be taken, and p is assigned the special value v in the direction map.

As an example, in Fig. 2 the fingerprint used as running example in this paper is shown to the left, and the computed initial direction map is given in the middle. Not all pixels of the image have been assigned one of the possible directions, some of them are assigned the special value v. In particular, the special value v is assigned not only to pixels that, actually, are not part of the fingerprint, but also to all pixels in the zones, circled in Fig. 2 middle, corresponding to the ridge breaking areas. Thus, no direction information is available in the ridge breaking areas; moreover, the initial direction map shows a too complex distribution of directions to be easily used, and a suitable updating of the direction map is necessary.

The updating of the direction map is done, as suggested in [15], by using a 45*45 window. For each pixel p, we count in the window the occurrences of each direction and assign to p the direction with the maximal occurrence. The final direction map can be seen in Fig. 2, right. Almost all pixels of the fingerprint have been assigned a direction and the obtained final direction map is noticeably smoother than the initial map. The final direction map may include less directions with respect to those in the initial map.

3.2 Binarization and Thinning

Rather than directly connecting broken ridges in the fingerprint image, we resort to skeletonization to thin down the ridges to unit width and suggest a way to link to each other thin lines found in correspondence of broken ridges.

A preliminary thresholding of the fingerprint image is performed to distinguish the ridges (foreground) from the background. To this purpose, a pixel p is taken as a foreground pixel if its gray-level is smaller than or equal to the average gray-level in a 9*9 window centered on p. Otherwise, p is taken as a background pixel. Skeletonization is accomplished by using the algorithm [16], which also includes a post-processing phase to prune non-significant branches and to reduce the zig-zags created during reduction to unit width. For the running example, the result of skeletonization is shown in Fig. 3, where the binarized fingerprint image is shown to the left and the resulting skeleton in the middle.

Fig. 3. The binarized fingerprint, left, the skeleton, middle, and the watershed transform, right

3.3 Linking Paths Guided by the Watershed Transform

Skeleton parts found in correspondence of broken ridges consist of a number of components. To link these components, we need to build linking paths connecting their extremes (end points of skeleton branches or isolated pixels of the skeleton). Naturally, not all skeleton components have to be linked to each other, which implies a selection of a proper subset of extremes, called *significant extremes*. To this purpose, we use the watershed transform [17-19].

The computation of the watershed transform of an image implies the detection of a set of pixels in the image, the *seeds*, from which to perform *region growing*. Region growing associates to each seed s those image pixels that are closer to s than to any other seed. In our case, we compute the watershed transform of the binary image, where the *seeds*, i.e., the extremes of all skeleton components, have value 1, and all remaining pixels have value 0. The growing process provides a partition of the image, where each region surrounded by watershed lines represents the area of influence of a seed. See Fig. 3 right. In this way, in correspondence of the ridge breaking areas, the watershed lines will be mostly placed midway between the extremes of skeleton components that we would like to connect, and the watershed lines can be seen as the barriers where the linking paths starting from the extremes terminate. Depending on the oriented directions of pairs of paths terminating on the same watershed line, and on the distance between the termination points of the paths, we can decide whether the extremes from which the paths originate are significant extremes.

To add to the skeleton the path associated to each pixel p that is one of the extremes, the direction associated to p in the final direction map is taken into account. Obviously, if p is an isolated pixel, two paths in are built in the two opposite ways of the direction, while if p is an end point, a unique path is built, which is the prolongation of the skeleton branch in the direction associated to p. The 9*9 discrete directional map shown in Fig. 1 is centered on the pixel p and all pixels along the direction associated to p in the appropriate way(s) are assigned to the path. If any of the pixels ascribed to the path belongs to a watershed line, path building from p is interrupted at that pixel, since the termination point of the path has been reached. Otherwise, the 9*9 window is centered on the last pixel ascribed to the path, and the path building process is repeated starting from it, still in the direction of p.

Initially, a list of the end points is constructed and only paths built from the end points are considered. To decide whether p is a significant end point and, hence, the path built from it, *path_p*, has to be actually used for broken ridge connection, we analyze *path_p* and any other path, *path_q*, originated from other extremes and terminating on the same watershed line. Two main cases are possible for the termination point of the path associated to p, which can be a *simple termination point*, or a *complex termination point*. A termination point is simple, white circles in Fig. 4, if it is adjacent to only two regions of the watershed partition. A termination point is complex, black circles in Fig. 4, when the termination point is adjacent to more than two regions. A different criterion is used to decide if *path_p* has to be taken or has to be removed, depending on whether q is an end point or an isolated pixel.

Fig. 4. Simple termination points (white circles) and complex termination points (black circles)

Let us suppose that the termination point for *path_p* is simple and that the path has been built in positive way. The termination point of *path_p* separates only two areas of influence, which are associated to p and to q, (see Fig. 4 left). The procedure is different depending on whether q is an end point or an isolated pixel. In the first case, if *path_q* has been built in negative way, and the distance between the termination points of *path_p* and *path_q* is smaller than an a priori fixed threshold θ, both *path_p* and *path_q* are interpreted as necessary to connect a broken ridge; if the distance overcomes the threshold, p is regarded as not placed in a ridge breaking area; finally, if also *path_q* has been built in positive way, decision on the significance of *path_p* can not yet be taken. An example in which *path_q* and *path_p* are built in the same way is shown Fig. 4 right, where the two paths *path_p* and *path_q* were built in correspondence with skeleton components belonging to two mostly parallel ridges that should not be reconnected. In the case that q is an isolated pixel, the criterion to establish if p and q should be linked to each other is the following: only if q is located along the same discrete direction associated to p, the two pixels p and q have to be linked to each other. If this is the case, linking occurs by taking *path_p* and by prolonging it to reach q, along the direction assigned to p. If q is not along the discrete direction associated to p, the decision on the significance of *path_p* can not yet be taken.

Let us now suppose that the termination point for *path_p* is complex. The termination point of *path_p* separates more than two areas of influence, which are associated to p and to q_1, q_2, etc. (see Fig. 4 middle). A decision must be taken to select, among the paths, *path_q₁*, *path_q₂* etc., terminating on the crossing watershed lines, which one should be possibly accepted together with *path_p*. Paths generated by end points q_i are considered first. Only paths, built in opposite way with respect to *path_p* and such that the distance between their termination points and the termination point of *pah_p* is under the threshold θ, are taken into account. Among them, the path with the minimal distance is taken, together with *path_p*, for reconnecting a broken ridge. Of course, if no *path_q_i* in opposite way exists or the threshold is overcome, the q_i that are isolated pixels, if any, are considered and the same procedure followed in case of isolated pixels and simple termination point is followed.

Fig. 5. The regions associated to extremes that should be connected, stars, are not adjacent

Whenever linking paths are accepted as necessary for reconnecting ridges, an updating of the list of the end points is accomplished. In fact, when an end point is linked to an isolated pixel, a new end point, coinciding with the isolated pixel, is generated in the skeleton, from which a new path can be built. The process of path building and identification of significant paths is iterated as far as new end points are added to the list.

The above process works correctly if the partition regions associated to two significant extremes are adjacent. However, this is not always the case. For example, the extremes denoted by stars in Fig. 5 should be linked to each other, but the corresponding partition regions are separated by a partition region associated to the extreme denoted by a cross, with whom (correctly!) linking was not accomplished during the above process.

A second step of path building, allowing a path to cross the barriers and continue until the watershed line of the next partition region is met, is necessary. Also the second step is performed starting only from the end points, and the end points that are taken into account are those that during the previous phase were not classified as significant extremes, i.e., a decision on their associated paths was not taken. The second step is done by using the same process accomplished in the first step, the only difference being that the areas of influence of the pixels that we are going to link are not adjacent. Isolated pixels of the skeleton possibly remaining at the end of the reconnection process are disregarded and are considered as noise.

3.4 Results and Conclusion

The performance of our method, when applied to the datasets used for FVC, has been evaluated by an expert of the Police Headquarters of Naples, Italy, who found the results very good for a more reliable identification of the minutiae. For space limitation, in Fig. 6 only four images with reconstructed ridges are shown, where the image to left is for the fingerprint used as running example.

Fig. 6. Reconstructed ridges (red color denotes reconstructed pixels)

Fig. 7. From left to right: a fingerprint, its artificially corrupted version, the fingerprint reconstructed by using a 45*45 window for updating the direction map, and the ROC curve

To test the method also for images largely corrupted, we have artificially increased the number of ridge breaking areas in the fingerprints of the dataset. The original images have been compared with the results obtained by processing the artificially corrupted images to verify the ability of our method in reconnecting broken ridges. Windows of different size, ranging from 9*9 to 73*73, have been used for the computation of the final direction map in order to build a ROC curve and so evaluate the goodness of the method. About 50 artificially corrupted images have been used and in all cases, the area under the ROC curve is larger than 0.90, indicating the effectiveness of the proposed method. Again for space limitation, only one example is given in Fig. 7.

It might appear that, besides the analogy as concerns the construction of the direction map, yet another analogy exists between our method and the one in [15] since both methods use the watershed transform. However, we stress that the watershed transform is used for different aims in the two methods. For [15], the watershed transform of the fingerprint image is used to associate partition regions with valleys and ridges. Then, two direction maps are computed, for the fingerprint image and for the watershed transform, and the directions in these two maps that are perpendicular to each other are used to identify the ridge breaking areas. In our case, instead, the watershed transform is only used to guide the path building process.

Our method has been implemented in C on a standard PC, by using OpenCV libraries. Future work will be done to improve the construction of the direction map, especially as concerns pixels placed at peripheral parts of the fingerprint.

Acknowledgements

We are gratefully indebted to Dr. Luigi Bisogno, Head Detective Inspector, Department of Judicial Dactyloscopy of the Scientific Police, Police Headquarters of Naples, for his precious help in evaluating the results of our method.

References

[1] Wu, C., Shi, Z., Govindaraju, V.: Fingerprint image enhancement method using directional median filter. In: Proc. SPIE 2004, vol. 5404, pp. 66–75 (2004)
[2] Hong, L., Wan, Y., Jain, A.: Fingerprint image enhancement: algorithm and performance evaluation. IEEE Trans. PAMI 20(8), 777–789 (1998)

[3] Areekul, V., Watchareeruetai, U., Suppasriwasuseth, K., Tantaratana, S.: Separable Gabor filter realization for fast fingerprint enhancement. In: Proc. ICIP 2005, vol. 3,
pp. 253–256 (2005)

[4] Yang, J., Liu, L., Jiang, T., Fan, Y.: A modified Gabor filter design method for fingerprint image enhancement. Pattern Recognition Letters 24(12), 1805–1817 (2003)

[5] Sherlock, B.G., Monro, D.M., Millard, K.: Fingerprint Enhancement by Directional Fourier Filtering. IEEE Proc. – Visual Image Signal Processing 241(2), 87–94 (1994)

[6] Ikonomopoulos, A., Unser, M.: A Directional Filtering Approach to Texture Discrimination. In: Proc. Seventh International Conference on Pattern Recognition, pp. 87–89 (1984)

[7] Willis, A.J., Myers, L.: A Cost-Effective Fingerprint Recognition System for Use with
Low-Quality Prints and Damaged Fingertips. Pattern Recognition 34, 255–270 (2001)

[8] Jain, A.K., Lin, H., Bolle, R.: On-line Fingerprint Verification. IEEE Transactions on Pattern Analysis and Machine Intelligence 19(4), 302–314 (1997)

[9] Hong, L.: Automatic Personal Identification Using Fingerprints, Ph.D Dissertation (1998)

[10] Rao, A.: A Taxonomy for Texture Description and Identification. Springer, Heidelberg
(1990)

[11] Stock, R.M., Swonger, C.W.: Development and Evaluation of a Reader of Fingerprint
Minutiae, Technical Report CAL No. XM-2478-X-1, pp. 13–17 (1969)

[12] Candela, G.T., Grother, P.J., Watson, C.I., Wilkinson, R.A., Wilson, C.L.: PCASYS – A
Pattern-Level Classification Automation System for Fingerprints, Technical Report
(1995)

[13] Eun-Kyung, Y., Sung-Bae, C.: Adaptive Fingerprint Image Enhancement with Fingerprint Image Quality Analysis. Image and Vision Computing 24, 101–110 (2006)

[14] Madhusoodhanan, P., Sumantra Dutta, R.: Robust Fingerprint Classification Using an Ei-
gen Block Directional Approach. In: Indian Conference on Computer Vision, Graphics
and Image Processing, ICVIGIP 2004 (2004)

[15] Oliveira, M.A., Leite, N.J.: A Multiscale Directional Operator and Morphological Tools
for Reconnecting Broken Ridges in Fingerprint Images. Pattern Recognition 41(1),
367–377 (2008)

[16] Sanniti di Baja, G., Thiel, E.: Skeletonization Algorithm Running on Path- Based Distance Maps. Image and Vision Computing 14, 47–57 (1996)

[17] Roerdink, J.B.T.M., Meijster, A.: The Watershed Transform: Definitions. Algorithms and
Parallelization Strategies, Fundamenta Informaticae 41, 187–228 (2001)

[18] Beucher, S., Meyer, F.: The Morphological Approach to Segmentation: the Watershed
Transformation. In: Mathematical Morphology in Image Processing, ch. 12, pp. 433–481.
Marcel Dekker, New York (1992)

[19] Meyer, F.: Color Image Segmentation. In: Proceedings of the International Conference on
Image Processing and its Applications, pp. 303–306 (1992)

Optimum Sensors for 'Chromaticity' Constancy in the Pixel

Sivalogeswaran Ratnasingam and Steve Collins

Department of Engineering Science,
University of Oxford, OX1 3PJ, Oxford, United Kingdom
{siva,collins}@robots.ox.ac.uk

Abstract. In machine vision systems recording the colour of an object is crucial for applications such as skin detection while it will enhance applications including colour based recognition and image retrieval. Unfortunately, almost none of the existing colour constancy algorithms have been designed to deal with the high dynamic ranges that can occur in external, naturally illuminated scenes. One algorithm that can deal with these scenes has been proposed by Finlayson and Drew. In this paper a method of assessing the performance of this algorithm, and equivalent algorithms, are proposed. The performance of this algorithm is then significantly improved by optimising the spectral response of the sensors used to obtain the data required by algorithm. Since the resulting performance is comparable to that of the human visual system it appears that this algorithm is capable of obtaining useful chromaticity information under highly varying illumination conditions.

Keyword: sensor optimisation, chromaticity constancy.

1 Introduction

The high dynamic range (HDR) of illuminant causes difficulties in capturing a scene independent of lighting conditions. This large variation in intensity (10^9 [1]) of an illuminant makes the performance of the state of the art colour constancy algorithms to degrade in HDR scenes [2]. Recent research shows that the most advanced algorithms are not able to provide stable chromaticity that can be used in colour based recognition applications [3]. In HDR scenes the effect of scene illuminant should be discounted at pixel level and this is difficult with three sensor linear responses.

Foster states that the conventional colour measurement methods concentrate not on colour constancy but on complementary aspects [4]. This suggests that to achieve better chromaticity constancy, the imaging sensors should be optimised. Ohta [5] shows that exact colour reproduction is impossible with currently available dyes. It is proved by Verhel et al. [6] that four sensors are required for accurate colour reproduction. Based on the above discussion, four sensor imaging system was chosen for solving the lighting effect in HDR scenes and optimise the sensitivity of the sensors for better chromaticity constancy. Finlayson and Drew's [7] algorithm is investigated for identification of similar colours and the sensor parameters are optimised for better

P. Foggia, C. Sansone, and M. Vento (Eds.): ICIAP 2009, LNCS 5716, pp. 748–756, 2009.
© Springer-Verlag Berlin Heidelberg 2009

performance. In this work a new method of sensor optimisation for chromaticity constancy, error metric for optimisation, and a method for comparing the ability of identifying similar chromaticities and illuminant independent chromaticity space are proposed.

In this research work, the organic dyes are to be used in implementing the optimised imaging device for achieving chromaticity constancy in HDR scenes. As most of the organic sensors have a full width at half maximum of 100 nm this work focuses on the performance of the algorithm at 100 nm width sensors. Finlayson and Drew's algorithm is described and its performance is investigated in section 2. Section 3 discusses the optimisation of sensor parameters and the ability of similar colour separability of the algorithm. In section 4, the effect of quantisation on the algorithm's performance is investigated. Finally, based on the results, conclusions have been made in section 5.

2   The Algorithm

Based upon a model in which it is assumed that Planck's blackbody equation models the illuminant spectrum and that the sensors spectral response can be modeled by the Dirac delta function Finlayson and Drew have proposed a color constancy algorithm that only uses information from 4-sensor responses [7]. The responses from each of these sensors are proportional to the logarithm of the incident photon flux in a different spectral range. The first step of the algorithm is to use either one of these logarithmic sensor responses or the geometric mean of all four responses as a normalising channel to compensate for possible changes in geometry and more importantly the brightness of the illuminant [7]. When a single logarithmic response is used as the normalising channel this automatically reduces the dimension of the space of possible responses by one. Alternatively, when the geometric mean is used as the normalising channel one of the normalised channels can be discarded. In either case the result is a three dimensional space of normalised response ratios. The results presented in this paper are for the first case. In this three dimensional space each colour follows a trajectory as the spectrum of the illuminant varies. To remove this illuminant induced variation, the 3-dimensional space is projected into a 2-dimensional space in which the variations due to changing illuminant spectrum are minimised. The resultant 2-dimensional space is approximately independent of shading, scene geometry and scene illuminant [7].

To test this algorithm's ability to extract data that can be used to distinguish perceptually similar colours the algorithm has been implemented in MATLAB. The algorithm was then applied to the simulated responses of sensors whose inputs were obtained from the reflectance spectra of Munsell colours[8] illuminated by 6 different CIE standard daylight illuminants (D40, D45, D50, D55, D60 and D65) [9], Both the reflectance spectra of the Munsell colours and the standard daylights are sampled at 1nm intervals in the range between 400nm and 700nm and the spectral sensitivity of the sensors was modeled using a Lorentzian function.

Initial investigations of the algorithm were performed with sensors that have a full width half maximum of 100nm and peak spectral responses at 437.5nm, 512.5nm, 587.5nm and 662.5nm. Figure 1 shows the two dimensional chromaticity space formed by the algorithm when the sensor with the lowest peak wavelength response was used to normalise the other responses. In this figure the colour of each cross matches the Munsell colour used to generate the corresponding data point. This representation means that the results clearly show a smooth variation in chromaticity across the space with white at its centre. The other noticeable feature of these results is that dark colours are spread across the space however, a closer inspection of these results shows that they have the similar reflectance spectra (chromaticity) to their neighbours but with a low reflectivity.

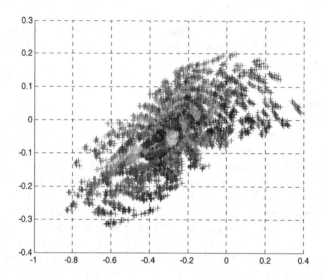

Fig. 1. The chromaticity space with 1269 munsell colours projected when applying 6-CIE standard daylight illuminants. Assuming the white point as the centre of the space, colour red is projected on the positive y-axis, orange is in the second quadrant, yellow is on the negative x-axis, green is in the third quadrant, blue is projected on the negative y-axis, purple is on the positive x-axis and brown is in the first quadrant.

A key feature of the algorithm is that it normalises the sensor responses in order to accommodate variations in the brightness of the illuminant. This also normalises the brightness component of a colour preserving only the chromaticity. This feature of the algorithm has been confirmed by scaling the reflectance representing each Munsell colours by different factors to create families of chromaticities, such as the one shown in Figure 2. As expected each of these families are projected to the same point in the two dimensional space created by the algorithm, for example the scaled reflectances in Figure 2 are all mapped to the same point which is circled in Figure 2.

A closer inspection of the space (figure 1) shows that each colour sample creates a small cluster of six points in the chromaticity space, one for each of the six day light illuminants. This space therefore has the basic characteristics required to separate different chromaticities. It is important to use a perceptually relevant scale to quantify the similarity between neighbouring chromaticities. For this the separability of the projected areas different colour samples has been tested.

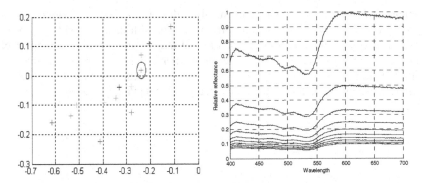

Fig. 2. Illustrates the chromaticity space, all synthetic reflectances shown in figure are projected as a single point (shown with in the circle) with some neighbor colours. These synthetic reflectance spectra were obtained by scaling the spectra with different factors.

The CIELab space is one colour space that has been designed so that distances in the space are proportional to the perceptual differences between colours. Although the method of calculating a colour co-ordinates in this space have been agreed there are several slightly different qualitative descriptions of colours separated by different distances in CIELab space. One example of a set of qualitative descriptions is that due to Abrardo et al. who describe colours that differ by between 1.0 and 3.0 CIELab units as a very good colour match to each other, whilst colours separated by distances between 3.0 and 6.0 units are a good colour match to each other [10].

Since the algorithm is expected to differentiate the chromaticity between different surfaces the Munsell colours used to test the algorithm were taken for a small range of L values in CIELab space. After examining a histogram of the L values within the Munsell colours those colours with L values between 47.8 and 50.2 were chosen to obtain the largest possible set of colours that differ mainly in their chromaticity. From these colours two sets of test samples with 100 pairs of colours in each set were chosen in such a way that the Euclidean distance between members of each pair in CIELab space was either in the range between 1.0 and 4.0 units or between 4.6 and 6.0 CIELab units. These distance ranges were chosen considering the available data.

In testing the performance of the algorithm 6-CIE standard illuminants (D41, D46, D51, D56, D61 and D64) and these two test sets (reflectance spectra) are used to generate the spectra of light incident on the simulated sensors. The algorithm is then applied to project each reflectance spectrum and illuminant pair into the chromaticity space. As expected each of the six illuminants meant that each reflectance sample created a cluster of six points in the chromaticity space. The first step in our method of determining the seperability of these spectra is to determine the smallest circle that encloses each of these clusters. If the centre distance between the two circles enclosing the members of each pair is larger than the sum of radii of the two circles then this pair of spectra is considered to be separable. Using this definition of seperability the performance of the algorithm was investigated for widths (full width at half maximum) of the sensor responses from 20 nm to 200 nm. The algorithm was tested with all four options of normalising the sensor responses and the results for the best choice of normalizing channel (see section 3) are reported in this paper.

Figure 3 shows the performance of the algorithm when used to separate perceptually similar colours with data obtained from sensors with different widths. Since the algorithm was used upon a mathematical model that assumed a very narrow spectral response it is not surprising that the algorithms performance decreases as the sensor width increases. Despite this tendency these results suggest that with this algorithm it is possible to separate colours that represent a good match to each other.

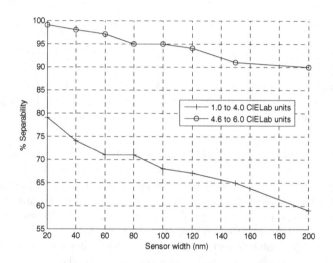

Fig. 3. Illustrates the test results of both test sets when applying the unquantised channel response to the algorithm. Width of the sensors is varied from 20 nm to 200 nm.

3   Sensor Optimisation

The sensors used to obtain the data for the results in Figure 3 were positioned uniformly but there is no reason to believe that this is the best choice of sensors. The sensor spectral characteristics was therefore optimised using a steepest descend algorithm. In this optimization process the position of the peak spectral responses of each sensor was allowed to vary while keeping all four widths equal and constant. There is a possibility that if the parameters are chosen to minimise the average size of the cluster of points from each colour it would merge the different colours. To overcome this problem, 100 pairs of training samples were chosen in the same way as the test sets but with the members of each pairs separated by 6.0 to 7.1 units in the CIELab space. The success of the algorithm means that the separability of these colours will not improve significantly. The error measure used in this optimisation was therefore the ratio between the average of the largest dimension of both clusters of a pair and the distance between the cluster centres. This ratio is averaged over all 100 pairs of samples in the training set. This error measure was chosen to measure the spread of a colour due to variation of illuminant on the chromaticity space relative to the separation between similar colours and the sensor parameters were chosen to minimise this ratio. In this optimisation six CIE standard daylight illuminants are applied to illuminate the training samples. Figure 4 illustrates the chromaticity space formed by the optimised sensor response. The optimised sensors (peak positions: 422.1, 452.8, 523.1 and 557.2 nm) were obtained by starting the optimisation process with initial sensor positions used in section 1 and full width at half maximum of 100 nm.

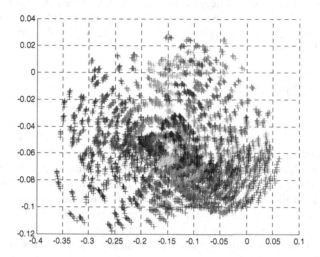

Fig. 4. Chromaticity space formed by the optimised sensor set. Six different CIE standard daylight illuminant spectra and 1269 munsell data were applied in generating this space.

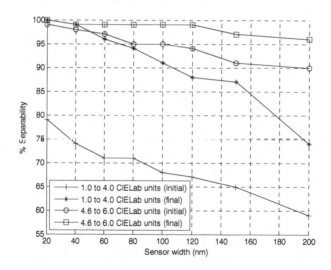

Fig. 5. Illustrates the initial and final performance of the algorithm when testing with both test sets. The channel responses applied in this test are unquantised sensor responses.

The chromaticity space formed by the optimised sensors (figure 4) shows a smooth variation of colour across the space and the average cluster spread compared to the total area of the space is 40 % smaller than in the initial space. This simple measure suggests that samples should be more easily separated.

Again the ability to separate different reflectances at different sensor widths has been tested. The results in figure 5 show that optimisation of the position of the peak spectral response of each sensor improves the performance of the algorithm in separating similar colours. A significant improvement is achieved in separating the most similar colours (that is those separated by between 1.0 and 4.0 CIELab units). In fact these results suggest that the algorithm can show a comparable performance to the human visual system.

4 Quantisation

One aspect of a real camera that has not been included in the model used to obtain the results in Figure 5 is the quantization of the sensor responses by the analogue-to-digital converter (adc). To study the effect of quantisation on the performance of the algorithm, the algorithm was optimised with different quantisers. The first stage in representing the quantiser is to determine the maximum sensor response. The CIE standard daylight illuminant (D65) was used to determine the maximum response and since the optimisation process changes the effective position of the sensor, the maximum sensor response was found by shifting the sensor's peak response from 400nm to 700 nm in 1 nm steps. The maximum response was calculated for each of the sensor widths of interest and the maximum response for each width was divided by 2^n, n is the number of bits in the quantiser which was varied between 6 and 16. Each sensor response was then equated to the nearest of these quantized values.

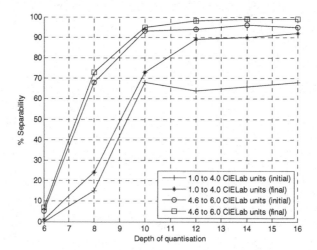

Fig. 6. Illustrates the initial and final seperability of colours as a function of quantisation depth. Full width at half maximum of all four sensors was kept at 100 nm.

Figure 6 shows the separability of similar colours with varying numbers of bits used to represent the sensor responses for two sets of data and two sets of sensors peak positions. These results show that in all four cases the performance of the algorithm increases rapidly when the number of quantisation bits increases from 6 to 10.

This suggests that the least significant bit of a 10 bits quantiser is small enough to capture the information required to separate perceptually similar colours. These results also show that optimizing the sensor positions can result in a significant increase the in separability of similar colours, especially when more than 10 bits are used to represent the output from each sensor.

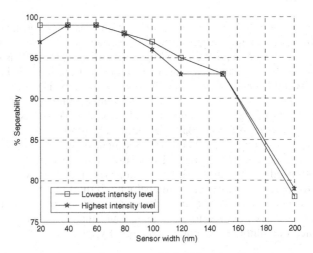

Fig. 7. Shows the test results of both test sets with initial and optimised sensor sets. The channel responses are quantised with a 10-bits quantiser.

Although the results in Figure 6 suggest that there might be some advantage from using a 12 bit adc to represent the response of sensors most cameras are currently supplied with either an 8 bit or a 10 bit adc. The final aspect of the impact of quantization that has been investigated is to confirm colour seperability despite the high dynamic range of illuminants. For this investigation a 6-decade intensity range of the illuminant was represented by dividing the daylight illuminant spectra by 10^6. The seperability of colours for the highest and lowest illuminant intensities are shown in Figure 7. This figure shows the results obtained with data quantised to 10-bits when separating pairs of colours that differ by between 4.6 and 6.0 CIELab units. The first significant feature of these results is that the performance of the algorithm drops at larger width. This is because as the sensor width increases the correlation between the sensor responses to the two members in each pair will increase and eventually the difference between the two responses will be smaller than the difference represented by the quantized sensor responses. When this occurs the quantized data will not contain the information needed to separate the member of each pair. These results suggest that any sensors used to obtain the data for this algorithm should have a full width half maximum of 100nm or less.

Another important conclusion that can be drawn from results such as those in Figure 7 is that the results obtained are almost identical for the two simulated illumination intensities. Since these differ by a factor of 10^6 these results suggest that this combination of sensors and algorithm is capable of dealing with HDR scenes. Furthermore, these results show that using the data for sensors with a full-width half maximum of less than 100nm it is possible to separate almost all the colours that would be described as representing either a good [10] or acceptable [11] match to each other. This suggests that using data from sensors with optimised spectral responses, the performance of the algorithm in separating similar chromaticities is comparable to the human visual system.

5 Conclusion

An existing algorithm has been investigated for chromaticity constancy. The algorithm uses the ratios of the outputs from four sensors to accommodate potentially large variations in the amount of reflected light falling on a sensor. This normalization process results in three normalized sensor responses that are independent of the illuminant intensity but dependant upon the illuminant spectrum. This illuminant dependence is then removed by extracting a two dimensional illuminant independent chromaticity descriptor from these three normalized responses. A method of assessing the resulting space has been proposed based upon the ability to easily separate perceptually similar colours. Using this method of assessment it has been shown that colours are more easily separated if the spectral response of the sensors used to gather the image are optimized. Furthermore, this is particularly important when the effects of quantization to represent the effect of an analogue to digital converter in the camera are taken into account. However, using a 10 bit adc and sensors with optimized peak spectral responses it is possible to separate colours that are good matches to each other even when the illuminant brightness changes by 10^6.

References

1. Holst, G.C., Lomheim, T.S.: CMOS/CCD Sensors and camera systems. SPIE press, Washington (2007)
2. Ebner, M.: Color constancy. Wiley- IS&T Series in Imaging Science and Technology (2007)
3. Funt, B., Barnard, K., Martin, L.: Is colour constancy good enough? In: Burkhardt, H.-J., Neumann, B. (eds.) ECCV 1998. LNCS, vol. 1406, pp. 445–459. Springer, Heidelberg (1998)
4. Foster, D.: Does colour constancy exist? Trends in Cognitive Science 7, 439–443 (2003)
5. Ohta, N.: Optimisation of Spectral Sensitivities. Phot. Sci. Eng. 27, 193–201 (1983)
6. Vrhel, M.J., Trussell, J.H.: Optimal color filters in the presence of noise. IEEE Trans. Image Processing 4, 814–823 (1995)
7. Finlayson, G.D., Drew, M.S.: 4-sensor camera calibration for image representation invariant to shading, shadows, lighting, and specularities. In: ICCV, pp. 473–480 (2001)
8. Database – Munnsell Colours Matt,
   ftp://ftp.cs.joensuu.fi/pub/color/spectra/mspec/
9. Colorpro Communications,
   http://www.colorpro.com/info/data/daylites.html
10. Abrardo, A., Cappellini, V., Cappellini, M., Mecocci, A.: Art-works colour calibration using the VASARI scanner. In: Proceedings of IS&T and SID's 4th Color Imaging Conference: Color Science, Systems and Applications, pp. 94–97 (1996)
11. Hardeberg, J.Y.: Acquisition and reproduction of color images: colorimetric and multispectral approaches. PhD dissertation, Paris (1999)

An Improved Adaptive Smoothing Method

Xin Hu[1], Hui Peng[2], Joseph Kesker[3], Xiang Cai[4], William G. Wee[4],
and Jing-Huei Lee[5]

[1] Microsoft Corporation
Redmond, Washington, United States, 98052
{huxin82}@gmail.com
[2] Advantest America, INC
Santa Clara, California, United States, 95054
{h.peng}@advantest.com
[3] Sheet Dynamic Ltd.,
Cincinnati, Ohio, United States, 45212
{jmkesler}@gmail.com
[4] Department of Electrical and Computer Engineering,
University of Cincinnati, Cincinnati, Ohio, United States, 45221
{caixg,wwee}@ececs.uc.edu
[5] Department of Biomedical Engineering,
University of Cincinnati, Cincinnati, Ohio, United States, 45221
{leej8}@ucmail.uc.edu

Abstract. An improvement of the Chen's method has been provided through the calculation of a more accurate H map. The H map is the pixel's contextual inhomogeneity value reflecting its proximity position with respect to an edge feature, and a more accurate H value leads to the more accurate smoothing speed for the pixel. While experiments on 5 real images show slight improvements in SNRs of our method over that of the Chen method, edge features preserving capability has been enhanced with low FARs (false alarm rates) for edge feature extracted from applying the Sobel filter to the image. Furthermore, parameter values have been determined through an exhaustive searching process resulting in the suggestions of h=0.4 and l=4 for practical applications where the original noise free image is not available and/or no viewer to visually make a selection of the final smoothed image as the output.

1 Introduction

Image smoothing is an image enhancement method with the objective of reducing and/or removing image noise. In a general case, it is impossible to completely remove image noise and recover the original noise free image. Generally, the image smoothing algorithm will blur the image edge features while removing the image noise [3].

In smoothing operations, images are assumed to have an approximately piecewise constant gray level distribution [2,3]. Based on this widely adopted assumption, an image can be viewed as the combination of many local regions with constant intensity. The separations of these local regions are edge features comprised of connected edge pixels. These edge features are of great importance in characterizing

P. Foggia, C. Sansone, and M. Vento (Eds.): ICIAP 2009, LNCS 5716, pp. 757–766, 2009.

image content. Therefore, a desirable quality of an image smoothing algorithm is to preserve image edge features while removing the image noise. Most of the current image smoothing algorithms do not incorporate edge feature preservation in their designs and cannot effectively separate edge pixels from other image pixels in their smoothing processes. Thus, either the smoothing result blurs out edge features or the image noise is not effectively removed. The contextual based smoothing algorithms in general have better performance over non-contextual ones with respect to edge preservation and noise removal and the scale based algorithms are superior in performance over the non-scale based algorithms [1,3]. It has been shown in [2] that Chen's algorithm can effectively remove noise while preserving image features. There are three parameters, h, S, and T that are needed to be selected in the algorithm. Parameters h and S control the impact of inhomogeneity value H and the gradient on the smoothing speed respectively and parameter T is the total number of iterations. While S is not sensitive to the final results and can set between 10 and 20, h and T have to be carefully selected in order to give quality smoothing results. In many of our simulations, SNR drops off rather rapid after T number of iterations. In this paper, an improved algorithm is proposed to further improve edge feature preservation feature and also provide a practical way to select values of parameter h and T.

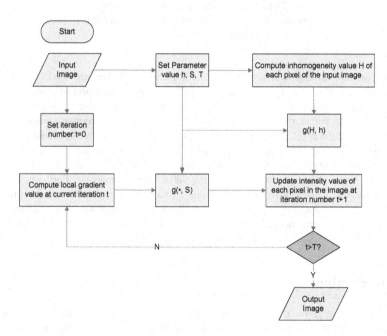

Fig. 1. A functional flowchart of chen's smoothing algorithm

2 Problem Statement

As discussed in the introduction section, Chen adaptive smoothing algorithm is conceptually attractive. Our aim is to improve upon his algorithm. Here a brief presentation of Chen's algorithm is provided. It is a pixel based adaptive smoothing algorithm where pixels with smoother neighborhood have larger smoothing actions while pixels with rougher neighborhood have smaller smoothing actions. The iterative smoothing action for a pixel (x,y) is defined as.

$$I^{t+1}_{(x,y)} = I^t_{(x,y)} + \Delta I (H_{(x,y)}, \nabla I^t_{(x,y)}, \Delta f^t_{(x,y)})^t_{(x,y)} \tag{1}$$

The $\Delta I(\cdot)^t_{(x,y)}$ determines the amount of smoothing action in a given iteration, and it is jointly determined by inhomogeneity $H_{(x,y)}$, gradient $\nabla I^t_{(x,y)}$, and which is the intensity difference of pixel (x,y) and its 8 adjacent neighbors. The $H_{(x,y)}$ is a measurement of pixel (x,y)'s contextual discontinuity, and $\nabla I^t_{(x,y)}$ is a measurement of its local discontinuity. Both discontinuity measurements are combined to determine the appropriate smoothing action or speed for the pixel. H is calculated by averaging the disconnectedness values among a pixel and its 8 adjacent pixels where the disconnectedness value between the pixel and one of its neighbors is calculated using a square shape homogeneous neighborhood (HN). Since HN is restricted to a square shape and often does not represent the actual homogenous area around the pixel. For a smaller neighborhood, the size and shape errors may lead to error in H. The smallest HN of 3 by 3 may not reflect the true size and shape of the homogeneous area when the adjacent pixel is an edge pixel. Furthermore, H does not reflect the direction of the edge which may be important when the pixel under consideration is adjacent to an edge feature pixel rather than a noisy pixel. It is rather important that we have a correct H map to reflect the real contextual discontinuity value of the pixel. In addition, our numerous experiments on real images (5 in number) have indicated that the SNR of the resulting image is rather sensitive to the value of parameter h and T. The fact that the SNR drops off rather rapidly as the number of iteration increases is rather important. These difficulties are limiting the practical applicability of the algorithm to any noise contaminated image where the original image is not available.

It is obvious that a correct H map is the key in getting a good smoothing result since the algorithm aggressively smoothing out homogenous regions of an image while at the same time limiting the smoothing operation in edge feature rich regions. In this paper, a modified procedure to compute the H map is provided. Parameter settings are to be estimated through an experimental searching operation.

3   Approach

A good H map depends on a correct HN and correct HN depends on having a correct shape of homogeneity neighborhood which is not a square in general. Here, we propose the following two improvements:

3.1   Generation of a Correct Homogeneity Neighborhood(HN)

A correct neighborhood has the following properties: it takes the shape of homogeneous neighborhood and is not necessarily a square one, meets a selected smoothness criterion, and finally, has the largest neighborhood area (larger than 3 by3). The larger is the HN size the better (more accurate) is the statistics on the intensity calculations. The level set method is used to search for the HN since the method is an iterative process derived from a selected smoothness criterion and guarantees a connected region from an initial starting local region around a pixel. The smoothness criterion is embedded in the deforming speed function in deforming the HN. The speed function used in our implementation is the commonly adopted inverse of a gradient function. The initial contour is placed around the interested pixel and consists of its 4 neighbors. To reduce the computation time, the maximum number of iterations is set to be 5, and the maximum size of HN is set to be 150 pixels. A morphological erosion operation is applied to the resulting close region to produce a smoother HN. H value of each pixel is the average brightness of the pixels in its HN. Obviously, with this modification, the problem of having 3 by 3 HN in Chen's algorithm is overcome.

3.2 Incorporation of the Directional Information in the H Map Computation

The H map is derived from the HN map to extract the inhomogeneity (context discontinuity) of a pixel and its 8 neighboring pixels. As stated earlier, it reflects whether a pixel is adjacent to an edge element or not. The directional information is an important knowledge needed in the adaptive method to identify the neighboring edge pixels as illustrated in Fig. 2. A large average intensity difference between two adjacent pixels' HNs in a particular direction is an indication of either the presence of a large noise pixel or an adjacent edge segment. To distinguish these two situations, a threshold value is used to compare with these directional differences. If three or more adjacent pixels differences exceed this threshold, then the present of an edge segment is declared and smoothing weights are changed accordingly. To accomplish this, $\Delta HN(i)$ is computed as the average intensity difference of the center pixel's HN and the HN of its ith adjacent pixel with i being from 1 to 8.

$$H(*) = \sum \omega_i \Delta HN(i); \sum \omega_i = 1; i = 1 \sim 8;. \tag{2}$$

The $\Delta HN(i)$ indicates the directional intensity difference. As illustrated in Fig.2, the $\Delta HN(i)$ in the diagonal direction will be larger than all other directions. The weight wi will be set larger to emphasize the directional discontinuity.

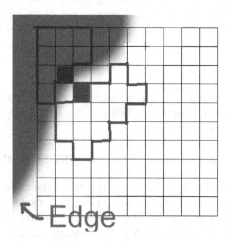

Fig. 2. An illustration of two HN neighborhoods of the edge

All the improvements are concentrated in producing an improved H map so that a better smoothing result can be obtained with edge features being properly preserved. The rest of the adaptive iterative smoothing algorithm stays the same as Chen original algorithm.

4   Experimental Results

Experiments are designed to show comparisons of performances of our proposed method and Chen method based on SNR, DR(edge feature detection rate) and FAR(edge feature false alarm rate) on a set of 5 real images (shown in Fig.3) contaminated with various degrees of additive noise. In addition, parameter settings of h and T are experimentally determined using the 5 real images.

4.1   Performance Comparison between Our Algorithm and Chen's Algorithm

Chen's algorithm has been considered to give better performance in terms of SNR than most other adaptive methods. Chen's algorithm is implemented and verified per [3] by us to produce more experiment results beyond reported results. In our experiments, Gaussian noise with zero mean and different standard deviations (Std) is added to an original image. The comparisons are based on two key objectives – high SNR and edge preservation. For edge preservation evaluation, we have devised the following procedure:

i)   Use the Sobel edge operator with a threshold to extract all edge pixels from an image.
ii)   Use the resulting edge pixels from an original image as the ground truth.
iii)   Calculate detection rate (DR) and false-alarm rate (FAR) as measures of the edge preservation capability.

DR and FAR are defined as:

DR = (Total number of edge pixels matched between the smoothed image and the original image) / (Total number of edge pixels of the original image).

FAR = (Total number of edge pixels found in the smoothed image and not in the original image) / (Total number of edge pixels of the original image).

It is desirable that a good smoothing method will have a high DR together with a very low FAR. It is possible for the FAR to be much larger than 1 when the total number of true edge pixels is much smaller than the image size under noisy condition. The main reason of selecting Sobel operator is that it is a simple and non-smoothing edging method. Although different threshold values give different sets of edges, it has been shown in our experiments that the results are consistent when comparing the performances of the two methods using different threshold values (In comparison different threshold values, one same threshold value will be applied in both methods each time).

The 5 images in Fig. 3 are selected to reflect a broader class of images to provide a more critical comparison of performance. These images are carefully selected to reflect different image data collection situations from an object with a smooth to a

Fig. 3. Images: a) Lena; b) Cameraman; c) Scene; d) Human face; e) Peppers

highly texture image, from a single person image to a very dense crowd, and from an in-door image to an out-door scene. It is expected that the experimental results derived from these images can provide a preliminary and practical conclusion on the applicability of the two algorithms. Additive Gaussian noise of STD of 10 and 20 are considered like most others reported in the literature.

The ground truth edge pixels are extracted using the Sobel operator with a threshold on the original image. Note that different threshold settings give different total number of edge pixels. Our experiments have indicated that the comparison results of performances are consistence using different threshold values(Applying the same threshold value to generate comparing result each time and changing the threshold value to produce a set of comparison results). Be noted that Sobel operator preserves high frequency texture edge features. The results are presented in Table 1 and 2. The results show slight improvements on SNRs and significant improvements on FARs in all 5 cases when comparing the two methods. While our method provides lower DRs when compared to that of original images, they are consistently higher than using the Chen method. Furthermore, the DRs are reduced by 10% to 20% due to the smoothing operation with the order of magnitude improvements in the FARs which maybe significant to any further image segmentation operations. Note that some high frequency texture pixels are also eliminated in the process in producing lower DRs, and therefore, the DRs are even lower for more complicated or busy images like Fig.3d and 3e. These Low DR numbers should not affect the true edge pixels for most object segmentation applications since they are non-texture data. We also have the results on an MRI brain image with various degrees of added noise with significant improvements in SNR. We do not have DR and FAR figures in this case.

Table 1. Smoothing results comparison for 5 real images (without small region removal process)

Image		Fig. 3a		Fig. 3b		Fig. 3c		Fig. 3d		Fig. 3e	
Test Setting		*	**	*	**	*	**	*	**	*	**
A	SNR	125	32	185	48	63	17	170	43	272	71
	DR	0.93	0.91	0.85	0.83	0.83	0.84	0.89	0.84	0.95	0.92
	FAR	1.7	2.17	0.07	0.65	0.12	0.74	0.17	0.24	0.0	1.1
B	SNR	220	139	456	185	121	82	224	117	443	267
	DR	0.68	0.58	0.69	0.58	0.68	0.5	0.68	0.63	0.81	0.73
	FAR	0.11	0.14	0.05	0.13	0.1	0.08	0.08	0.1	0.12	0.32
C	SNR	248	149	462	199	128	87	243	129	454	281
	DR	0.79	0.63	0.75	0.62	0.7	0.52	0.73	0.69	0.86	0.74
	FAR	0.09	0.10	0.02	0.03	0.04	0.05	0.03	0.04	0.06	0.09

*: Gaussian noise with 0 mean and std 10; **: Gaussian noise with 0 mean and std 20.
A: Noisy image; B: Smoothed image with Chen's method; C: Smoothed Image with our method.

Table 2. Smoothing results comparison for 5 real images (with small region removal process)

Image		Fig. 3a		Fig. 3b		Fig. 3c		Fig. 3d		Fig. 3e	
Test Setting		*	**	*	**	*	**	*	**	*	**
A	SNR	125	32	185	48	63	17	170	43	272	71
	DR	0.94	0.93	0.93	0.88	0.89	0.86	0.93	0.88	0.96	0.93
	FAR	1.76	1.9	0.17	0.82	0.25	1.04	0.17	0.37	0.81	0.98
B	SNR	220	139	456	185	121	82	224	117	443	267
	DR	0.73	0.6	0.8	0.64	0.77	0.56	0.75	0.70	0.84	0.75
	FAR	0.09	0.11	0.11	0.2	0.09	0.12	0.1	0.2	0.1	0.21
C	SNR	248	149	462	199	128	87	243	129	454	281
	DR	0.81	0.67	0.86	0.72	0.79	0.58	0.79	0.74	0.88	0.77
	FAR	0.07	0.08	0.06	0.06	0.08	0.1	0.04	0.09	0.05	0.08

*: Gaussian noise with 0 mean and std 10; **: Gaussian noise with 0 mean and std 20.
A: Noisy image; B: Smoothed image with Chen's method; C: Smoothed Image with our method.

4.2 Experimental Determination of h and T Parameter Values

The main purpose of the experiment is to enhance the applicability of our proposed smoothing method and Chen method. Both methods require the selections of two significant parameter values – "h" and "T" (the total iteration number). Experiments have shown the resulting smoothed image is not sensitive to selection of S value as long as it stays within the range between 10 and 40. If we can show experimentally that the smoothing results do not change very much in SNRs, i.e., SNR figures are within a narrow band, for ranges of h and T will improve the applicability of our proposed method. Be noted that on real images, the SNRs drop off rather rapidly after T iterations. Our experimental approach is to do an exhaustive search of h and T in obtaining the best SNR figures of all 5 images under the contamination of an additive Gaussian noise.

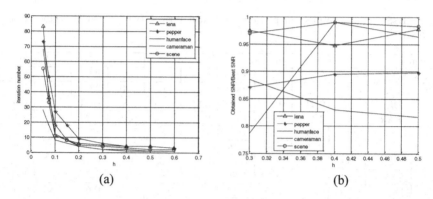

Fig. 4. Our algorithm, (a): besting stopping iteration number versus h; (b): obtained SNR/best SNR versus h

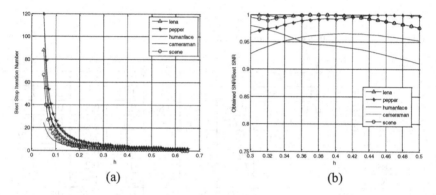

Fig. 5. Chen's algorithm, (a): besting stopping iternation number versus h; (b): obtained SNR/best SNR versus h

For all 5 images in Fig.3, SNRs are computed for different values of h and T with each incoming image being contaminated with Gaussian noise of standard deviation of 20. Our experiments show that the SNR peaks for higher h values with smaller T values, and they drop off rather rapidly for larger h and larger T. For parameter value range selection results, we have Fig.4a and Fig.4b. Fig.4a shows the plots of the T (number of iterations for the best SNR) versus the h. One can see that T is less than 8 iterations in all 5 images for h ranging from 0.2 to 0.6. Fig.4b shows the plot ratios of the obtained SNR versus best SNR figure (maximum of 1) for each image versus h ranging from 0.3 to 0.5. There is only one best SNR for each image. While the resulting SNRs are better than 80% of the best SNR, and they stay rather close range the SNR performances for the whole range of h. Therefore, one can draw a conclusion that for these 5 images, and for T ranges from 3 to 6 and h ranges from 0.3 to 0.5, our smoothing method will provide SNRs of over 80% of the best SNRs. After the computation of the H map, one needs only a very few iterations to obtain a smoothed image in practice as shown in these 5 images. We also conduct the same experiments using Chen's algorithm and very similar results for h and T are shown in Fig.5a and 5b.

5 Conclusion

Our modified algorithm shows slight improvements in SNR when compared to that of Chen's algorithm as can be seen in Tables 1 and 2 for 5 selected images shown in Fig. 3 with different degrees of added noise. These tables show also large improvements in preserving edge features when comparing the same two algorithms. Furthermore, experimental results shown in Fig. 4 and 5 allow us to select the two key parameters of h ranging from 0.3 to 0.5 and T ranging from 3 to 6 that provide comparable smoothing results (higher than 80% from the best SNR) in all 5 images shown in Fig. 3 for both our algorithm and Chen's algorithm. The best combination set for any specific application can visually be determined experimentally using a small number of combinations of different h and T. For practical applications without the knowledge of the noise free image and/or a viewer, we suggest the set of h=0.4 and T=4.

Acknowledgement

The authors wish to thank Dr. Ke Chen for clarifying his smoothing algorithm and also for providing the source code.

References

1. Udupa, J.K., Samarasekera, S.: Fuzzy Connectedness and Object Definition: Theory, Algorithms, and Applications in Image Segmentation. Graphical Models Image Processing 58(3), 246–261 (1998)
2. Chen, K.: Adaptive Smoothing via Contextual and Local Discontinuities. IEEE Trans. on Pattern Analysis and Machine Intelligence 27(10), 1552–1567 (2005)
3. Gonzalez, R.C., Woods, R.E.: Digital Image Processing, 2nd edn. Prentice Hall, Upper Saddle River (2002)
4. Perona, P., Malik, J.: Scale-Space and Edge Detection Using Anisotropic Diffusion. IEEE Trans. Pattern Analysis and Machine Intelligence 12, 629–639 (1990)
5. Black, M.J.: Robust Anisotropic Diffusion. IEEE Trans. Image Processing 7, 421–432 (1998)
6. Saha, P.K., Udupa, J.K.: Scale-Based Diffusive Image Filtering Preserving Boundary Sharpness and Fine Structures. IEEE Trans. Medical Imaging 20, 1140–1155 (2001)
7. Chen, K.: A feature preserving adaptive smoothing method for early vision. Journal of Pattern Recognition Society 13 (2000)
8. Saha, P.K., Udupa, J.K.: Scale-Based Fuzzy Connected Image Segmentation: Theory, Algorithms, and Validation. Computer Vision and Image Understanding 77, 145–174 (2000)
9. Saha, P.K., Udupa, J.K.: Scale-based filtering of medical images. In: Proc. SPIE: Medical Imaging, vol. 3979, pp. 735–746 (2000)
10. Saha, P.K., Udupa, J.K.: Optimum Image Thresholding via Class Uncertainty and Region Homogeneity. IEEE Trans. Pattern Analysis and Machine Intelligence 23, 689–706 (2001)
11. Pednekar, A.S., Kakadiaris, I.A.: Image Segmentation Based on Fuzzy Connectedness Using Dynamic Weights. IEEE Transaction on Image Processing 15(6), 1555–1562 (2006)

12. Vu, R.H.: Fuzzy algorithms: Application to adipose tissue quantification on MR images. Biomedical Signal Processing and Control 2(3), 239–247 (2007)
13. Peng, H.: Modification and Implementation of a 2D Context-Sensitive Adaptive Smoothing Algorithm and its Extension to 3D, master thesis in University of Cincinnati (2006)
14. Hou, Y.: Application of a 3D Level Set Method in MRI Surface Segmentation, Master thesis in University of Cincinnati (2005)
15. Sethian, J.A.: Level Set Methods and Fast Marching Methods: Evolving Interfaces in Computational Geometry, Fluid Mechanics, Computer Vision and Materials Science. Cambridge University Press, Cambridge (1999)
16. McInerney, T., Terzopoulos, D.: Deformable models in medical image analysis: a survey. Medical Image Analasis 1, 91–108 (1996)
17. Pednekar, A.S., Kakadiaris, I.A.: Image Segmentation Based on Fuzzy Connectedness Using Dynamic Weights. IEEE Transaction on Image Processing 15(6), 1555–1562 (2006)
18. Herman, G.T., Carvalho, B.M.: Multiseeded segmentation using fuzzy connectedness. IEEE Trans. on Pattern Anal. Mach. Intell. 23, 460–474 (2001)
19. Vu, R.H.: Fuzzy algorithms: Application to adipose tissue quantification on MR images. Biomedical Signal Processing and Control 2(3), 239–247 (2007)
20. Bloch, I.: Fuzzy spatial relationships for image processing and interpretation: a review. Image and Vision Computing 23(2), 89–110 (2005)

Objective Quality Assessment Measurement for Typhoon Cloud Image Enhancement

Changjiang Zhang, Juan Lu, and Jinshan Wang

College of Mathematics, Physics and Information Engineering,
Zhejiang Normal University, Jinhua, China
zcj74922@zjnu.edu.cn

Abstract. There are kinds of enhancement methods for satellite image, however, visual quality of them are basically assessed by human eyes. This can result in wrong identification. This will result in wrong prediction for center and intensity of the typhoon. It is necessary to find an objective measure to evaluate the visual quality for enhanced typhoon cloud image. In order to solve this problem, we give an objective assessment measurement based on information, contrast and peak-signal-noise-ratio. We design an experiment to certify the proposed measure by using the typhoon cloud images which are provided by China Meteorological Administration, China National Satellite Meteorological Center.

Keywords: Assessment; typhoon; satellite image; enhancement.

1 Introduction

There are many kinds of noise in a typhoon cloud image. If they cannot be efficiently reduced, they may affect the overall image quality to the extent that it is impossible to extract some important information. For example, the noise may disturb the procedure of locating the center position, when we try to predict the moving path of the typhoon. In addition, the contrast of some typhoon cloud images may be poor, which may affect to accurately segment the helical cloud band from the typhoon cloud image. Therefore, it is important to efficiently reduce the noise and enhance the contrast in a typhoon cloud image.

Recently, much good work has been carried out in satellite cloud image enhancement. Ref. [1] developed an approach by merging the data from several satellite images of the same area in order to improve the spatial resolution of the sensor. This enhancement technique is called Data Cumulation. The paper starts with the theory of sampling image data over a scene, discusses the theoretical background of the approach and describes it implementation. Simulated Data Cumulation has been carried out using both artificial targets and satellite image data as well. Ref. [2] pointed out that threshold selection is an important problem for the purpose of image enhancement. Image enhancement consists of subdividing the intensity gray levels into bands, such that the resulting image presents more contrast, and less gray levels. One means of achieving threshold selection is through the use of gray tone spatial dependency

P. Foggia, C. Sansone, and M. Vento (Eds.): ICIAP 2009, LNCS 5716, pp. 767–776, 2009.

matrices. A function of gray levels is computed from a co-occurence matrix of the image and then a threshold is chosen which corresponds to the etrema of this function. This article describes the algorithm of GTRLM and the results of the application of this technique to some satellite images. Ref. [3] presented a method for the improvement of the visual quality of satellite and aerial images. It helps geographers in their visual interpretation of urban growth in developing countries. This method is based on local contrast estimation. Results of the application of the algorithms to aerial and satellite images are discussed. Ref. [4] accomplished satellite image enhancement and smoothing towards automatic feature extraction through an effective serial application of anisotropic diffusion processing and alternating sequential filtering. A robust anisotropic diffusion filtering is used with Tukey's biweight robust error norm for "edge-stopping" function. A well-known class of morphological filters, alternating sequential filtering is applied afterwards for a more extended enhancement and smoothing.

Recently, the wavelet transform has been widely applied to the image enhancement. Some image enhancement algorithms only consider the enhancement and do not care about noise reduction. For example, Fu, J.C. and Wan, Y. used the improved histogram equalization in wavelet domain to enhance the image Ref. [5]. Temizel, A. proposed two algorithms to enhance an image resolution by the estimation of detail wavelet coefficients at high resolution scales and cycle-spinning methodology in the wavelet domain respectively [6]. Xiao, D. respectively presented an algorithm to enhance the contrast of an image by modifying both coarse and detail coefficients[7]. Heric, D. introduced a novel image enhancement technique based on the multiscale singularity detection with an adaptive threshold whose value is calculated via the maximum entropy measure in the directional wavelet domain [8]. Some image enhancement algorithms only consider noise reduction and do not care about detail enhancement. For example, Ercelebi, E. proposed a method by applying lifting-based wavelet domain Wiener filter to enhance the contrast of an image [9]. The proposed method transforms an image into the wavelet domain using lifting-based wavelet filters and then applies a Wiener filter in the wavelet domain and finally transforms the result into the spatial domain. Many enhancement algorithms consider both detail enhancement and noise reduction. For example, Pengxin Zeng proposed a wavelet-based algorithm for image contrast enhancement [10]. The approach treats the correlation between wavelet planes as an indication of the likelihood that noise is present. Then, it modifies the wavelet transform coefficients at different scales in different degrees by a pointwise nonlinear transformation. The algorithm achieves an excellent balance between the enhancement of subtle image detail, and the avoidance of noise amplification. Luo, Gaoyong presented a new method of x-ray image denoising based on fast lifting wavelet thresholding for general noise reduction and spatial filtering for further denoising by using a derivative model to preserve edges [11]. Belousov, Artem A. described a developed two-phase full-color image enhancement algorithm [12]. During the first phase the picture is denoised based wavelet thresholding. During the second phase brightness and contrast are automatically tuned up using evolutionary algorithm.

Although many above methods have been proposed to enhance image, however, most of methods assess the image quality by subjective measure. This will result in different assessment for different men. It is necessary to develop an efficient objective assessment measure for an image. Especially, for typhoon cloud image, this is very necessary because this will affect the center location of the typhoon and main body segmentation of cloud series of the typhoon. Further, this will result in an incorrect prediction for moving path or intensity of the typhoon.

2 Objective Assessment Measure for Typhoon Cloud Image

Digital images are subject to a wide variety of distortions during acquisition, processing, compression, storage, transmission and reproduction, any of which may result in a degradation of visual quality. For applications in which images are ultimately to be viewed by human beings, the only "correct" method of qualifying visual image quality is through subjective evaluation. In practice, however, subjective evaluation is usually too inconvenient, time-consuming and expensive [13]. The goal of research in objective image quality assessment is to develop quantitative measures that can automatically predict perceived image quality.

An objective image quality metric can play a variety of roles in image processing applications. First, it can be used to dynamically monitor and adjust image quality. Second, it can be used to optimize algorithms and parameter settings of image processing systems. Third, it can be used to benchmark image processing systems and algorithms. We construct a quality measure from the perspective of image information in order to assess the enhanced image quality. The system separates the task of enhanced image quality measurement into three comparisons: information entropy, contrast and signal-noise-ratio. First, the information entropy of each enhanced image is compared. The better the enhanced image quality is, the bigger the information entropy is. Second, the contrast of each enhanced image is compared. Assuming a discrete signal, the mean intensity can be written as

$$\mu_x = \frac{1}{N}\sum_{i=1}^{N} x_i \tag{1}$$

We remove the mean intensity from the signal. In discrete form, the resulting signal $x - \mu_x$ corresponds to the projection of vector x onto the hyperplane defined by

$$\sum_{i=1}^{N} x_i = 0 \tag{2}$$

We used the standard deviation (the square root of variance) as an estimate of the signal contrast. An unbiased estimate in discrete form is given by

$$c = \left(\frac{1}{N-1} \sum_{i=1}^{N} \left(x_i - \mu_x \right)^2 \right)^{\frac{1}{2}} \tag{3}$$

The better the enhanced image quality is, the bigger c is.

Third, the peak-signal-noise-ratio (PSNR) of enhanced image is compared.

$$p = 10 \cdot \log \left(\frac{MN \cdot \max\left(F_{ij}^{2}\right)}{\sum_{i=1}^{M}\sum_{j=1}^{N}\left(F_{ij} - G_{ij}\right)^{2}} \right) \tag{4}$$

Where F_{ij} and G_{ij} are gray level value at (i, j) in original image and enhanced image respectively. M and N are width and height of the original image respectively. The better the enhanced image quality is, the bigger p is. Finally, the three components are combined to yield an overall measure

$$S = f\left(e, c, p\right) \tag{5}$$

Generally, the better the enhanced image quality is, the bigger p is. However, the PSNR may become small after an image is enhanced and reduced noise although the overall quality of an image is good. Therefore we construct following overall measure to assess the quality of an enhanced image:

$$S = e^{\alpha} \cdot c^{\beta} \cdot \left[sign(\mathrm{p}) \cdot |\mathrm{p}|^{\gamma} \right] \tag{6}$$

where $\alpha > 0$, $\beta > 0$ and $\gamma > 0$ are parameters used to adjust the relative importance of the three components. In order to simplify the expression and above analysis to PSNR, we set $\alpha = \beta = 1$ and $\gamma = \frac{1}{5}$ in this paper. This results in a specific form of the following index

$$S = e \cdot c \cdot \left[sign(\mathrm{p}) \cdot |\mathrm{p}|^{\frac{1}{5}} \right] \tag{7}$$

The better the enhanced image quality is, the bigger S is.

3   Experimental Results

In experiments, nine infrared typhoon cloud images, which are provided by China Meteorological Administration, China National Satellite Meteorological Center, are used to verify the efficiency of proposed algorithm, where three typhoon cloud images are corrupted by additive gauss white noise (GWN). We will compare the performance between the proposed algorithm (ZCJ) [14], histogram equalization (HE), AFL method [15], WYQ method [16], XLZ method [17] and un-sharpened mask method (USM). Fig.1 (a)-(b) respectively represent original typhoon cloud image (typhoon No. 0425) and the corresponding noisy one (peak-signal-noise-ratio is 10dB). Fig.1 (c)-(h) respectively shows denoising and enhancement results by HE, AFL, WYQ, XLZ, USM and ZCJ.

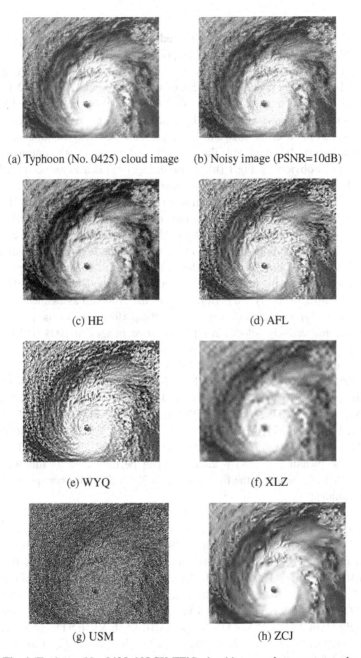

(a) Typhoon (No. 0425) cloud image   (b) Noisy image (PSNR=10dB)

(c) HE   (d) AFL

(e) WYQ   (f) XLZ

(g) USM   (h) ZCJ

Fig. 1. Typhoon (No. 0425- NOCK-TEN) cloud image enhancement results

According to Fig.1, we can see that HE method, AFL method and USM only considers enhancing contrast of an image while noise is also enhanced while enhancing the contrast of the typhoon cloud image. AFL method, which is proposed based on the classical discrete wavelet transform, has a better result than HE method and USM method, however, there are some undesired spot in the enhanced typhoon cloud image. Both WYQ method and XLZ method consider noise suppression while enhancing the contrast of the typhoon cloud image. WYQ method has enlarged the background bur while enhancing contrast of the typhoon cloud image. XLZ method has a good denoising result. However, the details in the typhoon cloud image are blurred. Noise in the enhanced image by USM method is greatly enlarged. The eye and cloud bands in the cloud image are emerged into the background. Compared with five other methods, ZCJ method is the best in visual quality. Both contrast and details are good, this is obvious in Fig.1 (h). Noise in Fig.1 (b) is also reduced well and eye region and main cloud bands of the typhoon are well kept.

In order to objectively assess the enhanced images quality, Equation (7) is used to accomplish the work. Table 1 lists the scores of enhanced images with different peak-signal-noise-ratio (PSNR). According to Table 1, we can see that the scores of enhanced images are becoming lower and lower with the increasing of standard deviation of noise. Compared with five other methods, the scores of enhanced images using the proposed algorithm are the highest. This exactly proves the advantage of the proposed algorithm. In order to certify the performance of the proposed assessment measure, we give thirty other typhoon cloud images to test the performance of the proposed measurement. We respectively select ten typhoon cloud images in 2004 (0401- SUDAL, 0402-NIDA, 0404-CONSON, 0406-DIANMU, 0409-KOMPASU, 0413- MERANTI, 0414-RANANIM, 0418-AERE, 0422-MEARI, and 0423-MA-ON), 2005 (0502-ROKE, 0503-SONCA, 0504-NESAT, 0505-HAITANG, 0509-MATSA, 0511-MAWAR, 0514-NABI, 0516-VICENTE, 0518-DAMREY, and 0522-TEMBIN) and 2006 (0601- CHANCHU, 0603-EWINIAR, 0606-PRAPIROON, 0611-SONAMU, 0613- SHANSHAN, 0616-BEBINCA, 0617-RUMBIA, 0619-CIMARON, 0621-DURIAN, and 0623-Trami) to test the performance of the proposed assessment measure. The meaning of "0401- SUDAL" can be explained as follows: name of typhoon is SUDAL, which is the first typhoon in 2004. Similar other spellings have the similar meanings.

Fig.2-Fig.4 show the test typhoon cloud images from 2004 to 2006. The five cloud images of the first row in Fig.2 are respectively 0401- SUDAL, 0402-NIDA, 0404-CONSON, 0406-DIANMU, and 0409-KOMPASU. The five cloud images of the second row in Fig.2 respectively show 0413- MERANTI, 0414-RANANIM, 0418-AERE, 0422-MEARI, and 0423-MA-ON. The five cloud images of the first row in Fig.3 are respectively 0502-ROKE, 0503-SONCA, 0504-NESAT, 0505-HAITANG, and 0509-MATSA. The five cloud images of the second row in Fig.3 respectively show 0511- MAWAR, 0514-NABI, 0516-VICENTE, 0518-DAMREY, and 0522-TEMBIN. The five cloud images of the first row in Fig.4 are respectively 0601-CHANCHU, 0603-EWINIAR, 0606-PRAPIROON, 0611-SONAMU, and 0613- SHANSHAN. The five cloud images of the second row in Fig.4 respectively show 0616-BEBINCA, 0617-RUMBIA, 0619-CIMARON, 0621-DURIAN, and 0623-Trami.

Table 1. Scores of enhanced images with different PSNR (0425- NOCK-TEN)

PSNR	HE	AFL	WYQ	XLZ	USM	ZCJ
2	150.36	-328.45	-263.02	195.06	-1215.60	**200.90**
4	168.49	-268.79	-212.06	194.99	-1073.30	**205.89**
6	180.84	-196.56	100.21	194.89	-953.32	**210.99**
8	190.35	183.54	192.16	194.81	-856.23	**217.64**
10	197.57	213.16	209.92	194.74	-784.43	**223.52**
12	203.22	223.31	218.31	194.67	-727.54	**231.00**
14	207.19	228.17	223.27	194.61	-688.84	**235.21**
16	210.18	230.51	226.28	194.57	-660.16	**239.20**
18	212.10	231.77	228.37	194.53	-643.19	**241.95**
20	213.36	232.58	229.74	194.49	-632.31	**243.26**

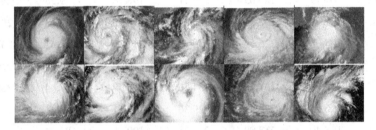

Fig. 2. Test typhoon cloud images (2004)

Fig. 3. Test typhoon cloud images (2005)

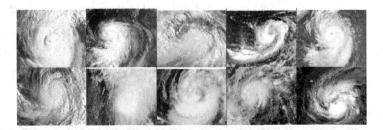

Fig. 4. Test typhoon cloud images (2006)

In order to test the efficiency of the proposed measure, Table 2-Table 4 gives the scores of enhanced cloud images with different methods. Here all the PSNR of the test cloud images are set as 12 dB. From Table 2-Table 4, we can see that the scores of ZCJ method is the highest compared with other five methods. Although some scores are higher than ZCJ method, for example, the two scores of AFL method and WYQ method are higher than ZCJ method in Table 3 and Table 4, the overall visual quality of the ZCJ method is the best. In a sum, the proposed assessment measure can be used to assess the visual quality of the enhanced typhoon cloud images. The visual quality is agreed with the objective index with the proposed assessment measure.

Table 2. Scores of enhanced images with different typhoon cloud images (2004)

No.	HE	AFL	WYQ	XLZ	USM	ZCJ
0401	205.11	238.28	242.92	226.94	-696.57	**244.70**
0402	170.91	190.61	179.01	153.05	-689.87	**191.65**
0404	207.79	232.63	228.11	198.76	-739.28	**235.14**
0406	181.99	202.88	206.96	190.30	-642.83	**208.42**
0409	204.08	226.69	230.59	217.20	-682.41	**237.79**
0413	202.93	238.98	238.00	216.05	-737.93	**250.60**
0414	198.93	237.18	234.26	215.47	-737.64	**250.18**
0418	196.05	225.90	229.36	232.51	-680.41	**248.17**
0422	196.40	218.09	220.41	199.78	-682.74	**223.01**
0423	214.44	270.91	264.49	250.06	-798.26	**291.14**

Table 3. Scores of enhanced images with different typhoon cloud images (2005)

No.	HE	AFL	WYQ	XLZ	USM	ZCJ
0502	137.73	166.98	165.33	131.92	-654.88	**167.13**
0503	202.15	251.57	244.09	214.70	-774.18	**259.29**
0504	212.19	248.39	248.37	228.13	-753.06	**265.26**
0505	208.90	237.52	239.85	217.80	-724.94	**245.66**
0509	191.77	209.57	168.76	158.38	-762.65	**215.83**
0511	178.79	181.53	185.12	164.04	-636.87	**184.64**
0514	-123.29	144.11	137.94	114.88	-627.51	**144.15**
0516	174.07	184.54	166.53	140.15	-711.63	**183.38**
0518	166.57	180.96	177.49	161.89	-656.87	**183.11**
0522	219.32	268.87	269.63	252.78	-769.90	**288.14**

Table 4. Scores of enhanced images with different typhoon cloud images (2006)

No.	HE	AFL	WYQ	XLZ	USM	ZCJ
0601	181.59	209.34	207.33	197.45	-697.45	**223.66**
0603	217.83	277.90	279.32	282.33	-763.85	**308.88**
0606	-143.59	135.56	130.63	101.38	-598.92	**134.04**
0611	215.47	289.18	278.46	280.66	-830.80	**323.91**
0613	200.05	224.99	225.54	208.87	-716.88	**233.71**
0616	191.49	208.76	198.07	168.64	-732.27	**207.34**
0617	198.95	253.81	254.60	237.10	-768.42	**269.16**
0619	190.78	250.30	254.45	248.88	-722.94	**269.75**
0621	203.10	238.60	234.37	208.03	-737.45	**249.29**
0623	216.32	279.25	279.98	281.41	-765.18	**310.79**

4 Conclusion

This paper proposed an objective measure to assess the visual quality for typhoon cloud image enhancement. The measure can be used to evaluate the visual quality for satellite cloud image, especially for typhoon cloud image. It has a good assessment results by our designed experiments. This can provide accurate information for center and intensity prediction of the typhoon.

Acknowledgments

Part of the research is supported by the Grants for China Natural Science Foundation (40805048), China Zhejiang Province Natural Science Foundation (Y506203), Typhoon Research Foundation of Shanghai Typhoon Institute/China Meteorological Administration (2008ST01), Research foundation of State Key Laboratory of Severe Weather/Chinese Academy of Meteorological Sciences (2008LASW-B03). China Meteorological Administration, China National Satellite Meteorological Center is acknowledged for providing all the typhoon cloud images in this manuscript.

References

1. Albertz, J., Zelianeos, K.: Enhancement of satellite image data by data cumulation. Journal of Photogrammetry and Remote Sensing 45 (1990)
2. Fernandez-Maloigne, C.: Satellite images enhancement. In: Proceedings-International Symposium on Automotive Technology & Automation, vol. 3, pp. 210–215 (1990)
3. Bekkhoucha, A., Smolarz, A.: Technique of images contrast enhancement: an application to satellite and aerial images. Automatique Productique Informatique Industrielle 26, 335–353 (1992)

 4. Karantzalos, K.G.: Combining anisotropic diffusion and alternating sequential filtering for satellite image enhancement and smoothing. In: Proceedings of SPIE – Image and Signal Processing for Remote Sensing IX, vol. 5238, pp. 461–468 (2004)
 5. Wan, Y., Shi, D.: Joint Exact Histogram Specification and Image Enhancement Through the Wavelet Transform. IEEE Transactions on Image Processing 16, 2245–2250 (2007)
 6. Temizel, A., Vlachos, T.: Wavelet domain image resolution enhancement. IEEE Proceedings Vision, Image and Signal Processing 153, 25–30 (2006)
 7. Xiao, D., Ohya, J.: Contrast enhancement of color images based on wavelet transform and human visual system. In: Proceedings of the IASTED International Conference on Graphics and Visualization in Engineering, pp. 58–63 (2007)
 8. Heric, D., Potocnik, B.: Image enhancement by using directional wavelet transform. Journal of Computing and Information Technology – CIT 14, 299–305 (2006)
 9. Ercelebi, E., Koc, S.: Lifting-based wavelet domain adaptive Wiener filter for image enhancement. IEEE Proceedings Vision, Image and Signal Processing 153, 31–36 (2006)
10. Zeng, P., Dong, H., Chi, J., Xu, X.: An approach for wavelet based image enhancement. In: 2004 IEEE International Conference on Robotics and Biomimetics, pp. 574–577 (2004)
11. L. Gaoyong, O. David, H. Chris: Real-time wavelet denoising with edge enhancement for medical x-ray imaging. Proceedings of SPIE - The International Society for Optical Engineering, vol.6063, pp. 606303 (2006)
12. Belousov, A.A., Spitsyn, V.G., Sidorov, D.V.: Applying Wavelets and Evolutionary algorithms to automatic image enhancement. In: Proceedings of SPIE - The International Society for Optical Engineering, vol. 6522, pp. 652210 (2006)
13. Wang, Z., Bovik, A.C., Skith, H.R., Simoncelli, E.P.: Simoncelli: Image quality assessment: from error visibility to structural similarity. IEEE Transactions on Image Processing 13, 600–612 (2004)
14. Changjiang, Z., Xiaodong, W., Haoran, Z., Chunjiang, D.: An anti-noise algorithm for enhancing global and local contrast for infrared image. International Journal of Wavelet, Multi-resolution and Information Processing 5(1), 101–112 (2007)
15. Laine, A.F., Schuler, S., Fan, J., Huda, W.: Mammographic feature enhancement by multiscale analysis. IEEE Transactions on Medical Imaging 13(4), 725–752 (1994)
16. Ying-Qian, W., Pei-Jun, D., Peng-Fei, S.: Research on wavelet-based algorithm for image contrast enhancement. Wuhan University Journal of Natural Sciences 9, 46–50 (2004)
17. Zong, X., Laine, A.F.: De-noising and contrast enhancement via wavelet shrinkage and nonlinear adaptive gain. In: Published in wavelet applications III, proceedings of SPIE, vol. 2762, pp. 566–574 (1996)

Fuzzy Smoothed Composition of Local Mapping Transformations for Non-rigid Image Registration

Edoardo Ardizzone, Roberto Gallea, Orazio Gambino, and Roberto Pirrone

Università degli studi di Palermo
DINFO - Dipartimento di Ingegneria Informatica
Viale delle Scienze - Ed.6 - 3° piano - 90128 Palermo (Italy)
{ardizzon,robertogallea,gambino,pirrone}@unipa.it

Abstract. This paper presents a novel method for medical image registration. The global transformation is obtained by composing affine transformations, which are recovered locally from given landmarks. Transformations of adjacent regions are smoothed to avoid blocking artifacts, so that a unique continuous and differentiable global function is obtained. Such composition is operated using a technique derived from fuzzy C-means clustering. The method was successfully tested on several datasets; results, both qualitative and quantitative, are shown. Comparisons with other methods are reported. Final considerations on the efficiency of the technique are explained.

Keywords: free form deformation, image registration, fuzzy clustering, function interpolation.

1 Introduction

Image Registration is a recent research field in medical imaging with a rapid evolution in the latest years. Indeed, it is a very important task for many applications such as image fusion to integrate data acquired with different modalities (for example MR and PET), therapy evaluation by observing the changes in two images acquired in different times, segmentation purposes, and so on. The problem consists in applying spatial transformations to an *input* image so that it can be superimposed to a *target* one. At the end of the automatic process, corresponding pixels will be in the same positions on both the images.

Feature-based approaches recover the global transformation using a sparse set of data such as points or lines that have a correspondence in the two images. The information about the relative positions of these elements allows the registration method to interpolate a global transformation function.

A well known landmark based method used in literature is the Thin-Plate Spline (TPS) surface fitting [1] along with its variants, such as [2], [3], [4] and [5].

This method models a surface constrained to contain several node points. This is done by decomposing the whole transformation in a linear (affine) part, and the superposition of the so-called principal warps that are mutually independent.

P. Foggia, C. Sansone, and M. Vento (Eds.): ICIAP 2009, LNCS 5716, pp. 777–786, 2009.

This paper proposes a novel landmark-based registration method. The presented procedure computes independently several local deformations, which are composed subsequently in a global transformation function, which exhibits continuity and smoothness properties. The algorithm is based on concepts derived from Fuzzy C-means clustering [6]. Even though C-means relies on the determination of the clustering centroids, thus requiring an iterative minimization procedure, here the centroids are given as a starting condition, so just membership functions need to be computed. As a result, the optimization step is removed allowing the recovering of the global displacement function composition to be simply the result of quick and efficient sum and product operations.

The landmark-based approach was chosen for several reasons. Firstly, the system is intended just to assist the expert, keeping its role fundamental for the diagnosis process; in addition it allows a fast single-pass computation. Lastly, in our approach, since each local transformation is independent from the others, it is possible to achieve additional speedups by exploiting parallel elaborations.

The paper is arranged as follows: in sect. 2 some thoretical remarks required for the understanding of the work are given. In sect. 3, the registration algorithm steps are presented. Sect. 4 shows the tests performed to validate the algorithm and describes the results, comparing them with the TPS approach. Sect. 4 contains considerations on the algorithm performance and the evaluation of the obtained results. Sect. 5 discusses how the performance can be improved and states the roadmap for further development of the method.

2   Theoretical Remarks

Before proceeding with the description of the proposed registration algorithm, some remarks about Fuzzy c-means clustering technique and Thin Plate Spline are required. The former is used for determining a weighting function for composing local transformations, while the latter is a well-known literature method used for landmark-based registration and it is used in this paper for comparative purposes.

2.1   Fuzzy C-Means

Fuzzy C-means is a powerful and efficient data clustering method. Each data sample, represented by some feature values, is associated to the clusters of the feature space using some membership degree. Each cluster is identified by its centroid, a point where the feature values are representative for its own class. The original algorithm is based on the minimization of the following objective function:

$$J_s = \sum_{j=1}^{m} \sum_{i=1}^{k} (u_{ij})^s d(\mathbf{x_i}, \mathbf{c_j})^2 , \quad 1 \leq s \leq \infty \tag{1}$$

where $d(\mathbf{x_i}, \mathbf{c_j})$ is a distance function between each observation vector $\mathbf{x_i}$ and the cluster centroid $\mathbf{c_j}$, m is the number of clusters, which should be chosen a priori,

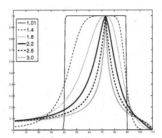

Fig. 1. Example of 1-d membership function plot for different values of s

k is the number of observations, u_{ij} is the membership degree of the sample $\mathbf{x_i}$ belonging to cluster centroid $\mathbf{c_j}$ and $s > 1$ is a parameter which determines the amount of clustering fuzziness, i.e. the form of membership function Fig. (1), having a value that for common task generally lies in the interval around 2. An additional constraint is that the membership degrees should be positive and structured such that $u_{i,1} + u_{i,2} + ... + u_{i,m} = 1$. The method proceeds as an iterative procedure where, given the membership matrix $\mathbf{U} = [u_{ij}]$ of size k by m, the new positions of the centroids are updated as:

$$\mathbf{c_j} = \frac{\sum_{i=1}^{k} (u_{ij})^s \mathbf{x_i}}{\sum_{i=1}^{k} (u_{ij})^s} \qquad (2)$$

The algorithm ends after a fixed number of iterations or when the improvement of each iteration is substantially small and the new membership values are given by the following equation:

$$u_{ij} = \frac{1}{\sum_{l=1}^{m} \left(\frac{d(\mathbf{x_i}, \mathbf{c_j})}{d(\mathbf{x_i}, \mathbf{c_l})} \right)^{\frac{2}{s-1}}} \qquad (3)$$

2.2   Thin Plate Spline

One of the classical approaches to image registration is the Thin Plate Spline (TPS). The name is derived from the physical analogy, which involves the bending of a thin metal sheet. In the context of spatial coordinates transformation and image registration, lifting the plate corresponds to displace the image in one direction (i.e. x, y or z axis). The Thin Plate Spline is a parametric interpolation function which is defined by $D(K + 3)$ parameters, where D is the number of spatial dimensions of the datasets and K is the number of the given landmark points where the displacement values are known. The function is a composition of an affine part, defined by 3 parameters, and K radial basis functions, defined by an equal number of parameters. In $2d$ its analytic form is defined as:

$$g(\mathbf{p}) = ax + by + d + \sum_{i=1}^{K} \rho \left(\|\mathbf{p} - \mathbf{c_i}\|^2 \right) w_i; \quad \mathbf{p} = \begin{bmatrix} x \\ y \end{bmatrix}; \quad \mathbf{c_i} = \begin{bmatrix} c_x \\ c_y \end{bmatrix} \qquad (4)$$

where $\mathbf{p}$ is the input point, $\mathbf{c_i}$ are the landmark points and $\rho\left(r\right) = \frac{1}{2}r^2\log r^2$ is the radial basis function. All of the TPS parameters are computed solving a linear system defined by a closed-form minimization of the bending energy functional. Such functional is given by:

$$E_{tps} = \sum_{i=1}^{K}\|y_i - g\left(\mathbf{p}_i\right)\|+\lambda \int\int\left[\left(\frac{\partial^2 g}{\partial x^2}\right)^2 + 2\left(\frac{\partial^2 g}{\partial xy}\right)^2 + \left(\frac{\partial^2 g}{\partial y^2}\right)^2\right]dxdy. \quad (5)$$

The functional is composed by two terms: the data term and the regularization term. The former minimizes the difference between known and recovered displacements at landmark points, the latter minimizes the bending energy of the recovered function, i.e. maximises its smoothness and it is weighted by the parameter λ. As mentioned before, for this expression a closed-form analytical solution exists, from which is possible to recover all of the required spline function parameters. The main characteristic of this function is that it exhibits minimum curvature properties.

3   The Registration Algorithm

The proposed method takes as inputs the target image, the input one, and two sets of control points with their correspondences. The resulting output is the function which implements the mapping between all the points in the two images. The determination of the mapping function is constrained by the displacement of the control points, which can be chosen manually or automatically. Since the purpose of the method is just to find the transformation that achieves the registration, no considerations are reported about control points determination. However, in sect. 5 some clues are given on this topic. The registration procedure is composed of four processing steps (Fig. 2): image space subdivision, local mapping estimation, weighting function computation and global mapping composition. The first step consists in subdividing the whole image into separate regions. For this purpose the adopted strategy is the classic Delaunay triangulation [7] of the given control points, which is optimal in the sense it maximizes all the angles in the generated triangles. With a proper choice of the landmarks, Delaunay triangulation avoids the generation of very thin triangular regions whose vertices are almost collinear, this will produce numerical instability when obtaining local transformations. An example of the output of this procedure is shown in Fig. 3. Once the triangular regions resulting from Delaunay algorithm

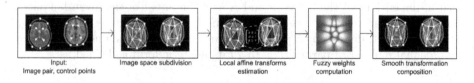

| Input: | Image space subdivision | Local affine transforms | Fuzzy weights | Smooth transformation |
| Image pair, control points | | estimation | computation | composition |

Fig. 2. System block diagram

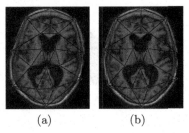

(a)   (b)

Fig. 3. From left to right: Delaunay triangulation for input image (a), and target image (b)

are available, the affine transform which best maps each region into the other is recovered by solving the linear system defined by the constraints over the coordinates of the three triangle vertices (6):

$$
\begin{bmatrix} x \\ y \\ 1 \end{bmatrix} = \begin{bmatrix} a\ b\ c \\ d\ e\ f \\ 0\ 0\ 1 \end{bmatrix} \begin{bmatrix} x_{0,n} \\ y_{0,n} \\ 1 \end{bmatrix} = \begin{bmatrix} ax_0 + by_0 + c \\ dx_0 + ey_0 + f \\ 1 \end{bmatrix} \Rightarrow \begin{cases} x_1 = a_1 x_{0,1} + b_1 y_{0,1} + c_1 \\ y_1 = d_1 x_{0,1} + e_1 y_{0,1} + f_1 \\ x_2 = a_2 x_{0,2} + b_2 y_{0,2} + c_2 \\ y_2 = d_2 x_{0,2} + e_2 y_{0,2} + f_2 \\ x_3 = a_3 x_{0,3} + b_3 y_{0,3} + c_3 \\ y_3 = d_3 x_{0,3} + e_3 y_{0,3} + f_3 \end{cases}
$$
$$(6)$$

Direct composition of such transformations produces a triangle mesh, and, even though it is spatially congruent and the final global transformation function is continuous, it does not provide good results, because in correspondence of the triangles' boundaries it obviously exhibits crisp edges (Fig. 4a). The surfaces displayed in Fig. 4 represents the resulting displacement along the horizontal direction of the pixel in position (i, j) when it is transformed from the input image to the target one, respectively using direct composition (a), the proposed method (b), and TPS (c). The global transformation is thus completely defined by a couple of surfaces, one for each dimension. We need a further processing in order to make the global transform function smooth. To achieve this purpose, we weigh the local mapping functions in a proper way, using concepts related to Fuzzy c-means clustering technique. In sec. 2.1 such technique is recalled in more details. Even though centroids and fuzzy membership concepts are useful for our purposes, no clustering process is required, and no minimization is performed actually. If we assume the center of mass of each triangle as a cluster centroid in the feature space defined by the pixel spatial coordinates (i, j) (in [8] the landmarks coordinates are roughly used for this purpose), then membership values relative to each cluster can be assigned to each pixel in the image. Membership values will be more or less strong according to its displacement w.r.t. each centroid. Due to the summation constraint, it is possible to use membership values as weighting terms for the local mapping functions. The amount of decay related to distance variation, and consequently the membership value itslef, is controlled by means of the s exponent, which is the unique tunable parameter in this registration scheme (see sec. 4 for further details).

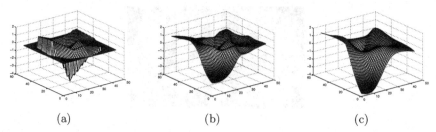

(a)   (b)   (c)

Fig. 4. From left to right: an example of the resulting mapping function with affine direct composition (a), fuzzy smoothed composition (b), TPS surface fitting (c)

Given the above conditions, the new coordinate vector $\mathbf{v_{ij}}$ of the pixel at position (i, j) is given by:

$$\mathbf{v_{ij}} = \sum_n u_{ij,l} \left(\mathbf{T_n} \cdot \mathbf{x_{ij}}\right) \tag{7}$$

where $u_{ij,l}$ is the membership degree of the pixel of coordinates $\mathbf{x_{ij}}$ for the l-th centroid while $\mathbf{T_n}$ is the affine transformation for the l-th centroid, recovered in the previous step.

This results in a smooh transformation function with no discontinuities, and governable smoothness by adjusting the s parameter. An example is shown in Fig. 4b. For comparisons purposes, in Fig. 4c, the transformation obtained from TPS approximation using the same inputs is also shown.

Another remarkable advantage of our approach is that the time-consuming minimization procedure required to fit a global transformation function is replaced by solving analitically at most $2n - 2 - b$ linear systems of three equations, where n is the total number of control points and b is the number of vertices of the convex hull defined by the control points. What needs to be computed is just the membership matrix $\mathbf{U}$ using (7). The metric used to compute the distance function is the Euclidean distance because it is sufficient to take into account just spatial closeness between pixels and control points. Such method can be used both for 2-D images and 3-D volumes. The only difference is in the number of transformation functions to be computed that is one for each dimension.

4   Results and Discussion

The proposed method has been implemented and tested on sets of both real (100 sample pictures) and synthetic medical images provided by Brainweb [9,10,11,12] (50 sample pictures). Some preliminary tests were conducted on a template pattern. The image contains a white circle on black background, Fig. 5a. The image was strongly deformed as in Fig. 5b. Then the registration procedure was applied using a different number of landmarks both with our algorithm, and the TPS one. The results are shown in Fig. 5c and Fig. 5d. Differences between the two methods are shown in Fig. 5e, where the dark contour represents the TPS approximation scheme, while the bright one refers to the proposed method.

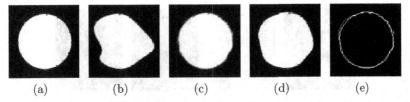

(a)   (b)   (c)   (d)   (e)

Fig. 5. From left to right: results on a template image using 18 control points. Base image (a), input image (b), registered image using our method (c), and using TPS approach (d), difference between the two approaches (e) where the bright contour represents our method, while the dark one is related to the TPS approach.

The figure shows that a better image recovery is obtained using the proposed method, though differences are quite subtle, just in correspondence of the area of large deformations, which are better modelled by local transformations. (like in the middle part of the pattern).

The second class of tests consists in the use of synthetic medical images manually deformed and then registered back onto their original version. In this case the performance has been evaluated using several similarity metrics: sum of squared difference (SSD), mean squared error (MSE) and mutual information (MI) as objective measures, and Structural Similarity ($SSIM$) [13] as a subjective one. The algorithm was run using different values for the s parameter. Visual results for the proposed method applied to a sample image are depicted in Fig. 6, while the measures are summarized in Table 1. Comparisons with TPS approach are also presented. The outcomes point out that the presented method performs better than TPS irrespectively to the similarity measure taken into account.

Other merely visual tests were performed on various photographic images in order to evaluate the performance of the algorithm for other purposes, such as morphing. In Fig. 7 the results obtained morphing two sample images are shown.

As results from the tests reported, in the average case comparisons with TPS approach resulted in a better performance of our method. In addition, it results even more efficient and faster: as an example on a P4 machine equipped with MS Windows Vista and Matlab R2008a, the registration of a 208x176 pixels image using 18 landmarks (Fig.3 and Fig.6), took around 40% of the time taken by

Table 1. Results summary for different values of s and λ, best measures underlined

	Fuzzy Approximation				**TPS Approximation**			
s	MSE	SSD	MI	SSIM	λ	MSE	SSD	MI	SSIM
1.2	29.3167	1073225	1.6627	0.7985	0.0001	30.8739	1359829	1.2067	0.7918
1.4	29.2199	1069683	1.6649	0.8001	0.0006	30.4943	1149111	1.2487	0.8135
1.6	<u>29.0541</u>	<u>1063612</u>	<u>1.6725</u>	<u>0.8021</u>	0.0011	31.0487	<u>1136312</u>	1.2502	<u>0.8145</u>
1.8	29.9451	1096229	1.6570	0.7935	0.0016	30.2244	1168397	<u>1.2505</u>	0.8142
2.0	30.4536	1114847	1.6488	0.7886	0.0021	29.6988	1181151	1.2494	0.8139
2.2	31.2665	1144603	1.6281	0.7716	0.0026	29.9593	1171422	1.2501	0.8139
2.4	31.7396	1161925	1.6154	0.7593	0.0031	<u>29.2244</u>	1165640	1.2496	0.8137
2.6	32.2610	1181010	1.6022	0.7491	0.0036	30.9593	1172249	1.2489	0.8132
2.8	32.6101	1193790	1.5934	0.7413	0.0041	30.9593	1174901	1.2485	0.8130
3.0	32.9059	1204621	1.5853	0.7339	0.0046	30.2244	1168803	1.2490	0.8095

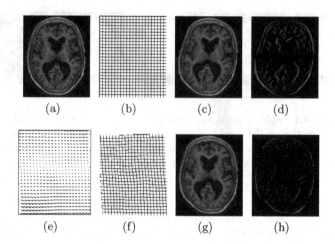

Fig. 6. From left to right: ground truth (a), initial registration grid (b), deformed version of the image (c), initial error image (d), deformation field (e), deformed registration grid (f), registered version with 18 landmark points (g), final error image (h)

Fig. 7. From left to right, qualitative results on a photographic image: input image (a), registered image using 31 landmark points (b), target image (c)

TPS approximation (execution times are approximately 14.8 seconds versus 37.2 seconds). Notwithstanding for both methods is required the solution of linear systems, in the case of TPS, the system to solve is as larger as the number of control points. The computational burden of our technique is much smaller, since simple (and parallelizable) systems of just six equations need to be solved. The results have then to be combined with simple distance measures and weighted sums. As regards the tuning of the smoothing parameter s, experiments shown that the optimal value generally lies in a range between 1.4 and 2, and a few one-dimensional search attempts (3-4 trials on average) using bisection strategies such as golden ratio, are enough to find the right solution, keeping the method convenient. In addition, similar problems exist in the TPS approach where the regularization parameter λ should be determined.

Comparing the size of data structures for the whole spatial transformation, it can be seen that our approach is linear in the number of triangles (which are at most $2M - 2 - b$, see sec. 3), and as a consequence, of control points. Storing space for affine transformation parameters (six for each triangle) is in the order of $12M$, where M is the number of control points. Moreover, $2M$ values, i.e. one for each triangle, for the membership degrees of each point are needed. However, once every single pixel has been transformed, its membership degree can be dropped, so the total data structure is $14M$ large. TPS approximation has a little more compact structure, because it needs just to maintain the $2(M + 3)$ x and y surface coefficients (M for the non-linear part and 3 for the linear one in each dimension). However, the storing complexity is $O(M)$ in both cases, i.e. linear in the number of control points used, and thus equivalent.

5   Conclusions and Future Work

A novel method aimed to free form deformation and registration has been presented. This technique computes the whole global transformation by composing several local transformation. Such composition is kept continuous and smooth by means of applying weighting functions to each pixel, depending on its position. Such weighting term is obtained from fuzzy membership of each pixel to each region in the image. Fuzzy C-means clustering algorithm is used for this purpose. However, since just the concepts of centroids and fuzzy membership degree are used, no clustering operation needs to be performed actually. The performance of the proposed method was evaluated with several tests using both objective and subjective measures, and the results were compared to free form deformation technique based on TPS surface approximation. From this study, it resulted that the presented method provides better results. In addition, it is substantially faster due to its straightforward computation requiring no optimization.

Future work will be oriented towards the use of the same technique for registering 3-D medical volume datasets using parallelization of computations and an automatic feature detection. The feature information are intended to be chosen by means of contour curvature evaluation and similarity considerations on the inner structures. Subsequently, the control points-based approach will be left towards a fully automatic pixel-based elastic registration framework.

References

1. Bookstein, F.L.: Principal warps: thin-plate splines and the decomposition of deformations. IEEE Transactions on Pattern Analysis and Machine Intelligence 11(6), 567–585 (1989)
2. Arad, N., Dyn, N., Reisfeld, D., Yeshurun, Y.: Image warping by radial basis functions: Application to facial expressions. Computer Vision, Graphics, and Image Processing. Graphical Models and Image Processing 56(2), 161–172 (1994)
3. Rohr, K., Stiehl, H.S., Sprengel, R., Buzug, T.M., Weese, J., Kuhn, M.H.: Landmark-based elastic registration using approximating thin-plate splines. IEEE Transactions on Medical Imaging 20(6), 526–534 (2001)

4. Bartoli, A., Perriollat, M., Chambon, S.: Generalized thin-plate spline warps. IEEE International Conference on Computer Vision and Pattern Recognition, cvpr (2007)
5. Johnson, H.J., Christensen, G.E.: Consistent landmark and intensity-based image registration. IEEE Transactions on Medical Imaging 21, 450–461 (2002)
6. Bezdek, J.C.: Pattern Recognition with Fuzzy Objective Function Algorithms (Advanced Applications in Pattern Recognition). Springer, Heidelberg (1981)
7. Delaunay, B.N.: Sur la sphère vide. Bulletin of Academy of Sciences of the USSR (6), 793–800 (1934)
8. Ardizzone, E., Gallea, R., Gambino, O., Pirrone, R.: Fuzzy c-means inspired free form deformation technique for registration. In: WILF, International Workshop on Fuzzy Logic and Applications (2009)
9. Cocosco, C.A., Kollokian, V., Kwan, R.K.S., Pike, G.B., Evans, A.C.: Brainweb: Online interface to a 3d mri simulated brain database. NeuroImage 5, 425 (1997)
10. Kwan, R.K.S., Evans, A.C., Pike, G.B.: Mri simulation-based evaluation of image-processing and classification methods. IEEE Transactions on Medical Imaging 18(11), 1085–1097 (1999)
11. Kwan, R.K.-S., Evans, A.C., Pike, G.B.: An extensible mri simulator for post-processing evaluation. In: Höhne, K.H., Kikinis, R. (eds.) VBC 1996. LNCS, vol. 1131, pp. 135–140. Springer, Heidelberg (1996)
12. Collins, D.L., Zijdenbos, A.P., Kollokian, V., Sled, J.G., Kabani, N.J., Holmes, C.J., Evans, A.C.: Design and construction of a realistic digital brain phantom. IEEE Trans. Med. Imaging 17(3), 463–468 (1998)
13. Wang, Z., Bovik, A.C., Sheikh, H.R., Simoncelli, E.P.: Image quality assessment: From error visibility to structural similarity. IEEE Transactions on Image Processing 13, 600–612 (2004)

Many-to-Many Matching under the l_1 Norm

M. Fatih Demirci and Yusuf Osmanlıoğlu

TOBB University of Economics and Technology,
Computer Engineering Department,
Sogutozu Cad. No:43 , 06560 Ankara, Turkey
{mfdemirci,yosmanlioglu}@etu.edu.tr

Abstract. The problem of object recognition can be formulated as matching feature sets of different objects. Segmentation errors and scale difference result in many-to-many matching of feature sets, rather than one-to-one. This paper extends a previous algorithm on many-to-many graph matching. The proposed work represents graphs, which correspond to objects, isometrically in the geometric space under the l_1 norm. Empirical evaluation of the algorithm on a set of recognition trails, including a comparison with the previous approach, demonstrates the efficacy of the overall framework.

Keywords: graph embedding, Earth Mover's Distance, graph matching, object recognition.

1   Introduction

Object matching is one of the core problems in computer vision. Given two objects, the objective of this problem is to establish a correspondence between their features. This objective consists of two steps: extracting features from objects and matching these features. The overall matching process results in a similarity (or, dissimilarity) value, which can be used for classifying an unknown object (query) as an instance of a particular class from a database. In a simple experimental setup, this can be achieved by a linear search, i.e., computing the similarity between the query and each database object and locating the database object with the highest similarity score.

Due to their representational power, graphs have been widely used in several domains such as pattern recognition, computational and molecular biology, linguistics , computer networks, and physics. A graph $G = (V, E)$ is composed of a finite set of vertices (V) and set of connections (edges) (E) between the vertices. Two vertices u and $v \in V$ are adjacent if there exists an edge $e = (u, v) \in E$. In computer vision and pattern recognition, graphs have been used to represent complex structures such as 3D objects, medical images, and fingerprints. In these structures, vertices correspond to regions or features of the object and edges show the relationships between the vertices. When graphs are used to represent the objects, object matching problem is reformulated as that of graph matching.

P. Foggia, C. Sansone, and M. Vento (Eds.): ICIAP 2009, LNCS 5716, pp. 787–796, 2009.

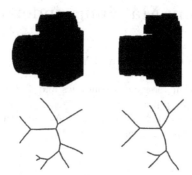

Fig. 1. The need for many-to-many matching. Although the silhouettes of two camera objects are similar, no one-to-one matching exists between their shock graphs.

The problem of finding the similarity between pairs of objects using their graph representations has been the focus of many researchers in the computer vision and pattern recognition communities for over twenty years. To obtain a good correspondence between two graphs, a lot of work focuses on the search for the best isomorphism between two graphs or subgraphs (e.g., [18,12,11]). Given two graphs $G_1 = (V_1, E_1)$ and $G_2 = (V_2, E_2)$, the isomorphism of G_1 and G_2 is defined as a bijection between the vertex sets of G_1 and G_2, $f : V(G_1) \rightarrow V(G_2)$ such that any two vertices u and $v \in G$ are adjacent if and only if $f(u)$ and $f(v)$ are adjacent in G_2.

While it is still an open question whether the detection of graph isomorphism can be done in polynomial time, the subgraph isomorphism problem is known to be NP-complete [7]. Some researches, such as [10], achieve polynomial time algorithms on the problem of graph isomorphism detection by imposing certain restrictions on graphs. Despite the fact that (sub)graph isomorphism detection algorithms have been successfully applied to various problems in computer vision, due to noise, segmentation and articulation errors, and scale differences no significant isomorphism may exist between graphs of similar objects. The limitations of the exact graph matching is depicted in Figure 1, where the silhouettes of two shapes and their undirected shock graphs [15] are shown at the top and bottom rows, respectively. Although the camera silhouettes are similar, no graph or subgraph isomorphism exist between their graphs. As a result of segmentation errors or scale differences, a feature of a shape may correspond to a group of features in the other. Thus, to encode such feature correspondences in the matching, the graph matching problem is expressed rather as that of inexact (or, error tolerant, error correcting) graph matching. The proposed work is focused on the inexact graph matching, whose goal is to find many-to-many vertex correspondences of two graphs. Heuristic based graph traversing [17], graph editing [5,16], and linear programming [3] are only some examples of inexact graph matching algorithms.

Given two graphs, establishing their many-to-many correspondences cannot be done in linear or polynomial time without imposing a restriction on the graph. In the worst case, a collection of vertices, which are not connected to each other, may match to a collection of vertices of the other graph. A number of all possible subgraphs of a graph is defined by a Bell number [4]. The objective of this paper is to find a pair of subgraphs, one from each input graph and compute the correspondences between their vertices. Each vertex correspondence contributes to the similarity between the input graphs. The similarity values also show the structural relations between the vertices.

In previous work [6], we presented an inexact graph matching that established many-to-many correspondences between vertex sets of two graphs. By transforming graphs into alternative domains, our framework showed that the many-to-many graph matching can be approximately solved in polynomial time. More specifically, the framework represented vertices as $d-$dimensional points by embedding graphs into geometric space. This embedding ensures that the shortest path distances between the vertices reflect the Euclidean distance between their corresponding points. Using graph embedding techniques, many-to-many graph matching was reformulated as many-to-many point matching. The approach then computed the correspondences between the points using the Earth Mover's Distance (EMD) [14] algorithm. Although the approach provides good retrieval and matching results, it suffers from a major drawback. Namely, the graph embedding under the l_2 norm results in distortion, i.e., the distance between the vertices is not preserved by their corresponding points in the geometric space. In this paper, we overcome this problem through an isometric graph embedding technique. Drawing on an important theorem from the field of graph theory, the graph embedding under l_1 ensures that the distances in the input graphs (trees) are preserved exactly in the geometric space. Experimental evaluation of the proposed paper presents the effectiveness of the approach over the previous work.

The rest of the paper is organized as follows. After providing a brief overview of the previous many-to-many matching algorithm in Section 2, we describe the extension of this algorithm in Section 3. The experiments are presented in Section 4. Finally, we finish the paper with the conclusion in Section 5.

2   Overview of the Many-to-Many Matching Algorithm

The previous work on many-to-many matching is based on representing graphs in geometric spaces. This step is performed by graph embedding techniques. More specifically, the algorithm uses a graph embedding technique to represent each vertex as a point. Here, the objective is to ensure that the distance between any pair of vertices equals to that between their corresponding points. The most important advantage of the embedding used in the previous work comes from the fact that the graphs are embedded into the geometric space of predefined dimensionality.

The embedding approach mentioned above does not work for any type of graphs; it only works for trees. Thus, the many-to-many graph matching approach first represents the graphs as trees and embeds the resulting trees into the $d-$dimensional geometric space. This two-step transformation reduces the problem of many-to-many graph matching to that of many-to-many point matching,

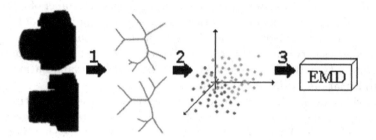

Fig. 2. Overview of the many-to-many matching algorithm. After representing silhouettes as shock graphs (transition 1), graphs are embedded into geometric spaces of the same dimensionality (transition 2). To compute the matching between the two distributions the Earth Mover's Distance (EMD) algorithm is used (transition 3).

for which the EMD algorithm is used. Note that computing the tree representation of a graph is beyond the scope of this paper. However, the reader is referred to the taxonomy problem [1] in the literature.

The EMD is based on a well-known *transportation problem* [2] and computes the dissimilarity between two distributions. Assume that each element in the first distribution indicates supplies and each element in the second distribution indicates demands at their positions. The EMD then computes the minimum amount of work required to transform one distribution into the other. Formally, let $P = \{(p_1, w_{p1}), \ldots, (p_n, w_{pn})\}$ be the first distribution of size n, $Q = \{(q_1, w_{q1}), \ldots, (q_m, w_{qm})\}$ be the second distribution of size m, where p_i (or q_i) is the position of the ith element and w_{pi} (or w_{qi}) is the weight, and let d_{ij} denote the the ground distance between points p_i and q_j. The objective of this problem is to find a flow matrix $F = [f_{ij}]$ with f_{ij} being the flow between p_i and q_j, which minimizes the overall cost:

$$EMD(P, Q) = \sum_{i=1}^{n} \sum_{j=1}^{m} f_{ij} d_{ij}$$

such that $\sum_{i=1}^{n} f_{ij} \leq w_{pi}$, $\sum_{j=1}^{m} f_{ij} \leq w_{qj}$, $\sum_{i=1}^{n} \sum_{j=1}^{m} f_{ij} = \min(\sum_{i=1}^{n} w_{pi}, \sum_{j=1}^{m} w_{qj})$, and $f_{ij} \geq 0$.

The EMD is formulated as a linear programming problem and its solution provides the many-to-many point correspondences. Applying these correspondences back to the original graphs, many-to-many graph matching is obtained. It should be noted that the solution also presents the distance between the point sets. The distance is then used as a dissimilarity score between the original graphs. Thus, given a query and database, the database graph, which most resembles the query can be retrieved by computing the dissimilarity score between the query and each database graph. In the proposed work, the weights of the points are derived from the vertices. In shock graphs, the weight of a vertex represents the maximal bi-tangent circle centered at the vertex. This graph format is outlined in Section 4. The overview of the many-to-many matching algorithm is given in Figure 2.

3   Embedding Graphs into the l_1 Norm and Many-to-Many Point Matching

The matching algorithm outlined in the previous section suffers from a major drawback. Namely, after representing graphs as trees, embedding the resulting trees into the l_2 norm introduces distortion. As a result, the distance between vertex pairs is not equal to that between their corresponding points in the geometric space. The following theorem, which appeared in [9] specifies this distortion.

Theorem 1. *For a tree T with $l(T)$ leaves, there exists an embedding ϕ : $V(T) \rightarrow l_2^d$ with distortion:*

$$D(\phi) \leq O(l^{1/(d-1))}(min\{\log l(T), d\})^{1/2}) \tag{1}$$

where d is the dimension of the geometric space.

As stated in [6], the graph embedding approach introduces on average 17% of distortion in a 100 dimensional space. Consequently, the graphs are not represented exactly in the geometric space and the many-to-many matching between the points may result in wrong correspondences.

This paper overcomes this problem by embedding graphs into l_1. It is well known that any tree can be embedded isometrically in the l_1 norm [8]. Using this fact, we ensure that no distortion is introduced when moving from the graph domain to the geometric domain. In a $d-$dimensional geometric space, the distance, U_1, between two points $X = \{x_1, x_2, ..., x_d\}$ and $Y = \{y_1, y_2, ..., y_d\}$ can be computed under the l_1 norm as follows :

$$U_1 = \sum_{k=1}^{d} |x_k - y_k|. \tag{2}$$

For each vertex in the graph, the coordinate of its corresponding point in the geometric space is computed using the concept of caterpillar decomposition, which captures the topological structure of the graph. Caterpillar decomposition is the collection of the edge-disjoint (sub)root-leaf paths. This concept is described in a sample tree shown in Figure 3. The three paths between a and c, a and g, a and m are called level 1 paths and represent first three paths in caterpillar decomposition. If we remove these three level 1 paths from the tree, we are left with the 3 edge-disjoint paths. These are the paths between e and f, i and j, k and l, called level 2 paths, which represent the other three paths in caterpillar decomposition. If removing the level 2 paths had left additional connected components, the process would be repeated until all the edges in the tree had been removed. The union of the paths is called the caterpillar decomposition, denoted by $\mathfrak{P}$. The total number of paths in $\mathfrak{P}$ specifies the dimensionality of the geometric space into which the graph is embedded.

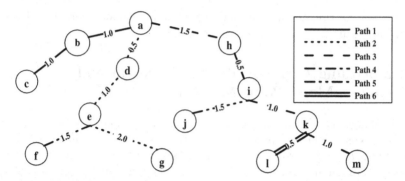

Fig. 3. Edge-disjoint paths extracted from caterpillar decomposition of a tree

To compute the coordinate of vertex v in the geometric space, we first find the unique path $P(v)$ between v and the root r. Assume that the first segment of $P(v)$ of weight l_1 follows some path $P^1 \in \mathfrak{P}$, the second segment of weight l_2 follows a path $P^2 \in \mathfrak{P}$, and the last segment of weight l_a follows a path $P^a \in \mathfrak{P}$. Let the sequences $\langle P^1, \ldots, P^a \rangle$ and $\langle l_1, \ldots, l_a \rangle$ be the decomposition sequence and the weight sequence of $P(v)$, respectively. Since each path in $\mathfrak{P}$ corresponds to a coordinate axis, the following process is used to find the coordinate of v. If the decomposition sequence of $P(v)$ consists of a path $P^i \in \mathfrak{P}$, its corresponding coordinate will have a value of l_i as defined in the weight sequence. Otherwise, the corresponding coordinate will have 0. It is easy to see that the embedding obtained through this procedure is isometric under the l_1 norm. To illustrate this procedure, we turn back to Figure 3 in which the tree is embedded into a 6-dimensional space. For example, to compute the coordinates of vertex f, observe that the path between a and f consists of one level 1 path (between a and e) of weight 1.5 and one level 2 path (between e and f) of weight 1.5. Since these paths correspond to the 2nd and 4th paths in caterpillar decomposition of the tree, only 2nd and 4th coordinate of the point representing f will be non-zero. Thus, the coordinates of vertex f in the geometric space are $(0, 1.5, 0, 1.5, 0, 0)$. Although caterpillar decomposition $\mathfrak{P}$ is not unique, the resulting embeddings are all isometric under l_1. However, to be consistent in our embedding procedure, the order in which the paths in caterpillar decomposition are selected is done by their weights.

It is important to note that embeddings produced by the above algorithm can be of different dimensions. Therefore, in order to match the two embeddings, we must first perform a registration step, whose objective is to project the two distributions into the same normed space. In general, this step can be done in two different ways. The first one is to project the distributions onto the first K right singular vectors of their covariance matrices. This technique is based on Principal Component Analysis and retains the maximum information about the original vectors among all projections onto subspaces of dimension K. Although this technique equalizes the dimensions of the two distributions while

Fig. 4. Sample silhouettes from the dataset

loosing minimal information, it still introduces distortion in the geometric space. Since our objective is to perform a distortion-free embedding, this method is not used in the proposed paper. Given two distributions of different dimensions, the second technique equalizes their dimensions simply by padding zeros to lower dimensional distribution. Despite the fact that this increases the complexity of the EMD algorithm, we use the second technique in the paper. As indicated in the following paragraph, a more efficient implementation of this technique is employed in our framework.

Having isometrically embedded the graphs into the same dimension, we can now proceed with finding the matching between the points. As mentioned before, this step is performed by the EMD algorithm. To generate the many-to-many matching efficiently under l_1, we use the EMD-L_1 approach presented in [13], which has a simplified structure and better time complexity than the original EMD formulation. In addition, the authors formally proved that the EMD-L_1 is equivalent to the original EMD with l_1 ground distance without approximation.

3.1   Complexity

Since the proposed algorithm consists of several components, we first state the complexity of each component. Computing the tree for a given graph takes $O(|V|^2)$(see [1] for details). Performing an isometric embedding of trees into the geometric space under l_1 can be done in linear time using depth first search. The EMD is formulated as a linear programming problem and can be solved using a network flow algorithm in $O(|V|^3)$. Finally, mapping the EMD solution back to the graph is $O(|V|)$. Thus, the overall complexity of the proposed approach is bounded by $O(|V|^3)$. Although the complexity of the previous work is not improved theoretically, the experiments presented in the next section demonstrate the effectiveness of the framework on a 2D recognition task.

4   Experiments

In this section, we perform the experimental evaluation of the proposed method and its comparison with the previous work [6]. In our dataset, there are 1620 silhouettes of 9 objects, with 180 views for each. Example silhouettes are shown in Figure 4. Each silhouette is represented by an undirected shock tree, whose nodes represent shocks [15] and whose edges connect adjacent shock points.

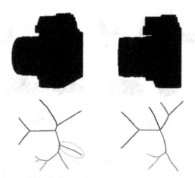

Fig. 5. The result of applying the proposed algorithm to the graphs in Figure 1. Many-to-many correspondences have been colored the same. The portion shown in an ellipse in the first graph represents unmatched vertices.

Each shock point p on the skeleton is associated with a 3-dimensional vector $v(p) = (x, y, r)$, where (x, y) are the Euclidean coordinates of the point and r is the radius of the maximal bi-tangent circle centered at the point. Each shock point becomes a node in the shock graph. Each pair of shock points is connected by an edge whose weight reflects the Euclidean distance between them. The graph is converted into a tree by computing its minimum spanning tree. Thus, tree nodes correspond to shock points, and tree edges connect nearby shock points. We choose the root of the tree to be the node that minimizes the sum of the tree-based shortest path distances to all other nodes.

As an illustration of our approach, we first use the example shown in Figure 1, where the need for many-to-many matching is observed. The result of applying our method to these graphs is given in Figure 5 in which many-to-many correspondences are colored the same. The portion shown in an ellipse in the first graph represents unmatched vertices.

To provide a more comprehensive evaluation of our framework, we conducted the following experiment. We first use each database graph as a query (with replacement) to the remaining database. Then, we compute the distance between each query and each of the remaining database graphs using our proposed algorithm. Ideally, given a query view of an object, the matching algorithm should return a neighboring view of the same object. We classify this as a correct pose estimation. According to the results, our framework and the previous work obtain 93.1% and 90.8% pose estimation rates, respectively. In a second experiment, we measure the object recognition rates for both algorithm. Namely, if the algorithm returns a database graph, which belongs to the same object as the query regardless of whether it is a neighboring view, we classify this as a correct object recognition. While our framework achieves 97.5%, the previous work results in 95.3% object recognition rates. The results clearly demonstrate the improved performance offered by the isometric embedding technique.

One important point to consider is that many of the objects are symmetric, and if a query neighbor has an identical view elsewhere on the object, that view might be chosen and scored as an error. Thus, the pose estimation rates, in these experiments, should be considered as worst-case. In addition, by improving the sampling resolutions of the viewing sphere, we expect that both pose estimation and object recognition rates increase.

5   Conclusions

Matching object features many-to-many is a critical process for object recognition and classification. One-to-one matching algorithms cannot handle segmentation/articulation errors or scale difference, which may exist between features of similar objects. This paper computes the dissimilarity between object pairs represented as graphs by computing the many-to-many matching between their vertices. The proposed framework embeds the input graphs isometrically into a geometric space under the l_1 norm. Unlike the previous algorithm, graph embedding used in the proposed method is distortion-free. After computing the EMD between the distributions, desired many-to-many matchings are obtained. Experimental evaluation of the framework represents more effective results over the previous work. Performing a more comprehensive experimental test using a larger dataset, studying different isometric embedding techniques under various norms, and employing other distribution-based matching algorithms in our framework are our future plans.

References

1. Agarwala, R., Bafna, V., Farach, M., Paterson, M., Thorup, M.: On the approximability of numerical taxonomy (fitting distances by tree metrics. SIAM Journal on Computing 28(2), 1073–1085 (1999)
2. Ahuja, R.K., Magnanti, T.L., Orlin, J.B.: Network Flows: Theory, Algorithms, and Applications, pp. 4–7. Prentice Hall, Englewood Cliffs (1993)
3. Almohamad, H.A., Duffuaa, S.O.: A linear programming approach for the weighted graph matching problem. IEEE Transactions on Pattern Analysis and Machine Intelligence 15(5), 522–525 (1993)
4. Bell, E.T.: Exponential numbers. American Mathematics Monthly 41, 411–419 (1934)
5. Bunke, H.: Error correcting graph matching: On the influence of the underlying cost function. IEEE Transactions on Pattern Analysis and Machine Intelligence 21(9), 917–922 (1999)
6. Demirci, F., Shokoufandeh, A., Keselman, Y., Bretzner, L., Dickinson, S.: Object recognition as many-to-many feature matching. International Journal of Computer Vision 69(2), 203–222 (2006)
7. Garey, M.R., Johnson, D.S.: Computers and Intractability: A Guide to the Theory of NP-Completeness. W. H. Freeman & Co, New York (1979)
8. Gupta, A.: Embedding tree metrics into low dimensional euclidean spaces. In: STOC 1999: Proceedings of the thirty-first annual ACM symposium on Theory of computing, pp. 694–700. ACM, New York (1999)
9. Gupta, A.: Embedding tree metrics into low-dimensional euclidean spaces. Discrete & Computational Geometry 24(1), 105–116 (2000)

10. Hoffmann, C.M.: Group-theoretic algorithms and graph isomorphism. Springer, Berlin (1982)
11. Horaud, R., Skordas, T.: Structural matching for stereo vision. In: Nineth International Conference on Pattern Recognition, Rome, Italy, pp. 439–445 (1988)
12. Lee, S.W., Kim, J.H.: Attributed stroke graph matching for seal imprint verification. Pattern Recognition Letters 9, 137–145 (1989)
13. Ling, H., Okada, K.: An efficient earth mover's distance algorithm for robust histogram comparison. IEEE Transactions on Pattern Analysis and Machine Intelligence 29(5), 840–853 (2007)
14. Rubner, Y., Tomasi, C., Guibas, L.J.: The earth mover's distance as a metric for image retrieval. International Journal of Computer Vision 40(2), 99–121 (2000)
15. Siddiqi, K., Shokoufandeh, A., Dickinson, S., Zucker, S.: Shock graphs and shape matching. International Journal of Computer Vision 35(1), 13–32 (1999)
16. Wang, Y.K., Fan, K.C., Horng, J.T.: Genetic-based search for error-correcting graph isomorphism. IEEETSMC: IEEE Transactions on Systems, Man, and Cybernetics 27 (1997)
17. Williams, M.L., Wilson, R.C., Hancock, E.R.: Deterministic search for relational graph matching. Pattern Recognition 32(7), 1255–1271 (1999)
18. Wong, E.K.: Model matching in robot vision by subgraph isomorphism. Pattern Recognition 25(3), 287–303 (1992)

Evaluation of a Foreground Segmentation Algorithm for 3D Camera Sensors

Luca Bianchi, Piercarlo Dondi, Riccardo Gatti, Luca Lombardi, and Paolo Lombardi

University of Pavia, Dept. of Computer Engineering and System Science,
Via Ferrata 1, 27100 Pavia Italy
{luca.bianchi,piercarlo.dondi,riccardo.gatti,
luca.lombardi}@unipv.it

Abstract. Our interest is focusing on the innovative time-of-flight (TOF) cameras. In this paper we present our approach to foreground segmentation, based on smart-seeded region growing. The seeding strategy makes use of the characteristic intensity signal provided by TOF cameras, and growing is proved by experimental measurements to produce a pixel-wise segmentation of 82%-92% quality. Compared to background subtraction, our approach uses more explicitly the unique capacity of TOF cameras to isolate foreground objects on the basis of their distance. Our work will find an application in gate monitoring and passage surveillance.

Keywords: region growing, tracking, gate monitoring, time-of-flight cameras.

1 Introduction

The development of time-of-flight (TOF) scanner-less cameras has started a set of new research in computer vision and imaging applications [1]. Realtime grid measurement of depth is now possible using a single compact sensor, whereas traditionally it has been achieved with multi-camera systems.

TOF cameras are active imaging sensors using laser light to measure distances from sensor to scene objects. They are based either on pulsed light or modulated light. In the first case, a coherent wavefront hits the target and high frequency photon gating measures the return time-of-flight. In the latter, the emitted light is modulated and time-of-flight is measured by phase delay detection.

TOF cameras evidently present some advantages. Opposite to laser scanners and active illumination stereo, TOF cameras acquire distance data without employing any moving mechanical part. They can reach video rate, are insensible to shadows, and can measure 3D distance in textured as well as untextured scenes. On the other hand, their measurement range is limited to a few meters and, until today, have a limited resolution. Also, they suffer from noise depending on the amount of incident active light and this causes problems for using multiple TOF cameras. Figure 1 shows the pictures of some TOF cameras currently on the market.

Detection and tracking of people is one application that can benefit from TOF cameras. The third dimension gives trackers more informative measurements and, in principle, this should increase their reliability and precision. Also, 3D sensing adds

P. Foggia, C. Sansone, and M. Vento (Eds.): ICIAP 2009, LNCS 5716, pp. 797–806, 2009.

Fig. 1. Different manufacturers provide sensors with diversified aspect ratios and resolutions, as well as sensors based on different physical principles: MESA Imaging SR4000 (top left), PMD[vision]® (top right), and Canesta (bottom left) are phase-based, whereas Zcam by 3DV Systems (bottom right) is based on photon gating

a feature (distance) to help characterizing individual targets and disambiguating between targets in case of mutual occlusions.

The application of TOF cameras to people tracking is limited by the maximum measurement range of these sensors. In contrast with laserscanners – that reach hundreds of meters, TOF cameras have nominal ranges of up to 10m. The practical range is even shorter, as noise caused by scattering, multi-paths and ambient light severely limits this range to a few meters (2-5m) [10].

We are investigating the potential application of TOF cameras to gate monitoring and passage surveillance. The typical setup would have the camera overlooking the entrance to a room or hall from the ceiling with an angle of 0°-45° from the vertical. Depending on the angle, a camera may capture just heads and shoulders of passers-by from above (0°) or also their facial features if they are facing the camera (>0°). For traditional color-based systems, vertically aligned cameras improve the tracking because people reduce to blobs moving parallel to a 2D plane and occlusions are basically eliminated. However, information on faces and on people's heights is lost unless multiple cameras are used. The vice versa is true if the angle between camera axis and the vertical grows.

The 3D information coming from TOF cameras can help conjugate reliable tracking with face/height detection from a single sensor. In gate monitoring the height of ceiling restricts the operating range within the maximum discussed above. For applications requiring face verification, the near future reserves TOF cameras integrating color and depth pixels (at least two manufacturers have announced or already commercialize such sensors). Instead for the setting with a 0° angle TOF cameras can determine the height of passers-by and hence distinguish adults from children. This characterization can be of use in some specific scenarios, like when counting resourceful customers that enter or exit a shopping center.

In this paper we present our work on foreground segmentation for TOF images. We propose an approach founded on seed-based region growing that fully exploits the depth keying capability of TOF sensors. Integration of the segmentation algorithm with a Kalman tracker is straightforward, as the tracker naturally provides a set of seeds for the next image. Our system features both components, i.e. region-based segmentation and Kalman filtering, but in this work we disable the tracking algorithm with the purpose of evaluating the precision and reliability of segmentation. We report the results obtained on video sequences acquired in a controlled environment and labeled manually by a human operator to define ground truth.

Section 2 presents some previous works related to people detection with TOF cameras. Section 3 describes our foreground segmentation. Section 4 illustrates the experimental results, and Section 5 concludes the paper.

2 Related Work

Most TOF-based systems for foreground segmentation up to date have focused on two techniques, namely distance thresholds and background subtraction. The first method sets a "cube of interest" by defining minimum and maximum distances for foreground [2]. All objects falling within the cube are labeled as foreground. If the minimum threshold is set to 0 (camera sensor), the second threshold can be dynamically set after the first object. For our scenario, this approach suffers from problems if the camera angle from the vertical is greater than $0°$, for instance $30°$. Only one person at a time would be segmented and so a second person partially occluded, would be labeled as background. Furthermore, additional processing is needed because selected pixels are to be clustered into objects.

The second method is inherited by motion detection techniques used in computer vision, notably in video surveillance applications. It consists in creating a model of the object-free scene by means of statistical analysis. The background model is most often pixel-based and only rarely region-based. Then, frame by frame, newly acquired images are compared to the model and pixels which differ significantly are marked as foreground. This technique provides aggregated foreground clusters of objects in motion and includes a noise rejection criterion implicitly in its statistical nature. To our knowledge, it is the most popular approach implemented to date for TOF cameras [4-7], sometimes using both depth and intensity values to build the model.

However, background subtraction suffers from known problems: i) ghosts appearing when background objects leave the scene, ii) absorption of still persons, iii) bootstrapping requiring a few frames, and so on. We propose an approach that more closely exploits the benefits of augmented 3D sensing and the intrinsic characteristics of the signal acquired by light-modulated TOF cameras.

3 Segmentation

We employ the SR3000 in our project, the model previous to the SR4000 shown in Figure 1 in the MESA Imaging line [3]. The SR3000 is a modulated-light camera that we use at 20MHz. Active sources emit in the near infrared (around 850nm) so that no emission is perceivable in the visible spectrum. The SR3000 delivers two maps per frame: the first contains distance information and the other measures the intensity of reflected light (hereafter indicated with D and I, respectively). Figure 2 shows a typical frame sequence taken by the SR3000 device. The images of the first line are the distance maps D, and the images of the second line are the intensity maps I, both at 16 bits. The intensity image depicts the intensity of light reflected by objects in the near

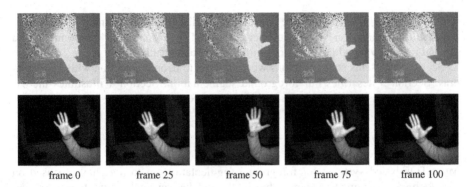

| frame 0 | frame 25 | frame 50 | frame 75 | frame 100 |

Fig. 2. Some frames of one of the sequences analyzed: distance images (top) and intensity images (bottom)

infrared. Almost all of this intensity derives from the internal light sources. Typically, objects near the sensor get more illuminated, while faraway objects receive less light. Hence, peaks in the intensity image tend to correspond to nearby objects. Because in our scenario targets are always closer than the background (the floor or objects shorter than people), we make use of the above observation on the intensity signal to our advantage.

Our approach to segmentation consists in growing regions of foreground objects on the distance map, starting from seeds planted on peaks of the intensity map. The advantages of region growing will be further discussed in Section 5, but briefly they can be summarized in good quality of boundaries (intrinsic noise rejection), independence of background models, and independence of shape models.

To start region growing, we apply a threshold on the intensity image to find some connected components, which then serve as seeds for the distance map D. In practical terms we use peaks of the intensity map I as seeds, under the assumption that the objects to track are the most reflective. In our experiments the threshold will be varied as a parameter to evaluate the performance and robustness of segmentation. We grow a region and then exclude the grown pixels from successive growths. We proceed this way for all seeds in order of descending intensity.

Growing on the distance map has proven experimentally to provide more precise results. Distance data on well illuminated objects (or persons) are homogeneous or smoothly changing (see Figure 2 left). Conversely, growing on the intensity map can be unreliable because its variations are sensible and uncorrelated to object boundaries. For example, folds of the sweater on the arm in Figure 2 (right) reflect light at very different shades.

After experimenting with centroid region growing [8], DBSCAN [9] and other approaches, we have obtained satisfying results with a customized similarity measure. A similarity S between a cluster pixel x and a neighboring pixel y is defined as:

$$S(x, y) = |\mu_x - D_y| \qquad (1)$$

In (1), D_y is the distance value of pixel y and μ_x is a local parameter related to the mean distance value around x, to be explained soon. The lower is S, the more similar the pixels. In our tests we use 4-connected neighborhoods of radius 1.

After defining with I_y the intensity value of pixel y, and given two constant thresholds θ and λ, a pixel x belonging to a cluster C absorbs a neighbor y according to the following predicate:

$$\{ x \in C, S(x, y) < \theta, I_y > \lambda \} \rightarrow \{ y \in C \} \tag{2}$$

When a seed is planted, μ_x in (1) is initialized to D_x. When a neighbor y of seed x is absorbed, we compute the average distance value μ_y in an incremental manner as follows:

$$\mu_y = (\mu_x \cdot \alpha + D_y) / (\alpha + 1) \tag{3}$$

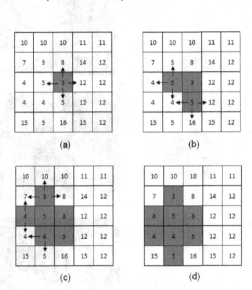

Fig. 3. Starting with a seed in a pixel map (a), the algorithm checks new pixels as shown by the arrows. The example refers to a threshold $\theta = 3$ and $\alpha = 1$. As pixels are absorbed (b), (c), note that the algorithm never tests twice the same pixel from a given direction. (d) is the final segmentation.

Parameter α is a *learning factor* of the local mean of D. If pixel y had exactly α neighbors in the cluster, and if the mean of D in these neighbors were exactly μ_x, then μ_y becomes the mean of D when y is added to the cluster.

When compared to methods that use global region statistics, like e.g. in centroid region growing, our approach is faster: μ_y depends only on the history of pixel absorptions until y is first reached by a growing front, and not from later steps. Thus, as soon as a pixel y is reached by the cluster boundary, it can be tested for absorption. Conversely, in centroid region growing, the addition of a pixel alters the global cluster mean and so the order in which boundary pixels are tested is significant.

Besides, the locality of our approach tolerates greater variations of map values inside a cluster because it produces transitive closures of the similarity S. Both head and shoulders of the same person, lying at slightly different distance from the camera, are more likely to be segmented as the same cluster, rather than two different clusters.

4 Experimental Evaluation

We used a SR3000 TOF camera to test our algorithms. Images are 176x144 pixels and the aperture is 47.5x39.6 degrees. We have observed an acquisition rate of 20 fps when the camera is in pure acquisition mode, without any further elaboration. When our algorithms are run on a 2.0 GHz Intel Xeon PC, the rate is still high, at 18 fps.

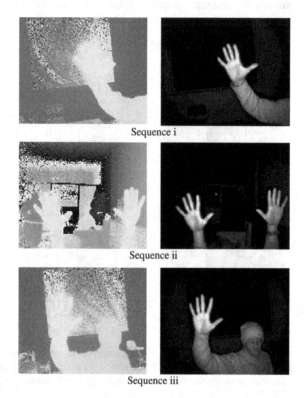

Sequence i

Sequence ii

Sequence iii

Fig. 4. Distance (left) and intensity (right) of one frame for each of the three sequences used

To assess the performance of our region growing approach, we have manually labeled a set of videos featuring very different conditions: i) a waving hand, ii) two well-separated waving hands, iii) a body and a hand that moves to side (figure 4). The videos have been acquired in different lighting conditions in order to better estimate algorithm performances. Each video consists of 150 frames. The tests have shown that our segmentation algorithm has good performance both with static and moving objects.

As our approach depends upon two parameters, i.e. the similarity threshold θ and the intensity threshold λ, we compute the performance for various values of $\{\theta, \lambda\}$. We vary θ in $[0.5, 2]*2^{10}$ with step $0.125*2^{10}$ and λ in $[0.5, 2]*10^3$ with step $0.1*10^3$. For each set of parameters, we run the segmentation algorithm on the full sequence and record its performance in terms of the number of pixels correctly labeled as foreground with respect to the ground truth drawn manually. In order to test the specific influence of each parameter independently, we run the segmentation algorithm with varying θ and a fixed λ, and then with varying λ and a fixed θ.

Specifically, using three pixel-wise indices, true positive (TP), false negative (FN) and false positive (FP) – each referred to the number of pixels detected with respect to a manual segmentation taken as ground truth – , we compute the following measures:

- *completeness* = TP / (TP + FN). Completeness is the percentage of the reference data that is explained by the extracted data. The optimal value is 1.
- *correctness* = TP / (TP + FP). Correctness represents the percentage of correctly extracted foreground data. The optimal value is 1.
- *quality* = TP / (TP + FP + FN). Quality is a more general measure combining completeness and correctness into a single measure. The optimal value is 1.

We compute these values on individual frames, and we take the average on the entire test sequence.

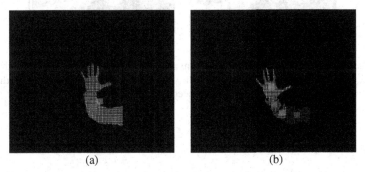

(a)   (b)

Fig. 5. An example of segmentation with θ over (a) and under threshold (b). In the second case the algorithm find four clusters instead of one. The red quads are the centroid of the clusters.

We have observed that generally for a given video there is a threshold over which a further increase in 0 has a negligible contribution, and under which the segmentation failed and the algorithm finds more clusters than those which are really (Figure 6).

On the contrary, a variation of λ has always a big impact on the results. Figure 6 shows a clear example of this effect. Observe that for low values of λ (Figures 6a, 6b) the cluster is more complete but less precise, whereas for high values of λ (Figures 6c, 6d) there is an increase in precision (i.e. better correctness) at the expense of loss of pixels (i.e. worse completeness). In this case the best value of λ for a good segmentation is near λ=1000 (b).

The completeness/correctness plot in Figure 7 highlights the impact of λ. Each dot represents a run with a given value of λ. All dots referring to the same sequence share the same threshold θ. In fact, given the premises above, for each sequence we have selected a θ far enough from the threshold that guaranteed target's compactness.

The plot shows that, in optimal conditions (broken and continuous lines), for the larger part tests have scored between 94% and 97% in correctness and between 92% and 96% in completeness. Those two videos were recorded in a room without sunlight

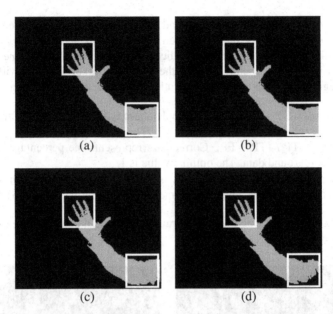

(a)   (b)

(c)   (d)

Fig. 6. The result of our segmentation algorithm applied to one frame of the seq. i with different value of λ: (a) is the result with λ=500, (b) with λ =1000, (c) with λ=1500 and (d) with λ=2000. Notice that, with growing of λ, the fingers become more precise and the shoulder gradually disappears.

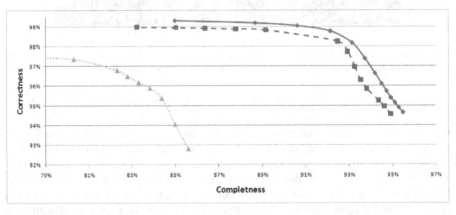

Fig. 7. Correctness/completeness at varying λ with a θ fixed, plot for the three video sequences: red broken line = seq. i; green dotted line = seq. ii; blue continuous line = seq. iii. Every point represents a run of the algorithm throughout the entire sequence with a different parameter set.

to reduce illumination interference. In the worst conditions (dotted line), with much noise generated by sunlight, in spite of a predictable reduction of completeness (82%-85%), tests have scored high values of correctness between 93% and 97%, like in the better case. This means that, also in bad condition, the program is able to minimize the number of false positive pixels outside the shape of segmented objects.

A quantitative measure of goodness for this algorithm is provided by quality. The average quality factor varies between 82% and 92%.

Although a specific sensitivity study has not yet been done, the graph of Figure 7 suggests that the algorithm is robust enough to parameter changes.

5 Discussion and Conclusion

We have presented an approach to foreground segmentation and tracking of objects in video sequences acquired by TOF cameras, envisioning a future application to gate monitoring and passage surveillance. Our approach exploits the intrinsic characteristic of the intensity and distance signals generated by modulated-light TOF to seed a region growing algorithm.

Region growing carries some advantages with respect to other approaches. Our tests on thresholding and histogram-based tracking have confirmed the low noise-resilience inherent to these methods, above all near boundaries because the spatial connection of pixels is neglected. Compared to edge detection (e.g. Canny) region growing guarantees closed regions. As for background subtraction, we use the natural depth-keying feature provided by TOF cameras to eliminate the computational burden of maintaining a background model.

We use a region growing based on cumulative differences rather than on global statistics. Cumulative differences are smoothed by a parameter called neighborhood size, which, for high values, makes the approach similar to a global-statistics approach. The proposed region growing method aggregates regions of smoothly changing distance values, as in the case of head and shoulders or arms and shoulders of the same person. By smart planting of seeds we manage to segment foreground objects with very little processing. Each foreground pixel is visited only once and background pixels are never visited, save for pixels along borders of foreground clusters.

Through testing on sequences manually labeled for ground truth, we have found that the segmentation algorithm presents only a limited sensitivity to the similarity threshold parameter θ. However the intensity threshold parameter λ has been found to play a key role. Overall the quality of pixel-wise segmentation ranges from 82% to 92% in our tests.

Future work includes the mapping of the segmentation results onto color images coming from webcams, and further refinement of segmentation in the color space.

Acknowledgements

Financial support for this project was provided by PRIN 2006: "Ambient Intelligence: event analysis, sensor reconfiguration and multimodal interfaces".

References

1. Kolb, A., Barth, E., Koch, R.: ToF-Sensors: New Dimensions for Realism and Interactivity. In: CVPR 2008, Workshop On Time of Flight Camera based Computer Vision, TOF-CV (2008),
http://www-video.eecs.berkeley.edu/Proceedings/CVPR_WS2008/data/workshops16.htm

2. Gvili, R., Kaplan, A., Ofek, E., Yahav, G.: Depth Key. In: SPIE Electronic Imaging 2003 Conference, Santa Clara, CA (2003)
3. Oggier, T., Lehmann, M., Kaufmann, R., Schweizer, M., Richter, M., Metzler, P., Lang, G., Lustenberger, F., Blanc, N.: An all-solid-state optical range camera for 3D real-time imaging with sub-centimeter depth resolution (SwissRanger). In: Mazuray, L., Rogers, P.J., Wartmann, R. (eds.) Optical Design and Engineering, Proceedings of the SPIE, vol. 5249, pp. 534–545 (2004)
4. Felder, J., Weiss, S.: Time-of-Flight Imaging for Industrial Applications, Master Thesis, ETH Swiss Federal Institute of Technology Zurich (2007)
5. Witzner, D., Mads, H., Hansen, S., Kirschmeyer, M., Larsen, R., Silvestre, D.: Cluster Tracking with Time-of-Flight Cameras, CVPR 2008, Workshop On Time of Flight Camera based Computer Vision, TOF-CV (2008),
   http://www-video.eecs.berkeley.edu/Proceedings/CVPR_WS2008/data/workshops16.htm
6. Guðmundsson, S.A., Larsen, R., Aanæs, H., Pardàs, M., Casas, J.R.: TOF Imaging in Smart Room Environments towards Improved People Tracking. In: CVPR 2008 Workshop On Time of Flight Camera based Computer Vision, TOF-CV (2008),
   http://www-video.eecs.berkeley.edu/Proceedings/CVPR_WS2008/data/workshops16.htm
7. Bevilacqua, A., Di Stefano, L., Azzari, P.: People tracking using a time-of-flight depth sensor. In: IEEE International Conference on Video and Signal Based Surveillance, pp. 89–94 (2006)
8. Adams, R., Bischof, L.: Seeded Region Growing. IEEE Transactions on Pattern Analysis and Machine Intelligence 16(6), 641–647 (1994)
9. Ester, M., Kriegel, H.P., Sander, J.: A density-based algorithm for discovering clusters in large spatial databases with noise, pp. 226–231. AAAI Press, Menlo Park (1996)
10. Oprisescu, S., Falie, D., Ciuc, M., Buzuloiu, V.: Measurements with ToF Cameras and Their Necessary Corrections. In: Proc. of ISSCS 2007 (2007)

Image Quality Assessment Based on Multi-scale Geometric Analysis

Mingna Liu[1], Xin Yang[1], and Yanfeng Shang[2]

[1] Institute of Image Processing and Pattern Recognition,
Shanghai Jiaotong University, P.R. China
[2] Department of Electronics and Informatics, Vrije Universiteit Brussel,
IBBT, 1050 Brussel, Belgium
{mingnal,yangxin}@sjtu.edu.cn, yshang@etro.vub.ac.be

Abstract. A novel objective full-reference image quality assessment metric based on Multi-scale Geometric Analysis (MGA) of contourlet transform is proposed. Contourlet transform has excellent properties for image representation, such as multiresolution, localization and directionality, which are the key characteristics of human vision system. Utilizing multiresolution and directionality of MGA, we extract the distortion of structural information from different vision scale and edge direction. The degradation of image quality is evaluated based on the defined energy of structural distortion. Performance experiments are made on professional image quality database with five different distortion types. Compared with some state-of-the-art measures, the results demonstrate that the proposed method improves accuracy and robustness of image quality prediction.

Keywords: Image quality assessment, contourlet transform, image structure.

1 Introduction

Image Quality Assessment (QA) is of fundamental importance in image processing systems, such as image acquisition, compression, enhancement, de-noising, reproduction, and etc.. Generally the approaches for image QA can be categorized into two main classes: subjective and objective ways. The former surveys the opinion of human observers through subjective tests, where a group of persons evaluate several corrupted images, with appropriate criteria, methodologies and hardware. However, it is difficult to implement the time-consuming subjective evaluation in many cases, for example in real-time system. Thus, in this paper, we are focusing on the objective image QA which intends to automatically quantify image degradation in a perceptual manner.

Current approaches to quantifying the visual fidelity of a distorted image can roughly be divided into the following paradigms: 1) metrics based on the statistics of pixels: they assess pixel-based brightness difference between distorted and reference images, such as Mean-Squared Error (MSE), Peak Signal-to-Noise Ratio (PSNR). They are attractive image QA measures due to the simplicity and

P. Foggia, C. Sansone, and M. Vento (Eds.): ICIAP 2009, LNCS 5716, pp. 807–815, 2009.
© Springer-Verlag Berlin Heidelberg 2009

mathematical convenience. However, they present poor correlation with subjective ratings for ignoring the inter-dependence among pixels[6]. 2) metrics based on Human Vision System (HVS): these approaches are constructed on the mathematical models of HVS[1]. However, although they are mostly accepted, the limited understanding of HVS and the complexity of simulation models keep them from going much further. 3) metrics based on overarching principles: this kind of metrics capture structural feature or information loss from distorted images, which are believed to be the HVS preferred top-down characteristics[2,3,4,5]. Among them, the Structural SIMilarity (SSIM) index attracts a lot of attention for its first puts forward the assumption that *human visual perception is highly adaptive for extracting structural features from natural scene*[2]. Furthermore, Considering the dependence of image quality on viewing conditions (such as viewing distance and display resolution), in [7] the single-scale SSIM index is developed into a multi-scale method. In light of this, we intend to implement a multi-scale image quality measure to deal with structural information change and provide a better approximation to perceived image distortion.

Recently, a theory for high dimensional signals called Multi-scale Geometric Analysis (MGA) has been developed. Several MGA tools were proposed, such as ridgelet[8], curvelet[10], and contourlet[9,11]. Those methods present better directional sensitivity than wavelet transform, i.e. they possess *anisotropy*, so that they could describe the edge feature better, then adaptive to HVS. So in our scheme for structural information extraction, except multiresolution, the direction information is another consideration.

In this paper, we propose a Multi-Scale Directional Difference (MSDD) metric utilizing contourlet transform, capturing the directional structure features in different scales. Firstly the reference and distorted images are decomposed into three level and up to twenty subbands. Every subband represents the image structure of different scale and direction. We evaluate the image perception information loss by calculating the difference between every corresponding subbands of distorted and reference images. The sum up of all these difference are defined as the Energy of Structural Distortion(ESD). Finally, the image quality score is obtained by applying Weber-Fechner law to ESD. Compared with other image QA metric, the validation experiment displays that the proposed metric is a novel and successful scheme for objective image quality predicting.

The organization of this paper is given as follow. The contourlet transform is introduced in section 2. The definition and characteristics of MSDD metric for image QA is presented in section 3. In section 4, the performance of the proposed image quality metric is validated through subjective evaluation experiment with five distortion types. Section 5 concludes the study.

2   Contourlet Transform

In 2001, contourlet was pioneered by Do and Vetterli as the latest MGA tool[11]. Contourlet is a true 2-D sparse representation for 2-D signals like images. The overall result of contourlet transform is a sparse image expansion expressed by

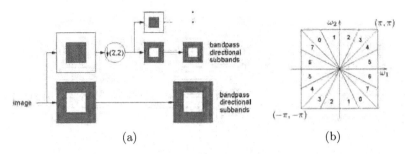

Fig. 1. The scheme of contourlet transform. (a) The block diagram; (b) The frequency partition.

contour segments, so it can capture 2-D geometrical structures in visual information much more effectively than traditional multiresolution analysis methods.

Contourlet can be described as Pyramidal Directional Filter Bank (PDFB), which include the Laplacian Pyramid (LP) and the Directional Filter Bank (DFB). In each scale decomposition, the Laplacian pyramid is used to capture the point discontinuities, and then followed by the DFB to link point discontinuities into linear structures, so that directional information can be captured with a rich set of basis oriented at various directions and scales. This allows contourlets to efficiently approximate a smooth contour at multipleresolutions and multidirections. Contourlet can effectively capture the intrinsic contours and edges in natural images whose traditional multiresolution analysis methods are difficult to handle. Fig. 1 depicts the block diagram of contourlet decomposition and frequency partition of contourlet transform. Here 8-direction directional decomposition is applied in the finest scale, subbands 0-3 correspond to the mostly horizontal directions, while subbands 4-7 correspond to the mostly vertical directions. Contourlet offers a much richer subband set of different directions and shapes, which helps to capture geometric structures in images much more efficiently. In the frequency domain, the contourlet transform provides a multiscale and directional decomposition.

Specifically, let $a_0[\mathbf{n}]$ be the input image. The output after the LP stage is J bandpass images $b_j[\mathbf{n}]$, $j = 1, 2, \ldots, J$ (in the fine-to-coarse order) and a lowpass image $a_J[\mathbf{n}]$. That means, the j-th level of the LP decomposes the image $a_{j-1}[\mathbf{n}]$ into a coarser image $a_j[\mathbf{n}]$ and a detail image $b_j[\mathbf{n}]$. Each bandpass image is further decomposed by an l_j-level DFB into 2^{l_j} bandpass directional images $c_{j,k}^{l_j}[\mathbf{n}]$, $k = 0, 1, \ldots, 2^{l_j} - 1$. Thus the whole decomposition can be represented as

$$a_0[\mathbf{n}] \rightarrow \{a_J[\mathbf{n}], b_1[\mathbf{n}], b_2[\mathbf{n}], \ldots, b_J[\mathbf{n}]\}$$
$$b_j[\mathbf{n}] = \{c_{j,0}[\mathbf{n}], c_{j,1}[\mathbf{n}], \ldots, c_{j,2^{l_j}-1}[\mathbf{n}]\} \tag{1}$$

3   Multi-scale Directional Difference (MSDD) Metric

Natural image signals are highly structured. They contain intrinsic geometrical structures that are key features in visual information[11]. Thus, a good image QA

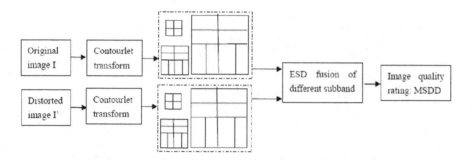

Fig. 2. The block diagram of MSDD

metric should capture the key structural features and present image fidelity ratings well coherent with subjective scores. Contourlet can offer better anisotropy, multiresolution, directionality and localization properties for 2-D signals than existing image representation methods, so better image QA performance can be expected. In this paper, considering the direction and texture information, we develop a new set of characteristics of the structural information by contourlet transform, extracting the directional structure feature in different scales, named Multi-Scale Directional Difference (MSDD) Metric. The block diagram is illustrated in Fig 2.

Firstly, taking the original and distorted images as the inputs, the system iteratively applies a LP decomposition on the images and generated lowpass images and bandpass images. The bandpass images are decomposed by DFB to achieve the multidirectionality. This step finish the extraction of multi-scale structural feature as well as direction and texture information. Secondly, the difference between the subbands for distorted and original images is calculated individually, quantifying the Energy of Structural Distortion (ESD) for the distorted image. Thirdly, the ESD of lowpass and bandpass images is fused weighted. Finally, employing the Weber-Fechner law[12], objective image quality score of our measure is obtained.

Suppose the original and distorted images are I and I', with size $P \times Q$. They are decomposed by contourlet transform and represented as:

$$
\begin{aligned}
I[\mathbf{n}] &\rightarrow \{a_J[\mathbf{n}], b_1[\mathbf{n}], b_2[\mathbf{n}], \dots, b_J[\mathbf{n}]\} \\
b_j[\mathbf{n}] &= \{c_{j,0}[\mathbf{n}], c_{j,1}[\mathbf{n}], \dots, c_{j,2^{l_j}-1}[\mathbf{n}]\}
\end{aligned}
\tag{2}
$$

$$
\begin{aligned}
I'[\mathbf{n}] &\rightarrow \{a'_J[\mathbf{n}], b'_1[\mathbf{n}], b'_2[\mathbf{n}], \dots, b'_J[\mathbf{n}]\} \\
b'_j[\mathbf{n}] &= \{c'_{j,0}[\mathbf{n}], c'_{j,1}[\mathbf{n}], \dots, c'_{j,2^{l_j}-1}[\mathbf{n}]\}
\end{aligned}
\tag{3}
$$

ESD of the lowpass and bandpass subbands for distorted image are:

$$
\mathrm{ESD}_J = \frac{1}{M \times N}\left(\sum_{m=1}^{M}\sum_{n=1}^{N}(a_J(m,n) - a'_J(m,n))^2\right)^{\frac{1}{2}}
\tag{4}
$$

$$\text{ESD}_{j,k} = \frac{1}{W_{j,k} \times H_{j,k}} \left(\sum_{w=1}^{W_{j,k}} \sum_{h=1}^{H_{j,k}} (c_{j,k}(w,h) - c'_{j,k}(w,h))^2 \right)^{\frac{1}{2}} \tag{5}$$

where $M \times N$ is the size of decomposed lowpass subband, $W_{j,k} \times H_{j,k}$ is the size of decomposed bandpass subband in j-th level and k-th direction ($j = 1, 2, \ldots, J$; $k = 0, 1, \ldots, 2^{l_j} - 1$).

In the ESD fusion step, the weights of lowpass and bandpass subbands for ESD fusion deserve some consideration. In our method, to balance the contribution of different frequency bands, we utilize the subband size to define the weights:

$$D = < \boldsymbol{w} \cdot \boldsymbol{ESD} >$$
$$= w_J * \text{ESD}_J + \sum_{j=1}^{J} \sum_{k=0}^{2^{l_j}-1} (w_{j,k} * \text{ESD}_{j,k}) \tag{6}$$

where w_J and $w_{j,k}$ are the weights for the distortion of lowpass and bandpass subbands in j-th level and k-th direction:

$$w_J = \frac{P \times Q}{M \times N}, w_{j,k} = \frac{P \times Q}{W_{j,k} \times H_{j,k}} \tag{7}$$

Based on the Weber-Fechner law [12], the relationship between the physical magnitude of stimuli and the perceived intensity of the stimuli is logarithm, the quality measurement is defined in terms of "visual decibels", coincident with the traditional error metrics[13]:

$$MSDD = log_{10}(1 + D), \quad D > 0 \tag{8}$$

where the constant 1 is included to avoid negative value of quality score.

MSDD models any distortion as the difference of ESD and measure the difference between the original and distorted images by the decomposing processing. Here the structural vector a_J and b_j are desired to describe the shape, edge, texture and others by themselves. The difference of structural information, which are gained by computing the ESD, are desired to represent the variation of the images' degradation along different scales and directions. Then we compare the difference of MSDD values to measure the distortion magnitude. The typical MSDD values range between 0 and 1.3. The actual value is meaningless, but the comparison between two values for different test images gives one measure of quality. The lower the predicted score of MSDD is, the better the image quality is. When $a_J = a'_J$ and $b_j = b'_j$, the distorted and the original images are identical, so MSDD = 0. The metric satisfies the following conditions:

1. symmetry: MSDD(x,y) = MSDD(y,x);
2. boundedness: MSDD(x,y) $\geq$ 0;
3. unique minimum: MSDD(x,y) = 0 if and only if x = y.

4 Experimental Results and Discussion

4.1 Performance in Predicting Visual Fidelity

In this section, the performance of the MSDD metric is analyzed in terms of its ability to predict image quality fidelity in a manner that agrees with subjective

Fig. 3. Some original images in LIVE database

ratings. Specifically, the professional LIVE image database is utilized[15]. The LIVE image database consists of 29 original 24-bits/pixel color images, and 779 distorted images. Five subdatabases with different types of distortions are tested: 1) JPEG2000 compression(JP2K), 2) JPEG compression(JPEG), 3) Gaussian white noise(WM), 4) Gaussian blurring(GBlur), and 5) Rayleigh-distributed bit-stream errors of a JPEG2000 compressed stream(FF). The distortion varies at a broad range of quality, from imperceptible levels to high levels of impairment. The subjective ratings are obtained from about 25000 individual human quality judgments. Fig 3 shows some original images in LIVE database.

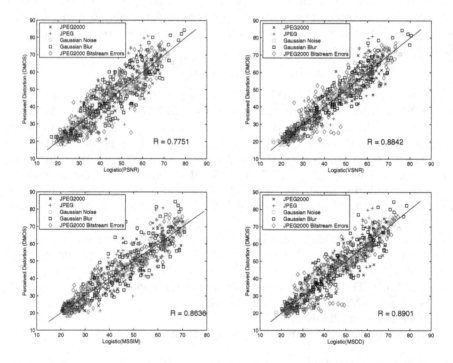

Fig. 4. Subjective ratings of perceived distortion for the 779 images of the LIVE database plotted against predicted values from each of the four metrics. In all graphs, the vertical axis denotes perceived distortion (Difference Mean Opinion Score) as reported by subjects[6]. The horizontal axes correspond to the normalized four metrics' outputs.

For comparison, these same sets of images from LIVE are analyzed by PSNR, Mean SSIM (MSSIM)[2] and Visual Signal-to-Noise Ratio (VSNR) metric[5]. In MSDD, considering the computation cost, we choose the decomposing scale $J = 3$, the decomposing direction $l_j = 3, for j = 1, 2$. MSSIM is computed on filtered and down sampled versions of the images which the downsampling factor is chosen based on the height of each image as described at [14]. VSNR are applied using their default implementations provide at [5]. After a logistic transformation for the outputs normalization[6], Some validation criteria exploited by Video Quality Experts Group (VQEG) for objective quality metric validation are utilized for our experiments[16], such as linear Correlation Coefficient, Root-Mean-Square-Error(RMSE) and Spearman Rank Order Correlation Coefficient (SROCC). And for LIVE database, the four metrics are applied to grayscale versions of the images which are obtained via a pixel-wise transformation of $I = 0.2989R + 0.5870G + 0.1140B$, where R, G and B denote the 8-bit grayscale, red, green and blue intensities, respectively.

The results are listed in Table 1 and Fig 4. For considering the combination of low-level visual property of perceived contrast and the mid-level visual property of global precedence, VSNR shows the best prediction performance on all subdatabases except FF. And MSDD is a strong competitor. It acquires close performance with VSNR across the five distortion types, even better in WN. MSSIM does much better on FF subdatabase than the other three metrics, while much worse in GBlur. PSNR acts well on WN distortion type when errors are statistically independent. While for the other four distortion types, it is not adaptable well. In the cross-distortion validation (all 779 distorted images taken as a whole, much more complicated than subdatabases), PSNR degrades worst for the loss of structural information consideration. MSSIM and VSNR performs better than PSNR while still worsen by a sizable margin. MSDD displays the

Table 1. Correlation Coefficient, RMSE and Rank-Order Correlation Coefficient between subjective ratings and normalized four metrics' outputs

Measure	Metric	JP2K	JPEG	WN	GBlur	FF	All
Correlation	PSNR	0.9338	0.8918	0.9578	0.8757	0.8598	0.7751
Coefficient	MSSIM	0.9367	0.9282	0.9747	0.8739	0.9448	0.8633
	VSNR	0.9517	0.9420	0.9741	0.9371	0.8947	0.8842
	MSDD	0.9369	0.9320	0.9832	0.9119	0.8852	0.8901
RMSE	PSNR	5.7976	7.2352	4.5900	7.5932	8.3995	10.1760
	MSSIM	5.6703	5.9482	3.5668	7.6445	5.3877	8.1264
	VSNR	4.9751	5.3654	3.6135	5.4867	7.3477	7.5230
	MSDD	5.6618	5.7957	2.9125	6.4534	7.6513	7.3397
Rank Order	PSNR	0.9282	0.8703	0.9562	0.8711	0.8661	0.7692
Correlation	MSSIM	0.9317	0.9025	0.9630	0.8943	0.9409	0.8510
Coefficient	VSNR	0.9447	0.9077	0.9745	0.9449	0.8994	0.8834
	MSDD	0.9324	0.8967	0.9813	0.9195	0.8852	0.8928

best capability dealing with the complicated situations. Finally, we can draw the conclusion that MSDD exhibits the better general performance than the other three state-of-the-art measures, showing the robustness and feasibility for image QA.

4.2 Discussion

In fact, for the appealing characteristics of contourlet transform, MSDD avoids the usual limitation of most the other image QA metrics. The decomposing coefficients have the corresponding locations as the spatial locations. So the MSDD can be expanded to be a distortion map to describe the spatially localized fidelity. A primary shortcoming about MSDD is that the metric is limited to grayscale images. An extension of the MSDD metric might include an additional stage which accounts for perceived distortion due to degradations in color. The MSDD metric has relatively high computational complexity. Using a MATLAB implementation, the metric requires for a 512×512 image approximately 1s on a 1.80-GHz Intel Pentium machine.

5   Conclusion

This paper presented a multi-scale directional structural difference metric for quantifying the visual fidelity of natural images. Via multiscale geometric analysis of contourlet transform, the proposed MSDD metric operates based on structure distortion in different scales and directions. Multiresolution, localization and multidirectionality are modeled as subband decomposition of contourlet transform. Finally MSDD is determined based on the weighted sum of the ESD. This metric is well adaptable for five typical distortion types, especially outstanding in cross-distortion validation. MSDD could be extended for colorful image quality evaluation. There should be a lot of work to investigate potential improvements in the future.

References

1. Watson, A.B.: DCT quantization matrices visually optimized for individual images. Human Vision, Visual Processing, and Digital Display IV (1993)
2. Wang, Z., Bovik, A.C., Sheikh, H.R., Simoncelli, E.P.: Image quality assessment: From error measurement to structural similarity. IEEE Trans. Image Process 13(4), 600–612 (2004)
3. Sheikh, H.R., Bovik, A.C., de Veciana, G.: An Information Fidelity Criterion for Image Quality Assessment Using Natural Scene Statistics. IEEE Trans. Image Process 14(12), 2117–2128 (2005)
4. Sheikh, H.R., Bovik, A.C.: Image information and visual quality. IEEE Trans. Image Process 15(2), 430–444 (2006)
5. Chandler, D.M., Hemami, S.S.: VSNR: A Wavelet-Based Visual Signal-to-Noise Ratio for Natural Images. IEEE Trans. Image Process 16(9), 2284–2298 (2007)

6. Sheikh, H.R., Sabir, M.F., Bovik, A.C.: A Statistical Evaluation of Recent Full Reference Image Quality Assessment Algorithms. IEEE Trans. Image Process 15(11), 3440–3451 (2006)
7. Wang, Z., Simoncelli, E.P., Bovik, A.C.: Multi-scale structural similarity for image quality assessment. In: Proceedings of the 37th IEEE asilomar conference on signals, systems and computers, November 9-12 (2003)
8. Cands, E.J.: Ridgelets:Theory and Applications. Department of statistics, Stanford University, USA (1998)
9. Do, M.N.: Contourlets and Sparse Image Expasions. Proceedings of SPIE - The International Society for Optical Engineering 5207(2), 560–570 (2003)
10. Donoho, D.L., Duncan, M.R.: Digital curvelet transform: strategy, implementation and experiments. In: Proc. Aerosense 2000, Wavelet Applications VII, SPIE, vol.4056, pp. 12-29 (2000)
11. Do, M.N., Vetterli, M.: The Contourlet Transform: An Efficient Directional Multiresolution Image Representation. IEEE Trans. Image Process 14(12), 2091–2106 (2005)
12. Levine, M.W.: Fundamentals of sensation and perception, 3rd edn. Oxford University Press, New York (2000)
13. van den branden Lambrecht, C.J., Verscheure, O.: Perceptual quality measure suing a spatio-temporal model of the huamn visual system. In: Bhaskaran, V., Sijstermans, F., Panchanathan, S. (eds.) Digital Video Compression: Algorithms and Technologies, proc. SPIE, San Jose, CA, vol. 2668, pp. 450–461 (1996)
14. SSIM website, http://www.ece.uwaterloo.ca/~z70wang/research/ssim/
15. Sheikh, H.R., Wang, Z., Cormack, L., Bovik, A.C.: Image and Video Quality Assessment Research at LIVE, http://live.ece.utexas.edu/research/quality
16. VQEG, Final Report From the Video Quality Experts Group on the Validation of Objective Models of Video Quality Assessment, Phase II (August 2003), http://www.vqeg.org/

Connected Component Labeling Techniques on Modern Architectures

Costantino Grana, Daniele Borghesani, and Rita Cucchiara

Dipartimento di Ingegneria dell'Informazione, Università degli Studi di Modena e Reggio Emilia, Via Vignolese 905/b, 41100 Modena, Italy
{costantino.grana,daniele.borghesani,rita.cucchiara}@unimore.it

Abstract. In this paper we present an overview of the historical evolution of connected component labeling algorithms, and in particular the ones applied on images stored in raster scan order. This brief survey aims at providing a comprehensive comparison of their performance on modern architectures, since the high availability of memory and the presence of caches make some solutions more suitable and fast. Moreover we propose a new strategy for label propagation based on a 2x2 blocks, which allows to improve the performance of many existing algorithms. The tests are conducted on high resolution images obtained from digitized historical manuscripts and a set of transformations is applied in order to show the algorithms behavior at different image resolutions and with a varying number of labels.

Keywords: connected component labeling, comparison, union-find.

1 Introduction

Connected component labeling is a fundamental task in several computer vision applications. It is used as a first step in the task chain in many problems, e.g for assigning labels to segmented visual objects, and for this reason a fast and efficient algorithm is undoubtedly very useful. A lot of techniques have been proposed in literature in the past; most of them referred to specific hardware architectures to take advantage of their characteristics, but nowadays, modern architectures do not suffer anymore of such limitations that constitute a design priority of some of these algorithms. In this paper, a brief survey of traditional and new labeling techniques is presented and a comparison of some labeling techniques is reported in order to find out the real performances of these proposals on modern computer architectures.

Moreover, Intel has released a precious set of libraries as an open source project named OpenCV. These libraries contain an implementation of all the main algorithms useful in computer vision applications and include two strategies for connected component analysis: a contour tracing (cvFindContours) followed by a contour filling (cvDrawContours), or a flood fill approach (cvFloodFill) which can be applied sequentially to all foreground pixels. We will also consider these two approaches in the comparison.

P. Foggia, C. Sansone, and M. Vento (Eds.): ICIAP 2009, LNCS 5716, pp. 816–824, 2009.

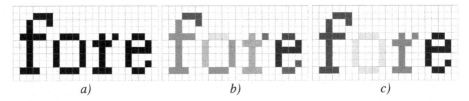

Fig. 1. Example of binary image depicting text (*a*), its labeling considering 4-connectivity (*b*), and 8-connectivity (*c*)

Beside an extensive review of labeling algorithms, the main contribution of this work is a new block based scanning strategy, which allows to substantially improve the performance of the most common class of algorithms, namely the raster scan one.

We will exclude two wide classes of algorithms from our analysis. The first one is the class of parallel algorithms which has been extensively studied up to the first half of the '90s. These algorithms were aimed to specific massively parallel architectures and do not readily apply to current common workstations, which provide more and more parallelism (instruction level, thread level and so on), but substantially different from the parallelism exploited in those algorithms. The second class is given by algorithms suitable for hierarchical image representations (for example quadtrees) initially studied for accessing large images stored in secondary memory. We excluded them because the vast majority of images is currently stored in sequential fashion, since they can often be fully loaded in main memory.

After formalizing the basic concepts needed, we review of some of the most used labeling algorithms, the newest ones and then we detail our proposal. The different algorithms performance are evaluated on a high resolution image dataset, composed of documental images with a large number of labels. Different modifications are performed to test these algorithms in several situations in order to show which is the most effective algorithm in different conditions.

2 Neighborhood and Connectivity

Two pixels are said to be 4-*neighbors* if only one of their image coordinates differs of at most one, that is if they share a side when viewed on a grid. They are said to be *8-neighbors* if one or both their image coordinates differ of at most one, that is if they share a side or a corner when viewed on a grid.

A subset of a digitized picture, whose pixels share a common property, is called *connected* if for any two points P and Q of the subset there exists a sequence of points $P = P_0, P_1, \ldots, P_{n-1}, P_n = Q$ of the subset such that P_i is a neighbor of $P_{i-1}, 1 \leq i \leq n$ [1].

The common choice in binary images, where the property of interest is to be part of the "foreground" with respect to the "background", is to choose 8-connectivity, that is connectivity with 8-neighbors, for the foreground regions, and 4-connectivity for background regions. This usually better matches our usual perception of distinct objects, as in Fig. 1.

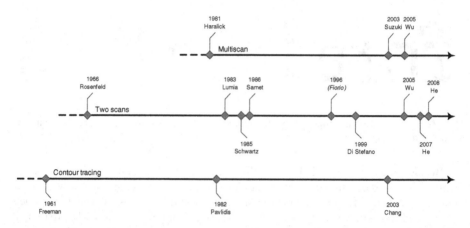

Fig. 2. Timeline showing the evolution of the labeling algorithms

In binary images, the "labeling" procedure is the process of adding a "label" (an integer number) to all foreground pixels, guaranteeing that two points have the same label if and only if they belong to the same connected component.

3   The Evolution of Labeling Algorithms

The problem of labeling has been deeply studied since the beginning of Computer Vision science. In the following we try to provide a historical view of the different approaches, discussing how they contributed to current approaches and if their purposes are still applicable to modern architectures.

The first work proposed for image labeling date back to Rosenfeld *et al.* in 1966 [1], and this can be considered the very classical approach to labeling. It is based on a raster scan of the image and, rather than generate an auxiliary picture, the "redundancies" of the labels are stored in an equivalences table with all the neighborhood references. The redundancies are solved processing the table by repeatedly using an unspecified sorting algorithm and removing redundant entries, consequently requiring an high amount of CPU power. Finally the resulting labels are updated in an output image with a single pass, exploiting the solved equivalences table.

A problem of the original algorithm is the use of a second image to store labels and of another structure to store equivalences. To tackle this problem an improvement has been proposed by Haralick *et al.* [2]. This algorithm does not use any equivalences table and no extra space, by iteratively performing forward and backward raster scan passes over the output image to solve the equivalences exploiting only local neighborhood information. This technique clearly turns out to be very expensive when the size of the binary image to analyze increases.

Lumia *et al.* [3] observe that both previous algorithms perform poorly on '83 virtual memory computers because of page faults, so they mix the two approaches trying to keep the equivalences table as small as possible, saving memory usage. In this algorithm a forward and a backward scan are sufficient to complete the labeling, but at the end of each row the collected equivalences are solved and another pass immediately updates that row labels. This suggests that four passes over the data are indeed used by this algorithm. The technique to solve label equivalences is left unspecified.

Schwartz et al.[4] further explored on this approach, in order to avoid the storage of the output image, which would have required too much memory. Thus they use a sort of run length based approach (without naming it so), which produces a compact representation of the label equivalences. In this way, after a forward and a backward scan, they can output an auxiliary structure which can be used to infer a pixel label.

Samet and Tamminen [5] are the first researchers who clearly named the equivalence resolution problem as the *disjoint-set union problem*. This is an important achievement, since a quasi linear solution for this problem is available: the so called *union-find* algorithm, from the name of the basic operations involved. The algorithm is executed in two passes. The first pass creates an intermediate file consisting of image elements and equivalence classes while the second pass processes this file in reverse order, and assigns final labels to each image element. Their proposal is definitely complex, since it also targets quad-tree based image representations and is aimed at not keeping the equivalences in memory. In particular in [6] a general definition of this algorithm for arbitrary image representations has been proposed.

The Union-Find algorithm is the basis of a more modern approach for label resolution. As a new pixel is computed, the equivalence label is resolved: while the previous approaches generally performed first a collection of labels and at the end the resolution and the Union of equivalence classes, this new approach guarantees that at each pixel the structure is up to date.

A relevant paper in this evolution is [7] where Di Stefano and Bulgarelli proposed an online label resolution algorithm with an array-based structure to store the label equivalences. The array-based data structure has the advantage to reduce the memory required and to speed up the retrieval of elements without the use of pointer dereferencing. They do not explicitly name their equivalences resolution algorithm as Union-Find, and their solution requires multiple searches over the array at every Union operation.

In 2003, Suzuki [8] resumed Haralick's approach, including a small equivalence array and he provided a linear-time algorithm that in most cases requires 4 passes. The label resolution is performed exploiting array-based data structures, and each foreground pixel takes the minimum class of the neighboring foreground pixels classes. An important addition to this proposal is provided in an appendix in the form of a LUT of all possible neighborhoods, which allows to reduce computational times and costs by avoiding unnecessary Union operations.

In the same year, Chang et al. [9] proposed a radically different approach to connected components labeling. Their approach is an improvement of [10] and [11], and it is based on a single pass over the image exploiting contour tracing technique for internal and external contours, with a filling procedure for the internal pixels. This technique proved to be very fast, even because the filling is cache-friendly for images stored in a raster scan order, and the algorithm can also naturally output the connected components contours.

In 2005, Wu in [12] proposed a strategy to increase the performances of the Suzuki's approach. He exploited a decision tree to minimize the number of neighboring pixels to be visited in order to evaluate the label of the current pixel. In fact in a 8-connected components neighborhood, often only one pixel is needed to determine the label of the new one. In the same paper, Wu proposed another strategy to improve the Union-Find algorithm of Fiorio and Gustedt [13] exploiting an array-based data structure. For each equivalence array a path compression is performed to compute the root, in order to directly keep the minimum equivalent label within each equivalence array.

In 2007, He (in collaboration with Suzuki) proposed another fast approach in the form of a two scan algorithm [14]. The data structure used to manage the label resolution is implemented using three arrays in order to link the sets of equivalent classes without the use of pointers. By using this data structure, two algorithms have then been proposed: in [15] a run-based first scan is employed, while in [16] a decision tree is used to optimize the neighborhood exploration and to apply merging only when needed. The He and the Chang proposals can be considered the state-of-the-art methods for connected components labeling, being the latest evolution of two different approaches to solve the problem, and obtaining similar performances in terms of computation time. With the dataset used by He in [16], the Chang algorithm was shown to be slightly slower.

4   Speeding Up Neighbors Computation

The algorithms analyzed so far differ each other on the way neighboring pixels are analyzed, how many passes are performed and in the way the resolution of equivalences is managed. While the number of passes depends on the underline idea of the algorithm, and the label resolution is based on a limited amount of data structures and optimization proposed in literature, there is still something to say about the neighborhood computation. In [16], besides the efficient data structure used for label resolution, He proposed an optimization of the neighborhood computation deeply minimizing the number of pixel needed to access.

In this paper, we provide another optimization for the neighboring computation based on a very straightforward observation: when using 8-connection, the pixels of a 2x2 square are all connected to each other. This implies that they will share the same label at the end of the computation. For this reason we propose to logically scan the image moving on a 2x2 pixel grid. To allow this, we have to provide rules for the connectivity of 2x2 blocks.

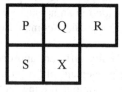   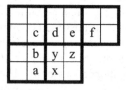

Blocks   Pixels in blocks

Referring to the figure, we can define the following rules:

- P is connected to X if c and y are foreground pixels
- Q is connected to X if (d or e) and (y or z) are foreground pixels
- R is connected to X if f and z are foreground pixels
- S is connected to X if (a or b) and (y or x) are foreground pixels

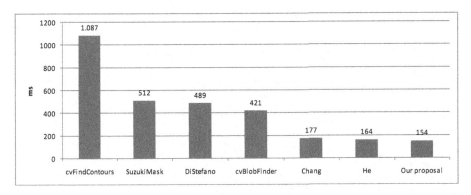

Fig. 3. Results of Test 1

By applying these connectivity rules, we obtain two advantages: the first one is that the number of provisional labels created during the first scan, is roughly reduced by a factor of four, and the second is that we need to apply much less unions, since equivalences are implicitly solved within the blocks. Another advantage is that a single label is stored for the whole block. On the contrary the same pixel needs to be checked multiple times, but this is easily solved by the use of local variables and caching, and the second scan requires to access again the original image to check which pixels in the block require their label to be set. Overall the advantages greatly overcome the additional work required in the following stage.

This method may be applied to different connected component labeling algorithms, and, depending from the algorithms, can improve performances from 10% to 20% based on the way they consider the neighborhood of the current pixel.

5 Comparison

The main focus of this comparison is to evaluate the performance of the algorithms under stress, that is when working with high resolution images with thousands of labels. Besides, we also tested their scalability, varying the image sizes and the number of labels.

To this purpose, we produce three datasets coming from the binarized version of high resolution documentary images. The first dataset is composed by 615 images, with a resolution of 3840x2886 pixels. For each algorithm, a mean value of the processing times will indicate which one has the best overall performance. The second dataset is composed by 3,173 images derived by the first dataset by a sequence of 10 subsequent dilations with a 3x3 pixels square structuring element. In this way we preserve the image size (total amount of pixel processed) but we decrease the number of labels thanks to the dilations (that merges little by little an increasing amount of blobs). This test will show which algorithm has the best scalability varying the number of labels, and at the same time which algorithm performs better with lower and higher amount of labels. Finally the third dataset is composed by 3807 images obtained from a 160x120 downscaled version of the first dataset, increasingly upscaled with 11 4:3 formats (up to the original image size). This dataset will be useful to

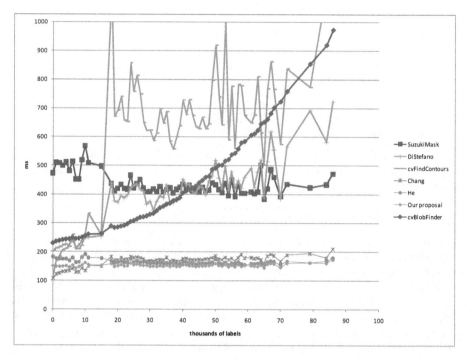

Fig. 4. Results of Test 2

evaluate the scalability of these algorithms with a small fixed number of blobs, but a larger number of pixels.

In all tests we applied our 2x2 block optimization to a raster scan algorithm which uses He's technique for handling equivalences and applies a *union* operation every time two different labeled blocks are connected.

The results of the first test are shown in Fig. 3. On high resolution images, our approach provides the best performances, by using the block optimization. Suzuki and DiStefano proposals are superior to the OpenCV standard contour tracing method, but cannot beat the other technique based on flood fill. After our proposal, the overall best techniques are Chang's and He's.

The results of the second test are shown in Fig. 4. Even in this case, the performace of OpenCV algorithms, as well as Suzuki and DiStefano ones, result to be not quite good (even if their proposal proves to have a good scalability). Chang's and He's algorithms and our proposal are still the approaches with the best performances. It is important to highlight that the behaviour of these algorithms is somehow different below and above the 150 labels: in this case the OpenCV contour tracing technique stays close to the other techniques. Chang algorithm is a clear winner with less then 10000 labels, while our proposal has the best performance in other cases.

Finally the results of the latest test are shown in Fig. 5. In this case, where the average number of labels is 473, OpenCV contour tracing proved to have a great scalability increasing the size of the image, while Chang and our method still perform very well. Nevertheless, zooming in at lower images sizes, up to 1024x768, we can notice that our approach and Chang's provide the best performance.

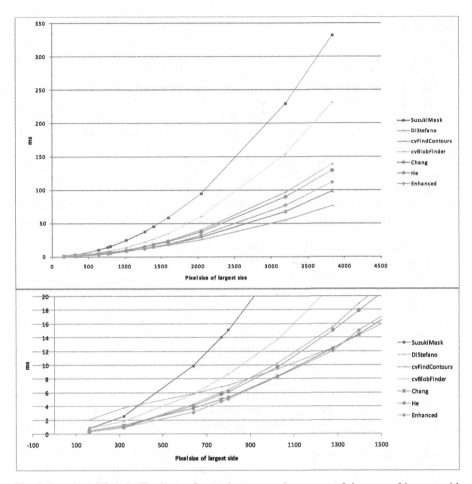

Fig. 5. Results of Test 3. The lower figure shows an enlargement of the area of images with widths below 1500 pixels.

6   Conclusions

We have given a comprehensive overview of the different strategies which have been proposed for the connected component labeling problem, pointing out relations and evolution of the single optimization proposals.

A new strategy for label propagation has been proposed, based on a 2x2 block subdivision. This strategy allows to improve the performance of many existing algorithms, given that the specific connection rules are satisfied.

Experimental results have stressed a few points of the different algorithms, in particular showing how the Cheng approach is a clear winner when the number of labels is small, compared to the image size, while our proposal can obtain around 10% of speedup when the number of labels is high.

References

1. Rosenfeld, A., Pfaltz, J.L.: Sequential Operations in Digital Picture Processing. Journal of the ACM 13(4), 471–494 (1966)
2. Haralick, R.M.: Some neighborhood operations. In: Real Time Parallel Computing: Image Analysis, pp. 11–35. Plenum Press, New York (1981)
3. Lumia, R., Shapiro, L.G., Zuniga, O.A.: A New Connected Components Algorithm for Virtual Memory Computers. Computer Vision Graphics and Image Processing 22(2), 287–300 (1983)
4. Schwartz, J.T., Sharjr, M., Siegel, A.: An efficient algorithm for finding connected components in a binary image. Robotics Research Technical Report 38. New York Univ. New York (1985)
5. Samet, H., Tamminen, M.: An Improved Approach to connected component labeling of images. In: International Conference on Computer Vision And Pattern Recognition, pp. 312–318 (1986)
6. Dillencourt, M.B., Samet, H., Tamminen, M.: A general approach to connected-component labeling for arbitrary image representations. Journal of the ACM 39(2), 253–280 (1992)
7. Di Stefano, L., Bulgarelli, A.: A simple and efficient connected components labeling algorithm. In: 10th International Conference on Image Analysis and Processing, pp. 322–327 (1999)
8. Suzuki, K., Horiba, I., Sugie, N.: Linear-time connected-component labeling based on sequential local operations. Comput. Vis. Image Underst. 89(1), 1–23 (2003)
9. Chang, F., Chen, C.J.: A component-labeling algorithm using contour tracing technique. In: 7th International Conference on Document Analysis and Recognition, pp. 741–745 (2003)
10. Freeman, H.: Techniques for the Digital Computer Analysis of Chain-Encoded Arbitrary Plane Curves. In: 17th National Electronics Conference, pp. 412–432 (1961)
11. Pavlidis, T.: Algorithms for graphics and image processing. Computer Science Press, Rockville MD (1982)
12. Wu, K., Otoo, E., Shoshani, A.: Optimizing connected component labeling algorithms. In: SPIE Conference on Medical Imaging, vol. 5747, pp. 1965–1976 (2005)
13. Fiorio, C., Gustedt, J.: Two Linear Time Union-Find Strategies for Image Processing. Theor. Comput. Sci. 154, 165–181 (1996)
14. He, L., Chao, Y., Suzuki, K.: A Linear-Time Two-Scan Labeling Algorithm. In: IEEE International Conference on Image Processing, vol. 5, pp. 241–244 (2007)
15. He, L., Chao, Y., Suzuki, K.: A Run-Based Two-Scan Labeling Algorithm. IEEE Transactions on Image Processing 17(5), 749–756 (2008)
16. He, L., Chao, T., Suzuki, K., Wu, K.: Fast connected-component labeling. Pattern Recognition (2008) (in press)

Estimation of Object Position Based on Color and Shape Contextual Information

Takashi Ishihara, Kazuhiro Hotta, and Haruhisa Takahashi

The University of Electro-Communications,
1-5-1 Chofugaoka Chofu-shi Tokyo, 182-8585, Japan
{ishihara,hotta,takahasi}@ice.uec.ac.jp
http://www.htlab.ice.uec.ac.jp/

Abstract. This paper presents a method to estimate the position of object using contextual information. Although convention methods used only shape contextual information, color contextual information is also effective to describe scenes. Thus we use both shape and color contextual information. To estimate the object position from only contextual information, the Support Vector Regression is used. We choose the Pyramid Match Kernel which measures the similarity between histograms because our contextual information is described as histogram. When one kernel is applied to a feature vector which consists of color and shape, the similarity of each feature is not used effectively. Thus, kernels are applied to color and shape independently, and the weighted sum of the outputs of both kernels is used. We confirm that the proposed method outperforms conventional methods.

Keywords: color context, shape context, object detection, support vector regression, Pyramid Match Kernel, summation kernel.

1 Introduction

It becomes increasingly important to detect specific target from still images or videos as the first step of object tracking and recognition. Although conventional methods detected a target by clipping part of an image, the scenery around and objects it belongs exists a strong relationship with each other. Human detects the object using contextual information obtained from the image as well as information obtained from the object.

Recently, the methods using contextual information to estimate the position of object were proposed [1][2]. Conventional methods were based on only shape contextual information, though the color information is effective to describe scenes. Therefore, we propose the contextual information based on both color and shape information. Color information is robust to background changes and less computational cost in comparison to the shape information.

As a contextual information based on color information, we use color histograms which are computed in subregions of various sizes. We also use Gabor feature which was used in convention methods [1][2] to extract shape information. After extracting a Gabor feature from an image, we construct histograms

P. Foggia, C. Sansone, and M. Vento (Eds.): ICIAP 2009, LNCS 5716, pp. 825–834, 2009.

which are computed in subregions of various sizes, and they are used as shape contextual information.

Torralba [1] used generative model to estimate the position of object from contextual information. Suzuyama et al. [2] has shown effective use of Support Vector Regression (SVR) instead of using generative model to estimate the position from contextual information, and achieved the high accuracy in comparison to Torralba's method. From these reasons, we select SVR. The generalization ability of SVR depends on the selection of a kernel function. We choose the Pyramid Match Kernel [3] based on the similarity between histograms, because our contextual information is based on histogram.

If we apply one kernel to a feature vector which consists of color and shape contextual information, then it is hard to reflect the similarity of only shape or color. To avoid this problem, we apply a kernel to each color and shape information independently, and the outputs of kernels are integrated by summation [4][5].

In the experiments, we estimate the position of car in an image from only contextual information. To compare the accuracy with the conventional method [2], we use the same image database as the conventional method. Experimental results show that the proposed method which integrates color and shape information outperforms the conventional method based on only shape contextual information. To confirm the effectiveness of the use of Pyramid Match Kernel, we compare the Pyramid Match Kernel and polynomial kernel which was used in conventional method [2]. It turns out that Pyramid Match Kernel achieves the higher accuracy in comparison to polynomial kernel.

This paper is organized as follows. In section 2, we describe color and shape contextual information. Section 3 explains how to estimate the position of object from contextual information. Experimental results are shown in section 4. Finally, conclusion and future works are described in section 5.

2   Contextual Information

To extract shape contextual information, we use Gabor feature which was also used in conventional methods [1][2]. Although conventional methods applied principal component analysis to Gabor feature, the shape contextual information depends heavily on the position of objects. The positions of objects are not stable in the same scene. Thus, the proposed method develops histograms from Gabor feature to be robust to position changes of objects. They are used as shape contextual information. We also use color histogram as color contextual information. This is also robust to position changes of objects. The details of shape contextual information is explained in section 2.1. Section 2.2 explains color contextual information.

2.1   Shape Contextal Information

In this section, we explain how to extract the shape contextual information. First, we explain Gabor feature.

The Gabor filters [8][9] used in this paper are defined as

$$v_{\mathbf{k}}(\mathbf{x}) = \frac{\mathbf{k}^2}{\sigma} \exp(\frac{-\mathbf{k}^2\mathbf{x}^2}{2\sigma^2}) \cdot (\exp(i\mathbf{k}\mathbf{x}) - \exp(-\frac{\sigma^2}{2})), \tag{1}$$

where $\mathbf{x} = (x, y)^T, \mathbf{k} = k_v \exp(i\phi), k_v = k_{max}/f^v, \phi = \mu \cdot \pi/4, f = \sqrt{2}, \sigma = \pi$. In the following experiments, Gabor filters of 4 different orientations $\mu = (0, 1, 2, 3)$ with 3 frequency levels ($v = 0, 1, 2$) are used. Thus, we obtain 12 output images of Gabor filters from one image. The size of Gabor filters of 3 different frequency levels is set to 9 9, 13 13 and 17 17 pixels respectively.

After extracting Gabor feature, we take the average within unoverlapped local regions of 2×2 pixels to reduce the computational cost. Fig.1, 2 and 3 show the outputs of Gabor filters (the norm of real and imaginary parts) of each scale parameter. Red pixels represent high output and blue pixels represent low output. It turns out that Gabor filters of specific orientation emphasize the specific edges. Since Gabor filter of small v is sensitive to fine edges, the outputs of Gabor filters in Fig.1 is more clear than those in Fig.3.

Fig. 1. Example of Gabor feature of v=0

Fig. 2. Example of Gabor feature of v=1

Fig. 3. Example of Gabor feature of v=2

The output images of Gabor filters depend heavily on the position of objects in images. Namely, they are not robust to position changes of objects. Since the composition and the position of objects in the same scenes are not stable, the robustness to position of objects is required. Thus we develop the histogram from the outputs of Gabor filters. However, we do not know appropriate sizes for computing histograms. If we develop the histogram from whole output image, it is robust to position changes of objects but does not work well to estimate the position. We can consider that both the robustness to position changes and rough topological information are effective. Therefore, we prepare some subregions for

Fig. 4. Subregions for shape histogram and example of histogram

compute histograms. Fig.4 shows the subregions used in the experiments. We divide the output images of Gabor filters into 1×1 and 2×2 subregions, and compute one histogram from one subregion. The histograms are robust feature to position changes. In addition, they have rough topological information. The number of bins of one histogram is set to 256 because 256 bins are appropriate for Pyramid Match Kernel. Each histogram with 256 bins is normalized so that sum of value is 1. The image on rightside in Fig.4 shows the example of shape histogram. The dimention of multi-resolution histogram obtained from an input image is 15,360 (=256(bins)×3(scales)×4(orientations)×5(subregions)).

2.2   Color Contextual Information

The color information is also important to describe scenes as well as shape information. We convert images from RGB color space to HSV color space and histogram is computed in each color independently. To use the local and global feature, we develop the color histogram from subregions of various sizes. In this paper, the image is divided into 1×1, 2×2 and 4×4 subregions, and histogram with 256 bins of each color is developed from each subregion. Each histogram is normalized so that the sum of values is 1. Fig.5 shows examples of the subregions and color histograms. We define color histograms as color contextual information. The dimention of multi-resolution color histogram obtained from an input image is 16,128 (=256(bins)×3(H, S, V)×21(subregions)).

Fig. 5. Subregions for color histogram and example of histogram

3   Position Estimation Using SVR

We select SVR to estimate the position of object, because Suzuyama [2] reported that SVR outperforms generative model [1]. SVR must be trained to estimate the position of objects from only contextual information. To develop the estimator by SVR, the teacher signal (correct position of objects) obtained manually and contextual information are used.

We want to develop the good estimator with high generalization ability. However the generalization ability of SVR depends on the selection of a kernel function. We choose the Pyramid Match Kernel [3] based on the similarity between histograms, because our contextual information is based on histogram. When the Pyramid Match Kernel is adopted to a feature which consists of color and shape contextual information, the similarity of each color or shape is not used effectively. To use the similarity of each feature, we use the weighted summation kernel. First, we explain the Pyramid Match Kernel in section 3.1. Section 3.2 explains the weighted summation kernel.

3.1 Pyramid Match Kernel

Pyramid Match Kernel [3] measures the similarity between histograms, by changing the bin size in a hierarchically fashion. Kernel function is defined as

$$K(y, z) = \sum_{i=0}^{L} \frac{1}{2^i} (L(H_i(y), H_i(z)) - L(H_{i-1}(y), H_{i-1}(z))), \tag{2}$$

where H_i is histogram at level i. $L(H(y), H(z))$ is the function for measuring the similarity between histograms, and counts the overlapped value in the correspoinding bin. In the experiments, L is set to 3.

3.2 Weighted Summation Kernel

We can adopt one kernel to a feature vector which consists of color and shape contextual information. However, in that case, the similarity of each feature is not used effectively. To avoid this problem, we use the summation kernel [4][5]. By assigning kernels to each feature independently and calculating the summation of each output, we obtain a new kernel function which uses the similarity of each feature effectively. The summation function K_{sum} is defined as

$$K_{sum}(x, z) = K_c(x_c, z_c) + K_s(x_s, z_s), \tag{3}$$

where K_c and K_s are the kernels for color and shape. In this paper, Pyramid Match Kernel is used as kernel function. In [5], all kernels are integrated with equal weights. However, the summation kernel with non-negative weight also satisfies Mercer's theorem [6]. In this paper, we use weighted sum of the two kernels as

$$K_{sum}(x, z) = \alpha K_c(x_c, z_c) + (1 - \alpha)K_s(x_s, z_s), \tag{4}$$

where α is a constant between 0 and 1. In the following experiments, we set α to 0.5 empirically.

4 Experiments

In the experiments, we estimate the position of car in an image. 990 images are used for training and 330 images are used for evaluation. The size of an input

Fig. 6. Examples of images used in test

image for extracting color contextual information is 128 128 pixels. This is the same images as the conventional method [2]. The size of an input image for extracting shape contextual information is 64 64 pixels to reduce the computational cost. Fig.6 shows the examples of images. A variety of scenes can be seen, and cars appear in different poses, scales and positions. The estimation of car position from those images is not easy task.

First, we explain how to train SVR. To develop the estimator of car location by SVR, we need the teacher signal of car location and contextual information obtained from images. The same teacher signals as Suzuyama's method are used. They were obtained manually by positioned the center point of cars in images. Suzuyama had labeled the location of car on the same manner so as not to make a large difference between training and test. SVR is trained by the teacher signals and contextual information of training images. In general, the output of SVR is only one. Thus, we train two SVRs for X and Y coordinates. As previously mentioned, we use weighted summation of Pyramid Match Kernel of color and shape contextual information.

Table 1. Comparison of the proposed method and convention methods

	X-coordinate	Y-coordinate
Proposed method with Pyramid Match Kernel	22.08(pixel)	7.54(pixel)
Suzuyama [2]	22.23(pixel)	8.68(pixel)
Generative model	26.61(pixel)	11.04(pixel)

Table 2. Evaluation of X-Y root mean squared error while changing α

α	0.0	0.1	0.2	0.3	0.4	0.5	0.6	0.7	0.8	0.9	1.0
X-coordinate	24.42	24.03	23.14	22.61	22.29	22.08	21.95	21.88	21.78	21.67	21.64
Y-coordinate	8.51	7.70	7.57	7.54	7.54	7.54	7.70	7.64	7.71	7.81	8.09

Fig. 7. Examples of in which the proposed method works well

Fig. 8. Examples of failure in prediction

The proposed method estimates the center position (X and Y coordinates) of cars in test images by using SVR. Since we have the correct position of cars in test images, we can calculate root mean squared error between estimated position and correct position. That is used as a measure of accuracy. The conventional method [2] also evaluates the accuracy with the same manner. Table 1 shows result of the root mean squared error of both methods. Since the cars in images line up side-by-side, it is difficult to estimate the position in X-coordinate. On the other hand, the estimation in Y-coordinate is easier than that in X-coordinate because it is rare that cars line up vertically. Thus, the error in X-coordinate is larger than those in Y-coordinate. Table 1 demonstrates that the proposed method outperforms the conventional method. To compare the accuracy with the another method [1], Suzuyama developed the estimator based on generative model of shape contextual information [2]. The result is also shown in Table 1. Our method also outperforms the approach using generative model.

Fig.7 shows the examples in which the proposed method works well. Cross point of green lines on the images indicates the correct position selected manually. The correct position is set to the center of group of cars because cars line up side-by-side. Cross point of red lines on the images indicates the car location estimated by the proposed method. The proposed method works well when it is easy for human to recognize the car location in color. This result suggests the importance of color contextual information as well as shape information. Fig.7 demonstrates that our method works well, though the images used in test include quite different scene such as weather changes, brightness, point of view, graphic resolution and cars appearance, poses, scales and positions.

Next, we show the examples of failure in prediction in Fig.8. The SVR estimates the position by the weighted sum of kernels. Since the kernel computes the similarity with training samples, the proposed method estimates the position based on the similarities with contextual information of training images. Thus, it does not work well to the images which are not included in training samples.

Table 2 demonstrates the evaluation result of X-Y root mean squared error between estimated position and correct position while changing the weight α in equation (4). $\alpha = 0$ means that only shape contextual information is used, and $\alpha = 1$ means that only color contextual information is used. Estimation of Y-coordinate works well when $\alpha = 0.5$ or 0.4, which suggests the importance of using both color and shape contextual information to estimate the position of Y-coordinate. On the other hand, estimation of X-coordinate works well when $\alpha = 1.0$ which suggests the importance of using color contextual information to estimate the position of X-coordinate.

5   Conclusion

We proposed the method to estimate the position of object based on only color and shape contextual information obtained from the images. In conventional methods, only shape contextual information was used to estimate object position but color information is effective to describe scenes. Thus, we use color and shape contextual information. Since they are described as histograms, we use Pyramid Match Kernel to reflect the similarity of histograms effectively. The results show that the proposed method outperformed the conventional method using only shape contextual information.

Since the proposed method estimates the rough position of objects, it is useful to speed up the object detection. However, current method estimates only one position. We will extend our method to estimate all positions of objects in an image. This is a subject for future works.

References

1. Torralba, A.: Contextual Priming for Object Detection. International Journal of computer Vision 53(2), 169–191 (2003)
2. Suzuyama, Y., Hotta, K., Haruhisa, T.: Context Based Prior Probability Estimation of Object Appearance. The Institute of Electrical Engineers of Japan 129-C(5) (2009) (in Japanese)
3. Grauman, K., Darrell, T.: The Pyramid Match Kernel: Discriminative Classification with Sets of Image Features. In: Proc. International Conference on Computer Vision, pp. 1458–1465 (2005)
4. Nomoto, A., Hotta, K., Takahashi, H.: An asbestos counting method from microscope images of building materials using summation kernel of color and shape. In: Proc. International Conference on Neural Information Processing (2008)
5. Hotta, K.: Robust Face Recognition under Partial Occlusion Based on Support Vector Machine with Local Gaussian Summation Kernel. Image and Vision Computing 26(11), 1490–1498 (2008)

6. Shawe-Taylor, J., Cristianini, N.: Kernel methods for Pattern Analysis. Cambridge University Press, Cambridge (2004)
7. Label Me, http://labelme.csail.mit.edu/
8. Hotta, K.: Object Categorization Based on Kernel Principal Component Analysis of Visual Words. In: Proc. IEEE Workshop on Applications of Computer Vision (2008)
9. Lades, M., Vorbruggen, J.C., Buhmann, J., Lange, J., Van de Malsburg, C.: Distortion invariant object recognition in the dynamic link architecture. IEEE Transactions on Computer 42(3), 300–311 (1993)

Hallucinating Faces: Global Linear Modal Based Super-Resolution and Position Based Residue Compensation

Xiang Ma[1], Junping Zhang[2], and Chun Qi[1]

[1] School of Electronics& Information Engineering, Xi'an Jiaotong University, Xi'an, China
[2] Department of Computer Science and Engineering, Fudan University, Shanghai, China
maxiangmail@163.com

Abstract. A learning-based face hallucination method is proposed in this paper for the reconstruction of a high-resolution face image from a low-resolution observation based on a set of high- and low-resolution training image pairs. The proposed global linear modal based super-resolution estimates the optimal weights of all the low-resolution training images and a high-resolution image is obtained by applying the estimated weights to the high-resolution space. Then, we propose a position based local residue compensation algorithm to better recover subtle details of face. Experiments demonstrate that our method has advantage over some established methods.

Keywords: Face hallucination; Super-resolution; Residue compensation.

1 Introduction

Super-resolution addresses various applications in a variety of important sectors, as diverse as medical imaging, satellite imaging, surveillance system, image enlarging in web pages, and restoration of old historic photographs. Super-resolutions are roughly separated into two classes [8]: general super-resolution [4], which extracts a single high-resolution image from a sequence of general low-resolution images, and domain specific super-resolution[1], [2], [5], [6], [8], which extracts high-resolution image details from a restricted class of high-resolution images, such as in the face domain. In this study, we focus on face image super-resolution, which is also known as face hallucination. Face hallucination is to reconstruct a high-resolution face image from a low-resolution one based on a set of high- and low-resolution training image pairs.

Baker *et al.* [1] was the first to develop a face hallucination method under a Bayesian formulation and proposed the term face hallucination. In this method, it generates the high frequency details from a parent structure with the assistance of training samples. Liu *et al.* [2] adopted a two-step approach integrating a global parametric model with Gaussian assumption and a local nonparametric model based on Markov random field (MRF). Both of the two methods used complicated probabilistic models and were based on an explicit down-sampling function, which is sometimes unavailable in practice. Inspired by locally linear embedding (LLE), a well-known manifold learning

P. Foggia, C. Sansone, and M. Vento (Eds.): ICIAP 2009, LNCS 5716, pp. 835–843, 2009.

method, Chang *et al.* [3] proposed Neighbor Embedding algorithm based on assumption that small patches in the low- and high-resolution images form manifolds with similar local geometry in two distinct spaces. Wang *et al.* [6] suggested a face hallucination method using principal component analysis (PCA) to represent the structural similarity of face images. Zhuang *et al.* [5] developed a two-phase face hallucination. The locality preserving hallucination algorithm combines locality preserving projection (LPP) and Radial basis function (RBF) regression together to hallucinate the global high-resolution face. The details of the synthetic high-resolution face are further improved by residue compensation based on Neighbor Embedding. Jia *et al.* [8] applied hierarchical tensor algebra to face hallucination to solve different facial modalities. His super-resolution approach still integrates probability models with Gaussian assumption. Park *et al.* [9] proposed a novel example-based face hallucination method with an extended morphable face model. This method has advantages in enhancing the resolution of face image and improving the performance of face recognition.

A global linear modal based super-resolution is proposed in our study to reconstruct the face image keeping the main characteristics of the ground truth face instead of using a manifold learning or extended morphable face model. Furthermore, a residual face containing the high-frequency information was produced and piled onto the result of step one by proposed local residue compensation algorithm based on position to better the final result.

The rest of the paper is organized as follows: In Section 2, we will describe the proposed method in detail. Section 3 shows experiments results, and Section 4 concludes the paper.

2   Proposed Face Hallucination Method

2.1   Global Linear Modal Based Super-Resolution

In [8], a novel face image was represented by a linear combination of prototypes [9]. In our method, all training images are used as a linear combination to represent a new facial image input. A low-resolution face image input is denoted as I . Suppose that H^m are the high-resolution training images, whose low-resolution correspondences are represented as L^m , $m = 1,...,M$, where M is the number of training image pairs. Face image is represented as a column vector of all pixel values in algorithm.

We expect

$$I \cong \sum_{m=1}^{M} w_m L^m = P \tag{1}$$

where P is the reconstructed image estimated with the linear combination of all the low-resolution training images. $w_1, w_2, ... w_M$ are the reconstruction weights of the low-resolution training images which are constrained to have a sum of one.

The reconstruction error $E(w)$ is defined as follows:

$$E(w) = \|I - P\|^2$$

(2)

Equation (2) represents the difference between the input facial image and its reconstructed equivalent

The optimal reconstruction weights are based on the minimization of the reconstruction error $E(w)$:

$$w = \arg \min_{w_m} \|I - P\|^2$$

(3)

where w is a M-dimensional weight vector by stacking each reconstruction weights.

Let $\mathbf{Z} = (X - \mathbf{Y})^T (X - \mathbf{Y})$, where $X = L \cdot C^T$, C is a column vector of ones and $\mathbf{Y}$ is a matrix with its columns being the training images $L^1, L^2, ..., L^M$.

Equation (3) is a constrained least squares problem which has the following solution

$$w = (\mathbf{Z}^{-1}C) / (C^T \mathbf{Z}^{-1} C)$$

(4)

The estimated weight w maintains the minimization of the reconstruction error $E(w)$, however, the variance of w is relatively large, which makes the reconstructed image unsmooth. To reduce the variance of w, we let $\mathbf{Z} = \mathbf{Z} + \mathbf{I} \cdot a$, where a is a large number and $\mathbf{I}$ is a diagonal matrix of ones. Thus, the solution for w is no longer optimal but deviated.

Replacing each low-resolution image L^m by its corresponding high-resolution sample H^m in (1), the result is denoted as $\tilde{P}$, we have

$$\sum_{m=1}^{M} w_m H^m = \tilde{P}$$

(5)

Equation (5) shows that $\tilde{P}$ is the linear combination of the high-resolution training image, so it should be approximately face-like at a high-resolution level.

The acquisition process can be expressed as [1], [2]:

$$I_L = \frac{1}{q^2} \sum_{k=0}^{q-1} \sum_{l=0}^{q-1} I_H \left(qi + k, qj + l \right) + n$$

(6)

where I_H is the ground truth high-resolution image which is q^2 times larger than I_L, q is a positive integer and n is the random noise.

For notation simplification, if I_H, I_L and n are respectively vectors, equation (6) can be rewritten as:

$$I_L = AI_H + n$$

(7)

where A is a matrix. Equation (7) combines a smoothing and a down-sampled step.

From (7) and (5), without consideration of noise disturbance, we have

$$A\tilde{P} = \sum_{m=1}^{M} w_m AH^m = w_1 AH^1 + w_2 AH^2 + ... + w_M AH^M$$

$$= w_1 L^1 + w_2 L^2 + ... + w_M L^M = \sum_{m=1}^{M} w_m L^m = P \qquad (8)$$

From (1) and (8), we have

$$A\tilde{P} = P \cong I \qquad (9)$$

Equation (9) shows that the degradation of $\tilde{P}$ is close to the low-resolution input image I. Since the weight w is not computed from high-resolution training images, the image $\tilde{P}$ needs further step to better recover face subtle details.

2.2 Local Residue Compensation Based on Position

In this section, we propose the residue compensation algorithm based on position. In this step, a residue image $\tilde{T}$ is estimated and the final result H^* is obtained by adding $\tilde{T}$ to $\tilde{P}$.

The input of residue compensation is obtained by subtracting the degradation version of the result $\tilde{P}$ from the original low-resolution input face I:

$$T = I - A(\tilde{P}) \qquad (10)$$

The low-resolution training image R_L^m for residue compensation can be obtained by the following equation:

$$R_L^m = L^m - A(H_1^m) \qquad (11)$$

where H_1^m is the result gained by global face modal based face hallucination method using L^m as low-resolution image input, of course, the training pair number is changed from M to $M-1$.

The high-resolution training image R_H^m for residue compensation can be obtained by the following equation:

$$R_H^m = H^m - H_1^m \qquad (12)$$

The obtained training images are respectively considered as a patch matrix composed of overlapping square patches: $\left\{ R_L^{mP}(i, j) \right\}_{m=1}^{N}$、$\left\{ R_H^{mP}(i, j) \right\}_{m=1}^{N}$, where N is the number of the patches in image. The patch located at row i and column j in the patch matrix can be denoted as $R_L^{mP}(i, j)$ or $R_H^{mP}(i, j)$. The patch $R_L^{mP}(i, j)$ and its adjacent patches are shown in Fig. 1.

Suppose that the patch covers $n \times n$ pixels. To low-resolution image training set, if n is an odd number , the patch $R_L^{mP}(i, j)$ overlaps with its adjacent patches by size $[(n-1)/2] \times [(n-1)/2]$, and its corresponding high-resolution patch $R_H^{mP}(i, j)$ which covers $qn \times qn$ pixels overlaps with its adjacent patches by size $[q(n-1)/2] \times [q(n-1)/2]$; if n is an even number , the patch $R_L^P(i, j)$ overlaps with its adjacent patches by size $(n/2) \times (n/2)$,and its corresponding high-resolution patch $R_H^{mP}(i, j)$ covering $qn \times qn$ pixels overlaps with its adjacent patches by size $[qn/2] \times [qn/2]$.

T is also represented in patches: $\{T^{mP}(i, j)\}_{m=1}^N$. From (1), for each image patch located at position (i, j) , we have:

$$T^{mP}(i, j) \cong \sum_{m=1}^M w_m(i, j) \cdot R_L^{mp}(i, j) \qquad (13)$$

where $w_m(i, j)$ represent the reconstruction weights of the low-resolution training image patches, which are constrained to have a sum of one.
From (1)-(5), $w_m(i, j)$ are obtained by the following equation:

$$w(i, j) = (\mathbf{Z}^{-1}C) / (C^T \mathbf{Z}^{-1}C) \qquad (14)$$

where $\mathbf{Z} = (X - \mathbf{Y})^T (X - \mathbf{Y})$, $X = T^P(i, j) \cdot C^T$, C is a column vector of ones and $\mathbf{Y}$ is a matrix with its columns being the training images $R_L^{1P}(i, j), R_L^{2P}(i, j),..., R_L^{MP}(i, j)$, $w(i, j)$ is a M-dimensional weight vector by stacking each reconstruction weights $w_m(i, j)$.
Replacing each low-resolution image patch $R_L^{mP}(i, j)$ by its corresponding high-resolution patch $R_H^{mP}(i, j)$ in (13), the result is denoted as:

$$\sum_{m=1}^M w_m(i, j) \cdot R_H^{mp}(i, j) = \tilde{T}^{mP}(i, j) \qquad (15)$$

where $\tilde{T}^{mP}(i, j)$ represents the reconstructed image patch estimated by the linear combination of the high-resolution training image patches.

According to their original positions, all the reconstructed patches are integrated to form the final image $\{\tilde{T}^{mP}(i, j)\}_{m=1}^N$, which is also denoted in global image $\tilde{T}$. Pixels of the overlapping regions in the result are obtained by averaging the pixels value in the overlapping regions between two adjacent patches.

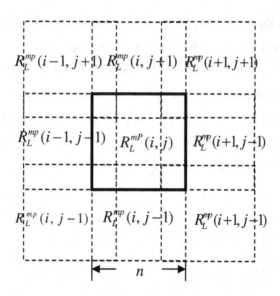

Fig. 1. Image patch $R_L^{mP}(i, j)$ with its adjacent image patches

The final result X^* is obtained by adding the $\tilde{T}$ to the step-one result $\tilde{P}$.

$$X^* = \tilde{P} + \tilde{T} \tag{16}$$

where X^* is the final hallucinated image.

The proposed face hallucination method is summarized as follows:

Step1. Approximate the low-resolution face input by the linear combination of all the low-resolution training images.

Step2. Compute the reconstruction weight w_m and synthesize the result image $\tilde{P}$.

Step3. Obtain the face residue input $\{T^{mP}(i, j)\}_{m=1}^{N}$ and generate the pair-wise training images $\left\{R_L{}^{mP}(i, j)\right\}_{m=1}^{N}$ and $\left\{R_H{}^{mP}(i, j)\right\}_{m=1}^{N}$ for residue compensation.

Step4. For each patch $T^{mP}(i, j)$ located at (i, j):

(a) Compute the reconstruction weight $w_m(i, j)$.

(b) Reconstruct the patch $\tilde{T}^{mP}(i, j)$.

Step5. Integrate all the hallucinated residue patches to form a residue image $\tilde{T}$.

Step6. Add the residue image $\tilde{T}$ to $\tilde{P}$, the final hallucinated image X^* is produced.

3 Experiment Results

Our face hallucination method was performed on the CAS-PEAL Face Database [7]. The 290 normal expression images of different peoples under the same light condition were randomly selected and aligned manually according to the locations of 3 points: centers of left and right eyeballs and center of the mouth. We cut out the region of the face according to interesting. All faces were standardized to the size of 128×96.

The 20 high-resolution images were blurred using a 7×7 Gaussian filter with σ =0.85, and down-sampled to 32×24 for test. The rest of the images were used as high-resolution training images, and down-sampled to 32×24 for using as low-resolution training images.

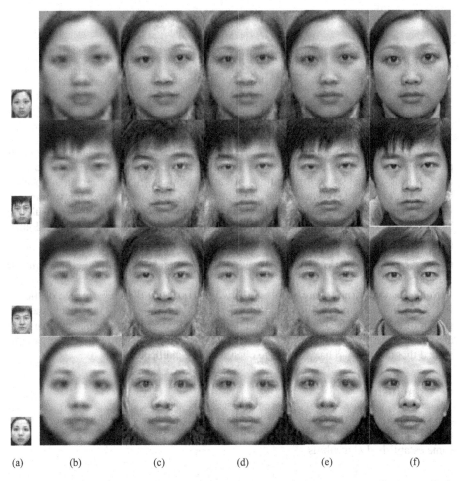

(a)   (b)   (c)   (d)   (e)   (f)

Fig. 2. The hallucination results. (a) The input 24×32 low-resolution faces. (b) Cubic B-Spline. (c) Wang's method. (d) Zhuang's method. (e) Our method. (f) The original 96×128 high-resolution faces.

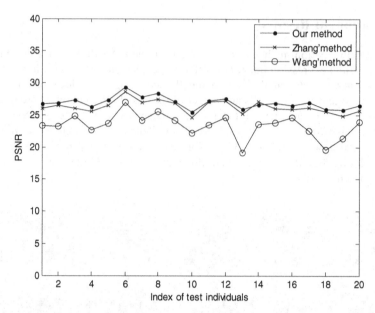

Fig. 3. PSNR values of the hallucinated results from three different methods

The size of 3×3 low-resolution patch was used in residue compensation. We compared our method with some methods based on the same training set. These methods are Cubic-B-Spine, Wang's eigentransformation method [6] and Zhuang's Locality Preserving method [5]. The image pairs of 150 people were used for training in Zhuang's method [5] and our method. In order to achieve the optimal results in Wang's method [6], we used image pairs of 270 for training and let Variance contribution rate of PCA be 0.9999; We selected h =135, $K_1 = 8$, $K_2 = 5$ mentioned in [5] to optimize the results of Zhuang's method [5]. The size of the image patch in our method is 3×3.

Some resultant images are shown in Fig. 2. To quantify the performance of the results, we also computed the peak signal-to-noise ration (PSNR) of each method shown in Fig. 3. It can see that our method has the highest PSNR values compared to the values from other methods for all test faces. Based on the comparisons, it is concluded that our method has advantage over current established methods.

4   Conclusion

A novel approach to hallucinating faces is presented in this study. Experiments show that the proposed method generates results with the best image quality compared to some established algorithms.

Acknowledgments

This work was supported in part by the grants from the National Natural Science Foundation of China under number 60641002 and in part by the National High- Tech

Research and Development Program ("863"program) of China under number 2007AA01Z176 .

The research in this paper use the CAS-PEAL-R1 face database collected under the sponsorship of the Chinese National Hi-Tech Program and ISVISION Tech. Co. Ltd.

References

[1] Baker, S., Kanade, T.: Hallucinating Faces. In: IEEE Inter. Conf. on Automatic Face and Gesture Recognition, pp. 83–88. IEEE Press, France (2000)

[2] Liu, C., Shum, H.Y., Zhang, C.S.: A two-step approach to hallucinating faces: global parametric model and local nonparametric model. In: Inter. Conference on Image and Graphics, pp. 192–198. IEEE Press, New York (2001)

[3] Chang, H., Yeung, D.-Y., Xiong, Y.: Super-resolution through neighbor embedding. In: Inter. Conference on Computer Vision and Pattern Recognition, pp. 1275–1282. IEEE Press, Washington (2004)

[4] Costa, G.H., Bermudez, J.C.M.: Statistical analysis of the LMS algorithm applied to super resolution image reconstruction. IEEE Transactions on Signal Processing 11, 2084–2095 (2007)

[5] Zhuang, Y., Zhang, J., Wu, F.: Hallucinating faces: LPH super-resolution and neighbor reconstruction for residue compensation. Pattern Recognition 40, 3178–3194 (2007)

[6] Wang, X., Tang, X.: Hallucinating Face by Eigentransformation. IEEE Transactions on Systems Man and Cybernetics 35, 425–434 (2005)

[7] Gao, W., et al.: The CAS-PEAL Large-Scale Chinese Face Database and Baseline Evaluations. IEEE Transactions on System Man, and Cybernetics (Part A) 38, 149–161 (2008)

[8] Jia, K., Gong, S.G.: Generalized face super-resolution. IEEE Transactions on Image Processing 17, 873–886 (2008)

[9] Park, J.S.S., Lee, W.: An Example-Based Face Hallucination Method for Single-Frame, Low-resolution Facial Images. IEEE Transactions on Image Processing 17, 1806–1816 (2008)

Joint Affine and Illumination Estimation Using Scale Manipulation Features

Kobi Bentolila[1] and Joseph M. Francos[1]

Electrical and Computer Engineering Department,
Ben-Gurion University, Beer Sheva 84105, Israel

Abstract. We present a novel image transform called Scale Manipulation Features (SMF). The transform calculates affine invariant features of objects in a global manner and avoids using any sort of edge detection. The transform can be used for registration of affine transformed images in the presence of non homogenous illumination changes and for estimation of the illumination changes. The computational load of the method is relatively low since it is linear in the data size. In this paper we introduce the transform and demonstrate its applications for illumination compensation and for object registration in the presence of an affine geometric transformation and varying illumination.

Keywords: Geometric distortion, Affine invariance, Illumination invariance, Affine invariant features, image transform.

1 Introduction

The general problem of object registration when seen from different points of view and under different illumination conditions is a very complex problem in computer vision. In many cases, the change in point of view is modeled as a geometric transformation like shift, rotation or scale of the image coordinates. Illumination changes, on the other hand can be modeled by a linear combination of basis images.

The idea of representing illumination changes by a linear combination of images was proposed by Shashua [1]. Hallinan [2] represented illumination changes by a linear combination of base images, and used PCA to find an approximation of the basis images. Belhumer and Kreigman [3] showed that the illumination cone of a convex lambertian surface can be constructed from as few as three images. Further work was done by Basri and Jacobs [4] who used spherical harmonics to show that set of images produced by a lambertian surface lies close to a 9 dimensional space.

The most popular methods for image registration today are local methods, such as IBR and EBR [5], SIFT [6], and MSER [7]. These methods identify features of small regions in the image and extract the transformation from the correspondence of the features. Most local methods can handle small non uniform illumination changes but they are sensitive to changes in light source direction. Since the features are local they are sensitive to noise.

P. Foggia, C. Sansone, and M. Vento (Eds.): ICIAP 2009, LNCS 5716, pp. 844–852, 2009.

Global methods for affine invariant features include MSA [8], affine invariant moments [9], CW moments [10] and trace transform [11]. However, None of these methods can handle illumination changes. Affine and illumination invariance features are presented in [12] however the illumination changes are global and not location dependent.

A global method for registration in the presence of general a multi dimensional geometric homeomorphism was proposed by [13]. The method was extended in [14] to affine registration with illumination variation using hyper-spectral data.

In this paper we propose a novel transform called Scale Manipulation Features (SMF). The transform calculates features of isolated objects in a global manner and does not rely on any type of edge detection. The transform can be used for illumination compensation and for registration in the presence of an affine geometric transformation. The computational complexity of the transform is relatively low and grows linearly with the size of the object.

The paper is organized as follows: Section 2 defines the problem of estimating jointly the illumination and affine geometric changes. Section 3 defines the SMF transform, shows its invariance to affine geometric transformations and the linear properties of the transformation. Section 4 describes the illumination estimation scheme. Section 5 defines SMF moments and demonstrates their usage for affine registration. Section 6 describes an experiment of affine registration under varying illumination of real images.

2 Problem Definition

In this section we introduce the mathematical model used to describe the problem of object registration in the presence of varying illumination. The mathematical model described here was first defined at [13] and [14].

We begin by defining the geometric deformation. Let G be the group of the allowed geometric deformations and $S = \{f : R^2 \rightarrow R\}$, f is integrable with bounded support, be the space of the image functions. The action of G on S is defined by $G \times S \rightarrow S$ such that for $\phi \in G, f \in S$, ϕ acts on f by $(\phi, f) \equiv f \circ \phi$ (composition of functions). Loosely speaking, each member of G acts on an image f by changing the coordinates system of f. Thus, in the absence of illumination variation, the registration problem is formulated as follows: Given the functions (images) h and f, such that $h = f \circ \phi$, find ϕ.

We will restrict the discussion to affine geometric transformation. We define G_{aff} to be the group of affine invertible transformation $G = \{\phi(\mathbf{A}, \mathbf{b}); \mathbf{A} \in GL(2), \mathbf{b} \in R^2\}$, where $\phi(\mathbf{x}) = \mathbf{A}\mathbf{x} + \mathbf{b}$. The group action of $\phi(\mathbf{A}, \mathbf{b})$ is defined as $(\phi, f)(\mathbf{x}) = f(\mathbf{A}\mathbf{x} + \mathbf{b})$.

The radiometric changes are modeled as different linear combinations of a number of basis images. Let by f_i , i=1,..,n be a set of basis functions, then $f = \sum_{i=1}^{n} a_i f_i$ describes the image of an object viewed at a certain illumination state.

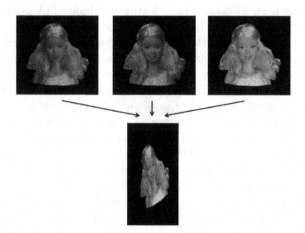

Fig. 1. Different illuminations of an image and an affine transformed linear combination

The problem of joint affine geometric transformation estimation and radiometric change estimation discussed in this paper is therefore defined as

$$h = (\sum_{i=1}^{n} a_i f_i) \circ \phi \tag{1}$$

Given only the observation h and the illumination basis images f_i , i=1,..,n we wish to find the coefficients a_i and the geometric transformation ϕ. Figure 1 display an affine transformed mixture of illuminated images.

We use the same notations ϕ, f, f_i, h throughout this paper to describe the affine transformation, the illuminated image, the basis illumination functions and the observation respectively.

3   Scale Manipulation Features

In this section, we introduce an affine invariant image transform called Scale Manipulation Features (SMF) and explain the properties of the transform.

3.1   The Definition of SMF

Let

$$sp_f(\mathbf{x}) = \begin{cases} 1 \text{ if } f(\mathbf{x}) > 0 \\ 0 \text{ else} \end{cases} \tag{2}$$

be the support function of an image intensity function f, $\mathbf{x} \in R^2$. We define the center of mass of the support by

$$\mu_f = \frac{1}{\|sp_f\|_{L_1}} \int_{R^2} \mathbf{x} sp_f(\mathbf{x}) d\mathbf{x} \tag{3}$$

Let α be a scale factor, $\alpha \in (0,1]$ and let

$$sp_{f,\alpha}(\mathbf{x}) = sp_f(\frac{1}{\alpha}(\mathbf{x} - \mu_f) + \mu_f) \tag{4}$$

be the scale of sp_f around the center of mass μ_f. Using the above definition we can now define the SMF transform

$$F(\alpha) = \frac{1}{\|sp_f\|_{L_1}} \int_{R^2} f(\mathbf{x}) \cdot sp_{f,\alpha}(\mathbf{x})d\mathbf{x} \tag{5}$$

The SMF transformation calculates the weight of an image intensity function in regions determined by α. Fig 2 shows an illustration of the selected region. Each α value correspond to a region centered at the image support center of mass.

Fig. 2. Original image and scaled integration area, $\alpha = 0.6$

3.2 SMF Invariance to Affine Transformation

Let f be an image intensity function, $\phi(\mathbf{A}, \mathbf{b})$ an affine transformation and $h = f \circ \phi$ the affine transformed image. Let $F(\alpha)$ and $H(\alpha)$ denote the SMF of f and h respectively.

Theorem 1. $F(\alpha) = H(\alpha)$

Proof. See [15].

Since $F(\alpha) = H(\alpha)$ regardless of the affine transformation, we can use the SMF to extract affine invariant features. Each value of α yields an additional feature.

3.3 SMF Linear Properties

Let f_i, i=1,..,n be some image intensity functions representing an object in the same pose under different illuminations, and let $F_i(\alpha)$ be their corresponding SMF transforms. Let a_i, i=1,..,n be a set of non negative coefficients, and let $f = \sum_{i=1}^{n} a_i f_i$ be a linear combination of the images, representing the object under some arbitrary illumination condition. As above, let $F(\alpha)$ denote the SMF transform of f .

Theorem 2. $F(\alpha) = \sum_{i=1}^{n} a_i F_i(\alpha)$

Proof.

$$F(\alpha) = \frac{1}{\|sp_f\|_{L_1}} \int_{R^2} \sum_{i=1}^{n} a_i f_i(\mathbf{x}) \cdot sp_{f,\alpha}(\mathbf{x}) d\mathbf{x} = \sum_{i=1}^{n} a_i \frac{1}{\|sp_f\|_{L_1}} \int_{R^2} f_i(\mathbf{x}) \cdot sp_{f,\alpha}(\mathbf{x}) d\mathbf{x}$$

Since f_i represents the object in the same pose, under a different illumination, we have that for each i,j $\in \{1,...,n\}$, $sp_{f_i} = sp_{f_j} = sp_f$. Therefore

$$F(\alpha) = \sum_{i=1}^{n} a_i \frac{1}{\|sp_{f_i}\|_{L_1}} \int_{R^2} f_i(\mathbf{x}) \cdot sp_{f_i,\alpha}(\mathbf{x}) d\mathbf{x} = \sum_{i=1}^{n} a_i F_i(\alpha)$$

4 SMF for Estimating Illumination in the Presence of Affine Transformation

By theorems 1 and 2

$$H(\alpha) = \sum_{i=1}^{n} a_i F_i(\alpha) \tag{6}$$

Let $\alpha_1, ..., \alpha_m$ be a set of m different coefficients. Evaluating the SMF in (6) for these coefficients results in the following set of linear equations in $a_1, ... a_m$

$$\begin{pmatrix} F_1(\alpha_1) & \cdots & F_n(\alpha_1) \\ \vdots & \ddots & \vdots \\ F_1(\alpha_m) & \cdots & F_n(\alpha_m) \end{pmatrix} \cdot \begin{pmatrix} a_1 \\ \vdots \\ a_n \end{pmatrix} = \begin{pmatrix} H(\alpha_1) \\ \vdots \\ H(\alpha_m) \end{pmatrix} \tag{7}$$

In the absence of noise, using $m = n$ coefficients provides a linear system with n equations and n unknowns that can be solved by matrix inversion. In the presence of noise, using $m > n$ equations leads to a linear regression problem. An estimation of $a_1, ..., a_n$ is then obtained by a least square method.

Once $a_1, ..., a_n$ are known, the illumination changes can be compensated for and the problem is reduced to a strictly geometric form of $h = f \circ \phi$ where f is known and is given by $f = \sum_{i=1}^{n} a_i f_i$.

5 Affine Transformation Estimation Using First and Second Order SMF Moments

We define the first order moment SMF of f, $\mathbf{F}^1(\alpha)$, $\mathbf{F}^1 \in R^2$ as

$$\mathbf{F}^1(\alpha) = \frac{1}{\|sp_f\|_{L_1}} \int_{R^2} (\mathbf{x} - \mu_f) \cdot f(\mathbf{x}) \cdot sp_{f,\alpha}(\mathbf{x}) d\mathbf{x} \tag{8}$$

and the second order moment SMF of f, $\mathbf{F}^2(\alpha)$, $\mathbf{F}^2 \in R^{2\times2}$ as

$$\mathbf{F}^2(\alpha) = \frac{1}{\|sp_f\|_{L_1}} \int_{R^2} (\mathbf{x} - \mu_f) \cdot (\mathbf{x} - \mu_f)^T \cdot f(\mathbf{x}) \cdot sp_{f,\alpha}(\mathbf{x}) d\mathbf{x} \tag{9}$$

The first and second order moments SMF are the first and second order moments of the image function at regions determined by α.

Theorem 3. $\boldsymbol{F}^1(\alpha) = \boldsymbol{A} \cdot \boldsymbol{H}^1(\alpha)$

Theorem 4. $\boldsymbol{F}^2(\alpha) = \boldsymbol{A} \cdot \boldsymbol{H}^2(\alpha) \cdot \boldsymbol{A}^T$

Proof. See [15].

The second order moment SMF does not lead directly to linear constraints, but linear constraints can be derived from it: Using theorem 4 we have

$$\mathbf{F}^2(\alpha) \cdot \mathbf{A}^{-T} = \mathbf{A} \cdot \mathbf{H}^2(\alpha)$$

Using the notation $\mathbf{A} = \begin{pmatrix} a_{11} & a_{12} \\ a_{21} & a_{22} \end{pmatrix}$, the matrix A^{-T} can be written as

$$\mathbf{A}^{-T} = \frac{1}{|det(A)|} \begin{pmatrix} a_{22} & -a_{21} \\ -a_{12} & a_{11} \end{pmatrix} = \frac{\|sp_h\|_{L_1}}{\|sp_f\|_{L_1}} \begin{pmatrix} a_{22} & -a_{21} \\ -a_{12} & a_{11} \end{pmatrix}$$

Thus first and second order moments SMF yield six linear constraints on the values of $\mathbf{A}$ for each value of α. By using linear methods such as least squares we can extract the parameters of the matrix $\mathbf{A}$. Once the parameters of $\mathbf{A}$ are known, the shift term $\mathbf{b}$ can be easily calculated.

6   Experiment - Joint Estimation of Illumination and Affine Geometric Deformation

In this experiment we demonstrate SMF ability for registration of images in presence of location dependent illumination changes.

6.1   Experiment Settings

We use an array of 14 light sources to illuminate a glossy toy airplane. PCA is performed on 100 gray-scale images of the airplane. The images are taken at the same pose, with a random illumination power of each light source distributed uniformly in the range of 10% to 90% of the maximal power. 10 basis images, $f_1, .., f_{10}$ are extracted from the PCA.

Fig. 3. Registration results - rotation -40 , pan -30

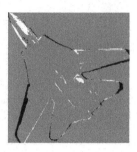

Fig. 4. Registration results - rotation -40 , pan 30

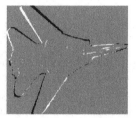

Fig. 5. Registration results - rotation 80 , pan 0

Fig. 6. Illustration of the illuminated plane

We connect the plane to a two axis motorized stage for rotation and pan. The observations h are images of the plane taken at various poses, in each image the illumination power of each of light source is chosen randomly as above. The registration problem is described as $h = \left(\sum_{i=1}^{n} a_i f_i\right) \circ \phi$.

6.2   The Registration Process

For each image, we first estimate the illumination coefficients, a_i, using the method described in section 4 and reduce the problem to the form $h = \widehat{f} \circ \phi$, where $\widehat{f} = \sum_{i=1}^{10} a_i f_i$. After the illumination changes are compensated for, an estimation of the affine transformation, $\widehat{\phi}$, is performed using the constraints described is section 5.

The registration results of various illumination and pose conditions are illustrated in figures 3,4 and 5. The leftmost images show the observations, h. The middle images show $\widehat{h} = \widehat{f} \circ \widehat{\phi}$ - the estimated affine transform applied to the estimated illuminated template image. The rightmost images show the difference image of the support between the observation h and $\widehat{h}$.

7   Conclusion

We have introduced a novel image transformation, SMF, and demonstrated its properties and usage. We showed that the transformation can be used for registration in the presence of harsh illumination changes. The method is simple and requires only integrations of the image and linear equations solving, therefore it is computationally inexpensive.

References

1. Shashua, A.: Geometry and Photometry in 30 Visual Recognition. PhD thesis, MIT Dept of Brain and Cognitive Science (August 1992)
2. Hallinan, P.W.: A low-dimensional representation of human faces for arbitrary lighting conditions. In: Proceedings of the IEEE Conference on Computer Vision and Pattern Recognition, pp. 995–999 (1994)
3. Belhumeur, P., Kriegman, D.: What Is the Set of Images of an Object under All Possible Lighting Conditions. Intl J. Computer Vision 28, 245–260 (1998)
4. Basri, R., Jacobs, D.W.: Lambertian Reflectance and Linear Subspaces. IEEE Transactions on Pattern Analysis and Machine Intelligence 25(2), 218–233 (2003)
5. Tuytelaars, T., Van Gool, L.: Matching Widely Separated Views Based on Affine Invariant Regions. Intl J. Computer Vision 1(59), 61–85 (2004)
6. Lowe, D.G.: Distinctive image features from scale-invariant keypoints. International Journal of Computer Vision 60(2), 91–110 (2004)
7. Matas, J., Chum, O., Urban, M., Pajdla, T.: Robust wide baseline stereo from maximally stable extremal regions. In: Proc. of British Machine Vision Conference, pp. 384–396 (2002)
8. Rahtu, E., Salo, M., Heikkila, J.: Affine invariant pattern recognition using multi-scale autoconvolution. IEEE Transactions on Pattern Analysis and Machine Intelligence 27(6), 908–918 (2005)
9. Flusser, J., Suk, T.: Pattern recognition by affine moment invariants. Pattern Recognition 26(1), 167–174 (1993)
10. Yang, Z., Cohen, F.S.: Cross-weighted moments and affine invariants for image registration and matching. IEEE Trans. Pattern Analysis and Machine Intelligence 21(8), 804–814 (1999)
11. Petrou, M., Kadyrov, A.: Affine invariant features from the trace transform. IEEE Trans. Pattern Analysis and Machine Intelligence 26(1), 30–44 (2004)

12. Mindru, F., Tuytelaars, T., van Gool, L., Moons, T.: Moment Invariants for Recognition under Changing Viewpoint and Illumination. Computer Vision and Image Understanding 94, 3–27 (2004)
13. Francos, J.M., Hagege, R., Friedlander, B.: Estimation of Multi-Dimensional Homeomorphisms for Object Recognition in Noisy Environments. In: Thirty Seventh Asilomar Conference on Signals, Systems, and Computers (2003)
14. Frenkel, R., Francos, J.: Registration of geometric deformations in the presence of varying illumination. In: Proc. IEEE International Conference on Image Processing 2007, vol. 3, pp. 489–492 (2007)
15. Bentolila, K., Francos, J.: Affine and Illumination Estimation Using Scale Manipulation Transform (to appear)

Real-Time Descriptorless Feature Tracking*

Antonio L. Rodríguez, Pedro E. López-de-Teruel, and Alberto Ruiz

[1] Dpto. Ingeniería y Tecnología de Computadores, University of Murcia (Spain)
[2] Dpto. Lenguajes y Sistemas, University of Murcia (Spain)
arodriguez@ditec.um.es, {pedroe,aruiz}@um.es

Abstract. This paper presents a simple and efficient estimator of long-term sparse optical flow. It is supported by a novel approach to feature tracking, essentially based on global coherence of local movements. Expensive invariant appearance descriptors are not required: the locations of salient points in successive frames provide enough information to create a large number of accurate and stable tracking histories which remain alive for significantly long times. Hence, wide-baseline matching can be achieved both in extremely regular scenes and in cases in which corresponding points are photometrically very different. Our experiments show that this method is able to robustly maintain in real time hundreds of trajectories in long video sequences using a standard computer.

1 Introduction

Robust detection and tracking of a large number of features along video sequences is a fundamental issue in many computer vision systems. Applications such as visual navigation, 3D reconstruction, visual SLAM or augmented reality, among many others, commonly base their operation on precise landmark tracking. Physical points are usually chosen for this task, as there are many well known efficient algorithms for detecting them from scratch (see [1] for a good review) as well as for tracking them in time (based mainly in the local photometric structure of the image around the detected point, such as in the classical approach [2]). Another reason is their superior geometrical relevance, which allows to get more interimage constraints. Using the 2D position of the tracked points along the sequence, the 3D structure of the original landmarks can be inferred, taking advantage of well established multiple view geometry results [3] [4] and on-line bayesian approaches [5] [6].

More recently, new multiscale interest point detectors and associated descriptors for matching have also been developed, perhaps being SIFT [7] and MSER [8] the most known and widely used. These are clearly more powerful for wide baseline matching, but are also more computationally expensive and hence less amenable for real time systems running in standard low cost off-the-self hardware. (Considerable research effort is being devoted to obtain efficient implementations in alternative computing platforms like GPUs [9] or FPGAs [10]). In

---

* This work has been supported by the Spanish MEC and European FEDER funds under grants "TIN2006-15516-C04-03" and Consolider "CSD2006-00046".

P. Foggia, C. Sansone, and M. Vento (Eds.): ICIAP 2009, LNCS 5716, pp. 853–862, 2009.
© Springer-Verlag Berlin Heidelberg 2009

any case, their multiscale invariance makes these features more appropriate for object recognition and classification under very different viewpoints.

In this paper, however, we are interested in continuous tracking, where the key issues are (a) precise localization of points at the finest possible scale, (b) a fast and robust detection/tracking procedure and (c) the ability to track large number of points along the maximum possible number of frames. Point matching algorithms are classically based on comparisons of local image patches (whether using the original, normalized, filtered, gradient, or other kind of more or less complex preprocessing of each patch). This adds some computational load to the tracking system which does not scale well with the number of features. Thus, they are commonly used for off-line video processing applications [3], but are less amenable for real time continuous tracking. Anyway, when largely simplified [6], or when used only on a small and well conditioned set of selected points [5], such methods are remarkably successful.

In contrast, we focus on pure 2D location to improve efficiency and scalability in the number of tracked points[1]. We completely discard the local photometric structure of the environment of each point, exploiting continuity and global coherence of the movement to guide matching. The proposed method uses a *detection stage* based on aggregated salience of the Determinant of Hessian (DoH) operator [1], followed by the estimation of a coarse *holistic* feature motion model based on a variation [11] of RANSAC [12]. Our experiments show that this *descriptorless* approach is viable, efficient and scalable, allowing for long-term tracking of 3D points whose 2D appearance changes along the sequence.

The paper is organized as follows. Section 2 gives an overview of the proposed method. Then, sections 3 and 4 respectively describe in detail the two main stages, saliency detection and robust tracking. In section 5 we present performance measurements in realistic scenarios, which justify the validity of the approach. Finally, section 6 provides the main conclusions of this work.

2   General Overview of the Approach

The proposed feature tracker works in three stages:

- First, salient points are detected in the input image to obtain an initial set of features suitable to be tracked. Any kind of point detector could in principle be used in this stage, but for better performance the detector should be repeatable and stable, and must obtain accurate point locations. This is important for our *descriptorless* approach, as the posterior matching process will be based only in position information. In order to get a good balance between speed and accuracy, we will use a simple saliency operator based on local maxima of aggregated image nonlinearity, as measured by the DoH operator [1], which shows remarkable repeatability. This detector will be further discussed in Sec. 3.

---

[1] The system described in [6] also focuses on scalability, but rather in the map of tracked 3D features and the associated uncertainty management procedure than in the process of detection and tracking of 2D points itself.

Fig. 1. Illustration of the alignment process. Left and center: salient points and a rectangle indicating the best metric transformation relating two frames. (For clarity we only show a few points and very distant, non successive frames). Right: Green points aligned and superimposed on the red points. Observe that most points are closely aligned, while for some others there is no matching.

– In a second stage we estimate the 2D metric motion model which best aligns the points detected in successive frames. This is a clearly incorrect model for the 2D projection of most movements in a real 3D scene. Even so, a 2D projective model for the local movement of image features is approximately correct if the camera centers are close in successive images. If the angles between optical axes are also small, such homography approximately reduces to a metric transformation. Therefore, these approximations are acceptable for reasonably continuous interframe movements.

   Note that due to point detection failures and the limitations of the simplified motion model, in many cases some of the detected points will not have a matching counterpart in the previous image. Some kind of sample consensus estimation [12] is required. To allow for real-time computation, only a reduced set of the most salient points is used at this stage (much like in the PROSAC technique described in [11]). A simple motion predictor assuming constant velocity guides and bounds the search. Section 4 describes this robust estimator in detail.

– In the last stage we compute the largest set of point correspondences consistent with the estimated metric transformation. Figure 1 illustrates point alignment for two sample images.

3   Salient Point Detector

Our point detector is based on the Determinant of the Hessian (DoH) filter. For an input image $I(x, y)$, the value of the response image is defined as follows:

$$H(x,y) = \begin{vmatrix} \frac{\partial^2 I(x,y)}{\partial^2 x} & \frac{\partial^2 I(x,y)}{\partial x \partial y} \\ \frac{\partial^2 I(x,y)}{\partial x \partial y} & \frac{\partial^2 I(x,y)}{\partial^2 y} \end{vmatrix} \quad (1)$$

The determinant is strongly positive on blob-like regions [1,7], and negative on saddle points. Both cases indicate significant non-linearity in the locality of a point and are equally important for feature detection. We are interested in regions which, due to the presence of a blob, a corner, a textured zone, or similar

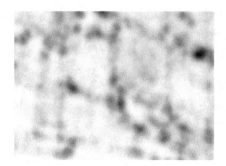

Fig. 2. Illustration of the saliency operator. Left: output of the smoothed absolute value of the DoH (σ_{post}=6). Darker zones correspond to locally nonlinear regions. Right: strong local maxima of the operator indicate stable and repeatable features.

situations, cannot be well approximated linearly. Poorly localized structures like flat gray level zones and simple straight edges must be discarded. In order to detect strongly salient nonlinear regions we take a local average of the absolute value of the DoH response in (1). We apply a previous gaussian filter to the input image with σ_{pre} to reduce noise and select the working scale. In practice $\sigma_{pre} \approx 2.0$ or 4.0 is acceptable in most cases, and in principle the algorithm is not very sensitive to this value.

After obtaining the absolute DoH response image, we estimate the aggregated local saliency by a second gaussian filter, this time using a larger σ_{post}. The effect of this parameter is grouping small textured zones in a unique maximum response point. Thus, increasing σ_{post} will hopefully make the position of the local maxima of the response more stable, possibly at the cost of diminishing the number of totally tracked points. In practice, σ_{post} should be chosen such that the positive and negative contiguous DoH peaks in a corner are joined in just one output peak. Values of σ_{post} around 6.0 or 8.0 are in principle adequate for small/medium scale point detection, though this parameter can be tuned to work at varying levels of detail (more on this on the experiments section). Figure 2 illustrates our saliency operator on a sample image.

As we will see in the next section, the alignment process requires detected points being sorted by relevance. The smoothed absolute value of the DoH filter response at each point, which is closely related to detection repeatability in successive frames, can be directly used for this task.

4   Robust Mapping Estimation

Simplified metric 2D motion model. Under the global metric model assumed for feature motion, the locations of two corresponding points $(x, y, 1)$ and $(x', y', 1)$ are related by the following expression:

$$\begin{pmatrix} x' \\ y' \\ 1 \end{pmatrix} = \begin{pmatrix} s\cos(\alpha) & -s\sin(\alpha) & \Delta x \\ s\sin(\alpha) & s\cos(\alpha) & \Delta y \\ 0 & 0 & 1 \end{pmatrix} \begin{pmatrix} x \\ y \\ 1 \end{pmatrix} \qquad (2)$$

This model has four parameters: global scale s, rotation α, and displacements Δx and Δy. They are completely determined from just two point correspondences.

PROSAC motion model estimation. Robust estimation proceeds as follows. In order to increase the probability of finding a valid motion model earlier in the search procedure, we initially select only the (hopefully) most repeatable points from each image. In our case, we use the N_{max} points with greater absolute value of the local maxima of the DoH. A naive initial approach would result then in a maximum of $N_{max} \times N_{max}$ candidate pairs[2], though in practice, as we will see shortly, we will reduce this number by more than an order of magnitude using a simple and efficient heuristic.

To get an initial guess for interimage correspondence, we assume that the camera performs a smooth movement. Therefore, the metric mapping to be estimated for the current image will be similar to that of the previous one[3]. Given a candidate point correspondence $(x, y) \mapsto (x', y')$, and the current metric motion model $E^{(t)} = (z^{(t)}, \alpha^{(t)}, \Delta x^{(t)}, \Delta y^{(t)})$, we define the following distance:

$$\mathcal{D}\left(E^{(t)}, (x, y) \mapsto (x', y')\right) = \left\| \begin{pmatrix} x' \\ y' \\ 1 \end{pmatrix} - \begin{pmatrix} z^{(t)} \cos(\alpha^{(t)}) & -z^{(t)} \sin(\alpha^{(t)}) & \Delta x^{(t)} \\ z^{(t)} \sin(\alpha^{(t)}) & z^{(t)} \cos(\alpha^{(t)}) & \Delta y^{(t)} \\ 0 & 0 & 1 \end{pmatrix} \begin{pmatrix} x \\ y \\ 1 \end{pmatrix} \right\|$$

Instead of using every possible matching in the search, we can use only the matchings between each point p_0 in the previous image and the n points (where n is a constant value) closer to its estimated location $E^{(t)} p_0$ in the current image. This speeds-up the search considerably, because the number of candidate matchings is reduced from $N_{max} \times N_{max}$ to $n \times N_{max}$. Our tests indicate that a value of $n = 4$ is enough to obtain the same results as using the whole $N_{max} \times N_{max}$ candidate matchings set in the PROSAC search[4].

The $n \times N_{max}$ candidates are then sorted according to the following simple heuristic value:

$$\mathcal{L}\left(E^{(t)}, (x, y) \mapsto (x', y')\right) = e^{-\mathcal{D}\left(E^{(t)}, (x,y) \mapsto (x',y')\right)}$$

A high value of $\mathcal{L}$ for a given matching indicates that the correspondence is more likely to be valid, and should be used earlier in the sample consensus search.

In each step, two possible correspondence pairs are taken from the list of sorted candidates to compute a new tentative metric movement model $E^{(t+1)}$.

---

[2] For example, a value of $N_{max} = 50$ leads to 2500 candidate matchings.

[3] A more elaborate Kalman filter estimator could also be used, possibly taking into account angular and linear velocities. In practice, our simple constant velocity predictor works remarkably well even for moderate camera accelerations, and our tests indicate that the Kalman filter does not produce a significant improvement in the tracker accuracy.

[4] For $N_{max} = 50$ and $n = 4$, this reduces the number of candidates matching from 2500 to only 200.

Fig. 3. Wide baseline matching after continuous tracking of 100 frames. For clarity only a small number of correspondences are shown. Observe the very different local photometric structure of corresponding points in most matchings.

This model is evaluated against the remaining correspondences in the list. If the model explains (up to a given distance threshold τ) the motion of a sufficient number (N_{min}) of features, the search finishes and the model is considered to be valid. Again, any sensible approximate choice of these parameters will work without affecting too much the behaviour of the algorithm (say, for example, $\tau \approx 10$ pixels, and $N_{min} \approx 0.5 N_{max}$, depending also on the quality of the optics and the clarity of the images obtained by the camera). Observe that local feature descriptors are not required for matching, even if the interframe displacements are larger than the typical distances between features in a given frame. Global motion coherence is sufficient to estimate an initial set of valid correspondences just from position information.

This is a straightforward application of PROSAC [11], a variation of the RANSAC robust estimation technique which uses heuristic information to significantly increase the probability of finding a valid model earlier in the search. This is mandatory in real-time applications.

Global set of matches and model refinement. The estimated motion model is finally used to find the largest set of valid correspondences in the whole list of points (i.e., not limited to the N_{max} most salient ones). We consider a correspondence $p_i \mapsto q_j$, (with p_i in the first image, and q_i in the second) to be valid if (a) the closest point to $E^{(t+1)}p_i$ in the second image is q_j, (b) the closest point to $E^{(t+1)^{-1}}q_j$ in the first image is p_i, and (c) the distance between $E^{(t+1)}p_i$ and

Fig. 4. Sample frames taken from test videos. Left to right: *floor-texture.avi, paper-mountain.avi, table-1.avi, table-2.avi, template-2.avi.*

the q_j is smaller than a given threshold (we can use τ again in this step). The resulting matches can be used to reestimate the metric interframe motion model.

Continuous operation and matching hysteresis. Only features that are tracked through a sufficient number of frames are considered as correctly matched. This way, remaining outliers due to spurious features are finally discarded, while all the correctly tracked inliers remain stable even if their local image patches have radically changed (see Fig. 3).

An additional advantage of this approach is that it allows for easy recovery of lost features due to occlusion or temporary detection failure. If a feature is not detected in a given frame, the tracker keeps on estimating its location at each new frame using the global motion model. If it appears again early in the video sequence, tracking continues as if the point was never lost. Otherwise, after a given number of frames (UF_{max}, for maximum number of unmatched frames) tracking for this point is utterly finished.

5   Experimental Results

Robustness and efficiency of the proposed tracking algorithm have been evaluated in several realistic scenarios and operating conditions. Figure 4 shows a few sample frames taken from five test videos available at [13]. Unless otherwise stated, we used the following parameter values: in the point detection stage, the final corner response image was thresholded with an absolute value of 1000, to quickly eliminate low-response points. To obtain a feature point list with a reasonable size, it will contain at most 300 of the points with best corner response

Table 1. Performance of different stages of the algorithm. Central columns values are in milliseconds. The last column indicates the mean number of points per frame used in the matching stage.

	Size	Detection	Alignment	Matching	#points
	320x240	10.871	0.575	5.931	299.115
floor-texture.avi	480x360	21.218	0.641	5.655	300
	640x480	37.596	0.824	5.062	300
	320x240	8.961	0.493	2.483	138.869
paper-mountain.avi	480x360	17.716	0.516	5.566	277.777
	640x480	32.268	0.513	6.069	300
	320x240	8.24	0.537	2.766	152.401
table-1.avi	480x360	18.443	0.547	6.007	293.754
	640x480	32.227	0.528	5.989	300
	320x240	9.166	0.527	2.327	131.038
table-2.avi	480x360	18.414	0.597	5.383	262.102
	640x480	32.014	0.571	6.38	299.86
	320x240	8.71	0.487	2.931	149.431
template-2.avi	480x360	18.28	0.506	5.531	256.965
	640x480	32.629	0.553	6.156	285.374

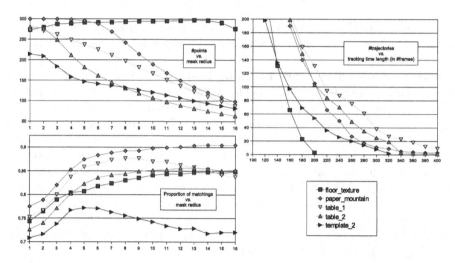

Fig. 5. Analysis of dynamic behaviour of the tracker: (Top left) σ_{pre} vs. mean number of points per frame. (Bottom left) σ_{pre} vs. mean proportion of matched points between consecutive frames. (Right) Total number and time lengths of the tracking trajectories.

image. The UF_{max} parameter for point hysteresis is set to 2 frames in the tests. The parameters σ_{pre}, σ_{post} and τ were set to 4.0, 8.0 and 8.0 respectively. Finally, the values $N_{max} = 30$, $N_{min} = 15$ achieve a good compromise between accuracy and computing time in the PROSAC stage.

All tests were performed on a 2.4 GHz Intel processor, using optimized low-level image processing routines from the Intel Integrated Performance Primitives (IPP) library.

Computing time performance: Table 1 shows the mean execution time per frame of the main computation stages, for three different typical input image sizes. Even for the largest 640×480 size, in every case the total computing time keeps below 40 ms (25 fps). The execution time also depends on the total number of points, so very textured videos, such as *floor-texture.avi*, show slightly slower processing rates. Anyway, the low level computation of saliency takes most of the computing time, so for smaller sizes (480×360 and 320×240), the detection stage becomes much faster. The posterior alignment and matching time depends on the total number of features rather than image size (though obviously these magnitudes are implicitly related).

Influence of σ_{post}: Obviously, this parameter has also a direct influence on the total number of points extracted in each frame. Figure 5 illustrates how smaller values of σ_{post} tend to increment the number of points (Fig. 5, top left), at the cost of making the detector less repeatable[5]. This clearly affects the proportion of matched points in successive frames (Fig. 5, bottom left).

---

[5] The X axis in top and bottom left graphs of Fig. 5 actually corresponds to the mask radius in pixels, equal to $2.5\sigma_{pre}$.

Fig. 6. Tracking examples (for clarity only a few trajectories are displayed). Left: Translation. Center: Zoom. Right: Rotation. By exploiting motion coherence we can track a large number of features in extremely regular textured scenes.

Tracking evaluation: Figure 5 (right) plots the number of tracked points vs. tracking time length (measured as consecutive frames). The algorithm obtains hundreds of correct trajectories during long time periods even in difficult scenes with large uniformly textured zones (*paper-mountain.avi*, *floor-texture.avi*). Note that classical approaches based on local patch descriptors are prone to fail in such situations. The shortest tracking trajectories were obtained in the *floor-texture.avi* and *template-2.avi* test videos, where, in the worst case, more than 100 points were tracked during more than 140 frames. Longer trajectories are obtained in sequences which focus on a specific object (*paper-mountain.avi*, *table-1.avi* and *table-2.avi*). The best results are obtained in the *table-1.avi* test, where most objects never get out of sight, nor are occluded by other objects. More than 60 points are tracked for more than 280 frames, and up to 10 points for more than 400 frames. Figure 6 shows some snapshots of the tracking algorithm in action. We encourage the reader to download from [13] recorded real-time demonstrations of the dynamic behavior of this method.

6   Conclusion

This work demonstrates that appearance descriptors are not required for long-term, stable estimation of sparse optical flow. Global motion coherence is sufficient to remove feature matching ambiguity, even in scenes with undifferentiated texture. This is an advantageous alternative for wide-baseline matching, since invariant keypoint characterization is achieved just by spatio-temporal continuous history.

The proposed tracking method is remarkably efficient in computation time: our experiments show that hundreds of points can be tracked during dozens of seconds in video sequences with rich camera movements. This approach opens up new possibilities for applying in real-time many geometric reconstruction algorithms based on interframe relationships.

References

1. Schmid, C., Mohr, R., Bauckhage, C.: Evaluation of interest point detectors. International Journal of Computer Vision 37(2), 151–172 (2000)
2. Shi, J., Tomasi, C.: Good features to track. Proc. of IEEE Computer Vision and Pattern Recognition Conference, 593–600 (1994)
3. Pollefeys, M., VanGool, L.: Visual modeling: from images to images. Journal of Visualization and Computer Animation 13, 199–209 (2002)
4. Hartley, R., Zisserman, A.: Multiple View Geometry in Computer Vision, 2nd edn. Cambridge University Press, Cambridge (2003)
5. Davison, A.J., Molton, N.D.: MonoSLAM: Real-time single camera SLAM. IEEE Trans. on PAMI 29(6), 1052–1067 (2007)
6. Rosten, E., Drummond, T.: Fusing points and lines for high performance tracking. In: Proc. of the IEEE ICCV conference, pp. 1508–1515 (2005)
7. Lowe, D.: Distinctive image features from scale-invariant keypoints. International Journal of Computer Vision 20, 91–110 (2003)
8. Matas, J., Chum, O., Urban, M., Pajdla, T.: Robust wide baseline stereo from maximally stable extremal regions. In: Proc. of the BMVC, pp. 384–393 (2002)
9. Heymann, S., Maller, K., Smolic, A., Froehlich, B., Wiegand, T.: SIFT implementation and optimization for general-purpose GPU. In: Proc. of Int. Conf. in Central Europe on Computer Graphics, Visualization and Computer Vision (2007)
10. Se, S., Nge, H., Jasiobedzki, P., Moyung, T.: Vision based modeling and localization for planetary exploration rovers. In: Proc. of Int. Astronautical Congress (2004)
11. Chum, O., Matas, J.: Matching with PROSAC - Progressive sample consensus. In: Proc. of the IEEE CVPR, pp. 220–226 (2005)
12. Fischler, M.A., Bolles, R.C.: Random sample consensus: A paradigm for model fitting with applications to image analysis and automated cartography. Communications of the ACM 24(6), 381–395 (1981)
13. PARP Group homepage (2009), http://perception.inf.um.es/tracker/

Adaptive Sharpening with Overshoot Control

Antonio Buemi, Gaetano Santoro, Arcangelo Bruna, and Mirko Guarnera

ST Microelectronics, AST Catania Lab, Imaging Group
Stradale Primosole, 50 - 95121 Catania, Italy
{antonio.buemi, gaetano.santoro, arcangelo.bruna,
mirko.guarnera}@st.com

Abstract. This paper presents the Adaptive Sharpening with Overshoot Control (ASOC), an algorithm for digital image contrast enhancement. The ASOC exploits a properly defined band-pass filter in order to better discriminate the "uniform/not uniform" zones of the input (blurred) image. A more aggressive sharpening is then performed on the textured zones, whilst the homogeneous regions are preserved.

Keywords: sharpening, gradients, band pass filters, overshoot.

1 Introduction

The principal target of the sharpening in digital images [1] is to highlight fine details in an image or to enhance blurred images. Since not only edges or details but any discontinuity in the image could be enhanced by a trivial approach, one of the most important objectives in a sharpening algorithm design is providing sharpening without introducing noise amplification and the so-called ringing effects. Considering the typical horizontal profile of an edge (Fig.1), the target is making steeper such intensity profile. Several approaches have been presented in literature. The simplest algorithms (both conceptually and computationally) to the problem are the Unsharp Masking (UM) techniques [2],[3],[4]. Such methods are based on the idea of adding a high passed version Z of the original image I to the input image, yielding the enhanced image Y:

$$Y(m,n)=I(m,n)+Z(m,n)\bullet \lambda \qquad (1)$$

where λ is an "enhance factor", used in order to modulate the strength of the filter. Different methods of UM for image enhancement are compared in the same condition in [2]. The results of such analysis show that the majority of the UM algorithms are very sensitive to the enhancement factor λ thus, for a good sharpening algorithm, this parameter must be adapted pixel by pixel with a recursive estimation, taking into account the statistics of neighboring pixel values. It increases the computational cost of the algorithm. An appropriate filter definition is a basic issue for the sharpening approach that uses sharpening masks in order to perform spatial filtering able to enhance the high contrast areas much more than the low contrast areas of the image. Using a filter properly defined, a good estimation of the local dynamics of the input

P. Foggia, C. Sansone, and M. Vento (Eds.): ICIAP 2009, LNCS 5716, pp. 863–872, 2009.
© Springer-Verlag Berlin Heidelberg 2009

Fig. 1. Horizontal graylevel profile of an edge

image may be obtained performing an adaptive sharpening and avoiding noise amplification too. In [5], [6] are described several methods that exploit the Human Visual System properties and accurate filter definition in order to achieve contrast enhancement. An ad hoc sharpening filter definition method is described in [7].

The histogram equalization algorithms for contrast enhancement [1] represent a good tradeoff between simplicity and effectiveness. Global histogram equalization methods define a transform function depending on the whole image histogram information. Such transform allows stretching the contrast of high histogram region and compressing the contrast of the low histogram region. The simplicity of such procedure makes it appreciable for the efficiency of the algorithm, but limits the contrast improvement. The local histogram equalization approaches provide better results in terms of image quality because they allows to adapt the contrast strength to local brightness features of the input images, even if such improvement involves all pixels in the image and implies a consequent complexity grow. Nevertheless, the complexity could be reduced by splitting the histogram in partially overlapped sub-blocks and processing them independently [8]. Overlapping of such sub regions allow to avoid undesired blocking effects, too. Other approaches tried exploiting other image domains. A solution for sharpening compressed images in the Discrete Cosine Transform domain has been proposed in [9]. Such technique is applied to images compressed using the JPEG standard. The sharpening is achieved by suitably scaling each element of the encoding quantization table to enhance the high-frequencies of the image. The modified version of the encoding table is then transmitted in lieu of the original, thus the sharpening is performed without affecting compressibility. The wavelet domain is also suitable for sharpening algorithm development since allows local adaptation in smooth and non-smooth parts due to the theoretical link between wavelets and smoothness spaces, as discussed in [10]. Since conventional 2D wavelet transforms are separable, do they cannot represent non-separable structures of the image, e.g. directional curves, Nezhadarya et alii [11] proposed an innovative method to improve the sharpening of the input image using the so-called *contourlet* transform, whose directionality feature makes it suitable for representation of curves and edges in the image. Several solutions based on fuzzy logic have been also developed. In [11] a fuzzy bidirectional flow framework based on generalized fuzzy sets is proposed. A fuzzy operator is also defined in [13]. An adaptive fuzzy method for image contrast enhancement has been recently proposed in [14]. It is based on defining adaptively smooth and sharp parameters calculating the difference between the gray value of each pixel and the median of its neighborhood. The main goal of such approach is discerning among noisy, flat and high frequencies region of the image and joining noise reduction and contrast enhancement steps.

Traditional edge sharpening methods mainly increases the intensity differences across an edge, but the edge width remains unchanged, thus this kind of approaches produce only limited effects for wide and very blurred edges. An algorithm that performs the sharpening across the edge and also reduces the edge width is presented in [15]. The algorithm discussed in this paper is an efficient solution based on a 5x5 band-pass filter and designed to reduce the main drawbacks of most of the sharpening techniques: the noise amplification and the ringing effects. Since the contrast of edge in the image is usually achieved by raising the intensity of the brighter side of an edge and lowering the intensity of the darker side (Fig. 1), overshoots are introduced along both sides of the edges yielding the ringing effect. Solutions for this problem are also proposed in [16] and [17]. The algorithm ADSOC proposed in [17], in particular, is based on a 5x5 filter mask and it retrieves directions information to obtain a better sharpening along the edges. Our solution reduces the noise amplification thanks to a band-pass filter and using a simply noise control, whilst an over/undershoot control block has been developed in order to manage the ringing effect.

The rest of the document is organized as follows: the section 2 describes the ASOC; the section 3 presents an analysis of the algorithms performances in comparison with other techniques; the section 4 includes conclusions and final remarks.

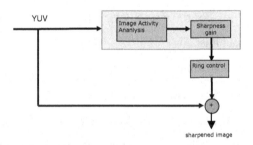

Fig. 2. Adaptive sharpening basic scheme

2   Algorithm Description

The Fig. 2 shows a simplified scheme of the Adaptive Sharpening with Overshoot Control (ASOC) algorithm. It consists on three basic steps:

- *Image Activity Analysis*: a band-pass filter is applied in order to discern the homogeneous and the textured regions of the image. A noise check is also enabled in order to avoid noise amplification.
- *Sharpness Gain computation*: the sharpness gain is the band-pass filter response that should be added to the input image in order to achieve sharpening.
- *Ringing Control*: an undershoot/overshoot control system is implemented in order to reduce unpleased ringing effects.

2.1 Image Activity Analysis

This is the main step of the algorithm because it allows to find the zones of the image where the sharpening should be performed. Since the real borders and edges in images are not abrupt transitions but heavy gradients (due to optics and preprocessing on the camera), the ASOC uses Band Pass Filters. In fact this kind of filters is able to:

- highlight less the very high frequencies than the medium frequencies (border slopes);
- reduce the noise amplification;
- preserve gradients;

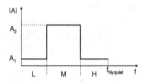

Fig. 3. Band Pass Filter frequency response

the noise amplification is reduced according to the following considerations. Let the image signal $\hat{s}(x, y)$ affected by a additive noise $\eta(x,y)$ be:

$$\hat{s}(x, y) = s(x, y) + \eta(x, y) \tag{2}$$

In the frequency domain it is:

$$\hat{S}(u, v) = S(u, v) + N(u, v). \tag{3}$$

If we consider the signal as sum of band signal:

$$S(u, v) = S_L + S_M + S_H \quad \text{and} \quad N(u, v) = N_L + N_M + N_H. \tag{4}$$

Where L, M and H represent the Low, Medium and High Signal components.
Let now consider a pseudo-ideal HPF as shown in fig.3, with $A_2 \gg A_1$. If we apply the HPF to $\hat{s}(x, y)$, then:

$$HPF \cdot \hat{S} = (S_L + N_L)A_1 + (S_M + N_M)A_2 + (S_H + N_H)A_1 \cong (S_M + N_M)A_2. \tag{5}$$

The Sharpening is normally:

$$S_{SHARP} = \hat{S} + \alpha(HPF \cdot \hat{S}) \cong S + N + \alpha(S_M + N_M)A_2. \tag{6}$$

In the Edge zones the S_M signal has an amplitude greater than the N_M noise, then in edge zones:

$$S_{SHARP} \cong S + N + \alpha A_2 S_M \tag{7}$$

In non edge zones the residual $A_2 N_M$ can be minimized by using proper edge detection techniques.

Fig. 4 shows the frequency response and the mask of the 5x5 band-pass filter used in the ASOC. Only the pixels of the images whose the filter response is greater than a given threshold *th* are processed, because they are assumed falling in textured regions of the image. This threshold resolve the problem of the above residual noise term. The main drawback of the thresholding is that some residual noise may remain, and thus highlighted. This noise is no more Gaussian, because it becomes "salt and pepper" and thus a median based analysis or morphological is required [18].

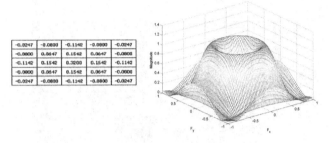

Fig. 4. The 5x5 band-pass filter used in the second step of the ASOC algorithm

We analyze the surrounding in order not to remove this "generated" noise but to identify it and do not highlight it through the HPF. For this reason we define a new noise level *noise_th* . For each pixel P under examination (Fig. 5), the minimum and the maximum of eight pixels of the 5x5 block are computed. If the condition:

$$(max\text{-}min) < noise\_th \quad \text{with} \quad Max=max\{X1,...,X8\}, \; Min=min\{X1,...,X8\} \tag{8}$$

is true, the luminance of the pixel P remains unchanged. Otherwise, the sharpening is performed.

X1	X2	X3
X4	P	X5
X6	X7	X8

Fig. 5. 5x5 window used in the noise control block

When the noise control is activated, the number of isolated processed pixels decreases, whilst the quality of the final image increases. The improvement is much more visible in the enlarged detail showed in Fig. 6.

2.2 Sharpness Gain Computation

The ASOC mainly depends on two parameters:

Threshold: the region classification of the images depends on the chosen threshold, which affects the noise sensitivity of the algorithm according to a coring function. If the energy (that is the BFP applied to a pixel surrounding) is lower than this threshold, the pixel analyzed is left unsharpened.

The noise threshold can be a function of the estimated noise variance of the image [19]: *Threshold* = $f(\sigma_{noise})$

Gain: sharpness boost. For each pixel P_{in}, the sharpened value is given by:

$$P_{out}=P_{in}+(sharp*gain) \tag{9}$$

Obviously the sharpness effect grows with the gain.

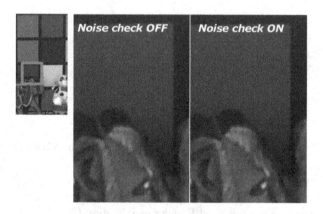

Fig. 6. Output of the ASOC with the noise check

2.3 Ringing Control

The under/overshoots control is performed exploiting the information concerning the local dynamic of the image which are used to reduce the sharpening side effects.

The value "sharp" to be added (for each pel) to the original luminance value P_{in} is computed as in the algorithm discussed in the previous section, that is the response of the band-pass filter computed by a mask of size n x n.

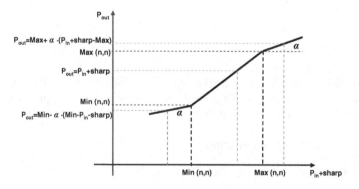

Fig. 7. Ringing effect control scheme

If the sharpened value $P_{out}=P_{in}+sharp$ falls in the range *[Min,..., Max]*, with *Min=minimum(n,n)* and *Max=maximum(n,n)*, it remains unchanged (Fig. 7). If P_{out} is out of range, the overshot effect is reduced simply making smaller the gain between the sharpened value and the maximum (or minimum) of the block. The number of "control levels" *l* could be fixed arbitrary. The *"strength"* of the overshot is the parameter that allows to vary the distance between the maximum/minimum value of the block and the sharpened value. The chart showed in Fig. 7 describes the ringing control geometry. Thus, the sharpened value Pout is given by:

$$P_{out} = \begin{cases} Max + \alpha \cdot (Pin + sharp\text{-}Max) & \text{if} & Pin + sharp > Max(n,n) \\ Pin + sharp & \text{if} & Pin + sharp \in [Min(n,m), Max(n,n)] \\ Min\text{-} \alpha(Min\text{-}Pin\text{-}sharp) & \text{if} & Pin + sharp < Min(n,n) \end{cases} \quad (9)$$

where

$$\alpha = \begin{cases} 0 & \text{if} & strength = 0 \\ \dfrac{strength}{l} & \text{if} & strength \in [1,...l] \end{cases} \quad (10)$$

Thus, if $\alpha = 0$ then $P_{out}=Max$ and no overshot is created, whilst if is $\alpha = 1$, the ringing control is disabled.

Observe that a slight ring makes the image more natural, whilst the absence of ringing may produce the unpleased effect of a flat image, thus in general is advised to enable a minimum overshoot.

3   Experimental Results

In order to evaluate the performances of the ASOC, the algorithm has been compared with several sharpening techniques. In particular, the following methods have been implemented and compared: AUM: Adaptive Unsharp Masking [3], RUM: Rational Unsharp Masking [4], ADSOC: Adaptive Sharpening with Overshoot Control [17]. The AUM is based on the idea of applying a different contrast level enhancement depending on the local dynamics of the images of interest. It employs a Gauss-Newton strategy to update the parameters needed to modify the contrast level and some Laplacian operators to estimate the local dynamics of the image. The RUM is a non-linear method that uses a rational control term to balance the enhancement intensity. It avoids noise amplifications using a rational control factor to measure the local activity level in the image in order to distinguish high, medium and low contrasted areas. The AUM algorithm yields a well-balanced sharpening effect at the expense of a high computational complexity, while the RUM overcomes this disadvantage, but it suffers from a minor flexibility. The ADSOC is based on a 5x5 High-pass filter and exploits directional information extracted by the response of a filters' bank in order to yield the sharpened image. It exploits some directional information in order to perform a stronger sharpening across the directions of the edges in the input image. In particular the response of a 5x1 band-pass filter banks

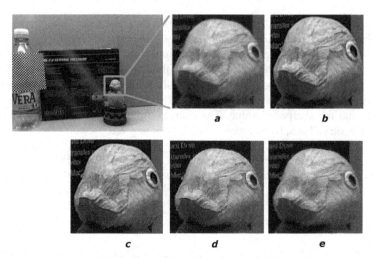

Fig. 8. Comparative tests (a) Input image. (b) Outputo of ADSOC. (c) Output of ASOC. (d) Output of the RUM. (e) Output of AUM.

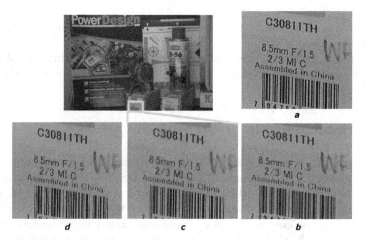

Fig. 9. (a) Image sharpened using ASOC. (b) Output of the ADSOC. (c) Output of the AUM. (d) Output obtained applying the RUM algorithm.

(see [17] for details) is used to compute the sharpness gain. If the pixel p under examination yields at least a filter response d_i greater than a fixed threshold $th2$, it corresponds to an edge region of the image, thus the intensity of p is adjusted to achieve sharpening. The estimated gain to be added to p is the response of the 5x1 filter corresponding to the direction orthogonal respect to d_i. The Fig. 8 shows comparative tests among the four algorithms described above. Note that both ADSOC and ASOC perform a strong sharpening, avoiding unpleasant ringing effects on the writing in the background. The RUM is not adaptive, so the contrast is enhanced indiscriminately in the whole image. The AUM algorithm allows to avoid ringing and artifacts, but the sharpening effect is reduced. Since the ringing effect is completely removed the image appears quite unnatural. Moreover the additional cost of the recursive process required by the AUM implies a large amount of additional resources, so it could be applied only in post-processing applications, whilst the other solutions are less expensive in terms of computational and memory cost.

The further example showed in Fig. 9 highlights the different performances of the ASOC and ADSOC in a critical case. The ADSOC introduces some artifact along the borders of the writing. Such undesired effect is produced by the directional tests that may give a different response for adjacent pixel, e.g. along a curve. A possible solution of this problem could be the use of high-pass filters in the directional test in order to obtain a more accurate response from the filters' bank. In the same example, the AUM provides a limited sharpening effect, the RUM introduces some unpleasant effect in the bottom of the picture.

4 Conclusions

An efficient sharpening algorithm has been presented. It is based on a band-pass filter able to discern uniform and detailed zones of the image in order to apply a balanced contrast enhancement. The proposed approach allows achieving sharpening with reduced noise amplification and ringing effect.

References

[1] Gonzales, R.C., Woods, R.E.: Digital Image Processing. 2, pp. 91-109/125-141. Prentice Hall, Englewood Cliffs (2002)
[2] Badamchizadeh, M.A., Aghagolzadeh, A.: Comparative Study Of Unsharp Masking Methods For Image Enhancement. In: Proceedings of the Third International Conference on Image and Graphics, ICIG 2004 (2004)
[3] Polesel, A., Ramponi, G., Mathews, V.J.: Image Enhancement via Adaptive Unsharp Masking. IEEE Trans. on Image Processing 9(3), 505–510 (2000)
[4] Ramponi, G., Polesel, A.: A Rational Unsharp Masking Technique. Journal of Electronic Imaging 7(2), 333–338 (1998)
[5] Baldrich, R., Vanrell, M., Benavente, R., Salvatela, A.: Color Image Enhancement Based On Perceptual Sharpening. In: Proceedings of International Conference on Image Processing (ICIP), September 14-17, vol. 3, pp. III–401–III–404 (2003)
[6] Marsi, S., Ramponi, G., Carrato, S.: Image Contrast Enhancement Using a Recursive Rational Filter. In: IEEE International Workshop on Imaging System and Techniques, Stresa, Italy (IST), May 14 (2004)
[7] Murphy, N.P.: Determining a Sharpening Filter for a Digital Image, European Patent, EP1411470A2, April 21 (2004)
[8] Kim, J.-Y., Kim, L.-S., Hwang, S.-H.: An Advanced Contrast Enhancement Using Partially Overlapped Sub-block Histogram Equalization. In: Proceedings of IEEE International symposium on Circuits and Systems (ISCAS 2000), May 28-31 (2000)
[9] Konstantinides, K., Bhaskaran, V., Beretta, G.: Image Sharpening in the JPEG Domain. IEEE Transactions On Image Processing 8(6) (June 1999)
[10] Berkner, K., Gormish, M.J., Schwartz, E.L., Bolielc, M.: A New Wavelet-Based Approach to Sharpening and Smoothing of Images in Besov Spaces with Applications to Deblurring, September 10-13, vol. 3, pp. 797–800 (2000)

[11] Nezhadarya, E., Shamsollahi, M.B.: Image Contrast Enhancement by Contourlet Transform. In: 48th International Symposium ELMAR-2006, June 07-09 (2006)

[12] Fu, S.: Fuzzy Bidirectional Flow for Adaptive Image Sharpening. In: IEEE International Conference on Image Processing, ICIP 2005, September 11-14, vol. 1, pp. 917–920 (2005)

[13] Russo, F., Ramponi, G.: A Fuzzy Operator for the Enhancement of Blurred and Noisy Images. IEEE Transactions on Image Processing 4(8) (August 1995)

[14] Chen, D., Qian, Y.: An Improved Algorithm of Adaptive Fuzzy Image Enhancement. In: International Symposium on Computer Science and Computational Technology (2008)

[15] Chung, M.K., Kee, D., Leu, J.-G.: Edge sharpening through ramp width reduction. Image and Vision Computing 18(6), 501–514 (2000)

[16] Li, X.: Luminance Enhancement With Overshoot Reduction Control Based on Chrominance Information, US Patent 6453068, September 17 (2002)

[17] Buemi, A., Santoro, G., Bruna, A., Guarnera, M.: Adaptive Directional Sharpening with Overshoot Control. Electronic Imaging, January 27-31 (2008)

[18] Wang, Z., Zhang, D.: Progressive switching median filter for the removal of impulse noise from highly corrupted images. Circuits and Systems II: IEEE Trans on Analog and Digital Signal Processing 46(1), 78–80 (1999)

[19] Bruna, A., Bosco, A., Smith, S., Tomaselli, V.: Fast noise level estimation using a convergent multiframe approach. In: IEEE International conference on image processing (ICIP 2006), October 8-11 (2006)

Applying Visual Object Categorization and Memory Colors for Automatic Color Constancy

Esa Rahtu[1], Jarno Nikkanen[2], Juho Kannala[1],
Leena Lepistö[2], and Janne Heikkilä[1]

[1] Machine Vision Group
University of Oulu, Finland
[2] Nokia Corporation
Visiokatu 3, 33720 Tampere, Finland
esa.rahtu@ee.oulu.fi,jarno.nikkanen@nokia.com

Abstract. This paper presents a framework for using high-level visual information to enhance the performance of automatic color constancy algorithms. The approach is based on recognizing special visual object categories, called here as memory color categories, which have a relatively constant color (e.g. the sky). If such category is found from image, the initial white balance provided by a low-level color constancy algorithm can be adjusted so that the observed color of the category moves toward the desired color. The magnitude and direction of the adjustment is controlled by the learned characteristics of the particular category in the chromaticity space. The object categorization is performed using bag-of-features method and raw camera data with reduced preprocessing and resolution. The proposed approach is demonstrated in experiments involving the standard gray-world and the state-of-the-art gray-edge color constancy methods. In both cases the introduced approach improves the performance of the original methods.

Keywords: object categorization, category segmentation, memory color, color constancy, raw image.

1 Introduction

Color constancy is a characteristic feature of human visual system which causes the perceived color of objects to remain relatively constant under varying illumination conditions. It is also a desired property of digital cameras, which typically aim to reproduce the colors of the scene to look similar as they appeared to a human observer standing behind the camera when the image was taken. However, the response of digital camera sensors depends on the chromaticity of the illumination and this effect has to be compensated in order to achieve visually pleasing reproduction of colors. Therefore most cameras apply computational color constancy algorithms, also known as automatic white balancing algorithms, which estimate the illumination of the scene so that color distortions can be compensated [1,2].

P. Foggia, C. Sansone, and M. Vento (Eds.): ICIAP 2009, LNCS 5716, pp. 873–882, 2009.

The existing computational color constancy algorithms can be divided into two categories: the ones that require characterization of camera sensor response and the ones that do not. Examples of the former category are color by correlation [3] and gamut mapping algorithms [4], whereas the gray-world [5] or gray-edge [6] algorithms exemplify the other class. In large scale mass production of camera sensors, the color response of the sensors can vary from sample to sample. Having very strict limits for the color response would mean reduced yield and hence higher cost per sensor. Sample specific characterization is also possible, but that would have an impact on the sensor price as well. Consequently, the color constancy algorithms which do not rely heavily on accurate characterization information are useful in such cases in which the cost of the camera sensor is a very critical parameter. On the other hand, the accuracy of illumination estimates is typically better for the algorithms which utilize sensor characterization.

The common factor in the most of previous works on color constancy is that they are based on low-level image information. The use of object recognition in color constancy is considered in [7], but their approach requires that one or more of the exact training objects appear in the analyzed image. According to our knowledge the use of visual object categories is considered only in [8]. However the estimation method they present is based on purely utilizing the mean color values of the categories without any further analysis in the chromaticity domain. Moreover the evaluation method introduced there is rather expensive to compute.

The color constancy application that is considered in this paper is consumer photography with digital cameras, including mobile phone cameras. In this application visually pleasing color quality is more important than very precise color reproduction. Therefore, instead of sensor characterization, we investigate an approach which is based on analyzing the semantic content of images. That is, we aim to detect such object categories from the images which have memory colors associated with them. Such categories are, for example, foliage, grass, sky, sand and human skin [9]. Each of such objects have a limited range of chromaticities associated with them, referred to as memory color clusters hereinafter. Consequently, the initial estimate of white point, which can have error due to inaccurate characterization or poor algorithm performance, can be improved by modifying the white point in such way that the chromaticities of detected objects or surfaces fall closer to their corresponding memory color clusters.

In addition, many color constancy algorithms have difficulties in estimating the illumination chromaticity when there are only a few colors present in the image. This is the case for example for gamut mapping algorithms or gray-world and similar algorithms for obvious reasons. By utilizing the approach proposed in this paper it is possible to increase robustness also in these kinds of situations.

2   Memory Color Categories

The concept of memory color refers to such colors that are associated with familiar object categories in long term memory [10]. This concept is particularly useful in our application, where the goal is to provide visually pleasing colors and it is preferred to reproduce colors close to the corresponding memory colors. An essential characteristic of a memory color is the fact that it is defined in a relatively compact domain in the chromaticity space. In the following we describe how the memory colors used in this paper are learned from correctly white balanced sample images.

We collected a training dataset of 53 images illustrating the tested categories in different locations, time instants, and illuminations. For each training image we also associated a reference white point, which was based on illumination chromaticity measurements with Konica-Minolta CL-200 chroma meter. The reference points were used to white balance each training image according to the von Kries model [11,12]:

$$x_{wb} = G x_{raw} = s \begin{bmatrix} \frac{1}{w_R} & 0 & 0 \\ 0 & \frac{1}{w_G} & 0 \\ 0 & 0 & \frac{1}{w_B} \end{bmatrix} x_{raw}, \tag{1}$$

where w_R, w_G and w_B are the corresponding RGB-coordinates of the reference white point, $s = \max(w_R, w_G, w_B)$, and $x_{raw} = [R_{raw}, G_{raw}, B_{raw}]^T$ and $x_{wb} = [R_{wb}, G_{wb}, B_{wb}]^T$ are RGB-vectors of the raw and the white balanced pixels respectively. The scaling s is introduced to prevent the colorization of the saturated areas of the image.

After the white balancing the images need to be further converted from the sensor color space to a sensor-independent reference color space, which in our case is the linear RGB space (RGB_{lin}) with $sRGB$ [13] primaries (i.e. transformation from RGB_{lin} to $sRGB$ is obtained by applying the gamma correction [12]). The conversion is done using 3×3 sensor specific conversion matrix C_C as $x_{lin} = C_C x_{wb}$, where $x_{lin} = [R_{lin}, G_{lin}, B_{lin}]^T$ is the vector of the resulting RGB_{lin} values.

The RGB_{lin} training images were roughly hand segmented by defining a set of bounding boxes that capture the memory color categories. The pixels in these segments were converted to chromaticity space $[R_{lin}/G_{lin}, B_{lin}/G_{lin}]^T$ [12], where a mean value was computed for each category in each image. The final memory color domain was defined by an ellipse $(x - m_{ell})^T C_{ell}^{-1} (x - m_{ell}) = r_m^2$, where m_{ell} is the weighted mean of the segmented pixels over all training images and C_{ell} is the corresponding covariance matrix. The size r_m of the ellipse remained as a parameter. The weighting used was the number of segmented pixels per image. Figure 1(a) illustrates some examples of the training images and segmentations.

3   Proposed Framework

In this section we describe the details of the proposed approach. We start from the recognition of the memory color categories and then continue by introducing a method for the refinement of the initial color constancy estimate. The overall process is illustrated in Figure 1(b).

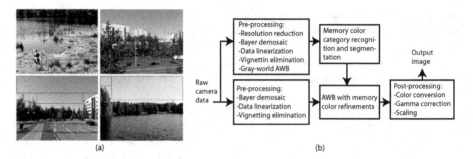

(a)   (b)

Fig. 1. (a) Examples of the training images and segmentations. (b) The overall image processing pipeline proposed in this paper (cf. [12]).

3.1   Category Recognition

The first step in the proposed process is to recognize the memory color categories. For this task we apply the widely used bag-of-words (BOW) method combined with a SVM classifier [14]. In BOW approach the image is described as a distribution over visual words, which are learned from the local visual descriptors of the training images using vector quantization. The local descriptors are computed from circular patches with radius 4, 8, and 12 pixels extracted on a regular grid with 10 pixel spacing. Each patch is described by one of the following three descriptors, gray scale SIFT [15], W-SIFT [16], or Centile [17], depending on the experiment. In the case of SIFT and W-SIFT the feature vectors were further reduced to 40 dimension using principal component analysis.

The vector quantization is performed by K-means clustering resulting in a vocabulary of 1000 words. In the SVM classifier we used Chi-squared kernel defined as $K(x,y) = e^{-\gamma \chi^2 (x,y)}$, where γ is a learned parameter and $\chi^2(x,y) = \sum_j (x_j - y_j)^2 / (x_j + y_j)$. The three different descriptors were chosen to examine the effects of different modalities in the recognition performance with our image data. SIFT, W-SIFT, represent two state-of-the-art texture based descriptor, where the first one applies only gray scale information and the second one includes also color modality. The Centile feature represents a simple method that exploits only color information.

Since we are interested in applying high-level color constancy estimation as an integral part of the camera's image processing pipeline (Fig. 1), we aim to make a fast recognition using the original raw data with clearly downscaled resolution. The data for the recognition may be achieved from the corresponding viewfinder image that is captured before the final image is taken. However due to the properties of raw camera data, some preprocessing is still essential.

The reduced pipeline we applied was the following: 1) remove the possible offset from the pixel raw values, 2) perform linear interpolation based Bayer pattern demosaicing, 3) downscale the image to 240 × 320, 4) perform gray-world white balancing. The normalization in step four was introduced in order to equalize the differences in color response between different models of camera sensors. The size 240 × 320 was selected to match the size of the viewfinder image in our camera system. One can refer to [12] for more comprehensive discussion and examples of camera systems.

3.2 Refining Color Constancy Approximation

The color constancy refinement takes place in the automatic white balancing stage of the processing pipeline illustrated in Figure 1(b). There we first make an initial estimation of the balance with some standard method, which in our experiments was taken to be either gray-world or gray-edge. These two reference algorithms were selected since they do not need any sensor characterization, which could be prohibitive in the case of low cost equipment. Furthermore the gray-edge algorithm [6] has been reported to achieve comparable results with the state of the art methods like gamut mapping [4] and color-by-correlation [3].

After the white balancing with the reference method, we take the category recognition result into account. If a memory color category is found, we perform fast approximate segmentation to the image. This is done by first converting the image pixels to RGB_{lin} and then to the chromaticity space $[R_{lin}/G_{lin}, B_{lin}/G_{lin}]^T$. In this space we take all pixels into the segment that lay inside the extended memory color ellipse. The ellipse is achieved from the corresponding memory color domain by extending the original ellipse size from r_m to r_s. For a satisfactory segmentation we must assume that chromaticities of the pixels are not too far from their true values. However we are only refining the result of the reference method, and we can assume that the solution is already reasonably close to the correct one. The experiments later illustrate that usually even the simple gray-world method produces an initial estimate that is close enough. Figure 2(a) illustrates results of the segmentation step.

Before refining the color constancy estimate, we verify that the memory color category covers more than given proportion p of the image area. The limitation is set in order to have enough support for the memory color for reliable refinement and to detect some of the missclassifications. If the support of the category is larger than the limit p, we compute the mean value m_{oRB} of the segmented pixels in $[R_{lin}/G_{lin}, B_{lin}/G_{lin}]^T$. The initial white balancing is then refined so that m_{sRB} moves to the closest point e_{sRB} at the corresponding memory color ellipse, if not inside the ellipse already. Given m_{sRB} and e_{sRB} the refined white balancing matrix is calculated as

$$p_1 = C_C^{-1} \left[e_{sRB}(1)\ 1\ e_{sRB}(2) \right]^T, \quad p_2 = C_C^{-1} \left[m_{sRB}(1)\ 1\ m_{sRB}(2) \right]^T, \quad (2)$$

$$G_{ref} = s \begin{bmatrix} p_1(1)/p_2(1) & 0 & 0 \\ 0 & p_1(2)/p_2(2) & 0 \\ 0 & 0 & p_1(3)/p_2(3) \end{bmatrix} G_{init}, \quad (3)$$

where $x(i)$ refers to i-th component of a vector x, G_{init} and G_{ref} are the initial and refined white balance matrices respectively, and s is such constant that the minimum value at the diagonal of G_{ref} is equal to one. From here the processing pipeline continues normally using now the estimated G_{ref} instead of G_{init} as a white balancing transformation.

(a)   (b)

Fig. 2. (a) Example results of the category segmentation. The pixels not included into segment are shown as white. (b) Samples of the final white balanced images in $sRGB$. The columns from left to right illustrate the white point estimation using gray-edge, refined gray-edge, and ground truth, respectively.

4   Experiments

To demonstrate the performance of our framework, we performed two kind of experiments. First we evaluated the memory color categorization and then the method for color constancy refinement. We begin with the categorization experiments.

4.1   Memory Color Categories

In these experiments we evaluate the method using two memory color categories, namely grass & foliage and sky. We collected seven datasets of raw images, each taken by different person with different sensor in a wide variety of time instants and places. The number of images in these sets were 377, 518, 508, 506, 319, 108, and 508. The images in the training sets were processed using the pipeline in Section 3.1 and hand labeled so that if the image contains significant portion of the memory color category it was tagged with the category label and otherwise not. This differs slightly from the traditional categorization, but since our goal at the end was to refine the color constancy estimation we were only interested in images, where the support for the category was large enough. Figures 2 and 3 illustrate some images used in the experiment.

The categorization system described in Section 3.1 was trained using six of the image sets, and then tested using the seventh one. For each of the descriptors, SIFT, W-SIFT, and Centile, we calculated the mean performance over the all seven combinations of test and training sets. The resulting classification performances are listed in Table 1. Each column gives the result for a train-test-split where the given set is used for testing.

Table 1. Mean classification performances for grass & foliage and sky categories. Each column gives the results for a train-test-split where given set is used as a test set.

Grass & foliage category:								
SIFT descriptor	set 1	set 2	set 3	set 4	set 5	set 6	set 7	**average**
True positive	74.3 %	83.7 %	85.9 %	88.0 %	74.2 %	66.7 %	92.6 %	**86.2 %**
False positive	8.8 %	4.8 %	2.7 %	15.7 %	7.5 %	13.1 %	12.6 %	**7.7 %**
W-SIFT descriptor								
True positive	82.9 %	80.6 %	93.7 %	96.4 %	81.8 %	54.2 %	96.3 %	**91.5 %**
False positive	3.3 %	2.6 %	1.1 %	15.2 %	5.9 %	8.3 %	15.1 %	**5.7 %**
Centile descriptor								
True positive	69.5 %	81.6 %	88.0 %	91.3 %	74.2 %	58.3 %	75.6 %	**81.2 %**
False positive	4.0 %	5.5 %	5.2 %	12.7 %	15.4 %	3.6 %	5.7 %	**7.4 %**
Sky category:								
SIFT descriptor	set 1	set 2	set 3	set 4	set 5	set 6	set 7	average
True positive	68.2 %	59.2 %	76.5 %	66.4 %	63.4 %	77.8 %	87.6 %	**73.7 %**
False positive	5.7 %	3.2 %	4.5 %	3.2 %	3.0 %	9.7 %	11.6 %	**5.1 %**
W-SIFT descriptor								
True positive	78.8 %	75.0 %	67.9 %	77.3 %	68.3 %	94.4 %	93.6 %	**81.1 %**
False positive	4.9 %	2.5 %	2.3 %	1.9 %	2.5 %	4.2 %	12.7 %	**4.1 %**
Centile descriptor								
True positive	50.8 %	68.4 %	71.6 %	64.8 %	61.0 %	80.6 %	91.4 %	**71.9 %**
False positive	3.8 %	2.5 %	4.5 %	4.2 %	3.8 %	5.6 %	8.4 %	**4.3 %**

The overall performance with the sky category seems to be lower than with grass & foliage category. This probably follows from the characteristic texture of the latter category compared to almost textureless sky. Furthermore we can observe that texture based features are performing better, but still computationally simple Centile features result relatively high recognition rate especially with grass & foliage category. In some cases one can also observe near 10% false positive rate. A closer look reveals that almost all of these images contain a little portion of the memory color category, but not enough to be labeled as positive in the ground truth. These images however rarely cause problems in the color constancy refinement, because of the limit in the segment size.

4.2 White Balance Refinements

For the fifth image set in the categorization experiment we also measured the illumination chromaticity with similar methods as in Section 2. These values were

Table 2. Relative improvements achieved. The left result refers to gray-world and right to gray-edge method as initial approximation.

Category	Δerr_{mean}	Δerr_{median}	number of images improved
grass & foliage	2.6 % / 5.6 %	14.3 % / 2.7 %	51.9 % / 61.4 %
sky	25.2 % / 1.9 %	29.1 % / 15.0 %	76.9 % / 57.5 %

Fig. 3. Samples of the final white balanced images in $sRGB$. The columns from left to right illustrate the white point estimation using gray-world, refined gray-world, and ground truth, respectively.

used as a ground truth in the following automatic white balancing experiment, where the initial color constancy, provided by a low-level reference method, was refined for those images, which were recognized to contain a memory color category. As reference methods we used both gray-world and gray-edge algorithms. The category labeling for the test set was taken from the results achieved with SIFT descriptor in the previous section. We selected SIFT instead of W-SIFT for this experiment since it was faster to evaluate. The framework used in the experiment was the one described in Section 3.2 with parameter values $r_m = 0.5$, $r_s = 3.0$, and $p = 10\%$, for the grass & foliage category and $r_m = 0.6$, $r_s = 2.0$, and $p = 25\%$, for the sky category. For the gray-edge method we applied parameter values $n = 1$, $p = 1$, and $\sigma = 6$, according to [6].

As an error measure we calculated angle difference of the white point coordinates $err = \cos^{-1}(\hat{w}_{true} \cdot \hat{w}_{estim})$, where $\hat{a} = a/\|a\|_{L^2}$, and w_{true} and w_{estim} are vectors containing the ground truth and the estimated coordinates of the white point respectively. The results are shown in Table 2. The relative improvements reported there are calculated as follows $\Delta err_{mean} = (mean(err_{init}) - mean(err_{ref}))/mean(err_{init}) \cdot 100\%$, where err_{init} and err_{ref} refer to errors of the initial and refined approximations respectively, and $mean$ is the mean over all positively classified images. The median error Δerr_{median} is achieved by replacing $mean$ with median operator. Finally the number of images improved indicates the portion of the positively classified images, that resulted in the same or better estimation than with the reference method. Some images of the results are also illustrated in Figures 2(b) and 3.

It can be observed, that according to all measures, the application of memory color correction achieves a considerable improvement in both categories, and especially in the case of sky. This is probably due to the fact that the memory color domain for sky is more compact than that of grass & foliage. Further improvements may be achieved by dividing the grass & foliage category in several sub classes for which more compact memory color clusters are available. Finally also visual results indicate a clear improvement in the subjective quality of the white balancing.

5   Conclusions

In this paper we presented a framework for applying visual category recognition results to improve automatic color constancy. The approach was based on so called memory color categories, which are known to occupy a compact region in the chromaticity space. The category recognition was performed by using the bag-of-features approach for low resolution input images which were first roughly white balanced with the simple and fast gray-world algorithm. Then, the categorization was used for adjusting the white balance produced by a low-level method, such as the gray-world or gray-edge algorithms. The experiments indicate that the proposed approach constantly improves the result of both low-level methods. Hence, utilizing semantic information of object categories is a promising new direction for automatic color constancy.

Acknowledgments

The Academy of Finland is gratefully acknowledged for providing the funding for this research.

References

1. Barnard, K., Martin, L., Coath, A., Funt, B.: A comparison of computational color constancy Algorithms. II. Experiments with image data IEEE Transactions on Image Processing 11(9), 985–996 (2002)
2. Barnard, K., Cardei, V., Funt, B.: A comparison of computational color constancy algorithms. I: Methodology and experiments with synthesized data. IEEE Transactions on Image Processing 11(9), 972–984 (2002)
3. Finlayson, G., Hordley, S., Hubel, P.: Color by correlation: a simple, unifying framework for color constancy. IEEE Transactions on Pattern Analysis and Machine Intelligence 23(11), 1209–1221 (2001)
4. Forsyth, D.: A novel algorithm for color constancy. International Journal of Computer Vision 5(1), 5–36 (1990)
5. Buchsbaum, G.: A spatial processor model for object color perception. J. Frank. Inst. 310 (1980)
6. van de Weijer, J., Gevers, T., Gijsenij, A.: Gray edge Edge-based color constancy. IEEE Transactions on Image Processing 16(9), 2207–2214 (2007)
7. Obdrzalek, Š., Matas, J., Chum, O.: On the Interaction between Object Recognition and Colour Constancy. In: Proc. International Workshop on Color and Photometric Methods in Computer Vision (2003)
8. van de Weijer, J., Schmid, C., Verbeek, J.: Using high-level visual information for color constancy. In: Proc. International Conference on Computer Vision, pp. 1–8 (2007)

9. Fairchild, M.: Colour appearance models, 2nd edn. John Wiley & Sons, Chichester (2006)
10. Bodrogi, P., Tarczali, T.: Colour memory for various sky, skin, and plant colours: effect of the image context. Color Research and Application 26(4), 278–289 (2001)
11. Barnard, K.: Practical color constancy. PhD Dissertation, School of Computing Science, Simon Fraser Univ., Bumaby, BC, Canada (1999)
12. Nikkanen, J., Gerasimow, T., Lingjia, K.: Subjective effects of white-balancing errors in digital photography. Optical Engineering 47(11) (2008)
13. Stokes, M., Anderson, S., Chandrasekar, S., Motta, R.: A standard default color space for the internet-sRGB (1996), http://www.w3.org/Graphics/Color/sRGB
14. Csurka, G., Dance, C., Fan, L., Williamowski, J., Bray, C.: Visual categorization with bags of keypoints. In: Proc. European conference on Computer Vision, pp. 59–74 (2004)
15. Lowe, D.: Distinctive image features from scale-invariant keypoints. International Journal of Computer Vision 60(2), 91–110 (2004)
16. van de Sande, K., Gevers, T., Snoek, C.: Evaluation of color descriptors for object and scene recognition. In: Proc. IEEE Conference on Computer Vision and Pattern Recognition (2008)
17. Silvén, O., Kauppinen, H.: Color vision based methodology for grading lumber. In: Proc. 12th International Conference on Pattern Recognition, vol. 1, pp. 787–790 (1994)

Anomaly-Based Detection of IRC Botnets by Means of One-Class Support Vector Classifiers*

Claudio Mazzariello and Carlo Sansone

University of Napoli Federico II
Dipartimento di Informatica e Sistemistica
via Claudio 21, 80125 Napoli (Italy)
{claudio.mazzariello,carlo.sansone}@unina.it

Abstract. The complexity of modern cyber attacks urges for the definition of detection and classification techniques more sophisticated than those based on the well known *signature detection* approach. As a matter of fact, attackers try to deploy armies of controlled *bots* by infecting vulnerable hosts. Such bots are characterized by complex executable command sets, and take part in cooperative and coordinated attacks. Therefore, an effective detection technique should rely on a suitable model of both the envisaged networking scenario and the attacks targeting it.

We will address the problem of detecting *botnets*, by describing a behavioral model, for a specific class of network users, and a set of features that can be used in order to identify *botnet*-related activities. Tests performed by using an anomaly-based detection scheme on a set of real network traffic traces confirmed the effectiveness of the proposed approach.

1 Introduction

Computer networks and networked hosts have always been targeted by cyber-attacks. The nature of such attacks has evolved alongside with technology and protocol improvements: modern attacks exploit stealthy techniques for breaking into systems and controlling or disrupting their resources. In fact, the aim of malicious users is often to collect a large number of infected hosts in order to make them cooperate toward a common malicious objective. Furthermore, attackers' motivations have changed over time. While in the past system vulnerabilities were exploited more for the sake of research curiosity and bug exposure, nowadays huge amounts of money are often driving the trends in attack perpetration. The potential damage caused by a well crafted Denial of Service attack on a competitor's activities, the valuable personal information harvested by going out *phishing* ingenuous and unexperienced users, or the significant saving in marketing investment obtained by spamming millions of users at a *ridiculous*

---

* This work has been partially supported by the European Community's Seventh Framework Programme (FP7/2007-2013) under grant agreement no. 216585 (INTERSECTION Project).

P. Foggia, C. Sansone, and M. Vento (Eds.): ICIAP 2009, LNCS 5716, pp. 883–892, 2009.

cost are some of the reasons pushing dishonest investors to spend money in this sort of underground competition for customers and resources.

In this framework *botnets* have recently gained increasing interest by the scientific community, the industry, and the media. Like worms, they are able to spread over thousands of host at a very high rate, infecting them using a wide set of known vulnerabilities. Unlike worms, botnets reach a further step in putting network security at danger due to their ability to coordinate themselves, and to cooperate towards a common malicious objective. For that reason, botnets are nowadays one of the preferred means to spread spam all over the Internet [1].

A *Botnet* can be in fact regarded as a distributed platform for performing malicious actions. Botnets are made by *zombie* hosts, named *bots* in this context, which are controlled by the attacker, also known as the *botmaster*, by means of a Command & Control (C&C) channel used to issue commands to, and eventually get responses back from the bots. Bots are usually common hosts, usually not very well protected, infected by means of several techniques.

Many works try to propose a botnet taxonomy [2,3], built by taking into account properties such as the propagation mechanism, the vulnerability exploitation strategy, the type of command and control channel used, or the set of commands available to the botmaster. Dagon et al., in [4] analyze time patterns characterizing botnet activity. The type of channel most often addressed so far is based on the IRC protocol. That is because originally, bots were benign programs used by IRC channel operators to monitor and manage their own channels automatically. In [5] the authors present some metrics based on flow analysis aimed at detecting botnets. After filtering out IRC session from the rest of the traffic, they apply flow based methods in order to discriminate between benign and malicious IRC channels. In [6] and [7] methods are proposed, which combine both application and network layer analysis. In [8] the authors propose to correlate information about IRC channel activity at the application layer, with information coming from the monitoring of network activity. Some authors also address the problem of botnet detection by using machine learning techniques [9]. The intuition behind this idea is that machine learning can provide a good means of characterizing botnets, once a good set of representative features has been selected. In [10] Rajab et al. propose a multifaceted approach, based on distributed monitoring, to detect botnets from the network behavior point of view. Others propose monitoring of services such as DNS for blacklisting botnet related domain [11].

In this paper a proposal for a system analyzing IRC traffic for botnet detection is presented. Differently from other approaches [5], where the analysis is performed at the network layer, our approach addresses the problem of application layer behavior modeling. Our system sniffs network traffic, extracts a behavior model of IRC traffic, and uses pattern recognition techniques for detecting the expected differences between a normal and a malicious user. Similarly to other network security approaches [12], we propose an anomaly-based detection schema, since "clean" IRC channels are easily available for training, while botnet-infected ones could be very difficult to obtain.

The paper is structured as follows: in Section 2 some background and technical information are given about the botnet phenomenon; the IRC traffic model and the features proposed for distinguishing between normal and botnet-related activities are described in Section 3; in Section 4 some experimental results show the detection performance of the proposed botnet detection system; finally, in Section 5 some conclusive remarks are given.

2   Understanding the Botnet Phenomenon

In the botnet model we decided to address, any infected host scans a defined subset of the whole IP space looking for known vulnerabilities. Once a vulnerable host is found, the vulnerability is exploited, and the host gets eventually infected. Once infected, the new bot contacts a server where it downloads the bot binary. The first examples of bots used to have the botmaster and command and control IP hardcoded, therefore once either of those was discovered, the botnet was made completely useless. For both flexibility and resiliency matters, though, bots started using symbolic names for contacting both the command and control channel and the botmaster. That is why a new bot, once infected, will issue a number of DNS queries to resolve the symbolic names associated to the entities it has to contact. By describing the finite state automaton describing the typical botnet behavior, specific stages of a bot's and botnet's lifecycle are targeted, in order to perform the detection and disruption operations.

Experiments show that known bots are characterized by a propagation profile similar to that of popular Internet worms. That is because many bots inherited their own propagation strategies from some popular worms of the past, which proved very quick and effective [10]. Under this assumption, it can be assumed that the number of infected hosts, and hence of DNS requests issued, varies according to a sigmoidal law. At the beginning, very few hosts are infected. Few hosts, then, perform scans, and the probability of clean hosts to get infected is really low. Once the number of infected hosts increases, they are spread all across the IP space. In this phase, the propagation speed is very high, and increases very quickly. Beyond a certain number of infected hosts, instead, the propagation speed decreases. This happens because the probability of finding a non infected host during scans decreases, and also due to some administrators' reaction. Once the vulnerability and its exploitation are discovered, in fact, some of the bots will be sanitized and removed from the botnet. Hence, it's difficult to identify properties which can allow to detect a botnet during the initial and the final phases of its life. By observing DNS traffic properties during the phase associated to the steepest part of the sigmoid, it is possible to imagine features which can allow to effectively discriminate between legitimate and botnet-related requests. The definition of such features, however, depends on the application context and on the problem we are willing to address.

Once the botnet is established and in a steady state as to its spreading, it becomes more difficult to detect its activity from the network activity point of view. In fact, its related statistics will look steady and hardly distinguishable from background traffic characteristics. Therefore, it might make sense to think about some detection techniques based on packet inspection, which exploit information at the application layer. In order to be able to do that effectively, however, we have to consider all the well known drawbacks related to packet inspection, which has been criticized lately. In general, application level payload decoding is not feasible in high speed networks, since it's very hard to keep up with network traffic's pace with a detailed analysis. Hence, we need to filter out the largest portion of traffic not of any interest for our botnet hunting purpose.

Starting from these considerations in this paper we decide to analyze botnets characterized by a centralized command and control channel based on IRC protocol, so as to exclude from our analysis any traffic flow not using such protocol.

3   The Proposed Architecture for Detecting IRC Botnets

As stated in the Introduction, IRC has been one of the first protocols exploited to implement a command and control channel for botnets. IRC bots are sets of scripts connecting to IRC channels, and performing automated functions inside such channels. Initially, the bots functions were very simple and related to a small set of automated tasks. Over time, such functions evolved and allowed the bots to perform a wide range of tasks, from channel maintenance to gaming support and activity logging. The introduction of remote control for IRC bots was the preliminary step to the creation of IRC-based bot armies. Malicious bots connect autonomously to IRC channels used by botmasters to issue commands.

In the case of botnet activity detection in an IRC channel, the main steps involved in the detection process can be described as follows (see also Fig. 1). A trace containing IRC traffic is collected from the Internet. An IRC decoder detects the presence of traffic related to the IRC protocol, and decodes it according to the protocol specifications. Since we are willing to reveal the nature of IRC channels, such channels are identified and separated. A feature vector describing, at any time t, the current status of the channel under consideration is extracted and finally a classifier is fed by the feature extractor.

3.1   The Considered Features

The aim of this work is to find features which allow us to discriminate between human and botnet-related activity in an IRC channel, and test their effectiveness. The key observation here is that human users of a normal IRC channel will exhibit a behavior very different from that of automated bots waiting for, and responding to, commands from the botmaster, and the difference in such behaviors can emerge by analyzing them by means of natural language recognition techniques. The intuition is that a bot, due to its limited set of commands, will have a limited dictionary, resulting in a limited number of used terms, and a low variability of each sentence's properties. Since bot commands are structured as common shell commands, we expect to find a very structured set of sentences in a botnet channel. To be more specific, we expect most of the sentences of a

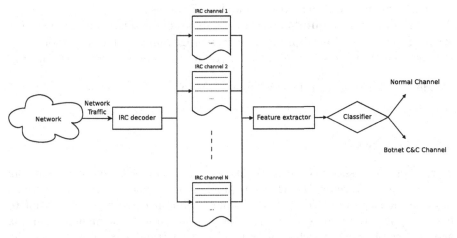

Fig. 1. Scheme of the proposed architecture for detecting IRC botnets

bot-related conversation to look like a command followed by a sequence of arguments or (argument, value) couples. On the other hand, a human conversation
should be characterized by a higher variability of sentence properties, a different
interaction pattern among chatters, and possibly a broader dictionary.

Based on the above considerations, a numeric model of IRC activity has been
defined. Such a model consists of a number of features, which describe the degree
of activity in an IRC channel, the variability and complexity of the vocabulary
used in sentences typed by users and the degree of activity due to both users
and control mechanisms in the channel. A feature vector is associated to each
observed channel, and its values are updated at the occurrence of each event
within such channel. Significant events may be related to user activity, or channel control activity. At each moment in time, a feature vector can be regarded
as describing the channel status, according to the properties described by the
features. In particular, the features we used have been defined as follows:

Average words number: average number of unique words in a sentence
Words number variance: variance of the number of unique words in a sen-
 tence
Unusual Nickname: percentage of unusual nicknames of channel users, de-
 fined with respect to the definitions in [13]. Such nicknames usually contain
 characters such as "|,%,−,_"
IRC Commands Rate: overall IRC command rate with respect to overall
 channel activity
PRIVMSG Rate: percentage of PRIVMSG commands with respect to overall
 channel activity
WHO Rate: percentage of WHO and NAMES commands with respect to over-
 all channel activity
AVG word length: average word length in a PRIVMSG command
Word length variance: word length variance in a PRIVMSG command

Average vowel number: average number of vowels in a message
Average consonant number: average number of consonants in a message
Average punctuation signs number: average number of punctuation
String distance: Levenshtein distance [14] among words in the same message

Additional details regarding the description of the used features can be found in [15].

3.2 The Classifier

As regards the classifier of the architecture shown in Fig. 1, we propose to use an anomaly-based detector. Our choice is justified by the fact the it is quite trivial to obtain normal and "clean" IRC channels, while it could be very difficult to find really infected channels. In computer security, in fact, the main assumption at the base of anomaly detection is the fact that fraudulent activities usually deviates from legitimate activities and then can be detected comparing them to the model of normal behaviors [12].

In order to build a good model of normal channels, we propose to use a one-class classifier, the ν-SVC presented in [16] which is inspired by the Support Vector Machine classifier proposed by Vapnik in [17]. The one-class classification problem is formulated so as to find a hyperplane that separates a desired fraction, say ν, of the training patterns from the origin of the feature space. Such a hyperplane cannot always be found in the original feature space, thus a mapping function from it to a kernel space must be used. In particular, it can be proved that when the Gaussian kernel given by:

$$K(\mathbf{x}, \mathbf{y}) = \exp\left(-\frac{\|\mathbf{x} - \mathbf{y}\|^2}{\gamma}\right), \tag{1}$$

is used, it is always possible to find a hyperplane that solves the separation problem [12]. The parameter γ, together with ν, has to be determined during the training phase of the ν-SVC.

4   Experimental Results

The results presented here were obtained by analyzing IRC logs. The normal channel logs were collected by sniffing traffic produced by activity in several real IRC channels; the botnet-related logs, instead, were collected at the Georgia Institute of Technology, in the Georgia Tech Information Security Center (GTISC) labs. The complete dataset consists of about $1,250,000$ samples, respectively belonging to eight normal rooms and nine infected rooms, as reported in Table 1.

In order to evaluate the best values for the ν and γ parameters presented in Section 3.2, we performed a grid search, by fixing different values for ν, and allowing γ's value to change in the range $(2^{-1}, 2^{-11})$. So, the best values for ν

Table 1. The considered dataset

	# of channels	# of patterns
Normal channels	8	55,000
Botnet channels	9	1,192,376

and γ have been fixed to 2^{-3} and 2^{-5}, respectively, since those values gave the best accuracy on the training data.

The tests we performed can be roughly divided into three categories. First of all, we performed a per-pattern evaluation of our approach. Then, we tested the detection ability of the proposed system, when trained with a certain number of normal channels. Finally, we investigate how the introduction of a suitable threshold can affect the performance of the system in detecting normal and infected channels.

Independent patterns. For the first set of tests, we consider the whole dataset as merely composed of patterns, without taking the nature of the problem into account. Classification is performed on a per-pattern basis. We evaluate how classification accuracy changes by increasing the percentage of patterns selected from the whole dataset for training. In Table 2 the first column indicates the percentage of patterns randomly selected from the dataset for training. As it is evident, when training the system with 50% of the normal data (about 28,000 patterns) we have very good results in terms of detection of botnet-related patterns. An higher number of normal patterns for training do not increase the overall performance.

Indivisible channels. In the second set of tests, we consider the problem's nature for the first time, both during the training and the test phase. Such tests are performed by dividing the dataset into subsets, each composed of patterns associated with the same IRC channel. In this case, training and test set are not selected randomly. In each of the tests we use all the patterns referring to a defined number of normal IRC channels for training, and the remaining channels (both normal and infected) for tests. The experimental evaluation of the system is again performed on a per-pattern estimation of classification accuracy.

Table 2. Classification accuracy on a per-pattern basis, as the number of training patterns varies

Percentage of the dataset selected for training	*Normal* channels	*Botnet* channels
50%	87.22%	99.86%
60%	87.18%	99.85%
70%	87.22%	99.86%
80%	87.20%	99.86%
90%	87.15%	99.85%

Table 3. Classification accuracy on a per-pattern basis, as the number of training channels varies

Training channels	*Normal* channels	*Botnet* channels
1	72.36%	99.70%
3	77.90%	100.00%
5	85.96%	99.45%
7	90.23%	99.98%

Therefore, in the second and third column of Table 3 we report the percentage of patterns relative to test channels which were correctly classified individually. In order to have a more robust estimate of the system performance, results on each row are the average values obtained by considering all the training sets that can be built with a specific number of normal channels. In general, it's worth pointing out that normal channel classification accuracy is lower than botnet channel classification accuracy. This may depend on the fact that botnet channels exhibit a regularity in connected users behavior patterns which is not peculiar to normal channels. The latter, in fact, may have different characterizations depending on the channel topic, the users type and the inherent variability of human conversations.

Channel's anomaly score thresholding. In this experiment, we define a per-channel anomaly score, and a thresholding mechanism for assigning a class label to each channel. The anomaly score of a channel is represented by the ratio of the number of patterns, associated to the same channel, identified as botnet-related, with respect to the number of patterns describing the same channel which are identified as describing a normal user behavior. The channel is assigned a class label, depending on the current value of the anomaly score, compared to the fixed thresholding value. In Table 4 we report the overall per-channel classification accuracy; once again values have been averaged on all the possible training sets that can be built with a specific number of normal channels. As it can be expected, experimental results show that the classification accuracy increases with the number of channels used for training. However, the accuracy decreases when the anomaly score threshold increases. In fact, a higher value for the anomaly score requires more confidence in assigning the class label. So, it is not always possible to correctly classify a channel with a too high threshold, since training

Table 4. Accuracy in channel classification by thresholding the anomaly score, as the number of training channels varies

Training channels	Threshold				
	6%	12%	25%	50%	75%
1	89.84%	89.55%	85.93%	74.22%	69.53%
3	97.27%	95.79%	94.64%	92.35%	83.93%
5	99.70%	97.17%	96.87%	96.28%	92.41%
7	100.00%	98.75%	98.75%	98.75%	97.50%

data may not be perfectly representative of all possible normal channels. On the other hand, it is very interesting to note that just one channel seems to be sufficient for training a system that is able to correctly classify about the 90% of the test channels, both normal and infected ones.

5   Conclusions and Future Work

In this paper, we presented the model of IRC user behavior in a channel in order to distinguish between normal and botnet-related activity. On this model we built a classification system based on a one-class Support Vector Classifier. The proposed approach demonstrated its effectiveness on a dataset of about 1,250,000 patterns extracted from 17 different IRC channels. The next step will be the deployment of the system in order to work online on a real network, sniffing traffic from the wire, and producing live and hopefully timely alerts in real-time.

References

1. Ramachandran, A., Feamster, N.: Understanding the network-level behavior of spammers. SIGCOMM Comput. Commun. Rev. 36(4), 291–302 (2006)
2. Barford, P., Yegneswaran, V.: An inside look at botnets. In: Christodorescu, M., Jha, S., Maughan, D., Song, D., Wang, C. (eds.) Special Workshop on Malware Detection. Advances in Information Security, vol. 27. Springer, Heidelberg (2007)
3. Puri, R.: Bots and botnets: An overview. Technical report, SANS institute (2003)
4. Dagon, D., Zou, C., Lee, W.: Modeling botnet propagation using time zones. In: NDSS, The Internet Society (2006)
5. Strayer, W.T., Walsh, R., Livadas, C., Lapsley, D.: Detecting botnets with tight command and control. In: Proceedings 2006 31st IEEE Conference on Local Computer Networks, November 2006, pp. 195–202 (2006)
6. Akiyama, M., Kawamoto, T., Shimamura, M., Yokoyama, T., Kadobayashi, Y., Yamaguchi, S.: A proposal of metrics for botnet detection based on its cooperative behavior. In: SAINT-W 2007: Proceedings of the 2007 International Symposium on Applications and the Internet Workshops, Washington, DC, USA, p. 82. IEEE Computer Society, Los Alamitos (2007)
7. Binkley, J.R., Singh, S.: An algorithm for anomaly-based botnet detection. In: SRUTI 2006: Proceedings of the 2nd conference on Steps to Reducing Unwanted Traffic on the Internet, Berkeley, CA, USA, p. 7. USENIX Association (2006)
8. Cooke, E., Jahanian, F., Mcpherson, D.: The zombie roundup: Understanding, detecting, and disrupting botnets, June 2005, pp. 39–44 (2005)
9. Livadas, C., Walsh, R., Lapsley, D., Strayer, W.: Using machine learning technliques to identify botnet traffic. In:31st IEEE Conference on Local Computer Networks, pp. 967–974 (November 2006)
10. Rajab, M.A., Zarfoss, J., Monrose, F., Terzis, A.: A multifaceted approach to understanding the botnet phenomenon. In: Almeida, J.M., Almeida, V.A.F., Barford, P. (eds.) Internet Measurement Conference, pp. 41–52. ACM, New York (2006)
11. Ramachandran, A., Feamster, N., Dagon, D.: Revealing botnet membership using dnsbl counter-intelligence. In: SRUTI 2006: Proceedings of the 2nd conference on Steps to Reducing Unwanted Traffic on the Internet, Berkeley, CA, USA, p. 8. USENIX Association (2006)

12. Giacinto, G., Perdisci, R., Del Rio, M., Roli, F.: Intrusion detection in computer networks by a modular ensemble of one-class classifiers. Information Fusion 9(1), 69–82 (2008)
13. Goebel, J., Holz, T.: Rishi: identify bot contaminated hosts by irc nickname evaluation. In: HotBots 2007: Proceedings of the first conference on First Workshop on Hot Topics in Understanding Botnets, Berkeley, CA, USA, p. 8. USENIX Association (2007)
14. Levenshtein, V.I.: Binary codes capable of correcting deletions, insertions, and reversals. Soviet Physics Doklady 10(8), 707–710 (1966)
15. Mazzariello, C.: Irc traffic analysis for botnet detection. In: Fourth International Conference on Information Assurance and Security, IAS 2008, September 2008, pp. 318–323 (2008)
16. Schlkopf, B., Platt, J.C., Shawe-Taylor, J., Smola, A.J., Williamson, R.C.: Estimating the support of a high-dimensional distribution. Neural Computation 13(7), 1443–1471 (2001)
17. Vapnik, V.: Statistical Learning Theory. Wiley, Chichester (1998)

Detection of Duplicated Regions in Tampered Digital Images by Bit-Plane Analysis

Edoardo Ardizzone and Giuseppe Mazzola

Dipartimento di Ingegneria Informatica (DINFO) - Università degli Studi di Palermo
Viale delle Scienze, building 6, 90128, Palermo, Italy
ardizzon@unipa.it, mazzola@dinfo.unipa.it

Abstract. In this paper we present a new method for searching duplicated areas in a digital image. The goal is to detect if an image has been tampered by a copy-move process. Our method works within a convenient domain. The image to be analyzed is decomposed in its bit-plane representation. Then, for each bit-plane, block of bits are encoded with an ASCII code, and a sequence of strings is analyzed rather than the original bit-plane. The sequence is lexicographically sorted and similar groups of bits are extracted as candidate areas, and passed to the following plane to be processed. Output of the last planes indicates if, and where, the image is altered.

Keywords: Image Forensics, Image Analysis, Bit-Plane Decomposition, Duplication Detection, Image Forgeries.

1 Introduction and Previous Works

A picture is worth a thousand words. But sometimes it does not tell the truth. Nowadays new digital techniques and tools (i.e. Adobe Photoshop) make it relatively easy to alter the content of a digital image. Digital Image Forensics is a form of Image Analysis which deals with the problem of certifying the authenticity of a picture, or its origin. It can be roughly subdivided in to three branches:

- Image source identification, which aims to identify which device was used to capture an image (different models of scanner, digital camera, etc.);
- Computer generated image recognition, to detect if an image is natural or synthetic;
- Image tampering detection, to discover if an image has been intentionally modified by human intervention.

In this paper we focused on the problem of detecting duplicated regions in digital images. The region-duplication (or Copy-Move, see [1][2]) is one of the most common forgery used for image tampering: a part of an image is copied and pasted into another part of the same image. This process is used to delete some objects from the scene, and to substitute information with some other taken from "good regions", e.g. highly-textured areas or uniform ones. To make alterations harder to detect, post-processing techniques (i.e. smooth filters) are used, especially in the edges of the tampered areas. On the other hand, although these techniques may cause no visual

P. Foggia, C. Sansone, and M. Vento (Eds.): ICIAP 2009, LNCS 5716, pp. 893–901, 2009.
© Springer-Verlag Berlin Heidelberg 2009

artifacts, they usually alters some image features. State of the art approaches proposed different features to be analyzed in order to detect these alterations.

Nevertheless the need of digital techniques for image authentication has been widely recognized, Digital Image Forensics is still a new research field in the Image Processing area. With regard to the image forgery detection problem, Farid proposed several statistical methods, based on color filter interpolation [3] and re-sampling [4]. Fridrich presented a solution to detect copy-move type of forgery [1]. Ng and Chang proposed a model for image splicing to detect photomontage [5].

To detect duplicate areas, the simplest approach is exhaustive search, but it is computationally expensive. To speed up the process, often digital images are not analyzed in the spatial domain, but projected in a different representation domain, and block-matching approaches are used. Some features are extracted from each block, and matched with those extracted by other blocks, in order to find those similar. In this paper we present a new method to find duplicated areas in digital images, by using bit-plane decomposition and block-matching analysis.

2   The Proposed Approach

In order to make the analysis process faster, images need to be represented in a convenient domain. We use bit-plane slicing to decompose images to analyze.

Our solution can be divided into three steps:

- Image decomposition by bit-plane slicing;
- Bit block encoding;
- Search for duplicated areas.

The next sub-sections will describe in detail each of these steps.

2.1   Bit Plane Decomposition

Bit-plane slicing is a well known technique used to represent the content of a grayscale image. It is mostly used for applications in the fields of digital watermarking [6] and image compression [7][8]. In [9] bit-planes are used to classify grayscale textures. In one of our previous works we used bit-plane representation for an image restoration application [10].

A n-bit grayscale image can be split in n different planes, one for each bit used to represent them. The higher bit-planes contain the most significant bits, that is the most part of the image information, while the lower ones usually contain noise (fig.1).

For our purposes, images to analyze are first grayscaled, therefore only the brightness component is processed. Image is then split in its bit-planes and Gray- coding is applied, to decorrelate information between different planes. We observed that working with block of bits in the bit-plane domain is simpler and faster than working with blocks of pixels of the image. Furthermore our method let the user to select the starting plane, to avoid processing less significant planes, speeding-up the execution time. In section 3 we will show how results are affected by setting the starting plane.

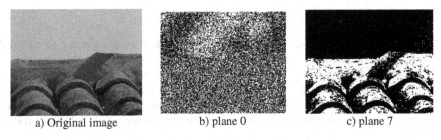

| a) Original image | b) plane 0 | c) plane 7 |

Fig. 1. The most (c) and the less (b) significant bit-planes of an image (a)

2.2 Bit Block Encoding

Once the image has been decomposed in its bit planes, the next step is to use a suitable representation to simplify the following analysis step.

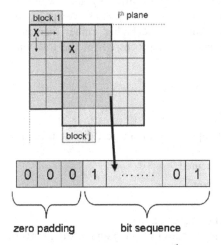

Fig. 2. Two overlapping blocks in i^{th}-plane. An m x m block is created from a starting point X (top part). Bit-blocks are rasterized and zero-padded (bottom).

We start from a user-selected plane and proceeds towards the most significant ones. The starting plane (size NxM) is analyzed in scan order (from top left to bottom right), and divided into m x m (m is also set by the user) overlapping blocks, each one shifted rightward by 1, and downward by 1 after processing a row. Image border bits are included only in the last blocks of each row. Therefore we have N' x M' blocks where N'=(N-m-1) and M'=(M-m-1).

Each block is a m x m binary matrix, and is rasterized in a array of m^2 bits. This array is zero-padded, in order to make its size multiple of 8 (fig.2). Bits are taken from the array 8 per time, and converted in a single char using ASCII code. Each block is coded into a string of $k=m^2/8$ chars (considering zero padding). Therefore the bit-plane is represented with a sequence of N' x M' strings with size k. Each string contains information about a block of bits. Note that there is a lot of redundancy, because blocks overlap, and closer ones differ only for a column or for a row. Bit-planes are analyzed in this coded domain, rather than bit per bit. We tested different types of coding (decimal, octal, hexadecimal), but ASCII code showed to be the most suitable for our goals. Bit-planes are represented in a very compact form, and larger blocks was used for our experiments. Starting plane is the only one to be entirely encoded. In the next section we will see that for the following planes only part of each plane is encoded, saving a lot of execution time (see section 2.3).

2.3 Searching for Duplicated Areas

With the previous steps, the starting plane is represented as a sequence of encoded strings. We sort this sequence, lexicographically, in order to have identical strings side by side. Then we analyze the whole sorted sequence, searching for groups of consecutive identical strings, and we mark these groups as possible candidate areas. The coordinates of the candidates are then passed up to the next plane, and bit-block encoding is applied only for bits in these candidate areas (see fig. 3), while the rest of the plane is simply ignored.

The process of encoding – searching candidates is repeated until the most significant plane is processed. The output of the last plane processing indicates the duplicated areas of the input image.

Choosing a starting plane different from the first one (plane 0) we can set the tolerance about the similarity measure used to search duplicated areas. If the starting plane is zero, detected areas are identical in the original grayscale image.

Note that the probability to have identical areas in less significant planes, which are typically similar to noise, is much lower than in most significant ones, except in case of tampering. Therefore starting from lower planes to the higher, rather than from higher to lower, reduce the number of candidates to be processed for the following planes, speeding up the process.

3   Experimental Results

We tested our method on a set of about 20 tampered color images, different both in their size and tampered area size.

For each test image, two types of test are executed:

- fixing the starting plane and varying block size;
- fixing block size and varying starting plane.

For each test we measured both accuracy and execution time.

As regards the accuracy, we created our image dataset copying and pasting parts of an image onto other parts of the same image. We saved source and destination area positions in a binary mask (see fig. 4.c, 5.c, 6.c), which represents our reference area A_R. Best results are those in which the detected area A_D is most similar to A_R. In particular we measured the detection precision DP as follows:

$$A_{In} = \frac{n(A_D \cap A_R)}{n(A_R)} \tag{1}$$

$$A_{Out} = \frac{n(A_D \cap \overline{A}_R)}{n(A_D)} \tag{2}$$

$$DP = A_{In} \cdot (1 - A_{Out}) \tag{3}$$

where:

- A_{In} is the ratio between the number of pixels in the intersection of the detected area A_D and the reference area A_R, and the number of pixels in A_R. When it tends to 1,

A_D covers the whole A_R, but nothing can be said about pixels outside A_R; if it tends to 0 A_D and A_R have smaller intersection;

- A_{Out} is the ratio between the number of pixels in A_D, which are not in A_R, and the number of pixels in A_D. When this parameter tends to 1, the whole detected area has no intersection with the reference. If it tends to 0, fewer pixels of A_D are labeled outside A_R. Nevertheless this parameter will not assure that the whole reference area has been covered.
- DP combines these two parameters: DP is high if A_D both covers A_R and has few outliers, and it is low if A_D and A_R are only partially overlapped or, though when A_R is well covered, A_D contains many pixels which are not in A_R.

Fig. 3 shows the effects of varying starting bit-plane (fig. 3.a) or block size (fig. 3.b), in detection precision. In the first case, if block size is fixed, we observed that the lower the starting plane, the higher the accuracy of our method. The drawback is an higher execution time because more planes have to be processed. In fact, the higher the starting plane, the looser the tolerance in searching similar areas, and therefore the larger the number of false positives (zones labeled as identical which are not identical) ($A_{Out} \rightarrow 1$). The "cut-off" starting plane P, that is the higher starting plane which gives best accuracy, depends on image resolution and typically is in [2,4].

If we vary block size, fixing the starting plane, two overlapping effects are observed:

- If the block size is larger than the tampered areas, $A_{In} \rightarrow 0$. In fact, whatever block we consider in a plane, it will contain bits which do not belong to the tampered area. Therefore no matches can be found.
- If block size is small $A_{Out} \rightarrow 1$, because the probability to have natural similarities in an image, so that the number of false positives, increases.

The "steady state", [B'',B'], with the best accuracy, depends both on image resolution, and tampered area size and shape. B' is the largest block size to achieve best accuracy, B'' is the smallest one. For high-resolution images and smooth tampered area shape B' is larger than 16 and B'' 7-8. For low-resolution image with high-detailed tampered area shapes, B' is typically 6-7 and B'' 4, so that the "steady state" is very tight. In our experiments we measured an average accuracy in the "steady state" of 98,7%.

Fig.4 shows some detection results. Note that processing only the starting plane (fig.4.d), many false positives are detected. After processing some more planes, false positives are fewer. Final results is very similar to the reference area mask. For this image we measured an accuracy of 99,6%.

Fig.5 shows results obtained varying starting plane. Best results are achieved starting from plane 2 or lower (fig. 5. d, accuracy 97%). The higher the starting plane, the larger the number of false positives (fig. 5. e-i).

Fig.6 shows results obtained varying block size. Note that using larger block size (fig. 6.d,e,f) only part of the tampered area is detected. Best results with block size 8 (fig. 6.g), with an accuracy of 99,3%. Using smaller blocks (fig. 6.h,i), causes the detection of false positives.

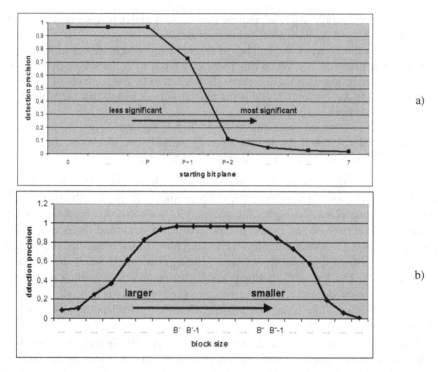

Fig. 3. Detection precision vs starting bit-plane (a) and vs block size (b). P is the "cut off" starting plane and depends on image resolution. B' and B'' are the two "cut off" block sizes, and depend on image resolution and on tampered area size.

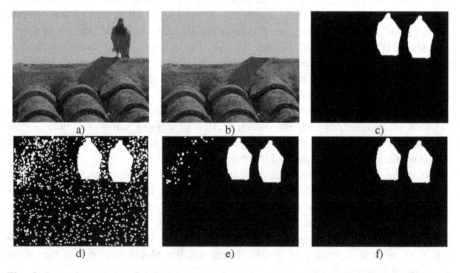

Fig. 4. Detection results. Original image (a), tampered image (b), reference area mask (c), detected duplicated areas after processing the starting plane (d), intermediate result (e), final result (f).

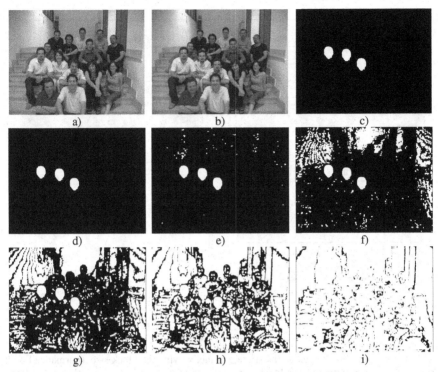

Fig. 5. Results varying starting plane. Original image (a), tampered (b), reference area mask (c), results with starting plane 2 (d), 3 (e), 4 (f), 5 (g), 6 (h), 7 (i).

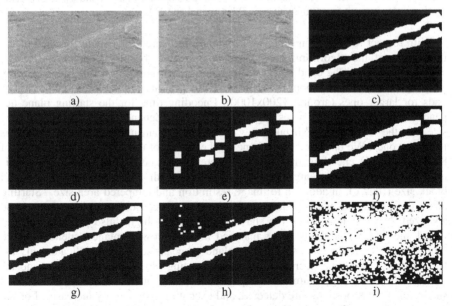

Fig. 6. Results varying block size. Original image (a), tampered (b), reference area mask (c), results with block size 16 (d), 14 (e), 10 (f), 8 (g), 4 (h), 3 (i).

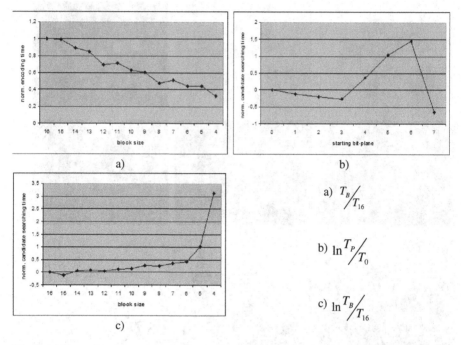

Fig. 7. (a) Execution time to encode the starting plane, varying the block size. (normalized with respect to the value measured for block size 16). (b) Candidate searching time vs starting plane. T_P is the time measured starting from bit plane P and T_0 is that for plane 0. (c) Candidate searching time vs block size. T_B is the time measured using block size B and T_{16} is that using block size 16. (we use for testing values of B between 4 and 16).

With respect to execution time, we separately measured time spent for each of the three parts of the algorithm: bit-plane decomposition, bit-block encoding (for the starting plane), and the candidate area searching. Decomposition time depends only on image size and takes about 0,5 s for small images (around 250x200) and few seconds for larger ones (around 1200x1000). Encoding time for the starting plane depends on image and block sizes (fig. 7.a), and it is independent from tampered area size. For the "steady state" it takes few seconds for small images up to few minutes for larger ones. We observed that whenever the square of the block size is multiple of 8 (e.g. 12, 8, 4) encoding time slightly decrease, because no zero padding step is needed. Candidate area searching time depends on both starting plane (fig.7.b), and block size (fig.7.c), in addition to image resolution and tampered area size. Starting analysis from higher planes reduces execution time, because fewer planes have to be analyzed. Nevertheless, when the starting plane is too high, false positives are detected and a larger area has to be analyzed in the following planes, spending more time. Starting from the most significant (plane 7) means searching duplicates only for that plane, so that time decreases again. Decreasing block size, execution time increases, because a larger number of duplicated areas is found. When block size is too small, many false positives are detected, and execution time rapidly increases. For the "steady state", candidate searching phase takes few seconds for small images up to half a minute for larger ones.

4 Conclusions and Future Works

Copy-move is one of the most used form of tampering to alter a digital image. Highly textured areas, or homogeneous ones, are typically used to delete objects from a scene or to replicate an object into the image.

In this paper we presented a new method to detect duplicated areas in a digital image. Our method analyzes a digital image in the bit-plane domain. Block of bits are encoded, using the ASCII code, into strings of characters, in order to find identical sequences in each bit plane. Detected candidate areas in a plane are processed in the following planes. Output of the last processed plane indicates tampered areas.

Experimental results showed that the proposed solution proves to reach very high accuracy without spending much execution time.

There are some drawbacks in our approach. First, it does not work with JPEG images, because JPEG compression alters (not uniformly) the intensity value of the pixels in an image. To our knowledge, there are no works about the relationship between JPEG compression and bit-plane representation. This is an interesting open problem. Moreover our method cannot be applied if the duplicated area is rotated or scaled. Solutions to detect other types of tampering will be the focus of our future studies. Furthermore our approach can be easily adapted to several more application fields: image compression, digital watermarking, image segmentation, etc.

References

1. Fridrich, J., Soukal, D., Lukas, J.: Detection of Copy-Move Forgery in Digital Images. In: Proc. Digital Forensic Research Workshop, Cleveland, OH (August 2003)
2. Mahdian, B., Saic, S.: Detection of Copy–Move Forgery Using a Method Based on Blur Moment Invariants, Forensic Science International, vol. 171(2), pp. 180–189
3. Popescu, A., Farid, H.: Exposing digital forgeries in color filter array interpolated images. IEEE Transactions on Signal Processing 53(10), 3948–3959 (2005)
4. Popescu, A.C., Farid, H.: Exposing Digital Forgeries By Detecting Traces of Re-Sampling. IEEE Transactions on Signal Processing 53(2), 758–767 (2005)
5. Ng, T.T., Chang, S.F., Sun, Q.: Blind Detection of Photomontage Using Higher Order Statistics. In: IEEE International Symposium on Circuits and Systems, Vancouver, Canada (May 2004)
6. Wang, R.Z., Lin, C.F., Lin, J.C.: Image hiding by optimal LSB substitution and genetic algorithm. Pattern Recognition 34, 671–683 (2001)
7. Kamata, S., Eason, R.O., Kawaguchi, E.: Depth-First Coding For Multivalued Pictures Using Bit-Plane Decomposition. IEEE Transactions on Communications 43(5), 1961–1969 (1995)
8. Galatsanos, N.P., Yu, S.S.: Binary Decompositions For High-Order Entropy Coding of Grayscale Images. IEEE Transactions on Circuits And Systems For Video Technology 6, 21–31 (1996)
9. García-Sevilla, P., Petrou, M., Kamata, S.: The use of Boolean model for texture analysis of grey images. Computer Vision and Image Understanding 74, 227–235 (1999)
10. Ardizzone, E., Dindo, H., Mazzola, G.: Texture Synthesis for Digital Restoration in the Bit-Plane Representation. In: The Third IEEE International Conference on Signal-Image Technology & Internet–Based Systems 2007, Shangai, China, December 16-19 (2007)

Color Features Performance Comparison for Image Retrieval

Daniele Borghesani, Costantino Grana, and Rita Cucchiara

Dipartimento di Ingegneria dell'Informazione, Università degli Studi di Modena e Reggio Emilia, Via Vignolese 905/b, 41100 Modena, Italy
{daniele.borghesani, costantino.grana,
rita.cucchiara}@unimore.it

Abstract. This paper proposes a comparison of color features for image retrieval. In particular the UCID image database has been employed to compare the retrieval capabilities of different color descriptors. The set of descriptors comprises global and spatially related features, and the tests show that HSV based global features provide the best performance at varying brightness and contrast settings.

Keywords: color features, HSV, image retrieval, feature comparison.

1 Introduction

The increasing availability of multimedia digital libraries (publicly shared or personal) and low cost devices to produce them, raised the need of appropriate tools for the search within this enormous amount of data. Classical search methodologies in desktop and web contexts are based on textual keywords. In order to reuse the majority of all preexisting searching techniques with multimedia data, the most immediate solution is tagging, but it is generally boring from the user prospective and unfeasible if the amount of data to annotate is too high. The search and retrieval based on content (CBIR) is the most difficult but at the same time the most effective and elegant way to solve the problem. A lot of literature background has been produced so far, focusing on specific components (like the learning algorithms, the features to use, the way to select the most effective features, etc...), sometimes specialized on some real world context (news, sports, etc...). A lot of functioning systems have also been proposed. Columbia University proposed its semantic video search engine (CuVid [1]), including 374 visual concept detectors and using different combinations of input modalities (keyword, image, near-duplicate and semantic concepts). IBM multimedia search and video system (Marvel [2]) uses multimodal machine learning techniques for bridging the semantic gap, recognizing entities such as scenes, objects, events and people. University of Amsterdam also proposed a semantic video search system [3] featuring a fascinating user interface (RotorBrowser) and 500 automatically detected semantic concepts. We also proposed a general framework called PEANO (Pictorially Enriched ANnotation with Ontologies) which allows to automatically annotate video clips by comparing their similarity to a domain specific set of prototypes [4].

P. Foggia, C. Sansone, and M. Vento (Eds.): ICIAP 2009, LNCS 5716, pp. 902–910, 2009.
© Springer-Verlag Berlin Heidelberg 2009

Considering the way scientific community tried to solve the problem, we can highlight two fundamental functionalities we would like in a CBIR system:

- The ability to search and retrieve specific visual objects: given an image, we want to retrieve in our digital library all images containing the object depicted within the query, that is "I want to find my friend John in all my image library"
- The ability to search and retrieve images by appearance similarity: given a sample image or a keyword (textual representation of a pictorial prototype), we want to retrieve the most similar images to the query, that is "I like this seaside landscape, I want to find all similar images I've got in my image library".

The global appearance similarity task, especially if it is fast to compute, has also an important side effect, that is the possibility to prune from the digital library all images that will not likely matter for other more specific retrieval techniques. This is a major advantage even because usually the local features exploited for the objects recognition or other more sophisticated global features, and the learning algorithms employed, are quite weighty to compute.

The most straightforward representation for global features is the histogram. It allows a scale independent representation, suitable both for color and gradient information, and it has a robust and easy metric to evaluate similarity, that is histogram intersection. Besides, one of the most discriminative characteristic for global features is undoubtedly the color. It brings information about the nature of what we see, it allows inferences about environment depending on brightness conditions, and the way humans perceive the chromatic appearance helps recognition process of an object and changes understanding of the environment self.

In this paper, we aim at analyzing in detail the discriminative capabilities of several well known color descriptors. We adopt a standard image database called UCIDv.2, freely available and complete with ground truth. To test their performance, we modify the brightness characteristic of images in order to test the behavior of these features in extreme conditions.

2 Color Features for Image Retrieval

The standard definition of HSV histogram is proposed as MPEG-7 scalable color description [5]: a 256-bins histogram providing 16 different values for H, and 4 different values for S and V. Normally, H is defined in the range [0..360], while S and V are defined in [0..1]. HSV36 has been presented in [6]. This procedure aims to improve the representation power of HSV color space. Firstly a non uniform quantization of hue has been introduced, dividing the entire spectrum into 7 classes: red, orange, yellow, green, cyan, blue and purple. Then another quantization has been proposed for S-V plane, in order to distinguish the black area (V <= 0.2), and the grey area (S <= 0.2), providing a fixed general subdivision of the chromatic area of the plane into 4 subparts.

The RGB histogram is a standard color histogram based on RGB components of the image. Each component is subsampled into 8 values, resulting in a 512-bin histogram.

Firstly introduced by [7], the color correlogram describes the spatial correlation of colors using an arbitrary spatial distance. It consists in a table indexed by color couple (c_i, c_j) so that the k-th entry designates the probability p of finding a pixel of color c_j at a distance k from a pixel of color c_i in the image. So let I be an $n \times n$ image, with m quantized colors $c_1, \ldots, c_m$ and let a distance $d \in [n]$ be fixed a priori. The correlogram of I is defined for $i, j \in [m], k \in [d]$ as

$$\gamma_{c_i, c_j}^{(k)}(I) \triangleq P\left\{\exists\, p_1 \in I_{c_i}, p_2 \in I_{c_j} : |p_1 - p_2| = k\right\} \tag{1}$$

In particular autocorrelograms are a subset of correlograms capturing the spatial correlation between identical colors only:

$$\alpha_c^{(k)}(I) \triangleq \gamma_{c,c}^{(k)}(I) \tag{2}$$

Correlograms may be computed on RGB or HSV color information [8].

Spatial chromatic histograms, were introduced in [9]. This feature proposes to merge spatial information with color information, in order to take in account spatial distribution of color blobs along the image: for each color bin add the center of mass and the average distance from it. The similarity between two queries is given by:

$$f_s(Q, I) = \sum_{i=1}^{c} \min(h_Q(i), h_I(i)) \cdot \left(\frac{\sqrt{2} - d(b_Q(i), b_I(i))}{\sqrt{2}} + \frac{\min(\sigma_Q(i), \sigma_I(i))}{\max(\sigma_Q(i), \sigma_I(i))} \right) \tag{3}$$

The similarity function f_s acts also as a weighting function, increasing importance of large areas with equally colored pixels.

Color opponent process [10] is a well known color theory that exploits, instead of raw RGB channel information, color cones in an antagonistic matter. The motivation is that their respective wavelengths have some overlap, so it's more efficient to record differences between these cones than the original entire signal. The theory proposes three opponent channels: reddish green (red versus green), yellowish blue (blue versus yellow) and luminance (black versus white). An original 24 bin RGB pixel information can now be described as a compressed 8 bit color opponent pixel information, using 3 most significant bits for chrominance components and 2 most significant bits for luminance component. A 256-bins histogram may be computed to provide a color opponent histogram.

Edge detection is very used in content based retrieval: edge features locally extract more significant points in the image, that are perceptually more relevant from a human point of view, using only brightness information. A common and effective way to represent edge features is edge histogram [11], which globally describes the frequency and the directionality of edges and (as histogram itself) it's invariant to translations, rotations and scaling.

3 HSV Histogram with Achromatic Selection

Regarding achromaticity issues in HSV color space, different solutions have been proposed. In [12] two regions are defined and separately treated, one for the chromatic and one for the achromatic colors. These areas are obtained with a complicated set of thresholds in the IHS color space. Similarly, in [13] a fuzzy technique has been proposed in order to distinguish among chromatic, achromatic, and black colors. Sural et al. [14] propose a histogram modification that takes into account the above mentioned regions. In particular, they identify the achromatic region by thresholding the saturation coordinate with a linear function of the intensity value and based on the outcome chose to represent the color with its hue or its value only. In [15] a detailed comparison of the MPEG-7 color descriptors can be found, proving that the Scalable Color Descriptor is not suitable for monochromatic images. Moreover in [6] an arbitrary subdivision of HSV color space has been proposed, in order to select an achromatic region and quantize the remaining chromatic one.

To solve the problem of achromatic images, we proposed an enhanced version of the HSV color space [16]. The Scalable Color Descriptor requires a quantization of the HSV color space, with 16 values in H and 4 values in each S and V (256 bins in total). Supposing every color channel in the range [0,1), the bin index may be obtained as:

$$\text{bin} = f(H,S,V) = \lfloor n_H H \rfloor n_S n_V + \lfloor n_S S \rfloor n_V + \lfloor n_V V \rfloor \qquad (4)$$

where n_H, n_S, n_V are the quantization levels devoted to every color channel. Usually these are chosen to be powers of 2 for ease of representation.

Adopting, as is usual, a linear quantization of each coordinate leads to have, for example, 64 different bins for the darkest colors characterized by the lowest values of V. A possible error could be the erroneous assignment to different bins with dark color: for this reason a visually uniform background can be split on different bins. We propose to add n_A bins to the HSV histogram that contains all the achromatic and dark colors. These n_A bins correspond to gray levels, from black to white; for convenience, we choose to set $n_A = n_V = 4$, as the number of levels assigned to the V axis in the MPEG-7 standard. The dark and achromatic colors are selected by imposing a unique threshold λ on the S and V coordinates respectively. The value of λ has been empirically set.

Moving some of the colors from the original bins to the n_A achromatic ones makes these original bins less used with respect to the others. In fact, it doesn't make sense anymore to uniformly subdivide the S and V channels, if part of it is then discarded. A better solution is to fully employ the chromatic bins to describe only the effective chromatic area (Fig. 1). To this aim we linearly quantize the remaining HSV space, by simply redefining the f function of Eq. 4:

$$f'(H,S,V) = f\left(H, \frac{S-\lambda}{1-\lambda}, \frac{V-\lambda}{1-\lambda}\right) \qquad (5)$$

A different approach could be used to reduce the number of bins in the histogram, without affecting the chromatic area. The threshold λ can be set to $1/n_V$, thus making the achromatic area exactly match the first set of bins for S and V. This forces these bins to 0, thus allowing their removal. This indeed induces a compression with respect to the color representation, but it is selectively applied to the least significant colors. For example with reference to the aforementioned 16,4,4 subdivision, this would lead to $16 \times 3 \times 3 = 144$ bins, plus 4 bins for the achromatic area.

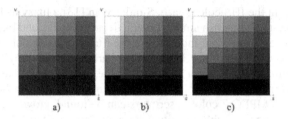

Fig. 1. a) original quantization of the SV plane with H = 0 (red); b) achromatic area detection (λ=0.2); d) Linear re-quantization of the chromatic area

HSV color space drawbacks are mostly significant in real world images and the consequent introduction of non-uniform brightness distribution. These phenomena is due to unprofessional cameras or indoor/outdoor situations, so the achromatic separation provided with aHSV can focus the descriptive power to the chromatic area.

4   Experimental Results

The database used for our test was UCIDv.2 (UnCompressed Image Database), provided by [17]. It contains 1338 real world 512x384 uncompressed images, together with a ground truth: for each query, a variable number of models is indicated. To obtain a more significant corpus of data and perform our tests in different working conditions, we modified the original database producing 25 different versions. Brightness and/or contrast values have been varied in a systematic way in order to simulate different light conditions, producing a total amount of 1338x25 images.

To evaluate the performance of the system, we used the same metric indicated in [17], that is a modified version of match percentile metric:

$$MP_Q = \frac{100}{S_Q} \sum_{i=1}^{S_Q} \frac{N - R_i}{N - i}, \quad \text{with } R_i < R_{i+1} \tag{6}$$

Where S_Q is the number of models for query Q, N is the total number of images in the database, i is the rank of the image in the ground truth and R_i is the rank of the image computed by the system. The average match percentile may then used as a global measure of performance of a retrieval system.

The first two columns of the Table 1 report the percentage of decrease in brightness and contrast for the entire database. HSV based histograms perform better than other features in all cases, and with different light conditions proposed. It performs better that standard RGB histograms, and it's more stable at varying light conditions, due to the nature of HSV histograms.

Gray histograms (that carries information only about the brightness) provide poor performance. The use of spatial information (with RGB and HSV histograms) have also proved to be less effective than using color histograms only. Their dependency on the color distribution, even if very useful for the classification of particular images with a similar color distribution, is not always useful for global appearance similarity.

Table 1. Comparison of different color features. HSV provides the best performance.

Brightness	Contrast	HSV	RGB	HistColOpp	Gray	SpatialHSV	SpatialRGB	cHSV	cRGB	EH
0	0	92,72	91,05	90,29	76,16	91,05	89,44	88,21	87,26	76,28
0	-20	92,66	90,11	89,93	76,35	90,53	88,72	88,71	87,17	75,83
0	-40	92,33	89,55	89,4	76,34	89,35	86,15	88,43	86,63	75,18
0	-60	92,24	88,04	88,98	76,45	85,74	83,4	87,67	82,78	74,58
0	-80	91,69	81,61	88,09	76,5	77,17	83,37	86,21	77,4	73,64
-20	0	92,71	90,34	89,72	76,26	90,34	88,48	88,2	86,97	76,01
-20	-20	92,72	90,47	89,76	76,35	90,36	88,09	89,08	86,65	75,76
-20	-40	92,42	89,3	89,45	76,34	90,18	87,44	88,62	85,05	75,19
-20	-60	91,99	87,92	89,14	76,45	87,58	82,9	88,29	84,14	74,62
-20	-80	89,87	83,26	88,04	76,5	78,77	74,13	85,98	79,24	73,65
-40	0	91,84	89,54	89,14	76,51	89,83	87,15	87,67	86,27	75,59
-40	-20	92,81	89,89	89,71	76,38	89,62	87,16	88,42	85,59	76,03
-40	-40	92,84	89,65	89,07	76,34	90,07	86,97	88,87	86,45	75,18
-40	-60	91,77	87,62	89,16	76,45	89,1	84,16	88,12	83,33	74,62
-40	-80	90,49	81,33	87,42	76,5	81,79	81,33	85,99	80,18	73,74
-60	0	91,31	88,36	88,4	76,5	88,25	85,53	87,18	86,09	75,75
-60	-20	92,14	88,33	88,66	76,73	88,89	85,05	87,02	85,78	74,99
-60	-40	92,68	88,7	89,26	76,33	89,37	84,22	88,38	84,91	75,4
-60	-60	92,67	88,12	88,78	76,45	88,98	83,44	88,68	82,74	74,58
-60	-80	92,28	82,36	88,42	76,5	85,29	84,19	87,42	78,23	73,64
-80	0	90,34	86,42	86,93	76,62	87,34	84,78	86,46	84,61	74,78
-80	-20	91,03	87,26	87,36	76,95	87,4	84,1	87	84,02	75,03
-80	-40	91,92	87,22	88,15	76,71	87,19	82,5	86,86	83,37	75,18
-80	-60	92,7	86,5	89,11	76,41	86,79	80,89	88,67	83,92	74,57
-80	-80	91,39	84,27	87,56	76,5	84	76,74	87,85	79	73,76

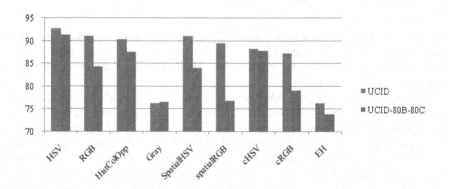

We tested color correlograms and edge histograms, in order to capture the aggregation level and the salient edges in the image respectively, but none of them reached the same performance of HSV histograms. Both of them are intrinsically connected to the spatial arrangements of color blobs, so the efficiency is more or less closed to spatial histograms. Lastly we also tested color opponent histograms, exploiting color opponent theory, that has proved to be not as powerful as HSV based histograms but very stable varying light conditions indeed.

The second section of this analysis regards in particular the direct comparison between standard HSV histograms and aHSV histograms. For completeness, we also show comparison with another enhanced HSV (here called HSV36) previously

Table 2. Comparison of different HSV color features. B and C indicates respectively the decrease of brightness and contrast in the modified images.

B	C	HSV	AHSV	HSV36
0	0	92,72	93,25	90,49
0	-20	92,66	92,93	89,97
0	-40	92,33	93	88,63
0	-60	92,24	91,69	84,38
0	-80	91,69	88,18	73,67
-20	0	92,71	93,1	89,73
-20	-20	92,72	93,06	89,79
-20	-40	92,42	93,01	89,55
-20	-60	91,99	92,27	86,56
-20	-80	89,87	88,61	76,61
-40	0	91,84	91,97	88,78
-40	-20	92,81	93,14	89,02
-40	-40	92,84	93,17	89,38
-40	-60	91,77	92,83	88,46
-40	-80	90,49	89,8	79,86
-60	0	91,31	90,93	87,68
-60	-20	92,14	92,28	88,32
-60	-40	92,68	93,04	88,7
-60	-60	92,67	92,76	88,05
-60	-80	92,28	91,52	83,66
-80	0	90,34	90,09	86,56
-80	-20	91,03	90,68	86,58
-80	-40	91,92	91,48	86,47
-80	-60	92,7	92,51	85,87
-80	-80	91,39	92,14	81,93

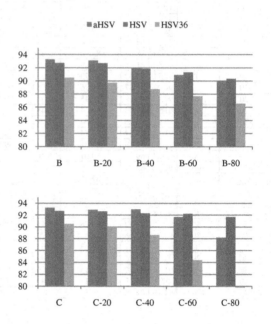

described. Results are shown in Table 2. Standard HSV outperforms HSV36 in all cases, staying up to 10 percentage points over the rival with a more stable behavior decreasing brightness and contrast. Moreover aHSV performs quite and slightly better than HSV itself in most cases.

The gap between respective AMP can seem quite small, but it's an average estimation sparse on the entire database, that takes account not only the "binary" retrieval result (if a model was found or not) but also the rank of this model in the retrieval (in which position the system outputs that model). For this reason, a small gap can lead to significant differences from the visual point of view in the retrieval output. aHSV histogram maintains its supremacy, and only when images become too dark HSV histogram performs better than aHSV: in these cases, the gap between the respective performances are quite similar. In these cases a more optimized value for n_A and λ should be necessary: appearance (in terms of hue, saturation and brightness) turns out to be closer to gray colors, so the separation between chromatic and achromatic area leads to a less efficient representation of the achromatic area in the image (now dominant). Even if in these cases image tends to grayscale, HSV still remains a more efficient retrieval feature than simple grayscale histograms. According to these tests, with real world images, in the best case scenario (generally with quite predictable and limited variations of brightness and quality), aHSV can potentially outperform standard HSV histogram. Instead in the worst case scenario aHSV turns out to have the same or just a little worse performance.

Fig. 2. The results page on the left has a MP=98.46, with 4 missing models of 16 in first 15 results. The one on the right has a MP=99.29, with 2 missing models of 7 in first 15 results.

Some examples of retrieval are reported in figure **2**. The first image in the sequence represents the query submitted to the system, the following images are the result of the query. Green bordered images corresponds to effective model images of the ground truth provided, red bordered images are misclassifications.

5 Conclusions

In this paper a single feature comparison between color features has been proposed in order to establish the respective discriminating value in a generic retrieval application. The analysis showed the advantages linked to the use of HSV color space in content retrieval application, and then the advantages linked to the use of the enhanced HSV color space. An improvement of performances in terms of quality of retrieval has been evidenced, without losing any advantages compared to the standard definition Test were conducted using a general images database, with unprofessional photos taken in different environment, with different light conditions, with variable zooming, framing and orientation.

References

1. Chang, S.-F., Kennedy, L.S., Zavesky, E.: Columbia University's semantic video search engine. In: Proceedings of the 6th ACM international conference on Image and video retrieval, Amsterdam, The Netherlands, pp. 643–643 (2007)
2. Natsev, A., Tešić, J., Xie, L., Yan, R., Smith, J.R.: IBM multimedia search and retrieval system. In: Proceedings of the 6th ACM international conference on Image and video retrieval, Amsterdam, The Netherlands, p. 645 (2007)
3. Rooij, C.G.M.: Mediamill: Semantic video browsing using the rotorbrowser. In: Proceedings of the ACM International Conference on Image and Video Retrieval, Amsterdam, The Netherlands (July 2007)

4. Grana, C., Vezzani, R., Bulgarelli, D., Barbieri, F., Cucchiara, R., Bertini, M., Torniai, C., Del Bimbo, A.: PEANO: Pictorial Enriched ANnotation of VideO. Accepted for publication. In: Proceedings of the 14th ACM international Conference on Multimedia, Santa Barbara, CA, United States, October 23-27 (2006)
5. Information technology - Multimedia content description interface - Part 3: Visual, ISO/IEC Std. 15 938-3:2003 (2003)
6. Lei, Z., Fuzong, L., Bo, Z.: A CBIR method based on color-spatial feature. In: TENCON 1999. Proceedings of the IEEE Region 10 Conference, vol. 1, pp. 166–169 (1999)
7. Huang, J., et al.: Image indexing using color correlogram. In: Proceedings of 1997 IEEE Computer Society Conference on Computer Vision and Pattern Recognition, pp. 762–768 (1997)
8. Ojala, T., Rautiainen, M., Matinmikko, E., Aittola, M.: Semantic image retrieval with HSV correlograms. In: Proc. 12th Scandinavian Conference on Image Analysis, Bergen, Norway, pp. 621–627 (2001)
9. Cinque, L., Levialdi, S., Olsen, K.A., Pellicano, A.: Color-based image retrieval using spatial-chromatic histograms. IEEE International Conference on Multimedia Computing and Systems 2, 969–973 (1999)
10. Hurvich, L., Jameson, D.: An opponent-process theory of color vision. Psychological Review 64, 384–390 (1957)
11. Won, C.S., Park, D.K., Park, S.-J.: Efficient Use of MPEG-7 Edge Histogram Descriptor. ETRI Journal 24(1), 23–30 (2002)
12. Tseng, D.C., Chang, C.H.: Color segmentation using perceptual attributes. In: Proceedings of 11th IAPR International conference on Pattern Recognition, Vol.III. Conference C: Image, Speech and Signal Analysis, pp. 228–231 (1992)
13. Seaborn, M., Hepplewhite, L., Stonham, J.: Fuzzy colour category map for content based image retrieval. In: Proceedings of the British Machine Vision Conference, BMVC 1999 (1999)
14. Sural, S., Qian, G., Pramanik, S.: Segmentation and histogram generation using the HSV color space for image retrieval. In: Proceedings of the International Conference on Image Processing, vol. 2, pp.II-589- II-592 (2002)
15. Eidenberger, H.: Statistical analysis of MPEG-7 image descriptions. ACM Multimedia Systems Journal 10(2), 84–97 (2004)
16. Grana, C., Vezzani, R., Cucchiara, R.: Enhancing HSV Histograms with Achromatic Points Detection for Video Retrieval. In: Proceedings of ACM International Conference on Image and Video Retrieval, CIVR 2007 pp.302–308 (2007)
17. Schaefer, G., Stich, M.: UCID - An Uncompressed Colour Image Database. In: Proc. SPIE, Storage and Retrieval Methods and Applications for Multimedia 2004, San Jose, USA, pp. 472–480 (2004)

An Adaptive Technique for Accurate Feature Extraction from Regular and Irregular Image Data

Sonya Coleman[1], Shanmuglingam Suganthan[2], and Bryan Scotney[3]

[1] University of Ulster, Magee, BT48 7JL, Northern Ireland
[2] Smart Sensors Ltd, University of Bath Innovation Centre, Broad Quay, Bath, BA1 1UD
[3] University of Ulster, Coleraine, BT52 1SA, Northern Ireland
SA.Coleman@Ulster.ac.uk, S.Suganthan@ieee.org,
BW.Scotney@Ulster.ac.uk

Abstract. We present a single multi-scale gradient-based feature extraction algorithm that can be directly applied to irregular or regular image data and hence can be used on both range and intensity images. We illustrate the accuracy of this approach using the Figure of Merit evaluation technique on real images, demonstrating that the application of this approach to both range and intensity images is more accurate than the equivalent approach of applying a gradient operator, such as Sobel, to an intensity image and, separately, the scan-line approximation approach to range images.

Keywords: Range Data, Gradient Operator, Feature Extraction.

1 Introduction

For many years, feature extraction techniques have been developed for use on intensity images, the earliest being the simple gradient operators of Sobel and Prewitt, and extensive efforts have been made to develop multi-scale feature extraction approaches, for example [8, 17]. Recently computer vision applications have increasingly begun to use range image data [11, 12] instead of, or in conjunction with, intensity image data [7]. This is largely because range imagery can be used to obtain reliable descriptions of 3-D scenes; a range image contains distance measurements from a selected reference point or plane to surface points of objects within a scene [4], allowing more information about the scenes to be recovered [3]. However, techniques that can be used for feature extraction directly from more than one image type and in particular that can be directly applied to both range and intensity images are not readily available [2, 9]. Typically approaches for feature extraction in intensity or range images can only be applied principally to that specific image type; none of the typical approaches can be readily applied to both image types without image pre-processing. As much research has been undertaken in trying to integrate 2D and 3D images [2], specifically in application areas such as medical imaging [6] and face recognition [5, 21], we believe that a single approach that can be used on both image types would greatly aid the process of image fusion.

When using range images the problem of data irregularity may be encountered [13, 14]. In [15, 16] we addressed the data distribution problem by generating directional

P. Foggia, C. Sansone, and M. Vento (Eds.): ICIAP 2009, LNCS 5716, pp. 911–919, 2009.

derivate operators that are shape adaptive, and hence can be applied directly to both irregularly and regularly distributed data, thus providing the facility for the operators to be applied directly to both range and intensity images. In [15, 16] we noted that the standard thresholding technique for finding edges, typically applied to intensity images, is not appropriate for use on range image data, as it does not identify edges, but surfaces in range images; to overcome this drawback, we identified a process of finding significant changes in the gradient response as a means of determining edges in range images.

In [16] we present multi-scale gradient operators for direct use on range images containing either irregularly or regularly distributed image data, designed within the finite element framework. In this paper we demonstrate how the flexibility of this approach enables us to apply our multi-scale technique to either range or intensity images, and the performance evaluation illustrates the accuracy of this approach. Section 2 provides a brief overview of the multi-scale algorithm published in [16] and discusses how such an approach can be readily applied to both intensity and range images. Section 3 provides initial Figure of Merit results for the approach, demonstrating that our single approach works better than the equivalent use of two separate feature extraction algorithms, and Section 4 provides a summary and details of future work.

2 Overview of Adaptive Bilinear-Gaussian (BG) Operators

In order to address the use of either intensity or range images, we consider an image to be represented by a spatially irregular sample of values of a continuous function $u(x,y)$ of depth value on a domain Ω. Our operator design is then based on the use of a quadrilateral mesh in which the nodes are the sample points. With each node i in the mesh is associated a piecewise bilinear basis function $\phi_i(x, y)$ which has the properties $\phi_i(x_j, y_j) = 1$ if $i = j$ and $\phi_i(x_j, y_j) = 0$ if $i \neq j$, where (x_j, y_j) are the coordinates of the nodal point j in the mesh. Thus $\phi_i(x, y)$ is a "tent-shaped" function with support restricted to a small neighbourhood centred on node i consisting of only those elements that have node i as a vertex. The image function u is approximately represented by a function

$$U(x, y) = \sum_{j=1}^{N} U_j \phi_j(x, y)$$

in which the parameters $\{U_1,...,U_N\}$ are mapped from the image pixel values (either intensity or range) at the N irregularly located nodal points.

The complete operator design is described in detail in [16] whereby we formulate image operators that correspond to weak forms in the finite element method; for example, corresponding to a first directional derivative $\partial u / \partial b \equiv \underline{b} \cdot \underline{\nabla} u$ we may use a test function $v \in H^1(\Omega)$ to define the weak form

$$E(u) = \int_{\Omega} \underline{b} \cdot \underline{\nabla} u v d\Omega,$$

where $\underline{b} = (\cos\theta, \sin\theta)$ is the unit direction vector. Since we are focussing on multi-scale operators that can explicitly embrace the concept of size and shape variability, the design procedure in [16] uses a finite-dimensional test space $T_\sigma^h \subset H^1$ that explicitly embodies a size parameter σ that is determined by the local data distribution. Using such test functions, the first order functional is defined as

$$E_i^\sigma(U) = \int_{\Omega_i^\sigma} \underline{b}_i \cdot \nabla U \psi_i^\sigma \, d\Omega_i \,,$$

where sets of test functions $\psi_i^\sigma(x, y)$, $i=1,\ldots,N$, are used when defining irregular derivative-based operators and the chosen test function is a Gaussian basis function. Hence we refer to our technique as the use of Bilinear-Gaussian operators. Further details of operator construction can be found in [16].

Figure 1 illustrates a local "3×3" neighbourhood on an irregular mesh. When using range image data, within each neighbourhood a different size parameter is computed for each quadrant of the neighbourhood, enabling the Gaussian test function to adapt to the local area more accurately. However, when using an intensity image, the data distribution will be regular and therefore $W_\sigma^{e_1} = W_\sigma^{e_2} = W_\sigma^{e_3} = W_\sigma^{e_4}$. As illustrated in Figure 1, $W_\sigma^{e_m}$ is chosen as the "diagonal" of the neighbourhood from the operator centre (x_i, y_i), and in each case the quadrant scale parameter $\sigma_m = W_\sigma^{e_m}/1.96$ ensures that the diagonal of the quadrant through (x_i, y_i) encompasses 95% of the cross-section of the Gaussian.

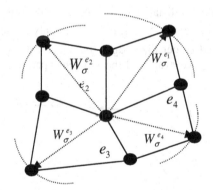

Fig. 1. Local 3×3 operator neighbourhood

In the case where intensity images are used, the 3×3 (or any other sized) operator needs to be computed only once and applied appropriately across the image plane; however, as suggested by the change in $W_\sigma^{e_m}$ within any neighbourhood, construction of the operators on an irregular quadrilateral grid, and hence when using range image data, differs in that it is no longer appropriate to build an entire operator, as each operator throughout an irregular mesh will differ with respect to the operator neighbourhood shape. When using an irregular grid with a range image, we work on an element-by-element basis, taking advantage of the flexibility offered by the finite element method as a means of creating irregular operators to encompass the data available in any local neighbourhood.

3 Results

In order to obtain features after application of our technique to range and intensity images, two different methods of thresholding must be used. In the case of using intensity images, features are found using the standard thresholding approach. However, when gradient operators are applied to range images, standard thresholding yields object surfaces rather than edges; hence we must look for significant changes in the gradient responses of the range image.

For evaluation purposes, we use the well-known Figure of Merit (FoM) measure [1] and compare our proposed technique (further denoted as BG) with that of the well-known scan-line approximation algorithm [10] (further denoted as SA). Pratt [1] considered three major areas of error associated with the determination of an edge: missing valid edge points; failure to localise edge points; and classification of noise fluctuations as edge points. Pratt therefore introduced the FoM technique as one that balances these three types of error, defined as

$$R = \frac{1}{\max(I_A, I_I)} \sum_{i=1}^{I_A} \frac{1}{1 + \alpha d^2}$$

Here I_A is the actual number of edge pixels detected, I_I is the ideal number of edge pixels, d is the separation distance of a detected edge point normal to a line of ideal edge points, and α is a scaling factor, most commonly chosen to be $\frac{1}{9}$, although this value may be adjusted to penalize edges that are localized but offset from the true edge position. Initially we evaluated the gradient operators with respect to their use

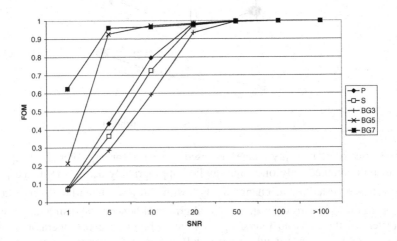

Fig. 2. FoM values vs SNR for operators on a vertical edge

on intensity images. Figure 2 presents comparative results on a vertical ramp edge using the Prewitt and Sobel operators (denoted P and S) and the proposed 3×3, 5×5 and 7×7 Bilinear-Gaussian gradient operators (denoted as BG3, BG5 and BG7). The results illustrate that the multi-scale approach works well on intensity images when compared with the well-known operators of Prewitt and Sobel.

In order to evaluate the accuracy of using just one approach for feature extraction on both intensity and range images, we initially apply the operators to the intensity image (Figure 3(a)) and select the visually best edge map for each operator, an example of which is illustrated in Figure 4.

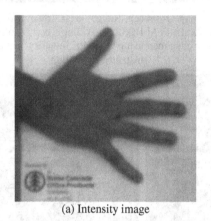

(a) Intensity image

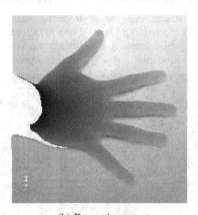

(b) Range image

Fig. 3. Original images

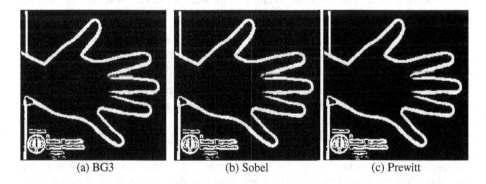

     (a) BG3   (b) Sobel   (c) Prewitt

Fig. 4. Example of edge maps (ground truth) using the intensity image in Figure 3(a)

We then run a series of experiments whereby we apply each technique, 3×3, 5×5 and 7×7 Bilinear-Gaussian gradient operators (denoted as BG3, BG5 and BG7) and the scan-line approach of [10], to the corresponding range image (Figure 3(b)) over a range of practical thresholds. Using each intensity image feature map as a possible ground truth match, we compute the FoM value at each threshold for every operator

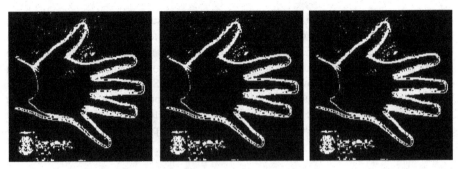

(a) Range edge map from (b) Range edge map from (c) Range edge map from
BG3, providing best FoM BG3, providing best FoM BG3, providing best FoM
using BG3 intensity edge map using Sobel intensity edge map using Prewitt intensity edge
as ground truth   as ground truth   map as ground truth

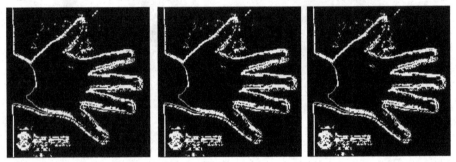

(d) Range edge map from SA, (e) Range edge map from SA, (f) Range edge map from SA,
providing best FoM using providing best FoM using providing best FoM using
BG3 intensity edge map as Sobel intensity edge map as Prewitt intensity edge map as
ground truth   ground truth   ground truth

Fig. 5. Edge maps corresponding to maximum FoM value, using the ground truth in Figure 4:
(a)-(c)BG3 operator; (d)-(f) SA approach [10]

in order to determine the range image feature map than provides the best FoM value
and hence the best match between intensity and range edge maps; an example of such
optimal edge maps are presented in Figure 5.

It should be noted in the Figure 5 that the edge maps generated using the scan-line
approach that provide the best FoM value are relatively noisy in comparison to the
corresponding edge maps using the BG3 operator. It's also worth noting that our
technique automatically finds all features, whereas the approach in [10] does not
automatically find the object boundary via the scan line approximation but instead
assumes the boundary at the transition between data and no data in the range image.

Table 1 provides the maximum computed FoM values when each range image feature map is compared to the corresponding ground truth intensity image. We can
see that in each case the proposed adaptive Bilinear-Gaussian approach provides a
higher FoM value than the scan-line approach. Moreover, and the main focus of the
paper, using a single operator (BG3) on both the intensity image and the range image

Table 1. Computed FoM values and % match values

Operator used for ground truth on intensity image		New Bilinear-Gaussian technique (BG)	Scan line approach (SA)
BG3	FoM	**0.8229**	**0.7953**
	Total pixel match	90.07%	89.39%
	Edge pixel match	61.99%	59.38%
	Background pixel match	94.30%	93.91%
BG5	FoM	**0.8223**	**0.8022**
	Total pixel match	88.67%	88.71%
	Edge pixel match	62.02%	62.02%
	Background pixel match	93.36%	93.40%
BG7	FoM	**0.8201**	**0.7789**
	Total pixel match	88.01%	87.74%
	Edge pixel match	64.16%	62.93%
	Background pixel match	92.78%	92.70%
Sobel	FoM	**0.8056**	**0.7965**
	Total pixel match	90.14%	89.41%
	Edge pixel match	60.89%	59.41%
	Background pixel match	94.57%	93.96%
Prewitt	FoM	**0.7977**	**0.7965**
	Total pixel match	90.11%	89.34%
	Edge pixel match	60.62%	61.06%
	Background pixel match	94.64%	93.68%

provides a higher FoM value than the equivalent individual use of either Sobel or Prewitt on the intensity image followed by using BG3 on the range image. Table 1 also provides details on overall pixel matching in the edge maps for both edge and background pixels.

4 Summary

With the increase in imaging modalities available, image matching and image fusion have become prominent issues in recent years. We have demonstrated, via our evaluation, that the multi-scale technique presented in [16] for feature extraction on range images can be accurately used for feature extraction on both intensity and range images, regularly and irregularly distributed. The performance evaluation demonstrates that use of the proposed technique for edge detection on range and intensity images performs better than the combination of two different detection algorithms: one suitable for range images and one suitable for intensity images. We have thus provided a one-step approach to processing both image types, removing the need for application of two individual techniques.

Acknowledgment

This work was supported by the U.K Research Council EPSRC under grant number EP/C006283/1. We would like to thank Professor Horst Bunke for providing us with the code for the scan line approximation algorithm in [10].

References

1. Abdou, I.E., Pratt, W.K.: Quantitative Design and Evaluation of Enhancement/ Threshold Edge Detectors. Proc. of IEEE 67(5) (May 1979)
2. Alshawabkeh, Y., Haala, N., Fritsch, D.: 2D-3D Feature Extraction and Registration of Real World Scenes. In: ISPRS Commission V Symposium Image Engineering and Vision Metrology, pp. 32–37 (2006)
3. Bellon, O., Silva, L.: New Improvements on Range Image Segmentation by Edge Detection Techniques. In: Proc. of Workshop on Artificial Intelligence and Computer Vision (November 2000)
4. Besl, P.J.: Active, optical range imaging sensors. Machine Vision and Apps. 1, 127–152 (1988)
5. Colombo, A., Cusano, C., Schettini, R.: Face3 a 2D+3D Robust Face Recognition System. In: Proc. of IEEE Int. Conf. on Image Analysis and Processing, pp. 393–398 (2007)
6. Cyr, C.M., Kamal, A.F., Sebastian, T.B., Kimia, B.B.: 2D-3D Registration Based on Shape Matching. In: IEEE Workshop Mathematical Methods in Biomedical Image Analysis, pp. 198–203 (2000)
7. Dias, P., et al.: Combining Intensity and Range Images for 3D Modelling. Proc. of the IEEE Int. Conf. on Image Processing (2003)
8. Ferreira, M., Kiranyaz, S., Gabbouj, M.: Multi-Scale Edge Detection and Object Extraction for Image Retrieval. In: Proc IEEE Int. Conf. on Acoustics, Speech and Signal Processing, vol. 2 (2006)
9. Gachter, S.: Results on Range Image Segmentation for Service Robots. Technical Report, Switerland
10. Jiang, X.Y., Bunke, H.: Fast Segmentation of Range Images into Planar Regions by Scan Line Grouping. Machine Vision and Applications 7(2), 115–122 (1994)
11. Katsoulas, D., Werber, A.: Edge Detection in Range Images of Piled Box-like Objects. In: Proc. Int. Conf. on Pattern Recognition pp.80–84 (2004)
12. Marshall, D., Lukas, G., Martin, R.: Robust Segmentation of Primitives from Range Data in the Presence of Geometric Degeneracy. IEEE Trans. PAMI 23(3), 304–314 (2001)
13. Maas, H.-G.: Planimetric and height accuracy of airborne laserscanner data - User requirements and system performance. In: Fritsch, D. (ed.) Proceedings of Photogrammetric Week, vol. 49. Wichmann Verlag (2003)
14. Lee, B.K., Yu, K., Pyeon, M.: Effective Reduction of Horzontal Error in Laser Scanning Information by Strip-Wise Least Squares Adjustments. ETRI Journal 25(2), 109–120 (2003)
15. Suganthan, S., Coleman, S.A., Scotney, B.W.: Range Image Feature Extraction with Varying Degrees of Data Irregularity. In: International Machine Vision and Image Processing Conference, pp. 33–40 (2007)

16. Suganthan, S., Coleman, S.A., Scotney, B.W.: Scalable Operators for Feature Extraction on 3-D Data. Springer Tracts in Advanced Robotics 44, 263–272 (2008)
17. Tremblais, B., Augereau, B.: A fast multi-scale edge detection algorithm. Pattern Recognition Letters 25(6), 603–618 (2004)
18. Tsalakanidou, F., Malassiotis, S., Strintzis, M.G.: Integration of 2D and 3D Images for Enhanced Face Authentication. In: Proc. 6th IEEE Int. Conf. Automatic Face and Gesture Recognition (2004)

Processing Hexagonal Images in a Virtual Environment

Sonya Coleman[1], Bryan Scotney[2], and Bryan Gardiner[1]

[1] School of Computing and Intelligent Systems, University of Ulster,
Magee, BT48 7JL, Northern Ireland
[2] School of Computing and Information Engineering, University of Ulster,
Coleraine, BT52 1SA, Northern Ireland

Abstract. For many years the concept of using hexagonal pixels for image capture has been investigated, and several advantages of such an approach have been highlighted. Recently there has been a renewed interest in the use of hexagonal images, representation of architectures for such images and general hexagonal image processing. Therefore, we present multiscale hexagonal gradient operators, developed within the finite element framework, for use directly on hexagonal pixel-based images. We demonstrate these operators using two environments: a *virtual hexagonal environment* and the direct use of simulated hexagonal pixel-based images. In both scenarios, we evaluate the proposed operators and compare them with the use of standard image processing operators on typical square pixel-based images, demonstrating improved results in the case of simulated hexagonal pixel-based images.

Keywords: Hexagonal pixel-based images, hexagonal gradient operators.

1 Introduction

Image processing tasks have traditionally involved the use of square operators on rectangular images lattices. A more recent concept that has been investigated is the use of hexagonal pixels for image capture, introducing the area of hexagonal image processing. Although hexagonal lattices have been explored for approximately 40 years [6, 12, 14], recent improvements in charged coupled device (CCD) technology have made hexagonal sampling attractive for practical applications and a renewed interest has been developed in this area [8, 9]. The hexagonal structure is considered to be preferable to the standard rectangular structure typically used for images in terms of the improved accuracy and efficiency that can be achieved for a number of image processing tasks. There are a number of reasons why this is the case, and one major advantage is the consistency available in terms of neighbouring pixel distances when tiling an image plane, thus creating a condition that will facilitate the implementation of circular symmetric kernels that is associated with an increase in accuracy when detecting edges, both straight and curved [1]. Additionally, sampling on a hexagonal grid has proven to achieve greater efficiency than on a square lattice. Vitulli [13] concluded that the sampling efficiency of hexagonal sampling exceeds that of square sampling, as approximately 13% fewer pixels are needed to obtain the same performance as achieved using square sampling. With 13% fewer pixels needed to

P. Foggia, C. Sansone, and M. Vento (Eds.): ICIAP 2009, LNCS 5716, pp. 920–928, 2009.

represent a hexagonal image with the same information, less storage in memory will be needed for the image data, and hence potentially less computational time to process the image. Although there are obvious benefits with hexagonal based images, image representation in a hexagonal structure can currently be achieved only through square to hexagonal image conversion [5, 12, 14, 16], though the emergence of genuine hexagonal-based sensor systems and image capture devices is crucial for the benefits of hexagonal structure to be fully appreciated and exploited.

Taking all this into consideration, few attempts have been made to process such hexagonal images. Although many feature detection operators exist for square lattices [2, 7], due to the structure of the hexagonal lattice these operators are not directly compatible with hexagonal pixel images. Only the simplest operators such as Sobel and Prewitt have, to date, been extended for use on hexagonal images [9, 12, 15], and only one gradient operator has been explicitly designed for use on hexagonally structured images [4]. However, more recently attempts have been renewed to apply processing techniques directly to hexagonal images, for example bi-lateral filtering based edge detection [15], introducing the possibility for significant development in the area of feature detection on these lattices.

In recent work [11] the finite element framework has been used to design and implement novel near-circular derivative operators that have been shown to improve edge orientation angular error. This paper builds on the finite element framework used in [11] to facilitate hexagonally structured images. We present an approach to the development of multiscale gradient operators explicitly for use directly on hexagonal grids. In order to obtain hexagonal pixel based images, regular rectangular images must be resampled to a hexagonal lattice, and the procedure that we use to do so is described in Section 2. Sections 3 and 4 discuss how hexagonal pixels are represented in an image, giving a brief overview of how the gradient operators are implemented. In Section 5 we apply our hexagonal gradient operators in the *virtual hexagonal* environment for processing only, and then resample into a square pixel-based image for display and evaluation. Section 6 summarises the benefits obtained in the processing environment and discusses future work.

2 Creating a Hexagonal Pixel

To date, a hexagonal image can only be obtained by resampling a standard square pixel-based image. We have chosen to use the approach of [16] whereby hexagonal pixels are created through clusters of square sub-pixels. We have modified this technique slightly by representing each pixel by a $n \times n$ pixel block, as in [8], in order to create a sub-pixel effect to enable the sub-pixel clustering; this modification limits the loss of image resolution. Each pixel of the original image is represented by a 7×7 pixel block, Fig. 1(a), of equal intensity in the new image [8]. This creates a resized image of the same resolution as the original image with the ability to display each pixel as a group of $n \times n$ sub-pixels. The motivation for image resizing is to enable the display of sub pixels, which is not otherwise possible. With this structure now in place, a cluster of sub-pixels in the new image, closely representing the shape of a hexagon, can be created that represents a single hexagonal pixel in the resized image, Fig.1(b).

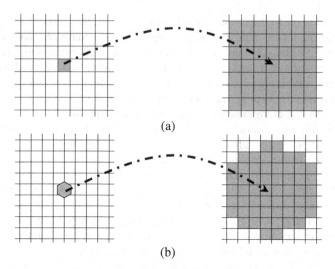

(a)

(b)

Fig. 1. Resizing of image to enable display of image at sub pixel level

3   Representing a Hexagonal Pixel-Based Image

It is possible to represent the hexagonal image by using an array of samples of a continuous function $u(x, y)$ of image intensity on a domain Ω. Fig. 2 represents hexagonal pixels with nodes placed in the centre of each pixel. These nodes are the reference points for the computation of finite element based techniques throughout the domain Ω.

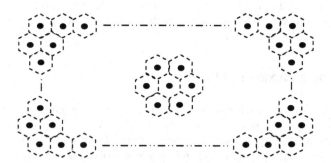

Fig. 2. Representation of a hexagonal image

4   Multiscale Hexagonal Operator Design

We propose an operator for use on a hexagonal pixel based image as illustrated in Fig. 2. The operator design procedure is based on the use of a "virtual mesh" illustrated in Fig. 3, consisting of equilateral triangular elements, which overlays the pixel array shown in Fig. 2.

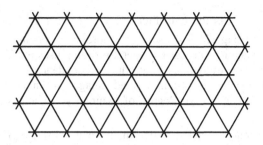

Fig. 3. Virtual mesh of equilateral triangular elements

With any node in the virtual mesh, say node i, with co-ordinates (x_i, y_i) we associate a piecewise linear basis function $\phi_i(x, y)$ which has the properties $\phi_i(x_j, y_j) = 1$ if $i = j$ and $\phi_i(x_j, y_j) = 0$ if $i \neq j$ where (x_j, y_j) are the co-ordinates of the nodal point j. $\phi_i(x, y)$ is thus a "tent-shaped" function with support restricted to a small neighbourhood centred on node i consisting of only those triangular elements that have node i as a vertex. To construct an operator centred on node i, we define a neighbourhood Ω_i^σ consisting of a compact subset of six elements. Denoting by D_i^σ the set of nodes contained in or on the border of Ω_i^σ, we may approximately represent the image u over the neighbourhood Ω_i^σ by a function $U(x, y) = \sum_{j \in D_i^\sigma} U_j \phi_j(x, y)$ in which the parameters $\{U_j\}$ are mapped from the hexagonal image intensity values. The approximate image representation is therefore a simple piecewise linear function on each element in the neighbourhood Ω_i^σ and having intensity values $\{U_j\}$ at nodes $j \in D_i^\sigma$.

As in [11], we formulate operators that correspond to weak forms of operators in the finite element method. Operators used for smoothing may be based simply on a weak form of the image function. In this case it is assumed that the image function $u \equiv u(x, y)$ belongs to the Hilbert space $H^0(\Omega)$; that is, the integral $\int u^2 d\Omega$ over Ω is finite. Edge detection and enhancement operators are often based on first or second derivative approximations, for which it is necessary that the image function $u \equiv u(x, y)$ belongs to the Hilbert space $H^1(\Omega)$; i.e., the integral $\int (|\nabla u|^2 + u^2) d\Omega$ over Ω is finite, where ∇u is the vector $(\partial u / \partial x, \partial u / \partial y)^T$. We are currently concerned only with first order derivative operators and, therefore, to obtain a weak form of the first directional derivative $\partial u / \partial b \equiv \underline{b} \cdot \nabla u$ the derivative term is multiplied by a test function $v \in H^1$ and the result integrated over the image domain Ω to give

$$E(u) = \int_\Omega \underline{b} \cdot \nabla u v d\Omega \tag{1}$$

where $\underline{b} = (\cos\theta, \sin\theta)$ is the unit direction vector. This enables us to design our hexagonal operator using either a Cartesian coordinate system or the three axes of symmetry of the hexagon. Our current operator design uses the Cartesian coordinate system as the three axes of symmetry introduces redundancy [8]. However, the symmetric hexagonal coordinate system has advantages when applied to tasks such as rotation that involve a large degree of symmetry [8] and so may be used in future work.

In the finite element method a finite-dimensional subspace $S^h \subset H^1$ is used for function approximation; in our design procedure S^h is defined by the virtual finite element mesh in Fig. 3. Our general design procedure incorporates a finite-dimensional test space $T_\sigma^h \subset H^1$ that explicitly embodies a scale parameter σ and this test space T_σ^h comprises a set of Gaussian basis functions $\psi_i^\sigma(x, y)$, $i=1,..., N$. Each test function $\psi_i^\sigma(x, y)$ is restricted to have support over the neighbourhood Ω_i^σ, centred on node i. In general the size of Ω_i^σ may be explicitly related to the scale parameter σ [3], as illustrated by the six-element and 24-element hexagonal neighbourhoods in Fig. 4.

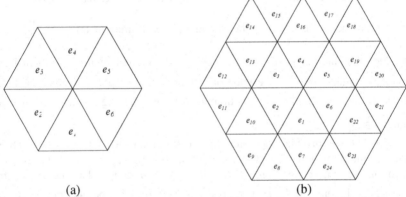

(a)   (b)

Fig. 4. Hexagonal operator structures: (a) six-element neighbourhood; (b) 24-element neighbourhood

The sets of test functions $\psi_i^\sigma(x, y)$, $i=1, ..., N$, are then used in the weak forms of the first derivative in (2). In particular we note that the integrals need to be computed only over the neighbourhood Ω_i^σ, rather than the entire image domain Ω, since ψ_i^σ has support restricted to Ω_i^σ. Hence the approximate image representation over Ω_i^σ may be used, providing the functional

$$E_i^\sigma(U) = \int_{\Omega_i^\sigma} \underline{b}_i \cdot \nabla U \psi_i^\sigma d\Omega_i \cdot \tag{2}$$

To illustrate the implementation of the first order hexagonal operator on a virtual mesh as shown in Fig. 3, a local co-ordinate reference system for a general equilateral triangular element will be used. Here one of the nodes α, β, λ, is a central node i of a neighbourhood Ω_i^σ. For example, the neighbourhood Ω_i^σ, in Fig. 4(a) covers a set of six elements $\{e_m\}$; a Gaussian basis function ψ_i^σ is associated with the central node i which shares common support with the surrounding seven basis functions ϕ_j. Hence $E_i^\sigma(U)$ needs to be computed over the six elements in the neighbourhood Ω_i^σ. Substituting the image representation into the functional $E_i^\sigma(U)$ in (2) yields

$$E_i^\sigma(U) = b_{i1} \sum_{j=1}^{N} K_{ij}^\sigma U_j + b_{i2} \sum_{j=1}^{N} L_{ij}^\sigma U_j \tag{3}$$

where $K_{ij}^\sigma = \sum_{m|e_m \in S_i^\sigma} k_{ij}^{m,\sigma}$ and $L_{ij}^\sigma = \sum_{m|e_m \in S_i^\sigma} l_{ij}^{m,\sigma}$ and $k_{ij}^{m,\sigma}$ and $l_{ij}^{m,\sigma}$ are the element integrals $k_{ij}^{m,\sigma} = \int \frac{\partial \phi_j}{\partial x} \psi_i^\sigma dxdy$ and $l_{ij}^{m,\sigma} = \int \frac{\partial \phi_j}{\partial y} \psi_i^\sigma dxdy$. In order to calculate $k_{ij}^{m,\sigma}$ and $l_{ij}^{m,\sigma}$, we introduce co-ordinates ξ and η such that $\xi \geq 0$, $\eta \geq 0$ and $1 - \xi - \eta \geq 0$. Mapping these global co-ordinates to local co-ordinates can be obtained by means of a co-ordinate transformation from e_m to $\hat{e}$ defined by (4) and (5).

$$x = (x_2^m - x_1^m)\xi + (x_3^m - x_1^m)\eta + x_1^m, \tag{4}$$

$$y = (y_2^m - y_1^m)\xi + (y_3^m - y_1^m)\eta + y_1^m. \tag{5}$$

5   Processing in a Virtual Hexagonal Environment

In this section we present the results obtained when we resample a standard square pixel-based to a hexagonal pixel-based image, the *virtual hexagonal environment*, solely for the purpose of image processing and then resample back to the original square pixel-based image for display and evaluation as illustrated in Fig. 5. Within the *virtual hexagonal environment* feature extraction is performed using the multiscale hexagonal operators presented in Section 3.

The purpose of this is to determine whether, in the current absence of hexagonal image sensors, there is benefit to be gained by processing in a *virtual hexagonal environment*. Initially we provide Figure of Merit results in Fig. 6 using a ramp edge

Fig. 5.

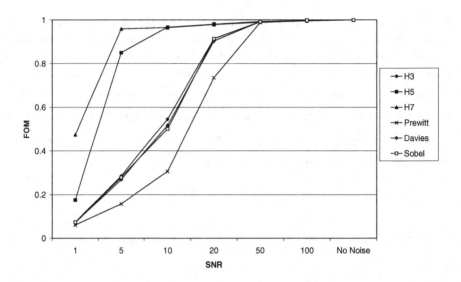

Fig. 6. Figure or merit results using a 60° oriented edge

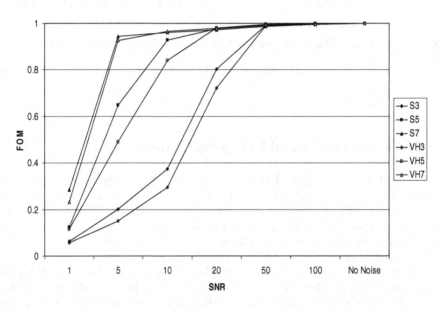

Fig. 7. Figure of merit results computed on a horizontal edge

oriented at 60°, comparing our proposed multiscale gradient operators (denoted H3, H5 and H7) with existing operators that can be directly used on hexagonal images, namely Davies [4], Prewitt and Sobel. The results show that our proposed approach provides improved edge localisation, over a range of signal-to-noise ratios, compared with the existing hexagonal operators.

In addition, we compute Figure of Merit results using the proposed hexagonal operators in the *virtual environment* (denoted VH3, VH5 and VH7) and the equivalent use of finite element based standard square operators [10] on standard images (denoted S3, S5 and S7). The results presented in Fig. 7 demonstrate that processing in a *virtual environment* provides results that are comparable to, and in some cases slightly better than, the equivalent use of typical operators on standard square pixel based images. We also illustrate real edge maps in Fig. 8, again illustrating that both approaches provide comparable results. These initial results are promising given that a hexagonal pixel-based image contains 13% fewer pixels than a standard square pixel-based image. Although computation is required to resample the original square pixel-based image to a hexagonal pixel-based image, the hexagonal operators designed on a Cartesian axis contain fewer operator values than the corresponding square operators, thus generating a significant overall reduction in computation. For example, for a given 256×256 image, removing boundary pixels, 63504 pixels will be processed. Using a 5×5 operator there will be 63504×25 multiplications totalling 1587600. If the same image is re-sampled onto a hexagonal based image there will be 55566 pixels processed by an equivalent hexagonal gradient operator containing only 19 values. Therefore there will be only 1055754 multiplications, corresponding to 66.5% of the computation required to generate a similar feature map using an equivalent traditional square pixel-based image. The increase in accuracy when using our proposed hexagonal operators combined with the increase in efficiency when directly applying these operators will counteract the time taken to resample to a hexagonal grid.

(a) Original square pixel-based image

(b) Edge map using 5×5 standard square operator

(c) Edge map using 19-point hexagonal operator within the *virtual hex-environment*

Fig. 8. Edge maps obtained using Lena image

6 Conclusion

The use of hexagonal pixel-based images has received much attention in recent years with respect to both image architecture and processing. We have presented a design procedure for multi-scale gradient operators developed explicitly for use on hexagonal pixel-based images, created within the finite element framework. Using the Figure of Merit evaluation technique, we have demonstrated that the proposed operators can provide better feature localisation than currently existing operators for processing hexagonal images. In addition, we have demonstrated the use of such operators in a *virtual hexagonal environment,* and the initial results obtained are promising. Therefore, we conclude that given the potential computational gain of using hexagonal images through both the fact that a hexagonal pixel-based image contains 13% fewer pixels than the equivalent square pixel-based image and the fact that hexagonal operators contain fewer operator values than their square-lattice counterparts, the use of hexagonal pixel-based images has potential be significantly beneficial to the computer vision and image processing communities. Future work will encompass the use of the spiral architecture in our operator implementation with the overall aim of providing an overall design and implementation framework that can reduce further the computation complexity of the approach. Hence the hexagonal image framework should become more appealing for use in real-time imaging applications.

References

[1] Allen, J.D.: Filter Banks for Images on Hexagonal Grid. Signal Solutions (2003)
[2] Canny, J.F.: A Computational Approach to Edge Detection. IEEE Trans on Pattern Analysis and Machine Intelligence 8(6) (November 1986)
[3] Davies, E.R.: Circularity – A New Design Principle Underlying the Design of Accurate Edge Orientation Filters. Image and Vision Computing 5, 134–142 (1984)
[4] Davies, E.R.: Optimising Computation of Hexagonal Differential Gradient Edge Detector. Electronic Letters 27(1)
[5] He, X.: 2-D Object Recognition with Spiral Architecture. University of Technology, Sydney (1999)
[6] He, X., Jia, W.: Hexagonal Structure for Intelligent Vision. In: Information and Communication Technologies, ICICT, pp. 52–64 (2005)
[7] Marr, D., Hildreth, E.: Theory of Edge Detection. In: Proceedings of the Royal Society of London, Series B, vol. 207, pp. 187–217 (1980)
[8] Middleton, L., Sivaswamy, J.: Hexagonal Image Processing; A Practical Approach. Springer, Heidelberg (2005)
[9] Middleton, L., Sivaswamy, J.: Edge Detection in a Hexagonal-Image Processing Framework. Image and Vision Computing 19, 1071–1081 (2001)
[10] Scotney, B.W., Coleman, S.A., Herron, M.G.: Device Space Design for Efficient Scale-Space Edge Detection. In: Sloot, P.M.A., Tan, C.J.K., Dongarra, J., Hoekstra, A.G. (eds.) ICCS-ComputSci 2002. LNCS, vol. 2329, pp. 1077–1086. Springer, Heidelberg (2002)
[11] Scotney, B.W., Coleman, S.A.: Improving Angular Error via Systematically Designed Near-Circular Gaussian-based Feature Extraction Operators. Pattern Recognition 40(5), 1451–1465
[12] Staunton, R.C.: The design of hexagonal sampling structures for image digitisation and their use with local operators. Image Vision Computing 7(3), 162–166 (1989)
[13] Vitulli, R.: Aliasing Effects Mitigation by Optimized Sampling Grids and Impact on Image Acquisition Chains. Geoscience and Remote Sensing Symposium, 979–981 (2002)
[14] Wu, Q., He, X., Hintz, T.: Virtual Spiral Architecture. In: Int. Conf. on Parallel and Distributed Processing Techniques and Applications, pp. 339–405 (2004)
[15] Wu, Q., He, X., Hintz, T.: Bi-lateral Filtering Based Edge Detection on Hexagonal Architecture. In: Proc. of Int. Conf. on Acoustic, Sound an Signal Processing, vol 2, pp. 713–716 (2005)
[16] Wuthrich, C.A., Stucki, P.: An Algorithm Comparison between Square and Hexagonal Based Grids. In: CVGIP: Graphical Models and Image Processing, vol. 53, pp. 324–339 (1991)

Pixel Coverage Segmentation for Improved Feature Estimation

Nataša Sladoje[1] and Joakim Lindblad[2]

[1] Faculty of Engineering, University of Novi Sad, Serbia
sladoje@uns.ns.ac.yu
[2] Centre for Image Analysis, SLU, Uppsala, Sweden
joakim@cb.uu.se

Abstract. By utilizing intensity information available in images, partial coverage of pixels at object borders can be estimated. Such information can, in turn, provide more precise feature estimates. We present a pixel coverage segmentation method which assigns pixel values corresponding to the area of a pixel that is covered by the imaged object(s). Starting from any suitable crisp segmentation, we extract a one-pixel thin 4-connected boundary between the observed image components where a local linear mixture model is used for estimating fractional pixel coverage values. We evaluate the presented segmentation method, as well as its usefulness for subsequent precise feature estimation, on synthetic test objects with increasing levels of noise added. We conclude that for reasonable noise levels the presented method outperforms the achievable results of a perfect crisp segmentation. Finally, we illustrate the application of the suggested method on a real histological colour image.

1 Introduction

By utilizing grey-levels in digital object representations, the loss of information associated with the process of image segmentation can be significantly reduced. In our previous work, we explored grey level discrete object representations corresponding to pixel coverage. Such representations are characterized by pixel values proportional to the (relative) area of a pixel covered by the imaged (presumably crisp continuous) object. Therefore, pixel values range from 0 (assigned to pixels having empty intersection with the object) to 1 (pixels completely covered by the object). The pixel values strictly between 0 and 1 appear on the (one pixel thick) border of an object. We conducted a number of studies showing advantages of this type of object representations, *pixel coverage representation*, [9], compared to crisp (binary) digital image representations, especially when it comes to the precision and accuracy of feature estimations, [8,9].

Encouraging results, proven both theoretically and by empirical studies on synthetic objects, direct our interest to applications of the developed estimators on real images. The first step required for such use is an appropriate image segmentation method, i.e., a segmentation method which results in a pixel coverage representation. In [9] we presented a simple pixel coverage segmentation method,

P. Foggia, C. Sansone, and M. Vento (Eds.): ICIAP 2009, LNCS 5716, pp. 929–938, 2009.

primarily as a proof of concept, at that moment leaving fairly unexplored the potentially wide field of pixel coverage segmentation methods.

In this paper we present a more general approach for pixel coverage segmentation. After giving a brief overview of the existing related results in Section 2, we introduce in Section 3 the main result of the paper – a novel pixel coverage segmentation method. The method consists of the combination of an arbitrary crisp segmentation method with an additional step where pixels on the border of the object(s) are revisited and their coverage values are computed. In Section 4 we present results of evaluation of the proposed segmentation method, based on a study performed on synthetic data. Finally, in Section 5 we illustrate application of the proposed segmentation method for quantitative analysis of a histological image. Section 6 concludes the paper.

2 Background

Image segmentation aims at partitioning the image into a number of components characterized by a certain intra-component homogeneity and inter-component discontinuity. In an ideal case a one-to-one correspondence between the set of intensities and the set of the image components exists and a partitioning can be based on a straightforward classification of pixel intensities. However, even in such an ideal case, discretization of the continuous object leads to ambiguous situations where one pixel—the Voronoi region associated to a point in an integer grid—may be partly covered by more than one object in the image. The intensity value of such a pixel is a mixture of the intensities of the corresponding "pure" components. However, crisp segmentation methods do not allow partial belongingness of a pixel to an object, and therefore a hard decision of the belongingness has to be made. For the general case, more or less complex and task-dependent segmentation methods are used, often combining spatial and intensity information, or/and some a priori knowledge. Different segmentation methods may deal with (different types of) noise in different ways; however, the issue of mixed border pixels remains, being caused by discretization itself.

It is not surprising that the issue of mixed pixels is thoroughly addressed in remote sensing applications (see, e.g., [3,4,11]). Pixels in remotely sensed images are of sizes that very often lead to individual pixels being covered by different classes/objects imaged on the ground. Sub-pixel proportion estimation, leading to so-called fraction images, is a widely studied problem. Most often used approaches are linear mixture models and neural networks, the former due to their simplicity, and the latter when the mixtures in the pixels are non-linear and more complex, [4].

Interest for sub-pixel segmentation approaches exists in cases of images of higher resolution as well. In particular, 3D medical image analysis often requires treatment of partial volume voxels, i.e., voxels that contain not a single tissue, but rather a mixture of two or more tissue types, [5]. The issue is particularly studied for MR and PET images of the human brain; it is shown in [6] that consistently misplacing the tissue borders, in a brain volume having voxels of size $1\,\mathrm{mm}^3$, by only one voxel resulted in volume errors of approximately 30%, 40%, and 60% for white matter, grey matter and cerebrospinal fluid (CSF), respectively. A number of methods were suggested to overcome this limitation, and to address the issue of partial volume effect corrections. Often used are methods based on expectation-maximization, e.g. [5], scale-space approaches [12], wavelets [1], Markov random fields [2], fuzzy techniques, e.g. [10], etc.

Theoretical results derived in [8,9] increase the interest for sub-pixel segmentation approaches in 2D images of higher resolution as well, with a particular goal to utilize such segmentations for precise feature estimation. Studies and development of general and easily accessible pixel coverage segmentation methods and tools for subsequent analysis have, however, not attracted very much attention by now. These observations motivate the study reported here of a general approach, with minimal ties to any particular imaging modality or application, for augmenting any given crisp segmentation to a pixel coverage segmentation, providing an easily accessible tool for improved feature estimates for a large range of applications.

3 Pixel Coverage Segmentation

Let a square grid in 2D be given. The Voronoi region associated to a grid point $(i,j) \in \mathbb{Z}^2$ is called pixel $p_{(i,j)}$. Pixel coverage digitization is defined in [9] as:

Definition 1. *For a given continuous object $S \subset \mathbb{R}^2$, inscribed into an integer grid with pixels $p_{(i,j)}$, the pixel coverage digitization of S is*

$$\mathcal{D}(S) = \left\{ \left((i,j), \frac{A(p_{(i,j)} \cap S)}{A(p_{(i,j)})}\right) \middle| (i,j) \in \mathbb{Z}^2 \right\},$$

where $A(X)$ denotes the area of a set X.

A pixel coverage representation corresponding to a crisp real object, with a well defined continuous border is, ideally, characterized by homogeneous regions of "pure" pixels, completely covered by either object or background, which are separated by a one pixel thick layer of "mixed" pixels, partially covered by both object and background. Pure pixels are assigned values 0 (background) and 1 (object), while mixed pixels are assigned values between 0 and 1, in accordance to their pixel coverage.

A *pixel coverage segmentation* of an image I into m components $c_k, k \in \{1, 2, \ldots, m\}$ is

$$\mathcal{S}(I) = \left\{ ((i,j), \alpha_{(i,j)}) \,\middle|\, (i,j) \in I_D \right\},$$

where

$$\alpha_{(i,j)} = (\alpha_1, \ldots, \alpha_m), \quad \sum_{k=1}^{m} \alpha_k = 1, \quad \alpha_k = \frac{A(p_{(i,j)} \cap S_k)}{A(p_{(i,j)})},$$

and where $S_k \subset \mathbb{R}^2$ is the extent of the component c_k and $I_D \subseteq \mathbb{Z}^2$ is the image domain. The continuous sets S_k are, in general, not known, and the values α_k therefore have to be estimated from the image data.

To obtain a pixel coverage segmentation, we propose a method composed of four steps: (i) application of a crisp segmentation method, appropriately chosen for the particular task; (ii) selection of pixels to be assigned partial coverage; (iii) application of a local linear mixture model for "de-mixing" of partially covered pixels and assignment of pixel coverage values; (iv) ordered thinning of the set of partly covered pixel to provide one pixel thin 4-connected regions of mixed pixels.

The first step in the proposed method is expected to provide correct assignment of class belongingness/area coverage to pure pixels. Crisp segmentation methods are numerous and can be selected to fit the application at hand. We suggest to utilize any appropriate existing segmentation method, and assume that the resulting segmentation provides a trustworthy result for all but boundary pixels. Each pixel $p(i, j)$, inner for the component c_k, is assigned segmentation-vectors $\alpha_{(i,j)}$ such that $\alpha_k = 1$ and $\alpha_{l \neq k} = 0$. Even though it is clear that in the presence of noise inner region pixels are not of accurate reference intensity of a pure class, but are often exhibiting properties of mixed pixels, the idea is to have confidence in the used crisp segmentation method up to the dichotomization into the inner/pure and border pixels. The pixels detected as inner will therefore not be revisited, or reassigned.

In the second step of the suggested segmentation method, pixels possibly being intersected by the boundaries of continuous imaged objects are to be detected. Such pixels are assumed to be mixed, with partial coverage by two or more image components. In the crisp segmentation in step (i), however, they are assigned to only one of the components, and are therefore to be revisited and reassigned. The set B of pixels considered for step (iii) are all pixels which are 4-connected to a pixel with a different label.

The third step in the pixel coverage segmentation process is computation of partial coverage values of the (potentially mixed) pixels of the set B. We suggest to use a linear model, due to its simplicity, and the fact that it corresponds to the ideal (noise-free) pixel coverage assignment that arises when integrating spatially distinct signals over finite sized detector elements (e.g. in a digital camera). This model assumes that the value of a mixed pixel is a convex combination of the values corresponding to the pure classes c_k covering the observed pixel, where the coefficients in the combination correspond to the proportions of the pure classes appearing. Note that for imperfect imaging devices, the assumption on spatially distinct signals may not hold. Given a particular imaging situation, it is recommended to verify this assumption and possibly act accordingly, e.g. by incorporating a deconvolution step into the process.

In general, the intensity values of the pure classes are not known, but have to be estimated from the image data. We suggest to use a local approach when estimating the values of a class c_k. For each pixel observed in the process of partial coverage assignment, the local pure class representation c_k (we use the same symbol for the class and its intensity representation) is estimated as the mean value of the pixels in a local neighbourhood of a suitable size which are classified, according to steps (i) and (ii), as completely belonging to the observed class c_k. This approach, in our opinion, has two main advantages: i) only the classes relevant – existing in the neighbourhood of the observed pixel are considered for a mixture in that pixel, and ii) sensitivity of the pure class description to intensity variations over the image is decreased; in general, the local within class variance is smaller than the global one.

The image values of a mixed pixel $p = (p_1, p_2, \ldots, p_n)$ (n being the number of channels of the image) are assumed, in a noise-free environment, to be a convex combination of the (locally estimated) pure classes c_k:

$$p = \sum_{k=1}^{m} \alpha_k c_k, \quad \sum_{i=k}^{m} \alpha_k = 1, \quad \alpha_k \geq 0, \tag{1}$$

where each coefficient α_k corresponds to the coverage of the pixel p by an object of a class c_k. In a noise-free environment, and if the number m of classes (variables) is not bigger than the number $n + 1$ of equations (including the equation $\sum_{k=1}^{m} \alpha_k = 1$), the problem of partial coverage is solved as a system of linear equations.

In real imaging conditions noise has to be considered. In the presence of noise, it is not certain that there exists a (convex) solution to the linear system (1). Therefore we reformulate the problem to the following optimization problem: Find a point p^* of the form $p^* = \sum_{k=1}^{m} \alpha_k^* c_k$, such that p^* is a *convex* combination of c_k and the distance $d(p, p^*)$ is minimal. We solve the constrained optimization problem by using Lagrange multipliers method, and we minimize the function

$$F(\alpha_1, \ldots, \alpha_m, \lambda) = \|p - \sum_{k=1}^{m} \alpha_k c_k\|_2^2 + \lambda(\sum_{k=1}^{m} \alpha_k - 1)$$

over all $\alpha_k \geq 0$, for a given pixel $p = (p_1, \ldots, p_n)$ and classes $c_1, \ldots, c_m$. The obtained solution $\alpha^* = (\alpha_1^*, \ldots, \alpha_m^*)$ provides estimated partial coverage of the pixel p by each of the observed classes $c_k, k \in \{1, \ldots, m\}$.

The partial coverage values are computed for all pixels of B. However, since the set B is not necessarily a one pixel thick set, it may happen that some of its elements, which should be pure, are assigned partial coverage due to presence of noise. To reduce the impact of noise, we, in the fourth step, perform thinning of the set of mixed pixels. We iteratively assign the simply 4-connected pixel of the current set of mixed pixels which is at a smallest distance to one of the crisp class vectors to that particular crisp class. The resulting set of pixels is a 4-connected one pixel-thick border between the neighbouring regions.

4   Evaluation and Results

In the previous section we introduced the pixel coverage segmentation method. Its evaluation addresses accuracy of the proposed assignment of partial coverage values to the pixels on the border between two objects. Note that in the ideal case, assuming continuous pixel coverage values and a noise-free environment, the suggested model provides exact partial coverage segmentation. In a real situation, errors are introduced due to quantization and the presence of noise.

Being interested in pixel coverage segmentation primarily for its further use for precise and accurate feature estimations, we have, in addition to directly testing the performance of the proposed segmentation method, also evaluated perimeter and area estimates based on such segmentations. Perimeter is estimated using the method presented in [9], and area is estimated according to [8].

A synthetic object (Fig. 1(a)) is randomly placed (rotated and translated) at 100 different positions in the square grid (the side of the object is 100 pixels long) and digitized using pixel coverage digitization. A zoomed-in part of the resulting object, with a (one-pixel thick) partial coverage at its boundary, as well as its superimposed crisp discretization, is shown in Fig. 1(b). Each digitization is subsequently corrupted by increasing levels of additive uncorrelated Gaussian noise (standard deviation between 0 and 40% of the foreground/background contrast) providing a total of 900 test images.

To keep the evaluation independent of any particular segmentation method, tests with synthetic objects are performed using an ideal error free crisp segmentation; a Gauss centre point digitization of the continuous object is used both as a reference and as a starting crisp segmentation for the proposed method.

A 2D Gaussian weighted neighbourhood with a standard deviation of 2 pixels (truncated at 10 pixels) is used when estimating the pure class values c_k.

To evaluate the pixel coverage segmentation, the assigned coverage values are, per pixel, compared with the true ones, for increasing amounts of added noise. The average absolute error,

$$\varepsilon = \frac{1}{N} \sum_{p \in B} |\hat{A}(p) - A(p)|$$

where B is the set of evaluated boundary pixels, N is the cardinality of B, and $\hat{A}(p)$ and $A(p)$ are, respectively, assigned and true coverage for a pixel $p \in B$, is computed and presented in Fig. 1(d); 100 random displacements of the object are observed for each level of noise. In Fig. 1(e) we show the relative error of perimeter estimation for the observed synthetic object for increasing levels of noise, whereas Fig. 1(f) presents the area estimation on the same test object, under the same conditions.

As it is visible from the plots in Fig. 1(d-e), the improvement when using the suggested method, compared to the results obtained for an ideal (noise free) crisp segmentation, is significant when the standard deviation of the present noise does not exceed 20%. Above that level, the suggested method does not provide any improvement in terms of accuracy. It is, however, worth noting that the precision of the feature estimates (exhibited as low variation of the obtained results) is significantly higher for the proposed method, and in the case of area estimation provides improvement of the result for all the observed noise levels. We note that the perimeter of the test object is overestimated in the presence

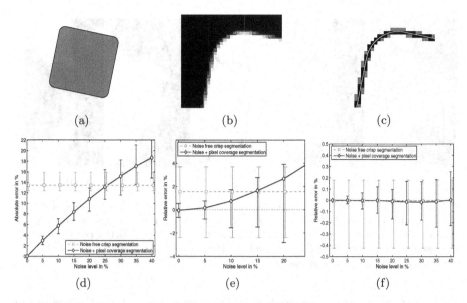

Fig. 1. (a) Continuous synthetic test object. (b) Part of a pixel coverage segmentation of (a), with superimposed border of its crisp segmentation. (c) Part of the set B. Grey pixels are removed in the thinning step. Superimposed is the border of the original continuous object. (d) Average absolute error of pixel coverage values in B for increasing levels of noise, lines represent means of 100 observations and bars show max and min errors. (e) and (f) Relative error for the estimated object perimeter and area, respectively.

of noise (Fig 1(e)). This is not surprising; noise, in almost all cases, leads to a less smooth boundary of the object, and therefore a longer perimeter.

5   Quantitative Analysis of a Histological Image

In this section we verify applicability of the suggested method on a real image and compute precise feature estimates based on the resulting segmentation.

The image shown in Fig. 2(a) is a part of material used in a histomorphometrical study described in [7]. It contains three regions: a screw-shaped implant, bone region, and soft tissue. Quantification is performed by measuring the length of the contact between the implant and the bone region, relative to the overall length of the implant border, and by measuring the percentage of bone area in the vicinity of the implant; for a detailed description see [7]. Measurements obtained manually, by an expert using integrated microscope software and with higher magnification available, are used as a ground truth.

We applied the proposed pixel coverage segmentation method to segment the RGB image. First step was to perform a crisp segmentation of the image. For this illustrative example, it was done manually, to get a good starting segmentation and to not mix errors from the crisp segmentation process with errors from the

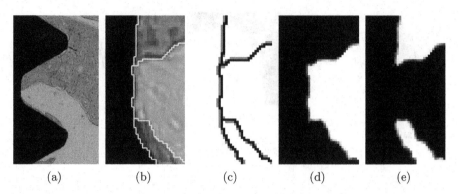

(a)	(b)	(c)	(d)	(e)

Fig. 2. (a): The screw-shaped implant (black), bone (purple with a number of hollow spaces) and soft tissue (light blue). (b) Part of a crisp (manual) segmentation of (a) into the three regions. (c) The set B of (grey and black) pixels. Partial coverage values are assigned to the black pixels. (d) and (e) Pixel coverage segmentations of the soft tissue and the bone region, respectively.

pixel coverage estimation. A part of the manual segmentation is presented in Fig. 2(b). The extracted set B is shown in Fig. 2(c) as the union of black and grey pixels. The grey pixels are detected as pure in the thinning step and only the one-pixel thick 4-connected region in black is assigned partial coverage values. The result of the suggested pixel coverage segmentation method is presented in Fig. 2(d) and 2(e). The first presents segmented soft tissue, whereas the second shows segmented bone. Grey values, visible on the borders between the regions, correspond to partial pixel coverage.

Our goal is to obtain bone-implant contact length estimates, as well as bone area estimates, which provide an improvement in terms of accuracy and precision, compared to those obtained in [7]. We apply the length estimation method presented in [9], and the area estimation method presented and analysed in [8], to the pixel coverage segmentation obtained by the suggested method. While the estimation of area is straightforward, some adjustments of the length estimation method are required. The method, as presented in [9], is applicable for estimation of the border between two classes, whereas in the observed example there may exist pixels which are partly covered by three classes. To adjust the method appropriately, we observe the border line as being between the two classes - implant and non-implant (soft tissue and bone together) - where the

Table 1. Feature estimation results for manual (using integrated microscope software), crisp [7], and the herein suggested method. See [7] for notation details.

Method	Contact length	Bone area R	Bone area M
Manual	79%	48%	78%
Crisp	88%	50%	81%
Suggested	85%	49%	81%

existing method is directly applicable. After the border line within a pixel is estimated, it is distributed to the two non-implant classes proportionally to their coverage of that pixel. This approach is attractive due to its simplicity, and is acceptably accurate. Due to very low number of pixels in the image which are covered by three classes, potentially introduced errors have minimal impact on the result. Pixels covered by more than two classes are presumably rare in most applications.

The results of feature estimates are presented in Table 1. It is clear that the proposed method provides feature estimates closer to the manual measurements, here considered to be the ground truth.

6   Conclusions

We present a novel approach for extending an existing crisp segmentation to a pixel coverage segmentation, where pixels on object boundaries are assigned values proportional to their coverage by the image components. The evaluation performed on synthetic images shows that features estimated from the pixel coverage segmentation are more accurate than what is achieved from the starting crisp segmentation, for reasonable noise levels. The example performed on a histological image shows the successful application of the method to a real world problem. The presented examples are in 2D, but the method is directly applicable also to higher dimensional image data.

Acknowledgements. Prof. Carina B. Johansson is acknowledged for providing the histological data. Nataša Sladoje is financially supported by the Ministry of Science of the Republic of Serbia through the Projects ON144018 and ON144029 of the Mathematical Institute of the Serbian Academy of Science and Arts.

References

1. Bousion, N., Hatt, M., Reilhac, A., Visvikis, D.: Fully automated partial volume correction in PET based on a wavelet approach without the use of anatomical information. In: Proc. of IEEE Nuclear Science Symposium, pp. 2812–2816. IEEE Society, Los Alamitos (2007)
2. Choi, H.S., Haynor, D.R., Kim, Y.: Partial volume tissue classification of multichannel magnetic resonance images - a mixed model. IEEE Trans. on Medical Imaging 10(3), 395–407 (1991)
3. Foody, G.M., Lucas, R.M., Curran, P.H., Honzak, M.: Non-linear mixture modeling without end-members using an artificial neural network. Int. Journal of Remote Sensing 18(4), 937–953 (1997)
4. Jua, J., Kolaczykb, E.D., Gopa, S.: Gaussian mixture discriminant analysis and sub-pixel land cover characterization in remote sensing. Remote Sensing and Environment 84(4), 550–560 (2003)
5. Leemput, K.V., Maes, F., Vandermeulen, D., Suetens, P.: A unifying framework for partial volume segmentation of brain MR images. IEEE Trans. on Medical Imaging 22(1), 105–119 (2003)

6. Niessen, W.J., Vincken, K.L., Weickert, J., ter Haar Romeny, B.M., Viergever, M.A.: Multiscale segmentation of three-dimensional MR brain images. International Journal of Computer Vision 31(2/3), 185–202 (1999)
7. Sarve, H., Johansson, C.B., Lindblad, J., Borgefors, G., Franke Stenport, V.: Quantification of bone remodeling in the proximity of implants. In: Kropatsch, W.G., Kampel, M., Hanbury, A. (eds.) CAIP 2007. LNCS, vol. 4673, pp. 253–260. Springer, Heidelberg (2007)
8. Sladoje, N., Lindblad, J.: Estimation of moments of digitized objects with fuzzy borders. In: Roli, F., Vitulano, S. (eds.) ICIAP 2005. LNCS, vol. 3617, pp. 188–195. Springer, Heidelberg (2005)
9. Sladoje, N., Lindblad, J.: High-precision boundary length estimation by utilizing gray-level information. IEEE Trans. on Pattern Analysis and Machine Intelligence 32(2), 357–363 (2009)
10. Souza, A., Udupa, J.K., Saha, P.K.: Volume rendering in the presence of partial volume effects. IEEE Trans. on Medical Imaging 24(2), 223–235 (2005)
11. Verbeiren, S., Eerens, H., Piccard, I., Bauwens, I., Van Orshoven, J.: Sub-pixel classification of SPOT-VEGETATION time series for the assessment of regional crop areas in Belgium. Int. Journal of Applied Earth Observation and Geoinformation 10(4), 486–497 (2008)
12. Vincken, K.L., Koster, A.S., Viergever, M.A.: Probabilistic segmentation of partial volume voxels. Pattern Recognition Letters 15, 477–484 (1994)

A Generic Method of Line Matching for Central Imaging Systems under Short-Baseline Motion

Saleh Mosaddegh[1], David Fofi[1], and Pascal Vasseur[2]

[1] Le2i UMR CNRS 5158, Université de Bourgogne, Le Creusot, France
[2] MIS, Université de Picardie Jules Verne, Amiens, France

Abstract. Line matching across images taken by a central imaging system (perspective or catadioptric) with focus on short baseline motion of the system is proposed. The relationship between images of lines on unitary sphere is studied and a simple algorithm for matching lines are proposed assuming the rotation of the system is known apriori or it can be estimated from some correspondences in two views. Two methods are discussed for retrieving R in the case it is not known apriori. Experimental results on both synthetic and real images are also presented.

1 Introduction

Line Matching is simply finding the corresponding images of the same 3D line across two or multiple images of a scene. It is often the first step in the reconstruction of scenes such as an urban scene. The images can be captured by any types of imaging systems. This work address central imaging systems e.g. a perspective camera or a catadioptric system. Our method for line matching consists of 3 main steps. First, lines of interest have to be detected in both images. Second, the line segments are projected from 2D to 3D by lifting to unitary sphere. Locating corresponding lines using the relation derived in the following section is the final stage of the line matching algorithm. The geometric relation between two images required a priori here is the rotation of imaging system. This can directly be recorded during image acquisition or later by different available methods such as methods based on matching corresponding vanishing points [9, 10]. In this work, we are interested in the last step of the matching algorithm. In [11, 15] we presented a pipeline for automatic line matching with focus on paracatadioptric systems under the short-baseline motion of the system by employing line intersections correspondences as input to RANSAC in order to compute the rotation of the imaging system. In this work however we employ two different methods for estimating rotation; one is an already developed and robust method of retrieving the rotation using vanishing points direction and second one is a simple alternative method which will shortly be explained. We aim to formulate a generic method of matching lines for all central imaging systems under the short-baseline motion including perspective cameras. The latest work which significantly improves on the state of the art for line matching across two or more perspective views can be found in [1]. They also assume that the

P. Foggia, C. Sansone, and M. Vento (Eds.): ICIAP 2009, LNCS 5716, pp. 939–948, 2009.

motion of the camera is apriori known (through fundamental matrix) and the problem is then reduced to finding corresponding lines by help of fundamental matrix and epipolar geometry. The most related work to line matching in cata-dioptric imaging systems is done in [5] for visual servoing/tracking purposes by tracking line features during the camera (and/or the object) motion. The paper is mainly concerned with the use of projected lines extracted from central cata-dioptric images as input of a visual servoing control loop. The method is based on the estimation of the partial camera displacement between two views, given by the current and desired images and it is entirely different from the problem of matching lines across views in which there is considerable motion between corresponding lines which is the subject of our work. While in the perspective case line matching is rather efficiently solved, to the best of our knowledge, this is the first work dealing with this problem in catadioptric images.

2   Proposed Method

The rest of this text is organized as follows. In the next section, we derive the relation between normal vector of the great circle of any 3D line represented in the first unitary sphere coordinate system and its corresponding vector ex-pressed in the second system which in return gives us an adequate tool to match lines. Then, we recall the sphere equivalence followed by a brief description of the two algorithms for recovering the rotation of the imaging system. We skip giving the definition of catadioptric imaging systems and unitary sphere model due to space restrictions. General readers are referred to references [2, 3, 4] for explanations and details. Finally some experimental results of applying the pro-posed algorithm on both synthetic and real images are presented. For extracting line segments, we use the line extraction algorithm of [6]. For recovering R, along with our proposed method we also explain attitude estimation method of [10]. We will shortly give a brief explanation of these algorithms.

2.1   The Relation between Images of 3D Lines on Unitary Sphere

Having the intrinsic parameters of the imaging system, the key idea is to project the image on the unitary sphere, turning the conic curves (images of the lines on the image plane) into their corresponding great circles on the unitary sphere. Knowing that a great circle is fully defined by normal vector of its plane, the problem of matching conics is then reduced to matching these vectors. In this section we show that under short range motion, two corresponding great circle are mainly related by rotation part of the imaging system motion. Consider a line in 3D scene with two separate 3D points X_1 and X_2 on it. Suppose n_1 is the non-normalized vector of the plane which passes through these two points and the origin of the first unitary sphere and n_2 is corresponding vector expressed in the second model (Fig. 1). Then:

$$n_2 = (RX_1 + t) \times (RX_2 + t) = det\,(R)\,R^{-t}\,(X_1 \times X_2) + [t]_\times\,R\,(X_1 - X_2) =$$
$$det\,(R)\,R^{-t}n_1 + [t]_\times\,R\,(X_1 - X_2) = Rn_1 + [t]_\times\,R\,(X_1 - X_2)$$

Where metric transformation of the imaging system (represented by two unitary spheres in Fig. 1) is defined by the rotation matrix R and translation vector t and R^{-t} is inverse transpose of R. Note that for a rotation matrix, $det(R) = 1$ and transpose inverse is the same as R. Above relation coincides with the relation obtained in [7,8] in which equivalent Euclidean Plücker representation of the line is used to derive a similar formula:

$$n_2 = Rn_1 + [t]_\times Rl, \ l = \frac{(X_1 - X_2)}{\|X_1 - X_2\|}$$

Where the 3D line segment is represented by its infinite supporting line represented by two vectors l and n. l is a unit vector parallel to the line, and n is a non-normalized vector to the plane defined by the line and the origin of the coordinate system and its norm is equal to the distance of the line to the origin, e.g.$\|n\| = d$, see Fig. 1. Therefore if transformation between two positions of the imaging system is a pure rotation ($t = 0$) or the movement of the system in comparison to its distance to the scene is very small (short baseline, for example aerial imaging), we can neglect the second term in the above equations and conclude that under the pure rotation or short base line motion, n_1 and n_2 are related by the rotation matrix:

$$n_2 = Rn_1 \tag{1}$$

This equation can also be visually verified as shown in Fig 2. One immediate result is that for the case of short-baseline, after estimating the rotation matrix, for each line in the first image, all which is needed to find its corresponding line in the second image is to multiply R at normal vector of great circle of the line. The result vector is pointing at same direction as the normal vector of great circle of corresponding line is pointing (inside a reasonable angular distance error).

2.2   Lifting from Image Plane to Unitary Sphere

The necessary equations for lifting a pixel on the image onto the unitary sphere are already derived in several slightly different formulations in literature. We use

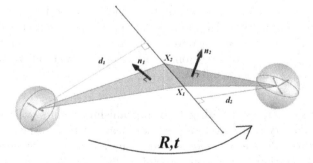

Fig. 1. A 3D Line in the scene and its projections on a unitary sphere at two different positions. n_1 and n_2 are normal vectors of related great circles.

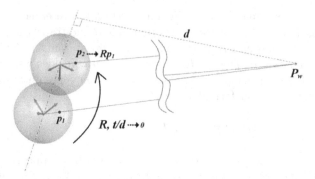

Fig. 2. If the motion of the imaging system is a short range motion (pure rotation), the images of a world point on the unitary sphere at two different positions are approximately (absolutely) related by the rotation of the system. Note that there is a considerable arbitrary rotation between two unitary sphere coordinate systems.

the projection model of [14] which is an extension of the model proposed by [12, 13] as follows:

Consider the pixel (i, j) on the image plane(of our interest are the pixels belonging to conic segments, the images of 3D lines on the image plane). The pixel coordinates after lifting are:

$$X_s = \Omega \times m, \qquad Y_s = \Omega \times n, \qquad Z_s = \Omega - \xi$$

where $\Omega = \frac{\xi + \sqrt{1 + (1 - \xi^2)(i^2 + j^2)}}{i^2 + j^2 + 1}$, $\qquad n = \frac{i - v_0}{\gamma r}$, $\qquad m = \frac{j - u_0 - ns\gamma}{\gamma}$

ξ is a parameters describing the mirror shape, s is skew parameter, r is aspect ratio,γ is generalized focal lengths and (u_0, v_0) is principal point . All these parameters are available as the result of calibration. The same above equations can be used in reverse to project a point on unitary sphere into image plane.

2.3   Recovering R

There are several methods for estimating R applicable to all types of central imaging systems (cf. [9] for a review on these methods and their pros and cons). Regarding the simplicity and robustness we have experimented with two automatic methods, one from [9] which works in urban scene with at least two groups of 3D parallel lines and the other one is our proposed method which is suitable for short-baseline motion as follows.

Recovering R using Vanishing Points. Vanishing Points (VP) are points on the plane at infinity and therefore they are invariant to translation. A rotation matrix has three degree of freedom and each vanishing point correspondence provides two rotation constraints. Therefore for estimating R, it is sufficient to have two enough distinct VP correspondences in the two views. Reference [10] has exploited above facts to estimate the rotation of an imaging system in

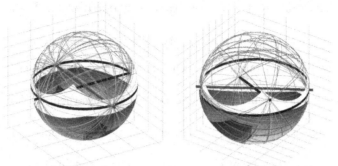

Fig. 3. Projection of two paracatadioptric images on the unitary sphere, their extracted great circles and two dominant vanishing directions. For a better demonstration, half of the great circles are hidden.

two steps, extraction of vanishing points followed by recovering R by matching these points. For the sake of completeness, we briefly explain their method for extracting VP. For matching part, interested readers are referred to [9]. Consider two great circles corresponding to two parallel 3D lines. The intersection of these two great circles (say vector u) corresponds to the common direction of the lines. u should also point at the direction of any other line parallel to these two lines (inside a similarity threshold). Therefore checking for all lines, we can find the number of lines that may share the same direction u. Repeating this procedure for each combination of two great circles we can compute the vector that corresponds to the highest number of parallel lines (the vanishing point of those lines). To detect the second dominant direction, we remove the lines belong to the first dominant direction and repeat the above steps (See Fig 3).

Recovering R using points correspondences and RANSAC. The idea behind this approach is already depicted in Fig 2. In the case of short-baseline motion, the image of the scene on the unitary sphere goes under the same rotation as imaging system. Exploiting this fact, we suggest the following simple method for extracting the R:

- Manually or by means of automatic algorithms such as SIFT feature extractor, extract enough point correspondences between two views.
- Lift these correspondences to their unitary spheres.
- Using RANSAC or similar fitting algorithms, find the best rotation matrix which relates these corresponding points.

Note that this method is only feasible when the imaging system goes under a short range motion. Note also that theoretically, having the images of two salient 3D points (which are not collinear with the center of unitary sphere) and their correspondences is sufficient to estimate the rotation matrix. However we employ RANSAC to be able to automatically extract some interest points and their correspondences without being concerned about the errors in detection of positions of these points in the image planes and also any possible mismatches.

3   Implementation Details and Experimental Results

The proposed method is composed of the following main steps:

1. Given two images taken by a central imaging system under short range motion, extract their line segments (cf. [6]).
2. Extract two dominant vanishing directions and use them to estimate R (cf. section 2 and [9]).
3. Project line segments onto the unitary sphere and compute normal vectors of their great circles.
4. Find corresponding great circle of each line segment in the other image by using the relation (1) derived in section 2.1.

Fig. 4 along with Fig. 3 demonstrates the steps of our algorithm on a pair of synthetic images. We have applied the R on whole first sphere for the sake of demonstration. In practice and during the implementation only normal vector and two end points of each segment (necessary to find the segment bounding box for the case there are ambiguities) are affected. In the last step, for some segments, matching great circles using the relation (1) is not enough and one ambiguity may occur when more than one segment are lying on corresponding infinite line because these segments are all located on the same 3D scene plane (as it is shown in Fig. 5). To resolve this ambiguity we also find the corresponding bounding box of the segment in the first image and we chose the candidate segment which is inside the bounding box or is intersecting it. During our experiments, the calibration method of [14] was employed to calibrate the imaging system. As the first approach we used the framework of [2] to detect the lines, extract the vanishing points and estimate R. This approach is especially of interest since the method uses already extracted lines (great circles on the unitary sphere) to estimate R in comparing to the second approach which includes extra steps of extracting salient point correspondences and fitting a rotation matrix to them. Therefore in our experiments, we used the first approach since we had enough vanishing points available.

Synthetic images. Fig. 5 shows the line segments extracted on two synthetic aerial images (upper row) and matched lines (lower row). There is a 110 degree rotation around the optical axis of the system and 30 and 20 degree around two other axes all measured w.r.t. a fixed coordinate system. Translation of the system is neglectable. Only lines of length 15 pixels or more are considered. The angular threshold for matching great circles is set to one degree. 261 and 226 segments are obtained for the left and right images, respectively. The algorithm outputs the matches displayed at the bottom row of the figure. All of the 121 matches obtained are correct.

Real Images. Fig. 6 shows the result of applying our algorithm on two real perspective images. Note that this method is far simpler than an approach such in [1] in which photometric properties of the segments neighborhoods along with

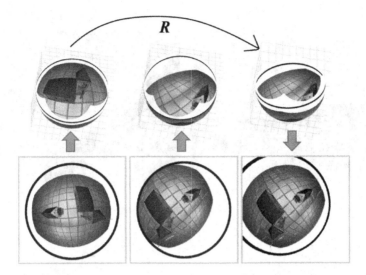

Fig. 4. Steps of the proposed algorithm: Lifting images onto unitary sphere, recovering R and rotating the first image according to R. Segments on the back projected image now coincident with their correspondings in the second image.

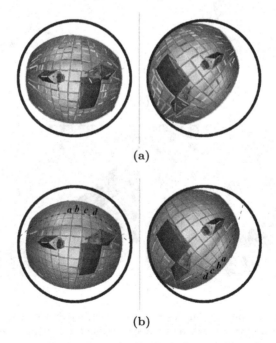

(a)

(b)

Fig. 5. Top: Two paracatadioptric images and their extracted segments. Bottom: matched lines (each color represents one correspondence. All of the 121 matches shown are correct. Note that segments a, b, c and d share the same great circle (dashed line). The end points of each segment are used to find the correct correspondence.

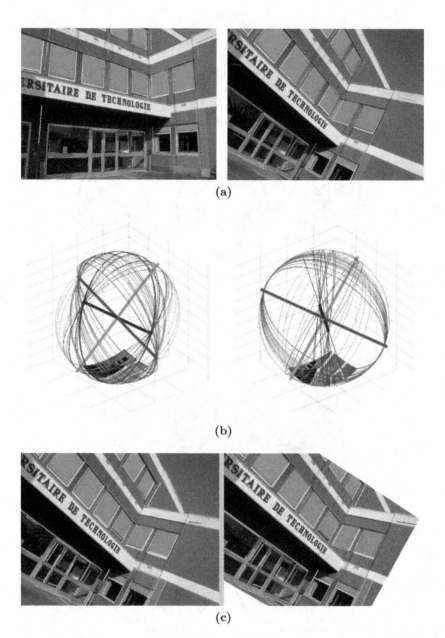

Fig. 6. Top: Two perspective images and their extracted segments. Middle: related great circles onto unitary sphere and three dominant vanishing directions (75 % of lines are hidden). Bottom: matched lines (each color represents one correspondence. Note that the image on the left is the second view and the image on the right is the first view after applying the R on it). 93% of 129 matches shown are correct.

epipolar geometry are exploited to do the same job. For this experiment, rotating imaging system around its focal point was not easy since this point is somewhere inside the camera and we needed a special flexible fixture to carry out the job. However, rotating (while trying to avoid translating) of imaging system can be considered as a short-baseline motion. Images of Fig. 6 are taken by a random rotation of the imaging system in this way. Even though matching 2 vanishing points is enough to recover R, we use 3 vanishing points to reduce the overall error. The recovered R is composed of an approximately 31 degree rotation around the optical axis of the system and 4 degree and 4.5 degree around two other axes all measured w.r.t. a fixed coordinate system. For this example, the numbers of segments extracted are 284 and 245 for the left and right images. Obtained Matches are shown at the bottom row of the figure. 93% of the 129 matches are correct. The performance of the proposed method has decreased not only because the motion of the system is not a real short-baseline motion (we found that there is also a small translation of the imaging system) but mainly because perspective imaging systems suffer from a limited field of view. The wider field of view of a perspective camera results in the better extraction of lines and the longer line segments. Note that the larger error in the computing the position of the lines causes larger error in the estimation of the vanishing points and therefore a less accurate recovery of R and eventually more mismatches. The second method of recovering R by matching salient points rather than vanishing points, however, can overcome this problem since it does not depend on the images of the lines.

4   Conclusion

This work dealt with the problem of matching lines for all types of central imaging system under a short baseline motion by presenting a generic and simple line matching approach. The method is composed of three main steps of extracting line segments, recovering R and matching lines respectively. Two methods for retrieving R, one based on matching vanishing points and the other based on matching any two feature points were also presented. The evaluation and optimization of the method on the real catadioptric systems and extension of the method to long baseline motion are the subjects of future works.

References

1. Schmid, C., Zisserman, A.: Automatic line matching across views. In: Proceedings of the IEEE Conference on Computer Vision and Pattern Recognition, pp. 666–672 (1997)
2. Barreto, J.P., Araujo, H.: Issues on the geometry of central catadioptric image formation. In: International Conference Computer Vision 01, Hawaii, pp. 422–427 (2001)
3. Baker, S., Nayar, S.: A theory of catadioptric image formation. In: Proc. of IEEE International Conference on Computer Vision, Bombay, pp. 35–42 (1998)

4. Geyer, C., Daniilidis, K.: Catadioptric projective geometry. International Journal of Computer Vision 45(3), 223–243 (2001)
5. Mezouar, Y., Haj Abdelkader, H., Martinet, P., Chaumette, F.: Central catadioptric visual servoing from 3d straight lines. In: IEEE/RSJ Int. Conf. on Intelligent Robots and Systems, IROS 2004, Sendai, Japan, September 2004, vol. 1, pp. 343–349 (2004)
6. Bazin, J.C., Demonceaux, C., Vasseur, P.: Fast central catadioptric line extraction. In: Martí, J., Benedí, J.M., Mendonça, A.M., Serrat, J. (eds.) IbPRIA 2007. LNCS, vol. 4478, pp. 25–32. Springer, Heidelberg (2007)
7. Navab, N., Faugeras, O.D.: The Critical Sets of Lines for Camera Displacement Estimation: A Mixed Euclidean-Projective and Constructive Approach. International Journal of Computer Vision 23(1), 17–44 (1997)
8. Bartoli, A., Sturm, P.: The 3D line motion matrix and alignement of line reconstructions. International Journal of Computer Vision 57(3) (May/June 2004)
9. Bazin, J.C., Kweon, I.S., Demonceaux, C., Vasseur, P.: Spherical region-based Matching of Vanishing Points in Catadioptric Images. In: OMNIVIS 2008, in conjunction with ECCV 2008, Marseille, France. Octobre (2008)
10. Bazin, J.C., Kweon, I.S., Demonceaux, C., Vasseur, P.: UAV Attitude Estimation by Vanishing Points in Catadioptric Image. In: IEEE International Conference on Robotics and Automation 2008 (ICRA 2008), Pasadena, CA, Mai (2008)
11. Mosaddegh, S., Fofi, D., Vasseur, P., Ainouz, S.: Line Matching across Catadioptric Images. In: OMNIVIS 2008, in conjunction with ECCV 2008, Marseille, France (October 2008)
12. Barreto, J.P., Araujo, H.: Issues on the geometry of central catadioptric image formation. In: CVPR, vol. 2, pp. 422–427 (2001)
13. Geyer, C., Daniilidis, K.: A unifying theory for central panoramic systems and practical implications. In: Vernon, D. (ed.) ECCV 2000. LNCS, vol. 1843, pp. 445–461. Springer, Heidelberg (2000)
14. Mei, C., Rives, P.: Single view point omnidirectional camera calibration from planar grids. In: ICRA 2007 (April 2007)
15. Mosaddegh, S.: Line Matching across Catadioptric Images. Master's thesis, Le2i laboratory, Université de Bourgogne, France (June 2008)

Reconstructing 3D Facial Shape
Using Spherical Harmonics

Chengming Zou[1,2], Guanghui Zhao[1], and Edwin R. Hancock[2]

[1] School of Computer Science, Wuhan University of Technology,
Wuhan, Hubei, 430070, China
{zoucm,zhaogh}@hotmail.com
[2] Department of Computer Science, The University of York, York, YO10 5DD, UK
{zoucm,erh}@cs.york.ac.uk

Abstract. It is now well established that 3D facial shape can be effectively and conveniently reconstructed using spherical harmonics. This paper extends the state-of-the-art by showing how to recover a 3D facial shape reconstruction using a spherical parameterization and minimizing a Harmonic Energy based on spherical medians. The solution is formulated as a linear system and we propose an iterative residual fitting algorithm (LSQR-IRF) to solve it. We demonstrate the effectivenss of the method on range-data.

Keywords: Spherical Harmonics, Reconstruction, 3D Facial Shape.

1   Introduction

Recently, it has been shown that statistical models based on the distribution of surface normals can offer a powerful means of representing an recognising facial shape. The reasons for this are two-fold. First, the needle map (or Gauss map) offers a representation that is rich in terms of differential geometry, and hence can potentially be used to capture subtle variations in facial shape. Secondly, surface reflectance is determined by the relative orientation of the surface and the light source. Hence, given a description of skin reflectance then a surface normal model can be fitted to image brightness data to recover 3D shape from a 2D facial image.

There are a number of approaches to capturing the statistics of surface normal direction. For instance, Smith and Hancock [1] project the surface normals into a tangent space to construct a statistical model using principal geodesic analysis. This work has recently been extended to gender recognition [2], but has proved too cumbersome for expression recognition. Bronstein, Bronstein and Kimmel [3] develop a spherical embedding, that allows faces to represented in a manner that is invariant to expression. Parameterising the distribution of surface normals, Kazhdan et al. [4] use the fact that the spherical harmonics of a given frequency form a subspace which is a rotationally invariant and which can be applied to the extended gaussian image (EGI). to create a rotationally invariant shape descriptor.

P. Foggia, C. Sansone, and M. Vento (Eds.): ICIAP 2009, LNCS 5716, pp. 949–957, 2009.
© Springer-Verlag Berlin Heidelberg 2009

In this paper we present a novel approach for 3D facial shape reconstruction using spherical harmonics. Our main contribution is to develop a robust spherical parameterization for mapping of facial shape meshes onto a unit sphere. The spherical harmonic representation decomposes polar functions into the frequency domain. Thus, we can reconstruct the 3D facial shape with a linear combination of spherical harmonics.

2 Spherical Harmonics

The spherical harmonic H_n^m of degree n and order m is defined as[5]

$$
H_n^m(\theta, \phi) = \begin{cases} c_n^m P_n^{|m|}(\cos\theta)\sin(|m|\phi), & -n \le m \le -1 \\ \frac{c_n^m}{\sqrt{2}} P_n^m(\cos\theta), & m = 0 \\ c_n^m P_n^m(\cos\theta)\cos(m\phi), & 1 \le m \le n \end{cases} \tag{1}
$$

where $c_n^m = \sqrt{\frac{2n+1}{2n}\frac{(n-|m|)!}{(n+|m|)!}}$ and the associated Legendre polynomials P_n^m are the solutions of the differential equation $P_n^m(x) = \frac{(-1)^n}{2^n n!}(1-x^2)^{\frac{m}{2}}\frac{d^{n+m}}{dx^{n+m}}(x^2-1)^n$.

Any spherical continuous function $f(\theta, \phi)$ can be be represented by a linear combination of spherical harmonics $H_n^m(\theta, \phi)$ as follows:

$$
f(\theta, \phi) = \sum_{n=0}^{\infty} \sum_{m=-n}^{n} a_n^m H_n^m(\theta, \phi) \tag{2}
$$

where the coefficients a_n^m are uniquely determined by[5]

$$
a_n^m = \int_0^{\pi} \int_0^{2\pi} H_n^m(\theta, \phi)^* f(\theta, \phi)\sin\theta d\phi d\theta \tag{3}
$$

where $H_n^m(\theta, \phi)^*$ is the complex conjugate of $H_n^m(\theta, \phi)$.

The spherical harmonic expansion described above is essentially the Fourier transform for functions defined on the sphere, and it transforms spherical scalar signals into the frequency domain. Spherical harmonics are orthonormal, complete, and can be used to construct a coarse-to-fine hierarchy. This makes them a natural choice as basis functions to reconstruct complex object surfaces including faces [6]. We denote a 3D facial surface mesh M as $s(\theta, \phi)$. In order to describe $s(\theta, \phi)$, we just need to expand these spherical functions using spherical harmonics[7]:

$$
s(\theta, \phi) = \sum_{n=0}^{\infty} \sum_{m=-n}^{n} A_n^m H_n^m(\theta, \phi) \tag{4}
$$

where $A_n^m = (a_{xn}^m, a_{yn}^m, a_{zn}^m)^T$ is vector encoding the Cartesian coordinates a_{xn}^m, a_{yn}^m, a_{zn}^m of the vertices of M.

Spherical harmonics reconstruct a surface in a coarse-to-fine hierarchy. With increasing degree n the spherical harmonics seem to capture increasing detail. If we truncate the the maximal degree at N_{max}, the surface is approximated by

$$s(\theta, \phi) \approx \sum_{n=0}^{N_{max}} \sum_{m=-n}^{n} A_n^m H_n^m(\theta, \phi) \tag{5}$$

3   Spherical Parameterization

The first step in constructing spherical harmonics is to calculate the spherical signal as a function of θ and ϕ, and this process is referred to as spherical parameterization.

3.1   The Geodesic Distance

A unit vector $m \in R^3$ may be considered as a point lying on a spherical manifold $n \in S^2$, where S^2 is the unit sphere, and the two representations are related by $m = \Phi(n)$, where $\Phi : S^2 \to R^3$ is an embedding. If $v \in T_n S^2$ is a vector on the tangent plane to the manifold at $n \in S^2$ and $v \neq 0$, then the exponential map, denoted Exp_n, of v is the point on S^2 along the geodesic in the direction of v at distance $\| v \|$ from n. The inverse of the exponential map is the log map, denoted by Log_n. The geodesic distance between two points $n_1 \in S^2$ and $n_2 \in S^2$ can be expressed in terms of the log map, and is denoted by[1,8]

$$d(n_1, n_2) = \| Log_{n_1}(n_2) \| \tag{6}$$

Since a unit sphere is a Riemannian manifold and great circles are geodesics, arc length is the Riemannian distance between a pair of points and hence[1],

$$d(n_1, n_2) = \arccos(\Phi(n_1) \cdot \Phi(n_2)) \tag{7}$$

3.2   Spherical Medians

If we consider the distribution of unit vectors as a distribution of points on a spherical manifold $n_1, \cdots, n_k \in S^2$, it is clear that the mean direction is dependent on the embedding Φ and is the extrinsic mean of a distribution of spherical data[1]:

$$\mu_\Phi = \arg \min_{n \in S^2} \sum_{i=1}^{k} \| \Phi(n) - \Phi(n_i) \|^2 \tag{8}$$

In other words, the extrinsic mean is the Euclidean average (or center of mass) of the distribution of points in R^3, projected back onto the closest point on the sphere. A more natural definition of the average of a distribution of points on the unit sphere uses arc length as the choice of geodesic distance measure. Using (7), we can define the intrinsic mean[1]:

$$\mu = \arg \min_{n \in S^2} \sum_{i=1}^{k} d(n, n_i) \tag{9}$$

For spherical data, this is known as the spherical median.

3.3 Harmonic Energy

Suppose h is a homeomorphism between R^3 and S^2, we define the harmonic energy as [9]:

$$E(h) = \sum_{[u,v] \in K} k_{u,v} \parallel h(u) - h(v) \parallel^2 \tag{10}$$

where K are the edges of M, and $k_{u,v}$ are the spring constants computed as in [10]. Given 3D facial shape data in the form of unit vectors, we use h to map these vectors onto a unit sphere. In order to avoid folding, h should be harmonic. If h is harmonic, then $E(h)$ acquire a minimal value. In other words, in order to diffuse h to harmonic, we should minimize $E(h)$.

For $k_{u,v}$ are constants, so in order to simplify calculation, we let $k_{u,v} \equiv 1$. We know that $h(u) \in S^2$, so $\parallel h(u) - h(v) \parallel$ is the geodesic distance the point $h(u)$ to the point $h(v)$. Thus minimizing $E(h)$ can be denoted as follow:

$$\arg\min \sum_{[u,v] \in K} d(n_{h(u)}, n_{(h(v))})^2 \tag{11}$$

The edges $[u, v] \in K$ of the mesh form a 1-ring for the neighbors of u, denoted $Star(u)$. From (9), the intrinsic mean μ is such that the total distance between μ and $Star(u)$ will be minimum. For every u, we may calculate the intrinsic mean of $Star(u)$, and if we move u close to μ, then $\sum_{v \in Star(u)} d(n_{h(u)}, n_{h(v)})^2$ will be reduced. Thus if every u is the intrinsic mean of $Star(u)$, Eq. (11) will be minimum. Thus h is harmonic and can be used for spherical parameterization.

3.4 Spherical Parameterization Algorithm

In summary, we give our algorithm for spherical parameterization as follow:

Algorithm 1. Spherical Parameterization

Input: mesh M, step length δt
Output: spherical signal θ and ϕ
Step 1) Compute the spherical barycentric map b from M to S^2, $h \leftarrow b$.
Step 2) Compute the harmonic energy $E(h)$, if $\delta E < \varepsilon$ then goto 7).
Step 3) Compute intrinsic mean μ of every point of h, and set $\Delta h = \delta t \cdot \mu$.
Step 4) Update h using $h \leftarrow h - \Delta h$.
Step 5) Shift the center of mass of $h(M)$ to origin and normalize $h(v), v \in K$ to the unit vector.
Step 6) Repeat 2) through 5).
Step 7) Compute Euler angles θ and ϕ by h.
Step 8) return θ and ϕ.

In order to ensure the convergence of the algorithm, Step 5) is added so that the solution is unique. It is executed to force the centre-of-mass of the surface to remain at the origin during entire update process.

4 Computing Spherical Harmonics

4.1 Calculating Associated Legendre Polynomial

In SPHARM, the efficient computation of the Associated Legendre Polynomial (ALP) is an important issue. One popular method is the Recursive Algorithm (RA) which easy to implement, but it is not efficient. To overcome this limitation we use a non recursive algorithm. We note the following properties of ¿From the definition of ALP, we know that $P_n^m(x) = 0$ when $n < |m|$ and from Ref.[11]:

$$P_n^m(x) = ((2n-1)xP_{n-1}^m(x) + (n+m-1)P_{n-2}^m(x))/(n-m) \qquad (12)$$

$$P_{n+1}^{n+1}(x) = -(2n+1)(1-x^2)^{1/2}P_n^n(x) \qquad (13)$$

$$P_n^{n-1}(x) = (2n-1)xP_{n-1}^{n-1}(x) \qquad (14)$$

Based on these properties our algorithm for calculating ALP as follow (where $|x| < 1$ is:

Algorithm 2. Calculate Associated Legendre Polynomial

Input: x, n, where $|x| < 1, n > 0$
Output: $P_0^0, P_1^0, P_1^1, \cdots, P_n^0, P_n^1, \cdots, P_n^n$
Step 1) Set $P_0^0(x) = 1.0$.
Step 2) Use formula (13) to calculate $P_1^1(x), P_2^2(x), \cdots, P_n^n(x)$.
Step 3) Use formula (14) to calculate $P_1^0(x), P_2^1(x), \cdots, P_n^{n-1}(x)$.
Step 4) Use the result of 2) and 3) and formula (12) to calculate $P_n^m, \forall |m| \le n-2$.
This is a non-recursive algorithm and although it uses more memory than the recursive algorithm, for a given x and degree n, it can calculate all the $P_n^m(x)$ in one pass with greatly improved the efficiency.

4.2 LSQR[12] Iterative Residual Fitting

We focus our discussion on expanding a spherical scalar signal $f(\theta, \phi)$. For the SPHARM case, we can apply the same method three times and expand $x(\theta, \phi)$, $y(\theta, \phi)$ and $z(\theta, \phi)$ separately. Given a function $f(\theta, \phi)$ and a user-specified maximum degree L_{max}, we can reconstruct the original function as follows:

$$\hat{f}(\theta, \phi) = \sum_{l=0}^{L_{max}} \sum_{m=-l}^{l} \hat{a}_l^m Y_l^m(\theta, \phi) \approx f(\theta, \phi) \qquad (15)$$

The higher the degrees the more accurate the reconstruction $\hat{f}(\theta, \phi)$. Unfortunately, with increasing L_{max}, the above linear system becomes intractable. To overcome this problem we exploit the properties of the spherical harmonic transform. First, we make use of the coarse-to-fine hierarchy provided by SPHARM's. If we use a just a few low degree SPHARM's to expand a spherical function

$f(\theta, \phi)$, we obtain a low-pass filtered reconstruction. If we use a higher degree representation, then the reconstruction is more detailed. Taking advantage of this coarse-to-fine hierarchy, we start from a low degree reconstruction and then iteratively add higher degree SPHARM's to increase the reconstructed detail. Since, SPHARM's form an orthonormal basis the reconstruction residual from a low frequency representation (i.e., $f(\theta, \phi)$-its reconstruction) encode the unreconstructed high frequnecy detail. To add in more detail to our model, we can simply use a few higher degree harmonics to fit the residual.

To develop this idea, we first introduce some notation:

$$A_n = \begin{pmatrix} Y_n^{-n}(\theta_1, \phi_1) & Y_n^{-n+1}(\theta_1, \phi_1) & \cdots & Y_n^n(\theta_1, \phi_1) \\ Y_n^{-n}(\theta_2, \phi_2) & Y_n^{-n+1}(\theta_2, \phi_2) & \cdots & Y_n^n(\theta_2, \phi_2) \\ \vdots & \vdots & \vdots & \vdots \\ Y_n^{-n}(\theta_w, \phi_w) & Y_n^{-n+1}(\theta_w, \phi_w) & \cdots & Y_n^n(\theta_w, \phi_w) \end{pmatrix} \tag{16}$$

$$b_n = (\hat{a}_n^{-n}, \hat{a}_n^{-n+1}, \cdots, \hat{a}_n^n)^T, M = (b_0^T, b_1^T, \cdots, b_{L_{max}}^T)^T \tag{17}$$

$$f = (f(\theta_1, \phi_1), f(\theta_2, \phi_2), \cdots, f(\theta_w, \phi_w))^T \tag{18}$$

where A_n is a matrix of degree n spherical harmonic values for w sampling points, b_n contains the estimated degree n coefficients, f is a vector of spherical function values at w sampling points, and M is a spherical harmonic model containing coefficients of up to degree L_{max}. Note that the model M minimizes

$$\sum_{i=1}^w (f(\theta_i, \phi_i) - \sum_{n=0}^{L_{max}} \sum_{m=-n}^n \hat{a}_n^m Y_n^m(\theta_i, \phi_i))^2 \tag{19}$$

We can now formally present our algorithm as follows:

Algorithm 3. LQSR Iterative Residual Fitting(LQSR-IRF)

Input: A spherical function f with w sampled values $\{\theta_i, \phi_i, f(\theta_i, \phi_i) | 1 \leq i \leq w\}$, the maximal SH expansion degree L_{max}
Output: Reconstruct model M
Step 1) $r = (f(\theta_1, \phi_1), f(\theta_2, \phi_2), \cdots, f(\theta_n, \phi_n))^T$
Step 2) $M = (0, 0, \cdots, 0)^T \{Initialization, |M| = (1 + L_{max})^2\}$
Step 3) Solving $A_0 x_0 = r$ by LSQR get x_0', set $b_0 = x_0', r = r - A_0 x_0'$
Step 4) Set $d = 1$
Step 5) while $d \leq L_{max}$ do
Step 6) Solving $A_d x_d = r$ by LSQR get x_d', set $b_d = x_d', r = r - A_d x_d'$
Step 7) Set $d = d + 1$
Step 8) Set $M = M + (b_0^T b_1^T \cdots b_{L_{max}}^T)^T$
Step 9) return model M

5   Experiments

We have performed extensive experiments on several 3D facial range data-sets. Our algorithm is implemented in VC2005. The experiments are performed on a computer with a 1GHZ AMD Athlon Processor and 1GB of RAM, running WinXP. We have performed three experiments. The first is the reconstruction of face01 with a neutral facial expression which degree=58. The second is reconstruction face01 with six facial expressions, which degree=58. The final experiment is a reconstruction of face02 with neutral facial expression using in varying degree, and specifically degree=5,18,28,32,38,48,58,68.

5.1   Results

Each of the experimental runs completes in 5 minutes. The reconstructions obtained are shown in Figure 1 to Figure 3.

Fig. 1. Reconstruction face01 with neutral facial expression,left is source

Fig. 2. Reconstruction face01 with six facial expressions

Fig. 3. Reconstruction face02 with neutral facial expression in several degrees

5.2   Modeling Accuracy

Let $f(\theta, \phi)$ be raw 3D facial range image and $s(\theta, \phi)$ be its SPHARM reconstruction. In order to measure the SPHARM modelling accuracy, we calculate the mean squared distance(msd) and the maximal squared distance(xsd) between the n mesh vertices on the original surface and their reconstructions as follows.

$$msd = \frac{1}{w} \sum_{i=1}^{w} \| f(\theta_i, \phi_i) - s(\theta_i, \phi_i) \|^2 \tag{20}$$

$$xsd = \max\{\| f(\theta_i, \phi_i) - s(\theta_i, \phi_i) \|^2 | \ 1 \le i \le w\} \tag{21}$$

Table 1. The *msd* and *xsd*

Experiment	*msd*	*xsd*	*Degree*	*Expression*
1	0.000523	0.003588	58	neutral
2	0.000523	0.003588	58	neutral
2	0.000767	0.006114	58	smile
2	0.001041	0.013198	58	laugh
2	0.000301	0.002516	58	sad
2	0.000279	0.067474	58	surprised
2	0.000178	0.004020	58	pleased
3	0.001323	0.020878	5	neutral
3	0.000837	0.012049	18	neutral
3	0.000781	0.007028	28	neutral
3	0.000772	0.006274	32	neutral
3	0.000764	0.005928	38	neutral
3	0.000759	0.006263	48	neutral
3	0.000756	0.006256	58	neutral
3	0.000755	0.006058	68	neutral

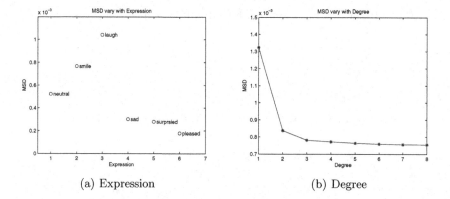

(a) Expression   (b) Degree

Fig. 4. MSD varying with expression and maximum degree of spherical harmonics

The values of *msd* and *xsd* found in our experiments are given in Table 1 and Figure 4. From Table 1 and Figure 4, it is clear that the reconstruction is accurate and we can reconstruct different facial expressions. As expected where the degree increases, the error decreases. Finally Figure 4 explores the structure of the error. The left-hand plot shows the embedding obtained, when multidimensional scaling is applied to the Euclidean distance between the vectors of fitted SPHARM co-efficients for the different expressions. The embeding reveals that the co-efficient distance increases with increasing departure from the neutral expression. The right-hand plot of Figure 4 shows the MSD as a function of the degree of the fitted SPARM model. As expected, the error decreases with increasing model order.

6   Conclusions

We have presented a novel framework for 3D facial shape reconstruction based on spherical harmonics. We used the intrinsic mean and harmonic map to implement a spherical parameterization. We provided an efficient non-recursive algorithm for calculating the associated Legendre polynomials. We also gave an iterative residual fitting method (LQSR-IRF) for reconstructing facial shape using spherical harmonics. Experimental results have shown that our method for 3D facial shape reconstruction is feasible and effective.

References

1. Smith, W.A.P., Hancock, E.R.: Facial Shape-from-shading and Recognition Using Principal Geodesic Analysis and Robust Statistics. Int. Journal Computer Vision 76, 71–91 (2008)
2. Wu, J., Smith, W.A.P., Hancock, E.R.: Weighted principal geodesic analysis for facial gender classification. In: Rueda, L., Mery, D., Kittler, J. (eds.) CIARP 2007. LNCS, vol. 4756, pp. 331–339. Springer, Heidelberg (2007)
3. Bronstein, A., Bronstein, M., Kimmel, R.: Expression invariant face recognition via spherical embedding. In: Image Processing, ICIP, vol. 3, pp. 756–759 (2005)
4. Kazhdan, M., Funkhouser, T., Rusinkiewicz, S.: Rotation Invariant Spherical harmonic representation of 3D shape descriptors. Proceedings of the 2003 Eurographics 43, 126–164 (2003)
5. Chung, M.K., Dalton, K.M., Shen, L., et al.: Weighted Fourier Series Representation and Its Application to Quantifying the Amount of Gray Matter. IEEE Transactions on Medecal Imaging 26(4), 566–581 (2007)
6. Ballard, D.H., Brown, C.M.: Computer Vision. Prentice-Hall, Englewood Cliffs (1982)
7. Shen, L., Chung, M.K.: Large-Scale Modeling of Parametric Surfaces using Spherical harmonics. In: Third International Symposium on 3D Data Processing, Visualization and Transmission (3DPVT) (2006)
8. Fletcher, P.T., Lu, C., Pizer, S.M., et al.: Principal Geodesic Analysis for the Study of Nonlinear Statistics of Shape. IEEE Transactions on Medical Imageing 23(8), 995–1005 (2004)
9. Gu, X., Yau, S.-T.: Computing Conformal Structures of Surfaces. Communications in Information and Systems 2(2), 121–146 (2002)
10. Eck, M., DeRose, T., Duchamp, T., et al.: Multiresolution Analysis of Arbitrary Meshes. In: Proceedings of SIGGRAPH 1995, pp. 173–182 (1995)
11. Ye, Q., Shen, Y.: Practical Handbook of Mathematics, 2nd edn. Science Press, China (2006)
12. Paige, C.C., Saunders, M.A.: LSQR: An Algorithm for Sparse Linear Equations and Sparse Least Squares. ACM Transactions on Mathematical Software 8(1), 43–71 (1982)

Retinex Combined with Total Variation for Image Illumination Normalization

Luigi Cinque and Gabriele Morrone

Dipartimento di Informatica, "Sapienza" Università di Roma
Via Salaria 113 00198 Roma, Italy
{cinque,morrone}@di.uniroma1.it

Abstract. This paper presents a method for the normalization of human facial images in arbitrary illumination conditions. The enhanced image is suitable to be used as an input to a face recognition system.

1 Introduction

Illumination normalization is an important task in the field of computer vision and pattern recognition. Face recognition is one of its most important applications and its accuracy depends heavily on how well the input images have been compensated for illumination, indeed the differences caused by varying illumination are more significant than the inherent differences between individuals.

Various methods have been proposed for face recognition under varying illumination: the Illumination Cone methods [3], a simplified Lambertian model [11,13,14], shape from shading [12] and quotient image based approaches [15]. However the performances of most of them are still far from ideal and many of these methods require either knowledge of the light source or a large number of training data, which are not suitable for most real world scenarios.

This paper presents an effective approach for illumination normalization based on the Land's "Retinex" model [1], which estimed the reflectance R as the ratio of the image I using a low pass filter to remove the effect of the illuminance L. To improve the effect of the Retinex (its goodness to remove shadows and specularities is already known [4]) in illumination normalization, we have combined it with the Total Variation Quotient Image model $(TVQI)$[6]. With this approach applied on standard database we have raised the accuracy of the recognition from 68,89% to 97,46% using only a single training image for each individual. Then, applying the histogram matching before the $TVQI$ and Retinex, we were able to realize the 100% accuracy under variable lighting conditions.

In subsequent sections methodology and experiments are outlined.

2 Methodology

The method proposed uses the Histogram matching to bring the intensity distribution of an image to a specific one of a target image, the TVQI to remove noise keeping the edges in the faces, and the SSR to remove shadows and specularities. The next sections explain the methods one by one.

P. Foggia, C. Sansone, and M. Vento (Eds.): ICIAP 2009, LNCS 5716, pp. 958–964, 2009.

2.1 Single Scale Retinex

Retinex is a human based image-processing algorithm, which provides color constancy and dynamic range compression. The color in the recorded images is strongly influenced by spectral shifts in the entire spectrum.

An image $I(x, y)$ is regarded as a product of reflectance R and the illuminance effect L. Assuming L changes slowly compared to R, the Retinex try to extract R by filtering the source image. Many variants of the Retinex have been published over the years. The last version is now referred to as the Single Scale Retinex (SSR) [2] is defined for a point (x, y) in an image as:

$$R_i(x, y) = \log I_i(x, y) - \log[F(x, y) \bigotimes I_i(x, y)] \qquad (1)$$

where $R_i(x, y)$ is the Retinex output, $I_i(x, y)$ is the image distribution in the i spectral band, the symbol $\bigotimes$ represents the convolution operator.

$F(x, y)$ is the Gaussian surround function given by Equation (2):

$$F(x, y) = Ke^{-(x^2+y^2)/\sigma^2} \qquad (2)$$

where σ is the Gaussian surround constant, that represent the standard deviation and that is referred to as the scale of the SSR.

A small value provides very good dynamic range compression but at the cost of poorer color rendition, causing greying of the image in uniform areas of color. Conversely, a large scale provides better color rendition but at the cost of dynamic range compression [2] .

Since face recognition is performed on grey-scale images we can ignore the greying effect, moreover we observed that the best illumination normalization is gained by small scales. Figure 1 illustrates the effect of Retinex processing on a facial image, I, for different values of σ

2.2 Total Variation Quotient Image

In order to improve the accuracy of the recognition, we applied the Total Variation Quotient Image before the SSR. As formalized in [6], an image f is modelled as the sum of large-scale output u and small-scale output v, where f, u and v are

(a)   Original (b) SSR, $\sigma = 2$ (c) SSR, $\sigma = 4$ (d) SSR, $\sigma =$
Image   10

Fig. 1. SSR application

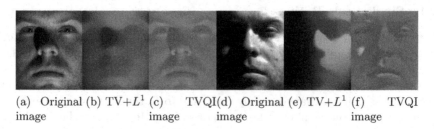

(a) Original (b) TV+L^1 (c)   TVQI(d) Original (e) TV+L^1 (f)   TVQI
image   image   image   image

Fig. 2. Sample TV images

defined as functions in $\mathbb{R}^2$. u contains background hues and important boundaries as sharp edges. The rest of the image, which is texture, is characterized
by small-scale patterns. Since the level sets of large-scale signal u have simpler
boundaries than those of small-scale signal v, we can obtain u from f by solving
a variational regularization problem:

$$\min \int_{\Omega} |\nabla u| + \lambda ||t(u, f)||_B \qquad (3)$$

where $\int_{\Omega} |\nabla u|$ is the total variation of u over its support Ω, $||t(u, f)||_B$ is some
measure of the closeness between u and f, and λ is a scalar weight parameter. The
choice of the measure $|| \cdot ||_B$ depends on applications. The first use of this model
was for image denoising [7] with the measure $||t(u, f)||_B = ||f - u||_{L^2}$. The L^2
term $||f - u||_{L^2}$ penalizes big $f(x) - u(x)$ values much more than small $f(x) - u(x)$
values, so the TV+L^2 model allows most small point-wise values (like most noise)
in $f - u$. The use instead of the L^1 measure $||f - u||_{L^1}$ penalizes the difference
between f and u in a linear way. The L^1 term lets $f - u$ contain nearly all the
signals with scale $<= 1/\lambda$ w.r.t. G-norm and with their original amplification.
So the TV+L^1 model with an appropriate λ can successfully extract small-scale
signals like the edges, lines, and corners of facial features from a face image, but
it has some limitation if it is directly applied for normalizing illumination. The
signal of the intrinsic structures in the image are not normalized, so before we
use the SSR we applied the total variation based quotient image (TVQI) model.
The intuition of the TVQI model is the Lambertian surface model. According
to the Lambertian model, the intensity at the (x, y) position of an image f is
defined as:

$$f_{x,y} = A_{x,y} \rho_{x,y} \cos \theta_{x,y} \qquad (4)$$

where A is the strength of the light source, ρ, the albedo (texture) of the image, is
the surface reflectance associated with each point in the image, and θ is the angle
between the surface normal and the light source. The intensity of image point
(x, y) is proportional to the strength A of the received light at this point. Therefore, the intensity and the variance of the small-scale signals are proportional
to the intensity of the background in their vicinities. For recognition purpose,

we approximate the normalized image by $v'_{x,y} = f_{x,y}/u_{x,y}$ for every point (x,y) using the output u of the TV+L^1 model. So the TVQI model result as:

$$TVQI = \frac{f}{u} \qquad (5)$$

To solve the variational regularization problem of TV we adopted the method proposed by Chambolle [8] using the L^1 term instead of L^2 and we chose λ based on the dimension of the face image [6] . See fig. 2 to observe the result of TV+L^1 with $\lambda = 0.4$ and the sequent TVQI image.

2.3   Histogram Matching

It's useful for the process of recognition to normalize a poorly illuminated image via histogram fitting to a similar, well-illuminated image. The reference histogram is taken from a frontal illuminated facial image: the histogram of each image to enhance will fit to the one of reference(see fig. 3).

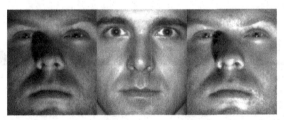

(a) Original im-(b) Reference im-(c) Image after
age   age   the   histogram
                                matching

Fig. 3. Histogram matching

By defining the histogram of a digital image with levels of intensity in $[0, L-1]$ as a function $h(r_k)$:

$$h(r_k) = n_k \qquad (6)$$

with r_k the k intensity value and n_k the number of pixel of the image with intensity r_k, and the normalized histogram as:

$$p(r_k) = \frac{r_k}{MN} \qquad (7)$$

with MN the product of rows number and columns number, the procedure is as follows:

1. Get the histogram $p_r(r)$ from source image, and use it to find the function $T(r_k)$

$$s_k = T(r_k) = (L-1) \sum_{j=0}^{k} p_r(r_j) \qquad (8)$$

2. Calculate the function G

$$G(z_q) = (L-1) \sum_{i=0}^{q} p_z(z_i)$$ (9)

where $p_z(z_i)$ are the values of the reference histogram
3. Calculate the inverse function

$$z_q = G^{-1}(s_k)$$ (10)

4. With functions $T(r_k)$ and $G^{-1}(sk)$, map all the values r_k on z_q

$$z_q = G^{-1}(T(r_k))$$ (11)

5. Update the pixel of the image, changing the n_k pixel from value r_k to value z_q with k and q in $[0, L-1]$

Figure 4 shows the application of the procedure on the image histogram of fig. 3 (a): center histogram come from image in fig. 3 (b), the rightmost is the result of the matching.

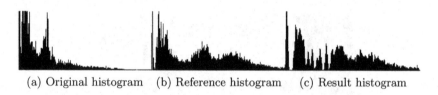

(a) Original histogram   (b) Reference histogram   (c) Result histogram

Fig. 4. Histogram matching: the histograms

3   Experiments

The feasibility and the validity of the proposed scheme is confirmed by the experimental results in this section. We have tested our algorithms using the extended Yale face database B cropped [9]. Five subjects, each with 64 different illumination frontal face images, have been chosen. We picked the frontal illumination images, one for each subject, as training set, we left the others for testing set (315 images, 192x168 pixel).

Support Vector Machines (SVM) were used for the face recognition experiments. An SVM with a linear kernel was trained for each set of experiments using the libSVM [10].

In order to normalize all the images in the database, three different experiments have been performed. First we have tested the SSR without any other enhancement to find the best value for the parameter σ obtaining the best accuracy in the face recognition (68,89%) with $\sigma = 4$ (see table 1). In the second experiment, we have normalized the database with the TVQI, $\lambda = 0.4$, and SSR with $\sigma = 4$. In this case the accuracy was 97,46% (only 8 images misclassified).

Finally, we applied all the proposed illumination correction methods (Histogram matching, TVQI and SSR sequencely), obtaining an accuracy of 100% . Performed test with relative accuracy are summarized in table 2.

Table 1. SSR results varying σ

	SSR			
σ	ok	%	err	%
1	215	68,25	100	31,75
2	215	68,25	100	31,75
3	215	68,25	100	31,75
4	217	68,89	98	31,11
5	213	67,62	102	32,38
6	213	67,62	102	32,38
7	212	67,30	103	32,70
8	210	66,67	105	33,33
9	206	65,39	109	34,61
10	205	65,08	110	34,92

In fig. 5 are presented the results of applying the different methods, either in isolation (TVQI fig. 5 (b) and (e)), or together (fig. 5 (c) and (f)).

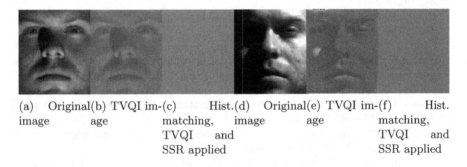

(a)   Original (b) TVQI im- (c)   Hist. (d)   Original (e) TVQI im- (f)   Hist.
image   age   matching,   image   age   matching,
             TVQI   and   TVQI   and
             SSR applied   SSR applied

Fig. 5. Sample images

Table 2. Average recognition Rate (%) comparison

Methodology	SSR	TVQI+SSR	Hist. match.+TVQI+SSR
Average	68,88	97,46	100

4   Conclusion

In this paper we have proposed a new methodology to normalize the facial images in order to improve the performance of a face recognition system. With the Histogram Matching we were able to compensate the difference in the intensity distribution between a poorly illuminated image and a well-illuminated one. The TVQI has enhanced the edges that are on the face and has removed most of the noise. At the end, with the SSR we have removed almost all the shadows in the image obtaining also a good dynamic compression. With the combined use of these three methods we were able to realize the 100% accuracy under variable lighting conditions in the process of face recognition.

Acknowledgments. This work was partially supported by the Italian Ministry of University and Scientific Research within the framework of the project "Ambient Intelligence: event analysis, sensor reconfiguration and multimodal interfaces"(PRIN - 2006-2008).

References

1. Land, E.H., McCann, J.J.: Lightness and Retinex Theory. J. Opt. Soc. Am. 61(1) (1971)
2. Jobson, D.J., Rahman, Z., Woodell, G.A.: A Multiscale Retinex for Bridging the Gap Between Color Images and the Human Observation of Scenes. IEEE Transactions on Image Processing 6(3), 965–976 (1997)
3. Belhumeur, P.N., Kriegman, D.J.: What is the set of images of an object under all possible lighting conditions? IEEE International Conference on Computer Vision and Pattern Recognition (1996)
4. Bhattacharyya, J.: Detecting Removing Specularities and Shadows in Images. Masters Thesis, Department of Electrical and Computer Engineering, McGill University (June 2004)
5. Rammamorthi, R., Hanrahan, P.: A Signal-Processing Framework for Inverse Rendering. In: ACM SIGGRAPH (2001)
6. Chen, T., Yin, W., Zhou, X.S., Comaniciu, D., Huang, T.S.: Illumination normalization for face recognition and uneven background correction using total variation based image models. In: Proceedings of the IEEE Computer Society CVPR, pp. 532–539 (2005)
7. Rudin, L., Osher, S., Fatemi, E.: Nonlinear total variation based noise removal algorithms. Physica D 60, 259–268 (1992)
8. Chambolle, A.: An algorithm for total variation minimization and applications. J. Math. Imaging Vis. 20, 89–97 (2004)
9. Lee, K.C., Ho, J., Kriegman, D.: Acquiring Linear Subspaces for Face Recognition under Variable Lighting. IEEE Trans. Pattern Anal. Mach. Intelligence 27(5), 684–698 (2005)
10. Chang, C.C., Lin, C.J.: LIBSVM: a library for support vector machines (2001), http://www.csie.ntu.edu.tw/~cjlin/libsvm
11. Hayakawa, H.: Photometric stereo under light source with arbitrary motion. Journal of Optical Society of America A, 11 (1994)
12. Horn, B., Brooks, M. (eds.): Shape from Shading. MIT Press, Cambridge (1989)
13. Shashua, A.: On photometric issues in 3d visual recognition from a single 2D image. International Journal of Computer Vision 21, 99–122 (1997)
14. Yuille, A.L., Snow, D., Epstein, R., Belhumeur, P.N.: Determining generative models of objects under varying illumination: Shape and albedo from multiple images using svd and integrability. International Journal of Computer Vision 35, 203–222 (1999)
15. Wang, H., Li, S.Z., Wang, Y.: Generalized quotient image. IEEE International Conference on Computer Vision and Pattern Recognition (2004)

A Color-Based Interest Operator

Marta Penas[1] and Linda G. Shapiro[2]

[1] Dpt. of Computer Science, University of A Coruña. 15071, A Coruña. Spain
mpenas@udc.es
[2] Dpt. of Computer Science and Engineering, University of Washington. US
shapiro@cs.washington.edu

Abstract. In this paper we propose a novel interest operator robust to photometric and geometric transformations. Our operator is closely related to the grayscale MSER but it works on the HSV color space, as opposed to the most popular operators in the literature, which are intensity based. It combines a fine and a coarse overlapped quantization of the HSV color space to find maximally stable extremal regions on each of its components and combine them into a final set of regions that are useful in images where intensity does not discriminate well. We evaluate the performance of our operator on two different applications: wide-baseline stereo matching and image annotation.

Keywords: interest operators, feature matching, HSV color space, wide-baseline stereo, image annotation.

1 Introduction

Feature matching is an important challenge in Computer Vision, with broad applications to image retrieval [1,2], video analysis [3,4] and motion tracking [5,6]. Local regions are well suited for matching, since they are robust to occlusion and background clutter. For this reason, several papers in the recent literature describe the use of interest operators [7,8,9,10] to detect image regions suitable for feature matching purposes. Such regions must exhibit some desirable properties such as: distinctiveness and invariability to scaling, rotation, 3D camera viewpoint or changes in illumination.

The interest operators in the literature can be divided in two main categories: those based on edges and corners that detect structured and highly textured regions and those based on intensity that detect blob like features. Examples of the first category are the Harris affine [8] and EBR [7] detectors. The MSER [9], Kadir [10] SIFT [11] and IBR [7] detectors fall in the second category. In many cases, the operators detect complementary image regions and, thus, it is common to find applications that combine their outputs [7,12].

The Harris affine operator [8] detects the interest points in the image through the Harris corner detector, then selects an adequate scale through the LoG kernel and estimates the affine shape of the interest region in the point neighborhood. The Edge Based Regions (EBR) [7] operator starts from interest points, also

P. Foggia, C. Sansone, and M. Vento (Eds.): ICIAP 2009, LNCS 5716, pp. 965–974, 2009.
© Springer-Verlag Berlin Heidelberg 2009

detected using the Harris detector, and the edges that meet at each point to build an interest region that, as opposed to the Harris affine regions, is not centered at the interest point. The Kadir operator [10] defines the interest regions as those exhibiting unpredictability, in terms of the Shannon entropy, both in their local attributes and their spatial scale. Finally, the Scale Invariant Feature Transform (SIFT) operator [11] detects interest points as those locations invariant to scale changes, defined as the scale-space extrema in the DoG kernel. All the operators just mentioned detect ellipse or circle-shaped regions starting from the initial interest points. In contrast, the following interest operators detect arbitrary-shaped regions through the analysis of the image intensity.

The IBR (Intensity Based Regions) operator [7] defines the interest points as local extrema of the image intensity. The algorithm analyzes the intensity along several rays emanating from the initial interest points. On each of these rays, the point where the intensity changes significantly is selected and, by linking these points, the interest region is determined.

The MSER (Maximally Stable Extremal Regions) operator [9] detects a set of regions that exhibit some desirable properties for feature matching: covariance to adjacency preserving transformations and invariance to scale changes and affine transformations of image intensities. The detection of MSER regions starts with the thresholding of the image intensity at all the 256 gray values. At each threshold level, the pixels below the threshold are colored in black, while the pixels over the threshold are colored in white. The set of connected white components are the maximal regions of the level. Those maximal regions that are stable over a range of thresholdings constitute the maximally stable extremal regions of the image. The algorithm also computes the MSER regions in the inverted image. The performance of the operator is governed by three parameters: the minimum size of a region ms, the maximum size of a region as a percentage of the image size per and the minimum margin of the region mm, this is, the minimum stability of the maximal regions to be considered MSER regions.

A color variant of the MSER that operates in the RGB space was introduced in [13]. The extension to color is made by looking at successive time steps of an agglomerative clustering of image pixels. The selection of time steps is performed by analyzing the evolution of the color differences between neighboring image pixels, with the aim to process a uniform number of pixels per time step. This is not intuitive and not necessarily optimal in the general case, which is why our operator follows a different approach. It works on the HSV color space and imposes hard constraints on the color differences that largely increase the robustness of the method to parameter changes, as demonstrated in sec. 2.

Several color descriptors [14,15] have also been proposed recently. Though the use of color information in the region description could add value to our results, this analysis is beyond the scope of the current paper, where we have used the widely known SIFT descriptor [11] in our experiments.

We are mainly interested in the interest operators that are able to detect regions of arbitrary shape and, to the best of our knowledge, only [13] analyzes the image color, even though it contains important information that could be of great use for feature matching. For this reason, in sec. 2, we introduce a new interest operator, closely related to the MSER detector, that operates on color and improves the results of the grayscale detector on those images where the intensity is not discriminative enough. Sec. 3 describes some practical applications that test the performance and robustness of our operator, and sec. 4 summarizes the conclusions from our work.

2   Color Based MSER

The MSER operator designed by J. Matas [9] operates on intensity, which is not always discriminative enough, as shown in figure 1. MSER was run on the grayscale version of the input color image and it could only find some of the green areas, which stand out well in the color image, but not in grayscale. Also, the stability of the regions is fragile and very dependent on the input parameters. In this paper we present a color interest operator, called COLOR, based on the same principles as the MSER. Our operator detects interest regions in the HSV color space and is less sensitive to changes in the input parameters and small interconnections among regions, as will be demonstrated.

Fig. 1. From left to right: input image; output MSER regions with $mm = 5$ and 7, respectively. MSER was run on the grayscale version of the input.

The HSV color model has been chosen, since it is quite similar to the way humans perceive color. It defines color in terms of three components: the *hue* that ranges from 0 to 360 degrees and defines the color type, the *saturation* that defines the percentage of gray, and the *value* that defines the brightness of the color, both ranging from 0 to 1.

In order to detect interest regions in the HSV color space, an adequate quantization of its components must be first chosen. To do so, two important principles must be taken into account: a value of 0 represents the black color regardless of the hue and the saturation, and a saturation of 0 represents a gray color defined by the value regardless of the hue. Based on these principles, several quantizations can be found in the literature. Smith [16] designed a uniform quantization scheme of the color space into 166 colors. Zhang et al [17] suggest a non-uniform quantization into 36 colors. Huang et al. [18] also suggest a non-uniform quantization into 166 colors.

In this work, we have combined a fine and a coarse overlapped quantization of the HSV diagram. The COLOR operator produces sets of regions from all three bands: value V, saturation S and hue H. The V-band is quantized into 125 bins and processed with a variant of the MSER operator that does not join pixels if their hues or saturations are very different. These additional constraints have been added in order to avoid joining regions with clear differences in color. We have found that a maximum difference of 0.125 in saturation and 15° in hue, which is a rather coarse quantization of these components, produces good results. Fig. 2 depicts a simplified pseudocode of the interest region detection in the V-band, which yields *value regions*.

```
1. Quantize the V-space
2. Sort pixels according to value.
3. Initialize an empty image I.
4. For each V-bin
   4.1. Place the pixels in the V-bin into the image I
   4.2. Compute the extremal regions in I, connecting two neighboring
        pixels only if their difference in hue is below 15 degrees and
        their difference in saturation is below 0.125.
5. Find minima of the rate of change of the area function
```

Fig. 2. Pseudocode for interest region detection in value

A pixel is analyzed according to its hue and saturation when its value is above 0.2 and its saturation above 0.1, since below these thresholds, the pixel can be considered gray or black and its hue and saturation are undefined. The S-band and the V-band are also quantized into 180 and 125 bins, respectively, and processed with a variant of the MSER that does not join pixels with similar saturation if they have very different hues and vice-versa. Again, the maximum difference in saturation is 0.125 and the maximum difference in hue is 15°. Processing the S-band yields *saturation regions*, while processing the H-band yields *hue regions*. Finally, a postprocessing stage produces the final set of COLOR regions, which is a union of the value, saturation and hue regions in which regions that are approximately the same have been combined; if two regions of similar size overlap by more than 95%, the larger is used.

Fig. 3 depicts a simplified pseudocode of the interest region detection in saturation. The pseudocode for interest region detection in hue is very similar to the one depicted in fig. 3 and, for this reason, it has not been included. As in [9], the current implementation details include the use of the efficient union-find algorithm to store and merge the regions in each bin.

In [9], the author states that the MSER regions can be defined on pixels that come from a totally ordered set, which is not the case with the hue, since it has circular continuity. Despite this fact, the regions detected on hue have proven to contain useful information. Also, since the regions are computed in two directions as in the MSER operator, the effect of the circular continuity can be mitigated by analyzing the hue clockwise starting from 0° and anti-clockwise starting from 180°.

```
1. Quantize the S-space
2. Sort pixels according to saturation (only if value > 0.1 and
   saturation > 0.2)
3. Initialize an empty image I.
4. For each S-bin
   4.1. Place the pixels in the S-bin into the image I
   4.2. Compute the extremal regions in I, connecting two neighboring
        pixels only if their difference in hue is below 15 degrees
5. Find minima of the rate of change of the area function
```

Fig. 3. Pseudocode for interest region detection in saturation

We have previously stated that the regions detected by our operator are more stable to changes in the input parameters than the regions detected by MSER. Figure 4 demonstrates this point since our operator detects the most relevant features in the image regardless of a large variation in the input parameters. The regions detected in the intensity are in fact less stable to parameter changes than the regions detected in the HSV, due to the additional restrictions we have applied on its components.

Fig. 4. Interest regions detected by our operator with different input parameters. $ms = 100$, $per = 0.05$, $mm_H = 6, 12, 18$, $mm_S = 5, 10, 15$ and $mm_S = 3, 5, 8$, respectively.

Our interest operator has been tested on several applications and compared with the operators described in sec. 1. The results of these tests have been summarized on the next section.

3   Evaluation of the Operator

In order to test the robustness of our interest operator to several image transformations in a real application, we have implemented a wide-baseline stereo matching system very similar to that in [7]. The goal of such a system is to find the homography that defines the transformation between two scenes. To this end, first a set of interest regions are extracted from the input images and then a descriptor is assigned to each of these regions. We have used the SIFT descriptor [11] in our experiments. Since the SIFT descriptor applies to elliptical regions, and not all the interest operators produce ellipse-shaped regions, the outputs of such operators have been approximated by the best-fitting ellipse.

Fig. 5. Top row: reference images for the 'bikes', 'leuven' and 'ubc' image series, respectively. Bottom row: last image of each series.

In order to establish correspondences between regions, a nearest-neighbor based scheme has been used. A tentative match is established between two regions if they are mutual nearest neighbors in terms of Euclidean distance, and this distance is below a predefined threshold. In order to reject false initial matches, a geometric constraint is applied next. The homography transforming two image patches is computed and the match is retained only if its homography is compatible with that defined by at least min_c other matches. We have found that, as stated in [7], $min_c = 8$ produces good results. Finally, the homography between images is computed applying RANSAC on the retained matches.

The wide-baseline stereo matching has been tested on the set of images listed in http://www.robots.ox.ac.uk/~vgg/research/affine/ since these images are subject to several common transformations like blur or viewpoint change, and the groundtruth for such transformations is available. In total, eight series of six images are available, each composed of a reference image and its successive transformations from easiest to hardest. The homographies between the reference image and the other images in the series are available.

Fig. 5 shows two images of three series subject to photometric transformations with the matching regions detected by our operator superimposed. Our operator is able to solve the correspondences between all the images in each of these series, which proves its robustness to transformations such as blur, illumination changes, and JPEG compression.

Fig. 6 shows two images of three series subject to geometric transformations. In this case, our operator is not always able to find the correspondences between images; for this reason its performance has been compared with the operators described in sec. 1 in order to determine if these operators are more robust than ours to geometric transformations. The results of this comparison are summarized in table 1.

Fig. 6. Top row: reference images for the 'boat', 'graf' and 'wall' image series, respectively. Bottom row: second image of each series.

On the 'bark' series, our operator is not able to find any correspondence, in fact, only the Harris affine operator is able to find one of the five correspondences. On the 'boat' series, our operator is able to find two correspondences, the same number found by all the other operators. On the 'graph' series, our operator finds three correspondences, the same as the MSER and the Harris affine operator, while the Kadir, IBR and EBR operators find only two correspondences. Finally, on the 'wall' series, our operator finds all the correspondences, the same as the other operators except the IBR, which is only able to find three correspondences.

These results show that the proposed operator is robust to both, geometric and photometric transformation, which is of great importance when its outputs are used for feature matching, as will be the case with the following example.

Our operator has also been tested on an image annotation framework. To this end, it has been used as the base region detector in a Spatial Pyramid Matching annotation system [19]. Such a system operates in several stages: first, the

Table 1. Scene matching results for images subject to geometric transformations

	2	3	4	5	6	2	3	4	5	6	2	3	4	5	6	2	3	4	5	6
	Bark					Boat					Graf					Wall				
Harris	✗	✗	✗	✓	✗	✓	✗	✗	✓	✗	✓	✓	✗	✓	✗	✓	✓	✓	✓	✓
Kadir	✗	✗	✗	✗	✗	✓	✗	✗	✓	✗	✓	✓	✗	✗	✗	✓	✓	✓	✓	✓
EBR	✗	✗	✗	✗	✗	✓	✗	✗	✓	✗	✓	✓	✗	✗	✗	✓	✓	✓	✓	✓
IBR	✗	✗	✗	✗	✗	✓	✗	✗	✓	✗	✓	✓	✗	✗	✗	✓	✓	✓	✗	✗
MSER	✗	✗	✗	✗	✗	✓	✗	✗	✓	✗	✓	✓	✗	✓	✗	✓	✓	✓	✓	✓
COLOR	✗	✗	✗	✗	✗	✓	✗	✗	✓	✗	✓	✓	✗	✓	✗	✓	✓	✓	✓	✓

Table 2. Results obtained by different interest operators on a subset of the Caltech 256 dataset

	252	253	251	145	129	182	140	130	Mean
Kadir	**98.36**	92.29	85.64	98.42	**99.65**	81.14	79.10	73.30	**72.71**
Harris	98.11	93.07	**90.54**	95.29	99.17	76.39	**79.68**	70.90	70.48
MSER	97.47	92.80	87.33	**99.14**	93.73	**81.30**	75.63	67.80	69.67
COLOR	98.35	**94.13**	86.41	98.69	96.59	79.86	79.44	**74.07**	71.53

interesting regions of an image are detected and a descriptor is assigned to each of these regions; again the SIFT descriptor has been used. Then, a vocabulary is generated based on a subset of the training images. Each image region is assigned to a dictionary bin, and the image signature is generated by the concatenation of a set of histograms counting the number of regions per bin in several recursive partitions of the input image. Finally, a spatial pyramid matching kernel that weights the differences between histogram bins according to their partition level and position, is used to compute the differences between signatures, which are finally used as the input kernel for an SVM based annotation.

This annotation framework has been applied to a subset of the Caltech 256 dataset. Concretely, the 50 object categories that produce the best results, according to [20], have been used to test the performance of our operator and compare it with the operators introduced in sec. 1. It should be noted that these operators retrieve different image regions, and the best results would probably be obtained through a combination of their results, as is common in annotation frameworks nowadays [12]. This application is just a comparison to determine if our operator is competitive with those most widely used in the literature. Two disjoint sets of 30 and 50 images have been used for training and testing, respectively. The accuracy of the system has been measured in terms of the percentage average precision, which ranges from 0 to 100, and reflects the performance on the relevant images, rewarding systems that retrieve the relevant images quickly. Table 2 shows the results obtained by the operators, Kadir, Harris affine, MSER and COLOR operator, on a subset of the selected categories. The last column in table 2 is the global mean result on the 50 categories analyzed.

The first thing to note is that, on average, the results produced by the four operators are very similar. The Kadir operator has the highest mean average precision, followed by our operator, though it is not robust to affine changes. This could be the case because the "easiest" categories on the Caltech 256 dataset do not contain large viewpoint changes that could affect its performance. Each operator works best on different categories, for example, our color operator produces the best results on 13 categories, the second best result on 20, the third best on 11 and the worst on 6 categories.

Since our operator was designed to improve the original grayscale MSER operator, the comparison to MSER is the most important. Our operator outperforms the MSER operator on 37 of the 50 selected categories, and it achieves a 6.13% gain in performance measured in terms of mean average precision.

4   Discussion and Conclusions

In this paper we have introduced an interest operator based on the MSER operator designed by Matas [9] that operates on color, concretely on the HSV space, where it combines a fine and a coarse quantization in order to find the maximally stable regions present in each component. It detects the most important and distinctive features in the input images and produces high quality results in both structured and non-structured images.

We have tested our operator on two different application. First, a wide-baseline stereo matching applied to scenes undergoing different photometric and geometric deformations has been used to test the robustness of our operator to such deformations. Then, an image annotation application, where our operator produced the best results on some categories and achieved a comparable performance to the most widely used operators in the literature. Our operator outperformed the MSER operator in most of the categories and in terms of average performance. Both applications assess the suitability of our interest operator for feature matching.

Acknowledgements

This work has been funded by the Xunta de Galicia and the *Secretaría de Estado de Universidades e Investigación* of the Ministry of Science and Education of Spain, and partially supported by the U. S. National Science Foundation under grant No. IIS-0705765.

References

1. Schmid, C., Mohr, R.: Local grayvalue invariants for image retrieval. IEEE Trans. on Pattern Analysis and Machine Intelligence 19(5), 530–535 (1997)
2. Tuytelaars, T., Gool, L.V.: Content-based image retrieval based on local affinely invariant regions. In: International Conference on Visual Information Systems, pp. 493–500 (1999)
3. Sivic, J., Zisserman, A.: Video google: a test retrieval approach to object matching in videos. In: International Conference on Computer Vision (2003)
4. Schaffalitzky, F., Zisserman, A.: Automated location matching in movies. Computer Vision and Image Understanding 92, 236–264 (2003)
5. Harris, C.: Geometry from visual motion. Active Vision, 263–284 (1992)
6. Torr, P.: Motion segmentation and outlier detection. PhD thesis, University of Oxford (1995)
7. Tuytelaars, T., Gool, L.V.: Matching widely separated views based on affine invariant regions. International Journal on Computer Vision 59(1), 61–85 (2004)
8. Mikolajczyk, K., Schmid, C.: Scale and affine invariant interest point detectors. International Journal on Computer Vision 60 (2004)
9. Matas, J., Chum, O., Urban, M., Pajdla, T.: Robust wide baseline stereo from maximally stable extremal regions. In: British Machine Video Conference, pp. 384–393 (2002)

10. Kadir, T., Zisserman, A., Brady, M.: An affine invariant salient region detector. In: European Conference on Computer Vision, pp. 404–416 (2004)
11. Lowe, D.G.: Distinctive image features from scale-invariant keypoints. International Journal of Computer Vision 60(2), 91–110 (2004)
12. Marszałek, M., Schmid, C., Harzallah, H., van de Weijer, J.: Learning object representations for visual object class recognition. In: Visual Recognition Challenge Workshop, in conjunction with ICCV (October 2007)
13. Forssen, P.: Maximally stable colour regions for recognition and matching. In: IEEE Conference on Computer Vision and Pattern Recognition, pp. 1–8 (2007)
14. Van de Weijer, J., Schmid, C.: Coloring local feature extraction. In: European Conference on Computer Vision, pp. 334–348 (2006)
15. Van de Sande, K., Gevers, T., Snoek, C.: Evaluation of color descriptors for object and scene recognition. In: IEEE Conference on Computer Vision and Pattern Recognition, pp. 1–8 (2008)
16. Smith, J.R.: Integrated spatial and feature image system: retrieval, analysis and compression. PhD thesis, Columbia University (1997)
17. Zhang, L., Lin, F., Zang, B.: A CBIR method based on color-spatial feature. In: IEEE Region 10 International Conference TENCON, pp. 166–169 (1999)
18. Huang, C., Yu, S., Zhou, J., Lu, H.: Image retrieval using both color and local spatial feature histograms. In: Int. Conference on Communications, Circuits and Systems, pp. 927–931 (2004)
19. Lazebnik, S., Schmid, C., Ponce, J.: Beyond bags of features: spatial pyramid matching for recognizing natural scene categories. In: IEEE Conference on Computer Vision and Pattern Recognition, vol. 2, pp. 2169–2178 (2006)
20. Griffin, G., Holub, A., Perona, P.: Caltech-256 object category dataset. Technical report 7694, California Institute of Technology (2007)

An Evaluation of Scale and Noise Sensitivity of Fibre Orientation Estimation in Volume Images

Maria Axelsson

Centre for Image Analysis, Swedish University of Agricultural Sciences,
Box 337, SE-751 05, Uppsala, Sweden
maria@cb.uu.se

Abstract. Fibre orientation influences many important properties of fibre-based materials, for example, strength and stiffness. Fibre orientation and the orientation anisotropy in paper and other wood fibre-based materials have previously been estimated using two-dimensional images. Recently, we presented a method for estimating the three-dimensional fibre orientation in volume images based on local orientation estimates. Here, we present an evaluation of the method with respect to scale and noise sensitivity. The evaluation is performed for both tubular and solid fibres. We also present a new method for automatic scale selection for solid fibres. The method is based on a segmentation of the fibres that also provides an estimate of the fibre dimension distribution in an image. The results show that the fibre orientation estimation performs well both in noisy images and at different scales. The presented results can be used as a guide to select appropriate parameters for the method when it is applied to real data. The applicability of the fibre orientation estimation to fibre-based materials with solid fibres is demonstrated for a volume image of a press felt acquired with X-ray microtomography.

1 Introduction

Fibre orientation is an important property of many fibre-based materials. In paper and wood fibre composite materials it influences other physical properties such as strength, stiffness, and hygroexpansion. If the microscopical material properties can be correlated to macroscopical material properties, new materials with more specialised properties can be designed.

Previously, methods for estimating fibre orientation in both two-dimensional (2D) images and three-dimensional (3D) images have been presented. In [1] a sheet splitting method including a 2D gradient image analysis method of the scanned sheets was presented. This is the predominant method used in the paper industry to estimate fibre orientation. Today, fibre orientation estimates can be obtained for A4 or A3 sheet sizes with a spatial resolution of 2 × 2 mm. For a review see for example [2]. However, only orientations in the plane of the sheet can be estimated, since the 3D information is lost in the splitting.

Material properties can be studied in 3D using volume images. In 2001 Samuelsen et al. [3] demonstrated that synchrotron X-ray microtomography provides a tool to acquire volume images of materials such as paper. The technique

P. Foggia, C. Sansone, and M. Vento (Eds.): ICIAP 2009, LNCS 5716, pp. 975–984, 2009.

is the same as for Computed Tomography (CT) used in medical applications, but the resolution is in the micrometer range, which makes X-ray microtomography suitable to image material microstructure. Today, desktop X-ray microtomography scanners are also available. However, they provide lower resolution compared to synchrotron X-ray microtomography.

2D methods, such as stereological and cross sectional methods, have been proposed for estimating fibre orientation in volume images. However, such methods are not suited to estimate fibre orientation in wood fibre based materials such as paper and wood fibre composites, due to the large shape and size variation of wood fibres after they have passed the pulping process.

Few image analysis methods have been proposed for estimating 3D fibre orientation. A method for synthetic fibres was presented in [4]. A fixed number of filters with different orientations were used and the orientation corresponding to the filter with the largest filter response was selected as the fibre orientation in each voxel. This approach is computationally heavy when many filters are used to obtain good angular resolution. In [5] we presented a method for estimating the 3D fibre orientation in volume images. The method is based on local orientation estimates using quadrature filters and structure tensors. This method provides detailed estimates of the fibre orientation using only six quadrature filters that can estimate any orientation in 3D. Here, we evaluate the robustness of the method with respect to noise and scale using synthetic data. The error estimates for both tubular fibres, such as wood fibres, and for solid fibres, such as synthetic polymer fibres, is evaluated. In addition, we present a novel method for automatic scale selection for solid fibres. We also demonstrate the applicability of the 3D fibre orientation estimation to press felts, which is a material made of solid polymer fibres.

The method for estimating 3D fibre orientation is outlined in Section 2 and the new method for automatic scale selection for solid fibres is presented in 3. The evaluation of the orientation estimation with experiments and results is presented in Section 4 and a discussion and conclusion are found in Section 5.

2   3D Fibre Orientation Estimation

The fibre orientation in a material can be estimated using the local orientation of the material microstructure in volume images. The method presented in [5] is based on a framework for local orientation estimation using quadrature filters and structure tensors, which is thoroughly described in [6].

The local 3D orientation of the structure in a neighbourhood of a voxel can be estimated using a set of at least six quadrature filters, where each filter is sensitive to signal variation in a certain orientation. The filters are phase invariant where the real part of each filter corresponds to a line detector and the complex part corresponds to an edge detector. The centre frequency of the radial function of the filters should be selected to correspond to the size of the interesting image structures. Small filters that correspond to edges in the image provide better estimates than large filters that correspond to large structures such as the fibre walls.

The volume image is convolved with the quadrature filters and the filter responses are combined to a structure tensor in each voxel. The structure tensor is represented by a 3×3 symmetric matrix in 3D. There are thus six independent components. To reduce local errors and obtain better estimates the tensor field is smoothed by convolving each component image with a small Gaussian kernel. The standard deviation for the Gaussian distribution is denoted σ_s. The fibre orientation is a large scale property that is assumed to vary slower than the small scale variations and noise that is reduced by the smoothing.

As described in [6] the local orientation and local structure anisotropy in each voxel neighbourhood can be obtained from the eigenvectors and the eigenvalues of the tensor. The eigenvalues are sorted according to size in descending order. The sorted eigenvalues are denoted λ_1, λ_2, and λ_3 and the corresponding eigenvectors $\mathbf{e}_1$, $\mathbf{e}_2$, and $\mathbf{e}_3$. The orientation of the largest signal variation in a neighbourhood, $\mathbf{e}_1$, is referred to as the local orientation. Certainty estimates for the estimated local orientation and the other two orientation estimates are given by

$$c_1 = \frac{\lambda_1 - \lambda_2}{\lambda_1}, \quad c_2 = \frac{\lambda_2 - \lambda_3}{\lambda_1}, \quad c_3 = \frac{\lambda_3}{\lambda_1}$$

The fibre orientation is modelled as the orientation with the least signal variation. The fibre orientation can thus be estimated using the eigenvector $\mathbf{e}_3$. The c_2 measurement is used as certainty for the fibre orientation. The certainty is large in neighbourhoods where there is large signal variation in two main orientations and small signal variation in the third orientation. When the orientation estimates are weighted by the c_2 measurement and also by the probability of the voxel to contain a fibre, the estimation error is reduced [5]. The obtained orientation estimates can be averaged over parts of the sample, like layers of a paper sheet, or over the whole sample depending on the desired output.

3   Automatic Scale Selection for Solid Fibres

Fibre orientation estimates from different parameter setups can be combined to improve the estimation result for materials with different fibre dimensions. Here, a method for selecting scale by weighting the orientation estimates from volumes with solid fibres is presented. The method is intended for application to raw data volume images from X-ray microtomography and similar images.

A segmentation of the fibres, where each voxel contains the approximate fibre radius, is calculated using the raw volume image. First noise is reduced using bilateral filtering [7], which is an edge preserving filtering method. Then the volume is segmented into fibre and void using hysteresis thresholding to binarise the samples [8]. The distance transform [10] is applied to the fibres where the shortest distance to the background is calculated for all voxels inside the fibres. Then the watershed segmentation algorithm [9] is applied to the distance transformed image. This creates a regionalisation of the fibres where each maximum in the distance transform generates one region. The distance transform is smoothed before the watershed algorithm is applied to reduce over-segmentation due to noise and small shape variations of the fibres. A segmented image where each voxel contains the approximate fibre radius is obtained by setting all voxels in a region to the value of the corresponding distance maximum. The distance maxima in the segmented image are used to weight orientation results obtained using different parameter setups for different fibre dimensions. This is exemplified for three fibre diameters in Section 4.2. If the diameters are not known exactly or assumed to vary, results obtained using a range of parameter setups can also be combined using this method. In addition, the presented segmentation of the fibre dimensions directly provides an estimate of the fibre dimension distribution by summing the number of voxels for each fibre radius and weighting the result with the corresponding radius.

4   Experiments and Results

The evaluation of the orientation estimation using synthetic data is presented in Section 4.1 and the applicability of the orientation estimation to real data with solid fibres is illustrated in Section 4.2.

4.1   Synthetic Data

Synthetic test volumes with randomly positioned straight fibres were used to evaluate the fibre orientation estimation. Volumes with either tubular or solid fibres were generated with specific fibre dimensions and known fibre orientation. To evaluate the difference between tubular and solid fibres, pairs of volumes with the same fibre positions and fibre orientation but different fibre interior were used. The volumes were $250 \times 250 \times 250$ voxels with approximately 150–500 fibres in each volume, depending on the fibre diameter. The fibre length was constant in all volumes. Six different fibre diameters, D_f, were used. These correspond to volumes with different fibre dimensions or different scales. A test set with ten volumes for each fibre diameter was generated to provide good statistics. Noise was also added to the volumes in the test set to evaluate the robustness of the method. The original pixel values range from 0 to 1 with the background close to 0 and the fibres close to 1. Gaussian noise with zero mean and standard deviation, σ_n, of 0.2, 0.4, and 0.6 was added to each volume.

Fibre orientation was estimated in the four test sets; in the images without noise and in the images with the three different noise levels. The spatial filter size was $7 \times 7 \times 7$ voxels, the centre frequency $\pi/2$, and the bandwidth 2 octaves. The weighted mean error for the estimated fibre orientation is calculated as

$$E_{s(\sigma_s)} = \frac{\sum_I wc_2 \arccos(|\mathbf{v_{gt}} \cdot \mathbf{e_3}|)}{\sum_I wc_2}, \tag{1}$$

where σ_s is the standard deviation used for the Gaussian in the smoothing of the tensor field, w is a weight depending on the image intensity or the probability of the voxel to contain fibres, c_2 is the certainty value, $\mathbf{v_{gt}}$ is the ground truth orientation, and $\mathbf{e_3}$ is the estimated orientation. The weighted mean error was

Table 1. Comparison of the estimation error for tubular fibres of different dimensions. No noise. Average over ten volumes.

D_f	E	$E_{s(0)}$	$E_{s(1)}$	$E_{s(2)}$	$E_{s(3)}$	$E_{s(4)}$	$E_{s(5)}$	$E_{s(6)}$	$E_{s(7)}$	$E_{s(8)}$
6	15.85	9.55	3.85	**2.30**	3.00	4.58	6.72	9.10	11.48	13.75
8	15.68	12.99	5.26	**1.40**	1.89	3.03	4.65	6.56	8.59	10.63
10	12.80	14.05	8.14	2.63	**1.64**	2.41	3.57	5.07	6.76	8.53
12	19.01	17.89	12.15	4.92	**1.74**	1.97	2.77	3.82	5.09	6.51
14	21.18	20.16	14.47	8.20	3.29	**1.90**	2.39	3.20	4.20	5.36
16	21.78	23.43	18.05	11.58	5.08	2.21	**2.19**	2.85	3.64	4.60

Table 2. Comparison of the estimation error for solid fibres of different dimensions. No noise. Average over ten volumes.

D_f	E	$E_{s(0)}$	$E_{s(1)}$	$E_{s(2)}$	$E_{s(3)}$	$E_{s(4)}$	$E_{s(5)}$	$E_{s(6)}$	$E_{s(7)}$	$E_{s(8)}$
6	9.56	6.72	3.31	**2.18**	3.04	4.74	6.91	9.26	11.62	13.86
8	11.94	10.28	5.94	3.03	**2.49**	3.49	5.05	6.90	8.88	10.88
10	13.88	14.73	9.44	5.38	3.19	**3.13**	4.16	5.58	7.20	8.90
12	23.94	20.66	14.50	9.16	5.42	**3.75**	**3.75**	4.58	5.74	7.06
14	28.77	23.94	18.00	12.53	8.03	5.09	**4.07**	4.27	5.07	6.09
16	31.39	26.65	21.68	16.17	11.39	7.48	5.29	**4.64**	4.89	5.63

Table 3. Comparison of the estimation error for tubular fibres of different dimensions. Noise with $\sigma_n = 0.2$ was added to the images. Average over ten volumes.

D_f	E	$E_{s(0)}$	$E_{s(1)}$	$E_{s(2)}$	$E_{s(3)}$	$E_{s(4)}$	$E_{s(5)}$	$E_{s(6)}$	$E_{s(7)}$	$E_{s(8)}$
6	24.83	19.10	6.17	**3.60**	4.02	5.45	7.53	9.90	12.33	14.65
8	29.24	25.08	8.31	**2.82**	**2.82**	3.72	5.20	7.07	9.10	11.16
10	32.14	28.65	12.30	4.07	**2.76**	3.22	4.18	5.55	7.18	8.93
12	35.68	33.59	18.48	6.92	3.22	**3.12**	3.67	4.56	5.73	7.09
14	39.29	38.25	22.58	11.01	4.94	**3.33**	3.50	4.09	4.93	5.98
16	41.05	41.07	27.63	15.53	7.13	3.90	**3.54**	3.92	4.56	5.39

Table 4. Comparison of the estimation error for solid fibres of different dimensions. Noise with $\sigma_n = 0.2$ was added to the images. Average over ten volumes.

D_f	E	$E_{s(0)}$	$E_{s(1)}$	$E_{s(2)}$	$E_{s(3)}$	$E_{s(4)}$	$E_{s(5)}$	$E_{s(6)}$	$E_{s(7)}$	$E_{s(8)}$
6	25.41	21.06	6.81	**3.65**	3.96	5.43	7.51	9.85	12.21	14.47
8	34.13	31.85	12.44	5.43	**4.05**	4.62	5.96	7.71	9.65	11.63
10	40.26	40.11	21.29	8.98	5.04	**4.46**	5.17	6.40	7.91	9.55
12	44.94	45.43	31.23	15.13	7.95	5.39	**5.07**	5.70	6.72	7.95
14	47.16	47.89	36.68	21.26	11.46	6.92	5.43	**5.41**	6.03	6.93
16	48.64	49.67	41.17	28.43	16.79	10.06	6.96	**6.00**	6.10	6.70

Table 5. Comparison of the estimation error for tubular fibres of different dimensions. Noise with $\sigma_n = 0.4$ was added to the images. Average over ten volumes.

D_f	E	$E_{s(0)}$	$E_{s(1)}$	$E_{s(2)}$	$E_{s(3)}$	$E_{s(4)}$	$E_{s(5)}$	$E_{s(6)}$	$E_{s(7)}$	$E_{s(8)}$
6	36.21	33.09	11.63	6.16	**5.88**	6.94	8.77	10.98	13.30	15.55
8	39.50	37.52	14.60	5.27	**4.45**	4.99	6.22	7.90	9.81	11.79
10	42.01	40.64	20.05	6.92	**4.64**	**4.64**	5.31	6.45	7.91	9.54
12	44.37	43.75	27.37	10.48	5.47	**4.77**	5.03	5.72	6.71	7.93
14	47.21	47.01	32.41	15.48	7.57	5.31	**5.03**	5.37	6.02	6.91
16	48.31	48.33	36.55	20.72	10.09	6.13	**5.24**	5.32	5.76	6.45

Table 6. Comparison of the estimation error for solid fibres of different dimensions. Noise with $\sigma_n = 0.4$ was added to the images. Average over ten volumes.

D_f	E	$E_{s(0)}$	$E_{s(1)}$	$E_{s(2)}$	$E_{s(3)}$	$E_{s(4)}$	$E_{s(5)}$	$E_{s(6)}$	$E_{s(7)}$	$E_{s(8)}$
6	39.57	37.34	14.38	7.04	**6.22**	7.12	8.82	10.91	13.10	15.23
8	45.12	44.16	24.12	9.98	6.86	**6.67**	7.55	9.00	10.73	12.57
10	48.39	48.13	33.77	14.99	8.34	**6.80**	6.93	7.78	9.03	10.48
12	50.58	50.59	40.56	22.93	11.97	8.16	**7.22**	7.43	8.18	9.23
14	51.68	51.79	43.93	29.73	16.22	9.98	7.76	**7.27**	7.55	8.22
16	52.60	52.75	46.74	36.52	22.66	13.76	9.70	8.23	**7.98**	8.29

Table 7. Comparison of the estimation error for tubular fibres of different dimensions. Noise with $\sigma_n = 0.6$ was added to the images. Average over ten volumes.

D_f	E	$E_{s(0)}$	$E_{s(1)}$	$E_{s(2)}$	$E_{s(3)}$	$E_{s(4)}$	$E_{s(5)}$	$E_{s(6)}$	$E_{s(7)}$	$E_{s(8)}$
6	44.01	42.69	20.22	9.92	**8.45**	8.99	10.44	12.36	14.45	16.55
8	45.27	44.62	22.79	8.45	**6.41**	6.51	7.46	8.93	10.69	12.55
10	47.42	47.00	28.87	11.00	6.93	**6.30**	6.64	7.54	8.80	10.27
12	49.04	48.92	35.39	15.86	8.34	6.65	**6.49**	6.92	7.73	8.81
14	51.14	51.12	39.71	22.08	11.38	7.85	6.91	**6.88**	7.29	8.00
16	51.77	51.83	42.33	27.48	14.55	9.07	7.32	**6.92**	7.09	7.58

Table 8. Comparison of the estimation error for solid fibres of different dimensions. Noise with $\sigma_n = 0.6$ was added to the images. Average over ten volumes.

D_f	E	$E_{s(0)}$	$E_{s(1)}$	$E_{s(2)}$	$E_{s(3)}$	$E_{s(4)}$	$E_{s(5)}$	$E_{s(6)}$	$E_{s(7)}$	$E_{s(8)}$
6	46.92	46.02	25.17	12.32	**9.77**	9.86	11.01	12.67	14.55	16.45
8	50.13	49.75	35.07	17.05	11.16	**9.81**	10.03	11.02	12.42	14.01
10	51.91	51.78	41.68	23.65	13.51	10.40	**9.66**	9.95	10.81	11.97
12	53.16	53.15	45.85	31.75	18.16	12.39	10.38	**9.90**	10.19	10.92
14	53.77	53.80	47.81	36.98	22.92	14.69	11.29	10.05	**9.82**	10.13
16	54.38	54.42	49.67	41.90	29.57	19.10	13.79	11.48	10.63	**10.53**

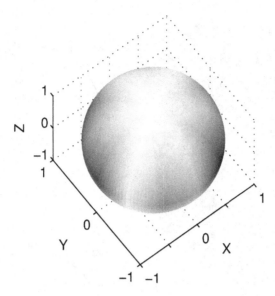

Fig. 1. Colour map for the estimated orientations. Hue varies with the X and Y coordinates and saturation with the Z coordinate.

calculated for each volume image both before smoothing the tensor field, $E_{s(0)}$, and after eight different amounts of Gaussian smoothing, $E_{s(\sigma_s)}$, with standard deviation σ_s. The mean error without weighting the estimates, E, was also calculated. The results for the noise free volumes are reported in Table 1 and Table 2, for the tubular and solid fibres, respectively. All errors are reported in degrees. The minimal error is indicated using bold face. The results for the three noise levels for both fibre types are reported in Table 3 to Table 8.

Smoothing the tensor field prior to estimating the orientation reduces the error for all fibre diameters, D_f, and all noise levels. Larger smoothing must be used for larger values of D_f to obtain the lower errors. The error increases with larger amounts of noise as expected, but the method still performs well for the largest amount of noise. The error is larger for solid fibres than for tubular fibres for larger fibre diameters. For smaller diameters, such as $D_f = 6$ voxels, the difference between solid fibres and tubular fibres is small. It is evident from the results that high resolution of the fibre cross section does not contribute to better estimates. As a result, high resolution images can be downsampled while maintaining the performance of the method.

4.2 Real Data

Press felts that are used in paper manufacturing are made of synthetic polymer fibres with different fibre diameters. They consist of both larger fibres, that form the base weave, and fibres with smaller diameters, called batt fibres, that are needled onto the base weave. A volume image of a press felt was acquired using desktop X-ray microtomography in a Skyscan 1172. Fibres with four different

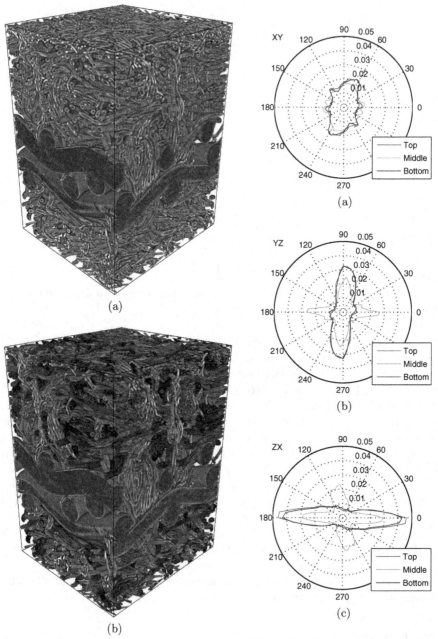

(a)

(b)

(a)

(b)

(c)

Fig. 2. (a) Volume rendering of a press felt, which consist of polymer fibres with four different fibre diameters. (b) Volume rendering of the 3D fibre orientation estimates in the same volume.

Fig. 3. The fibre orientation distribution for the top, middle, and bottom part of the sample. (a) Projection on the XY plane. (b) Projection on the YZ plane. (c) Projection on the ZX plane.

sizes were present in the image; the fibres in the base weave and batt fibres of three different diameters. As the results have shown that high resolution of individual fibre cross sections is not needed to estimate fibre orientation, the volume image was downsampled to match the fibre diameters in the experiments on synthetic data. The resulting image size was $467 \times 501 \times 642$ voxels, with batt fibre diameters of 6, 12, and 15 voxels. Figure 2(a) shows a volume rendering of the material. The difference in fibre diameter between the base weave and the batt fibres is clearly visible in the figure. The orientation of the fibres in the base weave are not estimated in this experiment, since they are large compared to the batt fibres and only partly visible in the image. Larger samples acquired at lower resolution are needed to obtain good estimates of the fibre orientation of the base weave fibres.

Fibre orientation was estimated in the volume image using the same parameter setup for the filters as in Section 4.1. Three values of σ_s, 2, 4, and, 6 voxels, corresponding to the three batt fibre diameters were selected using the three lowest error estimates from Table 2. The resulting tensor images were combined to a final result by selecting orientation estimates voxel-wise from each of the three images using the smallest difference between the optimal radius for each of the three scales and the fibre radius obtained using the method presented in Section 3. The fibres in the base weave were also masked using the estimated fibre radii. The final result of the estimated orientation is shown in Figure 2(b). The base weave is shown in gray and the batt fibres are pseudo coloured based on the estimated orientation as proposed in [5]. Hue varies with the X and Y coordinates and saturation with the Z coordinate, see Figure 1. Figure 3 shows the distribution of the estimated orientations projected on the XY, YZ, and ZX planes for the top, middle, and bottom part of the sample. More fibres are orientated in the X direction in all parts. In the middle part, the fibre orientations are limited by the batt fibres and the fibres are oriented both in the X direction and the Z direction.

5   Discussion and Conclusion

In this paper we have shown that the method for 3D fibre orientation estimation [5] is applicable to both tubular and solid fibres. The method was evaluated in a study on synthetic data with respect to noise and scale. Ten repetitions of each parameter setup was used to obtain reliable results. The results show that the method provides good orientation estimates for both tubular and solid fibres in both noise free and noisy images. It also performs well for a large range of fibre diameters which correspond to different scales. As the fibre orientation provides good estimates also for the smaller fibre diameters it is possible to use low resolution volumes of the fibre material to estimate fibre orientation. The model of the fibre orientation that is used in the method is valid also for small fibre cross sections. The results presented in this paper can be used as a guide to select appropriate parameters for real data. In addition, we have demonstrated the suitability of the method to materials based on solid fibres using press felt.

It was exemplified how parameter selection can be performed using real data. A new method for estimating the fibre radii for solid fibres, which can be used to select scale locally in the image, was also presented and exemplified.

It is left for future work to develop methods for automatic parameter selection, where suitable parameters are selected directly using image information. Another interesting topic is more advanced adaptive scale selection which is based on the local fibre dimensions. This is useful for materials that consist of fibres with different fibre dimensions.

Acknowledgements. The author acknowledges Prof. Gunilla Borgefors and Dr. Joakim Rydell for valuable scientific discussions. The press felt volume image was provided by Albany International AB in Halmstad, Sweden.

References

1. Erkkilä, A.-L., Pakarinen, P., Odell, M.: Sheet forming studies using layered orientation analysis. Pulp and Paper Canada 99(1), 81–85 (1998)
2. Hirn, U., Bauer, W.: Evaluating an improved method to determine layered fibre orientation by sheet splitting. In: 61st Appita Annual Conference and Exhibition, Gold Coast, Australia, May 6–9, pp. 71–79 (2007)
3. Samuelsen, E., Gregersen, Ø., Houen, P.J., Helle, T., Raven, C., Snigirev, A.: Three-dimensional imaging of paper by use of synchroton X-Ray microtomography. Journal of Pulp and Paper Science 27(2), 50–53 (2001)
4. Robb, K., Wirjandi, O., Schladitz, K.: Fiber orientation estimation from 3D image data: Practical algorithms, visualization, and interpretation. In: Proceedings of 7th International Conference on Hybrid Intelligent Systems, September 2007, pp. 320–325 (2007)
5. Axelsson, M.: Estimating 3D Fibre Orientation in Volume Images. In: Proceedings of 19th International Conference on Pattern Recognition (2008)
6. Granlund, G.H., Knutsson, H.: Signal Processing for Computer Vision. Kluwer Academic Publishers, Dordrecht (1995)
7. Tomasi, C., Manduchi, R.: Bilateral filtering for gray and color images. In: IEEE International Conference on Computer Vision 1998, pp. 836–846 (1998)
8. Canny, J.F.: A computational approach to edge detection. IEEE Transactions on Pattern Analysis and Machine Intelligence 8(6), 679–698 (1986)
9. Vincent, L., Soille, P.: Watersheds in digital spaces: An efficient algorithm based on immersion simulations. IEEE Transactions on Pattern Analysis and Machine Intelligence 13(6), 583–598 (1991)
10. Borgefors, G.: On Digital Distance Transforms in Three Dimensions. Computer Vision and Image Understanding 64(3), 368–376 (1996)

Real-Time Online Video Object Silhouette Extraction Using Graph Cuts on the GPU

Zachary A. Garrett and Hideo Saito

Department of Information and Computer Science, Keio University
3-4-1 Hiyoshi, Kohoku-ku, Yokohama, 223-8522 Japan
{zgarrett,saito}@hvrl.ics.keio.ac.jp

Abstract. Being able to find the silhouette of an object is a very important front-end processing step for many high-level computer vision techniques, such as Shape-from-Silhouette 3D reconstruction methods, object shape tracking, and pose estimation. Graph cuts have been proposed as a method for finding very accurate silhouettes which can be used as input to such high level techniques, but graph cuts are notoriously computation intensive and slow. Leading CPU implementations can extract a silhouette from a single QVGA image in 100 milliseconds, with performance dramatically decreasing with increased resolution. Recent GPU implementations have been able to achieve performance of 6 milliseconds per image by exploiting the intrinsic properties of the lattice graphs and the hardware model of the GPU. However, these methods are restricted to a subclass of lattice graphs and are not generally applicable. We propose a novel method for graph cuts on the GPU which places no limits on graph configuration and which is able to achieve comparable real-time performance in online video processing scenarios.

1 Introduction

Graph cutting is a technique that can be applied to energy minimization problems that occur frequently in computer vision. One of the most common applications of graph cuts is binary image segmentation, or object silhouette extraction. The groundwork for solving the push relabel maximum flow across graphs was laid through Goldberg and Tarjan's [1] reasearch, but the applicability to computer vision was not demonstrated until 1989 [2] and further expanded by Boykov et. al [3,4]. However, graph cuts have consistently been difficult to adapt to real-time scenarios due to the intensive computation required to construct and cut even a single graph.

Improving the speed of finding the *st*-mincut of a graph has been the goal of recent research on graph cuts. Research methods that have shown varying degrees of success include algorithms that re-use previous search trees [5], re-use of previous cuts to create a pseudo-flow which can be pushed and pulled through the graph [6], and finally implementations of push-relabel algorithms have been adapted to the GPU [7]. Currently, the fastest of these algorithms, presented by Vineet and Narayanan [8] in 2008, demonstrates a GPU implementation that

P. Foggia, C. Sansone, and M. Vento (Eds.): ICIAP 2009, LNCS 5716, pp. 985–994, 2009.

can compute the graph cut on a 640x480 image in approximately 6 milliseconds. This implementation exploits properties of the lattice graphs created from the input images and the hardware model in the graphics processor. Vineet and Narayanan admit that this approach makes the method only applicable to such graph types and not generally usable by any arbitrary maximum-flow calculation. Furthermore, these papers make no mention of the computation required for graph construction in the online video scenario.

In the case of online video, a graph must be constructed from each video frame as it arrives at the CPU. In contrast, offline methods layer all of the video frames into a 3D volume and cut once across the entire video sequence [9]. On traditional computing platforms, this necessitates techniques which speed up not only the cutting of the graph, but also the construction of the graph. One proposed method uses a laplacian pyramidal structure of decreasing resolutions of the input image to cut decreasingly coarse graphs [10]. This method works well for generally round objects without holes, but has difficulty with other input. We previously presented an online method for live video situations that uses the silhouette of the previous segmentation as a mask for graph construction, in effect shrinking the graph [11]. However, none of these methods compute faster than 100 milliseconds per QVGA frame. To realize real-time applications of graph cuts, large-scale parallel computing needs to be considered.

Recent advances in GPU hardware have given researchers access to low cost, large SIMD arrays which allow data level parallelization of algorithms. Research into how to harness the power of the graphics processor has lead to graphics card manufacturer's providing general purpose graphics processing unit (GPGPU) frameworks such as CUDA [12] by NVIDIA. In the field of computer vision, two such software libraries are CVGPU [13] and OpenVidia [14]. These libraries support many of the basic operations in computer vision with speed improvements of up to 100x, particularly in linear filtering tasks. Research has shown that the push-relabel algorithm is able to run in parallel due to the design of the method and various CPU based approaches having already been presented [15,16].

In this paper we present a fast, generic implementation of the push-relabel algorithm based on the lock-free method proposed by Hong [15] using the CUDA framework and the power of the GPU. Using this method in the system we proposed in [11], we are able to track images in online and offline video and obtains the silhouette of the tracked object at each frame. Our method is adaptable to any graph construction and runs at a 30 Hz frame rate for QVGA images and 4-5 Hz frame rate for HD TV images . By accepting any graph construction, the method is not restricted to lattice graphs, allowing the technique to be applied to maximum flow solutions in other problem spaces, such as graph cuts across spaces of greater than three dimensions [17].

Section 2 presents the GPU framework provided by CUDA and describes how programs are parallelized within this framework. In Section 3 we describe our GPU implementation of a lock-less generic push-relabel graph cut algorithm. Section 4 describes our experimental setup and discusses our experimental results. Finally, Section 5 gives concluding remarks and the direction for our future work.

2   GPU Programming Framework

GPGPU research initially focused on representing computations as graphics renderings. By encoding data arrays into textures and program kernels written in fragment or vertex shaders, computation could be performed by rendering the image. This method has limitations: read-back performance of the result was poor for early hardware, kernel operations were limited, and data structure sizes were limited to texture sizes [18]. To overcome these limitations, both NVIDIA and AMD released new high-level programming interfaces named CUDA and Stream SDK in 2007, respectively. These programming interfaces improved the memory access interface and created an easier to use programming environment, which led to an increase in popularity of porting existing programs to the GPU.

CUDA allows researchers to easily parallelize their computing task to take advantage of the GPU. CUDA provides a software library to interface with the graphics processor, and a specialized compiler to create executable code to run on the GPU. CUDA presents programmers with two other types of memory access, shared memory and global memory, on top of the texture cache units. Being able to access all the memory on the GPU (albeit with varying access speeds) has made it much easier to perform research into GPGPU computing. The method presented in this paper was built using the CUDA architecture and run on NVIDIA hardware. Vineet and Narayanan have previously explained the CUDA framework in detail [8], and there are many technical resources available on the NVIDIA CUDA homepage [19].

3   Graph Cuts

The traditional method for push-relabel graph cutting is outlined in [1]. The algorithm consists of two main operations: *discharge* (also called *push*) and *relabel* (also called *raise*). In push-relabel algorithms, vertices have two states: overflowing and inactive. Vertices contain information concerning the amount of *excess* and *height*. Edges hold information about their *residual capacity*. Typically a queue of overflowing vertices is checked each iteration, with the first vertex in the list being dequeued and either *discharged* or *relabeled*. The loop terminates once there are no more viable *discharge* or *relabel* operations to perform.

Discharging a vertex causes some of the excess to be pushed to neighboring vertices when the incident edge has not completely saturated (has residual capacity). The push decreases the excess in the current vertex, increasing excess in the destination, and decreases the residual capacity of the edge. The destination vertex is then enqueued into the overflowing list, along with the current vertex if it is still overflowing.

A vertex must be *relabeled* when it is overflowing but has no valid neighbors. A neighbor is valid if the edge incident to both vertices has remaining capacity, and the destination vertexs height is lower than the current vertex. The current vertex's height is increased to one more than the lowest neighbor, which allows further *discharging*.

3.1   Novel GPU Graph Cut Technique

To develop a GPU implementation of a traditional algorithm, both data structure layout (the graph representation in memory) and concurrency bottlenecks must be carefully considered before being able to realize the full potential of the GPU. CUDA implementations of graph cuts for image segmentation have traditionally paired the 2D lattice structure of graphs with the 2D grid structure of the CUDA programming model. However this leads to restrictions on the types of graphs that can be processed by the routine. Furthermore, traditional graph cut algorithms contain branching and looping. In CUDA, divergent code produces poor performance because the SIMD model cannot perform the instructions in parallel, making new techniques for graph cuts necessary.

Graph Representation. Vineet and Narayanan presented a method of graph cuts in CUDA which has shown improved performance by pairing the 2D lattice graphs with the CUDA programming model. They conceded that this method would not be feasible for other types of graphs [8]. We structure our graphs similar to the technique presented by Harish et. al [20] that improved performance in distance calculations on arbitrary graphs using the GPU by representing graph $G(V, E)$ as a vertex array V_a and an edge array E_a. Edges in the edge list will be grouped so that all edges that originate at a vertex are contiguous, and the vertex will contain a pointer to the first edge in the group, as in Figure 1. Each edge structure holds information about its capacity, current flow, and destination vertex.

GPU Maximum Flow. Due to the design of the traditional push relabel algorithm (conditionals and the looping over a queue), the algorithm is not immediately useable on the GPU. The first step is to convert the algorithm loop to the CUDA grid. This is a fairly simple process of creating a CUDA kernel

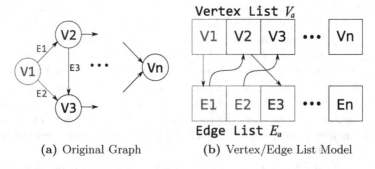

(a) Original Graph   (b) Vertex/Edge List Model

Fig. 1. Conversion of a direct graph into vertex and edge lists

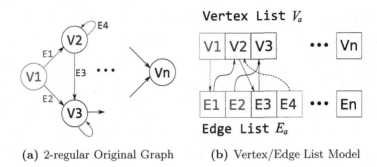

(a) 2-regular Original Graph   **(b)** Vertex/Edge List Model

Fig. 2. Addition of null edges to achieve a k-regular graph

that will perform either a *discharge* or *relabel* for a given vertex each invocation, and terminate once no discharging or relabeling is feasible. Another method is to create multiple CUDA kernels, typically consisting of a kernel that will push all possible flow from a vertex or mark it as needing relabeling, and another kernel that updates all the labels of vertices previously marked. In this method many different types of kernels must be coded and invoked many times.

3.2 Optimization Techniques

We improved upon the basic implementation of vertex and array lists. To make our list based graph representation more SIMD friendly, we first make the input graph *regular* by adding null edges to any vertex that has fewer edges than the vertex with the highest degree. Second, we simplify the code by only having one kernel, which performs both the discharging and relabeling steps.

Since the GPU is treated as an array of SIMD processors, it is important that the algorithm is able to perform the same operation across multiple data locations. However, we are assuming that any kind of graph configuration could be used as input, requiring that each vertex be treated uniquely, as the vertex set is not homogeneous. To overcome this problem, we propose adding extra edges to the graph so that each vertex has the same degree. In Figure 2, the dotted line of edge $E4$ is an example of a null edge. These null edges point back to the originating vertex and have a capacity of zero. This would cause the null edges to be ignored by the graph cut algorithm, as the destination of the edge would never have a height lower than the origin (a condition for discharging), and the capacity of the edge restricts the amount of flow discharged to zero.

Algorithm 1 details the steps of the computation that take place on the CPU. The *initialize* function starts by discharging the maximum possible amount of flow from the source to the neighboring vertices. Then the GPU kernel is invoked so that one thread is excuted for each non-source and non-sink vertex. The CPU continues to invoke the GPU kernel until no discharge or relabel operations can be performed. The GPU kernel is detailed in Algorithm 2. Since our graph is regular, the loop over the neighbors is fully unrolled. The null edges will be ignored because the height of u will never be less than the current vertex's

Algorithm 1. GPU_GraphCut(Graph $G(V, E)$)

```
finished ← false
Initialize(V, E)
while not finished do
    // GraphCutKernel() is performed in parallel on the GPU
    finished ← GraphCutKernel(V,E)
end
```

Algorithm 2. GPU_GraphCut_KERNEL($G(V, E)$)

```
tld ← GetThreadID()
amtPushed ← 0
foreach Neighbor u of V[tld] do
    if u.height < V[tld].height and (V[tld], u) ∈ E has capacity > 0 then
        amtPushed ← amtPushed + Discharge(V[tld], u)
    end
end
if amtPushed > 0 and V[tld].excess > 0 then
    V[tld].height = FindLowestNeighbor(V[tld]).height + 1
end
```

height (since they are equal). In addition the discharge can be modified to push a conditionally assigned amount of flow. Conditional assignment allows us to use the ternary operator, which prevents divergent code since it can be optimized to a zeroing of either operand of an addition.

4   Experimental Results

To test the performance of our proposed technique, we performed a comparison of a CPU implementation of image segmentation using graph cuts versus our proposed GPU implementation. The CPU implementation uses the open source library provided by Vladimir Kolmogorov [5], using OpenCV for data capture and graph construction. The test computer used was running Windows XP. The CPU implementation ran on an Intel Quad Core Xeon processor, and the GPU implement ran on an NVIDIA GTX 280 graphics card. All of these components are regularly available at any electronics retailer. A video sequence scaled to four different resolutions (QVGA, VGA, HD720, and HD1080) was used in testing the speed for video object silhouette extraction.

The speed for the cut only is presented in Figure 3. At higher resolutions the parallelism achieved by the GPU significantly increases the performance, as much as 2.5x. However, we begin to see real performance gains when the whole process, from frame acquisition to graph building and finally silhouette recovery, is considered. Since all of these steps can be done in parallel, we see major speed improvements of up to 10x times in full HD 1080 resolution (1920x1080), as shown in Figure 4. This emphasizes the overhead caused by the non-cut

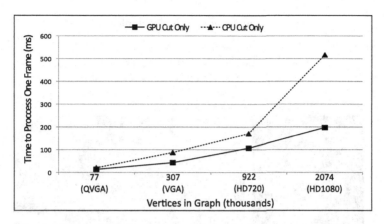

Fig. 3. Speed of graph cut (max-flow) calculation versus graph size

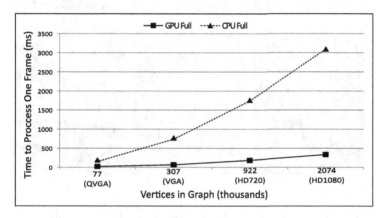

Fig. 4. Speed of frame silhouette retrieval versus graph size

operations, such as graph construction, in the cutting of image sequences. It is important to note that these tests do not use any kind of graph shrinking techniques, and that both implementations are cutting across the full HD TV image, which consists of over 2 millions vertices and 37 million edges.

In addition we chose a subset of images from the Berkeley Segmentation Dataset [21] to test the accuracy of the results between the two implementations. The dataset contains segmetations proposed by a set of human subjects, which we converted to silhouettes of the desired object so that they could be compared to our graph cut output. The test is designed to make sure that the silhouettes obtained are within a reasonable margin of error, and that the GPU algorithm is not returning erroneous results. Figure 5 gives three examples of the output from both the GPU and the CPU implementations. The border of the result silhouette is highlighted in cyan. Simple observation shows the cuts to be approximately visually equivalent.

Table 1. Accuracy of Graph Cut implementations

	Error	StdDev	Fp	Fn
GPU	4.3%	0.9%	2.3%	2.0%
CPU	3.4%	0.4%	1.9%	1.7%

Fig. 5. GPU (top) and CPU (bottom) output (border highlighted)

For a numerical comparison of the silhouettes, Table 1 shows the percentage of mislabeled pixels (the ratio of mislabeled pixels to total image pixels), the standard deviation (StdDev) of mislabeled pixels, as well as the mean rate of false positives and false negatives. The results demonstrate that both implementations give the same highly accurate segmentations.

5   Conclusions and Future Works

In this paper we have presented a new method for performing graph cuts on the GPU using CUDA. The method described is capable of handling arbitrary graph structures and is able to optimize them for the SIMD processing model employed on the GPU. We have shown that this technique enables large speedups in processing time, particularly for graphs with millions of vertices, achieving 10 frames-per-second processing High Definition video. Our future research directions include finding ways to use the results of this technique in higher end vision processing systems.

References

1. Goldberg, A.V., Tarjan, R.E.: A new approach to the maximum flow problem. Journal of the ACM 35, 921–940 (1988)
2. Greig, D.M., Porteous, B.T., Seheult, A.H.: Exact maximum a posteriori estimation for binary images. Journal of the Royal Statistical Society 51(2), 271–279 (1989)
3. Boykov, Y., Veksler, O., Zabih, R.: Markov random fields with efficient approximations. IEEE Conference on Computer Vision and Pattern Recognition, 648–655 (1998)
4. Boykov, Y., Veksler, O., Zabih, R.: Fast approximate energy minimization via graph cuts. IEEE Transactions on Pattern Analysis and Machine Intelligence 23 (2001)
5. Boykov, Y., Kolmogorov, V.: An experimental comparison of min-cut/max-flow algorithms for energy minimization in vision. IEEE Transactions on Pattern Analysis and Machine Intelligence 26, 359–374 (2004)
6. Juan, O., Boykov, Y.: Active graph cuts. IEEE Computer Society Conference on Computer Vision and Pattern Recognition 1, 1023–1029 (2006)
7. Hussein, M., Varshney, A., Davis, L.: On implementing graph cuts on cuda. First Workshop on General Purpose Processing on Graphics Processing Units (2007)
8. Vineet, V., Narayanan, P.: Cuda cuts: Fast graph cuts on the gpu. In: IEEE Conference on Computer Vision and Pattern Recognition: Workshop on Visual Computer Vision on GPUs, June 2008, pp. 1–8 (2008)
9. Boykov, Y., Funka-Lea, G.: Graph cuts and efficient n-d image segmentation. Int. J. Comput. Vision 70(2), 109–131 (2006)
10. Lombaert, H., Sun, Y., Grady, L., Xu, C.: A multilevel banded graph cuts method for fast image segmentation. In: Proceedings of the Tenth IEEE International Conference on Computer Vision (ICCV 2005), Washington, DC, USA, vol. 1. IEEE Computer Society, Los Alamitos (2005)
11. Garrett, Z., Saito, H.: Live video object tracking and segmentation using graph cuts. In: International Conference on Image Processing, pp. 1576–1579. IEEE, Los Alamitos (2008)
12. nVidia: NVIDIA CUDA Compute Unified Device Architecture - Programming Guide (2007)
13. Farrugia, J.P., Horain, P., Guehenneux, E., Alusse, Y.: Gpucv: A framework for image processing acceleration with graphics processors. In: 2006 IEEE International Conference on Multimedia and Expo., pp. 585–588 (2006)
14. Fung, J., Mann, S.: Openvidia: parallel gpu computer vision. In: Proceedings of the 13th annual ACM International Conference on Multimedia, pp. 849–852. ACM, New York (2005)
15. Hong, B.: A lock-free multi-threaded algorithm for the maximum flow problem. In: IEEE International Parallel and Distributed Processing Symposium, pp. 1–8. IEEE, Los Alamitos (2008)
16. Anderson, R., Setubal, J.C.: A parallel implementation of the push-relabel algorithm for the maximum flow problem. J. Parallel Distrib. Comput. 29(1), 17–26 (1995)

17. Yu, T., Xu, N., Ahuja, N.: Reconstructing a dynamic surface from video sequences using graph cuts in 4d space-time. In: 17th International Conference on Pattern Recognition, pp. 245–248. IEEE Computer Society, Los Alamitos (2004)
18. Harris, M.: Gpgpu: Beyond graphics. In: Game Developers Conference (2004)
19. nVidia: Cuda zone – the resource for cuda developers (2009), http://www.nvidia.com/object/cuda_home.html
20. Harish, P., Narayanan, P.J.: Accelerating large graph algorithms on the GPU using CUDA. In: Aluru, S., Parashar, M., Badrinath, R., Prasanna, V.K. (eds.) HiPC 2007. LNCS, vol. 4873, pp. 197–208. Springer, Heidelberg (2007)
21. Martin, D., Fowlkes, C., Tal, D., Malik, J.: A database of human segmented natural images and its application to evaluating segmentation algorithms and measuring ecological statistics. In: Proc. 8th Int'l Conf. Computer Vision, July 2001, vol. 2, pp. 416–423 (2001)

On a New Measure of Classifier Competence Applied to the Design of Multiclassifier Systems

Tomasz Woloszynski and Marek Kurzynski

Wroclaw University of Technology, Chair of Systems and Computer Networks,
Wyb. Wyspianskiego 27, 50-370 Wroclaw, Poland
marek.kurzynski@pwr.wroc.pl

Abstract. This paper presents a new method for calculating competence of a classifier in the feature space. The idea is based on relating
the response of the classifier with the response obtained by a random
guessing. The measure of competence reflects this relation and rates the
classifier with respect to the random guessing in a continuous manner.
Two multiclassifier systems representing fusion and selection strategies
were developed using proposed measure of competence. The performance
of multiclassifiers was evaluated using five benchmark databases from the
UCI Machine Learning Repository and Ludmila Kuncheva Collection.
Classification results obtained for three simple fusion methods and one
multiclassifier system with selection strategy were used for a comparison.
The experimental results showed that, regardless of the strategy used by
the multiclassifier system, the classification accuracy has increased when
the measure of competence was employed. The improvement was most
significant for simple fusion methods (*sum, product* and *majority vote*).
For all databases, two developed multiclassifier systems produced the
best classification scores.

1 Introduction

Onc of the most important tasks in optimizing a multiclassifier system is to select
a group of competent (adequate) classifiers from a pool of classifiers. There are
two main approaches to this problem: static selection scheme in which ensamble
of classifiers is selected for all test patterns, and dynamic selection method which
explores the use of different classifiers for different test patterns [6]. The most
dynamic classifier selection schemes use the concept of classifier "competence"
on a defined neighbourhood or region [7], such as the local accuracy a priori [11]
or a posteriori methods [2] or overall local accuracy and local class accuracy [10].

In this paper we present a new method of dynamic optimization scheme of
multiclassifier system based on a class-independent measure of classifier competence in the feature space. The value of the proposed measure of competence
is calculated with respect to the response obtained by random guessing. In this
way it is possible to evaluate a group of classifiers against a common reference
point. Competent (incompetent) classifiers gain with such approach meaningful
interpretation, i.e. they are more (less) accurate than the random classifier.

P. Foggia, C. Sansone, and M. Vento (Eds.): ICIAP 2009, LNCS 5716, pp. 995–1004, 2009.
© Springer-Verlag Berlin Heidelberg 2009

This paper is divided into five sections and organized as follows. In Section 2 the measure of classifier competence is presented and three different propositions of its functional form are given. In Section 3 two multiclassifier systems based on selection strategy and fusion strategy are developed. Computer experiments are described in Section 4 and Section 5 concludes the paper.

2   The Measure of Classifier Competence

Consider an n-dimensional feature space $\mathcal{X} \subseteq \mathcal{R}^n$ and a finite set of class labels $\mathcal{M} = \{1, 2, \ldots, M\}$. Let

$$\psi : \mathcal{X} \to \mathcal{M} \tag{1}$$

be a classifier which produces a set of discriminant functions $(d_1(x), d_2(x), \ldots, d_M(x))$ for a given object described by a feature vector x. The value of the discriminant function $d_i(x)$, $i = 1, 2, \ldots, M$ represents a support given by the classifier ψ for the i-th class. Without loss of generality we assume that $d_i(x) > 0$ and $\sum d_i(x) = 1$. Classification is made according to the maximum rule, i.e.

$$\psi(x) = i \Leftrightarrow d_i(x) = \max_{k \in \mathcal{M}} d_k(x). \tag{2}$$

We assume that, apart from a training and testing datasets, a validation dataset is also available. The validation dataset is given as

$$V_N = \{(x_1, i_1), (x_2, i_2), \ldots, (x_N, i_N)\}, \tag{3}$$

where $x_k \in \mathcal{X}$, $k = 1, 2, \ldots, N$ denotes the feature vector representing the k-th object in the dataset and $i_k \in \mathcal{M}$ denotes the object's class label.

The set (3) can be applied to the evaluation of classifier competence, i.e. its capability to correct activity (correct classification) in the whole feature space. For this purpose the *potential function* model will be used [7], [9]. In this approach feature space is considered as a "competence field" which is determined by the sources of competence located at the points x_k, $k = 1, 2, \ldots, N$.

We define the source competence $K_\psi(x_k)$ of the classifier ψ at a point $x_k \in \mathcal{X}$ from the set (3) as a function of class number M and the support of correct class $d_{i_k}(x_k)$ having the following properties:

1. $K_\psi(x_k)$ is strictly increasing function of $d_{i_k}(x_k)$ (for any M),
2. $K_\psi(x_k) = -1$ for $d_{i_k}(x_k) = 0$,
3. $K_\psi(x_k) = 0$ for $d_{i_k}(x_k) = 1/M$,
4. $K_\psi(x_k) = 1$ for $d_{i_k}(x_k) = 1$.

The idea of function K_ψ is based on relating the response of the classifier ψ with the response obtained by a random guessing. The source competence reflects this relation and rates the classifier with respect to the random guessing in a continuous manner. If the support for the correct class is lower than the probability of random guessing, then the source competence is negative and ψ is evaluated as an incompetent classifier. If in turn this support is greater than the probability

Table 1. The overview of the cases of the source competence

Support for the correct class	The source competence	Evaluation of the classifier ψ
$d_{i_k}(x_k) = 1$	$K_\psi(x_k) = 1$	The classifier is absolutely competent
$1 > d_{i_k}(x_k) > \frac{1}{M}$	$1 > K_\psi(x_k) > 0$	The classifier is competent
$d_{i_k}(x_k) = \frac{1}{M}$	$K_\psi(x_k) = 0$	The classifier is neutral (equivalent to the random guessing)
$\frac{1}{M} > d_{i_k}(x_k) > 0$	$0 > K_\psi(x_k) > -1$	The classifier is incompetent
$d_{i_k}(x_k) = 0$	$K_\psi(x_k) = -1$	The classifier is absolutely incompetent

of random guessing then K_ψ is positive and ψ is regarded as a competent classifier. The overview of different cases of values $d_{i_k}(x_k)$ and $K_\psi(x_k)$ and related interpretation of classifier competence at the point x_k is presented in Table 1.

The following functions will be considered as the source competence:

1. Logarithmic function:

$$K_\psi^{(1)}(x_k) = \begin{cases} 2 d_{i_k}(x_k) - 1 & \text{for } M = 2, \\ \frac{log[M(M-2) d_{i_k}(x_k)+1]}{log(M-1)} - 1 & \text{for } M > 2. \end{cases} \quad (4)$$

2. Exponential function:

$$K_\psi^{(2)}(x_k) = 1 - 2^{1 - \frac{(M-1)d_{i_k}(x_k)}{1 - d_{i_k}(x_k)}} \quad (5)$$

3. Piecewise linear function:

$$K_\psi^{(3)}(x_k) = \begin{cases} \frac{M}{M-1} d_{i_k}(x_k) - \frac{1}{M-1} & \text{for } \frac{1}{M} \le d_{i_k}(x_k) \le 1 \\ M d_{i_k}(x_k) - 1 & \text{for } 0 \le d_{i_k}(x_k) \le \frac{1}{M}. \end{cases} \quad (6)$$

The source competence also depends on the number of classes in the classification problem. This dependence is shown in Fig.1 for functions (4), (5) and (6).

The competence of the classifier ψ at any given point x is defined as the weighted sum of source competences $K_\psi(x_k)$, $k = 1, 2, \ldots, N$ with weights exponentially dependent on the distance $\|x - x_i\|$ between points x_k and x, namely:

$$C_\psi(x) = \sum_{k=1}^{N} K_\psi(x_k) \ exp[-\|x - x_i\|]. \quad (7)$$

Classifier ψ is competent in the given $x \in \mathcal{X}$ if $C_\psi(x) > 0$, otherwise ψ is regarded as an incompetent classifier.

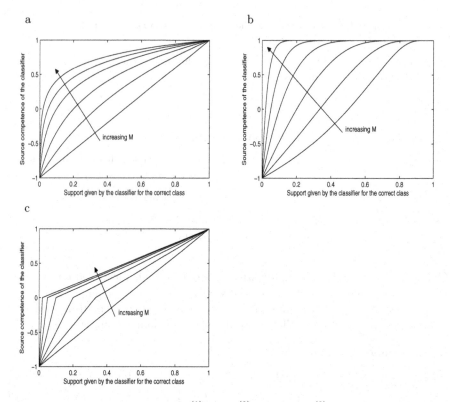

Fig. 1. The source competence $K^{(1)}$(a), $K^{(2)}$ (b) and $K^{(3)}$ (c) plotted against the support for the correct class for different number of classes ($M = 2, 3, 5, 10, 20, 50$)

Although any given metric can be used in the definition of the distance $\|x - x_i\|$ we propose a modified Euclidean distance in the following form:

$$\|x - x_k\| = \frac{0.5}{h_{opt}^2}(x - x_k)^T(x - x_k), \tag{8}$$

where the parameter h_{opt} is the optimal smoothing parameter obtained for the validation dataset V_N by the Parzen kernel estimation. The kernel estimation was used to normalize ranges of features and to ensure that each source competence will affect only its neighbourhood. Note that in this step no Parzen classifier is needed, i.e. only the value of the optimal smoothing parameter is calculated.

3   Application to Multiclassifier Systems

The measure of competence can be incorporated in virtually any multiclassifier system providing that $\mathcal{X}$ is an metric space. In this chapter we describe two multiclassifier systems based on proposed measure of competence, each one employing different strategy.

Let us assume that we are given a set (pool) of trained base classifiers $\mathcal{L} = \{\psi_1, \psi_2, \ldots, \psi_L\}$ and the validation dataset V_N. We define the multiclassifier $F_1(x)$ to be the classifier with the highest positive competence value at the point x:

$$F_1(x) = \psi_l(x) \Leftrightarrow C_{\psi_l}(x) > 0 \wedge C_{\psi_l}(x) = \max_{k=1,2,\ldots,L} C_{\psi_k}(x). \qquad (9)$$

The multiclassifier F_1 uses a selection strategy, i.e. for each object described by a feature vector x it selects a single classifier to be used for classification. In the case where all classifiers have negative values of competence classification is made according to the random classifier. The random classifier draws a class label using a discrete uniform distribution with probability value $\frac{1}{M}$ for each class.

The multiclassifier F_2 represents a fusion approach where the final classification is based on responses given by all competent classifiers:

$$F_2(x) = \sum_{l \in L_{pos}} C_{\psi_l}(x) \psi_l(x), \qquad (10)$$

where the set L_{pos} contains indices of classifiers with positive values of competence. Again, the random classifier is used in the case where all classifiers have negative values of competence. The classification is made according to the maximum rule given in (2).

4   Experiments

4.1   Benchmark Data and Experimental Setup

Benchmark databases used in the experiments were obtained from the UCI Machine Learning Repository [1] (*Glass, Image segmentation, Wine*) and Ludmila Kuncheva Collection [8] (*Laryngeal3* and *Thyroid*). Selected databases represent classification problems with objects described by continuous feature vectors. For each database, feature vectors were normalized for zero mean and unit standard deviation (SD). Three datasets were generated from each database, i.e. training, validation and testing dataset. The training dataset was used to train the base classifiers. The values of the competence for each base classifier were calculated using the validation dataset. The testing dataset was used to evaluate the accuracy of tested classification methods. A brief description of each database is given in Table 2.

For each database, 30 trials with the same settings were conducted. The accuracy of each classifier and multiclassifier used was calculated as the mean (SD) value of these 30 trials. In this way it was possible to evaluate both the accuracy and the stability of examined multiclassifier systems.

Table 2. A brief description of each database; *%training, %validation* and *%testing* indicate the percentage of objects used for generation of the training, validation and testing dataset, respectively

Database	#classes	#objects	#features	%training	%validation	%testing
Glass	6	214	9	30	40	100
Image segm.	7	2310	19	20	30	100
Wine	3	178	13	20	40	100
Laryngeal3	3	353	16	20	40	100
Thyroid	3	215	5	20	40	100

4.2 Classifiers

The following set of base classifiers was used in the experiments [3]:

1. LDC - linear discriminant classifier based on normal distributions with the same covariance matrix for each class;
2. QDC - quadratic discriminant classifier based on normal distributions with different covariance matrix for each class;
3. NMC - nearest mean classifier;
4. 1-NN - nearest neighbour classifier;
5. 5-NN - k-nearest neighbours classifier with $k = 5$;
6. 15-NN - k-nearest neighbours classifier with $k = 15$;
7. PARZEN1 - Parzen classifier with the Gaussian kernel and optimal smoothing parameter h_{opt};
8. PARZEN2 - Parzen classifier with the Gaussian kernel and smoothing parameter $h_{opt}/2$;
9. TREE - Tree classifier with Gini splitting criterion and pruning level set to 3;
10. BPNN1 - Feed-forward backpropagation neural network classifier with two hidden layers (2 neurons in each layer) and the maximum number of epochs set to 50;
11. BPNN2 - Feed-forward backpropagation neural network classifier with one hidden layer (5 neurons) and the maximum number of epochs set to 50.

Proposed multiclassifier systems were compared against a classifier selection method with class-independent competence estimation of each classifier (CS-DEC) [9]. This method was chosen because it is similar to the method presented in this paper, i.e. CS-DEC evaluates the competence of a classifier in a continuous manner with distance defined as a potential function. Although other approach is commonly used [2,10] (i.e. evaluation of competence using k-NN neighbourhood instead of potential functions), currently it is not known if these two methods produce significantly different results [7].

For a better evaluation of differences between proposed multiclassifiers and the method used for a comparison, 95% confidence intervals (CI) of accuracy were calculated. The intervals obtained for developed multiclassifiers were compared against the interval calculated for the CS-DEC. The accuracies of a given multi-classifier and CS-DEC were considered statistically significant if their respective 95% CI intervals were not overlapping.

The performances of four groups of simple fusion methods were also evaluated. The group A contained the *sum, product* and *majority vote* fusion methods used with all base classifiers. The groups B, C and D contained the same three fusion methods with the exception that only the base classifiers with positive value of competence $C_\psi(x)$ were used. This competence was calculated according to the source competence $K^{(1)}$ (group B), $K^{(2)}$ (group C) and $K^{(3)}$ (group D). If no competent base classifier for a given object x was available, the classification was made using the random classifier.

4.3   Results and Discussion

The results obtained for the base classifiers are shown in Table 3. It can be seen from the table that the set of base classifiers provided diversity needed in the multiclassifier systems, i.e. there was no single superior classifier and the range of classification scores was large (high values of the SD). The best overall accuracy averaged over all databases was achieved by the nearest neighbour classifier 1-NN (85.9%), followed shortly by two Parzen classifiers: PARZEN2 (85.8%) and PARZEN1 (85.2%). The lowest averaged classification scores were obtained for the quadratic discriminant classifier QDC (50.9%) and the neural network classifier BPNN1 (61.8%). The relatively low accuracy of the neural network classifier can be explained by the fact, that the learning process was stopped after just 50 epochs.

The results obtained for the multiclassifier systems are presented in Table 4. It can be noticed from the table that the group of fusion methods which used all base classifiers (group A) achieved the lowest classification accuracies. This indicates that weak classifiers from the pool can noticeably affect the *sum, product* and *majority vote* fusion methods. However, the same fusion methods combined

Table 3. The results obtained for the base classifiers. The best score for each database is highlighted.

| Classifier | Glass | Database / Mean (SD) accuracy [%] | | | |
		Image seg.	Laryngeal3	Thyroid	Wine
LDC	61.4(3.5)	90.8(0.7)	70.7(2.0)	91.7(2.3)	**95.9(1.4)**
QDC	27.1(10.8)	80.6(6.1)	31.5(15.6)	63.2(34.4)	52.1(20.1)
NMC	46.1(5.8)	84.2(1.1)	67.0(4.1)	92.7(2.7)	95.4(1.3)
1-NN	**76.0(2.1)**	**93.6(0.5)**	72.0(2.5)	93.6(1.9)	94.5(1.8)
5-NN	64.7(2.4)	90.3(1.0)	71.9(1.8)	88.0(4.4)	94.4(2.3)
15-NN	51.6(5.6)	85.8(1.0)	70.3(3.2)	73.3(3.6)	87.8(9.2)
PARZEN1	70.7(3.5)	93.2(0.7)	**75.1(1.9)**	92.1(2.9)	95.1(1.8)
PARZEN2	75.1(2.2)	93.1(0.5)	72.6(2.5)	**93.7(2.0)**	94.5(1.8)
TREE	60.2(5.1)	81.8(3.6)	67.5(3.7)	85.6(5.8)	81.1(5.7)
BPNN1	45.6(7.3)	40.8(5.3)	65.4(4.3)	85.5(7.3)	71.4(22.2)
BPNN2	48.7(8.0)	40.9(5.2)	66.6(4.4)	89.2(6.6)	83.2(13.4)

Table 4. The results obtained for the mutliclassifier systems (description in the text). The best score for each database is highlighted. Asterisks denote statistically significant differences with respect to the CS-DEC method.

Multiclassifier	Glass	Image seg.	Laryngeal3	Thyroid	Wine
		Database / Mean (SD) accuracy [%]			
Sum^A	41.9(15.3)	93.3(1.8)	73.5(9.2)	91.8(5.1)	96.3(1.4)
Product^A	28.9(8.8)	91.7(2.2)	43.0(15.7)	90.5(7.2)	83.3(9.4)
Majority vote^A	68.7(3.5)	93.5(0.9)	74.9(1.3)	92.5(2.8)	95.9(1.4)
Sum^B	74.3(2.6)	95.6(0.8)	81.6(1.4)	95.1(1.8)	97.8(1.1)
Product^B	74.3(2.4)	95.7(0.7)	80.8(1.5)	95.3(1.5)	96.5(2.4)
Majority vote^B	72.1(3.1)	94.1(0.9)	79.3(1.6)	94.2(2.0)	96.9(1.5)
Sum^C	74.3(2.5)	95.5(0.7)	81.3(1.4)	95.0(1.9)	97.8(1.1)
Product^C	74.2(2.4)	95.5(0.6)	80.7(1.4)	95.2(1.7)	96.6(2.5)
Majority vote^C	72.1(3.1)	94.1(0.9)	79.2(1.5)	94.2(2.2)	96.9(1.5)
Sum^D	74.3(2.6)	95.7(0.8)	81.6(1.6)	95.2(1.7)	97.8(1.1)
Product^D	74.3(2.5)	95.7(0.7)	80.7(1.6)	95.3(1.6)	96.5(2.4)
Majority vote^D	72.4(2.9)	94.1(1.0)	79.5(1.6)	94.4(2.0)	96.9(1.5)
CS-DEC	78.0(2.0)	94.6(0.4)	80.7(1.7)	95.5(1.8)	97.0(1.3)
$F_1^{(1)}$	**78.1(2.1)**	95.7(0.5)*	81.2(1.6)*	95.9(1.6)*	97.2(1.1)
$F_1^{(2)}$	76.7(2.6)*	95.7(0.5)*	81.0(1.5)	**96.0(1.5)** *	97.4(1.2)*
$F_1^{(3)}$	**78.1(1.9)**	95.7(0.5)*	81.2(1.7)*	**96.0(1.5)** *	97.1(1.1)
$F_2^{(1)}$	76.4(2.5)*	**95.9(0.6)** *	**82.0(1.6)** *	95.7(1.8)	97.8(1.0)*
$F_2^{(2)}$	76.0(2.3)*	**95.9(0.7)** *	81.8(1.5)*	95.6(1.8)	**97.9(1.0)** *
$F_2^{(3)}$	76.7(2.3)*	**95.9(0.6)** *	**82.0(1.7)** *	95.9(1.6)*	97.8(1.0)*

with the measure of competence (group B, C and D) produced the classification scores which were, on average, 10% higher (e.g. in the case of *product* multiclassifier and Glass database the improvement was over 45%). This can be explained by the fact, that for each input object x only classifiers that are assumingly more accurate than the random guessing were used in the classification process. It can be shown that a set of weak base classifiers, where each classifier performs just slightly better than the random classifier, can be turned into a powerful classification method. Such approach has been successfully used in boosting algorithms [4].

The multiclassifier CS-DEC used for comparison produced better classification scores averaged over all databases (89.1%) than the fusion methods from groups $A - D$. However, it was outperformed by two developed multiclassifier systems F_1 (89.6%) and F_2 (89.7%). The multiclassifiers F_1 and F_2 produced the best stability (the SD value of 1.4% averaged over all databases), followed by the CS-DEC and the group B and $Csum$ multiclassifiers (all 1.5%). Results obtained indicate that proposed measure of competence produced accurate and reliable evaluations of the base classifiers over all feature space. This in turn enabled multiclassifier systems to perform equally well for all input objects x. This can be explained by the fact, that the set of base classifiers was diversified, i.e. for each database and each object x to be classified, at least one competent classifier was always available (the random classifier in F_1 and F_2 methods was never used).

Statistically significant differences were obtained in 23 out of 30 cases (5 databases times 6 developed multiclassifiers). Four times these differences favored CS-DEC method (Glass database only). This shows that proposed multiclassifiers indeed display improvement in the class-independent competence measure over currently used approach.

It is interesting to note that results for all three forms of the source competence are almost identical, what suggests that character of dependence K_ψ on support d_{i_k} is rather negligible.

5   Conclusions

A new method for calculating the competence of a classifier in the feature space was presented. Two multiclassifier systems incorporating the competence were evaluated using five databases from the UCI Machine Learning Repository and Ludmila Kuncheva Collection. The results obtained indicate that the proposed measure of competence can eliminate weak (worse than random guessing) classifiers from the classification process. At the same time strong (competent) classifiers were selected in such a way that the final classification accuracy was always better than the single best classifier from the pool.

Simple fusion methods (*sum, product* and *majority vote*) displayed the greatest improvement when combined with the measure of competence. Two developed multiclassifier systems based on selection strategy (F_1) and fusion strategy (F_2) achieved both the best classification scores and stability, and outperformed other classification methods used for comparison. Experimental results showed that the idea of calculating the competence of a classifier by relating its response to the response obtained by the random guessing is correct, i.e. a group of competent classifiers provided better classification accuracy than any of the base classifiers regardless of the strategy which was employed in the multiclassifier system.

References

1. Asuncion, A., Newman, D.: UCI Machine Learning Repository. University of California, Department of Information and Computer Science, Irvine, CA (2007), http://www.ics.uci.edu/~mlearn/MLRepository.html
2. Didaci, L., Giacinto, G., Roli, F., Arcialis, G.: A study on the performance of dynamic classifier selection based on local accuracy estimation. Pattern Recognition 38, 2188–2191 (2005)
3. Duda, R., Hart, P., Stork, D.: Pattern Classification. Wiley-Interscience, Hoboken (2001)
4. Freund, Y., Schapire, R.: Experiments with a new boosting algorithm. In: Machine Learning: Proceedings of the Thirteenth International Conference, pp. 148–156 (1996)
5. Giacinto, G., Roli, F.: Design of effective neural network ensembles for image classification processes. Image Vision and Computing Journal 19, 699–707 (2001)

6. Ko, A., Sabourin, R., Britto, A.: From dynamic classifier selection to dynamic ensamble selection. Pattern Recognition 41, 1718–1733 (2008)
7. Kuncheva, L.: Combining Pattern Classifiers: Methods and Algorithms. Wiley-Interscience, New Jersey (2004)
8. Kuncheva, L.: Collection,
   `http://www.informatics.bangor.ac.uk/ kuncheva/activities/`
   `real_data_full_set.htm`
9. Rastrigin, L.A., Erenstein, R.H.: Method of Collective Recognition. Energoizdat, Moscow (1981)
10. Woods, K., Kegelmeyer, W.P., Bowyer, K.: Combination of multiple classifiers using local accuracy estimates. IEEE Transactions on Pattern Analysis and Machine Intelligence 19, 405–410 (1997)
11. Woloszynski, T., Kurzynski, M.: On a new measure of classifier competence in the feature space. Computer Recognition Systems 3 (2009) (in print)

Multi-class Binary Symbol Classification with Circular Blurred Shape Models

Sergio Escalera[1,2], Alicia Fornés[1,3], Oriol Pujol[1,2], and Petia Radeva[1,2]

[1] Computer Vision Center, Campus UAB, edifici O, 08193, Bellaterra, Spain
[2] Dept. Matemàtica Aplicada i Anàlisi, UB, Gran Via 585, 08007, Barcelona, Spain
[3] Dept. Computer Science, Campus UAB, Edifici Q, 08193, Bellaterra, Spain

Abstract. Multi-class binary symbol classification requires the use of rich descriptors and robust classifiers. *Shape* representation is a difficult task because of several symbol distortions, such as occlusions, elastic deformations, gaps or noise. In this paper, we present the Circular Blurred Shape Model descriptor. This descriptor encodes the arrangement information of object parts in a correlogram structure. A prior blurring degree defines the level of distortion allowed to the symbol. Moreover, we learn the new feature space using a set of Adaboost classifiers, which are combined in the Error-Correcting Output Codes framework to deal with the multi-class categorization problem. The presented work has been validated over different multi-class data sets, and compared to the state-of-the-art descriptors, showing significant performance improvements.

1   Introduction

Shape Recognition is one of the most active areas in Pattern Recognition, which consists in recognizing objects from a large set of classes (we use symbol and object indistinctly). Shape is one of the most important visual cues for describing objects, and with texture and color, it is widely used for describing the content of the objects. In the last years, there is an increasing interest in the developing of good shape recognition methods. Shape representation is a difficult task because of several object distortions, such as occlusions, elastic deformations, gaps or noise. In general, the desirable properties of a shape-based approach can be divided in two main groups: the definition of expressive and compact shape descriptors, and the formulation of robust classification methods.

A good shape descriptor should guarantee inter-class compactness and intra-class separability, even when describing noisy and distorted shapes. The main techniques for shape recognition are reviewed in [2]. They are mainly classified in continuous and structural approaches. Zernike moments and R-signature are examples of continuous approaches, which extract information from the whole shape region. Zernike moments [3] maintain properties of the shape, and are invariant to rotation, scale, and deformations. Contrary, other continuous approaches only use the external contour (silhouette) for computing the features, such as Curvature Scale Space (CSS) and Shape context. CSS [5] is a standard of the MPEG [4] that is tolerant to rotation, but it can only be used for close

P. Foggia, C. Sansone, and M. Vento (Eds.): ICIAP 2009, LNCS 5716, pp. 1005–1014, 2009.
© Springer-Verlag Berlin Heidelberg 2009

curves. Shape Context can work with non-closed curves, and has good performance in hand drawn symbols, because it is tolerant to deformations, but it requires point-to-point alignment of the symbols [6].

Concerning structural approaches, straight lines and arcs are usually the basic primitives. Strings, graphs or trees represent the relations between these primitives. The similarity measure is performed by string, tree or graph matching. Attributed graph grammars, Deformable models and Region Adjacency Graphs are a few examples of structural approaches. Attributed graph grammars [7] can cope with partially occluded symbols, while Region Adjacency Graphs [8] reach good performance in front of distortions in hand drawn documents.

Due to the large different kinds of problems in shape recognition applications, a shape descriptor usually reaches good performance in some aspects, but fails in others. In fact, some object descriptors, robust to some affine transformations and occlusions in some type of objects, are not enough effective in front of elastic deformations. For this reason, the research of a descriptor that can cope with elastic deformations and non-uniform distortions is still required. In the work of [11], the blurred shape model was presented. It is a descriptor that can deal with elastic deformations, variations in object styles and blurring, but it is sensible to rotations. In this paper, we present an evolution of the blurred shape model descriptor, which not only copes with distortions and noise, but also is rotationally invariant. The Circular Blurred Shape Model (CBSM) codifies the spatial arrangement of object characteristics using a correlogram structure. Based on a prior blurring degree, object characteristics are shared among correlogram regions. By rotating the correlogram so that the major descriptor densities are aligned to the x-axis, the descriptor becomes rotationally invariant.

Referring the categorization of object classes, many classification techniques have been developed. One of the most well-known techniques is the Adaboost algorithm, which has been shown to be good for feature selection, and it has shown to achieve high performance when applied to binary categorization tasks [9]. Afterwards, the extension to the multi-class case is usually solved by combining the binary classifiers in a voting scheme, such as one-versus-one or one-versus-all grouping schemes. Dietterich et. al. [10] proposed the Error Correcting Output Codes framework (ECOC) to benefit from error correction properties, obtaining successful results [15]. In this paper, we learn the CBSM features using Adaboost, and then, combine the binary problems in an ECOC configuration, which extends the system to deal with multi-class categorization problems. The comparison with the state-of-the-art descriptors and the high performance classifying multi-class problems with several categories show the robustness and better performance of the present methodology.

The paper is organized as follows: Section 2 describes the rotationally invariant Circular Blurred Shape Model descriptor. Section 3 describes the system of Error-Correcting Output Codes that uses the CBSM system to solve multi-class categorization problems. Section 4 presents the experimental evaluation of the methodology, and finally, Section 5 concludes the paper.

2   Circular Blurred Shape Model

In order to describe an object that can suffer from irregular deformations, the authors of [11] proposed a description strategy in which spatial arrangement of object parts is captured in a rectangular grid. Contiguous regions share information about the containing object points, and thus, the descriptor is tolerant to irregular deformations. The descriptor has shown to be suitable for the multi-class categorization of aligned symbols, outperforming state-of-the-art strategies [11].

In this section, we present a circular formulation of the Blurred Shape Model descriptor (CBSM). By defining a correlogram structure from the center of the object region, spatial arrangement of object parts is shared among regions defined by circles and sections. The method also allows a rotationally invariant description, rotating the correlogram by the predominant region densities. We divide the description of the algorithm into three main steps: the definition of the correlogram parameters, the descriptor computation, and the rotationally invariant procedure. We also include a fourth step to extend the CBSM methodology to solve symbol spotting problems.

Correlogram definition: Given a number of circles C, number of sections S, and an image region I, a centered correlogram $B = \{b_{\{1,1\}}, .., b_{\{C,S\}}\}$ is defined as a radial distribution of sub-regions of the image, as shown in Figure 1(a) and (b). Each region b has centroid coordinates defined by b^*. Then, the regions around b are defined as the neighbors of b. Note that depending of the spatial location of the analyzed region, different number of neighbors can be defined (Fig. 1(c)).

Descriptor computation: In order to compute the descriptor, first, a preprocess of the input region I to obtain the shape features is required. Working with document images, relevant *shape* information can be obtained by means of a contour map. However, based on the object properties, we can define another initial properties. In this paper, we use a Canny edge detector procedure.

Given the object contour map, each point from the image belonging to a contour is taken into account in the description process (Fig. 1(d)). First of all, the distances from the contour point $\mathbf{x}$ to the centroids of its corresponding region and neighbor regions are computed. The inverse of these distances are computed and normalized by the sum of total distances. These values are then added to the corresponding positions of the descriptor vector ν, including higher values to that positions corresponding to the nearest regions to $\mathbf{x}$ (Figure 1(e) bottom). This makes the description tolerant to irregular deformations.

At this point we have a description ν for an input image I, where the length of ν, defined by parameters C and S, defines the degree of spatial information taken into account in the description process. In Figure 2, a bat instance from the public MPEG7 data set [1] is described with different $C \times S$ correlogram sizes. In the way that we increase the number of regions, the description becomes more local. Thus, an optimal parameters of C and S should be obtained for each particular problem (i.e. via cross-validation).

Algorithm 1. Circular Blurred Shape Model Description Algorithm

Require: a binary image I, the number of circles C, and the number of sections S
Ensure: descriptor vector ν

Define $d = R/C$ and $g = 360/S$, where R is the radius of the correlogram, as the distance between consecutive circles and the degrees between consecutive sectors, respectively (Figure 1(a)).

Define $B = \{b_{\{1,1\}}, .., b_{\{C,S\}}\}$ as the set of bins for the circular description of I, where $b_{c,s}$ is the bin of B between distance $[(c - 1)d, cd)$ with respect to the origin of coordinates o, and between angles $[(s - 1)g, sg)$ to the origin of coordinates o and x-axis (Figure 1(b)).

Define $b^*_{\{c,s\}} = (d\sin\alpha, d\cos\alpha)$, the centroid coordinates of bin $b_{\{c,s\}}$, where α is the angle between the centroid and the x-axis, and $B^* = \{b^*_{\{1,1\}}, .., b^*_{\{C,S\}}\}$ the set of centroids in B (Figure 1(e)).

Define $X_{b_{\{c,s\}}} = \{b_1, .., b_{cs}\}$ as the sorted set of the elements in B^* so that $d(b^*_{\{c,s\}}, b^*_i) \le d(b^*_{\{c,s\}}, b^*_j)$, $i < j$.

Define $N(b_{\{c,s\}})$ as the neighbor regions of $b_{\{c,s\}}$, defined by the initial elements of $X_{b_{\{c,s\}}}$:

$$N(b_{\{c,s\}}) = \begin{cases} X', |X'| = S + 3 & \text{if } b_{\{c,s\}} \in IN \\ X', |X'| = 9 & \text{if } b_{\{c,s\}} \in MI \\ X', |X'| = 6 & \text{if } b_{\{c,s\}} \in EX \end{cases}$$

being X' the first elements of X, and IN, MI, and EX, the inner, middle, and extern regions of B, respectively (Figure 1(c)). Note that different number of neighbor regions appears depending of the location of the region in the correlogram. We consider the own region as the first neighbor.

Initialize $\nu_i = 0$, $i \in [1, .., CS]$, where the order of indexes in ν are:
$\nu = \{b_{\{1,1\}}, .., b_{\{1,S\}}, b_{\{2,1\}}, ..b_{\{2,S\}}, .., b_{\{C,1\}}, ..b_{\{C,S\}}\}$
for each point $\mathbf{x} \in I$, $I(\mathbf{x}) = 1$ (Figure 1(d)) **do**
  for each $b_{\{i,j\}} \in N(b_{\mathbf{x}})$ **do**
    $d_{\{i,j\}} = d(\mathbf{x}, b_{\{i,j\}}) = ||\mathbf{x} - b^*_{\{i,j\}}||^2$
  end for
  Update the probabilities vector ν positions as follows (Figure 1(f)):
  $\nu(b_{\{i,j\}}) = \nu(b_{\{i,j\}}) + \frac{1/d_{\{i,j\}}}{D_{\{i,j\}}}$, $D_{\{i,j\}} = \sum_{b_{\{m,n\}} \in N(b_{\{i,j\}})} \frac{1}{||\mathbf{x} - b^*_{\{m,n\}}||^2}$
end for
Normalize the vector ν as follows:
$d' = \sum_{i=1}^{CS} \nu_i$, $\nu_i = \frac{\nu_i}{d'}, \forall i \in [1, .., CS]$

Rotationally invariant descriptor: In order to make the description rotationally invariant, we look for the main diagonal G_i of correlogram B with the highest density. This diagonal is then the reference to rotate the descriptor. The orientation of the rotationally process, so that G_i is aligned with the x-axis, is that corresponding to the highest description density at both sides of G_i. This procedure is detailed in Algorithm 2. A visual result of the rotationally invariant process can be observed in Figure 2.

3   Multi-class Categorization

Error Correcting Output Codes are a meta-learning strategy that divides the multi-class problem is a set of binary problems, solves them individually and aggregates their responses into a final decision. ECOC classifiers combination have been shown to have interesting properties in statistical learning, reducing both the bias and variance of the base classifiers [12].

The ECOC meta-learning algorithm [13] consists in two steps: in the learning step, an ECOC encoding matrix is constructed in order to define the combination of the M binary classifiers. In the decoding step, the new sample $\mathbf{x}$ is classified

Algorithm 2. Rotationally invariant ν description
Require: ν, S, C
Ensure: Rotationally invariant descriptor vector ν^{ROT}

Define $\quad G \quad = \quad \{G_1, .., G_{S/2}\} \quad$ the $\quad S/2 \quad$ diagonals of $\quad B, \quad$ where
$G_i = \{\nu(b_{\{1,i\}}), .., \nu(b_{\{C,i\}}), .., \nu(b_{\{1,i+S/2\}}), .., \nu(b_{\{C,i+S/2\}})\}$

Select G_i so that $\sum_{j=1}^{2C} G_i(j) \geq \sum_{j=1}^{2C} G_k(j)$, $\forall k \in [1, .., S/2]$

Define L_G and R_G as the left and right areas of the selected G_i as follows:
$L_G = \sum_{j,k} \nu(b_{\{j,k\}}), j \in [1, .., C], k \in [i+1, .., i+S/2-1]$
$R_G = \sum_{j,k} \nu(b_{\{j,k\}}), j \in [1, .., C], k \in [i+S/2+1, .., i+S-1]$

if $L_G > R_G$ **then**
$\quad$ B is rotated $k = i + S/2 - 1$ positions to the left:
$\quad$ $\nu^{ROT} = \{\nu(b_{\{1,k+1\}}), .., \nu(b_{\{1,S\}}), \nu(b_{\{1,1\}}), .., \nu(b_{\{1,k\}}), ..,$
$\quad$ $.., \nu(b_{\{C,k+1\}}), .., \nu(b_{\{C,S\}}), \nu(b_{\{C,1\}}), .., \nu(b_{\{C,k\}})\}$
else
$\quad$ B is rotated $k = i - 1$ positions to the right:
$\quad$ $\nu^{ROT} = \{\nu(b_{\{1,S\}}), .., \nu(b_{\{1,S-k+1\}}), \nu(b_{\{1,1\}}), .., \nu(b_{\{1,S-k\}}), ..,$
$\quad$ $.., \nu(b_{\{C,S\}}), .., \nu(b_{\{C,S-k+1\}}), \nu(b_{\{C,1\}}), .., \nu(b_{\{C,S-k\}})\}$
end if

according to the set of M binary classifiers. The decoding algorithm finds the most suitable class label for the test sample using the output of this binary set of classifiers. Thus, given a set of N training samples $\mathbf{X} = \{\mathbf{x}_1, \ldots, \mathbf{x}_N\}$, where each $\mathbf{x}_i$ belongs to the class $C_i \in \{C_1, \ldots, C_K\}$, an ECOC encoding consists on constructing M binary problems using the original K classes. Each binary problem splits two meta-classes, and values $+1$ and -1 are assigned to each class belonging to the first or second meta-classes, respectively. If a class does not belong to any meta-class, the membership value is set to 0. This creates a $K \times M$ matrix $\mathbf{T}$. When a new sample must be classified, the outputs of the classifiers trained on each binary problem (columns of the matrix $\mathbf{T}$) are used to construct the codeword that is compared with each row of the matrix $\mathbf{T}$. The class codeword with the minimum distance is selected as the classifier output. The ECOC scheme allows to represent in a common framework well-known strategies such as one-versus-all or all-pairs, as well as more sophisticated problem dependent encodings, namely discriminant ECOC [14] or sub-class ECOC [15], without a significant increment of the codeword length. Literature shows that one of the most straightforward and well-performing approach disregarding of the properties of the particular base learner is the *one-versus-one* strategy.

The final part of the ECOC process is based on defining a suitable distance for comparing the output of the classifiers with the base codewords. The authors of [17] have recently shown that *weighted decoding* achieves the minimum error with respect to most of the state-of-the-art decoding measures. The weighted decoding strategy decomposes the decoding step of the ECOC technique in two parts: a weighting factor for each code position and any general decoding strategy. In [17] the authors show that for a decoding strategy to be successful, two

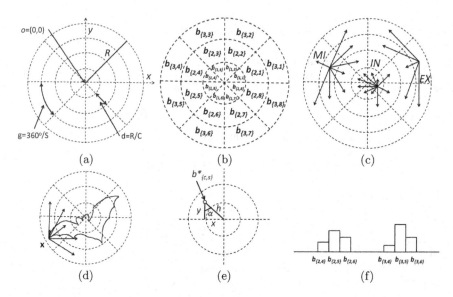

Fig. 1. (a) CBSM correlogram parameters, (b) regions distribution, (c) region neighbors, (d) object point analysis, (e) region centroid definition, and (f) descriptor vector update after point analysis

Bat1   Bat1 5×5 Bat1 24×24 Bat1 54×54   Bat2   Bat2 5×5 Bat2 24×24 Bat2 54×54

Fig. 2. Examples of image descriptions at different sizes for two object instances

conditions must be fulfilled: the bias induced by the zero symbol should be zero and the dynamic range of the decoding strategy must be constant for all the codewords. The complete decoding strategy weights the contribution of the decoding at each position of the codeword by the elements of W that ensures that both conditions are fulfilled. As such, the final decoding strategy is defined as $d(y, T(i, \cdot)) = \sum_{j=1}^{M} W(i, j) \cdot \mathcal{L}(T(i, j) \cdot h_j(x))$, where,

$$w(i, j) = \begin{cases} r_i(S, T(\cdot, j), T(i, j)) & T(i, j) \neq 0 \\ 0 & otherwise \end{cases} \qquad (1)$$

and $\sum_{j=1}^{M} W(i, j) = 1, \forall i \in \{1 \dots K\}$. We define the meta-class relative accuracy (r-value) of class k on the set S given the following definition,

$$r_k(S, \rho, i) = \frac{\#\text{elements of class } k \text{ classified as meta-class } i \text{ in the set } S}{\#\text{elements belonging to class } k \text{ in the set } S} \qquad (2)$$

where ρ defines which classes belong to which meta-class.

The second part of the weighting decoding lies in a base decoding strategy. In this article, we chose to use Linear Loss-based decoding as base strategy decoding. Linear Loss-based decoding was introduced by Allwein et al. [16] and is defined in the following way: given the input sample $\mathbf{x}$ and the binary code y result of applying all the dichotomizers $(h_1, h_2, \ldots, h_M)$ to the input test sample, the decoding value is defined as follows,

$$d(y, T(i, \cdot)) = \sum_{j=1}^{M} \mathcal{L}(T(i, j) \cdot h_j(x))$$

where $T(i, \cdot)$ denotes the codeword for class i, $h_j(x)$ is the prediction value for dichotomizer j, and $\mathcal{L}$ is a loss function that represents the penalty due to the miss-classification (we use $\mathcal{L}(\rho) = -\rho$).

4 Experimental Evaluation

In order to present the results, first, we discuss the data, methods, and validation of the experiments:

• *Data*: To test the multi-class symbol recognition system, we used two multi-class data sets: the public 70-class MPEG7 repository data set [1], which contains a high number of classes with different appearance of symbols from a same class, including rotation. And secondly, a 17-class data set of grey-level symbols, which contains the common distortions from real-environments, such as illumination changes, partial occlusions, or changes in the point of view.

• *Methods*: The methods used in the comparative are: SIFT [18], Zoning, Zernique, and CSS curvature descriptors from the standard MPEG [3] [19] [20]. The details of the descriptors used for the comparatives are the followings: the optimum grid size of the CBSM descriptors is estimated applying cross-validation over the training set using a 10% of the samples to validate the different sizes of $S = \{8, 12, 16, 20, 24, 28, 32\}$ and $C\{8, 12, 16, 20, 24, 28, 32\}$. For a fair comparison among descriptors, the Zoning and BSM descriptors are set to the same number of regions than the CBSM descriptor. Concerning the Zernique technique, 7 moments are used. The length of the curve for the CSS descriptor is normalized to 200, where the σ parameter takes an initial value of 1 and increases by 1 unit at each step. The descriptors are trained using 50 runs of Gentle Adaboost with decision stumps [9], and the one-versus-one ECOC design [16] with the Loss-Weighted decoding [17]. In order to show the benefits of the ECOC design, we also compare with a 3-Nearest Neighbor classifier.

• *Validation*: The classification score is computed by a stratified ten-fold cross-validation, testing for the 95% of the confidence interval with a two-tailed t-test.

4.1 MPEG7 Classification

In this experiment, we used the 70 object categories from the public MPEG7 binary object data set [1] to compare the descriptors in a multi-class categorization problem. Some examples of this data set are shown in Figure 3(a).

Table 1. Classification accuracy and confidence interval on the 70 MPEG7 symbol categories for the different descriptors using 3-Nearest Neighbor and the one-versus-one ECOC scheme with Gentle Adaboost as the base classifier

Descriptor	$3NN$	ECOC Adaboost
CBSM	**71.84(6.73)**	**80.36(7.01)**
BSM	65.79(8.03)	77.93(7.25)
Zernique	43.64(7.66)	51.29(5.48)
Zoning	58.64(10.97)	65.50(6.64)
CSS	37.01(10.76)	44.54(7.11)
SIFT	29.14(5.68)	32.57(4.04)

The classification results and confidence interval after testing using a stratified ten-fold cross-validation with a 3-NN and the ECOC configuration are shown in Table 1. Note that the best performance is obtained by our CBSM descriptor with the one-versus-one ECOC design with Loss-Weighted decoding and with 3-NN, followed by the original BSM. Moreover, the ECOC configurations always obtain higher performance than classifying with a nearest neighbor classifier.

4.2   Grey-Scale Symbol Classification

The second data set is composed by grey-level samples from 17 different classes, with a total of 550 samples acquired with a digital camera from real environments. The samples are taken so that there are high affine transformations, partial occlusions, background influence, and high illumination changes. Some examples of the 17 classes are shown in Fig. 3(b). The SIFT descriptor is a widely-used strategy for this type of images, obtaining very good results [18]. Hence, we compare the CBSM and SIFT descriptors in this experiment.

The performances and confidence intervals obtained in this experiment from a ten-fold cross-validation using the CBSM and SIFT descriptors in a

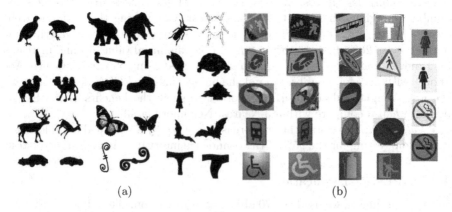

(a)   (b)

Fig. 3. (a) MPEG samples, and (b) Grey-scale symbol data set samples

Table 2. Performance and confidence interval of the CBSM and SIFT descriptors on the grey-scale symbols data set using a one-versus-one Adaboost ECOC scheme

CBSM	SIFT
77.82(6.45)	62.12(9.08)

one-versus-one ECOC scheme with Gentle Adaboost as the base classifier and Loss-Weighted decoding are shown in table 2. One can see that the result obtained by the CBSM descriptor adapted to grey-scale symbols significantly outperforms the result obtained by the SIFT descriptor. This difference is produced in this data set because of the high changes in the point of view of the symbols and the background influence, which significantly change the SIFT orientations.

5 Conclusion

In this paper, we presented the Circular Blurred Shape Model descriptor. The new descriptor is suitable to describe and recognize symbols that can suffer from several distortions, such as occlusions, rigid or elastic deformations, gaps or noise. The descriptor encodes the spatial arrangement of symbol characteristics using a correlogram structure. A prior blurring degree defines the level of degradation allowed to the symbol. Moreover, the descriptor correlogram is rotated guided by the major density so that it becomes rotationally invariant. The new symbol descriptions are learnt using Adaboost binary classifiers, and embedded in an Error-Correcting Output Codes framework to deal with multi-class categorization problems. The results over different multi-class categorization problems and comparing with the state-of-the-art descriptors show higher performance of the present methodology when classifying high number of symbol classes that suffer from irregular deformations.

Acknowledgements

This work has been supported in part by projects TIN2006-15308-C02, TIN2006-15694-C02-02, FIS PI061290, and CONSOLIDER-INGENIO CSD 2007-00018.

References

1. MPEG7 Repository Database,
   http://www.cis.temple.edu/latecki/research.html
2. Zhang, D., Lu, G.: Review of shape representation and description techniques. Pattern Recognition 37(1), 1–19 (2004)
3. Khotanzad, A., Hong, Y.H.: Invariant image recognition by Zernike moments. PAMI 12(5), 489–497 (1990)
4. Manjunath, B.S., Salembier, P., Sikora, T.: Introduction to MPEG-7: Multimedia Content Description Interface. Wiley, Chichester (2002)

5. Mokhtarian, F., Mackworth, A.K.: Scale-Based Description and Recognition of Planar Curves and Two-Dimensional Shapes. PAMI 8(1), 34–43 (1986)
6. Belongie, S., Malik, J., Puzicha, J.: Shape Matching and Object Recognition Using Shape Contexts. PAMI, 509–522 (2002)
7. Bunke, H.: Attributed programmed graph grammars and their application to schematic diagram interpretation. PAMI 4(6), 574–582 (1982)
8. Lladós, J., Martí, E., Villanueva, J.: Symbol Rec. by Error-Tolerant Subgraph Matching between Adjacency Graphs. PAMI 23(10), 1137–1143 (2001)
9. Friedman, J., Hastie, T., Tibshirani, R.: Additive logistic regression: a statistical view of boosting. Annals of Statistics 28(2), 337–374 (2000)
10. Dietterich, T.G., Bakiri, G.: Solving Multiclass Learning Problems via Error-Correcting Output Codes. JAIR 2, 263–286 (1995)
11. Fornés, A., Escalera, S., Lladós, J., Sánchez, G., Radeva, P.I., Pujol, O.: Handwritten symbol recognition by a boosted blurred shape model with error correction. In: Martí, J., Benedí, J.M., Mendonça, A.M., Serrat, J. (eds.) IbPRIA 2007. LNCS, vol. 4477, pp. 13–21. Springer, Heidelberg (2007)
12. Dietterich, T., Kong, E.: Error-correcting output codes corrects bias and variance. In: Prieditis, S., Russell, S. (eds.) ICML, pp. 313–321 (1995)
13. Dietterich, T., Bakiri, G.: Solving multiclass learning problems via error-correcting output codes. JAIR 2, 263–286 (1995)
14. Pujol, O., Radeva, P., Vitrià, J.: DECOC: A heuristic method for application dependent design of ECOC. PAMI 28, 1001–1007 (2006)
15. Escalera, S., Tax, D.M.J., Pujol, O., Radeva, P., Duin, R.P.W.: Subclass Problem-Dependent Design for Error-Correcting Output Codes. PAMI 30(6), 1041–1054 (2008)
16. Allwein, E., Schapire, R., Singer, Y.: Reducing multiclass to binary: A unifying approach for margin classifiers. JMLR 1, 113–141 (2002)
17. Escalera, S., Pujol, O., Radeva, P.: On the Decoding Process in Ternary Error-Correcting Output Codes. PAMI (2009)
18. Lowe, D.: Distinctive Image Features from Scale-Invariant Keypoints. JCV 60(2), 91–110 (2004)
19. Kim, W.Y., Kim, Y.S.: A new region-based shape descriptor. Hanyang University and Konan Technology (1999)
20. Standard MPEG ISO/IEC 15938-5:2003(E)

A Novel Recognition Approach for Sketch-Based Interfaces

Danilo Avola, Andrea Del Buono, Giorgio Gianforme, and Stefano Paolozzi

CSKLab National Research Center, Department of Advanced Research
Via Savoia 84, 00198 Rome, Italy
{danilo.avola,andrea.delbuono}@csklab.it
http://www.csklab.it/index.html.en
University of "Rome 3", Department of Computer Science and Automation
Viale della Vasca Navale 79, 00146 Rome, Italy
{gianforme,paolozzi}@dia.uniroma3.it
http://web.dia.uniroma3.it/

Abstract. Multimodal interfaces can be profitably used to support the more and more complex applications and services which support human activities in everyday life. In particular, sketch-based interfaces offer users an effortless and powerful communication way to represent concepts and/or commands on different devices. Developing a sketch-based interface for a specific application or service is a time-consuming operation that requires the re-engineering and/or the re-designing of the whole recognizer framework. This paper describes a definitive framework that allows users to define each kind of sketch-based interface, using freehand drawing only. The definition of the interface and its recognition process are performed using our developed Sketch Modeling Language (SketchML).

Keywords: Sketch-based interfaces, sketch-based interaction, sketch recognition, multi-domain, vectorization, segmentation, XML, SVG.

1 Introduction

Multimodal interfaces allow users to interact naturally with any desktop or mobile devices using multiple different modalities (e.g. sketch, gesture, speech, gaze). This kind of interaction provides a powerful tool that allows users to manage the more and more complex applications and services surrounding their activities in everyday life. In particular, sketch-based interfaces enable users to express concepts, to provide commands and to represent ideas in an immediate, intuitive and simple way.

Unlike the other modalities, sketch-based interaction has two advantageous features. The first one is the "robustness" respect outdoor and indoor environments. This means that both behavior and error level of other interfaces (e.g. speech-based, eye-based) are strongly tied to the specific environment in which these interfaces are used. In fact, several factors (e.g. noise, amount of light) can

P. Foggia, C. Sansone, and M. Vento (Eds.): ICIAP 2009, LNCS 5716, pp. 1015–1024, 2009.

influence the interpretation process of these interfaces. The second one is the quick "customization" of the concepts and/or commands and/or ideas used to manage a specific application or service. In fact, it is always possible to create a specific set of graphical symbols in order to manage several applications and/or services according to both specific graphical standards and user needs.

The main effort in building sketch-based interfaces regards the implementation of the recognizer framework able to distinguish every symbol allowed in the system (the set of those symbols is called application domain or library). The application domains are potentially unbounded, since they just depend on the customization. Developing a sketch-based interface (that is a specific set of symbols) for a specific application and/or service is a time-consuming operation that requires the re-engineering and/or the re-designing of the whole recognizer framework.

This paper describes a definitive framework that allows users to define each kind of sketch-based interface, using freehand drawing only. Interface definition and its recognition process are performed using our developed Sketch Modeling Language (SketchML). Compared to the actual adopted methodologies in sketch recognition, our developed approach (and related prototypes) has three advantageous main aspects that jointly put our results in the vanguard inside the sketch-based interfaces area. The first one regards the possibility to define each kind of application domain. Actual frameworks are focused recognize only a specific set of symbols. They can also recognize other kinds of application domains but this step, differently from our approach, involves the management of the recognition logic inside the framework itself. The second one regards the possibility to quickly define each kind of application domain simply using free hand-drawing. In fact, there are several frameworks based on multi-domain concept, but in order to build a new application domain it is necessary an expert user with a deep knowledge about standards and/or vectorial applications and/or programming languages and so on. The last one concerns the interface definition and its recognition process which are performed by using SketchML, a language based on XML (eXtended Markup Language) standard. This consolidated W3C (World Wide Web Consortium) standard ensures both compatibility on different devices and cooperation between different applications/services.

The paper is structured as follows. Section 2 proposes some remarkable related works in multi-domain sketch-based interfaces. Section 3 introduces the novel approach and the related developed framework. Section 4 shows experimental results on a wide application domain. Finally, Section 5 concludes the paper.

2   Related Works

As mentioned in the previous section, our approach has three advantages main aspects respect the actual methodologies (define each kind of library without manage the framework, use sketch to build any libraries, represent sketch and its recognition by SketchML). However, our results have been assisted by the study of some remarkable works about the multi-domain sketch recognition frameworks. For example, an interesting methodology is presented in [1]. In this work the authors show a framework that allows users to draw shapes in natural way. In particular, the framework is able to recognize a variety of defaults domains by exploiting several consolidate techniques able to catch information about: geometric, features, temporal, contextual, multi-modal and domain. A different approach is provided in [2]. In this work the authors present a novel form of dynamically constructed Bayesian network which uses a sophisticated recognition engine able to integrate information and domain knowledge to improve recognition accuracy across a variety of domains. Another interesting work is shown in [3], in this work the authors present a remarkable agent-based framework for sketched symbol interpretation that heavily exploits contextual information for ambiguity resolution. In particular, in this work the agents manage both the activity of low-level hand-drawn symbol recognizers and contextual information to obtain an efficient and precise interpretation of sketches. Another approach, features based, is shown in [4]. In this work the authors present an advanced heuristic based framework that offers the user more freedom for: free-style sketching, grouping the strokes, and reducing the complexity of recognition activity. Unlike previous approaches the authors in [5] introduce a primitive-based engine. Their prototype is designed to infer designers' intention and interprets the input sketch into more exact geometric primitives: straight lines, poly-lines, circles, circular arcs, and so on. An important work, tied to our approach, is explained in [6]. The authors introduce LADDER, the first language to describe how sketched diagrams in a domain are drawn, displayed, and edited. In this work the difficulties about a suitable choice of a set of predefined entities that is broad enough to support a wide range of domains are faced. This language consists of predefined shapes, constraints, editing behaviors, and display methods, as well as a syntax for specifying a domain description sketch grammar and extending the language, ensuring that shapes and shape groups from many domains can be described. The just mentioned work has been a real source of inspiration. Our proposed SketchML has several common points with LADDER language, but SketchML is more general and it can be used to represent any application domain. A different approach is shown in [7], where a framework for recognition of composite graphic objects, topological spatial relationships of their components play an important role is given. In this work the authors introduce the ternary relationship, which is a complement to the binary relationship, to describe composite graphic objects. Another remarkable approach is shown in [9] where the authors describe a statistical framework based on dynamic Bayesian networks that explicitly models the fact that objects can be drawn interspersed. We conclude this section showing an approach, among those available, based on HMMs (Hidden Markov Models). In fact, new interesting tendency on sketch recognition approaches is to use HMM to overcome several critical duties, such as: customization, shape learning, and so on. An innovative approach is proposed in [8] where the authors show that it is possible to view sketching as an interactive process in order to use HMM for sketch recognition process. All the described approaches depend on set of symbols and/or primitives that are tied to specific application domains. Our novel approach overcomes this kind of problems by using real general primitives.

3   Approach and Developed Framework

The developed framework provides two different environments. The first, shown in Figure 1-a, is the Library Editor Environment (LEE), where the user can define, by freehand drawing, the libraries. The second, shown in Figure 1-b, is the Sketch Recognition Environment (SRE), where the user can perform the recognition activity, on a drawing schema, after having loaded a previously created library. Both environments allow users to perform several useful activities, such as: deletions, restyling, and so on.

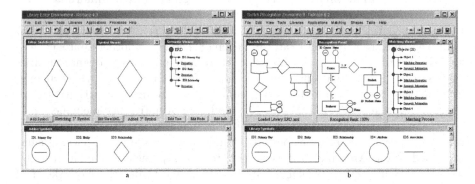

Fig. 1. a) Library Editor Environment b) Sketch Recognition Environment

In order to explain both the approach and the related framework functionalities a well known application domain, Entity Relationship Diagram (ERD), is introduced. In Figure 1-a the user has drawn the third symbol regarding the ERD domain, and the LEE has built the related vectorial representation. In Figure 1-b the user has performed a simple ERD schema, and the SRE has built the related vectorial schema. Both LEE and SRE work in off-line way, that is the user decides when the environments have to perform the recognition (and related vectorization) activity.

The approach and the algorithms designed to obtain the vectorial symbol/ schema from the sketched symbol/schema is the main aspect of our paper. In both environments our XML-based developed language (SketchML) is used to describe the vectorial representations.

The SRE exploits the knowledge of the symbols that make up the loaded library to improve the recognition process. In order to explain this concept in Figure 2 an example based on the five symbols belonging to the ERD library is shown. In Figure 2-a the user has correctly sketched an ERD instance. More precisely, the user has sketched the following sequence of ERD symbols: three primary keys, three entities, two relationships, three attributes and ten associations (twenty one objects). In Figure 2-b, all the drawn objects have been recognized. Indeed, the situation is more complex than the just mentioned one. In fact, taking into account the symbols belonging to the loaded library, it is possible to observe that the sketched symbol of association (shown in Figure 2-a

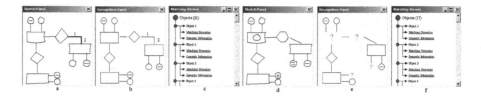

Fig. 2. Correct/Incorrect ERD Instance

by labels 1 and 2) is not a library symbol. It is recognized as an association symbol because it results as the composition of two symbols of the ERD library with a particular constraint (i.e. the two association symbols with an angle of ninety degrees). In Figure 2-c is shown the matching process of each symbol (explained in the relative section). This process allows the framework to map every object sketched by the user (in SRE) with a symbols belonging to the related library (defined in LEE).

Unlike the previous example, in Figure 2-d the user has incorrectly sketched an ERD instance. In fact, as it is possible to observe in Figure 2-e, seventeen objects have been recognized and four objects have not been recognized. In Figure 2-f is detailed each one of the matching process between the objects drawn by the user and the loaded library. This example highlights that four objects have not satisfied the matching requirements (in fact the matched objects are seventeen), this means that these four objects have not matched a respective symbol in the loaded library. The next two subsections describe the main aspects (approaches and algorithms) of the LEE and SRE.

3.1   Library Editor Environment

In order to explain the subsection content, it is necessary to introduce the following three definitions: stroke (set of pixels obtained during the pen action: pen down, pen drawing, pen up), sub-stroke (subpart of a stroke), generalized stroke (two, or more, joined sub-strokes coming from different strokes).

The LEE activity is performed by four sequential modules: the first module (First Layer Segmentation Algorithm, FLSA) is used to obtain, from the strokes drawn by user, two kind of objects: closed regions and poly-lines. The second module (Second Layer Segmentation Algorithm, SLSA) is used to obtain the set of primitives (ovals and lines) that make up each obtained object. The third module (Constraints Establishment, CE) is used to evaluate the relationships between the found primitives. The fourth module (SketchML Descriptor) is used "to translate" all the found information in a XML/SVG structure. In this subsection each module is detailed.

The aim of FLSA (first module) is to provide two different sets of objects: closed regions and poly-lines. This concept is not so simple as it might appear. In fact, there is not always a unique interpretation about two sketched strokes. For example, the strokes (S_1 and S_2) drawn in Figure 3-a-a can be interpreted as two overlapped closed regions (A_1 and A_2, Figure 3-a-b), otherwise the strokes can

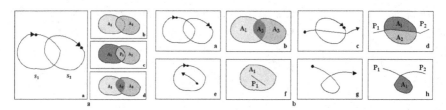

Fig. 3. a) Ambiguity Examples. b) Algorithm Interpretation.

be interpreted as two closed-regions (A_1 and A_2) and a poly-line (P_1), Figure 3-a-c. In another interpretation, Figure 3-a-d, the two strokes can be interpreted as three closed regions (A_1, A_2, A_3). Moreover, there are other available interpretations. This kind of issues, defined as ambiguity problems, is a crucial point of every sketch recognition system. To overcome the ambiguity problems, the developed FLSA works taking into account the following two definitions: closed region (the smallest area confined by a set of strokes and/or sub-Strokes and/or generalized strokes), poly-line (the smallest stroke or sub-Stroke). Following the introduced definitions every sketch can be interpreted in a unique way.

In order to highlight the algorithm approach in Figure 3-b some examples of developed algorithm interpretation are given. The two strokes drawn in Figure 3-b-a are interpreted, as shown in Figure 3-b-b, as three closed regions (A_1, A_2 and A_3). The two strokes drawn in Figure 3-b-c are interpreted, as shown in Figure 3-b-d, as two closed regions and two poly-lines (A_1, A_2 and P_1, P_1). The two strokes drawn in Figure 3-b-e are interpreted, as shown in Figure 3-b-d, as a closed region and a poly-line (A_1, P_1). Finally, the stroke drawn in Figure 3-b-g is interpreted, as shown in Figure 3-b-h, as a closed region and two poly-lines (A_1, P_1 and P_2).

In order to accomplish as just mentioned the FLSA works according to the following sequential two main steps. During the first step every stroke, without intersection points, is analyzed to check if it is closed or not. During the second step every stroke, with intersection points, is analyzed to detect every intersection point which is used to find the maximum number of disjoined areas. This last step is performed by an exhaustive sub-algorithm which, from every intersection point, searches every possible closed path. During the process the sub-algorithm considers, step by step, only the smallest areas that do not overlap (entirely or in part) other found areas.

Starting from the set of objects (closed regions and poly-lines) identified by the previous algorithm, the aim of the SLSA (second module) is to recognize, on each object, the set of primitives that makes it up. In our context, the term primitive means only two specific geometrical primitives: line and oval (and as particular arc and circle). The concept behind the developed algorithm is that every "segment" of a shape can be approximated by the mentioned geometrical primitives. In order to explain the just introduced concept in Figure 4 an example

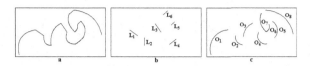

Fig. 4. Searching: Primitives

is shown. Deliberately the example regards a complex poly-line, our goal is to show that the proposed approach is very general, and it can be used on every kind of user sketch.

As shown in Figure 4-b, the algorithm first detects the lines $(L_1..L_6)$, the remaining searched primitives are the ovals or, as shown in this example (Figure 4-c), the sub-parts (arcs) of different ovals $(O_1..O_8)$. In order to accomplish this task on every closed-region and/or poly-line the algorithm works according to the following two main steps. During the first step (line detection) on every object the longest set points having a linearity property are searched. The term linearity property is used to indicate a contiguous set of points (having a prefixed minimum length, called L_{fix}) that, independently from the orientation, can be considered belonging to a same prefixed enclosing rectangle. During the second step (oval/arc, detection) every set of points discarded by the previous step is an oval (or arc) candidate. For this reason a curvature property is verified. The term curvature property is used to indicate a contiguous set of points in which, independently from the orientation, the linearity property is true but only on contiguous sub-set points having a length lower than L_{fix}. In order to obtain a suitable collocation of the found set of points as line and/or oval (or arc), the two steps are cooperatively applied several times. At the end of the developed algorithm it is possible to perform the vectorization step by replacing the set of points representing each detected primitive with the following basic SVG (Scalable Vector Graphics, which is an XML based language) shapes: primitive line with line SVG basic shape, primitive oval with ellipse SVG basic shape, primitive part of oval with path SVG basic shape.

Starting from the vectorial set of primitives (SVG basic shapes: lines, ellipses, and paths) that make up every object, the aim of the CE (third module) is to detect the spatial relationships between them. Our recognizer engine takes into account the following constraints classification: interiors (constraints evaluated on each single vectorial primitive, e.g. orientation, closure), internals (constraints evaluated between primitives of a same object, e.g. coincident, intersect), and externals (constraints evaluated between primitives of different objects, e.g. contain, vertical alignment). Every constraint has several attributes in order to specify the information needed to define the related spatial relationship.

When the recognition process reaches SketchML Descriptor (fourth module) every hard task has been performed. In fact, this module has only to include the vectorial information obtained previously about the SVG basic shapes (in SLSA), with the new information (suitably "translated" in XML) related to the found

Fig. 5. Vectorial Square Represented By SketchML

constraints. This enriched XML makes up the main constructs of our developed SketchML. In Figure 5 is shown a SketchML representation of a vectorial square. The amount of information needed to represent a simple and single symbol is very large, for this reason in Figure 5 only some constraints are shown.

In particular, the example shows that the square is considered as composed from four lines (Line-1, Line-2, Line-3, Line-4). These lines have several interior, internal and external constrains. More precisely, the main interior constraints explain the orientation of the lines, there is not main external constraints (because there are not others objects) and there are several internal constraints that explain the relationships between the mentioned four lines (for example, the GreaterLength constraint applied respectively to the arguments Line-1 and Line-2, describes that the second line (Line-2) is greater than the first line (Line-1) by about 40 percent.

3.2   Sketch Recognition Environment

This environment is used to recognize one or more than one library symbols. In the first case (i.e. when a user expresses a command) the environment works exactly as the LEE. In the second case (i.e. when a user expresses a concept) it is necessary a previous elaboration (based on context and spatial relationships) to recognize, first of all, how many possible symbols the user has drawn. To accomplish this task all the intersection points (of the sketch performed by the user) are evaluated. After this step the system detects the intersection points that do not have "correspondence" with the intersection points used to build the library, in this way a first evaluation about the number of the sketched objects can be performed. In both cases the next step is the matching process to map the performed "candidate" sketched symbols with the symbols contained in the loaded library.

3.3   Matching Process

The final purpose of matching between symbols sketched by the user in the SRE and the symbols represented in a specific library (made up by LEE) is to choose the right element inside the library that provides the suitable interpretation of the sketched symbols. As mentioned, every symbol of the loaded library inside the framework is described through an XML/SVG file. Also the user's sketch has been represented using XML/SVG file that contains information comparable to the symbols of the library. The matching algorithm performs an exhaustive search of the particular patterns created by the user during sketch activity. Every SVG basic primitive (that is, Line, Ellipse and Path), coming from library or user's sketch, is represented by both a node and a set of relationships (the constraints) between the nodes. Moreover, two or more related basic symbols (for example the containment constraint) are represented by two macro-nodes between which exist a macro-relation (in this case, the *containment*). The matching approach starts from a generic node (of the sketch representation), it performs a matching action with every node of the same kind (such as: line, ellipse or path) presents in the symbol of the loaded library. Obviously, the process appears exponentially complex specially when the first nodes are examined. The process ends when all the nodes are examined. When this happens several possible configuration will be identified by the system. Each one will have a rank depending on the quality of the accomplished matching. Several configuration will have a very low rank, others will have a suitable ranking profitable to identify the right pattern (i.e. the right symbol).

4   Experimental Results

This section shows the results obtained on a wide application domain designed to meet the needs of heterogeneous environments. As shown in Table 1 the application domain is made up from 178 different symbols. In this context it has to be taken into account that several symbols (e.g. arrow) can have up to eight different orientations (North, East, South, West, Northeast, Southeast, Southwest, Northwest) each of which is considered a different symbol. For each symbol has been performed an average of 75 tracking for a total of 11.570 tests. The percentage of recognition of each symbol is almost total. Indeed, this percentage tends to be slightly lower according to the complexity of the symbol. In fact, for symbols made up of more than 7 strokes some constraints may be ambiguous and misinterpreted. In order to overcome this problem, it is possible to introduce in the framework a more complex personalization concept. Moreover, it is possible to consider a new class of constraints (i.e. control constraints) able to oversee ambiguous potentially situations. The framework has been also tested on more traditional domains (i.e. entity relationship diagram, data flow diagram, electrical schemes, and so on) providing always a total level of reliability.

Table 1. Experimental Application Domain

N° Symbols 178 (Examples)	N° Tracing	Related Vectorization	% of Recognition	% Misinterpretation	N° Symbols 178 (Examples)	N° Tracing	Related Vectorization	% of Recognition	% Misinterpretation
[symbol]	72	[symbol]	100%	0%	[symbol]	100	[symbol]	95%	0%
[symbol]	80	[symbol]	96%	0%	[symbol]	67	[symbol]	99%	0%
----------	----------	----------	----------	----------	Tot: 11.570	Averange: 75	Tot: 11.570	Averange: 98%	0.5%

5   Conclusions

The proposed approach provides a concrete framework able to build and to recognize every kind of sketched symbol/schema. The key point is that a user, without special knowledge, can create a personalized library simply sketching the desired symbols. The simple and versatile language used to represent the sketch activity (SketchML) allows the cooperation of the proposed framework with a large number of applications, devices and services. The framework can be used on 2D and 3D library (adding another category of constraints 3D oriented). Moreover, the proposed algorithms allow the user to perform sketches with an high inaccuracy level (without ambiguity problems and/or unrecognized events).

References

1. Hammond, T., et al.: Free-sketch Recognition: Putting the CHI in Sketching. In: Proc. of CHI 2008 Extended Abstracts on Human Factors in Computing Systems, CHI 2008, pp. 3027–3032. ACM Press, Florence (2008)
2. Alvarado, C., Davis, R.: Dynamically Constructed Bayes Nets for Multi-Domain Sketch Understanding. In: Proc. of ACM SIGGRAPH 2007 courses, SIGGRAPH 2007, p. 33. ACM Press, California (2007)
3. Casella, G., Deufemia, V., Mascardi, V., Costagliola, G., Martelli, M.: An Agent-Based Framework for Sketched Symbol Interpretation. Journal of Visual Languages and Computing 19(2), 225–257 (2008)
4. Sahoo, G., Singh, B.K.: A New Approach to Sketch Recognition Using Heuristic. JCSNS International Journal of Computer Science and Network Security 8(2), 102–108 (2008)
5. Shu-Xia, W., Man-Tun, G., Le-Hua, Q.: Freehand Sketching Interfaces: Early Processing for Sketch Recognition. In: Jacko, J.A. (ed.) HCI 2007. LNCS, vol. 4551, pp. 161–170. Springer, Heidelberg (2007)
6. Hammond, T., Davis, R.: LADDER: a Language to Describe Drawing, Display, and Editing in Sketch Recognition. In: Proceedings of SIGGRAPH 2006: ACM SIGGRAPH 2006 Courses, p. 27. ACM Press, New York (2006)
7. Peng, B., Liu, Y., Wenyin, L., Huang, G.: Sketch Recognition Based on Topological Spatial Relationship. In: Fred, A., Caelli, T.M., Duin, R.P.W., Campilho, A.C., de Ridder, D. (eds.) SSPR&SPR 2004. LNCS, vol. 3138, pp. 434–443. Springer, Heidelberg (2004)
8. Sezgin, T.M., Davis, R.: HMM-Based Efficient Sketch Recognition. In: Proceedings of the 10th International Conference on Intelligent User Interfaces, IUI 2005, pp. 281–283. ACM Press, San Diego (2005)
9. Sezgin, T.M., Davis, R.: Sketch Recognition in Interspersed Drawings Using Time-Based Graphical Models. In: Proceedings of Computer Graphics, vol. 32(5), pp. 500–510. Pergamon Press, Inc., Elmsford (2008)

Simultaneous Document Margin Removal and Skew Correction Based on Corner Detection in Projection Profiles

M. Mehdi Haji, Tien D. Bui, and Ching Y. Suen

Centre for Pattern Recognition and Machine Intelligence, Concordia University, 1455 de Maisonneuve Blvd. West, Montreal, Quebec, Canada, H3G 1M8
{m_haji,bui,suen}@cs.concordia.ca

Abstract. Document images obtained from scanners or photocopiers usually have a black margin which interferes with subsequent stages of page segmentation algorithms. Thus, the margins must be removed at the initial stage of a document processing application. This paper presents an algorithm which we have developed for document margin removal based upon the detection of document corners from projection profiles. The algorithm does not make any restrictive assumptions regarding the input document image to be processed. It neither needs all four margins to be present nor needs the corners to be right angles. In the case of the tilted documents, it is able to detect and correct the skew. In our experiments, the algorithm was successfully applied to all document images in our databases of French and Arabic document images which contain more than two hundred images with different types of layouts, noise, and intensity levels.

Keywords: Document margin, layout analysis, projection profile, corner detection, skew correction.

1 Introduction

Document processing technologies are concerned with the use of computers for automatic processing of different kinds of media containing text data. Examples of the applications are Optical Character Recognition (OCR), digital searchable libraries, document image retrieval, postal address recognition, bank cheque processing and so on. In most of these applications, the source of data is an image of a document coming from a scanner or a photocopier. During the process of scanning or photocopying, an artifact, which we simply refer to as margin, is added to the image. These black margins are not only a useless piece of data and unpleasant when the page is reproduced (reprinted), but also can interfere with the subsequent stages of document layout analysis and page segmentation algorithms. Therefore, it is desirable or necessary to remove these margins before any subsequent stages in a document processing application. Despite its practical significance, this problem is often overlooked or not discussed thoroughly in papers. There are only a few studies which have addressed

P. Foggia, C. Sansone, and M. Vento (Eds.): ICIAP 2009, LNCS 5716, pp. 1025–1034, 2009.

the problem of document margin removal. Manmatha and Rothfeder in [1] have proposed a novel method using scale spaces for segmenting words in handwritten documents wherein they have used the basic technique of projection profiles for the detection of document margins. It is easy to obtain the margins from the projection profiles when the document is not tilted and the page is a perfectly straight rectangle. But as shown in Fig. 1, this is not always the case. The page may be skewed, and it may not be a perfect rectangle. Also, any of the four margins may be present or not. The basic technique discussed in [1], is not able to handle these cases. Peerawit and Kawtrakul in [2] have proposed a marginal noise removal method based upon edge detection. They have used the edge density property of the noise and text areas to detect the border between them. This method is designed to remove left and right margins only, and is incapable of handling skewed pages.

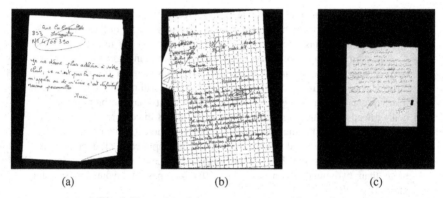

(a)   (b)   (c)

Fig. 1. Examples of documents images with margins

In [3], Fan et al. have proposed a top-down approach to margin removal. Firstly, the image is divided by locating possible boundaries between connected blocks. Next, the regions corresponding to marginal noise are identified by applying some heuristics based upon shape length and location of the split blocks and finally these regions are removed. Fan et al.'s algorithm is able to remove marginal noise from skewed pages, but it can not correct the page skew. Moreover, it does not find the page borders, i.e. it only removes the marginal noise and if portions of a neighboring page are present in the image, they will not be removed.

In [4, 5], Shafait et al. have used a geometric matching algorithm to find the optimal page frame. Their method is based on extraction and labeling of connected components at the first stage. Text lines and text zones must be identified prior to margin detection. However, extracting text lines from a page is a challenging task, especially for unconstrained handwritten types of documents [6, 7]. In fact, Shafait et al.'s algorithm is designed for machine printed documents. Moreover, it assumes the page frame is an axis-aligned rectangle (i.e. again, it can not handle skewed pages).

In [8], Stamatopoulos et al. have proposed a border detection algorithm for camera document images. Their method is based upon projection profiles combined with a connected component labeling process. But again, it needs the document skew to be corrected prior to margin removal.

There are several other published works concerning the problem of margin removal [9-12], but to the best of our knowledge, the algorithm we present in this paper is the first to address the problem of margin removal in presence of document skew.

(a) Input Document Image   (b) Vertical Projection Profile   (c)   Horizontal   Projection Profile

Fig. 2. A document image with margin and the corresponding vertical and horizontal projection profiles

2   Document Margin Removal and Skew Correction Using Projection Profiles

In this section we explain the margin removal algorithm, starting with the case of straight pages and then generalizing it to handle skewed pages.

2.1   Margin Removal for Straight Pages

The basic function of the algorithm is to find the corners which correspond to the page margins from the projection profiles of the input image. For a straight page, the left-most and right-most sharp corners in the horizontal profile of the image correspond to the left and right margins, and the left-most and right-most sharp corners in the vertical profile of the image correspond to the upper and lower margins (Fig. 2). Carrying out this task may appear simple, however the difficulty of implementation lies in corner detection, which is one of the most studied and open problems in computer vision. But in our case, by searching for the corners in 1-D projection profiles, rather than a 2-D image, we encounter a problem which can be easily solved.

Much research has been conducted upon the subject of corner detection in computer vision literature. This research can be broadly classified into two categories: grey-level and boundary-based [13]. In the first category, corners are found by using corner templates or computing the gradient at edge pixels. In the second category, corners are found by analyzing the properties of boundary pixels. For our case, we have chosen a boundary-based approach because we want to obtain corners from 1-D profiles which correspond to the document boundaries. We use a modification of the K-Cosine measure presented in [13] which is a new and robust algorithm for position, orientation, and scale invariant boundary-based corner detection for 2-D images.

The K-Cosine measure for a set of boundary points S = { $P_i \mid i = 1, 2, ..., m$ } is defined for each point i as follows:

$$c_i(K) = \cos\theta_i = \frac{\vec{a}_i(K)\vec{b}_i(K)}{\|\vec{a}_i(K)\|.\|\vec{b}_i(K)\|} \tag{1}$$

Where $\vec{a}_i(K) = \vec{P}_{i+K} - \vec{P}_i$ and $\vec{b}_i(K) = \vec{P}_{i-K} - \vec{P}_i$ are the two vectors connecting the point i to the Kth point before and after it, and θ_i denotes the angle between these two vectors. Therefore, K-cosine provides a measure of the curvature of boundary points over a region of support specified by K.

The overall performance of the 2-D corner detection algorithm based on the K-Cosine measure greatly depends on K. In [13], a careful analysis and a method of choosing a proper value for K is discussed, which is based on some geometric properties of the input set of boundary points. But, in our simplified 1-D version of the problem, where we are looking for corners in 1-D profiles, even a fixed value of K will work fine. Because, firstly, the corners of interest are almost right angles, secondly, they are located near the left and right ends of the boundary (i.e. projection profile), thirdly, there is only zero or one corners at each end (depending on whether or not the margin is present).

As the value of K is fixed in our application, we modify the definition of the K-Cosine measure in order to make sure that the corner detection scheme is robust against profile noise. We simply use a low-pass filtering which can be implemented as an averaging operation. More precisely, for each point of a projection profile, now we take the average of the K-Cosine measure over a local neighborhood of K. This new curvature measure is defined as follows:

$$C_i(K) = \frac{1}{K}\sum_{k=K/2}^{3K/2} c_i(k) \tag{2}$$

Having defined the curvature measure, we apply it to all points of the projection profile to obtain the corresponding Averaged K-Cosine Curvature Curve (AKC2). Now, the first zero-crossings of AKC2, scanning from left to right and right to left, correspond to the left and right corners of the projection profile. This is due to the fact that K-Cosine values vary between $-1 = \cos(\pi)$ and $1 = \cos(0)$, and thus the AKC2 curve has to cross the axis at the left and right rising edges of the corresponding profile. Please note that, even if the projection profile is not an exact rectangle function (i.e. it does not have 90-degree corners), the AKC2 curve still has two zero crossings which correspond to the left and right (or top and bottom) margins. Fig. 3 shows the document image of Fig. 2 with the corresponding AKC2 curves which determine the four margins of the image and the final result of margin removal.

2.2 Margin Removal for Skewed Pages

For skewed pages we observe that horizontal and vertical projection profiles have an isosceles trapezoidal shape as shown in Fig. 4. In this case, we need to estimate the base angle of the corresponding trapezoid to be able to correct the page skew. Let $T_{vpp}(I)$ and $T_{hpp}(I)$ denote the trapezoids corresponding to the vertical and horizontal

(a) Input Document Image

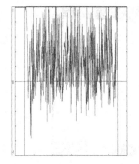

(b) Vertical AKC2 Curve

(c) Horizontal AKC2 Curve

(d) Result of Margin Removal Algorithm

Fig. 3. A document image with margin and the corresponding AKC2 curves and the result of margin removal algorithm

projection profiles of the input document image I respectively. The base angle of T_{vpp} which is the angle that the two non-parallel sides of it make with vertical axis, or equivalently, the base angle of T_{hpp} which is the angle that the two non-parallel sides of it make with horizontal axis is equal to the page skew angle.

In order to estimate the base angle, we use the same technique discussed in the previous section for finding corners in projection profiles. However in this case, we need all the four corners (i.e. the four vertices of the corresponding trapezoid).

Let V_1, V_2, V_3 and V_4 denote the four vertices of T_{vpp}, and H_1, H_2, H_3 and H_4 denote the four vertices of T_{hpp} as shown in Fig. 5. V_2 and V_3, and H_2 and H_3 can be found from the corresponding AKC2 curves, exactly the same way we did in the previous section. However, for H_1 and H_4, and V_1 and V_4, it should be noted that these corners may be very close to, or exactly lie on, the two ends (boundaries) of the corresponding profiles. Therefore, the AKC2 may not provide an appropriate measure of curvature to find them. We can easily handle this boundary problem by padding the profiles with enough ($> K$) number of zeros, corresponding to fictitious black margins on the four sides of the input document image.

Having obtained the coordinates of the vertices of T_{hpp} and T_{vpp}, we can calculate the absolute value of the page skew angle, but not the sign of it. As shown in Fig. 6, an axis-aligned rectangle when tilted to the left and to the right by the same skew angle θ, result in the same horizontal and the same vertical projection profiles. The

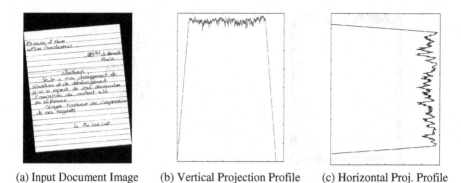

(a) Input Document Image   (b) Vertical Projection Profile   (c) Horizontal Proj. Profile

Fig. 4. A skewed document page with margin and the corresponding vertical and horizontal projection profiles

(a) T_{vpp} (b) T_{hpp}

Fig. 5. Trapezoids corresponding to vertical and horizontal projection profiles of a skewed document page with margin

proof is trivial by noting that the areas of the triangles $L_1L_2T_1'$ and $R_1R_2S_2'$; $L_3L_4T_3'$ and $R_3R_4S_4'$; $L_1L_4T_4'$ and $R_1R_4S_1'$; and $L_2L_3T_2'$ and $R_2R_3S_3'$ are equal by symmetry; and so are the areas of the parallelograms $T_4'L_2T_2'L_4$ and $R_1S_3'R_3S_1'$; and $L_1T_1'L_3T_3'$ and $S_2'R_2S_4'R_4$. Where T_1' is the intersection of the line segments L_1T_1 and L_2L_3; T_2' is the intersection of the line segments L_2T_2 and L_3L_4; T_3' is the intersection of the line segments L_3T_3 and L_1L_4; and T_4' is the intersection of the line segments L_4T_4 and L_1L_2; and similarly for S_1', S_2', S_3' and S_4'.

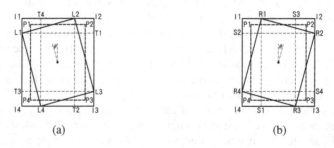

(a)   (b)

Fig. 6. An axis-aligned rectangle tilted to the left and to the right by the same angle

In Fig. 6, the inner rectangle $P_1P_2P_3P_4$ can correspond to the bounding box of a page of document without skew and margin. Then, the rectangles $L_1L_2L_3L_4$ and $R_1R_2R_3R_4$ are the skewed versions of it, and the triangles $I_1L_1L_2$, $I_2L_2L_3$, $I_3L_3L_4$, $I_4L_4L_1$, $I_1R_1R_4$, $I_2R_2R_1$, $I_3R_3R_2$ and $I_4R_4R_3$ correspond to the black (dark) margins around the page.

In our problem, given the horizontal and vertical projection profiles, we want to find the page corners (i.e. the coordinates of the rectangle $P_1P_2P_3P_4$). We do this by first obtaining the coordinates of $L_1L_2L_3L_4$ and $R_1R_2R_3R_4$ and then determining the sign of the skew angle. Let V_{1x}, V_{2x}, V_{3x} and V_{4x} be the indices of the four columns of the image corresponding to the four corners of the vertical projection profile as shown in Fig. 5(a). Let H_{1y}, H_{2y}, H_{3y} and H_{4y} be the indices of the four rows of the image corresponding to the four corners of the horizontal projection profile as shown in Fig. 5(b). Now, when $L_1L_2L_3L_4$ and $R_1R_2R_3R_4$ correspond to the left-skewed and right-skewed versions of the image, from Fig. 6, we can easily see:

$$L_{1x} = R_{4x} = V_{4x} ; L_{4x} = R_{1x} = V_{1x} ; L_{2x} = R_{3x} = V_{2x} ; L_{3x} = R_{2x} = V_{3x}$$
$$L_{2y} = R_{1y} = H_{1y} ; L_{1y} = R_{2y} = H_{2y} ; L_{3y} = R_{4y} = H_{3y} ; L_{4y} = R_{3y} = H_{4y}$$

(3)

Or,

$$L_1 = (V_{4x}, H_{2y}); L_2 = (V_{2x}, H_{1y}); L_3 = (V_{3x}, H_{3y}); L_4 = (V_{1x}, H_{4y})$$
$$R_1 = (V_{1x}, H_{1y}); R_2 = (V_{3x}, H_{2y}); R_3 = (V_{2x}, H_{4y}); R_4 = (V_{4x}, H_{3y})$$

(4)

Therefore we have obtained the coordinates of the skewed versions of the page from the projection profiles of it. Now, it is straightforward to calculate the absolute value of the skew angle θ. From Fig. 6, obviously we can obtain the absolute value of θ, by computing the slope of any of the eight sides of the rectangles $L_1L_2L_3L_4$ and $R_1R_2R_3R_4$. But as we pointed out earlier, the projection profiles are noisy and the page may not be a perfect rectangle; consequently, the coordinates of the skewed rectangles that we obtain from the above set of equations are estimates and not exact. Therefore, we make use of all the eight sides of the two rectangles to obtain the Maximum Likelihood (ML) estimate for the absolute value of θ:

$$|\theta| = \frac{1}{8} \left\{ \left| \tan^{-1}(\frac{L_{2y} - L_{1y}}{L_{2x} - L_{1x}}) \right| + \left| \tan^{-1}(\frac{L_{3x} - L_{2x}}{L_{3y} - L_{2y}}) \right| + \left| \tan^{-1}(\frac{L_{4y} - L_{3y}}{L_{4x} - L_{3x}}) \right| + \left| \tan^{-1}(\frac{L_{1x} - L_{4x}}{L_{1y} - L_{4y}}) \right| + \right.$$
$$\left. \left| \tan^{-1}(\frac{R_{2y} - R_{1y}}{R_{2x} - R_{1x}}) \right| + \left| \tan^{-1}(\frac{R_{3x} - R_{2x}}{R_{3y} - R_{2y}}) \right| + \left| \tan^{-1}(\frac{R_{4y} - R_{3y}}{R_{4x} - R_{3x}}) \right| + \left| \tan^{-1}(\frac{R_{1x} - R_{4x}}{R_{1y} - R_{4y}}) \right| \right\}$$

(5)

As we mentioned earlier, from the projection profiles we can not determine the sign of the skew angle. Therefore, we need another source of information to resolve the ambiguity of whether $L_1L_2L_3L_4$ or $R_1R_2R_3R_4$ corresponds to the true bounding box of the page. We use the fact that the local deviation of image pixels along the two sides (left and right, or up and down) of any of the four borders of the page is "high", and any border of the page corresponds to one side of the true bounding box. More precisely, the deviation of image pixels along the two sides of a line segment belonging to the true bounding box is "higher" than the other candidate line segment belonging to the other bounding box. Let $ALD_w(I, L)$ be the Average Local Deviation function which maps an area of the image I specified by the line segment L and thickness w to an integer in [0, 255], assuming the input image is an 8-bit grayscale one. The output of the function is the average of the absolute differences of the sum of w image pixels on the left and right, or top and bottom, along the line segment. If the line slope is great than 1, meaning the line segment is more vertical than horizontal, we look at the left and right side of it for computing the local deviation. Otherwise, the line slope is less than 1, meaning the line segment is more horizontal than vertical, we look at the top and bottom of it for computing the local deviation. Let $\{ L_i \mid i = 1, 2, ..., n \}$ be the set of coordinates of the image pixels corresponding to the line segment L. We obtain these coordinates by using the Bresenham's line algorithm [14]. Now, the function $ALD_w(I, L)$ can be formally defined as follows:

$$ALD_w(I,L) = \frac{1}{w.n} \left(H\left(\frac{|L_{ny} - L_{1y}|}{|L_{nx} - L_{1x}|} - 1 \right) \left| \sum_{i=1}^{n} \sum_{t=1}^{w} I(L_{iy}, L_{ix} - t) - \sum_{i=1}^{n} \sum_{t=1}^{w} I(L_{iy}, L_{ix} + t) \right| + \right.$$
$$\left. H\left(\frac{|L_{nx} - L_{1x}|}{|L_{ny} - L_{1y}|} - 1 \right) \left| \sum_{i=1}^{n} \sum_{t=1}^{w} I(L_{iy} - t, L_{ix}) - \sum_{i=1}^{n} \sum_{t=1}^{w} I(L_{iy} + t, L_{ix}) \right| \right) \tag{6}$$

Where $H(x)$ is the Heaviside step function.

Having defined the ALD function, we can check which of the rectangles $L_1L_2L_3L_4$ or $R_1R_2R_3R_4$ corresponds to the true bounding box of the page. If $L_1L_2L_3L_4$ is the true bounding box, then $ALD_w(I, L_1L_2)$ is higher than $ALD_w(I, R_1R_2)$, and vice versa. The same proposition holds true for the other three pairs of sides: L_2L_3 and R_2R_3, L_3L_4 and R_3R_4, and L_4L_1 and R_4R_1. As we do not assume the document page must have perfectly straight borders (look at the top border of the document page of Fig. 1(c) for example), we use all the four propositions to calculate the sign of the skew angle by taking a simple majority vote. We never encountered a case of a draw in our experiments. But if it happens, for example when the ALD function for two sides of $L_1L_2L_3L_4$ is higher than the two corresponding sides of $R_1R_2R_3R_4$ and is lower for the other two sides, it is either because 1) the skew angle is too small, and so we do not need to correct the skew at all, or 2) the page borders are very jagged, in which case we can try a larger value for w, for example we can multiply it by 2, and then calculate the ALD propositions again.

Having obtained the absolute value of the skew angle and the sign of it, we can correct the page skew by rotating the image by $-\theta$ around the center of the page which is the intersection of the diagonals of the bounding box.

The coordinates of the bounding box after skew correction, P_1, P_2, P_3 and P_4 (according to the naming convention of Fig. 6), determine the page margins. We again use the ML estimates:

$$\text{left margin} = (P_{1x} + P_{4x})/2 \tag{7}$$

$$\text{right margin} = (P_{2x} + P_{3x})/2 \tag{8}$$

$$\text{top margin} = (P_{1y} + P_{2y})/2 \tag{9}$$

$$\text{bottom margin} = (P_{3y} + P_{4y})/2 \tag{10}$$

3 Experimental Results

We tested our proposed algorithm on a database containing 219 French and Arabic document images with different types of margin noise, layouts and back-ground/foreground intensity levels. As only a small percentage of the documents were skewed (25 documents in total), we added some artificially generated skewed document images to the database by randomly selecting a set of the real documents and rotating each one by a random angle within $-\pi/6$ to $\pi/6$. There were 63 of these artificially skewed samples so we obtained an equal number of straight and skewed document images. With $K = 30$ and $w = 10$ fixed throughout all the experiments, our proposed algorithm successfully estimated the skew angle (with a standard deviation of less than 0.25 degrees) and removed margins in all cases. It should be mentioned that the algorithm performance is not very sensitive to the values of K and w. We expect the algorithm to have the same performance for a wide range of values for these two parameters.

4 Conclusion

In this paper, we proposed an original algorithm for simultaneous skew correction and margin removal for document images, based upon the detection of document corners from projection profiles. The algorithm is fast (linear in the number of image pixels) and robust. We designed the algorithm in such a way that it can handle any type of document image without making any restrictive assumptions. The algorithm doest not need the input page of document to be a perfect and axis-aligned rectangle. The algorithm can handle skew, non-right-angled corners, and jagged page borders. We verified the efficiency of the algorithm by applying it to a collection of document images with different types of margin noise, layouts and intensity levels and the algorithm was successful in all cases.

Acknowledgments

The authors would like to thank Ms. Teresa Bowyer for proofreading a previous draft of this manuscript. They would also like to thank the anonymous reviewers for their insightful comments.

References

1. Manmatha, R., Rothfeder, J.L.: A Scale Space Approach for Automatically Segmenting Words from Historical Handwritten Documents. IEEE Trans. Pattern Anal. Mach. Intell. 27, 1212–1225 (2005)
2. Peerawit, W., Kawtrakul, A.: Marginal noise removal from document images using edge density. In: 4th Information and Computer Engineering Postgraduate Workshop, Phuket, Thailand (2004)
3. Fan, K.-C., Wang, Y.-K., Lay, T.-R.: Marginal noise removal of document images. Pattern Recognition 35, 2593–2611 (2002)

4. Shafait, F., van Beusekom, J., Keysers, D., Breuel, T.: Page Frame Detection for Marginal Noise Removal from Scanned Documents. In: Ersbøll, B.K., Pedersen, K.S. (eds.) SCIA 2007. LNCS, vol. 4522, pp. 651–660. Springer, Heidelberg (2007)
5. Shafait, F., van Beusekom, J., Keysers, D., Breuel, T.M.: Document cleanup using page frame detection. International Journal of Document Analysis and Recognition 11, 81–96 (2008)
6. Du, X., Pan, W., Bui, T.D.: Text Line Segmentation in Handwritten Documents Using Mumford-Shah Model. In: Proceedings of the 11th International Conference on Frontiers in Handwriting Recognition (ICFHR 2008), Montreal, Canada (2008)
7. Li, Y., Zheng, Y., Doermann, D., Jaeger, S.: Script independent text line segmentation in freestyle handwritten documents. IEEE Trans. Pattern Analysis and Machine Intelligence 30, 1313–1329 (2008)
8. Stamatopoulos, N., Gatos, B., Kesidis, A.: Automatic Borders Detection of Camera Document Images. In: 2nd International Workshop on Camera-Based Document Analysis and Recognition (CBDAR 2007), Curitiba, Brazil, pp. 71–78 (2007)
9. Le, D.X., Thoma, G.R., Wechsler, H.: Automated Borders Detection and Adaptive Segmentation for Binary Document Images. In: Proceedings of the International Conference on Pattern Recognition (ICPR 1996) Volume III-Volume 7276, p. 737. IEEE Computer Society, Los Alamitos (1996)
10. Ávila, B.T., Lins, R.D.: Efficient Removal of Noisy Borders from Monochromatic Documents. In: Campilho, A.C., Kamel, M.S. (eds.) ICIAR 2004. LNCS, vol. 3212, pp. 249–256. Springer, Heidelberg (2004)
11. Cinque, L., Levialdi, S., Lombardi, L., Tanimoto, S.: Segmentation of page images having artifacts of photocopying and scanning. Pattern Recognition 35, 1167–1177 (2002)
12. Zhang, Z., Tan, C.L.: Recovery of Distorted Document Images from Bound Volumes. In: Proceedings of the Sixth International Conference on Document Analysis and Recognition, p. 429. IEEE Computer Society, Los Alamitos (2001)
13. Te-Hsiu, S., Chih-Chung, L., Po-Shen, Y., Fang-Chih, T.: Boundary-based corner detection using K-cosine. In: IEEE International Conference on Systems, Man and Cybernetics, 2007. ISIC, pp. 1106–1111 (2007)
14. Bresenham, J.E.: Algorithm for computer control of a digital plotter. IBM Systems Journal 4(1), 25–30 (1965)

Dense Two-Frame Stereo Correspondence by Self-organizing Neural Network

Marco Vanetti, Ignazio Gallo, and Elisabetta Binaghi

Department of Computer Science and Communication
Università degli Studi dell'Insubria
via Mazzini 5, Varese, Italy

Abstract. This work aims at defining an extension of a competitive method for matching correspondences in stereoscopic image analysis. The method we extended was proposed by Venkatesh, Y.V. *et al* where the authors extend a Self-Organizing Map by changing the neural weights updating phase in order to solve the correspondence problem within a two-frame area matching approach and producing dense disparity maps. In the present paper we have extended the method mentioned by adding some details that lead to better results. Experimental studies were conducted to evaluate and compare the solution proposed.

Keywords: Stereo matching, self-organizing map, disparity map, occlusions.

1 Introduction

Stereoscopic image analysis deals with the reconstruction of the three-dimensional shape of objects in a physical scene from multiple 2-D images captured from different viewpoints [1,2]. The accuracy of the overall reconstruction process depends on the accuracy with which the correspondence problem is solved. It concerns the matching of points or other kinds of primitives in two (or more) images such that the matched image points are the projections of the same point in the scene. The disparity map obtained from the matching stage is then used to compute the 3D positions of the scene points given the imaging geometry. A substantial amount of work has been done on stereo matching usually explored using area-based and feature-based approaches. Other types of stereo matching methods such as Bayesian, phase-based, wavelet-based and diffusion-based techniques have also been developed [3]. Despite important achievements, the high accuracy demand in diversified application domains such as object recognition, robotics and virtual reality [4] create the premise for further investigation. In previous works we investigated the potentialities of Neural Networks in Stereomatching basing our solutions on supervised learning [5,6].

Motivated by the acknowledged biological plausibility of unsupervised neural learning, Venkatesh et al. in [7] explored the potential of Self Organizing Maps (SOM) to solve the correspondence problem conceived as imitation of the stereo-perception ability of the human visual system (HVS). In order to take care of stereo constraints, the authors introduced certain modifications within the original SOM model giving rise to the modified SOM (MSOM) model in which the estimation of the disparity map from a stereo pair of images is obtained by computing the amount of deformation required

P. Foggia, C. Sansone, and M. Vento (Eds.): ICIAP 2009, LNCS 5716, pp. 1035–1042, 2009.

to transform it into the other image. As seen in our experiments, the MSOM model has many special properties and potentialities, but also highlight limitations especially in dealing with occluded areas. Proceeding from these results, in this paper we proposed an extension of the MSOM for the estimation of stereo disparity. The salient main aspects of the solution proposed are the extension of matching primitives from pixel intensity to a weighted composition of RGB values, the definition of a contextual strategy within the matching cost computation task and finally the explicit handling of occlusions and direct processing within occlusion edges. The improved MSOM model was experimentally evaluated basing on the analysis of well known test images including data with true disparity maps. The aim of the experiment is twofold: to measure the performances of the model as functions of the most important parameters, and to compare performances with those obtained by well known approaches recently published in literature.

2   The MSOM Model

This section describes the MSOM model proposed in [7] where the authors extend a Self-Organizing Map (SOM) neural network [8] by changing the neural weights updating phase. The base idea of the model MSOM is the following: *the matching between pixels of I_L and I_R, the left or reference image and the right or matching image in the stereo pair, is expressed in terms of the winning neurons in the network MSOM.*

The Algorithm 1 summarize the MSOM method through three main steps: *initialization*, *winner neuron selection* and *weights update*. During *initialization*, the neurons in the competitive layer are initialized with position and gray level of the pixels in the reference image I_L. During learning the input to the network is a randomly selected pixel $I_R(m, n)$ of the matching image. The learning phase proceeds searching the global minimum of a "Euclidean distance" between the input vector and the weights of the neurons (see equation (1)). If the coordinates of the winning neuron are (φ_r, φ_c), then we expect a matching between pixels $I_L(\varphi_r, \varphi_c)$ and $I_R(m, n)$. Finally, the *weights update* step, where only the first two components w_1 and w_2 of each neuron are updated (see equation (2)). From the trained MSOM model we can build the two disparity maps d^{hor} and d^{ver} of horizontal and vertical disparities respectively. In particular from the equation (4) is possible to construct the disparity values using the weights w_1 and w_2 of each neuron.

3   The StereoMSOM Model

The method proposed here, the StereoSOM, extends the MSOM algorithm with the main aims to speed up the convergence and increase the precision of the computed disparity map. The complete description of StereoSOM model is showed in Algorithm 2.

To reduce the convergence time of the StereoSOM algorithm we adapted the algorithm MSOM to work with epipolar images and confined the search for the corresponding pixel in a limited area $\{n + d_{min}, \ldots, n + d_{max}\}$ (see the requirements of Algorithm 2 and equation (5)). Moreover the learning algorithm of our method is divided into two distinct phases that we called the *ordering phase* and the *tuning phase*,

Algorithm 1. The MSOM algorithm

Require: To selection a reference image I_L and the corresponding matching image I_R having dimension $W \times H$;

Require: to create a matrix of neurons $n_{rc} = [w_1^{rc}, w_2^{rc}, w_3^{rc}]$ where $r = 1 \ldots H$ and $c = 1 \ldots W$;

Require: $\forall r$ and $\forall c$ initialize neurons n_{rc}: $w_1^{rc} = r$, $w_2^{rc} = c$ and $w_3^{rc} = I_L(r, c)$;

1: **for** $i = 1$ to $Iterations$ **do**
2:     randomly extract a pixel $I_R(m, n)$, $m = 1 \ldots H$ and $n = 1 \ldots W$;
3:     construct the corresponding input pattern $(i_1^{mn}, i_2^{mn}, i_3^{mn})$ where $i_1^{mn} = m$, $i_2^{mn} = n$ and $i_3^{mn} = I_R(m, n)$;
4:     discover the coordinates (φ_r, φ_c) of the winning neuron as follows:

$$(\varphi_r, \varphi_c) = \underset{r \in \{1, \ldots, H\}, c \in \{1, \ldots, W\}}{\arg \min} \sqrt{\sum_{k=1}^{3} (w_k^{rc} - i_k^{mn})^2} \tag{1}$$

5:     update the weights of neurons n_{rc} as follows:
6:     **for** $r = 1$ to H and $c = 1$ to W **do**
7:       **for** $k = 1$ to 2 **do**
8:       update the weight w_k^{rc} of neuron n_{rc} as follows:

$$w_k^{rc} \leftarrow w_k^{rc} + h_k(r, c) \, g_k(r, c) \left(i_k^{(r-(\varphi_r - m))(c-(\varphi_c - n))} - w_k^{rc} \right) \tag{2}$$

    where

$$h_k(r, c) = \eta \exp \left(-\frac{(r - \varphi_r)^2 + (c - \varphi_c)^2}{2\sigma_h^2} \right) \tag{3}$$

    and $g_k(r, c) = \exp \left(-\frac{(w_3^{rc} - w_3^{\varphi_r \varphi_c})^2}{2\sigma_g^2} \right)$

9:     **end for**
10:    **end for**
11: **end for**
12: compute horizontal and vertical disparity maps:

$$\begin{cases} d^{hor}(r, c) = c - w_2^{rc} \\ d^{ver}(r, c) = r - w_1^{rc} \end{cases} \tag{4}$$

characterized simply by different values of the configuration parameters. The parameters setting in the ordering phase leads to an approximate solution in a very short time leaving to the subsequent tuning phase its refinement. In particular the tuning phase improves the first rough calculation, updating the neural weights with small entities.

The StereoSOM model considers as matching primitives the color attributes. For color images encoded in RGB, color information will be presented in input to the network with $i_{C_1}^{rc} = R$, $i_{C_2}^{rc} = G$, $i_{C_3}^{rc} = B$. The overall matching primitives are processed within the network weighting the relative importance of the individual components by means of appropriate weights ρ_k (see equation (5)).

Within the weight updating procedure, an explicit definition of the winner neuron's neighborhood is included. In particular the new function defined in (7) depends from three parameters α, β e n_{size} considering that the function $\theta\,(r,c)$ has the following form:

$\theta\,(r,c) = \alpha\exp\left(-\frac{(r-\varphi_r)^2+(c-\varphi_c)^2}{2\sigma_h^2}\right)$ with $\sigma_h^2 = \frac{n_{size}^2}{-2\ln\left(\frac{\beta}{\alpha}\right)}$. Assigning a value to these

three parameters means that only an area of size $(2n_{size}+1)^2$ around the winning neuron will be updated.

The following subsections describe two relevant modifications of the MSOM algorithm. The first one concerns the introduction of a new strategy for the search of winning neuron called *Search Eye* (SE), while the second, called *Quality of Search* (QS) concerns the management of occluded areas.

3.1   Search Eye

The winning neuron strategy was updated basing on a moving window procedure: insted of comparing only the weights of the candidate neuron w^{rc}, an overall set of weights within a window is considered in the searching strategy (see (9)).

It is plausible to think that groups of neurons belonging to a single object on the scene have similar intensity and then similar disparities; adjusting the search window to neurons belonging to a single object will then improve the quality of the search process. The winning neuron search function is formalized as follows:

$$(\varphi_r,\varphi_c) = \left(m,\ \underset{c\in\{1,...,W\}}{\arg\min}\ \sum_{\Delta r=-\xi}^{\xi}\sum_{\Delta c=-\xi}^{\xi}\sqrt{\rho_1\left(w_1^{rc}-i_1^{mn}\right)^2+S(r,c,\Delta r,\Delta c)}\right)(9)$$

with $S(r,c,\Delta r,\Delta c) =$

$\sum_{k=2}^{K+1}\left[g_s\left(r+\Delta r,c+\Delta c\right)\rho_k\left(w_k^{(r+\Delta r)(c+\Delta c)}-i_k^{(m+\Delta r)(n+\Delta c)}\right)^2\right]$

and $g_s\,(r,c) = \exp\left(-\frac{\sum_{k=1}^{K}\left(i_{C_k}^{rc}-i_{C_k}^{mn}\right)^2}{2\sigma_s^2}\right)$

3.2   Quality of Search

In order to deal with occlusions and false matching the StereoMSOM algorithm implements a Bidirectional Matching strategy. In the case in which the backward matching, from I_R to I_L fails, the algorithm nullify the weight updating and continue with the next input.

4   Experiments

The experimental activity was supported by test data available on the Web at http:// vision.middlebury.edu/stereo. We selected four test data sets named *Tsukuba*, *Venus*, *Teddy* and *Cones* including stereo image pairs and true disparity (see Fig. 1).

Algorithm 2. The proposed StereoSOM algorithm for epipolar images

Require: To selection a reference image I_L and the corresponding matching image I_R having dimension $W \times H$;

Require: to create a matrix of neurons $n_{rc} = \left[w_1^{rc}, w_{C_1}^{rc} \ldots, w_{C_K}^{rc} \right]$ for generic images having K channels and where $r = 1 \ldots H$ and $c = 1 \ldots W$;

Require: $\forall r$ and $\forall c$ initialize neurons n_{rc}: $w_1^{rc} = c$, and $w_{C_k}^{rc} = I_L\left(r, c, C_k\right)$;

1: **for** $i = 1$ to $Iterations$ **do**
2:    randomly extract a pixel $I_R\left(m, n\right)$;
3:    construct the corresponding input pattern $\left(i_1^{mn}, i_{C_1}^{mn}, \ldots, i_{C_K}^{mn}\right)$ where $i_1^{mn} = n$;
4:    discover the coordinates $\left(\varphi_r, \varphi_c\right)$ of the winning neuron as follows:

$$(\varphi_r, \varphi_c) = \left(m, \underset{c \in \{n+d_{min}, \ldots, n+d_{max}\}}{\arg\min} \sqrt{\sum_{k=1}^{K+1} \left[\rho_k \left(w_k^{rc} - i_k^{mn}\right)^2\right]} \right) \tag{5}$$

5:    update the weights of neurons n_{rc} as follows:
6:    **for** $r = \varphi_r - n_{size}$ to $\varphi_r + n_{size}$ and $r = \varphi_c - n_{size}$ to $\varphi_c + n_{size}$ **do**
7:       update the weight w_1^{rc} of neuron n_{rc} as follows:

$$w_1^{rc} \leftarrow w_1^{rc} + h\left(r, c\right) g\left(r, c\right) \left(i_1^{r(c-(\varphi_c-n))} - w_1^{rc}\right) \tag{6}$$

where

$$h\left(r, c\right) = \begin{cases} \theta\left(r, c\right) & if \ \beta < \theta\left(r, c\right) < 1 \\ 1 & if \ \theta\left(r, c\right) \geq 1 \\ 0 & if \ \theta\left(r, c\right) \leq \beta \end{cases} \tag{7}$$

and $g\left(r, c\right) = \exp\left(-\dfrac{\sum_{k=1}^{K}\left(w_{C_k}^{rc} - w_{C_k}^{\varphi_r\varphi_c}\right)^2}{2\sigma_g^2}\right)$

8:    **end for**
9: **end for**
10: to compute the disparity map:

$$d^{hor}\left(r, c\right) = c - w_1^{rc} \tag{8}$$

Among the quality measures proposed by Scharstein and Szelinski in their papers [3,9] we adopted the percentage of bad matching pixels between the computed disparity map $d_C(x, y)$ and the ground truth map $d_T(x, y)$:

$$PBP_{\delta_d} = \left(\frac{1}{N} \sum (|d_C(x, y) - d_T(x, y)| > \delta_d)\right) \tag{10}$$

In this experiment the proposed StereoSOM algorithm was configured with the following set of parameters tuned with a trial and error procedure: for the ordering phase $\{\xi = 5, \sigma_s^2 = 700, g(r, c) = 1, \rho_1 = 0.001, \rho_2 = \cdots = \rho_{K+1} = 1, n_{size} = [80, 10], \alpha = 1, \beta = 1\}$ and for the tuning phase $\{\xi = 5, \sigma_s^2 = 700, \sigma_g^2 = 80, \rho_1 = 0.05, \rho_2 = \cdots = \rho_{K+1} = 1, n_{size} = 20, \alpha = [6, 1], \beta = [0.5, 0.005]\}$. The parameter expressed as $[a, b]$ vary linearly from a to b during the iterations.

reference image   ground truth   reference image   ground truth

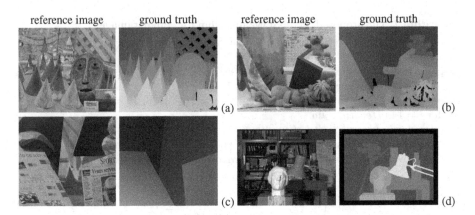

(a)   (b)

(c)   (d)

Fig. 1. Reference image and true disparity map of (a) *Cones*, (b) *Teddy*, (c) *Venus* and (d) *Tsukuba* test

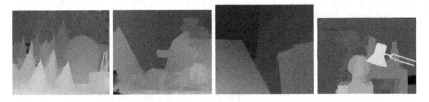

Fig. 2. Best disparity maps of the four dataset considered obtained by applying the proposed StereoSOM algorithm

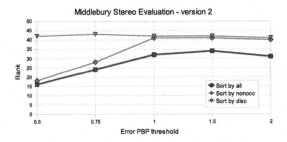

Fig. 3. Rank of StereoSOM algorithm obtained with the Middlebury Stereo Evaluation framewok. The comparison was made with the results of 54 different algorithms, already stored in the database of the framewok.

Fig. 2 shows the final disparity after 10000 iterations of ordering phase and 500000 iterations of tuning. As regard the execution time, the average time over all the four dataset considered is approximatively 100 sec. with 50000 iterations of tuning, running the algorithm over a laptop with an AMD 1800 MHz processor.

The disparity maps obtained (Fig. 2) were submitted to the Middlebury Stereo Evaluation tool, available on the Web at http://vision.middlebury.edu/stereo/eval, computing the PBP_{δ_d} measure over the whole image (ALL), in non occluded

Table 1. Results obtained by StereoSOM algorithm in terms of PBP_{δ_d} after 10000 iterations of ordering

Test image	δ_d	NOCCL	ALL	DISC	Iterations	NOCCL	ALL	DISC	Iterations
Tsukuba	0.5	19.99	20.52	32.26	50000	15.20	15.82	29.33	500000
	0.75	17.35	17.77	28.44		13.28	13.75	26.29	
	1	3.38	3.76	14.54		3.80	4.12	15.16	
	1.5	2.79	3.09	12.09		3.24	3.50	13.00	
	2	2.22	2.47	9.44		2.52	2.73	9.99	
Venus	0.5	6.78	7.43	19.65	50000	5.12	5.83	18.98	500000
	0.75	1.66	2.22	12.35		1.27	1.75	11.03	
	1	0.98	1.42	10.31		0.83	1.19	9.24	
	1.5	0.66	0.99	7.53		0.53	0.83	6.23	
	2	0.53	0.79	6.20		0.44	0.65	5.09	
Teddy	0.5	17.14	23.58	34.36	50000	16.24	22.68	32.50	500000
	0.75	12.50	18.49	26.28		11.94	17.92	24.95	
	1	10.41	15.73	22.39		10.26	15.54	21.30	
	1.5	7.77	12.06	17.42		8.02	12.20	16.26	
	2	6.15	9.82	13.80		6.30	9.89	12.47	
Cones	0.5	12.3	18.74	26.89	50000	10.9	17.25	22.61	500000
	0.75	7.96	14.34	20.04		6.76	12.99	16.30	
	1	6.31	12.40	16.57		5.35	11.33	13.61	
	1.5	4.91	10.51	13.32		4.15	9.71	11.10	
	2	4.11	9.35	11.35		3.46	8.65	9.30	

Table 2. Results obtained by MSOM algorithm in terms of PBP_{δ_d} after 10000 iterations of ordering and 1000000 iterations of tuning

Test image	δ_d	NOCCL	ALL	DISC	Test image	δ_d	NOCCL	ALL	DISC
Tsukuba	0.5	43.39	43.9	60.5	Teddy	0.5	33.76	38.72	54.82
	0.75	39.94	40.41	56.61		0.75	26.66	31.54	44.7
	1	22.97	23.6	45.9		1	23.62	28.11	39.72
	1.5	19.3	19.88	38.3		1.5	20.6	24.29	33.71
	2	9.16	9.68	27.38		2	18.75	22.07	29.73
Venus	0.5	31.57	32.36	53.98	Cones	0.5	40.56	44.95	62.9
	0.75	20.66	21.48	42.45		0.75	32.44	37.24	54.35
	1	15.17	15.91	36.24		1	27.93	32.83	48.66
	1.5	10.93	11.58	29.3		1.5	22.84	27.73	41.31
	2	7.97	8.46	22.82		2	19.6	24.37	35.67

regions (NOCCL) and in depth discontinuity regions (DISC). The evaluation tool automatically compared other stereo matching algorithms whose performances are available on the same Web site.

The Fig. 3 shows the rank of our algorithm compared with the results of 54 different algorithms. Observing this figure we see a sharp rise in our ranking algorithm varying the threshold δ_d. This behavior leads us to believe that the proposed algorithm is particularly suitable in the management of disparity maps with real values. In order to improve furtherly the performance of the StereoSOM algorithm new solutions have to be investigated for managing discontinuity areas.

The complete set of results obtained is shown in Table 1. The StereoSOM algorithm shows a globally satisfactory competitive behavior, even if it did not prevail on some of the algorithms involved in the comparison. The comparison with the MSOM model was done using an our implementation of the algorithm and evaluating the disparity map through the same tool available from the Middlebury website. The comparison result is available on the Table 2.

5   Conclusions and Future Works

Our objective in this study was to investigate an extension of the existing method MSOM, aimed at solving the correspondence problem within a two-frame area matching approach and producing dense disparity maps. The new StereoSOM model was tested on standard data sets and compared with several stereo algorithms available in the Middlebury Web site. The proposed StereoSOM algorithm shows globally a satisfactory competitive behavior. Salients aspects of our solution are the local processing of the stereo images, the use of a limited set of directly available features and the applicability without the image segmentation.

In future works we want to improve the behavior of the StereoSOM method in discontinuities and occluded areas. Moreover a further investigation of the robustness under non epipolar conditions will be investigated.

References

1. Ballard, D.H., Brown, C.M.: Computer Vision. Prentice-Hall, Englewood Cliffs (1982)
2. Faugeras, O.: Three-dimensional computer vision: a geometric viewpoint. MIT Press, Cambridge (1993)
3. Scharstein, D., Szeliski, R.: A taxonomy and evaluation of dense two-frame stereo correspondence algorithms. International Journal of Computer Vision 47, 7–42 (2002)
4. Bishop, C.M.: Neural Networks for Pattern Recognition. Oxford University Press, Oxford (1995)
5. Binaghi, E., Gallo, I., Marino, G., Raspanti, M.: Neural adaptive stereo matching. Pattern Recognition Letters 25, 1743–1758 (2004)
6. Gallo, I., Binaghi, E., Raspanti, M.: Neural disparity computation for dense two-frame stereo correspondence. Pattern Recogn. Lett. 29(5), 673–687 (2008)
7. Venkatesh, Y.V., Raja, S.K., Kumar, A.J.: On the application of a modified self-organizing neural network to estimate stereo disparity. IEEE Transactions on Image Processing 16(11), 2822–2829 (2007)
8. Kohonen, T.: Self-organizing formation of topologically correct feature maps. Biological Cybernetics 43(1), 59–69 (1982)
9. Scharstein, D., Szeliski, R.: High-accuracy stereo depth maps using structured light. In: Proceedings. 2003 IEEE Computer Society Conference on Computer Vision and Pattern Recognition, vol. 1, pp. I–195–I–202 (2003)

Towards a Linear Combination of Dichotomizers by Margin Maximization

Claudio Marrocco, Mario Molinara,
Maria Teresa Ricamato, and Francesco Tortorella

DAEIMI - Università degli Studi di Cassino, Cassino, Italy
{c.marrocco,m.molinara,mt.ricamato,tortorella}@unicas.it

Abstract. When dealing with two-class problems the combination of several dichotomizers is an established technique to improve the classification performance. In this context the margin is considered a central concept since several theoretical results show that improving the margin on the training set is beneficial for the generalization error of a classifier. In particular, this has been analyzed with reference to learning algorithms based on boosting which aim to build strong classifiers through the combination of many weak classifiers. In this paper we try to experimentally verify if the margin maximization can be beneficial also when combining already trained classifiers. We have employed an algorithm for evaluating the weights of a linear convex combination of dichotomizers so as to maximize the margin of the combination on the training set. Several experiments performed on publicly available data sets have shown that a combination based on margin maximization could be particularly effective if compared with other established fusion methods.

Keywords: Multiple Classifier Systems, Two-class classification, Margins, Linear Combination.

1   Introduction

In order to improve the classification performance a widely used technique to construct effective systems in many real world problems consists in combining more classifiers so as to take advantage of the strengths of the single classifiers and avoid their weaknesses. Combination is therefore considered a profitable solution in applications where some single classifiers are already available and their fusion could represent a convenient way to obtain a more proficient classification systems without building a new classifier from the scratch.

A huge number of possible combination rules has been proposed up to now [10]. Among them, the linear combination is certainly the most popular choice for application purposes due to both its simplicity and effectiveness [6] and for this reason it has been thoroughly studied to provide a theoretical model of its behavior with respect to the performance of the combined classifiers and the correlation among their outputs [6,16].

This can be particularly useful in two-class problems that require highly discriminating classifiers. In this context linear combiners are generally built at the

P. Foggia, C. Sansone, and M. Vento (Eds.): ICIAP 2009, LNCS 5716, pp. 1043–1052, 2009.

aim of minimizing the classification error and guarantee a good generalization degree of the recognition/verification system.

In machine learning field the issue of generalization has been particularly analyzed to explain the reduction of the generalization error achieved by Adaboost. To this aim, Schapire et al. [14] introduced the concept of margin which can be considered as a measure of the classification confidence. More precisely, while the sign of the margin indicates the correctness of the classifier, the magnitude estimates the confidence of the classifier in making its prediction on a given sample. Moreover, the margin has a direct connection with the generalization capability of the classifier as proved in several papers [1,3,15] which suggested upper bounds on generalization error expressed in terms of the classifier margin.

In [12] we focused on the concept of margin to evaluate the weights of a convex combination able to maximize the minimum margin of the combination on the training set of a multibiometrics problem. Starting from this point we further analyze the concept of margin to increase the generalization performance of the algorithm. To this aim, in this paper we introduce a soft margin-based combination rule that relaxes the constraint of the optimization problem allowing the system to achieve much better generalization results. Maximizing the smallest soft margin, we do not force outlier values to be assigned to their possible wrong label but we allow for some errors so as to find a trade off between margin and the contribution of each pattern to the decision. Several experiments performed on publicly available data sets have shown that this method is particularly effective if compared with other established linear fusion methods.

The rest of the paper is organized as follows: in sect. 2 the concept of margin and the difference between hard and soft margin are briefly shown while in sect. 3 the method for maximizing the minimum soft margin is described. In sect. 4 the results obtained on some benchmark data sets are presented and discussed. and finally, in sect. 5 some conclusions and an outline of further researches are briefly reported.

2   Margins and Generalization

We consider a standard two-class classification problem defined on a training set S containing N samples $(\mathbf{x}_i, y_i), i = 1, \cdots, N$ where $\mathbf{x}_i$ belongs to an instance space X and the labels y_i to the set $\{-1, +1\}$. A classifier f can be described as a mapping from X to the interval $[-1, +1]$ such that a sample $\mathbf{x}_i \in X$ is assigned to one of the classes according to $\mathrm{sgn}\,(f(\mathbf{x}_i))$. If we assume that y_i is the correct label of $\mathbf{x}_i$, the *sample margin* (or *hard margin*) associated to $\mathbf{x}_i$ is given by $y_i f(\mathbf{x}_i)$. As a consequence f provides a wrong prediction for $\mathbf{x}_i$ if the sample margin is negative and therefore the margin can be interpreted as a measure of the confidence in the prediction of the combined classifier.

The margin theory has been widely used in ensemble learning to analyze the generalization effectiveness of Adaboost. As it is well known, this algorithm generates weak classifiers via dinamically reweighting training samples on the basis of previous classification results; the final classifier is obtained by a convex combination of the constructed weak classifiers. In particular, in [14] it has been observed that AdaBoost continues to train even after the training error of the combination is zero that implies an improvement in the generalization error. It has been also proved that this behavior is due to the continue increasing of the margins of the samples in the training set. Some theoretical bounds have been determined on the generalization error of linear classifiers [14,4,9] showing that it improves with the *classifier margin* (or *minimum margin*), i.e. with the smallest margin of a sample over the training set S: $\mu(f) = \min_i y_i f(\mathbf{x}_i)$. The classifier margin has an intuitive meaning [5]: it measures the distance that the classifier can travel in the feature space without changing the way it labels any of the sample points. Therefore the size of the minimum margin (i.e. the margin related to the worst result on the training set) appears to be the most relevant factor for improving generalization.

On this basis, some experiments have been done aimed at improving the generalization performance of Adaboost by using a combination of the generated classifiers explicitly based on minimum margin maximization [7]. In [4] Breiman proposed a modified algorithm, called Arc-GV, suitable for this task showing that it asymptotically maximizes the margin. However, the results showed that these modified versions of Adaboost perform generally worse than the original one. A possible reason is that the boosting approach tries to improve their margins focusing on the most difficult samples but with a significant possibility of overfitting when dealing with very difficult samples [13]. This problem could be further emphasized by a minimum margin maximization combination which would give higher weights to the classifiers with higher minimum margins, but more prone to overfitting. Therefore, we need to relax the hard margin and allow for a possibility of mistrusting the data. To this aim, it is possible to introduce a non-negative quantity $\xi(\mathbf{x}_i)$ which expresses the possible mistrust on a sample $\mathbf{x}_i$ and define the *soft margin* as a trade off between the hard margin and $\xi(\mathbf{x}_i)$: $y_i f(\mathbf{x}_i) + C\xi(\mathbf{x}_i)$. In this way we can again focus on the minimum margin but considering now the smallest soft margin so expecting to observe less overfitting with respect to the hard margin. As a final remark it is worth noting that the idea of minimizing margins is reminiscent of the idea of support vector machines [18]. There, however, one tries to find a linear combination that achieves the best worst separation in the sense of Euclidean and therefore it turns out that SVMs maximize margins using quadratic rather than linear programs.

However, all these studies have only been focused on Boosting algorithms which construct from scratch an ensemble of classifiers as different instances of the same base learning algorithm. As far as we know, the potential effectiveness of such a combination has not yet been examined when the classifiers of the ensemble are built independently and not according to a boosting approach.

3   Soft Margin Maximization via Linear Programming

Let us now extend the concept of margin to the combination of K already trained classifiers $f_j(\mathbf{x}) \to [-1, +1]$ with $j = 1, \cdots, K$. The hard margin provided by the j-th classifier over the i-th sample is defined as:

$$\mu_{ij} = y_i \cdot f_j(\mathbf{x}_i) \quad \forall i = 1, \ldots, N, \quad \forall j = 1, \ldots, K \tag{1}$$

so that the f_j correctly classifies $\mathbf{x}_i$ iff $\mu_{ij} > 0$. If we now consider the linear convex combination of the K classifiers:

$$f_c(\mathbf{x}) = \sum_{j=1}^{K} w_j f_j(\mathbf{x}) \tag{2}$$

where $w_j \geq 0$ and $\sum_{j=1}^{K} w_j = 1$, the hard margin provided by f_c over the i-th sample is

$$\mu_i = y_i \cdot \left(\sum_{j=1}^{K} w_j f_j(\mathbf{x}_i) \right) = \sum_{j=1}^{K} w_j \mu_{ij} \quad \forall i = 1, \ldots, N \tag{3}$$

while the hard margin of f_c is $\mu = \min_i \mu_i$. However, as said in the previous section, the hard margin could not generalize well on noisy data and therefore we consider the maximization of the soft margin. Since μ depends on the weights $\mathbf{w} = \{w_1, w_2, \cdots, w_K\}$, we can choose such weights to make the hard margin as large as possible penalizing it with positive slack variables ξ_i. In this way we have a max-min problem which can be written as:

$$\text{maximize} \left(\min_i \sum_{j=1}^{K} w_j \mu_{ij} - C \sum_{i=1}^{N} \xi_i \right)$$

$$\text{subject to} \quad \sum_{j=1}^{K} w_j = 1$$

$$w_j \geq 0 \qquad \forall j = 1, \ldots, K$$
$$\xi_i \geq 0 \qquad \forall i = 1, \ldots, N$$

The penalizing term in the objective function is introduced to avoid large values for the slack variables ξ. This allows that some samples have margins larger than μ according to the value of the trade off constant C.

The problem can be recast as a linear problem [17] if we introduce the margin μ as a new variable:

$$\text{maximize} \quad \mu - C \sum_{i=1}^{N} \xi_i$$
$$\text{subject to}$$

$$\sum_{j=1}^{K} w_j \mu_{ij} \geq \mu - \xi_i \quad \forall i = 1, \ldots, N$$

$$\sum_{j=1}^{K} w_j = 1$$

$$w_j \geq 0 \qquad \forall j = 1, \ldots, K$$
$$\xi_i \geq 0 \qquad \forall i = 1, \ldots, N$$

Let us now collect the margins in a $N \times K$ matrix $\mathbf{M} = \{\mu_{ij}\}$, the weights in a vector $\mathbf{w}$, the slack variables in a vector $\boldsymbol{\xi}$ and let us define $\mathbf{e}_t$ as the column vector consisting of t ones and $\mathbf{z}_t$ as the column vector consisting of t zeros. We can then rewrite the problem in vectorial notation:

$$\text{maximize} \quad \mu - C\mathbf{e}_N^T \boldsymbol{\xi}$$

$$\text{subject to}$$

$$\mu \mathbf{e}_N - \mathbf{M}\mathbf{w} - \boldsymbol{\xi} \leq \mathbf{z}_N$$
$$\mathbf{e}_K^T \mathbf{w} = 1$$
$$\mathbf{w} \geq \mathbf{z}_K$$
$$\boldsymbol{\xi} \geq \mathbf{z}_N$$

Finally, considering $\mathbf{I}_t$ as the t-dimensional identity matrix we can write the problem in block-matrix form:

$$\text{maximize} \quad \begin{bmatrix} \mathbf{z}_K^T & -C\mathbf{e}_N^T & 1 \end{bmatrix} \begin{bmatrix} \mathbf{w} \\ \boldsymbol{\xi} \\ \mu \end{bmatrix}$$

$$\text{subject to} \tag{4}$$

$$\begin{bmatrix} -\mathbf{M} & -\mathbf{I}_N & \mathbf{e}_N \\ \mathbf{e}_K^T & \mathbf{z}_N^T & 0 \end{bmatrix} \begin{bmatrix} \mathbf{w} \\ \boldsymbol{\xi} \\ \mu \end{bmatrix} \begin{matrix} \leq \\ = \end{matrix} \begin{bmatrix} \mathbf{z}_N \\ 1 \end{bmatrix}$$

$$\mathbf{w} \geq \mathbf{z}_K$$
$$\boldsymbol{\xi} \geq \mathbf{z}_N$$

As a final remark, it is worth noting that to solve this problem we could use any one of the numerous linear programming methods available. However, it should be taken into account that the number of constraints could be very large since it equals the number of training samples.

4   Experiments

The effectiveness of the proposed fusion rule has been evaluated on 10 two-class data sets taken from the UCI Repository of Machine Learning Database [2] with different sizes and class skew. The features were previously scaled so as to have zero mean and unit standard deviation. To avoid any bias due to the particular partition of data set, 10 runs of a multiple hold out procedure have been performed for each data set. In each run, the data set has been parted into three sets: a training set to train the classifier, a tuning set to estimate the optimal weights (i.e. to train the combiner) and a test set to evaluate the compared combination methods.

The soft margin fusion rule (hereafter called SM) has been compared to the hard margin fusion rule (HM) and to two single combination rules: the simple

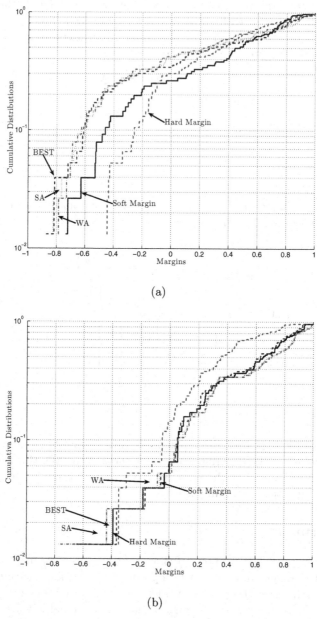

Fig. 1. Margin distributions graphs for the employed combination rules on the House data set when using WRLC (a) and ADAR (b) classifiers. The scale on y-axis is logarithmic.

average (SA) and the weighted average (WA) defined as $f(x) = \sum_{j=1}^{K} w_j f_j(x)$ where $w_j = \frac{Error_j}{\sum_{j=1}^{K} Error_j}$, i.e. where the classifiers are weighted according to the provided error rate. For the sake of completeness the results obtained by the best base classifier (BEST in the following tables) employed in each combination have been reported. All the data in input to the combiner have been normalized using the min-max normalization [8]. Then, to assign a sample to the positive or negative class a threshold to be imposed on the output of the combiner has been evaluated on the tuning set. In particular, using the Receiver Operating Characteristic (ROC) curve we determined the threshold value that minimizes the empirical error rate on the tuning set.

As base classifiers, we choose two different models. The first one is a random linear classifier, called *Weak Random Linear Classifier (WRLC)* [11] that allows us to easily build several simple classifiers by randomly assigning the coefficients of the linear discriminant function. If the error rate evaluated on the training set is lower than or equal to 0.5 the coefficients are held, otherwise the signs of the coefficients are reversed so as to invert the outputs of the classifier and ensure an error rate lower than 0.5. The second model is an AdaBoost classifier, implemented by means of the *Modest AdaBoost* algorithm [19]. The used weak learner is a CART decision tree with maximum depth equal to 3 and decision

Table 1. Mean error rate obtained using 4 base classifiers

Data Sets	SM	HM	SA	WA	BEST
			WRLC		
Australian	0.278 (0.013)	0.290 (0.022)	0.286 (0.011)	0.286 (0.011)	0.280 (0.005)
Balance	0.197 (0.023)	0.206 (0.034)	0.309 (0.032)	0.330 (0.025)	0.410 (0.015)
Breast	0.041 (0.003)	0.067 (0.010)	0.043 (0.005)	0.044 (0.005)	0.061 (0.003)
Cleveland	0.244 (0.010)	0.265 (0.014)	0.249 (0.011)	0.254 (0.009)	0.279 (0.011)
Hayes	0.325 (0.017)	0.361 (0.023)	0.353 (0.019)	0.354 (0.016)	0.371 (0.016)
Housing	0.273 (0.010)	0.308 (0.021)	0.314 (0.016)	0.324 (0.017)	0.309 (0.014)
Ionosphere	0.279 (0.014)	0.314 (0.025)	0.317 (0.013)	0.323 (0.013)	0.326 (0.008)
Liver	0.432 (0.010)	0.436 (0.013)	0.446 (0.011)	0.449 (0.009)	0.437 (0.005)
Pima	0.299 (0.013)	0.347 (0.016)	0.328 (0.011)	0.332 (0.013)	0.321 (0.018)
Sonar	0.346 (0.013)	0.376 (0.026)	0.370 (0.015)	0.369 (0.015)	0.359 (0.010)
			ADAR		
Australian	0.140 (0.004)	0.180 (0.013)	0.142 (0.004)	0.143 (0.004)	0.145 (0.004)
Balance	0.080 (0.004)	0.096 (0.007)	0.078 (0.004)	0.078 (0.004)	0.089 (0.004)
Breast	0.040 (0.001)	0.067 (0.004)	0.037 (0.002)	0.038 (0.002)	0.047 (0.001)
Cleveland	0.202 (0.009)	0.247 (0.015)	0.227 (0.009)	0.226 (0.009)	0.240 (0.006)
Hayes	0.215 (0.011)	0.278 (0.026)	0.211 (0.010)	0.209 (0.010)	0.240 (0.016)
Housing	0.133 (0.004)	0.164 (0.008)	0.138 (0.004)	0.138 (0.004)	0.143 (0.004)
Ionosphere	0.080 (0.003)	0.155 (0.013)	0.083 (0.004)	0.085 (0.005)	0.112 (0.003)
Liver	0.285 (0.009)	0.334 (0.020)	0.286 (0.011)	0.289 (0.011)	0.321 (0.010)
Pima	0.250 (0.008)	0.284 (0.015)	0.273 (0.016)	0.273 (0.017)	0.262 (0.006)
Sonar	0.216 (0.013)	0.248 (0.019)	0.222 (0.009)	0.225 (0.009)	0.206 (0.006)

Table 2. Mean error rate obtained using 7 base classifiers

Data Sets	SM	HM	SA	WA	BEST
		WRLC			
Australian	0.272 (0.009)	0.298 (0.017)	0.287 (0.009)	0.288 (0.009)	0.286 (0.009)
Balance	0.137 (0.016)	0.440 (0.012)	0.302 (0.025)	0.309 (0.022)	0.422 (0.021)
Breast	0.040 (0.002)	0.084 (0.010)	0.040 (0.003)	0.041 (0.004)	0.062 (0.001)
Cleveland	0.229 (0.009)	0.276 (0.019)	0.248 (0.009)	0.252 (0.009)	0.271 (0.012)
Hayes	0.314 (0.010)	0.440 (0.021)	0.342 (0.019)	0.345 (0.015)	0.373 (0.018)
Housing	0.268 (0.008)	0.303 (0.031)	0.323 (0.014)	0.333 (0.016)	0.294 (0.017)
Ionosphere	0.261 (0.011)	0.320 (0.033)	0.315 (0.009)	0.316 (0.008)	0.321 (0.007)
Liver	0.423 (0.014)	0.430 (0.013)	0.440 (0.013)	0.440 (0.011)	0.437 (0.007)
Pima	0.291 (0.080)	0.358 (0.018)	0.324 (0.008)	0.325 (0.008)	0.313 (0.017)
Sonar	0.348 (0.010)	0.361 (0.017)	0.382 (0.009)	0.387 (0.009)	0.357 (0.009)
		ADAR			
Australian	0.137 (0.003)	0.214 (0.013)	0.145 (0.002)	0.143 (0.003)	0.145 (0.004)
Balance	0.081 (0.004)	0.100 (0.008)	0.076 (0.003)	0.078 (0.003)	0.089 (0.005)
Breast	0.040 (0.001)	0.073 (0.006)	0.036 (0.001)	0.036 (0.001)	0.046 (0.001)
Cleveland	0.196 (0.007)	0.271 (0.016)	0.228 (0.007)	0.230 (0.007)	0.235 (0.005)
Hayes	0.202 (0.009)	0.339 (0.030)	0.205 (0.008)	0.199 (0.008)	0.230 (0.011)
Housing	0.130 (0.006)	0.184 (0.011)	0.137 (0.003)	0.137 (0.003)	0.143 (0.004)
Ionosphere	0.079 (0.003)	0.174 (0.011)	0.080 (0.003)	0.081 (0.005)	0.114 (0.004)
Liver	0.291 (0.008)	0.379 (0.015)	0.289 (0.010)	0.287 (0.010)	0.325 (0.011)
Pima	0.247 (0.004)	0.287 (0.010)	0.280 (0.014)	0.280 (0.013)	0.267 (0.006)
Sonar	0.215 (0.005)	0.253 (0.016)	0.221 (0.007)	0.222 (0.009)	0.207 (0.005)

stumps as nodes functions. The number of boosting steps is equal to 10. In order to obtain a lower correlation among different built classifiers, we have slightly modified the learning algorithm by providing an uniformly distributed random weight initialization. For this reason, we will refer to this classifier as *ADAR (AdaBoost with Random weight inizialization)*. It is worth noting that in this way, we are considering two different scenarios for the classification models involved in the combination: a set of weak classifiers that independently would not achieve an high margin and a set of robust classifiers able to achieve high margins on the training set.

Our first experiment show the behavior of the margin-based fusion rule on the training set. To this aim, we considered the cumulative distributions of margins on the training set provided by SM and the other employed fusion rules. In fig. 1 we report the margin cdfs for the proposed approach in comparison with the other rules for the Housing data set when using 4 WRLC (fig. 1.a) or 4 ADAR (fig. 1.b) classifiers. Looking at these graphs, we can evaluate that the hard margin exhibits an higher minimum margin than our rule since we relax the constraint of the maximization problem to try to achieve better performance on the test set. It is also worth noting that the minimum margin evaluated by SM is always higher than SA and WA.

In the second experiment, we have considered combinations with a number K of dichotomizers equal to 4 and 7. For each K, we have generated 30 different K-ples of dichotomizers and we have evaluated the mean error rate on the 10 runs of the hold out procedure for each combination. Tables 1-2 we report the results obtained on the 10 data sets in terms of mean and standard deviation.

Let us analyze the results for WRLC classifiers (first half of the tables). In this case the soft margin rule is able to outperform the other rules in all the considered cases. When using ADAR classifiers (second half of the tables), instead, the results are slightly worse. There are two data sets (Breast and Hayes) where SA and WA are always better than SM independently on the number of combined classifiers. Moreover, when increasing to 7 classifiers even on Balance and Liver data sets WA and SA outperform SM. In all the other cases SM is better than the other rules (if we exclude Sonar data set where the BEST has higher performance than all the combined rules) and in particular, it is better than HM. This different behavior with ADAR is probably due to the better performance (both in terms of margin and generalization error) achieved by the base classifiers that lead to simple combination rules with high performance.

5   Conclusions and Future Work

We have proposed a framework for the linear combination of dichotomizers based on the margin maximization. Our approach relies on the evaluation of the weights of a convex combination of classifiers such that the margin of the combination on the training set is maximized. In the margin evaluation we relaxed the constraint using slack variables so as to achieve a bettergeneralization than the hard margin approach. The obtained results in comparisons with other recent and commonly employed approaches both on margin distribution and on classification performance encourage a deeper analysis of the proposed method. In particular, it could be useful to consider combination rules that maximize the average or the median margin rather than the minimum one. Moreover, a more extensive experimentation involving a real application (e.g. multibiometrics) could be employed to better verify the effectiveness of this approach.

References

1. Anthony, M., Bartlett, P.L.: Neural Network Learning: Theoretical Foundations. Cambridge University Press, Cambridge (1999)
2. Asuncion, A., Newman, D.J.: UCI machine learning repository (2007)
3. Bartlett, P.L.: The sample complexity of pattern classification with neural networks: the size of the weights is more important than the size of the network. IEEE Transactions on Information Theory 44(2), 525–536 (1998)
4. Breiman, L.: Prediction games and arcing algorithms. Neural Computation 11(7), 1493–1517 (1999)
5. Crammer, K., Gilad-Bachrach, R., Navot, A., Tishby, N.: Margin analysis of the LVQ algorithm. In: Advances in NIPS, vol. 15, pp. 462–469 (2003)

6. Fumera, G., Roli, F.: A theoretical and experimental analysis of linear combiners for multiple classifier systems. IEEE Transactions on Pattern Analysis and Machine Intelligence 27(6), 942–956 (2005)
7. Grove, A.J., Schuurmans, D.: Boosting in the limit: maximizing the margin of learned ensembles. In: Proc. AAAI 1998/IAAI 1998, pp. 692–699. American Association for Artificial Intelligence (1998)
8. Jain, A.K., Nandakumar, K., Ross, A.: Score normalization in multimodal biometric systems. Pattern Recognition 38(12), 2270–2285 (2005)
9. Koltchinskii, V., Panchenko, D.: Empirical margin distributions and bounding the generalization error of combined classifiers. Annals of Statistics 30, 1–50 (2002)
10. Kuncheva, L.I.: Combining Pattern Classifiers. Methods and Algorithms. John Wiley & Sons, Chichester (2004)
11. Kuncheva, L.I., Whitaker, C.J.: Measures of diversity in classifier ensembles. Machine Learning 51, 181–207 (2003)
12. Marrocco, C., Ricamato, M.T., Tortorella, F.: Exploring margin maximization for biometric score fusion. In: da Vitoria Lobo, N., Kasparis, T., Roli, F., Kwok, J.T., Georgiopoulos, M., Anagnostopoulos, G.C., Loog, M. (eds.) S+SSPR 2008. LNCS, vol. 5342, pp. 674–683. Springer, Heidelberg (2008)
13. Ratsch, G., Onoda, T., Muller, K.R.: Soft margins for adaboost. Machine Learning 42(3), 287–320 (2001); NeuroCOLT Technical Report NC-TR-1998-021
14. Schapire, R.E., Freund, Y., Bartlett, P., Lee, W.S.: Boosting the margin: A new explanation for the effectiveness of voting methods. The Annals of Statistics 26(5), 1651–1686 (1998)
15. Shawe-Taylor, J., Bartlett, P.L., Williamson, R.C., Anthony, M.: Structural risk minimization over data-dependent hierarchies. IEEE Transactions on Information Theory 44(5), 1926–1940 (1998)
16. Tumer, K., Ghosh, J.: Analysis of decision boundaries in linearly combined neural classifiers. Pattern Recognition 29, 341–348 (1996)
17. Vanderbei, R.J.: Linear Programming: Foundations and Extensions, 2nd edn. Springer, Heidelberg (2001)
18. Vapnik, V.N.: Statistical Learning Theory. John Wiley & Sons, Chichester (1998)
19. Vezhnevets, A., Vezhnevets, V.: Modest adaboost - teaching AdaBoost to generalize better. In: Graphicon-2005, Novosibirsk Akademgorodok, Russia (2005)

Author Index

Printed in the United States
By Bookmasters